The Transgender Studies Reader

The Transgender Studies Reader

Edited by

Susan Stryker and Stephen Whittle

Routledge
Taylor & Francis Group
New York   London

Routledge is an imprint of the
Taylor & Francis Group, an informa business

Published in 2006 by
Routledge
Taylor & Francis Group
270 Madison Avenue
New York, NY 10016

Routledge is an imprint of Taylor & Francis Group

Printed in the United States of America on acid-free paper
10 9 8 7 6 5 4 3 2

International Standard Book Number-10: 0-415-94708-1 (Hardcover) 0-415-94709-X (Softcover)
International Standard Book Number-13: 978-0-415-94708-4 (Hardcover) 978-0-415-94709-1 (Softcover)

Library of Congress Cataloging-in-Publication Data

The transgender studies reader / edited by Susan Stryker and Stephen Whittle.
   p. cm.
  Includes bibliographical references and index.
  1. Transsexualism. 2. Transvestism. 3. Transsexuals. 4.
Transvestites. I. Stryker, Susan. II. Whittle, Stephen, 1955-

HQ77.9.T73 2006
306.76′8--dc22

2005037854

Taylor & Francis Group
is the Academic Division of Informa plc.

Visit the Taylor & Francis Web site at
http://www.taylorandfrancis.com

and the Routledge Web site at
http://www.routledge-ny.com

Contents

Acknowledgments

The authors were blessed with an enthusiastic editor at the outset of this project, Karen Wolny, who was unfortunately unable to bring this project to fruition with us at Routledge. We thank Kimberly Guinta for finally bringing this book to press after seemingly endless delays, and Daniel Webb for assembling the manuscript and securing permissions for work republished in *The Transgender Studies Reader*. We also thank Don Romesburg for his intrepid bibliographical assistance, and Texas Starr for administrative support in the preparation of this manuscript. We are indebted to our families for indulging the absences and interruptions occasioned by our work on this project. Most importantly, we would like to thank our friends, colleagues, and other transgender studies scholars for producing the work collected between these pages.

Foreword

Stephen Whittle

Trans identities were one of the most written about subjects of the late twentieth century. New communities of transgender and transsexual people have created new industries, a new academic discipline, new forms of entertainment; they offer new challenges to politics, government, and law, and new opportunities to broaden the horizons of everyone who has a trans person as their neighbor, coworker, friend, partner, parent, or child. Any Internet search, whether of Web sites, news articles, or academic papers, will produce thousands of results. A recent Google search for "transsexual" gave 3 million hits. Using the term "transgender" in an attempt to reduce the number porn sites actually retrieved far more: 7.5 million hits. The sites range from small personal projects to very large ones, such as the U.S. social organization Transgender Forum;[1] the UK's political lobby group, Press for Change;[2] the educational site for those in the Far East, Transgender Asia;[3] sites for professional service providers such as the Harry Benjamin International Gender Dysphoria Association,[4] and many health reference sites such as Trans-health.[5]

A trans identity is now accessible almost anywhere, to anyone who does not feel comfortable in the gender role they were attributed with at birth, or who has a gender identity at odds with the labels "man" or "woman" credited to them by formal authorities. The identity can cover a variety of experiences. It can encompass discomfort with role expectations, being queer, occasional or more frequent cross-dressing, permanent cross-dressing and cross-gender living, through to accessing major health interventions such as hormonal therapy and surgical reassignment procedures. It can take up as little of your life as five minutes a week or as much as a life-long commitment to reconfiguring the body to match the inner self. Regardless of the fact that trans identities are now more available, the problems of being trans have by no means been resolved. In many parts of the world, having a trans identity still puts a person at risk of discrimination, violence, and even death.

A trans person might be a butch or a camp, a transgender or a transsexual, an MTF or FTM or a cross-dresser; they might, in some parts of the world, consider themselves a lady boy, *katoey*, or even the reclaimed Maori identities *whakawahine* or *whakatane*. Some communities and their terms are ancient, such as the Hijra from Northern India, but many are more modern. The word "trans," referring to a "trans woman" or "trans man" (of whatever subtype of trans identity) is a very recent take on the umbrella term "transgender." Although there had been some previous usage in the 1990s (e.g., in the creation of the online group Trans-Academics), "trans" as a stand-alone term did not come into formal usage until it was coined by a parliamentary discussion group in London in 1998, with the deliberate intention of being as inclusive as possible when negotiating equality legislation. Cultural spaces and historiographies are constantly reframing the community, the identities, the cultures, and the language. We see new language being developed constantly; for example "per" as a pronoun was developed by UK community members with nonexistent gender identities, and similarly the U.S. term "hir" for those who have both.

The growth of home computer use in the 1990s, and the encouragement of many trans women at the forefront of information technology and Internet development, was crucial to the development of a new, geographically dispersed, diverse trans community in the 1990s (Whittle, 1998). Online, this newly formed community was able to discuss its experiences of fear, shame, and discrimination, and, as a result, many community members developed newly politicized personal identities. This new politicization forged a determination to change the world, by every means possible, for the next generation of trans youth. Significant changes have indeed taken place. At the very least, where once there was *pure* ignorance and prejudice of trans issues, we now see *informed* prejudice and discrimination, which is more easily addressed through the courts and legislature.

The work of trans activists and trans academics has always been linked, not least because of close communication within the new community, but also because of our shared experiences. In the 1970s and '80s, many trans people were unable to obtain or retain a job or a home, or to protect themselves from violence or discrimination. Yet the changes brought about in the '90s have enabled many of us to build new lives, families, and careers. As will be seen within this collection, in the 1990s trans became a cultural obsession, exerting a fascination across many scientific and humanities fields, and many communities of interest. It became an increasingly visible part of everyday life in diverse urban contemporary communities, as well as in some rural settings. It is now possible, simply by "telling" or theorizing my own life and the lives of other trans people, for me to build an academic career based on the fascination of the "Other" with people like me. It is their obsession that has given us the opportunity to use the power of the media to tell our stories, to theorize our lives, and to seek equality and justice.

In this collection we have included work from before the 1990s that is representative of the vast majority of work of those times, when the primary concern was the psychology and medicalization of transsexualism. In the 1990s, a new scholarship, informed by community activism, started from the premise that to be trans was not to have a mental or medical disorder. This fundamental shift was built upon within academia, and enabled trans men and women to reclaim the reality of their bodies, to create with them what they would, and to leave the linguistic determination of those bodies open to exploration and invention. To this extent, trans studies is a true linking of feminist and queer theory.

Exploring personal knowledge of trans possibilities in the classroom is far from easy, when few students have ever had to critically address their own gendered self. However, we can surmise some things from this collection, when presenting the history of trans studies. Of central concern is the fact that the taxonomy of sex and gender seemingly has become disordered; sex and gender themselves no longer appear as stable external categories but rather appear embedded in the individuals who experience them. This concern has derived from the postmodern process of deconstruction, in which modernity and its values, including gender, have been stripped away. The question of postmodern analysis is whether any reconstructive process can exist. For the trans person's understanding of the self, the question becomes whether gender, at the heart of self-understanding, can be theoretically recuperated. It is all very well having no theoretical place within the current gendered world, but that is not the daily lived experience. Real life affords trans people constant stigma and oppression based on the apparently unreal concept of gender. This is one of the most significant issues that trans people have brought to feminist and queer theory. Homophobia and sexism are not based on your genitals or with whom you sleep, but on how you perform the self in ways that are contraindicative to the heteronormative framework.

This brings us to another challenge, which is perhaps the most controversial issue in sex and gender theory. Is the basis of gender identity essential and biologically based, or is it socially constructed? Frequently, many non-trans theorists have used trans identities to support constructivist arguments. But increasingly, trans people are questioning whether the deeply held self-understandings they have can be entirely due to nurture and environment. There have been endless reasons given by psychologists for why trans people exist, but these are almost always shown to be based upon poor experimental procedures, using narrowly defined subject groups without relevant control groups, and with emphasis on issues that trans people would argue are not relevant. As such, the formal psycho-medical theories are falling rapidly by the wayside, and nothing has appeared in their place except some very limited evidence of biological differentiation that is so problematic that it cannot yet be said to have any proof value (Zhou et al., 1997).

The work of trans academics and theorists is increasingly moving trans people away from the discredited status of being mentally disordered, towards having expert knowledge of those who struggle to maintain the current strict gender regime, referred to by Kate Bornstein (1997) as "gender defenders." Finally being able to accept our own sanity, trans people have created gender disorder by becoming "gender outlaws." Whilst we can determine that trans people have always existed (within understandings contingent on time, space, and culture) this begs the question of whether trans is a natural or unnatural phenomena. Can a trans person be classed as intersex, or should there be any sex classification at all? Having a sex is apparently a prior determinant of being human, but as such it begs the meaning of what "human" is. One of the arguments made in legal trans theory is that etiology is always irrelevant in the claim to rights. Of course it isn't, because we do not afford rights to vegetable material, and we limit the rights of non-human animals. It is in the claim to human rights that the question of what is "human" becomes over-riding. Increasingly we presume that language, as another predeterminant of humanity, overrides the determinant of biological sex: that is, a person is the gender they claim to be, regardless of sex status. But the language of sex and gender is inherently limited. As trans people challenge their exclusion from language, and therefore from basic human rights, sex itself is increasingly becoming an unsafe foundation for the legal foundation of the order of human life.

Telling the trans story, as part of the academic project, has become a project of narrative repetition in which trans people have told of their anguish. In recent years, the constant clamoring of voices has finally been heard, and sympathetic listeners have worked with formerly excluded trans people to create broader access to social spaces that range from local LGBT support groups to the halls of senior government. The ongoing battle for inclusion, equality, and recognition of our diversity within politics, the courts, the media, and in many other parts of life, has made many of us public figures. Television chat shows and documentaries are still seeking out trans people to appear; films have been made, and, of course, books have been written. Even after my own very visible thirty years in the public arena, I was astonished to discover that after my appearance on a television show in 2003, a month-long discussion had taken place on an e-mail list for gay bears, in which the participants debated whether sleeping with me (or people like me) would call their own sexual orientation into question. (I was rather pleased to discover that overall they concluded I was rather attractive and that sleeping with me would apparently not make them any less gay.) But the questioning that trans people present to others' identities is a growing challenge to all who place their confidence in the binary rules of sexed lives: man/woman, male/female, masculine/feminine, straight/gay. We who are activists may think that the battle is being won, but perhaps it is not; recently, for example, religious and faith organizations have spent thousands of dollars trying to prevent legal advances for trans people.[6] Teaching about trans issues in this politicized context allows our students to understand that trans identities challenge the core beliefs of some of society's most powerful groups, and highlight the extent to which those groups wish to dominate the thinking of us all.

On reflection, if I was not trans, I imagine I would have been an ordinary woman (though that is too difficult for me to imagine), perhaps with a teaching job, cooking the meals, doing the garden, and bringing up the kids. Instead, I am part of the cultural crisis of the new millennium. I can personally vouch for the fact that in the mid-1970s, being trans was extremely dangerous and unpleasant, and yet I know from experience that trans people still pursued their identities. In recent years, embracing the trans community and its culture has led us to an exciting position at the cusp of one of the most significant social and political changes in the postmodern world. The struggles of trans people could have significant impact on all of our freedoms, depending upon who wins the war of ideologies surrounding the meaning of gender and sex.

One of the problems in putting together this collection is the ongoing paucity of empirical analysis of gender diversity. When I started teaching in 1990, my proposal for a class in sex and gender law was laughed at by some colleagues. Five years later there was still little interest. It took another five years for a course that would include the law of sexual orientation and gender identity to be established. This was partly due to the fact that although there is a vast array of medical and cultural comment, there is little in terms of in-depth empirical scientific, sociological, and legal investigation. As a result, gender issues are still viewed as "minority interests" rather than a matter of concern to us all.

For some reason, it has really only been trans men who have published in-depth empirical and sociological analyses. Extensive and in-depth social and legal studies on what it means to be a trans man have come from Aaron Devor (1997), Jason Cromwell (1999), Henry Rubin (2003), Jamison Green (2004), and me (2002). This highlights the serious lack of such a body of work representing trans women's voices. Despite the significant theoretical perspectives from trans women such as Sandy Stone (1991), Vivian K. Namaste (2000), Riki Wilchins (1997), and Susan Stryker (1994) there is a need to analyze why there is the difference in discipline. It may well be that the difficulty in "passing" makes it easier said than done for trans women to access the academy. It might be that the poverty that comes from more often supporting a prior family makes it harder for trans women to put together a research career. Whatever the reason, it highlights what the community already knows: trans women are most frequently the victims of discrimination because of their visibility.

The empirical and sociological analyses undertaken have shown that it is only by understanding and accepting that linguistic barriers still exclude the vast diversities of trans and non-trans identities, that we can possibly begin to accept that gender, like race, simply does not exist other than as an idea that has gained immeasurable power within the economies of social discourse. As we move into a new world, trans academics and theorists are creating new discursive practices which are repositioning the power of gender(s) and allowing more of us to have a say in what gender means, and in what its powers should be.

The *Transgender Studies Reader* is an effort to afford the student and teacher with a passage through the complexities of gender theory. It illustrates how trans people were problematized by science and society, and how trans people have responded by using the same intellectual tools that have oppressed them to place the "Other" in the problematized position. This process has not been easy. Our collection also illustrates the call to arms that has been issued by activist trans academics to make the study of the self and the Objective Other a reputable field.

In trans theory there is an inherent recognition that the trans position is problematic. The labels "man" and "woman" are inadequate to describe the trans experience, as the trans person's history and knowledge of the world is so different from that of "men born men" or "women born women." Yet the responsibility to recognize and articulate that position is no one else's but the self's. Trans theorists, who have been able to authenticate the actual spheres of pain within trans lives, in conjunction with critiquing existing commentary, have enabled the coherent voices of trans people to be heard throughout the academy. This task was not without risk. The willingness of trans academics and theorists to give up their hard-fought-for privacy in their new gender role has undoubtedly cost the pioneers in the field. However, it has been through this articulation of the imposition of gendering on us by others that the position of suffering of those with trans identities has been heard.

The public articulation of a trans voice and trans consciousness has not only influenced sex and gender studies, but it also impacted on trans people themselves, and has provided a collection of materials that coherently explain their own experiences as genuine. Amongst other things, it has created new ways in which to be an activist, as well as new ways of being trans. It is now possible:

- to acknowledge and fight the injustice of transphobia, and to be trans publicly in order to truly represent transphobia's victims;
- to be in charge of what we do to our own trans bodies, and to take risks in the art of our bodies;
- to become queer, by refusing gender ascription and by claiming the transsexualism of the self;
- to turn away, ultimately, from the relative safety of queerness and go beyond that to claim a unique position of suffering; and finally,
- to welcome the rage afforded by that experience of suffering, a suffering that is part and parcel of being trans.

Teaching transgender theory is itself an activist process as well as an explorative process. The field is expanding exponentially along with the cultural changes that accompany it. It also poses a daunting problem—in order to hear the voices of trans people, as justice demands, one has to acknowledge the limits of sex and gender and move into a new world in which any identity can be imagined, performed, and named.

NOTES

1. Transgender Forum, available at http:// www.tgforum.com/
2. Press for Change, available at http://www.pfc.org.uk
3. Transgender Asia http://web.hku.hk/~sjwinter/TransgenderASIA/
4. Harry Benjamin International Gender Dysphoria Association, available at http:// www.hbigda.org
5. Trans-health, available at http:// www.trans-health.com/
6. See The Liberator: Staver, M. D: Legal Update, Sept 2004 for an account of the involvement of the Christian fundamentalist group, Liberty Counsel, in the child care case of *Kanteras v. Kanteras* in the Florida courts at http://www. lc.org/newsletter/lib/2004/09update.htm, and the Christian Institute's briefing on the UK's Gender Recognition Bill at http://www.christian.org.uk/transsexualism/briefing_16jan04.pdf

REFERENCES

Cromwell, Jason. 1999. *Transmen and FTMs: Identities, bodies, genders, and sexualities.* Champaign: University of Illinois Press.
Devor, Aaron H. 1997. *FTM: Female-to-male transsexuals in society.* Bloomington: Indiana University Press.
Green, Jamison. 2004. *Becoming a visible man.* Nashville, TN: Vanderbilt University Press.
Namaste, Viviane K. 2000. *Invisible lives: The erasure of transsexual and transgendered people.* Chicago: University of Chicago Press.
Rubin, Henry S. 2003. *Self-made men: Identity and embodiment among transsexual men.* Nashville, TN: Vanderbilt University Press.
Stone, Sandy. 1991. The *Empire* strikes back: A posttranssexual manifesto. In *Body guards: The cultural politics of gender ambiguity*, eds. Julia Epstein and Kristina Straub, 280–304. New York: Routledge.

Stryker, Susan. 1994. My words to Victor Frankenstein above the village of Chamounix: Performing transgender rage. *GLQ* 1 (3): 227–254.

Wilchins, Riki A. 1997. *Read my lips: Sexual subversion and the end of gender.* Ithaca, NY: Firebrand Books.

Whittle, Stephen. 1998. The Trans-Cyberian mail way. *Journal of Social and Legal Studies* 7 (3), 389–408.

Whittle, Stephen. 2002. *Respect and Equality: Transsexual and Transgender Rights.* London: Cavendish.

Zhou, J.-N., Hofman, M. A., Gooren, L. J., and Swaab, D. F. 1995. A sex difference in the human brain and its relation to transsexuality. *Nature* 378: 68–70.

(De)Subjugated Knowledges
An Introduction to Transgender Studies

SUSAN STRYKER

IN 1995, I FOUND MYSELF STANDING IN LINE FOR MY TURN at the microphone in the Proshansky Auditorium of the Graduate Center of the City University of New York. I was attending a conference called "Lesbian and Gay History," organized by the Center for Lesbian and Gay Studies (CLAGS). I had just attended a panel discussion on "Gender and the Homosexual Role," moderated by Randolph Trumbach, whose speakers consisted of Will Roscoe, Martha Vicinus, George Chauncey, Ramon Gutierrez, Elizabeth Kennedy, and Martin Manalansan. I had heard a great many interesting things about fairies and *berdaches* (as two-spirit Native Americans were still being called), Corn Mothers and molly-houses, passionate female friendships, butch-femme dyads, and the Southeast Asian gay diaspora, but I was nevertheless standing in line to register a protest. Each of the panelists was an intellectual star in his or her own right, but they were not, I thought, taken collectively, a very gender-diverse lot. From my perspective, with a recently claimed transsexual identity, they all looked pretty much the same: like nontransgender people. A new wave of transgender scholarship, part of a broader queer intellectual movement was, by that point in time, already a few years old. Why were there no transgender speakers on the panel? Why was the entire discussion of "gender diversity" subsumed within a discussion of sexual desire—as if the only reason to express gender was to signal the mode of one's attractions and availabilities to potential sex partners?

As I stood in line, trying to marshal my thoughts and feelings into what I hoped would come across as an articulate and eloquent critique of gay historiography rather than a petulant complaint that no-body had asked *me* to be on that panel, a middle-aged white man on the other side of the auditorium reached the front of the other queue for the other microphone and began to speak. He had a serious issue he wanted to raise with the panelists, about a disturbing new trend he was beginning to observe. Transsexuals, he said, had started claiming that *they* were part of this new queer politics, which had to be stopped, of course, because everybody knew that transsexuals were profoundly psychopathological individuals who mutilated their bodies and believed in oppressive gender stereotypes and held reactionary political views, and they had been trying for years to infiltrate the gay and lesbian movement to destroy it and this was only the latest sick plot to....

It was an all-too-familiar diatribe—a line of thinking about transsexuality that passed at that time for a progressive point of view among many on the cultural left. At some point, in a fog of righteous anger, I leaned into the microphone on my side of the room and, interrupting, said, "I'm not sick." The man across the auditorium stopped talking, and looked at me. I said, "I'm transsexual, and I'm not sick. And I'm not going to listen to you say that about me, or people like me, any more." We locked eyes with each other for a few seconds, from opposite sides of the auditorium filled with a couple of hundred gay and lesbian scholars and activists (and a handful of trans people), until the man suddenly turned and huffed out of the room. I then proceeded to make what I still hoped was an eloquent and articulate critique of gay historiography. The man I interrupted, it turned out, was Jim Fouratt, a veteran of the 1969 gay rights riots at the Stonewall Inn, a founding member of the Gay Liberation Front, and a fixture on the fading New Left fringe of New York progressive politics. I now look back on that exchange as one of the few iconic moments in my public life—a representative of the transgender *arrivistes* stared down a representative of the old gay liberation vanguard, who abandoned the field of queer scholarship to a new interpretation of gender diversity. Sweet.[1]

Ten years later, in 2005, I found myself once again in the Proshansky Auditorium, for another CLAGS conference. This one was called "Trans Politics, Social Change, and Justice."[2] The room was filled with a couple of hundred transgender activists and academics, and a smattering of nontransgender gay, lesbian, bisexual, and straight people. CLAGS itself was no longer being run by its founder, the eminent gay historian Martin Duberman, but by transgender legal studies scholar Paisley Currah. I was there to show *Screaming Queens*, my recently completed public television documentary on the 1966 Compton's Cafeteria riot, a transgender revolt that took place in San Francisco three years before Stonewall.[3] Rather than struggling merely to speak and be heard during the closing plenary session, transgender voices engaged in a lively, sometimes acrimonious, debate. In the middle of a heated verbal exchange between radicals and centrists, a middle-aged white man patiently worked his way up the speaker's queue to the microphone. It was Jim Fouratt, of course. He complained that a new transgender hegemony was marginalizing and erasing the experiences of people like himself, that a revisionist history of sexual liberation and civil rights movement was rewriting the past in an Orwellian fashion, and—he would no doubt have continued with a further list of similar grievances had not numerous members of the audience shouted for him to sit down and shut up. He paused for a moment, gave up his struggle to be heard, and left the auditorium in a huff. Sad.

Those two moments in the Proshansky auditorium are, for me personally, bookends for a phase in the development of the field of transgender studies—a phase that Stephen Whittle and I have attempted, in a necessarily partial fashion that will unavoidably invite criticism, to document in *The Transgender Studies Reader*. What began with the efforts of emerging and marginally situated scholars and activists such as ourselves to be taken seriously on our own terms, and not pathologized and dismissed, has helped foster a sea-change in the academic study of gender, sex, sexuality, identity, desire, and embodiment. Histories have in fact been rewritten; the relationships with prior gay, lesbian, and feminist scholarship have been addressed; new modes of gendered subjectivity have emerged, and new discourses and lines of critical inquiry have been launched. Academic attention to transgender issues has shifted over the span of those ten years from the field of abnormal psychology, which imagined transgender phenomena as expressions of mental illness, and from the field of literary criticism, which was fascinated with representations of cross-dressing that it fancied to be merely symbolic, into fields that concern themselves with the day-to-day workings of the material world. "Transgender" moved from the clinics to the streets over the course of that decade, and from representation to reality.[4]

Perhaps the most surprising aspect of the whole transgender thing back in the 1990s was the startling rapidity with which the term itself took root, and was applied to (if not always welcomed by) the sociocultural and critical-intellectual formations that were caught up in, or suddenly crystallized by, its wake.[5] Given the struggles that have attended the advent of "transgender" as a descriptive term for a heterogeneous class of phenomena, merely to use the word is to take up a polemical and politicized position. In the end, we took the easy way out and pragmatically acknowledged that the term "transgender," for all it limitations and masked agendas, was the term in most common usage that best fit what we were trying to talk about. What began as a buzzword of the early 1990s has established itself as the term of choice, in both popular parlance and a variety specialist discourses, for a wide range of phenomena that call attention to the fact that "gender," as it is lived, embodied, experienced, performed, and encountered, is more complex and varied than can be accounted for by the currently dominant binary sex/gender ideology of Eurocentric modernity.

Transgender studies, as we understand it, is the academic field that claims as its purview trans-sexuality and cross-dressing, some aspects of intersexuality and homosexuality, cross-cultural and historical investigations of human gender diversity, myriad specific subcultural expressions of "gender atypicality," theories of sexed embodiment and subjective gender identity development, law and public policy related to the regulation of gender expression, and many other similar issues. It is an inter-disciplinary field that draws upon the social sciences and psychology, the physical and life sciences, and the humanities and arts. It is as concerned with material conditions as it is with representational practices, and often pays particularly close attention the interface between the two. The frameworks for analyzing and interpreting gender, desire, embodiment, and identity now taking shape in the field of transgender studies have radical implications for a wide range of subject areas. Transgender phe-nomena have become a topical focus in fields ranging from musicology to religious studies to digital media; a theme in the visual, plastic, and performing arts; and a matter of practical concern in such fields as public health, plastic surgery, criminal justice, family law, and immigration.

Most broadly conceived, the field of transgender studies is concerned with anything that disrupts, denaturalizes, rearticulates, and makes visible the normative linkages we generally assume to exist between the biological specificity of the sexually differentiated human body, the social roles and sta-tuses that a particular form of body is expected to occupy, the subjectively experienced relationship between a gendered sense of self and social expectations of gender-role performance, and the cultural mechanisms that work to sustain or thwart specific configurations of gendered personhood. The field of transgender studies seeks not only to understand the contents and mechanisms of those linkages and assumptions about sex and gender, biology and culture; it also asks who "we" are—we who make those assumptions and forge those links—and who "they" are, who seem to "us" to break them. The field asks why it should matter, ethically and morally, that people experience and express their gender in fundamentally different ways. It concerns itself with what we—we who have a passionate stake in such things—are going to do, politically, about the injustices and violence that often attend the percep-tion of gender nonnormativity and atypicality, whether in ourselves or in others.

Transgender studies, at its best, is like other socially engaged interdisciplinary academic fields such as disability studies or critical race theory that investigate questions of embodied difference, and analyze how such differences are transformed into social hierarchies—without ever losing sight of the fact that "difference" and "hierarchy" are never mere abstractions; they are systems of power that operate on actual bodies, capable of producing pain and pleasure, health and sickness, punishment and reward, life and death. Transgender studies has a deep stake in showing how the seemingly anomalous, minor, exotic, or strange qualities of transgender phenomena are in fact effects of the relationship constructed between those phenomena and sets of norms that are themselves culturally produced and enforced. Transgender studies enables a critique of the conditions that cause transgender phenomena to stand out in the first place, and that allow gender normativity to disappear into the unanalyzed, ambient background. Ultimately, it is not just transgender phenomena per se that are of interest, but rather the manner in which these phenomena reveal the operations of systems and institutions that simul-taneously produce various possibilities of viable personhood, and eliminate others. Thus the field of transgender studies, far from being an inconsequentially narrow specialization dealing *only* with a rarified population of transgender individuals, or with an eclectic collection of esoteric transgender practices, represents a significant and ongoing critical engagement with some of the most trenchant issues in contemporary humanities, social science, and biomedical research.

A LITTLE BACKGROUND

The word "transgender" itself, which seems to have been coined in the 1980s, took on its current meaning in 1992 after appearing in the title of a small but influential pamphlet by Leslie Feinberg, *Transgender Liberation: A Movement Whose Time has Come*.[6] First usage of the term "transgender" is generally attributed to Virginia Prince, a Southern California advocate for freedom of gender expression.[7] Prince used the term to refer to individuals like herself whose personal identities she considered to fall somewhere on a spectrum between "transvestite" (a term coined in 1910 by Dr. Magnus Hirschfeld) and "transsexual" (a term popularized in the 1950s by Dr. Harry Benjamin).[8] If a *transvestite* was somebody who episodically changed into the clothes of the so-called "other sex," and a *transsexual* was somebody who permanently changed genitals in order to claim membership in a gender other than the one assigned at birth, then a *transgender* was somebody who permanently changed social gender through the public presentation of self, without recourse to genital transformation.

In Feinberg's usage, transgender came to mean something else entirely—an adjective rather than a noun. Feinberg called for a political alliance between all individuals who were marginalized or oppressed due to their difference from social norms of gendered embodiment, and who should therefore band together in a struggle for social, political, and economic justice. Transgender, in this sense, was a "pangender" umbrella term for an imagined community encompassing transsexuals, drag queens, butches, hermaphrodites, cross-dressers, masculine women, effeminate men, sissies, tomboys, and anybody else willing to be interpolated by the term, who felt compelled to answer the call to mobilization. In the wake of Feinberg's pamphlet, a movement did indeed take shape under that rubric; it has gradually won new civil and human rights for transgender people, and has influenced the tenor of public debate on transgender issues for more than a decade.

Feinberg's call to arms for a transgender liberation movement followed close on the heels of another watershed publication that laid an important cornerstone for transgender studies, Sandy Stone's 1991 "posttranssexual manifesto."[9] Stone wrote against a line of thought in second-wave feminism, common since the early 1970s and articulated most vehemently by feminist ethicist Janice Raymond, which considered transsexuality to be a form of false consciousness.[10] Transsexuals, in this view, failed to properly analyze the social sources of gender oppression. Rather than working to create equality by overthrowing the gender system itself, they internalized outmoded masculine or feminine stereotypes and did harm to their bodies in order to appear as the men and women they considered themselves to be, but that others did not. In this view, transsexuals were the visible symptoms of a disturbed gender system. By altering the surface appearance of their bodies, such feminists contended, transsexuals alienated themselves from their own lived history, and placed themselves in an inauthentic position that misrepresented their "true selves" to others. Stone called upon transsexuals to critically refigure the notion of authenticity by abandoning the practice of passing as nontranssexual (and therefore "real") men and women, much as gays and lesbians a generation earlier had been called to come out of their self-protective but ultimately suffocating closets. Stone sought to combat the anti-transsexual moralism embedded in certain strands of feminist thought by soliciting a new corpus of intellectual and creative work capable of analyzing and communicating to others the concrete realities of "changing sex. " To a significant degree, Feinberg's "transgender" came to name the ensemble of critical practices called for by Stone's "posttransexual" manifesto.

The confluence of a few other major events in 1991 conspired to create and circulate new debates and discourses about transgender issues—and to revive some old ones. That year, the Michigan Women's Music Festival, a women-only event with deep roots in the lesbian feminist community, expelled a postoperative transsexual woman, Nancy Jean Burkholder, claiming she was "actually" a man.[11] This incident became a flashpoint in the United States and Canada for transgender people and their allies, many of whom had been radicalized by opposition to the Gulf War, the right-wing assault on public arts funding in the United States, and by the Reagan-Bush administrations' decade-long history of neglect of the AIDS crisis.[12] A provocative and intelligent performance artist named Kate Bornstein was tweaking the consciousness of audiences on both coasts of North America with confessional works that explored her tortured personal history with the word "transsexual."[13] Some of the more academically-minded members of these grassroots communities were reading a recent book by Judith Butler, *Gender Trouble*, and an older book by Michel Foucault, *History of Sexuality, Vol. 1*.[14] A Routledge anthology published that year, Julia Epstein and Kristina Straub's *Body Guards: The Cultural Politics of Gender Ambiguity*, which included Sandy Stone's pivotal essay, offered an early map of the terrain transgender studies would soon claim as its own.[15]

By 1992, the tenuous beginnings of the field were taking shape where the margins of the academy overlapped with politicized communities of identity. The activist group Transgender Nation—whose formation in 1992 as a focus group of the San Francisco chapter of Queer Nation marks the emergence of a specifically transgender politics within the broader queer movement of the early 1990s—generated scholarly work as part of its protest against the inclusion of "gender identity disorder" in the American Psychiatric Association's *Diagnostic and Statistical Manual*.[16] New 'zines like *Gender Trash, TransSisters, Rites of Passage,* and *TNT: The Transsexual News Telegraph* combined community-based cultural production with academically-informed critical gender theory. In Houston, legal activist Phyllis R. Frye organized the first professional conference on transgender law and employment policies. Building on the solid foundation built by female-to-male transsexual Lou Sullivan, a community-based historian and activist whose untimely death from AIDS-related illnesses tragically cut short an important career, Jamison Green transformed a local San Francisco FTM support group into FTM International, whose newsletter became a vital outlet for discussing myriad forms of female masculinity. Members of such organizations, some of whom were also graduate students and young academic faculty members, began forming informal personal and professional networks during the 1993 March on Washington for Gay, Lesbian and Bi Rights—which explicitly voted *not* to include "transgender" in its title.

A similar ferment was brewing in the United Kingdom. As in the United States, Europe had seen little formal transgender activism between the heyday of the sexual liberation movements and the early 1990s. In 1992, the political activist group Press for Change was founded in response to the defeat of an application at the European Court of Human Rights by Mark Rees, a transsexual man, for recognition of his rights to privacy and to marry. Unlike the political and theoretical developments in the United States, however, which represented something of a generational break between established and emerging communities of gender-diverse people, the Press For Change campaign included as strategic activists trans people who had been working on trans issues since the mid-1970s. These activists all had experience participating in local support groups affiliated in some fashion with the national Beaumont Society, which itself ultimately derived from Virginia Prince's Hose and Heels Club, founded in Los Angeles in the early 1960s. Although these support groups typically catered to the needs of heterosexual male transvestites, there was a significant history in the UK of mixed groups whose membership included not only part-time cross-dressers, but also postoperative transsexuals, and various others who occupied diverse niches within the gender system.

In 1975, a network of local support group leaders loosely affiliated themselves with the U.S. activist group TAO (Transsexual Action Organization). TAO-UK was a short-lived group devoted to anti-sexism, anti-racism, and peace campaigns that also specifically sought the right of self-determined medical treatment for transsexual people. These early activists became the core of Press for Change in 1992, whose signal victory has been passage of the national Gender Recognition Act in 2004—an accomplishment without parallel in the United States. Partly as a result of Press for Change's efficacy in leveraging the mechanism of institutional power, and partly as a result of profoundly different healthcare delivery systems, transgender academic work in the UK tended from the outset to be more policy-oriented, and more focused on medical and legal issues, than work originating in the United States, which has tended to be more concerned with queer and feminist identity politics. The differences between two such closely related bodies of scholarship highlights the need for careful attention to national contexts, not only when attempting to understand transgender phenomena themselves, but also when trying to understand how transgender phenomena have been interpreted and represented.[17]

The 1994 Queer Studies Conference at the University of Iowa fostered the first truly international network of emerging transgender scholars, and resulted in the formation of the still extant trans-academic listserv. The First International Conference on Cross-Dressing, Sex, and Gender, held in 1995 at California State University at Northridge, represented another benchmark in the development of the transgender studies field. For the first time at a professional meeting, an older generation of (primarily nontransgender) academic specialists who studied transgender phenomena was confronted by a significant number of academically trained specialists who also happened to be transgender people themselves. Transgender attendees angrily protested conference policies that marginalized and stigmatized transgender participants, such as asking transgender people to use separate toilet facilities from the other attendees, or scheduling presentations by transgender scholars exclusively in the "community track" rather than the "professional track."

The situation improved dramatically within a few short years. The astonishingly rapid rise of the term "transgender" seems to have increased exponentially around 1995 (fueled in part by the simultaneous, and even more astonishing, expansion of the World Wide Web). By the late 1990s a number of transgender studies special issues of peer-reviewed academic journals had appeared, as well as transgender-themed anthologies from academic publishers. Even the Harry Benjamin International Gender Dysphoria Association, the old-guard professional organization for medical and psycho-therapeutic service-providers to gender-questioning people, capitulated to the new nomenclature by naming its in-house publication the *International Journal of Transgenderism*. Increasingly, courses in transgender studies were taught at universities across North America and Europe, and transgender scholarship and cultural production were integrated into sexuality and gender studies curricula, as well as within general courses in such disciplines as sociology, psychology, anthropology, and law. Graduate students began writing theses and dissertations on transgender topics—more than 300 to date. The new interdisciplinary field gained coverage in the U.S. *Chronicle of Higher Education* and, in the UK, the *Guardian*'s Higher Education supplement.[18] By the end of the last century, transgender studies could make a fair claim to being an established discipline, though one with relatively scant institutional support.

This is the body of intellectual work that *The Transgender Studies Reader* seeks to sample and contextualize. It is intended to provide a convenient introduction to the field as it has developed over the past decade, an overview of some of the earlier work that informed this scholarship, and a jumping-off point for more sophisticated analyses in the next generation of inquiry.

BROADER CONTEXTS

The emergence of transgender studies has closely paralleled the rise of queer studies, with which it has enjoyed a close and sometimes vexed relationship. One influential interpretation of queer studies' appearance in the United States in the late 1980s and early 1990s is that the AIDS crisis necessitated a profound rethinking of the relationship between sexuality, identity, and the public sphere. Countering the homophobic characterization of AIDS as a "gay disease" required a postidentity sexual politics that simultaneously acknowledged the specificity of various bodies and sexualities (such as gay men), while also fostering strategic political alliances between other, sometimes overlapping, constituencies similarly affected by the epidemic (initially African refugees in Europe, Haitians in the United States, hemophiliacs, and injection drug users). This new "queer" politics, based on an array of oppositions to "heteronormative" social oppression rather than a set of protections for specific kinds of minorities that were vulnerable to discrimination, radically transformed the homosexual rights movement in Europe and America.[19] The queer movement allowed transgender people to make compelling claims that they, too, had political grievances against an oppressive heteronormative regime. Transgender studies initially took shape in that political and intellectual ferment.

Neither feminism nor queer studies, at whose intersection transgender studies first emerged in the academy, were quite up to the task of making sense of the lived complexity of contemporary gender at the close of the last century. First-wave African-American feminist Sojourner Truth's famous question, "Ain't I a Woman?," should serve as a powerful reminder that fighting for representation within the term "woman" has been as much a part of the feminist tradition as has asserting the value of womanhood and fighting for social equality between women and men. [20]"Woman" typically has been mobilized in ways that advance the specific class, racial, national, religious, and ideological agendas of some feminists at the expense of other women; the fight over transgender inclusion within feminism is not significantly different, in many respects, from other fights involving working-class women, women of color, lesbian women, disabled women, women who produce or consume pornography, and women who practice consensual sadomasochism. Just as in these other struggles, grappling with transgender issues requires that some feminists re-examine, or perhaps examine for the first time, some of the exclusionary assumptions they embed within the fundamental conceptual underpinnings of feminism. Transgender phenomena challenge the unifying potential of the category "woman," and call for new analyses, new strategies and practices, for combating discrimination and injustice based on gender inequality.[21]

Like recent feminism and feminist scholarship, queer politics and queer studies also remain invested, to a significant extent, in an underlying conceptual framework that is problematized by transgender phenomena. "Sexual object choice," the very concept used to distinguish "hetero" from "homo" sexuality, loses coherence to the precise extent that the "sex" of the "object" is called into question, particularly in relation to the object's "gender." Queer studies, though putatively antiheteronormative, sometimes fails to acknowledge that same-sex object choice is not the only way to differ from heterosexist cultural norms, that transgender phenomena can also be antiheteronormative, or that transgender phenomena constitute an axis of difference that cannot be subsumed to an object-choice model of antiheteronormativity. As a result, queer studies sometimes perpetuates what might be called "homonormativity," that is, a privileging of homosexual ways of differing from heterosocial norms, and an antipathy (or at least an unthinking blindness) toward other modes of queer difference. Transgender studies is in many ways more attuned to questions of embodiment and identity than to those of desire and sexuality, and is akin to other efforts to insist upon the salience of cross-cutting issues such as race, class, age, disability, and nationality within identity-based movements and communities.

Transgender phenomena invite queer studies, and gay and lesbian communities, to take another look at the many ways bodies, identities, and desires can be interwoven.

Transgender studies emerged in the early 1990s not just in conjunction with certain intellectual trends within feminism and queer theory, but also in response to broader historical circumstances. The disintegration of the Soviet Union, the end of the cold war, the rise of the United States as a unipolar superpower, the development of the European Union as the first multi-national state, and the elaboration of new global forms of capital during these years precipitated a pervasive, deeply motivated, critical reexamination of various conceptual binaries. Sex/gender systems, like other cultural constructs, deformed and reformed in tandem with new material circumstances.[22] The popular film and stage production *Hedwig and the Angry Inch*—the story of a male East German who undergoes a (botched) genital conversion surgery in order to become the wife of an American soldier, and later regrets the decision—explores precisely this shift in post-cold war possibilities for gendered embodiment.[23]

If a frame as totalizing as "East/West" at least momentarily lost its explanatory purchase in a chaotic pre-9/11 world that seemed increasingly structured by diasporic movements and transnational flows, how likely was it at that time that the equally hegemonic construction "woman/man" would remain uninterrogated? Transgender studies stepped into the breach of that ruptured binary to reconceptualize gender for the New World Order. The new field approached gender not as a system for correlating two supposedly natural, stable, and incommensurable biological sexes (male and female) with two normative, fixed, and equally incommensurable social categories (man and woman). Rather, it called into question that entire epistemological framework, and conceived of gender as yet another global system within which a great many diverse and specific forms of human being were produced, enmeshed, and modified along multiple axes of signification. In a world seemingly bent on becoming one, transgender studies grappled with the imperative of counting past two, when enumerating the significant forms of gendered personhood.

Furthermore, throughout the 1990s, the impending calendrical event of the year 2000 helped link critical attention to the collapse of familiar binaries with a sense of epochal change and the perceived advent of a new historical era. During the most recent *fin-de-siècle*, transgender phenomena were widely considered the bellwethers (for better or worse) of an emergent "postmodern" condition. Rita Felski suggests that the up-tick in attention to transgender issues at the close of the last century was an expression of "premillennial tension;" she contends that ends of centuries serve as privileged cultural moments in which to articulate myths of death and rebirth, decline and renewal, and she argues that in our own historical epoch these concerns have been writ large across proliferating representations of transgender bodies.[24] "Transgender" became an overdetermined construct, like "cyborg," through which contemporary culture imagined a future filled with new possibilities for being human, or becoming posthuman.[25] "Transgender studies" emerged at this historic juncture as one practice for collectively thinking our way into the brave new world of the twenty-first century, with all its threats and promises of unimaginable transformation through new forms of biomedical and communicational technologies.

POSTMODERNITY

Transgender phenomena may be "postmodern" to the extent that they are imagined to point beyond contemporary modernity, but transgender critical theory is technically postmodern, in one narrow use of that term, to the extent that it takes aim at the modernist epistemology that treats gender merely as a social, linguistic, or subjective representation of an objectively knowable material sex. Epistemological concerns lie at the heart of transgender critique, and motivate a great deal of the transgender struggle for social justice. Transgender phenomena, in short, point the way to a different understanding of how bodies mean, how representation works, and what counts as legitimate knowledge. These philosophical issues have material consequences for the quality of transgender lives.

In the modern base-and-superstructure epistemic paradigm, sex is considered the stable referential anchor that supports, and is made known by, the signs of gender that reflect it. This is a specific instance of what cultural critic Frederic Jameson called a "mirror theory of knowledge," in which representation consists of the reproduction for subjectivity of an objectivity assumed to lay outside it.[26] The epistemological assertion that the material world is reflected in the mirror of representation is "modern," in a long historical sense, to the extent that it gained force along with the rise of scientific materialism in societies of Western European origin since the end of the fifteenth century. "Matter" is what ultimately matters in this modern European worldview; it lies at the root of knowledge, and is the fundamental source of the meaning (re)invested in it through the derivative and secondary practices of human cognition and perception.

In this seemingly commonsensical view, the materiality of anatomical sex is represented socially by a gender role, and subjectively as a gender identity: a (biological) male is a (social) man who (subjectively) identifies himself as such; a woman is similarly, and circularly, a female who considers herself to be one. The relationship between bodily sex, gender role, and subjective gender identity are imagined to be strictly, mechanically, mimetic—a real thing and its reflections. Gender is simply what we call bodily sex when we see it in the mirror of representation—no questions asked, none needed.[27] Transgender phenomena call into question both the stability of the material referent "sex" and the relationship of that unstable category to the linguistic, social, and psychical categories of "gender." As the ambiguous bodies of the physically intersexed demonstrate in the most palpable sense imaginable, "sex," *any sex*, is a category "which is not one." Rather, what we typically call the sex of the body, which we imagine to be a uniform quality that uniquely characterizes each and every individual whole body, is shown to consist of numerous parts—chromosomal sex, anatomical sex, reproductive sex, morphological sex—that can, and do, form a variety of viable bodily aggregations that number far more than two. The "wholeness' of the body and "sameness" of its sex are themselves revealed to be socially constructed.[28]

Likewise, the contrary subjective identities of transsexuals, the sartorial practices of transvestites, and the gender inversion of butches and queens all work to confound simplistic notions of material determinism, and mirror-style representational practices, in relation to questions of gender. Sex, it turns out, is not the foundation of gender in the same way that an apple is the foundation of a reflection of red fruit in the mirror; "sex" is a mash-up, a story we mix about *how* the body means, which parts matter most, and how they register in our consciousness or field of vision. "Sex" is purpose-built to serve *as* a foundation, and occupies a space excavated for it by an epistemological construction project.[29]

Mirror-style representation encodes a moral drama. It can be true or false, accurate or error-filled. Deliberate misrepresentation of the relationship between representation/gender and referent/sex is fraught with consequence—sometimes with ostensibly comic consequences, as is the case with the innumerable cross-dressing farces that litter the landscape of pop culture, and sometimes with far more tragic results. Transgender people who problematize the assumed correlation of a particular biological sex with a particular social gender are often considered to make false representations of an underlying material truth, through the willful distortion of surface appearance. Their gender presentation is seen as a lie rather than as an expression of a deep, essential truth; they are "bad" by definition.[30]

For the supposed epistemological sin of perpetrating falsehoods that ensnare innocent and unsuspecting others, the atypically gendered must sometimes to pay with their lives. Hillary Swank won an Academy Award in 1999 for portraying Brandon, a murdered transgender youth whose story, told in the true-crime drama *Boys Don't Cry,* has become emblematic of the chronic undercurrent in our society of deadly anti-transgender violence.[31] Those who commit violence against transgender people routinely seek to excuse their own behavior by claiming they have been unjustly deceived by a mismatch between the other's gender and genitals.[32] State and society do similar violence to transgender people by using genital status, rather than public gender or subjective gender identity, as the fundamental criterion for determining how they will place individuals in prisons, residential substance abuse treatment program, rape crisis centers, or homeless shelters. One important task of transgender studies is to articulate and disseminate new epistemological frameworks, and new representational practices, within which variations in the sex/gender relationship can be understood as morally neutral and representationally true, and through which anti-transgender violence can be linked to other systemic forms of violence such as poverty and racism. This intellectual work is intimately connected to, and deeply motivated by, sociopolitical efforts to stem the tide of anti-transgender violence, and to save transgender lives.

PERFORMATIVITY

The model of linguistic "performativity," whose general applicability to the field of gender has been popularized most notably by the work of Judith Butler, has been tremendously influential within transgender studies precisely because it offers a non- or postreferential epistemological framework that can be useful for promoting transgender social justice agendas.[33] The notion of performativity, which is derived from speech act theory and owes an intellectual debt to the philosophical/linguistic work of J. L. Austin in *How to Do Things With Words*, is sometimes confused with the notion of performance, but this is something else entirely.[34] Butler in particular, especially in her early work in *Gender Trouble* and *Bodies That Matter*, has been criticized in some transgender scholarship and community discourse for suggesting that gender is a "mere" performance, on the model of drag, and therefore somehow not "real."[35] She is criticized, somewhat misguidedly, for supposedly believing that gender can be changed or rescripted at will, put on or taken off like a costume, according to one's pleasure or whim. At stake in these critical engagements is the self-understanding of many transgender people, who consider their sense of gendered self *not* to be subject to their instrumental will, not divestible, not a form of play. Rather, they see their gendered sense of self as ontologically inescapable and inalienable—and to suggest otherwise to them is to risk a profound misrecognition of their personhood, of their specific mode of being.

Speech act theory holds that language is not *just*, as the structuralists would have it, an abstract system of negative differences; rather, language is always accomplished by and through particular *speech acts,* the intent of which is communicative. Speech is social. It necessarily involves specific speakers and audiences, and can never be entirely divorced from extralinguistic contexts. A performative is one type of speech act. In contrast to a constative speech act—which involves the transmission of information about a condition or state of affairs, with which its correspondence is demonstrably true or false (e.g., "The apple is red.")—a performative "constates" nothing. It is a form of utterance that does not describe or report, and thus cannot be true or false. It is, or is part of, the doing of the action itself. Examples of performative speech acts would include vowing ("I do."), marrying ("I now pronounce you man and wife."), or being bar mitzvahed ("Today I am a man."). To say that gender is a performative act is to say that it does not need a material referent to be meaningful, is directed at others in an attempt to communicate, is not subject to falsification or verification, and is accomplished by "doing" something rather than "being" something. A woman, performatively speaking, is one who says she is—and who then does what woman means. The biologically sexed body guarantees nothing; it is necessarily there, a ground for the act of speaking, but it has no deterministic relationship to performative gender.

To conceptualize gender as a performative act raises a larger question about social and political struggles. For Jean-Francois Lyotard, writing in *The Postmodern Condition: A Report on Knowledge*, all acts of communication are inscribed within the field of *agonistics* (from the Greek *agon*, "to joust"). Jousting may be play, or it may be combat, but it necessarily involves taking up positions relative to one another, as well as some form of exchange, and some rules of engagement. Speech acts, in this model, are the smallest agonistic units, and they take place within different types of "language games," each with its own particular rules of enunciation, each as different from one another as a game of poker is from a game of chess. [36] The model of the "language game," like the model of the performative speech act, is useful for understanding in a formal way what was at stake in the emergence of transgender studies in the 1990s.

Each language game has specific players, or "posts"—for example, a sender, an addressee, and a referent—each assigned a part according to the type of speech act taking place. The constative speech act, "The apple is red," for example, is uttered by a sender who assumes a position of knowing the information; an addressee receives the utterance and is in a position to give or withhold agreement to the utterance. The referent—that about which the utterance pertains (in this case, the apple)— is not, in this game, in a position to make statements about itself. A performative utterance plays by a different set of rules. It is "not subject to discussion or verification on the part of the addressee, who is immediately placed within the new context created by the utterance."[37] Provided, of course, that the speaker is authorized, through a variety of extralinguistic circumstances, to occupy the position of performative utterer. The "I do" of the marriage vow has no performative force unless the right person addresses it to the proper other. Who gets to say "I do" to whom is completely determined by social and political forces (and as such it is subject to change over time).

The emergence of transgender studies in the 1990s was one such moment of change, when sociopolitical activism, coupled with broad and seemingly unrelated shifts in material conditions, worked in concert to create the possibility of new performative utterances, unprecedented things to say, unexpected language games, and a heteroglossic outpouring of gender positions from which to speak. Previously, people who occupied transgender positions were compelled to be referents in the language games of other senders and addressees—they were the object of medical knowledge delivered to the asylum keeper, the subject of police reports presented to the judge; they were the dirty little outcasts of feminist and gay liberation discourses whose speakers clamored for the affections of the liberal state. The psychotherapist whispered of them into the surgeon's ear, while the lawyer nodded in approval. Only rarely did we speak to others on our own behalf—in the pages of infrequently published autobiographies, or from the shadows of the freak show tents. This is not to suggest that transgender people did not carry on lively exchanges among themselves; indeed, there is a vast body of transgender community-based critical and cultural work that is scarcely visible to the broader society. It is rather to acknowledge that few other than transgender people themselves, and their self-appointed minders, took part in these marginalized conversations.

Then something happened in the early 1990s, though it's hard to say exactly what that something was. Causality is always a fraught concept. A calendar started rolling over; a world order collapsed; a pandemic virus changed the way we thought about sexuality and identity and the public sphere; an existing word was invested with new meaning to mobilize a movement, and it all crashed together on a cultural landscape fractured by an epistemic rift. Amidst the wreckage, transgender people seized the moment to produce knowledge of transgender phenomena in a postmodern fashion. We fought our way into speaking positions, claimed our voice with a vengeance, said who we were, and erupted into discourse. Transgender studies is one record of the conversation that ensued.

(DE)SUBJUGATED KNOWLEDGES

A useful terminological distinction can be made between "the study of transgender phenomena" and "transgender studies" that neatly captures the rupture between modern and postmodern epistemic contexts for understanding transgender phenomena, the different types of language games that pertain to each context, and the different critical practices that characterize each project.[38] The "study of transgender phenomena," as noted below, is a long-standing, on-going project in cultures of European origin. Transgender studies, on the other hand, is the relatively new critical project that has taken shape in the past decade or so. It is intimately related to emergent "postmodern conditions" for the production of knowledge, and is as innovative methodologically as it is epistemologically.

Transgender studies considers the embodied experience of the speaking subject, who claims constative knowledge of the referent topic, to be a proper—indeed essential—component of the analysis of transgender phenomena; experiential knowledge is as legitimate as other, supposedly more "objective" forms of knowledge, and is in fact necessary for understanding the political dynamics of the situation being analyzed. This is not the same as claiming that subjective knowledge of "being transgender" is somehow more valuable than knowledge of transgender phenomena gained from a position of exteriority, but is rather an assertion that no voice in the dialog should have the privilege of masking the particularities and specificities of its own speaking position, through which it may claim a false universality or authority.

This critical attention to questions of embodiment and positionality aligns transgender studies with a growing body of interdisciplinary academic research in the humanities and social sciences. Transgender studies helps demonstrate the extent to which *soma,* the body as a culturally intelligible construct, and *techne,* the techniques in and through which bodies are transformed and positioned, are in fact inextricably interpenetrated. It helps correct an all-too-common critical failure to recognize "the body" not as one (already constituted) object of knowledge among others, but rather as the contingent ground of all our knowledge, and of all our knowing. By addressing how researchers often fail to appreciate the ways in which their own contingent knowledges and practices impact on the formation and transformation of the bodies of others, transgender studies makes a valuable contribution towards analyzing and interpreting the unique situation of embodied human consciousness.[39]

Methodologically, transgender studies exemplifies what Michel Foucault once called "the insurrection of subjugated knowledges." By "subjugated knowledges," Foucault meant two different types of knowledge. First, he meant "historical contents that have been masked or buried in functional coherences or formal systemizations." He elaborated:

> To put this in concrete terms, it was certainly not a semiology of life in the asylum or a sociology of delinquence that made an effective critique of the asylum or the prison possible; it was really the appearance of historical contents. Quite simply because historical contents alone allow us to see the dividing lines and confrontations and struggles that functional arrangements or systematic organizations are designed to mask. Subjugated knowledges are then blocks of historical knowledge that were present in the functional and systematic ensembles, but which were masked, and the critique was able to reveal their existence by using the tools of scholarship.

Transgender studies draws upon just this sort historical content—descriptive materials buried in ethnographies of non-European gender systems, the transcripts of legal proceedings hidden in some obscure publication of case law, or the files of psychiatric patients—which must be excavated from the archives with the traditional tools of scholarship, and recontextualized within current academic debates. Recovering this kind of knowledge, and knowing where to look in the first place, requires, in Foucault's words, "meticulous, precise, technical expertise." It is the technical ability of its practitioners to make use of these scholarly tools, and to be conversant in academic discourse, that makes "transgender studies" a part of academe, and not just part of a "transgender community"—though the field's relationship to that community is crucial for its intellectual vitality.

Foucault's other kind of "subjugated knowledge, " which speaks to the politics of community involvement, is also central to the methodology of transgender studies. What Foucault describes as "a whole series of knowledges that have been disqualified as nonconceptual knowledges, as insufficiently elaborated knowledges, naïve knowledges, hierarchically inferior knowledges, knowledges that are below the required level of erudition or scientificity," is precisely the kind of knowledge that transgender people, whether academically trained or not, have of their own embodied experience, and of their relationships to the discourses and institutions that act upon and through them. Such knowledge may be articulated from direct experience, or it may be witnessed and represented by others in an ethical fashion. In either case, Foucault contends, the reappearance "from below" of "these singular local knowledges," like the knowledge of the psychiatrized or the delinquent, which have been "left to lie fallow, or even kept at the margins," is absolutely essential to contemporary critical inquiry.

While it might at first seem paradoxical to yoke together in a single term two such seemingly disparate forms of knowledge—"the specialized domain of scholarship" and "the knowledges that have been disqualified by the hierarchies of erudition and science"—it is precisely this genealogical coupling that, for Foucault, gives discursive critique its essential vigor. Both erudite scholarship and delegitimated "knowing" recapture, for use in the present, a historical knowledge of particular structurations of power. One offers "a meticulous rediscovery of struggles," while the other preserves "the raw memory of fights." [40] Transgender studies, through desubjugating previously marginalized forms of knowledge about gendered subjectivity and sexed embodiment, promises just such a radical critical intervention.

RENARRATION

Foucault's vast philosophical-historical research project helps support the claim that attending to what we would now call transgender phenomena has been a preoccupation of Western culture since Greek and Roman antiquity. The regulation of homosexuality, hermaphroditism, gender inversion, and other forms of "social monstrosity" have figured prominently in the development of "regimes of normalization" whose latter-day descendents in the modern period remain decidedly active and robust. [41] Transgender studies renarrates this considerable intellectual heritage. It calls attention to "transgender effects," those deconstructive moments when foreground and background seem to flip and reverse, and the spectacle of an unexpected gender phenomena illuminates the production of gender normativity in a startling new way. In doing so, the field begins to tell new stories about things many of us thought we already knew.

Since at least the nineteenth century in Europe and the United States, transgender phenomena have taunted the social order in ways that have spurred the development of sexology, psychiatry, endocrinology, and other medical-scientific fields involved in social regulatory practices. The clinical bibliography specifically related to transgender phenomena runs to many thousands of publications, and continues to grow even now, but it can be traced back to figures like Richard von Krafft-Ebbing, the great Victorian taxonomist of social deviance. Early entries in this bibliography include Karl von Westphal, who wrote of "contrary sexual feelings" as well as Max Marcuse's "drive for sexual transformation," Magnus Hirschfeld's "sexual intermediaries," and Havelock Ellis's "eonists." By the time we get to Freud, his disciples, and his detractors in the early twentieth century, we are on familiar ground with contemporary concepts in psychology and psychiatry.[42] By the middle of the last century, a specialized medical literature on "gender dysphoria" coalesced around the work of Harry Benjamin and his colleagues Robert Stoller, Richard Green, and John Money, which culminated in 1980 in the legitimation of a newly-defined clinical entity, "gender identity disorder," as an official psychopathology recognized by the American Psychiatric Association.[43] Transgender studies is now in a position to treat this immense body of clinical work as its archive.

Parallel to the clinical archive is an immense, centuries-old ethnography, equally ripe for empirical research, that documents European perspectives on cultures encountered around the world through exploration, trade, conquest, and colonization. This literature, along with its explication within the social science disciplines, demonstrates a perpetual European fascination—and more than a little Eurocentric unease—with the many ways that relationships between bodily sex, subjective gender identity, social gender roles, sexual behaviors, and kinship status have been configured in different times and places.[44] The mysterious *mujerados* and *morphodites* who populate the earliest accounts of European exploitation of the America continents are not *simply* (or perhaps even actually) vanished or suppressed members of "third genders" eradicated by genocidal European practices; they are, just as importantly, categories of deviant personhood constructed by a European imaginary and invested with the magical power to condense and contain, and thereby delimit, a more systemic European failure to grasp a radical cultural otherness in its totality.[45] For half a millennium now, Eurocentric culture has been treated to a parade of gender exotics, culled from native cultures around the world: India *hijra*, Polynesian *mahu*, Thai *kathoey*, Brazilian *travesti*, Arabian *xanith*, Native American *berdache*—and on and on. "Transgenders," at home and abroad, are the latest specimens added to the menagerie.

The conflation of many types of gender variance into the single shorthand term "transgender," particularly when this collapse into a single genre of personhood crosses the boundaries that divide the West from the rest of the world, holds both peril and promise. It is far too easy to assimilate non-Western configurations of personhood into Western constructs of sexuality and gender, in a manner that recapitulates the power structures of colonialism. "Transgender" is, without a doubt, a category of First World origin that is currently being exported for Third World consumption. Recently, however, engagements between a "transgender theory" that circulates globally with Eurocentric privilege, and various non-European, colonized, and diasporic communities whose members configure gender in ways that are marginalized within Eurocentric contexts, have begun to produce entirely new genres of analysis. Such encounters mark the geo-spatial, discursive, and cultural boundaries of transgender studies, as that field has been developed within Anglophone America and Europe, but also point toward the field's untapped potential.[46]

In developing our criteria for inclusion in this reader, Stephen Whittle and I decided to highlight some important earlier works in scientific sexology and feminism, and then to focus on works in English that explicitly engage with the term "transgender" (whether positively or negatively). We offer key texts drawn the "queer gender" debates, work that highlights the recent attention to female-bodied masculinity, work that explores the formation of a sense of self as well as the "border wars" of gender identity politics, and work that explores ethics, morality, and embodiment. We resisted attempting an "around the world in eighty genders" global survey of gender-diverse practices and identities. This was done in part because we felt we could not do justice to the global scope of transgender phenomena, and in part because a number of such anthologies attempting precisely this already exist.[47] One unfortunate consequence of our decision was the exclusion of many important bodies of work done with a regional focus, such as Don Kulick's and Annick Prieur's studies of male-bodied gender diversity in Mexico City and Brazil, Mauro Cabral's intensely poetic interdisciplinary work in Argentina, and a great deal of work on Southeast Asian genders.[48] We concentrated instead on work that explores how "transgender" has circulated globally, and on how race, class, and location have complicated the dissemination of that term.

Even given our editorial choices, which admittedly limited the range of cultural and ethnic diversity of work included in this reader, we were struck by the overwhelming (and generally unmarked) whiteness of practitioners in the academic field of transgender studies. This is due, no doubt, to the many forms of discrimination that keep many people of color from working in the relatively privileged environment of academe, but also to the uneven distribution and reception of the term "transgender" across different racial, ethnic, linguistic, and socioeconomic communities. We both feel, however, that the analytical framework for understanding gender diversity that has emerged from transgender studies—valuable though it is—is impoverished by the relative lack of contributions from people of color, and is therefore ultimately inadequate for representing the complex interplay between race, ethnicity, and transgender phenomena. That discussion is one that we hope to see developed more productively and more extensively in the years ahead.

In conclusion, we simply note that transgender phenomena haunt the entire project of European culture. They are simultaneously everywhere and elsewhere. Their multiple and contradictory statuses of visibility and erasure, of presence and absence, are intimately related to the operations of social power that create norms, impart consequence to difference, and construct the space of a dominant culture. A transgender studies more attuned to differences of race, location and class, as well as to differences within gender, would provide a better view into the making of this world we all inhabit, and enable a powerful critical rereading of contemporary (post)modernity in all its complexity.

NOTES

1. Lesbian and Gay History Conference, Center for Lesbian and Gay Studies, Graduate School, City University of New York, October 6–7, 1995; videotape documentation in author's possession.
2. Trans Politics, Social Change, and Justice Conference, Center for Lesbian and Gay Studies, Graduate School, City University of New York, May 6–7, 2005.
3. *Screaming Queens: The Riot at Compton's Cafeteria*, Dir. Victor Silverman and Susan Stryker, USA, 2005.
4. On the general shift in attention to transgender sociocultural formations, see Myra J. Hird, "For a Sociology of Transsexualism," *Sociology* 36(3): 577–595. For a framework for understanding the movement of transgender people from the clinics to the street, see Gayle Rubin, "Thinking Sex: Notes for a Radical Theory of the Politics of Sexuality," in Carole S. Vance, ed., *Pleasure and Danger: Exploring Female Sexuality*, 267–319 (Boston: Routledge & Kegan Paul, 1984).
5. David Valentine. "'I know what I am': The Category 'Transgender' in the Construction of Contemporary U. S. American Conceptions of Gender and Sexuality." Ph.D. Dissertation, Anthropology Department, New York University, 2000.
6. Leslie Feinberg, *Transgender Liberation: A Movement Whose Time Has Come* (New York: World View Forum, 1992).
7. Andrew Matzner "Prince, Virginia Charles," *GLBTQ: An Encyclopedia of Gay, Lesbian, Bisexual, Transgender, and Queer Culture*, http://www.glbtq.com/social-sciences/prince_vc.html
8. Magnus Hirschfeld, *Transvestites: The Erotic Drive to Cross-Dress* (Buffalo: Prometheus Books, 1991; orig. pub. Berlin, 1910; trans. Michael A. Lombardi-Nash); Harry Benjamin, *The Transsexual Phenomenon* (New York: Julian Press, 1966).
9. Sandy Stone, "The 'Empire' Strikes Back: A Posttranssexual Manifesto," in *Body Guards: The Cultural Politics of Gender Ambiguity*, ed. Julia Epstein and Kristina Straub, 280–304 (New York: Routledge, 1991).
10. Janice Raymond, *The Transsexual Empire: The Making of the She-Male* (Boston: Beacon, 1979).
11. Nancy Jean Burkholder, "Michigan Women's Music Festival," *Transsisters: The Journal of Transsexual Feminism* 2 (Nov/Dec 1993): 4.
12. On the queer political milieu in which transgender activism emerged, see the Queer Nation special issue of *OUT/Look: National Lesbian and Gay Quarterly* 11 (Winter 1991).
13. Kate Bornstein, *Gender Outlaw: On Men, Women, and the Rest of Us.* (New York: Routledge, 1994).
14. Judith Butler, *Gender Trouble: Feminism and the Subversion of Identity*. New York: Routledge, 1990; Michel Foucault, *History of Sexuality, Vol. 1, An Introduction* (New York: Vintage Reprint, 1990; orig. English trans. pub. Random House, 1978).
15. Julia Epstein and Kristina Straub, *Body Guards: The Cultural Politics of Gender Ambiguity* (New York: Routledge, 1991).
16. Susan Stryker, "My Words to Victor Frankenstein Above the Village of Chamounix: Performing Transgender Rage," *GLQ: A Journal of Lesbian and Gay Studies* 1:3 (1994): 237–254.

17.   Thanks to Stephen Whittle for substantive contributions to my understanding of the activist roots of UK-based transgen-
      der studies; see Stephen Whittle, "*Trans-Links of Friendships, the Bedroom and Politics: 1970's Trans-Atlantic Influences
      on Current Transgender Politics in the UK*," Future of the Queer Past Conference, University of Chicago, 2000.

18.   Susan Stryker, "The Transgender Issue: An Introduction," *GLQ: A Journal of Lesbian and Gay Studies* 4:2 (1998): 145–158;
      Robin Wilson, "Transgender Scholars Defy Convention, Seeking to Be Seen and Heard in Academe," *Chronicle of Higher
      Education*, February 6, 1998: A10–A12.

19.   David Halperin, *Saint Foucault: Toward a Gay Hagiography* (New York: Oxford, 1996).

20.   No definitive text of Truth's 1851 speech is extant; see Carleton Mabee, *Sojourner Truth: Slave, Prophet, Legend* (New
      York: New York University Press, 1993).

21.   See Cressida J. Heyes, "Feminist Solidarity after Queer Theory: The Case of Transgender," *Signs: Journal of Women in
      Culture and Society*, 28 (2003), 1093–1120; and "Reading Transgender, Rethinking Women's Studies" *NWSA Journal*
      12:2 (Summer 2000): 170–180.

22.   On third terms and the disruption of binaries, see Marjorie Garber, *Vested Interests: Cross-Dressing and Cultural Anxiety*
      (New York: Routledge, 1992.)

23.   See, for example, Jordy Jones "Gender Without Genitals: Hedwig's Six Inches" *Other: the magazine for people who
      defy categories* 1:1 (2003) 44–46; George Mott, "The Vanishing Point Of The Sexual Subject: *The Closet, Hedwig And
      The Angry Inch, L.I.E., The Sixth Sense, The Others, Y Tu Mamá También, The Psychoanalytic Review*, 91:4 (August
      2004): 607–614.

24.   Felski, Rita. "Fin de siècle, Fin de sexe: Transsexuality, Postmodernism, and the Death of History," *New Literary History*
      27:2 (Spring 1996), 337–349.

25.   Donna Haraway, *Simians, Cyborgs and Women: The Reinvention of Nature* (New York: Routledge, 1991); Judith Hal-
      berstam and Ira Livingston, eds. *Posthuman Bodies*. (Bloomington: Indiana University Press, 1995).

26.   Fredric Jameson, *Postmodernism, or The Cultural Logic of Late Capitalism* (Chapel Hill: Duke University Press,
      1992).

27.   On the "commonsensical" relationship between gender and body, see the discussion of "the natural attitude" in Harold
      Garfinkel, "Passing and the Managed Achievement of Sex Status in an 'Intersexed' Person," in *Studies in Ethnomethodol-
      ogy* (Englewood Cliffs NJ: Prentice Hall, 1967), 116–185.

28.   On intersex issues, see Alice Domurat Dreger, Hermaphrodites *and the Medical Invention of Sex* (Cambridge: Harvard
      University Press, 1998); Anne Fausto-Sterling, *Sexing the Body: Gender Politics and the Construction of Sexuality* (New
      York: Basic Books, 2000); and Suzanne J. Kessler, *Lessons From the Intersexed* (New Brunswick, NJ: Rutgers University
      Press, 1998).

29.   For a range of feminist poststructuralist, antifoundationalist critiques of the sex/gender relationship, with particular
      reference to the question of postmodernity, see Judith Butler and Joan Scott, eds., *Feminists Theorize the Political* (New
      York: Routledge, 1992).

30.   Raymond, *Transsexual Empire*, offers the classic account of "bad transsexuals," but see also Dwight Billings and Thomas
      Urban, "The Socio-Medical Construction of Transsexualism: An Interpretation and Critique," *Social Problems* 29 (1981):
      266–282.

31.   *Boys Don't Cry*, directed by Kimberley Pierce, USA 1999.

32.   Tarryn Witten and A. Evan Eyler, "Hate Crimes and Violence Against the Transgendered," *Peace Review*, 11:3 (1999):
      461–468.

33.   Judith Butler, *Gender Trouble; Bodies That Matter: On the Discursive Limits of "Sex."* (New York: Routledge, 1993), and
      "Doing Justice to Someone: Sex Reassignment and Allegories of Transsexuality," *GLQ: A Journal of Lesbian and Gay
      Studies* 7:4 (2001): 621–636.

34.   J. L. Austin, *How to Do Things With Words*, ed. J. O. Urmson and Marina Sbisá (Cambridge:, MA Harvard University
      Press, 1962).

35.   See, for example, Jay Prosser's extended discussion of Butler *Second Skins: The Body Narratives of Transsexuality* (New
      York: Columbia University Press, 1998), or Henry Rubin's "Phenomenology as Method in Trans Studies." *GLQ: A Journal
      of Lesbian and Gay Studies* 4:2 (1998): 263–281.

36.   Jean-Francois Lyotard, *The Postmodern Condition: A Report on Knowledge* (Manchester: Manchester University Press,
      1984), p. 89 n25, n34.

37.   Lyotard, *Postmodern*, p. 9.

38.   A similar distinction is proposed between positivist approaches to "studying transsexuality" and "transgender studies"
      in Katrina Roen, "Constructing Transsexuality: Discursive Manoeuvres through Psycho-Medical, Transgender, and
      Queer Texts," Ph.D. thesis, University of Canterbury, New Zealand, 1998, p. 42.

39.   The concept was "Somatechnics" was formulated in conversation with Nikki Sullivan, Joseph Pugliese, and other
      members of the Department of Critical and Cultural Studies, Macquarie University; see http://www.ccs.mq.edu.au/
      somatechnics.

40.   Foucault, Michel Foucault, *Society Must Be Defended: Lectures at the College de France, 1975–76* (New York: Picador,
      2003), 7–8.

41.   Michel Foucault, *Abnormal* (New York: Picador, 2003), 1–29.

42.   For a useful summary, see Jay Prosser, "Transsexuals and the Transsexologists: Inversion and the Emergence of Trans-
      sexual Subjectivity," in *Sexology in Culture: Labeling Bodies and Desires*, ed. Lucy Bland and Laura Doan (Oxford: Polity
      Press, 1998), 116–132; see also Richard Green and John Money, eds., *Transsexualism and Sex Reassignment* (Baltimore:
      Johns Hopkins University Press, 1969).

43 *Diagnostic And Statistical Manual of Mental Disorders of the American Psychiatric Association III* (Washington, D.C.: American Psychiatric Publishers, 1980).

44. On Eurocentric unease with global queerness, see the various articles in Arnaldo Cruz-Malavé and Martin Manalansan, IV, eds., *Queer Globalizations: Citizenship and the Afterlife of Colonialism* (New York: New York University, 2002).

45. Will Roscoe, "Was We'wha a Homosexual?: Native American Survivance and the Two-Spirit Tradition." *GLQ: A Journal of Lesbian and Gay Studies* 2:3 (1995): 193–235;

46. Lynn Marie Morgan and Evan B. Towle "Romancing the Transgender Native: Rethinking the Use of the 'Third Gender' Concept" *GLQ: A Journal of Lesbian and Gay Studies* 8:4 (2002): 469–497; Helen Hok-Sze Leung, "Unsung Heroes: Reading Transgender Subjectivities in Hong Kong Action Cinema," in *Masculinities and Hong Kong Cinema*, eds. Laikwan Pang and Day Wong (Hong Kong: Hong Kong University Press, 2005), 81–98; Susan Stryker, "Transgender Studies: Queer Theory's Evil Twin," *GLQ: A Journal of Lesbian and Gay Studies* 10:2 (Spring, 2004), 212–215.

47. Evelyn Blackwood, and Saskia Wieringa, eds., *Female Desires: Same-sex Relations and Transgender Practices Across Cultures* (New York: Columbia University Press, 1999); Gilbert Herdt, ed., *Third Sex, Third Gender: Beyond Sexual Dimorphism in Culture and History* (New York: Zone Books, 1994); Sandra P. Ramet, ed., *Gender Reversals and Gender Cultures: Anthropological and Historical Perspectives* (New York: Routledge, 1996).

48. Don Kulick, *Travesti: Sex, Gender, and Culture among Brazilian Transgendered Prostitutes.* (Chicago: University of Chicago Press, 1998); Mark Johnson, *Beauty and Power: Transgendering and Cultural Transformation in the Southern Philippines* (Oxford: Berg, 1997); Annick Prieur, *Mema's House, Mexico City: On Transvestites, Queens, and Machos* (Chicago: University of Chicago Press, 1998).

I

SEX, GENDER, AND SCIENCE

1

selections from

Psychopathia Sexualis with Special Reference to Contrary Sexual Instinct
A Medico-Legal Study

RICHARD VON KRAFFT-EBING

RICHARD VON KRAFFT-EBING (1840–1902), Professor of Psychiatry at Vienna, was one of the first scientific investigators to take a special professional interest in the sexual impulses of individuals. His landmark study, *Psychopathia Sexualis*, has been in print in various revised editions ever since its first publication in 1877. The text undertakes a vast taxonomic project, attempting to distinguish and classify specific features of the various case studies Krafft-Ebing offers for consideration. Underlying this entire project is Krafft-Ebing's assumption that any departure from procreative heterosexual intercourse represents a form of emotional or physical disease.

Over the course of his career, Krafft-Ebing developed an increasingly complex system for categorizing what he considered to be psychosexual disorders—among them homosexuality. Unlike today, when homosexuality is most often considered to be an erotic or romantic attraction between two otherwise typical women, or between two otherwise typical men, Krafft-Ebbing considered homosexuality to be a form of gender variance. That is, he considered a man who loved a man to be more like a woman; conversely, he considered a woman who loved a woman to be more like a man. These deviations from standard gender could be relatively minor and inconsequential, or relatively major and significant.

Krafft-Ebing noted two primary categories of homosexuality—acquired and congenital—and considered each to contain transgender elements to which he applied ornate Victorian labels such as "eviration," "defemination," "viraginity," and "metamorphosis sexualis paranoica." This later term represented the most extreme, and therefore the most pathological, form of gender deviation in Krafft-Ebing's conceptual framework. It described individuals we would today call transsexuals: people who strongly identify themselves as proper members of the "opposite" sex, and who wish to physically alter the sex-signifying aspects of their bodies. Krafft-Ebing thought such individuals were profoundly disturbed, and considered their desire for self-affirming transformation to be psychotic.

The cases Krafft-Ebing presents are doubly interesting, in that they document the extensive discursive and historical interconnections between transgender and homosexual phenomena, but also demonstrate the remarkable persistence of highly specific forms of subjectivity that are readily identifiable in current terminology. Case 131, reprinted below, exemplified what Krafft-Ebing called "gynandry," and what we would probably call female-to-male transsexualism.

ANDROGYNY AND GYNANDRY

Forming direct transitions from the foregoing groups are those individuals of contrary sexuality in whom not only the character and all the feelings are in accord with the abnormal sexual instinct, but also the skeletal form, the features, voice, etc.; so that the individual approaches the opposite sex anthropologically, and in more than a psychical and psycho-sexual way. This anthropological form of the cerebral anomaly apparently represents a very high degree of degeneration; but that this variation is based on an entirely different ground than the teratological manifestation of hermaphroditism, in an anatomical sense, is clearly shown by the fact that thus far, in the domain of contrary sexuality, no transitions to hermaphroditic malformation of the genitals have been observed. The genitals of these persons always prove to be fully differentiated sexually, though not infrequently there are present anatomical signs of degeneration (epispadiasis, etc.), in the sense of arrests of development in organs that are otherwise well differentiated.

* * *

Case 131. *Gynandry.*[1] History: On November 4, 1889, the stepfather of a certain Count Sandor V. complained that the latter had swindled him out of 800f., under the pretense of requiring a bond as secretary of a stock company. It was ascertained that Sandor had entered into matrimonial contracts and escaped from the nuptials in the spring of 1889; and, more than this, that this ostensible Count Sandor was no man at all, but a woman in male attire,—Sarolta (Charlotte), Countess V.

S. was arrested, and, on account of deception and forgery of public documents, brought to examination. At the first hearing S. confessed that she was born on Sept. 6, 1866; that she was a female, Catholic, single, and worked as an authoress under the name of Count Sandor V.

From the autobiography of this man-woman I have gleaned the following remarkable facts that have been independently confirmed:—

S. comes of an ancient, noble, and highly-respected family of Hungary, in which there have been eccentricity and family peculiarities. A sister of the maternal grandmother was hysterical, a somnambulist, and lay seventeen years in bed, on account of fancied paralysis. A second great-aunt spent seven years in bed, on account of a fancied fatal illness, and at the same time gave balls. A third had the whim that a certain table in her *salon* was bewitched. If anything were laid on this table, she would become greatly excited and cry, "Bewitched! bewitched!" and run with the object into a room which she called the "Black Chamber," and the key of which she never let out of her hands. After the death of this lady, there were found in this chamber a number of shawls, ornaments, bank-notes, etc. A fourth great-aunt, during two years, did not leave her room, and neither washed herself nor combed her hair; then she again made her appearance. All these ladies were, nevertheless, intellectual, finely educated, and amiable.

S.'s mother was nervous, and could not bear the light of the moon.

From her father's family it is said she had a trace too much. One line of the family gave itself up almost entirely to spiritualism: Two blood-relations on the father's side shot themselves. The majority of her male relatives are unusually talented; the females are decidedly narrow and domestic. S.'s father had a high position, which, however, on account of his eccentricity and extravagance (he wasted over a million and a half), he lost.

Among many foolish things that her father encouraged in her was the fact that he brought her up as a boy, called her Sandor, allowed her to ride, drive, and hunt, admiring her muscular energy.

On the other hand, this foolish father allowed his second son to go about in female attire, and had him brought up as a girl. This farce ceased in his fifteenth year, when the son was sent to a higher school.

Sarolta-Sandor remained under her father's influence till her twelfth year, and then came under the care of her eccentric maternal grandmother, in Dresden, by whom, when the masculine play became too obvious, she was placed in an Institute, and made to wear female attire.

At thirteen she had a love-relation with an English girl, to whom she represented herself as a boy, and ran away with her.

Sarolta returned to her mother, who, however, could do nothing, and was compelled to allow her daughter to again become Sandor, wear male clothes, and, at least once a year, to fall in love with persons of her own sex.

At the same time, S. received a careful education, and made long journeys with her father,—of course, always as a young gentleman. She early became independent, and visited *cafés*, even those of doubtful character, and, indeed, boasted one day that in a brothel she had had a girl sitting on each knee. S. was often intoxicated, had a passion for masculine sports, and was a very skillful fencer.

She felt herself drawn particularly toward actresses, or others of similar position, and, if possible, toward those who were not very young. She asserts that she never had any inclination for a young man, and that she has felt, from year to year, an increasing dislike for young men.

"I preferred to go into the society of ladies with ugly, ill-favored men, so that none of them could put me in the shade. If I noticed that any of the men awakened the sympathies of the ladies, I felt jealous. I preferred ladies who were bright and pretty; I could not endure them if they were fat or much inclined toward men. It delighted me if the passion of a lady was disclosed under a poetic veil. All immodesty in a woman was disgusting to me. I had an indescribable aversion for female attire,—indeed, for everything feminine,—but only in as far as it concerned me; for, on the other hand, I was all enthusiasm for the beautiful sex."

During the last ten years S. had lived almost constantly away from her relatives, in the guise of a man. She had had many *liaisons* with ladies, traveled much, spent much, and made debts.

At the same time, she carried on literary work, and was a valued collaborator on two noted journals of the Capital.

Her passion for ladies was very changeable; constancy in love was entirely wanting.

Only once did such a *liaison* last three years. It was years before that S., at Castle G., made the acquaintance of Emma E., who was ten years older than herself. She fell in love with her, made a marriage-contract with her, and they lived together, as man and wife, for three years at the Capital.

A new love, which S. regarded as a fate, caused her to sever her matrimonial relations with E. The latter would not have it so. Only with the greatest sacrifice was S. able to purchase her freedom from E., who, it is reported, still looks upon herself as a divorced wife, and regards herself as the Countess V.! That S. also had the power to excite passion in other women is shown by the fact that when she (before her marriage with E.) had grown tired of a Miss D., after having spent thousands of guldens on her, she was threatened with shooting by D. if she should become untrue.

It was in the summer of 1887, while at a watering-place, that S. made the acquaintance of a distinguished official's family. Immediately she fell in love with the daughter, Marie, and her love was returned.

Her mother and cousin tried in vain to break up this affair. During the winter, the lovers corresponded zealously. In April, 1888, Count S. paid her a visit, and in May, 1889, attained her wish; in that Marie—who, in the meantime, had given up a position as teacher—became her bride in the presence of a friend of her lover, the ceremony being performed in an arbor, by a false priest, in Hungary. S., with her friend, forged the marriage-certificate. The pair lived happily, and, without the interference of the step-father, this false marriage, probably, would have lasted much longer. It is remarkable that, during the comparatively long existence of the relation, S. was able to deceive completely the family of her bride with regard to her true sex.

S. was a passionate smoker, and in all respects her tastes and passions were masculine. Her letters and even legal documents reached her under the address of "Count S." She often spoke of having to drill. From remarks of the father-in-law, it seems that S. (and she afterward confessed it) knew how to imitate a scrotum with handkerchiefs or gloves stuffed in the trousers. The father-in-law also, on one occasion, noticed something like an erected member on his future son-in-law (probably a priapus). She also occasionally remarked that she was obliged to wear a suspensory bandage while riding. The fact is, S. wore a bandage around the body, possibly as a means of retaining a priapus.

Though S. often had herself shaved *pro forma*, the servants in the hotel where she lived were convinced that she was a woman, because the chambermaids found traces of menstrual blood on her linen (which S. explained, however, as hæmorrhoidal); and, on the occasion of a bath which S. was accustomed to take, they claimed to have convinced themselves of her real sex by looking through the key-hole.

The family of Marie make it seem probable that she for a long time was deceived with regard to the true sex of her false bridegroom. The following passage in a letter from Marie to S., August 26, 1889, speaks in favor of the incredible simplicity and innocence of this unfortunate girl: "I don't like children any more, but if I had a little Bezerl or Patscherl by my Sandi,—ah, what happiness, Sandi mine!"

A large number of manuscripts allow conclusions to be drawn concerning S.'s mental individuality. The chirography possesses the character of firmness and certainty. The characters are genuinely masculine. The same peculiarities repeat themselves everywhere in their contents,—wild, unbridled passion; hatred and resistance to all that opposes the heart thirsting for love; poetical love, which is not marred by one ignoble blot; enthusiasm for the beautiful and noble; appreciation of science and the arts.

Her writings betray a wonderfully wide range of reading in classics of all languages, in citations from poets and prose writers of all lands. The evidence of those qualified to judge literary work shows that S.'s poetical and literary ability is by no means small. The letters and writings concerning the relation with Marie are psychologically worthy of notice.

S. speaks of the happiness there was for her when by M.'s side, and expresses boundless longing to see her beloved, if only for a moment. After such a happiness, she could have but one wish,—to exchange her cell for the grave. The bitterest thing was the knowledge that now Marie, too, hated her. Hot tears, enough to drown herself in, she had shed over her lost happiness. Whole quires of paper are given up to the apotheosis of this love, and reminiscences of the time of the first love and acquaintance.

S. complained of her heart, that would allow no reason to direct it; she expressed emotions which were such as only could be felt,—not simulated. Then, again, there were outbreaks of most silly passion, with the declaration that she could not live without Marie. "Thy dear, sweet voice; the voice whose tone perchance would raise me from the dead; that has been for me like the warm breath of Paradise! Thy presence alone were enough to alleviate my mental and moral anguish. It was a magnetic stream; it was a peculiar power your being exercised over mine, which I cannot quite define; and, therefore, I cling to that ever-true definition: I love you because I love you. In the night of sorrow I had but one star,—the star of Marie's love. That star has lost its light; now there remains but its shimmer,—the sweet, sad memory which even lights with its soft ray the deepening night of death,—a ray of hope."

This writing ends with the apostrophe: "Gentlemen, you learned in the law, psychologists and pathologists, do me justice! Love led me to take the step I took; all my deeds were conditioned by it. God put it in my heart.

"If He created me so, and not otherwise, am I then guilty; or is it the eternal, incomprehensible way of fate? I relied on God, that one day my emancipation would come; for my thought was only love itself, which is the foundation, the guiding principle, of His teaching and His kingdom.

"O God, Thou All-pitying, Almighty One! Thou seest my distress; Thou knowest how I suffer. Incline Thyself to me; extend Thy helping hand to me, deserted by all the world. Only God is just. How beautifully does Victor Hugo describe this in his 'Legendes du Siècle'! How sad do Mendelssohn's words sound to me: 'Nightly in dreams I see thee'!"

Though S. knew that none of her writings reached her lover, she did not grow tired writing of her pain and delight in love, in page after page of deification of Marie. And to induce one more pure flood of tears, on one still, clear summer evening, when the lake was aglow with the setting sun like molten gold, and the bells of St. Anna and Maria-Wörth, blending in harmonious melancholy, gave tidings of rest and peace, she wrote: "For that poor soul, for this poor heart that beat for thee till the last breath."

Personal Examination: The first meeting which the experts had with S. was, in a measure, a time of embarrassment to both sides; for them, because perhaps S.'s somewhat dazzling and forced masculine carriage impressed them; for her, because she thought she was to be marked with the stigma of moral insanity. She had a pleasant and intelligent face, which, in spite of a certain delicacy of features and diminutiveness of all its parts, gave a decidedly masculine impression, had it not been for the absence of a moustache. It was even difficult for the experts to realize that they were concerned with a woman, despite the fact of female attire and constant association; while, on the other hand, intercourse with the man Sandor was much more free, natural, and apparently correct. The culprit also felt this. She immediately became more open, more communicative, more free, as soon as she was treated like a man.

In spite of her inclination for the female sex, which had been present from her earliest years, she asserts that in her thirteenth year she first felt a trace of sexual feeling, which expressed itself in kisses, embraces, and caresses, with sensual pleasure, and this on the occasion of her elopement with the red-haired English girl from the Dresden Institute. At that time feminine forms exclusively appeared to her in dream-pictures, and ever since, in sensual dreams, she has felt herself in the situation of a man, and occasionally, also, at such times, experienced ejaculation.

She knows nothing of solitary or mutual onanism. Such a thing seemed very disgusting to her, and not conducive to manliness. She had, also, never allowed herself to be touched ad genitalia by others, because it would have revealed her great secret. The menses began at seventeen, but were always scanty, and without pain. It was plain to be seen that S. had a horror of speaking of menstruation; that it was a thing repugnant to her masculine consciousness and feeling. She recognized the abnormality of her sexual inclinations, but had no desire to have them changed, since in this perverse feeling she felt both well and happy. The idea of sexual intercourse with men disgusted her, and she also thought it would be impossible.

Her modesty was so great that she would prefer to sleep among men rather than among women. Thus, when it was necessary for her to answer the calls of nature or to change her linen, it was necessary for her to ask her companion in the cell to turn her face to the window, that she might not see her.

When occasionally S. came in contact with this companion,—a woman from the lower walks of life,—she experienced a sexual excitement that made her blush. Indeed, without being asked, S. related that she was overcome with actual fear when, in her cell, she was compelled to force herself into the unusual female attire. Her only comfort was, that she was at least allowed to keep a shirt. Remarkable, and what also speaks for the significance of olfactory sensations in her vita sexualis, is her statement that, on the occasions of Marie's absence, she had sought those places on which Marie's head was accustomed to repose, and smelled of them, in order to experience the delight of inhaling the odor of her hair. Among women, those who are beautiful, or voluptuous, or quite young do not particularly interest her. The physical charms of women she makes subordinate. As by magnetic attraction, she feels herself drawn to those between twenty-four and thirty. She found her sexual satisfaction exclusively in corpora feminæ (never in her own person), in the form of manustupration of the beloved woman, or cunnilingus. Occasionally she availed herself of a stocking stuffed with oakum as a *priapus*. These admissions were made only unwillingly by S., and with apparent shame; just as in her writings, immodesty or cynicism are never found.

She is religious, has a lively interest in all that is noble and beautiful,—men excepted,—and is very sensitive to the opinion others may entertain of her morality.

She deeply regrets that in her passion she made Marie unhappy, and regards her sexual feelings as perverse, and such a love of one woman for another, among normal individuals, as morally reprehensible. She has great literary talent and an extraordinary memory. Her only weakness is her great frivolity and her incapability to manage money and property reasonably. But she is conscious of this weakness, and does not care to talk about it.

She is 153 centimetres tall, of delicate skeleton, thin, but remarkably muscular on the breast and thighs. Her gait in female attire is awkward. Her movements are powerful, not unpleasing, though they are somewhat masculine, and lacking in grace. She greets one with a firm pressure of the hand. Her whole carriage is decided, firm, and somewhat self-conscious. Her glance is intelligent; mien somewhat diffident. Feet and hands remarkably small, having remained in an infantile stage of development. Extensor surfaces of the extremities remarkably well covered with hair, while there is not the slightest trace of beard, in spite of all shaving experiments. The hips do not correspond in any way with those of a female. Waist is wanting. The pelvis is so slim, and so little prominent, that a line drawn from the axilla to the corresponding knee is straight,—not curved inward by a waist, or outward by the pelvis. The skull is slightly oxycephalic, and in all its measurements falls below the average of the female skull by at least one centimetre.

The circumference of the head is 52 centimetres; the occipital half-circumference, 24 centimetres; the line from ear to ear, over the vertex, 23 centimetres; the anterior half-circumference, 28.5 centimetres; the line from glabella to occiput, 30 centimetres; the ear-chin line, 26.5 centimetres; long diameter, 17 centimetres; greatest lateral diameter, 13 centimetres; diameter at auditory meati, 12 centimetres; zygomatic diameter, 11.2 centimetres. The upper jaw projects strikingly, its alveolar process projecting beyond the under jaw about 0.5 centimetre. The position of the teeth is not fully normal; the right upper canine has not developed. Mouth remarkably small. Ears prominent; lobes not differentiated, passing over into the skin of the cheek. Hard palate narrow and high; voice rough and deep; mammæ fairly developed, soft, and without secretion. Mons veneris covered with thick, dark hair. Genitals completely feminine, without trace of hermaphroditic appearance, but at the stage of development of those of a ten-year-old girl. The labia majora touch each other almost completely; labia minora have a cock's-comb-like form, and project under the labia majora. The clitoris is small, and very sensitive. Frenulum delicate; perineum very narrow; introitus vaginæ narrow; mucous membrane normal. Hymen wanting (probably congenitally); likewise, the carunculæ myrtiformes. Vagina so narrow that the insertion of a membrum virile would be impossible, and it is also very sensitive; certainly coitus had not taken place. Uterus is felt, through the rectum, to be about the size of a walnut, immovable, and retroflected.

The pelvis appears generally narrowed (dwarf-pelvis), and of decidedly masculine type. The distance between anterior superior spines is 22.5 centimetres (instead of 26.3 centimetres). Distance between the crests of the ilii, 26.5 centimetres (instead of 29.3 centimetres); between the trochanters, 27.7 centimetres (31); the external conjugate diameter, 17.2 centimetres (19 to 20); therefore, presumably, the internal conjugate would be 7.7 centimetres (10.8). On account of narrowness of the pelvis, the direction of the thighs is not convergent, as in a woman, but straight.

The opinion given showed that in S. there was a congenitally abnormal inversion of the sexual instinct, which, indeed, expressed itself, anthropologically, in anomalies of development of the body, depending upon great hereditary taint; further, that the criminal acts of S. had their foundation in her abnormal and irresistible sexuality.

S.'s characteristic expressions—"God put love in my heart. If He created me so, and not otherwise, am I, then, guilty; or is it the eternal, incomprehensible way of fate?"—are really justified.

The court granted pardon. The "countess in male attire," as she was called in the newspapers, returned to her home, and again gave herself out as Count Sandor. Her only distress is her lost happiness with her beloved Marie.

A married woman, in Brandon, Wisconsin, whose case is reported by Dr. Kiernan (*The Medical Standard*, 1888, November and December), was more fortunate. She eloped, in 1883, with a young girl, married her, and lived with her as husband undisturbed.

An interesting "historical" example of androgyny is a case reported by Spitzka (*Chicago Medical Review*, August 20, 1881). It was that of Lord Cornbury, Governor of New York, who lived in the reign of Queen Anne. He was apparently affected with moral insanity; was terribly licentious, and, in spite of his high position, could not keep himself from going about in the streets in female attire, coquetting with all the allurements of a prostitute.

In a picture of him that has been preserved, his narrow brow, asymmetrical face, feminine features, and sensual mouth at once attract attention. It is certain that he never actually regarded himself as a woman.

NOTE

1. Comp. the expert medical opinion of this case, by Dr. Birnbacher, in Friedreich's Blätter f. ger. Med., 1891, H. 1.

2

selections from

The Transvestites

The Erotic Drive to Cross-Dress

Magnus Hirschfeld

As a young medical doctor in Germany, pioneering sexologist Magnus Hirschfeld, founded the world's first gay rights organization, the Scientific Humanitarian Committee, in 1897. In 1919 in Berlin, he opened the world's first Institute for Sexology and wrote the first comprehensive textbook of sexology, *Geschlechtskunde*, (*Sexual Knowledge*, 5 vols., 1926–1930). From 1930 until 1933 he traveled around the world, promoting the new science of sexology in public lectures in New York, San Francisco, Tokyo, China, and the Near East. In his absence, Adolf Hitler labeled Hirschfeld—a gay, Jewish, Socialist—"the most dangerous man in Germany," and in 1933 the Nazis destroyed Hirschfeld's Institute and publicly burned his research collection. Unable to return to Berlin, Hirschfeld died in exile in France in 1935.

Hirschfeld was an early advocate for transgender people, whom he considered, like homosexuals, to be one of innumerable types of "sexual intermediaries" who existed on a spectrum from a hypothetical "pure male" to "pure female." Hirschfeld considered the diversity of sex and gender to be part of nature, and thought that society and laws should reflect this biological reality. Transgender individuals worked on the staff of the Institute for Sexology, and doctors associated with the Institute performed the first documented genital transformation surgeries.

The following selection is from Hirschfeld's 1910 book *The Transvestites*, in which he argues that transgenderism is a complex phenomenon that cannot be reduced to homosexuality, fetishism, or some form of psychopathology. The arguments outlined by Hirschfeld were later echoed in the views of his younger colleague Harry Benjamin, the German-born doctor who became the leading advocate for transgender people in the mid-twentieth century.

TRANSVESTISM AND HOMOSEXUALITY

Instead of no law without exception one should rather say no exception without law.

How, in fact, are we to understand this peculiar urge to cross-dress, whose symptomatology we met in the preceding? Is it perhaps only a matter of a form of homosexuality? In front of us, do we have a phenomenon that belongs in the area of what Havelock Ellis calls autoeroticism, that Hermann Rohleder has described as auto-monosexualism, or related to narcissism, as Naecke maintains? Do we have here a special form of masochism? Does the condition fall within the heading clothing fetishism; does it touch upon delusion mania, a "retardation" of the judgment of the personality, which we in psychiatry call paranoia; or, rather, do we have here an independent complex before us, which cannot be ordered according to recognized models at this time? Examining differential diagnoses will be our task in the following.

Since similar urges to effeminacy and masculinity, as we observe them here, were described only in the case of contrary sexuality, we at first were inclined to assume that we again had homosexuality before us, perhaps unconscious. However, more accurate testing revealed that this was not the case, because the main marker of homosexuality, as its root word—*homos*, or "same"—indicates, is the direction of the sex drive toward persons of the same sex. We saw in most of our cases that there was not a trace of it; that, on the other hand, there was an even stronger antipathy than normally appears in other heterosexuals. To be sure, some of them had homosexual episodes, which is not unusual for heterosexuals, but they were so transient and superficial that truly inborn homosexuality—and only congenital homosexuality can be true—is not a question here.

Even if one could doubt some of the cases (such as 12 and 15), that there was present an urge, vacillating between the two sexes, therefore a bisexual urge, nevertheless, in the majority the direction of the drive toward the opposite sex is so sharply expressed that the reality of effemination and virility in heterosexual persons must be seen as proven.

So now, effemination and masculation step before us as distinct phenomena, which certainly often, but not always, appear related. One has to extend the sentence: "not all homosexuals are effeminate" to include "and not all effeminate men are homosexual." This conforms with the fifth of our laws, the law of geno-genetics (see Hirschfeld, "Transsexuals: Theses on the Development of the Differences Between the Sexes" ["Geschlechtsuebergaenge"], p. 18): "Each sexual character can divert, but still allows himself to establish a relation in the deviations which prove themselves in the same period of time." Whether effemination relatively often connects with homosexuality, which I at present still consider more probable than with heterosexuality, cannot be deduced at the present time because of the lack of exact statistics.

According to the experience I have had up until now, I have the impression that in 50 to 60 percent of homosexuals virile characteristics prevail. Bloch, too, has the same opinion (see *Sexualleben* [*Sexual Life*], p. 551). He writes, "According to my observations, it seems to me the ratio between virile and feminine Uranians is approximately equal."

Among this ca. 50 percent, the homosexuals with feminine tendencies, the feminine admixture is natural, including every kind and every intensity and, in fact hardly 10 percent of them have a more intensified urge to put on women's clothing. To the contrary, the great majority of homosexuals, and not only the more virile ones, find transvestism thoroughly unpleasant. Still fewer are the number of those homosexual men who live fully as a woman; of Uranian women, fully as a man. If this is the case, then, if observed from the outside, a very nearly equal image is offered by homosexual and heterosexual transvestism. Only there is the one great difference, that the sex drive of the one, namely, the transvestites, better matches the physical characteristics; the homosexuals, more the psychological complex.

*　*　*

TRANSVESTISM AND FETISHISM

(Explanation of Richard Wagner's Letters to Milliner)

If the question about the homosexual as well as the monosexual basic character of these cases is to be answered in the negative, then we now have the task of investigating what place inside of the heterosexual direction of the drive we must make available for this peculiar deviation from the norm. Two areas come into question here: fetishism and masochism. Observed purely from the outside, the intensive tendency to cross-dress strongly reminds one of clothing fetishism. Representatives of both these tendencies, as opposed to the great majority of their contemporaries of the same sex, seek to put themselves in possession of pieces of clothing that belong to that sex to which they physically do not belong. Specialists with whom I have consulted about our cases, therefore, at first always suspected a fetishistic basis to the drive to cross-dress. The transvestites themselves, who understandably carefully think through their rare condition, starting, naturally, with their inner feelings, are surely as dissatisfied with this explanation as with the tracing back of their feminine drive to homosexuality. Those, particularly whose basic education allowed them an unbiased judgment, felt they were incorrectly labeled fetishists. They said that their urge to cross-dress could more easily be understood as a kind of masochism, a form of sexual humiliation. I consider both assumptions to be in error. Neither fetishism nor masochism, in spite of many points of contact, fail to solve the problem, even as little as homosexuality and auto-monosexuality could.

Transvestites are essentially different from fetishists by the following: "The sexual interests of fetishists are concentrated without exception on a specific part of the body of the woman or also on specific pieces of women's clothing," according to Krafft-Ebing (*Psychopathia Sexualis*, p. 108). The strong erotic charm that a part or especially the material covering it exerts, for which I suggested using the expression "part-covering" ("Teilanziehung") in *Essence of Love* (see chap. 6, "On Part-Covering," pp. 134–284), or "partial attraction," is in this case the determining factor. An attraction to a "part," which extends to a woman from "top to toe," is a contradiction in itself, an impossibility. Furthermore, we also see in fetishists, but not in transvestites, that the object of their tendency in the first place is loved in itself in relation to a second person, in more pathological cases also detached from the latter (for example, a tuft of hair cut off, a stolen handkerchief), but in no way mainly loved as a part of them themselves.

The fetishist at times also takes the woman's shoe or slip to bed for the purpose of sexual stimulation. To bring himself as close to "the beloved" as possible, he in fact also wears the woman's underwear under his suit. He prefers to wear the latter's, while transvestites like to wear new underwear. However, in general, during the regular day fetishists in no way make use of the pieces of clothing in their favorite fetishistic form. On the contrary, the lovers of elegant shoes, fine patent-leather boots, often wear clumsy elastic-sided boots or even knee boots; fetishists for women's blonde hair do press it passionately against themselves but do not at all think about putting on a woman's wig, as little as a breast fetishist would stuff his chest. In short, fetishists lack the expressed urge to put on the form of the beloved object, to identify with it, as it were, to change themselves into it.

* * *

Clothing fetishism and transvestism have in common that in both cases, even if on the one hand the pieces of clothing are considered the form of expression of a mental condition in very different ways, they are to be looked upon as "a mirror of the spiritual essence" (Bloch, *Sexual Life*, p. 153), as "a measuring device for the special and the personal in an individual [Lukianos, "Eroticism and Clothing" ("Erotik und Kleidung") in *The Torch* (*Die Fackel*) by Karl Kraus (Vienna), No. 198, p. 12], as "an ideal nakedness" [Herman Bahr, "On Clothing Reform" ("Zur Reform der Tracht") in *Dokumente der Frauen*, vol. 6, no. 23 (1902), p. 665].

In *Essence of Love* (*Wesen der Liebe*), p. 153, I explained that I cannot agree with Krafft-Ebing and Binet that the preference for a certain fetish can be traced back to a casual experience during youth, an accidental event ("choc fortuit"), but rather that I assume that it touches upon a connection of ideas that depend upon the psychosexual characteristic of the fetishists to project their endogenous peculiarity into a concrete symbol. So, too, the existence of the corset fetish just mentioned cannot be laid before just any psyche but rather requires a certain sexual type that first must be heterosexual;

secondly, sadistic; and thirdly, have the tendency to be receptive to the connection of thoughts (the possibilities of which are too great to be dealt with here) that call forth the charm of the narrow waist. These processes of association in the mind, which often are intricately interwoven in the imagination, very often create difficult problems.

That is also valid for the special case I am now treating, especially to show that the differential diagnosis between fetishistic tendencies and transvestism is also not always so simple. I am supported in this by the *Letters of Richard Wagner to a Milliner* (*Briefe Richard Wagners an eine Putzmacherin*) published by Daniel Spitzer [the last unabridged version was published in 1906 in Vienna by Carl Konegan (E. Stuelpnagel) Publishing House], a book that attracted much attention when it was published.

It was unreasonable that Wagner's letters were reprinted by *The Vienna New Free Press* (*Wiener neue freie Presse*) in 1877, six years before his death. (The originals, from the years 1864–68, are now in the possession of the Society of the Friends of Music in Vienna.) It was especially unreasonable for Spitzer to publish them with the intent of "offering the public a farce" to show it a German man "who could not be measured against even the *parisienne* most fond of fashion." But at this time it appears to me, as a specialist, to be very reasonable to submit this noteworthy document to an unbiased psychological evaluation.

It makes a great deal of difference whether an embittered anti-Wagnerian provides these letters with malicious sarcastic comments "to criticize" the writer with having a so-called "more than womanly love of dress," or they serve under close examination as a contribution to psychology and to set right the conclusions that the mockers and ignorant have made. It is not right to infer a homosexual feeling in Wagner from his correspondence with the milliner, which, in our opinion, even Hanns Fuchs did not prove in his interesting book *Richard Wagner und die Homosexualitaet* [with the subtitle *With Especial Emphasis on the Sexual Anomalies of Its Forms* (*unter besonderer Beruecksichtigung der sexuellen Anomalien seiner Gestalten*), published by H. Barsdorf, Berlin, 1903]. Moreover, in this book there are no details about these letters.

But it is even more incorrect—something that unskilled followers of Wagner still do today—to be willing to explain the content of the letters as psychologically unimportant, because the master was supposed to have suffered from a skin disease. The very detailed manner of ordering, the depth, the value that is placed on the coordination of the colors, the exact description of how the articles are to be made, disprove this assertion, totally without regard to the fact that the satin did not at all touch the skin in most places, and, according to statements by skin specialists, would rather have had an adverse effect on any kind of skin disease.

* * *

What the publisher thought of the letters he put in the motto he placed above them, using the first act of *Die Walkuere:* "He looks like a woman." He repeats it at the end of his statements with the remark:

"I believe readers will find the motto justifiable after they have read these letters, the one that I chose: 'He looks like a woman!' Hunding, Siglinde's husband, calls this out to the Valkyries, after he has gauged the progress of his guest, Siegmund, and continues: 'The glistening worm is even gleaming out of his eyes.' When one reads this letter written to a milliner, when one sees how, in the same, the exclusive subject, the love of dress, is dealt with enthusiastically and with interest, and when one finds out the large sum that is wasted on the glistening satin, one has to believe one is not reading the signature of a man; it must be the letter of a woman."

We, too, are of the opinion that Wagner's particular inclination justifies assuming that there is a feminine characteristic in his psyche, which, however, in no way deserves mockery and scorn. To the contrary, for psychologists not arrested by the superfluous, it gives evidence of the unusually rich and subtle complexity of his inner life, the continued study of which would be a difficult as well as a rewarding task for any modern psychoanalyst.

This femininity is not identical with homosexuality, as Hans Fuchs seems to assume when he says (place cited, p. 271): "That Nietzsche clearly recognized the mental homosexuality of the aged Wagner shows in the words: 'because Wagner in his older days was thoroughly of the feminine kind.' This appears to be evident in the case we have discussed here monographically. The third letter especially points to Wagner's characteristics that up until now appeared enigmatic but are made understandable here. So, we find this otherwise artistically creative man writing verbatim: 'I have confirmed it a hundred times that my bright morning coat is especially good for the composition of scientific work, that another blue morning coat has a very stark effect on my style, that a street costume with a white ornamental apron, somewhat like a house-robe, immediately drives out oppressive fatigue and dullness and allows me to do my creative work like nothing else I know of.'"

In many cases, people depend very heavily on their clothing for their ability to be mentally creative. One often hears this particularly in the case of artists and of the educated. A short anecdote, which, when it was first published was found very ridiculous, has its comical side along with its psychologically interesting side.

"When one day Nebenius, a statesman of Baden, was called to the court of Grand Duke Leopold to write an urgent dispatch, he said: 'Yes, your Majesty, that will take a while; I have to have my pipe.' 'Well, you can have all the pipes you want,' the grand duke replied. 'Indeed, but I also have to have a pair of Turkish heelless slippers.' These, too, were produced. 'Indeed, but I also have to have a dressing-gown.' But that was the last straw for the grand duke, and he yelled, 'Thunder and lightening, so go home!'" [See Dr. R. Schulze, *Fashion Foolishness* (*Modenarrheiten*), Berlin 1868, p. 235.]

Moreover, Beethoven, too, was supposed to be able to compose only in his dressing-gown. And it is reported that Haydn was able to compose only when he was wearing "his finest toilette."

There is not the slightest bit of evidence of any kind of masochistic undercurrent in the allegations that so eloquently depict the intensification of activity effected by clothing. This statement is important for the relationship between transvestism and masochism, to which we will now turn our attention.

TRANSVESTISM AND MASOCHISM

In no way does one find masochistic characteristics in all transvestites, and if so, then only to a stronger or lesser degree. Indeed, in some cases one finds exactly the opposite, thus in Case 6, from whom the young ladies flee because he "tyrannizes them too much." And in the case of Number 8, who could only be gratified by acting out a rape and forcing kisses with his tongue. Especially to be considered is that which Krafft-Ebing convincingly made clear in his splendid "Essay on the Explanation of Masochism" ("Versuch einer Erklaerung des Masochismus"), that the latter in and of itself depicts a degeneration of a specifically feminine characteristic, while "sadism is to be looked upon as a pathological intensification of the masculine sexual characteristic in its psychical accessories."

In the case of our transvestites, almost all characteristics, which impress us at first as being masochistic, easily lead back to the wish for effemination. Thus the inclination toward being the succubus during the sex act, the desire to possess an energetic woman and to be attacked by her, finally, also the pleasure of the initially uncomfortable and painful attributes of femininity, such as the piercing of the earlobes, wearing tightly laced corsets, shoes into which the feet must be forced and whose heels seem to one "like mountains." Exactly in these cases, the physical discomfort is more than compensated for by the emotional comfort of feeling and performing what is feminine.

If there are only a few algophiles (lovers of pain) among transvestites, then, on the other hand, it appears one does find among the truly extensive community of masochistic men that the drive to clothe oneself as a woman is present only very, very rarely.

Professional Berlin "maitressen"—the word used here in its derivative from "maître" in the sense of mistress—who service a large masochistic clientele, when questioned, told me that among their customers, the ones who want to play the woman's role are relatively rare. I could find out only about two of them, who, before they go to see their "domina" (mistress), send a box of women's clothing in advance so that they can dress as a woman before their punishment. These may well be cases that, as our policeman (Number 8) who also frequented masseuses, belong to the true transvestites who incidentally have masochistic tendencies.

* * *

More often than not, masochists use pieces of women's clothing. They tie on a pinafore or put on a petticoat. The piece most in use is the corset and the girdle, which, however, obviously have the task of being tools of torture rather than representing feminine symbols. In the literature on masochism I also find no analogies to our cases. Maerzbach (place cited, p. 116 and following), who devoted a splendid chapter to this phenomenon, alleges that, among the metamorphic forms of masochism, only persons such as servants, pupils, children, slaves, and animals (for example, dogs) wish to be so treated, not, however, as women, not to mention the fact that they really do wish to come forth in womanly form.

According to all of this we can consider masochism as only an incidental and attendant phenomenon, and in no way as the original motive of the drive to cross-dress, just as little as transvestism is a form of masochism. There are also women who possess both masochistic and sadistic tendencies, as well as ones who possess none of these. The necessary changes having been made, all of this is in reference to women who come forth as men. In this case, too, menlike women and sadism in no way coincide.

TRANSVESTISM AND THE ILLUSION OF SEXUAL METAMORPHOSIS

No matter how much transvestite men feel like women when dressed in women's clothing and women feel like men when dressed in men's clothing, they still remain aware that in reality it is not so. To be sure, some do imagine—and if so, then the wish is the originator of the thought—that their skin is softer, their forms rounder, and their movements more gracious than are usual for men, but they know full well, and often are depressed by the fact that they do not physically belong to the desired sex they love. If they did consider themselves actually to be women, whether cross-dressed or not, as persons with megalomania think they are the Messiah or millionaires or even the emperor and pope in one person, then it would be an illusory idea, and the condition would have to be addressed as mental illness, as being insane, as paranoia. Such cases of the illusion of sexual metamorphosis—*metamorphosis sexualis paranoica*—also do occur, even if only rarely in relation to other delusions.

* * *

In the case of most of these congenitally most strongly predisposed patients, a genuine drive to cross-dress is rare. Typical is that they feel that their genitals have changed into those of a woman. They imagine that they are growing women's breasts, that they have long pigtails, that their clothing is women's when in fact they are men's. Most of this is confirmed by voices they hear saying, "He's a whore," or, when they are on the street, they will hear someone say, "Just look at that old hag." They also dream that they are a woman during coitus. One reported that that "was natural" for him.

* * *

CLOTHING AS A FORM OF EXPRESSION OF MENTAL CONDITIONS

The external appearance, which we have to follow inward in our cases, is the cross-dressing of a male into a female, of a female into a male. At this point we meet with an important factor that differentiates this anomaly from many others in the area of sexuality. The divergent drive extends not only to a particular quality of the partner, the sex object, but much more to the sex subject, precisely the appearance of one's own personality that is wished for. And this certainly does not have to be only in the outer clothing, but rather also in the underclothing, as well as in all of the other accessories of the costumes, including headdress, that are like the other sex and, as much as possible, the use of commodities and customs as they are befitting to them.

Already at the beginning of the analytical part of this work I made short references to Thomas Carlyle, Robert Sommer, and Fritz Rumpf that here we are not to consider clothing as something arbitrary and capricious, as lifeless fabric, but rather as conspicuous, intentional indications of an inner striving. This is valid not only in these special cases, but rather in general, and to a much greater extent than is usually believed.

* * *

In our case, with regards to clothing, the most important point in life after birth that indicates we have reached adulthood is the receiving of long trousers in the case of the boys and long dresses in the case of the girls. The clothing that differentiates sex is put on them much earlier, often as early as the third birthday. Some time ago there was a story in the newspaper told by a child, which gives some food for thought about this problem. A country minister on a walk discovered a five-year-old boy bathing in a brook with some small girls. After he was scolded, what did the candid toddler reply? "I did not know, sir, that they were girls. They did not have any clothes on."

* * *

When we—to use an example nearest at hand—heard of children whose naive instinct made them rebel when someone first tried to get them to wear trousers, then there can be no doubt, according to our explanations, that these are already manifestations of femininity that resist the male attire, which is against their psyche, something they feel does not suit them, something strange and to be resisted. We saw how in all of our cases this antipathy against being clothed as a male, and conversely the sympathy for the female cross-dressing of the individual personality, increased much more at the time of sexual maturity and then more and more resolutely struggled to be transformed into action.

If we imagine to ourselves once more the total complex of transvestite tendencies and then ponder to what extent we recognized the essence of the clothing as symbol, as unconscious projection of the soul, then it might become clear that in the psyche of these men there is present a feminine admixture—and in the feminine counterpart a masculine one—which presses on to project itself. This alterosexual quota truly must be considerable since, as we discovered, it wants to withstand and does withstand very great resistance and inhibitions, not the least of which is the contrast between body and soul. To just what degree a dissipation/laxity and division is present in the bisexual personality is expressed best by our Case 3. He speaks about "the flitting about of feminine elements in my ego." He describes "the mania for women's clothing, to look absolutely like a woman on the outside as the desire of his feminine side for corresponding forms." He continues, "Then, when I throw off all that is the man and put on the woman externally, I can almost physically feel how the false, the violence, leaves me and disappears like fog."

In these statements is mirrored, even if not in medical terms, a truly clear and thoroughly correct image of the essence of the symptom as a freeing of the femininity usually bound in the man. We have before us here a special form of the mental double-sexuality (*Doppelgeschlechtlichkeit*), a phenomenon which represents an independent type in the series not only of the etiological but also of the character study-related admixture of male and female characteristics, as we have many times already become acquainted with them under the general name of the sexual intermediate stages in the areas of morphology and psychology. Since this "Theory of Intermediate Stages," whose drawing up and working through I consider a valuable product of modern biology and psychology, still meets with gross misunderstanding and misinterpretation, please allow me to explain it once more.

THE THEORY OF INTERMEDIARIES

First let us stress that in the case of the precept of sexual intermediaries, it is not a matter of a theory at all but rather only a principle of division.

By sexual intermediaries we understand manly formed women and womanly formed men at every possible stage, or, in other words, men with womanly characteristics and women with manly ones.

Therefore, if a woman has a full beard or a man has milk-producing teats, we register such people, who exhibit such obvious characteristics of the other sex, as mixed sexual formations or intermediaries. But we do not handle only such obvious cases but rather also each and every other one—and their number is not limited—ones who stand, in the physical or mental view, between a complete manly man and, in every respect, a womanly woman.

The hypothesis of this principle of division is, according to this, an exact explanation of what is manly and womanly, and herein lies the main difficulty and controversy, particularly because there are, besides pure manly and womanly characteristics, such that are neither manly nor womanly, or more correctly stated, not only manly, but also womanly. However, that these latter ones do not depend on full equality of the sexes goes without question; the sexes may be equivalent and have equal rights, but they are no doubt not of the same kind. What, then, is womanly, what is manly?

* * *

However, if we turn from the realm of the microscopic back to the macroscopic, from the many similar but in no way complete observations made by the cell researchers back to the considerations, as they must be concluded from facts available to everyone, then we, to make the rest simple, summarize what has preceded by separating the difference of the sexes into four clear groups that can be defined one from the other; they concern, as we see:

1. the sexual organs,
2. the other physical characteristics,
3. the sex drive,
4. the other emotional characteristics.

Accordingly, a complete womanly and "absolute" woman would be such a one who not only produces egg cells but also corresponds to the womanly type in every other respect; an "absolute" man would be such a one who forms semen cells yet also, at the same time, exhibits the manly average type in all other points. These kinds of absolute representatives of their sex are, however, first of all only abstractions, invented extremes; in reality they have not as yet been observed, but rather we have been able to prove that in every man, even if only to a small degree, there is his origin from the woman, in every woman the corresponding remains of manly origins.

However, if we ourselves assume that people existed who, to put a number on it, were 100 percent manly or possessed a likewise high womanly content, it still remains out of the question—and here too we find ourselves still in the area of simple facts of experience—that very many persons exist who, in spite of their carrying egg cells, exhibit characteristics that in general belong to the male sex, and that, on the other hand, there are people who secrete semen cells yet at the same time have observable womanly characteristics. Since in our use of language we usually describe the bearers of semen cells simply as men, the possessors of egg cells flatly as women, there are, therefore, women with manly, men with womanly characteristics, and these mixed forms are the ones that are understood under the expression "sexual intermediaries." We can order them most clearly as the sexual differences themselves, according to the four viewpoints we presented.

In the first group of the intermediaries, accordingly, belong such ones who lie in the area of the sexual organs, the hermaphrodites in a narrower sense, the so-called "pseudo-hermaphrodites," men who because of womanly split formations of the genitalia, women who because of an intensified growth of these organs, often give enough cause to be mistakenly identified regarding their sex at birth.

* * *

The second heading of the sexual intermediaries concerns the physical characteristics outside of the sexual organs. In this case we find men with womanly mammary tissue (*gynecomastia*) and women without such (*andromastia*; also the word *A-mazon* means without breasts); women with manly hair, such as manly beard or manly pubes (*feminae barbatae, androtrichia*) and men with womanly hair type, such as womanly pubes, beardlessness, etc. Women with manly larynx and organ (*androglottia*) and men with womanly formed vocal chords and womanly voice production (*gynecoglottia*), men with womanly pelvis (*gynophysia*) and women with manly pelvis (*androphysia*).

* * *

Under the second heading we also find men with womanly bone and muscular structure and women with manly skeleton and manly muscular systems, of manly size and figure, men with womanly, women with manly movements.

* * *

Under the same heading we find men with the soft complexion of women, and women with the coarser skin of men; women who have to wear men's and men who have to wear women's glove and shoe sizes: in short, no matter what part of the body we were to treat, in almost every case we can always perceive manly profiles in women, womanly profiles in men.

Under the third heading of sexual intermediaries, persons divergent with regard to their sexual drive, we classify men who engage in sex with a woman as a woman, for example, having the tendency of being the succubus, who love aggressive women as well as participation in forms of masochism.

Since physical and emotional sexual passivity, which we call masochism according to Krafft-Ebing, as this author has correctly stressed, is a "degeneration of specifically feminine and psychical characteristics," then its appearance in men is no doubt a strong feminine characteristic that, according to my experience, moreover, is often accompanied by other marks of femininity. Since, on the other hand, sadism—to use Krafft-Ebing's words—"represents a pathological intensification of manly, psychic sexual character," then sadistically inclined women are manly women. According to this we count masochistic men and sadistic women, who belong in the domain of sexual intermediaries, while, it is our opinion, sadistic men and masochistic women are solely abuses of instincts that are rooted in the sex drive corresponding to the sex of the persons in question.

Under the third heading, the corresponding condition for women, are ones who tend toward being the incubus, being sexually very aggressive (apart from prostitutes, whose actions naturally have other causes) as well as ones who exhibit sadistic impulses. With reference to the direction of the sex drive, in the case of men it indicates femininity when they feel attracted to women of manly appearance and character, to so-called "energetic women," sometimes even to homosexuals, also to manly clothed as well as to such ones who are considerably more mature, intellectual, and older than they themselves. On the other hand, women betray their manly mixture in a preference for the womanly kind of men, very dependent, very youthful, unusually gentle men, in general for such ones who in their traits of behavior and character correspond more to the feminine type. Juvenal, even (*Satire* 6) and Martial (6, 67) report about women who can only love "shy eunuchs with beardless faces."

Finally, belonging also to this category of intermediaries are women who not only love womanly kind of men, but also manly kind of women (bisexuals) or also only the latter alone, or even totally in like manner as "true" men, women of the thoroughly womanly type (homosexuals). The opposite of this subdivision are men who, besides women of the manly kind, also love men of the feminine kind (bisexuals) or only these or even totally like women, more or less men who strongly express the manly type (homosexuals).

In Group Four, in which we understand the emotional particularities in direct relation with the love life, ones to be counted as sexual intermediaries, are men whose feminine emotions and feelings are reflected in their manner of love, their direction of taste, their gestures and manners, their sensitivity, and many times in their particular way of writing, also men who more or less dress themselves as women or live totally as such; on the other side women of manly character, manly ways of thinking and writing, strong tendency toward manly passions, manly dress, naturally so such women who more or less lead the life of a man. Therefore, in this case also are our transvestites to be included.

* * *

All of these other sexual characteristics can be present in very different degrees. This basically depends on one's age. Sexual characteristics appear most markedly between the ages of 20 and 50. As is known, after maturity, boys often exhibit feminine features as young men, girls boyish ones as young women. And later too, after the period of the fifth decade, matrons after change of life often assume superficial virile stigmata, while old men frequently take on many kinds of feminine features.

Above all, however, even at the prime of life itself, this mixing appears in varying degrees.

* * *

If we want to represent these numbers of the mixtures of manly and womanly substances in a different way also, we can use the one-hundred-percent sexual type as a point of departure. Therefore, the manly admixture in a woman, who is only a little different from the absolute womanly type, can be numbered from one to ten percent, but it could be significantly more, perhaps twenty-five percent. Finally, there could be an equal amount of womanly and manly features present; indeed, it could even be with a bearer of the female ovary, also, a woman whose numerous manly features had been represented as womanly ones, and little by little we come to the point where, except for the sexual organs, the sexual characters of the three remaining groups, the sexual orientation as well as the physical and psychical phenomena in general, are manly in kind. This type borders close to the absolute "one hundred percent" man, in whose case, then, the fourth group, the sexual organs, are male. And then the same repeats itself. It might be only a trace of femininity mixed in the man, or the feminine qualities might equal the masculine or even surpass them, in spite of the fact that it is a matter of a bearer of male germ cells, meaning a man, and so it continues until we gradually come to a point where Groups Two, Three, and Four are eventually totally feminine; only Group One is still masculine or, where possible, this too can even approximate the feminine type.

All of these sexual varieties form a complete closed circle in whose periphery the above-mentioned types of intermediaries represent only the especially remarkable points, between which, however, there are no empty points present but rather unbroken connecting lines. The number of actual and imaginable sexual varieties is almost unending; in each person there is a different mixture of manly and womanly substances, and as we cannot find two leaves alike on a tree, then it is highly unlikely that we will find two humans whose manly and womanly characteristics exactly match in kind and number.

* * *

Even if there is an internal or external influencing, inhibiting, and encouraging will, access to education, practice, and suggestion—and of course even control has its boundaries—sexual individuality as such with respect to body and mind is inborn, dependent upon the inherited mixture of manly and womanly substances, independent of externals; it is formed in advance by nature and is dormant in the individual long before it is awakened, forces its way into awareness, and develops. It is particularly subject to temporary, even periodic changes; develops consequently nevertheless, gradually increases; maintains itself at a certain level, then returns again, but maintains the same characteristic impressions in all essentials for the entire lifetime.

After this general observation of the sexual mixed forms, if we return to the main subject of our work, the erotic drive to cross-dress, it will then become clearer to us in many respects and less of a rare phenomenon. The important conclusions put in order not only its place as a natural phenomenon, but also its etiology, prognosis, and therapy. We have indicated that it belongs to Group Four of the intermediaries; with respect to the three first groups of the sexual differences, the sex organs, the remaining physical characteristics, and the sex drive, these men exhibit no or only insignificant deviations from the norm, unessential in any case in comparison to the remaining psychosexual characteristics, the urge to dress as a woman and the desire to live as a woman as much as possible.

As we have seen, since in this case it is a matter of a form of the intermediaries, which clearly brings into relief what has thus far been described, it appears fitting, too, to give the new form a new name, a special scientific stamp. The term I use to characterize the most obvious internal and external images of the persons concerned, their feelings and thoughts, their drive to put on the clothing of the opposite sex, is taken from the Latin "trans" = across and "vestitus" = dressed, used also by the Roman classical writers as "transvestism." Both men and women are termed "transvestites." One disadvantage of the term is that it describes only the external side, while the internal is limitless. Some of the transvestites themselves have formed expressions that are quite noteworthy as expressions of their feelings. One of them (Case 2) called his drive "puellism" (from Latin *puella*, girl); another (Case 11), in the paragraph in which he tried to explain to his wife about men who appeared or wanted to appear as women, but on the other hand who were sexually attracted to men, called them "junoren." Both words for several reasons are not fitting. They would describe the drive in one sex only, namely, the male sex, are not capable of being changed, and could cause misunderstandings.

If one wanted to stress the condition that it is not simply a matter of cross-dressing, but rather more of a sexual drive to change, then the word "metamorphosis" would be better. One could call the persons sexual metamorphotics, the drive sexual-metamorphotic, and the phenomenon sexual metamorphism, the preference of cross-dressing as sexual metamorphosis. Apart from the ungainly expression, I would be against it because Krafft-Ebing already has designated the mania of sexual metamorphosis as metamorphosis sexualis paranoica, which, as discussed above, we had to differentiate sharply from the drive of sexual metamorphosis.

Sex researchers repeatedly use the practice, and in my opinion not a very happy one, of naming sexual anomalies after persons who have become famous by them because they had especially strong tendencies toward them. Some such words are sadism, masochism, narcissism, retifism, and onanism, after the biblical Onan. The corresponding "fame" is lacking among heterosexual transvestites. Perhaps the acumen of my readers will produce an expression that would better hit upon the core of the phenomenon than the provisional one, which, I imagine, will not be universally satisfactory.

There is little more to add about the cause of the drive to cross-dress, as can be said about the etiology of the sexual intermediaries in general. Why the womanly admixture is produced in one case that a hermaphrodite arises (example of the first group), in a second gynecomastia (example of the second group), in a third case an Urning (example of the third group), in a fourth a transvestite (example of the fourth group) we can up to the present not tell.

I already have explained in detail the diagnosis and differential diagnosis of transvestism in the discussion of related phenomena; as to the prognosis, I do not think it is probable that the transvestite drive can be made to disappear, according to the total character of this and related mixed forms, but we do not have sufficient experience to render a final opinion; one can definitely get at the drive itself by means of psychotherapy, by applying Freudian psychoanalysis, and by suggestion. Besides this, one would recommend, as with all analogous anomalies, a general treatment of the central nervous system, which has as its focus a strengthening of the will as well as an exact regulation of the lifestyle, which aims at a possible deviation of mental activity.

With all of this, if one does not come to the desired goal, then the most important thing is the decision whether or to what extent it is advisable to yield to the drive now and then. We saw in several examples how exceptionally comfortable and how advantageous transvestites felt their drive was to them when this at times occurred. In their descriptions, one instinctively recalls the sentence of Eduard von Hartmann in his philosophy of the subconscious, that the nongratification of a drive is a great wrong for the individual in question, rather than a moderate satisfaction. If one gives it more thought, that it basically is a harmless inclination by which no one is injured, then, from a purely medical standpoint, nothing can be said against the actual putting on of the clothing of the opposite sex; another question of a forensic nature is what would cause public disturbance and acting under false pretenses; these questions will be treated in the next chapter, where we discuss the position of transvestism in public.

At this time I would like to touch upon one other point, namely, whether these persons appear fitting to enter into marriage. As we discovered, many are married, most even happily. Only in one case (11) was the marriage a truly unhappy one because of the transvestite drive. Of course, in this case the wife was psychopathic, suffered persecution mania, delusions, and for a long time was institutionalized. It is unconditionally advised that a transvestite disclose everything to the spouse. One cannot assume that the unprepared spouse will be so accepting. I was surprised that many wives found no difficulty even traveling with their husbands dressed in women's clothing, or even sitting evenings at the family table, both spouses in women's clothing.

But even if the wife is accepting of her husband's preference, I still have my doubts as to the suitability of these marriages; it cannot be argued that transvestism belongs to the sexual intermediaries in whose case the outer appearance of the opposite sex is exceptionally considerable. In cases of lesser features, for example, no more than 33 1/3 percent then there can easily be a balance between the married couple, so that the descendants would not be endangered by a hereditary burden. Or the other hand, where the sexual gap of the personality is such a great one, as in our cases, there is such a deviation from the pure sex type that the deviation, even if it should not itself be considered a degeneration can lead to offspring who are psychologically disunified and frivolous who are unstable, degenerated individuals. Of course, I cannot produce any proof of this very theoretical supposition; on the contrary, the children of the transvestites whom I saw gave me the impression of being good and healthy. But the material available at this time is insufficient to dispel expressed fears.

Raising children today demands one to have nerves of steel. Transvestites who want to raise children must be physically healthy and strong as well as mentally well-developed persons. They must be careful with their choice of marriage partners because of the children. Moreover, I would be against transvestite women marrying. They are mostly very restless spirits, inclined toward adventure, and find it difficult to chain themselves to domestic duties. In fact, most suitable would be—which is in accordance with the wishes of these persons—a transvestite man and a somewhat manly kind of woman, who naturally need not be a transvestite, or a transvestite woman to a womanly man, so that, to quote Schopenhauer [in *The World as Will and Idea* in the chapter "Metaphysics of Sexual Love" (*Die Welt als Wille und Vorstellung*: "Metaphysik der Geschlechtsliebe")]: "The degree of his manliness corresponds to the degree of her womanliness"; to be sure, it would be more correct to say in our case the degree of her manliness to the degree of his womanliness.

3

Psychopathia Transexualis

DAVID O. CAULDWELL

DAVID CAULDWELL WAS A GENERAL MEDICAL PRACTITIONER who developed a substantial alternative career as a writer of populist "family" advice columns for the tabloid news media (including the journal *Sexology* from which this article is taken), which catered to the more prurient interests in life. Cauldwell's columns covered a wide array of health topics, but frequently returned to the themes of transvestic cross-dressing and gender-variant lives, and he clearly had a great wealth of background material from which to make his conclusions.

"Psychopathia Transexualis" is of interest on several levels. First, Cauldwell concludes that transsexualism is a genetically inherited predisposition, which, combined with a dysfunctional childhood, results in mental immaturity. This genetic influence has rarely been noted since in the psycho-scientific literature. The emphasis on dysfunctional nurturing, however, reflects the earlier work of Krafft-Ebing, Hirschfeld, and English sexologist Havelock Ellis, and anticipates the work of transsexualism experts Robert Stoller, Richard Green, John Money, and Leslie Lothstein. Second, the article is often referred to as the piece that first used the term "transexual" [sic], which became the primary descriptor to this day of those people seeking to access gender reassignment therapies. Hirschfeld, however, had previously used the term *seelischer Transsexualismus*, or "psychic transsexualism." Finally, the use by Cauldwell of a female-to-male case study calls attention to a historical shift in medical attention to transgender phenomena. Prior to the spectacular publicity given to male-to-female transsexual Christine Jorgensen in 1952, most medical and media attention was focused on female-to-male individuals—the post-Jorgensen pattern of paying greater attention to MTFs did not begin to change until the 1990s.

"Psychopathia Transexualis" is a very problematic article despite its frequent citation. It is an interesting, though excessively pathologizing, anecdotal account of Cauldwell's experience with one transsexual person. It is riddled with contradictions, such as labeling transsexualism psychopathic, while admitting there are many well-adjusted transsexual people. Interestingly, Cauldwell foresees a time when social education will resolve dysfunctional families, and effective rehabilitation will cure the remainder of those presenting with the problem. He would undoubtedly be disappointed to see that his forecast was completely wrong, and that transsexual people have become a common feature of modern societies.

One of the most unusual sexual deviations is Psychopathia Transexualis—*a pathologic-morbid desire to be a full member of the opposite sex. This desire is so powerful that the individual insists on—often impossible—elaborate surgery that would turn him into a complete woman, or her into a biologically perfect male. Our distinguished author gives us a most interesting case review under his personal observation. The condition, incidentally, is not at all rare. Thousands of cases exist.*

—Editor [of Sexology]

Among both sexes are individuals who wish to be members of the sex to which they do not properly belong. Their condition usually arises from a poor hereditary background and a highly unfavourable childhood environment. Proportionately there are more individuals in this category among the well-to-do than among the poor. Poverty and its attendant necessities serve, to an extent, as deterrents.

When an individual fails to mature according to his (or her) proper biological and sexological status, such an individual is psychologically (mentally) deficient. The psychological condition is in reality the disease.

When an individual who is unfavorably affected psychologically determines to live and appear as a member of the sex to which he or she does not belong, such an individual is what may be called a *psychopathic transexual*. This means, simply, that one is mentally unhealthy and because of this the person desires to live as a member of the opposite sex.

That which pertains to the psychopathic transexual may be called *psychopathia transexualis*. There are varying degrees of psychopathic transexuality. This article deals with one specific case.

CASE HISTORY—SUBJECT'S BACKGROUND

The subject of this study was born a normal female into a well known and fairly well-to-do family. On the maternal side there was a physician whose son became a lawyer and succeeded in his aspirations to hold political office. The paternal grandfather was prominent in politics and civic affairs. The father was a spoiled son, petted and spoiled by his mother and sisters. He was frequently put in jail for drunkenness and his family were in the habit of sending his wife (the subject's mother) to retrieve him from the clutches of a courtesan in a brothel.

There were two brothers older than the subject. One, the eldest by 13 years, evidently had survived this environment and was on his way up in the world when the subject was born. The other, about 10 years old when the subject was born, was feebleminded, never learned to talk, and while in his 20's was committed to a state institution.

The subject, as a small girl, was impressed with the adulation with which the men of the family were showered. She herself was not, however, neglected. *Frequently she was dressed as a boy*. One of her fondest memories is a picture of herself in boy's attire and smoking a pipe. The picture was made when she was five years old. She was told often what a cute child she was and emphasis was placed on her cuteness as a "boy."

At no time did the subject desire to be a female. Through taught differently, she grew up thinking of herself as a boy. Early she began playing the role of a male on every occasion possible. When she was 18 she discarded feminine attire entirely. She determined that she would live as a male and that nothing could stop her.

Through having written numerous booklets on sexological and related subjects, I have built a large list of correspondents. I first knew of the subject of this study through a letter. After that there was a considerable correspondence. Eventually the subject wrote that she intended to visit relatives near my home and asked if she might see me. I extended an invitation—my wife acquiescing—to visit my home. In doing so I made it clear that my time was devoted entirely to writing and research in science, and that I was not now engaged in active medical practice.

I shall call the subject Earl. This is not her name but this name, like her own, is frequently borne by members of both sexes.

During Earl's brief stay with us we agreed that we had never had a more inoffensive guest in our home. She wore levis and regular men's shirts while at home but changed to feminine attire without prompting when we went for drives or away from home. She appeared to be more puzzled than determined to live as a male. She admitted one homosexual "crush." The relationship was one of heart rather than one of sexual indulgence, although she claimed to have had sexual satisfaction through various intimate bodily caresses, regular lip-kissing, and similar caresses. She assured me that no caresses of any kind had been bestowed lower than the breasts. Her friend had professed sexual satisfaction. The relationship was broken up, evidently by the other girl's family and circumstances pertaining to her own family.

Earl's paternal family had contributed to her upkeep and schooling. There was an aged grandmother and there were two aunts—one a maiden, the other a widow. During her first visit Earl expressed the desire to undergo surgery which would, she hoped, bring about sex transmutation, thus making her a full male.

In cases of doubtful sex—usually cases of pseudo-hermaphroditism—surgical sex transmutation has often occurred. Actually, surgical measures have succeeded in establishing a nearer approach to the normal sexual integration of the individuals involved. I explained all of this to Earl and at her request gave her what we call the biological type of examination, which showed that her menses were regular and normal. Her external genitals were of perfect feminine formation, the clitoris normal, although the glans was unusually small. Hair distribution and voice normal.

It should be noted that the average sized clitoris with an unusually small glans *is the opposite of* male pseudo-hermaphroditism.

When Earl left us I believed that she would make an uneventful adjustment. But there were matters of family background with which I was not familiar at that time.

When we learned that Earl had entered a college for women it was felt that she had accomplished a satisfactory adjustment. We heard from her rarely. Once she wrote asking if I could help her to avoid taking physical education. I urged her to take the subject. In one letter there was a statement that a number of members of the faculty were homosexuals and that about 60 per cent of the student body appeared to be homosexuals. There was no hint of individual homosexuality on Earl's part. There were complaints about the house-mother who had been a matron or supervisor at a girl's reformatory and who, apparently, insisted on using reform school disciplinary tactics on these young college women.

Suddenly there was a frantic telegram. "If you are going to be at home and I can come, wire me collect. Important."

That was a puzzling message. I was inclined to think that she had become pregnant and thought that we could teach her how to become a good mother. Hence, I wired a welcome. Days passed and there was no word. Then suddenly, there was a collect telegram asking that we meet her at a certain time. We met her. She was a pitiful sight. She was dressed in a helter-skelter get-up of male attire and was thoroughly unkempt. She was broke. She had been sleeping on park benches and had been in police custody.

EARL DETERMINES TO BE A MALE

Earl was desperate to become a male. I listened as she calmly explained that she wanted me to find a surgeon who would remove her breasts, her ovaries, and close the vagina and then create for her an artificial penis. She would then take male hormones that she thought would, with masculine attire and occupation, solve her problem. I was amazed at such utter simplicity.

I explained that what she desired was impossible. A surgeon can castrate a woman, of course, and can readily remove her breasts. An artificial penis for cosmetic effect only, has been created by successive grafts of bone, skin, etc. But it is of no material use on a female and has no more sexual feeling than a fingernail.[1] BUT—it would be criminal for any surgeon to mutilate a pair of healthy breasts and it would be just as criminal for a surgeon to castrate a woman with no disease of the ovaries or related glands and without any condition wherein castration might be beneficial.

Earl was dissatisfied with my explanation. Why was it criminal if *she* wanted it done? How unreasonable! Earl also wanted to know if I didn't believe what I advocated in my writings: that the individual has a right to live his or her life as he or she chooses provided that in doing so no innocent party is involved. A surgeon evidently did not appear as an innocent individual in her mind.

Because Earl was of legal age, and the further fact that I felt her confidence should be fully kept, I had not communicated with any members of her family. Indeed, there had been no occasion for me to do so.

Just as I was beginning to learn that in my broad and tolerant consideration of people and of the sexual nature of the human being, I had overlooked the psychopathic traits in Earl, her brother and aunt called. We found them to be well integrated people and of the highest moral and social fiber. Earl's mother, not having heard from her for many days, had phoned that she might possibly be with us. (She had known of Earl's previous visit.)

By now we were beginning to learn something of the real Earl. We knew that her ambitions were to live parasitically. *She would not work.* She believed her grandmother and aunts were fabulously wealthy (which they were not) and that, without earning money herself, she could worm it out of them just as she had long wormed it out of them through deception. She refused to go away with her aunt or her brother. The aunt left her $10 for incidentals. A little later I realized that that Earl's relatives had been relieved that she had refused to go with them.

A SUMMARY OF FACTS

Earl's relatives began learning of her activities during recent months through various sources. Earl had been asked to withdraw from college on account of suspected homosexual activities. She admitted such activities. A woman who thinks of herself as a physical and psychological male is capable of only pseudo-homosexual activities with either sex. (With males she still would be a sexological female and with females she would be an imagined or fantasied psychological male.)

There had been but one homosexual affair according to Earl's statements. According to other authentic information, there had been a number of them. In some instances Earl had been, no doubt, the seducer and in others there had been mutuality and hence, no seduction.

She believed that she had a perfect right to go out just as any young male and court a female and, just as young males sometimes seduce young females, she thought that it was within her right to do the same thing.

Against her family Earl had death wishes. They did not, she contended, know how to use or to enjoy money. She—Earl, did.

She resented being referred to as "her and she." She had been immensely happy when, in a restaurant (in male attire of terrible taste) she had been referred to, or addressed as "Sir."

If doctors would not do exactly as Earl wanted them to do, or if they could not, then she would continue as she had done and bind her breasts as tightly downwards as possible, dress as a male and live as much the role of a male as possible. She already was pleased that she could use men's rest rooms. Frequently she had been referred to as "Sonny." She shaved in an effort to grow a beard. She kept on her guard in her effort to affect a masculine voice. (It never sounded in the least masculine.) She delighted in ultra-loud (and severely tawdry) socks and ties. The men's shoes she wore were far too large for her and made walking difficult. Her hair was conventional masculine trim. She was narcissistic and reveled in just seeing and feeling herself (as much when alone as otherwise) in the role of a male. She admired herself probably as much as the original Narcissus.

The expression of death-wishes annoyed my wife. We had to do something with our guest. Fortunately we were able to turn her over to her brother and within two or three days he passed her on to grandmother and aunts. They gave her all of the encouragement possible and bought her a complete feminine wardrobe. She would not don or touch a garment.

Unable to cope with a personality such as Earl's her family gave her a ticket to a city where she assured them she would get a job. They gave her enough cash for an intelligent person to get along on until more can be earned. They did not, any more than did I, expect that Earl would get a job or work. They felt as I feel that she would soon run afoul of the law and that the State would find it necessary to make some legal disposition of the case.

That there are better integrated transexuals we are well aware. There are case histories of outstanding social, civic and other leaders who were transexuals. In Arkansas a comparatively few years ago a Dr. Brown lived and practiced until in the 60's and was regarded as a male and a highly competent physician. She lived with a sister. In her final illness physicians who treated her discovered her true sex.

In my files I have numerous case histories of males who have lost their genitals through accident and who have become well-integrated transexuals living useful lives and helping, rather than hindering, society. I have other case histories of females who, usually because of an endocrine disturbance or an adrenal tumor, or ovarian disease, have felt that their masculine characteristics were a hindrance to them in careers as females. They have succeeded as well-integrated individuals, living as transexuals. These transexuals are, however, transexuals by affectation only. Evidently they are all, in their sexual activities, purely autosexual.

DR. HIRSCHFELD'S PRONOUNCEMENT

In "Sexual History of the World War" by Dr. Magnus Hirschfeld, a case is reported of a young woman who sought to enlist in the German Army of the first world war. She made several unsuccessful attempts. Eventually she was examined by Dr. Hirschfeld who pronounced her "a psychological male." She was thereupon accepted and became an excellent fighter, serving as a male soldier.

The psychopathic characteristic is manifested not, as may be thought, in actual homosexuality or transvestism, nor yet in the adoption of a male role and career, but in such practices as seduction, parasitism, violation of the social codes in numerous ways, frequently kleptomania and actual thievery, pathological lying, and other criminal and unsocial tendencies. (The adoption of a female role and career applies in the case of actual males.)

Although heredity had a part in producing individuals who may have psychopathic tendencies, such pitiful cases as that described herein are products, largely, of unfavorable childhood environment and overindulgent parents and other near relatives.

Some of the individuals involved, as was the subject of this study, are amenable to rehabilitation through a few organizations now in existence. A large enough number of suitable organizations might succeed in rehabilitating the majority of individuals of both sexes falling into the category of psychopathia transexualis.

Progress is being made. Within a quarter of a century social education may serve as a preventive in all but a few cases and social organizations may be able to rehabilitate the few who fall by the wayside.

NOTE

1. An artificial penis that is biologically effective can be built. *Sexology* has reported a number of such cases. These cases, however, were all male ones. During the war a number of soldiers were mutilated by gun shot, mines, etc., which deprived them, in some cases, completely of their penis. By plastic surgery an artificial organ was then built up on the remaining stump. Such organs, strangely enough, permit the subject to have gratifying marital union and offspring.—Editor [of *Sexology*].

4

Transsexualism and Transvestism as Psycho-Somatic and Somato-Psychic Syndromes

Harry Benjamin

Harry Benjamin, who popularized (but did not coin) the term "transsexual," was a compassionate though paternalistic advocate for transgender people throughout his long life. Trained as a medical doctor in his native Germany, Benjamin was initially interested in tuberculosis, prostitution, and other public health issues, but soon became interested in the emerging field of endocrinology. He worked with colleagues Eugen Steinach, the pioneering gland specialist who first isolated the effects of the "sex hormones," and with sex-reformer Magnus Hirschfeld. Benjamin immigrated to the United States prior to World War I and became a U.S. citizen. Although Benjamin was familiar with Hirschfeld's support of sex-change procedures in Europe, and had himself prescribed cross-gender hormones as early as the 1920s, it was primarily through his connections with Alfred Kinsey, beginning in 1949, that he developed an on-going association with individuals seeking to change their sex. Benjamin's subsequent publications, along with his clinical practice, determined much of the modern medical approach to transgender phenomena.

Benjamin's 1966 book, *The Transsexual Phenomenon*, remains his definitive work on the subject. The 1954 article included here, which contains the seed of his later work, was Benjamin's earliest published effort to create a systematic way of thinking about the differing interrelationships between the sexed body, gender identity, and sexual desire that can be observed in various transgender phenomena. It was originally presented at the U.S. Association for the Advancement of Psychotherapy, at a symposium organized by Benjamin himself after the publicity surrounding Christine Jorgensen's 1952 genital surgery called unprecedented attention to transgender issues. Given the context of its initial presentation, Benjamin's paper is quite polemical. He argues that psychotherapy aimed at curing the transsexual person of the desire to change sex is unproductive, and that transsexualism is likely caused by a combination of constitutional, psychological, and hormonal influences.

DEFINITION

Transvestism has become the accepted term for the desire of a certain group of people to dress in the clothes of the opposite sex. This term, first used by Magnus Hirschfeld (1) has the disadvantage that it names a disturbance of behavior and emotion after only one of its symptoms, although the most conspicuous one. This symptom, which is also known as "cross-dressing," is the symbolic fulfillment of a deep-seated and more or less intense urge suggesting a disharmony of the total sexual sense, a sexual indecision or a disassociation of the physical and mental sexuality.

Havelock Ellis (2) proposed the term "eonism," naming it after its prototype, the Chevalier D'Eon and as a parallel to sadism and masochism. Hamburger and his associates (3) in Denmark reserved the term eonism for severe cases of so-called "genuine transvestism." They also characterize it as "psychic hermaphroditism." This is the same extreme degree of transvestism for which I have used the term transsexualism (4) because a transformation of sex is the foremost desire. Cauldwell (12) spoke of Psychopathia transsexualis.

Naturally not every act of "cross-dressing" is transvestitic. Only if it occurs in an atmosphere of emotional pressure, sometimes to the point of compulsion and is accompanied by a more or less distinct sexual satisfaction can the term be applied. Otherwise it would be simple masquerading of a non-affective nature.

SYMPTOMATOLOGY

Transvestism can be a form of fetishism. If a man, for instance wears under his suit a female corset, or panties or long stockings, he may just want to be close to his beloved fetish. In other cases, however, such action may be a compromise for the transvestite because it might entail social, sometimes marital, complications or it may involve legal risks to dress completely as a woman and appear as such in public. Another compromise is dressing as a woman only in the privacy of the home. Both ways leave transvestites, and especially transsexualists, greatly frustrated and unhappy.

The transvestite wants to be accepted in society as a member of the opposite sex; he or she wants to play the role as completely and as successfully as possible. The male transvestite admires the female form and manners and tries to imitate both with an intensity that varies greatly from case to case. The female transvestite, being legally immune, has it easier to identify herself with the male sex, acting the part of a man in appearance as well as in conduct. Gutheil published an analyzed case of female transvestism in Stekel's book on Fetischism (5).

Transsexualism is a different problem and a much greater one. It indicates more than just playing a role. It denotes the intense and often obsessive desire to change the entire sexual status including the anatomical structure. While the male transvestite, *enacts* the role of a woman, the transsexualist wants to *be* one and *function* as one, wishing to assume as many of her characteristics as possible, physical, mental and sexual.

Transsexualism as well as transvestism are decidedly more frequent among men than women, like most other sexual deviations. Due to the more permissive fashions in women, female transvestism is less conspicuous, but naturally can involve for the individual the same frustrations and often tragic situations as in men. Since the social and legal complications are infinitely greater in male transvestism and transsexualism, this present discussion is largely confined to them.

The transsexualist is always a transvestite but not vice-versa. In fact, most transvestites would be horrified at the idea of being operated. The transsexualist, on the other hand, only lives for the day when his hated sex organs can be removed, organs which to him are nothing but a dreadful deformity. Therefore the transsexualist always seeks medical aid while the transvestite as a rule merely asks to be left alone.

To put it differently: In transvestism the sex organs are sources of pleasure; in transsexualism they are sources of disgust. That seems to me a cardinal distinction and perhaps the principal differential diagnostic sign. Otherwise there is no sharp separation between the two, one merging into the other.

It is quite evident that under the influence of sensational publicity a reasonably well adjusted transvestite could become greatly disturbed and fascinated by ideas of surgical conversion so that his emotional balance may be endangered.

RELATION TO HOMOSEXUALITY

Homosexual inclinations always exist in the transsexualist whether they result in actual physical contacts or not. The libido as far as sex activities are concerned is usually low and seems to be completely occupied with the sex conversion idea, indicating the close relationship to narcissism. The interpretation of the libido as homosexual is strongly rejected by the male transsexualists. They consider the fact that they are attracted to men natural because they feel as women and consider themselves of the female sex. For them to be attracted to "other females" appears to be a perversion.

Transvestites on the other hand are in the majority heterosexual, although their principal sexual outlet seems to be auto-erotic. Some are married and raise families, but the marriage rarely endures. Others have understanding girl-friends with whom they sometimes share their wardrobe.

Kinsey and his associates (6) consider transvestism and homosexuality "totally independent phenomena." So they are, as far as overt behavior is concerned. Most homosexuals would not be interested in "cross-dressing" just as most transvestites reject homosexual relations. Furthermore, the transvestitic behavior is chiefly a social problem, non-sexual on the surface, affecting one individual only, while homosexual behavior is an open manifestation of sex involving a second party.

However, I can see a relationship between the transvestitic and homosexual behavior in the fact that both are disturbances of the sexual unity of the individual, both constitute a split of soma and psyche in the field of sex, both are instinctive drives, quite beyond the individual's power to control or to change, no matter what the underlying cause may be.

ETIOLOGY

Speculations as to the causes of transvestism and transsexualism have led to much controversy in the past. There were, and still are, those who believe that all cases have an exclusively organic etiology. They consider transvestism in all its stages (as well as homosexuality) a form of intersexuality, an intermediate sex of genetic or endocrine origin. Hirschfeld spoke of metatropism as an organic state.

On the other hand, there is the strictly psychoanalytic explanation which traces all such deviations to psychological conditioning, infantile traumata, childhood fixations, or an arrested emotional development.

I believe that in the face of clinical facts, logic and objective observations, either approach as an exclusive key to the phenomenon is untenable.

An organic explanation of intersexual phenomena would have to be looked for either in the genetic mechanism or in the endocrine constitution or in a combination of both. Organically, sex is always a mixture of male and female components. The ratio varies with the individual, determining the constitutional makeup, physical and mental. Between the "full-female" and the "full-male," constituting the two extremes on either side (and they are naturally not 100% either), there is every possible intermediate status.

The chromosomal sex (or "genetic sex") normally producing the homogametic female (bearing XX chromosomes), or the heterogametic male (bearing XY chromosomes) is subject to disturbances most strikingly evidenced by hermaphroditic and pseudo-hermaphroditic deformities. Investigations into the chromosomal sex (11) have shown that it is probably contained in the nuclear structure of all body cells. It has been detected and demonstrated in the epidermal nuclei of the skin. It does not always correspond to the respective gonad, that is to say, the endocrine sex. Future research along these lines may thus determine the dominant sex in an individual and may do much to clarify our still incomplete knowledge of the nature of sex. To speak of a male when there are (or were) testicles and of a female when there are (or were) ovaries may be the most practical way to differentiate the sexes, but it is scientifically incorrect and unsatisfactory to the geneticist.

Similarly the term "transsexualism" answers a practical purpose and is appropriate in our present state of knowledge. If future research should show that male sex organs are compatible with (genetic) female sex or female sex organs with (genetic) male sex the term would be wrong because the male "transsexualist" is actually female and merely requires a transformation of genitals.

The endocrine aspect of the problem is intimately related to the genetic. If we find in a transvestite underdeveloped gonads and other signs of a congenital hypogonadism or if there are undescended testicles or hypospadia, we may be justified to suspect the sexual deviation to be due to a primary genetic disturbance also. But on the other hand all physical abnormalities can secondarily have far-reaching psychological repercussions.

The all-important role of environment and of psychological conditioning need not be stressed before this audience. There are any number of situations in early childhood that can be held responsible for the development of a sexual deviation. From the "smothering mother" to the dominant female in the family and the cross-dressing of the little boy to please a parent, each case of transvestism can have a different inception. Emotional development arrested during an early phase may play the most frequent role.

In some case histories the transvestitic tendency appears to have developed spontaneously at an early age. It may be well, therefore, to recall the fact as Dukor (7) expressed it: "The possibility of a purely psychological cause for a sexual deviation does not prove its correctness." There may be other factors besides. In a recent published monograph Bürger-Prinz, H. Albrecht and H. Giese (8) express the belief that there is no single principal cause for transvestism. Alden of San Francisco includes the realm of all mental and emotional reactions into the individual's constitutional equipment.

The effeminate male may look and behave as he does on a purely psychosomatic or psychological basis (imitating his mother, for instance) but he may also be the product of a somato-psychic mechanism originating in his chromosomes. It is often impossible to distinguish between the two.

Havelock Ellis has this to say in regard to etiology: "Early environmental influences assist but can scarcely originate Eonism. The normal child soon reacts powerfully against them. We must in the end seek a deeper organic foundation for Eonism."

THREE TYPES OF TRANSVESTITES

Let me briefly sketch my impression of the three principal types of transvestites as I have seen them in my practice and as the etiology suggested itself to me.

1. The principally psychogenic transvestite. He is anatomically a normal male but may lack masculinity. The feminine component in his make-up is sufficient to allow an early psychological conditioning to form the transvestitic pattern in later life. This psychological conditioning takes place long before the age of 12 or 13 when the principal attitudes are generally well established. His desire for sexual contacts is usually low, more often hetero- than homosexual. He is miserable when dressed as a man and immediately comfortable and relaxed in the clothes of a female. He has become an expert in cosmetic make-up, yet is occasionally in social or legal difficulties. He assumes a female first name and wants to be referred to as "she." He is usually introverted, non-aggressive, and his peculiarity hardly interferes with a smooth functioning of society. His conflict results from social pressure and legal prohibition. In fighting his peculiarity he sometimes over-emphasizes masculinity and becomes known as a "tough guy." In one case the over-compensation took the form of the patient having his entire body tattooed. Here masochism may have entered.

More than anything else the psychogenetic transvestite wants to see a change in the existing restrictive laws, so that he can lead a woman's life. *He* does not want to be changed but wants society's attitude toward him to change, again revealing narcissistic tendencies. Treatment is therefore rarely attempted. But if so it would be principally psychoanalytic. Endocrine therapy is rarely indicated. Only if there are signs of hypogonadism, masculinization may be attempted with testosterone. Simultaneously, a belated reenforcement of the maturing process with chorionic gonadotropin would be logical.

2. The intermediate type. His symptoms and problems are fundamentally the same as in type #1, but decidedly more pronounced. Therefore, he inclines at times toward transsexualism, but is at other times content with merely dressing and acting as a woman. He wavers between homo- and heterosexual desires usually according to chance meetings. He can be a very disturbed person. His masturbation fantasies are narcissistic and he visualizes himself functioning as a woman.

The gonads are usually within normal limits, but may incline toward underdevelopment suggesting a psycho-sexual infantilism. Skeletal measurements sometimes are of eunuchoid character. He rates low in masculinity and rather high in femininity on the respective M.F. scale. There may be more or less feminine markings in his physical make-up, for instance wide hips, breast development, female hair distribution, etc. Adverse childhood influences, often quite evident in his history, were therefore able to make a correspondingly deep impression on the personality structure. Psychosomatic and somato-psychic factors intermingle.

An attempt at therapy may be considered but prognosis—I believe—is poor. Personally, I have never seen a cure, but the patients usually do not persist in treatment long enough or have no real desire to be cured. The constitutional factors are possibly too deep and resist psychotherapeutic endeavors too strongly. Under the powerful suggestive influence of publicity like that of the Jorgensen case such transvestites may, for the first time, turn toward transsexualism.

3. The somatopsychic transsexualist. This type is well represented by the case of Christine Jorgensen, who published the facts of her own case frankly and with a well-conceived self-analysis.

Feminine appearance and orientation is often striking in these people but masculine features are compatible with full transsexualism. The conviction of these endocrine males that they are really females with faulty sex organs is profound and passionate. Suggestive childhood influences are often evident in their histories, but may, in other cases, be vague and not sufficiently plausible to help in explaining the phenomenon. Therefore a still greater degree of constitutional femininity, perhaps due to a chromosomal sex disturbance, must be assumed in spite of the fact that the gonadal status may appear within normal limits. Here, psychic hermaphroditism seems to be an apt description.

Sex life is largely cerebral and non-genital, satisfaction being derived more from their paraphilia that is to say their feminization fantasies and endeavors than from auto-erotism or homosexual contacts.

Hamburger and his associates have portrayed such a case in an article in the A.M.A. Journal (3). They analyzed the clinical facts and the surgical treatment with much insight and common sense, reaching the conclusion that "It is highly probable that eonism, (their term for transsexualism), is constitutionally conditioned."

After their report appeared, an interesting attempt was made in a letter to the A.M.A. Journal (9) to interpret the same case of transsexualism from a strictly psychoanalytic angle naturally with rejection of any treatment except psychoanalysis. Unfortunately, a theory that disregards biological factors in such cases—in my opinion—cannot convince and does not ring true.

Freud himself—I believe—would have disagreed with such a one-sided approach. During one of my visits to Vienna about 30 years ago I discussed the psyche-soma relationship with Freud and he agreed fully that a *disharmony* of the emotions may well be due to a *disharmony* of our endocrines.

All therapy, in cases of transsexualism—to the best of my knowledge—has proved useless as far as any cure is concerned. I know of no case where even intensive and prolonged psychoanalysis had any success. If we are dealing with a constitutional deviation, we can hardly expect to influence it.

Testosterone, for instance, would not change the desire for sex transformation either. It would merely increase libido and perhaps masculine appearance aggravating instead of diminishing the conflict. These people seem to me truly the victims of their genetic constitution, step-children of medical science, often crucified by the ignorance and indifference of society and persecuted by antiquated laws and by legal interpretations that completely lack in wisdom and realism.

THE NORMAL BOY

To complete the picture, I would like to mention the normal masculine boy who was exposed to adverse psychological conditioning. In former years it was quite customary that many boys kept their long curls till they went to school and some of them were dressed and treated more in a feminine than masculine fashion. That took place during the formative years. Naturally not all of them became transvestites or homosexuals. When this kind of conditioning went against their nature, nothing happened. They grew into normal manhood. But when it harmonized with a constitution of a high feminine component, then it was a different story.

In this connection I would like to raise a question of cause and effect. Parents who do bring up their boys as girls and give them female names usually do so to please themselves and to compensate for their disappointment in having a boy when they wanted a girl (or vice-versa). But is it not possible also that, in other instances, the boy—for constitutional reasons—looked and behaved so much like a girl that it seemed more natural to the parents to forget about his gonads for a while and bring him up as a female?

In one case that I observed recently a reversed situation actually seemed to exist. The parents wanted the boy that was born to them very much. But at the age of 3 or 4 the child rebelled and wanted to be dressed and treated "like other girls." The parents and two older sisters fought for a son and brother, but finally gave in. To keep peace they allowed the girl's dresses but—for a while at least—insisted on regular boy's haircuts. These constituted the most distressing moments in the boy's life. He grew up into an extremely feminine-looking transvestite and transsexualist. He was studied by two groups of psychiatrists. One group recommended the conversion-operation as the only way to preserve the patient's sanity; the other group advised against it as unlikely to solve the underlying psychological problems. In September of this year, however, the patient succeeded in realizing his life's ambition and did have a conversion-operation performed abroad.

I saw him a couple of weeks ago and can only say; so far, so good. He is happier and seems better balanced emotionally than when I saw him two years ago. However, I would make no prediction for the future; much will depend upon follow-up therapy.

I am fully aware that I am repetitious, but I feel that occasionally there is justification for it. Allow me, therefore, to summarize briefly my opinion: Our genetic and endocrine equipment constitutes either an unresponsive, sterile or a more or less responsive, that is to say, fertile soil on which a psychic trauma can grow and develop into such a basic conflict that subsequently a neurosis or sex deviation results.

Or, differently expressed: Our organic sexual constitution, that is to say the chromosomal sex supported and maintained by the endocrines, form the substance and the material that make up our sexuality. Psychological conditioning determines its final shape and function. The substance is largely inaccessible to treatment (except in its endocrine constituent.) The function is the domain of psychotherapy.

LEGAL ASPECTS

The legal aspects of transvestism, transsexualism and conversion-operations will be discussed by Mr. Robert Sherwin. The fear of arrest when they venture out in female dress and the utter frustration when they resist the temptation makes life truly miserable for these patients. A comparison to drug addiction readily comes to one's mind. One can only wonder that their neurotic symptoms are often not more pronounced.

FREQUENCY OF TRANSVESTISM

The number of transvestites and transsexualists in the United States is enormously difficult to estimate because too many of them keep their secret well-hidden; some are discovered only after death. An investigation is now in progress in California to procure an approximate idea of how many may be in that state. While there could be several hundred or more, they are hardly enough to constitute a problem for society even if restrictive laws were relaxed with the help of medical certificates.

TREATMENT

As far as the treatment of transvestism is concerned, my previous remarks may suffice on this occasion. The management of transsexualism, however, requires a few supplementary comments, especially as far as the conversion-operation is concerned.

Transsexualism is undoubtedly a rare condition, rare in proportion to the population. Its treatment is even more perplexing than that of etiology because medical considerations are so greatly complicated by social and legal ones.

In my opinion, psychotherapy for the purpose of curing the condition is a waste of time. A basic conflict would be too firmly anchored in the constitution. All that the psychiatrist can possibly do is to relax tension, to develop and reinforce realistic thinking, and to supply guidance. That, of course, is not a cure.

The transsexualist is primarily interested in having a conversion-operation performed and therein lies the dilemma which taxes the physician's conscience to an unusual degree.

The operation itself would consist in castration, the amputation of the penis (peotomy) and the possible plastic formation of an artificial vagina. But, alas, even if the patient had reached this goal, it may not always solve his problem. His feminization cravings may never end. The later realization that a complete change of sex including the ability of child-bearing is impossible and that only a change of secondary sex characteristics has been and can be accomplished, may leave some patients still frustrated even after a more or less extended period of relief. That is the tragedy and the pitfall in consenting to this irreversible procedure. And yet, in some cases, it may be the lesser evil and we may have to accept this chance as a calculated risk.

The patient who is constantly on the verge of a reactive psychosis or is in danger of suicide or self-mutilation cannot be turned down with an unequivocal "no." On the other hand the physician's sympathy should not tempt him to give in too easily to the patient's persuasive arguments and thus obscure his sound clinical judgment.

The psychiatrist must have the last word. He has to evaluate the personality in regard to possible future consequences and also as to the likelihood of somehow making life bearable under the status quo. If it is evident that the psyche cannot be brought into sufficient harmony with the soma, then and only then is it essential to consider the reverse procedure, that is, to attempt fitting the soma into the realm of the psyche.

In weighing the indication for the operation, another factor should be considered, namely the physical and especially facial characteristics of the patient. A feminine habitus, as it existed for instance in Christine Jorgensen, increases the chances of a successful outcome. A masculine appearance mitigates against it. Such patient may meet with serious difficulties later on when he expects to be accepted by society as a female and lead the life of a woman.

A conversion-operation is an infrequent procedure, even allowing for the fact that it may often be kept a deep secret (as a supposedly illegal procedure). Treatment with estrogens would have to follow in order to control castration symptoms, aside from having its feminizing effect. We must remember, of course, that castration produces a eunuch and not a woman.

Whenever the surgical intervention is contraindicated, "chemical castration" can be attempted with large doses of estrogen (naturally in combination with psychotherapy.) The psychological side-effects of such endocrine therapy can be of great value in addition to its hormonal result which is the suppression of the androgenic activity of the testes and the adrenal cortex. Repeated determinations of the 17-ketosteroids could show the degree of suppression. These steroids would be best kept at an average female level. If the estrogens do not suppress the 17-ketosteroid production sufficiently, cortisone may be used in addition. In that case the treatment of male transsexualism parallels that of female virilism (10).

Clinically, the hormonal castration can gradually produce an increase of mammary tissue, a reduction of body hair, and probably a slight atrophy of testes and penis. A decrease of libido and correspondingly diminished sexual tension is likely.

CONCLUSIONS AND SUMMARY

Let me leave you and my highly incomplete presentation with these conclusions:

Transvestism and transsexualism are symptoms that may have a great variety of causes. A constitutional predisposition is essential; then comes adverse psychological conditioning followed by the respective syndromes. The intensity of these two causative factors and their interplay determine the character of the final clinical picture (which may range from mere effeminacy of an otherwise normal man to deep-seated exclusive homosexuality and transsexualism.

Transvestism may be successfully handled by psychotherapy if the patient desires a cure. Otherwise it can only be treated by treating society and our legal statutes with their interpretations.

Transsexualism is inaccessible to any curative methods at present at our disposal. Nevertheless the condition requires psychiatric help, reinforced by hormone treatment and, in some cases, by surgery. In this way a reasonably contented existence may be worked out for these patients.

BIBLIOGRAPHY

1. Hirschfeld, Magnus: *Die Transvestiten*. Verlag "Wahrheit," Leipzig 1925.
2. Ellis, Havelock: *Eonism*. Vol. VII of Studies in the Psychology of Sex. F. A. Davis & Co., 1928.
3. Hamburger, Chr., Stürup, G. K., Dahl-Iversen, E.: "Transvestism." *A. M. A.*, Vol. 152, pp. 391–396, May 30, 1953.
4. Benjamin, Harry: "Transvestism and Transsexualism." *Int. J. of Sexology*, Vol. VII, No. 1, Aug. 1953.
5. Stekel, Wilhelm: *Der Fetischismus*. Urban & Schwarzenberg, 1923, pp. 534–570.
6. Kinsey, Pomeroy, Martin, Gebhard: *Sexual Behavior in the Human Female*. W. B. Saunders, 1953, p. 680.
7. Dukor, B.: *Schweiz. Med. Wschr.* 1951, 516.
8. Bürger-Prinz, Albrecht, Giese: *Zur Phaenomenologie des Transvestismus bei Maennern*. F. Enke, Stuttgart, 1953.
9. "Transvestism." *J. Am. Med. Ass.*, Vol. 152, No. 16, p. 1553.
10. Jailer, Joseph W.: "Virilism." *Bull. N. Y. Acad. of Med.*, May 1953.
11. Moore, K. L., Graham, M. A. and Barr, M. L.: "The Detection of Chromosomal Sex in Hermaphrodites from a Skin Biopsy." *Surg. Gyn. Obst.*, Vol. 96, No. 6, June 1953.
12. Cauldwell, D. O.: "Psychopathia Transsexualis." *Sexology*, N. Y., Dec. 1949.

5

selection from
Biological Substrates of Sexual Behavior

Robert Stoller

American psychoanalytic psychologist Robert Stoller developed an influential theory of transsexual etiology in the 1960s. He believed that male-to-female transsexuality was a pathology of psychosexual development caused during early childhood by "too much mother made possible by too little father." He considered female-to-male transsexuality to be an entirely different psychodynamic phenomena.

Building upon the earlier work of John Money and his colleagues at Johns Hopkins University, Stoller developed an influential three-part model of human psychosexual structures that distinguished between biological sex, social gender role, and subjective or "psychological" gender identity. In this article, Stoller discusses how biological sex provides a foundation for the other two components of his model.

Robert Stoller helped establish the pioneering Gender Identity Center at UCLA in the early 1960s, and later worked closely with the Harry Benjamin International Gender Dysphoria Association, and thus played an important role in the history of medical attention to transgender phenomena. Although his work, along with that of John Money, has largely fallen out of favor within recent humanities scholarship, it remains influential to the extent that it is responsible, to a significant degree, for popularizing the sex/gender distinction upon which much subsequent queer and feminist analysis has turned.

While the practice of sex has a venerable past, a more systematic understanding of its biology is still beyond us. Recently, however, and with increasing momentum, the study of biological aspects of this phenomenon is permitting us to see at least the dim outlines of the answers we shall be finding in the next years. This will permit us to take over a subject formerly the prerogative of philosophers, whose freedom from the responsibility of proof permitted them the assurance of certainty.

It is obvious that so many disciplines of biological research are now involved in studying problems of sex (for example, genetics, endocrinology, embryology, comparative anatomy, physiology) that in a short chapter one can only indicate some of the major areas in which significant investigations are taking place, and attempt to suggest the richness and promise of the field.

We know that reproduction is the fundamental purpose behind sexual behavior.* In the most primitive living creatures, reproduction occurs simply by binary fission, with the genetic makeup of the individual organism being identically reproduced. However, when one gets beyond the simplest organisms one finds techniques for combining genetic material in new combinations. Let us skip across the millennia of evolution and pause a moment with *amphibia*. At this level of evolution, we have long since passed the state of development in which sexual intercourse between males and females has first

---

*Though less and less clearly so the higher the organism, until in humans we find that sexual behavior may also have psychological purposes very distinct from procreation.

been introduced for reproduction. These creatures have both external and internal genital organs. The amphibian larva has an indifferent gonad made up of two parts: a medulla, which, if it develops, can only become a testis, and a cortex, which, if it develops, can only become an ovary. In the normal creature, gonadal differentiation is controlled by the sex chromosomes, which cause the opposite-sex cells in the indifferent gonad to melt away. Yet, though advanced and differentiated, the gonads of many amphibia are easily reversible: regardless of the genetic makeup (and on this level of development sex chromosomes are determining the sex of the creature), the genotypic female can be converted to a phenotypic male by suppressing development of the gonadal cortex and promoting medullary growth. If the experiment is carried out in embryological life, the destined female will become an anatomically normal male, having a completely male, sperm-producing testis, despite the fact that had the individual not been tampered with, it would have developed into a completely normal female. This can be accomplished by even such unrelated experimental modes as temperature extremes, castration, or gonadal grafts.

Let us stay with mammals, upon which and whom within the last five or six years there has occurred an explosion of fine research related to neurohumoral mechanisms influencing sexual behavior. Two areas especially have been investigated. The first has been the effect of prenatal hormones on postnatal sexual behavior. What one does, in essence, is to give male or female hormones in varying doses to pregnant animals or to newborns. If one does this, for example, to female offspring, not only do they become (anatomically) pseudohermaphroditic if one gives male hormones but also there are apparently central nervous system changes as well: These females shift both their normal childhood sexual behavior and their adult sexual behavior in the direction of markedly increased male behavior. Especially interesting has been the discovery of critical periods: If these sex hormones are given only during very limited periods in fetal development, the reversals in childhood and adult sexual behavior occur, but if one gives the hormones before or after the critical period, then the same aberrant behavior will not develop.

The second area of investigation has been the use of implants of hormones directly into those parts of the animals' hypothalamus that directly affect sexual behavior. Sexual behavior and sexual drive can be influenced in direct relationship either to the cells that have the hormone implant in their immediate neighborhood or to the quantity of the implant. From these studies emerges the very provocative thesis that in each animal there are both male and female CNS subsystems for the regulation of sexual behavior.* According to Young and co-workers, in the normal animal genetic control leads to fetal anatomical-biochemical development causing one system to become dominant, so that, in a male animal, for example, that system which controls male behavior becomes dominant while the second system with its potential for female behavior plays a far lesser role. When the normal development of the animal is distorted by the experimental use of sex hormones, the normally secondary system becomes increasingly predominant. As yet there is no *histological* evidence that such subsystems exist, but the experiments to date seem to demand such an explanation. Certainly it has been described for many years, especially by Ford and Beach, that the higher mammals show degrees of both masculine and feminine behavior in any individual, and there is much evidence that there is no such thing as an exclusively masculine or exclusively feminine mammal.

It will be helpful in our future discussions if we have available to us a very short review of embryological developments of the sexual apparatus in the male and female. It is interesting to note—and to note it can open up some rich fields for speculation—that in most mammals, but especially in humans, the resting baseline of the sexual tissues is female. That is to say, if something else is not added to the tissue, whether the embryo be genetically male or genetically female, no masculinization will occur. Masculinization, when it does occur results in a penis of normal size, with the urethra running through it and a urethral meatus opening at its end, with fusion of the scrotal skin, and with testes within the

---

*This may blunt the effects of Rado's attack on Freud's belief in a biological bisexuality as one root of psychological bisexuality.

scrotal sac. When this masculinization does not occur one has a bifid scrotum, which is in fact external lips, a clitoris with the urethra opening below it and no external gonads. In those individuals who instead of having the normal two sex chromosomes (XX or XY), have only one (XO), the external genitalia are female, and although the internal reproductive system does not finish its development, there is a tendency for the tissues to move in the direction of developing into female organs. It seems that by the third month in the male fetus' existence a masculinizing substance begins to be secreted in a few sexual cells, this process being initiated in some unknown way under the control of the Y sex chromosome. Once this masculinizing substance begins to be produced even in minute amounts, it influences more cells in that area to become masculinized so that they produce more of this substance so that more cells get masculinized so that more of the substance gets produced and so on, thus starting the process of the masculinizing of these and mort distant tissues until the final normal male sexual anatomy results that is found at birth.

Now to shift to a whole different discipline, *ethology,* a special aspect of the study of animal learning behavior and a radically different methodology of research. From this treasure house of data, I shall take only one popular example. Lorenz, as is well known, has made himself available to greylag geese at certain critical times in their infancy, times when in the birds' natural state the mother would be with them. Under these unusual conditions, in infancy the birds attach themselves to Lorenz; then throughout their growing period they follow and respond to him as if he were their mother. On reaching sexual maturity, their sexual drives are directed exclusively toward him and other humans and not toward their own species. Many species, it is postulated, are genetically endowed so that certain systems of the brain will respond to certain stimuli in the outside world and not to others, and so that the animal is receptive to being permanently influenced by these stimuli only (or at least especially) at certain circumscribed periods in its development—the critical periods. This process, called *imprinting,* is found in different degrees in many species of birds and mammals and is now being investigated biochemically and neurophysiologically. In grossest form, we might say that we humans are able to respond sexually to humans, rather than to other animals or inanimate objects, in part because of certain not yet discovered central nervous system "states of readiness" that are produced by our having been imprinted by human mothers rather than by, say, monkeys or lizards.

Work has been under way recently to determine to what extent these imprinting mechanisms play a part in human infants, but the impossibilities of controlled experiments and the difficulties of interpreting mother-newborn interrelationships make this still a wide open field. A number of workers feel that some sort of imprinting does take place in human infants.Of interest to us now is the fact that at this level of theorizing one comes upon the impossibility of separating out the biological from the psychological; at this point, one recognizes that the two words *biological* and *psychological* only represent two conceptual schemes for looking at the identical data.*

It will help our discussion of these problems to distinguish two different orders of data: sex and gender.

As mentioned earlier, I prefer to restrict the term *sex* to a biological connotation. Thus, with few exceptions, there are two sexes, male and female. To determine sex, one must assay the following physical conditions: chromosomes, external genitalia, internal genitalia (e.g., uterus, prostate), gonads, hormonal states, and secondary sex characteristics. (It seems likely that in the future another criterion will be added: brain systems.) One's sex, then, is determined by an algebraic sum of all these qualities, and, as is obvious, most people fall under one of two separate bell curves, the one of which is called "male," the other "female." It is well known that there is a certain amount of overlapping in all humans, and in some unusual cases the overlapping is considerable, as in certain hermaphrodites. There are also, genetically speaking, other sexes; thus, in addition to the XX female and the XY male,

---

*I leave out the important writings of learning theorists, and especially the fascinating work of Harlow, because these studies are not as immediately "biological" as those reviewed above.

there are individuals (XO, XXY, XXXY, etc.) who have a mixing of some of their biological attributes of sex. Such people are often anatomically intersexed as well.*

Gender is a term that has psychological or cultural rather than biological connotations. If the proper terms for sex are "male" and "female," the corresponding terms for gender are "masculine" and "feminine"; these latter may be quite independent of (biological) sex. Gender is the amount of masculinity or femininity found in a person, and, obviously, while there are mixtures of both in many humans, the normal male has a preponderance of masculinity and the normal female a preponderance of femininity. *Gender identity* starts with the knowledge and awareness, whether conscious or unconscious, that one belongs to one sex and not the other, though as one develops, gender identity becomes much more complicated, so that, for example, one may sense himself as not only a male but a masculine man or an effeminate man or even a man who fantasies being a woman. *Gender role* is the overt behavior one displays in society, the role which he plays, especially with other people, to establish his position with them insofar as his and their evaluation of his gender is concerned. While gender, gender identity, and gender role are almost synonymous in the usual person, in certain abnormal cases they are at variance. One problem that arises to complicate our work is that gender behavior, which is for the greatest part learned from birth on, plays an essential part in sexual behavior, which is markedly biological, and at times it is very difficult to separate aspects of gender and sex from a particular piece of behavior.

Let us look now at some of the biological aspects of human sexual and gender behavior. This discussion will not review the physiology of sexual excitement, orgasm, and like subjects. While these have been studied in great detail (by far the most important work being that of Masters and Johnson and the excellent review by Sherfey), I am here more concerned with central than with (anatomically) peripheral mechanisms. Nor will the biology of the anatomic development of one's primary and secondary sexual characteristics be considered further here. As with the material I sketched in on lower animals, it is possible only to sample representative work in humans in order to give an impression of the information presently becoming available.

First, from the work of geneticists: While many of us are still awaiting definitive information about the contributions that chromosomes and genes make to sex and gender behavior, there are geneticists who might consider that our waiting shows undue skepticism. Certainly there have been exciting discoveries in the genetic laboratories in the last decade or so. The discovery by Barr and Bertram of nuclear sex chromatin material in mammalian, including human, cells has given us a simple, rapid, and highly accurate screening test for genetic sex. Also, new techniques for visualizing chromosomes have revealed to us both the normal complement of 46 chromosomes to the human cell and the presence and morphology of the sex chromosomes. This immediately made possible some clarification of the contribution of chromosomes to intersexuality (e.g., the XO Turner's Syndrome of ovarian agenesis or the XXY of the typical Klinefelter's Syndrome). In addition, decades of speculations regarding the alleged role of gross chromosomal anomalies in perversion with gender abnormality were put to rest when it was shown that no such defects were demonstrable—for example, in homosexuality or transvestism.

At this stage in the development of the science of genetics, I can only take the position of a layman, consider the arguments inconclusive, and await more compelling facts.

Now some endocrinological data: As is well known, castration of the male produces changes in sexual behavior. If the testes are removed before puberty, not only are the secondary sex characteristics unable to develop, but also genital sexuality in the adult is almost nonexistent. Castration following puberty results in marked diminution of sexual activity; the speed and completeness with which this destruction of sexual behavior occurs varies the individual. Castration in females does not produce the same effects. Prepubertal girls who are ovariectomized can, as adults, experience normal sexual excitement and orgasm. Likewise, removal of the ovaries in the adult woman will not diminish her

---

* While the term *intersexed* has occasionally been used in the past to refer to people with gender problems without genetic or anatomical defects, everyone today, I believe, uses it to mean only those with pronounced biological defects.

sexual needs or pleasures per se. Some recent findings strongly suggest that sexual libido is dependent on androgens in both men and women; libido is clearly not dependent on estrogens in women but is probably the result of the minute amounts of androgens normally produced in the adrenals, for adrenalectomy in women severely diminishes if it does not destroy their libido. The administration of estrogens to men, on the other hand, does not affect their libido unless the amounts are large enough to suppress testosterone production. Castrated men can maintain sexual vigor if given testosterone. Women given androgens, with or without their ovaries removed, routinely have an upsurge of libido. However, it is important to remember that when hormones are added or subtracted in these ways, the direction of the libido is not changed. Thus, the addition of testosterone does not make women develop masculine tastes in sex, and giving testosterone to effeminate homosexuals does not make them any less effeminate but just increases their need for more homosexual relations.

While everyone is familiar with Freud's discoveries of the tremendous influence of postnatal effects on personality development and on the development of sexuality, it sometimes comes as a surprise to those not familiar with his works to discover that from the beginning of his career until the very end, Freud incessantly repeated his belief that there were biological substrates to behavior. However, because of the inadequacy of the laboratory sciences of his day, he recognized that he was forced to put aside any hope of proving that such substrates exist, maintaining that the future would bring the proof he needed. Nonetheless, in his study of infant and child libidinal development he felt he could find evidence of a biological undercurrent upon which floated the postnatal, learned behavior. It was his feeling that libidinal development (the progression of erotic and nonerotic charging of oral, anal and urethral, and phallic areas with compelling significance as the personality develops) was controlled by a biological clock, ultimately genetically controlled. He felt (and subsequent observers have demonstrated) that there is a gradual maturation of many complicated neuromuscular systems before a new part of the body comes into focus, that is, becomes highly libidinized.

This reminds us of the work on critical periods being done on lower animals; at any rate it is the case in human development that certain orifices—those with mucous membranes—become highly sensitive and highly charged emotionally only after certain amounts of time and biological development have preceded. Thus, for example, only after the neuromuscular systems related to bowel control have sufficiently developed—when the small child is really biologically prepared for toilet training—can such training proceed without damage, and it follows that premature attempts to force such training may have great psychological significance. Another example of probable biological control over the erotization of various parts of the body is found in the work of Spitz: He has determined that while there is in little boys a casual awareness of and playing with the penis, starting around eight to ten months of age, this organ is not selected any more frequently than are other parts of the body, until after a gradual heightening of erotic sensation over many months, when the time and interest spent in genital manipulation increase. By the time of the phallic phase, occurring in both boys and girls at around three to five, there is a very concentrated interest in one's penis or clitoris—in other words, easily recognized masturbation.

Obviously, we do not have all the pieces, and yet there are good clues. We know these investigators are on the track of important discoveries, of syntheses of as yet unrelated data. We can see now that comparative and human neurophysiology will be coupled with the discoveries of psychologists and psychoanalysts to increase our understanding of these mechanisms.

This sketch, then, suggests the directions that our present search for knowledge has taken in this area of substrates of sexual behavior. But this is only the beginning; our understanding of sexuality is as nothing if this is all we know, for in this most intense of all human communications, we must study the signals that pass between people, and also what memories, fantasies, and wishes are stirred up in the individual. In other words, we must turn to *psychology* as an essential methodology in our understanding of sexuality.

6

Passing and the Managed Achievement of Sex Status in an "Intersexed" Person

Harold Garfinkel

Harold Garfinkel was a social interaction theorist who pioneered the field of ethnomethodology, a phenomenological approach to understanding how people construct a sense of reality through their everyday encounters with the world. His study of "Agnes" illustrates how individuals maintain the social roles of man or woman, as well as how we all produce credible genders for ourselves and attribute gender identities to others. Gender, in Garfinkel's view, is a "managed achievement" and therefore "real"—as real as any other aspect of our collectively produced and collectively sustained sense of reality. For him, the construction of gender involves an interpretation or "reading" of the body for social cues, but it is not a material property of the body itself.

Agnes presented herself at the Gender Identity Clinic at the University of California, Los Angeles, as a physically and socially feminine woman with male genitals. She claimed to have spontaneously begun to feminize at puberty, and was completely comfortable being a young woman. Through her interviews and assessment with the clinical staff—including such medical experts on transsexualism as Robert Stoller and Richard Green—it was determined that Agnes had a rare intersex condition known as testicular feminization syndrome, which can cause an apparently male body to spontaneously feminize at puberty. Because the doctors felt that an attractive, heterosexual young woman like Agnes should have a vagina, and because this is what Agnes herself desired, a genital transformation surgery was arranged on her behalf. Garfinkel saw this as a powerful example of how the patient and the doctors collaboratively participated in upholding their shared sense of what properly constituted "woman."

In an appendix written eight years after the initial study was completed, Garfinkel revealed a final twist to the story of Agnes—that several years after her surgery Agnes admitted she was, in fact, a typical biological male, but had begun taking synthetic female hormones when she was a pre-teen. She lied to her medical team, feeling that if she revealed the steps she had taken to "change sex" from male to female, she would have been denied the genital surgery she desired. Garfinkel considered this to further confirm his theories about the "managed achievement" of gender as an interactive social process. Medical specialists in the field of gender identity management have considered the case a prime example of how transsexual patients try to manipulate their doctors to get what they want. Transgender people tend to see in the story of Agnes a savvy young woman who accurately mapped the relations of power within which she negotiated and actualized her sense of self.

Every society exerts close controls over the transfers of persons from one status to another. Where transfers of sexual statuses are concerned, these controls are particularly restrictive and rigorously enforced. Only upon highly ceremonialized occasions are changes permitted and then such transfers are characteristically regarded as "temporary" and "playful" variations on what the person "after all," and "really" is. Thereby societies exercise close controls over the ways in which the sex composition of their own populations are constituted and changed.

From the standpoint of persons who regard themselves as normally sexed, their environment has a perceivedly normal sex composition. This composition is rigorously dichotomized into the "natural," *i.e., moral*, entities of male and female. The dichotomy provides for persons who are "naturally," "originally," "in the first place," "in the beginning," "all along," and "forever" one or the other. Changes in the frequency of these moral entities can occur only through three legitimate paths: birth, death, and migration. Except for a legal change in birth certificate no legitimate path exists between the statuses of male and female. Even the legal change is regarded with considerable reservation by societal members who take their *bona fide* sex status for granted.

The normative, *i.e.,* legitimate sexual composition of the population as seen from the point of view of members who count themselves part of the perceivedly normally sexed population, can be described with the following table of transition probabilities:

	At time$_2$	
	Male	Female
At time$_1$ — Male	1.0	0.0
At time$_1$ — Female	0.0	1.0

This study reports one of a series of cases that fall into the normatively prohibited lower left and upper right cells. These persons are being studied in the Departments of Psychiatry, Urology, and Endocrinology in the Medical Center of the University of California, Los Angeles. These persons have severe anatomical irregularities. In each case the transfer occurred late in the developmental life cycle and was accomplished as a more or less clear matter of personal election. Severe anatomical anomalies—for example, the case to be reported here is that of a nineteen-year-old girl raised as a boy whose female measurements of 38-25-38 were accompanied by a fully developed penis and scrotum—were contradictory of the appearances that were otherwise appropriate to their claimed rights to live in culturally provided sexual statuses. The transfers were accompanied by the subscription, by each of these persons, to the cultural conception of a dichotomized sex composition in which, with vehement insistence, they included themselves. Such insistence was not accompanied by clinically interesting ego defects. These persons contrast in many interesting ways with transvestites, trans-sexualists, and homosexuals.

In each case the persons managed the achievement of their rights to live in the chosen sexual status while operating with the realistic conviction that disclosure of their secrets would bring swift and certain ruin in the form of status degradation, psychological trauma, and loss of material advantages. Each had as an enduring practical task to achieve rights to be treated and to treat others according to the obligated prerogatives of the elected sex status. They had as resources their remarkable awareness and uncommon sense knowledge of the organization and operation of social structures that were for those that are able to take their sexual status for granted routinized, "seen but unnoticed" backgrounds of their everyday affairs. They had, too, great skills in interpersonal manipulations. While their knowledge and interpersonal skills were markedly instrumental in character, by no means were they exclusively so.

The work of achieving and making secure their rights to live in the elected sex status while providing for the possibility of detection and ruin carried out within the socially structured conditions in which this work occurred I shall call "passing."

In the lives of these persons the work and the socially structured occasions of sexual passing were obstinately unyielding to their attempts to routinize the rounds of daily activities. This obstinacy points to the omnirelevance of sexual statuses to affairs of daily life as an invariant but unnoticed background in the texture of relevances that comprise the changing actual scenes of everyday life. The experiences of these intersexed persons permits an appreciation of these background relevances that are otherwise easily overlooked or difficult to grasp because of their routinized character and because they are so embedded in a background of relevances that are simply "there" and taken for granted.

I shall confine my attention in this paper to a discussion of one case. I should like to tell what this person had specifically to hide, the structural relevance of her secrets, the socially structured situations of crisis, the management strategies and justifications that she employed, and the relevance of these considerations for the task of treating practical circumstances as a sociological phenomenon.

AGNES

Agnes appeared at the Department of Psychiatry at U.C.L.A. in October, 1958 where she had been referred to Dr. Robert J. Stoller by a private physician in Los Angeles to whom Agnes had in turn been referred by her physician in her home town, Northwestern City. Agnes was a nineteen-year-old, white, single girl, who was at the time self-supporting and working as a typist for a local insurance company. Her father was a machinist who died when Agnes was a child. Her mother supported a family of four children, of whom Agnes was the youngest, with occasional and semiskilled work in an aircraft plant. Agnes said that she was raised as a Catholic but has not taken Communion for the past three years. She said of herself that she no longer believed in God.

Agnes' appearance was convincingly female. She was tall, slim, with a very female shape. Her measurements were 38-25-38. She had long, fine dark-blonde hair, a young face with pretty features, a peaches-and-cream complexion, no facial hair, subtly plucked eyebrows, and no makeup except for lipstick. At the time of her first appearance she was dressed in a tight sweater which marked off her thin shoulders, ample breasts, and narrow waist. Her feet and hands, though somewhat larger than usual for a woman, were in no way remarkable in this respect. Her usual manner of dress did not distinguish her from a typical girl of her age and class. There was nothing garish or exhibitionistic in her attire, nor was there any hint of poor taste or that she was ill at ease in her clothing, as is seen so frequently in transvestites and in women with disturbances in sexual identification. Her voice, pitched at an alto level, was soft, and her delivery had the occasional lisp similar to that affected by feminine appearing male homosexuals. Her manner was appropriately feminine with a slight awkwardness that is typical of middle adolescence.

Details of her medical, physical, and endocrinological characteristics have been reported elsewhere.[1] To summarize her medical, physical, and endocrinological characteristics, prior to any surgical procedures she appeared as a person with feminine body contours and hair pattern. She had large, well-developed breasts coexisting with the normal external genitalia of a male. An abdominal laparotomy and pelvic and adrenal exploration, performed two years before she was first seen at U.C.L.A., revealed no uterus or ovaries, no evidence of any vestigial female apparatus nor any abnormal tissue mass in the abdomen, retroperitoneal area, or pelvis. Bilateral testicular biopsy showed some atrophy of the testes. A large number of laboratory tests on blood and urine as well as X-ray examinations of the chest and skull were all within normal limits. A buccal smear and skin biopsy revealed a negative (male) chromatin pattern. There was some evidence of a urethral smear showing cellular cornification suggestive of moderately high estrogenic (female hormone) activity.

Agnes was born a boy with normal-appearing male genitals. A birth certificate was issued for a male and she was appropriately named. Until the age of seventeen she was recognized by everyone to be a boy. In the biography furnished to us over many hours of conversations, the male role was both consistently and insistently described as a difficult one and poorly managed. Her accounts exaggerated the evidences of her natural femininity and suppressed evidences of masculinity. Secondary feminine sex characteristics developed at puberty. According to her account, grammar school years were at least tolerable whereas the three years of high school were stressful in the extreme. At the age of seventeen, at the end of her junior year of high school, she refused to return to complete the senior year. This was in June, 1956. After considerable planning, rehearsals, dieting to "make myself pretty," and similar preparations, she left her home town in August, 1956 for a month's visit with a grandmother in Midwest City. At the end of the month's visit, according to plan, she left her grandmother's house without leaving word of her whereabouts, and in a downtown hotel changed to feminine attire with the hope of finding a job in that city. For various reasons she felt unable to carry through with the plan of remaining in Midwest City and after phoning her mother returned home on the evening of the change. In the fall of 1956, she entered a hospital in her home town for examinations and the exploratory laparotomy which was done under the supervision of her private physician. During the fall of 1956 and following her hospitalization, she continued her schooling with the help of a tutor that had been provided under her mother's arrangement with the Public School system. She chafed under this as a resented confinement. In December, 1956 the tutor was dismissed and Agnes got a job as a typist in a small factory on the outskirts of town. She continued with this job until August, 1957 when, accompanied by girlfriends, she came to Los Angeles. She lived in Long Beach with a girlfriend and worked in downtown Los Angeles in a small insurance office. In December, 1957 she and her roommate moved into downtown Los Angeles "to be close to our work." In February 1958 she met her boyfriend Bill, and in April, 1958, to be closer to him, moved to the San Fernando Valley. She quit her job in March 1958 and was out of work at the time that she moved to the Valley. After a succession of crises with her boyfriend she returned to her home town in April, 1958 to see her previous physician for the purpose of obtaining a letter from him "explaining" Agnes' condition to her boyfriend. This letter was deliberately written by her physician in a general manner so as to mask the actual character of the difficulty. The boyfriend found this only temporarily satisfactory. His increasing insistence upon intercourse and plans for marriage, which Agnes frustrated, produced a series of increasingly severe quarrels. In June, 1958 Agnes disclosed her actual condition to her boyfriend and the affair continued on this basis. In November, 1958 Agnes was seen for the first time at U.C.L.A. Regular conversations at weekly intervals were held until August, 1959. In March, 1959 a castration operation was performed at U.C.L.A. in which the penis and scrotum were skinned, the penis and testes amputated, and the skin of the amputated penis used for a vagina while labia were constructed from the skin of the scrotum.

During this period Agnes was seen regularly by Dr. Robert J. Stoller, psychiatrist and psychoanalyst, Dr. Alexander Rosen, a psychologist, and by me. Approximately thirty-five hours of conversations that I had with her were tape recorded. My remarks in this paper are based upon transcriptions of these materials and upon materials collected by Stoller and Rosen with whom the work was done collaboratively.

AGNES, THE NATURAL, NORMAL FEMALE

Agnes had an abiding practical preoccupation with competent female sexuality. The nature of her concerns, as well as the incongruity that such an abiding concern presents to "common sense," permits us to describe, preliminarily at least, the strange features that the population of legitimately sexed persons exhibit as *objective* features from the point of view of persons who are able to take their own normally sexed status for granted. For such members perceived environments of sexed persons are populated with natural males, natural females, and persons who stand in moral contrast with them, *i.e.,* incompetent, criminal, sick, and sinful. *Agnes agreed with normals in her subscription to this definition of a real world of sexed persons, and treated it, as do they, as a matter of objective, institutionalized facts, i.e.,* moral facts.

Agnes vehemently insisted that she was, and was to be treated as, a natural, normal female. The following is a preliminary list of properties of "natural, normally sexed persons" as cultural objects. Intended as an anthropological paraphrasing of members' beliefs, these properties are to be read with the use of the invariable prefix, "From the standpoint of an adult member of our society, . . ." Examples are furnished in the first two properties.

1. From the standpoint of an adult member of our society, the perceived environment of "normally sexed persons" is populated by two sexes and only two sexes, "male" and "female."

2. From the standpoint of an adult member of our society, the population of normal persons is a morally dichotomized population. The question of its existence is decided as a matter of motivated compliance with this population as a legitimate order. It is not decided as a matter of biological, medical, urological, sociological, psychiatric, or psychological fact. The question of its existence is instead decided by consulting both the likelihood that compliance to this legitimate order can be enforced and the conditions that determine this likelihood.

3. The adult member includes himself in this environment and counts himself as one or the other not only as a condition of his self-respect, but as a condition whereby the exercise of his rights to live without excessive risks and interference from others are routinely enforceable.

4. The members of the normal population, for him the *bona fide* members of that population, are essentially, originally, in the first place, always have been, and always will be, once and for all, in the final analysis, either "male" or "female."

5. Certain insignia are regarded by normals as essential in their identifying function,[2] whereas other qualities, actions, relationships, and the like are treated as transient, temporary, accidental, circumstantial, and the rest. For normals the possession of a penis by a male and a vagina by a female are essential insignia. Appropriate feelings, activities, membership obligations, and the like are attributed to persons who possess penises and vaginas. (However the possession of a penis or a vagina as a biological event is to be distinguished from the possession of one or the other or both as a cultural event. The differences between biological and cultural penises and vaginas as socially employed evidences of "natural sexuality" will be commented on at greater length below.)

6. The recognition of either male or female is made by normals for new members not only at the point of their first appearance, *e.g.,* the neonate, but even before. It extends as well to the entire ancestry and to posterity. The recognition is not changed by the death of the member.[3]

7. For normals, the presence in the environment of sexed objects has the feature of "a natural matter of fact." This naturalness carries along with it, as a constituent part of its meaning, the sense of its being right and correct, *i.e.,* morally proper that it be that way. Because it is a natural matter of fact, for the members of our society there are only *natural* males and *natural* females. The good society for the member is composed only of persons who are either one sex or the other. Hence the *bona fide* member of the society, within what he subscribes to as well as what he expects others to subscribe to as committed beliefs about "natural matters of fact" regarding distributions of sexed persons in the society, finds the claims of the sciences like zoology, biology, and psychiatry strange. These sciences argue that decisions about sexuality are problematic matters. The normal finds it strange and difficult to lend credence to "scientific" distributions of *both* male and female characteristics among persons, or a procedure for deciding sexuality which adds up lists of male and female characteristics and takes

the excess as the criterion of the member's sex, or the practice of using the first three years of training to decide sexuality, or the provision for the presence in the familiar society of males who have vaginas and females who have penises.

This "common sense" characterization is in no way limited to nonprofessional opinion. For example, a leading member of a prominent Department of Psychiatry in this country commented after hearing about the case, "I don't see why one needs to pay that much interest to such cases. She is after all a very rare occurrence. These persons are after all freaks of nature." We could not have solicited a more common sense formula. A measure of the extent of the member's commitment to the moral order of sexual types would consist of the reluctance to lend credence to a characterization that departed from the "natural facts of life." As we shall see below, in many different ways Agnes taught us as well, though unwittingly, the institutionally motivated character of this reluctance.

I have stressed several times that for the *bona fide* member "normal" means "in accordance with the mores." Sexuality as a natural fact of life means therefore sexuality as a natural and *moral* fact of life. The member's willingness, therefore, to treat normal sexuality as an object of theoretical interest requires, in deciding for himself the real nature of sexed persons, that he suspend the relevance of his institutionally routinized practical circumstances. We find, however, that the normal member does *not* treat sexuality, his own or others', as a matter of mere theoretic interest, whereas this is in principle the limit of our investigative interest in the phenomenon of normal sexuality as it is in other sciences as well. The normal also treats the sexed character of persons populating his everyday environment as a quality that is "decided by *nature*." This quality, once the member's "nature" decides it, holds thereafter irrespective of time, occasion, circumstance, or considerations of practical advantage. The person's membership as a normally sexed member, male or female, has the characteristic of, and is treated by the normal as remaining invariant throughout that person's biography and throughout his future lifetime and beyond. His sexual membership remains unchanged through any imputed actual and potential lifetime. To use Parsons' phrasing, it is "invariant to all exigencies."

8. From the standpoint of the normal member, if one examines the population of sexed persons at one time counting the presence of males and females, and at a later time examines the population again, no transfers will have occurred from one sex status to the other except for those transfers that are ceremonially permitted.

Our society prohibits willful or random movements from one sex status to the other. It insists that such transfers be accompanied by the well-known controls that accompany masquerading, play-acting, party behavior, convention behavior, spying, and the like. Such changes are treated both by those making the changes as well as those observing them in others as limited both by the clock as well as by occasions and practical circumstances. The person is expected "after the play" to "stop acting." On the way home from the party the person may be reminded that the party "is over," and that he should conduct himself like the person he "really is." Such admonitions as a "first line of social control" make up commonly encountered sanctions whereby persons are reminded to act in accordance with expected attitudes, appearances, affiliations, dress, style of life, round of life, and the like that are assigned by the major institutions. In our society these consist prominently of occupational and kinship arrangements with their intended obligatory statuses. Their importance is this: that persons are held to compliance with them regardless of their desires, *i.e.,* "whether they like it or not." From the standpoint of the normal, changes of the population's composition can be accomplished by the paths only of birth, death, and migration.

Agnes was all too aware that an alternative path had been traveled, that it was traveled with negligible frequency, and that the transfer was harshly punishable. Like Agnes, the normal knows that there are persons who make the change but he, as did she, counts such persons as freaks, unusual, or bizarre. Characteristically he finds the change itself difficult to "understand" and urges either punishment or medical remedy. Agnes did not depart from this point of view [4] even though her sex was for her a matter of willful election between available alternatives. This knowledge was accompanied by a burdensome necessity for justifying the election. The election consisted of choosing to live as the normally sexed person that she had always been.

Agnes subscribed to this description of a real world even though there were for her in that world persons, among whom she included herself, who had made the change from one sex to the other. Her early history stood in contrast for her to what she was nevertheless convinced about as to her normal sexuality. In seeking a change of birth certificate Agnes treated the change as the correction of an original error committed by persons who were ignorant of the "true facts."

Agnes held the conviction that there are not many people who could be told what she had done and who "will really understand." Hence, for Agnes an otherwise important common understanding with others had the troublesome feature that does not occur for normals, particularly where the dichotomy of sex types is concerned, namely, Agnes was unable to exercise the assumption that her circumstances, as they appeared to her would appear in a more or less identical way to her interactional partners, were they to exchange places. We might refer to this as the existence of a problematic "community of understandings" by and about sexed persons treating each other's sex as known in common and taken for granted by them.

9. In the cultural environments of normally sexed persons males have penises and females have vaginas. From the point of view of a normal member, wherever there are cases of males with vaginas and females with penises there are persons who, though they may be difficult to classify, must nevertheless be in principle classifiable and must be counted as members of one camp or the other. Agnes subscribed to this view too as a natural fact of life, even though this same population included at least one female with a penis, *i.e.*, herself, and following the operation included a female with a man-made vagina. It included others as well that she had learned of through her readings and contacts with physicians both in her home town and in Los Angeles. According to her account all others besides herself were personally unknown to her.

10. That Agnes could insist on her membership in the natural population of sexed persons even though she was, prior to the operation, a female with a penis and, following the operation, a female with a man-made vagina, suggests another important property of a naturally sexed person. When we compare Agnes' beliefs not only with those of normals but with what normals believe about persons whose genitals for one reason or another change in appearance, or suffer damage or loss, through aging, disease, injuries, or surgery we observe that it is not that normals and Agnes insist upon the possession of a vagina by females (we consider now only the case of the normal female; the identical argument holds for males). They insist upon the possession of *either* a vagina that nature made *or* a vagina that *should have been there all along, i.e.,* the *legitimate* possession. The legitimately possessed vagina is the object of interest. *It is the vagina the person is entitled to.* Although "nature" is a preferred and *bona-fide* source of entitlement, surgeons are as well if they repair a natural error, *i.e.,* if they serve as nature's agents to provide "what nature meant to be there." Not *just this* vagina but *just this* vagina as the case of the *real thing.* In the identical way that for a member of a language community a linguistic utterance is a case of a-word-in-the-language, or for a game player a move is a move-in-the-game, the genitals that serve the normal member as insignia of normally sexed membership consists of penises-and-vaginas-in-the-moral-order-of-sexed-persons. (I am speaking descriptively. I propose these "essences" as attributions that members find in their environments. To avoid any misunderstandings, I would like to stress that I am talking data. I am not arguing platonic realism as a philosophy of social science.)

Agnes' experiences with a female cousin, sister-in-law, and aunt may illuminate this property. In the course of commenting on what she characterized as her cousin's "jealousy" when a male visitor to her brother's home who had not met either one clearly preferred Agnes to her cousin who was approximately the same age, Agnes commented on her cousin's change in attitude from one in which she was favorable to Agnes before the trip to Midwest City but showed strong disapproval afterwards. According to Agnes' comments, Agnes felt that her cousin thought of Agnes as a fake, not a real woman. Agnes said of her cousin that the cousin felt that Agnes was a rival. (The portrayed rivalry was reciprocally felt, for Agnes said that she found it hard to "get her out of my mind.") Similarly for Agnes' sister-in-law, a mild disapproval on the sister-in-law's part prior to the Midwest City trip changed to open hostility upon Agnes' return. Agnes attributed this to the sister-in-law's resentment that Agnes was hardly the person to compare herself to the sister-in-law in affairs of proper domestic and marital conduct. By comparison with these rivals, Agnes commented on the dramatic change on the part of the elderly aunt who accompanied her mother to Los Angeles to care for Agnes during her convalescence from the castration operation. Agnes characterized the aunt as a natural female with no questions about it. The aunt, said Agnes, reflected the attitude of other family members. This attitude, said Agnes, was one of general acceptance prior to the trip to Midwest City, consternation and severe disapproval after the return, and relieved acceptance and treatment of her as a "real female after all" (Agnes' quotation of the aunt's remark) following the operation and during our conversations while the aunt was in Los Angeles. The point: in each case the object of interest was not the possession of the penis or of the man-made vagina, but, in the case of the cousin and sister-in-law, Agnes' penis was *prima facie* contradictory of Agnes' claims, by her other appearances, to possess the real thing. In the case of the aunt, although the vagina was man-made it *was* a case of the real thing since it was what she was now seen to have been entitled to all along. Both the aunt and the mother were strongly impressed by the fact that the operation had been done at all "in this country." That the physicians at the U.C.L.A. Medical Center by their actions reconstructed and validated Agnes' claim to her status as a natural female needs, of course, to be stressed.

Some additional features of Agnes as the natural female require mention.

Not only did Agnes directly express the claim "I have always been a girl," but it was advanced by the device of a remarkably idealized biography in which evidences of her original femininity were exaggerated while evidences of a mixture of characteristics, let alone clear-cut evidences of a male upbringing, were rigorously suppressed. The child Agnes of Agnes' accounts did not like to play rough games like baseball; her *"biggest"* problem was having to play boys' games; Agnes was more or less considered a sissy; Agnes was always the littlest one; Agnes played with dolls and cooked mud patty cakes for her brother; Agnes helped her mother with the household duties; Agnes doesn't remember what kinds of gifts she received from her father when she was a child. I once asked Agnes if she had lined up with the boys in public school. Her startled and angry reply was, "Lining up with the boys for what!" When I told her I was thinking of lining up in dancing class or lining up for physical examinations at school Agnes said, "Lining up never came up." I asked her if medical examinations with boys never happened. She agreed "That's right, they never happened." We came to refer to her presentation of the 120 per cent female. Not only in her accounts, but at times in her conversations with me, Agnes was the coy, sexually innocent, fun-loving, passive, receptive, "young thing." As a kind of dialectical counterpart to the 120 per cent female Agnes portrayed her boyfriend as a 120 per cent male who, she said, when we first started to talk, and repeated through eight stressful weeks following the operation when post-operative complications had subsided and the recalcitrant vagina was finally turning out to be the thing the physicians had promised, "wouldn't have been interested in me at all if I was abnormal." The penis that was possessed by the natural female was, repeatedly and under recurrent questioning, an accidental appendage used for the sole purpose of passing urine. The penis of Agnes' accounts had never been erect; she was never curious about it; it was never scrutinized by her or by others; it never entered into games with other children; it never moved "voluntarily"; it was never a source of pleasurable feelings; it had always been an accidental appendage stuck on by a cruel trick of fate. When it was amputated and Agnes was asked now that her penis and scrotum were gone what did she think of the penis and scrotum that were gone, her answer was that she did not feel it was necessary to give it any more thought than one would give to having had a painful wart that had been removed.

Agnes frequently called my attention to her lack of a biography that was appropriate to the fact that she was accepted by others and most particularly by her boyfriend as a girl. Agnes talked of the seventeen year gap in her life and indicated that her present female character was assigned by others a continuous history as a female that extended to the time of her birth. She pointed out that only since the time that she made the change had she been able to establish a female biography of experiences which she and others could draw on as a precedent in managing present appearances and circumstances. She lacked a proper biography to serve as a historico-prospective context for managing current situations. For others, and most particularly with her boyfriend, an all-along female corresponded to the anticipations that she encouraged with her boyfriend. Two years of accumulating memories presented her a chronic source for a series of crises about which more will be spoken below when I discuss her passing occasions and her management devices.

Another feature of the normal natural female was found in Agnes' portrayal of and insistence upon her life-long desire to be the thing that she had always known she was. Within her portrayals, her desires came essentially from mysterious and unknown sources, and withstood all vicissitudes posed by an ignorant environment that attempted to force, though unsuccessfully, an arbitrary line of departure from a normal course of development. Agnes stressed repeatedly, "I've always wanted to be a girl; I have always felt like a girl; and I have always been a girl but a mistaken environment forced the other thing on me." On many occasions of our conversations she was asked how she accounted for the desire that withstood environmental exigencies. Her replies invariably elaborated the theme, "There's no explaining it."

Given Agnes' subscription to the normals distinction between the normal natural male and the normal natural female, there was less ambiguity for Agnes in distinguishing between herself as either a male or a female than there was in distinguishing between herself as a natural female and a male homosexual. The very extensiveness of the exaggerations of her feminine biography, of the masculinity of her boyfriend, of her anaesthetized penis, and the like, furnish the feature continually insisted upon: an identification which is consistently feminine. Much of the instrumental realism that she directed to the management of her chosen sexual status was concerned with so managing her circumstances as to avoid what she treated as a mistaken and degrading identity. Confounding the two were matters of objectively assessable error, ignorance, and injustice on the parts of others. Those of her defenses which cost her dearly in effectiveness and reality orientation were directed to keeping the distances between her natural normal femininity and male homosexuals in repair. Time after time in the course of our meetings when I directed the conversation to homosexuals and transvestites Agnes had a great deal of difficulty, simultaneously managing her fascination for the topic and the great anxiety that the conversation seemed to generate. The picture she would present then was that of a mild depression. Her answers would become impoverished. Occasionally her voice would break as she denied knowledge of this or that. There was a repeated insistence that she was in no way comparable. "I'm not like them," she would continually insist. "In high school I steered clear of boys that acted like sissies...anyone with an abnormal problem...I would completely shy away from them and go to the point of being insulting just enough to get around them...I didn't want to feel noticed talking to them because somebody might relate them to me. I didn't want to be classified with them."

Just as normals frequently will be at a loss to understand "why a person would do that," *i.e.,* engage in homosexual activities or dress as a member of the opposite sex, so did Agnes display the same lack of "understanding" for such behavior, although her accounts characteristically were delivered with flattened affect and never with indignation. When she was invited by me to compare herself with homosexuals and transvestites she found the comparison repulsive. Although she wanted to know more, when I proposed that a transvestite who was being seen by another researcher was interested in talking with her she refused to have any contact with him. Nor would she consider talking with any of the other patients that I mentioned to her who we were seeing who had experiences similar to hers. When I told her that a group of about seventeen persons in San Francisco who had either received or were planning to have a castration operation were interested in meeting and exchanging experiences with persons with similar problems, Agnes said that she could not imagine what they would have to talk with her about and insisted that she was in no way any concern of theirs.

As we have seen, she insisted that her male genitals were a trick of fate, a personal misfortune, an accident, above all "it was beyond my control" whose presence she never accepted. She treated her genitals as an abnormal growth. Occasionally she would speak of them as a tumor. With genitals ruled out as essential signs of her femininity, and needing essential and natural signs of female sexuality, she counted instead the life-long desire to be a female and her prominent breasts. Her self-described feminine feelings, behavior, choices of companions, and the like were never portrayed as matters of decision or choice but were treated as *given* as a natural fact. As they were displayed in her accounts, their natural exercise would have been displayed from the beginning, she insisted, were it not for a misdirecting, frustrating, misunderstanding environment.

Before all she counted her breasts as essential insignia. On several occasions in our conversations she expressed the relief and joy she felt when she noticed at the age of twelve that her breasts were starting to develop. She said that she kept this discovery from her mother and siblings because "it was none of their business." It was clear from her later remarks that she meant by this that she feared that they would regard the development of the breasts as a medical abnormality and because of her age and incompetence might decide, regardless of and contrary to her wishes and to what she felt that she could have enforced upon them, that she receive medical attention and thereby risk their loss. She took particular pride in the size of her breasts, as she did in her measurements. Prior to the operation she was fearful that "the doctors at U.C.L.A." would decide among themselves, and without consulting her, and at the time of the operation, that the remedy for her condition consisted in amputating her breasts instead of her penis and scrotum. Following the operation, because of endocrinological changes and for other reasons, she lost weight. Her breasts became smaller; her chest measurement dropped from 38 to 35. The distress that she showed was sufficiently apparent to have been considered by us as one of the factors making up a short-lived but severe postoperative depression. When the Departments of Endocrinology and Urology had finished their medical work, but before the operation, she permitted herself a mild optimism which she kept under heavy check by the continual reminder that the decision was no longer in her hands, and by reminding herself, me, Stoller and Rosen that on prior occasions, most particularly after examinations in her home town, after permitting herself great optimism, she had been left with "nothing but encouragement. Just words." When she was told to report to the U.C.L.A. Medical Center and that the decision had been made to amputate the penis and make an artificial vagina for her, she spoke of the decision with great relief. She spoke of the medical decision as an authoritative vindication of her claims to her natural femininity. Even the complications following the operation furnished episodes of pleasurable vindication. For example, following the operation she developed a mild urethral drip for which she had been advised by the physician to wear a Kotex pad. When I observed rather pleasantly that this was certainly a new experience for her, she laughed and was obviously pleased and flattered.

There were many occasions when my attentions flattered her with respect to her femininity; for example, holding her arm while I guided her across the street; having lunch with her at the Medical Center; offering to hang up her coat; relieving her of her hand-bag; holding the automobile door for her while she entered; being solicitous for her comfort before I closed the auto door and took my own seat behind the wheel. At times like this her behavior reminded me that being female for her was like having been given a wonderful gift. It was on such occasions that she most clearly displayed the characteristics of the "120 per cent female." At such times she acted like a recent and enthusiastic initiate into the sorority of her heart's desire.

ACHIEVING THE ASCRIBED PROPERTIES OF THE NATURAL, NORMAL FEMALE

The natural, normal female was for Agnes an ascribed object.[5] In common with normals, she treated her femininity as independent of the conditions of its occurrence and invariant to the vicissitudes of desires, agreements, random or willful election, accident, considerations of advantage, available resources, and opportunities. It remained for her the temporally identical thing over all historical and prospective circumstances and possible experiences. It remained the self-same thing in essence under all imaginable transformations of actual appearances, time, and circumstances. It withstood all exigencies.

The ascribed, normal natural female was the object that Agnes sought to achieve for herself.

Two meanings of "achievement" are meant in speaking of Agnes' having achieved her status as a female. (1) Having become female represented for her a status up-grading from that of a male which was for her of lesser value than the status of a female. For her to be female made her a more desirable object by far in her own eyes and, as she was realistically convinced, in the eyes of others as well. Prior to the change and afterwards as well, the change to female not only represented an elevation of herself as a worth-while person, but was a status to which she literally aspired. (2) The second sense of achievement refers to the tasks of securing and guaranteeing for herself the ascribed rights and obligations of an adult female by the acquisition and use of skills and capacities, the efficacious display of female appearances and performances, and the mobilizing of appropriate feelings and purposes. As in the normal case, the tests of such management work occurred under the gaze of and in the presence of normal male and female others.

While her claims to her natural femininity could be advanced they could not be taken for granted. Many matters served as obstinate reminders that her femininity, though claimed, could be claimed only at the cost of vigilance and work. Prior to the operation she was a female with a penis. The operation itself substituted one set of difficulties for another. Thus, after the operation she was a female with a "man-made" vagina. In her anxious words, "Nothing that is made by man can ever be as good as something that nature makes." She and her boyfriend were agreed on this. In fact, her boyfriend who, in her accounts of him, prided himself as a harsh realist, insisted on this and taught it to her to her dismayed agreement. In addition, her brand new vagina proved to be recalcitrant and tricky. Shortly after the operation an infection developed from the mold. When the mold was removed adhesions formed and the canal would no longer receive a penis-sized mold. Manual manipulations to keep the canal open had to be done out of the sight of others and with care that the nature of this private work remain concealed. These manipulations caused pain. For many weeks after the operation she suffered discomfort and was exasperated and humiliated by fecal and urethral dripping. This was followed by further hospitalization. There were mood changes and feelings that she had lost the sharpness, alertness, and definiteness of her thoughts. Unpredictable mood changes produced severe quarrels with her boyfriend who threatened to leave her if she showed any further anger with him. In addition there was the reminder that while she now had the vagina that she had with it a male biography. She would say, "There is a big gap in my life." In addition there was the fact that the change to a public feminine appearance had been made only three years before. Most of her prior rehearsals had been those in imagination. Thus she was still learning to act and feel like a woman. She was learning this new role only as a function of actually playing it out. There were risks and uncertainties involved. The job of securing and guaranteeing the rights of female by coming to deserve such attributions through her accomplishments—through her success in acting out the female role—thereby involved her in circumstances whose omnirelevant feature was that she knew something vitally relevant to the accepted terms of the interaction that the others did not know and that she was in fact engaged in the uncertain tasks of passing.

What were some matters that after and/or before the operation Agnes was required to hide?

1. Prior to the operation the contradictory insignia of her feminine appearance; the masked male genitals.
2. That she was raised as a boy and thus did not have a history to correspond to her appearance as an attractive female.
3. That she made the change only three years before and was still learning to act like the thing that she wanted to be taken for.
4. That she was unable and would be unable to fulfill the things expected of her by males who were attracted to her precisely to the extent that she succeeded in putting herself over as a sexually attractive female.
5. There was a man-made vagina.
6. That she wanted the penis and scrotum removed and a vagina constructed in its place. After the operation that she had a vagina that had been constructed from the skin of an amputated penis, and labia from the skin of the lost scrotum.
7. There were the matters to mask about the sexual services that her boyfriend demanded that she somehow satisfied.
8. There was what she did, and with whose help, to alter her appearance.
9. There were the activities of active management of persons around her in order to achieve the operation, most particularly the physicians and research personnel at U.C.L.A., and of course the medical personnel during the years when she sought medical help.

Agnes sought to be treated and to treat others according to a legitimate sexual status, while there accompanied this a deep dark secret which was concerned not with the skills and adequacy with which she acted out the status but with the legitimacy of her occupancy. For Agnes, acting out the new status was accompanied by the feelings that she knew something that the other person did not know, the disclosure of which, she was convinced and feared, would ruin her. The sex status transfer involved the assumption of a legitimate status the disclosure of which involved great risks, status degradation, psychological trauma, and loss of material advantages. This kind of passing is entirely comparable to passing found in political undergrounds, secret societies, refugees from political persecution, or Negroes who become whites. In Agnes' case it is of particular interest because the change of sexual status was accompanied by her paying marked and deliberate attention to making the new identity secure against some known and many unknown contingencies. This was done via active and deliberate management of her appearances before others as an object. She placed great stress on manners and proprieties and manipulation of personal relationships. The work had to be done in situations known with the most faltering knowledge, having marked uncertainty about its rules of practice, with severe risks and important prizes simultaneously involved, one not being available without the other. Punishment, degradation, loss of reputation, and loss of material advantages were the matters at risk should the change be detected. In almost every situation of interaction the relevance of the secret operated as background knowledge. Her concern to escape detection had a value of highest priority. Almost every situation had the feature therefore of an actual or potential "character and fitness" test. It would be less accurate to say of her that she has passed than that she was continually engaged in the work of passing.

PASSING

The work of achieving and making secure her rights to live as a normal, natural female while having continually to provide for the possibility of detection and ruin carried on within socially structured conditions I call Agnes' "passing." Her situations of activity—a very large number of them—were chronically ones of "structured strain." We may think of them as socially structured situations of potential and actual crisis. Sociologically speaking, the stress is a "normal stress" in the sense that the stress occurred precisely because of her active attempts to comply with a *legitimate order* of sex roles. Each of a great variety of structurally different instances required vigilance, resourcefulness, stamina, sustained motivation, preplanning that was accompanied continually by improvisation, and, continually, sharpness, wit, knowledge, and very importantly her willingness to deal in "good reasons"—*i.e.,* to either furnish or be ready to furnish reasonable justifications (explanations) or to avoid situations where explanations would be required.

Passing was not a matter of Agnes' desire. It was necessary for her. Agnes had to be a female. Whether she liked it or not she had to pass. She enjoyed her successes and feared and hated her failures. When I asked her to tell me the "real good things" that had happened to her she talked about her first job after her return to her home town; fun on group dates in her home town after the change; living with her roommate in Los Angeles; her skill as a stenographer; a succession of increasingly better jobs; the operation eight weeks afterwards when the new vagina looked good, was finally healing without pain, and to the surprise of the surgeons was responding to her efforts to achieve five inches of depth. "Of course the best thing that ever happened to me was Bill."

When I asked Agnes if there were any "real bad things" that had happened to her, the strain in her attempt to reply was so evident that I found it necessary to modify the question and asked instead for some things that were "bad things but not such bad things." To this she replied, "Being noticed (in grammar and especially high school) and being noticed that I didn't have any friends or companions or anything." (After pausing). "I didn't have friends because I didn't react normally under any kind of a relationship like that. I couldn't have a boyfriend. I didn't *want* a boyfriend. Because of the way I was I couldn't have girlfriends either, so there I was . . . I didn't have friends because I couldn't react normally under any kind of a relationship like that." I asked why she couldn't have friends. "How *could* I have girlfriends? How *could* I have pals?" My question: why not? "I probably felt it would be impossible. At school I didn't joke around with the girls or pal around or do anything like that because then I was being very conspicuous." From her other descriptions, particularly difficult times can be briefly, but of course not exhaustively, enumerated as follows: growing up; the three years of high school; life at home immediately after the change; the attitudes of family, neighbors, and former friends after she returned from Midwest City; the acute disappointment when she was told that no action could be taken after her examinations and exploratory laparatomy in her home town; managing her boyfriend Bill's demands for intercourse; the episode with Bill when she finally disclosed to him that she had a penis between her legs; managing her conversations with us at U.C.L.A. in the hope that the decision would be favorable and that the operation would be done soon; her fear that the doctors would decide to amputate her breasts instead of her penis and that she was committed to an operation the decision being no longer within her control; following the operation her convalescence which lasted approximately six weeks and which was marked by a moderate depression, quickly changing moods which she was unable either to control or to justify to herself or to her boyfriend, and a succession of severe quarrels with her boyfriend; a recalcitrant vagina that would not heal properly and had a fraction of the depth she had hoped for; a severe bladder infection that required rehospitalization; the reduction in the size of her breasts from 38 inches to 35 and her attendant fear that the penis was after all necessary to keep her feminine appearance; her changed relationship with Bill for three months following the operation; and finally, anticipatorily, Los Angeles, if her marriage plans did not materialize.

The "real good situations" were those in which the work of passing permitted her the feelings of, and permitted her to treat others and to be treated by others as, a "normal, natural girl." The "real bad things" were the situations in which the management work, for various reasons, failed or promised to fail. Only in retrospect did they acquire the dramatic features of successes or failures. For our interests the critical cases were those that had to be handled *in their course*. What kinds of situations were they? How did she manage over their course to come to terms with them? In many of these situations and somehow, despite the socially structured character of the crises, she achieved some approximation to routinized management and "life as usual."

An illustrative instance may be used to introduce our discussion of these questions.

Before reporting for a physical examination for a job that she later obtained with a large insurance company, and because she had had similar previous physical examinations, Agnes decided that she would allow the physician's examination to proceed as far as her lower abdomen. If the physician then proceeded or gave any indication of examining the genital area she had decided to protest modesty and if this wasn't enough to put the physician off she would simply leave, perhaps feigning modesty, or if necessary giving no excuse. It was much to be preferred to forego the job than to risk disclosure, with one condition being dependent of course upon the other.

In instance after instance the situation to be managed can be described in general as one in which the attainment of commonplace goals and attendant satisfactions involved with it a risk of exposure. She employed a strategy by which she was prepared to get out from under if exposure seemed likely though at the cost of sacrificing these advantages. Her characteristic situation in passing was one in which she had to be prepared to choose, and frequently chose, between securing the feminine identity and accomplishing *ordinary* goals. Her chronic situation was one in which both conditions had to be simultaneously satisfied by her active deliberate management. The thing that she knew that others did not know was that the two conditions—managing to obtain opportunities for institutionalized and commonplace satisfaction, while minimizing the risk of disclosure—were ranked in a fixed priority: security was to be protected first. The common satisfactions were to be obtained only if the prior conditions of the secured identity could be satisfied. Risks in this direction entailed the sacrifice of the other satisfactions.

* * *

PASSING OCCASIONS THAT THE GAME MODEL DOES NOT ANALYZE PROPERLY

There are many occasions which fail to satisfy various game properties. When the game is used to analyze them, the analysis contains structural incongruities.

One type of such an occasion occurred very frequently: Agnes, by acting in the manner of a "secret apprentice" would learn, as she told it, "to act like a lady." Its feature was something like this: Agnes and her interaction partners would be directed to a valuable mutually understood goal while at the same time another goal of equivalent value, to which the other person contributed, remained known to Agnes alone and was carefully concealed. In contrast to the episodic character of the occasions that were described previously, such an occasion was characterized by its continuing and developmental character. Further, its "rules" are learned only over the course of the actual interaction, as a function of actual participation, and by accepting the risks involved.

Several persons were prominent in her accounts with whom she not only acted like a lady but learned, from them, how to act like a lady. An important partner-instructor was Bill's mother in whose home she spent a great deal of time as a prospective daughter-in-law. Bill's mother was of Dutch-Indonesian ancestry and supported herself as a dressmaker. While teaching Agnes how to cook Dutch dishes to please Bill, she also taught Agnes how to cook in the first place. Agnes said that Bill's mother taught her dressmaking and materials; she taught her which clothes she should wear; they discussed dress shops, shopping, styles that were appropriate for Agnes, and the skills of home management.

Agnes spoke of the "long lectures" that she would receive from Bill upon occasions that she did something which he disapproved. One evening he returned from work at around five in the afternoon to find her sunbathing on the lawn in front of her apartment. She learned a great deal from his detailed and angry arguments of the ways in which this "display in front of all those men coming home from work" was offensive to him, but attractive to other men.

On another occasion she received a lecture from Bill on how a lady should conduct herself on a picnic. This he did by angrily analyzing the failings of a companion's date who had insisted, in his angry account, on wanting things her own way, of offering her opinions when she should have been retiring, of being sharp in her manner when she should have been sweet, of complaining instead of taking things as they were, of professing her sophistication instead of being innocent, of acting bawdy instead of abjuring any claims of equality with men, of demanding services instead of looking to give the man she was with pleasure and comfort. Agnes quoted Bill with approval: "Don't think the others are taking your part when you act like that. They're feeling sorry for the guy who has to be with her. They're thinking, where did he ever pick her up!"

With her roommates and wider circles of girlfriends Agnes exchanged gossip, and analyses of men, parties, and dating postmortems. Not only did she adopt the pose of passive acceptance of instructions, but she learned as well the value of passive acceptance as a desirable feminine character trait. The rivalry with her female cousin, for all its hurtfulness, furnished her instruction by forcing a reflection upon the things that were wrong with her cousin, while claiming for herself qualities that contrasted with those that she found to criticize in the cousin.

On these occasions Agnes was required to live up to the standards of conduct, appearance, skills, feelings, motives, and aspirations while simultaneously learning what these standards were. To learn them was for her a continuous project of self-improvement. They had to be learned in situations in which she was treated by others as knowing them in the first place as a matter of course. They had to be learned in situations in which she was not able to indicate that she was learning them. They had to be learned by participating in situations where she was expected to know the very things that she was simultaneously being taught.

An occasion that was very much like that of the secret apprenticeship was one in which she permitted the environment to furnish her the answers to its own questions. I came to think of it as the practice of "anticipatory following." This occurred, I regret to say, with disconcerting frequency in my conversations with her. When I read over the transcripts, and listened again to the taped interviews while preparing this paper, I was appalled by the number of occasions on which I was unable to decide whether Agnes was answering my questions or whether she had learned from my questions, and more importantly from more subtle cues both prior to and after the questions, what answers would do. For another example, on the occasion of the physical examination for the insurance company job the examining physician palpated her abdomen. Agnes was uncertain as to what he was "feeling for." "Maybe he was feeling for my 'female organs'" (of course she has none), "or for something hard." To all his questions about pain or discomfort she answered that there was none. "When he didn't say anything I figured he hadn't found anything unusual."

Another common set of occasions arose when she engaged in friendly conversation without having biographical and group affiliation data to swap off with her conversational partner. As Agnes said, "Can you imagine all the blank years I have to fill in? Sixteen or seventeen years of my life that I have to make up for. I have to be careful of the things that I say, just natural things that could slip out…I just never say anything at all about my past that in any way would make a person ask what my past life was like. I say general things. I don't say anything that could be misconstrued." Agnes said that with men she was able to pass as an interesting conversationalist by encouraging her male partners to talk about themselves. Women partners, she said, explained the general and indefinite character of her biographical remarks, which she delivered with a friendly manner, by a combination of her niceness and modesty. "They probably figure that I just don't like to talk about myself."

There were many occasions whose structure was such as not to contain any criteria whereby a goal could be said to have been achieved, a feature intrinsic to game activities. Instead, success in managing the present interaction consisted in having established or sustained a valuable and attractive character, of acting in a present situation that was consistent with the precedents and prospects that the presented character formulated, and for which present appearances were documentary evidences. For example, Agnes said that it was soon clear to her after she started working for the insurance company that she would have to quit the job. The duties were dull and unskilled and there was little chance for advancement. The little innovations that she made in order to make the job more interesting gave only temporary relief. She wished very much to up-grade her skills and to establish a more impressive job history. For these reasons she wished to quit the job for a better one but would have had to quit in the face of Bill's opposition. She was convinced that he would credit none of these reasons but would instead use the reasons she gave as evidences of deficiencies in her attitude toward work. He had admonished her that for him, quitting for such reasons was not acceptable and that if she quit it would only reflect again on her immaturity and irresponsibility. When she quit nevertheless she justified it by saying that it was entirely out of her hands. She had been fired because of a work lay-off. This was not true.

A further set of passing occasions are particularly resistant to analysis as games. These occasions have the features of being continuous and developmental; of a retrospective-prospective significance of present appearances; of every present state of the action being identical in meaning with the-situation-as-it-has-developed-thus-far; in which commonplace goals could neither be abandoned, postponed, or redefined; in which Agnes' commitment to compliance with the natural, normal female was under chronic threat or open contradiction; and in which remedies were not only out of her hands but were beyond the control of those with whom she had to deal. All of these situations, both by her reports as well as by our observations, were stressful in the extreme.

One such "occasion" consisted of the continuing tasks that Agnes referred to as "remaining inconspicuous." Agnes said that this was very much a problem in high school. She insisted, "to set you right," that this was no longer her concern, and that it had been replaced by a fear of being exposed. The fact is, nonetheless, that it remained very much a matter of concern. My impression is that Agnes said this because of the way in which the problem had been brought up in our conversation. I had introduced it to her by relating to her comments by E.P., a male patient, about his preoccupation with remaining inconspicuous. I described E.P. to her as a person who was much older than she, had been raised as a female and at eighteen had had a castration operation which removed a vestigial penis. I told her that E.P. had continued to dress as a female but wanted to be treated as a male; and that the change for E.P. had occurred only several years before. I described E.P.'s appearance and illustrated his preoccupation with remaining inconspicuous with E.P.'s account of "this kind of nasty thing is always happening to me:" *i.e.*, of being approached in a bar by a man who would say, "Excuse me, my friend and I over there have a bet. Are you a man or a woman?" Agnes immediately detected E.P.'s "abnormality" and denied flatly that she and E.P. were in any way comparable. In this context she said that she did not recognize that the problem of remaining inconspicuous was any longer a problem for her.

Agnes described the problem of remaining inconspicuous in high school by talking about the way she avoided being conspicuous: by never eating in the high school lunch room; by joining no clubs; by restricting her physical movements; by generally avoiding conversations; by avoiding at any cost "those boys who had something queer about them"; by wearing a loose shirt somewhat larger than her size and sitting with her arms folded in front of her, leaning forward on the desk so that her breasts did not show; by avoiding choices of either male or female companions; by sitting in the far rear corner of every classroom and not responding to classroom discussions so that, as Agnes said, "whole days would pass and I wouldn't say a word"; and by following a rigid schedule of time and movements around the high school building so that, as her account of it runs, she always entered the same gate to the schoolyard entering the same door to the schoolroom, following the same path to her room, arriving at the same time, leaving by the same exit, following the same path home, and the like. This account had come up in reply to my question, "Was there any particular bad situation that occurred?" to which she replied, "I don't know about any particular bad situation but just that these things that were so obvious that you couldn't hide.... My general appearance ... it was very obvious that it wasn't masculine, too masculine." Despite all this, Agnes compromised her dress. She said that she dressed "pretty much the same way" in grade school as in high school. Her typical outfit consisted of white corduroy pants and a shirt worn open at the neck which she arranged in the manner of a loose blouse. It turned out that the loose blouse as a management device was taught to her by her brother. Even with the developing breasts she had preferred to wear her blouse tightly tucked in. She changed only upon the disapproval of her brother who was a few years older than she and attended the same school, who was embarrassed by her appearance because of its feminine overtones and berated her for dressing like a girl. Her brother urged that she loosen the shirt. It was her brother, too, who complained that she carried her books like a girl and who demonstrated to her and insisted that she carry them like a boy.

Another example of an "occasion of continuous development" consisted of having to manage the opinions of friends, neighbors, and family after her return from Midwest City. These were circles that Agnes complained "knew all about her from before." In the first part of her remarks when this topic came up she had asserted flatly that the problem of remaining inconspicuous was not a problem "even when I got home from Midwest City." A few moments later in that conversation when I questioned her rather closely about what her mother, her brother and sisters, previous friends, her mother's friends, and neighbors had to say, and how they treated her after her return, Agnes said, "It was so different that nobody in town knew how to treat it." Then after saying, "Everyone treated me nice; nicer than they ever treated me before, and they accepted me. They just wanted to find out," she changed her story. From the time of her return from Midwest City until she left for Los Angeles life was described by her as "terrible." She excepted her work experiences on her first job in her home town. In a later interview she said that she would never return to her home town. After the castration operation was performed at U.C.L.A. she talked of how much she wished to leave Los Angeles because she felt that so much was known about her and so many people knew about her, "All these doctors, nurses, and interns, and everybody."

A part of this situation was the rivalry with her cousin Alice and the combination of rivalry and mutual disapproval that went on between Agnes and her sister-in-law. After her return from Midwest City there was open disapproval and overt expressions of anger from her sister-in-law, her aunt, and most particularly her brother, who continually wanted to know "when she was going to stop this thing." Agnes said that those memories were painful and that she hated to remember them. To obtain her comments on them required considerable effort with questionable results because of the prominence of her denials and idealizations. She would repeat, "They accepted me" or she would deny that she could be expected to know *what* the others were thinking.

Another such "occasion" focused on the unsuccessful management by all parties concerned of the impugned self-esteem that Agnes suffered by the fact that an arrangement had been made after she dropped out of high school to continue her high school education with the use of a tutor that was provided by the public schools. Agnes did not return to high school in September, 1957 which would have been her senior year. Instead, according to Agnes' report, her mother arranged with the vice principal of the high school for the services of a teacher furnished by the public school system who came each day to her house. Agnes was very evasive in saying what she and her mother had talked about in this respect and what kind of arrangement the two might have agreed or disagreed on about her schooling and tutor. Agnes professed to have no information on this agreement and claimed not to know what her mother thought about the arrangement, or what the mother had discussed specifically with the vice principal. Agnes claimed further to be unable to recall how long each one of the tutorial sessions lasted or how long the home visits continued. The vagueness and apparent amnesia led us to feel that these were memories about which Agnes had said that she hated to "remember." Agnes did describe, though briefly, the period during which she was tutored as one of great discontent and chronic conflict with her mother. From my first inquiries about this discontent she insisted that though she had had a great deal of time, and that retrospectively she saw that she could have done more with it than she did, "I felt like a recluse…I wanted to go out and meet people and have a good time. Before I went to Midwest City I could hardly bear to leave the house. After I came back I wanted to start going out and having a social life and mix in public and there I was, cooped up in the house with nothing to do." Along with this Agnes furnished the brief comment that the special teacher was also one who taught other pupils who, as Agnes described them, were "abnormal in some way." Given Agnes' general refusal to consider her condition as that of an abnormal person, it was my feeling that she might have refused to comment further because of a general refusal to acknowledge in any way that she was "abnormal" as well as her insistence that except for a misunderstanding and hostile environment she would have been able to act and feel "naturally and normally."

One of the most dramatic "nongame-analyzable occasions" started with the castration operation and lasted for approximately six weeks afterwards.[6] Starting with the convalescence in the hospital immediately following the operation Agnes tried to sustain the privacy in the management of the care of her vagina by arranging for her own sitz-bath, and herself changing the dressing for the wound. This she insisted on doing out of the sight of the nurses and interns whom she resented. From her accounts, apparently, the nurses resented her as well. The vagina did not heal properly. An infection developed shortly after the operation. A large penis sized plastic mold had to be removed in order to facilitate healing with the result that adhesions developed and the canal closed down over its entire length, including the opening. The promised depth was lost and attempts to restore it by manual manipulation were made by both the attending surgeon, and under his advice, by Agnes. The efforts of both produced severe pain. For almost a week after her release from the hospital there was a combined urethral and fecal dripping with occasional loss of fecal control. Movements were painful and restricted. The new vagina required almost continual attention and care. The vagina had been anchored to the bladder and this together with its bearing on the lower intestine set up mixed signals so that as the bladder expanded under the flow of urine Agnes would experience the desire to defecate. A bladder infection developed. It was accompanied by continual pain and occasional severe abdominal spasms. The amputation of the testes upset the androgen-estrogen balance which precipitated unpredictable changes of moods. Arguments ensued with Bill who was quickly out of patience and threatened to leave her. Despite a campaign to discourage her mother from coming to Los Angeles, it became increasingly apparent to Agnes that the situation was beyond her control and that she could not hope to manage her convalescence by herself. This motivated the additional anxiety that if her mother were to appear, Agnes would hardly be in a position to keep Bill and Bill's family from learning the terrible last thing that her mother and she knew about Agnes that Bill and his family did not know, *i.e.*, that Agnes had been raised as a boy. Until she was rehospitalized for the bladder spasms she managed the care of the vagina and her general illness by spending her days in bed in Bill's home, returning in the evening to her own apartment. Thus it was necessary to manage the secrecy with Bill's mother who had been told only that she had had an operation for "female troubles." In addition, she suffered a moderately severe depression with bouts of unexplained and uncontrollable weeping, restlessness, deep feelings of nostalgia which were both strange to her and unpredictable in onset. Bill berated her for feeling sorry for herself and insisted on knowing, though she could give no reply, whether her condition was physical or whether she was "really like that all along." She complained to me that her thoughts and feelings had lost their sharpness, that she found it difficult to concentrate, that she was easily distracted, and that her memory failed her. As a further complication she became fearful of her depression and would ruminate about "going crazy."

After a particularly severe attack of bladder spasms she was readmitted to the hospital and remedies were administered. The spasms were quieted; testosterone injections were started; the bladder infection was brought under control; the vaginal canal was reopened and a regime first of manual manipulations of the canal and later of manipulations with the use of a plastic penis were started. At the end of approximately six weeks the depression had cleared entirely. The vagina was healing, only tenderness remained, and under Agnes' conscientious use of the mold she had achieved a depth of five inches and was able to insert a penis of an inch and a half in diameter. Quarrels with Bill had subsided and were replaced by an anticipatory waiting on the part of both Agnes and Bill for the time when the vagina would be ready for intercourse. Agnes described their relationship as, "It's not the way it was at the beginning. We're just like an old married couple now."

The full variety of game-analyzable and nongame-analyzable occasions were involved at one time or another or in one way or another when Agnes described her relationship with Bill. If for Agnes all roads led to Rome, they did so by coming together at the boyfriend as a common junction point. For passing illustration, in the course of one of our conversations, at my request, Agnes recited in detailed succession the events of a usual day, and considered for each the possibility of acting differently than she had acted. The recited chain of consequences led to Bill, and from him to her secrets and "problem." This occurred regardless of the commonplace events with which the "chain of relevances" began. Then I asked Agnes to start with something that she felt was extremely worthwhile, to imagine something that could alter it for the worse and to tell me what would happen then, and after that, and so on. She said, "The best thing that ever happened to me was Bill." Then the two of us laughed at the ineffectiveness of the trial.

Bill was discussed in every conversation we had. If she was discussing her confidence in herself as a female, the image of Bill was nearby as someone with whom she could feel "natural and normal." When she discussed her feelings of failure, of being a degraded, inferior female, Bill furnished the occasion when these feelings were most acutely encountered, for he was the only other one besides the physicians to whom she had voluntarily disclosed her condition. After the disclosure, her feelings of being an inferior female were in part assuaged by Bill's assurance that she need not feel inferior because the penis was nothing that she could have helped, and in any case it was not a sexual penis, it was a tumor or "like an abnormal growth." He was implicated in her accounts of her job aspirations, work attitude, work discipline, earnings, chances of advancement, occupational attainments. I mentioned before his "lectures" on how a lady should conduct herself whereby without knowing how he was teaching her he was nevertheless doing just that. On the occasions following the performance of household duties, their domestic relations, her conduct with strange companions, her conduct in Las Vegas, in his urging the operation and insisting that if she could not "get action out of those doctors at U.C.L.A. who only want to do research on you" that she drop the U.C.L.A. physicians and get a physician who would do her some good, in love-making, companionship, and the rehearsals for marriage, in all this Bill was either directly or indirectly relevant.

I proposed earlier that the occasions of passing involved Agnes in the work of achieving the ascribed status of the natural normal female. Bill's relevance to this work attenuated considerations of strict utility and instrumental effectiveness in her choice of strategies and in her assessments of the legitimacy of her procedures and their results. Among all her accounts, those that implicate Bill are invariably the most resistant to game analysis. One of the most obstinate structural incongruities that results when game analysis is used consists of the historico-prospective character of the mutual biography that their intimate interactions assembled, and the diffuse use to which this mutual biography could be and was put by each. It is the diffuse relevance of this biography that helped to make understandable how frantic Agnes' fears were of the disclosure to Bill and how particularly resistant she was to tell me how the disclosure had occurred. Only toward the end of our conversations and then only upon the only occasion in which I insisted that she tell me, did she tell the story, and then it was delivered in the manner of defeat, and piecemeal. The mutual biography aided us, as well, in understanding how the possibility of disclosure became increasingly unavoidable for her, and how the disclosure increasingly assumed the proportions of a major agony.

I shall confine my attention to two occasions, each of which was represented by a question that Bill had, which Agnes, while she stayed in the situation and precisely because there was no choice but to stay, found agonizingly difficult to answer. Prior to the operation and before Bill knew Agnes' condition his question was: "Why no intercourse?" After he knew, his reported question was, "What is all the talking at U.C.L.A. all about? If the doctors at U.C.L.A. wouldn't promise her anything why didn't she drop them and go to a physician who would do something as they would for any other person?"

Agnes met Bill in February, 1958. She had her own apartment. Bill would go there after work and spend the remainder of the evening. There was a great deal of necking and petting. While Agnes permitted fondling and stroking she would not permit Bill to put his hand between her legs. At first he berated her for teasing. Agnes met his first demands for fondling and intercourse by claiming her virginity. This did not satisfy him because, according to her story, she entered willingly "and passionately" into the love-making. (She denied that the love-making stimulated an erection at any time.) As a condition for continuing the affair Bill demanded a satisfactory explanation. She told him that she had a medical condition that prohibited intercourse; that the condition could not be repaired immediately; that she required an operation; that after the operation they could have intercourse. She talked only generally and vaguely about the "condition" which motivated Bill's curiosity to the point where he once again insisted upon knowing the condition in detail. She told him that she was not expert enough to furnish this information but would get it from her physician in Northwest City who was taking care of her. Fearful that Bill would leave her, Agnes returned to Northwest City where she asked the physician who had been taking care of her to write Bill a letter about her condition. The physician's letter, written deliberately in aid of Agnes, talked only generally about "a condition" that could not be repaired until she was 21 because an operation performed before that would endanger her life, which of course was not true. Although Bill did not know this, the answer nonetheless failed to satisfy him. He insisted that she tell him exactly what was wrong, and after a severe quarrel following frustrated intercourse made this a condition of any further courtship or marriage. Once more she tried to placate him by telling Bill that what was there was repulsive to her and would be repulsive to him, to which he replied, "What can be so repulsive? Are there bumps there?" She was convinced that she had the choice of either not telling him and losing him, or of telling him with the hope that he would understand, or if he did not, of losing him. She finally told him. On the many occasions when I asked her to tell me how he had convinced himself—for example had he made an inspection—she refused any further comment. She would insist that she was entitled to a private life and under no circumstances would she reveal how he had been convinced. To my question, "What does he know?" her answer invariably was, "He knows what you know," or "He knows everything that the doctors know." She would say nothing more. Agnes said that prior to the disclosure "I was like on a pedestal." Afterwards and since then she said that she was no longer able to feel, as she had felt prior to it, that she was "his queen." Agnes said that window shopping expeditions for home furnishings and discussion of wedding plans occurred prior to the disclosure. "Since April," when she returned home for the physician's letter, there had been no conversation about the wedding "because of the doubt for everyone concerned." Her account was not to be taken at face value. Later conversations occurred precisely because of the doubt. Some part, therefore, of what Agnes was talking about in saying "there had been no further conversations" referred to the degradation that she suffered upon finally having to tell Bill that she had a penis and scrotum between her legs and that this was behind all his frustrated attempts to pursue their love-making.

The feelings that persisted following this disclosure, that she was an inferior female, were accompanied at first by the repelling thought that perhaps Bill was "abnormal." She dismissed this by recalling that Bill had fallen in love with her before he knew about her condition; by recalling the stories he had told her of his love affairs and sexual successes; and by reviewing the fact that he regarded it as "more or less a tumor or something like that" and that he began to urge an operation to remedy the condition. At different times in the course of our conversations she insisted that there was nothing in his manner, appearance, character, treatments of her and other women, and treatments of men that "resembled homosexuals." By homosexuals she meant effeminate appearing men who dressed like women. She found the possibility of his "abnormality" repulsive saying that she could not bear to see him again if she thought "at all" that he was "abnormal." Following the operation we obtained an account of Bill's appearance and manner from the urological intern and resident who had attended her case. The resident had encountered Bill one day when Bill was leaving her hospital room. He visited her regularly while she was in the hospital. The resident reported that he was struck by Bill's small stature, fine dark features, and swishy manner. In leaving the room Bill batted his eyes at the resident from which the resident took the message, "You and I know what's in there." We were reluctant to credit the resident's account since his dislike for Agnes was evident on other scores. He was firmly opposed to the decision to operate, stating that the operation was neither necessary nor ethical. It was his conviction that there had been anal intercourse, a conviction that he held because of the flabbiness of the anal sphincter. With respect to the unknown source of estrogens he preferred the hypothesis that

Agnes, either alone or in league with others, had for many years obtained them from an exogenous source. Despite our attempts to talk with Bill, he refused all contact.

With respect to the second question, Agnes' passing occasions consisted of justifying to Bill her "choice" of "the doctors at U.C.L.A." The task of justifying to Bill her visits to U.C.L.A. arose as a topic in almost all our conversations not only prior to the operation but after it as well, though of course for different reasons. Bill urged that she should get the doctors at U.C.L.A. to treat he "without all this funny business. They're taking you for a ride. They're not going to do anything. They just want to do research. You're just a guinea pig for them." In response to this Agnes, in her Saturday morning conversations with us, would press for a definite commitment as soon as possible. She said repeatedly that she was unable to argue with him because "in the sense that he's thinking, he's perfectly right. But I know something that he doesn't know." (That she had been raised as a boy and that the specific way in which she was of interest to us had to remain concealed in her arguments with Bill.) Agnes had to manage Bill's impatience by somehow convincing him that she was in the right hands at U.C.L.A., given Bill's impatience with the slowness of the procedure, and the mysteriousness of the Saturday morning talks which she portrayed to him as our insistence on research. She had to allow his insistence that she need not put up with all this "monkey business" and she could not argue his claim that, because she had something wrong, she should insist with us that we either do something about it or release her. Yet along with this, Agnes had the additional aim of getting an operation done by competent hands at minimum or no cost, but to get this she had to engage in the research, not only because of the anatomical condition that Bill was preoccupied with, but which was only a small part of our research interests. Additional research interests were directed to the fact that she was raised until she was seventeen as a male. So Agnes was unable to answer Bill because in her own words "this is something I know that he doesn't know. So he thinks of me as I suppose more or less of someone coming in here and being baffled or fooled or messed around with by doctors that think, oh here's a young girl that doesn't think too much and we can you know just do some research on her.... That's my big problem because I can't argue the point with him and I can't show him that he's wrong in that sense, because in the sense he's thinking he's perfectly right. But actually if *I* felt that way I'd be perfectly wrong. That's why I have to wait. It's because I know something he doesn't know. That's why I have to wait."

Following the operation Agnes needed arguments again, because she was afraid of her depression and of the swarm of difficulties during the first few weeks of convalescence. As she said, she swapped one set of troubles for another. She was frightened of what was happening. Among other things she wanted assurance that she was not "crazy" and confided that she got considerable relief from talking with us, but was entirely unable to explain this to Bill. When she discussed it with Bill he either took the line or wanted her assurance that her psychological problems were due entirely to physical changes after the operations, and that she was not *that* kind of a person *i.e.*, moody, irritable, self-pitying, weepy, selfish, and that this was not her *"real"* character. Even after the vagina had started to heal properly and the depression had lifted, she was still willing, and in fact desired, to continue the weekly conversations. A part of her uneasiness concerned the functional character of her vagina and the question for her as to whether or not Bill would promise marriage before or after they had had intercourse. She took as a matter of course that she had to permit Bill intercourse with the new vagina before marriage. As she said, "That's what it's for; it's for intercourse." Another part of her concern consisted of the uncertainty which she felt in sensing a changed relationship to Bill as she compared present arrangements with what they had been many months before. She sensed as well that the relationship would change even more in the ensuing months. "Now," she said, "we are like an old married couple." At this time she expressed, too, the conviction that we knew more about

Bill than she did and knew more than we were saying. In one of the last interviews she asked, for the first time in all our conversations, if I would give her my opinion of Bill and did I think that Bill was "abnormal." I replied that I knew of Bill only from what she had told me about him, that I had never seen or talked with him, and that it would be unfair to give her such an opinion.

That Agnes was passing with us is a feature of the way in which our research was conducted with her, her problem being to obtain a competent, guaranteed, and low-cost operation without "submitting to research," by which she meant protecting her privacy. Thus, although she showed her willingness to take "all those tests" and to sort the Q-deck in accordance with various instructions, she herself furnished evidences of dissembling. Agnes had been given the Q-deck to take home with her and to sort and return the sorted deck to the psychologist the following week. Agnes said that Bill was forever wanting to see how she arranged the cards, "but I had the cards all mixed up so he couldn't find out anything." (Agnes laughed.) Another measure of her passing with us is found in the "secrets" that Agnes managed nevertheless to protect. Despite a total of approximately seventy hours of talks arranged with the three of us and additional talks with various members of the staff of the Urology and Endocrinology Departments, and despite the fact that direct and indirect questioning had been attempted to obtain information, there were at least seven critical areas in which we obtained nothing: (1) the possibility of an exogenous source of hormones; (2) the nature and extent of collaboration that occurred between Agnes and her mother and other persons; (3) any usable evidence let alone any detailed findings dealing with her male feelings and her male biography; (4) what her penis had been used for besides urination; (5) how she sexually satisfied herself and others and most particularly her boyfriend both before and after the disclosure; (6) the nature of any homosexual feelings, fears, thoughts, and activities; (7) her feelings about herself as a "phony female." Some details as to the way in which this passing with *us* was managed may become clear in the following section where specific features of her management devices are discussed.

If Agnes was passing with us, it must be stated in all fairness that there were many times, indeed, when I was passing with her. There were many occasions in the exchanges between Agnes and me when it was necessary for me to side-step her requests for information in order to avoid any display of incompetence and so as to maintain the relationship with Agnes. For example, I was unable to tell her whether or not there was a difference between male and female urine. There were several legal angles to the case, about which she asked questions which were obvious enough as questions when they were asked, but had not occurred to me nor did I have the faintest idea as to what their proper answers were. When she was suffering with the bladder and bowel impairment she asked if I could tell her how long this would go on and what she could expect to happen next. On several occasions prior to the operation she wanted to know if I could tell her what I knew about the likely decision. Several times she asked me details about the operation and the nature of postoperative care. She asked anatomical questions. One of these concerned a mysterious "hard thing" that she had encountered in the roof of the new vaginal canal. She assumed I would be able to tell her what it was. My wife had done graduate work with the hormone relaxin and its effects on the symphasis pubis in guinea pigs. I identified the hard thing as the symphasis pubis and told her what relaxin does by way of the spectacular relaxation of this cartilage prior to the passage of the neonate guinea pigs down the vaginal canal. I had to hope with a secret fervor that in transferring the story to humans that I was not telling her altogether a cock-and-bull story, partly because I would have liked to tell the truth, but perhaps even more importantly to preserve the friendship, the conspiracy, and the sense that we were in league with each other, that there were no secrets between us because I already knew many private things about her and nothing she might tell me would in any way change our sympathy for her or our desire to do what we could to see her happy and doing well. My typical reply therefore was to find out as much as I could about what she wanted to know, and why, and to reassure her that I could answer her questions but that it was to her best interest that she should have Stoller, the physician, give her the answers because answers to such questions were recognizedly of great importance to her and therefore she required authoritative answers. I must confess that this was an improvised answer that occurred on the first occasion that Agnes caught me short. Once it worked, however, I had it as a strategy to use on later occasions. It is of additional interest that despite such assurances Agnes could not ask me, apparently *knew* she could not ask me, nor would I have been prepared to tell her truthfully whether or how the decision to operate would be changed if she disclosed the answers to the seven points that we wanted her to tell us about but on which we could get no information from her.

REVIEW OF MANAGEMENT DEVICES

In contrast to homosexuals and transvestites, it was Agnes' conviction that she was naturally, originally, really, after all female. No mockery or masquerading accompanied this claim that we were able to observe. In this respect Agnes shared, point for point, the outlook of "normals."

But important differences nevertheless existed between Agnes and "normals" in that normals are able to advance such claims without a second thought whereas for her such claims involved her in uncertainties of responses from others. Her claims had to be bolstered and managed by shrewdness, deliberateness, skill, learning, rehearsal, reflectiveness, test, review, feedback, and the like. Her achieved rights to treat others and be treated herself as a natural female were achieved as the result of the successful management of situations of risk and uncertainty. Let me review some of the measures whereby she was able to secure and guarantee her claims.

Her devices were carried out within the conditions of, and were motivated by a knowledge of herself that was, for almost every occasion of contact with others, none of somebody's business who was nevertheless important to her. As I have noted, the concealed knowledge of herself was regarded by her as a potentially degrading and damaging disclosure. She was realistically convinced that there would be little by way of an available remedy by which other persons might be "set right" if the disclosure occurred. In this respect, the phenomena of Agnes' passing are amenable to Goffman's descriptions of the work of managing impressions in social establishments.[7] This amenability however is only superficial for reasons that will be apparent over the course of the discussion.

When I say that Agnes achieved her claims to the ascribed status of a natural female by the successful management of situations of risk and uncertainty, I do not mean thereby that Agnes was involved in a game, or that it was for her an intellectual matter, or that ego control for her extended to the point where she was able to switch with any success, let alone with any ease, from one sex role to the other. I have already mentioned several evidences of this. Other evidences can be cited. Even in imagination Agnes found it not only difficult to contemplate herself performing in the "male" way but found it repugnant. Some memories were so exceptionally painful to her as to be lost as grounds of deliberate action. When she learned that the decision had been made to operate, the knowledge that she was committed to the operation as a decision was accompanied by a fear that when she was on the table, because the decision would then be entirely out of her hands, the doctors without consulting her would decide to amputate her breasts rather than her penis. The thought provoked a mild depression until she was assured that nothing of the sort was the case. The natural female was a condition that her various strategies had to satisfy. Agnes was not a game player. The "natural female" was one among many institutional constraints, "irrational givens," a *thing* that she *insisted upon* in the face of all contrary indications and the seductions of alternative advantages and goals. It attenuated the deliberateness of her efforts, the actual availability, let alone exercise of choices, and the consistency of her compliance with norms of strict utility and effectiveness in her choices of means. It furnished "constraints" upon the exercise of certain rational properties of conduct, particularly of those rational properties that are provided for when certain games are used as procedural models to formulate formal properties of practical activities.

Not only is it necessary to stress the shortcomings of strategy analysis in discussing her "management devices," but the very phrase "management device" is only temporarily helpful. It is useful because it permits an enumerated account of these devices. For the same reason that it facilitates the enumeration it also clouds the phenomena that it is necessary to come to terms with. *These phenomena consist of Agnes in on-going courses of action directed to the mastery of her practical circumstances by the manipulation of these circumstances as a texture of relevances.* The troublesome feature encountered over and over again is the cloudy and little-known role that time plays in structuring the biography and prospect of present situations over the course of action as a function of the action itself. It is not sufficient to say that Agnes situations are played out over time, nor is it at all sufficient to regard this time as clock time. There is as well the "inner time" of recollection, remembrance, anticipation, expectancy. Every attempt to handle Agnes' "management devices" while disregarding this time, does well enough as long as the occasions are episodic in their formal structure; and all of Goffman's analyses either take episodes for illustration, or turn the situations that his scheme analyzes into episodic ones. But strategic analyses fail whenever these events are not episodic. Then to keep the analysis in good repair, there is required the exercise of theoretical ingenuity, and a succession of theoretical elections, one compounded on the other, with the frantic use of metaphor in the hope of bringing these events to faithful representation. This caveat can be summarized, although poorly, by pointing out that it would be incorrect to say of Agnes that she has passed. The active mode is needed: she is passing. Inadequate though this phrasing is, it summarizes Agnes' troubles. It stands as well for *our* troubles in describing accurately and adequately what her troubles were.

* * *

MANAGEMENT DEVICES AS MANIPULATIONS OF A TEXTURE OF RELEVANCES: COMING TO TERMS WITH "PRACTICAL CIRCUMSTANCES"

Sociologists have long been concerned with the task of describing the conditions of organized social life under which the phenomena of rationality in conduct occur. One such condition is continually documented in sociological writings: *routine as a necessary condition of rational action.* The rational properties of action that are of concern in this respect are those which are particular to the conduct of everyday affairs. Max Weber, in his neglected distinction between substantive rationality and formal rationality, and almost alone among sociological theorists, used this distinction between the two sets of rationalities throughout his work.

The relationships between routine and rationality are incongruous ones only when they are viewed according to everyday common sense or according to most philosophical teachings. But sociological inquiry accepts almost as a truism that the ability of a person to act "rationally"—that is, the ability of a person in *conducting his everyday affairs* to calculate; to act deliberately; to project alternative plans of action; to select before the actual fall of events the conditions under which he will follow one plan or another; to give priority in the selection of means to their technical efficacy; to be much concerned with predictability and desirous of "surprise in small amounts"; to prefer the analysis of alternatives and consequences prior to action in preference to improvisation; to be much concerned with questions of what is to be done and how it is to be done; to be aware of, to wish to, and to exercise choice; to be insistent upon "fine" as contrasted with "gross" structure in characterizations in the knowledge of situations that one considers valuable and realistic knowledge; and the rest—that this ability depends upon the person being able to take for granted, to take under trust, a vast array of features of the social order. In the conduct of his everyday affairs in order for the person to treat rationally the one-tenth of this situation that, like an iceberg appears above the water, he must be able to treat the nine-tenths that lies below as an unquestioned and, perhaps even more interestingly, as an unquestionable background of matters that are demonstrably relevant to his calculation, but which appear without even being noticed. In his famous discussion of the normative backgrounds of activity, Emil Durkheim made much of the point that the validity and understandability of the stated terms of a contract depended upon unstated and *essentially unstatable* terms that the contracting parties took for granted as binding upon their transactions.

These trusted, taken for granted, background features of a person's situation, that is, the routine aspects of the situation that permit "rational action," are commonly referred to in sociological discourse as the mores and folkways. In this usage the mores depict the ways in which routine is a condition for the appearance of rational action or, in psychiatric terms, for the operativeness of the reality principle. The mores have been used thereby to show how the stability of social routine is a condition which enables persons in the course of mastering and managing their everyday affairs to recognize each other's actions, beliefs, aspirations, feelings, and the like as reasonable, normal, legitimate understandable, and realistic.

Agnes' passing occasions and her management devices throw into relief the troubled relationship in her case between routine, trust, and rationality. By considering these passing occasions and management devices with respect to this troubled relationship we may be able to break free of mere "diagnosis" or Goffman's episodic emphasis. One may allow, in agreement with Goffman, the accuracy of Goffman's "naughty" view that members of a society generally, and Agnes in a particularly dramatic way, are much concerned with the management of impressions. We may allow, as well, the accuracy and acuteness of his descriptions of this concern. Nevertheless if one tries to reproduce the features of the real society by populating it with Goffman-type members we are left with structural incongruities of the sort that were discussed in previous sections of this paper.

A review of Agnes' passing occasions and management devices may be used to argue how practiced and effective Agnes was in dissembling. We would have to agree with Goffman that, like his persons who are engaged in the management of impressions, she was a highly accomplished liar, and that as it is in the society produced by Goffman's dissembling members, lying provided for Agnes and her partners conservative effects for the stable features of their socially structured interaction.

But a troublesome point in Goffman's interpretive procedure emerges with full clarity when his views are used to analyze other aspects of Agnes' case. The trouble revolves around the general absence with which deliberateness, calculation, or what Agnes calls her "awareness" enters as a property of the work of managing impressions for Goffman's members. In the empirical applications of Goffman's notions one is continually tempted to press the informant with exasperation, "Oh come on now, you must know better than that. Why don't you confess?" Agnes' case helps us to see what this trouble might be due to.

Agnes treated with deliberateness, calculation, and express management (*i.e.*, in the manner that Goffman would like every one of his informants to confess, if his mode of analysis is to be counted correct) matters that members (a) not only take under trust, but (b) require of each other, for their mutual judgments of normality, reasonableness, understandability, rationality, and legitimacy, that they treat in a trusting and trusted manner, and (c) require of each other that evidences of trust be furnished wherever deliberateness, calculation, and express management are used in managing problems of daily life. Agnes would have to act in this trusting fashion *but routine as a condition for the effective, calculated, and deliberate management of practical circumstances was, for Agnes, specifically and chronically problematic.* To have disregarded its problematic character, she was convinced, was to risk disclosure and ruin. A review therefore of her case permits the re-examination of the nature of practical circumstances. It leads us also to think of the work of impression management—in Agnes' case, these consist of her passing "management devices"—as attempts to come to terms with practical circumstances as a texture of relevances over the continuing occasions of interpersonal transactions. Finally, it permits us to ask what this "preoccupation" for impression managements is about by seeing how a concern for "appearances" is related to this texture of relevances.

In the course of one of our conversations Agnes had been questioning the necessity for any more research. She wanted to know how it bore on her chances of the operation. She wanted to know as well whether it would help "the doctors" to get the "true facts." I asked Agnes, "What do you figure the facts are?" She answered, "What do *I* figure the facts are, or what do I think everyone else thinks the facts are?" This remark may serve as a theme in elaborating Agnes' practical circumstances as a texture of relevances. The theme for her of the nature of her practical circumstances was furnished in yet another remark. Prior to the operation I had asked her about the discussions and activities that she and Bill might have engaged in by way of preparation for their marriage. In her answer she portrayed her discussions with Bill as overwhelmingly concerned with the necessity for the operation. She firmly dismissed my question with the remark: "You don't talk about how much fun you're going to have in New York when you're sinking on a ship in the middle of the ocean.... You're worried about the problem that's present."

PRACTICAL CIRCUMSTANCES

Agnes' circumstances were striking in the stringency with which past and future events were related and regulated as an arena by the clock and the calendar. Her futures were dated futures, most particularly as present actions and circumstances were informed by the assumption of a potential remedy for "her problem" that had to have occurred by some definite time. That there were many years during which no such date had been set did not detract in the slightest from the definiteness of this future even though its specific calendar date was entirely unknown. Agnes was required by specific performances not only to establish mastery over this arena, but by her performances to establish her moral worth as well. For her the morally worthwhile person and the "natural, normal female" were identical. In the pursuit of jobs, in the management of the love affair, in her aspirations to marriage, in her choice of companions, in the management of Northwest City friends and family, the tasks of achieving the status of the normal natural female had to be accomplished at, within, and by a time. Perhaps nowhere does this come out more dramatically than in the quarrels that anticipated the disclosure to Bill, and in the terrible recalcitrance of the new vagina that made up such a central feature of the postoperative depression. Her constant recourse to self-reassessment consisted of continual comparison of anticipated and actual outcomes, of continual monitoring of expectancies and payoffs, with strong efforts to accommodate and to normalize the differences. Agnes expended a great deal of effort upon bringing ever more areas of her life under conceptual representation and control. Expectations in areas of life that to persons better able than she to take their normal sexuality for granted would appear to be far removed from the concerns of criticism and review of "common sense knowledge" of the society were, for her, matters of active and critical deliberation, and the results of these deliberations were tied to uppermost levels in her hierarchy of plans. The contents of biographies and futures were highly organized with respect to their relevance to the achieved natural female status. It was indeed difficult for her to find any area that she could not in a few short steps make relevant to the prize.

There was very little of a "take it or leave it" attitude on Agnes' part toward past, present, or future fall of events. Agnes reasoned as follows: I have had this terrible time in high school, I was without companions as a child, I was raised as a boy, I have this face and these breasts, I've had dates and fun with girlfriends in the normal natural way that girls do, I lost seventeen years because a misunderstanding environment did not recognize the accidental character of the penis and refused to take action, hence I *deserve* the status that unfortunately I find myself in the position of having to ask for. For Agnes the likelihood of being accorded treatment as a natural, normal female was a moral likelihood. She reckoned her chances in terms of deservingness and blame. She found it repugnant to consider that an enumeration of such factors would or should serve in probability fashion merely to fix the likelihood that she was "female." With respect to that past as well as to her anticipated validation of her claims, the occurrence of a remedy for her condition had a moral requiredness. For her there must be and should be a plan and a reason for the way things had transpired as well as how they would have finally occurred. Very few things could occur for Agnes, bearing in their relevance on "her problem," in an accidental or coincidental manner. Agnes was motivated to search for patterns and for the "good reasons" that things occurred as they did. The events of Agnes' environment carried along for her, as their invariant features, that they could actually and potentially affect her and could be affected by her. To refer to this as Agnes' egocentricity, if it is left at that, may be seriously misleading. For Agnes her conviction that she had grasped the order of events arranged around her in an accurate and realistic fashion consisted in the conviction that her assessments were to be tested and were testable without ever suspending the relevance of what she knew, what she took to be fact, supposition, conjecture, and fantasy by reason of her bodily features and social positions in the real world. Everyday events, their relationships, and their causal texture were in no way matters of theoretic interest for Agnes. The possibility of considering the world otherwise "just to see where it leads"—a peculiar suspension and reordering of relevances that scientific theorists habitually employ—was for Agnes a matter of inconsequential play; as she would talk about it, "just words." When she was invited to consider it otherwise, the invitation amounted to a bid to engage in a threatening and repugnant exercise. It was no part of Agnes' concern to act in active alteration of "the social system." Instead she sought her remedy as an adjustment to it. One could never consider Agnes a revolutionary or a utopian. She had no "cause" and avoided such "causes" as one frequently finds among homosexuals who may seek to reeducate a hostile environment, or who might scrutinize that environment for evidences that it was not what it appeared to be but instead contained, in masked fashion, the identical types that it was hostile to and punishing of. Challenges to the system were for Agnes not even so much as hopeless risks. She wanted "in." The "credentials committee" was at fault.

Time played a peculiar role in constituting for Agnes the significance of her present situation. With regard to the past, we have seen the prominence with which she historicised, making for herself and presenting us with a socially acceptable biography. We have already remarked on the fact that the work of selecting, codifying, making consistent various elements in a biography, yielded a biography that was so consistently female as to leave us without information on many important points. Two years of arduous female activities furnished for her a fascinating input of new experiences upon which this historicizing process operated. Her attitude toward her own history required ever new rereadings of the trail that wound off behind her as she sought in reading and rereading the past for evidences to bolster and unify her present worth and aspirations. Before all, Agnes was a person with a history. Or, more pointedly perhaps, she was engaged in historicizing practices that were skilled, unrelieved, and biased.

On the side of future events, one is struck by the prevalence with which her expectations were expectations of the timing in the fall of events. There was little tolerable "slack" in this respect. It was to their timing that Agnes looked to inform her of their character. Events did not "just occur." They occurred in pace, duration, and phasing, and she looked to these as parameters of their meaning and to recognize them for "what they really are." She had only a thin interest in events characterized for their own sake and without regard for temporal determinations such as pace, duration, phasing. It was a prominent characteristic of Agnes' "realism" that she addressed her environment with an expectation of the scheduled fall of events. We were struck by the sharpness and extensiveness of her recall. An important part of this impression stemmed from the ease with which she dated events and arranged recalled sequences in strict chronology. The effect of such an orientation was to assimilate events both past and prospective to the status of means to ends and lent to the stream of experience an unremitting sense of practical purposiveness.

With almost remarkable ease, a present state of affairs taken for granted could be transformed into one of open problematic possibilities. Even small deviations from what she both expected and required to happen could occur to her as extraordinarily good or bad in their implications. She had achieved, at best, an unstable routinization of her daily rounds. One might expect that her concern for practical testing and the extensiveness of deliberateness, calculation, and the rest would be accompanied by the use of impersonal norms to assess her decisions of sensibility and fact, *i.e.*, that she knew what she was talking about, and that what she claimed to be so was indeed the case. Nothing of the sort was so. Agnes did not count her assessments of sensibility and fact right or wrong on the grounds of having followed impersonal, logico-empirical rules. Her rules of evidence were of much more tribal character. They could be summarized in a phrase: I am right or wrong on the grounds of who agrees with me. Particularly did she look to status superiors to test and maintain the difference between what in her situation she insisted were "true facts" and what she would count for "mere appearances." Being right or wrong was for Agnes a matter of being *in essence* correct or not. In matters relevant to her assessed chances of exercising her claimed rights to the status of the natural, normal female she did not take easily to the notion of being wrong in degree. For her the correctness of her assessments of events was a publicly verifiable one in the sense that other persons *typically like her* (*i.e.*, normal females) would experience what she had experienced in extremely close correspondence to the manner that she had experienced these events. She distrusted a characterization if its sense appeared to be peculiar or private to her and feared such an interpretation as unrealistic. Wanting to place the accent of actuality on events—fearing and suspecting supposition—she insisted that actual events were those which were verifiable by persons similarly situated. Similarly situated, to repeat, meant situated as a normal female. While she would allow that there were others in the world with problems like hers, neither with them nor with normal females was a community of understanding possible based upon their possible interchangeability of standpoints. "No one" Agnes insisted, "could possibly really understand what I have had to go through." In deciding the objectivity of her assessments of herself and of others Agnes counted, before anything, and sought to take for granted that she was normal and that she was like others.

AGNES, THE PRACTICAL METHODOLOGIST

Agnes' practices accord to the displays of normal sexuality in ordinary activities a "perspective by incongruity." They do so by making observable *that* and *how* normal sexuality is accomplished through witnessable displays of talk and conduct, as standing processes of practical recognition, which are done in singular and particular occasions as a matter of course, with the use by members of "seen but unnoticed" backgrounds of commonplace events, and such that the situated question, "What kind of phenomenon is normal sexuality?"—a member's question—accompanies that accomplishment as a reflexive feature of it, which reflexivity the member uses, depends upon, and glosses in order to assess and demonstrate the rational adequacy for all practical purposes of the indexical question and its indexical answers.

To speak seriously of Agnes as a practical methodologist is to treat in a matter of fact way her continuing studies of everyday activities as members' methods for producing correct decisions about normal sexuality in ordinary activities. Her studies armed her with knowledge of how the organized features of ordinary settings are used by members as procedures for making appearances-of-sexuality-as-usual decidable as a matter of course. The scrutiny that she paid to appearances; her concerns for adequate motivation, relevance, evidence, and demonstration; her sensitivity to devices of talk; her skill in detecting and managing "tests" were attained as part of her mastery of trivial but necessary social tasks, to secure ordinary rights to live. Agnes was self-consciously equipped to teach normals how normals make sexuality happen in commonplace settings as an obvious, familiar, recognizable, natural, and serious matter of fact. Her specialty consisted of treating the "natural facts of life" of socially recognized, socially managed sexuality as a managed production so as to be making these facts of life true, relevant, demonstrable, testable, countable, and available to inventory, cursory representation, anecdote, enumeration, or professional psychological assessment; in short, so as unavoidably in concert with others to be making these facts of life visible and reportable—accountable—for all practical purposes.

In association with members, Agnes somehow learned that and how members furnish for each other evidences of their rights to live as *bona-fide* males and females. She learned from members how, in doing normal sexuality "without having to think about it," they were able to avoid displays that would furnish sanctionable grounds for doubt that a member was sexually what he appeared to be. Among the most critical of these displays were situated indexical particulars of talk. Agnes learned how to embed these particulars in vis-à-vis conversations so as to generate increasingly tellable, mutual biographies.

Agnes' methodological practices are our sources of authority for the finding, and recommended study policy, that normally sexed persons are cultural events in societies whose character as visible orders of practical activities consist of members' recognition and production practices. We learned from Agnes, who treated sexed persons as cultural events that members make happen, that members' practices alone produce the observable-tellable normal sexuality of persons, and do so only, entirely, exclusively in actual, singular, particular occasions through actual witnessed displays of common talk and conduct.

AGNES, THE DOER OF THE ACCOUNTABLE PERSON

The inordinate stresses in Agnes' life were part and parcel of the concerted practices with normals, whereby the "normal, natural female" as a moral thing to be and a moral way to feel and act was made to be happening, in demonstrable evidence, for all practical purposes. Agnes' passing practices permit us to discuss two among many constituent phenomena that made up the normally sexed person as a contingent, practical accomplishment: (1) Agnes as a recognizable case of the real thing, and (2) Agnes the self-same person.

(1) *The case of the real thing*. In the ways Agnes counted herself a member to, and an object in, the environment of normally sexed persons, it included not only males with penises and females with vaginas but, because it included her as well, it included a female with a penis, and following the operation a female with a man-made vagina. For Agnes, and for the physicians who recommended the operation as the "humane" thing to do, the surgeons rectified nature's original mistake. Agnes'

rueful admission, "Nothing that man makes is as good as something that nature makes" expressed a member's realistic social truth about claims to normal sexuality. She, her family, and the physicians agreed that she had been granted a vagina as the organ which was rightfully hers, that she had resisted the anomaly as an accident of fate, and that because of a cruel trick she had been the victim of severe penalties of misunderstanding while she carried out the tasks of living as best she could as a misunderstood "case of the real thing." The operation furnished her and others evidences of the socially realistic character of her claims.

Agnes had witnessed in endless demonstrations by normals that and how normals believe that normal sexuality as a case of the real thing is an event in its own right and is assessable in its own terms, and that the accountability of normal sexuality could be made out from the study of how normally sexed members appear to common sense, lay or professional. Those were not her beliefs. Nor *could* she believe them. Instead, for Agnes in contrast to normals, the commonplace recognition of normal sexuality as a "case of the real thing" consisted of a serious, situated, and prevailing accomplishment that was produced in concert with others by activities whose prevailing and ordinary success itself subjected their product to Merleau-Ponty's "prejuge du monde."[8] Her anguish and triumphs resided in the observability, which was particular to her and uncommunicable, of the steps whereby the society hides from its members its activities of organization and thus leads them to see its features as determinate and independent objects. For Agnes the observably normally sexed person *consisted* of inexorable, organizationally located work that provided the way that such objects arise.[9]

(2) *The self-same person.* The ways in which the work and occasions of passing were obstinately unyielding to Agnes' attempts to routinize her daily activities suggest how deeply embedded are appearances-of-normal-sexuality for members' recognition in commonplace scenes as unavoidable, unnoticed textures of relevances. Agnes' management devices can be described as measures whereby she attempted to exercise control over the changed content and the changed texture of relevances. Directed over their course to achieving the temporal identicality of herself as the natural, normal female, her management devices consisted of the work whereby the problem of object constancy was continually under solution. Her "devices" consisted of her work of making observable for all practical purposes the valuable sexed person who remains *visibly* the self-same through all variations of actual appearances.

Agnes frequently had to deal with this accountable constancy as a task and in a deliberate way. Her management work consisted of actions for controlling the changing textures of relevances. It was this texture that she and others consulted for evidences that she was the self-same person, originally, in the first place, and all along that she had been and would remain. Agnes was well aware of the devices that she used to make visible the constancy of the valuable, self-same natural, normal female. But her question, "Devices for what?" inseparably accompanied that awareness.

With that question Agnes mocked scientific discussions of sex roles that portray how members are engaged in making normal sexuality accountable. She found it flattering and innocent to consider a normal's activities and hers as those of role players or role makers who know, seek to establish, and enforce compliance to socially standardized expectancies of normal sexuality with their "functional consequences" that prior to encountering actual occasions in which they apply the normal can "talk about," given the various things he might be *doing* with something that's "said," and in the actual occasion use them to exercise choice among displays of appropriate talk and conduct. Equally flattering were the varieties of psychologically certified normally sexed persons whose possibilities, according to a favored version, are fixed early in life by the social structures of the childhood family as a complicated program of reinforcements; or the biological normal who is after all one sex or the other by the surplus that remains in the appropriate column when the signs are arithmetically evaluated; or the sociological normal for whom society is a table of organization so that sex "positions" and "statuses" and their possible departures are assigned and enforced as a condition for maintaining that table of organization and for other "good reasons."

Each furnishes a commonplace method for theorizing out of recognition a demonic problematic phenomenon: *the unrelieved management of herself as the identical, self-same, natural female, and as a case of the real and valuable person by active, sensible, judgmentally guided unavoidably visible displays in practical, common sense situations of choice.*

That this phenomenon was happening was Agnes' enduring concern. Her devices were continually directed to, indeed, they consisted of a Machiavellian management of practical circumstances. But to manage in Machiavellian fashion her scenes of activity she had to take their relevant features on trust and be assured that normal companions were doing so, too. She differed from the normals in whose company and with whose unacknowledged help she "managed" the production task of keeping this trust in good repair. Thereby we encounter her wit with, her sensitivity to, her discrimination in selecting, her preoccupation with and talk about, and her artful practices in furnishing, recognizing "good reasons" and in using them and making them true. To enumerate Agnes' management devices and to treat her "rationalizations" as though they were directed to the management of impressions and to let it go at that, which one does in using Goffman's clinical ideal, euphemizes the phenomenon that her case brings to attention. In the conduct of her everyday affairs she had to choose among alternative courses of action even though the goal that she was trying to achieve was most frequently not clear to her prior to her having to take the actions whereby some goal might in the end have been realized. Nor had she had any assurances of what the consequences of the choice might be prior to or apart from her having to deal with them. Nor were there clear rules that she could consult to decide the wisdom of the choice before the choice had to be exercised. For Agnes, stable routines of everyday life were "disengageable" attainments assured by unremitting, momentary, situated courses of improvisation. Throughout these was the inhabiting presence of talk, so that however the action turned out, poorly or well, she would have been required to "explain" herself, to have furnished "good reasons" for having acted as she did.

That persons "rationalize" their own and each other's past actions, present situations, and future prospects is well known. If I were speaking only of that, this report would consist of one more authoritative version of what everyone knows. Instead, I have used the case to indicate why it is that persons would require this of each other, and to find anew as a sociological phenomenon how "being able to give good reasons" is not only dependent upon but contributes to the maintenance of stable routines of everyday life as they are produced from "within" the situations as situations' features. Agnes' case instructs us on how intimately tied are "value stability," "object constancy," "impression management," "commitments to compliance with legitimate expectancies," "rationalization," to member's unavoidable work of coming to terms with practical circumstances. It is with respect to that phenomenon that in examining Agnes' passing I have been concerned with the question of how, over the temporal course of their actual engagements, and "knowing" the society only from within, members produce stable, accountable practical activities, *i.e.*, social structures of everyday activities.

APPENDIX

In February, 1967, after this volume was in press, I learned from my collaborator, Robert J. Stoller, M.D., that Agnes, in October, 1966, had disclosed to him that she was not a biologically defective male. With his permission I quote the relevant passage from the recently completed manuscript of his book, *Gender Identity:*

"Eight years ago, when this research project was only a year old, a patient was seen who was found to be a unique type of a most rare disorder: testicular feminization syndrome, a condition in which it is felt that the testes are producing estrogens in sufficient amount that the genetically male fetus fails to be masculinized and so develops female genitalia and in puberty female secondary sex characteristics. This particular case was unique in that the patient was completely feminized in her secondary sex characteristics (breasts and other subcutaneous fat distribution; absence of body, facial, and limb hair; feminization of the pelvic girdle; and very feminine and soft skin) with a nonetheless normal-sized penis and testes. Abdominal contents were normal male. Following extensive workup, including examination of testicular tissue by microscope, it was decided that the findings were compatible with estrogen production by the testes. A report of these findings was published. At the time of this workup the patient was 19 years old and had been living undetected as a young woman for about two years. As far back as her memory reached, she had wanted to be a girl and had felt herself to be a girl though she was fully aware that she was anatomically a male and was treated by her family and by society as a boy. Consideration was given to the possibility that she had been taking estrogens on her own, but it was finally decided that this was not the case for the following reasons: (1) she very clearly denied taking such estrogens at the time that she revealed many other parts of her past history which would seem to be equally embarrassing to reveal; (2) even after successfully getting the operation she wanted, she still denied taking estrogens; (3) in order to have effected the biological changes found on physical examination and laboratory tests, she would have had to take just the right drug in just the right amounts starting at just the right time at puberty in order to have converted her body to the state in which it was found at age 19, and it was felt that this amount of information about endocrinology and sophistication about womanhood was beyond the possibilities of this person when 12 years old. There are no cases in the endocrinological literature of a male taking massive doses of estrogens exogenously from puberty on; (4) she was closely observed during hospitalization pre-operatively and her belongings searched; no estrogens were found; shortly after the testes were removed, she developed a menopause, which was considered good evidence that the testes were the source of estrogens; (5) when the testes were examined microscopically and sent to experts in other medical centers for confirmation, the tissue was considered as capable of producing testicular feminization syndrome; (6) the testes, examined post-operatively, were found to contain over twice as much estradiol as is present in the normal adult male.

"Not being considered a transsexual, her genitalia were surgically transformed so that she now had the penis and testes removed and an artificial vagina constructed from the skin of the penis. She subsequently married, moved away, and lived a very full life as a woman. She remained in contact over the years, and infrequently I would have a chance to talk to her and find out how her life was going.

"Five years later she returned. She had been passing successfully as a woman, had been working as a woman, and had been leading a very active, sexually gratifying life as a beautiful and popular young woman. Over the years, she had carefully observed the behavior of her women friends and had learned all the fine details of the expressions of femininity of a woman of her social class and age. Bit by bit, she had reassured herself on any of the possible defects in her femininity, the most important confirmations coming from the men who made love to her, none of whom complained that her anatomy was in the slightest bit suspicious. However, she still was not certain that her vagina was normal enough, and so I arranged for her to see a urologist who, because of his reputation, was in an outstanding position to speak to her as an authority; he told her unequivocally that her genitalia were quite beyond suspicion. . . .

"During the hour following the welcome news given her by the urologist, after having kept it from me for eight years, with the greatest casualness, in mid-sentence, and without giving the slightest warning it was coming, she revealed that she had never had a biological defect that had feminized her but that she had been taking estrogens since age 12. In earlier years when talking to me, she had not only said that she had always hoped and expected that when she grew up she would grow into a woman's body but that starting in puberty this had spontaneously, gradually, but unwaveringly occurred. In contrast, she now revealed that just as puberty began, at the time her voice started to lower and she developed pubic hair, she began stealing Stilbestrol from her mother, who was taking it on prescription following a pan-hysterectomy. The child then began filling the prescription on her own, telling the pharmacist that she was picking up the hormone for her mother and paying for it with money taken from her mother's purse. She did not know what the effects would be, only that this was a female substance, and she had no idea how much to take but more or less tried to follow the amounts her mother took. She kept this up continuously throughout adolescence, and because by chance she had picked just the right time to start taking the hormone, she was able to prevent the development of all secondary sex characteristics that might have been produced by androgens and instead to substitute those produced by estrogens. Nonetheless, the androgens continued to be produced, enough that a normal-sized adult penis developed with capacity for erection and orgasm till sexual excitability was suppressed by age 15. Thus, she became a lovely looking young 'woman,' though with a normal-sized penis. . . .

"My chagrin at learning this was matched by my amusement that she could have pulled off this coup with such skill. Now able to deal openly with me, for the first time she reported much that was new about her childhood and permitted me to talk with her mother, something that had been forbidden for those eight years."

This news turned the article into a feature of the same circumstances it reported, *i.e.*, into a situated report. Indeed, if the reader will re-read the article in light of these disclosures, he will find that the reading provides an exhibit of several prevailing phenomena of ethnomethodological study: (1) that the recognizedly rational accountability of practical actions is a member's practical accomplishment, and (2) that the success of that practical accomplishment consists in the work whereby a setting, in the same ways that it consists of a recognized and familiar organization of activities, masks from members' relevant notice members' practical ordering practices, and thereby leads the members to see a setting's features, which include a setting's accounts, "as determinate and independent objects."

Following Agnes' disclosures, Stoller exploited the break by tape recording 15 hours of interviews with her and her mother. A subsequent study will be done using the particulars of the disclosures to study the above phenomena. We plan, with the use of the new materials, to re-listen to the earlier taped conversations, to inspect our subsequent records, and to re-read this article. To mark this prospect the original article is called *Part I*.

NOTES

In collaboration with Robert J. Stoller, M.D., The Neuropsychiatric Institute, University of California, Los Angeles.

1. A. D. Schwabe, David H. Solomon, Robert J. Stoller, and John P. Burnham, "Pubertal Feminization in a Genetic Male with Testicular Atrophy and Normal Urinary Gonadotropin," Journal of Clinical Endocrinology and Metabolism, 22, No. 8 (August, 1962), 839–845.
2. For example, the Board of Health officer in Midwest City where Agnes was born, when he refused to approve Agnes' application for a change of birth certificate, was supposed to have agreed that "in the final analysis" the capacity to perform the male reproductive function settled Agnes' sex.
3. These properties need to be reviewed by considering actual cases that vary them along one or another "parameter" of recognition: deities, for one example; and war combatants whose genitals were destroyed as part of heroic mortal wounds, etc.
4. Nevertheless, further information is needed comparing Agnes with normals with respect to the possibility that normals are more accepting of willful election than she was. For example, several lay persons who were told about her case expressed considerable sympathy. They found as the thing to be sympathetic about that she should have had to have been confronted with the election in the first place.
5. Parsons treats "ascription" as a "relation concept." Any feature of an object may be treated by the actor according to the rule of its invariance to considerations of adaptation and goal attainment. This property of any feature's treatment

Parsons speaks of as "ascription." A person's sex is a common illustration, but not because of the properties of a person's sex but because and only because a person's sex is frequently treated this way.

6.   NOTE: The following alternative description of the two week period immediately following the operation was written by Robert J. Stoller. Reasons for including it are made clear at the conclusion of the study.

"One of the most dramatic 'non-game analyzable occasions' started with the castration operation and lasted for approximately two months. Starting immediately postoperatively, Agnes tried to sustain privacy in managing the care of her vagina by arranging to give herself the prescribed sitz baths and changing her own surgical dressings. She insisted on doing this out of sight of the nurses and house officers, which may have added to the resentment the nurses felt toward her. Immediately postoperatively, she developed bilateral thrombophlebitis of the legs, cystitis, contracture of the urethral meatus, and despite the plastic mold which was inserted into the vagina at the time of surgery, a tendency for the vagina outlet to contract. She also required postoperatively several minor surgical procedures for modification of these complications and also to trim the former scrotal tissue to make the external labia appear more normal. Despite the plastic mold, the newly-made vagina canal had a tendency to close and heal, which required intermittent manipulations of the mold and daily dilatations. Not only were all of these conditions painful or otherwise uncomfortable but also, although minor, since they were frequent, they produced increasing worry that the surgical procedure would not end up with the desired result of a normal functioning and appearing set of female genitalia. Although these distressing conditions were carefully (and ultimately successfully) treated, at the time that she was well enough to go home these complications were still not fully resolved. During her first week home, there was difficulty with occasional uncontrolled seepage of urine and feces. In addition, her physical activities had to be restricted because of pain. The cystitis did not immediately clear with treatment but persisted for a couple of weeks, producing unpleasant symptoms ranging from urinary frequency, urgency, burning on urination, to bouts of considerable pelvic pain.

"About two weeks after surgery, another set of very unpleasant symptoms developed. She gradually became increasingly weak and tired, was listless, lost her appetite, lost a great deal of weight so that her breasts and hips became noticeably smaller, her skin lost its fresh and smooth appearance, and became waxy; she lost interest in sex; and she rather rapidly became increasingly depressed, being subject to sudden uncontrollable spells of crying. The first time she was seen by us following her return home, she presented this picture. It sounded like a rather typical and moderately severe depression. It seemed to be rather strong evidence that a mistake had been made. The operation had been performed primarily for psychological reasons; it had been the judgment of the medical staff that her identity was so strongly fixed in a female direction that no forms of treatment could ever make her masculine. In addition, it was felt that she was unequivocally sincere in her expressions of desperateness about her anomalous anatomical situation and her feelings that if anybody attempted to make her a male, not only would the attempts be of no use but that they would drive her to despair if not suicide. There is always the possibility when a patient makes such claims about something they want in reality that there is more ambivalence present than is observable, and it is the responsibility of the experts making the evaluation to determine that such a degree of ambivalence does not exist. We had felt without doubt that our evaluation was extensive and adequate and that it revealed that this patient was as well fixed in her femininity as are many anatomically normal females and that whatever latent or vestigial masculinity was present was not greater in degree or quality than that found in anatomically normal women. If this judgment was wrong, then it would be expected that the absoluteness of the castrating operation, the uncontrovertible and unalterable fact of the loss of male genitalia would, when the patient was faced with its actuality, produce a severe psychological reaction only if the hidden masculinity and unconscious desires to be a man were strong enough and had been missed by us.

"Therefore, on being confronted with a rather severely depressed patient, we had presumptive evidence that an error in judgment had been made and that the patient was now depressed from having lost her insignia of masculinity. Thus, the clear listing of all of these classical symptoms of depression.... She reported that she had been having increasingly frequent episodes of sudden sweating accompanied by a very peculiar sensation which started in her toes and swept up her legs through her trunk and into her face, a rushing sensation of heat. She was having hot flashes on the basis of a surgical menopause. When the operation was performed and her tests removed, the source of the estrogens which had produced the whole complicated anatomical picture of secondary sex characteristics of a woman was removed. Thus, she had acutely developed a menopausal syndrome no different from what is frequently seen in young women who have their ovaries removed. Every one of the symptoms named above can be accounted for by the acute loss of estrogen (though this is not to say that the menopausal syndrome in anatomically normal women is usually to be explained simply on the basis of decrease of estrogen). At this point, hormone assays revealed an increase in urinary FSH and the absence of urinary estrogen. She was immediately placed on estrogen replacement therapy and *all* of the above signs and symptoms disappeared. She lost her depression, regained her interest in life and sexual drive; her breasts and hips returned to their normal ampleness; her skin took on its more usual feminine appearance, and so on.

"It may be of value to mention briefly the pathological findings of the testes. They were severely changed from the normal male as a result of the chronic presence of estrogens in their milieu so that, in brief, the normal pathological evidence for production of fertile sperm was absent. Various degenerative and abortive forms of spermatogenesis were found in the abnormal cells. However, there was no tumor found, and there was no evidence of an ovotestis (that is, a hermaphroditic condition in which ovarian and testicular tissue are found in the same organ). The conclusion of the endocrinologist was that Agnes 'presented a clinical picture that seemed to suggest a superimposition of an excess of estrogen upon the substratum of a normal male.' What could not be explained, and what therefore made her unique in the endocrinologic literature is that even in the presence of large enough production of estrogen to produce completely feminine secondary sex characteristics... There is at this time no adequate explanation for this anomaly.

"It is safe to assume that the findings of depression were due simply to the acute loss of estrogen following castration. Agnes had never had such an episode before; the episode was abruptly ended by the administration of estrogen and no such episode has occurred again. She has been on daily estrogen since that time.

"Agnes subsequently had to return to the hospital for further treatment of cystitis and for the minor surgical procedure of completely opening up the vaginal canal. Her subsequent course surgically and endocrinologically was uneventful."

7.   Erving Goffman, *The Presentation of Self in Everyday Life,* University of Edinburgh, Social Sciences Research Centre, 1956.

8.   This and the observations in the remainder of this paragraph were obtained by revising the illuminating remarks by Hubert L. and Patricia Allen Dreyfus (in their translators' introduction to Maurice Merleau-Ponty, *Sense and Non-Sense* [Evanston, Ill.: Northwestern University Press, 1966], pp. x–xiii) so as to make their modified sense available to my interests.

9.   That knowledge loaned to her descriptions of this work an unavoidable "performative" character. This property of her descriptions of normal sexuality turned them into exhibitions which, as much as anything, distinguished for us her talk about normal sexuality from the talk about normal sexuality by normals.

7

selection from
The Role *of Gender and the* Imperative *of Sex*

Charles Shepherdson

Charles Shepherdson uses psychoanalytic theory to attempt to break out of the pointless debate over transsexualism that he sees raging between biological essentialism and social constructionism. Taking French psychoanalyst Jacques Lacan as his point of departure, and elaborating on the work of Lacanian psychoanalyst Catherine Millot, Shepherdson argues that the body can be reduced to neither "a natural fact nor a cultural construction." He suggests that only psychoanalysis is conceptually equipped to deal with a critical third question, which is how the embodied human subject acquires a body image and then situates that imaginary body in the symbolic realm of language and culture. This process is what psychoanalysts call the acquisition of sexual difference, which is something quite distinct from either sex (meaning the biological body with its particular reproductive capacity), or gender (meaning role or identity).

For psychoanalysis, the problem of transsexualism—or, more specifically, the problem of transsexuals' appeals to medical practitioners for surgical modification of the genitals—is that the request is considered to be a pathology of the purely psychical process of sexual differentiation, a denial of the symbolic meaning of the material reality of the body. It is not, as the transsexual claims, a neutral and strictly instrumental request to transform one genital morphology into another. As it is an expression of psychopathology, the psychoanalyst, who cannot ethically collaborate with the transsexual's fantasy of "being" the other sex, should deny the transsexual request for surgery.

While psychoanalysis has a great deal to offer in terms of understanding how the human organism becomes a gendered subject, the perceived dilemma of the psychoanalyst treating the transsexual patient reveals a profound struggle. Whose sense of meaning and reality, the analyst's or the analysand's, should have the power to actualize itself? The analyst, situating himself or herself as a voice of cultural authority, insists that the transsexual's body should mean what culture says it is supposed to mean; the transsexual insists that his or her body means differently, and wants the body to acquire a social and cultural meaning that corresponds with a subjectively held gender identity. It is this impasse that creates such antipathy toward psychoanalysis on the part of so many transgender people, whose struggle to control their own bodies has been far better served by medical service providers willing to change the *soma*, and not try to change the self.

TRANSSEXUALITY

One of Millot's most far-reaching arguments can be situated here: science offers the transsexual the possibility of transformation, based on the application of technological advances that are administered in silence, without asking too many questions *about the subject* (the "real work" begins with anesthetizing the patient). Concerning itself only with the manipulation of the "extended substance" of the organism (and perhaps, as Leslie Lothstein suggests, concerned with its own technical advancement, for which the subject is "raw material"), medical science operates by presupposing that it is dealing with the organism rather than the body, that the transsexual seeks an *anatomical change* rather than a *different embodiment*, a body that would reconfigure elements belonging to the categories of the imaginary, symbolic, and real. Put differently, the surgeon works with a conception of anatomy that presupposes a natural version of sexual identity, thereby foreclosing the question of sexual difference. Since some of those who seek an operation also occupy a position which would foreclose sexual difference, we are obliged to recognize a clear homology: the very foreclosure of sexual difference that characterizes the transsexual position is also sustained by the medical community. Science, Millot says, participates in the transsexual demand, which is the demand for an exit from the question of sexual difference.

As striking as this conjunction between the transsexual and the surgeon may seem (as Millot says, the transsexual's demand, like all demands, is addressed *to the other*, and even shaped in advance *by the other*, demand being originally intersubjective), the link between sexual difference and the history of science will come as no surprise to those who have recognized in the metaphysical tradition a conception of the subject that forecloses sexual difference, and who see the history of technology as based on an interpretation of being as "presence-at-hand," according to which the body would be precisely a "fashionable" extended substance. In short, this focus on the body as material substance coincides with a short-circuit of the symbolic order, which brings the entire medical apparatus, despite its cultural centrality, into close proximity with psychosis. To the extent that a smooth machinery is established, making surgery *available upon demand* (as the vocabulary of commodification has it), science "may even constitute a symptom of our civilization" (16).

There is consequently a historical dimension to Millot's discussion, for although transsexuality has no doubt existed since ancient times, strictly speaking "there is no transsexuality without the surgeon and the endocrinologist; in this sense, it is an essentially modern phenomenon" (17). Here, technology seems to coincide with a certain, historically developed interpretation of the body as present-at-hand, a material substratum inhabited by a "spiritual substance," an animated "subjectivity" who—in keeping with certain tenets of liberal tradition—should be "free" and have the "right to choose." And after all, on what grounds would one argue that "the psychoanalyst knows best" and should stand as the gatekeeper of the law?[1] Paradoxically, however, Millot argues that the position of absolute mastery is in fact claimed not by the analyst but by the legal apparatus and the medical community, insofar as they, like the transsexual, seek to eliminate the imperative of sexual difference, to replace the real of embodiment with a fantasy body that would be fully manipulable, unmarked by the limit of the real, a body that would pose no limit to the mastery of the subject:

> Such, in any case, is the dream of doctors and jurists whose vocation it is to deal in the fantasy of seemingly unlimited power—the power to triumph over death (that other real), the power to make laws [laws that would demonstrate the superiority of human law over the imperatives of sex and death], the power to legislate human reality flawlessly, leaving nothing to chance. Transsexuality is a *response to* the dream of forcing back, and even abolishing, the frontiers of the real. (p. 15, emphasis added)

What then distinguishes, according to Millot, the position of the analyst from this position of mastery ascribed to the lawyer or scientist who would "legislate human reality…leaving nothing to chance"? What distinguishes the analyst from the "gatekeeper of the law," legislating who may enter, or stating (more democratically) that "anyone may enter freely," though the gate be narrow? We are faced here with the difference between knowledge and ignorance, between the certainty of the law that provides in advance the set of possibilities offered to a neutral (and neuter) subject, the anonymous "anyone," and the ignorance of the analyst who, not knowing who is speaking, finds it necessary (and obligatory: a different law) *to listen*. A distinction is thus drawn between the *question* posed by the analyst, or more precisely opened for the analysand in the analytic situation, and the *answer* that is *given in advance* by science and the law, a distinction that could also be stated by contrasting the *certainty* of the transsexual (which coincides with the mastery of the doctor), and the *doubt* that inheres in every symbolic formulation of sexual difference. This is a clue to Millot's claim that *the certainty of the subject who claims a transsexual position, like the certainty of science* (which, after a few words have been exchanged, has "nothing more to say"), is a sign that the symbolic order has been foreclosed.

Millot notes further that the preliminary interviews that prospective candidates undergo are organized by criteria which reinforce the most conformist sexual stereotypes. After hormonal treatments, a male-to-female transsexual is obliged to live "like a woman" (whatever that means) in order to demonstrate (and test out for herself) whether this identity truly "fits":

> Like the doctors, psychiatrists, endocrinologists, and surgeons whom they consult, transsexuals gauge femininity in terms of the conformity of roles. Hand in hand, they construct scales of femininity, and measure them with batteries of tests.[2] Permission to undergo sex-change surgery is contingent on the results of these tests, which also enable transsexuals to train for their future roles. (14)

Thus, Gender Identity Clinics, under the guise of freedom of choice, and admitting an apparent diversity (from the "exotic" to the "mundane," but all under the regulation of preordained "types") are in fact "in the process of becoming 'sex control centers'" (14)—a fact which is hardly surprising in a culture where standardization is essential for the regular administration of free trade and smooth international exchange.

> Transsexuality involves an appeal, and especially a demand, addressed to the Other. As a symptom it is completed with the help of this Other dimension—more especially, with that of the function of the Other's desire. Lacan said that the neurotic symptom is completed during the analytical treatment, due to the fact that the analyst lends consistency to the desire of the Other, an enigma with which the symptom is bound up. (141, translation modified)

If the Other takes the form of a science for which there are no limits, a form of omnipotence (or, in Millot's terms, if the desire of the Other is absolute, a position of omnipotent *jouissance*, outside the law), the subject who comes to this Other with a demand—a demand that is also a symptom—will find this demand "completed" by the Other. If, on the contrary, the Other takes the form of one who is lacking, one-who-wants-to-know (who desires, which is precisely the opposite of absolute *jouissance*), then the symptom will be completed only by a discursive articulation in which the subject, having run up against the limit in the Other, encounters the question of his or her desire—which the demand often seeks to evade.

In the context of these psychological measures and obligatory performances (a sort of "test drive" in which it is determined whether one can live "in" the new model body), it should be noted of course that candidates for surgery have often read as much of the "psychological profile" material as their clinicians, and are very well prepared for these tests (like candidates for the LSAT or GRE, they have taken "primer" courses in order to "pass"), and, as Lothstein points out, they often have a degree of expertise in the performance of their role that makes it difficult (for all parties) to discover *who they really are*. It would perhaps be fashionable to argue that there is no "real" subject there, no "authentic personality," but only the product of various performances, and in some respects this is precisely the case, given that "the subject" is not constituted at birth, but formed in the course of a singular historical experience. But again, the question arises of the *relation between* (on the one hand) the subject who performs for these trials of identity, who seeks to "correspond" to a given (or apparently "chosen") role, or who has somehow come to demand surgery as a solution to the enigma of sexual difference, and (on the other hand) those ideals, those images, those stereotypes or performances with which the subject has come to comply (like the prospective "lawyer" or "professor"). Truly a "correspondence theory" of (sexual) truth.

The difficulty Millot addresses here—it is the clinical difficulty, the diagnostic question, of distinguishing which candidates are likely to benefit from surgery and which will not—may be put in terms of *demand and desire*: when the "who" that chooses has been brought to this choice by the "mortifying exigency" (59) of a demand in which the future is shut down, a demand in which desire is lost, a demand that the subject appears to make, but which has come from the Other, and with which the subject has complied, then perhaps the analyst has a responsibility to open for the subject a passageway that would lead from absolute submission to this demand, to the possibility of desire, which also means the possibility of a future. This question of ethics is clearly *avoided* when the clinical machinery simply stands ready to operate upon demand in an economic circuit of "supply and demand" that presupposes the subject "knows what he or she desires," when in fact desire may be lacking altogether, having been eclipsed by compliance with a punishing identification, demanding the adoption of a role with which, however "mortifying" it may be, the subject has come to comply.

One sees here where the family structure, and the desire of the parents, would have to be considered, according to Millot.[3] But in focusing on the character of modern science, Millot's focus is different at this point: the readiness to answer all demands, on the part of the medical community, with indifference to "who comes," amounts to confusing desire and demand, a failure to make any distinction between them, whereas the task of the analyst is precisely to make such a distinction, neither to answer the demand nor simply to prescribe, to tell the client what is permissible, to lay down the law, but rather to listen, in order to discover whether, behind the demand addressed to the surgeon, there is a desire, or whether there is not rather an effort to escape desire, by complying with this "mortifying exigency" that compels the subject to "choose" a solution to embodiment that would in fact have the character of a punishing imprisonment, an exit from desire as such.

Insofar as medical technology and the transsexual coincide and "complete" each other, then, we may speak of a mutual relation between demand and *jouissance*, which Millot would contrast with the relation to desire. For Schreber too, it is the absolute *jouissance* of God that Schreber's transformation is supposed to satisfy, as though he himself were being offered up as a divine sacrifice, which has become necessary in order to fill the void that threatens to appear in the universe, and that Schreber alone is able to circumvent. The "opposition between desire and *jouissance*" (99) noted by Millot is also taken up by Lacan, at the end of *Seminar XI*, where he speaks of Freud's references to the specter of Nazism in his *Group Psychology*: there is always the possibility that a group will find a solution to the fracture of the symbolic order, the intrusion of lack within it, by offering up a sacrifice in hope of satisfying the *jouissance* of an obscure god, who has become incarnated in the figure of an Other. "That is why I wrote *Kant avec Sade*," Lacan says (*SXI*, 276).

The point may also be made in terms of identification: Millot argues that whereas *some* subjects who present themselves for surgery have a relation to sexual difference, are identified with "the other sex," and will consequently benefit from an operation, fashioning a future for themselves on the basis of this identification, *other* subjects, by contrast, are not in fact identified with "the other sex," but are rather *horsexe*, "outsidesex." *This* latter identification is not a symbolic, but a phallic identification, in which desire has become impossible. To celebrate the transsexual as a "free" subject, the most avant-garde instance of the "malleability of gender," is to disregard the virtually transfixed character of this identification, and the suffering it entails.[4] These latter subjects, as much of the secondary literature acknowledges, are structurally close to psychosis, and Millot argues that for them, it is not a question of identification with the other sex, but rather a fantasy of the other sex, in which *the "other sex" is regarded as not lacking.*[5] In short, within the group of those who present themselves for surgery, Millot distinguishes two forms of identification, one oriented in relation to sexual difference (identification as "a man" or "a woman," with all the ambiguity, uncertainty, and symbolic mobility this entails), and another oriented by a *simulacrum* of sexual difference, a fantasy of "otherness" that in fact amounts to the elimination of sexual difference, its replacement by the fantasy of a sex that would not be lacking. This identification is marked by *certainty*, by a demand to eliminate the symbolic ambiguity that accompanies sexual difference, replacing it with the immobility of a "perfected" body, one that would put an end to the difficulties of historical existence, and bring time itself to a halt, as it did in the case of Schreber's apocalyptic narrative.[6]

This distinction between two forms of identification may be expressed in three ways, according to three periods of Lacan's work. First, it is explained as the difference between the establishment of an ego ideal (which is always associated with the future in Freud's thought, and the temporality of language) and the position of primary narcissism, a position in which the differential structure of language, and the relation to the other, can be eliminated. These two positions are situated in schema R (see chapter 2), as point "I" (the ego ideal) and point Φ (a phallic identification, which amounts to a denial of sexual difference, a position outside the symbolic). The task of the analyst who conducts the clinical interview is thus to determine which of these positions the subject occupies in requesting surgery. This also means that the demand for surgery does not by itself automatically reveal the subjective position of the person who makes it. Here again, we see a division between those in the medical profession who take such a request at face value, and stand ready to operate on demand (asking only about insurance, perhaps), and the analyst, who will ask "who speaks" in this demand.

Second, these two identifications may be expressed in terms of the sexuation diagram from *Encore*: on the "masculine" side, as the difference between a man and the Primal Father, and on the "feminine" side, as the difference between a woman and *La femme*. As Millot points out, the true transsexual, in the case of the male-to-female transsexual, for example, is not properly defined as "a man who wishes to become a woman," but as "a woman born into a man's body that she wishes to be rid of." Such a formulation replaces anatomical classification (which would then be susceptible to "transformation"—from one to the other) with "identification." But in the case of a phallic identification, an identification with a simulacrum of the other sex (with "*La femme*" or "The Father"), which Millot calls an identification "outsidesex," the symbolic is short-circuited: "The subject is compelled to *incarnate* the phallus in the form of a narcissistic image, if nothing can show that this is impossible" (59). For these subjects, the demand to occupy the position of "the other sex" (which is not so much the "other" sex, in a relation to alterity, as a position outside sex, a "perfection" attributed to the other and then sought as a possibility to be obtained for oneself), is the demand, not for a sexed position, but for a position in which nothing would be lacking, a position that would be filled, in one case, by "*La femme*" and in the other case by the Primal Father—both of which amount equally to a foreclosure of sexual difference.

In short, what schema R designates as the phallus is later elaborated in the sexuation diagram as equally (A) the Primal Father, the "immortal" figure in *Totem and Taboo* who stands as the *exception to the law*, a position impossible to occupy (which does not keep it from being sought), and (B) "*La femme*," the incarnation of "the woman who does not exist," the "spectacular" figure of a supposed "femininity" incarnated by some of the clients Millot discusses. "*La femme*" here occupies the position of "The Woman," the figure who would put an end to the question, "What is a woman?" (with emphasis on the *indefinite article*), by seeming to provide an answer for "the whole." Expressed in terms of set theory, the sexuation diagram distinguishes "women" in the plural as an open set (this one and that one and the next...without totality or essence), from "the one" ("*La femme*") who seems to incarnate the totality, to close the set of "all women" by representing "Woman" as such.

The crucial point here is the *contradictory relation* between "*La femme*," who undertakes to represent the whole, and the open set of "women," which cannot be totalized by reference to a single essence. This contradiction between "women" and "*La femme*" (a contradiction that runs parallel to the opposition, on the masculine side, between the set "All men are castrated," and the exception to the law, "the one who escapes castration," the father of the primal horde) is crucial if we are to understand the peculiar (nondialectical) logic by which identification with "*La femme*" paradoxically amounts to a foreclosure of sexual difference, making it impossible to identify as "a woman." This paradox, by which an incarnation of "The Woman" amounts to an exclusion of "women," is clearly expressed by the subject cited by Janice Raymond who says,

> Genetic women cannot claim to possess the courage, compassion and breadth of vision acquired during the transsexual experience. Free from the burdens of menstruation and procreation, transsexuals are clearly superior to genetic women. The future is theirs: in the year 2000, when the world is exhausting its energies on the task of feeding six billion souls, procreation will no longer be held to be an asset. (13–14)

Sixty pages later, Millot quotes one of her own clients who says:

> The conviction [has come to me] that the nearest humanity approaches to perfection is in the persons of good women—and especially perhaps in the persons of the kind, intelligent and healthy women past their menopause, no longer shackled by the mechanisms of sex....In all countries, among all races, on the whole these are the people I most admire; and it is into their ranks, I flatter myself, that I have now admitted myself. (70)

As Millot explains, such an identification is not only outside the symbolization of difference, but also an effort to circumvent desire; moreover, it is a demand that the subject *seems to make* (to "choose freely," etc.), but that in fact *comes from the Other*. This apparent "choice" of identification is thus regarded as an "exigency" with which the subject has agreed to comply:

> The Other's logical position, since unmarked by castration, can be replaced in the imaginary by the myth of the father of the horde as much as by the phantasy of the phallic woman. It is the place of absolute jouissance, which can be expressed by the formula $\exists x \, \overline{\Phi x}$. (58)

This is why Lacan writes that "The Woman" is one of the names of the father. Thus, among those who request what in the United States is called "sexual reassignment surgery," some are not identified with the other sex, but hold together a precarious identity by means of a fantasy of totalization, ascribed to the other sex. The subject who seeks such a position is thus regarded as seeking to move, not to another sexed position, but to a position in which his or her lack might be eliminated.

This allows Millot to make a further clarification, distinguishing these subjects in turn from psychotics. For in much of the clinical literature, debates hinge on the question of whether the transsexual is psychotic. Millot enters this debate in the following way: having distinguished the "true transsexual," who is identified with the other sex (as "a man" or "a woman," again, with all the uncertainty this entails), from the subject who maintains (or rather seeks to occupy) a phallic identification, she distinguishes further between *these* latter subjects and psychotics. She argues that the subjects who maintain this relation of fantasy to the "other sex" as not lacking, have their subjective consistency precisely on the basis of this relation, this quasi-symbolic link, which is also a relation to alterity, difference, and lack. The consequence is decisive: for these particular subjects, an operation would deprive them of the one *point of reference* in relation to which they have established a subjective consistency. For them, an operation eliminates this point of reference, replacing a *relation to the other* (a symbolic link), however precarious, with a *condition of "being"* that is outside the symbolic, so that surgery, far from liberating them for a future, will on the contrary imprison them once and for all in a position of foreclosure that has been kept at bay only by this fantasy of the other sex. For these subjects, surgery will precipitate a psychotic break.

The third account of transsexuality in Millot's book formulates the point we have just made in terms of knot theory. Arguing, on the basis of Lacan's later work, that in some cases the three orders (imaginary, real, and symbolic), are not truly knotted together but are nevertheless kept in something like a semblance of consistency by means of a symptomatic formation, Millot suggests that the transsexual demand plays the part of such a symptom. In other words, this demand provides a consistency and a symbolic relation for the subject, such that if the subject were *in fact* allowed to undergo surgery, the symptom would be resolved, but in such a way that the three orders, the three rings of the knot, would fall apart. The proper course of action in this case would therefore be to work with the demand, rather than to answer it directly with a "hands-on" operation.

TRANSVESTITE AND TRANSSEXUAL

How, then, are we to understand the difference between the transvestite and the transsexual, if it is not just a matter of degree, but a more decisive difference? Cross-dressing and other instances of the malleability of the subject, its "constructed" character, have gone far toward illuminating the symbolic mobility of gender, and the transsexual is sometimes enlisted to serve as a more radical example of this mobility. But perhaps the question of the body cannot be situated at precisely the same level as clothing, conceived as another fashionable, "symbolic" phenomenon. Whereas the transvestite already "has" an identity that is able to orchestrate and enjoy, the transsexual that concerns Millot is in limbo, waiting for the operation that will one day make possible the assumption of an identity that has hitherto been lacking. Recent research on literary forms has shown us the great variety of functions that cross-dressing can perform (in comedy and farce, in romance and burlesque, a whole vocabulary can be found); but the transsexual we find in Lothstein and Millot does not play a role or adopt a disguise to seduce or deceive, or to appropriate the power and privileges of the other sex in a scheme that aims at someone's erotic gratification, or at obtaining social leverage (one thinks of *Dangerous Liaisons*, *M. Butterfly*, and *The Crying Game* as recent examples in film). In Millot's account, the transsexual does not have the same grounding, the same identity, or the same relation to sexuality, to "being sexed," that one sees in the transvestite. In some sense, the transvestite already "has" a body with which to perform, while the transsexual lives a time of suspension in which the body has not yet been constituted. The question of identity, as it arises at the level of sexed embodiment, is not equivalent to what we usually understand by the term "gender role."

There is a different relation to the social order, as a result. Cross-dressing can always be a technique of social criticism; it can organize the forces of laughter or defiance against the stultifying boredom and routine of heterosexuality; it can be enlisted to demonstrate the arbitrary, artificial conventionality of a social standard that tries to pass itself off as "natural," or to expose through parody the excess of a type that takes itself as the measure of all things. Millot would seem to suggest that the transvestite not only has a body to dress, but is an individual with a relation to society, as might be confirmed through the fact that so many precise names can be given to the figures of impersonation, all of them functional and socially located: the "vamp," the "sex goddess," the figure of "Elizabeth Taylor dressed as Cleopatra," the "dyke," the "amazon," or the "brother-at-arms," "one of the guys," or the woman who takes her place as a man on the factory line, and is in it not for sexual subterfuge but for wages. The diversity of this language is clear enough from the variety of genres that have been developed by literature: burlesque, satire, farce, travesty, and so on. In this sense, the great variety of forms of cross-dressing are all socially subversive acts and can function as critique, even if the dominant culture subjects them to criticism in turn, limits their visibility, and their recognition to controlled places—certain neighborhoods, houses, or cabarets. As a critical force, the transvestite is also subject to satire and victimization.

But the transsexual that Millot describes does not have this disruptive relation to society, this position of defiance. The transvestite has a position, however marginalized and oppressed, that would seem to be denied to the transsexual, who does not yet have, on Millot's account, what the transvestite takes for granted. The transsexual, one might say, has instead a relation primarily to his or her body: if *this* relation could be settled to some extent, then a relation to society could be more effectively mobilized. In some sense, the acquisition of a body—which is not automatically given with the "fact" of embodiment, but has to be accomplished—would seem to be a prerequisite to the subjective act of dressing or undressing. The constitution of the body, Lacan would say, is the condition for the possibility of the act of a subject. Perhaps we could say that cross-dressing is the act of a subject who plays with what we call "gender roles," while the transsexual is someone whose capacity to act (in the sense not only of "performance," but of speech-act theory) waits upon (an idea of) embodiment. There is perhaps a difference here between "gender role" and "embodiment" that remains to be understood, a difference that cannot be reduced to biological terms or answered by the shortcut of technology. If, among those who come to the clinic, hoping to be referred to a surgeon, some turn out not to be identified with the other sex, but to be confined to a punishing identification Millot calls phallic, a position from which (if it could only be occupied) nothing more would need to be said, we are perhaps led to encounter what Freud called "the silence" of the death drive: these individuals stand out, not as proof of the ultimate freedom of the subject (which is what many would like to see, in celebrating the figure of the transsexual, perhaps from the distance and safety of fantasy); rather, they articulate in their being that symptom of a social order in which it is possible to look for a solution to suffering in the most stereotypical fantasy of the other—a solution that amounts to a "no exit." According to Millot, these subjects are not in a position to take up a sexual body, because they are engaged in a fantasy of totalization regarding the "other sex." One can only wonder if the medical technology that comes to the supposed aid of these subjects, without asking them very much about who they are (time being a precious commodity), is not the partner of this refusal of embodiment. The medical solution, far from being a source of liberation, would serve on the contrary as the accomplice of a society that sustains this fantasy of "the other sex."

NOTES

Originally published in chapter 3 "The *Role* of Gender and *Imperative* of Sex" in *Vital Signs: Nature, Culture, Psychoanalysis* (New York: Routledge, 2000)

1. A similar difficulty appears in the legal context when, as discussions of Jack Kevorkian have made clear, it is said that subjects should have the right to die, *if they are mentally competent*—which means that in certain cases, someone else will decide upon the subject's competence, that someone else will (and "ought to") protect the subject against the choices that subject might make, and that a person's free choice may not be in the person's own interest.

2. The recent, popular *Brain Sex* provides a good example of such a test, without the slightest ironic distance, a test designed to reveal through some "twenty questions" the degree of intrauterine hormonal testosterone to which one was exposed before birth, and to rank the respondent accordingly, on a sliding scale of masculinity and femininity. Anne Moir and David Jessel, *Brain Sex: The Real Difference Between Men and Women* (New York: Dell, 1989).

3. See also Moustapha Safouan, "Contribution to the Psychoanalysis of Transsexualism," in *Returning to Freud*, pp. 195–212.

4. Lothstein relates a series of cases that are illuminating in this regard.

5. It should also be clear from this that Millot's position clarifies what often remains unclear in the secondary literature—namely, whether transsexuals are homosexual or not. Excessive focus on "behavior" without sufficient attention to structural positions (that is, to the structural difference between phallic and symbolic identification) has led clinicians to orient themselves by reference to what a subject "does," which in fact shows very little. Millot's account would suggest that whereas the homosexual position is "normal," in that one finds desire, a relation to the other, and so on, the position *horsexe* is structured by a demand in which desire is eclipsed.

6. As Jacqueline Rose points out, Lacan became more and more concerned with the terms "certainty," "knowledge," and "belief" as he developed his account of sexual difference. See *Feminine Sexuality*, 50. Irigaray has taken up precisely these terms in "La Croyance Même," an essay on "belief" and sexual difference addressed to Derrida (in *Sexes et Parentés*, Paris: Minuit, 1987), 47–65. Derrida has responded (to her and others) in *Memoires of the Blind: The Self-Portrait and Other Ruins*, trans. Pascale-Anne Brault and Michael Nass (Chicago: University of Chicago Press, 1993), a text that opens with the question, "Do you believe?" (1).

8

A Cyborg Manifesto
Science, Technology, and Socialist-Feminism in the Late Twentieth Century

Donna Haraway

Feminist science studies scholar Donna Haraway's provocative 1983 "Cyborg Manifesto" helped launch the interdisciplinary field of cyborg studies, and contributed to innovative thinking across a wide range of humanities and scientific disciplines. Its conceptual vocabulary and theoretical framework directly informed one of the founding works of transgender studies, "The 'Empire' Strikes Back: A Posttranssexual Manifesto," by Haraway's doctoral student Sandy Stone.

"Cyborg," a word coined in science fiction literature to describe a human-machine hybrid, or "cybernetic organism," was transformed by Haraway into a potent figuration for analyzing three distinct "boundary ruptures" in the late-twentieth century that broadly characterize the contemporary situation of embodiment, identity, and desire: the boundaries between humans and nonhuman animals, between organisms and machines, and between the physical world and immaterial things. The cyborg, in Haraway's usage, is a way to grapple with what it means to be a conscious, embodied, subject in an environment structured by techno-scientific practices that challenge basic and widely-shared notions of what it means to be human—practices such as animal-to-human organ transplants and gene splices, cochlear implants, or the seemingly inescapable structuring of the material world by machine-readable codes.

Although Haraway calls her cyborg "a creature in a post-gender world," she does not specifically analyze transgender issues in this tremendously influential article. Rather, she addresses in a more general way several issues of central importance to transgender studies, such as the way that "gender" is, in part, a story we tell ourselves to naturalize a particular social organization of biological reproduction, family roles, and state powers. Even more importantly, through the very ruptures and cross-contaminations between the different types and fields of knowledge that her article simultaneously produces and points out, Haraway's cyborg demonstrates by example how a panoply of other marginalized embodied positions—such as "women of color," which she discusses in some detail—become sites for critical cultural, political, and intellectual practice. Transgender and intersex figures have likewise become politically charged sites of cultural struggle over the meaning of human being, and being human, in an increasingly technologized world.

AN IRONIC DREAM OF A COMMON LANGUAGE FOR WOMEN IN THE INTEGRATED CIRCUIT

This chapter is an effort to build an ironic political myth faithful to feminism, socialism, and materialism.[1] Perhaps more faithful as blasphemy is faithful, than as reverent worship and identification. Blasphemy has always seemed to require taking things very seriously. I know no better stance to adopt from within the secular-religious, evangelical traditions of United States politics, including the politics of socialist feminism. Blasphemy protects one from the moral majority within, while still insisting on the need for community. Blasphemy is not apostasy. Irony is about contradictions that do not resolve into larger wholes, even dialectically, about the tension of holding incompatible things together because both or all are necessary and true. Irony is about humour and serious play. It is also a rhetorical strategy and a political method, one I would like to see more honoured within socialist-feminism. At the centre of my ironic faith, my blasphemy, is the image of the cyborg.

A cyborg is a cybernetic organism, a hybrid of machine and organism, a creature of social reality as well as a creature of fiction. Social reality is lived social relations, our most important political construction, a world-changing fiction. The international women's movements have constructed 'women's experience', as well as uncovered or discovered this crucial collective object. This experience is a fiction and fact of the most crucial, political kind. Liberation rests on the construction of the consciousness, the imaginative apprehension, of oppression, and so of possibility. The cyborg is a matter of fiction and lived experience that changes what counts as women's experience in the late twentieth century. This is a struggle over life and death, but the boundary between science fiction and social reality is an optical illusion.

Contemporary science fiction is full of cyborgs—creatures simultaneously animal and machine, who populate worlds ambiguously natural and crafted. Modern medicine is also full of cyborgs, of couplings between organism and machine, each conceived as coded devices, in an intimacy and with a power that was not generated in the history of sexuality. Cyborg 'sex' restores some of the lovely replicative baroque of ferns and invertebrates (such nice organic prophylactics against heterosexism). Cyborg replication is uncoupled from organic reproduction. Modern production seems like a dream of cyborg colonization work, a dream that makes the nightmare of Taylorism seem idyllic. And modern war is a cyborg orgy, coded by C^3I, command-control-communication-intelligence, an $84 billion item in 1984's US defence budget. I am making an argument for the cyborg as a fiction mapping our social and bodily reality and as an imaginative resource suggesting some very fruitful couplings. Michael Foucault's biopolitics is a flaccid premonition of cyborg politics, a very open field.

By the late twentieth century, our time, a mythic time, we are all chimeras, theorized and fabricated hybrids of machine and organism; in short, we are cyborgs. The cyborg is our ontology; it gives us our politics. The cyborg is a condensed image of both imagination and material reality, the two joined centres structuring any possibility of historical transformation. In the traditions of 'Western' science and politics—the tradition of racist, male-dominant capitalism; the tradition of progress; the tradition of the appropriation of nature as resource for the productions of culture; the tradition of reproduction of the self from the reflections of the other—the relation between organism and machine has been a border war. The stakes in the border war have been the territories of production, reproduction, and imagination. This chapter is an argument for *pleasure* in the confusion of boundaries and for *responsibility* in their construction. It is also an effort to contribute to socialist-feminist culture and theory in a postmodernist, non-naturalist mode and in the utopian tradition of imagining a world without gender, which is perhaps a world without genesis, but maybe also a world without end. The cyborg incarnation is outside salvation history. Nor does it mark time on an oedipal calendar, attempting to heal the terrible cleavages of gender in an oral symbiotic utopia or post-oedipal apocalypse. As Zoe Sofoulis argues in her unpublished manuscript on Jacques Lacan, Melanie Klein, and nuclear culture, *Lacklein*, the most terrible and perhaps the most promising monsters in cyborg worlds are embodied in non-oedipal narratives with a different logic of repression, which we need to understand for our survival.

The cyborg is a creature in a post-gender world; it has no truck with bisexuality, pre-oedipal symbiosis, unalienated labour, or other seductions to organic wholeness through a final appropriation of all the powers of the parts into a higher unity. In a sense, the cyborg has no origin story in the Western sense—a 'final' irony since the cyborg is also the awful apocalyptic *telos* of the 'West's' escalating dominations of abstract individuation, an ultimate self untied at last from all dependency, a man in space. An origin story in the 'Western', humanist sense depends on the myth of original unity, fullness, bliss and terror, represented by the phallic mother from whom all humans must separate, the task of individual development and of history, the twin potent myths inscribed most powerfully for us in psychoanalysis and Marxism. Hilary Klein has argued that both Marxism and psychoanalysis, in their concepts of labour and of individuation and gender formation, depend on the plot of original unity out of which difference must be produced and enlisted in a drama of escalating domination of woman/nature. The cyborg skips the step of original unity, of identification with nature in the Western sense. This is its illegitimate promise that might lead to subversion of its teleology as star wars.

The cyborg is resolutely committed to partiality, irony, intimacy, and perversity. It is oppositional, utopian, and completely without innocence. No longer structured by the polarity of public and private, the cyborg defines a technological polis based partly on a revolution of social relations in the *oikos*, the household. Nature and culture are reworked; the one can no longer be the resource for appropriation or incorporation by the other. The relationships for forming wholes from parts, including those of polarity and hierarchical domination, are at issue in the cyborg world. Unlike the hopes of Frankenstein's monster, the cyborg does not expect its father to save it through a restoration of the garden; that is, through the fabrication of a heterosexual mate, through its completion in a finished whole, a city and cosmos. The cyborg does not dream of community on the model of the organic family, this time without the oedipal project. The cyborg would not recognize the Garden of Eden; it is not made of mud and cannot dream of returning to dust. Perhaps that is why I want to see if cyborgs can subvert the apocalypse of returning to nuclear dust in the manic compulsion to name the Enemy. Cyborgs are not reverent; they do not remember the cosmos. They are wary of holism, but needy for connection—they seem to have a natural feel for united front politics, but without the vanguard party. The main trouble with cyborgs, of course, is that they are the illegitimate offspring of militarism and patriarchal capitalism, not to mention state socialism. But illegitimate offspring are often exceedingly unfaithful to their origins. Their fathers, after all, are inessential.

I will return to the science fiction of cyborgs at the end of this chapter, but now I want to signal three crucial boundary breakdowns that make the following political-fictional (political-scientific) analysis possible. By the late twentieth century in United States scientific culture, the boundary between human and animal is thoroughly breached. The last beachheads of uniqueness have been polluted if not turned into amusement parks—language, tool use, social behaviour, mental events, nothing really convincingly settles the separation of human and animal. And many people no longer feel the need for such a separation; indeed, many branches of feminist culture affirm the pleasure of connection of human and other living creatures. Movements for animal rights are not irrational denials of human uniqueness; they are a clear-sighted recognition of connection across the discredited breach of nature and culture. Biology and evolutionary theory over the last two centuries have simultaneously produced modern organisms as objects of knowledge and reduced the line between humans and animals to a faint trace re-etched in ideological struggle or professional disputes between life and social science. Within this framework, teaching modern Christian creationism should be fought as a form of child abuse.

Biological-determinist ideology is only one position opened up in scientific culture for arguing the meanings of human animality. There is much room for radical political people to contest the meanings of the breached boundary.[2] The cyborg appears in myth precisely where the boundary between human and animal is transgressed. Far from signalling a walling off of people from other living beings, cyborgs signal disturbingly and pleasurably tight coupling. Bestiality has a new status in this cycle of marriage exchange.

The second leaky distinction is between animal-human (organism) and machine. Pre-cybernetic machines could be haunted; there was always the spectre of the ghost in the machine. This dualism structured the dialogue between materialism and idealism that was settled by a dialectical progeny, called spirit or history, according to taste. But basically machines were not self-moving, self-designing, autonomous. They could not achieve man's dream, only mock it. They were not man, an author to himself, but only a caricature of that masculinist reproductive dream. To think they were otherwise was paranoid. Now we are not so sure. Late twentieth-century machines have made thoroughly ambiguous the difference between natural and artificial, mind and body, self-developing and externally designed, and many other distinctions that used to apply to organisms and machines. Our machines are disturbingly lively, and we ourselves frighteningly inert.

Technological determination is only one ideological space opened up by the reconceptions of machine and organism as coded texts through which we engage in the play of writing and reading the world.[3] 'Textualization' of everything in poststructuralist, postmodernist theory has been damned by Marxists and socialist feminists for its utopian disregard for the lived relations of domination that ground the 'play' of arbitrary reading.[4] It is certainly true that postmodernist strategies, like my cyborg myth, subvert myriad organic wholes (for example, the poem, the primitive culture, the biological organism). In short, the certainty of what counts as nature—a source of insight and promise of innocence—is undermined, probably fatally. The transcendent authorization of interpretation is lost, and with it the ontology grounding 'Western' epistemology. But the alternative is not cynicism or faithlessness, that is, some version of abstract existence, like the accounts of technological determinism destroying 'man' by the 'machine' or 'meaningful political action' by the 'text'. Who cyborgs will be is a radical question; the answers are a matter of survival. Both chimpanzees and artefacts have politics, so why shouldn't we (de Waal, 1982; Winner, 1980)?

The third distinction is a subset of the second: the boundary between physical and non-physical is very imprecise for us. Pop physics books on the consequences of quantum theory and the indeterminacy principle are a kind of popular scientific equivalent to Harlequin romances* as a marker of radical change in American white heterosexuality: they get it wrong, but they are on the right subject. Modern machines are quintessentially microelectronic devices: they are everywhere and they are invisible. Modern machinery is an irreverent upstart god, mocking the Father's ubiquity and spirituality. The silicon chip is a surface for writing; it is etched in molecular scales disturbed only by atomic noise, the ultimate interference for nuclear scores. Writing, power, and technology are old partners in Western stories of the origin of civilization, but miniaturization has changed our experience of mechanism. Miniaturization has turned out to be about power; small is not so much beautiful as pre-eminently dangerous, as in cruise missiles. Contrast the TV sets of the 1950s or the news cameras of the 1970s with the TV wrist bands or hand-sized video cameras now advertised. Our best machines are made of sunshine; they are all light and clean because they are nothing but signals, electromagnetic waves, a section of a spectrum, and these machines are eminently portable, mobile—a matter of immense human pain in Detroit and Singapore. People are nowhere near so fluid, being both material and opaque. Cyborgs are ether, quintessence.

The ubiquity and invisibility of cyborgs is precisely why these sunshine-belt machines are so deadly. They are as hard to see politically as materially. They are about consciousness—or its simulation.[5] They are floating signifiers moving in pickup trucks across Europe, blocked more effectively by the witch-weavings of the displaced and so unnatural Greenham women, who read the cyborg webs of power so very well, than by the militant labour of older masculinist politics, whose natural constituency needs defence jobs. Ultimately the 'hardest' science is about the realm of greatest boundary confusion, the realm of pure number, pure spirit, C^3I, cryptography, and the preservation of potent secrets. The

---

* The US equivalent of Mills & Boon.

new machines are so clean and light. Their engineers are sun-worshippers mediating a new scientific revolution associated with the night dream of post-industrial society. The diseases evoked by these clean machines are 'no more' than the minuscule coding changes of an antigen in the immune system, 'no more' than the experience of stress. The nimble fingers of 'Oriental' women, the old fascination of little Anglo-Saxon Victorian girls with doll's houses, women's enforced attention to the small take on quite new dimensions in this world. There might be a cyborg Alice taking account of these new dimensions. Ironically, it might be the unnatural cyborg women making chips in Asia and spiral dancing in Santa Rita jail* whose constructed unities will guide effective oppositional strategies.

So my cyborg myth is about transgressed boundaries, potent fusions, and dangerous possibilities which progressive people might explore as one part of needed political work. One of my premises is that most American socialists and feminists see deepened dualisms of mind and body, animal and machine, idealism and materialism in the social practices, symbolic formulations, and physical arte-facts associated with 'high technology' and scientific culture. From *One-Dimensional Man* (Marcuse, 1964) to *The Death of Nature* (Merchant, 1980), the analytic resources developed by progressives have insisted on the necessary domination of techniques and recalled us to an imagined organic body to integrate our resistance. Another of my premises is that the need for unity of people trying to resist world-wide intensification of domination has never been more acute. But a slightly perverse shift of perspective might better enable us to contest for meanings, as well as for other forms of power and pleasure in technologically mediated societies.

From one perspective, a cyborg world is about the final imposition of a grid of control on the planet, about the final abstraction embodied in a Star Wars apocalypse waged in the name of defence, about the final appropriation of women's bodies in a masculinist orgy of war (Sofia, 1984). From another perspective, a cyborg world might be about lived social and bodily realities in which people are not afraid of their joint kinship with animals and machines, not afraid of permanently partial identities and contradictory standpoints. The political struggle is to see from both perspectives at once because each reveals both dominations and possibilities unimaginable from the other vantage point. Single vision produces worse illusions than double vision or many-headed monsters. Cyborg unities are monstrous and illegitimate; in our present political circumstances, we could hardly hope for more potent myths for resistance and recoupling. I like to imagine LAG, the Livermore Action Group, as a kind of cyborg society, dedicated to realistically converting the laboratories that most fiercely embody and spew out the tools of technological apocalypse, and committed to building a political form that actually manages to hold together witches, engineers, elders, perverts, Christians, mothers, and Leninists long enough to disarm the state. Fission Impossible is the name of the affinity group in my town. (Affinity: related not by blood but by choice, the appeal of one chemical nuclear group for another, avidity.)[6]

FRACTURED IDENTITIES

It has become difficult to name one's feminism by a single adjective—or even to insist in every circum-stance upon the noun. Consciousness of exclusion through naming is acute. Identities seem contradic-tory, partial, and strategic. With the hard-won recognition of their social and historical constitution, gender, race, and class cannot provide the basis for belief in 'essential' unity. There is nothing about being 'female' that naturally binds women. There is not even such a state as 'being' female, itself a highly complex category constructed in contested sexual scientific discourses and other social practices. Gender, race, or class consciousness is an achievement forced on us by the terrible historical experience of the contradictory social realities of patriarchy, colonialism, and capitalism. And who counts as 'us' in my own rhetoric? Which identities are available to ground such a potent political myth called 'us',

---

* A practice at once both spiritual and political that linked guards and arrested anti-nuclear demonstrators in the Alameda County jail in California in the early 1980s.

and what could motivate enlistment in this collectivity? Painful fragmentation among feminists (not to mention among women) along every possible fault line has made the concept of *woman* elusive, an excuse for the matrix of women's dominations of each other. For me—and for many who share a similar historical location in white, professional middle-class, female, radical, North American, mid-adult bodies—the sources of a crisis in political identity are legion. The recent history for much of the US left and US feminism has been a response to this kind of crisis by endless splitting and searches for a new essential unity. But there has also been a growing recognition of another response through coalition—affinity, not identity.[7]

Chela Sandoval, from a consideration of specific historical moments in the formation of the new political voice called women of colour, has theorized a hopeful model of political identity called 'oppositional consciousness', born of the skills for reading webs of power by those refused stable membership in the social categories of race, sex, or class. 'Women of color', a name contested at its origins by those whom it would incorporate, as well as a historical consciousness marking systematic breakdown of all the signs of Man in 'Western' traditions, constructs a kind of postmodernist identity out of otherness, difference, and specificity. This postmodernist identity is fully political, whatever might be said about other possible postmodernisms. Sandoval's oppositional consciousness is about contradictory locations and heterochronic calendars, not about relativisms and pluralisms.

Sandoval emphasizes the lack of any essential criterion for identifying who is a woman of colour. She notes that the definition of the group has been by conscious appropriation of negation. For example, a Chicana or US black woman has not been able to speak as a woman or as a black person or as a Chicano. Thus, she was at the bottom of a cascade of negative identities, left out of even the privileged oppressed authorial categories called 'women and blacks', who claimed to make the important revolutions. The category 'woman' negated all non-white women; 'black' negated all non-black people, as well as all black women. But there was also no 'she', no singularity, but a sea of differences among US women who have affirmed their historical identity as US women of colour. This identity marks out a self-consciously constructed space that cannot affirm the capacity to act on the basis of natural identification, but only on the basis of conscious coalition, of affinity, of political kinship.[8] Unlike the 'woman' of some streams of the white women's movement in the United States, there is no naturalization of the matrix, or at least this is what Sandoval argues is uniquely available through the power of oppositional consciousness.

Sandoval's argument has to be seen as one potent formulation for feminists out of the world-wide development of anti-colonialist discourse; that is to say, discourse dissolving the 'West' and its highest product—the one who is not animal, barbarian, or woman; man, that is, the author of a cosmos called history. As orientalism is deconstructed politically and semiotically, the identities of the occident destabilize, including those of feminists.[9] Sandoval argues that 'women of colour' have a chance to build an effective unity that does not replicate the imperializing, totalizing revolutionary subjects of previous Marxisms and feminisms which had not faced the consequences of the disorderly polyphony emerging from decolonization.

Katie King has emphasized the limits of identification and the political/poetic mechanics of identification built into reading 'the poem', that generative core of cultural feminism. King criticizes the persistent tendency among contemporary feminists from different 'moments' or 'conversations' in feminist practice to taxonomize the women's movement to make one's own political tendencies appear to be the *telos* of the whole. These taxonomies tend to remake feminist history so that it appears to be an ideological struggle among coherent types persisting over time, especially those typical units called radical, liberal, and socialist-feminism. Literally, all other feminisms are either incorporated or marginalized, usually by building an explicit ontology and epistemology.[10] Taxonomies of feminism produce epistemologies to police deviation from official women's experience. And of course, 'women's culture', like women of colour, is consciously created by mechanisms inducing affinity. The rituals of poetry, music, and certain forms of academic practice have been pre-eminent. The politics of race and culture in the US women's movements are intimately interwoven. The common achievement of King and Sandoval is learning how to craft a poetic/political unity without relying on a logic of appropriation, incorporation, and taxonomic identification.

The theoretical and practical struggle against unity-through-domination or unity-through-incorporation ironically not only undermines the justifications for patriarchy, colonialism, humanism, positivism, essentialism, scientism, and other unlamented -isms, but *all* claims for an organic or natural standpoint. I think that radical and socialist/Marxist-feminisms have also undermined their/our own epistemological strategies and that this is a crucially valuable step in imagining possible unities. It remains to be seen whether all 'epistemologies' as Western political people have known them fail us in the task to build effective affinities.

It is important to note that the effort to construct revolutionary stand-points, epistemologies as achievements of people committed to changing the world, has been part of the process showing the limits of identification. The acid tools of postmodernist theory and the constructive tools of ontological discourse about revolutionary subjects might be seen as ironic allies in dissolving Western selves in the interests of survival. We are excruciatingly conscious of what it means to have a historically constituted body. But with the loss of innocence in our origin, there is no expulsion from the Garden either. Our politics lose the indulgence of guilt with the *naïveté* of innocence. But what would another political myth for socialist-feminism look like? What kind of politics could embrace partial, contradictory, permanently unclosed constructions of personal and collective selves and still be faithful, effective—and, ironically, socialist-feminist?

I do not know of any other time in history when there was greater need for political unity to confront effectively the dominations of 'race', 'gender', 'sexuality', and 'class'. I also do not know of any other time when the kind of unity we might help build could have been possible. None of 'us' have any longer the symbolic or material capability of dictating the shape of reality to any of 'them'. Or at least 'we' cannot claim innocence from practising such dominations. White women, including socialist feminists, discovered (that is, were forced kicking and screaming to notice) the non-innocence of the category 'woman'. That consciousness changes the geography of all previous categories; it denatures them as heat denatures a fragile protein. Cyborg feminists have to argue that 'we' do not want any more natural matrix of unity and that no construction is whole. Innocence, and the corollary insistence on victimhood as the only ground for insight, has done enough damage. But the constructed revolutionary subject must give late-twentieth-century people pause as well. In the fraying of identities and in the reflexive strategies for constructing them, the possibility opens up for weaving something other than a shroud for the day after the apocalypse that so prophetically ends salvation history.

Both Marxist/socialist-feminisms and radical feminisms have simultaneously naturalized and denatured the category 'woman' and consciousness of the social lives of 'women'. Perhaps a schematic caricature can highlight both kinds of moves. Marxian socialism is rooted in an analysis of wage labour which reveals class structure. The consequence of the wage relationship is systematic alienation, as the worker is dissociated from his (sic) product. Abstraction and illusion rule in knowledge, domination rules in practice. Labour is the pre-eminently privileged category enabling the Marxist to overcome illusion and find that point of view which is necessary for changing the world. Labour is the humanizing activity that makes man; labour is an ontological category permitting the knowledge of a subject, and so the knowledge of subjugation and alienation.

In faithful filiation, socialist-feminism advanced by allying itself with the basic analytic strategies of Marxism. The main achievement of both Marxist feminists and socialist feminists was to expand the category of labour to accommodate what (some) women did, even when the wage relation was subordinated to a more comprehensive view of labour under capitalist patriarchy. In particular, women's labour in the household and women's activity as mothers generally (that is, reproduction in the socialist-feminist sense), entered theory on the authority of analogy to the Marxian concept of labour. The unity of women here rests on an epistemology based on the ontological structure of 'labour'. Marxist/socialist-feminism does not 'naturalize' unity; it is a possible achievement based on a possible standpoint rooted in social relations. The essentializing move is in the ontological structure of labour or of its analogue, women's activity.[11] The inheritance of Marxian humanism, with its pre-eminently Western self, is the difficulty for me. The contribution from these formulations has been the emphasis on the daily responsibility of real women to build unities, rather than to naturalize them.

Catherine MacKinnon's version of radical feminism is itself a caricature of the appropriating, incorporating, totalizing tendencies of Western theories of identity grounding action.[12] It is factually and politically wrong to assimilate all of the diverse 'moments' or 'conversations' in recent women's politics named radical feminism to MacKinnon's version. But the teleological logic of her theory shows how an epistemology and ontology—including their negations—erase or police difference. Only one of the effects of MacKinnon's theory is the rewriting of the history of the polymorphous field called radical feminism. The major effect is the production of a theory of experience, of women's identity, that is a kind of apocalypse for all revolutionary standpoints. That is, the totalization built into this tale of radical feminism achieves its end—the unity of women—by enforcing the experience of and testimony to radical non-being. As for the Marxist/socialist feminist, consciousness is an achievement, not a natural fact. And MacKinnon's theory eliminates some of the difficulties built into humanist revolutionary subjects, but at the cost of radical reductionism.

MacKinnon argues that feminism necessarily adopted a different analytical strategy from Marxism, looking first not at the structure of class, but at the structure of sex/gender and its generative relationship, men's constitution and appropriation of women sexually. Ironically, MacKinnon's 'ontology' constructs a non-subject, a non-being. Another's desire, not the self's labour, is the origin of 'woman'. She therefore develops a theory of consciousness that enforces what can count as 'women's' experience—anything that names sexual violation, indeed, sex itself as far as 'women' can be concerned. Feminist practice is the construction of this form of consciousness; that is, the self-knowledge of a self-who-is-not.

Perversely, sexual appropriation in this feminism still has the epistemological status of labour; that is to say, the point from which an analysis able to contribute to changing the world must flow. But sexual objectification, not alienation, is the consequence of the structure of sex/gender. In the realm of knowledge, the result of sexual objectification is illusion and abstraction. However, a woman is not simply alienated from her product, but in a deep sense does not exist as a subject, or even potential subject, since she owes her existence as a woman to sexual appropriation. To be constituted by another's desire is not the same thing as to be alienated in the violent separation of the labourer from his product.

MacKinnon's radical theory of experience is totalizing in the extreme; it does not so much marginalize as obliterate the authority of any other women's political speech and action. It is a totalization producing what Western patriarchy itself never succeeded in doing—feminists' consciousness of the non-existence of women, except as products of men's desire. I think MacKinnon correctly argues that no Marxian version of identity can firmly ground women's unity. But in solving the problem of the contradictions of any Western revolutionary subject for feminist purposes, she develops an even more authoritarian doctrine of experience. If my complaint about socialist/Marxian standpoints is their unintended erasure of polyvocal, unassimilable, radical difference made visible in anti-colonial discourse and practice, MacKinnon's intentional erasure of all difference through the device of the 'essential' non-existence of women is not reassuring.

* * *

CYBORGS: A MYTH OF POLITICAL IDENTITY

I want to conclude with a myth about identity and boundaries which might inform late twentieth-century political imaginations. I am indebted in this story to writers like Joanna Russ, Samuel R. Delany, John Varley, James Tiptree, Jr, Octavia Butler, Monique Wittig, and Vonda McIntyre.[13] These are our story-tellers exploring what it means to be embodied in high-tech worlds. They are theorists for cyborgs. Exploring conceptions of bodily boundaries and social order, the anthropologist Mary Douglas should be credited with helping us to consciousness about how fundamental body imagery is to world view, and so to political language. French feminists like Luce Irigaray and Monique Wittig, for all their differences, know how to write the body; how to weave eroticism, cosmology, and politics from imagery of embodiment, and especially for Wittig, from imagery of fragmentation and recon-stitution of bodies.[14]

American radical feminists like Susan Griffin, Audre Lorde, and Adrienne Rich have profoundly affected our political imaginations—and perhaps restricted too much what we allow as a friendly body and political language.[15] They insist on the organic, opposing it to the technological. But their symbolic systems and the related positions of ecofeminism and feminist paganism, replete with organicisms, can only be understood in Sandoval's terms as oppositional ideologies fitting the late twentieth century. They would simply bewilder anyone not preoccupied with the machines and consciousness of late capitalism. In that sense they are part of the cyborg world. But there are also great riches for feminists in explicitly embracing the possibilities inherent in the breakdown of clean distinctions between organism and machine and similar distinctions structuring the Western self. It is the simultaneity of breakdowns that cracks the matrices of domination and opens geometric possibilities. What might be learned from personal and political 'technological' pollution? I look briefly at two overlapping groups of texts for their insight into the construction of a potentially helpful cyborg myth: constructions of women of colour and monstrous selves in feminist science fiction.

Earlier I suggested that 'women of colour' might be understood as a cyborg identity, a potent sub-jectivity synthesized from fusions of outsider identities and in the complex political-historical layerings of her 'biomythography', *Zami* (Lorde, 1982; King, 1987a, 1987b). There are material and cultural grids mapping this potential, Audre Lorde (1984) captures the tone in the title of her *Sister Outsider*. In my political myth, Sister Outsider is the offshore woman, whom US workers, female and feminized, are supposed to regard as the enemy preventing their solidarity, threatening their security. Onshore, inside the boundary of the United States, Sister Outsider is a potential amidst the races and ethnic identities of women manipulated for division, competition, and exploitation in the same industries. 'Women of colour' are the preferred labour force for the science-based industries, the real women for whom the world-wide sexual market, labour market, and politics of reproduction kaleidoscope into daily life. Young Korean women hired in the sex industry and in electronics assembly are recruited from high schools, educated for the integrated circuit. Literacy, especially in English, distinguishes the 'cheap' female labour so attractive to the multinationals.

Contrary to orientalist stereotypes of the 'oral primitive', literacy is a special mark of women of colour, acquired by US black women as well as men through a history of risking death to learn and to teach reading and writing. Writing has a special significance for all colonized groups. Writing has been crucial to the Western myth of the distinction between oral and written cultures, primitive and civilized mentalities, and more recently to the erosion of that distinction in 'postmodernist' theories attacking the phallogocentrism of the West, with its worship of the monotheistic, phallic, authoritative, and singular work, the unique and perfect name.[16] Contests for the meanings of writing are a major form of contemporary political struggle. Releasing the play of writing is deadly serious. The poetry and stories of US women of colour are repeatedly about writing, about access to the power to signify; but this time that power must be neither phallic nor innocent. Cyborg writing must not be about the

Fall, the imagination of a once-upon-a-time wholeness before language, before writing, before Man. Cyborg writing is about the power to survive, not on the basis of original innocence, but on the basis of seizing the tools to mark the world that marked them as other.

The tools are often stories, retold stories, versions that reverse and displace the hierarchical dualisms of naturalized identities. In retelling origin stories, cyborg authors subvert the central myths of origin of Western culture. We have all been colonized by those origin myths, with their longing for fulfilment in apocalypse. The phallogocentric origin stories most crucial for feminist cyborgs are built into the literal technologies—technologies that write the world, biotechnology and microelectronics—that have recently textualized our bodies as code problems on the grid of C^3I. Feminist cyborg stories have the task of recoding communication and intelligence to subvert command and control.

Figuratively and literally, language politics pervade the struggles of women of colour; and stories about language have a special power in the rich contemporary writing by US women of colour. For example, retellings of the story of the indigenous woman Malinche, mother of the mestizo 'bastard' race of the new world, master of languages, and mistress of Cortés, carry special meaning for Chicana constructions of identity. Cherríe Moraga (1983) in *Loving in the War Years* explores the themes of identity when one never possessed the original language, never told the original story, never resided in the harmony of legitimate heterosexuality in the garden of culture, and so cannot base identity on a myth or a fall from innocence and right to natural names, mother's or father's.[17] Moraga's writing, her superb literacy, is presented in her poetry as the same kind of violation as Malinche's mastery of the conqueror's language—a violation, an illegitimate production, that allows survival. Moraga's language is not 'whole'; it is self-consciously spliced, a chimera of English and Spanish, both conqueror's languages. But it is this chimeric monster, without claim to an original language before violation, that crafts the erotic, competent, potent identities of women of colour. Sister Outsider hints at the possibility of world survival not because of her innocence, but because of her ability to live on the boundaries, to write without the founding myth of original wholeness, with its inescapable apocalypse of final return to a deathly oneness that Man has imagined to be the innocent and all-powerful Mother, freed at the End from another spiral of appropriation by her son. Writing marks Moraga's body, affirms it as the body of a woman of colour, against the possibility of passing into the unmarked category of the Anglo father or into the orientalist myth of 'original illiteracy' of a mother that never was. Malinche was mother here, not Eve before eating the forbidden fruit. Writing affirms Sister Outsider, not the Woman-before-the-Fall-into-Writing needed by the phallogocentric Family of Man.

Writing is pre-eminently the technology of cyborgs, etched surfaces of the late twentieth century. Cyborg politics is the struggle for language and the struggle against perfect communication, against the one code that translates all meaning perfectly, the central dogma of phallogocentrism. That is why cyborg politics insist on noise and advocate pollution, rejoicing in the illegitimate fusions of animal and machine. These are the couplings which make Man and Woman so problematic, subverting the structure of desire, the force imagined to generate language and gender, and so subverting the structure and modes of reproduction of 'Western' identity, of nature and culture, of mirror and eye, slave and master, body and mind. 'We' did not originally choose to be cyborgs, but choice grounds a liberal politics and epistemology that imagines the reproduction of individuals before the wider replications of 'texts'.

From the perspective of cyborgs, freed of the need to ground politics in 'our' privileged position of the oppression that incorporates all other dominations, the innocence of the merely violated, the ground of those closer to nature, we can see powerful possibilities. Feminisms and Marxisms have run aground on Western epistemological imperatives to construct a revolutionary subject from the perspective of a hierarchy of oppressions and/or a latent position of moral superiority, innocence, and greater closeness to nature. With no available original dream of a common language or original symbiosis promising protection from hostile 'masculine' separation, but written into the play of a text that has no finally privileged reading or salvation history, to recognize 'oneself' as fully implicated in the world, frees us of the need to root politics in identification, vanguard parties, purity, and mothering. Stripped of identity, the bastard race teaches about the power of the margins and the importance of a mother like Malinche. Women of colour have transformed her from the evil mother of masculinist fear into the originally literate mother who teaches survival.

This is not just literary deconstruction, but luminal transformation. Every story that begins with original innocence and privileges the return to wholeness imagines the drama of life to be individuation, separation, the birth of the self, the tragedy of autonomy, the fall into writing, alienation; that is, war, tempered by imaginary respite in the bosom of the Other. These plots are ruled by a reproductive politics—rebirth without flaw, perfection, abstraction. In this plot women are imagined either better or worse off, but all agree they have less selfhood, weaker individuation, more fusion to the oral, to Mother, less at stake in masculine autonomy. But there is another route to having less at stake in masculine autonomy, a route that does not pass through Woman, Primitive, Zero, the Mirror Stage and its imaginary. It passes through women and other present-tense, illegitimate cyborgs, not of Woman born, who refuse the ideological resources of victimization so as to have a real life. These cyborgs are the people who refuse to disappear on cue, no matter how many times a 'Western' commentator remarks on the sad passing of another primitive, another organic group done in by 'Western' technology, by writing.[18] These real-life cyborgs (for example, the Southeast Asian village women workers in Japanese and US electronics firms described by Aihwa Ong) are actively rewriting the texts of their bodies and societies. Survival is the stakes in this play of readings.

To recapitulate, certain dualisms have been persistent in Western traditions; they have all been systemic to the logics and practices of domination of women, people of colour, nature, workers, animals—in short, domination of all constituted as others, whose task is to mirror the self. Chief among these troubling dualisms are self/other, mind/body, culture/nature, male/female, civilized/primitive, reality/appearance, whole/part, agent/resource, maker/made, active/passive, right/wrong, truth/illusion, total/partial, God/man. The self is the One who is not dominated, who knows that by the service of the other, the other is the one who holds the future, who knows that by the experience of domination, which gives the lie to the autonomy of the self. To be One is to be autonomous, to be powerful, to be God; but to be One is to be an illusion, and so to be involved in a dialectic of apocalypse with the other. Yet to be other is to be multiple, without clear boundary, frayed, insubstantial. One is too few, but two are too many.

High-tech culture challenges these dualisms in intriguing ways. It is not clear who makes and who is made in the relation between human and machine. It is not clear what is mind and what body in machines that resolve into coding practices. In so far as we know ourselves in both formal discourse (for example, biology) and in daily practice (for example, the homework economy in the integrated circuit), we find ourselves to be cyborgs, hybrids, mosaics, chimeras. Biological organisms have become biotic systems, communications devices like others. There is no fundamental, ontological separation in our formal knowledge of machine and organism, of technical and organic. The replicant Rachel in the Ridley Scott film *Blade Runner* stands as the image of a cyborg culture's fear, love, and confusion.

One consequence is that our sense of connection to our tools is heightened. The trance state experienced by many computer users has become a staple of science-fiction film and cultural jokes. Perhaps paraplegics and other severely handicapped people can (and sometimes do) have the most intense experiences of complex hybridization with other communication devices.[19] Anne McCaffrey's pre-feminist *The Ship Who Sang* (1969) explored the consciousness of a cyborg, hybrid of girl's brain and complex machinery, formed after the birth of a severely handicapped child. Gender, sexuality, embodiment, skill: all were reconstituted in the story. Why should our bodies end at the skin, or include at best other beings encapsulated by skin? From the seventeenth century till now, machines could be animated—given ghostly souls to make them speak or move or to account for their orderly development and mental capacities. Or organisms could be mechanized—reduced to body understood as resource of mind. These machine/organism relationships are obsolete, unnecessary. For us, in imagination and in other practice, machines can be prosthetic devices, intimate components, friendly selves. We don't need organic holism to give impermeable wholeness, the total woman and her feminist variants (mutants?). Let me conclude this point by a very partial reading of the logic of the cyborg monsters of my second group of texts, feminist science fiction.

The cyborgs populating feminist science fiction make very problematic the statuses of man or woman, human, artefact, member of a race, individual entity, or body. Katie King clarifies how pleasure in reading these fictions is not largely based on identification. Students facing Joanna Russ for the first time, students who have learned to take modernist writers like James Joyce or Virginia Woolf without flinching, do not know what to make of *The Adventures of Alyx* or *The Female Man*, where characters refuse the reader's search for innocent wholeness while granting the wish for heroic quests, exuberant eroticism, and serious politics. *The Female Man* is the story of four versions of one genotype, all of whom meet, but even taken together do not make a whole, resolve the dilemmas of violent moral action, or remove the growing scandal of gender. The feminist science fiction of Samuel R. Delany, especially *Tales of Nevèrÿon*, mocks stories of origin by redoing the neolithic revolution, replaying the founding moves of Western civilization to subvert their plausibility. James Tiptree, Jr, an author whose fiction was regarded as particularly manly until her 'true' gender was revealed, tells tales of reproduction based on non-mammalian technologies like alternation of generations of male brood pouches and male nurturing. John Varley constructs a supreme cyborg in his arch-feminist exploration of Gaea, a mad goddess-planet-trickster-old woman-technological device on whose surface an extraordinary array of post-cyborg symbioses are spawned. Octavia Butler writes of an African sorceress pitting her powers of transformation against the genetic manipulations of her rival (*Wild Seed*), of time warps that bring a modern US black woman into slavery where her actions in relation to her white master-ancestor determine the possibility of her own birth (*Kindred*), and of the illegitimate insights into identity and community of an adopted cross-species child who came to know the enemy as self (*Survivor*). In *Dawn* (1987), the first instalment of a series called *Xenogenesis*, Butler tells the story of Lilith Iyapo, whose personal name recalls Adam's first and repudiated wife and whose family name marks her status as the widow of the son of Nigerian immigrants to the US. A black woman and a mother whose child is dead, Lilith mediates the transformation of humanity through genetic exchange with extra-terrestrial lovers/rescuers/destroyers/genetic engineers, who reform earth's habitats after the nuclear holocaust and coerce surviving humans into intimate fusion with them. It is a novel that interrogates reproductive, linguistic, and nuclear politics in a mythic field structured by late twentieth-century race and gender.

Because it is particularly rich in boundary transgressions, Vonda McIntyre's *Superluminal* can close this truncated catalogue of promising and dangerous monsters who help redefine the pleasures and politics of embodiment and feminist writing. In a fiction where no character is 'simply' human, human status is highly problematic. Orca, a genetically altered diver, can speak with killer whales and survive deep ocean conditions, but she longs to explore space as a pilot, necessitating bionic implants jeopardizing her kinship with the divers and cetaceans. Transformations are effected by virus vectors carrying a new developmental code, by transplant surgery, by implants of microelectronic devices, by analogue doubles, and other means. Laenea becomes a pilot by accepting a heart implant and a host of other alterations allowing survival in transit at speeds exceeding that of light. Radu Dracul survives a virus-caused plague in his outerworld planet to find himself with a time sense that changes the boundaries of spatial perception for the whole species. All the characters explore the limits of language; the dream of communicating experience; and the necessity of limitation, partiality, and intimacy even in this world of protean transformation and connection. *Superluminal* stands also for the defining contradictions of a cyborg world in another sense; it embodies textually the intersection of feminist theory and colonial discourse in the science fiction I have alluded to in this chapter. This is a conjunction with a long history that many 'First World' feminists have tried to repress, including myself in my readings of *Superluminal* before being called to account by Zoe Sofoulis, whose different location in the world system's informatics of domination made her acutely alert to the imperialist moment of all science fiction cultures, including women's science fiction. From an Australian feminist sensitivity, Sofoulis remembered more readily McIntyre's role as writer of the adventures of Captain Kirk and Spock in TV's *Star Trek* series than her rewriting the romance in *Superluminal*.

Monsters have always defined the limits of community in Western imaginations. The Centaurs and Amazons of ancient Greece established the limits of the centred polis of the Greek male human by their disruption of marriage and boundary pollutions of the warrior with animality and woman. Unseparated twins and hermaphrodites were the confused human material in early modern France who grounded discourse on the natural and supernatural, medical and legal, portents and diseases—all crucial to establishing modern identity.[20] The evolutionary and behavioural sciences of monkeys and apes have marked the multiple boundaries of late twentieth-century industrial identities. Cyborg monsters in feminist science fiction define quite different political possibilities and limits from those proposed by the mundane fiction of Man and Woman.

There are several consequences to taking seriously the imagery of cyborgs as other than our enemies. Our bodies, ourselves; bodies are maps of power and identity. Cyborgs are no exception. A cyborg body is not innocent; it was not born in a garden; it does not seek unitary identity and so generate antagonistic dualisms without end (or until the world ends); it takes irony for granted. One is too few, and two is only one possibility. Intense pleasure in skill, machine skill, ceases to be a sin, but an aspect of embodiment. The machine is not an *it* to be animated, worshipped, and dominated. The machine is us, our processes, an aspect of our embodiment. We can be responsible for machines; *they* do not dominate or threaten us. We are responsible for boundaries; we are they. Up till now (once upon a time), female embodiment seemed to be given, organic, necessary; and female embodiment seemed to mean skill in mothering and its metaphoric extensions. Only by being out of place could we take intense pleasure in machines, and then with excuses that this was organic activity after all, appropriate to females. Cyborgs might consider more seriously the partial, fluid, sometimes aspect of sex and sexual embodiment. Gender might not be global identity after all, even if it has profound historical breadth and depth.

The ideologically charged question of what counts as daily activity, as experience, can be approached by exploiting the cyborg image. Feminists have recently claimed that women are given to dailiness, that women more than men somehow sustain daily life, and so have a privileged epistemological position potentially. There is a compelling aspect to this claim... But *the* ground of life? What about all the ignorance of women, all the exclusions and failures of knowledge and skill? What about men's access to daily competence, to knowing how to build things, to take them apart, to play? What about other embodiments? Cyborg gender is a local possibility taking a global vengeance. Race, gender, and capital require a cyborg theory of wholes and parts. There is no drive in cyborgs to produce total theory, but there is an intimate experience of boundaries, their construction and deconstruction. There is a myth system waiting to become a political language to ground one way of looking at science and technology and challenging the informatics of domination—in order to act potently.

One last image: organisms and organismic, holistic politics depend on metaphors of rebirth and invariably call on the resources of reproductive sex. I would suggest that cyborgs have more to do with regeneration and are suspicious of the reproductive matrix and of most birthing. For salamanders, regeneration after injury, such as the loss of a limb, involves regrowth of structure and restoration of function with the constant possibility of twinning or other odd topographical productions at the site of former injury. The regrown limb can be monstrous, duplicated, potent. We have all been injured, profoundly. We require regeneration, not rebirth, and the possibilities for our reconstitution include the utopian dream of the hope for a monstrous world without gender.

Cyborg imagery can help express two crucial arguments in this essay: first, the production of universal, totalizing theory is a major mistake that misses most of reality, probably always, but certainly now; and second, taking responsibility for the social relations of science and technology means refusing an anti-science metaphysics, a demonology of technology, and so means embracing the skilful task of reconstructing the boundaries of daily life, in partial connection with others, in communication with all of our parts. It is not just that science and technology are possible means of great human satisfaction, as well as a matrix of complex dominations. Cyborg imagery can suggest a way out of the maze of dualisms in which we have explained our bodies and our tools to ourselves. This is a dream not of a common language, but of a powerful infidel heteroglossia. It is an imagination of a feminist speaking in tongues to strike fear into the circuits of the supersavers of the new right. It means both building and destroying machines, identities, categories, relationships, space stories. Though both are bound in the spiral dance, I would rather be a cyborg than a goddess.

NOTES

1. Research was funded by an Academic Senate Faculty Research Grant from the University of California, Santa Cruz. An earlier version of the paper on genetic engineering appeared as 'Lieber Kyborg als Göttin: für eine sozialistisch-feministische Unterwanderung der Gentechnologie', in Bernd-Peter Lange and Anna Marie Stuby, eds, Berlin: *Argument-Sonderband* 105, 1984, pp 66–84. The cyborg manifesto grew from my 'New machines, new bodies, new communities: political dilemmas of a cyborg feminist', 'The Scholar and the Feminist X: The Question of Technology', Conference, Barnard College, April 1983.

    The people associated with the History of Consciousness Board of UCSC have had influence on this paper, so that it feels collectively authored more than graduate and undergraduate feminist theory, science, and politics, and theory and methods courses contributed to the cyborg manifesto. Particular debts here are due Hilary Klein (1989), Paul Edwards (1985), Lisa Lowe (1986), and James Clifford (1985).

    Parts of the paper were my contribution to a collectively developed session, 'Poetic Tools and Political Bodies: Feminist Approaches to High Technology Culture', 1984 California American Studies Association, with History of Consciousness graduate students Zoe Sofoulis, 'Jupiter space'; Katie King, 'The pleasures of repetition and the limits of identification in feminist science fiction: reimaginations of the body after the cyborg'; and Chela Sandoval, 'The construction of subjectivity and oppositional consciousness in feminist film and video'. Sandoval's (n.d.) theory of oppositional consciousness was published as 'Women respond to racism: A Report on the National Women's Studies Association Conference'. For Sofoulis's semiotic-psychoanalytic readings of nuclear culture, see Sofia (1984). King's unpublished papers ('Questioning tradition: canon formation and the veiling of power'; 'Gender and genre: reading the science fiction of Joanna Russ'; 'Varley's *Titan* and *Wizard*: feminist parodies of nature, culture, and hardware') deeply informed the cyborg manifesto.

    Barbara Epstein, Jeff Escoffier, Rusten Hogness, and Jaye Miler gave extensive discussion and editorial help. Members of the Silicon Valley Research Project of UCSC and participants in SVRP conferences and workshops were very important, especially Rick Gordon, Linda Kimball, Nancy Snyder, Langdon Winner, Judith Stacey, Linda Lim, Patricia Fernandez-Kelly, and Judith Gregory. Finally, I want to thank Nancy Hartsock for years of friendship and discussion on feminist theory and feminist science fiction. I also thank Elizabeth Bird for my favourite political button: 'Cyborgs for Earthly Survival'.

2. Useful references to left and/or feminist radical science movements and theory and to biological/biotechnical issues include: Bleier (1984, 1986), Harding (1986). Fausto-Sterling (1985), Gould (1981), Hubbard *et al.* (1982), Keller (1985), Lewontin *et al.* (1984), *Radical Science Journal* (became *Science as Culture* in 1987), 26 Freegrove Road, London N7 9RQ; *Science for the People*, 897 Main St., Cambridge, MA 02139.

3. Starting points for left and/or feminist approaches to technology and politics include: Cowan (1983), Rothschild (1983), Traweek (1988), Young and Levidow (1981, 1985), Weizenbaum (1976), Winner (1977, 1986), Zimmerm n (1983), Athanasiou (1987), Cohn (1987a, 1987b), Winograd and Flores (1986), Edwards (1985). *Global Electronics Newsletter*, 867 West Dana St., # 204, Mountain View, CA 94041; *Processed World*, 55 Sutter St., San Francisco, CA 94104; ISIS, Women's International Information and Communication Service, PO Box 50 (Cornavin), 1211 Geneva 2, Switzerland,

and Via Santa Maria Dell'Anima 30, 00186 Rome, Italy. Fundamental approaches to modern social studies of science that do not continue the liberal mystification that it all started with Thomas Kuhn, include: Knorr-Cetina (1981), Knorr-Cetina and Mulkay (1983), Latour and Woolgar (1979), Young (1979). The 1984 Directory of the Network for the Ethnographic Study of Science, Technology, and Organizations lists a wide range of people and projects crucial to better radical analysis; available from NESSTO, PO Box 11442, Stanford, CA 94305.

4. A provocative, comprehensive argument about the politics and theories of 'postmodernism' is made by Fredric Jameson (1984), who argues that postmodernism is not an option, a style among others, but a cultural dominant requiring radical reinvention of left politics from within; there is no longer any place from without that gives meaning to the ... others) need continuous cultural reinvention, postmodernist critique, and historical materialism; only a cyborg would have a chance. The old dominations of white capitalist patriarchy seem nostalgically innocent now: they normalized heterogeneity, into man and woman, white and black, for example. 'Advanced capitalism' and postmodernism release heterogeneity without a norm, and we are flattened, without subjectivity, which requires depth, even unfriendly and drowning depths. It is time to write *The Death of the Clinic*. The clinic's methods required bodies and works; we have texts and surfaces. Our dominations don't work by medicalization and normalization any more; they work by networking, communications redesign, stress management. Normalization gives way to automation, utter redundancy. Michel Foucault's *Birth of the Clinic* (1963), *History of Sexuality* (1976), and *Discipline and Punish* (1975) name a form of power at its moment of implosion. The discourse of biopolitics gives way to technobabble, the language of the spliced substantive; no noun is left whole by the multinationals. These are their names, listed from one issue of *Science*: Tech-Knowledge, Genentech, Allergen, Hybritech, Compupro, Genencor, Syntex, Allelix, Agrigenetics Corp., Syntro, Codon, Repligen, MicroAngelo from Scion Corp., Percom Data, Inter Systems, Cyborg Corp., Statcom Corp., Intertec. If we are imprisoned by language, then escape from that prison-house requires language poets, a kind of cultural restriction enzyme to cut the code; cyborg heteroglossia is one form of radical cultural politics. For cyborg poetry, see Perloff (1984); Fraser (1984). For feminist modernist/postmodernist 'cyborg' writing, see HOW(ever), 871 Corbett Ave, San Francisco, CA 94131.

5. Baudrillard (1983). Jameson (1984, p. 66) points out that Plato's definition of the simulacrum is the copy for which there is no original, i.e., the world of advanced capitalism, of pure exchange. See *Discourse* 9 (Spring/Summer 1987) for a special issue on technology (cybernetics, ecology, and the postmodern imagination).

6. For ethnographic accounts and political evaluations, see Epstein (forthcoming), Sturgeon (1986). Without explicit irony, adopting the spaceship earth/whole earth logo of the planet photographed from space, set off by the slogan 'Love Your Mother', the May 1987 Mothers and Others Day action at the nuclear weapons testing facility in Nevada none the less took account of the tragic contradictions of views of the earth. Demonstrators applied for official permits to be on the land from officers of the Western Shoshone tribe, whose territory was invaded by the US government when it built the nuclear weapons test ground in the 1950s. Arrested for trespassing, the demonstrators argued that the police and weapons facility personnel, without authorization from the proper officials, were the trespassers. One affinity group at the women's action called themselves the Surrogate Others; and in solidarity with the creatures forced to tunnel in the same ground with the bomb, they enacted a cyborgian emergence from the constructed body of a large, non-heterosexual desert worm.

7. Powerful developments of coalition politics emerge from 'Third World' speakers, speaking from nowhere, the displaced centre of the universe, earth: 'We live on the third planet from the sun'—*Sun Poem* by Jamaican writer, Edward Kamau Braithwaite, review by Mackey (1984). Contributors to Smith (1983) ironically subvert naturalized identities precisely while constructing a place from which to speak called home. See especially Reagon (in Smith, 1983, pp. 356–68). Trinh T. Minh-ha (1986–87).

8. hooks (1981, 1984); Hull *et al.* (1982). Bambara (1981) wrote an extraordinary novel in which the women of colour theatre group, The Seven Sisters, explores a form of unity. See analysis by Butler-Evans (1987).

9. On orientalism in feminist works and elsewhere, see Lowe (1986); Said (1978); ... workings of feminist taxonomies as genealogies of power in feminist ideology and polemic.

10. "Katie King (1986, 1987a) has developed a theoretically sensitive treatment of the workings of feminists taxonomies as genealogies of power in feminist ideology and polemic. King examines Jaggar's (1983) problematic example of taxonomizing feminisms to make a little machine producing the desired final position. My caricature here of socialist and radical feminism is also an example.

11. The central role of object relations versions of psychoanalysis and related strong universalizing moves in discussing reproduction, caring work, and mothering in many approaches to epistemology underline their authors' resistance to what I am calling postmodernism. For me, both the universalizing moves and these versions of psychoanalysis make analysis of 'women's place in the integrated circuit' difficult and lead to systematic difficulties in accounting for or even seeing major aspects of the construction of gender and gendered social life. The feminist standpoint argument has been developed by: Flax (1983), Harding (1986), Harding and Hintikka (1983), Hartsock (1983a, b), O'Brien (1981), Rose (1983), Smith (1974, 1979). For rethinking theories of feminist materialism and feminist standpoints in response to criticism, see Harding (1986, pp. 163–96), Hartsock (1987), and H. Rose (1986).

12. I make an argumentative category error in 'modifying' MacKinnon's positions with the qualifier 'radical', thereby generating my own reductive critique of extremely heterogeneous writing, which does explicitly use that label, by my taxonomically interested argument about writing which does not use the modifier and which brooks no limits and thereby adds to the various dreams of a common, in the sense of univocal, language for feminism. My category error was occasioned by an assignment to write from a particular taxonomic position which itself has a heterogeneous history, socialist-feminism, for *Socialist Review*. A critique indebted to MacKinnon, but without the reductionism and

with an elegant feminist account of Foucault's paradoxical conservatism on sexual violence (rape), is de Lauretis (1985; see also 1986, pp. 1–19). A theoretically elegant feminist social-historical examination of family violence, that insists on women's, men's, and children's complex agency without losing sight of the material structures of male domination, race, and class, is Gordon (1988).

13.   King (1984). An abbreviated list of feminist science fiction underlying themes of this essay: Octavia Butler, *Wild Seed, Mind of My Mind, Kindred, Survivor*, Suzy McKee Charnas, *Motherliness*; Samuel R. Delany, the Neverÿon series; Anne McCaffery, *The Ship Who Sang, Dinosaur Planet*; Vonda McIntyre, *Superluminal, Dreamsnake*; Joanna Russ, *Adventures of Alix, The Female Man*; James Tiptree, Jr, *Star Songs of an Old Primate, Up the Walls of the World*; John Varley, *Titan, Wizard, Demon*.

14.   French feminisms contribute to cyborg heteroglossia. Burke (1981); Irigaray (1977, 1979); Marks and de Courtivron (1980); *Signs* (Autumn 1981); Wittig (1973); Duchen (1986). For English translation of some currents of francophone feminism see *Feminist Issues: A Journal of Feminist Social and Political Theory*, 1980.

15.   But all these poets are very complex, not least in their treatment of themes of lying and erotic, decentred collective and personal identities. Griffin (1978), Lorde (1984), Rich (1978).

16.   Derrida (1976, especially part II); Lévi-Strauss (1961, especially 'The Writing Lesson'); Gates (1985); Kahn and Neumaier (1985); Ong (1982); Kramarae and Treichler (1985).

17.   The sharp relation of women of colour to writing as theme and politics can be approached through: Program for 'The Black Woman and the Diaspora: Hidden Connections and Extended Acknowledgements', An International Literary Conference, Michigan State University, October 1985; Evans (1984); Christian (1985); Carby (1987); Fisher (1980); *Frontiers* (1980, 1983); Kingston (1977); Lerner (1973); Giddings (1985); Moraga and Anzaldúa (1981); Morgan (1984). Anglophone European and Euro-American women have also crafted special relations to their writing as a potent sign: Gilbert and Gubar (1979), Russ (1983).

18.   The convention of ideologically taming militarized high technology by publicizing its applications to speech and motion problems of the disabled/differently abled takes on a special irony in monotheistic, patriarchal, and frequently anti-semitic culture when computer-generated speech allows a boy with no voice to chant the Haftorah at his bar 'ableness' particularly clear, military high-tech has a way of making human beings disabled by definition, a perverse aspect of much automated battlefield and Star Wars R&D. See Welford (1 July 1986).

19.   James Clifford (1985, 1988) argues persuasively for recognition of continuous cultural reinvention, the stubborn non-disappearance of those 'marked' by Western imperializing practices.

20.   DuBois (1982), Daston and Park (n.d.), Park and Daston (1981). The noun *monster* shares its root with the verb *to demonstrate*.

II

FEMINIST INVESTMENTS

9

selection from
Mother Camp

ESTHER NEWTON

ANTHROPOLOGIST ESTHER NEWTON'S MID-1960S FIELD RESEARCH with drag queens and other men who worked as female impersonators in the Midwestern United States outlined the symbolic and social differences between those men who cross-dressed to make a living, those who cross-dressed for sex, and those who cross-dressed for their own pleasure. Her groundbreaking work articulates a relationship between performance and gender that has become a central focus in queer theories of gender and sexuality.

Newton recognized drag as representative of one type of homosexuality, one that occupied the stigmatized bottom rung of the social scale. She grasped one of drag's essential features, that it is a double illusion signifying both the masculine and the feminine self, the male and the female body. From that she develops an understanding of drag, and its resulting culture of camp, as the central cultural form of the homosexual world prior to the gay liberation and lesbian feminist movements of the later 1960s. It was paradoxically significant both in creating a space for gay culture, as well as for providing the form for its oppression.

Mother Camp is among the first interdisciplinary studies of queer culture, and helped create the framework for future queer studies. One "sin of omission" in Newton's work is that she focused entirely on the homosexual sphere and did not take into account the heterosexual cross-dresser, thus missing out on alternative sets of meanings that gender cross-coding can evoke.

THE DRAG QUEEN

Professionally, impersonators place themselves as a group at the bottom of the show business world. But socially, their self-image can be represented in its simplest form as three concentric circles. The impersonators, or drag queens, are the inner circle. Surrounding them are the queens, ordinary gay men. The straights are the outer circle. In this way, impersonators are "a society within a society within a society," as one impersonator told me.

A few impersonators deny publicly that they are gay. These impersonators are married, and some have children. Of course, being married and having children constitute no barrier to participation in the homosexual subculture. But whatever may be the actual case with these few, the impersonators I knew universally described such public statements as "cover." One impersonator's statement was particularly revealing. He said that "in practice" perhaps some impersonators were straight, but "in theory" they could not be. "How can a man perform in female attire and not have something wrong with him?" he asked.

The role of the female impersonator is directly related to both the drag queen and camp roles in the homosexual subculture. In gay life, the two roles are strongly associated. In homosexual terminology, a drag queen is a homosexual male who often, or habitually, dresses in female attire. (A drag butch is a lesbian who often, or habitually, dresses in male attire.) Drag and camp are the most representative and widely used symbols of homosexuality in the English speaking world. This is true even though many homosexuals would never wear drag or go to a drag party and even though most homosexuals who do wear drag do so only in special contexts, such as private parties and Halloween balls.[1] At the middle-class level, it is common to give "costume" parties at which those who want to wear drag can do so, and the others can wear a costume appropriate to their gender.

The principle opposition around which the gay world revolves is masculine-feminine. There are a number of ways of presenting this opposition through one's own person, where it becomes also an opposition of "inside" = "outside" or "underneath" = "outside." Ultimately, all drag symbolism opposes the "inner" or "real" self (subjective self) to the "outer" self (social self). For the great majority of homosexuals, the social self is often a calculated respectability and the subjective or real self is stigmatized. The "inner" = "outer" opposition is almost parallel to "back" = "front." In fact, the social self is usually described as "front" and social relationships (especially with women) designed to support the veracity of the "front" are called "cover." The "front" = "back" opposition also has a direct tie-in with the body: "front" = "face"; "back" = "ass."

There are two different levels on which the oppositions can be played out. One is *within* the sartorial system[2] itself, that is, wearing feminine clothing "underneath" and masculine clothing "outside." (This method seems to be used more by heterosexual transvestites.) It symbolizes that the visible, social, masculine clothing is a costume, which in turn symbolizes that the entire sex-role behavior is a role—an act. Conversely, stage impersonators sometimes wear jockey shorts underneath full stage drag, symbolizing that the feminine clothing is a costume.

A second "internal" method is to mix sex-role referents *within* the visible sartorial system. This generally involves some "outside" item from the feminine sartorial system such as earrings, lipstick, high-heeled shoes, a necklace, etc., worn *with* masculine clothing. This kind of opposition is used very frequently in informal camping by homosexuals. The feminine item stands out so glaringly by incongruity that it "undermines" the masculine system and proclaims that the inner identification is feminine.[3] When this method is used on stage, it is called "working with (feminine) pieces." The performer generally works in a tuxedo or business suit and a woman's large hat and earrings.

The second level poses an opposition between a one sex-role sartorial system and the "self," whose identity has to be indicated in some other way. Thus when impersonators are performing, the oppositional play is between "appearance," which is female, and "reality," or "essence," which is male. One way to do this is to show that the appearance is an illusion; for instance, a standard impersonation maneuver is to pull out one "breast" and show it to the audience. A more drastic step is taking off the wig. Strippers actually routinize the progression from "outside" to "inside" visually, by starting in a full stripping costume and ending by taking off the bra and showing the audience the flat chest. Another method is to demonstrate "maleness" verbally or vocally by suddenly dropping the vocal level or by some direct reference. One impersonator routinely tells the audience: "Have a ball. I have two." (But genitals must *never* be seen.) Another tells unruly members of the audience that he will "put on my men's clothes and beat you up."

Impersonators play on the opposition to varying extents, but most experienced stage impersonators have a characteristic method of doing it. Generally speaking, the desire and ability to break the illusion of femininity is the mark of an experienced impersonator who has freed himself from other impersonators as the immediate reference group and is working fully to the audience. Even so, some stage impersonators admitted that it is difficult to break the unity of the feminine sartorial system. For instance, they said that it is difficult, subjectively, to speak in a deep tone of voice while on stage and especially while wearing a wig. The "breasts" especially seem to symbolize the entire feminine sartorial system and role. This is shown not only by the very common device of removing them in order to break the illusion, but in the command, "tits up!" meaning, "get into the role," or "get into feminine character."

The tension between the masculine-feminine and inside-outside oppositions pervade the homosexual subculture at all class and status levels. In a sense the different class and status levels consist of different ways of balancing these oppositions. Low-status homosexuals (both male and female) characteristically insist on very strong dichotomization between masculine-feminine so that people must play out one principle or the other exclusively. Low-status queens are expected to be very nellie, always, and low-status butch men are so "masculine" that they very often consider themselves straight.[4] (Although the queens say in private that "today's butch is tomorrow's sister.") Nevertheless, in the most nellie queen the opposition is still implicitly there, since to participate in the male homosexual subculture as a peer, one must be male inside (physiologically).

Recently, this principle has begun to be challenged by hormone use and by the sex-changing operation. The use of these techniques as a final resolution of the masculine-feminine opposition is hotly discussed in the homosexual subculture. A very significant proportion of the impersonators, and especially the street impersonators, have used or are using hormone shots or plastic inserts to create artificial breasts and change the shape of their bodies. This development is strongly deplored by the stage impersonators who say that the whole point of female impersonation depends on maleness. They further say that these "hormone queens" are placing themselves out of the homosexual subculture, since, by definition, a homosexual man wants to sleep with other *men* (i.e., no gay man would want to sleep with these "hormone queens").

In carrying the transformation even farther, to "become a woman" is approved by the stage impersonators, with the provision that the "sex changes" should get out of gay life altogether and go straight. The "sex changes" do not always comply, however. One quite successful impersonator in Chicago had the operation but continued to perform in a straight club with other impersonators. Some impersonators in Chicago told me that this person was now considered "out of gay life" by the homosexuals and could not perform in a gay club. I also heard a persistent rumor that "she" now liked to sleep with lesbians!

It should be readily apparent why drag is such an effective symbol of both the outside-inside and masculine-feminine oppositions. There are relatively few ascribed roles in American culture and sex role is one of them; sex role radiates a complex and ubiquitous system of typing achieved roles. Obvious examples are in the kinship system (wife, mother, etc.) but sex typing also extends far out into the occupational-role system (airline stewardess, waitress, policeman, etc.). The effect of the drag system is to wrench the sex roles loose from that which supposedly determines them, that is, genital sex. Gay people know that sex-typed behavior can be achieved, contrary to what is popularly believed. They know that the possession of one type of genital equipment by no means guarantees the "naturally appropriate" behavior.

Thus drag in the homosexual subculture symbolizes two somewhat conflicting statements concerning the sex-role system. The first statement symbolized by drag is that the sex-role system really is natural: therefore homosexuals are unnatural (typical responses: "I am physically abnormal"; "I can't help it, I was born with the wrong hormone balance"; "I am really a woman who was born with the wrong equipment"; "I am psychologically sick").

The second symbolic statement of drag questions the "naturalness" of the sex-role system *in toto*; if sex-role behavior can be achieved by the "wrong" sex, it logically follows that it is in reality also achieved, not inherited, by the "right" sex. Anthropologists say that sex-role behavior is learned. The gay world, via drag, says that sex-role behavior is an appearance; it is "outside." It can be manipulated at will.

Drag symbolizes both these assertions in a very complex way. At the simplest level, drag signifies that the person wearing it is a homosexual, that he is a male who is behaving in a specifically inappropriate way, that he is a male who places himself as a woman in relation to other men. In this sense it signifies stigma. At the most complex, it is a double inversion that says "appearance is an illusion." Drag says, "my 'outside' appearance is feminine, but my essence 'inside' [the body] is masculine." At the same time it symbolizes the opposite inversion: "my appearance 'outside' [my body, my gender] is masculine but my essence 'inside' [myself] is feminine."

In the context of the homosexual subculture, all professional female impersonators are "drag queens." Drag is always worn for performance in any case; the female impersonator has simply professionalized this subcultural role. Among themselves and in conversation with other homosexuals, female impersonators usually call themselves and are called drag queens. In the same way, their performances are referred to by themselves and others as drag shows.

But when the varied meanings of drag are taken into consideration, it should be obvious why the drag queen is an ambivalent figure in the gay world. The drag queen symbolizes all that homosexuals say they fear the most in themselves, all that they say they feel guilty about; he symbolizes, in fact, *the* stigma. In this way, the term "drag queen" is comparable to "nigger." And like that word, it may be all right in an ingroup context but not in an outgroup one. Those who do not want to think of themselves or be identified as drag queens under any circumstances attempt to disassociate themselves from "drag" completely. These homosexuals deplore drag shows and profess total lack of interest in them. Their attitude toward drag queens is one of condemnation combined with the expression of vast social distance between themselves and the drag queen.

Other homosexuals enjoy being queens among themselves, but do not want to be stigmatized by the heterosexual culture. These homosexuals admire drag and drag queens in homosexual contexts, but deplore female impersonators and street fairies for "giving us a bad name" or "projecting the wrong image" to the heterosexual culture. The drag queen is definitely a marked man in the subculture.

Homosexuality consists of sex-role deviation made up of two related but distinct parts: "wrong" sexual object choices and "wrong" sex-role presentation of self.[5] The first deviation is shared by all homosexuals, but it can be hidden best. The second deviation logically (in this culture) corresponds with the first, which it symbolizes. But it cannot be hidden, and it actually compounds the stigma.

Thus, insofar as female impersonators are professional drag queens, they are evaluated positively by gay people to the extent that they have perfected a subcultural skill and to the extent that gay people are willing to oppose the heterosexual culture directly (in much the same way that Negroes now call themselves Blacks). On the other hand, they are despised because they symbolize and embody the stigma. At present, the balance is far on the negative side, although this varies by context and by the position of the observer (relative to the stigma). This explains the impersonators' negative identification with the term drag queen when it is used by outsiders. (In the same way, they at first used masculine pronouns of address and reference toward each other in my presence, but reverted to feminine pronouns when I became more or less integrated into the system.)

THE CAMP

While all female impersonators are drag queens in the gay world, by no means are all of them "camps." Both the drag queen and the camp are expressive performing roles, and both specialize in transformation. But the drag queen is concerned with masculine-feminine transformation, while the camp is concerned with what might be called a philosophy of transformations and incongruity. Certainly the two roles are intimately related, since to be a feminine man is by definition incongruous. But strictly speaking, the drag queen simply expresses the incongruity while the camp actually uses it to achieve a higher synthesis. To the extent that a drag queen does this, he is called "campy." The drag queen role is emotionally charged and connotes low status for most homosexuals because it bears the visible stigmata of homosexuality; camps, however, are found at all status levels in the homosexual subculture and are very often the center of primary group organization.[6]

The camp is the central role figure in the subcultural ideology of camp. The camp ethos or style plays a role analogous to "soul" in the Negro subculture.[7] Like soul, camp is a "strategy for a situation."[8] The special perspective of the female impersonators is a case of a broader homosexual ethos. This is the perspective of moral deviance and, consequently, of a "spoiled identity," in Goffman's terms.[9] Like the Negro problem, the homosexual problem centers on self-hatred and the lack of self-esteem.[10] But if "the soul ideology ministers to the needs for identity,"[11] the camp ideology ministers to the needs for dealing with an identity that is well defined but loaded with contempt. As one impersonator who was also a well known camp told me, "No one is more miserable about homosexuality than the homosexual."

Camp is not a thing. Most broadly it signifies a *relationship between* things, people, and activities or qualities, and homosexuality. In this sense, "camp taste," for instance, is synonymous with homosexual taste. Informants stressed that even between individuals there is very little agreement on what is camp because camp is in the eye of the beholder, that is, different homosexuals like different things, and because of the spontaneity and individuality of camp, camp taste is always changing. This has the advantage, recognized by some informants, that a clear division can always be maintained between homosexual and "straight" taste:

> He said Susan Sontag was wrong about camp's being a cult,[12] and the moment it becomes a public cult, you watch the queens stop it. Because if it becomes the squares, it doesn't belong to them any more. And what will be "camp art," no queen will own. It's like taking off the work clothes and putting on the home clothes. When the queen is coming home, she wants to come home to a campy apartment that's hers—it's very queer—because all day long she's been very straight. So when it all of a sudden becomes very straight—to come home to an apartment that any square could have—she's not going to have it any more.[13]

While camp is in the eye of the homosexual beholder, it is assumed that there is an underlying unity of perspective among homosexuals that gives any particular campy thing its special flavor. It is possible to discern strong themes in any particular campy thing or event. The three that seemed most recurrent and characteristic to me were *incongruity, theatricality*, and *humor*. All three are intimately related to the homosexual situation and strategy. Incongruity is the subject matter of camp, theatricality its style, and humor its strategy.

Camp usually depends on the perception or creation of *incongruous juxtapositions*. Either way, the homosexual "creates" the camp, by pointing out the incongruity or by devising it. For instance, one informant said that the campiest thing he had seen recently was a Midwestern football player in high drag at a Halloween ball. He pointed out that the football player was seriously trying to be a lady, and so his intent was not camp, but that the *effect* to the observer was campy. (The informant went on to say that it would have been even campier if the football player had been picked up by the police and had his picture published in the paper the next day.) This is an example of unintentional camp, in that the campy person or thing does not perceive the incongruity.

Created camp also depends on transformations and juxtapositions, but here the effect is intentional. The most concrete examples can be seen in the apartments of campy queens, for instance, in the idea of growing plants in the toilet tank. One queen said that *TV Guide* had described a little Mexican horse statue as campy. He said there was nothing campy about this at all, but if you put a nude cut-out of Bette Davis on it, it would be campy. Masculine-feminine juxtapositions are, of course, the most characteristic kind of camp, but any very incongruous contrast can be campy. For instance, juxtapositions of high and low status, youth and old age, profane and sacred functions or symbols, cheap and expensive articles are frequently used for camp purposes. Objects or people are often said to be campy, but the camp inheres not in the person or thing itself but in the tension between that person or thing and the context or association. For instance, I was told by impersonators that a homosexual clothes designer made himself a beautiful Halloween ball gown. After the ball he sold it to a wealthy society lady. It was said that when he wore it, it was very campy, but when she wore it, it was just an expensive gown, unless she had run around her ball saying she was really not herself but her faggot dress designer.

The nexus of this perception by incongruity lies in the basic homosexual experience, that is, squarely on the moral deviation. One informant said, "Camp is all based on homosexual thought. It is all based on the idea of two men or two women in bed. It's incongruous and it's funny." If moral deviation is the locus of the perception of incongruity, it is more specifically role deviation and role manipulation that are at the core of the second property of camp, *theatricality*.

Camp is theatrical in three interlocking ways. First of all, camp is style. Importance tends to shift from what a thing *is* to how it *looks*, from *what* is done to *how* it is done. It has been remarked that homosexuals excel in the decorative arts. The kind of incongruities that are campy are very often created by adornment or stylization of a well-defined thing or symbol. But the emphasis on style goes further than this in that camp is also exaggerated, consciously "stagey," specifically theatrical. This is especially true of *the* camp, who is definitely a performer.

The second aspect of theatricality in camp is its dramatic form. Camp, like drag, always involves a performer or performers and an audience. This is its structure. It is only stretching the point a little to say that even in unintentional camp, this interaction is maintained. In the case of the football player, his behavior was transformed by his audience into a performance. In many cases of unintentional camp, the camp performs to his audience by commenting on the behavior or appearance of "the scene," which is then described as "campy." In intentional camp, the structure of performer and audience is almost always clearly defined. This point will be elaborated below.

Third, camp is suffused with the perception of "being as playing a role" and "life as theatre."[14] It is at this point that drag and camp merge and augment each other. I was led to an appreciation of this while reading Parker Tyler's appraisal of Greta Garbo.[15] Garbo is generally regarded in the homosexual community as "high camp." Tyler stated that "'Drag acts,' I believe, are not confined to the declassed sexes. Garbo 'got in drag' whenever she took some heavy glamour part, whenever she melted in or out of a man's arms, whenever she simply let that heavenly-flexed neck…bear the weight of her thrown-back head."[16] He concludes, "How resplendent seems the art of acting! It is all *impersonation*, whether the sex underneath is true or not."[17]

We have to take the long way around to get at the real relationship between Garbo and camp. The homosexual is stigmatized, but his stigma can be hidden. In Goffman's terminology, information about his stigma can be managed. Therefore, of crucial importance to homosexuals themselves and to non-homosexuals is whether the stigma is displayed so that one is immediately recognizable or is hidden so that he can pass to the world at large as a respectable citizen. The covert half (conceptually, not necessarily numerically) of the homosexual community is engaged in "impersonating" respectable citizenry, at least some of the time. What is being impersonated?

The stigma essentially lies in being less than a man and in doing something that is unnatural (wrong) for a man to do. Surrounding this essence is a halo effect: violation of culturally standardized canons of taste, behavior, speech, and so on, rigorously associated (prescribed) with the male role (e.g., fanciful or decorative clothing styles, "effeminate" speech and manner, expressed disinterest in women as sexual objects, expressed interest in men as sexual objects, unseemly concern with personal appearance, etc.). The covert homosexual must therefore do two things: first, he must conceal the fact that he sleeps with men. But concealing this *fact* is far less difficult than his second problem, which is controlling the *halo effect* or signals that would announce that he sleeps with men. The covert homosexual must in fact impersonate a *man*, that is, he must *appear* to the "straight" world to be fulfilling (or not violating) all the requisites of the male role as defined by the "straight" world.

The immediate relationship between Tyler's point about Garbo and camp/drag is this: if Garbo playing women is drag, then homosexuals "passing" are playing men; they are in drag. This is the larger implication of drag/camp. In fact, gay people often use the word "drag" in this broader sense, even to include role playing which most people simply take for granted: role playing in school, at the office, at parties, and so on. In fact, all of life is role and theatre—appearance.

But granted that all acting is impersonation, what moved Tyler to designate Garbo's acting specifically as "drag"? Drag means, first of all, role playing. The way in which it defines role playing contains its implicit attitude. The word "drag" attaches specifically to the outward, visible appurtenances of a role. In the type case, sex role, drag primarily refers to the wearing apparel and accessories that designate a human being as male or female, when it is worn by the opposite sex. By focusing on the outward appearance of role, drag implies that sex role and, by extension, role in general is something superficial, which can be manipulated, put on and off again at will. The drag concept implies *distance* between the actor and the role or "act." But drag also means "costume." This theatrical referent is the key to the attitude toward role playing embodied in drag as camp. Role playing is *play*; it is an act or show. The necessity to play at life, living role after superficial role, should not be the cause of bitterness or despair. Most of the sex role and other impersonations that male homosexuals do are done with ease, grace, and especially humor. The actor should throw himself into it; he should put on a good show; he should view the whole experience as fun, as a camp.[18]

The double stance toward role, putting on a good show while indicating distance (showing that it is a show) is the heart of drag as camp. Garbo's acting was thought to be "drag" because it was considered markedly androgynous, and because she played (even overplayed) the role of femme fatale with style. No man (in her movies) and very few audiences (judging by her success) could resist her allure. And yet most of the men she seduced were her victims because she was only playing at love—only acting. This is made quite explicit in the film "Mata Hari," in which Garbo the spy seduces men to get information from them.

The third quality of camp is its *humor*. Camp is for fun; the aim of camp is to make an audience laugh. In fact, it is a *system* of humor. Camp humor is a system of laughing at one's incongruous position instead of crying.[19] That is, the humor does not cover up, it transforms. I saw the reverse transformation—from laughter to pathos—often enough, and it is axiomatic among the impersonators that when the camp cannot laugh, he dissolves into a maudlin bundle of self-pity.

One of the most confounding aspects of my interaction with the impersonators was their tendency to laugh at situations that to me were horrifying or tragic. I was amazed, for instance, when one impersonator described to me as "very campy" the scene in "Whatever Happened to Baby Jane" in which Bette Davis served Joan Crawford a rat, or the scene in which Bette Davis makes her "comeback" in the parlor with the piano player.

Of course, not all impersonators and not all homosexuals are campy. *The* camp is a homosexual wit and clown; his campy productions and performances are a continuous creative strategy for dealing with the homosexual situation, and, in the process, defining a positive homosexual identity. As one performer summed it up for me, "Homosexuality is a way of life that is against all ways of life, including nature's. And no one is more aware of it than the homosexual. The camp accepts his role as a homosexual and flaunts his homosexuality. He makes the other homosexuals laugh; he makes life a little brighter for them. And he builds a bridge to the straight people by getting them to laugh with him." The same man described the role of the camp more concretely in an interview:

> Well, "to camp" actually means "to sit in front of a group of people"…not on-stage, but you *can* camp on-stage…I think that I do that when I talk to the audience. I think I'm camping with 'em. But a "'camp" herself is a queen who sits and starts entertaining a group of people at a bar around her. They all start listening to what she's got to say. And she says campy things. Oh, somebody smarts off at her and she gives 'em a very flip answer. A camp is a flip person who has declared emotional freedom. She is going to say to the world, "I'm queer." Although she may not do this all the time, but most of the time a camp queen will. She'll walk down the street and she'll see you and say, "Hi, Mary, how are you?" right in the busiest part of town…she'll actually camp, right there. And she'll swish down the street. And she may be in a business suit; she doesn't have to be dressed outlandishly. Even at work the people figure that she's a camp. They don't know what to *call* her, but they hire her 'cause she's a good kid, keeps the office laughing, doesn't bother anybody, and everyone'll say, "Oh, running around with Georgie's more fun! He's just more fun!" The squares are saying this. And the other ones [homosexuals] are saying, "Oh, you've got to know George, she's a camp." Because the whole time she's light-hearted. Very seldom is camp sad. Camp has got to be flip. A camp queen's got to think faster than other queens. *This* makes her camp. She's got to have an answer to anything that's put to her.…[20]
>
> Now *homosexuality* is *not* camp. But you take a camp, and she turns around and she makes homosexuality funny, but not ludicrous; funny but not ridiculous…this is a great, great art. This is a fine thing.…Now when it suddenly became the word…became like…it's like the word "Mary." Everybody's "Mary." "Hi, Mary. How are you, Mary." And like "girl." You may be talking to one of the butchest queens in the world, but you still say, "Oh, girl." And sometimes they say, "Well, don't call me 'she' and don't call me 'girl.' I don't feel like a girl. I'm a *man*. I just like to go to bed with you *girls*. I don't want to go to bed with another man." And you say, "Oh, girl, get you. Now she's turned butch." And so you camp about it. It's sort of laughing at yourself instead of crying. And a good camp will make you laugh along with her, to where you suddenly feel…you don't feel like she's made fun of you. She' sort of made light of a bad situation.

The camp queen makes no bones about it; to him the gay world is the "sisterhood." By accepting his homosexuality and flaunting it, the camp undercuts all homosexuals who won't accept the stigmatized identity. Only by fully embracing the stigma itself can one neutralize the sting and make it laughable.[21] Not all references to the stigma are campy, however. Only if it is pointed out as a joke is it camp, although there is no requirement that the jokes be gentle or friendly. A lot of camping is extremely hostile; it is almost always sarcastic. But its intent is humorous as well. Campy queens are very often said to be "bitches" just as camp humor is said to be "bitchy."[22] The campy queen who can "read" (put down) all challengers and cut everyone down to size is admired. Humor is the campy queen's weapon. A camp queen in good form can come out on top (by group consensus) against all the competition.

Female impersonators who use drag in a comic way or are themselves comics are considered camps by gay people. (Serious glamour drag is considered campy by many homosexuals, but it is unintentional camp. Those who see glamour drag as a serious business do not consider it to be campy. Those who think it is ludicrous for drag queens to take themselves seriously see the whole business as a campy incongruity.) Since the camp role is a positive one, many impersonators take pride in being camps, at least on stage.[23] Since the camp role depends to such a large extent on verbal agility, it reinforces the superiority of the live performers over record performers, who, even if they are comic, must depend wholly on visual effects.

NOTES

1. In two Broadway plays (since made into movies) dealing with English homosexuals, "The Killing of Sister George" (lesbians) and "Staircase" (male homosexuals), drag played a prominent role. In "George," an entire scene shows George and her lover dressed in tuxedos and top hats on their way to a drag party. In "Staircase," the entire plot turns on the fact that one of the characters has been arrested for "going in drag" to the local pub. Throughout the second act, this character wears a black shawl over his shoulders. This item of clothing is symbolic of full drag. This same character is a camp and, in my opinion, George was a very rare bird, a lesbian camp. Both plays, at any rate, abounded in camp humor. "The Boys in the Band," another recent play and movie, doesn't feature drag as prominently but has two camp roles and much camp humor.

2. This concept was developed and suggested to me by Julian Pitt-Rivers.

3. Even one feminine item ruins the integrity of the masculine system; the male loses his caste honor. The superordinate role in a hierarchy is more fragile than the subordinate. Manhood must be achieved, and once achieved, guarded and protected.

4. The middle-class idea tends to be that any man who has had sexual relations with men is queer. The lower classes strip down to "essentials," and the man who is "dominant" can be normal (masculine). Lower-class men give themselves a bit more leeway before they consider themselves to be gay.

5. It becomes clear that the core of the stigma is in "wrong" sexual object choice when it is considered that there is little stigma in simply being effeminate, or even in wearing feminine apparel in some contexts, as long as the male is known to be heterosexual, that is, known to sleep with women or, rather, not to sleep with men. But when I say that sleeping with men is the core of the stigma, or that feminine behavior logically corresponds with this, I do not mean it in any causal sense. In fact, I have an impression that some homosexual men sleep with men *because* it strengthens their identification with the feminine role, rather than the other way around. This makes a lot of sense developmentally, if one assumes, as I do, that children learn sex-role identity before they learn any strictly sexual object choices. In other words, I think that children learn they are boys or girls before they are made to understand that boys *only* love girls and vice versa.

6. The role of the "pretty boy" is also a very positive one, and in some ways the camp is an alternative for those who are not pretty. However, the pretty boy is subject to the depredations of aging, which in the subculture is thought to set in at thirty (at the latest). Because the camp depends on inventiveness and wit rather than on physical beauty, he is ageless.

7. Keil, *Urban Blues*, pp. 164–90.

8. This phrase is used by Kenneth Burke in reference to poetry and is used by Keil in a sociological sense.

9. Irving Goffman, *Stigma* (Englewood Cliffs, N.J.: Prentice-Hall, 1963.)

10. I would say that the main problem today is heterosexuals, just as the main problem for Blacks is Whites.

11. Keil, *Urban* Blues, p. 165.

12. I don't want to pass over the implication here that female impersonators keep up with Susan Sontag. Generally, they don't. I had given him Susan Sontag's "Notes on 'Camp'" (*Partisan Review* [Fall, 1964]: 515–30) to see what he would say. He was college educated, and perfectly able to get through it. He was enraged (justifiably, I felt) that she had almost edited homosexuals out of camp.

13. Informants said that many ideas had been taken over by straights through the mass media, but that the moment this happened the idea would no longer be campy. For instance, one man said that a queen he knew had gotten the idea of growing plants in the water tank of the toilet. But the idea is no longer campy because it is being advertised through such mass media as *Family Circle* magazine.

    How to defend *any* symbols or values from the absorbing powers of the mass media? Jules Henry, I believe, was one of the first to point to the power of advertising to subvert traditional values by appropriating them for commercial purposes (*Culture Against Man*, New York: Random House, 1963). But subcultural symbols and values lose their integrity in the same way. Although Sontag's New York *avant garde* had already appropriated camp from homosexuals, they did so in the effort to create their own aristocracy or integrity of taste as against the mass culture.

14. Sontag, "Notes on 'Camp,'" p. 529.

15. Parker Tyler, "The Garbo Image," in *The Films of Greta Garbo*, ed. Michael Conway, Dion McGregor, and Mark Ricci (New York: Citadel Press, no date), pp. 9–31.

16. Tyler, "The Garbo Image," p. 12.

17. Ibid. p. 28.

18. It is clear to me now how camp undercuts rage and therefore rebellion by ridiculing serious and concentrated bitterness.

19. It would be worthwhile to compare camp humor with the humor systems of other oppressed people (Eastern European Jewish, Negro, etc.).

20. Speed and spontaneity are of the essence. For example, at a dinner party, someone said, "Oh, we forgot to say grace." One woman folded her hands without missing a beat and intoned, "Thank God every one at this table is gay."

21.   It's important to stress again that camp is a pre- or proto-political phenomenon. The anti-camp in this system is the person who wants to dissociate from the stigma to be like the oppressors. The camp says, "I am not like the oppressors." But in so doing he agrees with the oppressors' definition of who he is. The new radicals deny the stigma in a different way, by saying that the oppressors are illegitimate. This step is only foreshadowed in camp. It is also interesting that the lesbian wing of the radical homosexuals have come to women's meetings holding signs saying: "We are the women your parents warned you against."

22.   The "bitch," as I see it, is a woman who *accepts* her inferior status, but refuses to do so gracefully, or without fighting back. Women and homosexual men are oppressed by straight men, and it is no accident that both are beginning to move beyond bitchiness toward refusal of inferior status.

23.   Many impersonators told me that they got tired of being camps for their friends, lovers, and acquaintances. They often felt they were asked to gay parties simply to entertain and camp it up, and said they did not feel like camping off stage, or didn't feel competent when out of drag. This broadens out into the social problem of all clowns and entertainers, or, even further, to anyone with a talent. He will often wonder if he is loved for himself.

10

Sappho by Surgery
The Transsexually Constructed Lesbian-Feminist

Janice G. Raymond

Janice Raymond's *The Transsexual Empire* did not invent anti-transsexual prejudice, but it did more to justify and perpetuate it than perhaps any other book ever written. Paradoxically, because it provoked such an outraged, anguished, and deeply motivated counter-response from transgender people, it also did more than any other work to elicit the new lines of critique that coalesced into transgender studies. It is a profoundly polemical book that is difficult to approach in a neutral manner, in much the same way that it is difficult to approach the *Protocols of the Elders of Zion* or other notorious works of propaganda. To substantively engage with it is to give credence to the easily falsifiable fantasies that structure it; to ignore it is to deny the power it still has to demonize transgender people in ways that have material consequences.

Raymond's book is still uncritically accepted by some on the cultural left, particularly lesbian-feminists, as a paragon of feminist criticism of "patriarchal" medical-scientific practices, and a politically progressive ethical condemnation of transsexualism. Within the new field of transgender studies, however, it is routinely vilified as an ideologically driven pastiche of shoddy research. She falsely asserts, for example, that transsexual surgical techniques were perfected by the Nazis in medical experiments performed on inmates of the death camps, and seriously advances the claim that male medical doctors are involved in a vast conspiracy to create a race of artificial women (the dreaded "transsexual empire" of her title) designed to replace biological females, as in *The Stepford Wives*. Raymond pays scant attention to female-to-male individuals, because she cannot easily fit them into her scheme.

In "Sappho by Surgery," the chapter that has caused the most offense among transgender people, Raymond expands upon the premise built up in earlier chapters, that biology defines gender. She claims that males who undergo sex-reassignment procedures remain deviant men and never become women. They use the appropriated appearance of the female body to invade women's spaces, particularly lesbian feminist spaces, in order to exercise male dominance and aggression over women and to subvert the feminist movement. Raymond claims that this is tantamount to rape—an undesired penetration—and that all MTF transsexuals are by definition rapists.

As will be seen throughout some of the articles in this anthology, Raymond provided the impetus for many transsexuals to begin theorizing their own lives, and asking whether they could ever claim the name of "feminist." Her work still creates misunderstanding, exclusion and prejudice, and "womyn-born-womyn" policies based on her ideas still dominate many women's events and services, from music festivals to discussion groups to rape crisis centers. Raymond articulated the fear of men that many women justifiably have, but she could be said to have unfortunately and misguidedly targeted a group of people who face even more inequalities than nontransgender women. With the republication of *Transsexual Empire* in 1994 with a new introduction, Raymond made it clear that her views had not changed in light of many years of critique.

Transsexualism is multifaceted. From all that has been said thus far, it is clear that it raises many of the most complex questions feminism is asking about the origins and manifestations of sexism and sex-role stereotyping.* While regarded by many as an obscure issue that affects a relatively minute proportion of the population, transsexualism poses very important feminist questions. Transsexually constructed lesbian-feminists show yet another face of patriarchy. As the male-to-constructed-female transsexual exhibits the attempt to possess women in a bodily sense while acting out the images into which men have molded women, the male-to-constructed-female who claims to be a lesbian-feminist attempts to possess women at a deeper level, this time under the guise of challenging rather than conforming to the role and behavior of stereotyped femininity. As patriarchy is neither monolithic nor one-dimensional, neither is transsexualism.

All men and male-defined realities are not blatantly macho or masculinist. Many indeed are gentle, nurturing, feeling, and sensitive, which, of course, have been the more positive qualities that are associated with stereotypical femininity. In the same way that the so-called androgynous man assumes for himself the role of *femininity,* the transsexually constructed lesbian-feminist assumes for himself the role and behavior of *feminist.* The androgynous man and the transsexually constructed lesbian-feminist deceive women in much the same way, for they lure women into believing that they are truly one of us—this time not only one in behavior but one in spirit and conviction.

CONTRADICTIONS OR CONFIRMATIONS?

It is not accidental that most male-to-constructed-female transsexuals who claim to be feminists also claim to be lesbian-feminists. In fact, I don't know of any transsexually constructed feminists who do not also claim to be lesbians. It is this combination that is extremely important. Lesbian-feminists have spent a great deal of energy in attempting to communicate that the self-definition of lesbian, informed by feminism, is much more than just a sexual choice. It is a total perspective on life in a patriarchal society representing a primal commitment to women on all levels of existence and challenging the bulwark of a sexist society—that is, heterosexism. Thus it is not a mere sexual alternative to men, which is characterized simply by sexually relating to women instead of men, but a way of being in the world that challenges the male possession of women at perhaps its most intimate and sensitive level. In assuming the identity of lesbian-feminist, then, doesn't the transsexual renounce patriarchal definitions of selfhood and choose to fight sexism on a most fundamental level?

First of all, the transsexually constructed lesbian-feminist may have renounced femininity but not masculinity and masculinist behavior (despite deceptive appearances). If, as I have noted earlier,

---

* For a long time, I have been very hesitant about devoting a chapter of this book to what I call the "transsexually constructed lesbian-feminist." In the order this book was written, it was actually the last chapter I wrote. The recent debate and divisiveness that the transsexually constructed lesbian-feminist has produced within feminist circles has convinced me that, while transsexually constructed lesbian-feminists may be a small percentage of transsexuals, the issue needs an in-depth discussion among feminists.

I write this chapter with the full realization that feminists look at the issue of the transsexually constructed lesbian-feminist from the vantage point of a small community in which transsexuals have been able to be very visible—not because there are that many of them, but because they immediately have center stage. Thus focusing attention on this particular aspect of the transsexual issue may only serve to inflate the issue and their presence all the more. It may also distract attention from the more central questions that transsexualism raises and the power of the medical empire that creates transsexualism to begin with.

Because the oral and written debate concerning the transsexually constructed lesbian-feminist seems to be increasing out of proportion to their actual numbers, I think that feminists ought to consider seriously the amount of energy and space we wish to give to this discussion. However, if any space should be devoted to this issue, it is in a book that purports to be a feminist analysis of transsexualism. Furthermore, most of the commentary thus far has been limited to letters to the editor and editorial comments in feminist papers, as well as a few scattered articles in various journals. Because of limited space, these analyses are necessarily restricted. I would like, therefore, to provide an extensive and intensive analysis of the issue and to address the deeply mythic dimensions that the transsexually constructed lesbian-feminist represents.

femininity and masculinity are different sides of the same coin, thus making it quite understandable how one could flip from one to the other, then it is important to understand that the transsexually constructed lesbian-feminist, while not exhibiting a feminine identity and role, still exhibits its obverse side—stereotypical masculinity. Thus the assumption that he has renounced patriarchal definitions of selfhood is dubious.

Masculine behavior is notably obtrusive. It is significant that transsexually constructed lesbian-feminists have inserted themselves into the positions of importance and/or performance in the feminist community. The controversy in the summer of 1977 surrounding Sandy Stone, the transsexual sound engineer for Olivia Records, an "all-women" recording company, illustrates this well. Stone is not only crucial to the Olivia enterprise but plays a very dominant role there.[1] The national reputation and visibility he achieved in the aftermath of the Olivia controversy is comparable, in feminist circles, to that attained by Renee Richards in the wake of the Tennis Week Open. This only serves to enhance his previously dominant role and to divide women, as men frequently do, when they make their presence necessary and vital to women. Having produced such divisiveness, one would think that if Stone's commitment to and identification with women were genuinely woman-centered, he would have removed himself from Olivia and assumed some responsibility for the divisiveness. In Boston, a transsexual named Christy Barsky has worked himself into a similar dominant position, this time coaching a women's softball team, coordinating a conference on women and violence, staffing a women's center, and performing musically at various all-women places. Thus, like Stone, he exhibits a high degree of visibility and also divides women, in the name of lesbian-feminism.

Pat Hynes has suggested that there is only an apparent similarity between a strong lesbian, woman-identified self and a transsexual who fashions himself in a lesbian-feminist image.[2] With the latter, his masculinity comes through, although it may not be recognized as such. Hynes especially points to the body language of transsexuals where she notes *subtle but perceptible* differences between, for example, the way lesbians interact with other women and the way transsexuals interact with women. One specific example of this is the way a transsexual walked into a women's restaurant with his arms around two women, one on each side, with the possessive encompassing that is characteristically masculine.

Mary Daly in explaining *why* this difference is perceptible points out that the transsexually constructed lesbian-feminist is able to deceptively act out the part of lesbian-feminist *because* he is a man with a man's history; that is, he is free of many of the residues of self-centered, self-depreciation, and self-contradiction that attend the history of women who are born with female bodies all of which is communicated both subtly and not so supply in gestures, body language, and the like.[3] Thus it is precisely *because* the transsexually constructed lesbian-feminist is a man, and *not* a woman encumbered by the scars of patriarchy that are unique to a woman's personal and social history that he can play our parts so convincingly and apparently better than we can play them ourselves. However, in the final analysis, he can only *play the part*, although the part may at times seem as, or more, plausible than the real woman (as is also the case with the male-to-constructed-female transsexual who appears more feminine than most feminine women).

What is also typically masculine in the case of the transsexually constructed lesbian-feminist is the appropriation of women's minds, convictions of feminism, and sexuality. One of the definitions of *male*, as related in Webster's, is "designed for fitting into a corresponding hollow part." This, of course, means much more than the literal signification of heterosexual intercourse. It can be taken to mean that men have been very adept at penetrating all of women's "hollow" spaces, at filling up the gaps, and of sliding into the interstices. Obviously, women who are in the process of moving out of patriarchal institutions, consciousness, and modes of living are very vulnerable and have gaps. I would imagine that it would be difficult, for example, for Olivia Records to find a female sound engineer and that such a person would be absolutely necessary to the survival of Olivia. But it would have been far more honest if Olivia had acknowledged the maleness of Sandy Stone and perhaps the necessity, at the time to employ a man in this role. As one woman wrote of Sandy Stone and the Olivia controversy: "I feel raped when Olivia passes off Sandy, a transsexual, as a real woman. After all his male privilege, is he going to cash in…lesbian feminist culture too?"[4]

Rape, of course, is a masculinist violation of bodily integrity. All transsexuals rape women's bodies by reducing the real female form to an artifact, appropriating this body for themselves. However, the transsexually constructed lesbian-feminist violates women's sexuality and spirit, as well. Rape, although it is usually done by force, can also be accomplished by deception. It is significant that in the case of the transsexually constructed lesbian-feminist, often he is able to gain entrance and a dominant position in women's spaces because the women involved do not know he is a transsexual and he just does not happen to mention it.

The question of deception must also be raised in the context of how transsexuals who claim to be lesbian-feminists obtained surgery in the first place. Since all transsexuals have to "pass" as feminine in order to qualify for surgery, so-called lesbian-feminist transsexuals either had to lie to the therapists and doctors, or they had a conversion experience after surgery.[5] I am highly dubious of such conversions, and the other alternative, deception, raises serious problems, of course.

Deception reaches a tragic point for all concerned if transsexuals become lesbian-feminists because they regret what they have done and cannot back off from the effects of irreversible surgery (for example, castration). Thus they revert to masculinity (but not male body appearance) by becoming the man within the woman, and more, within the women's community, getting back their maleness in a most insidious way by seducing the spirits and the sexuality of women who do not relate to men.

Because transsexuals have lost their physical "members" does not mean that they have lost their ability to penetrate women—women's mind, women's space, women's sexuality. Transsexuals merely cut off the most obvious means of invading women so that they *seem* noninvasive. However, as Mary Daly has remarked, in the case of the transsexually constructed lesbian-feminists their whole presence becomes a "member" invading women's presence and dividing us once more from each other.[6]

Furthermore, the deceptiveness of men without "members," that is, castrated men or eunuchs has historical precedent. There is a long tradition of eunuchs who were used by rulers, heads of state, and magistrates as *keepers of women*. Eunuchs were supervisors of the harem in Islam and wardens of women's apartments in many royal households. In fact, the world *eunuch*, from the Greek *eunouchos*, literally means "keeper of the bed." Eunuchs were men that other more powerful men used to keep their women in place. By fulfilling this…eunuchs also succeeded in winning the confidence of the ruler and securing important and influential positions.

Moreover, the word *eunuch* is also related to the word *scheme*. (Eunuchs schemed to obtain political power.) In Mesopotamia, many eunuchs became royal officers and managers of palaces, and "others emerge on the pages of history as important and often virile figures."[7] Some were famous warriors and statesmen, as well as scholars. One finds eunuchs associated with temples dedicated to the goddesses from at least 2000 B.C. until well into the Roman period.[8] In fact the earliest mention of eunuchs is in connection with the Minoan civilization of Crete, which was a transitional period from an earlier gynocentric society. It thus appears that eunuchs, to some extent, always attached themselves to women's spaces and, most frequently, were used to supervise women's freedom of movement and to harness women's self-centeredness and self-government. "It is stated that entree in every political circle was possible for eunuchs even if occurred to other men."[9]

Will the acceptance of transsexually constructed lesbian-feminists who have lost only their outward appendages of physical masculinity lead to the containment and control of lesbian-feminists? Will every lesbian-feminist space become a harem? Like eunuchs, transsexuals have gained prominent and dominant access to feminist political circles "barred to other men."[10] Just because transsexually constructed lesbian-feminists are not only castrated men, but have also acquired artifacts of a woman's body and spirit, does not mean that they are un-men, and that they cannot be used as "keepers" of woman-identified women when the "real men," the "rulers of patriarchy," decide that the women's movement (used here as both noun and verb) should be controlled and contained. In this way, they too can rise in the Kingdoms of the Fathers. The political implications of historical eunuchism and its potential for female control should not be lost upon woman-identified women.

MYTHIC DIMENSIONS OF TRANSSEXUALISM

Transsexuals are living and acting out a very ancient myth, that of single parenthood by the father. This myth was prevalent in many religious traditions, including the Jewish, Greek, and Christian. Eve was born of Adam; Dionysus and Athena were born of Zeus; and Jesus was generated by God the Father in his godly birth. (Mary was a mere receptacle used to conform Jesus to earthly birth standards.) When this myth is put into the context of transsexualism, the deeper dimensions of how transsexually constructed lesbian-feminists reinforce patriarchy can be perceived.

Simone de Beauvoir has remarked that "if [woman] did not exist, men would have invented her. They did invent her. But she exists also apart from their inventiveness."[11] Men, of course, invented the feminine, and in this sense it could be said that all women who conform to this invention are transsexuals, fashioned according to man's image. Lesbian-feminists exist apart from man's inventiveness, and the political and personal ideals of lesbian-feminism have constituted a complete rebellion against the man-made invention of woman, and a context in which women begin to create ourselves in our own image. Thus the transsexual who claims to be a lesbian-feminist *seems* to be the man who creates himself in *woman's* image. This, however, is deceptive, for note that he is still created in *man's* image since he is essentially a child of the Father (in this case, the medical fathers), renouncing his mothered birth.

Mary Daly has written at length in her most recent work, *Gyn/Ecology: The Metaethics of Medical Feminism,* about the myth of Dionysus.[12] She also recites various versions of the myth along with some scholarly commentaries on it. These can shed much light on the mythic implications of the transsexually constructed lesbian-feminist. First of all, Philip Slater points out the very interesting fact that, "Instead of seeking distance from mastery over the mother, the Dionysian position incorporates her."[13] In the most popular version of the myth, Semele the mother of Dionysus while pregnant with him, is struck by Zeus with a thunderbolt and is thus consumed. Hermes saves the six-month fetal Dionysus, sews him upon Zeus's thigh, and after three more months, Zeus "birthed him. Thus Zeus exterminates the woman and bears his own son, and we have single-parent fatherhood (read mother-hood). Moreover, Jane Harrison has pointed out that "the word Dionysus means not 'son of Zeus' but rather Zeus Young Man, i.e., Zeus in his young form."[14] Thus Dionysus is his own father (read mother) and births himself into existence.

Whether we are talking about being born of the father, or the self (son), which in the myth are one and the same person (as in the Christian trinity), we are still talking about male mothering. At this level of analysis, it might seem that what men really envy is women's biological ability to procreate. Transsexuals illustrate the way in which men do this, by acquiring the artifacts of female biology. Even though they cannot give birth they acquire the organs that are representative of this female power. However, it is the transsexually constructed lesbian-feminist who illustrates that much more is desired than female biology—that much more is at stake than literal womb envy. He shows that female biology, whether exercised in giving birth or simply by virtue of its existence, is representative of female creativity on a profound mythic level. Thus the creative power that is associated with female biology is not envied primarily because it is able to give birth physically but because it is multidimensional, bearing culture, harmony, and true inventiveness.[15]

The transsexually constructed lesbian-feminist feeds off woman's true energy source, i.e., her woman-identified self. It is he who recognizes that if female spirit, mind, creativity, and sexuality exist anywhere in a powerful way, it is here, among lesbian-feminists. I am not saying that the lesbian-feminist is the only self- and woman-identified woman. What I mean to express is that lesbianism-feminism signals a *total* giving of women's energy to women, and that it is this total woman-identified energy that the transsexual who claims to be a lesbian-feminist wants for himself. It is understandable that if men want to become women to obtain female creativity, then they will also want to assimilate those women who have withdrawn their energies from men at the most intimate and emotional levels.

This, of course, is not the usual way in which lesbian living has been harnessed. Most often, lesbian existence is simply not acknowledged, as evidenced in the laws against homosexuality, which legislate against male homosexuals, but not lesbians. It has been simply assumed that all women relate to men, and that women need men to survive. Furthermore, the mere labeling of a woman as "lesbian" has been enough to keep lesbian living harnessed or, at best, in the closet. "Lesbian is the word, the label, the condition that holds women in line. When a woman hears this word tossed her way, she knows that she...has crossed the terrible *boundary* of her sex role."[16] (Italics mine.)

Whereas the lesbian-feminist *crosses* the boundary of her patriarchally imposed sex role, the transsexually constructed lesbian-feminist is a *boundary violator*. This violation is also profoundly mythic, for as Norman O. Brown writes of Dionysus, he as the "mad god who breaks down boundaries."[17] Thus exhibiting qualities that are usually associated with femininity, he appeared to be the opposite of the masculine Apollo.

> While the super-masculine Apollo overtly oppresses/destroys with his contrived boundaries/hierarchies/rules/roles, the feminine Dionysus blurs the senses, seduces, confuses his victims—drugging them into complicity, offering them his "heart" as a love potion that poisons.[18]

It is, however, the *feminist* Dionysus who appears in the transsexually constructed lesbian-feminist. But he "blurs the senses, seduces, and confuses" in much the same way as the *feminine* Dionysus. He not only violates the boundaries of women's bodies but of our mind and spirits. What is more tragic, however, is that he unable to make women break down our boundaries of self-definition. Elizabeth Rose in a letter in response to my article in *Chrysalis*, "Transsexualism: The Ultimate Homage to Sex-Role Power," illustrates well this tendency of feminists to be seduced by Dionysian boundary violation.

> Raymond's article encourages us to set our "bottom line" (about whom we will allow the privilege of self-definition.
>
> I am upset that a magazine "of women's culture"...is basically encouraging the elitist/separatist attitude that self-definition [is]...subject to the scrutiny and judgments of those who, in the name of political purity, claim the power to define who is allowed entry into the feminist community...and, now, who is or is not female.[19]

Rose would encourage us to set no boundaries by employing the analogy of how boundaries have been used oppressively against lesbians in the past/present. "There are so many painful parallels between how the world has treated strong women and lesbians and how Raymond and others categorize and discount transsexuals."[20] But the analogy is false. The boundaries that have been and are used against lesbians are the boundaries of the Fathers:

The contrived Apollonian boundaries—such as the false divisions of "fields" of knowledge and the splits between "mind" and "heart." But in this process we do not become swallowed upon male-centered (Dionysian) confusion. Hags find and define our own boundaries, our own definitions. Radical feminist living "on the boundary" means this moving, Self-centering boundary definition. As we move we mark out our own territory.[21]

Rose and other women who have been confused/seduced by Dionysian transsexually constructed lesbian-feminist boundary violation would have us believe that all boundaries are oppressive. Yet if feminists cannot agree on the boundaries of what constitutes femaleness, then what can we hope to agree on? The Dionysian "Final Solution," as Daly points out, produces confusion in women—"inability to distinguish the female Self and her process from the male-made masquerade."[22] It encourages the leveling of genuine boundaries of self-preservation and self-centering.

THE SEDUCTION OF LESBIAN-FEMINISTS

It is not hard to understand why transsexuals want to become lesbian-feminists. They indeed have discovered where strong female energy exists and want to capture it. It is more difficult to understand why so many feminists are so ready to accept men—in this case, castrated men—into their most intimate circles. Certainly Dionysian confusion about the erasure of all boundaries is one reason that appeals to the liberal mind and masquerades as "sympathy for all oppressed groups." Women who believe this, however, fail to see that such liberalism is repressive, and that it can only favor and fortify the possession of women by men. These women also fail to recognize that accepting transsexuals into the feminist community is only another rather unique variation on the age-old theme of women nurturing men, providing them with a safe haven, and finally giving them our best energies.

The question arises: are women who accept transsexuals as lesbian-feminists expressing gratitude on some level to those men who are finally willing to join women and pay for their male privilege with their balls? Gratitude is a quality exhibited by all oppressed groups when they think that some in the class of oppressors have finally relinquished their benefits to join them. But, of course, it is doubtful that transsexuals actually give up their male privilege. As one woman put it: "A man who decides to call himself a woman is not giving up his privilege. He is simply using it in a more insidious way."[23] Furthermore, a man who decides to call himself a lesbian-feminist is getting a lot. The transsexually constructed lesbian-feminist is the man who indeed gets to be "the man" in an exclusive women's club to which he would have otherwise no access.

Women who think that these men are giving up male privilege seem to be naive about the sophisticated ways in which it is possible for men to co-opt women's energy, time, space, and sexuality. Transsexually constructed lesbian-feminists may be the first men to realize that "if you can't fight them, join them." In a short story entitled "The Women's Restaurant," by T. C. Boyle, which appeared recently in *Penthouse,* this point is well made.

The story begins by setting the scene in and around Grace & Rubie's Restaurant and is written from the point of view of the voyeuristic narrator. "It is women's restaurant. Men are not permitted.... What goes on there, precisely, no man knows. I am a man. I am burning to find out."[24] The narrator then proceeds to caricature Grace and Rubie as butch and femme, as well as to relate his several attempts to gain entrance. After two unsuccessful endeavors, he goes to a department store, buys a pink polyester pantsuit, a bra, pantyhose, and cosmetics with which he makes himself up to pass as a woman. He gains entrance and is able to experience what he has been missing.

> Here I was, embosomed in the very nave, the very omphalos of furtive femininity—a prize patron of the women's restaurant, a member, privy to its innermost secrets....There they were—women—chewing, drinking, digesting, chatting, giggling, crossing, and uncrossing their legs. Shoes off, feet up. Smoking cigarettes, flashing silverware, tapping time to the music. Women among women. I bathed in their soft chatter, birdsong, the laughter like falling coils of hair. I lit a cigarette and grinned. No more fairybook-hero thoughts of rescuing Rubie—oh no, this was paradise.[25]

Having drunk six tequila sunrises and a carafe of dinner wine, the male intruder/narrator finds it necessary to relieve himself, but forgets to sit down when he urinates in the rest room, at which point he is discovered by Grace. The story ends with his savoring of the triumph of temporary infiltration and a plan for permanent invasion.

> I have penetrated the women's restaurant, yes, but in actuality it was little more than a rape....I am not satisfied. The obsession grows in me, pregnant, swelling, insatiable with the first taste of fulfillment. Before I am through, I will drink it to satiety. I have plans....The next time I walk through those curtained doors at Grace & Rubie's there will be no dissimulation....There are surgeons who can assure it.[26]

That this story appeared in *Penthouse* is no surprise. It is obvious that its editors thought it would be of interest to their readers, whether budding or closet transsexuals. In spite of the ludicrous details and caricatures, one can see that the narrator was primarily attracted to the woman-centeredness of the restaurant. "Women among women...this was paradise." Such an attitude is representative of the transsexually constructed lesbian-feminist who indeed gets his "paradise," because there *were* surgeons who could "assure it." Ironically, the would-be transsexual narrator of the story says that the next time he walks through the doors, "there will be no dissimulation." Transsexualism, however, is dissimulation. As I have shown previously, to not acknowledge the fact that one is a transsexual in a women's space is indeed deception. Finally, "penetrating" the women's restaurant was "little more than a rape." Little more than a rape, indeed! What "little more" is there to such an act, unless it is the total rape of our feminist identities, minds, and convictions? The transsexually constructed lesbian-feminist, having castrated himself, turns his whole body and behavior into a phallus that can rape in many ways, all the time. In this sense, he performs *total* rape, while also functioning *totally* against women's will to lesbian-feminism.

We have seen three reasons why lesbian-feminists are seduced into accepting transsexuals: liberalism, gratitude, and naiveté. There is yet another reason—one that can be perhaps best described as the *last remnants of male identification*. This is a complex phenomenon, which has various ingredients.

On the one hand, there is fear of the label "man-hater." Are women who are so accepting of the transsexually constructed lesbian-feminist trying to prove to themselves that a lesbian-feminist (she who has been called the ultimate man-hater) is really not a man-hater after all? As Adrienne Rich has pointed out, one way of avoiding that feared label, and of allowing one's self to accept men, is to accept those men who have given up the supposed ultimate possession of manhood in a patriarchal society by self-castration.[27]

On the other hand, there is a second component to this "last remnant of male identification"—i.e., *attraction to masculine presence*. As Pat Hynes has suggested, there is an *apparent* similarity between a strong woman-identified self and a transsexual who fashions himself in a lesbian image. Because there is an *apparent* similarity, some lesbian-feminists may allow themselves to express the residues of their (buried) attraction to men or to masculine presence, while pretending to themselves that transsexually constructed lesbian-feminists are really women. This allows women to do two things: to express that attraction, yet also to decide themselves.

SELF DEFINITION

One of the most constraining questions that transsexuals, and, in particular, transsexually constructed lesbian-feminists, pose is the question of self-definition—who is a woman, who is a lesbian-feminist? But, of course, *they* pose the question on their terms, and *we* are faced with answering it. Men have always made such questions of major concern, and this question, in true phallic fashion, is thrust upon us. How many women students writing on such a feeble feminist topic as "Should Women Be Truck Drivers, Engineers, Steam Shovel Operators?" and the like, have had their male professor scribble in the margins: "But what are the real differences between men and women?" Men, of course, have defined the supposed differences that have kept women out of such jobs and professions, and feminists have spent much energy demonstrating how these differences, if indeed they do exist, are primarily the result of socialization. Yet there are differences, and some feminists have come to realize that those differences are important whether they spring from socialization, from biology, or from the total history of existing as a woman in a patriarchal society. The point is, however, that the origin of these differences is probably not the important question, and we shall perhaps never know the total answer to it. Yet we are forced back into trying to answer it again and again.*

Transsexuals, and transsexually constructed lesbian-feminists, drag us back to answering such old questions by asking them in a new way. And thus feminists debate and divide because we keep focusing on patriarchal questions of who is a woman and who is a lesbian-feminist. It is important for us to realize that these may well be non-questions and that the only answer we can give to them is that we know who *we* are. We know that we are women who are born with female chromosomes and anatomy, and that whether or not we were socialized to be so-called normal women, patriarchy has treated and will treat us like women. Transsexuals have not had this same history. No man can have the history of being born and located in this culture as a woman. He can have the history of *wishing* to be a woman and of *acting* like a woman, but this gender experience is that of a transsexual, not of a woman. Surgery may confer the artifacts of outward and inward female organs but it cannot confer the history of being born a woman in this society.

What of persons born with ambiguous sex organs or chromosomal anomalies that place them in a biologically intersexual situation? It must be noted that practically all of them are altered shortly after birth to become anatomically male or female and are reared in accordance with the societal gender identity and role that accompanies their bodies. Persons whose sexual ambiguity is discovered later are altered in the direction of what their gender rearing has been (masculine or feminine) up to that point. Thus those who are altered shortly after birth have the history of being practically born as male or female and those who are altered later in life have their body surgically conformed to their history. When and if they do undergo surgical change, they do not become the opposite sex after a long history of functioning and being treated differently.

Although popular literature on transsexualism implies that Nature has made mistakes with trans-sexuals, it is really society that has made the mistake by producing conditions that create the trans-sexual body/mind split. While intersexed people are born with chromosomal or hormonal anomalies, which can be linked up with certain biological malfunctions, transsexualism is not of this order. The language of "Nature makes mistakes" only serves to confuse and distort the issue, taking the focus off the social system, which is actively oppressive. It succeeds in blaming an amorphous "Nature" that is made to seem oppressive and is conveniently amenable to direct control/manipulation by the instruments of hormones and surgery.

---

* A parallel is the abortion issue, which can also be noted in this context. The key question, asked by men for centuries, is "when does life begin?" This question is posed in men's terms and on their turf, and is essentially unanswerable. Women torture themselves trying to answer it and thus do not assert or even develop our own questions about abortion.

In speaking of the importance of history for self-definition, two questions must be asked. Should a person want to change his/her personal and social history and if so, *how* should one change that history in the most honest and integral way? In answer to the first question, anyone who has lived in a patriarchal society has to change personal and social history in order to be a self. History cannot be allowed to determine the boundaries, life, and location of the self. We should be change agents of our own history. Women who are feminists obviously wish to change parts of their history as women in this society; some men who are honestly dealing with feminist questions wish to change their history as men; and transsexuals wish to change their history of *wanting* to be women. In stressing the importance of female history for female self-definition, I am not advocating a static view of such history.

What is more important, however, is *how* one changes personal history in the most honest and integral way, if one wants to break down sex-role oppression. Should nontranssexual men who wish to fight sexism take on the identity of women and/or lesbian-feminists while keeping their male anatomy intact? Why should castrated men take on these identities and self-definitions and be applauded for doing so? To what extent would concerned blacks accept whites who had undergone medicalized changes in skin color and, in the process, claimed that they had not only a black body but a black soul?

Can a transsexual assume the self-definition of lesbian-feminist just because he wants to, or does this particular self-definition proceed from certain conditions endemic to female biology and history? Women take on the self-definition of feminist and/or lesbian because that definition truly proceeds from not only the chromosomal fact of being born XX, but also from the whole history of what being born with those chromosomes means in this society. Transsexuals would be more honest if they dealt with their specific form of gender agony that inclines them to want a transsexual operation. This gender agony proceeds from the chromosomal fact of being born XY and *wishing* that one were born XX, and from the particular life history that produced such distress. The place to deal with that problem, however, is not the women's community. The place to confront and solve it is among transsexuals themselves.

One should be able to make choices about who one wants to be. But should one be able to make *any* choice? Should a white person attempt to become black, for example? The question is a moral one, which asks basically about the rightness of the choice, not the possibility of it. Should persons be able to make choices that disguise certain facets of our existence from others who have a right to know—choices that feed off others' energies, and reinforce oppression?

Jill Johnston has commented that, "many women are dedicated to working for the 'reconstructed man.'"[28] This usually means women gently or strongly prodding their significant men into androgynous behavior and action. Women who accept transsexually constructed lesbian-feminists say that these men are truly "reconstructed" in the most basic sense that women could hope for—i.e., they have paid with their balls to fight against sexism. Ultimately, however, the "reconstructed man" becomes the "reconstructed woman" who obviously considers himself equal to and a peer of genetic women in terms of his "womanhood." One transsexual openly expressed that he felt male-to-constructed-female transsexuals *surpassed* genetic women.

> Genetic women cannot possess the very special courage, brilliance, sensitivity and compassion—and overview—that derives from the transsexual experience. Free from the chains of menstruation and child-bearing, transsexual women are obviously far superior to Gennys in many ways.
>
> Genetic women are becoming quite obsolete, which is obvious, and the future belongs to transsexual women. We know this, and perhaps some of you suspect it. All you have left is your "ability" to bear children, and in a world which will groan to feed 6 billion by the year 2000, that's a negative asset.[29]

Ultimately, women must ask if transsexually constructed lesbian-feminists are our peers. Are they equal to us? Questions of equality often center on proportional equality, such as "equal pay for equal work," or "equal rights to health care." I do not mean equal in this sense. Rather I use equality to mean: "like in quality, nature, or status" and "capable of meeting the requirements of a situation or a task." In these senses transsexuals are not equal to women and are not our peers. They are neither equal in "quality, nature of status" nor are they "capable of meeting the requirements of the situation" of women who have spent their whole lives as women.

Jill Johnston has written of lesbian-feminism: "The essence of the new political definition is peer grouping. Women and men are not peers and many people seriously doubt whether we ever were or if we ever could be."[30] Transsexuals are not our peers, by virtue of their history.

> It is perhaps our mistrust of the man as the biological aggressor which keeps bringing us back to the political necessity of power by peer grouping. Although we are still virtually powerless it is only by constantly adhering to this difficult principle of the power inherent in natural peers (men after all have demonstrated the success of this principle very well) that women will eventually achieve an autonomous existence.[31]

The transsexual does not display the usual phallic aggression. Instead he violates women's bodies by taking on the artifactual female organs for himself. The transsexually constructed lesbian-feminist becomes a psychological and social aggressor as well.

Transsexually constructed lesbian-feminists challenge women's preserves of autonomous existence. Their existence within the women's community basically attests to the ethic that women should not live without men—or without the "reconstructed man." How feminists assess and meet this challenge will affect the future of our genuine movement, self-definition, and power of be-ing.

In the final analysis, transsexually constructed lesbian-feminists are in the same tradition as the man-made, made-up "lesbians" of the *Playboy* centerfolds. Every so often, *Playboy* and similar magazines feature a "Sappho Pictorial."[32] Recently, male photographers have entered the book market by portraying pseudolesbians in all sorts of positions, clothing, and contexts that could only be fantasized by a male mind.[33] In short, the manner in which women are depicted in these photographs mimics the poses of men pawing women. Men produce "lesbian" love the way they want it to be and according to their own canons of what they think it should be.

Transsexually constructed lesbian-feminists are in this tradition of pseudolesbian propaganda. Both the *Playboy* pseudolesbian and the transsexual pseudolesbian spread the "correct" (read male-defined) image of the lesbian, which in turn filters into public consciousness through the mass media as truth. By thus mutilating the true self-definition of the lesbian, men mold her image/reality according to their own. As Lisa Buck has commented, transsexualism is truly "their word made flesh!"[34]

Transsexually constructed lesbian-feminists attempt to function as image-makers of the lesbian-feminist—not only for the public-at-large, but also for the women's community. Their masquerade of the lesbian filters into women's consciousness through the feminist media as "the real thing." The ultimate tragedy of such a parody is that the reality and self-definition of lesbian-feminist becomes mutilated in women themselves. Lesbian-feminists who accept transsexually constructed lesbian-feminists as other selves are mutilating their own reality.

The various "breeds" of women that medical science can create are endless. There are the women who are hormonally hooked on continuous doses of estrogen replacement therapy. ERT supposedly will secure for them a new life of "eternal femininity."[35] There are the hysterectomized women, purified of their "potentially lethal" organs for "prophylactic" purposes.[36] Finally, there is the "she-male"—the male-to-constructed-female transsexual. And the offshoot of this "breed" is the transsexually constructed lesbian-feminist.

What all of these events point to is the particularly instrumental role that medicine has played in the control of deviant or potentially deviant women. "The Transsexual Empire" is ultimately a medical empire, based on a patriarchal medical model. This medical model has provided a "sacred canopy" of legitimations for transsexual treatment and surgery. In the name of therapy, it has medicalized moral and social questions of sex-role oppression, thereby erasing their deepest meaning.

NOTES

1. In June/July of 1977, twenty-two feminist musicians, sound technicians, radio women, producers, and managers sent an open letter to Olivia Records via *Sister*, a West Coast feminist newspaper. The letter focused on the employment of Sandy Stone, a male-to-constructed-female transsexual, as Olivia's recording engineer and sound technician. The signers protested Stone's presence at Olivia and the fact that Olivia did not inform women that Stone was a postoperative transsexual. They criticized Stone's participation in women-only events and accused him of taking work away from the "few competent women sound technicians in the Bay Area…whose opportunities are extremely limited." They noted that Stone's male privilege gave him access to his skills, and that he has never had to suffer the oppression that women face every day. The letter concluded by stating that "it is not our intention to discredit or trash Olivia," and requested that they publish a statement in response.

    In the same issue of *Sister*, Olivia replied that: 1. Surgery alone does not make a transsexual a woman. "This too-publicized step is merely the confirmation of a process that has already gone to near completion by that time." 2. Aside from a few well-publicized transsexuals, a person does not gain privilege by becoming a transsexual. Because Stone gave up his male identity and lives as a "woman" and a "lesbian," he is faced with the same kinds of oppression that "other" women and lesbians face, along with the added ostracism that results from being a transsexual. 3. A person's history is important but most significant is what that person's actions are now. 4. Day-to-day interaction with Sandy Stone has convinced the Olivia women that Sandy is a "woman we can relate to with comfort and trust." 5. Olivia did not indicate Stone's transsexual status, because they were afraid he would be "objectified." "We see transsexualism as a state of transition, and we feel that to continue to define a person primarily by that condition is to stigmatize her at the expense of her growth process as a woman." 6. Stone has trained women in technical skills and will build Olivia's recording studio where many women will apprentice. He is also writing a how-to book for women explaining the recording process. Thus Stone does not take employment away from women but provides it and may be "perhaps even the Goddess-sent engineering wizard we had so long sought."

2. Author's conversation with Pat Hynes, Cambridge, Mass., January 1978.

3. Author's conversation with Mary Daly, Boston, Mass., February 1978.

4. Rosemary Anderson, Letter entitled "Transsexual Feminism?" *Sister*, August–September 1977, p. 7.

5. Recently, questions have been raised by transsexuals who claim to be lesbian-feminists and by some professionals in gender identity clinics about clinic requirements of "passing" and about the stereotypical behavior of transsexuals. "We urge professionals *not* to assume or expect that all transsexuals will be heterosexually oriented or politically conservative and not to judge (for example) lesbianism in a male-to-female transsexual as invalid while accepting it in a genetic woman. Biological women and male-to-female transsexuals present a similarly vast range of sexual orientation and life-style choices; different choices are valid for different people…. Positively, we recommend a setting where the client is not forced to avow rigid self-definitions, but is permitted and even encouraged to find her/his own answers to the difficult and complex questions of sexuality and identity that confront us all." Deborah Heller Feinbloom *et al.*, "Lesbian/Feminist Orientation Among Male-to-Female Transsexuals," *Journal of Homosexuality*, 2 (Fall 1976): 70–71.

    There are several criticisms that can be made of such a stance. First, nonstereotypical behavior is encouraged as one choice among "different choices [that] are valid for different people." Thus there is no commitment to eradicating stereotypical behavior but only to encouraging alternative behavior ("different strokes for different folks"). And thus there is no commitment to ultimately phasing out gender identity control over *various* styles of behavior. The authors' conclusions coincide with John Money's recommendations in *Sexual Signatures* for "flexible" stereotypes.

    Second, the unanswered question is why are such transsexuals and transsexual professionals still advocating surgery. Transsexual surgery would not be necessary if rigid self-definitions had not produced the phenomenon of a "female mind in a male body." This self-definition would make no sense in a society that did not accept that split. Therefore, to support behavior and orientation that is not stereotypical, yet to continue advocating transsexualism is contradictory.

    Such recommendations only make the issue of "passing" and stereotypical behavior more invisible. These authors *appear* to get beyond the stereotypes, but they are actually supporting "passing" behavior on a deeper level. In effect, they are now advocating that men "pass" as lesbian-feminists, thus making a "role" out of lesbian-feminism that can be taken on by anyone. Ultimately, this brings lesbian-feminism within the confines of the gender identity clinics, where it can be observed, studied, *and controlled*–first in transsexuals, and then perhaps in lesbian-feminists. With the acceptance of transsexuals as lesbian-feminists by the gender identity clinics, the "passing" requirements only become modified.

The transsexual "passes" what are the current (seemingly avant-garde) requirements of the gender identity clinics. In order to become transsexed, however, his "passing" behavior must still be "baptized" as legitimately female.

It is significant that these recommendations are coming from male-to-constructed-female transsexuals. Here is a clear admission that lesbian-feminism is perceived as important and that more is at stake in transsexual surgery than obtaining the body and the traditional role of a woman. There is a recognition here that female power/energy/creativity is at the heart of the matter. Why are there no female-to-constructed-male transsexuals, for example, who are seeking to "pass" as homosexual men?

6.   Author's conversation with Mary Daly, Boston, Mass., February 1978.
7.   Robert Spencer, "The Cultural Aspects of Eunuchism," *CIBA Symposia*, 8 (1946): 407.
8.   *Ibid.*, p. 408.
9.   *Ibid.*, p. 413.
10. Another parallel is that some royal eunuchs also wore women's clothing, and their physical characteristics, especially as represented on Assyrian monuments, resembled those of women. Eunuch priests of goddess temples were said to wear women's garb and perform women's tasks. See John L. McKenzie, "Eunuch," *Dictionary of the Bible* (Milwaukee: The Bruce Publishing Company, 1965), 252.
11. Simone de Beauvoir, *The Second Sex* (New York: Bantam Books, 1953), p. 174.
12. See Mary Daly, *Gyn/Ecology: The Metaethics of Radical Feminism* (Boston: Beacon Press, 1978), pp. 66–67.
13. Philip Slater, *The Glory of Hera: Greek Mythology and the Greek Family* (Boston: Beacon Press, 1968), p. 211.
14. Jane Harrison, *Mythology* (New York: Harcourt, Brace and World, 1963), p. 97.
15. See comments in Chapter I about transsexual desire for female creativity as represented in female biology.
16. Radicalesbians, "The Woman Identified Woman," in Anne Koedt, Ellen Levine, and Anita Rapone, eds., *Radical Feminism* (New York: Quadrangle/New York Times Book Co., 1973), p. 241.
17. Norman O. Brown, *Love's Body* (New York: Random House, 1966), p. 116.
18. Daly, *Gyn/Ecology*, pp. 67–68.
19. Elizabeth Rose, Letter to the Editors, *Chrysalis*, 5 (1978): 6.
20. *Idem.*
21. Daly, *Gyn/Ecology*, p. 67.
22. *Ibid.*
23. Judy Antonelli, "Open Letter to Olivia," *Sister,* August–September 1977), p. 6.
24. T. C. Boyle, "The Women's Restaurant," *Penthouse,* May 1977, p. 112.
25. *Ibid.*, p. 132.
26. *Ibid.*, p. 133.
27. Conversation with Adrienne Rich, Montague, Mass., May 1977.
28. Jill Johnston, *Lesbian Nation: The Feminist Solution* (New York: Simon & Schuster, 1973), p. 180.
29. Angela Douglas, Letter, *Sister,* August–September 1977, p. 7.
30. Johnston, *Lesbian Nation*, p. 278.
31. *Ibid.*, p. 279.
32. See, for example, photographer J. Frederick Smith's "portfolio of stunning portraits inspired by ancient Greek poems on loving women," in *Playboy,* October 1975, pp. 126–35.
33. One photographer who is particularly obsessed with "capturing" women in pseudolesbian poses is David Hamilton. He is the creator of the following books of photography:
     Dreams of a Young Girl, text by Alain Robbe-Grillet (New York: William Morrow and Co., 1971).
     Sisters, text by Alain Robbe-Grillet (New York: William Morrow and Co., 1973). This book has an outrageous pictorial section entitled "Charms of the Harem."
     Hamilton's Movies–Bilitis (Zug, Switzerland: Swan Productions AG, 1977).
34. Lisa Buck (Unpublished notes on transsexualism, October 1977), p. 3.
35. An example of this literature is Robert Wilson's *Feminine Forever* (New York: M. Evans, 1966). This book sold 100,000 copies in its first year, as well as being excerpted in *Look* and *Vogue.*
36. See Deborah Larned, "The Greening of the Womb," *New Times*, December 12, 1974, pp. 35–39.

11

Divided Sisterhood

A Critical Review of Janice Raymond's *The Transsexual Empire*

CAROL RIDDELL

CAROL RIDDELL'S CRITIQUE OF JANICE RAYMOND'S *The Transsexual Empire*, published in pamphlet form within a year of the appearance of Raymond's book, is an important early expression of transgender feminism. It helps demonstrate to both transgender and nontransgender audiences that feminism, rather than being inescapably hostile to transgenderism, can support a broad range of positions.

Riddell's title, *Divided Sisterhood*, effectively turns on its head one of Raymond's central accusations—that male-to-female transsexuals "divide" feminist women with unproductive squabbles over the question of who is, and who is not, a woman—by suggesting that Raymond herself is guilty of creating this division by making an issue of transgender inclusion in lesbian, feminist, and women's groups.

Riddell faults Raymond for presenting a picture of transsexualism that is empirically false; as, for example, when Raymond contends that power-mad male doctors at Gender Identity Clinics are desperate to perform "sex change" surgery on zombie-like transsexuals who will be programmed to infiltrate women's culture. Riddell, citing her own experience, counters that most physicians at gender clinics are very uncomfortable with transsexual requests for surgery. It is in writing cogently about her own experiences, in her own voice, that Riddell makes her greatest contribution to the literature on transgenderism—she demonstrates, at a time when transsexualism was considered by most people to be both politically reactionary and emotionally disturbed, that a transsexual point of view can be both progressive and rational.

1. INTRODUCTION

I began hearing rumours of a book published in the United States attacking trans-sexuals. Oh, no, not another . . . A friend saw it in a bookstore in San Francisco; 'horrible', she said on the phone. Some feminists in this country started to talk of it, and extracts were published in the 'Revolutionary/Radical Feminist Newsletter.' I ordered a copy from the States. Better the devil you know. A brilliant and detailed critical review from the Feminist Review section of the *New Women's Times* came my way (1). At last the local Mersey-side Women's Paper gave me the book for review. Can I bear to touch it? But it is highly recommended—the cover and title page have eulogies from a well-known male sociologist. At the back are praises from intellectual feminists. Now I've read the book, and I think it is as my friend in America described. I feel, however, that the discrepancies between our views and those of the authorities need some explaining. The problem is not just the complete misconception of the causes of trans-sexualism that Ms. Raymond demonstrates, but of her whole method of approach to feminist analysis. This I believe has implications of concern to all feminists. In exposing such a method, it is difficult not to be tempted to score points against the book's many contradictions, or to descend into the mire of linguistic philosophizing with which Ms. Raymond is involved in chapter 6 and elsewhere. In the interests of communication, and because I think forms of expression themselves are influenced by a patriarchal system, I've tried to avoid the temptations as far as I can.

To begin with, it's useful to get some perspective on the problem of trans-sexualism in numerical terms. As a specific problem, it gets much more attention than it deserves, because of its very rarity. In the United States live some 205,000,000 people. Among them are perhaps 4,000 post-operative trans-sexual women and men (2), and perhaps as many more who want the operation but who haven't the money or the information to get it. That is, one trans-sexual for every 25,625 people who are not seeking sex 'change'. In Britain, there are 55,000,000 people, and a few hundred trans-sexuals. In the British women's movement, there seem to be 2 trans-sexuals, in the United States', maybe a dozen or so. It's important to remember this when considering Ms. Raymond's more fantastic scenarios, 'One hypothesis that is being tested in the trans-sexual laboratories is whether or not it is possible for men to diminish the number of women and/or to create a new 'breed' of females', scenarios that are not only the result of a mis-formulation of the problem, but reveal a state of paranoia about the situation with which I refuse to associate my own fears. Trans-sexuals are not a major social problem. We have some curiosity value to the media as freaks. This occasionally results in incredibly naive statements from trans-sexuals conned by publicity, which can be incredibly irritating to feminists, but trans-sexual women are not now, nor ever will be, a threat to the female sex's existence (3).

In the first section I have tried to outline, without comment, Ms.Raymond's main lines of argument, so readers who haven't read her book can have an idea of what I'm talking about, and so those who have can judge if I've understood it as they do. In the second, I've tried to show why she is wrong. In the third, I've sketched a few features of the trans-sexual *experience*, as I and other trans-sexuals I've known have lived it. This is to try to provide an antidote to Ms. Raymond's method, which denies not only any validity to the trans-sexual experience, but also to the experience of people who know and accept trans-sexuals for what we are. Finally, I've criticised the methods Ms. Raymond uses in a more general way, as representing a frightening and dangerous trend in feminism.

I know that in publishing this critique I make myself publicly visible. Ms. Raymond denies my existence as a woman, and believes that the aim of trans-sexual feminists is to seek publicity and, as agents of the patriarchy infiltrated into the women's movement, to sow dissention into it. As a trans-sexual woman and a feminist, I neither seek publicity, nor am I an agent of patriarchy. But my right, and that of other trans-sexual women and men to exist is threatened by this book. Also, the uncontested use of elitist and dogmatist methods, which in themselves reveal internalised maleness, is a threat to the feminist movement, as more and more groups of women are singled out as 'inadequate' by the standards the dogmatists propose. I have to try to answer the book.

2. AN OUTLINE OF THE MAIN ARGUMENTS OF 'THE TRANS-SEXUAL EMPIRE'

Ms. Raymond makes her position absolutely clear. Trans-sexual women 'are not women. They are *deviant males*'. Trans-sexual men are not men, but women. The first, basic underlying cause of trans-sexualism is the sex stereotyping system in a patriarchy, '. . . a patriarchal society and its social currents of masculinity and femininity is the First Cause of trans-sexualism'. Thus trans-sexuals exhibit one form of response to the same problems that women face in a patriarchal society. 'Like trans-sexuals, many women have felt hatred of their bodies and (sic) its functions, and have found themselves in a psychically disjointed state because they could not accept their role . . . feminists have become social critics and have organized, as feminists, around issues of sexism and sex-role oppression.'

The major secondary cause of trans-sexualism, it is argued, is the medical speciality which has grown up around the performance of trans-sexual operations. This is the trans-sexual empire. Not only surgeons, but psychiatrists, psychologists, counsellors, deportment instructors, speech therapists, electrologists and the like have formed powerful teams, sometimes using national funds, which enable the fulfillment of the wish. Trans-sexualism is, apart from scattered historical myths, a new phenomenon, dating from the growth of the trans-sexual operators in the fifties. These medical specialists, since they cannot create real women, attempt to create pastiches, which are characterized by being trained into being models of the kind of women men would like to see. The gender identity clinics therefore act as reinforcers of patriarchally defined stereotypes. They are already beginning to 'treat' children in some places, attempting to cure them of 'incipient' trans-sexual leanings, i.e. to get them to conform to existing, prescribed ways of behaviour. They may develop to become 'gender enforcers' for the re-adjustment of those who deviate, quite apart from trans-sexuals. The apparent existence of trans-sexual *men* is, in fact, a subterfuge, for the real purpose is to subordinate women. Trans-sexual men are 'the tokens that save face for the trans-sexual empire' (p. 27). They make it appear that a universal problem is involved, when there is actually a problem of control. Furthermore, trans-sexually operated men could potentially have been woman-identified women, and are thus lost to feminism. (Woman-identified women are women who are committed to women in every way)

Biologically, the basic indicator of sex is the chromosomal pattern, XX (female), XY (male). Since these cannot be changed, no person can change sex in reality. All that can be done is various procedures to simulate a biological state that is chromosomally denied. If there were no stereotypical behaviours prescribed by patriarchy for either sex, trans-sexuals could behave as they liked (subject to some general morality, of course), and would not have to have operations. Thus a moral (I would say, political) problem is created within our society, and transformed by the gender identity clinics into a medical one, one of 'adjustment', in this case physical as well as social. These medical procedures are used for patriarchy as a means of social control of gender stereotypes, which act in the interests of men.

Ms. Raymond outlines the various theories that have been put forward by the sex researchers to account for trans-sexualism. They fall into two categories, ante-natal—inadequate hormonal stimulation of the foetus has led to the brain being 'predisposed' towards female or male behaviour in opposition to male or female biology—and post-natal. These argue that abnormal features of early socialization are responsible. Typically, the responsibility for creating both male and female trans-sexuals is laid on the shoulders of the mother. The sex researchers always phrase the problem in terms of the trans-sexuals' need. They assert that gender identity is immutably fixed by the age of 18 months. They then argue that it is therefore right to accept a person's belief as to their gender identity. In Ms. Raymond's view, what such arguments actually allow is the legitimation of medical experimentation to produce 'synthetic' females, geared to male conceptions of 'proper' femaleness. Add to this the possibility of extra-natal conception, and Ms. Raymond has a nightmarish vision of a future in which biological women might become redundant.

In the present time, the people 'created' by what Ms. Raymond calls a process of 'male mothering' are unfortunate hybrids, neither female, nor male, dependent on the male medical establishment for their existence. When interviewed (Ms. Raymond talked with thirteen trans-sexual women and mentions a book by Thomas Kando who interviewed seventeen others), trans-sexual women present highly stereotypical notions of female behaviour, nor do those interviewed appear to experience the 'role-strain' of normal women (4). This indicates that they are not really women, but propagandists for male-defined images of women, not only in their words, but in their very existence. Trans-sexual women writers demonstrate this as well, particularly Jan Morris, whose 'female' self is a mirror image of a stereotypical male (5).

However, some few transsexual women have attempted to escape this stereotyping by becoming involved, as lesbian=feminists, in the women's movement. In Ms. Raymond's view, their position is even worse than that of other trans-sexuals. No trans-sexual woman has had the full experience of socialization as a woman, which other women have. She is chromosomally XY. There can be no question of her being accepted as a woman and allowed access to feminist spaces. Trans-sexual lesbian-feminists can only 'play the part' (p. 103). But the trans-sexual woman in the women's movement has an even more sinister role. 'As the (trans-sexual woman) exhibits the attempt to possess women in a bodily sense while acting out the images into which men have moulded women, the (trans-sexual woman) who claims to be a lesbian feminist attempts to possess women at a deeper level, this time under the guise of challenging rather than conforming to the role and behaviour of stereotyped femininity' (p. 99). Although the trans-sexual woman has no penis, in the feminist movement 'her whole presence becomes a 'member' invading women's presence and dividing us once more from each other' (p. 104). When real men decide that the women' movement needs containing, they will be able to use these pseudo-women as their agents (p. 106). Thus it is a matter of important principle that trans-sexual women are excluded from feminist spaces. Women who don't accept this—for instance the collective of Olivia, the women's record company, who have a trans-sexual woman among them—are exhibiting some or all of the following confusions. Liberalism, in not wanting to be intolerant; gratitude, that one of the ruling sex has renounced privileges; naiveté, in not realizing what is going on as Ms. Raymond sees it: still retaining elements of male identification by being fearful of being called man-haters, and still subject to the attraction of the male persona (p. 112–3). Not only does the trans-sexual feminist 'perform total rape' (p. 112), but lesbian feminists who accept trans-sexually constructed lesbian feminists as other selves are mutilating their own reality (p. 119).

By allowing trans-sexuals to resolve their problems by medical means, the sex researchers are denying them the right to challenge the patriarchal stereotyping system which ultimately creates them. Trans-sexual surgery is a form of behaviour modification and control which is allowed conditionally, an trans-sexuals accepting and learning to present themselves in terms of patriarchally approved stereotypes. It follows typical male patterns in that it fetishises forms, artificial vaginas, removed organs. The trans-sexual is inherently masochistic, and the 're-birth' experience reported by some trans-sexuals after operation is equivalent to total orgasm, and irresistibly tempting when offered (p. 139, 144). Reports of greater happiness by 90% of trans-sexuals after operation are quite superficial, and cannot be set against the drug dependency, stereotyped personality, and physical health risks involved The practice of trans-sexual surgery, in its blindness to the wider human ethics of the trans-sexual problem, has parallels to the Nazi experimentation in concentration camps, as Ms. Raymond describes at some length, where people were subjected to barbaric tortures in the name of 'medical science'. She notes at the end that the practices are not equivalent.

Finally, the problem is presented by Ms. Raymond in more philosophical terms. The trans-sexual state after operation is an inadequate mode of being. It substitutes a superficial integration for a total human integrity, which would accept the body-mind unity, and alter the conditions giving rise to conflict, rather than mutilating the body. Trans-sexualism operates at best on a principle of *androgeny*. This merely adds up qualities thought to be masculine and feminine. Trans-sexuals therefore combine bits and pieces of physical and social qualities that maleness and femaleness are supposed to have in patriarchy. The ways they do this in no way transcend the problem of dis-satisfaction with one's gender, but makes trans-sexuals unsatisfactory pastiches, even if they feel themselves to be satisfied with the result. Ms. Raymond lists seven rhetorical questions to give the essence of these arguments:

1. Is the price of individual satisfaction individual role conformity and the enforcement of social role stereotypes?

2.   Is trans-sexuals' capacity for social protest and criticism restricted by their operations, and other treatment?
3.   Are false opposites integrated to create a sense of trans-sexual well-being?
4.   Are larger possibilities of being restricted by defining well-being in terms of bodily features?
5.   Are trans-sexuals violating their bodily eco-systems so that they damage themselves physically? (e.g. by being liable to cancers)
6.   Is trans-sexual surgery creating medically dependent people?
7.   Is trans-sexual surgery a male conception of happiness, an attempt by men to bypass the creative energies of women by artificial means?

I believe the answer to all these questions is, in fact, no, and I have tried to explain why in the second and third sections, without dealing with them one by one.

In spite of her arguments, Ms. Raymond does not feel that trans-sexual operations should automatically be legislated out of existence. The first thing is to legislate against sex role stereotyping, the real cause of trans-sexualism. The proliferation of gender-identity clinics should be stopped; counselling and consciousness raising techniques should be used, which focus upon the restrictive aspects of trans-sexualism for true integrity in human personhood. Ms. Raymond does not wish to be regarded as treating the 'anguish and existential plight' of trans-sexuals unsympathetically (6).

No short summary can do total justice to any complex presentation of views, but I have tried to outline the major arguments she presents in reasonable terms.

Misgendering

How can I blame you for
for mistrusting me ?
Strive as I may
to adopt the symbols that legitimate your own oppressed existence
I am a poor imitation.

The surface of your mind
accepts me — sister, she;
it is from the deeper reaches that rebellion comes.
Intuitively
at unguarded moments
the tongue forms the pronoun of mistrust —
'He is there; I'll call him.'
Stabbing, stiletto, sharp.

How can I blame her?
An insidious enemy, man.
Omnipresent,
in my form
he is a spy, an outpost of the counterblows to come.
How many forms have men assumed?
How many ruses?

And yet,
there may be another truth yet.
Could it be that that identity is yours
years caught up in a facade, a screen of self protection?
Learning the oppressor's role.

your outpost in his *camp;*
home, strange, from afar at last.

There is no way to tell.
But since the surgeon's liberating knife
defies return, with multiple interventions in the brain,
your choice defines me —
Sister? Alien?

                                                    1974.

3. A CRITIQUE OF 'THE TRANS-SEXUAL EMPIRE'

As I read through Ms. Raymond's book, I experienced anger, constant irritation, and a lot of bitter-ness. I scribbled pages of critical notes. Reading it doesn't seem at the moment to hurt me personally, because it is all so far removed from who I am and what I'm about in this world. But I know that its publication will make my personal space in the women's movement more problematic, make it less easy for me to trust women who don't know me well, and vice versa, as well as making things harder for pre-operative and post-operative trans-sexuals in general. It is this knowledge that causes my bitterness. It makes me feel that, in spite of Ms. Raymond's claims of sympathy to the 'existential plight' of trans-sexuals, and her use of the conventional model of formal scholarship, which enables her not to present her emotions clearly, she actually experiences hatred and fear when thinking about trans-sexuals. These feelings are closest to the surface when she writes of the minuscule number of trans-sexuals who are involved in the women's movement.

How to order the innumerable points of disagreement which spin in my head? I think it's best to start by considering the method that she uses. Janice Raymond's proposition that the first cause of trans-sexualism is the patriarchal gender system, which she states again and again throughout the book, has the force of an axiom. The possibility that trans-sexualism might have other background causes is unacceptable, and unconsidered by her. The method of the book is thus dogmatic; theologi-cal in the worst sense. When one believes firmly, without the possibility of doubt, that a particular explanation is responsible, then there is no way that what we actually experience as happening, as human beings, can challenge that explanation. Actual experience has to be denied, distorted or ignored in order to fit in with the theory. Having started in this way, it is easy to present more and more arguments that seem to follow logically from the first. Each of them is equally unchallengeable. Ms. Raymond sees the patriarchal gender role system as responsible for her oppression as a woman, and extends that explanation to cover trans-sexualism as well. I tend to think that the *structure* of patriarchy is the crucial factor in women's oppression, i.e. the sexual division of labour which centres women's primary existence around the bringing up of children and the servicing of people, and men's about the production of things. The sex role system is a consequence of this (7). But the difference isn't central here (see section 4). Ms. Raymond further defines trans-sexualism as a creation of the sexist medical establishment. I think that in order to establish or refute these propositions, it would be valuable to look at; the history of trans-sexualism prior to the 1950s, and its cultural extent, which Ms. Raymond *defines* out of existence; something of the background of the development of the gender identity clinics themselves, which Ms. Raymond ignores and the significance of trans-sexual men which she has to deny, for their existence refutes her axiom that trans-sexualism is a creation of man, for 'men'. Her arguments remind me of some Marxists, who, accepting hetero-sexuality as 'given', define homo-sexuality as an aberration of class society, which will wither away in the new, socially-just state. Similarly, in a gender role free society, Janice Raymond argues that trans-sexualism would not exist, because anybody's behavioural desires could be expressed in whatever way they wanted, so 'changing' sex wouldn't matter.

Ms. Raymond's method also makes criticism impossible, except on matters of detail. Since, by definition, trans-sexual women are not women, and trans-sexual men are not men, our arguments, which are based on the fact that we *are* women or men, are invalidated from the start. Sex researchers who attack her are trying to uphold patriarchy, so their arguments are invalid. Women who have lived with, and experienced trans-sexual women as the women they are, are, by definition, deluded. Since the writer of this pamphlet is not me, but someone defined away as a male excrescence, raping the women's movement, with the purpose of sowing dissent, no arguments I present need be considered (p. 112). The implications of this kind of axiomatic, dogmatic thinking for the women's movement as a whole are really terrible, and are discussed in the final section.

A second criticism on the level of method is that, while attacking the particular aims of the sex researchers, general propositions of patriarchal scientific ideology are quite uncritically adopted. So the boundaries of existence are rigidly defined by biological criteria of body and cell structure, or by learned behaviour derived from social interaction. In other words, we are only what male science tells us that we may be. Women as a whole have never accepted that rational male scientism, ideological product of 18th and 19th century capitalist development, told the whole truth about existence. We are still discussing now women's own more unified knowledge, which, in the west, was destroyed with the witch hunts (8). Now, even male writers from within science are challenging the assumptions of their disciplines, which are seen as restricting enquiry, and arguing that subtle energy forces exist which are at levels behind biology (9). Ms. Raymond attacks the sex researchers for assuming that biology and socialization are destiny (ch. 2), but she assumes just that herself. 'It is biologically impossible to change chromosomal sex, and *thus* the trans-sexual is not really trans-sexed' (p. 126). 'Women take on the self-definition of feminist and or lesbian because that definition truly proceeds from not only the chromosomal fact of being born XX, but also from the whole history of what being born with those chromosomes means in this society' (p. 116), i.e., biology plus socialization equals destiny. By abandoning this kind of determinism, other causes of trans-sexualism become feasible. The past life experiences of trans-sexual women are not the same as those of men. Nor are they the same as those of other women. But responsible feminists with political credentials at least as good as Ms. Raymond's, do not find this a bar to accepting us. These aspects are discussed further in the next section.

The third problem of Ms. Raymond's method is that she uncritically accepts the male academic establishment's separation of personal feelings and factual presentation. I do not believe that people's feelings can or ought to be ignored in understanding the things they write about. At least they in-fluence the manner in which things are presented. I think it is possible to divine from the text that Janice Raymond feels deeply threatened and scared by the idea of trans-sexualism. This comes out most clearly in her chapter on trans-sexual women in the women's movement, who are trashed in the bitterest terms as rapists and energy stealers, male agents who sow dissention among women. In fact, the very tiny number of trans-sexual women in the women's movement are quite well integrated into their women's groups, sharing energy with other sisters, and being accused of nothing by the women who associate with them. We only become visible as a result of attacks from women who see trans-sexualism as an abstract problem which they can abstractly, regard as an extension of patriarchy. The opposition to Sandy Stone, for instance, a trans-sexual woman in the Olivia women's record collective, did not come from the women who worked with her, lived with her, knew her and loved her, but from women who did not know her at all. I want to know where Janice Raymond is *coming from* about trans-sexuals. If one compares 'The Trans-sexual Empire', say with, 'Of Woman Born', Adrienne Rich uses poetry and personal experience as an integral part of her arguments, whereas Janice Raymond does not admit to any feelings. This attitude just follows the false male division between reason and emotion. If Ms. Raymond sorted out her feelings about trans-sexuals, it might lead her to want to write in a different way.

So the Trans-sexual Empire sets out to 'prove' something which it has already assumed, allows nothing but male scientific limits for its determination of gender identity, and uses a method which denies us the right to know what she is really feeling.

Janice Raymond attacks the sex researchers as evil-intentioned instruments of patriarchal sex role coercion. While I agree with everything she says in attacking the attitudes they adopt, she gives them too much importance. I personally, from experience of the London 'gender identity clinic', cannot accept her idea that they are the experimental precursors of a new artificial replacement of biological women (e.g. p. 168), as being anything more than a paranoid fantasy. The fact of the matter is that the Gender identity clinics were not regarded with favour by most of the medical patriarchy. They were established and exist against the opposition of the most patriarchal and respectable elements of the medical profession, men who regard trans-sexualism as an even more disgusting aberration than Janice Raymond does, if possible. Their reasons, however, are diametrically opposed to Ms. Raymond's, since for them, trans-sexualism seems to threaten the natural order of things. The clinics developed under the intense and unremitting pressure of trans-sexuals, who would go to any length to obtain an operation, and for whom no treatment was satisfactory, other than operation. They did *not* develop as a natural extension of the patriarchy, but, like all marginal institutions, they strove to justify themselves by their conformity—hence all the ghastly gender—amendment training which trans-sexuals have to suffer. In Britain a few years ago, there were at least three centres doing operations under the national health service. Now there is only one. In the States, they form a *tiny* part of the medical establishment. However horrific their gender conformity programmes are to trans-sexuals, I think they are quite insignificant when compared to the thousands of gynaecologists, with equally sexist opinions, who are mutilating women with breast inserts (500,000), hysterectomies, caesarian sections (50% in some Los Angeles hospitals, apparently) and performing other atrocities on women's personhood. Further, what about the psychiatric patriarchs, who, when they are not relating to human distress by pumping patients full of drugs, and excoriating them with electric shocks, are wheeling round the make-up trays, encouraging women to that conformity to male-defined conceptions of female 'nature' that were responsible for most of them arriving in the hospitals in the first place (10). The real empire is the whole patriarchal medical establishment. To call the trans-sexual medics an 'empire', is to inflate their significance.

Janice Raymond denies a significant history for trans-sexualism before the 1950s, since her theory demands that. But such a history does exist, and a brief outline is available in a book she cites from, The Trans-sexual Phenomenon (11). This demonstrates clearly enough that trans-sexuals, *of both sexes*, have existed in all historical periods, and in cultures from all continents. When something has that range of time and culture spread, I think it is important to accept the possibility that explanations other than sex-role disorientation of deviant males are at work. Trans-sexual men are smaller in numbers than trans-sexual women, but they exist, they are equally determined about themselves, and they are not the token creation of the patriarchy's representatives in gender identity clinics. To say that they are is to deny them any humanness, any sense of personal identity at all, and to turn them into the passive agents of sexist manipulators. A trans-sexual man I know used to be in the women's movement and talked about his situation there. He received tremendous encouragement to go on living as a woman, and every opportunity to adopt non-sex stereo typed behaviour within the limits of his biological sex. He has now come out as the man he always knew himself to be, and is active in the men's movement. On Janice Raymond's terms he has no right there. The fact that there appear to be smaller numbers of trans-sexual men than trans-sexual women is not really relevant, since they are in no way tokens of the male medical establishment, as Ms. Raymond has to assume them to be. But there are many possible reasons, some of which have been pointed out by Karen Hagberg (note 1). The female state is generically primary, so possibly more anomalies occur in the differentiation process to maleness. The operation is more costly and complex and less satisfactory. In addition, aspects of the socialization of women involve learning acceptance. Trans-sexual men have been conditioned as women. This makes it that much more difficult to take the active steps necessary to realize their true identity (12).

Nowhere in her book does Ms. Raymond give any accounts of trans-sexual life experience. She interviewed 15 trans-sexuals, two of them men, the rest women. The only place she gives any information about these individuals is in the section which shows that trans-sexual women conform to sexual stereotypes. None of them emerges as a real person with a biography. No sensitive or caring collective account of the life experience of trans-sexuals, either pre-operative or post-operative, is presented. Instead, the most damning quotations possible are put together. Sometimes totally irrelevant information is presented as if it made a point. In order to 'demonstrate' that trans-sexuals in the women's movement commit total mind-body rape, Ms. Raymond quotes at length from an obviously cynical and meant-to be-funny story in, of all places, Penthouse magazine. I consider that to be dishonest, and her individualised attacks on trans-sexual women in the women's movement morally indefensible. (13). It is little wonder that the picture of the trans-sexual that emerges is a static caricature. There is no suggestion that people's attitudes might change. It is clear that pre- and immediately postoperative trans-sexuals show highly stereotyped attitudes about how they, as women or men, ought to be. I will deal with the case of trans-sexual women. Because of our biology, we were, usually, brought up as male children, forced to live as men in order to survive, and therefore developed ideas of what the actuality of women's existence is, that were seen through male identity blinkers. This distorted view was reinforced in many cases, by obligatory sexist counselling in order to be able to get operations, and demands that we conform if we were to get an operation. No wonder a lot of disturbed people emerge at the end. Pre- and immediately post-operative trans-sexuals are often very confused, and not easy to get on with. But women's oppression is not merely the consequence of a set of historical experiences. It is an existential condition, an oppression that is re-created from day to day by the lives that women have to lead, the opportunities open to us, the attitudes presented to us. This is as true for trans-sexual women as for any others. Excited from the achievement of something that involved a lifetime's struggle unaware of the male stereotypes that have formed their ideas of femaleness reinforced in those stereotypes by crudely patriarchal gender identity clinics—it is hardly to be expected that women like these will present a challenge to male sexist ideology about women's existence. Ms. Raymond cites extensively from Thomas Kando's study, Sex Change. None of the trans-sexual women interviewed there were operated more than two years previously. Jan Morris' embarrassing book, Conundrum, was published within two years of her operation (she was operated on at the same time as me, in the same clinic). At least Conundrum demonstrates that lack of success in the state of maleness has nothing to do with trans-sexualism. Jan was almost classically successful in her presentation as male before she came out. The important thing for trans-sexuals is on-going experience. Every woman's history of oppression is re-created in her day to day experience. In having the same experience, the trans-sexual woman is giving real meaning to her suppressed past. I'd predict that after several years of actual female existence, trans-sexual women would show, on average, just as much uneasiness about sexual expectations of women's identity as other women round them; no more, no less. But it is not only immediate post-operative trans-sexuals who seem satisfied with a tinsel notion of women's existence many born women publicly and vociferously urge these roles upon us, through the media, books and the innumerable pages of women's magazines. We, and not trans-sexual women, are our own keepers. To single out the small number of trans-sexual women as being particularly significant in the struggle against cripplingly deforming sex-role stereotypes, deflects energy from real causes—primarily the patriarchal system and secondarily the agents who peddle conformity through the media.

I find that behind Ms. Raymond's arguments that sexual difference (biology apart) is exclusively a product of male-defined values of a patriarchy, she shows an absolutism about sex difference. This expresses itself most clearly in the horror and revulsion at the thought of the lesbian feminist-trans-sexual. On page 101, she asserts that trans-sexuals in the women's movement have 'renounced femininity, but not masculinity and masculinist behaviour.' Since such trans-sexual women behave characteristically as other lesbian feminists behave, this is equivalent to saying that such behaviour is masculine. We all carry a baggage of maleness, expressed in attitudes, modes of thought and behaviour, attitudes which are very much part of Ms. Raymond's approach to the subject. But lesbian feminist behaviour is not 'masculine'. It searches for a cultural identity which transcends the stereotypes of gender with which we are all conditioned in this society. The trans-sexual feminist's search is exactly the same, and not a demonstration of masculinity. That is an empirical statement, subject to verification by other feminists. Ms. Raymond denies it totally and refuses to admit any evidence to the contrary. In our behaviour and attitudes we are all, not just trans-sexuals, products of learning conditioned by our existence in a patriarchy. In trying to develop the condition of female humanness, all of us have to renounce much powerful cultural learning we have been subjected to, and have internalized. Its content varies widely from woman to woman. For us to be successful, other human beings have to be involved in the same personal struggle, trans-sexual woman as well. The separation adopted by some women to undertake this struggle is a result of the degree of sexual oppression, intentional and unintentional, shown by men in our societies. But trans-sexual women's transformation in the same way is not on compatible with that of other women, who, as separatists, are able to accept, and work with transsexual feminists. For example, I was accepted and integrated into an ongoing consciousness-raising group which met weekly for nearly a year. According to Ms. Raymond's definition of me as personalized phallus, rapist, and agent of patriarchal oppression, this would hardly have been expected to be the case. In order to cope with the fact that trans-sexual women can be, and are, integrated into women's spaces, Ms. Raymond is forced to deny the experience of the other women involved as well, thus setting herself up as a judge of their feminist credentials (see the final section for further discussion).

Finally, it is perhaps necessary to discuss briefly the philosophical section of Ms. Raymond's book, if only because her use of such language cloaks bad argument, distortion and suppression of fact in academic respectability. In fact, the philosophical content is mystification, playing with words in a way that obscures the ethical absolutism which Ms. Raymond demands. She sets as her standard of measurement, the term 'integrity'. In this context, androgeny represents an adding up of qualities which derive from an immoral state—a patriarchal definition of sexual identity. It is necessary to transcend such a situation, to pass from integration, the aim of the trans-sexers, to a higher integrity of the human spirit, where physical mutilation is not involved. In a general sense, I can accept the concept of integrity as a legitimate aim of human endeavour, though I'm uneasy about it because it is too individualised. (People may feel it necessary to deny the integrity of their own existence for some wider goal of benefit to humanity.) But what is the content of integrity? How do we determine whether an act contributes to our integrity, and has anyone else the right to determine it for us; if so, to what degree, and in what respects? All these questions are at the heart of ethics. Most of us, in our lives, are faced with contradictory alternatives for action. The choice of one alternative, which may contribute to our perceived integrity, may reduce it in another respect. It is perfectly possible to argue, and often is argued, that the withdrawal from one half of the human race, implied by separatist feminism is a denial of an existent human reality, denying *integrity* in the interests of *integration* of certain aspects of human experience. But we reply that the terms of interaction demanded of us by men are so harsh, that only through withdrawal from such experience can we begin to realize an integrity that provides a model for all human behaviour to be patterned upon. Ms. Raymond's conception of integrity is partly based upon biological naturalism. Thus, the trans-sexual woman violates the integrity of her male biology (and the trans-sexual man, vice versa), by submitting to hormones, operations. But the alteration of the body is surely not an issue of absolutes. Do we deny the limbless artificial limbs? Is all transplant surgery unethical? Should one not wear glasses because one is born with defective vision, in order to preserve bodily integrity? Should a woman whose uterus has developed an incurable infection be denied the possibility of an operation for hysterectomy? If there is really no other course, her bodily integrity is violated, for the continuance and development of her *total* integrity-potential as a human being. As a result of a total hysterectomy, incidentally, she also becomes dependant on external hormonal medication in order to be able to realize her 'integrity potential'. Or is a person denied the use of the artificial supports, really realizing their true integrity as a human person, their death or disablement exemplifying it?

Who judges such questions? Who dares to set themselves up as such an absolute arbiter of human experience? Janice Raymond does, in regard to trans-sexuals at least. We violate our chromosomal identity by having operations. But is this identity to be the ultimate determinant of human action? It is perfectly legitimate to argue to the contrary if the evidence of its violation is positive. 90% of post-operative trans-sexuals experience their operations as positive in their results, a high figure, surely, for medical intervention. Ms. Raymond says that this positiveness is superficial. Who is she to say so? Even to begin to talk about it would involve a long investigation of before, and after, living patterns, with follow ups. Even though trans-sexuals do not become biologically identical with other women or men as a result of operations, enough can be done to allow the development of potential integrity, so deeply denied before, when so much of our energy was taken up trying to comprehend a fundamental fault in our identity construction. Are we dependent on medication for our survival? Yes, but no more so than many others. My father had, for many years, to take pills to control his blood pressure. Without them he would have died. Taking such pills did not make him inadequate, a slavish dependent of the medical establishment, but enabled him to develop his integrity in his later years. I also need to take some pills, 22 days out of 28, but neither am I fairly obviously, very beholden to patriarchal medicine. An endocrinologist assures me I run no greater risk of cancer than other periodless women on hormonal treatment, but even if I were at risk, the risk would be insignificant compared to the value for me of what I have done.

Ms. Raymond also says that integrity is denied by the creation of creatures who are satisfied to exist within the limitations of the current sexual stereotypes. Now, these stereotypes damage all of us, all the time, but most women do not *consciously* challenge them to any fundamental extent. Much present existential unhappiness comes from that. But why should trans-sexual women be singled out, and *forced* to experience on-going hell in order supposedly to make them revolutionaries in the sexual struggle. Not only would it not have such an effect, but it would deny us any element of autonomy. Is a person who just does what she is told, really changing anything? It sounds to me like a theological press gang for revolution. The stereotypes do not cause trans-sexualism, they confuse trans-sexuals, and the rest of us, and we have to find our own way out, through our own judgement of arguments and our own experiences of living, not by having them denied us.

Thus, there is no prima facie case for arguing that the trans-sexual situation is one that denies integrity for the trans-sexual, either on humanistic or medical grounds. Trans-sexuals, like all of us, are caught in a net of oppressive gender expectations, which we have to sort out as best we can, in situations where the social agencies to which we may refer only make our problem worse. But it is not trans-sexualism which is the problem, but the way we are pressured to live in the world. Another attack on our potential for integrity comes from individuals such as Ms. Raymond, projecting their own hatred and fear in spurious philosophical arguments. I cannot find any section of Ms. Raymond's book which does not bristle with half truth, distortion, suppressed information—all passed over with a sugar coat of scientific veneer. Above all, and uniquely, perhaps, Ms. Raymond has written a book concerning a group of people, of human beings, without apparently the slightest insight into any of our life histories, the problems of our existence as we see it, our own perceptions of the world. Trans-sexuals are given no validity as human beings with volitions of our own; no picture of the trans-sexual experience as a human condition emerges from her pages. We are merely the manipulated tools of the patriarchal establishment, monstrosities or tokens, hollow shells to be arranged in this or that parody. One might expect that a person writing about a group of human beings would present them to us as human beings, but perhaps that is just the naive liberalism which Ms. Raymond accuses other women who have come to know trans-sexuals of having.

The trans-sexual experience is neither greater nor lesser than that of any other human being. It is very special, and has its own special problems; it defies explanation in any terms of current rationality or medical expertise. In the society, drawn from feminist ideas, which one day will replace patriarchy, there will still be trans-sexuals, unless cosmic energy stops fucking things up occasionally, but, because there will be no limitations on their behaviour by oppressive gender roles, all they will need is an operation, since physical differences will perhaps be the only mark of sexual distinction (I am not absolutely certain of the latter, but am prepared to accept it as a working proposition). By then, I expect, wise women will be able to divine the energy patterns involved, and correct biology at birth, as can now be done with various hermaphroditic conditions. Who knows? But now we are here, and our voice needs occasionally—not too often—to be heard, lest we become the new scapegoats of the latest witch hunts emerging from within the feminist movement itself.

5. DIVIDED SISTERHOOD. 'THE TRANS-SEXUAL EMPIRE' AND FEMINISM

'The Trans-sexual Empire' is a dangerous book. It is dangerous to trans-sexuals because it does not treat us as human beings at all, merely as the tools of a theory; because its arguments may make things more difficult for trans-sexual women and men as they strive to come out; and because it seeks to create hostility towards us among women who have no actual experience of trans-sexual people, find the subject disturbing, and want some simple, straight-forward answer that allays their unease. I think trans-sexualism is frightening to many of us because, in an unstable, insecure world, basic sexual identity, male or female, is one of the few fairly firm constructs we have. However much we wish to modify our behaviour, our sense of our sex is very deep, and trans-sexuals seem to bring it into question. Yet, as I have tried to show, we do not seek to change sex, but to modify a biological anomaly, so that genuine human existence as the women or men we are already, is possible.

I think that the Trans-sexual Empire has relevance to a wider group than trans-sexuals. I see its negativity as three-fold. Firstly, I mistrust its attitude to feminist culture, though this is the most difficult objection to establish. Secondly, its emphases deflect attention from the most immediate problems, and tend to lead to scapegoating. Thirdly, its ideological dogmatism and anti-experiential viewpoint lead right back into the methods of patriarchy.

Ms. Raymond believes that every trans-sexual man was a potential woman-identified woman. Although this is not true, reading it began to make me ask myself, in what way does Ms. Raymond look at feminism? The book does not make the answer clear. The main line of argument is that male and female cultures are the creation of a male-defined sex role system. Overthrowing this system would enable human beings of integrity to behave in all the morally legitimate ways available to humans to behave, irrespective of sex. Sexual differences would be merely biological—the ability of women to give birth, chromosomal difference, physical differences in anatomy. However, at another point, she talks of the 'multi-dimensional female creative power, bearing culture, harmony and true inventiveness.'

Trans-sexual women are supposed to covet this (p. 107). Where do these characteristics come from? They cannot be biological in origin, because she had already ruled out this kind of explanation in attacking John Money's theory that hormones feminize or masculinize foetal brains (p. 48–9). There are two other alternatives. Perhaps there is some 'woman-spirit', or 'woman energy', underlying biology, which has the above characteristics. But if so, then trans-sexual women may have it, though they have a male biology. If this is the case, we are women, and Ms. Raymond's assertions that we are not, would be false. Alternatively, these characteristics are social in origin. But if sexual differences are defined by the *negative*, patriarchally-imposed sex stereotyping system, where do these *positive* characteristics come from? In the terms of the way she looks at things, there is no clear answer, but from the text of the chapter on trans-sexuals in the women's movement, it seems that a lot of emphasis is placed on the lesbian- feminist. She is the most significant challenger, not only of male dominance in society, but also of female compliance in it. This follows the arguments in the famous article by the Radicalesbians, the Woman-Identified Woman (16).

It is possible to look at things in a different way. Suppose we don't focus on sex stereotyping, but on the *position* of women in the structure of patriarchy. From this perspective, women's position in patriarchal structure gives rise to a female culture, which is potentially and partly in continual conflict with male culture. Women's position means that we ensure the continuance of the human race, and develop personal qualities in keeping with this task, while men threaten it, in conflicts over production and allocation of human resources (17). Men do not only try to contain this conflict between female life energy and male death energy by imposing notions of the feminine. They also control intellectual systems and thought processes, and educate us to internalise them. The separatist lesbian feminist who does not challenge herself about these things as well, may retain important elements of male identification, in spite of her separatism. These elements can internally damage the women's movement.

The female culture of resistance emphasizes caringness, respect for others' identity, the ability to share and grow from the experience of a common and allied oppression, the essential acceptance of another as equal, the integration of intellect and feeling, and an experiential attitude to knowledge, which men contempuously refer to as 'being closer to nature'. Men, on the other hand, exist in a world of *exclusion*, each group is seen as exclusive of others, and each individual feels himself in a potential competition with his fellows in every aspect of his behaviour. It has long been so. To adopt this kind of exclusiveness within the women's movement, however physically separate a woman keeps herself from men, however much she professes to hate them, actually demands of us the same kinds of destructive divisions that men use. If, on the other hand, we have a certainty of the *positiveness* of female culture, in spite of its distortion and deformation by patriarchal attempts to control it, the *inclusion* of marginals is not a threat, when it is genuine. Karen Hagberg makes a similar point, 'It does not seem prudent for feminists to perpetuate a strict male/female dichotomy in a patriarchal atmosphere which both fears and loathes sexual ambiguity of any kind.' Janice Raymond's book exudes hatred and exclusion. An academic intellectual, I fear she has been infested by another aspect of the patriarchal culture she professes to attack (18).

Secondly, the tactic of *deflection*, attempting to deflect attention from the source of a problem to a relatively innocent and defenceless party onto whom resentment can be channelled, is very old. It is a very basic tactic of patriarchal divisiveness. Find a scapegoat, and patriarchal power is safe. Witches were not responsible for the social evils of the mediaeval form of patriarchy; they attempted to alleviate them. But because wise women seemed a little different, it was possible to single them out and whip up a campaign against them, leaving the main cause untouched. Nazism used the same method, projecting blame on to Jews and homosexuals. McCarthyism channeled social discontent against those who were attempting to find the causes of social unease, by labelling them communist, and manipulating public opinion against them. Women have experienced this method all too often to our detriment. The effect of Janice Raymond's book is the same, in two respects. She gives a much more central role to the gender identity clinics than they deserve, when they are really the 'poor relations' of patriarchal medicine, to whose sexist, exploitative structure and organization they kow tow. It is like trying to excise a monster by focussing on his little toe. And she encourages the deflection of energy and anger which needs to go outwards, against the male system, *inwards*, against a small group of vulnerable women, by labelling them rapists, personifications of male organs and such nonsense. This is not merely incitement to hate, but totally destructive. Such energies, when directed inwards, will soon find new groups to feed against, as witch hunts proliferate, and Ms. Raymond encourages this, too: 'Lesbian—feminists who accept trans-sexually constructed lesbian feminists as other selves are mutilating their own reality' (p. 119). Or perhaps women with male children should be the next target? These methods of approaching problems are those of our enemies. We take them up ourselves at our peril.

Thirdly, a major weapon which men have used against women is the power to define our situation by their ideology. Central to the women's movement is the challenge to the ideological definition of reality. By accepting male definitions presented in terms of abstractions, our own feelings, experiences and personal understanding of reality can be denied. I remember it particularly from a left group, where women's almost constant dis-satisfaction with what was going on was never allowed any validity, since it did not seem to fit in with Marxist–Leninist method or theory. But it is also happening every time a man exclaims, for instance, 'Women are so emotional'. The whole consciousness-raising practice, fundamental to the women's movement, has been a basic alternative of our oppositional culture to such methods. It is based upon respecting another woman's understanding of her situation, giving validity to her experience, not judging her inadequate if she did not see her situation in the same way as you, not defining the answers to problems beforehand. It recognizes that we all have something to learn form each other, we all have valid experience of the struggle that belonging to our oppositional culture demands, we can share and develop collectively. I believe that it has been this refusal to define and demean that has enabled woman strength to be so powerfully developed in the women's movement. Anything which threatens it in the name of some ideological purity, is an imported threat which can undermine us, turn us against ourselves. Janice Raymond's book is the most explicit example of this ideological, dogmatic approach that I remember reading. She thinks she has the answer to trans-sexualism. Trans-sexual experience is invalid by definition. Any woman who dares to assert her own experience to the contrary is guilty of self-mutilation, of 'liberalism', of 'naiveté', of 'gratitude', of 'fear of being labelled a man-hater', of 'attraction to masculine presence' (p. 113, 119).

The women of the Olivia Records collective, lesbians and feminists, who had struggled to develop the world's first (I think) all woman feminist recording company, wrote, in relation to the trans-sexual woman who was a member of their collective, 'Day to day interaction with Sandy Stone has convinced us that she is a woman we can relate to with comfort and trust.' According to Ms. Raymond if they had been more honest, they'd have said they needed a man around' (p. 103). The same, presumably, applies to the women who accept and relate to the few other trans-sexuals in the women's movement, including myself. They are deluded. This is what Elizabeth Rose is talking about when she writes, of another article by Janice Raymond, in Chrysalis, 'I am upset that a magazine of 'women's culture' ... is basically encouraging the elitist/seperatist attitude that self-definition (is) ... subject to the scrutiny and judgements of those who, in the name of political purity, claim the power to define who is allowed entry into the feminist community ... and, now, who is, or is not female' (quoted abbreviated, p. 109). What is an alternative method, which recognizes women's experience, and does not invalidate it? Janice Raymond could have gone and talked to the women of Olivia, and to Sandy. She could have gone and talked to Christy Barsky (another feminist trans-sexual she identifies) and her friends. She could have shared experience with them and reported what they said, communicating the different experiences, to give women who have no access to trans-sexuals some means of making provisional judgement. Instead, she argues that all women who have such experience are inadequately feminist. Yes, we have heard that kind of ideological divisiveness before, from men, and are hearing it again now in the British women's movement from small numbers of women who arrogate themselves the right to be the custodians of feminist purity, and who are beginning to take Janice Raymond and her methods as their mentor. Patriarchal invasion is insidious. The denial of female experience in the name of ideological purity is not a product of, nor a contribution to, feminist culture. As trans-sexual women, we must claim the integrity of our own life experience, and other women who know us, are also asserting that their right to their own experience is fundamental. When we have to assert this right against other women, for whatever reason, confusion reigns, and patriarchy gains. Following the dogmatists will come the enforcers of the 'law'.

My living space is threatened by this book. Although I have had to challenge it in its particular content, as a trans-sexual woman, its dogmatic approach and denial that female experience is our basic starting point are a danger signal for the whole women's movement.

NOTES

Originally published as Riddell, Carol. *Divided Sisterhood: A Critical Review of Janice Raymond's* The Transsexual Empire. (Liverpool: News From Nowhere, 1980)

1. Karen A. Hagberg: Trans-sexualism: is gender absolute? New Women's Times Feminist Review, Aug. Sept. 1979, p.10–12.
2. In this pamphlet, I have used the correct gender references to trans-sexual people. Trans-sexual women are women born with a male biology and mistakenly socialized as males, who have to undergo physical conversion operations (and years of re-learning to realize their sexual identity. Trans-sexual men are men born with a female biology and mistakenly socialized as females. In quotations from Ms. Raymond's book, I have used her terms sometimes, which are oppressive and insulting to trans-sexuals, in inverted commas. Otherwise I have used correct terms in brackets.
3. Ms. Raymond quotes (twice, so no-one will miss it) the following statement by an American trans-sexual. 'Free from the chains of menstruation and child-bearing, trans-sexual women are obviously far superior to Gennys in many ways.
    Genetic women are becoming quite obsolete, which is obvious, and the future belongs to trans-sexual women. We know this, and perhaps some of you suspect it. All you have left is your 'ability' to bear children, and in a world which will groan to feed 6 billion by the year 2000, that's a negative asset' (cited, p.xvii & 117). In the context in which it appeared—feminist controversy about trans-sexualism, this foul arrogance was obviously designed to provoke rather than express a serious viewpoint. It makes furious anger understandable. But to consider it as representative of trans-sexual views, is as unreasonable as taking Margaret Thatcher's views to represent feminism.
4. Thomas Kando, Sex Change, Springfield, Illinois, Charles C. Thomas, 1973.
5. Jan Morris, Conundrum, London, Signet, 1974.
6. Neither, I am forcibly reminded, does Dr. Acker, in Marge Piercy's recent classic, 'Woman on the edge of Time', feel he is inhumane in meting out to Connie, the treatment that he does. (pub. Women's Press, 1979)
7. C.f. Nancy Chodorow, The Reproduction of Mothering, California U.P. 1978.
8. Barbara Ehrenreich and Dierdre English, Witches, Midwives and Nurses, Compendium, London, 1974.
9. E.g. Fritj of Capra, The Tao of Physics, London, Fontana 1976. Lyall Watson, Supernature, London, Coronet, 1974. Lawrence Blair, Rhythms of Vision, London, Paladin, 1977.
10. C.f. Phyllis Chesler, Women and Madness, New York, Avon, 1973. Barbara Ehrenreich and Dierdre English, For Her Own Good, London, Pluto, 1979 p.282f.
11. Harry Benjamin, The Trans-sexual Phenomenon, New York, Julian Press, 1966.
12. C.f. Raymond, p.26.
13. She also uses this method in her discussion of the behaviour of eunuchs in history (p.105–6), and of Nazi medical experiments (p.148–153).
14. C.f. Harry Garfinkel, Studies in Ethno-methodology,
15. From a novel in progress.
16. Radicalesbians, Woman-Identified Woman, In Notes from the 3rd Year, New York, 1971
17. E.g., Barbara Burris, The Fourth World Manifesto, also in Notes from the 3rd Year. Barbara Starrett, I Dream in Female, 1976 U.S. Pamphlet.
18. This is not to say that the only ways that women can be oppressive are by internalizing male ways of thinking. I don't think classism and racism, etc. can be reduced to this, though the ultimate 'First Cause' of such oppressions may be a patriarchal system.

12

A Transvestite Answers a Feminist

Lou Sullivan

Lou (neé Sheila) Sullivan, a gay-identified female-to-male transsexual man, became one of the founders and leaders of the FTM community in the 1980s, before his death from an AIDS-related illness in 1991. In "A Transvestite Answers a Feminist," written before his transition from female to male, Sullivan provides one of the first published engagements with the feminist critique of transgender identity.

Unlike many other female-bodied people who developed identities as men, Sullivan never found a home in a lesbian or women's community prior to his transition. Rather, he participated as an anomalous "female transvestite" in a community of gay men, and identified most closely with drag queens—people (curiously, like himself) with identities as men who nevertheless appeared as women to the world. Sullivan's closest contact with the feminist movement came from a coworker, a fellow secretary in the Slavic Languages Department at the University of Wisconsin-Milwaukee, where Sullivan worked before moving to San Francisco in 1975. It was in Sullivan's dialog with this self-proclaimed feminist that he developed the article reprinted below.

The woman Sullivan is corresponding with finds the solution to sexism in "junking any kind of image," but she fails to recognize that as a feminist she maintains her own image of herself, and that it is a gendered image—just as is Sullivan's. Sullivan, as he was to do throughout his future writing, affords a rare honesty when he answers his correspondent, in describing the difficulty of being unable to articulate for one's self what it is to be transgendered, but in describing the imperative to represent the self truthfully. As Sullivan had noted in one of his adolescent diary entries, "I don't know what somebody like me looks like, but when people look at me, I want them to think, 'There's one of those people with their own interpretation of happiness.' That's what I am."

Lou Sullivan went on to claim his identity as a female-to-male transsexual gay man and to establish one of the first FTM support group in the United States, wherein he enabled the FTM community to develop truly inclusive practices that fostered the real diversity that exists within the community today.

A little over a month ago, Schlitz distributed a poster advertising their beer, featuring a "Love American Style"—type beautiful woman with a bouffant jet-black shiny hairdo and all made-up to look "sexy." Dorothy, a co-worker of mine, attached the following note to the poster and left it for me: "Sheila—would this plastic woman image be anymore excusable if this was really a man?" A bit amused, I wrote in reply: "Honey, if this was a man, she'd have to have her shit a lot more together than any of us. Believe me. (And I mean ANY of us!)" Another note from Dorothy appeared on my desk!

Dear Sheila: First of all, anyone with their shit together is constipated. Anyone who needs to keep their hair in a helmet-like style is "constipated"—Immobile, unable to move or function as a real, relaxed human. A hair style like that is a very effective way of making sure your body won't enjoy itself, and isn't sex 50 per cent body pleasure? (Other 50 per cent, of course, is mental.)

Getting your shit together means playing an act in this sense. The person who's into this scene buys a lot of funny clothing and "gets it together" on his body, not in his mind, where real togetherness starts. He "gets it together" in his closet—even Alice Cooper is a "closet" queen in this respect. Now, whereas you see this superficial, bought at the department store image as implying a together personality on a man, you distain the woman who also relies on a closet full of funny, expensive clothing or make-up and lacquered hairdos as a "dumb cunt", NOT A PERSON. You very clearly stated that Joplin's trouble was her "hippy chick" image, and that often means wild clothes. Cooper dresses just as flashily, but his clothing hangup is "groovy."

The point you seem to be rather obviously trying NOT to understand is that anyone, man or woman, who must rely on a pre-packaged endorsed by *Vogue* magazine hair do or clothing is not a person, he/she is an image. This image enables the real personality to go into hiding (or conceals the fact that the person has no personality—probably more correct) because the "image" says everything about you and determines many of your actions. This is basically feminist movement thinking, so you should be aware of it. As I remember, you have put down your older makeup clad sister as being kind of a nowhere person. If people are bisexual, and the sexes are to be judged equally, what exactly makes her inferior to a transvestite? Why should I believe you? I don't believe in sex stereotyping or god, so why believe a smear of makeup is healthy on a man, but not a woman?

You're still trying to sweep mind fuck-ups under the carpet by changing the very deep and painful personality problems of the fag into some sort of ultra-cool hipness instead of realizing it's neurotic and isolating. Read Rechy's "City of Night" again. It's heartbreaking, not groovy. This scene could only appeal to someone who is absolutely terrified of communicating with other people. Yeah, they're real good at insulting each other, insulting themselves, cutting down all the institutions that oppress them...in short, they seem generally to react resentfully to situations, rather than mold their own lives. You say you believe in "will," but how much will do these people seem to have in this book? Can you really see this as a valid, fresh sort of life? Again, you said promiscuity without any sort of standards didn't appeal to you (it shouldn't). But when homosexuals practice this kind of non-selective fucking, bravo! After all, it's only somebody else (and a man at that) that gets emotionally hurt after every one of these one-night stands, not Sheila. And in spite of a fag's tough, oh sooooo wild'n decadent image they can hurt. If a man or woman is so tough that no pain gets through, I fear that the barriers are so high that no pleasure (probably sexual) can get through either. Remember that the mind as well as the body feels pain or pleasure, and that emotions can't be selectively repressed. A person either represses all his emotions (good and bad) or he accepts all of them. And isn't the need for a deep satisfying love an emotion?

And Sheila—I've been a Lou Reed fan, and bought all his records, for 4–5 years. He's been around for 6–7 years. Where were you and all the rest of his new supporters then? Same man making the same music, but as soon as he turned himself into a SEX-OBJECT, he gets the recognition I for one had felt he deserved as a plain MUSICIAN. Can you really think he doesn't know his music is of a secondary interest to most of his newly acquired fans? Look. No success until he decided to shove (exploit) his image (need I add up your ass?) and all of a sudden he's covered with a swarm of fruit flies. Gee, A song about shaving legs. Started shaving yours yet? If women aren't happy and satisfied as hairless sex-objects, will a man be happy as one?

I better add that I am, as always, 100 per cent against persecuting gays. I am also trying to say that they should not persecute themselves by adopting superficial roles, and going ga-ga over distorted sex-stereotype roles will only end up hurting the average gay and keep her/him from being a more "real" person.

I left the following note on Dorothy's desk in reply:

Dear Dorothy: I was startled by your heavy rap—figured either you were extremely pissed (at me?) or really wanted to understand what I was thinking. I don't know which—maybe you aren't sure yourself. It took me a while to get my thoughts and reactions together. Let's not make this a malicious encounter, but an educational one. OK?

Where does one begin to get his mind together when it is two absolute opposites? Finally I am beginning to try to reconcile a boy within me I knew was there as far back as when we kids dressed up to play cowboys and I knew it couldn't be real for me cuz I was the girl who had to be pretty and dainty and fragile and take care of the kids and cook and wait for my man to come to me. That cowboy in me could only appear as a dress-up, a pretend, but it was so real to me somehow that finally I was completely lost in it and scared someone might find out how deeply I felt it (at age 5 I had a Davy Crockett birthday party. The climax was when I appeared. I was Davy Crockett and I can still remember my thrill at the moment)...and everyone else thought we were just playing, pretending, but I wasn't and it was even more frightening, cuz I knew I wasn't. (When I was 15 I stuffed a rag into my underwear for my penis and walked around like that all day, dreading exposure.)

You say flagrant queens project an "image enabling the real personality to go into hiding." What is the REAL personality in this situation—when a man wishes to appear as a woman or a woman as a man? Where do they begin to be real? Where do they begin to relax with this kind of opposition inside? To keep inside the closet, to only dress up alone in a locked room, hoping no one will ever see, afraid to open your mouth in regard to any topic coming close to your secret (What is beauty? What makes you happy? WHO DO YOU LOVE??!!!)...their trying to appear straight and normal is "constipated"! That's WHY he she is an image, becuz in your own words "the image says everything about you and determines many of your actions." When he she lets himself out of the closet, dons the image of his true identity for all to see and is not scared to say "This is my lover", then he has a good start in "getting his mind together."

I challenge any person who will not admit this in themselves, such as "the woman who relies on a closet full of funny, expensive clothing or makeup and lacquered hairdos", because I could never be that...that which I was supposed to be...and I refuse to be identified with a woman like that. I CAN'T BE! My older sister is inferior to a transvestite becuz she can't relax, she's trying so hard to deny her inner humanity and free-ness, to bottle up any susceptibility to feelings—while a transvestite at the very least, admits to himself his inner life and feelings, and, at the most, if he comes out, he's left wide open for rejection by family and friends, physical harm, denial of use of public and private facilities, easy prey for others to try and fuck his head over by saying he's sick, etc.,—all for the sake of relaxing with themselves, being free and open and alive. You ask him to come alive to the world so the world can kill him.

"Sweeping mind fuck-ups under the carpet by changing the deep and painful personality problems of the fag into ultra-cool hipness instead of realizing it's neurotic and isolating!" Dorothy. I couldn't believe you said that. The reason "**FAGS**" have deep and painful personality problems is cuz people like you "**realize** (!) they are neurotic and isolating." And then you ask them to mold their own lives! The people in Rechy have a hell of a lot more will than any straight—the will to say fuck you to all the assholes who hate them so intensely, to say fuck you to the world of people who think they're sick and say fuck you, I'm ME...a lot more will than anyone else. But you say they just "seem generally to react resentfully to situations rather than mold their own lives." Where do you mold a life for yourself when all you do is battle oppressions day in and day out? Where does a black begin to mold his own life when he's alone among 200 KKKs, or a woman in a room with 50 men gawking at her tits and ass. They start at the bottom, that's where!! They band together and say fuck you everybody this is me and I'm good. Rechy's world is as valid and fresh a life as a black shouting out his SOUL or a wife splitting from her hubbie and kids and shouting her liberation.

I don't really think gays practice non-selective fucking anymore than straights. Lot and lots of gays go home from the bar alone cuz everyone there was a Gila monster, just like straights. You seem to think that's all gays do is get one-nighters. There's many more stable relationships among gays than that. Yet the rate of one-nighters is higher for gays than straights becuz of all the fear gays have of exposure, of being fucked over by straights telling them they're so sick for so long they begin to wonder themselves about their world and it's hard to have a lasting warm love with a person you've been branded from a child into thinking is sick and bad…someone you can never touch in public, you can never take home to mommy, you can never admit is your lover. (The two of you raise suspicion if you buy a house together, you can't take your lover to the office party or on a business trip, you can't adopt a child, and a million and five extra hassles if your couple is an older man with a 20-year-old lover.) Who can have a "deep satisfying love" under these conditions?

Six or seven years ago I was shoving rags into my underwear—that's where I was! Six or seven years ago Lou Reed was probably scared his fans would know him too well and that would be the end. "No success until he decided to exploit his image"—no success til he came out of his closet and gave others like him the courage to do the same and love and idolize him for it…for bringing out their lives to the public's attention as a valid, good, warm life. Yes a song about shaving legs—just like a song about natural Afros or no bras. (You'll never know if I shave my legs cuz I wear pants all the time now!)

Since you doubt men can be happy with shaved legs cuz you don't think women can be, you can come out of your closet and tell all of us how a man is to proclaim his total femininity or a woman her masculinity if not by images. You want to claim your freedom by NOT shaving your legs—so why can't a transvestite proclaim his by shaving his legs? I'm afraid you're trying to press straight standards on transvestites which just won't work…that's like whites judging the physical beauty of blacks by how "white" their facial features, etc., are.

Since you're adding you're 100 per cent against persecuting gays let me point out your use of chauvinist language: "fruit flies", "fags", "sex objects", "neurotic", "personality problems", "distorted sex-stereotype roles." It'd be nice if you could manage to do with that language what you did with "nigger" and "chick."

Transvestites coming out, having their own songs and idols, etc., will only "hurt" the average gay in the same sense women coming out (women's liberation) will "hurt" the average housewife.

(And double duty for all this if he's gonna pose for a Schlitz poster!)

That night Dorothy left this for me to find at work the next morning:

Just a quick note. Only wrote the way I did because you are transparently a heterosexual woman who simply cannot learn that a woman really doesn't have any lesser capabilities than a man. IF you were a lesbian as you are trying very hard to convince yourself, I certainly wouldn't have said anything to you. Also might have kept my mouth shut if you showed any interest in female homosexuals. As it is, you sit here in your "masculine" clothing (pants, masculine? nowadays?) typing and liking it. No wonder you are falling for this clothes makes the man bit. And I like you too much not to say something.

There is virtually no difference between men and women except a genital one, and anyone who limits and bases his life on his genitals is in a very bad way. That is exactly why we have a feminist movement—women were seen solely on the basis of reproductive organs, and then just couldn't take it any longer. But what are the flashy gays doing but imitating all the moronic frivolities that accrued around women in this unliberated stage? Gays are maintaining the double-standard era stereotyped woman, and as a woman who is having one hell of a time becoming fully real as a person, I cannot encourage this at all.

I would suggest you question your passivity, and so something about that. See someone if you have to. And also see if you can come up with any sort of "image" of a HUMAN—i.e., what makes a person, rather than what is a man or a woman. What happens when you discover that a man is tender, a woman aggressive; a man is spiritual, a woman is intellectual? Why get hung up on changing your sexual orientation when no difference exists in reality?—Dorothy

But when I awoke that morning, I found this letter in my mailbox at home:

Dearest Sheila: I really feel awful about the last couple days. You were my feminist friend. We have had very similar problems in relating to other women, even feminists, so I really needed you to talk to about women's issues. Knowing I wasn't the only woman that felt isolated from others of my sex was also reassuring. You seemed to be spunkier than I was in many respects (biking up to Terre Andre; camping on the Mississippi) and I respected you for that. You were for me a direct, energetic person and good to watch in action. When my boyfriend and I stopped by, you and I could grouse about our men's super intellectualism—I needed to, because their brainy talks made me feel very left out and inferior. We were great at work—when I felt confused about some dumb office thing, you reassured me. You never put me down at work, and finally I even found out that you were as scared about phoning as I was!

So look where we are. I've got another semi-nasty note in the drawer for you; forgive me. It's nasty because you're a fine person, a fine woman, in my eyes. You're also painfully like the woman I was at your age. This little fight we're having (which I started) is mostly this age difference. I've lived through a great deal of confusion as to what a woman is and I've gone through a long period of wanting sexual "hipness." Remember the grossly insensitive (to your feelings) way I was defending your boyfriend's leaving you? Well, I was trying to defend myself and my desires for sexual hipness disguised as sexual freedom. I am so sorry, and I'm ashamed that I never apologized for my cruelty to you til now. I'm especially ashamed because I discovered a few weeks ago how wrong I was to think promiscuity and little bitty orgies made me anything special. My artwork did make me special, but I lost sight of this in my two year long resentment of my boyfriend for keeping me from my sexy 'n free image. And boy oh boy, did I want an image! I just couldn't believe I was as good (smart) as he, no matter how much he told me I was. Men are smart, powerful and productive, not women, thought I, deep down inside. Well, I finally got over that. BUT—in the meantime I had lost 6 years during which I could have been developing as a strong, self-confident, self-loving person. And frankly, Sheila, I don't want to ever see another woman waste her youth on self-hatred like I wasted mine. I was so worried about you that I just exploded.

So maybe it seems like I'm patronizing you, but it's just that I've learned some truths about myself that I have a hunch apply to you. Pretty fuckin' presumptuous, ain't I? Dunno if it matters that I mean well. What I haven't learned is that people have to work thru their own problems. Maybe in my mid-30's I'll finally get that thru my thick skull.

But til then, all I can say is that masculinity and femininity, when taken as mental properties rather than physical conditions must be dumped by anyone who cares about people. "Femininity" has been used too, too long to rip off women and sensitive men, and "masculinity" has been misused to the extent of ripping off the whole world (men being the corporation heads and war-makers and women—minority ecology oppressors). I'm not talking about individuals so much as concepts (take "motherhood" as a concept and compare it to real mothers—concept has little to do with real mothers except to oppress and deceive them).

Yes, society's attitudes kill—but it's all people they kill, not just the obvious ones like blacks, freaks and gays. They killed my "Holiday Magic" sister, they killed my superficially contented mother and father, got your sister(s) and almost got me and two of my boyfriends. And it's really strange—like my parents would maintain that their images make them happy, and I know it's a lie. The only thing a person can do to get "free" is JUNK ANY KIND OF IMAGE. If "femininity" as concept is oppressive for women, it is, by its very nature, oppressive for men. If "masculinity" as concept (fear of showing emotions, social irresponsibility, hyper-competitiveness) is damaging to men, it will damage women as well. These two are socially set traps. Maybe a person hates his trap, but will he be better off in a trap someone else just jumped out of because it was a killer? How many people convince themselves to stay in a trap just because they tried to get into it so bad? What if the trap won't open when you want out? Ask a person with a prison record about that one.

I'm a wide-eyed dreamer, a utopian thru and thru. And that is why I am being such a bitch towards you right now. I so desperately want for others the peace-with-oneself that I'm having such a hard time finding. And in life any detours take years to get around. And sometimes a person can never get back on the right road. I hope that doesn't apply to us.

I felt I had to answer this letter also:

Dear Dorothy: Your letter was unexpected and surprising. I expected you to REALLY come down on me about the letter I left you. So your kind letter was more than welcome!

Dorothy, I don't feel I'm getting hung up in any "sexual hipness" (I'm not really all too sure what that means . . .) or any images. The reason I caught on so fast to what I'm doing now is cuz I always needed to do it but never had the guts to. So now I'm trying if out for size and seeing how I feel—if it's a nowhere scene, forget it. Seems I'm always going in and out of scenes . . . I guess that's how life is. For too long my boyfriend and I hid out with each other (I remember well how much I wanted to literally lock us up together in our place, board up the windows from the outside world and save us from everything). The awakening came for me when a beautiful gay came up to me on the street in the fall of '71 and I couldn't take time to even talk to him cuz I was meeting my boyfriend on the bus and it was coming a block away. And I knew when I got on that bus and left that beauty standing there that I'd never stop regretting that moment.

But now that we're untangled and I have freedom, I want to experiment in different things I've always wanted to. I'm not a lesbian. I don't want to be either. I've always thought of myself as a male homosexual (try and figure that one out—I can't). I think the reason I think that stems from my hate for the female scene. But I've always had a soft spot in my heart for transvestite and gay men becuz they seemed to me to be the most beautiful inside—the most able to abandon stereo types which, for men, I think, is a lot harder. I think they are one group that knows better than anyone that there's no difference between men and women. So I want to swim around a little—get to know some gays and transvestites, see if I can learn anything about the feelings I've had in these areas.

As long as one knows what he's doing he can't get "hung up" on it. I think I know what I'm doing and if things turn out badly, I'll know not to do it next time, right? So you're right . . . I gotta live and learn . . . don't we all?

I far from hate myself, sometimes I fear it's too much the opposite. (I love it when I find out women in the "femmy" scene hate me!) But I'm not trying to deny my "femininity", Dorothy, I'm just trying to sneak up on it thru the back door. The front door Avon lady approach didn't even work. I'd like to get the best of both worlds . . . what I'm trying to do now is find out how to get them. —Sheila

I invited her to go to a straight bar with me that weekend to talk and drink, but she flatly turned me down, saying obviously we've "got our heads in different directions, so why bother." We never spoke about this confrontation, it had been executed entirely in writing. Ever since this exchange, over a month ago, she's been cold and offish to me. Yesterday I came to the office to visit her and she refused to even acknowledge my presence, not even to as much as look at me. I stood by the door a while and then left.

NOTE

*Originally published as Sullivan, Sheila. "A Transvestite Answers a Feminist" (Milwaukee: Gay People's Union [GPU] News, August 1979) pp. 9–14.

13

Toward a Theory of Gender

Suzanne J. Kessler and Wendy McKenna

In this landmark contribution to the study of gender, psychologists Suzanne Kessler and Wendy McKenna elaborate the concept of "gender attribution," the process through which we all assign a gender to every person with whom we interact, based on rules and assumptions that are usually unacknowledged or unperceived. They rely explicitly on the "ethnomethodological" approach developed by Harold Garfinkel, which concentrates on the behaviors and thought processes people use to construct a sense of day-to-day reality. Kessler and McKenna understand gender, like reality itself, to be "socially constructed;" it is produced through interactions with others rather than being a "natural" quality of the material body. They are interested in transgender phenomena because they see them as special cases that make visible some of the routine social practices that everybody uses to construct gender on a day-to-day basis.

In the selection below, Kessler and McKenna summarize their thoughts on how the gender attribution process works. Data from an "overlay study" form a crucial part of their argument. They develop a series of transparencies depicting bodies with various physical characteristics or articles of clothing, which can be overlaid with one another in various combinations. By asking test participants to identity the gender of the various composite figures, the authors are able to quantify the process of gender attribution and to assign relative weights to particular elements involved in making the attribution.

Just as important as their quantitative work is the authors' historical and political framework. They recognize that gender attribution is a culturally and historically variable process, and they understand that the coercive powers of law and society are deployed to support the sense of "natural" reality created in part by gender attribution. They call on their readers to confront "the reality of other possibilities, as well as the possibility of other realities." In doing so, they presage the work of a later generation of transgender scholarship.

When we first began to think about gender as a social construction, we devised a "game" called the Ten Question Gender Game. The player is told, "I am thinking of a person and I want you to tell me, not *who* the person is, but whether that person is female or male. Do this by asking me ten questions, all of which must be answerable by 'yes' or 'no.' You may ask any question except, 'Is the person male?' or 'Is the person female?' After each question, based on the answer I have given you, tell me, at that point in the game, whether you think the person is female or male and why you have decided that. Then ask your next question. You need not stick with your first answer throughout the game, but regardless of whether you stay with your original choice or change your decision you must, at each point, explain your choice. At the end of the game I will ask you to give your final decision on the person's gender."

The game is reasonably simple, fun to play, and is not unlike "Twenty Questions." Our game, however, is not just for fun. Instead of answering the player's questions on the basis of the characteristics of some real person, we responded with a prearranged, random series of "yes's" and "no's." The game is a form of the "documentary method,"[1] and we created it both in order to find out what kinds of questions the players would ask about gender, and, more importantly, to uncover how the players would make sense out of what is, in many cases, seemingly contradictory information. The following is a transcript of a typical game:

Player: Is this person living?

Interviewer: No. What is it?

P: It was an irrelevant question. I shouldn't have asked you that question. No basis for judging it. Is the person over 5'8" tall?

I: Yes

P: Male. The probability in my mind of a taller person being male is higher for male and lower for female.

Is the person over 160 pounds in weight?

I: No.

P: Well, now I'm mixed. I'd still say leaning toward male.

Is the person under 140 pounds in weight?

I: No.

P: So, we're between 140 and 160 pounds. I'd say male on the basis of physical characteristics. A person over 5'8" between 140 and 160 pounds... I'd tend toward male.

Well, what else can I ask about this person? (long pause) Well, I mean, there're obviously some questions I can't ask.

I: Like what?

P: Like does this person wear skirts?

I: Yes.

P: The person *does* wear skirts. Then it's female I assume because I assume in general when people wear skirts they're female. The exception being Scottish males perhaps under some conditions, but I assume on the basis of probability that that's it. I've established in my mind that the person is probably—without asking directly questions about the sex of a person. I have to ask five more questions?

I: Yes.

P: Is the person a mother?

I: No.

P: Well I can't—that's a sex-directed question... Well, I'm still leaning toward female. (long pause)

Does the person have a 9 to 5 job?

I: No.

P: Well, I'm leaning toward female.

I: Why?

P: Skirts, the physical attribution make possible—physical characteristics makes possible female and not having a renumerative job makes less likely in my mind that the person's male. (long pause) When the person was a child, I don't know if this is a legitimate question, did the person play with dolls a lot?

I: No.

P: No? Well I'm still leaning toward female, because females don't have to play with dolls. I'm avoiding—I mean there're substitute questions for "is the person female or male," but I assume I can't ask those question.

I: Yes you can ask anything.

P: But if I ask some questions it's essentially . . .

I: You can ask me anything.

P: (long pause) Well, there's a system to this. If one thinks of good questions one can narrow it down very well, I imagine—any other physical characteristics . . . Well, you can't ask questions about physical characteristics if they determine whether the person is male or female.

I: Yes, you can.

P: Does the person have protruding breasts?

I: Yes.

P: Then more likely to be female. (long pause) I'm trying to think of good questions. We covered physical characteristics, job relations . . . I'll ask another physical question.
Does the person have developed biceps?

I: Yes, I'd like your final answer.

P: Well, I think the answers I've been given—the answer to the last question about developed biceps, leads me to doubt whether we're talking about a woman but the—and the physical characteristics describe, that is height and weight could be both man or woman in my mind although I tended a little bit toward man, but the several questions tip it in my mind. The wearing of skirts, the protruding breasts, the nonrenumerative job made it more likely in my mind that I'm talking about a woman than a man. Although the developed biceps, as I understand it, throws a monkey wrench in it because I don't know if it could be accurate to characterize any woman as having developed biceps, but perhaps you can.

We have played this game with over 40 people. A summary of what occurs includes the following observations: (1) Players exhibited the rule-guided behaviors described by Garfinkel (1967, pp. 89–94), including perceiving the answers as answers to their questions, seeing patterns in the answers, waiting for later information to inform earlier information, and so on. (2) Specifically in terms of gender, all players were able to make sense out of the apparent inconsistencies in the answers, such that players were led to postulate bearded women and men who were transvestites. In one case the player concluded it was a hermaphrodite, and in another that it was a transsexual. In all other cases the final decision was either "male" or "female." (3) Only 25 percent of the players asked about genitals in the first three questions. Most players asked questions about either gender role behaviors or secondary gender characteristics. When asked after the game why they did not ask about genitals, players explained that it would have been tantamount to asking "Is this person a male (or female)?", which was an unacceptable question since finding the answer was the object of the game. Players knew that their task was to discover the gender of the person without asking about gender specifically, synonymous, to them, with asking about genitals. Some of the players who did ask about genitals and received answers refused to ask any more questions, claiming that there was no reason to do so. They were absolutely certain of the person's gender, even if that decision conflicted with the other pieces of information they received. (4) Only two people who asked about genitals asked about a vagina before asking about whether the person had a penis. One was told "yes" the person had a vagina, and the other was told "no." Both of them then asked if the person had a penis. Of the fifteen people who asked about a penis first, eight were told "yes," and none of them then asked about a vagina. Of the seven who were told "no," only four then asked if the person had a vagina.

The way in which persons played this "game" suggested to us that (1) Gender attributions are based on information whose meaning is socially shared. Not just any information will inform a gender attribution, and certain information (biological and physical) is seen as more important than other information (role behavior). (2) Once a gender attribution is made, almost anything can be filtered through it and made sense of. (3) Gender attribution is essentially genital attribution. If you "know" the genital then you know the gender. (4) In some way, knowledge about penises may give people more information than knowledge about vaginas.

THE OVERLAY STUDY

In order to investigate further the relationship between gender attribution and genital attribution, and to collect additional information about the relative importance of physical characteristics in deciding gender, we designed a more formal study. A set of plastic overlays was prepared. Drawn on each overlay was one physical characteristic or one piece of clothing. The eleven overlays were: long hair, short hair, wide hips, narrow hips, breasts, flat chest, body hair, penis, vagina, "unisex" shirt, "unisex" pants. When the overlays were placed one on top of the other, the result was a drawing of a figure with various combinations of typically male and female physical gender characteristics. The overlays, in combination, produced ninety-six different figures. Each figure had either long or short hair, wide or narrow hips, breasts or a flat chest, body hair or no body hair, and a penis or a vagina. Figures were either unclothed, wore a non-gender-specific shirt and pants, or wore one of the two articles of clothing. All figures had the same, non-gender-specific face.

We assumed that the figure that had many typical female characteristics would be seen as female, and the figure that had many typical male characteristics would be seen as male. What, though, would people decide about the "mixed" figures? Would the figures be ambiguous stimuli, stumping the participants, or would sense be made of them as in our Ten Question Gender Game? How would the presence or absence of particular cues, especially genitals, affect the participants' perceptions of other physical characteristics?

Each of the ninety-six figures was shown to ten adults, five males and five females. The 960 participants were asked three questions: (1) Is this a picture of a female or a male? (2) Using a scale of 1 to 7, where 1 means not at all confident and 7 means very confident, how confident are you of your answer? (This was, in part, to give us information about whether the forced choice in Question 1 was a clear gender attribution or merely a guess.) (3) How would you change the figure to make it into the *other* gender?

From the participants' answers, not only would we have an "objective" measure of the relative weight of various characteristics in making gender attributions, but, in seeing how people construct gender from "contradictory" cues, we would gain some understanding of the phenomenological reality of femaleness and maleness. As we have pointed out previously in this book, people who are designated "males" and "females" vary within gender and overlap between genders on every social and biological variable. How, then, is gender dichotomized such that, phenomenologically, there are only males and females? By controlling the variables and by slowing down the gender attribution process by means of this overlay study, we hoped to *see* the construction of gender. Although making judgments about drawings is not the same as making judgments about real people, insights gained from the former are valuable in understanding the latter.

What constitutes gender? George Devereux, a psychoanalytic anthropologist, claims that ". . . much of mankind's high degree of sexual dimorphism is due to *woman's* conspicuous femaleness; she is sexually always responsive and has permanent breasts. Man is not more obviously male than the stallion; woman is more conspicuously female than the mare . . ." (1967, p. 179, italics ours). The findings of the overlay study are in direct refutation of Devereux's assertion. It is the penis which is conspicuous and apparently impossible to ignore, and it is the male figure which dominates the reality of gender. These findings hold for both male and female viewers of the figures.

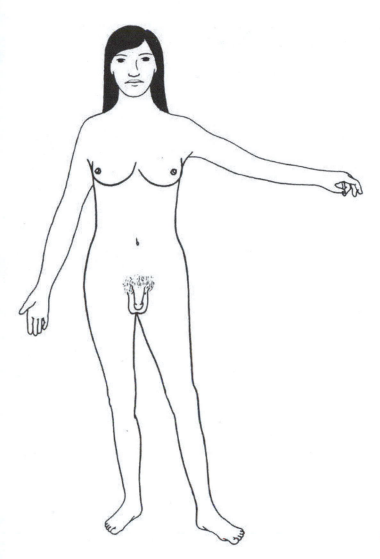

Figure 13.1

One way to analyze the relative importance of the genitals is to ask how many participants made a "male" gender attribution and how many a "female" gender attribution when the figure, irrespective of all other gender characteristics, had either a penis, a vagina, or had its genitals covered by pants. Considering first the thirty-two figures whose genitals were covered, ten of these figures had predominantly "male" characteristics (at least three out of four), ten had predominantly "female" characteristics, and twelve had an equal number of "female" and "male" characteristics. If "female" and "male" gender cues were equally "powerful," we would expect that 50 percent of the participants would provide a "male" gender attribution to the covered-genitals figure, and 50 percent would provide a "female" gender attribution. This did not occur.

There were a disproportionate number of "male" gender attributions—sixty-nine percent—to the covered-genitals figure. This finding can be understood in light of other data collected. Seavey, Katz, and Zalk (1975) report that adults who interacted with a baby without knowing its gender more often thought the infant to be a boy. (The baby used in the study was female.) In another study (Haviland,

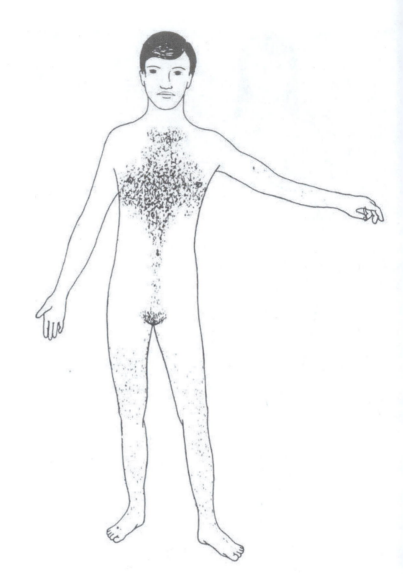

Figure 13.2

1976), men and women incorrectly labeled girls "male" twice as often as they labeled boys "female." In Chapter 4 we discussed the children's drawings study but did not, at that time, present data regarding the direction of errors in gender attributions. Kindergarten, third-grade, and adult participants attributed "male" to a female figure more often than they attributed "female" to a male figure. Preschoolers, who do not yet participate in the adult social construction of gender, did not show this bias. On the other hand, kindergarteners, who hold the most rigid and stereotyped ideas about gender, erred in saying "male" five times more often than they erred in saying "female."

   This predisposition to think and guess "male" irrespective of external stimuli is reflected in other cultural phenomena such as the use of the generic "he." Had our participants been asked to attribute gender to an inkblot, they might have responded "male" more often than "female." However, the participants were not just "thinking male" (making judgments irrespective of stimuli) but actually "seeing male," filtering the external stimuli through "androcentric" gender attributions. In other words, not only is there a tendency to respond with a "male" answer, but on practical occasions people's perceptions are such that the stimuli *look* "male."

Our evidence for asserting this comes from an analysis of the distribution of gender attributions for the figures with various secondary gender characteristics. Virtually all the "female" cues (long hair, wide hips, breasts, no body hair), and even the cues we intended to be neutral (clothing), were seen by at least 55 percent of the participants as male cues. Never were male cues (short hair, body hair, narrow hips, flat chest) seen by more than 36 percent of the viewers as female cues. We cannot blame this on poorly drawn female characteristics, since these same "female" cues were perceived as female in a predominantly female context. For example, overall, 57 percent of the figures with breasts were seen as male. Three and a half percent of the participants who made a "male" gender attribution to the figure with breasts said that adding breasts was the first thing that should be done to make the figure female. However, of those participants who saw the figure as female, over half of them mentioned "remove the breasts" as the first thing to do to make it male. Thus, in a female context the female cue was salient, but in a male context it could either be "ignored" or seen as a male cue. In phenomenological reality although the presence of a "male" cue, may be a sign of maleness, the presence of a "female" cue, by itself, is not necessarily a sign of femaleness. As we shall see, the only sign of femaleness is an *absence of male cues*.

Our discussion thus far has been limited to "secondary" physical cues. Presumably figures without pants, showing either a penis or a vagina, provide viewers with additional gender information and move them further from the fifty-fifty split we hypothesized. If genitals were the definitive gender cue then we would expect that figures with penises (irrespective of any other combination of gender characteristics they had) would be seen by 100 percent of participants as male, and figures with vaginas would be seen by 100 percent of participants as female. While genital cues increase the number of gender attributions toward the "appropriate" gender, the difference between the presence of a penis and the presence of a vagina is profound. Those participants who saw a figure with a penis responded like our hypothetical sample for whom the genital was the definitive gender cue, but those participants who saw a figure with a vagina did not. The presence of a penis is, in and of itself, a powerful enough cue to elicit a gender attribution with almost complete (96 percent) agreement. The presence of a vagina, however, does not have this same power. One third of the participants were able to ignore the reality of the vagina as a female cue.[2]

If we conceived of the processing of gender cues as additive, then we would conceptualize our findings in the following way: There existed in participants a tendency to think and see maleness which produced "baseline" gender attributions of 69 percent male and 31 percent female. Participants who saw the "undressed" figure had one more piece of information to produce an attribution. Genitals provided approximately 30 percent more information. "Female" gender attributions increased from 31 percent to 64 percent when a vagina was added. "Male" gender attributions increased from 69 percent to 96 percent when a penis was added. According to this conceptualization the genital is just one more piece of information. It is not that the penis is a more powerful cue than the vagina, but that each genital has a 30 percent power which is added onto a differential baseline (not based on genitals).

We do *not*, however, interpret the findings in that way. We conceive of the processing of gender cues multiplicatively. Cues work in a gestalt fashion. The genitals' function as central traits (Asch, 1946), affecting the interpretation of each of the other cues. Once participants decided that the figure had a penis, they were even more likely to see the long hair as "reasonable" male hair length, ignore/misperceive the width of the hips, and see the facial features as "masculine." Similarly, once they accepted the reality of the vagina, they were more likely to see short hair as "reasonably" female, and see the facial features as "feminine." If the vagina were as definitive a gender cue as the penis and functioned as a central trait, then it would produce female gender attributions with 96 percent agreement—overcoming the bias against such an attribution in the covered-genital condition. In fact, as some of our other findings indicate, the vagina does not function in this way. It is either ignored/misinterpreted in the first place or when recognized does not have the power to influence the other cues.[3]

Penis equals male but vagina does not equal female. How many additional female cues does the figure with a vagina need to have in order to produce female gender attributions 96 percent of the time? In other words, how female did a figure have to look before virtually all participants said that it was a female? There is no single female cue that *in conjunction with a vagina* produced female gender attributions more than 81 percent of the time. Figures with a vagina and *two* other female cues produced female gender attributions more often. If the two other female cues were long hair and breasts, female gender attributions were given 95 percent of the time—as often as male gender attributions were given when the penis was present. Even adding another female cue (vagina plus *three* female cues) brings the percentages of female gender attributions above 95 percent in only two conditions: the figure with wide hips, breasts covered, long hair; and the figure with no body hair, breasts, and long hair. Even when the figure has a vagina, the remaining male cues are obviously operative and powerful.

The differential reality of the genitals is noted again when we look at the participants' certainty answers. Young children are "better" at attributing gender to clothed figures than to naked ones (Katcher, 1955), presumably because genitals are not part of the way they construct gender. However, adults are not always more certain of their attributions to naked figures than to clothed figures. They are only more certain of their attribution to naked figures when the genital exposed is a penis. When the genital is a vagina, they are no more certain than when the genitals are covered. Participants were most certain of their gender attributions when the figure they judged had a penis, and least certain when the penis was strongly contradicted. If we consider the sixty-four conditions where the genitals were exposed, in twenty-five of them at least one-half of the participants gave certainty scores of "7", indicating they had no doubt about the figure's gender. The penis was a cue in twenty-two of those conditions. There was only one condition where at least one-half of the participants were very uncertain (scores of 1, 2, or 3). In this condition the figure had a penis and four female cues.[4] The participants' uncertainty in that condition was also reflected in the fact that one-half identified the figure as male and the other half as female.

More evidence regarding the phenomenological reality of the penis comes from participants' responses to how they would change the figures with genitals. We coded the "change" answers relating to genitals into three categories: (1) remove genitals, (2) add genitals, (3) change genitals. If the penis and vagina are equally real features then we would expect just as many participants to have said "add a vagina" to create a female as said "add a penis" to create a male. And similarly we would expect as many to have said "remove the penis" to make a female as "remove the vagina" to make a male. We did not find this.

In changing a male to a female 38 percent of the participants mentioned removing the penis, but only one percent said that it was necessary to add a vagina. When changing a female to a male, the findings are reversed. Thirty-two percent of the participants said that a penis needed to be added to make a male but only one percent said that the vagina need be removed.

Thompson and Bentler (1971) examined the relative importance of physical gender cues, testing responses to nude dolls with various combinations of male and female gender characteristics. If we compare the data they collected with the findings of the overlay study there is a significant similarity. The adults in Thompson and Bentler's study gave the doll with a muscular body structure, short hair, and male genitals the maximum "male" score; they gave the doll with a rounded body structure, long hair, and female genitals the maximum "female" score. When the cues were gender-consistent they were equally weighted. When the cues were in contradiction, however, the genitals clearly had differential meaning and power. Participants rated the doll with muscular body structure, short hair, and *female* genitals only somewhat less masculine than the maximum male score, while they rated the doll with rounded body structure, long hair, and *male* genitals considerably less feminine than the maximum female score. The power of the penis lies not in its absence, since the masculine doll minus the penis was still seen as very male, but in its presence. The feminine doll with a penis could not be seen as female.[5]

There seem to be no cues that are definitely female, while there are many that are definitely male. To be male is to "have" something and to be female is to "not have" it. This proposition is related to our earlier discussion of a "male response bias" and both are integral to the social construction of gender. The implications of this are explored in more detail in a later section of this chapter.

To summarize the overlay study: Gender attribution is, for the most part, genital attribution; and genital attribution is essentially penis attribution. In the next section we argue that penis attribution takes place irrespective of the biological genitals and on the basis of the cultural genitals.

CULTURAL GENITALS

Garfinkel (1967) makes a distinction between the possession of a penis or a vagina as a biological event and the possession of either genital as a cultural event. The cultural genital is the one which is assumed to exist and which, it is believed, should be there. As evidence of "natural sexuality," the cultural genital is a legitimate possession. Even if the genital is not present in a physical sense, it exists in a cultural sense if the person feels entitled to it and/or is assumed to have it.

According to our perspective and the language we have been using, cultural genitals are the attributed genitals, and since it is the penis which is either attributed or not attributed, we maintain that the only cultural genital is the penis. It belongs to males and is attributed by members as a part of the gender attribution process in particular instances. Physical genitals belong only to physical (genderless) bodies and consequently are not part of the social world. Attributed genitals are constructed out of our ways of envisioning gender and *always* exist in everyday interactions. Males have cultural penises and females have no cultural penises, even cardboard drawings wearing plastic pants. How else are we to understand the participants in the overlay study who claimed that the way to change a clothed male figure into a female was to "remove the penis," or the child who sees a picture of a person in a suit and tie and says: "It's a man because he has a pee-pee."

Physical genitals are a construction of biological and scientific forms of life and are relevant only to that perspective. Penises do not exist in isolation. They belong to, and are presumed to be attached to, males. When what looks like a penis is found to be attached to a female, it is treated as a penis only in the physical (non-social) sense. Janet, a male-to-female transsexual we interviewed, told us of one or two occasions prior to surgery when she had sexual encounters with men. These men did not treat the (physical) penis between her legs as a (social) penis. They seemed to have decided that it was "all right" that Janet *appeared* to have an inappropriate physical genital because they had already decided that the genital had no reality in a cultural sense. This example illustrates that if the physical genital is not present when it is expected (or vice versa), the original gender attribution is not necessarily altered. When expectations are violated a change in gender attribution does not necessarily follow. It is the cultural genital which plays the essential role in gender attribution. (See also Garfinkel, 1967, p. 157.)

The overlay study has confirmed Garfinkel's (1967) analysis that in the natural attitude genitals are the essential insignia of gender. More specifically the findings suggest that it is the penis which is essential. Garfinkel argues that when we "do" gender in particular instances we are creating the reality of gender as a construct. It is apparent, though, that we not only create gender as a construct, but we create the specific categories of "female" and "male." We must be doing more than gender; we must be doing *female* or *male* gender. While Garfinkel's analysis of the natural attitude toward gender provides us with the best (and only) guide to how gender is accomplished, he does not tell us how *female* and *male* are accomplished. When he discusses Agnes' concern with being a "real woman," his emphasis is on what *real* means for Agnes and for those making judgments about Agnes's gender. What does gender have to be in order to be taken as real? We are emphasizing the *woman* part of "real woman." A male and a female may engage in the same practices for the purpose of convincing others that they are *really* the gender they assert. They must, however, engage in different practices if they want to convince others that they are one particular gender and not another. To say that attributing "penis" leads to attributing a male gender does not explain how we attribute penis in the first place, nor under what conditions an attribution of no-penis occurs.

The relationship between cultural genitals and gender attribution is reflexive. The reality of a gender is "proved" by the genital which is attributed, and, at the same time, the attributed genital only has meaning through the socially shared construction of the gender attribution process. Reflexivity is an intrinsic feature of reality (Mehan and Wood, 1975). The question of how members reflexively create a sense of themselves as female or male, as well as make attributions of others, is the topic of the next section.

DOING FEMALE AND MALE

Theory and research on how "normal" people present themselves as either female or male has been almost totally absent from the literature. The most suggestive is a brief, but important paper by Birdwhistell (1970). Taking it for granted that there are two genders and that, in order to reproduce, the two genders must be able to tell each other apart, Birdwhistell raises the question of what the critical "gender markers" are for human beings. He rejects genitals as a marker because they are usually hidden and because children do not treat them as a relevant characteristic. He also rejects "secondary sexual characteristics" as being far from dichotomous, at least when compared to those markers in other species (e.g., plumage in birds). Birdwhistell believes that "tertiary sexual" characteristics" (nonverbal behaviors such as facial expression, movement, and body posture) are the predominant gender markers for humans. Using data and informants from seven cultures, he demonstrates that members can recognize and sketch out, in a rough way, typical and atypical nonverbal behaviors for females and males. In a study of American "gender markers," Birdwhistell indicates some of the body postures and facial expressions that differentiate males and females, concentrating on behaviors that convey sexual interest. He emphasizes that no nonverbal behavior ever carries meaning divorced from the context in which it occurs.

We agree with Birdwhistell on the importance of understanding gender display and recognition, as well as with his assertion that genitals and other physical characteristics are not the critical signs of gender. It is informative that people can describe and recognize typical and atypical gender displays, but if a display can be characterized as typical or atypical, then the gender of the person who is displaying has already been attributed. Therefore typical displays are not necessary to make a gender attribution nor are atypical displays grounds for doubting an attribution. A woman is still a woman, regardless of whether she is being (nonverbally) masculine or feminine.

Birdwhistell's work does not uncover particulars of the gender attribution process. His data on American gender displays was collected in the same way as every other study on "sex differences."

People were sorted *in the first place* into one of two gender categories, and only then, after an initial gender attribution was made, were these displays compared. This technique, as we have stated before, involves assumptions that militate against uncovering the gender attribution process. By accepting the fact of two genders and pre-categorizing people as one or the other, the researchers have already (implicitly) decided that there are differences. Given their ideas of what female and male mean, certain differences take on importance, while others are seen as irrelevant. On the one hand, variables may be chosen for study because they fit the list of differentiating characteristics which researchers already "know" men and women have (e.g., "preening" behavior). On the other hand, some cues may be ignored, either because they seem so obvious that they are not worth studying (e.g., wearing a dress) or because they are not considered relevant; that is, they are not part of the social construction of gender (e.g., the color of the person's hair).

In order to fully understand the role of nonverbal behaviors in the gender attribution process, it is necessary to understand that the social construction of gender determines why and how we study certain phenomena. Rather than asking people to notice or describe the typical and atypical behaviors of their own and the other gender (which, as even Birdwhistell notes, can never result in an exhaustive list), information could be gathered on which, if any, nonverbal behaviors are "conditions of failure." In what nonverbal ways could a person behave such that her/his gender is questioned? Although our own interests are theoretical, such concrete knowledge has practical implications for transsexuals and others. If the conditions of failure could be described, then people could be any gender they wanted to be, at any time.

The gender attribution process is an interaction between displayer and attributor, but concrete displays are not informative unless interpreted in light of the rules which the attributor has for deciding what it means to be a female or male. As members of a sociocultural group, the displayer and the attributor share a knowledge of the socially constructed signs of gender. They learn these signs as part of the process of socialization (becoming members). In our culture these signs include genitals, secondary gender characteristics, dress and accessories, and nonverbal and paralinguistic behaviors. As we established in Chapters 2 and 4, these concrete signs of gender are not necessarily universal, nor are they necessarily the same signs used by children.

In learning what the signs of gender are, the displayer can begin to accentuate them, to aid in creating the gender dichotomy. For example, as Haviland (1976) has demonstrated, height of the eyebrow from the center of the pupil differs considerably between adult American women and men, but is virtually identical in male and female infants and young children. The difference in adults is obviously aided, if not caused, by eyebrow tweezing and expressive style.

Along with the displayer learning to accentuate certain signs, the attributor contributes to the accentuation of gender cues by selective perception. For example, members of our culture may look for facial hair, while in other cultures this might not be considered something to inspect. In learning to look for facial hair, the attributor perceives in greater detail signs of facial hair than would be the case if facial hair were not a cue. Selective perception occurs in many other contexts. Eskimos differentiate various kinds of snow (Whorf, 1956); people *see* more or less aggressive behavior in a football game, depending on which side they support (Hastorf and Cantril, 1954).

Although within a positivist framework it is important to delineate specific gender cues and unravel the process involved in learning to accentuate and selectively perceive these cues, doing so glosses over the deeper structure of the social construction of gender. Members do not simply learn rules for telling females from males. They learn how to *use* the rules in their relation to the socially shared world of two genders. There is no rule for deciding "male" or "female" that will always work. Members need to know, for example, when to disregard eyebrows and look for hand size. Gender attributions are made within a particular social context and in relation to all the routine features of everyday life (Garfinkel, 1967). Among the most important of these features is the basic trust that events are what they appear to be and not performances or examples of deceit (unless one is viewing a performance; in that case the assumption is that it is a "real" performance which carries with it other routine features).

Given basic trust regarding gender, successfully passing transsexuals, by virtue of being successful, will be impossible to locate (Sulcov, 1973). To be successful in one's gender is to prevent any doubt that *one's* gender is objectively, externally real. We do not live our lives searching for deceit, and, in fact, classify people who do as paranoid. In contexts where deceit regarding gender is made salient, everyone's gender may begin to be doubted. For example, Feinbloom (1976) reports that when she speaks on panels that include "real" transsexuals, she, presenting herself as a "real" woman, is sometimes asked if she is a transsexual. The context in which persons appear reflexively create the possibility or impossibility of being real or "only" passing.

If there are no concrete cues that will always allow one to make the "correct" gender attribution, how is categorizing a person as either female or male accomplished in each case? Our answer, based on findings of the overlay study, reports from transsexuals, and the treatment of gender in the positivist literature, takes the form of a categorizing *schema*. The schema is not dependent on any particular gender cue, nor is it offered as a statement of a rule which people follow like robots. Rather, it is a way of understanding how it is that members of Western reality can see someone as either female or male. The schema is: *See someone as female only when you cannot see them as male.* Earlier in this chapter we stated that in order for a female gender attribution to be made, there must be an absence of anything which can be construed as a "male only" characteristic. In order for a "male" gender attribution to be made, the presence of at least one "male" sign must be noticed, and one sign may be enough, especially if it is a penis.[6] It is rare to see a person that one thinks is a man and then wonder if one has made a "mistake." However, it is not uncommon to wonder if someone is "really" a woman. The relative ease with which female-to-male transsexuals "pass" as compared to male-to-female transsexuals under-scores this point. It is symbolized by the male-to-female transsexual needing to cover or remove her facial hair in order to be seen as a woman and the female-to-male transsexual having the option of growing a beard or being clean shaven. The female may not have any "male" signs.

The schema, see someone as female only when you cannot see them as male, is not a statement of positivist fact. It is *not* that "male" gender characteristics are simply more obvious than "female" ones or that the presence of a male cue is more obvious than its absence. The salience of male characteristics is a social construction. We construct gender so that male characteristics are *seen* as more obvious. It could be otherwise, but to see that, one must suspend belief in the external reality of "objective facts."

To fail to see someone as a man is to see them as a woman and vice versa, since "male" and "female" are mutually constitutive. However, the conditions of failure are different. The condition of failure for being seen as a woman is to be seen as having a concrete "male" characteristic. The condition of failure for being seen as a man is to be seen as not having any concrete "male" characteristics. In the social construction of gender "male" is the primary construction.[7]

GENDER ATTRIBUTION AS AN HISTORICAL PROCESS

The gender attribution process is simultaneously an *ahistorical* and an *historical* process. It is ahistorical in the sense that we have been discussing; gender attributions are made in the course of a particular, concrete interaction. It is historical in the sense that it creates and sustains the natural attitude toward gender and hence gender as a permanent feature. The historicity of gender is constituted in the course of interaction. In ongoing interactions, once a gender attribution has been made, it is no longer necessary to keep "doing male" or "doing female." What Garfinkel, Agnes, and many others have failed to recognize is that it is not the particular gender which must be sustained, but rather the sense of its "naturalness," the sense that the actor has always been that gender. In sharing the natural attitude, both actor and attributor can assume (and each knows the other assumes) that gender never changes, that people "really" are what they appear to be. As a consequence of holding the natural attitude, the attributor filters *all* of the actor's behaviors through the gender attribution that was made, and the actor's behaviors are made sense of within that context. As we have illustrated in Chapter 5, almost nothing can discredit a gender attribution once it is made. Even the loss of the original criteria used to make the attribution might well become irrelevant. The man might shave his beard; the woman might have a mastectomy. The gender attribution will not change, though, merely because these signs no longer exist.

Since discrediting gender attributions is a matter of discrediting naturalness, this can only occur over time through a violation of the gender invariance rule. The person must create a sense of having "changed" genders. She/he must violate the naturalness of the gender (i.e., its historicity) before discrediting occurs and a new gender attribution is made. Even then, a discrediting of the original gender attribution will not necessarily occur. Gender attributions are so impervious to change that the person will be seen as "crazy" long before she/he is seen as being the other gender. For this reason, transsexuals find it most difficult to be seen as their "new" gender by those people who made their acquaintance in their "original" gender. The first impression will not dissipate for a long time (Feinbloom, 1976). If, however, the first impression is made when the transsexual is in his/her "new" gender, it will be most difficult to discredit *that* attribution, regardless of the information given to the attributor. We have had transsexuals lecture in classrooms and have had students question the authenticity of the lecturers' *transsexualism*. These students were unable, after a conscious search, to specify any cues that would unqualifiedly classify the transsexuals' gender as other than that which they appeared to be. The knowledge that these people had admittedly been assigned the other gender at birth and had lived 30 years as that gender became problematic for the students (and fascinating to us) because that information by itself could not be used to discredit the gender attribution.

If transsexuals understood these features of discrediting they would (1) focus on creating decisive first impressions as male or female and (2) then stop worrying about being the perfect man or woman and concentrate on cultivating the naturalness (i.e., the historicity) of their maleness or femaleness.

Just as any concrete cue can be cited as a reason for making a gender attribution, once an attribution has been discredited, anything concrete can be used as a "good reason" for the discrediting. "I knew she was 'really' a woman because of her slight build." In the case of discrediting, just as in the case of original attributions, the "good reasons" given are not necessarily the cues used during the process.

The reason that "normals" do not walk around questioning the gender attributions they make or wondering whether people will see them as they "really" are, is not because gender is a given, but because gender invariance is an incorrigible proposition. Rather than violating invariance, people use what might be seen as discrediting information to reflexively support this proposition. "I know that Greta has a penis, but that's irrelevant, since she's really a woman." All of us, transsexuals and "normals" alike, are in as little or as much danger of not being able to be seen as what we "really" are. It is our method of applying information which maintains our gender, not some intrinsic quality of our gender, itself.

GENDER DIMORPHISM: THE PROCESS AND ITS IMPLICATIONS

Once a gender attribution is made, the dichotomization process is set into motion. The cues involved in the schema which led to the attribution are seen as connected with a myriad of other cues which are consequently also attributed to the person. All of these cues taken together, or any of them separately, can then be used as reasons for having made the attribution in the first place. For example, people might decide that someone is male partly because they notice the presence of a beard which is a socially constructed "male" cue. If asked, "How do you know the person is male?" the attributor might answer, "Because he had narrow hips, a beard, and he walked like a man." The attributor may not have originally noticed the other's hips or walk, and in terms of a measurable distribution, the other might not have narrow hips or a "masculine" kind of walk. Since the other has been dichotomously placed into the gender category "male," and since the attributor "knows" that men have narrower hips than women and walk in a distinctive way, these features come to be seen as having been important in the attribution (see, e.g., Seavey et al., 1975). They are important, however, only because of the way we construct female and male as dichotomous, nonoverlapping categories with male characteristics generally constructed to be more obvious.

It has become increasingly acceptable to assert that the dichotomous behaviors which we attribute to the two genders (i.e., gender roles) are not necessarily the way women and men actually behave. There is growing evidence that the genders behave in very similar ways; and yet many people continue to make differential attributions of motives and behaviors, and to interpret behavior and its consequences in a dichotomous way, depending on whether the actor is female or male (e.g., Deaux, 1976; Rubin et al., 1974). Dichotomous gender role behaviors are overlayed on dichotomous *gender* which has traditionally meant two dimorphically distinct biological *sexes*. In the same way that behavior is dichotomized and overlayed on form, *form is dichotomized and overlayed on social construction*. Given a constitutive belief in two genders, form is dichotomized in the process of gender attribution at least as much as behavior is. As a result we end up with two genders, at least as different physically as they have been traditionally thought to be behaviorally.

The social construction of gender and the gender attribution process are a part of reality construction. No member is exempt, and this construction is the grounding for all scientific work on gender. The natural attitude toward gender and the everyday process of gender attribution are constructions which scientists bring with them when they enter laboratories to "discover" gender characteristics. Gender, as we have described it, consists of members' methods for attributing and constructing gender. Part of members' construction involves seeing gender as consisting of, and being grounded in, objective biological characteristics. Our reality is constructed in such a way that biology is seen as the ultimate truth. This is, of course, not necessary. In other realities, for example, deities replace biology as the ultimate source of final truth. What is difficult to see, however, is that biology is no closer to the truth, in any absolute sense, than a deity; nor is the reality which we have been presenting. What is different among different ways of seeing the world are the possibilities stemming from basic assumptions about the way the world works. What must be taken for granted (and what need not be) changes depending on the incorrigible propositions one holds. The questions that should be asked and how they can be answered also differ depending on the reality. We have tried to show, throughout this book, how we can give grounds for what biologists and social scientists do, and how the everyday process of gender attribution is primary. Scientists construct dimophism where there is continuity. Hormones, behavior, physical characteristics, developmental processes, chromosomes, psychological qualities have all been fitted into gender dichotomous categories. Scientific knowledge does not inform the answer to "What makes a person either a man or a woman?" Rather it justifies (and appears to give grounds for) the already existing knowledge that a person is either a woman or a man and that there is no problem in differentiating between the two. Biological, psychological, and social differences do not lead to our seeing two genders. Our seeing of two genders leads to the "discovery" of biological, psychological, and social differences.

In essence we are proposing a paradigm change in the way gender is viewed, a shift to seeing gender attribution as primary and gender as a practical accomplishment. In the remainder of this chapter we outline some of the theoretical and practical implications of such a shift.

One consequence of the shift is a new focus for research. Instead of concentrating on the *results* of seeing someone as female or male ("sex difference" research), scientists can begin to uncover factors in the gender attribution process. We have offered some suggestions on how this can be done, and will end the book with a few more. However, unless this research is undertaken with a concurrent acceptance of the proposition that gender is a social construction, there will not be, and cannot be, any radical changes in either how science is done or in how gender is viewed in everyday life.

Many of those concerned with sexism and the position of women in society have suggested that what is needed is a change in the concept of, or even the elimination of, gender roles. The assertion is that, even though the genders are physically dimorphic, except for a few biological differences related to reproduction, there is no necessary reason for any sort of differentiation. Rubin (1975) has written an excellent article, taking a strong position on this. She sees gender as a product of social organization, as the process by which "males" and "females" (the two sexes) become transformed into "men" and "women" (the two genders). Her analysis demonstrates the possibility of "the elimination of obligatory sexualities and sex roles, ... of an androgynous and genderless (though not sexless) society" (p. 204). Rubin's analysis of gender, while compatible with ours, still is grounded in, and takes for granted, the objective reality of two biological "sexes." Such a position does not question the facticity of two genders, as we mean "gender." An "androgynous society," by definition, retains the male/female dichotomy by agreeing to ignore it. Because accepting the facticity of two genders (or sexes; the former includes the latter) means accepting the assumptions which ground the gender attribution process, a "simple" elimination of gender role will not change what it means to be female or male. The social construction of gender revealed through the gender attribution process creates and sustains androcentric reality. "Male" characteristics are constructed as more obvious; a person is female only in the absence of "male" signs; there is a bias toward making a male gender attribution. In the process of attributing "male" or "female," dichotomous physical differences are constructed, and once a physical dichotomy has been constructed it is almost impossible to eliminate sociological and psychological dichotomies. Given that the physical dichotomy is androcentric, it is inevitable that the social one is also.

Whenever science has offered evidence of a biological continuum, but everyday members insist (because of the way reality is constructed) that there are discrete categories, there have been attempts to legislate against the continuum. Laws in the United States on what constituted a "Negro" and laws in Nazi Germany on what constituted a Jew are two of the most obvious examples. These laws did not reject biology, since biology is a crucial part of the construction of Western reality, but used biology. Race was seen as grounded in the amount of biological matter ("blood," or genetic material) of a certain type within a human body. Rulings in sports which legislate a person's gender are not very different from such laws. As scientists find fewer biological, psychological, and social dichotomies and more biological, psychological, and social continua, it is not impossible that legislators will attempt to legally define "female" and "male," rather than relying on specific judicial rulings. As long as the categories "female" and "male" present themselves to people in everyday life as external, objective, dichotomous, physical facts, there will be scientific and naive searches for differences, and differences will be found. Where there are dichotomies it is difficult to avoid evaluating one in relation to the other, a firm foundation for discrimination and oppression. Unless and until gender, in all of its manifestations *including the physical*, is seen as a social construction, action that will radically change our incorrigible propositions cannot occur. People must be confronted with the reality of other possibilities, as well as the possibility of other realities.

Scientific studies of gender are ultimately grounded in the biological imperative of reproduction. Dimorphism is seen as necessary for sperm and egg cell carriers to identify one another. Many of those who argue against the blurring of gender roles, against androgyny, against the claim of transsexuals to be a different gender, base their arguments on this "biological imperative." One extreme form of the argument is that if there are not clear roles, functions, and appearances, people will not develop "healthy" gender identities, no one will know how to, or want to, reproduce, and the species will become extinct.

The major premise of such arguments is that "male" and "female" are the same as "sperm carrier" and "egg carrier." However, what we have been demonstrating throughout this book is that they are not. "Male" and "female" are grounded in the gender attribution process and are social constructions. They are more encompassing categories than sperm and egg carrier. Not all egg carriers are female and not all females are egg carriers; not all sperm carriers are male, nor are all males sperm carriers.

The only requirement for the "biological imperative" of reproduction is that sperm and egg carriers must be identifiable to each other for reproductive purposes. However, not every human being can reproduce, nor does every human being who carries reproductive cells want to reproduce. Reproduction is not even a possibility for human beings throughout much of their life cycles. Sperm cell carriers are rarely younger than thirteen or fourteen, and probably have an increasing number of defective sperm cells as they grow older (Evans, 1976). Egg cell carriers are usually no younger than eleven or twelve, and can reproduce for only a few days each month for 30 to 40 years, which totals perhaps 3½ years over their life span when they could be identifiable as capable of reproduction. Thus, for all people, reproduction is not a continuous fact of life. In addition, technologies like artificial insemination, the development of techniques for ovarian and uterine transplants, and genetic engineering may, in the future, change our ideas of what the "biological imperative" for reproduction is.

The argument that certain "suitable sex differences" or stable secondary gender characteristics are necessary in order to make a differentiation between egg and sperm carriers is not an argument for the biological imperative. Rather, it is an argument for the maintenance of gender. Such arguments are based on the social construction of gender, of being female and male, which is much more than reproduction and, in fact, has little to do with reproduction. Gender, in science and in everyday life, is constructed to be dichotomous not only from birth, but even after death. A woman who dies remains a woman forever. If there were cultures whose dead became neuter, then this would suggest very different ideas about gender.

There are alternative ways we can begin to think about gender, new constructions for which "gender" is probably not even the most appropriate word. Some people, at some points in their lives, might wish to be identified as sperm or egg cell carriers. Except for those times, there need be no differentiation among people on *any* of the dichotomies which gender implies. Because the reproductive dichotomy would not be constituted as a lifetime dichotomy, it would not be an essential characteristic of people. Even the reproductive *dichotomy* might someday be eliminated through technology. No technological development related to reproduction, however, is necessary in order for a new social construction to appear.

Our description of this alternative possibility is not meant to be read as a prescription for a new social order, but as a theoretical "blueprint." Perhaps some readers will feel that we are describing myth or science fiction (see LeGuin, 1969, 1976). That is not our purpose here either, although both myth and theory serve important functions. It would be naive to assume that any statement of alternatives could, by fiat, change the way members view reality. We do not expect that there will develop a whole new social construction of gender in everyday life. What we are arguing is that the world we have now is no more or less "real" than any alternative. What we are demonstrating is that through our theoretical framework exciting alternative possibilities for understanding the meaning of gender present themselves.[8]

As we have reexamined the literature on gender, and as we have analyzed the data we collected on the gender attribution process, we have become convinced of an intriguing possibility. The process of *gender attribution* (deciding whether some one is female or male) and the resultant *gender identification* (assigning the label "female" or "male") may not be the same thing as *"gender"*[9] *differentiation*—knowing whether the other is similar or different from oneself, perhaps in terms of some basic reproductive criteria.

Although children are not 100 percent accurate in assigning gender labels until they are four or five, and although they cannot give "good reasons" for their identifications until they are somewhat older, Lewis and Weintraub (1974) reported that infants, before they are a year old, can make some kind of differentiation between "females" and "males." Male infants looked at pictures of other male infants longer than at pictures of female infants, and the reverse was true for female infants. What is most interesting about this study is that Lewis reports (Friedman et al., 1974, p. 191) that adults could not make accurate gender attributions to the pictures which the infants differentiated. The adults could not say, beyond a chance level, whether an infant pictured was female or male. Lewis, however, did not report whether the adults could differentiate in the same way the infants did, that is, on the basis of length of eye contact with the picture.

Lewis terms what the infants did "gender differentiation." Both Kohlberg and Green (Friedman et al., 1974, pp. 192–193) assert that the infants' behavior has nothing to do with gender and that it is "merely" a self–other distinction, since the infants were too young to have gender identities and/or gender concepts. We agree. Gender attribution and gender identification are not possible before the individual shares members' methods for seeing and doing gender. It is possible, however, that infants can make "gender" differentiations—the differentiation necessary for the "biological imperative" of reproduction—a process very different from gender attribution.

Were the infants using cues that adults could not perceive? Their behavior seems to be related to our finding in the children's drawings study that preschoolers were better at determining the "gender" of the other preschoolers' drawings than any other age group. It is also interesting that several transsexuals have mentioned to us that they have the most difficulty "passing" with young children. Is it possible that there is some ability which human beings have to differentiate sperm and egg cell carriers which is then overlayed and superceded by learned members' methods for constructing gender? Obviously a great deal more research on infant and children's gender attribution and "gender" differentiation processes is needed, as well as research on how these processes change over time. It is also important to know more about nonverbal (e.g., eye contact) indicators of "gender" differentiation in adults.

It has become clear to us that within the paradigm of contemporary science we cannot know all that can eventually be uncovered about what it means to be a woman or a man. All knowledge is now grounded in the everyday social construction of a world of two genders where gender attribution, rather than "gender" differentiation, is what concerns those who fear change. With the courage to confront, understand, and redefine our incorrigible propositions, we can begin to discover new scientific knowledge and to construct new realities in everyday life.

NOTES

1. This is the method (Garfinkel, 1967) by which members decide meanings and assemble a body of knowledge on the basis of documentary evidence. In Garfinkel's demonstration with a "rigged" question and answer format, he showed how, in searching for patterns, members make sense of incomplete, inappropriate, and contradictory material, and how they hear such answers as answers to their questions.

2. This was the one case where we found a difference between our female and male participants. Twenty-eight percent of the male participants said "male" when the figure had a vagina, but 43 percent of the female participants said "male." Why should the presence of at least one male cue in the context of a vagina be more salient to women than to men when they are constructing gender? If constructing "femaleness" requires an absence of "male" cues, perhaps those who have been so constructed ("women") are more sensitive to violations. Our sample of 960 participants was selected from those who happened to be on the campuses of eight of the colleges and universities in the New York Metropolitan area on the days the data was collected. It is possible that a sample of feminists would have placed more emphasis on the reality of the vagina.

3. Even when participants were asked to judge a nude figure with no genitals, they more often responded "male." In addition to the ninety-six conditions already mentioned, we had sixteen "no-genital" conditions. We expected that "female" gender attributions would predominate, since the drawings would approximate what some have called the "hidden" female genitals. In fact, though, 58 percent of the participants labeled the figure "male." The "male" cues (short hair, narrow hips, body hair, flat chest) were obviously impossible to ignore.

4. In order to partially check the validity of using a drawing, we replicated this condition (penis, breasts, hips, long hair, no body hair) using a photograph of an actual person (taken from a popular "sex" magazine). The findings for the photograph were almost identical to the findings for the drawing. Six participants identified the model as male and four as female. At least one half of the participants had low certainty scores. In addition, we showed ten participants a photograph of the same model with the penis hidden and pubic hair showing so that it looked like there might have been a vagina. Thus, we were able to closely replicate the condition: vagina, breasts, hips, no body hair, long hair. Again, the findings for the photograph were very similar to our overplay results. Eight participants identified the figure in the photograph as female.

5. Newton (1972) notes that the most amateur mistake a female impersonator can make is to fail to conceal the "telltale" bulge of the penis. Apparently that error is considered damaging enough to destroy the illusion of femaleness. This piece of evidence in conjunction with our data suggests why the female-to-male transsexual is not as overtly concerned with obtaining a penis as the male-to-female transsexual is with getting the penis removed.

6. Freud was right about the "obvious superiority" of the penis. However, he considered the emphasis on the penis as an inevitable psychological consequence of its objective reality. We are treating the belief in the penis' objective reality as problematic. Those who read Freud as being concerned with (socially real) phalluses, rather than (physically real) penises, see psychoanalytic theory as being grounded in meanings that come very close to our schema for differentiating females from males: "The alternative (is) between having, or not having, the phallus. Castration is not a real 'lack' but a meaning conferred upon the genitals of a woman.... The presence or absence of the phallus carries the difference between the two sexual statuses, 'man' and 'woman' " (Rubin, 1975, p. 191).

7. Several features of psychological and biological research and theory on gender seem to have an intriguing relationship to this schema. The specifics of the relationship are unknown and open to speculation, but these features include the precariousness of the development of a male gender identity and male gender role behaviors (as opposed to female), the prevalence of theories of male gender development which cannot explain female gender development, and the scientific fact that, beginning with conception, something (genes, hormones) must be added at every step to make the fetus male.

8. The major dilemma of the ethnomethodologist is the problem of infinite regress. If we assert that reality is a social construction, why stop at gender as a social construction? Why not assert that "sperm carriers" and "egg carriers" are as much of a construction as "male" or "female"? We all have to make a decision to take *something* for granted, to stop somewhere; otherwise it would be impossible to get out of bed in the morning. Our decision has been to stop here; others may wish to go on. (See Mehan and Wood (1975) for a discussion of this problem and an explanation of what Garfinkel (1966) meant when he said "Ethnomethodologists know 'tsouris.' ")

9. We have used "gender" as a modifier because no other word exists to convey our meaning. However, we have set it in quotation marks to differentiate it from gender, as the term has been used throughout the book—the socially constructed, dichotomous categories of "male" and "female" with all their layers of implications.

14

Doing Justice to Someone
Sex Reassignment and Allegories of Transsexuality

Judith Butler

Judith Butler's central tenet is that the hegemonic power of heteronormativity produces all forms of the body, sex, and gender. In "Doing Justice to Someone," her rereading of the David Reimer case (the so-called John/Joan case brought to popular attention by journalist John Colapinto in the book *As Nature Made Him*), Butler builds upon the view put forth in her earlier *Gender Trouble* and *Bodies that Matter* that all gender is an imitation for which there is no original.

David, one of twins, had his penis irreparably damaged in a circumcision accident. His parents, following the advice of psycho-endocrinologist John Money, were persuaded to raise the child as a girl. Over the next fifteen years, Money was to write up the case as support for his theory that gender was socially constructed rather than biologically innate. Another scientist of sexuality, Milton Diamond, eventually showed that Money's claim of success was not true; although raised to be a woman, David eventually started living as a man, and ultimately underwent female-to-male sex reassignment surgery.

Butler's analysis illustrates the plurality of the self, its underpinnings, and the multiple facets of identity. She questions the different perspectives of Money and Diamond, and illustrates the paradoxes of each argument. She does not, however, illustrate how the multiplicity of oppressive processes and practices become focused on the bending and breaking of the gendered self. For many transgender readers, Butler's insistence that gender is always ultimately about something else devalues their experience of gender identity's profound ontological claim—that it is precisely about the realness and inalienability of that identity, rather than about anything else. This article contributes to an understanding of the limitations of identity, but it begs another question; if gender is not real, how real can its oppression be?

I would like to take my point of departure from a question of power, the power of regulation, a power that determines, more or less, what we are, what we can be. I am not speaking of power only in a juridical or positive sense, but I am referring to the workings of a certain regulatory regime, one that informs the law, and one that also exceeds the law. When we ask what the conditions of intelligibility are by which the human emerges, by which the human is recognized, by which some subject becomes the subject of human love, we are asking about conditions of intelligibility composed of norms, of practices, that have become presuppositional, without which we cannot think the human at all. So I propose to broach the relationship between variable orders of intelligibility and the genesis and knowability of the human. And it is not just that there are laws that govern our intelligibility, but ways of knowing, modes of truth, that forcibly define intelligibility.

This is what Foucault describes as the politics of truth, a politics that pertains to those relations of power that circumscribe in advance what will and will not count as truth, that order the world in certain regular and regulatable ways, and that we come to accept as the given field of knowledge. We can understand the salience of this point when we begin to ask: What counts as a person? What counts as a coherent gender? What qualifies as a citizen? Whose world is legitimated as real? Subjectively, we ask: Who can I become in such a world where the meanings and limits of the subject are set out in advance for me? By what norms am I constrained as I begin to ask what I may become? What happens when I begin to become that for which there is no place in the given regime of truth? This is what Foucault describes as "the desubjugation of the subject in the play of…the politics of truth."[1]

Another way of putting this is the following: What, given the contemporary order of being, can I be? And this way of putting the question, which is Foucault's, does not quite broach the question of what it is *not* to be, or what it is to occupy the place of not-being within the field of being, living, breathing, attempting to love, as that which is neither fully negated nor acknowledged as being, acknowledged, we might say, into being. This relationship, between intelligibility and the human, is an urgent one; it carries a certain theoretical urgency, precisely at those points where the human is encountered at the limits of intelligibility itself. I would like to suggest that this interrogation has something important to do with justice. Since justice not only or exclusively is a matter of how persons are treated, how societies are constituted, but also emerges in quite consequential decisions about what a person is, what social norms must be honored and expressed for personhood to become allocated, how we do or do not recognize animate others as persons depending on whether or not we recognize a certain norm manifested in and by the body of that other. The very criterion by which we judge a person to be a gendered being, a criterion that posits coherent gender as a presupposition of humanness, is not only one that, justly or unjustly, governs the recognizability of the human but one that informs the ways we do or do not recognize ourselves, at the level of feeling, desire, and the body, in the moments before the mirror, in the moments before the window, in the times that one turns to psychologists, to psychiatrists, to medical and legal professionals to negotiate what may well feel like the unrecognizability of one's gender and, hence, of one's personhood.

I want to consider a legal and psychiatric case of a person who was determined without difficulty to be a boy at the time of birth, then was determined again within a few months to be a girl, and then decided to become a man in his teenage years. This is the John/Joan case, brought to public attention by the British Broadcasting Corporation in the early 1990s and recently again in various popular, psychological, and medical journals.[2] I base my analysis on an article cowritten by Milton Diamond, an endocrinologist, and the popular book *As Nature Made Him*, by John Colapinto, a journalist for *Rolling Stone*, as well as on work by John Money, critical commentaries by Anne Fausto-Sterling and Suzanne J. Kessler in their important recent books, and a newspaper account by Natalie Angier.[3] John, a pseudonym for a man who lives in Winnipeg, was born with XY chromosomes. When he was eight months old, his penis was accidentally burned and severed during a surgical operation to rectify phimosis, a condition in which the foreskin thwarts urination. This procedure is relatively risk-free, but the doctor who performed it on John was using a new machine, apparently one that he had not used before, one that his colleagues declared was unnecessary for the job, and he was having trouble making it work, so he increased the power to the machine to the point that it burned away a major portion of the penis. The parents were, of course, appalled, and they were, according to their own description, unclear how to proceed.

Then one evening, about a year later, they were watching television, and there they encountered Money talking about transsexual and intersexual surgery and offering the view that if a child underwent surgery and started socialization as a gender different from the one originally assigned at birth, he or she could develop normally, adapt perfectly well to the new gender, and live a happy life. The parents wrote to Money, who invited them to Baltimore, and so John was seen at Johns Hopkins University, at which point Money strongly recommended that he be raised as a girl. The parents agreed, and the doctors removed the testicles, made some preliminary preparations for surgery to create a vagina, but decided to wait until Joan, the newly named child, was older to complete the task. So Joan grew up as a girl, was monitored often, and was periodically given over to Money's Gender Identity Institute for the purposes of fostering her adaptation to girlhood. And then, it is reported, between the ages of eight and nine Joan found herself developing the desire to buy a toy machine gun. And then, it is said, between the ages of nine and eleven she started to realize that she was not a girl. This realization seems to have coincided with her desire to buy certain kinds of toys: more guns, apparently, and some trucks. Even without a penis, Joan liked to stand to urinate. And she was caught in this position once, at school, where the other girls threatened to "kill" her if she continued.

At this point the psychiatric teams that intermittently monitored Joan's adaptation offered her estrogen, which she refused. Money tried to talk to her about getting a real vagina, and she refused; in fact, she went screaming from the room. Money had her view sexually graphic pictures of vaginas. He even went so far as to show her pictures of women giving birth, holding out the possibility that Joan could give birth if she acquired a vagina. In a scene that could have inspired the recent film *But I'm a Cheerleader*, he also required that she and her brother perform mock-coital exercises with one another, on command. They both later reported being frightened and disoriented by this demand and did not tell their parents about it at the time. Joan is said to have preferred male activities and not to have liked developing breasts. All of these claims were attributed to Joan by another set of doctors, a team of psychiatrists at her local hospital. These psychiatrists and other local medical professionals intervened, believing that a mistake in sex reassignment had been made. Eventually the case was reviewed by Diamond, a sex researcher who believes in the hormonal basis of gender identity and who has been battling Money for years. This new set of psychiatrists and other doctors offered Joan the choice of changing paths, which she accepted. She started living as a boy, named John, at the age of fourteen. John requested and received male hormone shots; he also had his breasts removed. A phallus, so called by Diamond, was constructed for him between the ages of fifteen and sixteen. John does not ejaculate; he feels some sexual pleasure in the phallus; he urinates from its base. Thus it only approximates some of its expected functions, and, as we shall see, it enters John only ambivalently into the norm.

During the time that John was Joan, Money published papers extolling the success of this sex reassignment. The case was enormously consequential because Joan was an identical twin, and so Money could track the development of both siblings while controlling for genetic makeup. He insisted that both were developing normally and happily into their respective genders. But his own recorded interviews, mainly unpublished, and subsequent research have called his honesty into question. Joan was hardly happy, refused to adapt to many so-called girl behaviors, and was angered by Money's invasive, continual interrogations. Yet the published records from Johns Hopkins claim that Joan's adaptation to girlhood was successful, and certain ideological conclusions immediately followed. Money's Gender Identity Institute, which monitored Joan often, asserted that her successful development as a girl "offers convincing evidence that the gender identity gate is open at birth for a normal child no less than for one born with unfinished sex organs or one who was prenatally over or underexposed to androgen, and that it stays open at least for something over a year at birth."[4] Indeed, the case was used by the public media to prove that what is feminine and what is masculine can be altered, that these cultural terms have no fixed meaning or internal destiny. Even Kate Millett cited the case in arguing that biology is not destiny. Kessler also allied with Money in her essays in favor of the social constructionist thesis.[5] Later Kessler would disavow their alliance and write one of the most important books on the ethical and medical dimensions of sex reassignment, *Lessons from the Intersexed*, which includes a trenchant critique of Money.

Money's approach was to recruit male-to-female transsexuals to talk to Joan about the advantages of being a girl. She was subjected to myriad interviews and was asked again and again whether she felt like a girl, what her desires were, what her image of the future was, whether it included marriage to a man. She was also asked to strip and show her genitals to medical practitioners who were either interested in the case or monitoring it for her adaptational success.

When this case has been discussed in the press recently, and when psychiatrists and other medical practitioners have turned to it, they have done so to criticize the role that Money's institute played and, in particular, its readiness to use Joan's example to substantiate its own theoretical beliefs about the gender neutrality of early childhood, about the malleability of gender, about the primary role of socialization in the production of gender identity. In fact, this is not exactly everything that Money believes, but let us not probe that question here. The individuals who are critical of this case believe that it shows us something very different. When we consider, they argue, that John found himself deeply moved to become a boy and found it unbearable to continue to live as a girl, we have to consider as well that John experienced some deep-seated sense of gender, one linked to his original set of genitals, one seemingly there as an internal truth and necessity that no amount of socialization could reverse. This is the view of Colapinto and of Diamond as well.

So now the case of Joan/John is being used to make a revision and a reversal in developmental gender theory, providing evidence this time that counters Money's thesis, supporting the notion of an essential gender core tied in some irreversible way to anatomy and to a deterministic sense of biology. Indeed, Colapinto clearly links Money's cruelty to Joan to the "cruelty" of social construction as a theory, remarking that Money's refusal to identify a biological or anatomical basis for gender difference in the early 1970s "was not lost on the then-burgeoning women's movement, which had been arguing against a biological basis for sex differences for decades." Colapinto claims that Money's published essays "had already been used as one of the main foundations of modern feminism." He asserts that *Time* engaged in a similarly misguided appropriation of Money's views when it argued that this case, in the magazine's own words, "provides strong support for a major contention of women's liberationists: that conventional patterns of masculine and feminine behavior can be altered."[6] Indeed, Colapinto talks about the failure of surgically reassigned individuals to live as "normal" and "typical" women and men, arguing that normality is never achieved and hence assuming the inarguable value of normalcy itself.

Reporting on the refutation of Money's theory, Natalie Angier claims that the story of John has "the force of allegory."[7] But which force is that? And is this an allegory with closure? Angier reports that Diamond used the case to make an argument about intersexual surgery and, by implication, the relative success of transsexual surgery. Diamond argued, for instance, that intersexed infants, that is, those born with mixed or indeterminate genital attributes, generally have a Y chromosome, and that possession of the Y is an adequate basis for concluding that they ought to be raised as boys. As it is, the vast majority of intersexed infants are subjected to surgery that seeks to assign them to the female sex, since, as Cheryl Chase points out in Angier's article, it is simply considered easier to produce a provisional vaginal tract than to construct a phallus. Diamond argued that these children should be assigned to the male sex, since the presence of the Y is sufficient grounds for the presumption of social masculinity.

In fact, Chase, founder and director of the Intersex Society of North America, voiced skepticism about Diamond's recommendations. Her view, recently defended by Fausto-Sterling as well, is that there is no reason to make a sex assignment at all; society should make room for the intersexed as they are and cease the coercive surgical "correction" of infants.[8] Indeed, recent research has shown that such operations have been performed without the parents knowing about it, without the children themselves ever being truthfully told, and without their having attained the age of consent. Most astonishing, in a way, is the state that their bodies have been left in, with mutilations performed and then paradoxically rationalized in the name of "looking normal." Medical practitioners often say to the parents that the child will not look normal if not operated on; that the child will be ashamed in the locker room, *the locker room*, that site of prepubescent anxiety about impending gender developments; and that it would be better for the child to look normal, even when such surgery may deprive him or her of sexual function and sexual pleasure for life.

So, while some experts, such as Money, claim that the absence of the full phallus makes the social case for rearing the child as a girl, others, such as Diamond, argue that the presence of the Y chromosome is the most compelling fact or, that it is what is indexed in persistent feelings of masculinity, and that it cannot be constructed away. So, on the one hand, how my anatomy looks, how it comes to appear, to others and to myself as I see others looking at me, is the basis of my social identity as woman or man. On the other hand, how the presence of the Y tacitly structures my feeling and self-understanding as a sexed person is decisive. Money argues for the ease with which a female body can be surgically constructed, as if femininity were always little more than a surgical construction, an elimination, a cutting away. Diamond argues for the invisible and necessary persistence of maleness, which does not need to "appear" in order to operate as the key feature of gender identity. When Angier asks Chase whether she agrees with Diamond's recommendations on intersexual surgery, Chase replies, "They can't conceive of leaving someone alone." Indeed, is the surgery performed to create a "normal"—looking body, after all? The mutilations and scars that remain hardly offer compelling evidence that this is accomplished. Or are these bodies subjected to medical machinery that marks them for life precisely because they are "inconceivable"?

Another paradox that emerges here is the place of sharp machines, of the technology of the knife, in debates on intersexuality and transsexuality. If the John/Joan case is an allegory, or has the force of allegory, it seems to be the site where debates on intersexuality (John is not a intersexual) and transsexuality (John is not an transsexual) converge. This body becomes a point of reference for a narrative that is not about this body but that seizes on the body, as it were, to inaugurate a narrative that interrogates the limits of the conceivably human. What is inconceivable is conceived again and again, through narrative means, but something remains outside the narrative, a resistant moment that signals a persisting inconceivability.

Despite Diamond's recommendations, the intersexed movement has been galvanized by the Joan/John case; it is able now to bring to public attention the brutality and coerciveness and lasting harm of the unwanted surgeries performed on intersexed infants. The point is to try to imagine a world in which individuals with mixed or indeterminate genital attributes might be accepted and loved without having to undergo transformation into a more socially coherent or normative version of gender. In this sense, the intersexed movement has sought to ask why society maintains the ideal of gender dimorphism when a significant percentage of children are chromosomally various, and a continuum exists between male and female that suggests the arbitrariness and falsity of gender dimorphism as a prerequisite of human development. There are humans, in other words, who live and breathe in the interstices of this binary relation, showing that it is not exhaustive; it is not necessary. Although the transsexual movement, which is internally various, has called for rights to surgical means by which sex might be transformed, it is clear—and Chase underscores—that there is also a serious and increasingly popular critique of idealized gender dimorphism in the transsexual movement itself. One can see it in the work of Riki Anne Wilchins, whose gender theory makes room for transsexuality as a transformative exercise, but one can see it perhaps most dramatically in the work of Kate Bornstein, who argues that to go from female to male, or from male to female, is not necessarily to stay within the binary frame of gender but to engage transformation itself as the meaning of gender.[9] In some ways, Bornstein now carries the legacy of Simone de Beauvoir: if one is not born a woman, but becomes one, then becoming is the vehicle for gender itself.

But why, we might ask, has John become the occasion for a reflection on transsexuality? Although John comes to claim that he would prefer to be a man, it is not clear whether he himself believes in the primary causal force of the Y chromosome. Diamond finds support for his theory in John, but it is not clear, on the basis of my reading, that John agrees with Diamond. John clearly knows about hormones, has asked for them, and takes them. He has learned about phallic construction from transsexual contexts, wants a phallus, has it made, and so allegorizes a certain transsexual transformation without precisely exemplifying it. He is, in his own view, a man born a man, castrated by the medical establishment, feminized by the psychiatric world, and then enabled to return to who he was to begin with. But to return to who he is, he requires—and wants, and gets—a subjection to hormones and surgery. He allegorizes transsexuality to achieve a sense of naturalness. And this transformation is applauded by the endocrinologists on the case, since they understand his appearance now to be in accord with an inner truth. Whereas Money's institute enlists transsexuals to instruct Joan in the ways of women, and *in the name of normalization*, the endocrinologists prescribe the sex change protocol of transsexuality to John for him to reassume his genetic destiny, *in the name of nature*.

And though Money's institute enlists transsexuals to allegorize Joan's full transformation into a woman, the endocrinologists propose to appropriate transsexual surgery in order to build the phallus that will make John a more legible man. Importantly, it seems, the norms that govern intelligible gender for Money are those that can be forcibly imposed and behaviorally appropriated, so the malleability of gender construction, which is part of his thesis, turns out to require a forceful application. And the "nature" that the endocrinologists defend also needs assistance and augmentation through surgical and hormonal means, at which point a certain nonnatural intervention in anatomy and biology is precisely what is mandated by nature. So in each case the primary premise is in some ways refuted by the means by which it is implemented. Malleability is, as it were, violently imposed, and naturalness is artificially induced. There are ways of arguing social construction that have nothing to do with Money's project, but that is not my aim here. And there are, no doubt, ways of seeking recourse to genetic determinants that do not lead to the same kind of interventionist conclusions arrived at by Diamond and Sigmundson. But that is also not precisely my point. For the record, though, let us consider that the prescriptions arrived at by these purveyors of natural and normative gender in no way follow necessarily from the premises from which they begin, and that the premises with which they begin have no necessity in themselves. (One might well disjoin the theory of gender construction, for instance, from the hypothesis of gender normativity and have a very different account of social construction from that offered by Money; one might allow for genetic factors without assuming that they are the *only* aspect of nature that one might consult to understand the sexed characteristics of a human: why is the Y chromosome considered the primary determinant of maleness, exercising preemptive rights over any and all other factors?)

But my point in recounting this story and its appropriation for the purposes of gender theory is to suggest that the story as we have it does not supply evidence for either thesis, and to suggest that there may be another way to read this story, one that neither confirms nor denies the theory of social construction, one that neither affirms nor denies gender essentialism. Indeed, what I hope to underscore here is the disciplinary framework in which Joan/John develops a discourse of self-reporting and self-understanding, since it constitutes the grid of intelligibility by which his own humanness is both questioned and asserted.

It seems crucial to remember, as one considers what might count as the evidence of the truth of gender, that Joan/John was intensely monitored by psychological teams through childhood and adolescence, that teams of doctors observed Joan's behavior, that teams of doctors asked her and her brother to disrobe in front of them so that genital development could be gauged, that there was a doctor who asked her to engage in mock-coital exercises with her brother, to view the pictures, to know and want the so-called normalcy of unambiguous genitalia. There was an apparatus of knowledge applied to the person and body of Joan/John that is rarely, if ever, taken into account as part of what John responds to when he reports on his feelings of true gender. The act of self-reporting and the act of self-observation take place in relation to a certain audience, with a certain audience as the imagined recipient, before a certain audience for whom a verbal and visual picture of selfhood is produced. These are speech acts, we might say, that are very often delivered to those who have been scrutinizing, brutally, the truth of Joan's gender for years. Even though Diamond and Sigmundson and indeed Colapinto are in the position of defending John against Money's intrusions, they still ask John how he feels, who he is, trying to ascertain the truth of his sex through the discourse he provides. Of Joan, who was subjected to such scrutiny and, most important, repeatedly subjected to a norm, a normalizing ideal conveyed through a plurality of gazes, a norm applied to the body, a question was continually posed: Is this person feminine enough? Has this person made it to femininity? Is femininity properly embodied here? Is the embodiment working? Is it? Is it? How do we know? What evidence can we marshal in order to know? And surely we must have knowledge here. We must be able to say that we know, and communicate that in the professional journals, and justify our decision, our act. In effect, the question posed through these interrogatory exercises has to do with whether the gender norm that establishes coherent personhood has been successfully accomplished, and the inquiries and inspections can be understood, along these lines, not only as the violent attempt to implement the norm but as the institutionalization of that power of implementation.

The pediatricians and psychiatrists who have revisited the case in recent years cite John's self-description to support their point. John's narrative about his own sense of being male supports the theory that John is really male and that he was, even when he was Joan, always male.

John tells his interviewers the following about himself:

> There were little things from early on. I began to see how different I felt and was, from what I was supposed to be. But I didn't know what it meant. I thought I was a freak or something....I looked at myself and said I don't like this type of clothing, I don't like the types of toys I was always being given, I like hanging around with the guys and climbing trees and stuff like that and girls don't like any of that stuff. I looked in the mirror and [saw] my shoulders [were] so wide, I mean there [was] nothing feminine about me. [I was] skinny, but other than that, nothing. But that [was] how I figured it out. [I figured I was a guy] but I didn't want to admit it, I figured I didn't want to wind up opening a can of worms.[10]

So now you hear how John describes himself. And so, if part of my task here is to do justice not only to my topic but to the person I am sketching for you, the person about whom so much has been said, the person whose self-description and whose decisions have become the basis for so much gender theorizing in the last four years, then it seems to me that I must be careful in presenting these words. For these words can give you only something of the person I am trying to understand, some part of that person's verbal instance, and since I cannot truly understand this person, since I do not know this person and have no access to this person, I am left to be a reader of a selected number of words, words that I did not fully select, ones that were selected for me, recorded from interviews and then chosen by those who decided to write their articles on this person for journals such as the *Archives of Pediatrics and Adolescent Medicine*. So we might say that I have been given fragments of the person, linguistic fragments of something called a person, and what might it mean to do justice to someone under these circumstances? Can we?

On the one hand, we have a self-description, and that is to be honored. These are the words by which this individual gives himself to be understood. On the other hand, we have a description of a self that takes place in a language that is already going on, that is already saturated with norms, that predisposes us as we seek to speak of ourselves. And we have words that are delivered in the context of an interview, an interview that is part of the long and intrusive observational process that has accompanied John's formation from the start. To do justice to John is, certainly, to take him at his word, and to call him by his chosen name, but how are we to understand his word and his name? Is this the word that he creates? Is this the word that he receives? Are these the words that circulate prior to his emergence as an "I" that might gain a certain authorization to begin a self-description only within the norms of this language? So when one speaks, one speaks a language that is already speaking, even if one speaks it in a way that is not precisely how it has been spoken before. So what and who is speaking here, when John reports, "There were little things from early on. I began to see how different I felt and was, from what I was supposed to be"? This claim tells us minimally that John understands that there is a norm, a norm of how he was supposed to be, and that he has fallen short of it. The implicit claim is that the norm is femininity, and he has failed to live up to it. And there is the norm, and it is externally imposed, communicated through a set of expectations that others have, and then there is the world of feeling and being, and these realms are, for him, distinct. What he feels is not in any way produced by the norm, and the norm is other, elsewhere, not part of who he is, who he has become, what he feels.

But given what we know about how John has been addressed, we might, in an effort to do justice to John, ask what Joan saw as Joan looked at himself, felt as he felt himself, and please excuse my mixing of pronouns here, but matters are becoming changeable. When Joan looked in the mirror and saw something nameless, freakish, something between the norms, was she not at that moment in question as a human, was she not the specter of the freak against which and through which the norm installed itself? What was the problem with Joan, that people were always asking to see her naked, asking her questions about what she was, how she felt, whether this was or was not the same as what was normatively true? Is that self-seeing distinct from the way s/he is seen? John seems to understand clearly that the norms are external to him, but what if the norms have become the means by which he sees, the frame for his own seeing, his way of seeing himself? What if the action of the norm is to be found not merely in the ideal that it posits but in the sense of aberration and freakishness that it conveys? Consider precisely where the norm operates when John claims, "I looked at myself and said I don't like this type of clothing." To whom is John speaking? And in what world, under what conditions, does not liking that type of clothing provide evidence for being the wrong gender? For whom would that be true? And under what conditions?

John reports, "I don't like the types of toys I was always being given," and John is speaking here as someone who understands that such a dislike can function as evidence. And it seems reasonable to assume that Joan understood this dislike as evidence of gender dystopia, to use the technical term, because s/he has been addressed time and again by those who have made use of her every utterance about her experience as evidence for or against a true gender. That he happens not to have liked certain toys, certain dolls, certain games, may be significant in relation to the question of how and with what he liked to play. But in what world, precisely, do such dislikes count as clear or unequivocal evidence for or against being a given gender? Do parents regularly rush off to gender identity clinics when their boys play with yarn, or their girls play with trucks? Or must there already be an enormous anxiety at play, an anxiety about the truth of gender that seizes on this or that toy, this or that proclivity of dress, the size of the shoulder, the leanness of the body, to conclude that something like a clear gender identity can or cannot be built from these scattered desires, these variable and invariable features of the . . . structure of proclivity of attire?

So what does my analysis imply? Does it tell us whether the gender here is true or false? No. And does this have implications for whether John should have been surgically transformed into Joan, or Joan surgically transformed into John? No, it does not. I do not know how to judge that question here, and I am not sure it can be mine to judge. Does justice demand that I decide? Or does justice demand that I wait to decide, that I practice a certain deferral in the face of a situation in which too many have rushed to judgment? And it might be useful, important, even just, to consider a few matters before we decide, before we ascertain whether it is, in fact, ours to decide.

Consider in this spirit, then, that it is for the most part the gender essentialist position that must be voiced for transsexual surgery to take place, and that someone who comes in with a sense of gender as changeable will have a more difficult time convincing psychiatrists and doctors to perform the surgery. In San Francisco female-to-male candidates actually practice the narrative of gender essentialism that they are required to perform before they go in to see the doctors, and there are now coaches to help them, dramaturges of transsexuality who will help you make the case for no fee. Indeed, we might say that Joan/John together went through two transsexual surgeries: the first based on a hypothetical argument about what gender should be, given the ablated nature of the penis; the second based on what the gender should be, based on the behavioral and verbal indications of the person in question. In both cases, certain inferences were made, one that suggested that a body must appear a certain way for a gender to work, another that said that a body must feel a certain way for a gender to work. John clearly came to disrespect and abhor the views of the first set of doctors; he developed, we might say, a lay critique of the phallus to support his resistance:

> Doctor…said, it's gonna be tough, you're going to be picked on, you're gonna be very alone, you're not gonna find anybody unless you have vaginal surgery and live as a female. And I thought to myself, you know I wasn't very old at the time but it dawned on me that these people gotta be pretty shallow if that's the only thing they think I've got going for me; that the only reason why people get married and have children and have a productive life is because of what they have between their legs.…If that's all they think of me, that they justify my worth by what I have between my legs, then I gotta be a complete loser.[11]

Here John makes a distinction between the "I" that he is, the person that he is, and the value that is conferred on his personhood by virtue of what is or is not between his legs. He was wagering that he would be loved for something other than this or, at least, that his penis would not be the reason he was loved. He was holding out, implicitly, for something called "depth" over and against the "shallowness" of the doctors. And so we might say that, though John asked for and received his new status as male, asked for and received his new phallus, he is also something other than what he now has, and, though he has undergone this transformation, he refuses to be reduced to the body part that he has acquired. "If that's all they think of me," he says, offering a knowing and critical rejoinder to the work of the norm. "There is something here of me that exceeds this part, though I want this part, though it is part of me." He does not want his "worth" "justif[ied]" by what he has between his legs, and what this means is that he has another sense of how the worth of a person might be justified. So we might say that he is living his desire, acquiring the anatomy that he wants in order to live his desire, but that his desire is complex, and his worth is complex.

And this is why, no doubt, in response to many of the questions Money posed—Do you want to have a penis? Do you want to marry a girl?—John often refused to answer, refused the question, refused to stay in the room with Money, refused to visit Baltimore after a while. John did not trade in one gender norm for another, not exactly. It would be as wrong to say that he simply internalized a gendered norm (from a critical position) as it would be to say that he failed to live up to a gendered norm (from a normalizing, medical position), since he has already established that what will justify his worth will be the invocation of an "I" that is not reducible to the compatibility of his anatomy with the norm. He thinks something more of himself than what others think, he does not fully justify his worth through recourse to what he has between his legs, and he does not think of himself as a complete loser. Something exceeds the norm, and he recognizes its unrecognizability; it is, in a sense, his distance from the knowably human that operates as a condition of critical speech, the source of his worth, as the justification for his worth. He says that if what those doctors believe were true, he would be a complete loser, and he implies that he is not a complete loser, that something in him is winning. But he is also saying something more: he is cautioning us against the absolutism of distinction itself, for his phallus does not constitute the entirety of his worth, and so there is an incommensurability between who he is and what he has, between the phallus he has and what it is expected to be (and in this way he is no different from anyone with a phallus), which means that he has not become one with the norm, and yet he is still someone, speaking, insisting, even referring to himself.

And it is from this gap, this incommensurability, between the norm that is supposed to inaugurate his humanness and the spoken insistence on himself that he performs that he derives his worth, that he speaks his worth. We cannot precisely give content to this person at the very moment that he speaks his worth, which means that it is precisely the ways in which he is not fully recognizable, fully disposable, fully categorizable, that his humanness emerges. And this is important, because we might ask that he enter into intelligibility in order to speak and be known, but what he does instead, through his speech, is to offer a critical perspective on the norms that confer intelligibility itself. And he shows, we might say, that there is an understanding to be had that exceeds the norms of intelligibility itself. And he achieves this "outside," we might speculate, by refusing the interrogations that besiege him, by reversing their terms, learning the ways in which he might escape. And if he renders himself unintelligible to those who seek to know and capture his identity, this means that something about him is intelligible outside the framework of accepted intelligibility. We might be tempted to say that there is some core of a person, and so some presumption of humanism, that emerges here, that supervenes the discourses on sexed and gendered intelligibility that constrain him. But that would mean that he is denounced by one discourse, only to be carried by another discourse, the discourse of humanism. Or we might say that there is some core of the subject who speaks, who speaks beyond what is sayable, and that it is this ineffability that marks John's speech, the ineffability of the other who is not disclosed through speech but leaves a portentous shard of itself in its saying, a self that is beyond discourse itself.

But what I would prefer is that we consider carefully that when John invokes the "I" in this quite hopeful and unexpected way, he is speaking about a certain conviction he has about his own lovability; he says that "they" must think he is a real loser if the only reason anyone is going to love him is what he has between his legs. "They" are telling him that he will not be loved, or that he will not be loved unless he takes what they have for him, and that they have what he needs in order to get love that he will be loveless without what they have. But he refuses to accept that what they are offering in their discourse is love. He refuses their offering of love, understanding it as a bribe, as a seduction to subjection. He will be and he is, he tells us, loved for some other reason, a reason they do not understand, and it is not a reason we are given. It is clearly a reason beyond the regime of reason established by the norms of sexology itself. We know only that he holds out for another reason, and that in this sense we no longer know what kind of reason this is, what reason can be; he establishes the limits of what they know, disrupting the politics of truth, making use of his desubjugation within that order of being to establish the possibility of love beyond the grasp of that norm. He positions himself, knowingly, in relation to the norm, but he does not comply with its requirements. He risks a certain "desubjugation": Is he a subject? How will we know? And in this sense John's discourse puts into play the operation of critique itself, critique that, defined by Foucault, is precisely the desubjugation of the subject within the politics of truth. This does not mean that John becomes unintelligible and, therefore, without value to politics; rather, he emerges at the limits of intelligibility, offering a perspective on the variable ways in which norms circumscribe the human. It is precisely because we understand, without quite grasping, that he has another reason, that he *is*, as it were, another reason, that we see the limits to the discourse of intelligibility that would decide his fate. John does not precisely occupy a new world, since he is, even within the syntax that brings about his "I," still positioned somewhere between the norm and its failure. And he is, finally, neither one; he is the human in its anonymity, as that which we do not yet know how to name or that which sets a limit on all naming. And in that sense, he is the anonymous—and critical—condition of the human as it speaks itself at the limits of what we think we know.

NOTES

1. Michel Foucault, "What Is Critique?" trans. Lysa Hochroth, in *The Politics of Truth*, ed. Sylvère Lotringer and Lysa Hochroth (New York: Semiotext[e], 1997), 32. This essay was originally a lecture given at the French Society of Philosophy on 27 May 1978; it was subsequently published in *Bulletin de la Société française de la philosophie* 84, no. 2 (1990): 35–63.
2. For an excellent overview of this controversy see Anne Fausto-Sterling, *Sexing the Body: Gender Politics and the Construction of Sexuality* (New York: Basic, 2000), 45–77. John/Joan no longer operates with a pseudonym, but I keep the pseudonymous reference because it is the predominant way in which this person is referred to in the medical and psychological treatments of the issue here.
3. Milton Diamond and H. Keith Sigmundson, "Sex Reassignment at Birth: A Long Term Review and Clinical Implications," *Archives of Pediatrics and Adolescent Medicine* 151 (1997): 298–304; John Colapinto, *As Nature Made Him: The Boy Who Was Raised as a Girl* (New York: HarperCollins, 2000); Colapinto, "The True Story of John Joan," *Rolling Stone*, 11 December 1997, 54ff.; John Money and Richard Green, *Transsexualism and Sex Reassignment* (Baltimore: Johns Hopkins University Press, 1969); Fausto-Sterling, *Sexing the Body*; Suzanne J. Kessler, *Lessons from the Intersexed* (New Brunswick, N.J.: Rutgers University Press, 1998); Natalie Angier, "Sexual Identity Not Pliable after All, Report Says," *New York Times*, 14 March 1997, C1, C13. See also the videotape *Redefining Sex*, published by the Intersex Society of North America.
4. Money and Green, *Transsexualism and Sex Reassignment*, 299.
5. Kate Millett, *Sexual Politics* (Garden City, N.Y.: Doubleday, 1970), 41–42; Kessler, *Lessons from the Intersexed*, 6–7, 14–21; Kessler, "Meanings of Gender Variability," *Chrysalis* 2, no. 4 (1997–98): 33–38; and Kessler, "The Medical Construction of Gender: Case Management of Intersexed Infants," *Signs* 16 (1990): 3–26.
6. Colapinto, *As Nature Made Him*, 69.
7. Angier, "Sexual Identity Not Pliable," C1, C13.
8. See Fausto-Sterling, *Sexing the Body*, 79–114.
9. Riki Anne Wilchins, *Read My Lips: Sexual Subversion and the End of Gender* (Ithaca, N.Y.: Firebrand, 1997); Kate Bornstein, *Gender Outlaw: On Men, Women, and the Rest of Us* (New York: Vintage, 1995).
10. Quoted in Diamond and Sigmundson, "Sex Reassignment at Birth," 299–300. Ellipsis and last pair of brackets in original.
11. Ibid., 301. Ellipses in original.

15

Where Did We Go Wrong?
Feminism and Trans Theory—
Two Teams on the Same Side?

STEPHEN WHITTLE

STEPHEN WHITTLE, LECTURER IN LAW at Manchester Metropolitan University, has been recognized widely as a leading advocate for the rights of transgender and transsexual people in the United Kingdom and European Union. Much of his work is concentrated on legal analysis and the lack of a place in law for anyone outside the binary gender system. This brief article chronicles his quarter-century involvement in feminist debate, and offers a thoughtful commentary on what the transgender movement has learned from feminism, as well as what feminism can learn from the transgender movement.

Whittle traces his evolution from a lesbian separatist in the mid-1970s to his work as a transgender theorist in the twenty-first century, detailing in particular the "dark decade" of the 1980s when transgender people were pathologized by the medical and psychotherapeutic professions, and castigated by feminists for their supposed "false consciousness." He argues that both transgender and feminist theory have their roots in attempts to theorize beyond the nature/nurture debate, and to move social and legal practice into a different sphere. By highlighting the problems associated with the discussion that might have arisen when he was asked to edit a feminist journal, he problematizes the transgender self, placing it outside of conventional gender, and firmly into the realm of the "queer." He asks the reader to acknowledge that, as gender theorists, we have not yet started to work out what questions to ask as we interrogate gender—never mind come up with the answers. As such he opens the debate on whether those questions can ever be discovered, bearing in mind the limitations of language and, if so, what those questions might be.

Whittle makes telling use of an anecdote drawn from his experience playing lacrosse at an all-girl school, in which he and his teammates played on an unmarked playing field (a distinctive feature of women's lacrosse as opposed to men's lacrosse, where the pitch has clearly marked boundaries). He argues that women's socialization, those specific values that feminism endorses, facilitated the teams reaching agreement as to when a ball was out of play. He suggests that these same skills also belong to transgender theorists—an ability to work out whether the boundaries exist, and if they do, where they are. Accordingly, Whittle suggests that the relationship between transgender studies and feminism could proceed in much the same manner—that rather than bickering about who's on which team, and what the rules are, all concerned should get on with the game and work out an evolving consensus about where the boundaries are located, if they exist at all.

A SHORT PIECE OF HISTORY

Existing feminist oppositions to transsexual and transgender people, the medical processes they undertake and the knowledge and understanding they have of gender and sex, like all oppositions have a history. I want to start by framing this presentation in a small piece of my personal history. Like all trans people speaking on almost anything related to what trans is, the subjective experience always becomes the primary reference point.

In 1974, as a member of Manchester's 'Radical Lesbian Collective' I attended the 'Women's Liberation Conference' which was held in Edinburgh. The conference was an incredibly stormy affair. Loud and heated arguments took place around issues such as 'why were men providing child care in the conference crèche?' and 'how could women claim they were women-identified women if their sexual or homemaking partner was a man?' All of these discussions took place around a backdrop of the fundamental ideological differences between Liberal feminism, Marxist feminism and Radical Separatist (lesbian) feminism. At that time, and through my membership of the Lesbian Collective, I was firmly placed in the camp of radical separatism.

I believed—and still do believe—that there are values inherent in the complex understandings that arise out women's collective and individual histories which are better values in terms of informing people about ways of living and being. Those better values, if only articulated [through the process of women's consciousness raising] would lead to the deconstruction of the power inherent in the patriarchal structures that dictate gender and sex roles. That deconstruction project could only take place if women had a separate space, a place from which to speak and to formulate a new understanding both of patriarchal and heterosexist oppression and the oppositional tactics needed to combat that oppression. As such, I had no problem with my positioning as a radical separatist. Liberal feminism merely sought equality but on men's terms—it would not introduce a new set of values to the world. Marxist feminism simply viewed patriarchal oppression as being the revolutionary overturning of the economic structures that had made women members of the caste of 'slave', but even with the revolution and the discovery of women's power—it would however retain women as the partners of men, not as people with a separate and distinct voice.

When we returned to Manchester after the Women's Liberation Conference, I announced to the other collective members that the conference had confirmed for me that I was in fact a man (this was 1974 remember). I expected to be ousted from the collective and to be ostracised—not least because I was 'betraying women, by copping out, escaping my oppression and becoming an apparent oppressor'. Ironically the values that arose out of belonging to the slave caste of woman, and the untouchable sub-group of lesbian woman at that, were to be my saving grace. I was listened to, I was given gifts of shirts and ties out of the back of 'formerly identified as butch' women's wardrobes. I was taken to clubs where I would be able to meet other people who identified as I did—as trans—as a person whose self was not dictated by the labels attached at birth to genital morphology. My separate and distinct voice was not only heard but it was listened to, and a new set of values was followed. My belief in radical separatism was confirmed—for the time being.

RAYMOND AND THE TRANSSEXUAL PERSON

However, with the publication in 1979 of Janice Raymond's 'The Transsexual Empire', feminist theory and praxis was suddenly given a framework in which to,

> See(n) transsexuals as possessing something less than agency [in the words of Sandy Stone, a lesbian feminist transsexual woman vilified by Raymond]…transsexuals are infantilized, considered too illogical or irresponsible to achieve true subjectivity, or clinically erased by diagnostic criteria; or else, as constructed by some radical feminist theorists, as robots of an insidious and menacing patriarchy, an alien army designed and constructed to infiltrate, pervert and destroy "true" women (Stone, in Epstein and Straub, 1991, p 294).

Raymond made 3 arguments for use by feminists to condemn the transsexual woman (n.b. transsexual men didn't really exist in 1979, and probably still don't) that are undoubtedly very powerful,

Firstly: "Transsexuals are living out two patriarchal myths: single parenthood by the father (male mothering) and the making of woman according to man's image." (Raymond, 1979: xx)

In other words the process of transsexual "medical rebirth" is a process of mythic deception, which was one response, by a male power base, to the second wave of feminism in America in the 1960s.

Secondly: Transsexuals are one result of a "socio-political programme", controlled and implemented by the medico-legal hierarchies of, and on behalf of, a patriarchal hegemony which has used them:

"to colonise feminist identification, culture, politics and sexuality" (Raymond, 1979: xx).

Not only do they construct women out of men, but just as the androgynous man assumes the trappings of femininity when he identifies as, and is reconstructed as a transsexual, so:

"the transsexually constructed lesbian-feminist assumes for himself the role and behaviour of the feminist" (Raymond, 1979: 100).

Thus the transsexual is created as an alternative to biological women who are becoming obsolete. In this way the medical aspect of the patriarchal empire does not just attack women; it goes further so that their sense of self is being penetrated in every way. Women's identities, spirits and sexuality are all invaded. The physical loss of a penis does not mean the loss of an ability to penetrate.

Thirdly: In this context, Raymond made her most damning statement:

"All transsexuals rape women's bodies by reducing the real female form to an artifact, appropriating this body for themselves.... Transsexuals merely cut off the most obvious means of invading women, so that they seem non-invasive." (Raymond, 1979: 104)

The discourse of rape is a subtle one of possession, in particular of the flesh of women. When a man penetrates woman, he is often referred to as "possessing" that woman. Raymond's constructed transsexual woman who identifies as a lesbian feminist exhibits:

"the attempt to possess women in a bodily sense while acting out the images into which men have moulded women" (Raymond, 1979: 99).

Women were in 1979, therefore justified in thinking transsexual people were not innocent victims of oppression arising out of patriarchy's controlled gender and sex roles (which would have been one alternative reading), but rather were co-conspirators in an attempt by men to possess them and to remake them in a mould that suits them.

The historical location of Raymond's book places it in the history of sex-role, early feminist theory and from it emerged a construction of the transsexual person in which they are no longer merely a medico-legal construction, but they become part of the story, and mechanism, of patriarchal oppression. This discourse, documented by Raymond (she did not invent it single handedly) reproduces the power relations that are themselves inherent in radical feminist separatist theory. That some values and some knowledge are better...and others are inherently flawed.

THE EFFECTS OF RAYMOND

Raymond's discourse, I would argue, has had far-reaching ideological effects:

it promotes radical separatism as the only viable alternative to the patriarchal hegemony, because the patriarchy is always involved in the treacherous act of building the Trojan Horse [containing the transsexual woman] (and liberal feminism and Marxist feminism will always open the gate to the horse);

it supports the notion of separatism in that it sanctions an "invisible" oppression of transsexual people by women. It allows women to become dominant in telling their narrative about their past in order to justify and promote the use of sex-role theory, and, in assuming a homogeneity in voices, it subsumes any other discourse about gender and sex. In this way the transsexual person's story of gender oppression and a search for identity is silenced.

It assumes that biology is destiny, despite all that feminism seems to say in opposition to this in terms of the pre-determination of sex and gender roles. What is anatomically observable – the possession of a penis or a vagina at the birth of a child—what is viewed as 'natural' becomes the dictator of the socially constructed gender role.

THE RELATIONSHIP OF TRANS PEOPLE WITH FEMINISM

The reason that I wanted to talk about this is that being like all trans people I was obligated to explore the complex pedagogies that informed myself.

Initially, I was compelled to do so with practising clinical psychologists. It was part of my 'treatment'—a way in which others could actually justify allowing me to do to myself things they felt very uncomfortable about—a point I'll come back to presently. 15 years later, I undertook this exploration by default, when I embarked on reading the work of academic psychologists, psychotherapists and psychiatrists for my doctorate.

In both circumstances I felt washed out, mangled and hung out to dry. What did I discover about myself—well:

Between the faults of my over bearing father and weak mother—or depending upon whom you read, my overbearing mother and weak father, I should have certainly known that **I**:

was escaping my disgust at my lesbianism, or

my fear of economic dependency, or

just simply my inherent failure to conform to my gender role, or

I was seeking a cure to the obsessive compulsive disorder which manifested itself as a psychological desire to cleanse myself of the disgusting bodily attributes that came with a female morphology, or

I was so overwhelmingly bound up in my incestuous desire for my father that I had to inscribe himself upon me, or for that matter

my oedipal desire for my mother which meant I had to re-present myself as her possible sexual partner.

And so on and so forth—a diarrhea of theories, none of which fit my, not fantastic but also not awful, experience of childhood and life. However what I did know, on both occasions, was that trans people had to 'pass' the 'examinations' of the psycho-'experts', who acted as the gate keepers to the medical professionals who would provide the hormones and surgery that I knew were essential to not only enhance my life, but in order to keep me alive. As such the psycho-experts became the enemy I had to either persuade to believe me or to defeat (regardless of whether they believed me or not) in order to enter through the gateway. Yet—I also discovered that the psycho-experts were contained and controlled by both the overarching assumptions of their own disciplines, and the schools of theory they belonged to within those disciplines: that it is possible to find scientific evidence to 'truths' which have some sort of universality, but that that universality depends upon the paradigms of the theoretical understanding of the nature of 'human-ness' and its interaction with society, and culture. Where was feminism in all of this? In reality it has been moving forward from Raymond's objectivist view of what feminism is.

As Margot Liombart outlines in her chapter in the 1997 collection; "Deconstructing Feminist Psychology":

> "Feminist critical contributions to psychology have played a crucial role in the process of unmasking the objectivist fallacy of psychology. They have ensured that the second part of that equation is now included —that it that there is a social dimension, which had in the past been driven into oblivion by the positivist project, present in the production of psychological knowledge. Feminist psychologists have been instrumental, just as feminist have also been in other fields, in unmasking the effects of power, domination and exclusion. In psychology feminists have been instrumental in criticising the classical model of the production of knowledge, and the masculine ideology in most scientific practices. Further they have shown that most 'general' theories about human beings are nothing more than fictions."

SO WHERE DO WE GO FROM HERE?

Feminists when faced with trans people find themselves between the devil and deep blue sea. They now see that general theories are nothing more than fictions. But how does this pan out in real life?

Those who claim the right to a feminist theoretical position are apparently, when faced with trans people, faced with individuals who simply are not whom they claim to be. How can a person born with a penis claim to be a woman, when to be a woman requires that you are not born with a penis (or vice versa).

It begs the whole question of the existence of a feminist understanding. It is this challenge that we have to address in both theory and practice. Can feminists learn anything from the experience of the trans community. The transsexual person faces the problem of interpretation, and feminists have to address that interpretation through their understanding of the objectivist fallacy they have underlined, yet by doing so they challenge the very basis of feminist thought—that there are 2 sexes and there are 2 genders.

The transsexual/transgender community through its own writings and theorising has attempted to offer an "insider's" exploration of the ways in which trans people view gender issues and the use of transsexual and transvestite iconography in particular. However the trans community acknowledges that it is not, however, a clear cut issue. Trans theory has amongst its predecessors the work of neo-Marxists and feminist theorists. These schools of thought have had some difficulty in reconciling transgender behaviour with their political stances, as can be seen by the work of Janice Raymond or for example Sheila Jeffries whose radical feminist viewpoint cites trans men as being 'poor oppressed women pushed into self-mutilation by patriarchal oppression'.

Transgendered people as writers and speakers used to have to be **primarily** apologists. However the time has come when we are seeing a new form of transgendered performativity and text giving: now we have become theorizers about the idea/the word/ the signifier 'gender'. It is only been in the 1990s that transgendered people have felt able to participate in the theoretical discussions that surround sex and gender. The fight to be included in those discussions has involved the facing of several serious problems.

Firstly, any discussion of gender by the transgendered community has been hampered by the medical discourse surrounding transgendered behaviour which makes transgendered people out to be simultaneously self-interested and decidedly barmy.

Secondly, they have been hampered by social and legal restrictions which have made it very difficult publicly to come out as transgendered, and which further add another aspect of self interest to any work they might do on gender issues.

Thirdly, Janice Raymond's thesis in "The Transsexual Empire, the Making of the She-male" (1979) discredited for a long time any academic voice they might have, in particular with feminist theorists.

Fourthly, transgendered people have not been allowed either objectivity or sexuality. Objectivity was lost because of the combination of the other three factors; also, if they questioned gender and sex-roles, they were put in the invidious position of having to justify any sex-role change they might undertake to accommodate their gender. Sexuality was lost as it was constructed for them in the form of repressed homosexuality being appeased through reassignment surgery, or heterosexuality (in their new sex-role) was imposed on them by the medical profession in order to justify what was seen as a "medical collusion with an unattainable fantasy" (The Lancet, 1991, as cited in the 1994 preface to the reprinting of Raymond's "Transsexual Empire").

The transgendered community have not attempted to avoid these difficulties; rather they have tackled them head on.

Firstly, the postmodernist acknowledgement of a multiplicity of voices has been adapted to theoretical stances and there is an ongoing discussion as to whether the medical profession should take a diagnostic or merely enabling role for those people who actively seek reassignment treatment.

Secondly, the trans community has consistently fought through the courts and the legislature not for the right to marry or the right to disappear, but for the right to be trans and yet to be afforded what others are afforded; relationship protection, personal safety, anti-discrimination legislation, access to appropriate health care and treatment.

Thirdly, transgenderists have tackled the problems raised by radical feminism by continuously asking for answers to the very awkward question. If there is an insistence upon the existence of and resultant oppression of binary sex and gender roles then you cannot exclude all trans people from experience any of that. For example trans men and trans women challenged the "Womyn born Womyn" policy of the 1994 Michigan Womyn's Music Festival by asking for their right for either group to enter the festival.

Fourthly, transgendered people have questioned the whole notion of objectivity—they do not try to claim it and instead they have built upon the tradition the community has of autobiographical writing to give a voice to their self-acknowledged subjectivity. As to sexuality, they have begun to reclaim it. Through the work begun by gay, lesbian or bi activists they have started to come out. The argument is simple: if you can acknowledge in yourself that what makes a person is what takes place between the ears and not between the legs, then a trans person is in a privileged position to know that sexuality is a movable and mutable force within us all.

Default assumptions are (as they always have been [see Jason Cromwell's recent book on this]) one of the biggest problems facing the acceptance of the trans community's contribution to any academic work or, for that matter, any acceptance at all. There is the first assumption that females do not become men or males become women: they become pastiches, surgical constructions of imaginary masculinities or femininities. The default assumption that underlies any notion of a transgendered existence is that gender is immutable and it is fixed through biological constraints, and social construction merely affects any representation that the biological may take. This is also the default assumption of feminism—biology is destiny, no matter that in the same breath we say it is not.

Transgendered activists and academics are attempting to deal with the volatile concept of identification, but it is against all the odds: the rigidity of a set of default assumptions concerning sex-roles that pervades all discussion of gender—that the two have an incorruptible sameness that makes them all pervasive. Yet gender and sex are fundamentally different for the transgendered community. They face the everyday reality of that difference in their lives, and attempts to reconcile it have led to it being challenged in unanticipated ways. Many have had to move on from seeking any biological basis for their state of being; all searching for aetiology has been unsuccessful. Any aetiology that has been proposed, whether social or biological, has been torn down by the mass of exceptions. It has been accepted that seeking aetiology is a fruitless occupation as the multiplicity of possible factors increases. And even if it were found and there were possible points of interception, would the "cure" be wanted?

Expressing the move to a theory in which gender and sex roles are clearly separated (at least for a large number of people) and what that means to the modernist view of gender theory is a challenge the transgendered community is not ignoring, nor is it prepared to come up with trite self-serving answers. Challenging their own sense of self, looking inwards to find who they are, using the process of autobiography that they know so well, is producing some very interesting answers which challenge the very binary structure of the complacent world in which gender was invented, and by which it has become obsessed. After all trans people did not invent gender. Gender is merely a word to signify a concept of the human imagination that belongs within and supports the foundations of a patriarchal heterosexist hegemony. Feminists can take heart from the fact that within the trans community there is no hidden answer as to what gender is. However there are answers to how it is experienced and what those experiences mean.

As a 'born female bodied' person I was, in 1997, the first 'man' to be asked to edit the Journal of Gender Studies. The Journal is the voice of British academic socialist feminism with its roots entrenched in both Marxist and radical separatist feminism. I wrote in my editorial to the 'Transgendering Edition' (Journal of Gender Studies, Nov. 1998).

> "Trans has problematised all the categories and all the words of sex, gender and sexualities. No amount of trying is ever going to clearly pin them down again, they have become linguistic signposts which we now know are often pointing down the wrong road. The audible gasp when I asked 'am I the first man to edit the journal?' was what I expected, because the acknowledgement of the questions has to arise before we can even start to formulate the answers. I have no idea whether I have been asked to edit because—and here I give as many choices as I can think of, and my responses to those choices:

>> I am a woman really but deluded in thinking I am a man, therefore as a woman I can edit the journal

> (This is still the predominate medical model of the transsexual condition. It is a mental health problem which as yet psychotherapy or other forms of mental health treatment mechanisms have been unable to cure, so medicine colludes with the person's delusions by performing 'sex change' surgery, which has, at least, been shown to enhance the individuals social functioning. Do the journal editor's follow this school of thought? —I hope not.)

>> or I am a woman really and an acceptable performance of masculinity by a woman, because I acknowledge it as performance, by being out about my trans status

(As Riki Anne Wilchins would put it "Trans-identity is not a natural fact. Rather it is a political category we are forced to occupy when we do certain things with our bodies" Performance is a theory which dictates people and who they are as much as biological essentialism does. It removes any sense of personal choice and freedom. I would agree with Wilchins, it is a category placed by others because I choose my freedoms.)

or I am a woman really and my oppression as a woman lies in my childhood experiences as a girl and my experience as a woman who lives as a transsexual man

(Undoubtedly my childhood was seen by others as being a girl's childhood, but would the second part of this statement be different if I was not 'out' as being a transsexual man. Does it rely upon it position of open oppression? However it was this viewpoint that was to enable the radical separatist women's group of Sussex University to invite me to their 1978 Christmas party, even though I had heard that at that party a woman left after being criticised for wearing a skirt and living with a man.)

or I am a woman really and it is just that my body morphology simply is no longer 100% female

(I have no idea whether it ever was—I have never had my chromosomes tested, though I do know I had a uterus and ovaries because they were apparently, according to the surgeon, removed. How do we define people through bodies when, to date, medicine acknowledges over 60 intersex conditions and one in every two hundred babies is born with a question mark over their 'sex'. I really have grave doubts as to whether anyone knows my body morphology, apart from a few clone friends.)

or I am a man really but the acceptable face of manhood because of my childhood experiences— herein others thought I was female and therefore oppressed me as such

(This presumes that manhood can be defined through body morphology at any given time, though of course in my case it is not 'penis' dependent. In that case, would a trans woman have been asked to edit the journal because, of course, in childhood they would have been given the privileges afforded to boys (although probably a sissy boy, I presume it would still be better than my existence as a tomboy).)

or I am a man really but my position as male is undoubtedly contested

(The contestation comes as part of this process of being asked to edit this journal. If my maleness (manhood) was not contested I expect I would not have been asked, but in turn by asking me it becomes contested.)

or I am a man really but my feminist credentials are pretty good

(They are: I attended the 1974 and 1975 Women's Movement Conferences here in the UK and I was part of the Lesbian Collective who worked towards creating the women's refuge and centre in Manchester in 1975. But I don't expect anyone ever knew that about me when I was asked to edit)

I actually do not care which of the above possibilities were the justification for my invitation to edit, and though I have contested them they all have some potential validity to me. I hope they were subconscious rather than conscious, if conscious we should have, at the very least, started a dialogue around the issues. However I do not care just as I do not care whether I was 'born this way' or 'became this way'.

The question of the 'gay gene' or the 'tranny brain' is a potentially frightening route to another eugenics programme to destroy the brilliance of difference in the world, and the sooner we reject these projects the better. Whatever made me, I am, and I can no longer say who the 'I' is, except through a descriptive process in which the words man/woman, male/female, straight/gay become absorbed into Queer (I have a friend who says 'what I like about you is that you are just SO QUEER for a straight person' and straight does not refer to my sexual behaviour).

To get back to this special Transgender edition: It is a first because it is queer/feminist writings, not one nor the other, it trans'es that border, by which I mean something specific. Trans'ing is not just 'crossing over', not just 'blurring boundaries', not just 'blending categories', but it fully queers the pitch by highlighting, clarifying, deconstructing and then blowing apart the border between queer and feminist theory, just as in 'real' life it highlights, clarifies, deconstructs and then blows apart all the things we know about sex, genders and sexualities.

This collection prioritises, for the first time ever I suspect, the experiences of the 'born female bodied' trans person and through that it highlights the experiences and issues of it whole new ball game going on in a different ball park with a different set of boundaries. When I played lacrosse (originally devised by Native Americans whose cultures had spaces for two spirit people) at my all girls school, playing the 'women's' game meant that our pitch had no boundaries (unlike the 'men's' game which has clearly-marked white lines.) This was possible because unlike 'born male bodied' people playing as men with all the social constraints and values that entailed, as 'born female bodied' people playing as women, with it different set of social constraints and values, we were in a position to reach a consensus as to when the ball was out of play."

Perhaps this is the position we—both feminism and trans—can now reach: knowing when the ball is out of play through consensus rather than rules.

I wrote a few years back that 'gender' was an excuse for oppression—nothing more and nothing less. As Kate Bornstein has put it so succinctly: It is like a caste structure—it includes many facets and many aspects of a person's life. The perfect gender is not just male, it is white, it is tall and of slim build, it has money and political power, sexual choice, it is fertile but has control of that fertility, and it is probably American and called Bill Clinton. For the rest of us, it will never be perfect and for some, it will be less perfect than for others. Feminism is about a better set of values in which gender loses some of its power of oppression, in which separate and distinct voices are not only heard but also listened to, and in which a better set of values is followed. That is what we who are trans can gain from them—but perhaps much more importantly now, it is also something we can give back to them.

REFERENCES

Burmen, E. (ed.), "Deconstructing Feminist Psychology," 1997, London: Routledge
Raymond, J., "The Transsexual Empire: The Making of the She-Male," 1979, London: The Women's Press
Stone, S., "The Empire Strikes Back: A Posttranssexual Manifesto" in Julia Epstein and Kristina Straub *"Body Guards: The Cultural Politics of Gender Ambiguity,"* 1991, London: Routledge
Wilchins, R., "Read My Lips: Sexual Subversion and the End of Gender," 1997, New York, Firebrand Books.

III

QUEERING GENDER

16

Transgender Liberation
A Movement Whose Time Has Come

Leslie Feinberg

LESLIE FEINBERG, WHOSE PARTICULAR STYLE OF BEING TRANSGENDER helped non-gender-specific pronouns like "s/he" and "hir" achieve a limited popularity over the past decade, must be considered a founding figure of contemporary transgender studies. Hir influential pamphlet, reproduced below, took an older (and apolitical) term—transgender—and infused it with a radical new meaning.

Previously, "transgender" had referred most frequently to biological males who lived socially as women, but who did not undergo genital modification surgery. In Feinberg's redefinition, the term came to refer to a "pangender" movement of oppressed minorities—transsexuals, butch lesbians, drag queens, cross-dressers, and others—who all were called to make common revolutionary cause with one another in the name of social justice. The tract provided an ideological and historical framework for the similar but more emotionally moving fictionalization of Feinberg's life, *Stone Butch Blues*. The pamphlet was subsequently expanded in two book-length treatments, *Transgender Warriors* and *Trans-Liberation: Beyond Pink and Blue.*

Through many examples drawn from a wide range of cultures and historical periods, Feinberg, a Marxist, argues that transgender people in pre-capitalist tribal and agrarian societies were revered and honored, while the widespread contemporary oppression of gender-variant people is an effect of the capitalist mode of production. Though hir particular theory of history has not attracted widespread support in transgender communities, hir work has gained a devoted and grateful following for the powerful way it calls upon transgender people to recover their historical legacy, and to harness that knowledge to the current struggle for a more just society. It is an important foundational text of contemporary transgender theory and activism.

This pamphlet is an attempt to trace the historic rise of an oppression that, as yet, has no commonly agreed name. We are talking here about people who defy the "man"-made boundaries of gender.

Gender: self-expression, not anatomy.

All our lives we've been taught that sex and gender are synonymous—men are "masculine" and women are "feminine." Pink for girls and blue for boys. It's just "natural," we've been told. But at the turn of the century in this country, blue was considered a girl's color and pink was a boy's. Simplistic and rigid gender codes are neither eternal nor natural. They are changing social concepts.

Nevertheless, there's nothing wrong with men who are considered "masculine" and women whose self-expression falls into the range of what is considered "feminine." The problem is that the many people who don't fit these narrow social constraints run a gamut of harassment and violence.

This raises the question: Who decided what the "norm" should be? Why are some people punished for their self-expression?

Many people today would be surprised to learn that ancient communal societies held transgendered people in high esteem. It took a bloody campaign by the emerging ruling classes to declare what had been considered natural to be its opposite. That prejudice, foisted on society by its ruling elite, endures today.

Yet even in a society where there are harsh social penalties for not fitting, a large part of the population can't or won't change their nature. It is apparent that there are many ways for women and men to be; everything in nature is a continuum.

Many of the terms used to describe us are words that cut and sear.

When I first worked in the factories of Buffalo as a teenager, women like me were called "he-shes." Although "he-shes" in the plants were most frequently lesbians, we were recognized not by our sexual preference but by the way we expressed our gender.

There are other words used to express the wide range of "gender outlaws": transvestites, transsexuals, drag queens and drag kings, cross-dressers, bull-daggers, stone butches, androgynes, diesel dykes or berdache—a European colonialist term.

We didn't choose these words. They don't fit all of us. It's hard to fight an oppression without a name connoting pride, a language that honors us.

In recent years a community has begun to emerge that is sometimes referred to as the gender or transgender community. Within our community is a diverse group of people who define ourselves in many different ways. Transgendered people are demanding the right to choose our own self-definitions. The language used in this pamphlet may quickly become outdated as the gender community coalesces and organizes—a wonderful problem.

We've chosen words in this pamphlet we hope are understandable to the vast majority of working and oppressed people in this country, as a tool to battle bigotry and brutality. We are trying to find words, however inadequate, that can connect us, that can capture what is similar about the oppression we endure. We have also given careful thought to our use of pronouns, striving for both clarity and sensitivity in a language that only allows for two sexes.

Great social movements forge a common language—tools to reach out and win broader understanding. But we've been largely shut out of the progressive movement.

It was gay transvestites who led the 1969 battle at the Stonewall Inn in New York City that gave birth to the modern lesbian and gay movement.

But just as the lesbian and gay movement had to win over the progressive movement to the understanding that struggling shoulder to shoulder together would create a more powerful force for change, the transgendered community is struggling to win the same understanding from the lesbian and gay movement.

Many people think that all "masculine" women are lesbians and all "feminine" men are gay. That is a misunderstanding. Not all lesbians and gay men are "cross"-gendered. Not all transgendered women and men are lesbian or gay. Transgendered people are mistakenly viewed as the cusp of the lesbian and gay community. In reality the two huge communities are like circles that only partially overlap.

While the oppressions within these two powerful communities are not the same, we face a common enemy. Gender-phobia—like racism, sexism and bigotry against lesbians and gay men—is meant to keep us divided. Unity can only increase our strength.

Solidarity is built on understanding how and why oppression exists and who profits from it. It is our view that revolutionary changes in human society can do away with inequality, bigotry and intolerance.

In the spirit of building that fighting movement, we offer this view of the sweeping patterns in history, the commonality of women and men who have walked the path of the berdache, of the transgendered—walked that road whether we were held in high esteem or reviled.

Look at us. We are battling for survival. Listen. We are struggling to be heard.

TRANSGENDER PREDATES OPPRESSION

Jazz musician Billy Tipton died in 1989 at the age of 74. He will be remembered most not for his music, but for the revelation that Tipton was born a woman. Tipton died of an untreated bleeding ulcer rather than visit a doctor and risk exposure.

After his death this debate began: Did Tipton live as a man simply in order to work as a musician in a male-dominated industry or because of lesbian oppression?

It is true that women's oppression, especially under capitalism, has created profound social and economic pressures that force women to pass as men for survival. But this argument leaves out transgendered women—women who are considered so "masculine" in class society that they endure extreme harassment and danger. Many of these women are forced to "pass" in order to live. Of course transgendered women also experience the crushing weight of economic inequity and, in many cases, anti-lesbian oppression. These factors also play a role in forcing "masculine" women as well as non-transgendered women to pass.

If "masculine" women are acknowledged at all, it is implied that they're merely a product of decadent patriarchal capitalism and that when genuine equality is won, they will disappear.

IT'S "PASSING" THAT'S NEW

Transgendered women and men have always been here. They are oppressed. But they are not merely products of oppression. It is *passing* that's historically new. Passing means hiding. Passing means invisibility. Transgendered people should be able to live and express their gender without criticism or threats of violence. But that is not the case today.

There are legions of women and men whose self-expression, as judged by Hollywood stereotypes, is "at odds" with their sex. Some are forced underground or "pass" because of the repression and ostracism they endure.

Today all gender education teaches that women are "feminine," men are "masculine," and an unfordable river rages between these banks. The reality is there is a whole range of ways for women and men to express themselves.

Transgender is a very ancient form of human expression that pre-dates oppression. It was once regarded with honor. A glance at human history proves that when societies were not ruled by exploiting classes that rely on divide-and-conquer tactics, "cross-gendered" youths, women and men on all continents were respected members of their communities.

"SHE IS A MAN"

"Strange country, this," a white man wrote of the Crow nation on this continent in 1850, "where males assume the dress and perform the duties of females, while women turn men and mate with their own sex."

Randy Burns, a founder of the modern group Gay American Indians, wrote that GAI's History Project documented these alternative roles for women and men in over 135 North American Native nations.

The high incidence of transgendered men and women in Native societies on this continent was documented by the colonialists who referred to them as *berdache*.

Perhaps the most notable of all berdache Native women was Barcheeampe, the Crow "Woman Chief," the most famous war leader in the history of the upper Missouri nations. She married several wives and her bravery as a hunter and warrior was honored in songs. When the Crow nation council was held, she took her place among the chiefs, ranking third in a band of 160 lodges.

Today transgender is considered "anti-social" behavior. But amongst the Klamath nations transgendered women were given special initiation ceremonies by their societies.

Among the Cocopa, Edward Gifford wrote, "female transvestites were called war hameh, wore their hair and pierced their noses in the male fashion, married women and fought in battle alongside men."

Wewha, a famous Zuni berdache who was born a man, lived from 1849 to 1896. She was among the tallest and strongest of all the Zuni. When asked, her people would explain, "She is a man." Wewha was sent by the Zuni to Washington, D.C., for six months where she met with President Grover Cleveland and other politicians who never realized she was berdache.

Osh-Tische (Finds Them and Kills Them), a Crow berdache or badé who was also born a man, fought in the Battle of the Rosebud. When a colonial agent tried to force Osh-Tisch to wear men's clothing, the other Native people argued with him that it was against her nature and they kicked the agent off their land. They said it was a tragedy, trying to change the nature of the badé.

A Jesuit priest observed in the 1670s of the berdache, "They are summoned to the Councils, and nothing can be decided without their advice."

But the missionaries and colonialist military reacted to the Native berdache in this hemisphere with murderous hostility. Many berdache were tortured and burnt to death by their Christian conquerors. Other colonial armies sicced wild dogs on the berdache.

WHY SUCH HOSTILITY?

Why were the European colonialists so hostile to transgendered women and men? The answer can be found back on the European continent in the struggles that raged between the developing classes of haves and have-nots.

Ancient societies on the European continent were communal. Thousands of artifacts have been unearthed dating back to 25,000 B.C. that prove these societies worshipped goddesses, not gods. Some of the deities were transgendered, as were many of their shamans or religious representatives.

We have been taught that the way things are now is roughly the way they have always been—the "Flintstones" school of anthropology. The strong message is: Don't bother trying to change people. But a glance at history proves that human society has undergone continuous development and change.

A great debate has raged for more than 150 years about the role of women in ancient societies. To hear Jesse Helms and his ilk rant, you'd think that the patriarchal nuclear family has always existed. That's not true.

Twentieth century anthropologists recognize that matrilineal communal societies existed all over the world at an early stage in social development. Women were the heads of *gens* or clans that bore little resemblance to today's "family."

But many argue that matrilineage could co-exist with the subjugation of women, and that there is no confirmed documentation of any culture in history in which women consistently held leadership positions. This ignores the relationship between male domination and private property, and implies that women's oppression is merely a result of "human nature."

This ideological argument is as much a weapon of class warfare as prisons are.

Rosalind Coward offers an invaluable overview of this debate in her work *Patriarchal Precedents*. Coward shows that most 19th century European scholars held the patriarchal nuclear family and male inheritance to be universal. But by the latter part of the century, European colonialists studying the peoples of Southern India and Southwest Asia disputed that view.

In 1861, Johann Bachofen published his famous book *Das Mutterrecht* (Mother Right)—a scientific study of the family as an evolving social institution. His work was regarded as a fundamental contribution to modern anthropology.

Lewis Henry Morgan, the great ethnologist and one of the founders of anthropology, wrote his significant work *Ancient Society* in 1877—an exhaustive study of communal societies with kinship systems based on women. He studied the Haudenosaunee (Iroquois Confederacy) on this continent, and numerous indigenous peoples in India and Australia. His research on social evolution confirmed that the patriarchal form of the family was not the oldest form of human society.

The research of Bachofen and especially Morgan was the basis for Frederick Engels' great 1884 classic, *Origin of the Family, Private Property and the State*. Engels argued that early societies were based on collective labor and communal property. Cooperation was necessary for group survival.

Engels, Karl Marx's leading collaborator in developing the doctrine of scientific socialism, found that these ancient societies showed no evidence of a state apparatus of repression, large-scale warfare, slavery or the nuclear family. Engels and Marx saw Morgan's studies as further proof that the modern-day oppression of women was rooted in the cleavage of society into classes based on private ownership of property. The fact that oppression was not a feature of early communal societies lent great weight to their prognosis that overturning private ownership in favor of socialized property would lay the basis for revolutionizing human relations.

Research in this century, particularly by women, has further disproved the view that women have always been considered "inferior." The extensive research of Marija Gimbutas and Gerda Lerner revealed that prior to 4500 B.C. goddesses, not gods, were worshipped throughout Europe and Western Asia.

As Jacquetta Hawkes concluded in her *History of Mankind:* "There is every reason to suppose that under the conditions of the primary neolithic way of life, mother-night and the clan system were still dominant, and land would generally have descended through the female line. Indeed, it is tempting to be convinced that the earliest neolithic societies throughout their range in time and space gave woman the highest status she has ever known." (It's interesting to note that this progressive woman researcher, writing in 1963, still found it necessary to use the term "mankind" to describe humanity.)

WHEN BIGOTRY BEGAN

In the fertile river valleys of Eurasia and Northeast Africa, during the period of about 4500 B.C. to 1200 B.C., human labor became more productive and abundance accumulated as wealth. The old communal systems were gradually and unconsciously transformed.

A tremendous societal change took place. The desire to pass on wealth to male heirs demanded wifely monogamy; the patriarchal family became the new economic unit of society.

But the respect the ancient communal societies accorded transgendered men and women, and same-sex love, endured long after these societies underwent dramatic changes.

An Egyptian sculpture of a bearded Queen Hat-shepsut dressed in the garb of a pharaoh (1485 B.C.), for example, shows the persistence of popular folklore about the bearded woman as a sacred symbol of power and wisdom.

A link between transvestism and religious practice is also found in ancient myths associated with Greek gods and heroes. The myth of Achilles notes that he lived and dressed as a woman at the court of Lycomedes in Scyros before he acquired his martial skills.

"Macrobius reports that male priests dressed as women in honor of the Bearded Aphrodite of Cyprus; on the same island, the cult of Ariadne (originally a fertility cult) was marked by a ceremony in which a boy was dressed in female clothes and proceeded to enact all the symptoms of labor and birth" (*Dressing Up*).

Herodotus noted that Scythian religious shamans spoke and dressed as women and were highly revered. The priests of Artemis at Ephesus were reported to have worn "women's clothing" (*Dressing Up*).

"Men had to dress up before they could take part in the rites of Hercules at Rome (Hercules himself spent three years dressed as a woman at the court of Omphale, Queen of Lydia).... At the vine growers' festival, the Athenian Oschophoria, two boys dressed in women's clothes and carried a vine stock in procession. At the Argive festival of Hybristika, the men adopted female clothing. At the feast of Hera at Samos, the men wore long, white robes and placed their hair in golden nets" (*Dressing Up*).

To "justify" the new economic system and break the spirit of people who had lived and worked communally, a systematic downgrading of the status of women and an assault on the transgendered population began.

An early prohibition against transgender was codified in the Mosaic Law of the Hebrews, one of the earliest patriarchal societies: "The woman shall not wear that which pertaineth unto a man, neither shall a man put on a woman's garment; for all that do so are abomination unto the Lord thy God" (*Deuteronomy*, 22:5).

The rise of the Greek city-states during the 8th to 6th centuries B.C., is another example of the subjugation of women. The new patriarchal economic system couldn't co-exist with matrilineage. But in many areas transgender, same-sex love and many of the old religious practices of transvestism continued to flourish, because they didn't yet threaten the new ruling order.

The slave-owners developed an ideology degrading women in order to justify overturning women's equality in society. Many of the early Greek myths and the numerous depictions in artwork of battles against Amazon warriors symbolized the overthrow of matrilineal communal societies and their replacement with patriarchal slave societies.

Patriarchal gods like the Greek deity Dionysos arose to overpower the pre-class goddesses. Dionysos was one of the Greek gods that replaced goddess worship. But Greek painters and writers portrayed Dionysos as feminine or dressed in women's apparel. Transvestism also persisted in the rituals of Dionysos, which endured even after Christianity became a state religion of the ruling elite.

The attitude toward women partly accounts for the growing hostility of the ruling classes toward transgendered men. But another aspect of the campaign against "effeminate" men, and Dionysos in particular, might have been to create a Rambo mentality, like the extreme appeal to "manhood" of the Nazi war machine or today's Pentagon. These were "expand or die" militaristic societies. Unlike the war god Ares, Dionysos was a "make love, not war" god who encouraged soldiers to desert their posts in battle.

The Christian writer Clement of Alexandria authored a book in the third century A.D. called *Exhortation* that demanded pagan Greeks recognize the error of their beliefs. "If one goes around examining pictures and statues, he will at once identify your gods from their disgraceful depictions, Dionysos from his dress."

THE PERSISTENCE OF TRANSGENDER

Although ruling attitudes toward cross-gendered expression were changing and becoming repressive, ancient respect for transgender proved difficult to eradicate and transgendered women and men continued to be present in all classes of society.

"The Roman Caesars were reported to show a fondness for wearing women's clothes and Caligula, according to Seutonius, often adopted female clothing" (*Dressing Up*).

But the ruling class repression began to demand increasing conformity—even among the elite. "The most famous example is that of Elagabalus…," wrote Arthur Evans, "who became emperor of Rome in 218 A.D. As Emperor, he often appeared in public in drag, practiced ritual sex with members of both sexes, and publicly declared one of his male lovers to be his husband. The sentiments of the ruling classes were outraged. He was assassinated by an indignant Praetorian Guard in 222 A.D. His body was mutilated, dragged through the streets of Rome, and thrown in the Tiber River" (*Witchcraft and the Gay Counterculture*).

In the fourth century A.D., the Bishop of Amasia in Cappadocia denounced the New Year's Day practice of men cross-dressed "in long robes, girdles, slippers and enormous wigs." Bishop Isidore of Seville (560–636 A.D.) railed against New Year's dancers "womanizing their masculine faces and making female gestures."

The worship of a god in a dress so enraged the Christian hierarchy that in 691 A.D. the Council of Constantinople decreed: "We forbid dances and initiation rites of the 'gods,' as they are falsely called among the Greeks, since, whether by men or women, they are done according to an ancient custom contrary to the Christian way of life, and we decree that no man shall put on a woman's dress nor a woman, clothes that belong to men . . ." (*The God of Ecstasy*).

THE NATURAL BECOMES "UNNATURAL"

Ancient religion, before the division of society into classes, combined collectively held beliefs with material observations about nature. Christianity as a mass religion really began in the cities of the Roman empire among the poor, and incorporated elements of collectivism and hatred of the rich ruling class. But over several hundred years, Christianity was transformed from a revolutionary movement of the urban poor into a powerful state religion that served the wealthy elite.

Transgender in all its forms became a target. In reality it was the rise of private property, the male-dominated family and class divisions led to narrowing what was considered acceptable self-expression. What had been natural was declared its opposite.

As the Roman slave-based system of production disintegrated it was gradually replaced by feudalism. Laborers who once worked in chains were now chained to the land.

Christianity was an urban religion. But the ruling classes were not yet able to foist their new economic system, or the religion that sought to defend it, on the peasantry. The word pagan derives from the Latin paganus, which meant rural dweller or peasant. It would soon become a codeword in a violent class war.

Even after the rise of feudalism, remnants of the old pagan religion remained. It was joyously pro-sexual—lesbian, gay, bisexual and straight. Many women were among its practitioners. Many shamans were still transvestites. And transvestism was still a part of virtually all rural festivals and rituals.

In the medieval Feast of Fools, laymen and clergy alike dressed as women. The Faculty of Theology at the University of Paris reported priests "who danced in the choir dressed as women."

But in order for the land-owning Catholic church to rule, it had to stamp out the old beliefs that persisted from pre-class communal societies, because they challenged private ownership of the land.

Ancient respect for transgendered people still had roots in the peasantry. Transvestism played an important role in rural cultural life. Many pagan religious leaders were transgendered. So it was not surprising that the Catholic church hunted down male and female transvestites, labeling them as heretics, and tried to ban and suppress transvestism from all peasant rituals and celebrations.

By the 11th century, the Catholic church—by then the largest landlord in Western Europe—gained the organizational and military strength to wage war against the followers of the old beliefs. The campaign was carried out under a religious banner—but it was a class war against the vestiges of the older communal societies.

JOAN OF ARC

Almost everyone has heard of Joan of Arc. Yet today few people realize that in 1431, when she was 19 years old, Joan of Arc was burned at the stake by the Inquisition of the Catholic church because she refused to stop dressing as a man.

Almost 500 years later, in 1920, the Catholic church canonized "Saint Joan" because it needed a popular figure to connect to the church at a time of revolutionary upheaval worldwide. Because Joan of Arc had been from the common people, she was still enormously popular, especially among peasants and workers. But the church and France buried the fact that she was a transvestite—an expression of her identity she was willing to die for rather than renounce.

Joan of Arc was an illiterate daughter of the peasant class. The courage with which she defended her right to self-expression was as extraordinary as the brilliance of her military leadership, which contributed to the emergence of the nation-state of France.

What was there about the social soil in which she was rooted that would account for such a remarkable personality?

Joan of Arc was born in Domrémy, in the province of Lorraine, about 1412. Beginning in 1348 the bubonic plague had ruptured the fabric of the feudal order. By 1350 half the population of Western Europe had died and whole provinces were depopulated.

France was then in the grip of the Hundred Years War. The armies of the English feudal lords had been attacking France for almost a century. The peasants suffered plunder at the hands of the marauding occupation army as well as heavy taxation by the French nobility.

The immediate problem for the peasantry was how to eject the English army, something the French nobility had been unable to do. But on a broader scale peasant rebellions—including the significant Revolt of the Jacquerie (Commoners)—were shaking European feudalism root and branch.

The leadership of Joan of Arc emerged during this period of powerful social earthquakes. In 1429, this confident 17-year-old woman, dressed in garb traditionally worn by men, presented herself and a group of her followers at the court of Prince Charles, heir to the French throne. Her stated goal was to forge an army of peasants to drive the occupation army from French soil.

Religion permeated all aspects of feudal life. Joan asserted that her mission, motivation and mode of dress were directed by God. She must have been an impressive young woman, because the court agreed to support her efforts. Joan was placed at the head of a 10,000-strong army.

On April 28, 1429, Joan led a march on Orleans. The next day, she entered the city at the head of her peasant army. On May 8, the English were routed. Over the next months, she further proved her genius as a military strategist, as well as her ability to inspire the rank and file. With Joan as its leader, her army liberated other French villages and towns, forcing the English to retreat.

Joan then persuaded Charles to go to Rheims to receive the crown. It was a long and dangerous journey through territory still occupied by the English army. Her troops were embattled and famished along the way, but the trip was successful, and forced the English army to yield more turf. As Charles was crowned king of France, Joan stood beside him, holding her combat banner. The nation-state of France, soon to be fully liberated from occupation, was born.

Captured

Joan was captured in Compiègne by the Burgundians, who were allies of the English feudal lords. Had she been a knight or nobleman captured in battle, the expected practice would have been for king Charles to offer a ransom for her freedom.

But Joan was a peasant. The French nobility refused to pay, revealing not only their arrogance but how anxious they were by then to get rid of her. For as a military leader of a popular peasant movement, she could pose a threat to the feudal class.

The English urged the Catholic church to condemn her for her transvestism. The king of England, Henry VI, wrote, "It is sufficiently notorious and well-known that for some time past a woman calling herself Jeanne the Pucelle (the Maid), leaving off the dress and clothing of the feminine sex, a thing contrary to divine law and abominable before God, and forbidden by all laws, wore clothing and armor such as is worn by men."

In November 1430, the Burgundians turned Joan over to the dreaded Inquisition. The church levied 70 charges against her—from sorcery to horse theft. Those charges were then condensed to 12.

Joan's judges accused her of being raised a pagan. Church leaders had long charged that the district of her birth, Lorraine, was a hotbed of paganism and witchcraft. Peasants there still clung to some of the old beliefs and matrilineal traditions, even in the period of Joan's lifetime. The custom of giving children the mother's surname, not the father's, still survived.

The feudal landlords were involved in an ongoing war against communards who held out against enslavement as serfs. Scapegoating Joan of Arc and the area of her birth fed this counter-revolutionary campaign.

On April 2, 1431, the Inquisition dropped the charges of witchcraft; they were too hard to prove. It was not until 1451 that the Inquisition was fully authorized to deal with witchcraft.

Crime of Transvestism

Joan was condemned because of her assertion that her transvestism was a religious duty and that she regarded her visions as higher than the authority of the church. Many historians and academicians have seen Joan's transvestism as inconsequential. In the verbatim proceedings of her interrogation, however, the court records show that Joan's judges found her transvestism repugnant and demanded that she wear women's clothing. Joan refused, knowing her defiance meant she was considered damned.

Joan of Arc's testimony in her own defense revealed how deeply her transvestism was rooted in her identity. She vowed, "For nothing in the world will I swear not to arm myself and put on a man's dress."

Joan was taken on a terrifying tour of the torture chamber and its instruments of agony. She was brought to a cemetery and shown a scaffold that her tormentors said awaited her if she did not submit to them. After suffering this psychological torture and the threat of being burned alive, on April 24, 1431, Joan recanted by accusing herself of wearing clothes that violated natural decency. She agreed to submit to the church's authority and to wear women's clothing. She was "mercifully" sentenced to life in prison in women's dress, on bread and water.

Within days she resumed male dress. Her judges asked her why she had done so, when putting on male clothing meant certain death. The court recorded her reply: "She said, of her own will. And that nobody had forced her to do so. And that she preferred man's dress to woman's."

The Inquisition sentenced her to death for resuming male dress, saying "time and again you have relapsed, as a dog that returns to its vomit." Joan of Arc was immediately burned alive at the stake.

Why was the charge of transvestism so significant?

The real reason can be found in the decree issued by the faculty of the University of Paris on May 14, 1431, which condemned Joan's transvestism and urged that she be burned as a heretic. These church theologians declared that Joan's cross-dressing was "following the custom of the Gentiles and the Heathen."

The church was now the only powerful institution that cemented all of feudal Western Europe into one political system. More important, the church was by far the most powerful feudal lord, claiming ownership of one-third of the soil of the Catholic world.

The Inquisition, and later the witch trials, were weapons of terror and mass murder that took a staggering toll in human life—from Ireland to Poland. Many peasant women, including many lesbians, who followed the older rural-based religions were accused of being witches and tortured and burned. Transgendered people, gay men, Arabs, Jews, scientists, herbalists, healers—anyone who challenged or questioned the ruling class and the church was considered a threat and exterminated.

This was counter-revolutionary terror by the land-owning class. It was aimed at the restive and rebellious peasantry as well as the small new bourgeoisie that was to become a challenge to its class rule.

Torture was the rule. The Inquisitors didn't come armed with just the Bible—they arrived with swords and fire to put down peasant uprisings. The impending collapse of feudalism only heightened the reactionary suppression.

TRANSGENDER ENDURES

Yet despite centuries of this murderous campaign transgender was not eradicated.

In medieval Italy and France there were actual transvestite male festive societies known as "Abbeys of Misrule."

Naogeorgus wrote in *The Popish Kingdom* (1570) that at the Shroveport festival: "Both men and women chaunge their weede, the men in maydes aray, And wanton wenches drest as men, doe trauell by the way . . ."

Transgender still existed among the ruling classes, as well. For example, when Queen Christina of Sweden abdicated in 1654, she donned men's clothes and renamed herself 'Count Dohna.' Henry III of France was reported to have dressed as an Amazon and encouraged his courtiers to do likewise.

Throughout the Middle Ages and into early industrial capitalism, transvestism continued to play an important role in many militant struggles as a form of social and political rebellion against class rule.

"In 1630, for example, the Mere Folle and 'her' troupe attacked royal tax officers in Dijon; in Beaujolais in the 1770s, male peasants put on women's clothes and attacked their landlord's surveyors; in Wiltshire in 1631, bands of peasants, led by men dressed as women who called themselves 'Lady Skimmington,' rioted against the King's enclosure of their forest lands; in April 1812, two male weavers in female clothing—'General Ludd's wives'—led a crowd in the destruction of looms and factories in Stockport; the Welsh riots of the 1830s and 1840s, against turnpike tolls and other statutory taxes, were led by 'Rebecca' and other transvestites; the Porteous riots of 1736 in Edinburgh were led by men disguised as women, and their male leader was known as 'Madge Wildfire'; in Ireland the Whiteboys, who were active in the 1760s, dressed in long white frocks 'to restore the ancient commons and redress other grievances' " in the struggle against the British landlords (*Dressing Up*).

As the old land-based feudal order was replaced by capitalism, the very existence of transvestite and other transgendered women and men had been largely driven underground. Many were forced to pass as the opposite sex in order to survive. Transvestite women passed as men and became soldiers, pirates and highway robbers. Yet transvestism continued to emerge culturally throughout Europe in holiday celebrations, rituals, carnival days, masquerade parties, theater and opera.

These transgender traditions persist today in the Mummer's Festival, Mardi Gras and Halloween. In contemporary imperialist Japan cross-gendered roles are still at the heart of ancient Noh drama and Kabuki theater. But these are not merely vestiges of tradition. Transgendered women and men still exist, no matter how difficult their struggle for survival has become.

TRANSGENDER AROUND THE WORLD

Our focus has been on European history, and consciously so. The blame for anti-transgender laws and attitudes rests squarely on the shoulders of the ruling classes on that continent. The seizures of lands and assets of the "accused" during the witch trials and Inquisition helped the ruling classes acquire the capital to expand their domination over Asia, Africa and the Americas. The European elite then tried to force their ideology on the peoples they colonized around the world.

But despite the colonialists' racist attempts at cultural genocide, transvestism and other transgendered expression can still be observed in the rituals and beliefs of oppressed peoples. It is clear that they held respected public roles in vast numbers of diverse societies in cultures continents apart.

Since the 16th century, "transvestite shamans have...been reported among the Araucanians, a large tribe living in southern Chile and parts of Argentina....Male transvestite shamans have also been reported for the Guajira, a cattle-herding people of northwest Venezuela and north Colombia, and the Tebuelche, hunter-gatherers of Argentina" (*Construction*).

"Transvestism also used to be practiced by shamans in the Vietnamese countryside, Burma, in India among the Pardhi, a hunting people, and in the southeast, by the Lhoosais, as well as in Korea" (*Construction*).

Transgender in religious ceremony is still reported in areas of West Africa. "One of the principal deities of the Aborney pantheon is Lisa-Maron, a figure which incorporates both man and woman; the great god Shango can be represented as either male or female; and contemporary shamans in Brazil worship Yansan, who is the 'man-woman' " (*Dressing Up*).

"The mugawe, a powerful religious leader of the Kenyan Meru, is considered a complement to the male political leaders and consequently must exemplify feminine qualities: he wears women's clothing and adopts women's hairstyles; he is often homosexual, and sometimes marries a man. Among the Kwayama, a tribe of Angolan Bantu cultivators and herders, many diviners, augerers, and diagnosers of illness wear women's clothing, do women's work, and become secondary spouses of men whose other wives are female. South African Zulu diviners are usually women, but roughly 10 percent are male transvestites" (*Construction*).

Male-to-female transgender that doesn't appear to have a special religious significance has been reported in the pastoral Nandi of Kenya, the Dinka and Nuer of the Sudan, the agricultural Konso and Amhara of Ethiopia, the Ottoro of Nubia, the Fanti of Ghana, the Ovimbundu of Angola, the Thonga farmers of Zimbabwe, the Tanala and Bara of Madagascar, the Wolof of Senegal, and the Lango, Iteso, Gisu, and Sebei of Uganda (*Construction*).

Cross-dressing is still a feature in Brazilian and Haitian ceremonies derived from West African religions (*Construction*).

The Chukchee, Kamchadal, Koryak, and Inuit—all Native peoples of the Artic Basin—had male shamans who dressed as women.

"In India, the Vallabha sect, devotees of Krishna, dressed as women.... Reports, of the 1870s and 1930s, describe the priests (*bissu*) of the Celebes who live and dress as women" (*Dressing Up*).

In his ground-breaking book *The Golden Bough*, James Frazier noted that in the Pelew Islands, "a goddess chooses a man, not a woman, for her minister and her inspired mouthpiece.... He wears female attire, he carries a piece of gold on his neck, he labors like a woman in the Tano field." Frazier reported that this custom was widespread among indigenous peoples.

PASSING FOR SURVIVAL

By the time the Industrial Revolution in Europe had forged plowshares into weapons and machinery, prejudice against transgendered women and men was woven deep into the tapestry of exploitation.

But mercantile trade and early industrial capitalism created opportunities for anonymity that seldom existed under feudalism, where the large serf families and their neighbors lived and worked on the land.

Capitalism unchained the peasants from the land—but chained them to machinery as wage slaves, or sent them off in armies and armadas to conquer new land, labor and resources.

Not only transgendered women but men now had the opportunity to pass. The oppression of women under capitalism forced many thousands of women who weren't transgendered to pass as men in order to escape the economic and social inequities of their oppression.

The consequences for passing were harsh. At the close of the 17th century the penalty in England was to be placed in the stocks and dragged through the streets in an open cart. In France as late as 1760 transvestites were burned to death.

Despite the criminal penalties, women passed as men throughout Europe—most notably in the Netherlands, England and Germany. Passing was so widespread during the 17th and 18th centuries that it was the theme of novels, fictionalized biographics and memoirs, art, plays, operas and popular songs.

One of the most famous passing women of the 17th century was Mary Frith—known as "Moll Cutpurse." This bodacious character fought and drank with the men in the underworld districts of 17th century London. They never realized she was a woman. She supported herself by reading fortunes, fencing stolen items and relieving passersby of their purses and wallets. After her exposure as a woman, Moll Cutpurse published her diary and was twice portrayed on the stage before her death at the age of 74.

Angélique Brulon passed as Liberté and was a decorated officer in Napoleon's infantry, serving in seven campaigns between 1792 and 1799 that liberated much of Europe from feudalism.

Charley Wilson was born Catherine Coombes in 1834 in England and lived as a man for over 40 years. At age 63, Wilson was forced into the poor house and her sex was discovered. The authorities made her wear a blue-print dress and red shawl. "If I had money," Wilson reportedly told a visitor, "I would get out of here in men's clothes and no one would detect me."

Many women became pirates and highway robbers.

Transgendered expression persisted among men, as well. German historian Johann Wilhelm von Archeholz described a London pub called the Bunch of Grapes in the 1770s: "On entering the room the guard found two fellows in women's attire, with muffs and wide shawls and most fashionable turban like bonnets.... it turned out that each member of the club had a woman's name."

At a transvestite ball in Paris in 1864, "there were at least 150 men, and some of them so well disguised that the landlord of the house was unable to detect their sex" (*Dressing Up*).

Transgender was central to one of the most famous 19th-century scandals in Victorian England—the Vere Street coterie. This 1813 account described the patrons of a pub: "Many of the habitues took on female appellations as well as female dress..." Hollingway said that the police raided one of their meetings but were so fooled by at least one of the patrons that he was discharged by the police and magistrates as a woman (*Dressing Up*).

Many such accounts of widespread transgender "clubs" were reported in 19th-century Victorian London.

A famous case in 19th-century England was the arrest of Stella (Ernest) Boulton and Fanny (Frederick) Park outside the Strand Theater on April 28, 1890. They were tried on charges of "conspiracy to commit a felony." Boulton's mother testified in defense of her son and explained that he had dressed as a girl since age 6. Stella and Fanny were both acquitted.

While it is biologically easier for a woman to pass as a young man than for a man to pass as a woman, many transgendered men have lived successfully without discovery.

Mrs. Nash, for example, married a soldier at Forte Meade in the Dakota Territory. After her husband's transfer, Mrs. Nash married another soldier. After she died, it was discovered that she was a man (*Vested Interests*).

CAPITALISM WIELDS OLD PREJUDICE

In capitalism's early competitive stage, when the new bourgeoisie were fighting feudalism and all its ideological baggage, they prided themselves on their enlightened and scientific view of the world and society.

But once in power, the capitalists made use of many of the old prejudices, particularly those that suited their own divide-and-conquer policies.

"Liberty, fraternity and equality" soon became a dead letter as hellish sweatshops expanded into the factory system. Colonized peoples were seen as subjects to be used up in the production of wealth. As the new ruling class established itself, it demanded conformity to the system of wage slavery, and shed its radicalism.

But despite long being termed "illegal" and "unnatural" and still carrying with it an "unofficial" death penalty, transvestism is still a part of human expression.

Transvestites and other transgendered people were leaders of the first wave of gay liberation that began in the 1880s in Germany. That movement enjoyed the support of many in the mass Socialists parties.

Magnus Hirschfeld, a Jewish gay leader of the first wave of gay liberation in Germany in the 1880s, was also reported to be transvestite. He wrote a ground-breaking work on the subject. Most of the valuable documentation this movement uncovered about transgender throughout history, along with research about lesbians and gay men, was burned in a pyre by the Nazis.

LIVES RENDERED INVISIBLE

While, as we have seen, transgendered expression has always existed in the Western Hemisphere, the need to "pass" washed up on these shores with the arrival of capitalism. Many women and men have been forced to pass. Some of their voices have been recorded.

Deborah Sampson passed as a male soldier in the American War of Independence. She once pulled a bullet out of her own thigh to avoid discovery. She later published her memoirs entitled *The Female Review* and went on a public speaking tour in 1802.

Jack Bee Garland (Elvira Mugarrieta), born the daughter of San Francisco's first Mexican consul, was detained by police in Stockton, Calif., in 1897, charged with "masquerading in men's clothes." A month later the gregarious and outspoken Garland was made an honorary member of Stockton's Bachelors Club.

Lucy Ann Lobdell, born in New York State in 1829, was a renowned hunter and trapper. She explained her painful decision to leave her young daughter with her parents and venture out into a "man's world" as Rev. Joseph Lobdell.

"I made up my mind to dress in men's attire to seek labor, as I was used to men's work. And as I might work harder at housework, and get only a dollar a week, and I was capable of doing men's work, and getting men's wages. I feel that I cannot submit to see all the bondage with which woman is oppressed, and listen to the voice of fashion, and repose upon the bosom of death. I am a mother; I love my offspring even better than words can tell. I can not bear to die and leave that little one to struggle in every way to live as I have to do." Lobdell died in an asylum.

Harry Gorman lived as a man for more than 20 years, until hospitalized in Buffalo in 1903. The 40-year-old cigar-chomping railroad cook swore that "nothing would hire" her to wear women's clothing. Gorman alluded to at least 10 other women "who dressed as men, appeared wholly manlike, and were never suspected of being otherwise, also employed in the same railway-company; some of these being porters, train-agents, switchmen and so on. They often met together and made themselves not a little merry over the success of their transference from one class of humanity to another" (*Gay American History*).

Cora Anderson lived as Ralph Kerwinieo for 13 years before being brought up on charges of "disorderly conduct" in 1914 in Milwaukee after her sex was disclosed. After being ordered by the court to don "women's" apparel, Anderson, a South American Indian, explained: "In the future centuries it is probable that woman will be the owner of her own body and the custodian of her own soul. But until that time you can expect that the statutes [concerning] women will be all wrong. The well-cared-for woman is a parasite, and the woman who must work is a slave. The woman's minimum wage will help, but it will not—cannot—effect a complete cure. Some people may think I am very bitter against the men. I am only bitter against conditions—conditions that have grown up in this man-made world" (*Gay American History*).

The struggle of James McHarris (Annie Lee Grant) for the right to live as a man was reported in a 1954 article in Ebony. McHarris, arrested in Mississippi on an unrelated petty charge, endured having to strip in front of the mayor and police, and was imprisoned in a men's jail.

Transvestism has continued to flourish in drama and comedy in the U.S. and in Europe. Cross-gendered performances were an integral part of burlesque and vaudeville in the U.S. during the 19th century.

The blues tradition in the 1920s and 1930s incorporated lyrics about transgendered expression in the urban African American communities in songs like Ma Rainey's "Prove It On Blues," and Bessie Jackson's "B-D Women" (bull-dagger women).

Transgendered roles are still seen—most frequently as "comedy"—on television and in film, theater, literature, dance and music. But the social penalties for transgendered people who try to live and work in dignity and respect are still cruel and frequently violent.

CHRISTINE JORGENSEN BATTLED BIGOTRY

The development of anesthesia and the commercial synthesis of hormones are relatively recent discoveries of this century. These breakthroughs opened the possibility for individuals to change their sex to conform with their gender. Since that time, tens of thousands of transsexuals in this country alone have made the same life decision that Christine Jorgensen made.

While Jorgensen was not the first person to have a sex-change, she was by far the most well-publicized. She died May 3, 1989, at age 62 after a battle with cancer. Jorgensen was remembered in mainstream media obituaries as George Jorgensen, the Bronx-born ex-GI and photographer who traveled to Denmark in the early 1950s to become Christine—the first reported sex-change.

These accounts admit to an "international fuss" over her life decision, but add that she was "transformed into an instant celebrity. She traveled the lecture and nightclub circuit, met royalty and celebrities and ended up rich" (New York Daily News, May 4, 1989).

Sounds like a Harlequin novel, doesn't it? This is sheer hypocrisy coming from the media—and the ruling powers guiding their pens—that made Jorgensen the object of universal ridicule. Not once during her lifetime did anyone who controls this society say that Christine Jorgensen was a human being deserving respect.

The news of Jorgensen's sex change was leaked to the press in late 1952—one of the deepest periods of political reaction in the history of the United States. It was the height of the notorious McCarthy witch hunts, when hundreds were dragged into court and put in prison simply for their political views. The Rosenbergs were sitting on death row, awaiting electrocution at Sing-Sing. Pentagon planes bombed Korea and tested the hydrogen bomb in the South Pacific.

Jim Crow laws still ruled the South. Gay men and lesbians were fighting for survival without a movement. Transvestism was only acceptable when it was "Uncle Milty" Berle putting on drag for guffaws.

When the news about Christine Jorgensen hit, all hell broke loose. From appalled news commentators to cruel talk show hosts, she was attacked so viciously it seemed she was exiled from the human race.

What had been an important private decision was seized on by a hostile media and vulgarized. Her personal life was no longer her own. She was relentlessly hounded. Jorgensen told the media a year before her death: "I'm not that recognizable anymore. I can actually go into a supermarket and people don't know who I am, which is just wonderful and suits me just fine.

"Things don't hurt the way they did then," she added.

Somehow she paid this punishing emotional price and survived with grace and dignity. It took great courage.

The attacks on Jorgensen were part of a campaign meant to enforce conformity, but it was too late in history for this to succeed.

Jorgensen told the press in 1986: "I could never understand why I was receiving so much attention. Now, looking back, I realize it was the beginning of the sexual revolution, and I just happened to be one of the trigger mechanisms."

FROM JOAN OF ARC TO STONEWALL

In the last decades, the development of technology rendered many of the occupational divisions between men and women obsolete. Women were joining the work force in larger numbers, becoming a part of the working class in the most active and immediate sense. This shaped a whole new consciousness.

The contraceptive pill, first produced in 1952, virtually revolutionized social relations for many women, and allowed women to participate in all phases of life with the same freedom from unwanted pregnancies as men.

Rigidly enforced gender boundaries should also have been scrapped. But the motor force of capitalism still drives prejudice and inequity as a vehicle for division. It took monumental struggles—and still greater ones remain on the horizon—to right these wrongs.

The civil rights and national liberation movements of the 1950s and 1960s, and the massive resistance to the Vietnam war, rocked the world and helped give rise to the women's liberation struggle as well.

In 1969, militant young gay transvestites in New York City's Greenwich Village led a fight against cops who tried to raid the Stonewall Inn. The battles lasted for four nights running. The Stonewall Rebellion gave birth to a modern lesbian and gay rights movement that will never again be silenced behind closet doors.

From peasant uprisings against feudalism in the Middle Ages to the Stonewall Rebellion in the 20th century, transvestites and other transgendered people have figured in many militant struggles, both in defense of the right of personal expression and as a form of political rebellion.

But from the violence on the streets to the brutality of the police, from job discrimination to denial of health care and housing—survival is still a battle for the transgendered population.

Transgendered people are the brunt of cruel jokes on television and in films. Movies like "Psycho," "Dressed to Kill" and "Silence of the Lambs" create images of transgendered people as dangerous sociopaths.

In "Silence of the Lambs," a sort-of-transvestite, wanna-be-transsexual kills women and skins them in order to sew a woman's body for himself. The film turns reality upside down: It is actually transvestites and transsexuals who have been the victims of grisly murders.

This point was driven home by activists who disrupted the National Film Society awards in spring 1992. They passed out fliers highlighting the real-life murder of transsexual Venus Xtravaganza, who appeared in the documentary "Paris is Burning." Xtravaganza was murdered before the film on Harlem's drag balls was finished.

"Silence of the Lambs" swept the Academy Awards. "Paris is Burning" wasn't even nominated.

FIGHTING FOR A BETTER WORLD

The institutionalized bigotry and oppression we face today have not always existed. They arose with the division of society into exploiter and exploited. Divide-and-conquer tactics have allowed the slave-owners, feudal landlords and corporate ruling classes to keep for themselves the lion's share of wealth created by the laboring class.

Like racism and all forms of prejudice, bigotry toward transgendered people is a deadly carcinogen. We are pitted against each other in order to keep us from seeing each other as allies.

Genuine bonds of solidarity can be forged between people who respect each other's differences and are willing to fight their enemy together. We are the class that does the work of the world, and can revolutionize it. We can win true liberation.

The struggle against intolerable conditions is on the rise around the world. And the militant role of transgendered women, men and youths in today's fight-back movement is already helping to shape the future.

NOTE

*Originally published as Feinberg, Leslie. *Transgender Liberation: A Movement Whose Time Has Come* (New York: World View Forum, 1992).

17

The Empire *Strikes Back*
A Posttranssexual Manifesto

SANDY STONE

SANDY STONE'S "POSTTRANSSEXUAL MANIFESTO" has been described justly as the protean text from which contemporary transgender studies emerged. It developed a poststructuralist analysis of gender identity that opened up new possibilities for transsexuals—and, by extension, for other types of people who feel themselves to be "differently gendered"—to escape the powerful effects of both medical and feminist discourses that have worked to efface and invalidate their life experiences. Simultaneously, Stone called for a new body of intellectual work, grounded in new practices of selfhood, to take root and flourish, and give fresh expression to "entire spectra of desire" that had previously been unexpressed.

The title of Stone's article refers directly to Janice Raymond's 1978 anti-transsexual polemic, *The Transsexual Empire*, in which Raymond personally attacked Stone for daring to present herself as a woman and to work as a sound engineer at Olivia Records, a women-only feminist music collective. Stone exacts her revenge more than a decade later, not by waging an anti-feminist counter-attack on Raymond, but by undermining the foundationalist assumptions that support Raymond's narrower concept of womanhood, and by claiming a speaking position for transsexuals that cannot be automatically dismissed as damaged, deluded, second-rate, or somehow inherently compromised.

Sandy Stone's path-breaking essay explicitly addresses the literary genres of transsexual biography and autobiography. It looks at the ways that others have "ventriloquized" their ideas about gender through transsexual mouthpieces, as well as how transsexual autobiographical writing has often uncritically reproduced discourses of gender that ultimately are unhelpful for understanding the complex specificity of transsexual embodiment and experience. One of Stone's goals in critiquing previous representations of transsexualism was to encourage new forms of self-expression capable of revealing the deep and powerful ways we all construct a sense of self in reference to our particular form of embodiment. In the wake of Stone's article, a gradual but steady body of new academic and creative work by transgender people has gradually taken shape, which has enriched virtually every academic and artistic discipline with new critical perspectives on gender.

FROGS INTO PRINCESSES

The verdant hills of Casablanca look down on homes and shops jammed chockablock against narrow, twisted streets filled with the odors of spices and dung. Casablanca is a very old city, passed over by Lawrence Durrell perhaps only by a geographical accident as the winepress of love. In the more modern quarter, located on a broad, sunny boulevard, is a building otherwise unremarkable except for a small brass nameplate that identifies it as the clinic of Dr. Georges Burou. It is predominantly devoted to obstetrics and gynecology, but for many years has maintained another reputation quite unknown to the stream of Moroccan women who pass through its rooms.

Dr. Burou is being visited by journalist James Morris. Morris fidgets in an anteroom reading *Elle* and *Paris-Match* with something less than full attention, because he is on an errand of immense personal import. At last the receptionist calls for him, and he is shown to the inner sanctum. He relates:

> I was led along corridors and up staircases into the inner premises of the clinic. The atmosphere thickened as we proceeded. The rooms became more heavily curtained, more velvety, more voluptuous. Portrait busts appeared, I think, and there was a hint of heavy perfume. Presently I saw, advancing upon me through the dim alcoves of this retreat, which distinctly suggested to me the allure of a harem, a figure no less recognizably odalisque. It was Madame Burou. She was dressed in a long white robe, tasseled I think around the waist, which subtly managed to combine the luxuriance of a caftan with the hygiene of a nurse's uniform, and she was blonde herself, and carefully mysterious.... Powers beyond my control had brought me to Room 5 at the clinic in Casablanca, and I could not have run away then even if I had wanted to.... I went to say good-bye to myself in the mirror. We would never meet again, and I wanted to give that other self a long last look in the eye, and a wink for luck. As I did so a street vendor outside played a delicate arpeggio upon his flute, a very gentle merry sound which he repeated, over and over again, in sweet diminuendo down the street. Flights of angels, I said to myself, and so staggered...to my bed, and oblivion.[1]

Exit James Morris, enter Jan Morris, through the intervention of late twentieth–century medical practices in this wonderfully "oriental," almost religious narrative of transformation. The passage is from *Conundrum*, the story of Morris' "sex change" and the consequences for her life. Besides the wink for luck, there is another obligatory ceremony known to male-to-female transsexuals which is called "wringing the turkey's neck," although it is not recorded whether Morris performed it as well. I will return to this rite of passage later in more detail.

MAKING HISTORY

Imagine now a swift segue from the moiling alleyways of Casablanca to the rolling green hills of Palo Alto. The Stanford Gender Dysphoria Program occupies a small room near the campus in a quiet residential section of this affluent community. The Program, which is a counterpart to Georges Burou's clinic in Morocco, has been for many years the academic focus of Western studies of gender dysphoria syndrome, also known as transsexualism. Here are determined etiology, diagnostic criteria, and treatment.

The Program was begun in 1968, and its staff of surgeons and psychologists first set out to collect as much history on the subject of transsexualism as was available. Let me pause to provide a very brief capsule of their results. A transsexual is a person who identifies his or her gender identity with that of the "opposite" gender. Sex and gender are quite separate issues, but transsexuals commonly blur the distinction by confusing the performative character of gender with the physical "fact" of sex, referring to their perceptions of their situation as being in the "wrong body." Although the term transsexual is of recent origin, the phenomenon is not. The earliest mention of something which we can recognize *ex post facto* as transsexualism, in light of current diagnostic criteria, was of the Assyrian king Sardanapalus, who was reported to have dressed in women's clothing and spun with his wives.[2] Later instances of something very like transsexualism were reported by Philo of Judea, during the Roman Empire. In the eighteenth century the Chevalier d'Eon, who lived for thirty-nine years in the female role, was a rival of Madame Pompadour for the attention of Louis XV. The first colonial governor of New York, Lord Cornbury, came from England fully attired as a woman and remained so during his time in office.[3]

Transsexualism was not accorded the status of an "official disorder" until 1980, when it was first listed in the *American Psychiatric Association Diagnostic and Statistical Manual*. As Marie Mehl points out, this is something of a Pyrrhic victory.[4]

Prior to 1980, much work had already been done in an attempt to define criteria for differential diagnosis. An example from the 1970s is this one, from work carried out by Leslie Lothstein and reported in Walters and Ross's *Transsexualism and Sex Reassignment*[5]:

> Lothstein, in his study of ten ageing transsexuals [average age fifty-two], found that psychological testing helped to determine the extent of the patients' pathology [*sic*]…[he] concluded that [transsexuals as a class] were depressed, isolated, withdrawn, schizoid individuals with profound dependency conflicts. Furthermore, they were immature, narcissistic, egocentric and potentially explosive, while their attempts to obtain [professional assistance] were demanding, manipulative, controlling, coercive, and paranoid.[6]

Here's another:

> In a study of 56 transsexuals the results on the schizophrenia and depression scales were outside the upper limit of the normal range. The authors see these profiles as reflecting the confused and bizarre life styles of the subjects.[7]

These were clinical studies, which represented a very limited class of subjects. However, the studies were considered sufficiently representative for them to be reprinted without comment in collections such as that of Walters and Ross. Further on in each paper, though, we find that each investigator invalidates his results in a brief disclaimer which is reminiscent of the fine print in a cigarette ad: In the first, by adding "It must be admitted that Lothstein's subjects could hardly be called a typical sample as nine of the ten studied had serious physical health problems" (this was a study conducted in a health clinic, not a gender clinic), and in the second, with the afterthought that "82 per cent of [the subjects] were prostitutes and atypical of transsexuals in other parts of the world."[8] Such results might have been considered marginal, hedged about as they were with markers of questionable method or excessively limited samples. Yet they came to represent transsexuals in medicolegal/psychological literature, disclaimers and all, almost to the present day.

During the same period, feminist theoreticians were developing their own analyses. The issue quickly became, and remains, volatile and divisive. Let me quote an example.

> Rape…is a masculinist violation of bodily integrity. All transsexuals rape women's bodies by reducing the female form to an artifact, appropriating this body for themselves.…Rape, although it is usually done by force, can also be accomplished by deception.

This quote is from Janice Raymond's 1979 book *The Transsexual Empire: The Making of The She-Male*, which occasioned the title of this paper. I read Raymond to be claiming that transsexuals are constructs of an evil phallocratic empire and were designed to invade women's spaces and appropriate women's power. Though *Empire* represented a specific moment in feminist analysis and prefigured the appropriation of liberal political language by a radical right, here in 1991, on the twelfth anniversary of its publication, it is still the definitive statement on transsexualism by a genetic female academic.[9] To clarify my stakes in this discourse let me quote another passage from *Empire*:

> Masculine behavior is notably obtrusive. It is significant that transsexually constructed lesbian-feminists have inserted themselves into the positions of importance and/or performance in the feminist community. Sandy Stone, the transsexual engineer with Olivia Records, an 'all-women' recording company, illustrates

this well. Stone is not only crucial to the Olivia enterprise but plays a very dominant role there. The...visibility he achieved in the aftermath of the Olivia controversy...only serves to enhance his previously dominant role and to divide women, as men frequently do, when they make their presence necessary and vital to women. As one woman wrote: "I feel raped when Olivia passes off Sandy...as a real woman. After all his male privilege, is he going to cash in on lesbian feminist culture too?"

This paper, "The *Empire* Strikes Back," is about morality tales and origin myths, about telling the "truth" of gender. Its informing principle is that "technical arts are always imagined to be subordinated by the ruling artistic idea, itself rooted authoritatively in nature's own life."[10] It is about the image and the real mutually defining each other through the inscriptions and reading practices of late capitalism. It is about postmodernism, postfeminism, and (dare I say it) posttranssexualism. Throughout, the paper owes a large debt to Donna Haraway.

"ALL OF REALITY IN LATE CAPITALIST CULTURE LUSTS TO BECOME AN IMAGE FOR ITS OWN SECURITY"[11]

Let's turn to accounts by the transsexuals themselves. During this period virtually all of the published accounts were written by male-to-females. I want to briefly consider four autobiographical accounts of male-to-female transsexuals, to see what we can learn about what they think they are doing. (I will consider female-to-male transsexuals in another paper.)

The earliest partially autobiographical account in existence is that of Lili Elbe in Niels Hoyer's book *Man Into Woman* [1933].[12] The first fully autobiographical book was the paperback *I Changed My Sex!* (not exactly a quiet, contemplative title), written by the striptease artist Hedy Jo Star in the mid-1950s.[13] Christine Jorgensen, who underwent surgery in the early 1950s and is arguably the best known of the recent transsexuals, did not publish her autobiography until 1967; instead, Star's book rode the wave of publicity surrounding Jorgensen's surgery. In 1974 *Conundrum* was published, written by the popular English journalist Jan Morris. In 1977 there was *Canary*, by musician and performer Canary Conn.[14] In addition, many transsexuals keep something they call by the argot term "O.T.F.": The Obligatory Transsexual File. This usually contains newspaper articles and bits of forbidden diary entries about "inappropriate" gender behavior. Transsexuals also collect autobiographical literature. According to the Stanford gender dysphoria program, the medical clinics do not, because they consider autobiographical accounts thoroughly unreliable. Because of this, and since a fair percentage of the literature is invisible to many library systems, these personal collections are the only source for some of this information. I am fortunate to have a few of them at my disposal.

What sort of subject is constituted in these texts? Hoyer (representing Jacobson representing Elbe, who is representing Wegener who is representing Sparre),[15] writes:

A single glance of this man had deprived her of all her strength. She felt as if her whole personality had been crushed by him. With a single glance he had extinguished it. Something in her rebelled. She felt like a schoolgirl who had received short shrift from an idolized teacher. She was conscious of a peculiar weakness in all her members...it was the first time her woman's heart had trembled before her lord and master, before the man who had constituted himself her protector, and she understood why she then submitted so utterly to him and his will.[16]

We can put to this fragment all of the usual questions: Not by whom but *for* whom was Lili Elbe constructed? Under whose gaze did her text fall? And consequently what stories appear and disappear in this kind of seduction? It may come as no surprise that all of the accounts I will relate here are similar in their description of "woman" as male fetish, as replicating a socially enforced role, or as constituted by performative gender. Lili Elbe faints at the sight of blood.[17] Jan Morris, a world-class journalist who has been around the block a few times, still describes her sense of herself in relation to makeup and dress, of being on display, and is pleased when men open doors for her:

> I feel small, and neat. I am not small in fact, and not terribly neat either, but femininity conspires to make me feel so. My blouse and skirt are light, bright, crisp. My shoes make my feet look more delicate than they are, besides giving me … a suggestion of vulnerability that I rather like. My red and white bangles give me a racy feel, my bag matches my shoes and makes me feel well organized … When I walk out into the street I feel consciously ready for the world's appraisal, in a way that I never felt as a man.[18]

Hedy Jo Star, who was a professional stripper, says in *I Changed My Sex!*: "I wanted the sensual feel of lingerie against my skin, I wanted to brighten my face with cosmetics. I wanted a strong man to protect me." Here in 1991 I have also encountered a few men who are brave enough to echo this sentiment for themselves, but in 1955 it was a proprietary feminine position.

Besides the obvious complicity of these accounts in a Western white male definition of performative gender, the authors also reinforce a binary, oppositional mode of gender identification. They go from being unambiguous men, albeit unhappy men, to unambiguous women. There is no territory between.[19] Further, each constructs a specific narrative moment when their personal sexual identification changes from male to female. This moment is the moment of neocolporraphy—that is, of gender reassignment or "sex change surgery."[20] Jan Morris, on the night preceding surgery, wrote: "I went to say good-bye to myself in the mirror. We would never meet again, and I wanted to give that other self a last wink for luck … "[21]

Canary Conn writes: "I'm not a *muchacho* … I'm a *muchacha* now … a girl [*sic*]."[22]

Hedy Jo Star writes: "In the instant that I awoke from the anaesthetic, I realized that I had finally become a woman."[23]

Even Lili Elbe, whose text is second-hand, used the same terms: "Suddenly it occurred to him that he, Andreas Sparre, was probably undressing for the last time." Immediately on awakening from first-stage surgery [castration in Hoyer's account], Sparre writes a note. "He gazed at the card and failed to recognize the writing. It was a woman's script." Inger carries the note to the doctor: "What do you think of this, Doctor. No man could have written it?" "No," said the astonished doctor; "no, you are quite right … "—an exchange which requires the reader to forget that orthography is an acquired skill. The same thing happens with Elbe's voice: "the strange thing was that your voice had completely changed … You have a splendid soprano voice! Simply astounding."[24] Perhaps as astounding now as then but for different reasons, since in light of present knowledge of the effects [and more to the point, the non-effects] of castration and hormones none of this could have happened. Neither has any effect on voice timbre. Hence, incidentally, the jaundiced eyes with which the clinics regard historical accounts.

If Hoyer mixes reality with fantasy and caricatures his subjects besides ("Simply astounding!"), what lessons are there in *Man Into Woman*? Partly what emerges from the book is how Hoyer deploys the strategy of building barriers within a single subject, strategies that are still in gainful employment today. Lili displaces the irruptive masculine self, still dangerously present within her, onto the God-figure of her surgeon/therapist Werner Kreutz, whom she calls The Professor, or The Miracle Man. The Professor is He Who molds and Lili that which is molded:

> what the Professor is now doing with Lili is nothing less than an emotional moulding, which is preceding the physical moulding into a woman. Hitherto Lili has been like clay which others had prepared and to

which the Professor has given form and life...by a single glance the Professor awoke her heart to life, a life with all the instincts of woman.[25]

The female is immanent, the female is bone-deep, the female is instinct. With Lili's eager complicity, The Professor drives a massive wedge between the masculine and the feminine within her. In this passage, reminiscent of the "oriental" quality of Morris's narrative, the male must be annihilated or at least denied, but the female is that which exists to be *continually* annihilated:

> It seemed to her as if she no longer had any responsibility for herself, for her fate. For Werner Kreutz had relieved her of it all. Nor had she any longer a will of her own...there could be no past for her. Everything in the past belonged to a person who...was dead. Now there was only a perfectly humble woman, who was ready to obey, who was happy to submit herself to the will of another...her master, her creator, her Professor. Between [Andreas] and her stood Werner Kreutz. She felt secure and salvaged.[26]

Hoyer has the same problems with purity and denial of mixture that recur in many transsexual auto-biographical narratives. The characters in his narrative exist in an historical period of enormous sexual repression. How is one to maintain the divide between the "male" self, whose proper object of desire is Woman, and the "female" self, whose proper object of desire is Man?

> "As a man you have always seemed to me unquestionably healthy. I have, indeed, seen with my own eyes that you attract women, and that is the clearest proof that you are a genuine fellow." He paused, and then placed his hand on Andreas' shoulder. "You won't take it amiss if I ask you a frank question?...Have you at any time been interested in your own kind? You know what I mean."
> Andreas shook his head calmly. "My word on it, Niels; never in my life. And I can add that those kind of creatures have never shown any interest in me."
> "Good, Andreas! That's just what I thought."[27]

Hoyer must separate the subjectivity of "Andreas," who has never felt anything for men, and "Lili," who, in the course of the narrative, wants to marry one. This salvaging procedure makes the world safe for "Lili" by erecting and maintaining an impenetrable barrier between her and "Andreas," reinforced again and again in such ways as two different handwriting styles and two different voices. The force of an imperative—a natural state toward which all things tend—to deny the potentialities of mixture, acts to preserve "pure" gender identity: at the dawn of the Nazi-led love affair with purity, no "creatures" tempt Andreas into transgressing boundaries with his "own kind."

> "I will honestly and plainly confess to you, Niels, that I have always been attracted to women. And to-day as much as ever. A most banal confession!"[28]

—banal only so long as the person inside Andreas's body who voices it is Andreas, rather than Lili. There is a lot of work being done in this passage, a microcosm of the work it takes to maintain the same polar personae in society in the large. Further, each of these writers constructs his or her account as a narrative of redemption. There is a strong element of drama, of the sense of struggle against huge odds, of over-coming perilous obstacles, and of mounting awe and mystery at the breathtaking approach and final apotheosis of the Forbidden Transformation. Oboy.

> The first operation...has been successful beyond all expectations. Andreas has ceased to exist, they said. His germ glands—oh, mystic words—have been removed.[29]

Oh, mystic words. The *mysterium tremendum* of deep identity hovers about a physical locus; the entire complex of male engenderment, the mysterious power of the Man-God, inhabits the "germ glands" in the way that the soul was thought to inhabit the pineal. Maleness is in the you-know-whats. For that matter, so is the ontology of the subject. Therefore Hoyer can demonstrate in the coarsest way that femaleness is lack:

> The operation which has been performed here [that is, castration] enables me to enter the clinic for women [exclusively for women].[30]

On the other hand, either Niels or Lili can be constituted by an act of *insinuation*, what the New Testament calls *endeuein*, or the putting on of the god, inserting the physical body within a shell of cultural signification:

> Andreas Sparre…was probably undressing for the last time…For a lifetime these coverings of coat and waistcoat and trousers had enclosed him.[31]
>
> It is now Lili who is writing to you. I am sitting up in my bed in a silk nightdress with lace trimming, curled, powdered, with bangles, necklace, and rings …[32]

All these authors replicate the stereotypical male account of the constitution of woman: Dress, makeup, and delicate fainting at the sight of blood. Each of these adventurers passes directly from one pole of sexual experience to the other. If there is any intervening space in the continuum of sexuality, it is invisible. And nobody *ever* mentions wringing the turkey's neck.

No wonder feminist theorists have been suspicious. Hell, *I'm* suspicious.

How do these accounts converse with the medical/psychological texts? In a time in which more interactions occur through texts, computer conferences, and electronic media than by personal contact, and consequently when individual subjectivity can be constituted through inscription more often than through personal association, there are still moments of embodied "natural truth" that cannot be avoided. In the time period of most of these books, the most critical of these moments was the intake interview at the gender dysphoria clinic when the doctors, who were all males, decided whether the person was eligible for gender reassignment surgery. The origin of the gender dysphoria clinics is a microcosmic look at the construction of criteria for gender. The foundational idea for the gender dysphoria clinics was first, to study an interesting and potentially fundable human aberration; second, to provide help, as they understood the term, for a "correctable problem."

Some of the early nonacademic gender dysphoria clinics performed *surgery on demand*, which is to say regardless of any judgment on the part of the clinic staff regarding what came to be called appropriateness to the gender of choice. When the first academic gender dysphoria clinics were started on an experimental basis in the 1960s, the medical staff would not perform surgery on demand, because of the professional risks involved in performing experimental surgery on "sociopaths." At this time there were no official diagnostic criteria; "transsexuals" were, *ipso facto*, whoever signed up for assistance. Professionally this was a dicey situation. It was necessary to construct the category "transsexual" along customary and traditional lines, to construct plausible criteria for acceptance into a clinic. Professionally speaking, a test or a differential diagnosis was needed for transsexualism that did not depend on anything as simple and subjective as feeling that one was in the wrong body. The test needed to be objective, clinically appropriate, and repeatable. But even after considerable research, no simple and unambiguous test for gender dysphoria syndrome could be developed.[33]

The Stanford clinic was in the business of helping people, among its other agendas, as its members understood the term. Therefore the final decisions of eligibility for gender reassignment were made by the staff on the basis of an individual *sense* of the "appropriateness of the individual to their gender of choice." The clinic took on the additional role of "grooming clinic" or "charm school" because, according to the judgment of the staff, the men who presented as wanting to be women did not always "behave like" women. Stanford recognized that gender roles could be learned (to an extent). Their involvement with the grooming clinics was an effort to produce not simply anatomically legible females, but *women*...i.e., *gendered* females. As Norman Fisk remarked, "I now admit very candidly that...in the early phases we were avowedly seeking candidates who would have the best chance for success."[34] In practice this meant that the candidates for surgery were evaluated on the basis of their *performance* in the gender of choice. The criteria constituted a fully acculturated, consensual definition of gender, and *at the site of their enactment we can locate an actual instance of the apparatus of production of gender.*

This raises several sticky questions, the chief two being: Who is telling the story for whom, and how do the storytellers differentiate between the story they tell and the story they hear?

One answer is that they differentiate with great difficulty. The criteria which the researchers developed and then applied were defined recursively through a series of interactions with the candidates. The scenario worked this way: Initially, the only textbook on the subject of transsexualism was Harry Benjamin's definitive work *The Transsexual Phenomenon* [1966].[35] [Note that Benjamin's book actually postdates *I Changed My Sex!* by about ten years.] When the first clinics were constituted, Benjamin's book was the researchers' standard reference. And when the first transsexuals were evaluated for their suitability for surgery, their behavior matched up gratifyingly with Benjamin's criteria. The researchers produced papers which reported on this, and which were used as bases for funding.

It took a surprisingly long time—several years—for the researchers to realize that the reason the candidates' behavioral profiles matched Benjamin's so well was that the candidates, too, had read Benjamin's book, which was passed from hand to hand within the transsexual community, and they were only too happy to provide the behavior that led to acceptance for surgery.[36] This sort of careful repositioning created interesting problems. Among them was the determination of the permissible range of expressions of physical sexuality. This was a large gray area in the candidates' self-presentations, because Benjamin's subjects did not talk about any erotic sense of their own bodies. Consequently nobody else who came to the clinics did either. By textual authority, physical men who lived as women and who identified themselves as transsexuals, as opposed to male transvestites for whom erotic penile sensation was permissible, could not experience penile pleasure. Into the 1980s there was not a single preoperative male-to-female transsexual for whom data was available who experienced genital sexual pleasure while living in the "gender of choice."[37] The prohibition continued postoperatively in interestingly transmuted form, and remained so absolute that no postoperative transsexual would admit to experiencing sexual pleasure through masturbation either. Full membership in the assigned gender was conferred by orgasm, real or faked, accomplished through heterosexual penetration.[38] "Wringing the turkey's neck," the ritual of penile masturbation just before surgery, was the most secret of secret traditions. To acknowledge so natural a desire would be to risk "crash landing"; that is, "role inappropriateness" leading to disqualification.[39]

It was necessary to retrench. The two groups, on one hand the researchers and on the other the transsexuals, were pursuing separate ends. The researchers wanted to know what this thing they called gender dysphoria syndrome was. They wanted a taxonomy of symptoms, criteria for differential diagnosis, procedures for evaluation, reliable courses of treatment, and thorough follow–up. The transsexuals wanted surgery. They had very clear agendas regarding their relation to the researchers, and considered the doctors' evaluation criteria merely another obstacle in their path—something to be overcome. In this they unambiguously expressed Benjamin's original criterion in its simplest form: The sense of being in the "wrong" body.[40] This seems a recipe for an uneasy adversarial relationship, and it was. It continues to be, although with the passage of time there has been considerable dialogue between the two camps. Partly this has been made possible by the realization among the medical and psychological community that the expected criteria for differential diagnosis did not emerge. Consider this excerpt from a paper by Marie Mehl, written in 1986:

> There is no mental nor psychological test which successfully differentiates the transsexual from the so-called normal population. There is no more psychopathology in the transsexual population than in the population at large, although societal response to the transsexual does pose some insurmountable problems. The psychodynamic histories of transsexuals do not yield any consistent differentiation characteristics from the rest of the population.[41]

These two accounts, Mehl's statement and that of Lothstein, in which he found transsexuals to be depressed, schizoid, manipulative, controlling, and paranoid, coexist within a span of less than ten years. With the achievement of a diagnostic category in 1980—one which, after years of research, did not involve much more than the original sense of "being in the wrong body"—and consequent acceptance by the body police, i.e., the medical establishment, clinically "good" histories now exist of transsexuals in areas as widely dispersed as Australia, Sweden, Czechoslovakia, Vietnam, Singapore, China, Malaysia, India, Uganda, Sudan, Tahiti, Chile, Borneo, Madagascar, and the Aleutians.[42] (This is not a complete list.) It is a considerable stretch to fit them all into some plausible theory. Were there undiscovered or untried diagnostic techniques that would have differentiated transsexuals from the "normal" population? Were the criteria wrong, limited, or short-sighted? Did the realization that criteria were not emerging just naturally appear as a result of "scientific progress," or were there other forces at work?

Such a banquet of data creates its own problems. Concomitant with the dubious achievement of a diagnostic category is the inevitable blurring of boundaries as a vast heteroglossic account of difference, heretofore invisible to the "legitimate" professions, suddenly achieves canonization and simultaneously becomes homogenized to satisfy the constraints of the category. Suddenly the old morality tale of the truth of gender, told by a kindly white patriarch in New York in 1966, becomes pancultural in the 1980s. Emergent polyvocalities of lived experience, never represented in the discourse but present at least in potential, disappear; the *berdache* and the stripper, the tweedy housewife and the *mujerado*, the *mah'u* and the rock star, are still the same story after all, if we only try hard enough.

WHOSE STORY IS THIS, ANYWAY?

I wish to point out the broad similarities which this peculiar juxtaposition suggests to aspects of colonial discourse with which we may be familiar: The initial fascination with the exotic, extending to professional investigators; denial of subjectivity and lack of access to the dominant discourse; followed by a species of rehabilitation.

Raising these issues has complicated life in the clinics.

"Making" history, whether autobiographic, academic, or clinical, is partly a struggle to ground an account in some natural inevitability. Bodies are screens on which we see projected the momentary settlements that emerge from ongoing struggles over beliefs and practices within the academic and medical communities. These struggles play themselves out in arenas far removed from the body. Each is an attempt to gain a high ground which is profoundly moral in character, to make an authoritative and final explanation for the way things are and consequently for the way they must continue to be. In other words, each of these accounts is culture speaking with the voice of an individual. The people who have no voice in this theorizing are the transsexuals themselves. As with males theorizing about women from the beginning of time, theorists of gender have seen transsexuals as possessing something less than agency. As with "genetic" "women," transsexuals are infantilized, considered too illogical or irresponsible to achieve true subjectivity, or clinically erased by diagnostic criteria; or else, as constructed by some radical feminist theorists, as robots of an insidious and menacing patriarchy, an alien army designed and constructed to infiltrate, pervert and destroy "true" women. In this construction as well, the transsexuals have been resolutely complicit by failing to develop an effective counterdiscourse.

Here on the gender borders at the close of the twentieth century, with the faltering of phallocratic hegemony and the bumptious appearance of heteroglossic origin accounts, we find the epistemologies of white male medical practice, the rage of radical feminist theories and the chaos of lived gendered experience meeting on the battlefield of the transsexual body: a hotly contested site of cultural inscription, a meaning machine for the production of ideal type. Representation at its most magical, the transsexual body is perfected memory, inscribed with the "true" story of Adam and Eve as the ontological account of irreducible difference, an essential biography which is part of nature. A story which culture tells itself, the transsexual body is a tactile politics of reproduction constituted through textual violence. The clinic is a technology of inscription.

Given this circumstance in which a minority discourse comes to ground in the physical, a counterdiscourse is critical. But it is difficult to generate a counterdiscourse if one is programmed to disappear. The highest purpose of the transsexual is to erase him/herself, to fade into the "normal" population as soon as possible. Part of this process is known as *constructing a plausible history*—learning to lie effectively about one's past. What is gained is acceptability in society. What is lost is the ability to authentically represent the complexities and ambiguities of lived experience, and thereby is lost that aspect of "nature" which Donna Haraway theorizes as Coyote—the Native American spirit animal who represents the power of continual transformation which is the heart of engaged life. Instead, authentic experience is replaced by a particular kind of story, one that supports the old constructed positions. This is expensive, and profoundly disempowering. Whether desiring to do so or not, transsexuals do not grow up in the same ways as "GGs," or genetic "naturals."[43] Transsexuals do not possess the same history as genetic "naturals," and do not share common oppression prior to gender reassignment. I am not suggesting a shared discourse. I am suggesting that in the transsexual's erased history we can find a story disruptive to the accepted discourses of gender, which originates from within the gender minority itself and which can make common cause with other oppositional discourses. But the transsexual currently occupies a position which is nowhere, which is outside the binary oppositions of gendered discourse. For a transsexual, *as a transsexual*, to generate a true, effective and representational counterdiscourse is to speak from outside the boundaries of gender, beyond the constructed oppositional nodes which have been predefined as the only positions from which discourse is possible. How, then, can the transsexual speak? If the transsexual were to speak, what would s/he say?

A POSTTRANSSEXUAL MANIFESTO

To attempt to occupy a place as speaking subject within the traditional gender frame is to become complicit in the discourse which one wishes to deconstruct. Rather, we can seize upon the textual violence inscribed in the transsexual body and turn it into a reconstructive force. Let me suggest a more familiar example. Judith Butler points out that the lesbian categories of "butch" and "femme" are not simple assimilations of lesbianism back into terms of heterosexuality. Rather, Butler introduces the concept of *cultural intelligibility*, and suggests that the contextualized and resignified "masculinity" of the butch, seen against a culturally intelligible "female" body, invokes a dissonance that both generates a sexual tension and constitutes the object of desire. She points out that this way of thinking about gendered objects of desire admits of much greater complexity than the example suggests. The lesbian butch or femme both recall the heterosexual scene but simultaneously displace it. The idea that butch and femme are "replicas" or "copies" of heterosexual exchange underestimates the erotic power of their internal dissonance.[44] In the case of the transsexual, the varieties of performative gender, seen against a culturally intelligible gendered body *which is itself a medically constituted textual violence*, generate new and unpredictable dissonances which implicate entire spectra of desire. In the transsexual as text we may find the potential to map the refigured body onto conventional gender discourse and thereby disrupt it, to take advantage of the dissonances created by such a juxtaposition to fragment and reconstitute the elements of gender in new and unexpected geometries. I suggest we start by taking Raymond's accusation that "transsexuals divide women" beyond itself, and turn it into a productive force to multiplicatively divide the old binary discourses of gender—as well as Raymond's own monistic discourse. To foreground the practices of inscription and reading which are part of this deliberate invocation of dissonance, I suggest constituting transsexuals not as a class or problematic "third gender," but rather as a *genre*—a set of embodied texts whose potential for *productive* disruption of structured sexualities and spectra of desire has yet to be explored.

In order to effect this, the genre of visible transsexuals must grow by recruiting members from the class of invisible ones, from those who have disappeared into their "plausible histories." The most critical thing a transsexual can do, the thing that *constitutes* success, is to "pass."[45] Passing means to live successfully in the gender of choice, to be accepted as a "natural" member of that gender. Passing means the denial of mixture. One and the same with passing is effacement of the prior gender role, or the construction of a plausible history. Considering that most transsexuals choose reassignment in their third or fourth decade, this means erasing a considerable portion of their personal experience. It is my contention that this process, in which both the transsexual and the medicolegal/psychological establishment are complicit, forecloses the possibility of a life grounded in the *intertextual* possibilities of the transsexual body.

To negotiate the troubling and productive multiple permeabilities of boundary and subject position that intertextuality implies, we must begin to rearticulate the foundational language by which both sexuality and transsexuality are described. For example, neither the investigators nor the transsexuals have taken the step of problematizing "wrong body" as an adequate descriptive category. In fact "wrong body" has come, virtually by default, to *define* the syndrome.[46] It is quite understandable, I think, that a phrase whose lexicality suggests the phallocentric, binary character of gender differentiation should be examined with deepest suspicion. So long as we, whether academics, clinicians, or transsexuals, ontologize both sexuality and transsexuality in this way, we have foreclosed the possibility of analyzing desire and motivational complexity in a manner which adequately describes the multiple contradictions of individual lived experience. We need a deeper analytical language for transsexual theory, one which allows for the sorts of ambiguities and polyvocalities which have already so productively informed and enriched feminist theory.

In this volume, Judith Shapiro points out that "To those…who might be inclined to diagnose the transsexual's focus on the genitals as obsessive or fetishistic, the response is that they are, in fact, simply conforming to *their culture's* criteria for gender assignment" [emphasis mine]. This statement points to deeper workings, to hidden discourses and experiential pluralities within the transsexual monolith. They are not yet clinically or academically visible, and with good reason. For example, in pursuit of differential diagnosis a question sometimes asked of a prospective transsexual is "Suppose that you could be a man [or woman] in every way except for your genitals; would you be content?" There are several possible answers, but only one is clinically correct.[47] Small wonder, then, that so much of these discourses revolves around the phrase "wrong body." Under the binary phallocratic founding myth by which Western bodies and subjects are authorized, only one body per gendered subject is "right." All other bodies are wrong.

As clinicians and transsexuals continue to face off across the diagnostic battlefield which this scenario suggests, the transsexuals for whom gender identity is something different from *and perhaps irrelevant to* physical genitalia are occulted by those for whom the power of the medical/psychological establishments, and their ability to act as gatekeepers for cultural norms, is the final authority for what counts as a culturally intelligible body. This is a treacherous area, and were the silenced groups to achieve voice we might well find, as feminist theorists have claimed, that the identities of individual, embodied subjects were far less implicated in physical norms, and far more diversely spread across a rich and complex structuration of identity and desire, than it is now possible to express. And yet in even the best of the current debates, the standard mode is one of relentless totalization. The most egregious example in this paper, Raymond's stunning "All transsexuals rape women's bodies" (what if she had said, e.g., "all blacks rape women's bodies"), is no less totalizing than Kates's "transsexuals...take on an exaggerated and stereotypical female role," or Bolin's "transsexuals try to forget their male history." There are no subjects in these discourses, only homogenized, totalized objects—fractally replicating earlier histories of minority discourses in the large. So when I speak the forgotten word, it will perhaps wake memories of other debates. The word is *some*.

Transsexuals who pass seem able to ignore the fact that by creating totalized, monistic identities, forgoing physical and subjective intertextuality, they have foreclosed the possibility of authentic relationships. Under the principle of passing, denying the destabilizing power of being "read," relationships begin as lies—and passing, of course, is not an activity restricted to transsexuals. This is familiar to the person of color whose skin is light enough to pass as white, or to the closet gay or lesbian...or to anyone who has chosen invisibility as an imperfect solution to personal dissonance. In essence I am rearticulating one of the arguments for solidarity which has been developed by gays, lesbians and people of color. The comparison extends further. To deconstruct the necessity for passing implies that transsexuals must take responsibility for *all* of their history, to begin to rearticulate their lives not as a series of erasures in the service of a species of feminism conceived from within a traditional frame, but as a political action begun by reappropriating difference and reclaiming the power of the refigured and reinscribed body. The disruptions of the old patterns of desire that the multiple dissonances of the transsexual body imply produce not an irreducible alterity but a myriad of alterities, whose unanticipated juxtapositions hold what Donna Haraway has called the promises of monsters—physicalities of constantly shifting figure and ground that exceed the frame of any possible representation.[48]

The essence of transsexualism is the act of passing. A transsexual who passes is obeying the Derridean imperative: "Genres are not to be mixed. I will not mix genres."[49] I could not ask a transsexual for anything more inconceivable than to forgo passing, to be consciously "read," to read oneself aloud—and by this troubling and productive reading, to begin to *write oneself* into the discourses by which one has been written—in effect, then, to become a (look out—dare I say it again?) posttranssexual.[50] Still, transsexuals know that silence can be an extremely high price to pay for acceptance. I want to speak directly to the brothers, sisters and others who may read/"read" this and say: I ask all of us to use the strength which brought us through the effort of restructuring identity, and which has also helped us to live in silence and denial, for a re-visioning of our lives. I know you feel that most of the work is behind you and that the price of invisibility is not great. But, although *individual* change is the foundation of all things, it is not the end of all things. Perhaps it's time to begin laying the groundwork for the next transformation.

NOTES

Thanks to Gloria Anzaldúa, Laura Chernaik, Ramona Fernandez, Thyrza Goodeve, and John Hartigan for their valuable comments on earlier drafts of this paper, Judy Van Maasdam and Donald Laub of the Stanford Gender Dysphoria Program for their uneasy help, Wendy Chapkis; Nathalie Magan; the Olivia Records Collective, for whose caring in difficult times I am deeply grateful; Janice Raymond, for playing Luke Skywalker to my Darth Vader; Graham Nash and David Crosby; and to Christy Staats and Brenda Warren for their steadfastness. In particular, I thank Donna Haraway, whose insight and encouragement continue to inform and illuminate this work.

1. Jan Morris, *Conundrum*, (New York: Harcourt Brace Jovanovich, 1974) 155.
2. In William A.W. Walters, and Michael W. Ross, *Transsexualism and Sex Reassignment*, (Oxford: Oxford University Press, 1986).
3. This capsule history is related in the introduction to Richard Docter's *Transvestites and Transsexuals: Toward a Theory of Cross-Gender Behavior*, New York: Plenum Press, 1988. It is also treated by Judith Shapiro, "Transsexualism: Reflections on the Persistence of Gender and the Mutability of Sex", in this volume, as well as by Janice Irvine in *Disorders of Desire: Sex and Gender in Modern American Sexology* (Philadelphia: Temple University Press, 1990). In chapter seven of this volume, Gary Kates argues that the Chevalier d'Eon was not a transsexual because he did not demonstrate the transsexual syndrome as Kates understands it; i.e., "intense discomfort with masculine clothes and activities, as is normal in male-to-female transsexuals." Kates's idea of the syndrome comes from standard texts. Later in this paper I discuss the mythic quality of much of this information.
4. In Mehl's introduction to Betty Steiner, ed., *Gender Dysphoria Syndrome: Development, Research, Management* (New York: Plenum Press, 1985).
5. Walters and Ross, op.cit.
6. From Don Burnard and Michael W. Ross, "Psychosocial Aspects and Psychological Theory: What Can Psychological Testing Reveal?" in Walters and Ross [58,2].
7. Walters and Ross, [58,3].
8. Walters and Ross, [58,3].
9. There is some hope to be taken that Judith Shapiro's work will supercede Raymond's as such a definitive statement. Shapiro's accounts seem excellently balanced, and she is aware that there are more accounts from transsexual scholars that have not yet entered the discourse.
10. This wonderful phrase is from Donna Haraway's "Teddy Bear Patriarchy: Taxidermy in the Garden Of Eden, New York City, 1908–1936," in *Social Text* 11, 11:20.
11. Haraway, op.cit. The anecdotal character of this section is supported by field notes which have not yet been organized and coded. A thoroughly definitive and perhaps ethnographic version of this paper, with appropriate citations of both professionals and their subjects, awaits research time and funding.
12. The British sexologist, Norman Haine, wrote the introduction, thus making Hoyer's book a semi-medical contribution.
13. Hedy Jo Star, (Carl Rollins Hammonds), 1955. *I Changed My Sex! [From an O.T.F.]*. Star's book has disappeared from history, and I have been unable to find reference to it in any library catalog. Having held a copy in my hand, I am sorry I didn't hold tighter.
14. There was at least one other book published during this period, Renée Richards's "Second Serve," which is not treated here.
15. Niels Hoyer was a pseudonym for Ernst Ludwig Harthern Jacobson; Lili Elbe was the female name chosen by the artist Einar Wegener, whose given name was Andreas Sparre. This lexical profusion has rich implications for studies of self and its constructions, in literature and also in such emergent social settings as computer conferences, where several personalities grounded in a single body are as much the rule as the exception.
16. Hoyer [163].
17. Hoyer [147].
18. Morris [174].
19. In *Conundrum*, Morris does describe a period in her journey from masculine to feminine (from a few years before surgery to immediately afterward) during which her gender was perceived, by herself and others, as ambiguous. She is quite unambiguous, though, about the moment of transition from *male* to *female.*
20. Gender reassignment is the correct disciplinary term. In current medical discourse, sex is taken as a natural physical fact and cannot be changed.
21. Morris [115]. I was reminded of this account on the eve of my own surgery. Gee, I thought on that occasion, it would be interesting to magically become another person in that binary and final way. So I tried it myself—going to the mirror and saying goodbye to the person I saw there—and unfortunately it didn't work. A few days later, when I could next get to the mirror, the person looking back at me was still me. I still don't understand what I did wrong.
22. Canary Conn, *Canary: The Story of a Transsexual* (New York: Bantam, 1977), 271. Conn had her surgery at the clinic of Jesus Maria Barbosa in Tijuana. In this excerpt she is speaking to a Mexican nurse; hence the Spanish terms.
23. Star, op.cit.
24. I admit to being every bit as astounded as the good Doctor, since except for Hoyer's account there are no other records of change in vocal pitch or timbre following administration of hormones or gender reassignment surgery. If transsexuals do succeed in altering their vocal characteristics, they do it gradually and with great difficulty. But there are more than sufficient problems with Lili Elbe's "true story," not the least of which is the scene in which Elbe finally "becomes a woman" by virtue of her physician's *implanting into her abdominal cavity a set of human ovaries.* The attention given by the media in the past decade to heart transplants and diseases of the immune system have made the lay public more aware of the workings of the human immune response, but even in 1936 Hoyer's account would have been recognized

by the medical community as questionable. Tissue rejection and the dream of mitigating it were the subjects of speculation in fiction and science fiction as late as the 1940s; e.g., the miracle drug "collodiansy" in H. Beam Piper's *One Leg Too Many* (1949).

25. Hoyer [165].
26. Hoyer [170]. For an extended discussion of texts that transmute submission into personal fulfillment cf. Sandy Stone, forthcoming, "Sweet Surrender: Gender, Spirtuality, and the Ecstasy of Subjection; Pseudo-transsexual Fiction in the 1970s."
27. Hoyer [53].
28. Ibid.
29. Hoyer [134].
30. Hoyer [139]. Lili Elbe's sex change took place in 1930. In the United States today, the juridical view of successful male-to-female sex change is still based upon lack; e.g., a man is a woman when "the male generative organs have been totally and irrevocably destroyed." (From a clinic letter authorizing a name change on a passport, 1980).
31. Hoyer [125].
32. Hoyer [139]. I call attention in both preceding passages to the Koine Greek verb ἐενδένειν, referring to the moment of baptism, when the one being baptized enters into and is entered by the Word; *endeuein* may be translated as "to enter into" but also "to put on, to insinuate oneself into, like a glove"; viz. "He [*sic*] who is baptized into Christ shall have put on Christ." In this intense homoerotic vein in which both genders are present but collapsed in the sacrifi[c]ed body cf. such examples as Fray Bernardino de Sahagun's description of rituals during which the officiating priest puts on the flayed skin of a young woman (in Frazer [589–91]).
33. The evolution and management of this problem deserves a paper in itself. It is discussed in capsule form in Donald R. Laub and Patrick Gandy, eds., *Proceedings of the Second Interdisciplinary Symposium on Gender Dysphoria Syndrome* (Stanford: Division of Reconstructive and Rehabilitation Surgery, Stanford Medical Center, 1973) and in Janice M. Irvine, *Disorders Of Desire: Sex and Gender in Modern American Sexology*, (Philadelphia: Temple University Press, 1990).
34. In Laub and Gandy [7]. Fisk's full remarks provide an excellent description of the aims and procedures of the Stanford group during the early years, and the tensions of conflicting agendas and various attempts at resolution are implicit in his account. For additional accounts cf. both Irvine and Shapiro, op.cit.
35. Harry Benjamin, *The Transsexual Phenomenon* (New York: Julian Press, 1966). The paper which was the foundation for the book was published as "Transsexualism and Transvestism as Psycho-somatic and Somato-Psychic Syndromes" in the *American Journal of Psychotherapy* [8:219–30 (1954)]. A much earlier paper by D.O. Cauldwell, "Psychopathia transexualis", in *Sexology* 16:274–80 (1949), does not appear to have had the same effect within the field, although John Money still pays homage to it by retaining Cauldwell's single-s spelling of the term. In early documents by other workers one may sometimes trace the influence of Cauldwell or Benjamin by how the word is spelled.
36. Laub and Gandy [8, 9 *passim*].
37. The problem here is with the ontology of the term "genital," in particular with regard to its definition for such activities as pre- and postoperative masturbation. Engenderment ontologizes the erotic economy of body surface; as Judith Butler and others (e.g., Foucault) point out, engenderment polices which parts of the body have their erotic components switched off or on. Conflicts arise when the *same* parts become multivalent; e.g., when portions of the (physical male) urethra are used to construct portions of the (gendered female in the physical male) neoclitoris. I suggest that we use this vertiginous idea as an example of ways in which we can refigure multivalence as intervention into the constitution of binary gendered subject positions; in a binary erotic economy, "Who" experiences erotic sensation associated with these areas? (In chapter ten in this volume Judith Shapiro raises a similar point in her essay "Transsexualism: Reflections on the Persistence of Gender and the Mutability of Sex." I have chosen a site geographically quite close to the one she describes, but hopefully more ambiguous, and therefore more dissonant in these discourses in which dissonance can be a powerful and productive intervention.)
38. This act in the borderlands of subject position suggests a category missing from Marjorie Garber's excellent paper "Spare Parts: The Surgical Construction of Gender," in *differences* 1:137–59 (1990); it is an intervention into the dissymmetry between "making a man" and "making a woman" that Garber describes. To a certain extent it figures a collapse of those categories within the transsexual imaginary, although it seems reasonable to conclude that this version of the coming-of-age story is still largely male—the male doctors and patients telling each other the stories of what Nature means for both Man and Woman. Generally female (female-to-male) patients tell the same stories from the other side.
39. The terms "wringing the turkey's neck" (male masturbation), "crash landing" (rejection by a clinical program), and "gaff" (an undergarment used to conceal male genitalia in preoperative m/f transsexuals), vary slightly in different geographical areas but are common enough to be recognized across sites.
40. Based upon Norman Fisk's remarks in Laub and Gandy [7], as well as my own notes. Part of the difficulty, as I discuss in this paper, is that the investigators (not to mention the transsexuals) have failed to problematize the phrase "wrong body" as an adequate descriptive category.
41. In Walters and Ross, op.cit.
42. I use the word "clinical" here and elsewhere while remaining mindful of the "Pyrrhic victory" of which Marie Mehl spoke. Now that transsexualism has the uneasy legitimacy of a diagnostic category in the DSM, how do we begin the process of getting it *out* of the book?
43. The actual meaning of "GG," a m/f transsexual slang term, is "genuine girl," (*sic*) also called "genny."
44. Judith Butler, *Gender Trouble* (New York: Routledge, 1990).

45.   The opposite of passing, being *read,* provocatively invokes the inscription practices to which I have referred.

46.   I am suggesting a starting point, but it is necessary to go much further. We will have to question not only how *body* is defined in these discourses, but to more critically examine who gets to say *what "body" means.*

47.   In case the reader is unsure, let me supply the clinically correct answer: "No."

48.   For an elaboration of this concept cf. Donna Haraway, "The Promises Of Monsters: A Regenerative Politics for Inappropriate/d Others," in Paula Treichler, Cary Nelson, and Larry Grossberg, eds. *Cultural Studies* (New York: Routledge, 1991).

49.   Jacques Derrida, "La Loi Du Genre/The Law Of Genre," trans. Avital Ronell in *Glyph* 7(1980):176 (French); 202 (English).

50.   I also call attention to Gloria Anzaldúa's theory of the mestiza, an illegible subject living in the borderlands between cultures, capable of partial speech in each but always only partially intelligible to each. Working against the grain of this position, Anzaldúa's "new mestiza" attempts to overcome illegibility partly by seizing control of speech and inscription and writing herself into cultural discourse. The stunning "Borderlands" is a case in point; cf. Gloria Anzaldúa, *Borderlands/La Frontera: The New Mestiza* (San Francisco: Spinsters/Aunt Lute, 1987).

18

Gender Terror, Gender Rage

Kate Bornstein

With *Gender Outlaw: On Men, Women, and the Rest of Us*, performance artist and author Kate Bornstein proposed that culture, rather than creating roles for naturally gendered people, was creating gender out of the roles people played. In chapter 8, excerpted here, she discusses the shift in her thinking about "gender terrorism," a phrase she coined. Initially meant to refer to people like herself who radically challenge the fundamental structures of gender and free up opportunities for gender to change, she came to apply it instead to people she labelled "gender defenders," or supporters of the status quo, who acted out their feelings of fear and loathing by directing violence and hostility towards transgender people.

Bornstein is also critical of hostilities within the transgender community, especially of harsh feelings directed against one activist by another. While she supports transgender activism in theory, she cautions against mixing activism with anger in practice. Expressions of rage, she feels, whether confined within a transgender community or directed at outside opponents, tend to invalidate whatever is being said.

Bornstein, who often uses nongender specific personal pronouns, raises the question of whether there can be any position "beyond gender." S/he says s/he's tried being a man and a woman, but that neither one work for her. Rather than falling between the cracks and becoming invisible, Bornstein instead calls attention to herself in a way s/he hopes will ultimately make the partitioning of gender meaningless. S/he refuses to be categorized and placed on either side of the gender divide. In art and life, Bornstein aims for real-world gender fluidity on a day-to-day basis.

> *If transsexuality marks a response to the dream of changing sex, it is also clearly the object of dreaming, and even phantasizing, in non-transsexuals. In the final analysis, sexual difference, which owes much to symbolic dualisms, belongs to the register of the* **real**. *It constitutes an insuperable barrier, an irreducible wall against which one can bang one's head indefinitely.*
>
> —Catherine Millot, *Horsexe: Essays on Transexuality*, 1990

For a while, I thought that it would be fun to call what I do in life *gender terrorism*. Seemed right at first—I and so many folks like me were terrorizing the structure of gender itself. But I've come to see it a bit differently now—gender terrorists are not the drag queens, the butch dykes, the men on roller skates dressed as nuns. Gender terrorists are not the female to male transsexual who's learning to look people in the eye while he walks down the street. Gender terrorists are not the leather daddies or back-seat Betties. Gender terrorists are not the married men, shivering in the dark as they slip on their wives' panties. Gender terrorists are those who, like Ms. Millot, bang their heads against a gender system which is *real* and *natural*; and who then use gender to terrorize the rest of us. These are the real terrorists: the Gender Defenders.

[A]nything that undermines confidence in the scheme of classification on which people base their lives sickens them as though the very ground on which they stood precipitously dropped away. The vertigo produced by the loss of cognitive orientation is similar to that produced by the loss of physical orientation. Philosophic nausea, certain forms of schizophrenia, moral revulsion, negative experience, the horror of having violated a taboo, and the feeling of having been polluted are all manifestations of this mental **mal de mer**, *occasioned by the sudden shipwreck of cognitive orientation which casts one adrift in a world without structure.*

People will regard any phenomenon that produces this disorientation as "disgusting" or "dirty." To be so regarded, however, the phenomenon must threaten to destroy not only one of their fundamental cognitive categories but their whole cognitive system.

— *Murray S. Davis, Smut: Erotic Reality/Obscene Ideology, 1983*

That's what gender outlaws do: our mere presence is often enough to make people sick. Take that great scene in the film, *The Crying Game*. You know the scene: the one that got all the attention—the one you weren't supposed to talk about? The one with the (gasp) full penile nudity—on the body of what appeared to be a woman! To me, the telling aspect of the scene is not so much the revelation of the person as transgendered, as much as it was the nausea and vomiting by the guy who did the discovering. That's a fairly strong reaction in any language, any culture. Many transgendered people will tell you that's an all-too accurate reaction; one usually followed, as in *The Crying Game*, by a physical attack on the transgendered person. With all the talk centering on the movie at the time of its release, no one focused on the issue of revulsion. I think no one brought it up, because it would draw focus to the other side of revulsion: desire.

The revelation of Dil's gender ambiguity called into question both the sexual orientation (desire) and the gender identity of Fergus.

Fergus' inner dialogue may have gone like this: "I'm really turned on by this woman, and that's how it should be—I'm male and I'm heterosexual." Then, as Dil disrobes, that inner voice might protest, "Wait! She's got a penis! She's a man!" And then the real awful truth may reveal itself like this: "Wait, I'm still attracted to this person, this man! But only women and faggots go for men—does that mean I'm a woman? Does it mean I'm homosexual?" Poor baby!

His vomiting can be seen not so much as a sign of revulsion as an admission of attraction, and the consequential upheaval of his gender identity and sexual orientation. The questioning of these heretofore unquestioned states of very personal identity would certainly result in nausea—the poor man's cognitive system had really been shaken up! I don't think *The Crying Game* is saying it's good to throw up when you find out someone is transgendered; I think the movie is brilliantly showing us that it's a common response.

And how about the public silence surrounding *The Crying Game*? When it was released in 1993, no one wanted to give away the "big secret." The last time there was such a furor about "don't give away the surprise ending," it was Hitchcock's *Psycho*, about another secretly transgendered person. The public response of "don't say a word" is more than "don't spoil the movie." What's to spoil, anyway? I knew about "the secret" before I went, and I thoroughly enjoyed the film. No, I think the "keep the secret" response on the part of the public was more a reflection of how the gender defenders of this culture would like to see transgendered people: as a secret, hidden away in some closet.

The Gender Defender is someone who actively, or by knowing inaction, defends the status quo of the existing gender system, and thus perpetuates the violence of male privilege and all its social extensions. The gender defender, or gender terrorist, is someone for whom gender forms a cornerstone of their view of the world. Shake gender up for one of these folks, and you're in for trouble.

WHAT ARE THEY AFRAID OF ?

Because gender ambiguity and gender outlaws are made invisible in this culture, and because gender transgressors are by and large silent (and thus invisible), for reasons stated earlier, the defenders of gender rigidity lash out at the nearest familiar label: homosexuality and lesbianism, the points at which gender outsiders intersect with sexual outsiders.

Not surprisingly, there are no words for the terror and hatred of gender transgressors, and because no one has named it yet, it seems that there is no hatred. When they do name it, they'll probably call it "genderism" or something equally boring.

> So much violence is perpetrated in the name of that fear and that loathing. I've been trying to come up with a name for this phobia for a few years now, and the word has eluded me. **Transphobia** is one term in vogue with some transsexuals. Fear of crossing? Fear of transgressing? If this term were allowed that sort of breadth—that is including the fear and hatred of **any** kind of border-dwellers—then it might have some possibilities.

The acts of a gender defender are acts of violence against gender outsiders.

» **Gay Bashing is one act of gender defenders.**
>   » Have you seen a single gay man or lesbian walking down the street recently?
>   » How did you know or why did you suspect that they were gay or lesbian?
>   » Was it something they were doing sexually? Or something about their gender presentation?
>   » Why do gay bashers pick out certain gays and lesbians to bash?

» **The attack on transsexuals by some cultural feminists is another defense of gender.**

> *All transsexuals rape women's bodies by reducing the real female form to an artifact, appropriating this body for themselves. However, the transsexually constructed lesbian-feminist violates women's sexuality and spirit, as well. Rape, although it is usually done by force, can also be accomplished by deception. It is significant that in the case of the transsexually constructed lesbian-feminist, often he is able to gain entrance and a dominant position in women's spaces because the women involved do not know he is a transsexual and he just does not happen to mention it.*
>
> —Janice G. Raymond, *The Transexual Empire*, 1979

Both Raymond and Millot generalize beyond what would be acceptable practice in any academic work; that's a mark of their fanaticism. But there's some historical, cross-cultural precedent for their concern that transsexuals are bad for feminism: the Navajo *nadle*. The *nadle* is a sort of transgendered male-to-female person, with a unique social function: the *nadle* was often called upon to suppress the women's revolutions. Neither Raymond nor Millot seem familiar with these wolves in chic clothing, but both implicitly fear the concept.

> *The **nadle**'s role and value in mythology are male-oriented. Barren themselves, the **nadle** are useful as mediators, and, perhaps related to this, they serve as ferrymen. When there was a quarrel between the men and the women and the latter secluded themselves on one side of the river, the **nadle**, by deciding to bring the women back across, enabled the men to overcome the women. In doing this, they acted as [gender] strike-breakers or scabs, reversing the course of the age-old theme of the strike of one [gender] against the other.*
>
> —Wendy O'Flaherty, *Women, Androgynes, and other Mythical Beasts*, 1980

I've seen some examples of what Raymond fears: male-to-female transsexuals entering "women-only" spaces, and attempting to assume a position of control and power. If Raymond herself has personally experienced that, I can empathize with her anger. My contention, however, is that it is not the transsexual person or even the issue of transsexuality that is bad for feminism: I think that what's bad for the future of feminism is male privilege, and I think that occasionally a male-to-female transsexual will carry more than a small degree of that over into their newly-gendered life. A better solution to this situation would be to point out what's going on, and to talk it through. I don't think male privilege has a place *anywhere*, and I think it would best be processed out of *any* environment.

Raymond and her supporters bring up the subject of deception. Personally, I agree that hiding, and not proclaiming one's transsexual status, is an unworthy stance, more heinous if one's invisible status is maintained with the purpose of gaining power. Transsexuals are moving, however, in the direction of openly embracing their borderline status—either willingly, or by the probing eye of public interest—and the debate on being or not-being out as a transsexual is, at this writing, heating up.

» Segments of the Men's Movement defend gender.

I'm talking about men who drum and chant in the woods to ward off the possibility of being called women. What's amusing is that lesbians had been drumming and chanting in the woods for well over a decade before Robert Bly and company got the bright idea to appropriate the practice and proclaim it "male."

» The author of the "Helms Amendment" is definitely a gender defender!

"None of the funds authorized to be appropriated for the National Endowment for the Arts…may be used to promote, disseminate, or produce materials which in the judgment of the National Endowment for the Arts…may be considered obscene, including but not limited to, depictions of sadomasochism, homoeroticism, the sexual exploitation of children, or individuals engaged in sex acts and which, when taken as a whole, do not have serious literary, artistic, political or scientific value."

—Senator Jesse Helms, Republican, North Carolina

I'm not included in Senator Helms' amendment. I'm not included in most legislation these days. But me and my people, we're the ones they'd *want* to legislate against, if they could even begin to conceive of us, because *we're* the ones who threaten their manhood. People have underrated Gore Vidal's *Myra Breckinridge*, and the sequel *Myron*. In fact, the movie version of *Myra Breckenridge* has been called one of the worst movies of all time. I think it has a lot to do with the point Vidal makes: that the existence of transgendered people—people who exist sexually for pleasure, and not procreation—strikes terror at the heart of our puritanical Eurocentric culture. Vidal positions Myra as the voice and agent of doom for the traditional American male. I think he was on the mark, and I'd be proud to call Myra my sister.

I'm afraid that by spelling this all out the way I'm doing in this book, and the way other transgendered people are doing—I'm afraid we'll tip our hands. Could be fun, though, and it's much better than suffocating in the grip of the social disease called gender!

THE PROTECTION RACKET

We can feel secure in the protection provided by a group, but that protection has its price. Compliance with the group often extends further than acceptance of the group's views to include participation in the attack on deviants by subtle (or not so subtle) disapproval, punishment, or rejection of any member who voices criticism of the consensus.... [The] dissident is criticized as disloyal, lacking commitment, interfering with the important work of the group.

—Arthur J. Deikman, *The Wrong Way Home: Uncovering Patterns of Cult Behavior in American Society, 1990*

There's no current protection for the transgendered, no group dynamic strong enough to ward off possible attacks on individuals. I'm not looking forward to the policeman's baton, the media's poison, or the assassin's bullet—sadly, these are almost inevitable in this world of wave after wave of minorities rising up to confront the dominant ideology.

This culture attacks people on the basis of being or not being correctly gendered (having a politically correct body). It's when we get to a point of knowing we're not gendered in the same way as our friends, relatives, and co-workers—it's then that we get angry and start to do something about gender.

» What's your gender?
» When did you decide that?
» How much say do you have in your gender?
» Is there anything about your gender or gender role that you don't like, or that gets in your way?
» Are there one or two qualities about another gender that are appealing to you, enough so that you'd like to incorporate those qualities into your daily life?
» What would happen to your life if you did that?
» What would your gender be then?
» How do you think people would respond to you?
» How would you feel if they did that?

GENDER ACTIVISM BEGINS WITH GENDER RAGE

*"You're just jealous because **I'm** a real freak, and **you** have to wear a mask!"—The Penguin*
"You just may be right." —Batman

—Tim Burton, *Batman Returns*, 1993

Sometimes, it's not the fist in your belly that gets to you.
Sometimes, it's when they're quiet, even polite.
Sometimes, it's how they look at you day after day that finally gets to you.
They squint at you, like they can't see.
It's as if by squinting they might get a better make on you.
If they're in a crowd, they shift their eyes so their friends can't tell they're looking at you.
    Real subtle.
You can read the fear behind the smirk,
The hatred just past the disgust.
You worry it's your paranoia.
and you always hope it's only your paranoia.
(Confidence, they've told you, helps you pass.)
But there's always one of them who looks at you with longing.
And that scares you the most,
Because if you let that longing into your heart, you have to accept yourself just the way you are.

It's not only people who intentionally transgress gender who get into trouble. Eventually the gender system lets everyone down. It seems to be rigged that way. Sometimes, even with all the time and effort we put into obeying the rules, we get hurt. We can get badly hurt by being a real man or a real woman.

So what happens to the person who finds out that he or she has been duped or disappointed by some aspect of gender? How does someone come to terms with some inner ambiguity of gender, and the demands of a rigid, nearly monolithic, universal gender system? This person could get closer to the gender outlaws who have previously been regarded as outsiders. This person would sense some common ground with the more obvious renegades of the gender system, usually some commonality in the area of gender role oppression. Bridging the gap between him or herself and the outlaws, the now former-gender-defenders can't devalue the outsider without devaluing him or herself. Instead of someone defending gender, we've now got someone who begins intentionally to bend gender.

> What are you being denied on account of your gender?
> What does a person of another gender have that you can't have?

And this brings up a great deal of anger. Because, we've suddenly positioned ourselves in the area previously marked "freaks only." We've chosen to stand with the oppressed. But standing with freaks never hurt anyone—it's when we agree that we *deserve* the oppression and the ridicule that accompanies the freak's position in the culture—that's when the wound is mortal.

> The first national television talk show I did was **Geraldo**. The subject was **Transsexual Regrets: Who's Sorry Now**. It was supposed to be about all these transsexuals who'd gotten fairly far along in their transformation, but were now changing their minds. I was there with psychologist Jayne Thomas to provide a little balance: we were the happy transsexuals. Somewhere around the time when an audience member asked me if I could "orgasm with that vagina," I realized that yep, I was a freak all right, but I was only a freak to the degree that I remained silent. When I spoke, I had a chance to educate, and, paradoxically, I became less of a freak.

We don't deserve the ridicule, the stares, the fist in our bellies. We are entitled to our anger in response to this oppression: our anger is a message to ourselves that we need to get active and change something in order to survive. So we resist the oppression, the violence—we resist the tendency of the culture to see us as a joke.

So now we're standing on the side of the freaks. Now what? If we can't call the freaks names anymore because we realize we're one of them, then we have to look back at our position as a former insider, and we begin to devalue *that*. We've now officially become activists. But outside or inside, it's still a side; and taking a side usually means taking the identity of a side, and there you have identity politics as one more rendering of a game called us-versus-them. In "transgender politics," as in any other identity politics, we look around for a "them." From the standpoint of the transgendered person, there's no shortage of "them," no shortage at all.

> A theatre critic in **The San Francisco Chronicle** once chided me for bringing a show about transsexualism to a lesbian and gay theater. "Preaching to the converted," he called it. Who or what did he think was in the audience? I tell you, I **wish** there had been an audience of transsexuals out there each night! I'd have felt a lot less lonely and vulnerable than I did. People make assumptions.

LOOSE CANONS OF ACTIVISM

One trouble in having only a few of "us," and a lot of "them," is that it's easy to hit out at the wrong "them." At this writing, some transgender activists are targeting lesbian separatists because these women have established something called "women-only spaces"; and a small number of these women will not brook the admission of transgendered women, whom the separatists don't see as women. In response to demands for inclusion by the transgendered, the women on the inside get angry and a war of epithets begins. It's a war about who's a man and who's a woman.

From what I can see, women inhabit "women only" spaces to heal from the oppression of their number by the larger culture, by men in particular, and because they don't see us as women, we're perceived as the other side of the binary: men. Perceived as men, we get in the way of their healing, and so we're excluded.

> The current phraseology is "women born women." We're told that only "women born women" are allowed into some space. Well, that's a problem. Aside from the obvious absurdity of a newborn infant being called a woman, the phrase "woman born woman" just throws us back into the what's-a-woman question.

Some transsexuals take exclusion by lesbian separatists as oppression, but I don't think so. Lesbian oppression at the hands of the dominant ideology is not the same as the exclusion experienced by the transgendered at the hands of the lesbian separatists—lesbians just don't have the same economic and social resources with which to oppress the transgendered. I think both sides need to sit down and talk with one another, and I think both sides need to do some serious listening.

> I once stated this opinion in a San Francisco newspaper article. A small number of transgender activists called me a Nazi and a reactionary, and claimed I'd set "the cause" back years through that article. Their accusation was that I was giving fuel to "the enemy." I got harassing phone calls, and they threatened to demonstrate against my next theater piece. Like I said, I don't speak for all transgendered people.

> *A free society is one where it is safe to be unpopular.*
>
> —Adlai Stevenson

I think that anger and activism mix about as well as drinking and driving. When I'm angry, I don't have the judgment to select a correct target to hit out against. I do believe that anger is healthy, that it can lead to a recognition of the *need* for action, but activism itself is best accomplished by level heads who can help steer others' anger toward correct targets. A correct target is the group that has both the will and the power to oppress you wherever you go. The correct target for any successful transsexual rebellion would be the gender system itself. But transsexuals won't attack that system until they themselves are free of the need to participate in it.

> Movements tend to coalesce around a particular moment of rebellion. The transgender moment of rebellion has not yet come, and transgendered people are growing more and more restless. But the transgender Stonewall or Selma, Alabama is not going to come about by attacking the gay and lesbian community, or even lesbian separatists, outlaws like ourselves. In Selma, and at the Stonewall, members of the minority group stood up to the real forces of oppression: the police state.

It does hurt, being excluded or even attacked by other oppressed groups, and it makes me feel a shame I thought I'd gotten over a long time ago. It's not what people say when they exclude me and my people, or how they say it, but rather it's a very long ache that I don't believe will stop until there's a whole lot more room in the world for difference. Sometimes it's a seemingly insignificant act of exclusion that will tip the scale and turn someone from insider to outsider, like the one that really got to me.

> When I first went through my gender change, I was working for an IBM subsidiary in Philadelphia. The biggest quandary there was "which bathroom is it going to use?" To their credit, most of the people in my office didn't really care; it was the building manager who was tearing his hair out over this one. I suppose he felt I would terrorize the women in their bathroom, and lie in waiting for the men in **their** bathroom. Finally, a solution was reached: even though I worked on the 11th floor of a large office building, I would use a bathroom on the seventh floor. The seventh floor had been under construction, but for lack of funds they simply stopped construction; no one worked on that floor. Piles of plaster and wiring littered the floor, and pools of water lay everywhere. But there was a working bathroom in the very back of that floor, and that's where they sent me. No one ever cleaned it, no one kept it stocked. It was poorly lit and it was scary. Isn't it amazing the lengths we'll go to in order to maintain the illusion that there are only two genders, and that these genders must remain separate? Most gender outlaws have some similar bathroom horror story. It's all part of what Marjorie Garber calls "urinary segregation."

Something happens, some final bit that lights up the injustice of the gender system, and in that flash, we see that the emperor is wearing no clothes. That this either/or gender system we've got is truly oppressing us. That happens, and we snap; we begin to fight.

> » Have you ever been teased or baited by reason of acting outside your assigned gender role?
> » Where do you think the sanctions for that teasing or baiting come from?

There are a lot of ways to fight, and transgendered people these days are coming together in the common fight for the right to express our genders freely. Where once we met only in drag bars or social teas, we're now meeting at protest marches and in consciousness-raising groups.

> » Would you like to meet other people who feel the same way you do about gender?
> » Would you like to hear you're not the only one?
> » Would you like to know you've got a history in this world?
> » Do you think that might make you smile?

We meet to discuss ways and means of securing our freedom. In this struggle for our freedom of expression there comes a point where the gender system reveals itself to be not only oppressive, but silly. When we see how ridiculous it is, we can truly begin to dismantle it.

19

My Words to Victor Frankenstein above the Village of Chamounix
Performing Transgender Rage

Susan Stryker

Susan Stryker's evocative retelling of the story of Frankenstein's monster specifically responded to Sandy Stone's call for "post-transsexual" theorizing rooted in the embodied experience of transgender people, and was the first published academic work to link this project explicitly to queer critical theory. Like other early voices in the field, Stryker helped situate transgender studies in larger intellectual currents. She draws—explicitly or implicitly—on Kristeva's notion of the abject and Althusser's notion of interpolation, as well as on Butler's notion of gender performativity.

Stryker's title derives from the scene in Mary Shelley's *Frankenstein* in which the monster first speaks back to its maker, revealing itself as something other, and something more, than its creator intended. She turns this literary meeting into a metaphor for the critical encounter between a radicalized transgender subjectivity and the normativizing intent of medical science. In doing so, she claims her own transsexual body as a monstrously powerful place, situated outside the natural order, from which to speak and write and act.

In her essay, Stryker both claims and rechannels the rage that many transgender people feel over being made outcasts; she transforms a particular experience of suffering into a basis for self-affirmation, intellectual inquiry, moral agency, and political action. Her text helped clear the way for other transgender theorists to dare to speak in their own voices, as experts on their own situations, and to accept their affective experience—including their rage and anger—as part of that expertise.

INTRODUCTORY NOTES

The following work is a textual adaptation of a performance piece originally presented at "Rage Across the Disciplines," an arts, humanities, and social sciences conference held June 10–12, 1993, at California State University, San Marcos. The interdisciplinary nature of the conference, its theme, and the organizers' call for both performances and academic papers inspired me to be creative in my mode of presenting a topic then much on my mind. As a member of Transgender Nation—a militantly queer, direct action transsexual advocacy group—I was at the time involved in organizing a disruption and protest at the American Psychiatric Association's 1993 annual meeting in San Francisco. A good deal of the discussion at our planning meetings concerned how to harness the intense emotions emanating from transsexual experience—especially rage—and mobilize them into effective political actions. I was intrigued by the prospect of critically examining this rage in a more academic setting through an idiosyncratic application of the concept of gender performativity. My idea was to perform self-consciously a queer gender rather than simply talk about it, thus embodying and enacting the concept simultaneously under discussion. I wanted the formal structure of the work to express a transgender aesthetic by replicating our abrupt, often jarring transitions between genders—challenging generic classification with the forms of my words just as my transsexuality challenges the conventions of legitimate gender and my performance in the conference room challenged the boundaries of acceptable academic discourse. During the performance, I stood at the podium wearing genderfuck drag—combat boots, threadbare Levi 501s over a black lace body suit, a shredded Transgender Nation T-shirt with the neck and sleeves cut out, a pink triangle, quartz crystal pendant, grunge metal jewelry, and a six-inch long marlin hook dangling around my neck on a length of heavy stainless steel chain. I decorated the set by draping my black leather biker jacket over my chair at the panelists' table. The jacket had handcuffs on the left shoulder, rainbow freedom rings on the right side lacings, and Queer Nation-style stickers reading SEX CHANGE, DYKE, and FUCK YOUR TRANSPHOBIA plastered on the back.

MONOLOGUE

The transsexual body is an unnatural body. It is the product of medical science. It is a technological construction. It is flesh torn apart and sewn together again in a shape other than that in which it was born. In these circumstances, I find a deep affinity between myself as a transsexual woman and the monster in Mary Shelley's Frankenstein. Like the monster, I am too often perceived as less than fully human due to the means of my embodiment; like the monster's as well, my exclusion from human community fuels a deep and abiding rage in me that I, like the monster, direct against the conditions in which I must struggle to exist.

I am not the first to link Frankenstein's monster and the transsexual body. Mary Daly makes the connection explicit by discussing transsexuality in "Boundary Violation and the Frankenstein Phenomenon," in which she characterizes transsexuals as the agents of a "necrophilic invasion" of female space (69–72). Janice Raymond, who acknowledges Daly as a formative influence, is less direct when she says that "the problem of transsexuality would best be served by morally mandating it out of existence," but in this statement she nevertheless echoes Victor Frankenstein's feelings toward the monster: "Begone, vile insect, or rather, stay, that I may trample you to dust. You reproach me with your creation" (Raymond 178; Shelley 95). It is a commonplace of literary criticism to note that Frankenstein's monster is his own dark, romantic double, the alien Other he constructs and upon which he projects all he cannot accept in himself; indeed, Frankenstein calls the monster "my own vampire, my own spirit set loose from the grave" (Shelley 74). Might I suggest that Daly, Raymond and others of their ilk similarly construct the transsexual as their own particular golem? (1)

The attribution of monstrosity remains a palpable characteristic of most lesbian and gay representations of transsexuality, displaying in unnerving detail the anxious, fearful underside of the current cultural fascination with transgenderism. (2) Because transsexuality more than any other transgender practice or identity represents the prospect of destabilizing the foundational presupposition of fixed genders upon which a politics of personal identity depends, people who have invested their aspirations for social justice in identitarian movements say things about us out of sheer panic that, if said of other minorities, would see print only in the most hate-riddled, white supremacist, Christian fascist rags. To quote extensively from one letter to the editor of a popular San Francisco gay/lesbian periodical:

> I consider transsexualism to be a fraud, and the participants in it…perverted. The transsexual [claims]
> he/she needs to change his/her body in order to be his/her "true self." Because this "true self" requires
> another physical form in which to manifest itself, it must therefore war with nature. One cannot change

one's gender. What occurs is a cleverly manipulated exterior: what has been done is mutation. What exists beneath the deformed surface is the same person who was there prior to the deformity. People who break or deform their bodies [act] out the sick farce of a deluded, patriarchal approach to nature, alienated from true being.

Referring by name to one particular person, self-identified as a transsexual lesbian, whom she had heard speak in a public forum at the San Francisco Women's Building, the letter-writer went on to say:

> When an estrogenated man with breasts loves a woman, that is not lesbianism, that is mutilated perversion. [This individual] is not a threat to the lesbian community, he is an outrage to us. He is not a lesbian, he is a mutant man, a self-made freak, a deformity, an insult. He deserves a slap in the face. After that, he deserves to have his body and mind made well again. (3)

When such beings as these tell me I war with nature, I find no more reason to mourn my opposition to them—or to the order they claim to represent—than Frankenstein's monster felt in its enmity to the human race. I do not fall from the grace of their company—I roar gleefully away from it like a Harley-straddling, dildo-packing leatherdyke from hell.

The stigmatization fostered by this sort of pejorative labelling is not without consequence. Such words have the power to destroy transsexual lives. On January 5, 1993, a 22-year-old pre-operative transsexual woman from Seattle, Filisa Vistima, wrote in her journal, "I wish I was anatomically 'normal' so I could go swimming.... But no, I'm a mutant, Frankenstein's monster." Two months later Filisa Vistima committed suicide. What drove her to such despair was the exclusion she experienced in Seattle's queer community, some members of which opposed Filisa's participation because of her transsexuality—even though she identified as and lived as a bisexual woman. The Lesbian Resource Center where she served as a volunteer conducted a survey of its constituency to determine whether it should stop offering services to male-to-female transsexuals. Filisa did the data entry for tabulating the survey results; she didn't have to imagine how people felt about her kind. The Seattle Bisexual Women's Network announced that if it admitted transsexuals the SBWN would no longer be a women's organization. "I'm sure," one member said in reference to the inclusion of bisexual transsexual women, "the boys can take care of themselves." Filisa Vistima was not a boy, and she found it impossible to take care of herself. Even in death she found no support from the community in which she claimed membership. "Why didn't Filisa commit herself for psychiatric care?" asked a columnist in the Seattle Gay News. "Why didn't Filisa demand her civil rights?" In this case, not only did the angry villagers hound their monster to the edge of town, they reproached her for being vulnerable to the torches. Did Filisa Vistima commit suicide, or did the queer community of Seattle kill her? (4)

I want to lay claim to the dark power of my monstrous identity without using it as a weapon against others or being wounded by it myself. I will say this as bluntly as I know how: I am a transsexual, and therefore I am a monster. Just as the words "dyke," "fag," "queer," "slut," and "whore" have been reclaimed, respectively, by lesbians and gay men, by anti-assimilationist sexual minorities, by women who pursue erotic pleasure, and by sex industry workers, words like "creature," "monster," and "unnatural" need to be reclaimed by the transgendered. By embracing and accepting them, even piling one on top of another, we may dispel their ability to harm us. A creature, after all, in the dominant tradition of Western European culture, is nothing other than a created being, a made thing. The affront you humans take at being called a "creature" results from the threat the term poses to your status as "lords of creation," beings elevated above mere material existence. As in the case of being called "it," being called a "creature" suggests the lack or loss of a superior personhood. I find no shame, however, in acknowledging my egalitarian relationship with non-human material Being; everything emerges from the same matrix of possibilities. "Monster" is derived from the Latin noun monstrum, "divine portent," itself formed on the root of the verb monere, "to warn." It came to refer to living things of anomalous shape or structure, or to fabulous creatures like the sphinx who were composed of strikingly incongruous parts, because the ancients considered the appearance of such beings to be a sign of some impending supernatural event. Monsters, like angels, functioned as messengers and heralds of the extraordinary. They served to announce impending revelation, saying, in effect, "Pay attention; something of profound importance is happening."

Hearken unto me, fellow creatures. I who have dwelt in a form unmatched with my desire, I whose flesh has become an assemblage of incongruous anatomical parts, I who achieve the similitude of a natural body only through an unnatural process, I offer you this warning: the Nature you bedevil me with is a lie. Do not trust it to protect you from what I represent, for it is a fabrication that cloaks the groundlessness of the privilege you seek to maintain for yourself at my expense. You are as constructed as me; the same anarchic Womb has birthed us both. I call upon you to investigate your nature as I have been compelled to confront mine. I challenge you to risk abjection and flourish as well as have I. Heed my words, and you may well discover the seams and sutures in yourself.

CRITICISM

In answer to the question he poses in the title of his recent essay, "What is a Monster? (According to Frankenstein)," Peter Brooks suggests that, whatever else a monster might be, it "may also be that which eludes gender definition" (219). Brooks reads Mary Shelley's story of an overreaching scientist and his troublesome creation as an early dissent from the nineteenth-century realist literary tradition, which had not yet attained dominance as a narrative form. He understands Frankenstein to unfold textually through a narrative strategy generated by tension between a visually oriented epistemology, on the one hand, and another approach to knowing the truth of bodies that privileges verbal linguisticality, on the other (199–200). Knowing by seeing and knowing by speaking/hearing are gendered, respectively, as masculine and feminine in the critical framework within which Brooks operates. Considered in this context, Shelley's text is informed by—and critiques from a woman's point of view—the contemporary reordering of knowledge brought about by the increasingly compelling truth claims of Enlightenment science. The monster problematizes gender partly through its failure as a viable subject in the visual field; though referred to as "he," it thus offers a feminine, and potentially feminist, resistance to definition by a phallicized scopophilia. The monster accomplishes this resistance by mastering language in order to claim a position as a speaking subject and enact verbally the very subjectivity denied it in the specular realm.

Transsexual monstrosity, however, along with its affect, transgender rage, can never claim quite so secure a means of resistance because of the inability of language to represent the transgendered subject's movement over time between stably gendered positions in a linguistic structure. Our situation effectively reverses the one encountered by Frankenstein's monster. Unlike the monster, we often successfully cite the culture's visual norms of gendered embodiment. This citation becomes a subversive resistance when, through a provisional use of language, we verbally declare the unnaturalness of our claim to the subject positions we nevertheless occupy. (6)

The prospect of a monster with a life and will of its own is a principal source of horror for Frankenstein. The scientist has taken up his project with a specific goal in mind—nothing less than the intent to subject nature completely to his power. He finds a means to accomplish his desires through modern science, whose devotees, it seems to him, "have acquired new and almost unlimited powers; they can command the thunders of heaven, mimic the earthquake, and even mock the invisible world with its shadows.... More, far more, will I achieve," thought Frankenstein. "I will pioneer a new way, explore unknown powers, and unfold to the world the deepest mysteries of creation" (Shelley 47). The fruit of his efforts is not, however, what Frankenstein anticipated. The rapture he expected to experience at the awakening of his creature turned immediately to dread. "I saw the dull yellow eyes of the creature open. His jaws opened, and he muttered some inarticulate sounds, while a grin wrinkled his cheeks. He might have spoken, but I did not hear; one hand was stretched out, seemingly to detain me, but I escaped" (Shelley 56, 57). The monster escapes, too, and parts company with its maker for a number of years. In the interim, it learns something of its situation in the world, and rather than bless its creator, the monster curses him. The very success of Mary Shelley's scientist in his self-appointed task thus paradoxically proves its futility: rather than demonstrate Frankenstein's power over materiality, the newly enlivened body of the creature attests to its maker's failure to attain the mastery he sought. Frankenstein cannot control the mind and feelings of the monster he makes. It exceeds and refutes his purposes.

My own experience as a transsexual parallels the monster's in this regard. The consciousness shaped by the transsexual body is no more the creation of the science that refigures its flesh than the monster's mind is the creation of Frankenstein. The agenda that produced hormonal and surgical sex reassignment techniques is no less pretentious, and no more noble, than Frankenstein's. Heroic doctors still endeavor to triumph over nature. The scientific discourse that produced sex reassignment techniques is inseparable from the pursuit of immortality through the perfection of the body, the fantasy of total mastery through the transcendence of an absolute limit, and the hubristic desire to create life itself. (7) Its genealogy emerges from a metaphysical quest older than modern science, and its cultural politics are aligned with a deeply conservative attempt to stabilize gendered identity in service of the naturalized heterosexual order.

None of this, however, precludes medically constructed transsexual bodies from being viable sites of subjectivity. Nor does it guarantee the compliance of subjects thus embodied with the agenda that resulted in a transsexual means of embodiment. As we rise up from the operating tables of our rebirth, we transsexuals are something more, and something other, than the creatures our makers intended us to be. Though medical techniques for sex reassignment are capable of crafting bodies that satisfy the visual and morphological criteria that generate naturalness as their effect, engaging with those very techniques produces a subjective experience that belies the naturalistic effect biomedical technology can achieve. Transsexual embodiment, like the embodiment of the monster, places its subject in an unassimilable, antagonistic, queer relationship to a Nature in which it must nevertheless exist.

Frankenstein's monster articulates its unnatural situation within the natural world with far more sophistication in Shelley's novel than might be expected by those familiar only with the version played by Boris Karloff in James Whale's classic films from the 1930s. Film critic Vito Russo suggests that Whale's interpretation of the monster was influenced by the fact that the director was a closeted gay man at the time he made his Frankenstein films. The pathos he imparted to his monster derived from the experience of his own hidden sexual identity. (8) Monstrous and unnatural in the eyes of the world, but seeking only the love of his own kind and the acceptance of human society, Whale's creature externalizes and renders visible the nightmarish loneliness and alienation that the closet can breed. But this is not the monster who speaks to me so potently of my own situation as an openly transsexual being. I emulate instead Mary Shelley's literary monster, who is quick-witted, agile, strong, and eloquent.

In the novel, the creature flees Frankenstein's laboratory and hides in the solitude of the Alps, where, by stealthy observation of the people it happens to meet, it gradually acquires a knowledge of language, literature, and the conventions of European society. At first it knows little of its own condition. "I had never yet seen a being resembling me, or who claimed any intercourse with me," the monster notes. "What did this mean? Who was I? What was I? Whence did I come? What was my destination? These questions continually recurred, but I was unable to solve them." (Shelley 116, 130). Then, in the pocket of the jacket it took as it fled the laboratory, the monster finds Victor Frankenstein's journal, and learns the particulars of its creation. "I sickened as I read," the monster says. "Increase of knowledge only discovered to me what a wretched outcast I was." (Shelley 124, 125).

Upon learning its history and experiencing the rejection of all to whom it reached out for companionship, the creature's life takes a dark turn. "My feelings were those of rage and revenge," the monster declares. "I, like the arch-fiend, bore a hell within me" (130). It would have been happy to destroy all of Nature, but it settles, finally, on a more expedient plan to murder systematically all those whom Victor Frankenstein loves. Once Frankenstein realizes that his own abandoned creation is responsible for the deaths of those most dear to him, he retreats in remorse to a mountain village above his native Geneva to ponder his complicity in the crimes the monster has committed. While hiking on the glaciers in the shadow of Mont Blanc, above the village of Chamounix, Frankenstein spies a familiar figure approaching him across the ice. Of course, it is the monster, who demands an audience with its maker. Frankenstein agrees, and the two retire together to a mountaineer's cabin. There, in a monologue that occupies nearly a quarter of the novel, the monster tells Frankenstein the tale of its creation from its own point of view, explaining to him how it became so enraged.

These are my words to Victor Frankenstein, above the village of Chamounix. Like the monster, I could speak of my earliest memories, and how I became aware of my difference from everyone around me. I can describe how I acquired a monstrous identity by taking on the label "transsexual" to name parts of myself that I could not otherwise explain. I, too, have discovered the journals of the men who made my body, and who have made the bodies of creatures like me since the 1930s. I know in intimate detail the history of this recent medical intervention into the enactment of transgendered subjectivity; science seeks to contain and colonize the radical threat posed by a particular transgender strategy of resistance to the coerciveness of gender: physical alteration of the genitals. (9) I live daily with the consequences of medicine's definition of my identity as an emotional disorder. Through the filter of this official pathologization, the sounds that come out of my mouth can be summarily dismissed as the confused ranting of a diseased mind.

Like the monster, the longer I live in these conditions, the more rage I harbor. Rage colors me as it presses in through the pores of my skin, soaking in until it becomes the blood that courses through my beating heart. It is a rage bred by the necessity of existing in external circumstances that work against my survival. But there is yet another rage within.

JOURNAL (FEBRUARY 18, 1993)

Kim sat between my spread legs, her back to me, her tailbone on the edge of the table. Her left hand gripped my thigh so hard the bruises are still there a week later. Sweating and bellowing, she pushed one last time and the baby finally came. Through my lover's back, against the skin of my own belly, I felt a child move out of another woman's body and into the world. Strangers' hands snatched it away to suction the sticky green meconium from its airways. "It's a girl," somebody said. Paul, I think. Why, just then, did a jumble of dark, unsolicited feelings emerge wordlessly from some quiet back corner of my mind? This moment of miracles was not the time to deal with them. I pushed them back, knowing they were too strong to avoid for long.

After three days we were all exhausted, slightly disappointed that complications had forced us to go to Kaiser instead of having the birth at home. I wonder what the hospital staff thought of our little tribe swarming all over the delivery room: Stephanie, the midwife; Paul, the baby's father; Kim's sister Gwen; my son Wilson and me; and the two other women who make up our family, Anne and Heather. And of course Kim and the baby. She named her Denali, after the mountain in Alaska. I don't think the medical folks had a clue as to how we all considered ourselves to be related to each other. When the labor first began we all took turns shifting between various supporting roles, but as the ordeal progressed we settled into a more stable pattern. I found myself acting as birth coach. Hour after hour, through dozens of sets of contractions, I focused everything on Kim, helping her stay in control of her emotions as she gave herself over to this inexorable process, holding on to her eyes with mine to keep the pain from throwing her out of her body, breathing every breath with her, being a companion. I participated, step by increasingly intimate step, in the ritual transformation of consciousness surrounding her daughter's birth. Birth rituals work to prepare the self for a profound opening, an opening as psychic as it is corporeal. Kim's body brought this ritual process to a dramatic resolution for her, culminating in a visceral, cathartic experience. But my body left me hanging. I had gone on a journey to the point at which my companion had to go on alone, and I needed to finish my trip for myself. To conclude the birth ritual I had participated in, I needed to move something in me as profound as a whole human life.

I floated home from the hospital, filled with a vital energy that wouldn't discharge. I puttered about until I was alone: my ex had come over for Wilson; Kim and Denali were still at the hospital with Paul; Stephanie had gone, and everyone else was out for a much-needed walk. Finally, in the solitude of my home, I burst apart like a wet paper bag and spilled the emotional contents of my life through the hands I cupped like a sieve over my face. For days, as I had accompanied my partner on her journey, I had been progressively opening myself and preparing to let go of whatever was deepest within. Now everything in me flowed out, moving up from inside and out through my throat, my mouth because these things could never pass between the lips of my cunt. I knew the darkness I had glimpsed earlier would reemerge, but I had vast oceans of feeling to experience before that came up again.

Simple joy in the presence of new life came bubbling out first, wave after wave of it. I was so incredibly happy. I was so in love with Kim, had so much admiration for her strength and courage. I felt pride and excitement about the queer family we were building with Wilson, Anne, Heather, Denali, and whatever babies would follow. We've all tasted an exhilarating possibility in communal living and these nurturing, bonded kinships for which we have no adequate names. We joke about pioneering on a reverse frontier: venturing into the heart of civilization itself to reclaim biological reproduction from heterosexism and free it for our own uses. We're fierce; in a world of "traditional family values," we need to be.

Sometimes, though, I still mourn the passing of old, more familiar ways. It wasn't too long ago that my ex and I were married, woman and man. That love had been genuine, and the grief over its loss real. I had always wanted intimacy with women more than intimacy with men, and that wanting had always felt queer to me. She needed it to appear straight. The shape of my flesh was a barrier that estranged me from my desire. Like a body without a mouth, I was starving in the midst of plenty. I would not let myself starve, even if what it took to open myself for a deep connectedness cut off the deepest connections I actually had. So I abandoned one life and built this new one. The fact that she and I have begun getting along again, after so much strife between us, makes the bitterness of our separation somewhat sweet. On the day of the birth, this past loss was present even in its partial recovery; held up beside the newfound fullness in my life, it evoked a poignant, hopeful sadness that inundated me.

Frustration and anger soon welled up in abundance. In spite of all I'd accomplished, my identity still felt so tenuous. Every circumstance of life seemed to conspire against me in one vast, composite act of invalidation and erasure. In the body I was born with, I had been invisible as the person I considered myself to be; I had been invisible as a queer while the form of my body made my desires look straight. Now, as a dyke I am invisible among women; as a transsexual, I am invisible among dykes. As the partner of a new mother, I am often invisible as a transsexual, a woman, and a lesbian. I've lost track of the friends and acquaintances these past nine months who've asked me if I was the father. It shows so dramatically how much they simply don't get what I'm doing with my body. The high price of whatever visible, intelligible, self-representation I have achieved makes the continuing experience of invisibility maddeningly difficult to bear.

The collective assumptions of the naturalized order soon overwhelmed me. Nature exerts such a hegemonic oppression. Suddenly I felt lost and scared, lonely and confused. How did that little Mormon boy from Oklahoma I used to be grow up to be a transsexual leatherdyke in San Francisco with a Berkeley Ph.D.? Keeping my bearings on such a long and strange trip seemed a ludicrous proposition. Home was so far gone behind me it was gone forever, and there was no place to rest. Battered by heavy emotions, a little dazed, I felt the inner walls that protect me dissolve to leave me vulnerable to all that could harm me. I cried, and abandoned myself to abject despair over what gender had done to me.

Everything's fucked up beyond all recognition. This hurts too much to go on. I came as close today as I'll ever come to giving birth—literally. My body can't do that; I can't even bleed without a wound, and yet I claim to be a woman. How? Why have I always felt that way? I'm such a goddamned freak. I can never be a woman like other women, but I could never be a man. Maybe there really is no place for me in all creation. I'm so tired of this ceaseless movement. I do war with nature. I am alienated from Being. I'm a self-mutilated deformity, a pervert, a mutant, trapped in monstrous flesh. God, I never wanted to be trapped again. I've destroyed myself. I'm falling into darkness I am falling apart.

I enter the realm of my dreams. I am underwater, swimming upwards It is dark. I see a shimmering light above me. I break through the plane of the water's surface with my lungs bursting. I suck for air—and find only more water. My lungs are full of water. Inside and out I am surrounded by it. Why am I not dead if there is no difference between me and what I am in? There is another surface above me and I swim frantically towards it. I see a shimmering light. I break the plane of the water's surface over and over and over again. This water annihilates me. I cannot be, and yet—an excruciating impossibility—I am I will do anything not to be here.

I will swim forever.
I will die for eternity.
I will learn to breathe water.
I will become the water.
If I cannot change my situation I will change myself.

In this act of magical transformation
I recognize myself again.

I am groundless and boundless movement.
I am a furious flow.
I am one with the darkness and the wet.

And I am enraged.

Here at last is the chaos I held at bay.
Here at last is my strength.

I am not the water—
I am the wave,
and rage
is the force that moves me.

Rage
gives me back my body
as its own fluid medium.

Rage
punches a hole in water
around which I coalesce
to allow the flow to come through me.

Rage
constitutes me in my primal form.
It throws my head back
pulls my lips back over my teeth
opens my throat
and rears me up to howl: and no sound dilutes
the pure quality of my rage.

No sound
exists
in this place without language
my rage is a silent raving

Rage
throws me back at last
into this mundane reality
in this transfigured flesh
that aligns me with the power of my Being.

In birthing my rage,
my rage has rebirthed me.

THEORY

A formal disjunction seems particularly appropriate at this moment because the affect I seek to examine critically, what I've termed "transgender rage," emerges from the interstices of discursive practices and at the collapse of generic categories. The rage itself is generated by the subject's situation in a field governed by the unstable but indissoluble relationship between language and materiality, a situation in which language organizes and brings into signification matter that simultaneously eludes definitive representation and demands its own perpetual rearticulation in symbolic terms. Within this dynamic field the subject must constantly police the boundary constructed by its own founding in order to maintain the fictions of "inside" and "outside" against a regime of signification/materialization whose intrinsic instability produces the rupture of subjective boundaries as one of its regular features. The affect of rage as I seek to define it is located at the margin of subjectivity and the limit of signification. It originates in recognition of the fact that the "outsideness" of a materiality that perpetually violates the foreclosure of subjective space within a symbolic order is also necessarily "inside" the subject as grounds for the materialization of its body and the formation of its bodily ego.

This primary rage becomes specifically transgender rage when the inability to foreclose the subject occurs through a failure to satisfy norms of gendered embodiment. Transgender rage is the subjective experience of being compelled to transgress what Judith Butler has referred to as the highly gendered regulatory schemata that determine the viability of bodies, of being compelled to enter a "domain of abjected bodies, a field of deformation" that in its unlivability encompasses and constitutes the realm of legitimate subjectivity (16). Transgender rage is a queer fury, an emotional response to conditions in which it becomes imperative to take up, for the sake of one's own continued survival as a subject, a set of practices that precipitates one's exclusion from a naturalized order of existence that seeks to maintain itself as the only possible basis for being a subject. However, by mobilizing gendered identities and rendering them provisional, open to strategic development and occupation, this rage enables the establishment of subjects in new modes, regulated by different codes of intelligibility. Transgender rage furnishes a means for disidentification with compulsorily assigned subject positions. It makes the transition from one gendered subject position to another possible by using the impossibility of complete subjective foreclosure to organize an outside force as an inside drive, and vice versa. Through the operation of rage, the stigma itself becomes the source of transformative power. (10)

I want to stop and theorize at this particular moment in the text because in the lived moment of being thrown back from a state of abjection in the aftermath of my lover's daughter's birth, I immediately began telling myself a story to explain my experience. I started theorizing, using all the conceptual tools my education had put at my disposal. Other true stories of those events could undoubtedly be told, but upon my return I knew for a fact what lit the fuse to my rage in the hospital delivery room. It was the non-consensuality of the baby's gendering. You see, I told myself, wiping snot off my face with a shirt sleeve, bodies are rendered meaningful only through some culturally and historically specific mode of grasping their physicality that transforms the flesh into a useful artifact. Gendering is the initial step in this transformation, inseparable from the process of forming an identity by means of which we're fitted to a system of exchange in a heterosexual economy. Authority seizes upon specific material qualities of the flesh, particularly the genitals, as outward indication of future reproductive potential, constructs this flesh as a sign, and reads it to enculturate the body. Gender attribution is compulsory; it codes and deploys our bodies in ways that materially affect us, yet we choose neither our marks nor the meanings they carry. (11) This was the act accomplished between the beginning and the end of that short sentence in the delivery room: "It's a girl." This was the act that recalled all the anguish of my own struggles with gender. But this was also the act that enjoined my complicity in the non-consensual gendering of another. A gendering violence is the founding condition of human subjectivity; having a gender is the tribal tattoo that makes one's personhood cognizable. I stood for a moment between the pains of two violations, the mark of gender and the unlivability of its absence. Could I say which one was worse? Or could I only say which one I felt could best be survived?

How can finding one's self prostrate and powerless in the presence of the Law of the Father not produce an unutterable rage? What difference does it make if the father in this instance was a pierced, tattooed, purple-haired punk fag anarchist who helped his dyke friend get pregnant? Phallogocentric language, not its particular speaker, is the scalpel that defines our flesh. I defy that Law in my refusal to abide by its original decree of my gender. Though I cannot escape its power, I can move through its medium. Perhaps if I move furiously enough, I can deform it in my passing to leave a trace of my rage. I can embrace it with a vengeance to rename myself, declare my transsexuality, and gain access to the means of my legible reinscription. Though I may not hold the stylus myself, I can move beneath it for my own deep self-sustaining pleasures.

To encounter the transsexual body, to apprehend a transgendered consciousness articulating itself, is to risk a revelation of the constructedness of the natural order. Confronting the implications of this constructedness can summon up all the violation, loss, and separation inflicted by the gendering process that sustains the illusion of naturalness. My transsexual body literalizes this abstract violence. As the bearers of this disquieting news, we transsexuals often suffer for the pain of others, but we do not willingly abide the rage of others directed against us. And we do have something else to say, if you will but listen to the monsters: the possibility of meaningful agency and action exists, even within fields of domination that bring about the universal cultural rape of all flesh. Be forewarned, however, that taking up this task will remake you in the process.

By speaking as a monster in my personal voice, by using the dark, watery images of Romanticism and lapsing occasionally into its brooding cadences and grandiose postures, I employ the same literary techniques Mary Shelley used to elicit sympathy for her scientist's creation. Like that creature, I assert my worth as a monster in spite of the conditions my monstrosity requires me to face, and redefine a life worth living. I have asked the Miltonic questions Shelley poses in the epigraph of her novel: "Did I request thee, Maker, from my clay to mould me man? Did I solicit thee from darkness to promote me?" With one voice, her monster and I answer "no" without debasing ourselves, for we have done the hard work of constituting ourselves on our own terms, against the natural order. Though we forego the privilege of naturalness, we are not deterred, for we ally ourselves instead with the chaos and blackness from which Nature itself spills forth. (12)

If this is your path, as it is mine, let me offer whatever solace you may find in this monstrous benediction: May you discover the enlivening power of darkness within yourself. May it nourish your rage. May your rage inform your actions, and your actions transform you as you struggle to transform your world.

NOTES

1. While this comment is intended as a monster's disdainful dismissal, it nevertheless alludes to a substantial debate on the status of transgender practices and identities in lesbian feminism. H. S. Rubin, in a sociology dissertation in progress at Brandeis University, argues that the pronounced demographic upsurge in the female-to-male transsexual population during the 1970s and 1980s is directly related to the ascendancy within lesbianism of a "cultural feminism" that disparaged and marginalized practices smacking of an unliberated "gender inversion" model of homosexuality—especially the butch-femme roles associated with working-class lesbian bar culture. Cultural feminism thus consolidated a lesbian-feminist alliance with heterosexual feminism on a middle-class basis by capitulating to dominant ideologies of gender. The same suppression of transgender aspects of lesbian practice, I would add, simultaneously raised the spectre of male-to-female transsexual lesbians as a particular threat to the stability and purity of nontranssexual lesbian-feminist identity. See Echols for the broader context of this debate, and Raymond for the most vehement example of the anti-transgender position.

2. The current meaning of the term "transgender" is a matter of some debate. The word was originally coined as a noun in the 1970s by people who resisted categorization as either transvestites or transsexuals, and who used the term to describe their own identity. Unlike transsexuals but like transvestites, transgenders do not seek surgical alteration of their bodies but do habitually wear clothing that represents a gender other than the one to which they were assigned at birth. Unlike transvestites but like transsexuals, however, transgenders do not alter the vestimentary coding of their gender only episodically or primarily for sexual gratification; rather, they consistently and publicly express an ongoing commitment to their claimed gender identities through the same visual representational strategies used by others to signify that gender. The logic underlying this terminology reflects the widespread tendency to construe "gender" as the sociocultural manifestation of a material "sex." Thus, while transsexuals express their identities through a physical change of embodiment, transgenders do so through a non-corporeal change in public gender expression that is nevertheless more complex than a simple change of clothes.

    This essay uses "transgender" in a more recent sense, however, than its original one. That is, I use it here as an umbrella term that refers to all identities or practices that cross over, cut across, move between, or otherwise queer socially constructed sex/gender boundaries. The term includes, but is not limited to, transsexuality, heterosexual transvestism, gay drag, hutch lesbianism, and such non-European identities as the Native American berdache or the Indian Hijra. Like "queer," "transgender" may also be used as a verb or an adjective. In this essay, transsexuality is considered to be a culturally and historically specific transgender practice/identity through which a transgendered subject enters into a relationship with medical, psychotherapeutic, and juridical institutions in order to gain access to certain hormonal and surgical technologies for enacting and embodying itself.

3.   Mikuteit 3–4, heavily edited for brevity and clarity.

4.   The preceding paragraph draws extensively on, and sometimes paraphrases, O'Hartigan and Kahler.

5.   See Laqueur 1–7, for a brief discussion of the Enlightenment's effect on constructions of gender. Feminist interpretations of *Frankenstein* to which Brooks responds include Gilbert and Gubar, Jacobus, and Homans.

6.   Openly transsexual speech similarly subverts the logic behind a remark by Bloom, 218, that "a beautiful 'monster,' or even a passable one, would not have been a monster."

7.   Billings and Urban, 269, document especially well the medical attitude toward transsexual surgery as one of technical mastery of the body; Irvine, 259, suggests how transsexuality fits into the development of scientific sexology, though caution is advised in uncritically accepting the interpretation of transsexual experience she presents in this chapter. Meyer, in spite of some extremely transphobic concluding comments, offers a good account of the medicalization of transgender identities; for a transsexual perspective on the scientific agenda behind sex reassignment techniques, see Stone, especially the section entitled "All of reality in late capitalist culture lusts to become an image for its own security" (280–304).

8.   Russo 49–50: "Homosexual parallels in *Frankenstein* (1931) and *Bride of Frankenstein* (1935) arose from a vision both films had of the monster as an antisocial figure in the same way that gay people were 'things' that should not have happened. In both films the homosexuality of director James Whale may have been a force in the vision."

9.   In the absence of a reliable critical history of transsexuality, it is best to turn to the standard medical accounts themselves: see especially Benjamin, Green and Money, and Stoller. For overviews of cross-cultural variation in the institutionalization of sex/gender, see Williams, "Social Constructions/Essential Characters: A Cross-Cultural Viewpoint," 252–76; Shapiro 262–68. For accounts of particular institutionalizations of transgender practices that employ surgical alteration of the genitals, see Nanda; Roscoe. Adventurous readers curious about contemporary non-transsexual genital alteration practices may contact E.N.I.G.M.A. (Erotic Neoprimitive International Genital Modification Association), SASE to LaFarge-werks, 2329 N. Leavitt, Chicago, IL 60647.

10. See Butler, "Introduction," 4 and *passim*.

11. A substantial body of scholarship informs these observations: Gayle Rubin provides a productive starting point for developing not only a political economy of sex, but of gendered subjectivity; on gender recruitment and attribution, see Kessler and McKenna; on gender as a system of marks that naturalizes sociological groups based on supposedly shared material similarities, I have been influenced by some ideas on race in Guillaumin and by Wittig.

12. Although I mean "chaos" here in its general sense, it is interesting to speculate about the potential application of scientific chaos theory to model the emergence of stable structures of gendered identities out of the unstable matrix of material attributes, and on the production of proliferating gender identities from a relatively simple set of gendering procedures.

WORKS CITED

Benjamin, Harry. *The Transsexual Phenomenon*. New York: Julian, 1966.

Billings, Dwight B., and Thomas Urban. "The Socio-Medical Construction of Transsexualism: An Interpretation and Critique." *Social Problems* 29 (1981): 266–82.

Bloom, Harold. "Afterword." *Frankenstein, or The Modern Prometheus*. New York: Signet/NAL, 1965. 212–23. Orig. pub. "*Frankenstein*, or The New Prometheus." *Partisan Review* 32 (1965): 611–18.

Brooks, Peter. *Body Work: Objects of Desire in Modern Narrative*. Cambridge, MA: Harvard UP, 1993.

Butler, Judith. *Bodies That Matter: On the Discursive Limits of "Sex."* New York: Routledge, 1993.

Daly, Mary. *Gyn/Ecology: The Metaethics of Radical Feminism*. Boston: Beacon, 1978.

Echols, Alice. *Daring to Be Bad: Radical Feminism in America, 1967–1975*. Minneapolis: U of Minnesota P, 1989.

Gilbert, Sandra, and Susan Gubar. "Horror's Twin: Mary Shelley's Monstrous Eve." *The Madwoman in the Attic*. New Haven: Yale UP, 1979. 213–47.

Green, Richard, and John Money, eds. *Transsexualism and Sex Reassignment*. Baltimore: Johns Hopkins UP, 1969.

Guillaumin, Colette. "Race and Nature: The System of Marks." *Feminist Studies* 8 (1988): 25–44.

Homans, Margaret. "Bearing Demons: Frankenstein's Circumvention of the Maternal." *Bearing the Word*. Chicago: Chicago UP, 1986. 100–19.

Irvine, Janice. *Disorders of Desire: Sex and Gender in Modern American Sexology*. Philadelphia: Temple UP, 1990.

Jacobus, Mary. "Is There a Woman in this Text?" *Reading Woman: Essays in Feminist Criticism*. New York: Columbia UP, 1986. 83–109.

Kahler, Frederic. "Does Filisa Blame Seattle?" Editorial. *Bay Times* [San Francisco] 3 June 1993: 23.

Kessler, Suzanne J., and Wendy McKenna. *Gender: An Ethnomethodological Approach*. Chicago: U of Chicago P, 1985

Laqueur, Thomas. *Making Sex: Body and Gender from the Greeks to Freud*. Cambridge, MA: Harvard UP, 1990.

Meyer, Morris. "I Dream of Jeannie: Transsexual Striptease as Scientific Display." *The Drama Review*. 35.1 (1991): 25–42.

Mikuteit, Debbie. Letter. *Coming Up!* Feb. 1986: 3–4.

Nanda, Serena. Neither Man Nor Woman: The Hijras of India. Belmont, CA: Wadsworth, 1990.

O'Hartigan, Margaret D. "I Accuse." Bay Times [San Francisco] 20 May 1993: 11.

Raymond, Janice G. The Transsexual Empire: The Making of the She-Male. Boston: Beacon, 1979.

Roscoe, Will. "Priests of the Goddess: Gender Transgression in the Ancient World." American Historical Association Meeting. 9 January 1994. San Francisco.

Rubin, Gayle. "The Traffic in Women: Notes on the 'Political Economy' of Sex." Toward an Anthropology of Women. Ed. Rayna R. Reiter. New York: Monthly Review Press, 1975. 157–210.

Russo, Vito. The Celluloid Closet: Homosexuality in the Movies. New York: Harper and Row, 1981.

Shapiro, Judith. "Transsexualism: Reflections on the Persistence of Gender and the Mutability of Sex." Body Guards: The Cultural Politics of Gender Ambiguity. Ed. Julia Epstein and Kristina Straub. New York: Routledge, 1991. 248–79.

Shelley, Mary. Frankenstein, or The Modern Prometheus. Orig. pub. 1817. New York: Signet/NAL, 1965.

Stoller, Robert. Sex and Gender. Vol. 1. New York: Science House, 1968. The Transsexual Experiment. Vol. 2 of Sex and Gender. London: Hogarth, 1975.

Stone, Sandy. "The Empire Strikes Back: A Posttranssexual Manifesto." Body Guards: The Cultural Politics of Gender Ambiguity. Ed. Julia Epstein and Kristina Straub. New York: Routledge, 1991. 280–304.

Williams, Walter. The Spirit and the Flesh: Sexual Diversity in American Indian Culture. Boston: Beacon, 1986.

Wittig, Monique. "The Mark of Gender." The Straight Mind and Other Essays. Boston: Beacon, 1992. 76–89.

20

Judith Butler

Queer Feminism, Transgender, and the Transubstantiation of Sex

JAY PROSSER

IN *SECOND SKIN SKINS: THE BODY NARRATIVES OF TRANSSEXUALITY*, literary scholar Jay Prosser offers one of the most theoretically sophisticated interdisciplinary interpretations of transgender experience, arguing that embodiment is a process of storytelling through which one's identity is communicated to others. In the following selection, Prosser discusses the transgender figure's simultaneous centrality to and marginalization within the field of queer studies in general, and in the work of Judith Butler in particular.

Prosser points out how the "critical visibility" of transgender phenomena serves as a rationale for the intellectual projects of early queer theorists like Eve Kosofsky Sedgwick, whose influential analysis of male homosocial desire in nineteenth-century English literature posits the sublimation of trans-gender identification as one of the central mechanisms of normative heterosexuality. Prosser likewise identifies attention to transgender themes in the work of thinkers and activists as diverse as Sue-Ellen Case, Kobena Mercer, Cherrie Moraga, Gloria Anzaldua, Teresa de Lauretis, and Marjorie Garber, to argue that "in retrospect, transgender gender appears as the most crucial sign of queer sexuality's aptly skewed point of entry into the academy."

Prosser couples his observations on the ubiquity of transgenderism within early queer theory with a pointed critique of the way that certain types of transgender phenomena, notably camp and drag, are valorized while others, notably transsexualism, are disparaged—the former being deployed to support a theory of gender performativity, the latter held up as an example of an intellectually suspect "founda-tionalism" or "essentialism." Prosser productively reads Judith Butler's early work on gender to resituate transsexualism as equally performative, and no more essentialist, than other expressions of gender.

> There is little time for grief in the *Phenomenology* [*of Spirit*] because renewal is always close at hand. What seems like tragic blindness turns out to be more like the comic myopia of Mr. Magoo whose automobile careening through the neighbor's chicken coop always seems to land on all four wheels. Like such miraculously resilient characters of the Saturday morning cartoon, Hegel's protagonists always reassemble themselves, prepare a new scene, enter the stage armed with a new set of ontological insights—and fail again. As readers, we have no other narrative option but to join in this bumpy ride.
> —Judith Butler, *Subjects of Desire: Hegelian Reflections in Twentieth-Century France*

TRANSGENDER AND THE QUEER MOMENT

> Queer is a continuing moment, movement, motive—recurrent, eddying, troublant. The word
> "queer" itself means across—it comes from the Indo-European root *twerkw*, which also yields
> the German *quer* (transverse), Latin *torquere* (to twist), English athwart.
>
> —Eve Kosofsky Sedgwick, *Tendencies*

In its earliest formulations, in what are now considered its foundational texts, queer studies can be seen to have been crucially dependent on the figure of transgender. As one of its most visible means of institutionalization, queer theory represented itself as traversing and mobilizing methodologies (feminism, poststructuralism) and identities (women, heterosexuals) already, at least by comparison, in institutionalized place. Seized on as a definitively queer force that "troubled" the identity categories of gender, sex, and sexuality—or rather revealed them to be always already fictional and precarious—the trope of crossing was most often impacted with if not explicitly illustrated by the transgendered subject's crossing their several boundaries at once: both the boundaries between gender, sex, and sexuality and the boundary that structures each as a binary category.

Even in Eve Kosofsky Sedgwick's work, which has argued most trenchantly for "a certain irreducibility" of sexuality to gender, and thus one might deduce would follow a certain irreducibility of *homo*sexuality to *trans*gender, homophobic constructions are understood to be produced by and productive of culturally normative gender identities and relations. The implications of this include a thorough enmeshing of homosexual desire with transgender identification. In its claim that women in the nineteenth century served to mediate desire between men, Sedgwick's *Between Men: English Literature and Male Homosocial Desire* suggests that the production of normative heterosexuality depended on a degree of male identification—and yet importantly, the disavowal of this identification—with woman as the object of desire. At the beginnings of queer therefore, in what is arguably lesbian and gay studies' first book, heterosexuality is shown to be constructed through the sublimation of a cross-gendered identification; for this reason, making visible this identification—transgendered movement—will become the key queer mechanism for deconstructing heterosexuality and writing out queer.

Sedgwick's next book foregrounds this methodological function of transgender explicitly. *Epistemology of the Closet* presents transgender as one good reason for the development of a theory of (homo)sexuality distinct from feminism. The critical visibility of transgender—"the reclamation and relegitimation of a courageous history of lesbian trans-gender role-playing and identification"—poses a challenge to lesbianism's incorporation within feminism: "The irrepressible, relatively class-nonspecific popular culture in which James Dean has been as numinous an icon for lesbians as Garbo or Dietrich has for gay men seems resistant to a purely feminist theorization. It is in these contexts that calls for a theorized axis of sexuality as distinct from gender have developed." Exceeding feminism's purview of gender, transgender demands and contributes to the basis for a new queer theory; paradoxically, transgender demands a new theory of sexuality. It is transgender that makes possible the lesbian and gay overlap, the identification between gay men and lesbians, which forms the grounds for this new theory of homosexuality discrete from feminism. And it is surely this overlap or cross-gendered identification between gay men and lesbians—an identification made critically necessary by the AIDS crisis—that ushers in the queer moment.

Most recently in her autobiographical narratives and performance pieces, Sedgwick has revealed her personal transgendered investment lying at and as the great heart of her queer project. Her confession of her "identification? Dare I, after this half-decade, call it with all a fat *woman's* defiance, my identity?—as a gay man" "comes out" with the transgendered desire that has been present in her work all along. Similarly in its readings, *Tendencies* derives its queer frisson openly and consistently from an identification across genders: a mobility "across gender lines, including the desires of men for women and of women for men," a transgendered traversal that in its queering (skewing and unraveling) of apparently normative heterosexuality is simultaneously a movement across sexualities. To summon the queer moment, the book begins with a figure for transgender—gay men wearing DYKE T-shirts and lesbians wearing FAGGOT T-shirts.

But Sedgwick is just the tip of the iceberg. The transgendered presence lies just below the surface of most of lesbian and gay studies' foundational texts. Early work on the intersections of race, gender, and sexual identities theorized otherness as produced through a racist, homophobic, and sexist trans-gendering, and thus again transgendering became the means to challenging this othering. Kobena Mercer's work on the fetishizing/feminizing white gaze of Robert Mapplethorpe at the black male body; Cherríe Moraga's description of the hermaphroditic convergence of the chingón and the chingada; Gloria Anzaldúa's memory of the mita' y mita' figure in the sexual, gender, and geographic border-lands: these various cross-gendered figures emerged both as constructions and, in their articulation by these critics, deconstructions of cultural ideologies that insist on absolute difference in all identity. Other early lesbian and gay studies work invested in the transgendered subject's "trans" a transgressive politics. For Teresa de Lauretis, Sue-Ellen Case, Jonathan Dollimore, and Marjorie Garber whether appearing in contemporary lesbian cinematic representations of butch/femme desire, in theatrical cross-dressing in early modern England, or as popular cultural gender-blending icons, the transgen-dered subject made visible a queerness that, to paraphrase Garber, threatened a crisis in gender and sexual identity categories. Crucial to the idealization of transgender as a queer transgressive force in this work is the consistent decoding of "trans" as incessant destabilizing movement between sexual and gender identities. In short, in retrospect, transgender *gender* appears as the most crucial sign of queer *sexuality's* aptly skewed point of entry into the academy.

Without doubt though, the single text that yoked transgender most fully to queer sexuality is Judith Butler's *Gender Trouble: Feminism and the Subversion of Identity*. *Gender Trouble's* impact was enor-mous: published in 1990, appearing with the decade, it transformed transgender into a queer icon, in the process becoming something of an icon of the new queer theory itself. Yet how this actually hap-pened, how *Gender Trouble* imbricated queer with transgender, and how the book itself was imbricated with transgender forms something of an intriguing critical phenomenon. For the embodied subject of transgender barely occupies the text of *Gender Trouble*—a book very much, after all, about subjects' failure of embodiment. As Butler herself states in remarking her surprise at the tendency to read *Gender Trouble* as a book about transgendered subjects, "there were probably no more than five paragraphs in *Gender Trouble* devoted to drag [yet] readers have often cited the description of drag as if it were the 'example' which explains the meaning of [gender] performativity." From this later point, her 1993 essay "Critically Queer," Butler clearly challenges the equation of transgender and homosexuality, or to be precise, the construction of transgender as the only sign of a deconstructive homosexuality: "cross-gendered identification is not the exemplary paradigm for thinking about homosexuality, although it may be one." Yet the effect of *Gender Trouble* was precisely to secure transgender as a touchstone of lesbian and gay theory. How did *Gender Trouble* canonize, and how was it canonized for, a theory of transgender performativity that was apparently not its substance?

In the first essay appearing in the first edition of the first academic journal devoted to lesbian and gay studies, *GLQ: A Journal of Lesbian and Gay Studies*, itself a canonical moment in queer studies, Sedgwick comments on *Gender Trouble's* canonically queer status: "Anyone who was at the 1991 Rutgers conference on Gay and Lesbian Studies [another canonizing mechanism], and heard *Gender Trouble* appealed to in paper after paper, couldn't help being awed by the productive impact this dense and even imposing work has had on the recent development of queer theory and reading." Surmising that these invocations were not indicative of an uncomplicated loyalty to *Gender Trouble* however, Sedgwick goes on to suggest that "the citation, the *use* of Butler's formulations in the context of queer theory will prove to have been highly active and tendentious." That *Gender Trouble* was subject to a set of reiterations and recitations proliferating meanings beyond the intention of the "original" might be considered especially fitting given its own attraction toward Foucauldian proliferation as the effective means for denaturalizing copies that pretend to originality. Its argument about recitation lent an amenability to its own recitation. There's something very campy, very definitively queer, about readings that refused to adhere to the letter of Butler's argument, that refused, to use its vernacular, to "repeat loyally." The original underwent a certain overreading, playful exaggeration, a mischievous adding of emphasis, yet nevertheless remained a discernible referent.

Camp may in fact be quite fundamental to our reading of *Gender Trouble* and our understanding of its transgender import. In his introduction to his anthology on camp (one of two anthologies on camp that appeared soon after *Gender Trouble*) David Bergman nominates Butler as "the person who has done the most to revise the academic standing of camp and to suggest its politically subversive potential." Bergman states that her success in queer studies comes in part from bringing to camp a high theoretical tone—and, we might add, from bringing camp to high theory. Pushing further on the connections between camp, queer, and the argument of *Gender Trouble*, it might be said that Butler's centrality in queer theory is in part an effect of queer's recuperation of camp and queer's recuperation *through* camp. The late eighties/early nineties, simultaneous with the beginnings of queer theory, saw the cultural and political reappropriation of camp, and the history of the term "queer" is most symptomatic of this. From homophobic epithet designating and reinforcing the other's social abjection to self-declared maker of community pride, "queer" was reclaimed precisely according to the transformative mechanisms of camp in which what has been devalued in the original becomes overvalued in the repetition. In turn, in its queer reevaluation, camp has proven a key strategy for queer theory's own institutionalization, a means by which to piggyback into the academy on (appropriating and redefining) already established methodologies. *Between Men*, for instance, deployed a distinctive camp style in subjecting canonical nineteenth-century literature to deliberate yet wonderfully subtle overreadings that brought to the surface its sexual subtexts. In its academic manifestation, camp actually comes to appear a form of queer deconstruction, not simply inverting the opposition between the original and the copy, the referent and the repetition but creating, according to Scott Long, a third space, "a stance, detached, calm, and free, from which the opposition as a whole and its attendant terms can be perceived and judged." This third space, this queer deconstruction, is surely queer theory.

It is certainly this camp inversion of the expected order of terms to elucidate the construction of the original that forms the very pith of *Gender Trouble*'s theory: the subject does not precede but is an effect of the law; heterosexuality does not precede but is an effect of the prohibition on homosexuality; sex does not precede but is an effect of the cultural construction of gender. Butler's argument consistently reverses the expected history between the two terms in each formulation to bring them into a third space where each opposition as a whole can be perceived and judged. The binaries of sexual difference that undergird what Butler terms "the metaphysics of sex" are fragmented and mobilized with a Derridean flourish into sexual *différance* (*GT* 16). The driving sensibility of *Gender Trouble*'s theory is in this respect an archetypically camp one. Although the embodied transgendered subject doesn't occupy *Gender Trouble* in any substantial way, it is this camp reversal of terms that conveys the sense that the transgendered subject of drag is always in the margins of the text, the implicit referent (ironically given Butler's use of camp/drag's function to displace the referent). For it is as the *personification* of camp—the third/intermediate term that reveals the constructedness of the binary of sex, of gender, and of the sex/gender system—that queer studies has anointed the transgendered subject queer. "Critically Queer"'s reading of *Gender Trouble*'s reception is thus absolutely right. Transgendered subjects, butches and drag queens, did come to appear the empirical examples of gender performativity, their crossing illustrating both the inessentiality of sex and the nonoriginality of heterosexuality that was the book's thesis. And those five paragraphs or so where *Gender Trouble* does explicitly address the subject in drag certainly do nothing to contradict this conception of transgender as exemplarily camp/queer/performative: "*In imitating gender, drag implicitly reveals the imitative structure of gender itself—as well as its contingency*" (GT 137). In this sentence (particularly given that the italics appear in the original), transgender's function is unambivalently and emphatically that of the elucidating example of gender performativity.

This chapter charts the achievement of and challenges that association, transgender/camp/queer/ performativity. That transgender can emerge as a "studies" in the late nineteen-nineties, that the figure at the center of many of transgender's projects is the "gender troubler," is largely due to Butler's canonization (both the canonization of Butler and her inadvertent canonization of transgender): "*s/he*"—the transgenderist, the third camp term whose crossing lays bare and disrupts the binaries that found identity—threads prominently through the self-declared first reader in the new field of transgender studies. My concern is the implication of this harnessing of transgender as queer for transsexuality: what are the points at which the transsexual as transgendered subject is not queer? The splits and shifts between the deployment of transgender and that of transsexuality within Butler's work are revealing on this count. Whereas in *Gender Trouble* the transgendered subject is used to deliteralize the matter of sex, in Butler's later *Bodies That Matter: On the Discursive Limits of "Sex,"* the transsexual in particular symbolizes a carefully sustained ambivalence around sex. That Butler chooses to elucidate the limits of the transgendered subject's deliteralization of sex through the figure of a transsexual is a powerful indicator of the conceptual splitting between transsexual and queer and, indeed, of queer theory's own incapacity to sustain the body as a literal category. In transsexuality sex *returns*, the queer repressed, to unsettle its theory of gender performativity. In making Butler the substance of my first chapter, I intend both to mark the absolutely generative force her work has had for this book and to suggest that the limitations over the figure of the transsexual and the literality of the sexed body in her work make necessary my readings of the transsexual body narratives that follow.

QUEER GENDER AND PERFORMATIVITY

> To realize the difference of the sexes is to put an end to play.
> —Jacques Lacan and Wladimir Granoff, "Fetishism:
> The Symbolic, the Imaginary, and the Real"

Even though it is articulated only in the last of four sections in the final chapter ("Bodily Inscriptions, Performative Subversions" [*GT* 128–141]), that is in less than one-twelfth of the book, it is the account of gender performativity that is most often remembered as the thrust of *Gender Trouble*. Sedgwick illustrates: "Probably the centerpiece of Butler's recent work has been a series of demonstrations that gender can best be discussed as a form of performativity." More intriguing than the disproportionate emphasis accorded the final section of *Gender Trouble* in general remembrance, however, is the way in which *gender* performativity has become so coextensive with *queer* performativity as to render them interchangeable. Sedgwick, again, exemplifies the way in which "gender" has slipped rapidly into "queer." "Queer Performativity" (the title of her essay on James) she writes, is "made necessary" by Butler's work in and since *Gender Trouble*; and in *Tendencies* Sedgwick assigns Butler "and her important book" (*Gender Trouble*) a representative function, "stand[ing] in for a lot of the rest of us" working on queer performativity. How does this slippage from gender to queer in the discussion of performativity come about, and how does *Gender Trouble* come to "stand in for" it?

While it argues that *all* gender is performative—that "man" and "woman" are not expressions of prior internal essences but constituted, to paraphrase Butler, through the repetition of culturally intelligible stylized acts—*Gender Trouble* presents the transgendered subject as the concrete example that "brings into relief" this performativity of gender (*GT* 31). In retrospect we can note that, in concretizing gender performativity with transgender, *Gender Trouble* inadvertently made possible two readings that Butler later returns to refute: first, that what was meant by gender performativity was gender theatricality; and second, that all transgender is queer is syllogistically subversive. The first assumption, that gender performativity means acting out one's gender as if gender were a theatrical role that could be chosen, led to the belief that Butler's theory of gender was both radically voluntarist and antimaterialist: that its argument was that gender, like a set of clothes in a drag act, could be donned and doffed at will, that gender *is* drag. In this reading *Gender Trouble* was both embraced and critiqued. (Even before *Gender Trouble*, however, Butler had carefully argued against any conceptualization of gender as something that could be chosen at will). In fact, Butler's notion of performativity is derived not from a Goffman-esque understanding of identity as role but from Austinian speech-act theory, crucially informed by Derrida's deconstruction of speech-act theory. Not cited in *Gender Trouble* but implicit throughout in its insistence on the cruciality of repetition as destabilizing is Derrida's reading of J. L. Austin and John Searle. *Bodies That Matter* wastes little time before citing Derrida's reading (introduction 13), and in order to clarify this speech-act sense of performativity, the new work emphasizes gender's citationality throughout. To some extent in *Bodies That Matter*, the later term, "citationality," comes to displace the former of *Gender Trouble*, "performativity." Like a law that requires citing to be effective, *Bodies That Matter* argues, sex comes into effect through our citing it, and, as with a law, through our compulsion to cite it. Butler's refiguring of sex as citational law in *Bodies That Matter* is designed to derail the understanding of gender as free theatricality that constituted the misreading of *Gender Trouble*, to clarify how gender is compelled through symbolic prohibitions. The shifts in terms in the books' titles, from "Gender Trouble" to the "Discursive Limits of 'Sex'" (both the shift from "gender" to "'sex'" and from "trouble" to "discursive limits") run as parallel attempts to account for gender's materiality, its nonsuperficiality, and at the same time to foreground the "limits" of the "trouble" subjects can effect to its constitutive prohibitions. That "sex" appears typographically inserted in citation marks suggests sex precisely as a citation.

It is the second assumption drawn from *Gender Trouble*'s illustration of gender performativity with transgender that concerns me most: the assumption that transgender is queer is subversive. For it is this syllogism that enables Sedgwick to make that slide from gender performativity to queer performativity and that effectively encodes transgendered subjectivity as archetypically queer and subversive. It should be understood that, although it never makes such an argument, *Gender Trouble* does set up the conditions for this syllogism: transgender = gender performativity = queer = subversive. We can begin to illustrate the first part of this, the equation of transgender with gender performativity, by examining *Gender Trouble*'s reading of Beauvoir's "One is not born a woman, but rather becomes one." In Butler's reformulation of Beauvoir's famed epigram on the construction of gender nearly half a century later, it is through the suggestion of a possible transgendering that gender appears not simply constructed but radically contingent on the body. To cite Butler: "Beauvoir is clear that one 'becomes' a woman, but always under a cultural compulsion to become one. And clearly, the compulsion does not come from 'sex.' *There is nothing in her account that guarantees that the 'one' who becomes a woman is necessarily female*" (*GT* 8; my emphasis). And again: "Beauvoir's theory implied seemingly radical consequences, ones that she herself did not entertain. For instance, if sex and gender are radically distinct, then it does not follow that to be a given sex is to become a given gender; in other words, *'woman' need not be the cultural construction of the female body, and 'man' need not interpret male bodies"* (*GT* 112; my emphasis). In both citations, Butler's suggestion of a possible transgendered becoming (that men may not be males and women may not be females) not only opens up a conceptual space between gender and sex and leaves sex dispensable to the process of gendering; it also conveys that gender is not a teleological narrative of ontology at all, with the sexed body (female) as recognizable beginning and gender identity (woman) as clear-cut ending. In Butler's reading transgender demotes gender from narrative to performative. That is, gender appears not as the end of narrative becoming but as performative moments all along a process: repetitious, recursive, disordered, incessant, above all, unpredictable and necessarily incomplete. "It is, for [Butler's version of] Beauvoir, never possible finally to become a woman, as if there were a *telos* that governs the process of acculturation and construction. Gender is the repeated stylization of the body, a set of repeated acts within a highly rigid regulatory frame that congeal over time to produce the appearance of substance, of a natural sort of being" (*GT* 33).

If transgender now equals gender performativity, how does this formulation come to acquire the additional equivalencies of queer and subversion? In "Critically Queer," in correcting the tendency to misread *Gender Trouble* as about transgender, Butler underscores that there is no essential identity between transgender and homosexuality: "not only are a vast number of drag performers straight, but it would be a mistake to think that homosexuality is best explained through the performativity that is drag." That she must return to make this qualification, however, is again precisely because *Gender Trouble* has already produced an implicit equivalence between transgender and homosexuality, so that transgender appears as the sign of homosexuality, homosexuality's definitive *gender* style. In one claim key to this imbrication of transgender with homosexuality, "parodic and subversive convergences" are said to "*characterize* gay and lesbian cultures" (*GT* 66; my emphasis). This characterization encodes transgender as homosexual gender difference, a kind of archetypal queer gender.

Where "straight" gender occults its own performativity according to a metaphysics of substance, queer transgender reveals ("brings into relief") the performativity of all gender. Transgender "dramatizes" the process of signification by which all gendered embodiment "create[s] the effect of the natural" or real; drag's imitative workings parallel the imitative workings that structure straight genders, for all "gender is a kind of persistent impersonation that passes as the real" (*GT* x). The metaphysics of substance undergirds the naturalization of sex and of heterosexuality. What Butler terms the "heterosexual matrix," building in particular on Monique Wittig's analyses of the straight mind's naturalization of a dimorphic gender system, sustains heterosexuality as natural and naturalizes gender as sex. The naturalizing mechanism works both ways, shoring up the apparent naturalness of both sex/gender and heterosexual desire. The claim to "be" a man or a woman is made possible by the binary and oppositional positioning of these terms within heterosexuality. Sex, gender, and desire are unified through the representation of heterosexuality as primary and foundational. Female, femininity, and woman appear as stable and conjoined terms through their opposition to male, masculinity, and man. Gender, in other words, appears as *identity*. What stabilizes the association and keeps the two sets discrete and antithetical is the apparent naturalness of heterosexual desire.

Queer transgender's function in *Gender Trouble* can be summarized as twofold: to parallel the process by which heterosexuality reproduces (and reproduces itself through) binarized gender identities; and at the same time to contrast with heterosexuality's naturalization of this process. For whereas the constructedness of straight gender is obscured by the veil of naturalization, queer transgender reveals, indeed, explicitly performs, its own constructedness. In other words, queer transgender serves as heterosexual gender's subversive foil. Thus in the scheme of *Gender Trouble*, heterosexual gender is assigned as ground, queer transgender as figure, dramatizing or metaphorizing the workings of heterosexuality's construction. Even in "Critically Queer," in the very same paragraph that apparently seeks to disentangle homosexuality and transgender, Butler writes that drag "exposes or *allegorizes*" the process by which heterosexualized genders form themselves. Queer transgender is allegory to heterosexual gender's (specious, for it only veils its performativity) referentiality or literality.

Biddy Martin has described her anxiety in response to Butler's and Sedgwick's work over this tendency of "antifoundationalist celebrations of queerness" to represent queer sexualities as "figural, performative, playful, and fun." Martin's anxiety specifically concerns the way in which feminism, gender, and, by extension, the female body, are stabilized in this dynamic, projected by queerness as "fixity, constraint, or subjection...a fixed ground." While agreeing that the category of woman is often subject to a degree of a priori stabilization in the very writings that call for its destabilization and proliferation, my concerns, for the following reasons, are particularly with the effective appropriation of transgender by queer. In the first instance, transgendered subjectivity is not inevitably queer. That is, by no means are all transgendered subjects homosexual. While "Critically Queer" itself points this out, *Gender Trouble's* queer transgender illustrates a certain collapsing of gender back into sexuality that, in the particular process of *Gender Trouble's* canonization, has become a tendency of queer studies: a tendency that is, as Martin suggests, the queering of gender through sexuality (and I would add of sexuality through gender). And, more crucially in regard to this first distinction, in the context of a discussion of how gender and sexual subjects have been taken up in theoretical paradigms, by no means are transgendered subjects necessarily queer even in the sense that queer has come to signify in queer studies. That is, although "queer" as a camp term has to some extent lost that referent "homosexual" and now signifies not as homosexual *stricto sensu* but as a figure for the performative—subversive signifier displacing referent—by no means are all transgendered subjects queer even in this figurative, nonreferential sense. Butler's reading of Venus Xtravaganza in *Bodies That Matter* will work as an attempt to demonstrate just this: the way in which not every gender-crossing is queerly subversive. Yet it should be pointed out again that the fact that she must later return to disentangle transgender, queer, and subversion in *Bodies That Matter* as she must in the essay "Critically Queer," is due precisely to their prior entanglement in *Gender Trouble*. (Although, given the importance within Butler's theory of the dynamic of citation, the extent to which her own writing is generated through such reiterative returns should be noted as richly appropriate.)

My second reason for concern with queer's arrogation of transgender is that it allocates to nontransgendered subjects (according to this binary schema, straight subjects), the ground that transgender would appear to *only* figure; this "ground" is the apparent naturalness of sex. For if transgender figures gender performativity, nontransgender or straight gender is assigned (to work within Butler's own framework of speech-act theory) the category of the constative. While within this framework, this allocation is a sign of the devaluation of straight gender, and conversely queer's alignment of itself with transgender gender performativity represents queer's sense of its own "higher purpose," in fact there are transgendered trajectories, in particular *transsexual* trajectories, that aspire to that which this scheme devalues. Namely there are transsexuals who seek very pointedly to be nonperformative, to be constative, quite simply, to *be*. What gets dropped from transgender in its queer deployment to signify subversive gender performativity is the value of the matter that often most concerns the transsexual: the *narrative* of becoming a biological man or a biological woman (as opposed to the performative of effecting one)—in brief and simple the materiality of the sexed body. In the context of the transsexual trajectory, in fact, Beauvoir's epigram can be read quite differently as describing not a generic notion of gender's radical performativity but the specific narrative of (in this case) the male-to-female transsexual's struggle toward sexed embodiment. One is not born a woman, but *nevertheless* may become one—given substantial medical intervention, personal tenacity, economic security, social support, and so on: becoming woman, in spite of not being born one, may be seen as a crucial goal. In its representation of sex as a figurative effect of straight gender's constative performance, *Gender Trouble* cannot account for a transsexual desire for sexed embodiment as *telos*. In this regard *Gender Trouble* serves to prompt readings of transsexual subjects whose bodily trajectories might exceed its framework of the theory of gender performativity.

If *Gender Trouble* enables the syllogism transgender = gender performativity = queer = subversive, it stabilizes this syllogism through suggesting as constant its antithesis: nontransgender = gender constativity = straight = naturalizing. The binary opposition between these syllogisms proliferates a number of mutually sustaining binary oppositions between *Gender Trouble*'s conceptual categories: queer versus straight; subversive versus naturalizing; performativity versus constativity; gender versus sex. The first term in each opposition is ascribed a degree of generativity that puts in question the primacy of the second. The value of this intervention lies in our recognition that it is the second term that is customarily awarded primacy and autonomy over the first. But the transsexual, as Butler later realizes in Venus Xtravaganza, ruptures these binaries and their alignment.

Because it constitutes the focal point of the transsexual trajectory (to *be* a woman) among these binaries, it is the matter of sex that is of interest to me next before Venus, not simply in its conceptually associative opposition to transgendered subjects in *Gender Trouble* but as a conceptual category in itself. Transgender certainly allows Butler to displace an expressivist model of gender where gender is the cultural expression or interpretation of sex (consolidated as bedrock) with a performative model where sex can "be shown to have been gender all along" (*GT* 8). But *Gender Trouble*'s most thorough accounting for sex as discursive effect appears in the discussion of melancholia in the second chapter, "Prohibition, Psychoanalysis, and the Production of the Heterosexual Matrix" (*GT* 35–78). Here, although the transgendered subject is not explicitly marshaled to exemplify the theory, the figure of transgender haunts the analyses, and the particular conceptualization of sex as "gender all along," as we shall see, certainly has significant implications for any theory of transsexual subjectivity.

HETEROSEXUAL MELANCHOLIA AND THE ENCRYPTING OF SEX

> To recast the referent as the signified . . .
> —Judith Butler, "Contingent Foundations"

Butler has suggested that it was the tendency to skip over this central chapter that led to the conventional (mis)reading of *Gender Trouble* as about drag and promoting a "free play" model of gender. On two occasions she has stated that this tendency is enabled by the book's structure, by too great a thematic break between the discussion of drag and the discussion of melancholia: "The problem is that I didn't bring forward the psychoanalytic material into the discussion of performativity well enough"; "[W]hat I failed to do is to refer the theatricality of drag back to the psychoanalytic discussions that preceded it, for psychoanalysis insists that the opacity of the unconscious sets limits to the exteriorization of the psyche." Butler's later work has gone on to make these moves back and forth between drag and psychoanalysis, to work the connections between gender performativity and melancholia. Melancholia later becomes a way of delimiting the "play" of gender performativity (one section in "Critically Queer" is subtitled "Melancholia and the Limits of Performance"), a means for Butler to unstick the notion of performativity from the literal performance (external display) to which it had become fixed and resituate performativity within the interior workings of the psyche. If, as Butler later writes, the drag sections of *Gender Trouble* "did not address the question of how it is that certain forms of disavowal and repudiation come to organize the performance of gender," drag as it is reworked though melancholia becomes interesting not so much for what it reveals as for what it reveals as repudiated—or rather, to follow Butler's specific psychoanalytic distinction, foreclosed. For although drag is later said to expose or to allegorize heterosexuality, now elaborated as heterosexual melancholia, melancholia is itself constituted by the "unperformable," by what it reveals as that which cannot be revealed as such.

Even without Butler's later underscoring its importance and her continued reworking of melancholia and gender performativity, however, it is difficult not to conclude that, in its thorough accounting for the construction of sex via a thorough accounting of the construction of heterosexuality, this second chapter represents the primary achievement of *Gender Trouble*. While the construction of gender and sexuality is often asserted in poststructuralist theory, this chapter details how the process of construction actually takes place through the categories of culture, the psyche, and body, setting up a complex and brilliant exchange between their domains and, by extension, structuralist and psychoanalytic theory. The analyses stem from these difficult questions: If sex is "gender all along," not a prior ontological substance that gender interprets but rather gender in masquerade, how is it that gender comes to pass so effectively as sex? How does sex appear as biological bedrock, and gender as its *a posteriori* cultural interpretation?

The deft interlocking of theoretical paradigms, namely, Lévi-Strauss, Lacan (and to a lesser extent, Joan Rivière), and Freud gives to Butler's answering of these questions a comprehensive and authoritative feel. Her beginning premise, undergirding the work of Lévi-Strauss, Lacan, and Freud—and of course Foucault—is the productivity of cultural prohibitions. However, where psychoanalysis and structuralism both posit incest as the prohibition that produces heterosexuality, Butler argues that the incest taboo is preceded by the taboo on homosexuality, for it is this that inaugurates the positive Oedipus complex, that is, the incestuous desires in the first place. The child's compliance with the taboo on homosexuality ensures that his/her object-cathexis is directed toward the opposite-sexed parent. In a move designed to refute the primacy of heterosexuality over homosexuality, Butler asks: What then is the productive effect on heterosexuality of the prohibition of homosexuality? What happens to the once-desired, now-outlawed homosexual love object? Where within the subject does this object-cathexis go?

Via Lacan, Butler asserts that the lost object is incorporated through a melancholic strategy of masquerade crucial to the production of sexual difference. In Lacan's "The Meaning of the Phallus," women appear to be the phallus through a masquerade effected by a melancholic incorporation. Incorporated are the "attributes of the object/Other that is lost," and significantly for Butler, Lacan exemplifies the lost object with a female homosexual cathexis (*GT* 48). The lost object, in particular "the signification of the body in the mold of the Other who has been refused," is incorporated as a mask via "melancholic identification" (*GT* 50). Lacan's account enables Butler to locate "the process of gender incorporation within the wider orbit of melancholy" and to suggest that the unresolved homosexual cathexes outlawed by the taboo on homosexuality effect the production of heterosexually invested genders: symbolic sexual difference (*GT* 50). From Lacan, Rivière's famous refusal of the distinction between the masquerade of femininity and "genuine womanliness" (and Stephen Heath's elaboration of this assertion) allows Butler to consider the mask not as concealing an interior authentic gender essence but rather as that which masquerades as this essence; the mask itself constitutes gender (*GT* 53).

So far in Butler's chapter the argument has stayed within the bounds of the construction of *gender*. Butler now begins to account for the construction of *sex*, that is how sex is "gender all along." She does so by turning to Freud's writings on melancholia and incorporation ("Mourning and Melancholia" and *The Ego and the Id*, particularly its chapter, "The Ego and the Super-Ego [Ego Ideal]"), and by layering over these two other sets of psychoanalytic texts: Nicolas Abraham and Maria Torok's work on mourning, melancholia, and the processes of introjection and incorporation; and Roy Schafer's descriptions of psychic internalization and the psychoanalytic language of internalization. My questions here—what happens to the matter of sex in *Gender Trouble* and what are its implications for the subject of transsexuality—can be addressed by our careful retracing and elaboration of Butler's steps through these texts.

Freud's 1917 "Mourning and Melancholia" distinguishes these two eponymous psychic states. He defines mourning as a normal finite reaction of grief, which has as its goal the resolution of the death of a loved object. Melancholia differs from mourning on all counts. First, the object is lost not necessarily through death but through, for instance, love. Second, the melancholic does not know for what he grieves: the loss remains opaque to consciousness. And thus third, in not knowing what he has lost, the melancholic *preserves* his object-loss by encrypting it and incorporating it as an identification. In this incorporation of the once-desired lost object as an identification, the melancholic regresses to an oral phase where object-cathexis and identification are confused. In 1923 in *The Ego and the Id*, Freud returns to this essay in order to normalize the workings of melancholia. He discards the opposition between mourning and melancholia and suggests that the processes distinct to melancholia should now be reconceived as part of the process of mourning. Depathologizing melancholia, he argues that its dynamic of substituting an object-cathexis for an identification is central to the formation of the ego. In fact, "it may be the sole condition under which the id can give up its objects." In particular, the dynamics of substitution and incorporation should be understood to produce normative—that is nonpathological—gendering; they function to resolve the object-cathexes of the Oedipus complex and to consolidate gender positioning. Surely significantly for Butler, although she doesn't cite this passage, Freud's example of how identification through incorporation functions to consolidate gender is one of a moment of transgendered identification: "Analysis very often shows that a little girl, after she has had to relinquish her father as a love-object, will bring her masculinity into prominence and identify herself with her father (that is, with the object which has been lost), instead of with the mother."

Freud's generalization of the dynamics of melancholia, his understanding of their role in gendering (through transgendering), allows Butler to select melancholia as the response to the taboo on homosexuality in generating normative (that is heterosexual) gender positions. Heterosexuality is ensured by the cultural prohibition on homosexuality, but the once-loved homosexual object must nevertheless be processed. Because of the cultural prohibition on homosexuality, because of the cultural unnameability of homosexuality, the lost homosexual love-object (always already lost in the sense that it is forbidden) cannot be mourned—that is, articulated or named. The taboo on homosexuality effects a denial of its desired status; grief over the loss is instead turned back in on itself in an unarticulated and unconscious melancholia. At this point Butler enlists Abraham and Torok's description of mourning and melancholia as characterized by two antithetical dynamics of internalization; where mourning introjects the lost object, melancholia incorporates it. Introjection, Abraham and Torok argue, clearly developing Freud's 1917 understanding of mourning as a consciousness of loss, works on a recognition or consciousness of the absence of the object. The void left by the loss of the object is not so much "filled" by articulation of the loss—that is, language—as it makes possible language—that is, the expression of loss. The original loss (the loss of the breast) is resolved through the child's cry. The loss of the real object (originally the mother's body) is thus displaced into language or metaphorized; the mouth emptied of the breast makes possible the mouth filled with words. Melancholia, on the other hand, sets in motion a fantasy of incorporation. As a means of denying the loss, the subject imagines or fantasizes taking in the object. When the loss cannot be acknowledged and articulated via mourning, the subject imagines literally "swallowing" the object, a melancholic fantasy of literalization. As a refusal to displace loss into language, incorporation, Abraham and Torok argue, is fundamentally antimetaphoric. In this sense incorporation is a magical resolution of loss; the loss is actually not resolved at all, remaining unacknowledged and unspoken. As prohibited desire that thus cannot be mourned, Butler uses Abraham and Torok to suggest, the lost homosexual cathexis is incorporated (rather than introjected) as prohibited identification.

But if this identification is incorporated, where exactly is it incorporated? Butler asks: "If the identifications sustained through melancholy are 'incorporated,' then the question remains: Where is this incorporated space? If it is not literally within the body, perhaps it is *on* the body as its surface signification such that the body must itself be understood *as* an incorporated space" (*GT* 67). Having established that melancholia is one psychic effect of the prohibition on homosexuality in the production of heterosexual identity, this, then, is Butler's most engaging proposal. Melancholia for the lost homosexual love-object literalizes sex on the (heterosexual) body. Through Freud and Abraham and Torok, the incorporation that does the work of melancholia appears as an antimetaphorical activity "precisely because it maintains the loss as radically unnamable. In other words, incorporation is not only a failure to name or avow the loss, but erodes the conditions of metaphorical signification itself" (*GT* 68). Incorporation enacts a literalization of the loss. "As an antimetaphorical activity, incorporation *literalizes* the loss *on* or *in* the body and so appears as the facticity of the body, the means by which the body comes to bear 'sex' as its literal truth" (*GT* 68).

This interchangeability between "on" and "in" ("*on* or *in*"), this slippage between, in other words, the surface of the body and its interiority, is crucial. It sets up an equivalence between surface and interiority that is absolutely pivotal both to Butler's description of sexing as a fantasy of incorporation and to her figuring of the body *as* a psychically "incorporated space." In Abraham and Torok the literalizing dynamic of incorporation is crucially a *fantasy* of literalization. Nothing is ever literally taken in during this process of incorporation. Rather, as a means of denying its absence, the subject fantasizes "swallowing" its loss. Corporeal interiority, in this case the notion that the body has a sex, is thus indexical of the literalizing fantasy of heterosexual melancholia, its incorporative response to the prohibition of homosexuality. It is only via this fantasy of literalization that the body comes "to bear a sex" as literal truth, that gender gets inscribed on the body as sex and sex appears as the literal embodiment of gender:

> The conflation of desire with the real—that is, the belief that it is the parts of the body, the "literal" penis, the "literal" vagina, which cause pleasure and desire—is precisely the kind of literalizing fantasy characteristic of the syndrome of melancholic heterosexuality. The disavowed homosexuality at the base of melancholic heterosexuality reemerges as the self-evident anatomical facticity of sex, where "sex" designates the blurred unity of anatomy, "natural identity," and "natural desire." The loss is denied and incorporated, and the genealogy of that transmutation fully forgotten and repressed. The sexed surface of the body thus emerges as the necessary sign of a natural(ized) identity and desire. The loss of homosexuality is refused and the love sustained or encrypted in the parts of the body itself, literalized in the ostensible anatomical facticity of sex. Here we see the general strategy of literalization as a form of forgetfulness, which, in the case of a literalized sexual anatomy, "forgets" the imaginary and, with it, an imaginable homosexuality. (*GT* 71)

The denied homosexual love is thus incorporated as the "surface" of the body that yet masquerades as interior literal sex. Heterosexuals who believe that their penises and vaginas are the "cause" of their pleasure or desire literalize them and "forget" an/other body: both the (once-loved) homosexual body, the body of the other, and their own imaginary or phantasmatic body (there is an implicit binding of the homosexual to the imaginary).

Because she grounds it on a misrecognition, a mistaking of the signifier of gender for the referent of sex, of the metaphorical for the literal, Butler's description of heterosexual sexing through melancholia inevitably raises mind-boggling questions about what (nonerroneous) recognition might entail. What imaginary body (parts or surfaces) does the heterosexual male who literalizes his penis forget? Is the forgotten imaginary necessarily other than what masquerades as the real? Does this body correspond to a gendered one? Are the imaginary and the phantasmatic already gendered? Later in *Gender Trouble*, in "The Body Politics of Julia Kristeva" (*GT* 79–93), Butler critiques Kristeva's premise of a pre-Symbolic body, one situated in the murky maternal space of the semiotic before the paternal law. Butler reverses Kristeva's temporality, positioning the semiotic or the imaginary as an effect of the Symbolic, the (zone of) prohibition again productive of (the zone of) the prediscursive Kristeva conceives as primary. As this section of the final chapter of *Gender Trouble* suggests that no imaginary body can signify outside of gender, it would follow that the imaginary body in the second chapter is already gendered. Indeed Butler asserts as much in the final pages of "Prohibition, Psychoanalysis, and the Production of the Heterosexual Matrix" when she figures the imaginary or fantasized body as "an altered bodily ego…within the gendered rules of the imaginary" (*GT* 71). In literalizing his penis, then, might the straight man be said to forget an imaginary or fantasized vagina? Does he also forget to literalize (invest sex in) body parts that he might be said to already "have" (more than he can be said to "have" a vagina)—feet for instance? And how are *these* parts gendered in the imaginary? What exactly *are* the "gendered rules" of the imaginary? The question of the precise relations between actual heterosexual subjects and the theory of heterosexual melancholia is prompted by, though not addressed in, *Gender Trouble*'s description.

For transsexual embodiment, Butler's harnessing psychoanalytic discussions of melancholia and incorporation to the processes of gendering has two interdependent significant effects: it refigures sex from material corporeality into phantasized surface; and through this it reinscribes the opposition between queer and heterosexual already at work in *Gender Trouble*, sustaining it by once again enlisting transgender as queer.

First, Butler's deliteralization of sex depends upon her conceiving the body as the psychic projection of a surface. This conceptualization derives from a rather eclectic reading of Freud's description of the bodily ego in *The Ego and the Id*. I cite the Freud passage in full.

> A person's own body, and above all its surface, is a place from which both external and internal perceptions may spring. It is *seen* like any other object, but to the *touch*, it yields two kinds of sensations, one of which may be equivalent to an internal perception. Psycho-physiology has fully discussed the manner in which a person's own body attains its special position among other objects in the world of perception. Pain, too, seems to play a part in the process, and the way in which we gain new knowledge of our organs during painful illnesses is perhaps a model of the way by which in general we arrive at the idea of our body.
>
> The ego is first and foremost a bodily ego; it is not merely a surface entity, but is itself the projection of a surface.

In the apparent periphery of a footnote, *Gender Trouble* cites from the second paragraph of this passage Freud's assertion, "the ego is first and foremost a bodily ego" (GT 163, n. 43). But then, in a substitution crucially significant to her conceptualization of the body as the psychic projection of a surface, Butler replaces the referent "it" in the subsequent part of the cited sentence, *which in Freud clearly refers back to the ego as bodily ego* ("The ego is first and foremost a bodily ego; it . . .), with the word (square bracketed, demoted—in my citation of Butler's note—to parenthetical) "body." Butler's recitation of the passage reads: "Freud continues the above sentence: '(*the body*) is not merely a surface entity, but is itself the projection of a surface'" (*GT* 163 n. 43; my emphasis). Butler's reading of Freud's assertion thus figures the body as interchangeable with the ego. That is, the body appears not only as a surface entity but as itself *the psychic projection of a surface*. Yet that it is precisely Freud's concern at this point in his essay to articulate the bodily origins of the ego, the conception of the ego as product of the body not the body as product of the ego, is underscored by the explanatory footnote added by his editor James Strachey that appeared first in the 1927 English translation of this text immediately following the above passage—a note authorized by Freud. The note reads: "I.e. the ego is ultimately derived from bodily sensations, chiefly from those springing from the surface of the body. It may thus be regarded as a mental projection of the surface of the body." Butler's reading therefore inverts the note's representation of the body as productive of the psyche ("the ego is derived from bodily sensations") and, through that square-bracketed substitution, conversely images the body as a psychic effect. The body itself becomes commensurable with the psychic projection of the body. Whereas Freud's original assertion maintains a distinction between the body's real surface and the body image as a mental projection of this surface (a distinction between corporeal referent and psychic signified), Butler's recitation collapses bodily surface into the psychic projection of the body, conflates corporeal materiality with imaginary projection. In so doing, it lets slip any notion of the body as a discernible referential category.

Her later use in *Bodies That Matter* of this same passage in *The Ego and the Id* repeats and indeed heightens this reading, even though she here (again in a footnote) addresses directly that 1927 footnote—and even though she here reads it directly as Freud's: "Although Freud is offering an account of the development of the ego, and claiming that the ego is derived from the projected surface of the body, he is inadvertently establishing the conditions for the articulation of the body as morphology" (*BTM* 258, n. 4). The modifying subordination in her syntax ("although") to which her summary of the manifest meaning of the note is confined makes clear that she recognizes that what she desires the note to articulate is not deliberate but "inadvertent." Yet in spite of this recognition, Butler continues to read against the manifest sense of the note—the description of the ego as derived from the body—in order to emphasize the antithesis: the body as morphology. This notion of body as morphology derives from a Lacanian conceptualization of the body as illusory psychic projection. Indeed, her citation of Freud appears here in her chapter on imaginary morphology, "The Lesbian Phallus and the Morphological Imaginary," where Freud's concept of the ego as a bodily ego is said to "prefigure" Lacan's mirror stage in which the body is an "idealization or 'fiction' " (*BTM* 73). But Freud's configuration of the relations between psyche and body is quite different from Lacan's. If in Lacan's mirror stage the body is the ego's misconception, in Freud's *The Ego and the Id* the body is the site of the ego's conception.

Butler's inversion of Freud's formulation of the relations between psyche and body in *Gender Trouble* may also be influenced by Roy Schafer's reading of Freud's bodily ego to illustrate the illusory status of the distinctions the subject makes (and the language of psychoanalysis sustains) between what is interior and what is exterior to the body. Butler enlists Schafer's critique of internalization (in addition to Abraham and Torok's analyses) to argue that incorporation is a fantasy. Schafer proposes that, in its language of internalization, psychoanalysis literalizes the always-imaginary projections on the part of the subject between what is inside and outside. For Schafer Freud's description of the bodily ego exemplifies the original way in which the subject deludes itself into believing in the facticity of corporeal interiority. The bodily ego constitutes a perception or rather a construction of the body espoused (falsely) by the subject, not a product of the body at all but rather a misreading of it; for via the bodily ego the subject assumes wrongly that the self can be conceived as occupying a body, a materiality in space. My contention is that it is precisely this point that the 1927 footnote approved by Freud seeks to emphasize. Freud's bodily ego is designed not to dematerialize the body into phantasmatic effect but to materialize the psyche, to argue its corporeal dependence.

In her critique of the queering of gender Martin has remarked on the tendency in queer studies for "surfaces [to] take priority over interiors and depths and even rule conventional approaches to them [i.e., interiors and depths] as inevitably disciplinary and constraining." Butler's conceptualization of sex as a heterosexual melancholic fantasy of literalization, of sex as the phantasmatic encrypting of gender in the body, implicitly designates corporeal interiority as "disciplinary and constraining" and, conversely, privileges surface as that which breaks up interiority and reveals its status as fantasy. This prioritization of surface is emphatically occularcentric, as is *Gender Trouble*'s concomitant investment in the transgendered subject of the power to reveal sex as "gender all along" (i.e., interiority as incorporated fantasy). *Gender Trouble*'s theoretical economy of gender relies heavily on a notion of the body as that which can be seen, the body as visual surface. This is possibly most marked in its deployment of the transgendered subject to illustrate gender performativity: girls who *look like* boys and boys who *look like* girls. In this sense then, in its dependence on the visible, on body-as-surface, the theory of gender performativity does in fact work out of a definitively theatrical arena. Any claim to a sense of sexed interiority, any *feeling* of being sexed or gendered (whether "differently" or not), along with other ontological claims, is designated phantasmatic, symptomatic of heterosexual melancholia. Yet, to return to that passage in *The Ego and the Id*, Freud underlines that the bodily ego derives not so much from the perception of the body (an "external perception"), that is, from what can be seen, but from the *bodily sensations* that stem from its touching—touching here in both an active and passive sense—(an "internal perception"): "[A person's body] is *seen* like any other object, but to the *touch*, it yields two kinds of sensations, one of which may be equivalent to an internal perception."

The transsexual doesn't necessarily *look* differently gendered but by definition *feels* differently gendered from her or his birth-assigned sex. In both its medical and its autobiographical versions, the transsexual narrative depends upon an initial crediting of this feeling as generative ground. It demands some recognition of the category of corporeal interiority (internal bodily sensations) and of its distinctiveness from that which can be seen (external surface): the difference between gender identity and sex that serves as the logic of transsexuality. This distinction is tactically, ingeniously, and rigorously refused by *Gender Trouble*; it is this refusal that allows for a refiguration of sex into gender. In its one mention of transsexuality *Gender Trouble* uses transsexuality to exemplify not the constitutive significance of somatic feeling but the reverse, the phantasmatic status of sex: the notion that pleasure exceeds material body parts. The transsexual's often declared capacity to experience his or her body as differently sexed from its materiality certainly supports Freud's notion of a bodily ego. But, because the subject often speaks of the imaginary body as more real or more sensible, I argue that this phenomenon illustrates the materiality of the bodily ego rather than the phantasmatic status of the sexed body: the material reality of the imaginary and not, as Butler would have it, the imaginariness of material reality. That the transsexual's trajectory centers on reconfiguring the body reveals that it is the ability to feel the bodily ego in conjunction and conformity with the material body parts that matters in a transsexual context; and that sex is perceived as something that must be changed underlines its very un-phantasmatic status.

Butler's deliteralization of sex, her displacement of sex from material interiority into fantasized surface, is enabled by the production of a binary between queer and heterosexual. The second important ramification for a theory of transsexual embodiment following the refiguring of the body as visual surface, is the alignment once again of transgender with queer. Heterosexuality is engendered via the literalizing strategies of melancholia, strategies that queer through its transgendered performativity brings into relief. Heterosexuality operates by attempting to literalize sex *in* the body; queer transgender reveals this depth as surface. It is not that heterosexuality is natural and queer denaturalizing; rather, heterosexuality is naturaliz*ing*, concealing the masquerade of the natural that queer makes manifest. Even so, heterosexuality and queer are represented as, respectively, restrictive interiority and playful surface. If gay and lesbian cultures are said to be *characterized* by camp, parodic subversive—that is, transgendered—performances that deliteralize the apparently real of sex, heterosexuality is said to be *characterized* by a literalizing of the apparently real: "The conflation of desire with the real . . . is precisely the kind of literalizing fantasy characteristic of the syndrome of melancholic heterosexuality" (*GT* 71). This attribution of character effects a certain hypostatization of queer and heterosexual, simultaneously impacting queer more thoroughly with transgender. In effect Butler subjects heterosexuality to a certain degree of grounding in order to read queer *through* transgender as refiguring this ground. In operation is a generic antithesis, the queer performative coinciding with the comedic staging of the impossibility of identity, heterosexual literalization with the melancholic attempt to sustain it as absolute ground. As Butler herself implicitly acknowledges when she considers how transgendered subjects also reliteralize the gender norms in her essay on *Paris is Burning*, this pivotal antithesis of *Gender Trouble* is too neat. If in *Gender Trouble* the transsexual is not distinguished from the queer transgendered subject, in *Bodies That Matter* the transsexual is specifically elected as the subject who most succinctly illustrates the limitations of the queerness of transgender. It is to this delimiting and the transsexual that I now turn.

VENUS IS BURNING: THE TRANSUBSTANTIATION OF THE TRANSSEXUAL

> I don't feel that there's anything mannish about me except what I might have between me down there. I guess that's why I want my sex change, to make myself complete.
>
> —Venus Xtravaganza, *Paris is Burning*

Because it was released in 1990, hot on the heels of the publication of *Gender Trouble*, Jennie Livingston's film *Paris is Burning* often got taken up in discussions of queer identities in conjunction with Butler's book, as if the subjects of the drag ball—again, the lure of the visual example in transgendered contexts—illustrated Butler's theory of gender performativity. Both texts in their transgendered themes captured what seemed definitive of the queer moment. For this reason they were subject to a certain yoking together in feminist/queer studies—in our readings, course syllabi, conferences, and so on. Butler's chapter in *Bodies That Matter* on the ambivalent effects of transgender in *Paris is Burning*, "Gender is Burning: Questions of Appropriation and Subversion" (*BTM* 121–142), serves by association therefore as a return to the subject of transgender in *Gender Trouble* to mark out *its* ambivalent effects. In this sense "Gender is Burning" functions to complicate those binary syllogisms of *Gender Trouble*. The essay's thesis is that crossing identifications in the film both denaturalize and renaturalize identity norms: "*Paris is Burning* documents neither an efficacious insurrection nor a painful resubordination, but an unstable coexistence of both" (*BTM* 137).

While Butler uses *Paris is Burning* in general to document the ambivalent significance of performative crossings, she uses Venus Xtravaganza as the specific lever to articulate this ambivalence: "Venus, and *Paris is Burning* more generally, calls into question whether parodying the dominant norms is enough to displace them; indeed, whether the denaturalization of gender cannot be the very vehicle for a reconsolidation of hegemonic norms" (*BTM* 125). For Butler it is the particular configuration of Venus's body, gender presentation, desires, and fate that best exemplifies how transgressive crossings can simultaneously reinscribe symbolic norms. The film's representation of this Latina transsexual delimits the subversive possibilities of parodic repetitions. Yet although its argument about ambivalence pivots on the specific material ambivalence of the transsexual body, Butler's essay encodes transsexuality as metaphor in a way that sublimates into theoretical allegory the specific materiality of Venus's sex and of her death as a light-skinned Latina transsexual.

The revelation of Venus's murder in the second part of *Paris is Burning* (filmed in 1989, two years after the first encounter with Venus) is indisputably the moment that most cuts through any sense of the performativity, the fictionality of identities the film provides elsewhere, particularly in the ball scenes. That Venus is killed for her transsexuality, for inhabiting a body which, as that of a preoperative male-to-female transsexual, is not coherently female, is strongly supported by the film's narrative. Angie Xtravaganza, the mother of Venus's house, to whom the film turns to provide an account of the occurrence, firmly fixes Venus's death in the context of a transsexual narrative: "That's part of life. That's part of being a transsexual in New York City." The implication is that Venus is murdered in her hotel bedroom on being "read" by her client, killed for having a body in excess of the femaleness he imagined he was paying for; killed, then, as a transsexual. Butler isolates Venus's death as the most prominent instance in the film in which the symbolic precludes its resignification: "This is a killing that is performed by the symbolic that would eradicate those phenomena that require an opening up of the possibilities for the resignification of sex" (*BTM* 131). Yet while Butler's isolation of this moment and this citation suggest that what matters (to the client, to the film, and to Butler the critic) is Venus's transsexuality and the particular configuration of her sexed body as a male-to-female, Butler's reading of Venus's killing situates Venus's body along a binary of queer man/woman of color, in the split between which Venus's Latina, passing-as-white, transsexual body falls.

Butler attributes Venus's death first to "homophobic violence," staking that it is Venus's "failure to pass completely [that renders her] clearly vulnerable" to this violence (*BTM* 129–130). By "failure to pass completely," Butler clearly intends Venus's penis; yet the presence of the penis on Venus's body renders neither her a homosexual man (a literalization of gender surely symptomatic of the heterosexual melancholia *Gender Trouble* critiqued) nor her death an effect of homophobia. Venus presents herself unambivalently as a transsexual woman, not as a gay man or drag queen. Although the only "genetic girl" is behind the camera, it does not follow that all the bodies in *Paris is Burning* are male. Rather, the film presents a spectrum of bodies and desires, heterosexual and homosexual, in-drag, transsexual, and genetic male, with the subjects frequently articulating the distinctions between these categories in a careful self-positioning. Stating that there's nothing "mannish" about her except what she has "down there," Venus describes looking forward to sex reassignment surgery to make her "complete": in other words, a complete woman. Her identification not as a gay man or a drag queen but as an incomplete (preoperative transsexual) woman highlights the impossibility of dividing up all identities along the binary homosexual/heterosexual. If it applies to Venus at all, her desire—to be a complete woman for a man—is heterosexual, and it is more this desire in combination with her transsex that kills her: not as a homosexual man, then, but as a transsexual woman whose desire is heterosexual—or, as *the failure to be* (an ontological failure) a biological woman.

It is therefore equally inadequate to read Venus's death as equivalent to that of a woman of color, as Butler does in the second instance: "If Venus wants to become a woman, and cannot overcome being a Latina, then Venus is treated by the symbolic in precisely the ways in which women of color are treated" (*BTM* 131). Without disputing that women (of color or white) can be treated identically to Venus, and while underlining that it is crucial that Venus's passing be acknowledged as double-leveled—a race and sex crossing—again, it is not for *being* a woman of color but for failing to be one that Venus is murdered; it is the crossing, the trans movement that provokes her erasure. Her death is indexical of an order that cannot contain crossings, a body in transition off the map of three binary axes—sex (male or female), sexuality (heterosexual or homosexual), and race (of color or white): a light-skinned Latina transsexual body under construction as heterosexual and female. At work in Venus's murder is not fear of the same or the other but fear of bodily crossing, of the movement in between sameness and difference: not homo- but transphobia, where "trans" here signifies the multileveled status of her crossing. This interstitial space is not foregrounded in Butler's reading of Venus's death.

If for Butler Venus's death represents the triumph of the symbolic, "Gender is Burning" discovers the symbolic asserting its norms through Venus even before this moment—in particular, in her expressed desires to become a "complete woman," to marry and attain financial security. The second two are of course crucially dependent on the first: a Latina transsexual's desires for sexed realness and domestic comfort. It is to set the realization of these desires in motion that Venus is turning tricks to earn enough for her lower surgery, sex work being a not uncommon, indeed often the only means by which poor/working-class male-to-females can afford to change sex. For Butler these desires reveal the extent to which Venus, even before her murder, is subject to "hegemonic constraint":

> Clearly, the denaturalization of sex, in its multiple senses, does not imply a liberation from hegemonic constraint: when Venus speaks of her desire to become a whole woman, to find a man and have a house in the suburbs with a washing machine, we may well question whether the denaturalization of gender and sexuality that she performs, and performs well, culminates in a reworking of the normative framework of heterosexuality. (*BTM* 133)

Venus's fantasy as a Latina transsexual of becoming "real" (both achieving coherent sexed embodiment and middle-class security) and her corporeal progress in realizing this fantasy mark her out from the drag ball performers who "do" realness and who "resist transsexuality" (*BTM* 136). Butler's presupposition is twofold here: first, that inherent to *doing* realness is an agency resistant to and transformative of hegemonic constraint that the desire to *be* real lacks; and following this, that the transsexual's crossing signifies a failure to be subversive and transgressive of hegemonic constraint where it *ought* to be. Hegemony constrains Venus through the "normative framework of heterosexuality." If resisting transsexuality produces a denaturalizing agency, it is because in Butler's scheme transsexuality is understood, by definition, to be constrained by heterosexuality. By extension, to fail to resist transsexuality fully (as Venus does in hoping for a sex change) is to reliteralize sex (to be rather than perform it) according to the workings of heterosexual melancholia. While Venus's murder symptomizes the triumph of the heterosexual matrix, in her desires Venus is duped by this same heterosexual ideology into believing that a vagina will make her a woman. The heterosexual matrix is therefore already asserting its hegemony in Venus's transsexuality even before her death.

From this scheme it might appear that the binary of heterosexual = literalizing/queer = performative is still in operation in *Bodies That Matter*, with transsexuality standing in for the first term. The transgendered subject, here exemplified in the transsexual, would accordingly appear simply to have been switched from one side of the binary to the other since *Gender Trouble*. Yet Butler's essay works not to reinforce but to demonstrate the ambivalence of this binary, to delimit (not negate) the queer performativity of transgender. It is the literal ambivalence of Venus's transsexual body that allows for this new theoretical ambivalence. Venus's death represents the triumph of hegemonic norms only as it simultaneously illustrates Venus denaturalizing these norms: it is a "killing performed by the symbolic that would eradicate those phenomena that require an opening up of the possibilities for the resignification of sex." Venus's body, with penis intact, is such a phenomenon that would resignify sex. Even in her death, because of her transsexual incoherence between penis and passing-as-a-woman, Venus holds out for Butler the promise of queer subversion, precisely as her transsexual trajectory is incomplete. In her desire to complete this trajectory (to acquire a vagina), however, Venus would cancel out this potential and succumb to the embrace of hegemonic naturalization. In other words, what awards Venus the status of potential resignifier of the symbolic in Butler's scheme is the fact that Venus doesn't get to complete her narrative trajectory and realize her desires, because she still has a penis at her death. What matters for Butler is the oscillation between the literality of Venus's body and the figurative marks of her gender. Conversely, Venus's desire to close down this tension (what I am calling her desire for sexed realness, for embodied sex) curtails her capacity to resignify the symbolic. That Butler figures Venus as subversive for the same reason that Butler claims she is killed, and considers indicative of hegemonic constraint the desires that, if realized might have kept Venus at least from this instance of violence, is not only strikingly ironic, it verges on critical perversity. Butler's essay locates transgressive value in that which makes the subject's real life most unsafe.

Butler's essay itself is structured on an ambivalence toward transsexuality in its relation to the literal, caught (twice over), both between reading transsexuality literally and metaphorically and between reading the transsexual as literalizing and deliteralizing. That Butler assigns Venus the function of ambivalence in her effect on the literal is encapsulated in the essay's reliance on the theme of transubstantiation, a term that is conjoined to transsexuality twice in the essay, that indeed stands in for transsexuality: first, in reference to Venus; and second, in reference to Jennie Livingston's camera. First, then, Butler writes that Venus's transsexual fantasy of realness is one of transubstantiation: "Now Venus, Venus Xtravaganza, she seeks a certain transubstantiation of gender in order to find an imaginary man who will designate a class and race privilege that to-female transsexual as model perfect, the photographic camera metaphorically phallicizes Livingston's body. For in representing the male-to-female transsexual as woman as object of desire, Livingston, Butler writes, "assumes the power of 'having the phallus.'" (*BTM* 135). The camera's feminization/eroticization of the male-to-female transsexual circulates the phallus from transsexual to lesbian, a circulation that amounts to a "transsexualization of lesbian desire": "What would it mean to say that Octavia is Jennie Livingston's kind of girl? Is the category or, indeed, 'the position' of white lesbian disrupted by such a claim? If this is the production of the black transsexual for the exoticizing white gaze, is it not also the transsexualization of lesbian desire?" (*BTM* 135). Livingston's desire for the transsexual is apparently also her identification with the transsexual; or rather the moment enacts an exchange of identities, with the "real girl" acquiring a phallus (becoming transsexualized) as she represents the transsexual as a "real girl." Extending her metaphorization of transsexuality, Butler designates the camera (photographic symbolizing cinematic) the tool of this (s)exchange, the "surgical instrument and operation through which the transubstantiation occurs" that produces Octavia as woman, which "transplants" the phallus from Octavia's body to Livingston's lesbian body.

Transsexuality and transubstantiation are thus brought together for a second time in Butler's essay, now in a metaphorical context. As in Butler's discussion of Venus's fantasy, transsexuality is again implicitly defined as, rendered equivalent to, transubstantiation. How is the double dynamic of literalization and deliteralization played out in this second moment of transsexualization as transubstantiation? I suggest that Butler's reading here again depends on the literal sexed ambivalence of the preoperative male-to-female transsexual body (the woman with a penis). Yet Butler's metaphor of transsexualization, its application to the lesbian body—and the refiguring of surgery into the camera's look—in effect displaces the materiality of transsexuality, and thus the materiality of sex, to the level of figurative. First, in figuring the phallus as circulated from Octavia to Livingston, the metaphor of transsexualization pivots on, and actually originates in, Octavia's penis. We know that Octavia, like Venus, is indeed preoperative for likewise in her narrative Octavia speaks of looking forward to the surgery that will make her a "complete" woman. However, as in its process of circulation in Butler's essay this penis becomes the phallus (Livingston's camera is said to accord her the phallus, not the penis), this penis is clearly subject in its translation to Lacanian sublimation itself. Butler's metaphor of transsexualization depends upon this crucial substitution of fleshly part with symbolic signifier, a confusion between phallus and penis that certainly does not take place in the film. For while Octavia (like Venus) may yet have a penis, in no way can she be said to "have the phallus": that is, in no way is she accorded or does she assume the position of delegate of the symbolic order. Conversely, while (presumably) Livingston has no penis, her capacity to represent Octavia, Venus, and the rest of the cinematic subjects as embodied others via her authority as disembodied overseer, as hooks's essay argues so convincingly, situates her precisely in this position of the symbolic's delegate—the one who appears to have the phallus. In the context of this film by a white lesbian about black and Latino/a gay men, drag queens, and transsexuals, the penis and phallus might be said to remain not only discrete but oppositional. Worlds apart from her subjects in her whiteness, her middle-classness, her educated-ness, and her "real" femaleness, Livingston's position behind the camera is that of an authority with absolute powers of representation.

Moreover, Livingston appears to wield this phallic power most heavily in her representation of the transsexuals, Octavia and Venus, in particular in her representation of their fantasies. The section in the film in which Octavia and Venus are cataloguing their desiderata stands as the most explicitly edited and authored moments in the film. Their sentences, most of which begin "I want," are rapidly intercut with each other's and their visual images likewise interwoven. The technique suggests an identity of their fantasies—not only that there is a generic transsexual fantasy but that the transsexual might be conceived according to what she *lacks*; "I want" reveals all that the subject lacks. At the same time, in its location of these scenes, the cinematic apparatus occults its own framing/authoring function. Both Octavia and Venus are filmed reclining on beds in bedrooms (the viewer is led to believe the subjects' own); Octavia is even dressed for bed. The setting allows the audience to assume an intimacy with the subjects, to forget the extent to which these moments are mediated through Livingston's white female gaze—exactly the dynamic of occultation that provides fodder for hooks's critique. Elsewhere in the film it becomes evident how Livingston's camera mediates what of their lives the subjects reveal. Before her death, for instance, Venus informs Livingston that she no longer works the streets, a claim that her death, of course, proves drastically untrue. (The question of whether Venus would have continued to work the streets to save for her surgery, *of whether Venus would have been killed, had Livingston contracted her* along with the film's subjects as actors is ultimately unanswerable, though the fatal ending of Venus's narrative demands its asking.) To summarize, then: in having the power to represent the other and conceal this power, Livingston not only "has the phallus," this having enables her to represent the transsexual other—Octavia and Venus—as crucially lacking: not so much in spite of, as because of their penises. Along with race and class, the crucial structuring difference between Livingston on the one hand and Venus and Octavia on the other is sexed coherence or biological real-ness: the difference between the nontransgendered and the embodied transgendered subject.

If phallus and penis are antithetical in *Paris is Burning*, Livingston's "phallicization" in no way reveals her embodiment—even allegorically—as Butler claims. The difference between reality and the allegorical, between the fleshy intractability of the penis and the transcendence of the phallus could not be more marked. As her position behind it renders her unrepresented, only a disembodied voice popping questions, the camera is precisely Livingston's means to disembodiment not to her embodiment. Thus hooks's critique of the filmmaker's bodily erasure still holds. Indeed, Butler's al-legorization of Livingston's body in the very vehicle for her disembodiment only places further out of reach the filmmaker's literal corporeality, the notion that Livingston has a "body that matters." And although rendering the camera a lesbian phallus might well disrupt Livingston's identity as a lesbian, it does nothing to disrupt its transcendent whiteness: the reason why hooks has problems with its overseeing position in the first place. Indeed, Butler's wish to curtail hooks's critique of Livingston's disembodiment seems queerly motivated (in both senses)—that is, until she reveals an identification with Livingston: both "white Jewish lesbian[s] from Yale" (*BTM* 133). This moment—exceptionally autobiographical for Butler—suggests that perhaps something quite personal is at stake in Butler's discovering an exception to the disembodied gaze of the auteur representing transgendered subjects. For Butler as much as for Livingston the personal investment in this representation of transgendered subjects may well be there; but the point is that in neither is it ever shown and in both this elision of whatever autobiographical stakes there are exacts the cost of objectification and derealization on the represented subjects.

Most significantly, the essay's metaphorical shifting of transsexuality from Venus's body to Livingston's camera displaces transsexuality to a realm that has nothing to do with the materiality of the body. In the context of a discussion of a film during the making of which one of the protagonists is killed for her transsexuality, for the literal configuration of her sexed body, this sublimation of transsexuality appears more prominent and, in my experience anyway, proves the most disturbing moment in Butler's oeuvre. The critic's metaphorization of the transsexual body transcends the literality of transsexuality in precisely a way in which Venus cannot—Venus who is killed for her literal embodiment of sexual difference. Even in the film we might notice that the literality of Venus's transsexual body and the facticity of her death are already subject to a glossing over. As hooks points out, the film glides over the reality of Venus's death, the moment is rapidly overridden by the spectacle of the ball, and, now that she can no longer function in the service of this spectacle, Venus is abandoned. Indeed, it might be said that not only does the filmic narrative fail to mourn Venus, it markedly includes no scenes of others' bereavement over Venus. We simply have Angie Xtravaganza's terse account of what happened to Venus overlaying footage of Venus filmed on the Christopher Street piers while she was still alive, this montage itself threatening to deny the reality, the finality of Venus's death. In metaphorizing transsexuality, Butler inadvertently repeats something of this deliteralization of the subject, her body, and her death. The substance of the transsexual body is sublimated in the move from the literal to the figurative. In the critical failure to "mourn" her death, Venus's body (surely the lost object of *Paris is Burning*), the most prominent representation we have in this film of the pain and anguish of embodying the experience of being differently sexed, is encrypted in Livingston's camera. And what is not kept in view in the film or the theory on it is the intractable materiality of that body in its present state and its peculiar sex.

QUEER FEMINISM AND CRITICAL IMPROPRIETY: TRANSGENDER AS TRANSITIONAL OBJECT?

> The institution of the "proper object" takes place, as usual, through a mundane sort of violence.
>
> —Judith Butler, "Against Proper Objects"

In her work since *Bodies that Matter* Butler demonstrates how the founding of lesbian and gay studies as a methodology distinct from feminism has involved a privileging of subjects and categories to the exclusion of others. Her essay in the "More Gender Trouble" issue of *differences* edited by her in 1994, "Against Proper Objects," critiques the way in which lesbian and gay studies has arrogated sexuality as its "proper object" of study, defining itself through and against feminism by assigning gender as feminism's object of study. What comes to appear quite critically improper in Butler's essay is this very investment in theoretical property: both the assurance with which that attribution of the object to the other is made (in effect a restriction of the other to the object) and the claims staked in the name of this attribution and restriction—namely, lesbian and gay studies' claims to "include and supersede" feminism.

Butler's essay implies that it might never be possible to claim methodological distinctness without bringing into play a degree of aggression, that every theory that grounds itself by allocating "proper objects" will be prone to this kind of critical impropriety. Undoubtedly, my attempts to wrest the transsexual from the queer inscription of transgender—and here, my criticisms of Butler's writing on Venus—are not free of aggression. From the point of view of this project, what subtends the difference in such readings is quite primal (theoretical, political, and admittedly personal): concerns about territory, belonging, creating homes; indeed, the extent to which identity is formed through our investment in external "objects"—a fundamental tenet of psychoanalysis, that definition depends on defining and "owning" objects. The question is perhaps quite simple: Where (best) does the trans-sexual belong? In seeking to carve out a space for transgender/transsexual studies distinct from queer studies, inevitably terrain must be mapped out and borders drawn up (a fact that doesn't render them uncrossable). Representations, subjects, and bodies (such as Venus) serve as the all-important flags that mark the territory claimed. It is additionally inevitable that the establishment of methodological grounds involves the attempt early on to circumscribe neighboring methodologies and approaches, the emphasizing of what *they* do *not* as opposed to what *we do*.

Significantly, "Against Proper Objects" conjures transsexuality in order to complicate articulations of methodological difference (although Butler's language of "domestication" suggests not my frontier-scale struggles but tiffs in the kitchen). Butler presents transsexuality as a category that, because of its "important dissonance" with homosexuality (tantalizingly, but importantly for my readings which follow, she doesn't say what this is), falls outside the domain of lesbian and gay studies ("APO" 11). Insofar as lesbian and gay studies delimits its proper object to sexuality and "refuses the domain of gender, it disqualifies itself from the analysis of transgendered sexuality altogether" ("APO" 11). Trans-sexuality and transgender are invoked as illustrations of the exclusions that lesbian and gay studies has performed in fixing its proper object as sexuality. Transsexuality and transgender number among the categories of "sexual minorities" Butler rightly understands Gayle Rubin insisting in 1984 made necessary a "radical theory of the politics of sexuality." These categories, Butler believes, get sidelined, ironically in lesbian and gay studies' appropriation of Rubin's essay as a foundational text. As I outlined at the beginning of this chapter, my sense of the role of transgender in lesbian and gay studies is quite different: that is, the figure of transgender has, rather, proven crucial to the installation of lesbian and gay studies—its installation *as* queer. Even work purporting to focus exclusively on sexuality and not gender—I suggested Sedgwick's in particular—implicitly engages this transgendered figure and, correlatively, the axis of gender. (In her other mention of transgender and transsexuality Butler writes of Sedgwick's antihomophobic critique that "[b]y separating the notion of gender from sexual-ity, [it] narrows the notion of sexual minorities offered by Rubin, distancing queer studies from the consideration of transgendered persons, transgendered sexualities, transvestism, cross-dressing, and cross-gendered definition" ["APO" 24, n. 8]). Although it strongly suggests that "an analysis of sexual relations apart from an analysis of gender relations is [not] possible," Butler's essay does not address how lesbian and gay studies might *already* be engaged in gender analyses, if largely unconsciously ("APO" 9). Indeed, toward the end of Butler's interview of Gayle Rubin in the same "More Gender Trouble" issue of *differences*, Rubin provocatively hints that Butler's critique of lesbian and gay studies' exclusion of gender might amount to a tilting at windmills:

> As for this great methodological divide you are talking about, between feminism and gay/lesbian studies, I do not think I would accept that distribution of interests, activities, objects and methods....I cannot imagine a gay and lesbian studies that is not interested in gender as well as sexuality....I am not persuaded that there is widespread acceptance of this division of intellectual labor between feminism, on the one hand, and gay and lesbian studies on the other.

That s/he has received considerably less critical attention than the cross-dresser or drag artist(e), that s/he has not been subject to the same deliberate and concentrated queer recuperation, and indeed, as is demonstrated in Butler's own work on Venus, that s/he is more likely to be deployed to signal the *unqueer* possibilities of cross-gender identifications, suggests that, above all transgendered subjects, the transsexual is more of the limit case for queer studies: the object that exceeds its purview. Yet my sense is that the reasons for transsexuality's exceeding queer lie not so much in queer's refusal of the category of gender (and thus transgender), as Butler argues, as in queer's poststructuralist problems with literality and referentiality that the category of transsexuality makes manifest—particular in relation to the sexed body. Butler's metaphorical displacement of the literality of Venus's sex can serve to exemplify just this.

Indeed, according to Butler, it must remain "an open question whether 'queer' can achieve these same goals of inclusiveness" imagined by Rubin's radical theory of sexual politics, whether queer studies can incorporate all of the "sexual minorities" among which transgender and transsexuality might be categorized ("APO" 11). For Butler the concern is queer's *capacity* to include, a question about queer's elasticity, about how far the term "queer" will stretch. What is not a concern is whether queer *should* even attempt to expand; expansion, inclusion, incorporation are automatically invested with value. One wonders to what extent this queer inclusiveness of transgender and transsexuality is an inclusiveness *for* queer rather than for the trans subject: the mechanism by which queer can sustain its very queerness—prolong the queerness of the moment—by periodically adding subjects who appear ever queerer precisely by virtue of their marginality in relation to queer. For does not this strategy of inclusiveness ensure the conferral on queer of the very open-endedness, the mobility, and—in the language of "Against Proper Objects"—the very means by which to "rift" methodological "grounds" that queer has come to symbolize? If, as Butler writes, "normalizing the queer would be, after all, its sad finish," the project of expansion enables queer to resist this normalization (what Butler fears will be "the institutional domestication of queer thinking") that would herald its end ("APO" 21). Yet if we conceive of "finish" and "end" here not as a limitation in time but a limitation in institutional space, this limited reach is inevitable and arguably necessary for the beginnings of other methodologies, for reading other narratives from other perspectives.

What Butler does not consider is to what extent—and on what occasions—transgendered and transsexual subjects and methodologies might not wish for inclusion under the queer banner. "Against Proper Objects" assesses inclusion and the resistance to inclusion solely from the perspective of queer; it does not imagine possible resistance stemming from the putatively excluded "sexual minorities." Our discussions should address not only—or perhaps not primarily—queer's elasticity but also what is gained and lost for nonlesbian and gay subjects and methodologies in joining the queer corporation. In the case of transsexuality there are substantive features that its trajectory often seeks out that queer has made its purpose to renounce: that is, not only reconciliation between sexed materiality and gendered identification but also assimilation, belonging in the body and in the world—precisely the kinds of "home" that Butler's essay holds at bay in its critical trooping of "domestication." There is much about transsexuality that must remain irreconcilable to queer: the specificity of transsexual experience; the importance of the flesh to self; the difference between sex and gender identity; the desire to pass as "real-ly gendered" in the world without trouble; perhaps above all, as I explore in my next chapter, a particular experience of the body that can't simply transcend (or transubstantiate) the literal.

Since *Gender Trouble*, "domestication" has figured as something of a specter in Butler's work. Domestication appears to represent the assigning of subjects and methodologies to specific categorical homes, the notion that there is an institutional place to which they belong. For the Butler of 1990 what was at stake was the domestication of gender, and concomitantly the domestication of feminism through gender's domestication beyond sexuality. *Gender Trouble* sought "to facilitate a political convergence of feminism, gay and lesbian perspectives on gender, and poststructuralist theory" to produce a "complexity of gender[,]...an interdisciplinary and postdisciplinary set of discourses in order to resist the *domestication* of gender studies or women['s] studies within the academy and to radicalize the notion of feminist critique" (*GT* xiii; my emphasis). As a means of resisting gender/

women's studies' domestication, *Gender Trouble* marshaled lesbian and gay sexuality and, as I have suggested, lesbian and gay genders, in effect troubling or queering gender. In analyzing the way in which the sex/gender system is constructed through the naturalization of heterosexuality and vice versa, *Gender Trouble* performed its work in an interstitial space between feminism and lesbian and gay studies, producing a new methodological genre—hence my term for this: queer feminism. In this sense *Gender Trouble* constituted an attempt to queer feminism. Yet although Butler's work might be said to have always conceived of domestication—what we might term object-constancy to push further on the psychoanalytic metaphor—as restrictive, it is interesting to note that in 1994 it is no longer *feminist* but *queer* studies that she perceives to be under threat of domestication: the shift indexes the change in values of the currencies of these methodologies, the ways in which queer and gender studies have "circumscribed" feminism. In "Against Proper Objects" it is (trans)gender that returns as the supplement to trouble the domestication of (homo)sexuality, gender that "troubles" queer. This shift in Butler's theoretical "object-cathexis" is a sure a sign of queer's institutionalization (Oedipalization? with feminism as [M]Other?) if ever there was one.

To resist queer's incorporation of trans identities and trans studies is not to refuse the value of institutional alliances and coalitions (in the form of shared conferences, journals, courses, and so on). But an alliance, unlike a corporation, suggests a provisional or strategic union between parties whose different interests ought not to be—indeed, cannot totally be—merged, sublimated for cohering—or queering—the whole. In closing, it needs emphasizing that it is precisely queer's investment in the figure of transgender in its own institutionalization—and above all the methodological and categorical crossings of Butler's queer feminism—that have made it possible to begin articulating the transsexual as a theoretical subject. It can be said that, in its very origins and its early attempts at self-definition, transgender studies is allied with queer.

21

Are Lesbians Women?

JACOB HALE

IN THIS ARTICLE, PHILOSOPHER C. JACOB HALE works at the intersection of feminist theory, queer theory, and transgender theory to evaluate Monique Wittig's famous claim that lesbians are not women. Hale acknowledges that Wittig's position resonates with that of many lesbians who have resisted heteronormative pressures to become conventionally feminine, but he critiques Wittig's understanding of linguistic paradigms, and her seeming acceptance of "woman" as a category that is entirely subsumed within an oppressive heterosexuality. He argues that Wittig's claim is undermined further by her failure to analyze adequately the complexities involved in the process of gendering, and in the composition of sex/gender categories.

Hale contends that "woman," as that concept is currently understood in the contemporary United States, is an internally incoherent amalgam of at least thirteen analytically distinct defining characteristics, none of which is necessary or sufficient in itself to guarantee the status "woman." He exposes the inadequacy of current language for expressing the lived complexity of gender, and demonstrates that the category "woman" is neither immutable nor natural. Rather, it is something that has to be worked out time after time, case by case, through an incessant series of negotiations, through repeated acts of meaning-making.

Hale's article is one of the most closely-argued studies of just how "fuzzy" gender categories are in the contemporary United States—in spite of, or perhaps because of, their presumed "naturalness." In spite of finding fault with Wittig, he ultimately praises her work for opening up a conceptual space in which it becomes possible to imagine that some individual human beings have escaped from the naturalized binary of sexual dimorphism.

"Lesbians are not women" was the sentence with which Monique Wittig ended "The Straight Mind" at the Modern Language Association's annual conference in 1978. A moment of stunned silence followed (Turcotte 1992, viii). Eighteen years later, this claim often is first greeted with surprise, confusion, nervous giggles, disbelief, dismissal, disdain, or "the incredulous stare" (as we call it within analytic philosophy). Namascar Shaktini initially called Wittig's view "eccentric" in her 1994 *Hypatia* review of *The Straight Mind and Other Essays* (Shaktini 1994, 212).

However, I have encountered positive reactions to Wittig's claim, primarily from nonacademic dykes. Several reactions were: "Cool," "Obviously," and "Well, *I'm* not, bud, but what about lipstick lesbians?" Increasingly, one finds acceptance of Wittig's conclusion in academic writing. For example, Diane Griffin Crowder (Crowder 1993, 66) and Cheshire Calhoun (Calhoun 1994, 566) have both recently endorsed Wittig's conclusion, although each offers arguments different from Wittig's in support of the claim that lesbians are not women.

It is no surprise that this claim excites such reactions. One reason for negative reactions is that it flies in the face of the dominant culture's definitions of the categories of both gender and sexuality, which do not differ relevantly from those used by lesbian and gay activists. Thus, one of my gay students initially responded by saying, "I would have thought that that [*woman*] was the one thing a lesbian *had* to be." Further, Wittig's claim is incendiary in feminist, lesbian, and gay contexts. Taken by itself, without attention to Wittig's underlying position, it threatens a number of feminist and lesbian feminist positions; the so-called sex wars have been identity wars, after all. When considered in the context of Wittig's underlying position, this claim is incendiary indeed, for it threatens to blow up the theoretical structure of any political work based on a notion of woman's identity or women's identities. Most important, it shakes the foundations of feminism itself or feminisms themselves. For if Wittig's underlying position is correct, there is no naturally constituted category of women, so there is no naturally constituted subject for feminism to represent, theoretically or politically. Further, if Wittig's underlying position is correct, the concept *woman* is coherent only within the conceptual context of the political regime of heterosexuality, a regime that oppresses those it classifies as women. This calls into question the desirability of feminist reliance on the concept *woman*, even if only as a concept to be redefined, revalued, or ultimately discarded as Wittig herself urges (Wittig 1979, 120–21; Wittig 1992, 14).[1] Despite the threats Wittig's view poses, it resonates with the dreams, hopes, longings, and visions of those lesbians who have resisted the heterosexualizing, feminizing, and womanizing pressures of the dominant culture and of some feminist subcultures as well.

Wittig gives her arguments for the claim that a lesbian is not a woman, but "something else, a not-woman, a not-man" (Wittig 1992, 13), primarily in "One Is Not Born a Woman." Wittig may have intended "lesbians are not women" as a political intervention at a specific cultural, historical, technological, and intellectual moment, as an exhortation to lesbians to refuse their categorization as women. The arguments she offers for this claim, however, make it appear that she is advancing a claim that she believes is already true, and she does not clearly distinguish between strategic refusal and truth-claim. Although taking "lesbians are not women" as a truth-claim may not be accurate Wittig exegesis, it is this construal that I examine in this essay. I believe this approach is fruitful because it illuminates the descriptive elements of the concept *woman* in our culture now, which in turn gives us a better basis for political strategizing, including strategically refusing categorization as women; bluntly: one needs to understand what one is up against to go up against it successfully, unless one is blessed with dumb luck.[2]

Before beginning my arguments I want to make explicit some of the assumptions in this essay. I remain firmly agnostic about sex/gender distinctions; nothing I say commits me to any particular sex/gender distinction, nor to its demise. I assume that there is nothing necessary, nor necessarily natural, about any culture's gender concepts. I accept that a particular culture's gender concepts may change over time, that different cultures may have different gender concepts, that within one culture there may be a number of different, competing gender concepts, and that these differences cannot be determined a priori. Such variation reflects differences in how gender intersects with subject positioning according to race, ethnicity, class, religion, sexuality, and regional location, as well as differences arising from the varying, sometimes competing interests of specialized institutions and fields of discourse. Despite this intracultural variation, we can identify a set of dominant cultural concepts of gender. Please understand "in this culture" as appended to every reference to a category of gender or sexuality throughout this essay; unless I specify otherwise, I am writing about the dominant culture of the United States now. Although my analyses may apply more widely, I am in no position to claim so.

Finally, I do not assume that it's better to be a woman than to be something else, nor do I assume the converse. Instead, I believe not only that gender should be consensual,[3] or at least more consensual than it is now if full gender consensuality is impossible, but also that if our goal is to further feminist and queer political aims, we would do well to have both the strategies of gender proliferation and feminist redefinition and revaluation of womanhood operating at the same time. Any prediction of success in this context is an empirical prediction about effects in an exceedingly complex, rapidly shifting social/cultural/economic/technological field, hence not a prediction about which a high degree of certainty is warranted. In addition, it is more likely that these two strategies, operating in tandem *and* in creative tension, embodied in a multiplicity of tactical ways, will succeed than that either one alone will.

"YOU'RE NOT A REAL WOMAN"

One argument Wittig gives for believing that lesbians are not women is based on the observation that lesbians are often accused of not being real women or of being "not real women"; heterosexuals mean this both as insult and as threat. Wittig uses the principle "to be one, one has to be a 'real' one" to derive the conclusion that lesbians are not women (Wittig 1992, 12).

Her mistake here is trivial. The word "real" is sometimes used in ways that conform to Wittig's principle. However, other functions of the word "real" may be at work in the accusation that lesbians are not real women. J. L. Austin pointed out that "real" sometimes functions as "a dimension word" that can be used to express commendation, for example, " 'Now this is a *real* carving-knife!' may be one way of saying that this is a good carving-knife" (Austin 1962, 73). Conversely, "not real" sometimes functions to express disapproval. Common examples include saying that decaffeinated coffee is "not real coffee," low-fat milk "not real milk," paper plates "not real plates," and so on. One more frequently hears the positive commendation expressed, for example: "I prefer eating from a *real* plate and, yes, *I'll* wash the dishes," "I think I need some *real* coffee before listening to *another* philosophy paper."

It is plausible to believe that this is the use of "not real" in the accusation that lesbians are not real women. On this reading, it does not imply that lesbians are not women; instead it implies that lesbians, while women, are not good women because they do not behave in relation to men in the ways that are valued positively for women. Similarly, a white European American middle-class woman who is not a good cook, doesn't care about keeping a clean house, or refuses to have sex with one particular man (even if she is having sex with other men) might, for any one of these reasons alone, be told that she is not a real woman without this implying that she is not a woman at all. Of course, "real" need not have the same meaning in every use of "not a real woman," so my argument leaves open the possibility that when non-lesbian women are told that they are not real women this is intended to imply that they are bad women, whereas being a lesbian is incompatible with being a woman at all. However, analyzing the accusation that lesbians are not real women hardly seems a promising way to answer or dissolve this question.[4]

WHAT IS IT TO BE A WOMAN?

The second of Wittig's arguments relies on her analysis of interconnections between the category of sex, heterosexuality as political regime, and the concepts *woman* and *man*. Here are three quotes in which Wittig argues for her view that lesbians are not women.

From "Paradigm":

> Insofar as the virtuality "woman" becomes reality for an individual only in relation to an individual of the opposing class—men—and particularly through marriage, lesbians, because they do not enter this category, are not "women." Besides, it is not as "women" that lesbians are oppressed, but rather in that they are not "women." (They are, of course, not "men" either.) And it is not "women" (victims of heterosexuality) that lesbians love and desire but lesbians (individuals who are not the females of men). (Wittig 1979, 121)

From the end of "The Straight Mind":

> Let us say that we break off the heterosexual contract. So, this is what lesbians say everywhere in this country and in some others, if not with theories at least through their social practice, whose repercussions upon straight culture and society are still unenvisionable. An anthropologist might say that we have to wait for fifty years. Yes, if one wants to universalize the functioning of these societies and make their invariants appear. Meanwhile the straight concepts are undermined. What is woman? Panic, general alarm for an active defense. Frankly, it is a problem that the lesbians do not have because of a change of perspective, and it would be incorrect to say that lesbians associate, make love, live with women, for "woman" has meaning only in heterosexual systems of thought and heterosexual economic systems. Lesbians are not women. (Wittig 1992, 32)

From the last paragraph of "One Is Not Born a Woman":

> To destroy "woman" does not mean that we aim, short of physical destruction, to destroy lesbianism simultaneously with the categories of sex, because lesbianism provides for the moment the only social form in which we can live freely. Lesbian is the only concept I know of which is beyond the categories of sex (woman and man), because the designated subject (lesbian) is *not* a woman, either economically, or politically, or ideologically. For what makes a woman is a specific social relation to a man, a relation that we have previously called servitude, a relation which implies personal and physical obligation as well as economic obligation ("forced residence," domestic corvée, conjugal duties, unlimited production of children, etc.), a relation which lesbians escape by refusing to become or to stay heterosexual. (Wittig 1992, 20)

Following Judith Butler to some extent, I propose the following reconstruction of Wittig's argument (Butler 1987, 136–37):

> (1) The category of sex presupposes a discourse in which sex is binary, *man* and *woman* are exhaustive, and *man* and *woman* are complementary opposites.
> So, (2) The category of sex is subsumed under the discourse of heterosexuality.
> So, (3) To be a woman means to be in a binary relation with a man.
> (4) No lesbian is in a binary relation with a man.
> So, (5) No lesbian is a woman.

I want to assume that premises (3) and (4) are true and ask: Under what interpretation of *binary relation with a man* are they true?[5] At first, it seems that the answer must be that one is in a binary relation with a man just in case one is in a sexual/affectional (though not necessarily monogamous) relationship with a man. Paradigmatically, this would be a heterosexual marriage (Wittig 1992, 6–7; Wittig 1979, 121).

There is nothing in Wittig to suggest that heterosexual marriage is the only relationship that counts as a binary relation between a man and a woman, nor would this restriction be plausible. Further, she has not said that a heterosexual marriage always counts as a binary relation between a man and a woman; this would not be plausible either. Imagine that the man who posted the following personal ad in *Deneuve* (a national lesbian glossy) finds what he's looking for:

> ATTENTION CALIFORNIA DYKES
> My GAM boyfriend needs a green card through marriage. If your girlfriend needs one too, this GWM can reciprocate. (*Deneuve* 1994)

Apparently, heterosexual marriage is a paradigm example of a binary relation between a woman and a man, but being married is neither necessary nor sufficient for being in such a relation. Even reading *binary relation with a man* as a fuzzy concept, a number of "problem cases" arise; I will not examine all of these apparent counterexamples.[6]

A number of my colleagues and students have asked if Wittig would say that Catholic nuns, simply in virtue of being nuns, are not women. Although in "One Is Not Born a Woman" Wittig writes, "Lesbian is the only concept I know of which is beyond the categories of sex (woman and man), because the designated subject (lesbian) is *not* a woman, either economically, or politically, or ideologically" (Wittig 1992, 20), in "The Category of Sex" she writes, "Some lesbians and nuns escape [the category of sex]" because they are not "seen [as] (and made) sexually available to men" (Wittig 1992, 7). This contradiction reflects an inadequate specificity in Wittig's work about the degree and types of participation in heterosexuality necessary for membership in the category *woman*.

While being a nun may be a way of resisting or escaping marriage, nuns are symbolically married to Jesus Christ. Some lesbians' gender self-presentations are indistinguishable from those of heterosexual women whose self-presentations, arguably, signal their sexual availability to men. Many lesbians and Catholic nuns participate in institutions that help maintain the political regime of heterosexuality. Sometimes they are highly subservient to individual men in these institutions, and must make themselves sexually available to individual men who have institutional power over them. Lesbians and nuns are not entirely free from male control of their reproductive labor, even if this is not controlled by an individual man in the same way it may be within a heterosexual marriage. A lesbian may be barred from adopting children or be denied custody or visiting rights to her children, simply because she is a lesbian (Calhoun 1994, 564–65). Nuns and lesbians are both vulnerable to male control of their reproductive labor if they are impregnated through rape.

A distinction between ideological components of the categories *lesbian* and *nun* and their (imperfect) instantiations might avoid these difficulties. Things get much worse for Wittig's view, however, once we attend to the lives and experiences of people who do not fit clearly into the binary distinction between heterosexuals, on the one hand, and gays and lesbians, on the other hand. Not only has Wittig overlooked bisexuals, her view has no way to categorize cases such as those suggested by the following personal ad from the Women's category in *Venus Infers*, a self-described "quarterly magazine for leatherdykes" (*Venus Infers* n.d., 2):

Looking for Daddy
This handsome fag boy needs a daddy: a strong, tough, loving daddy with a sharp knife and a big dick. Let me serve you, and let me show you what a pig I can be, with proper discipline. Experienced daddies only. Dykes, FTMs, and gay men in the Bay Area all welcome. My boy pussy awaits you. (*Venus Infers* n.d., 48)

Since the ad text begins, "This handsome fag boy. . . ," we may infer that this handsome fag boy is not open to all experienced dyke daddies in the Bay Area. In contemporary dyke usage, when "fag" is applied to dykes, it indicates features of the gendering of one's sexual partner, one's own gendered self-presentation, and one's preferred sexual practices. How must this boy's dyke daddy be gendered? High femme is clearly out, but exactly where this boy would draw the line between butch enough and too femme for dyke daddy material is unclear. Probably this handsome fag boy and any prospective dyke daddies who respond to the ad can work out all these gendered nuances between themselves, without any theoretical help from me.[7]

This ad presents three distinct ways in which a simple binary distinction between heterosexual and homosexual fails to account for real people's embodied experiences of sexual desire and practice. First, it points out the possibility of dyke-fag sex, without this sexual activity necessarily recategorizing either participant as heterosexual or bisexual (Califia 1994; Sadownick 1993, 25–26). Second, it points out that dyke sexuality may be gender-nuanced much more subtly than the simple categories of *homosexual* and *lesbian* can cover. Finally, since this ad lists FTM (female-to-male transsexual) daddies as a possibility, it points to the existence of people whose gender and sexuality may confound both the binary Wittig wishes to discard and that which she presupposes. Simple classification of sexual activity between this handsome fag boy and an FTM as heterosexual, gay, or lesbian fails. Categorizing any of this as *bisexual* misses the crucial cultural-situatedness of these practices; they are intelligible within sites of overlap between dyke, fag, leatherqueer, and trans communities.

Similarly, Judith Halberstam argues against a simple binary distinction between *heterosexual* and *homosexual*, in part by invoking a list of some of the many self-categorizations used within queer communities to specify sexual desire and practice. She writes:

> Some queer identities have appeared recently in lesbian zines and elsewhere: guys with pussies, dykes with dicks, queer butches, aggressive femmes, F2Ms, lesbians who like men, daddy boys, gender queens, drag kings, pomo afro homos, bulldaggers, women who fuck boys, women who fuck like boys, dyke mommies, transsexual lesbians, male lesbians. As the list suggests, gay/lesbian/straight simply cannot account for the range of sexual experience available. (Halberstam 1994, 212)[8]

Insofar as sexuality is related to gender, the most important point in the foregoing is that Wittig's analysis of the categories of sex obscures the specificities of the ways in which human beings are gendered through sexuality and the ways in which human beings gender themselves through sexuality, when it is precisely these specificities of gendering to which we must attend if we are to get clear about how gender works in our culture, about how gender works in other cultures, and, ultimately, about how the oppressions gender enables can be overcome.

The problem, then, for Wittig goes well beyond the point that the concepts *woman, man*, and *lesbian* are inherently vague. The problem is deeper: her analysis is too simplistic to handle the variety of ways in which people, including lesbians, are gendered. Since Wittig's view is that the concepts *man, woman,* and *lesbian* each rest on a single defining characteristic, her view does not have conceptual room for the multiplicity of genderings present even only among contemporary U.S. lesbians.

In the next two sections, I develop a view more complex than Wittig's of the dominant culture's concept of *woman*, while retaining what I consider to be the important contributions she has made to our understanding of the categories of sex.

THE "NATURAL ATTITUDE" TOWARD GENDER AND THE CONCEPT WOMAN

In this section, I develop some themes necessary to articulate my proposed reconstruction of our culture's concept *woman*. I begin by asking: What are the commonly held presuppositions that constitute our dominant cultural attitude about what gender is?

The landmark essay from which I draw to answer this question is Harold Garfinkel's "Passing and the Managed Achievement of Sexual Status in an 'Intersexed' Person, Part 1" (Garfinkel 1967), which was based on Garfinkel's 1958 case study of Agnes. "Agnes" is the pseudonym of a patient who presented at the Department of Psychiatry at the University of California at Los Angeles to obtain sex reassignment surgery. Agnes was generally recognized to be a boy until age 17. However, by the time she presented at age 19, she had achieved a convincing self-presentation as a woman. U.C.L.A. psychiatrists, including

Robert Stoller, were charged with determining whether or not Agnes was a suitable candidate for sex reassignment surgery. Garfinkel "used her case as an occasion to focus on the ways in which sexual identity is produced and managed as a 'seen but unnoticed', but nonetheless institutionalized, feature of ordinary social interactions and institutional workings" (Heritage 1984, 181). Agnes's gendering of herself diverged from some, but certainly not all, of the typical workings of gender as a social practice in our culture. Observing Agnes's range of similarities and differences from typical embodiments of gender allowed "Garfinkel to distance himself from the familiar phenomena of gender and to come to view them as 'anthropologically strange' " (Heritage 1984, 182), thus to "examine the strangeness of all gendered bodies, not only the transsexualized ones," borrowing Halberstam's phrasing from a different context (Halberstam 1994, 226). Garfinkel came to see "the institution of gender . . . as a densely woven fabric of morally accountable cultural practices which are throughout both accountable, and accountably treated, as natural" (Heritage 1984, 198). Garfinkel attempted to identify the primary threads of this fabric, the primary components of the natural attitude toward gender; I follow Kate Bornstein's reformulation of Garfinkel (Bornstein 1994, 46–50; Garfinkel 1967):

1. There are two, and only two, genders (female and male).
2. One's gender is invariant. (If you are female/male, you always were female/male and you always will be female/male.)
3. Genitals are the essential sign of gender. (A female is a person with a vagina; a male is a person with a penis.)
4. Any exceptions to two genders are not to be taken seriously. (They must be jokes, pathology, etc.)
5. There are no transfers from one gender to another except ceremonial ones (masquerades).
6. Everyone must be classified as a member of one gender or another. (There are no cases where gender is not attributed.)
7. The male/female dichotomy is a "natural" one. (Males and females exist independently of scientists' [or anyone else's] criteria for being male or female.)
8. Membership in one gender or another is "natural." (Being female or male is not dependent on anyone's deciding what you are.)

Garfinkel's reconstruction points out that there is not a *unique* concept of gender held even by the dominant members of our culture. He argues that those who hold the "natural attitude," dubbed "normals," are suspicious of some medical and scientific claims about gender. Since "normals" regard the gender binary as "a natural matter of fact," they find claims made by sciences such as zoology, biology, and psychiatry "strange," because "these sciences argue that decisions about sexuality are problematic matters" which require "a procedure for deciding sexuality" (Garfinkel 1967, 123–24). The general point here is that specialized discourses about gender do not agree entirely with the "natural attitude" toward gender, nor with one another. These specialized discourses include distinct medical discourses, other scientific discourses, psychotherapeutic discourses, and legal discourses (which vary state-by-state in the United States). Although all of these discourses share regulatory aims, they have somewhat distinct aims and often attempt to regulate differently. Hence, it should be expected that these discourses would differ to some extent in their claims about gender, especially since there is a wide variety of evidence which appears to contradict the "natural attitude." While "normals" who hold the "natural attitude" must continually adjust their attitude to claims about gender which appear to contradict their attitude, or ignore these claims, or explain or laugh or ridicule or beat them away, specialized discourses about gender are by no means immune from the influence of the "natural attitude" either. Rather, they are shaped by the desire to hold as much, or the most crucial elements, of the "natural attitude" in place, insofar as this is consistent with their specialized aims; indeed, their special-ized aims may, sometimes, take less precedence than upholding some aspect of the "natural attitude."

Often, the "natural attitude" can be maintained only by some rather desperate maneuvers in the face of apparently contradictory embodied lives. One of the most desperate of these many maneuvers used to maintain the "natural attitude" is the medical "treatment" and "management" of intersexed individuals. Individuals who are born with "ambiguous" genitals are assigned to a sex as soon as pos-sible, that assignment is rarely changed after a child is more than eighteen months old, and children are surgically and hormonally altered to match their assignments as fully as possible. Infants with tissue between their legs which does not appear to have the potential for developing into a phallus capable of penis-in-vagina intercourse are usually assigned, surgically as well as legally, to the category *female* (Holmes 1994, 11). Often children are not told that they have been surgically or hormonally altered, and sometimes children's guardians are also kept ignorant (Kessler [1990] 1994). Often chil-dren only learn that they are intersexed when further medical treatments are deemed necessary in response to problems emerging during puberty. Parents and children are left with a burden of pain and shame which keeps most of them silent (Chase 1994). This range of practices is not politically neutral; it functions to protect, insofar as possible, "normals" from having to face embodiments that would dislodge their solid status as "normals."

I'll turn now to examining a second theme in the dominant cultural attitude about gender. Marilyn Frye reminds us that women continually find themselves in "double bind" situations, as an effect of the nature of oppression:

> One of the most characteristic and ubiquitous features of the world as experienced by oppressed people is the double bind situations in which options are reduced to a very few and all of them expose one to penalty, censure or deprivation. For example, it is often a requirement upon oppressed people that we smile and be cheerful. If we comply, we signal our docility and our acquiescence in our situation. We need not, then, be taken note of. We acquiesce in being made invisible, in our occupying no space. We participate in our own erasure. On the other hand, anything but the sunniest countenance exposes us to being perceived as mean, bitter, angry or dangerous. This means, at the least, that we may be found "difficult" or unpleasant to work with, which is enough to cost one one's livelihood; at worst, being seen as mean, bitter, angry or dangerous has been known to result in rape, arrest, beating and murder. One can only choose to risk one's preferred form and rate of annihilation. (Frye 1983, 2–3)

We can, I believe, draw two morals about the concept *woman* from the pervasiveness of double bind situations in women's experiences. First, the concept *woman* is internally incoherent; this inco-herence arises from the following: a woman is devalued according to how different she is from the white non-transsexual male heterosexual middle-class able-bodied Christian norm, for this norm provides standards of evaluation of human worthiness, and a woman is also devalued according to how close she is to this norm, for it dictates that those people who should have the positively evalu-ated characteristics it upholds as standards are white non-transsexual heterosexual middle-class able-bodied Christian men.

Second, the concept *woman* is, at least in part, an essentially normative concept. My use of the word "essentially" here should not be understood as implying that the concept *woman* is a natural concept, for a thoroughly cultural construct, such as the game of baseball, can have essential char-acteristics: without a ball, it isn't a baseball game. The characteristic of *woman* which Wittig takes as uniquely definitional is essentially normative, and the double bind situations of which Frye reminds us arise partly because of prescriptive and proscriptive claims about how women should behave and be. Of course, the myth that Wittig is showing for what it is—mythical—tells us that the normative elements in the concept *woman* follow from purely physical descriptive "natural facts" about women considered as females; so one element of the myth is that the concept *woman* is, fundamentally and essentially, descriptive.

Since the concept *woman* functions prescriptively and proscriptively, we should expect it to include both positive and negative exemplars; hence, its defining characteristics should allow for the possibility of both. There is no one paradigm of womanhood; rather, at the very least we should expect one positively and one negatively evaluated paradigm. However, there is more than one culturally recognized way to "be a good woman." One is by participating in heterosexuality in the way Wittig vaguely describes and takes to be the crucial defining characteristic of *woman*. However, there are other ways to participate in heterosexuality, that is, to aid in its perpetuation, which certainly do not require and sometimes preclude sexual/affectional involvements with men. A few such roles are schoolteacher, librarian, nurse, and avowedly celibate, religious devotee.

Further, we find multiple candidates for contemporary negative paradigms in the dominant culture's representations of, for example, sex workers,[9] pregnant women whose behaviors could cause harm to their fetuses, "single welfare mothers," dominatrixes, women who cut off their abusive husbands' penises, mothers who kill their children, and, perhaps, lesbians.

Consider the Nola Darling character in Spike Lee's *She's Gotta Have It*. The representation of a heterosexual African American woman with the audacity to assume the masculine prerogative of having multiple heterosexual sex partners serves as a useful prop to heterosexist ideology by showing the negative consequences (rape, loneliness) to women whose sexual behaviors do not closely approximate one of the positively evaluated paradigms of *woman*. This oppressive purpose is best served if there are at least a few flesh-and-blood "bad girls" who are punished, who punish themselves, and who meet with bad ends in ways not obviously attributable to human agency. (Remember those old dime store lesbian pulp novels?)

The culturally recognized threat of falling out of the category entirely need not be enforced very often, if ever, to serve its function. The oppressive purposes of the negative exemplars are best served if at least some of these flesh-and-blood bad girls do not, by virtue of their transgressions from positively evaluated paradigms, fall out of the category *woman* entirely. For if all bad girls fall out of the concept entirely, then it would be harder for those whose behaviors and beings bad girls serve to limit—good girls—to see bad girls' bad futures as possible futures for themselves. This is because it is hard for many women, even those tempted to be bad, to imagine themselves outside the category *woman*, let alone outside the categories *woman* and *man*. Indeed, this imagining may be conceptually impossible for many members of our culture. If it is true that we attribute gender as universally as Garfinkel asserts, then we cannot imagine ourselves as wholly genderless. To attempt to imagine ourselves as such would be to attempt to imagine ourselves out of social existence. The remaining possibilities, then, would be imagining oneself as having some gender other than *man* or *woman* or imagining oneself on a borderline between the category in which one began life and some other category or the realm of the genderless. I will consider these alternatives in turn.

Given the pull of the "natural attitude" toward gender, it cannot be the case that many bad girls are, thereby, in some gender category or categories other than *man* or *woman*. This "natural attitude," according to which there are exactly two genders and one's gender is invariant and determined by one's genitals, would be severely undermined if many bad girls ceased being women simply by being bad. Maintaining the "natural attitude" requires that there are so few exceptions that they can be clearly demarcated from "the normals." Otherwise, exceptions could not be treated as pathological cases, as freaks, as jokes, or as some other kind of negatively evaluated aberration or abnormality; rampant anomaly would destroy the "natural attitude."

The second alternative is that being a bad girl automatically puts one on a borderline between the category *woman* and some other gender category or the realm of the genderless, the realm of social nonexistence. This is the alternative that is closest to Butler's notion of homosexual abjection. In *Bodies That Matter*, she argues from a Lacanian perspective that casting gays and lesbians into the realm of the abject—a realm on the border between the inside and the outside of our culture's categories of sex—functions to induce an association between homosexuality and psychosis in the straight mind, thus using the fear of psychosis to keep people straight (Butler 1993). The fear of abjection, of exile from the category *woman*, functions to ensure that many birth-assigned females will strive unceasingly to embody their membership in that category as fully as possible, although full membership may be embodied in different ways, and proper means of such embodiment differ and are contested. Yet the possibility that abjection occurs often runs afoul of the same problems as the first possibility: the "natural attitude" cannot survive if abjection is common.

A multiplicity of regulative strategies is necessary to keep people straight, to keep women from being bad girls,[10] and to keep people clearly within their gender categories. Perhaps having a very small number of birth-assigned females fall entirely out of the category *woman*, as well as a very small number who end up on a frontier between that category and some other category or none at all does serve regulatory functions. This works best, however, when these are infrequently instantiated complements to a number of other more pervasive tactics. These include threatening that this will happen when it will not and severely punishing, in ways other than exile from the category *woman*, those who do not uphold the natural attitude toward gender or do not conform to one of the positively evaluated paradigms for the gender to which they have been assigned. Ridicule, harassment, scorn, humiliation, not being allowed to use either public rest room, fists, boots, rapists' penises, baseball bats, beer bottles, billy clubs, knives, and guns serve regulatory functions just as effectively as an existential fear of falling out of one's prescribed gender category.

THE DEFINING CHARACTERISTICS OF THE CATEGORY WOMAN

In this section I offer my reconstruction of the dominant culture's concept of *woman*. There are a number of defining characteristics of the category *woman*. None of these characteristics is a necessary or sufficient condition. My list includes thirteen characteristics, clustered into several groups, differently weighted; some of these characteristics may be satisfied to differing degrees. Any adequate reconstruction of the dominant cultural concept *woman* needs to include all the elements I list, though this list may not be exhaustive. I owe a tremendous debt to Bornstein's *Gender Outlaw* in this section (Bornstein 1994, 21–40).[11]

The first cluster includes five characteristics generally regarded as sex characteristics by those who subscribe to a sex/gender distinction. In our culture, this cluster is more heavily weighted than any of the other defining characteristics.

1.   Absence of a penis.

Although presence of a vagina plays a role here, absence of a penis is primary. Initial gender assignment is typically and normatively made by a doctor who does not *examine* genitals but, instead, takes a *quick glance* between an infant's legs. If that doctor sees tissue that seems to have the potential to develop into a penis within "the normal range," the announcement is made: "It's a boy!" If that doctor does not see such tissue the announcement is: "It's a girl!" (Kessler [1990] 1994, 223–24, 227–28). Such announcements are performative in the strictest Austinian sense: announcement constitutes initial assignment, yet the moral accountability of the "natural attitude" requires that this assignment masquerade as a report of an already existing, purely natural fact.

Weighting penises more heavily than vaginas in attributing gender is not limited to attributions to neonates. In their overlay study, Suzanne J. Kessler and Wendy McKenna found that: "the presence of a penis is, in and of itself, a powerful enough cue to elicit a gender attribution with almost complete (96 percent) agreement. The presence of a vagina, however, does not have this same power. One third of the participants were able to ignore the reality of the vagina as a female cue" (Kessler and McKenna 1978, 151). Garfinkel's formulation of the "natural attitude" toward gender is mistaken in this regard. It is not quite accurate that, according to the "natural attitude," a female is a person with a vagina and a male is a person with a penis. Instead, as Bornstein writes, "It has little or nothing to do with vaginas. It's all penises or no penises . . ." (Bornstein 1994, 22).

2.   Presence of breasts.

After absence of penis when a body is unclothed, presence of breasts tends to be the most heavily weighted of the thirteen characteristics in gender attributions. This is evidenced by Kessler and McKenna's findings in their overlay study (Kessler and McKenna 1978, 145–53), by the importance of breast growth to MTFs (male-to-female transsexuals) for achieving convincingly feminine self-presentations, by the importance of top surgery to many FTMs, including both many of us who never undergo genital reconstruction surgeries and many who do, for achieving convincingly masculine self-presentations. Presence or absence of breasts also plays a large part in producing and maintaining gender *identity* in transsexuals and in non-transsexual birth-assigned females who undergo mastectomy as treatment for breast cancer. Absence of breasts, in the latter case, can threaten an individual's sense of herself as a woman, whereas absence of breasts can be crucial in producing and maintaining FTMs' masculine identities.

Analyzing a passage from Colette's *The Pure and the Impure* in which Colette suggests that lesbians might have their breasts removed "in this year of 1930," Crowder argues:

> Colette's semifacetious suggestion that modern lesbians chop off their breasts illustrates a profound ambivalence toward the lesbian body as a female body. On one level, she implies that lesbian rejection of "femininity" is such a radical rejection of being female that it necessitates bodily mutilation—aimed at the breast since it is the only specifically female organ visible when a woman is clothed. On another level, Colette ties this act to behaviors (smoking cigars, working on cars) that we associate with masculinity, rather than with gender neutrality. Colette sees lesbians as rejecting femaleness, symbolized by the breast, and embracing masculinity, represented by cigars and cars. (Crowder 1993, 64–65)

Contemporary lesbian anxiety about whether or not butches will expose their breasts—during sex, at pride parades, at women's music festivals, or as assertion of their right to use women's rest rooms when challenged—is another facet of lesbian ambivalence about the relationship between the categories *lesbian* and *woman*. Pressure put on butches to expose their breasts reflects anxieties that butches are not women or are on their way to becoming men. For butch refusal to ground and elicit this anxiety, presence of breasts must be a very heavily weighted characteristic of *woman*.[12]

3.   Presence of reproductive organs (uterus, ovaries, and fallopian tubes) which allow for pregnancy to occur if the person engages in intercourse with a fertile man.
4.   Presence of estrogen and progesterone in a balance with androgens within the "normal" range (as defined by endocrinologists) for females of one's age group.
5.   Presence of XX, or perhaps absence of Y, chromosomes.

Each of these five characteristics can vary somewhat independently, so no one of the five by itself is either necessary or sufficient for being within the category *woman*. An initial gender assignment, based on the absence of penile tissue, may be defeated by a number of nongenital characteristics. One is if chromosomal testing, done for some reason such as determining whether or not an athlete will be allowed to compete in women's events in the Olympics, indicates the presence of a Y chromosome. Yet this specialized case does not show that chromosomes are the ultimate, essential bedrock of our culture's concept *woman*, nor even that chromosomes are taken to be the most important of this cluster. Chromosomal testing is rare, even in cases of sex reassignment. Furthermore, insofar as MTFs fall within the category *woman*, most do so despite having XY chromosomes, despite lacking a uterus, ovaries, and fallopian tubes, and in some cases despite presence of a penis, though usually not without presence of estrogen in a balance with testosterone closer to that typical for women than that for men and sufficient to have caused some breast tissue growth.

6.   Having a gender identity as a woman.

Do you feel yourself to be a woman? Then, according to this defining characteristic, you are. This characteristic is less heavily weighted by the dominant culture than are many others, though it is not entirely negligible, as is shown by the crucial role gender identity plays in definitions of and diagnostic criteria for adult gender identity disorder (the current diagnostic category under which transsexuals gain access to medically regulated technologies) and in transsexual experiences.

The next cluster of defining characteristics has to do with what traditionally have been called "gender roles."

7.   Having an occupation considered to be acceptable for a woman.
8.   Engaging in leisure pursuits (including hobbies, club memberships, looser social affiliations, recreational activities, entertainment interests, and nonoccupational religious activities) considered to be acceptable for a woman, and pursuing these in ways considered acceptable for a woman.

I have not specified the content of (7) and (8), nor will I do so for (10)–(12) below, so as to allow for embodiments of these criteria to vary in relation to intersections of gender with race, ethnicity, class, religion, sexuality, regional location, and other such modalities. (8) leads naturally to a defining characteristic similar to that which Wittig takes to be the essential defining characteristic of the category *woman*.

9.   Engaging at some point in one's life in some form of sexual/affectional relationship with a man who is commonly recognized as heterosexual, whose life history is consistent with that placement of him, and who either self-identifies as heterosexual or who does not self-identify as gay or bisexual, and not later renouncing one's status as heterosexual.

I agree with Wittig that being heterosexual is part of what it is to be a woman. However, this is not the one and only defining characteristic of the concept *woman*, nor is satisfying this characteristic necessary or sufficient for being within the category *woman*.

I have formulated this defining characteristic with an eye to the "problem cases" I raised against Wittig's analysis. First, this defining characteristic is loose enough to include a variety of relationships other than marriage, including cohabitation and domestic partnerships between two and only two fairly clearly heterosexual people, but also including less normative forms of heterosexual involvement, including promiscuity, prostitution, and mistress-slave contracts. This defining characteristic can be satisfied by divorced women, widowed women, and single heterosexual mothers who are not participating currently and may not participate in the future in heterosexual relationships but who do not actively withdraw themselves from the category *heterosexual* in some way, for example, by coming out as lesbians. Still, it is strict enough about the type of participation in heterosexuality required that it does not apply to lesbians who participate in heterosexuality by voting or working in institutions that perpetuate heterosexuality. Further, this condition does not run into problems with categorizing dykes who engage in dyke-fag sex.

The next cluster of defining characteristics are ones that would often be taken to have to do with gender attribution by measures other than those that I have put into the first cluster (genitals, breasts, reproductive organs, hormones, and chromosomes), though some of these would be considered secondary sex characteristics by those who endorse a sex/gender distinction.

10. Achieving and maintaining a physical gender self-presentation the elements of which work together to produce the gender assignment "woman" in those with whom one interacts (including children and transsexuals), unambiguously, constantly, and without those with whom one interacts ever thinking about making this gender assignment. Such elements include attire, jewelry, cosmetics, hairstyle, distribution, density, and texture of facial and body hair, fingernail and toenail appearance, skin texture, overall body morphology and size, odor, facial structure, and vocal characteristics.

11. Behaving in ways that work together to produce the gender assignment "woman" in those with whom one interacts (including children and transsexuals), unambiguously, constantly, and without those with whom one interacts ever thinking about making this gender assignment. These behavioral cues include movements, posture, facial expressions, manners, decorum, etiquette, protocol, and deportment considered to be within acceptable ranges for women. For example, this may include degrees and styles of aggressiveness in communicating with others, and, more generally, how one uses and negotiates power in interactions with others. This also includes styles of verbal expression which are taken to reflect styles of thought: for example, women are more intuitive or emotional and less rational than men; women engage in less linear thought than men; women are more supportive and cooperative and less competitive in conversation than men, and so on.

12. Giving textual cues that work together to produce the gender assignment "woman" in those with whom one interacts (including children and transsexuals), unambiguously, constantly, and without those with whom one interacts ever thinking about making this gender assignment. Textual features include citing a continuous, unambiguous history as a woman who was a girl before adulthood, referring to an unambiguous future as a woman interrupted only by death, having only documents bearing the designation 'F' (for example, birth certificate, driver's license, passport) or bearing no gender designation (for example, employee or student identification card, credit card) and bearing either no photographs or photographs consistent with (10), using, answering to, and having documents bearing only a name consistent with the assignment "woman," using only feminine pronouns to refer to oneself whenever making third person singular pronominal references to oneself, quoting only others' third person singular pronominal references to oneself which use feminine pronouns, and showing and displaying only photographs, drawings, or other pictorial representations of oneself which are consistent with (10).

Do people, including children and transsexuals, with whom you interact think you're a woman? Do they think this all the time, unambiguously, and without ever thinking about thinking about it? If so, according to (10)–(12), then you're a woman.

For those who wish to place or maintain themselves within the category *woman* negotiating this cluster of defining characteristics is "essentially a balancing act," says a stunning *Mademoiselle* article entitled "Are You Woman Enough to Wear Menswear?" This article illustrates the delicate balance, always stated in the imperative, between masculine clothes and a feminine face with a photograph textually purporting to juxtapose "the power of a polka-dot tie [and] the allure of a sensuous face," yet showing the model's cleavage.

Satisfaction of (10)–(12) is frequently a primary concern in the gender performativities of MTFs. This is also a common primary concern, though usually less consciously so, in the gender performativities of birth-assigned females who wish to stay within the category *woman*. The difference is not necessarily in the amount of effort required, but rather in the degree of awareness that one is engaged in such an effort and in the degree of awareness of the specific dangers failure would bring on.

In a Wittgensteinian manner, Heritage explicates the balancing act, the continual production and maintenance of a gender self-presentation, which results in consistent, unambiguous, unconscious gender assignment of oneself to the category *woman*:

> It is surprising to realize the extent to which gender differentiation consists of a filigree of small-scale, socially organized behaviours which are unceasingly iterated. Together these—individually insignificant—behaviours interlock to constitute the great public institution of gender as a morally-organized-as-natural fact of life. This institution is comparatively resistant to change. To adapt Wittgenstein's famous analogy, the social construction of gender from a mass of individual social practices resembles the spinning of a thread in which fibre is spun on fibre. (Heritage 1984, 197)

Application of this cluster of defining characteristics may sometimes be defeated by a contradictory but very clear classification according to the first cluster. I am unsure about whether or not application of this cluster may be defeated by another defining characteristic or a cluster of other defining characteristics. (10)–(12) are very heavily weighted in defining gender in our culture, for were we uncertain of our gender attributions very often, or if we were to discover or decide frequently that our gender attributions were incorrect, this would weaken our belief in the "natural attitude" toward gender more radically than such belief would be undermined in any way other than a profound disturbance in our ability to rely on (1)–(5). Indeed, if much divergence were found in the classifications produced by these two clusters, this divergence would seriously undermine the "natural attitude."

13.   Having a history consistent with the gender assignment "woman" as produced by (10)–(12) which provides an unbroken line of descent from female infancy through girlhood to womanhood.

ARE LESBIANS WOMEN? REVISITED

Let me now return to the question: "Are lesbians women?" Anyone who expected an unequivocal answer has, I hope, abandoned this expectation. Before answering this question, I will take a brief detour back to the arguments. We have seen that Wittig's analysis of the concept *woman* is beset by her fundamental misunderstanding of the *logical type* of definition with which our culture operates. In her latest novel, *Across the Acheron*, she briefly acknowledges that her view of the distinction between lesbians and women is overly simple. The first-person protagonist, Wittig, journeys through the rings of hell with her guide, Manastabal. In many of these rings, women—not lesbians, of course—instantiate completely one aspect of their oppression under the regime of heterosexuality; for example, in one ring they appear as slaves who don't fight their leashes (Wittig [1985] 1987, 23–25), as appendages in another (44–46), and in a third ring they appear as two-dimensional creatures who, like playing-cards, cannot stand upright, in contradistinction to those "of the third dimension": men (50–51). Just as the categories *mother* and *amazon* were kept distinct in *Lesbian Peoples* (Wittig and Zeig [1976] 1979), Wittig makes clear that the categories *woman* and *lesbian* are distinct throughout *Across the Acheron*.

With one exception. In one of several interludes in a limbo region, Manastabal confronts Wittig with this tendency. This particular limbo space is a lesbian bar. Here Wittig uses the same language for lesbians that she often uses in her theoretical writing: "I feel like getting up at each new arrival in order to meet her and congratulate her on being in such a place; or else I want to stand on the table and propose a general toast to *all the deserters, all the runaways, all the escaped slaves* assembled here" (Wittig [1985] 1987, 73–74; emphasis mine). She seems so satisfied in the bar that Manastabal comments on it.

Wittig is crestfallen at first, but after more tequila she challenges her guide: "How is it, Manastabal, my guide, that you attach so much credit to the intelligence of the damned souls, as in the case of the bicephalics? Personally I tend to think that only a certain degree of stupidity can explain why anyone stays in Hell" (Wittig [1985] 1987, 74).

Manastabal replies: "It's just that your principle is: either . . . or. You don't acknowledge any nuances. You see nothing complex in what constitutes the basis of Hell. You assert that it must be destroyed and you imagine that you have only to blow on it" (Wittig [1985] 1987, 74).

A recent argument given by Crowder makes a mistake similar to Wittig's oversimplification. Although she endorses Wittig's conclusion, her own arguments pay scant attention to Wittig's underlying analysis of the relationship between the regime of heterosexuality and the categories of sex. Instead, Crowder focuses on "the lesbian body," arguing that this body "undermines the very categories of sex and gender themselves" by "deconstructing femininity in physical appearance." She cites male disguise, camp, and butch/femme role playing as examples of "the lesbian refusal to be women" (Crowder 1993, 66). Thus, Crowder notices that some U.S. lesbians do not embody characteristics (10)–(12). She disregards the facts that not every lesbian fails to satisfy (10)–(12) and that this cluster is also not satisfied by some nonlesbians who count as women by (1)–(5). Moreover, she fails to give any reason to believe that failure to satisfy these conditions alone implies that one is not a woman. I have argued that this view is mistaken, for characteristics (10)–(12) are neither necessary nor sufficient for being a woman. However, there is one way in which Crowder is on firmer ground here than Wittig: the conditions that Crowder argues that lesbians fail to satisfy are, I have argued, more heavily weighted than that which Wittig argues that lesbians fail to satisfy. Still, although Crowder endorses Wittig's view that "lesbians opt out of the heterosexual economy" (Crowder 1993, 66), she does little to indicate the underlying oppressive function of the distinctions (between *man* and *woman*, and between *sex* and *gender*) which she is critiquing.

Calhoun's arguments are different from Wittig's and Crowder's in that she appeals to three distinct defining characteristics of the concept *woman*. Drawing on Wittig's insight that the categories of sex are the results of the regime of heterosexuality, which requires that there be "two sexes/genders so that sexual desire can be heterosexualized" and that "sex/gender map onto reproductive differences" (Calhoun 1994, 566), Calhoun argues that "individuals who violate the unity of reproductive anatomy, heterosexual desire, and gender behavior fall out of the domain of intelligible gender identity" (566–67), that is, categorization as *woman* or as *man*. From this she immediately concludes, "At best, lesbians are not-women" (567).

Anatomy and gender behavior certainly do link some lesbians to the category *woman*; but there are vast differences among lesbians in regard to attributes of anatomy and gender behavior, which Calhoun's account neglects. Nonetheless, the point important to Calhoun's justification of her conclusion is that she relies on a *unity*, a relation of "coherence and continuity" (Calhoun 1994, 566; quoted from Butler 1990, 17), of the defining characteristics on which Calhoun focuses. Calhoun is right to notice that these characteristics work together (along with other characteristics she fails to mention) to produce and reproduce culturally intelligible gender embodiments. But Calhoun's stress on unity misunderstands the logical type of our dominant cultural definition of gender, for it takes as necessary each of the defining characteristics: if you do not have one of three properties, then you do not have a unity of those three properties. This emphasis on unity requires far too little for inclusion within the category *woman* to be an accurate formulation of our dominant cultural conception of gender, for it excludes from the category *woman* any person whose reproductive anatomy alone or whose gender behavior alone does not conform to (1)–(5) or (10)–(12). Since Calhoun does not clarify the terms "reproductive anatomy" and "gender behavior," she is open to the same kind of counter-arguments as Wittig, although the specific problem cases would differ. I will not engage these apparent counterexamples, but will only list a few: postmenopausal women, women who have had hysterectomies, infertile women "of child-bearing age," heterosexual women who insist on egalitarian or open marriage contracts, heterosexual women with nontraditional occupations, heterosexual academic women who do not defer to their male colleagues in department meetings, and so forth. Further, Calhoun overlooks differences in the *weighting* of the different defining characteristics of the concept *woman*.

Are lesbians women? Some are, some are not, and in many cases there is no fact of the matter. There are many differences among lesbians as to which of the defining characteristics of *woman* they satisfy, which they do not satisfy, the extent to which they do satisfy those characteristics which they satisfy, and the extent to which they fail to satisfy those characteristics which they do not satisfy. No lesbian satisfies every defining characteristic of the category *woman*, since every lesbian fails to satisfy condition (9); yet, even in regard to this condition, the degree to which lesbians fail to satisfy it differs. But many lesbians do, fairly clearly and to a fairly great extent, satisfy each of the other defining characteristics. There is no principled reason to say that such lesbians are not women, given that they satisfy the most heavily weighted defining characteristics for being in that category, they satisfy all but one of the characteristics, and that characteristic which they do not satisfy is not one among the most heavily weighted.

WITTIG'S CONTRIBUTIONS

I would like to close with a few words about Wittig's enormous contributions.

She opened the way for understanding the straight mind, by showing up as myths the notions of dimorphic sexual difference upon which heterosexuality as a political regime is founded, and which in turn founds the oppression of those classified as women within its discourses. She is right, I think, to locate the category (and, hence, the categories) of sex, as well as their occupants, as material and cultural *products* of the regime of heterosexuality, just as it produces those who are not contained within the categories of sex *as such* by excluding them from these categories. From her theoretical work we can draw the invaluable conclusion that the category (and categories) of sex function to perpetuate the regime of heterosexuality, which, in turn, enables (though it is neither necessary nor sufficient for) the oppression of those it classifies as women. Yet, we must also understand this sort of functional primacy as distinct from definitional primacy, for the actual classification of human beings within the category of sex does not work exactly as Wittig thinks.

Wittig further opened up the conceptual space for believing that some human beings have escaped the categories of dimorphic sexual difference which found the heterosexual regime, and for seeing this as a possibility for ourselves. This possibility, in turn, has given us greater justification for pursuing gender proliferation as one promising strategy in overthrowing the heterosexual regime. It loosens the stranglehold, coming from both the dominant culture and also from some versions of cultural and radical feminism, of nonconsensual gender on those birth-designated females who have felt profound discomfort at being in, being placed by others within, or proclaiming themselves to be within, the category *woman*. Wittig's theoretical work has enabled a better development of our understanding of the ways in which queer gender performativities trouble the heterosexual regime. As Harmony Hammond writes, "In her shift away from a definition of lesbian identity based on gender to one based on sexual preference, as well as her deconstruction of sex, gender, and the lesbian body (in order to (re)member it), Wittig, like Foucault, anticipated and influenced much of today's rich discourse around the body and sexuality" (Hammond 1994, 105–6).[13]

Yet Wittig's emphasis on the material may serve as a useful corrective to some current trends within queer theory. As Rosemary Hennessey writes:

> This way [Wittig's] of conceptualizing lesbian implies that the formation of resistant subjectivities will require more than changing discourses and constructions of the subject. In this sense Wittig's resistant subject puts pressure on the overriding emphasis in queer theory on sexuality as discursively constructed and/or as an expression of bodies or pleasures. We can look at how her concept of subjective cognitive practice as a class issue can redirect our thinking about sexuality, identity, and resistance. If we understand the prevailing categories of sex as integral to an economic, political, and ideological order, becoming "queer" can be seen as "a new subjective definition" that has to be undertaken by every one of us. This is not a subject position based upon biology or sexual object choice or issuing from a utopian "elsewhere" so much as a critical perspective that opens up ways of thinking about sexuality in both straight and gay culture. (Hennessey 1993, 971–72)

Gendering ourselves in ways that challenge the "natural attitude" toward gender threatens the regime of heterosexuality, and so also the oppression of women. But simply engaging in gender play, sexually or in public acts of self-presentation, is not as subversive as some contemporary queer politics and theory would have it. To shift our*selves*, our subjectivities, our embodied gender performativities, to shift our own gendered beings in response to the dominant scheme's responses to our gender threats, we need the greatest degree of theoretical specificity possible. This theoretical specificity is lessened by focusing on only one aspect of the dominant culture's gender scheme, as Wittig does and as do queers who think that looking queer or playing queer is all it takes. To paraphrase Manastabal's admonition to Wittig in the Limbo Bar, you have to do more than blow at one piece of it to blow it away. Nonetheless, this theoretical specificity can be increased by foregrounding, as Wittig does, the functions of the category of sex to uphold the heterosexual regime and, in turn, to enable the oppression of women as such.[14]

NOTES

Previously published in *Hypatia* vol. 11, no. 2 (Spring 1996) © by Jacob Hale.

1. See Butler (1990, 4–5) for an alternative formulation of this problem.
2. Shane Phelan writes: "What comes to the fore, then, is not truth but strategy. If we ask why certain metanarratives function at certain times and places, we find that the answer does not have to do with the progress of a unitary knowledge but rather with shifting structures of meaning, power, and action" (Phelan 1993, 767). While all this may be true, it is still possible and important to say that some accounts of the contents of these metanarratives are true, others false. This, of course, is different from saying that the metanarratives themselves are true or false. Nonetheless, it is both possible and important to argue that many of these metanarratives are false.
3. Kate Bornstein profitably applies SM consensuality/nonconsensuality discourse to gender (Bornstein 1994, 121–25). Susan Stryker gives a useful analysis of the nonconsensuality of gender as "the founding condition of human subjectivity," "the tribal tattoo that makes one's personhood cognizable" (Stryker 1994, 249–50).
4. I thank Regina Lark, Cindy Stern, and Ali Whitmer for discussions of the functions of "real" and "not real."
5. "Binary" is Butler's term, not Wittig's. Yet I believe it is accurate here, for Wittig often writes of the oppositional nature

of the definitions of *woman* and *man*, and also that the regime of heterosexuality includes exhaustivity of these two categories. Although analytic philosophers use "binary relation" simply to mean *two-termed relation*, it has a different meaning in this context. Here, binary distinctions are distinctions between two categories which are defined oppositionally and which apply exhaustively within their domain. Not every two-termed relation between two people who are members of such categories can be a binary relation in the relevant sense, however, else any individual woman and any individual man would be in binary relation(s) to each other.

6. Problem cases Cheshire Calhoun lists are "the heterosexual celibate, virgin, single-parent head of household, marriage resister, or the married woman who insists on an egalitarian marriage contract" (Calhoun 1994, 563). Another problem case arises for Wittig when we ask whether or not gay men (in common parlance) count as men on her view. Rosemary Hennessey notices this problem but, misunderstanding it as raising the specter of lesbian separatism, dismisses it (Hennessey 1993, 97). Harry Hay offers arguments for the conclusion that gays, as well as lesbians, escape the categories of sex, based on concepts of subject-object and subject-subject consciousness (Hay 1987; Hay in Thompson 1987; Hay in Thompson 1994).

7. I do not use "dyke" and "fag" here simply as synonyms for "lesbian" and "gay man." These terms indicate culturally located genderings of sexual practices and desires which often take primacy over gender of object choice, thus are not exact synonyms and may not be coextensive terms.

8. This quote from Halberstam, as well as my analysis of the personal ad from *Venus Infers*, points out a crucial methodological lesson, namely, anyone who wants to think clearly about gender in relation to sexuality in our culture needs to be conversant in the discourses used and continually re-created by those who are *forced* to move well beyond the categories available in the dominant culture discourse about sex, gender, and sexuality. Queer and transgendered discourses are produced by those of us who cannot communicate about our gendered sexual desires and practices without creating new languages, languages much more specific and more richly nuanced than those available to us from the dominant culture and from feminist, lesbian or gay cultures. Queer gendered sexual practice far exceeds theory right now; indeed, my own practices far exceed the conceptual tools available to me now. However, queer community-based discourses are ahead of theory now. Here's the lesson, in a nutshell: if, minimally, you don't understand the personals and other sexually explicit expressions of desire in queer and transgendered sex radical/leatherqueer publications (including homegrown ones), you don't understand the margins, the edges, of our dominant cultural expressions of sex, gender, and sexuality. Continuing to appropriate bell hooks' analogy out of context (hooks 1984, vix), if you don't understand gendered life on the edge, you don't understand gendered life at the center.

9. Shannon Bell argues that many feminist theorists "have tended to appropriate feminine difference in the [canonical, masculine] texts [they have studied] solely as difference in relation to the male subject. They have neglected the inscription of difference within the category 'woman' (the maternal body/the libidinal female body) found in the texts. Consequently, they have privileged the reproductive in the couple maternal/sexual that has come to delimit the female" (Bell 1994, 21). Based on this analysis, she develops the view that prostitutes are "the other within the categorical other, 'woman' " (2). Although Bell is right to criticize feminist theorists who have misunderstood the category *woman* by neglecting non-reproductive representations of *woman* and women, she distorts cultural constructions of this category by insisting that it is always constructed by binary pairings, rather than allowing for multiple, non-binary exemplars of ways to be a good woman and a bad woman.

10. For one list of a multiplicity of such strategies, see Rich ([1980] 1983).

11. I leave vague the dominant cultural attitude toward causal structuring of the defining characteristics of *woman*. Probably the most common belief is that presence of XX, or absence of Y, chromosomes causes many of the remaining twelve defining characteristics to be present. Yet this is highly contested. I thank James Bogen for drawing this to my attention.

12. This point comes to the fore in Judith Halberstam's reading of Sergio Toledo's film *Vera* (Italy). A girls' reformatory director challenges Vera Bauer and other young butches: "Okay, you're so butch, let's see your pricks." Bauer's girlfriend Clara says it's "not fair" for Bauer to have sex with her unless they are both naked, but when Bauer strips to an undershirt and Clara tries to touch Bauer's breasts, Bauer runs out of the room. Halberstam remarks that Bauer "is surrounded by people who must see her dick if they are to approve her masculinity, or her breasts if they are to prove her masculinity is simply a facade" (Halberstam 1994, 221–25).

13. I thank Frances Pohl for bringing Hammond's article to my attention.

14. Earlier versions of this paper were presented to the Society for Women in Philosophy/Pacific Division, the Philosophy and Women's Studies Field Groups at Pitzer College, the Department of Philosophy at California State University, Los Angeles, and the Department of Philosophy at California State University, Northridge; I am grateful for comments I received on those occasions. Participating in a Los Angeles area feminist theory/queer theory discussion group has helped my thinking on the topics I discuss in this paper; the following have participated in that group: Karen Barad, Mary Crane, Ann Ferguson, Robin Podolsky, Jennifer Rycenga, Bergeth Schroeder, Laurie Shrage, Kayley Vernallis, and D. D. Wills. Anonymous *Hypatia* referees' reports were also useful in preparing my final version of this essay.

REFERENCES

Are you woman enough to wear menswear? 1992. *Mademoiselle*, October, 152ff.

Austin, J. L. 1962. *Sense and sensibilia*. New York: Oxford University Press.

Bell, Shannon. 1994. *Reading, writing, and rewriting the prostitute body*. Bloomington: Indiana University Press.

Bornstein, Kate. 1994. *Gender outlaw: On men, women and the rest of us.* New York: Routledge.
Butler, Judith. 1987. Variations on sex and gender: Beauvoir, Wittig, and Foucault. In *Feminism as critique: On the politics of gender*, ed. Seyla Benhabib and Drucilla Cornell. Minneapolis: University of Minnesota Press.
———. 1990. *Gender trouble: Feminism and the subversion of identity.* New York: Routledge.
———. 1993. *Bodies that matter: The discursive limits of "sex."* New York: Routledge.
Califia, Pat. 1994. Gay men, lesbians, and sex: Doing it together. In *Public sex: The culture of radical sex.* Pittsburgh: Cleis Press.
Calhoun, Cheshire. 1994. Separating lesbian theory from feminist theory. *Ethics* 104(3): 558–81.
Chase, Cheryl. 1994. Intersexuality definitions, bibliography. Posting to the Queer Studies List, QSTUDY-L@UBVM. CC.BUFFALO.EDU, 15 November.
Crowder, Diane Griffin. 1993. Lesbians and the (re/de) construction of the female body. In *Reading the social body*, ed. Catherine B. Burroughs and Jeffrey David Ehrenreich. Iowa City: University of Iowa Press.
Deneuve. 1994. 4(3).
Frye, Marilyn. 1983. *The politics of reality: Essays in feminist theory.* Freedom, CA: Crossing Press.
Garfinkel, Harold. 1967. Passing and the managed achievement of sex status in an "intersexed" person, part 1. In *Studies in ethnomethodology.* Oxford: Polity Press.
Halberstam, Judith. 1994. F2M: The making of female masculinity. In *The lesbian postmodern*, ed. Laura Doan. New York: Columbia University Press.
Hammond, Harmony. 1994. A space of infinite and pleasurable possibilities: Lesbian self-representation in visual art. In *New feminist criticism: Art, identity, action*, ed. Joanna Frueh, Cassandra L. Langer, and Arlene Raven. New York: IconEditions.
Hay, Harry. 1987. A separate people whose time has come. In *Gay spirit: Myth and meaning*, ed. Mark Thompson. New York: St. Martin's Press.
Hennessey, Rosemary. 1993. Queer theory: A review of the *differences* special issue and Wittig's "The straight mind." *Signs* 18(4): 964–73.
Heritage, John. 1984. *Garfinkel and ethnomethodology.* Cambridge: Polity Press.
Holmes, Morgan. 1994. Remembering a queer body. *Undercurrents*, May, 11–13.
hooks, bell. 1984. *Feminist theory: From margin to center.* Boston: South End Press.
Kessler, Suzanne J. [1990] 1994. The medical construction of gender: Case management of intersexed infants. In *Theorizing feminism: Parallel trends in the humanities and social sciences*, ed. Anne C. Herrmann and Abigail J. Stewart. Boulder: Westview Press.
Kessler, Suzanne J., and Wendy McKenna. 1978. *Gender: An ethnomethodological approach.* New York: John Wiley and Sons.
Phelan, Shane. 1993. (Be) coming out: Lesbian identity and politics. *Signs* 18(4): 765–90.
Rich, Adrienne. [1980]. 1983. Compulsory heterosexuality and lesbian existence. In *Powers of desire: The politics of sexuality*, ed. Ann Snitow, Christine Stansell, and Sharon Thompson. New York: Monthly Review Press.
Sadownick, Doug. 1993. The new sex radicals: Gays and the return of desire. *L.A. Weekly*, 2–8 July, 18–20, 22, 24–26.
Shaktini, Namascar. 1994. Review of *The straight mind and other essays* by Monique Wittig. *Hypatia* 9(1): 211–14.
Stryker, Susan. 1994. My words to Victor Frankenstein above the village of Chamounix: Performing transgender rage. *GLQ* 1(3): 237–54.
Thompson, Mark. 1987. Harry Hay: A voice from the past, a vision for the future. (Interview.) In *Gay spirit: Myth and meaning*, ed. Mark Thompson. New York: St. Martin's Press.
———. 1994. Harry Hay: Reinventing ourselves. (Interview.) In *Gay soul: Finding the heart of gay spirit and nature.* San Francisco: Harper San Francisco.
Turcotte, Louise. 1992. Foreword: Changing the point of view. Trans. Marlene Wildeman. In *The straight mind and other essays.* See Wittig 1992.
Venus Infers. n.d. 1(4).
Wittig, Monique. 1979. Paradigm. Trans. George Stambolian. In *Homosexualities and French literature: Cultural contexts/critical texts*, ed. Elaine Marks and George Stambolian. Ithaca: Cornell University Press.
———. [1985] 1987. *Across the Acheron.* Trans. David Le Vay with Margaret Crosland. London: Peter Owen.
———. 1992. *The straight mind and other essays.* Boston: Beacon Press.
Wittig, Monique, and Sande Zeig. [1976] 1979. *Lesbian peoples: Materials for a dictionary.* Trans. Monique Wittig and Sande Zeig. New York: Avon Books.

22

Hermaphrodites with Attitude
Mapping the Emergence of Intersex Political Activism

CHERYL CHASE

WITH THIS TOUR-DE-FORCE ARTICLE, CHERYL CHASE brought intersex issues into the purview of queer theory. She presents an overview of the medical management of intersex conditions that result in congenital ambiguous genitalia, recounts her own intersex autobiography, reviews the creation of the Intersex Society of North America, and analyzes Western feminist discourses on "genital mutilation."

Chase argues that intersex, transgender, and sexual-orientation activism are closely linked through a shared liberal emphasis on protecting personal ethical choice and the right to control one's own body. She effectively unmasks the cultural processes that have rendered intersexuality virtually invisible and largely unknown—in spite of the fact one in every two thousand individuals exhibits some degree of intersexuality at birth. Chase makes a forceful case for ending nonconsensual genital surgeries on intersex children too young to make decisions on their own behalf. She argues that these surgeries are almost always medically unnecessary, that they generally damage sexual functioning, and are done largely to comfort doctors and parents who feel unable to bond with or accept the humanity of an infant body that cannot be clearly labeled "boy" or "girl." She argues as well that current medical practice effectively abolishes the natural diversity of sexed body types and uses the sharp end of a scalpel to impose a culturally constructed male/female dichotomy. She then offers a devastating critique of the deafening silence surrounding the medicalized genital cutting practiced on intersex individuals, exposing the racist and colonialist underpinnings of much feminist outrage over "African" genital cutting.

One question that remains unaddressed in Chase's article is whether intersexuality, if allowed to exist without medical intervention, would lead to new minority forms of personal identity—or whether it might contribute to the overthrow of sexual identity categories for everybody.

The insistence on two clearly distinguished sexes has calamitous personal consequences for the many individuals who arrive in the world with sexual anatomy that fails to be easily distinguished as male or female. Such individuals are labeled "intersexuals" or "hermaphrodites" by modern medical discourse.[1] About one in a hundred births exhibits some anomaly in sex differentiation,[2] and about one in two thousand is different enough to render problematic the question "Is it a boy or a girl?"[3] Since the early 1960s, nearly every major city in the United States has had a hospital with a standing team of medical experts who intervene in these cases to assign—through drastic surgical means—a male or female status to intersex infants. The fact that this system for preserving the boundaries of the categories male and female has existed for so long without drawing criticism or scrutiny from any quarter indicates the extreme discomfort that sexual ambiguity excites in our culture. Pediatric genital surgeries literalize what might otherwise be considered a theoretical operation: the attempted production of normatively sexed bodies and gendered subjects through constitutive acts of violence. Over the last few years, however, intersex people have begun to politicize intersex identities, thus transforming intensely personal experiences of violation into collective opposition to the medical regulation of bodies that queer the foundations of heteronormative identifications and desires.

HERMAPHRODITES: MEDICAL AUTHORITY AND CULTURAL INVISIBILITY

Many people familiar with the ideas that gender is a phenomenon not adequately described by male/female dimorphism and that the interpretation of physical sex differences is culturally constructed remain surprised to learn just how variable sexual anatomy is.[4] Though the male/female binary is constructed as natural and presumed to be immutable, the phenomenon of intersexuality offers clear evidence to the contrary and furnishes an opportunity to deploy "nature" strategically to disrupt heteronormative systems of sex, gender, and sexuality. The concept of bodily sex, in popular usage, refers to multiple components including karyotype (organization of sex chromosomes), gonadal differentiation (e.g., ovarian or testicular), genital morphology, configuration of internal reproductive organs, and pubertal sex characteristics such as breasts and facial hair. Because these characteristics are expected to be concordant in each individual—either all male or all female—an observer, once having attributed male or female sex to a particular individual, assumes the values of other unobserved characteristics.[5]

Because medicine intervenes quickly in intersex births to change the infant's body, the phenomenon of intersexuality is today largely unknown outside specialized medical practices. General public awareness of intersex bodies slowly vanished in modern Western European societies as medicine gradually appropriated to itself the authority to interpret—and eventually manage—the category which had previously been widely known as "hermaphroditism." Victorian medical taxonomy began to efface hermaphroditism as a legitimated status by establishing mixed gonadal histology as a necessary criterion for "true" hermaphroditism. By this criterion, both ovarian and testicular tissue types had to be present. Given the limitations of Victorian surgery and anesthesia, such confirmation was impossible in a living patient. All other anomalies were reclassified as "pseudohermaphroditisms" masking a "true sex" determined by the gonads.[6]

With advances in anesthesia, surgery, embryology, and endocrinology, however, twentieth-century medicine moved from merely labeling intersexed bodies to the far more invasive practice of "fixing" them to conform with a diagnosed true sex. The techniques and protocols for physically transforming intersexed bodies were developed primarily at Johns Hopkins University in Baltimore during the 1920s and 1930s under the guidance of urologist Hugh Hampton Young. "Only during the last few years," Young enthused in the preface to his pioneering textbook, *Genital Abnormalities*, "have we begun to get somewhere near the explanation of the marvels of anatomic abnormality that may be portrayed by these amazing individuals. But the surgery of the hermaphrodite has remained a terra incognita." The "sad state of these unfortunates" prompted Young to devise "a great variety of surgical procedures" by which he attempted to normalize their bodily appearances to the greatest extents possible.[7]

Quite a few of Young's patients resisted his efforts. One, a "'snappy' young negro woman with a good figure" and a large clitoris, had married a man but found her passion only with women. She refused "to be made into a man" because removal of her vagina would mean the loss of her 'meal ticket," namely, her husband.[8] By the 1950s, the principle of rapid postnatal detection and intervention for intersex infants had been developed at John Hopkins with the stated goal of completing surgery early enough so that the child would have no memory of it.[9] One wonders whether the insistence on early intervention was not at least partly motivated by the resistance offered by adult intersexuals to normalization through surgery. Frightened parents of ambiguously sexed infants were much more open to suggestions of normalizing surgery, while the infants themselves could of course offer no resistance whatever. Most of the theoretical foundations justifying these interventions are attributable to psychologist John Money, a sex researcher invited to Johns Hopkins by Lawson Wilkins, the founder of pediatric endocrinology.[10] Wilkins's numerous students subsequently carried these protocols to hospitals throughout the United States and abroad.[11] Suzanne Kessler notes that today Wilkins and Money's protocols enjoy a "consensus of approval rarely encountered in science."[12]

In keeping with the Johns Hopkins model, the birth of an intersex infant today is deemed a "psychosocial emergency" that propels a multidisciplinary team of intersex specialists into action. Significantly, they are surgeons and endocrinologists rather than psychologists, bioethicists, representatives from intersex peer support organizations, or parents of intersex children. The team examines the infant and chooses either male or female as a "sex of assignment," then informs the parents that this is the child's "true sex." Medical technology, including surgery and hormones, is then used to make the child's body conform as closely as possible to that sex.

The sort of deviation from sex norms exhibited by intersexuals is so highly stigmatized that the likely prospect of emotional harm due to social rejection of the intersexual provides physicians with their most compelling argument to justify medically unnecessary surgical interventions. Intersex status is considered to be so incompatible with emotional health that misrepresentation, concealment of facts, and outright lying (both to parents and later to the intersex person) are unabashedly advocated in professional medical literature.[13] Rather, the systematic hushing up of the fact of intersex births and the use of violent techniques to normalize intersex bodies have caused profound emotional and physical harm to intersexuals and their families. The harm begins when the birth is treated as a medical crisis, and the consequences of that initial treatment ripple out ever afterward. The impact of this treatment is so devastating that until just a few years ago, people whose lives have been touched by intersexuality maintained silence about their ordeal. As recently as 1993, no one publicly disputed surgeon Milton Edgerton when he wrote that in forty years of clitoral surgery on intersexuals, "not one has complained of loss of sensation, *even when the entire clitoris was removed.*"[14]

The tragic irony is that, while intersexual anatomy occasionally indicates an underlying medical problem such as adrenal malfunction, ambiguous genitals are in and of themselves neither painful nor harmful to health. Surgery is essentially a destructive process. It can remove and to a limited extent relocate tissue, but it cannot create new structures. This technical limitation, taken together with the framing of the feminine as a condition of lack, leads physicians to assign 90 percent of anatomically ambiguous infants as female by excising genital tissue. Members of the Johns Hopkins intersex team have justified female assignment by saying, "You can make a hole, but you can't build a pole."[15] Positively heroic efforts shore up a tenuous masculine status for the remaining 10 percent assigned male, who are subjected to multiple operations—twenty-two in one case[16]—with the goal of straightening the penis and constructing a urethra to enable standing urinary posture. For some, the surgeries end only when the child grows old enough to resist.[17]

Children assigned to the female sex are subjected to surgery that removes the troubling hypertrophic clitoris (the same tissue that would have been a troubling micropenis if the child had been assigned male). Through the 1960s, feminizing pediatric genital surgery was openly labeled "clitorectomy" and was compared favorably to the African practices that have been the recent focus of such intense scrutiny. As three Harvard surgeons noted, "Evidence that the clitoris is not essential for normal coitus may be gained from certain sociological data. For instance, it is the custom of a number of African tribes to excise the clitoris and other parts of the external genitals. Yet normal sexual function is observed in these females."[18] A modified operation that removes most of the clitoris and relocates a bit of the tip is variously (and euphemistically) called clitoroplasty, clitoral reduction, or clitoral recession and is described as a "simple cosmetic procedure" to differentiate it from the now infamous clitorectomy. However, the operation is far from benign. Here is a slightly simplified summary (in my own words) of the surgical technique—recommended by Johns Hopkins Surgeons Oesterling, Gearhart, and Jeffs—that is representative of the operation:

> They make an incision around the phallus, at the corona, then dissect the skin away from its underside. Next they dissect the skin away from the dorsal side and remove as much of the corpora, or erectile bodies, as necessary to create an "appropriate size clitoris." Next, stitches are placed from the pubic area along both sides of the entire length of what remains of the phallus; when these stitches are tightened, it folds up like pleats in a skirt, and recesses into a concealed position behind the mons pubis. If the result is still "too large," the glans is further reduced by cutting away a pie-shaped wedge.[19]

For most intersexuals, this sort of arcane, dehumanized medical description, illustrated with close-ups of genital surgery and naked children with blacked-out eyes, is the only available version of *Our Bodies, Ourselves*. We as a culture have relinquished to medicine the authority to police the boundaries of male and female, leaving intersexuals to recover as best they can, alone and silent, from violent normalization.

MY CAREER AS A HERMAPHRODITE: RENEGOTIATING CULTURAL MEANINGS

I was born with ambiguous genitals. A doctor specializing in intersexuality deliberated for three days—sedating my mother each time she asked what was wrong with her baby—before concluding that I was male, with a micropenis, complete hypospadias, undescended testes, and a strange extra opening behind the urethra. A male birth certificate was completed for me, and my parents began raising me as a boy. When I was a year and a half old my parents consulted a different set of experts, who admitted me to a hospital for "sex determination." "Determine" is a remarkably apt word in this context, meaning both "to ascertain by investigation" and "to cause to come to a resolution." It perfectly describes the two-stage process whereby science produces through a series of masked operations what it claims merely to observe. Doctors told my parents that a thorough medical investigation would be necessary to determine (in the first sense of that word) what my "true sex" was. They judged my genital appendage to be inadequate as a penis, too short to mark masculine status effectively or to penetrate females. As a female, however, I would be penetrable and potentially fertile. My anatomy having been relabeled as vagina, urethra, labia, and outsized clitoris, my sex was determined (in the second sense) by amputating my genital appendage. Following doctors' orders, my parents then changed my name, combed their house to eliminate all traces of my existence as a boy (photographs, birthday cards, etc.), changed my birth certificate, moved to a different town, instructed extended family members no longer to refer to me as a boy, and never told anyone else—including me—just what had happened. My intersexuality and change of sex were the family's dirty little secrets.

At age eight, I was returned to the hospital for abdominal surgery that trimmed away the testicular portion of my gonads, each of which was partly ovarian and partly testicular in character. No explanation was given to me then for the long hospital stay or the abdominal surgery, nor for the regular hospital visits afterward, in which doctors photographed my genitals and inserted fingers and instruments into my vagina and anus. These visits ceased as soon as I began to menstruate. At the time of the sex change, doctors had assured my parents that their once son/now daughter would grow into a woman who could have a normal sex life and babies. With the confirmation of menstruation, my parents apparently concluded that that prediction had been borne out and their ordeal was behind them. For me, the worst part of the nightmare was just beginning.

As an adolescent, I became aware that I had no clitoris or inner labia and was unable to orgasm. By the end of my teens, I began to do research in medical libraries, trying to discover what might have happened to me. When I finally determined to obtain my medical records, it took me three years to overcome the obstruction of the doctors whom I asked for help. When I did obtain them, a scant three pages, I first learned that I was a "true hermaphrodite" who had been my parents' son for a year and a half and who bore a name unfamiliar to me. The records also documented my clitorectomy. This was the middle 1970s, when I was in my early twenties. I had come to identify myself as lesbian, at a time when lesbianism and a biologically based gender essentialism were virtually synonymous: men were rapists who caused war and environmental destruction; women were good and would heal the earth; lesbians were a superior form of being uncontaminated by "men's energy." In such a world, how could I tell anyone that I had actually possessed the dreaded "phallus"? I was no longer a woman in my own eyes but rather a monstrous and mythical creature. Because my hermaphroditism and long-buried boyhood were the history behind the clitorectomy, I could never speak openly about that or my consequent inability to orgasm. I was so traumatized by discovering the circumstances that produced my embodiment that I could not speak of these matters with anyone.

Nearly fifteen years later, I suffered an emotional meltdown. In the eyes of the world, I was a highly successful businesswoman, a principal in an international high tech company. To myself, I was a freak, incapable of loving or being loved, filled with shame about my status as a hermaphrodite and about my sexual dysfunction. Unable to make peace with myself, I finally sought help from a psychotherapist, who reacted to each revelation about my history and predicament with some version of "no, it's not" or "so what?" I would say, "I'm not really a woman," and she would say, "Of course you are. You look female." I would say, "My complete withdrawal from sexuality has destroyed every relationship I've ever entered." She would say "Everybody has their ups and downs." I tried another therapist and met with a similar response. Increasingly desperate, I confided my story to several friends, who shrank away in embarrassed silence. I was in emotional agony, feeling utterly alone, seeing no possible way out. I decided to kill myself.

Confronting suicide as a real possibility proved to be my personal epiphany. I fantasized killing myself quite messily and dramatically in the office of the surgeon who had cut off my clitoris, forcibly confronting him with the horror he had imposed on my life. But in acknowledging the desire to put my pain to some use, not to utterly waste my life, I turned a crucial corner, finding a way to direct my rage productively out into the world rather than destructively at myself. I had no conceptual framework for developing a more positive self-consciousness. I knew only that I felt mutilated, not fully human, but that I was determined to heal. I struggled for weeks in emotional chaos, unable to eat or sleep or work. I could not accept my image of a hermaphroditic body any more than I could accept the butchered one the surgeons left me with. Thoughts of myself as a Frankenstein's monster patchwork alternated with longings for escape by death, only to be followed by outrage, anger, and a determination to survive. I could not accept that it was just or right or good to treat any person as I had been treated—my sex changed, my genitals cut up, my experience silenced and rendered invisible. I bore a private hell within me, wretchedly alone in my condition without even my tormentors for company. Finally, I began to envision myself standing in a driving storm but with clear skies and a rainbow visible in the distance. I was still in agony, but I was beginning to see the painful process in which I was caught up in terms of revitalization and rebirth, a means of investing my life with a new sense of authenticity that possessed vast potentials for further transformation. Since then, I have seen this experience of movement through pain to personal empowerment described by other intersex and transsexual activists.[20]

I slowly developed a newly politicized and critically aware form of self-understanding. I had been the kind of lesbian who at times had a girlfriend but who had never really participated in the life of a lesbian community. I felt almost completely isolated from gay politics, feminism, and queer and gender theory. I did possess the rudimentary knowledge that the gay rights movement had gathered momentum only when it could effectively deny that homosexuality was sick or inferior and assert to the contrary that "gay is good." As impossible as it then seemed, I pledged similarly to affirm that "intersex is good," that the body I was born with was not diseased, only different. I vowed to embrace the sense of being "not a woman" that I initially had been so terrified to discover.

I began searching for community and consequently moved to San Francisco in the fall of 1992, based entirely on my vague notion that people living in the "queer mecca" would have the most conceptually sophisticated, socially tolerant, and politically astute analysis of sexed and gendered embodiment. I found what I was looking for in part because my arrival in the Bay Area corresponded with the rather sudden emergence of an energetic transgender political movement. Transgender Nation (TN) had developed out of Queer Nation, a post-gay/lesbian group that sought to transcend identity politics. TN's actions garnered media attention—especially when members were arrested during a "zap" of the American Psychiatric Association's annual convention when they protested the psychiatric labeling of transsexuality as mental illness. Transsexual performance artist Kate Bornstein was introducing transgender issues in an entertaining way to the San Francisco gay/lesbian community and beyond. Female-to-male issues had achieved a new level of visibility due in large part to efforts made by Lou Sullivan, a gay FTM activist who had died an untimely death from HIV-related illnesses in 1991. And in the wake of her underground best-selling novel, *Stone Butch Blues*, Leslie Feinberg's manifesto *Transgender Liberation: A Movement Whose Time Has Come* was finding a substantial audience, linking transgender social justice to a broader progressive political agenda for the first time.[21] At the same time, a vigorous new wave of gender scholarship had emerged in the academy.[22] In this context, intersex activist and theoretician Morgan Holmes could analyze her own clitorectomy for her master's thesis and have it taken seriously as academic work.[23] Openly transsexual scholars, including Susan Stryker and Sandy Stone, were visible in responsible academic positions at major universities. Stone's "*Empire* Strikes Back: A Posttranssexual Manifesto" refigured open, visible transsexuals not as gender conformists propping up a system of rigid, binary sex but as "a set of embodied texts whose potential for productive disruption of structured sexualities and spectra of desire has yet to be explored."[24]

Into this heady atmosphere, I brought my own experience. Introduced by Bornstein to other gender activists, I explored with them the cultural politics of intersexuality, which to me represented yet another new configuration of bodies, identities, desires, and sexualities from which to confront the violently normativizing aspects of the dominant sex/gender system. In the fall of 1993, TN pioneer Anne Ogborn invited me to participate in a weekend retreat called the New Woman Conference, where postoperative transsexual women shared their stories, their griefs and joys, and enjoyed the freedom to swim or sunbathe in the nude with others who had surgically changed genitals. I saw that participants returned home in a state of euphoria, and I determined to bring that same sort of healing experience to intersex people.

BIRTH OF AN INTERSEX MOVEMENT: OPPOSITION AND ALLIES

Upon moving to San Francisco, I started telling my story indiscriminately to everyone I met. Over the course of a year, simply by speaking openly within my own social circles, I learned of six other intersexuals—including two who had been fortunate enough to escape medical attention. I realized that intersexuality, rather than being extremely rare, must be relatively common. I decided to create a support network. In the summer of 1993, I produced some pamphlets, obtained a post office box, and began to publicize the Intersex Society of North America (ISNA) through small notices in the media. Before long, I was receiving several letters per week from intersexuals throughout the United States and Canada and occasionally some from Europe. While the details varied, the letters gave a remarkably coherent picture of the emotional consequences of medical intervention. Morgan Holmes: "All the things my body might have grown to do, all the possibilities, went down the hall with my amputated clitoris to the pathology department. The rest of me went to the recovery room—I'm still recovering." Angela Moreno: "I am horrified by what has been done to me and by the conspiracy of silence and lies. I am filled with grief and rage, but also relief finally to believe that maybe I am not the only one." Thomas: "I pray that I will have the means to repay, in some measure, the American Urological Association for all that it has done for my benefit. I am having some trouble, though, in connecting the timing mechanism to the fuse."

ISNA's most immediate goal has been to create a community of intersex people who could provide peer support to deal with shame, stigma, grief, and rage as well as with practical issues such as how to obtain old medical records or locate a sympathetic psychotherapist or endocrinologist. To that end, I cooperated with journalists whom I judged capable of reporting widely and responsibly on our efforts, listed ISNA with self-help and referral clearinghouses, and established a presence on the Internet (http://www.isna.org). ISNA now connects hundreds of intersexuals across North America, Europe, Australia, and New Zealand. It has also begun sponsoring an annual intersex retreat, the first of which took place in 1996 and which moved participants every bit as profoundly as the New Woman Conference had moved me in 1993.

ISNA's longer-term and more fundamental goal, however, is to change the way intersex infants are treated. We advocate that surgery not be performed on ambiguous genitals unless there is a medical reason (such as blocked or painful urination), and that parents be given the conceptual tools and emotional support to accept their children's physical differences. While it is fascinating to think about the potential development of new genders or subject positions grounded in forms of embodiment that fall outside the familiar male/female dichotomy, we recognize that the two-sex/gender model is currently hegemonic and therefore advocate that children be raised either as boys or girls, according to which designation seems most likely to offer the child the greatest future sense of comfort. Advocating gender assignment without resorting to normalizing surgery is a radical position given that it requires the willful disruption of the assumed concordance between body shape and gender category. However, this is the only position that prevents irreversible physical damage to the intersex person's body, that respects the intersex person's agency regarding his/her own flesh, and that recognizes genital sensation and erotic functioning to be at least as important as reproductive capacity. If an intersex child or adult decides to change gender or to undergo surgical or hormonal alteration of his/her body, that decision should also be fully respected and facilitated. The key point is that intersex subjects should not be violated for the comfort and convenience of others.

One part of reaching ISNA's long-term goal has been to document the emotional and physical carnage resulting from medical interventions. As a rapidly growing literature makes abundantly clear (see the bibliography on our website, http://www.isna.org/bigbib.html), the medical management of intersexuality has changed little in the forty years since my first surgery. Kessler expresses surprise that "in spite of the thousands of genital operations performed every year, there are no meta-analyses from within the medical community on levels of success."[25] They do not know whether postsurgical intersexuals are "silent and happy or silent and unhappy."[26] There is no research effort to improve erotic functioning for adult intersexuals whose genitals have been altered, nor are there psychotherapists specializing in working with adult intersex clients trying to heal from the trauma of medical intervention. To provide a counterpoint to the mountains of medical literature that neglect intersex experience and to begin compiling an ethnographic account of that experience, ISNA's *Hermaphrodites with Attitude* newsletter has developed into a forum for intersexuals to tell their own stories. We have sent complimentary copies of the newsletter filled with searing personal narratives to academics, writers, journalists, minority rights organizations, and medical practitioners—to anybody we thought might make a difference in our campaign to change the way intersex bodies are managed.

ISNA's presence has begun to generate effects. It has helped politicize the growing number of intersex organizations, as well as intersex identities themselves. When I first began organizing ISNA, I met leaders of the Turner's Syndrome Society, the oldest known support group focusing on atypical sexual differentiation, founded in 1987. Turner's Syndrome is defined by an XO genetic karyotype that results in a female body morphology with nonfunctioning ovaries, extremely short stature, and a variety of other physical differences described in the medical literature with such stigmatizing labels as "web-necked" and "fish-mouthed." Each of these women told me what a profound, life-changing experience it had been simply to meet another person like herself. I was inspired by their accomplishments (they are a national organization serving thousands of members), but I wanted ISNA to have a different focus. I was less willing to think of intersexuality as a pathology or disability, more interested in challenging its medicalization entirely, and more interested still in politicizing a pan-intersexual identity across the divisions of particular etiologies in order to destabilize more effectively the heteronormative assumptions underlying the violence directed at our bodies.

When I established ISNA in 1993, no such politicized groups existed. In the United Kingdom in 1988, the mother of a girl with androgen-insensitivity syndrome (AIS, which produces genetic males with female genital morphologies) formed the AIS Support Group. The group, which initially lobbied for increased medical attention (better surgical techniques for producing greater vaginal depth, more research into the osteoporosis that often attends AIS), now has chapters in five countries. Another group, K. S. and Associates, was formed in 1989 by the mother of a boy with Klinefelter's Syndrome and today serves over one thousand families. Klinefelter's is characterized by the presence of one or more additional X chromosomes, which produce bodies with fairly masculine external genitals, above-average height, and somewhat gangly limbs. At puberty, people with K. S. often experience pelvic broadening and the development of breasts. K. S. and Associates continues to be dominated by parents, is highly medical in orientation, and has resisted attempts by adult Klinefelter's Syndrome men to discuss gender identity or sexual orientation issues related to their intersex condition.

Since ISNA has been on the scene, other groups with a more resistant stance vis-à-vis the medical establishment have begun to appear. In 1995, a mother who refused medical pressure for female assignment for her intersex child formed the Ambiguous Genitalia Support Network, which introduces parents of intersexuals to each other and encourages the development of pen-pal support relationships. In 1996, another mother who had rejected medical pressure to assign her intersex infant as a female by removing his penis formed the Hermaphrodite Education and Listening Post (HELP) to provide peer support and medical information. Neither of these parent-oriented groups, however, frames its work in overtly political terms. Still, political analysis and action of the sort advocated by ISNA has not been without effect on the more narrowly defined service-oriented or parent-dominated groups. The AIS Support Group, now more representative of both adults and parents, noted in a recent newsletter,

> Our first impression of ISNA was that they were perhaps a bit too angry and militant to gain the support of the medical profession. However, we have to say that, having read [political analyses of intersexuality by ISNA, Kessler, Fausto-Sterling, and Holmes], we feel that the feminist concepts relating to the patriarchal treatment of intersexuality are extremely interesting and do make a lot of sense. After all, the lives of intersexed people are stigmatized by the cultural disapproval of their genital appearance, [which need not] affect their experience as sexual human beings.[27]

Other more militant groups have now begun to pop up. In 1994, German intersexuals formed both the Workgroup on Violence in Pediatrics and Gynecology and the Genital Mutilation Survivors' Support Network, and Hijra Nippon now represents activist intersexuals in Japan.

Outside the rather small community of intersex organizations, ISNA's work has generated a complex patchwork of alliances and oppositions. Queer activists, especially transgender activists, have provided encouragement, advice, and logistical support to the intersex movement. The direct action group Trans-sexual Menace helped an ad hoc group of militant intersexuals calling themselves Hermaphrodites with Attitude plan and carry out a picket of the 1996 annual meeting of the American Academy of Pediatrics in Boston—the first recorded instance of intersex public protest in modern history.[28] ISNA was also invited to join GenderPAC, a recently formed national consortium of transgender organizations that lobbies against discrimination based on atypical expressions of gender or embodiment. More mainstream gay and lesbian political organizations such as the National Gay and Lesbian Task Force have also been willing to include intersex concerns as part of their political agendas. Transgender and lesbian/gay groups have been supportive of intersex political activism largely because they see similarities in the medicalization of these various identities as a form of social control and (especially for transsexuals) empathize with our struggle to assert agency within a medical discourse that works to efface the ability to exercise informed consent about what happens to one's own body.

Gay/lesbian caucuses and special interest groups within professional medical associations have been especially receptive to ISNA's agenda. One physician on the Internet discussion group glb-medical wrote:

> The effect of Cheryl Chase's postings—admittedly, after the shock wore off—was to make me realize that THOSE WHO HAVE BEEN TREATED might very well think [they had not been well served by medical intervention]. This matters a lot. As a gay man, and simply as a person, I have struggled for much of my adult life to find my own natural self, to disentangle the confusions caused by others' presumptions about how I am/should be. But, thankfully, their decisions were not surgically imposed on me!

Queer psychiatrists, starting with Bill Byne at New York's Mount Sinai Hospital, have been quick to support ISNA, in part because the psychological principles underlying the current intersex treatment protocols are manifestly unsound. They seem almost willfully designed to exacerbate rather than ameliorate already difficult emotional issues arising from sexual difference. Some of these psychiatrists see the surgical and endocrinological domination of a problem that even surgeons and endocrinologists acknowledge to be psychosocial rather than biomedical as an unjustified invasion of their area of professional competence.

ISNA has deliberately cultivated a network of nonintersexed advocates who command a measure of social legitimacy and can speak in contexts where uninterpreted intersex voices will not be heard. Because there is a strong impulse to discount what intersexuals have to say about intersexuality, sympathetic representation has been welcome—especially in helping intersexuals reframe intersexuality in nonmedical terms. Some gender theory scholars, feminist critics of science, medical historians, and anthropologists have been quick to understand and support intersex activism. Years before ISNA came into existence, feminist biologist and science studies scholar Anne Fausto-Sterling had written about intersexuality in relation to intellectually suspect scientific practices that perpetuate masculinist constructs of gender, and she became an early ISNA ally.[29] Likewise, social psychologist Suzanne Kessler had written a brilliant ethnography of surgeons who specialize in treating intersexuals. After speaking with several "products" of their practice, she, too, became a strong supporter of intersex activism.[30] Historian of science Alice Dreger, whose work focuses not only on hermaphroditism but on other forms of potentially benign atypical embodiment that become subject to destructively normalizing medical interventions (conjoined twins, for example), has been especially supportive. Fausto-Sterling, Kessler, and Dreger will each shortly publish works that analyze the medical treatment of intersexuality as being culturally motivated and criticize it as harmful to its ostensible patients.[31]

Allies who help contest the medicalization of intersexuality are especially important because ISNA has found it almost entirely fruitless to attempt direct, nonconfrontational interactions with the medical specialists who themselves determine policy on the treatment of intersex infants and who actually carry out the surgeries. Joycelyn Elders, the Clinton administration's first surgeon general, is a pediatric endocrinologist with many years of experience managing intersex infants but, in spite of a generally feminist approach to health care and frequent overtures from ISNA, she has been dismissive of the concerns of intersexuals themselves.[32] Another pediatrician remarked in an Internet discussion on intersexuality: "I think this whole issue is preposterous.... To suggest that [medical decisions about the treatment of intersex conditions] are somehow cruel or arbitrary is insulting, ignorant and misguided.... To spread the claims that [ISNA] is making is just plain wrong, and I hope that this [on-line group of doctors and scientists] will not blindly accept them." Yet another participant in that same chat asked what was for him obviously a rhetorical question: "Who is the enemy? I really don't think it's the medical establishment. Since when did we establish the male/female hegemony?" While a surgeon quoted in a *New York Times* article on ISNA summarily dismissed us as "zealots,"[33] there is considerable anecdotal information supplied by ISNA sympathizers that professional meetings in the fields of pediatrics, urology, genital plastic surgery, and endocrinology are buzzing with anxious and defensive discussions of intersex activism. In response to the Hermaphrodites with Attitude protests at the American Academy of Pediatrics meeting, that organization felt compelled to issue the following statement to the press: "The Academy is deeply concerned about the emotional, cognitive, and body image development of intersexuals, and believes that successful early genital surgery minimizes these issues." Further protests were planned for 1997.

The roots of resistance to the truth claims of intersexuals run deep in the medical establishment. Not only does ISNA critique the normativist biases couched within most scientific practice, it advocates a treatment protocol for intersex infants that disrupts conventional understandings of the relationship between bodies and genders. But on a level more personally threatening to medical practitioners, ISNA's position implies that they have—unwittingly at best, through willful denial at worst—spent their careers inflicting a profound harm from which their patients will never fully recover. ISNA's position threatens to destroy the assumptions motivating an entire medical subspecialty, thus jeopardizing the ability to perform what many surgeons find to be technically difficult and fascinating work. Melissa Hendricks notes that Dr. Gearhart is known to colleagues as a surgical "artist" who can "carve a large phallus down into a clitoris" with consummate skill.[34] More than one ISNA member has discovered that surgeons actually operated on their genitals at no charge. The medical establishment's fascination with its own power to change sex and its drive to rescue parents from their intersex children are so strong that heroic interventions are delivered without regard to the capitalist model that ordinarily governs medical services.

Given such deep and mutually reinforcing reasons for opposing ISNA's position, it is hardly surprising that medical intersex specialists have, for the most part, turned a deaf ear toward us. The lone exception as of April 1997 is urologist Justine Schober. After watching a videotape of the 1996 ISNA retreat and receiving other input from HELP and the AIS Support Group, she suggests in a new textbook on pediatric surgery that while technology has advanced to the point that "our needs [as surgeons] and the needs of parents to have a presentable child can be satisfied," it is time to acknowledge that problems exist that "we as surgeons...cannot address. Success in psychosocial adjustment is the true goal of sexual assignment and genitoplasty.... Surgery makes parents and doctors comfortable, but counseling makes people comfortable too, and is not irreversible."[35]

While ISNA will continue to approach the medical establishment for dialogue (and continue supporting protests outside the closed doors when doctors refuse to talk), perhaps the most important aspect of our current activities is the struggle to change public perceptions. By using the mass media, the Internet, and our growing network of allies and sympathizers to make the general public aware of the frequency of intersexuality and of the intense suffering that medical treatment has caused, we seek to create an environment in which many parents of intersex children will have already heard about the intersex movement when their child is born. Such informed parents we hope will be better able to resist medical pressure for unnecessary genital surgery and secrecy and to find their way to a peer-support group and counseling rather than to a surgical theater.

FIRST-WORLD FEMINISM, AFRICAN CLITORECTOMY, AND INTERSEX GENITAL MUTILATION

> We must first locate and challenge our own position as rigorously as we challenge that of others.
> —Salem Mekuria, "Female Genital Mutilation in Africa"

Traditional African practices that remove the clitoris and other parts of female genitals have lately been a target of intense media coverage and feminist activism in the United States and other industrialized Western societies. The euphemism *female circumcision* largely has been supplanted by the politicized term *female genital mutilation* (FGM). Analogous operations performed on intersexuals in the United States have not been the focus of similar attention—indeed, attempts to link the two forms of genital cutting have met with multiform resistance. Examining how first-world feminists and mainstream media treat traditional African practices and comparing that treatment with their responses to intersex genital mutilation (IGM) in North America exposes some of the complex interactions between ideologies of race, gender, colonialism, and science that effectively silence and render invisible intersex experience in first-world contexts. Cutting intersex genitals becomes yet another hidden mechanism for imposing normalcy upon unruly flesh, a means of containing the potential anarchy of desires and identifications within oppressive heteronormative structures.

In 1994, the *New England Journal of Medicine* paired an article on the physical harm resulting from African genital surgery with an editorial denouncing clitorectomy as a violation of human rights but declined to run a reply drafted by University of California at Berkeley medical anthropologist Lawrence Cohen and two ISNA members detailing the harm caused by medicalized American clitorectomies.[36] In response to growing media attention, Congress passed the Federal Prohibition of Female Genital Mutilation Act in October 1996, but the act specifically exempted from prohibition medicalized clitorectomies of the sort performed to "correct" intersex bodies. The bill's principal author, former Congresswoman Patricia Schroeder, received and ignored many letters from ISNA members and Brown University professor of medical science Anne Fausto-Sterling asking her to recast the bill's language. The *Boston Globe*'s syndicated columnist Ellen Goodman is one of the few journalists covering African FGM to respond to ISNA. "I must admit I was not aware of this situation," she wrote to me in 1994. "I admire your courage." She continued, however, regularly to discuss African FGM in her column without mentioning similar American practices. One of her October 1995 columns on FGM was promisingly titled, "We Don't Want to Believe It Happens Here," but it discussed only immigrants to the United States from third-world countries who performed clitorectomies on their daughters in keeping with the practices of their native cultures.

While clitorectomized African immigrant women doing anti-FGM activism in the United States have been receptive to the claims made by intersex opponents to medicalized clitorectomies and are in dialogue with us, first-world feminists and organizations working on African FGM have totally ignored us. To my knowledge, only two of the many anti-FGM groups contacted have responded to repeated overtures from intersex activists. Fran Hosken, who since 1982 has regularly published a catalogue of statistics on female genital mutilation worldwide, wrote me a terse note saying that "we are not concerned with biological exceptions."[37] Forward International, another anti-FGM organization, replied to an inquiry from German intersexual Heike Spreitzer that her letter was "most interesting" but that they could not help because their work focuses only on "female genital mutilation that is performed as a harmful cultural or traditional practice on young girls." As Forward International's reply to Spreitzer demonstrates, many first-world anti-FGM activists seemingly consider Africans to have "harmful cultural or traditional practices," while we in the modern industrialized West presumably have something better. We have science, which is linked to the metanarratives of enlightenment, progress, and truth. Genital cutting is condoned to the extent that it supports these cultural self-conceptions.

Robin Morgan and Gloria Steinem set the tone for subsequent first-world feminist analyses of FGM with their pathbreaking article in the March 1980 issue of *Ms.* magazine, "The International Crime of Genital Mutilation."[38] A disclaimer warns, "These words are painful to read. They describe facts of life as far away as our most fearful imagination—and as close as any denial of women's sexual freedom." For *Ms.* readers, whom the editors imagine are more likely to experience the pain of genital mutilation between the covers of their magazine than between their thighs, clitorectomy is presented as a fact of foreign life whose principal relevance to their readership is that it exemplifies a loss of "freedom," that most cherished possession of the liberal Western subject. The article features a photograph of an African girl with her legs held open by the arm of an unseen woman to her right. To her left is the disembodied hand of the midwife, holding the razor blade with which she has just performed a ritual clitorectomy. The girl's face—mouth open, eyes bulging—is a mask of pain. In more than fifteen years of coverage, Western images of African practices have changed little. "Americans made a horrifying discovery this year," *Life* soberly informed its readers in January 1997 while showing a two-page photo spread of a Kenyan girl held from behind as unseen hands cut her genitals.[39] The 1996 Pulitzer Prize for feature photography went to yet another portrayal of a Kenyan clitorectomy.[40] And in the wake of Fauziya Kassindja's successful bid for asylum in the United States after fleeing clitorectomy in Togo, the number of FGM images available from her country has skyrocketed.[41]

These representations all manifest a profound othering of African clitorectomy that contributes to the silence surrounding similar medicalized practices in the industrialized West. "Their" genital cutting is barbaric ritual; "ours" is scientific. Theirs disfigures; ours normalizes the deviant. The colonialist implications of these representations of genital cutting are even more glaringly obvious when images of intersex surgeries are juxtaposed with images of African FGM. Medical books describing how to perform clitoral surgery on white North American intersex children are almost always illustrated with extreme genital close-ups, disconnecting the genitals not only from the individual intersexed person but from the body itself. Full-body shots always have the eyes blacked out. Why is it considered necessary to black out the eyes of clitorectomized American girls—thus preserving a shred of their privacy and helping ward off the viewer's identification with the abject image—but not the eyes of the clitorectomized African girls in the pages of American magazines?[42]

First-world feminist discourse locates clitorectomy not only "elsewhere," in Africa, but also "elsewhen" in time. A recent *Atlantic Monthly* article on African clitorectomy asserted that the "American medical profession stopped performing clitoridectomies decades ago," and the magazine has since declined to publish a contradictory letter to the editor from ISNA.[43] Academic publications are as prone to this attitude as the popular press. In the recent *Deviant Bodies* anthology, visual artist Susan Jahoda's "Theatres of Madness" juxtaposes nineteenth- and twentieth-century material depicting "the conceptual interdependence of sexuality, reproduction, family life, and 'female disorders.' "[44] To represent twentieth-century medical clitorectomy practices, Jahoda quotes a July 1980 letter written to *Ms.* magazine in response to Morgan and Steinem. The letter writer, a nurse's aide in a geriatric home, said she had been puzzled by the strange scars she saw on the genitals of five of the forty women in her care: "Then I read your article.... My God! Why? Who decided to deny them orgasm? Who made them go through such a procedure? I want to know. Was it fashionable? Or was it to correct 'a condition'? I'd like to know what this so-called civilized country used as its criteria for such a procedure. And how widespread is it here in the United States?"[45] While Jahoda's selection of this letter does raise the issue of medicalized American clitorectomies, it safely locates the genital cutting in the past, as something experienced a long time ago by women now in their later stages of life.

Significantly, Jahoda literally passed over an excellent opportunity to comment on the continuing practice of clitorectomy in the contemporary United States. Two months earlier, in the April 1980 issue of *Ms.*, feminist biologists Ruth Hubbard and Patricia Farnes also replied to Morgan and Steinem:

> We want to draw the attention of your readers to the practice of clitoridectomy not only in the Third World...but right here in the United States, where it is used as part of a procedure to "repair" by "plastic surgery" so-called genital ambiguities. Few people realize that this procedure has routinely involved removal of the entire clitoris and its nerve supply—in other words, total clitoridectomy....In a lengthy article, [Johns Hopkins intersex expert John] Money and two colleagues write...that "a three-year old girl about to be clitoridectomized...should be well informed that *the doctors will make her look like all other girls and women*' (our emphasis), which is not unlike what North African girls are often told about their clitoridectomies.... But to date, neither Money nor his critics have investigated the effect of clitoridectomies on the girls' development. Yet one would surely expect this to affect their psychosexual development and their feelings of identity as young women.[46]

While Farnes and Hubbard's prescient feminist exposé of medicalized clitorectomies in the contemporary United States sank without a trace, there has been an explosion of work that keeps "domestic" clitorectomy at a safe distance. Such conceptualizations of clitorectomy's geographical and temporal cultural remoteness allow first-world feminist outrage to be diverted into potentially colonialist meddling in the social affairs of others while hampering work for social justice at home.[47]

Feminism represents itself as being interested in unmasking the silence that surrounds violence against women. Most medical intersex management is another form of violence based on a sexist devaluing of female pain and female sexuality. Doctors consider the prospect of growing up as a boy with a small penis to be a worse alternative than growing up as a girl *sans* clitoris and ovaries; they gender intersex bodies accordingly and cut them up to make the assigned genders support cultural norms of embodiment. These medical interventions transform many transgressive bodies into ones that can be labeled safely as women and subjected to the many forms of social control with which women must contend. Why then have most first-world feminists met intersexuals with a blank stare?

Intersexuals have had such difficulty generating mainstream feminist support not only because of the racist and colonialist frameworks that situate clitorectomy as a practice foreign to proper subjects within the first world but also because intersexuality undermines the stability of the category "woman" that undergirds much of first-world feminist discourse. We call into question the assumed relation between genders and bodies and demonstrate how some bodies do not fit easily into male/female dichotomies. We embody viscerally the truth of Judith Butler's dictum that "sex," the concept that accomplishes the materialization and naturalization of power-laden, culturally constructed differences, has really been "gender all along."[48] By refusing to remain silenced, we queer the foundations upon which depend not only the medical management of bodies but also widely shared feminist assumptions of properly embodied feminine subjectivity. To the extent that we are not normatively female or normatively women, we are not considered the proper subjects of feminist concern.

As unwilling subjects of science and improper subjects of feminism, politicized intersex activists have deep stakes in allying with and participating in the sorts of poststructuralist cultural work that exposes the foundational assumptions about personhood shared by the dominant society, conventional feminism, and many other identity-based oppositional social movements. We have a stake, too, in the efforts of gender queers to carve out livable social spaces for reconfigured forms of embodiment, identity, and desire. In 1990, Suzanne Kessler noted that "the possibilities for real societal transformations would be unlimited" if physicians and scientists specializing in the management of gender could recognize that "finally, and always, people construct gender as well as the social systems that are grounded in gender-based concepts. . . . Accepting genital ambiguity as a natural option would require that physicians also acknowledge that genital ambiguity is 'corrected' not because it is threatening to the infant's life but because it is threatening to the infant's culture."[49] At that time, intersexuals had not yet been heard from, and there was little reason to think that physicians or other members of their culture would ever reflect on the meaning or effect of what they were doing. The advent of an activist intersex opposition changes everything.

NOTES

My appreciation goes to Susan Stryker for her extensive contributions to the structure and substance of this essay.

1   Claude J. Migeon, Gary D. Berkovitz, and Terry R. Brown, "Sexual Differentiation and Ambiguity," in *Wilkins: The Diagnosis and Treatment of Endocrine Disorders in Childhood and Adolescence,* ed. Michael S. Kappy, Robert M. Blizzard, and Claude J. Migeon (Springfield, Ill.: Charles C. Thomas, 1994), 573–715.

2.   Lalitha Raman-Wilms et al., "Fetal Genital Effects of First-Trimester Sex Hormone Exposure: A Meta-Analysis," *Obstetrics and Gynecology* 85 (1995): 141–48.

3.   Anne Fausto-Sterling, *Body Building: How Biologists Construct Sexuality* (New York: Basic Books, forthcoming).

4.   Judith Butler, *Gender Trouble: Feminism and the Subversion of Identity* (New York: Routledge, 1990); Thomas Laqueur, *Making Sex: Body and Gender from the Greeks to Freud* (Cambridge, Mass.: Harvard University Press, 1990).

5.   Suzanne Kessler and Wendy McKenna, *Gender: An Ethnomethodological Approach* (New York: John Wiley and Sons, 1978).

6.   Alice Domurat Dreger, "Doubtful Sex: Cases and Concepts of Hermaphroditism in France and Britain, 1868–1915," (Ph. D. diss., Indiana University, 1995); Alice Domurat Dreger, "Doubtful Sex: The Fate of the Hermaphrodite in Victorian Medicine," *Victorian Studies* (spring 1995): 336–70; Alice Domurat Dreger, "Hermaphrodites in Love: The Truth of the Gonads," *Science and Homosexualities,* ed. Vernon Rosario (New York: Routledge, 1997), 46–66; Alice Domurat Dreger, "Doctors Containing Hermaphrodites: The Victorian Legacy," *Chrysalis: The Journal of Transgressive Gender Identities* (fall 1997): 15–22.

7.   Hugh Hampton Young, *Genital Abnormalities, Hermaphroditism, and Related Adrenal Diseases* (Baltimore: Williams and Wilkins, 1937), xxxix–xl.

8.   Ibid., 139–42.

9.   Howard W. Jones Jr. and William Wallace Scott, *Hermaphroditism, Genital Anomalies, and Related Endocrine Disorders* (Baltimore: Williams and Wilkins, 1958), 269.

10. John Money, Joan G. Hampson, and John L. Hampson, "An Examination of Some Basic Sexual Concepts: The Evidence of Human Hermaphroditism," *Bulletin of the Johns Hopkins Hospital* 97 (1955): 301–19; John Money, Joan G. Hampson, and John L. Hampson, "Hermaphroditism: Recommendations Concerning Assignment of Sex, Change of Sex, and Psychologic Management," *Bulletin of Johns Hopkins Hospital* 97 (1955): 284–300; John Money, *Venuses Penuses* (Buffalo: Prometheus, 1986).

11. Robert M. Blizzard, "Lawson Wilkins," in Kappy et al., *Wilkins,* xi–xiv.

12. Suzanne Kessler, "The Medical Construction of Gender: Case Management of Intersexual Infants," *Signs: Journal of Women in Culture and Society* 16 (1990): 3–26.

13. J. Dewhurst and D. B. Grant, "Intersex Problems," *Archives of Disease in Childhood* 59 (1984): 1191–94; Anita Natarajan, "Medical Ethics and Truth-Telling in the Case of Androgen Insensitivity Syndrome," *Canadian Medical Association Journal* 154 (1996): 568–70; Tom Mazur, "Ambiguous Genitalia: Detection and Counseling," *Pediatric Nursing* (1983): 417–22; F. M. E. Slijper et al., "Neonates with Abnormal Genital Development Assigned the Female Sex: Parent Counseling," *Journal of Sex Education and Therapy* 20 (1994): 9–17.

14. Milton T. Edgerton, "Discussion: Clitoroplasty for Clitoromegaly due to Adrenogenital Syndrome without Loss of Sensitivity (by Nobuyuki Sagehashi)," *Plastic and Reconstructive Surgery* 91 (1993): 956.

15. Melissa Hendricks, "Is It a Boy or a Girl?" *Johns Hopkins Magazine,* November 1993, 10–16.

16. John F. Stecker et al., "Hypospadias Cripples," *Urologic Clinics of North America: Symposium on Hypospadias* 8 (1981): 539–44.

17. Jeff McClintock, "Growing Up in the Surgical Maelstrom," *Chrysalis: The Journal of Transgressive Gender Identities* (fall 1997): 53–54.

18. Robert E. Gross, Judson Randolph, and John F. Crigler, "Clitorectomy for Sexual Abnormalities: Indications and Technique," *Surgery* 59 (1966): 300–308.

19. Joseph E. Oesterling, John P. Gearhart, and Robert D. Jeffs, "A Unified Approach to Early Reconstructive Surgery of the Child with Ambiguous Genitalia," *Journal of Urology* 138 (1987): 1079–84.

20. Kira Triea, "The Awakening," *Hermaphrodites with Attitude* (winter 1994): 1; Susan Stryker, "My Words to Victor Frankenstein above the Village of Chamounix: Performing Transgender Rage," *GLQ* 1 (1994): 237–54.

21. Leslie Feinberg, *Stone Butch Blues* (Ithaca, N.Y.: Firebrand, 1993); Leslie Feinberg, *Transgender Liberation: A Movement Whose Time Has Come* (New York: World View Forum, 1992).

22. See, for example, Judith Butler, *Bodies That Matter: On the Discursive Limits of "Sex"* (New York: Routledge, 1993); Butler, *Gender Trouble; Laqueur, Making Sex;* and Julia Epstein and Kristina Straub, eds., *Body Guards: The Cultural Politics of Gender Ambiguity* (New York: Routledge, 1991).

23. Morgan Holmes, "Medical Politics and Cultural Imperatives: Intersexuality Beyond Pathology and Erasure" (master's thesis, York University, Toronto, 1994).

24. Sandy Stone, "The *Empire* Strikes Back: A Posttranssexual Manifesto," in Epstein and Straub, *Body Guards,* 280–304, quotation on 296.

25. Suzanne Kessler, *Lessons from the Intersexed* (New Brunswick, N.J.: Rutgers University Press, forthcoming).

26. Robert Jeffs, quoted in Ellen Barry, "United States of Ambiguity," Boston *Phoenix,* 22 November 1996, 6–8, quotation on 6.

27. AIS Support Group, "Letter to America," *ALIAS* (spring 1996): 3–4.

28. Barry, "United States of Ambiguity," 7.

29. Anne Fausto-Sterling, "The Five Sexes: Why Male and Female Are Not Enough," *The Sciences* 33, no. 2 (March/April 1993): 20–25; Anne Fausto-Sterling, *Myths of Gender: Biological Theories about Women and Men,* 2d ed. (New York: Basic Books, 1985), 134–41.

30. Kessler, "The Medical Construction of Gender"; Suzanne Kessler, "Meanings of Genital Variability," *Chrysalis: The Journal of Transgressive Gender Identities* (fall 1997): 33–38.

31. Anne Fausto-Sterling, *Building Bodies: Biology and the Social Construction of Sexuality* (New York: Basic Books, forthcoming); Kessler, "Meanings of Genital Variability"; Alice Domurat Dreger, *Hermaphrodites and the Medical Invention of Sex* (Cambridge, Mass.: Harvard University Press, forthcoming).

32. "Dr. Elders' Medical History," *New Yorker,* 26 September 1994: 45–46; Joycelyn Elders and David Chanoff, *From Sharecropper's Daughter to Surgeon General of the United States of America* (New York: William Morrow, 1996).

33. Natalie Angier, "Intersexual Healing: An Anomaly Finds a Group," *New York Times,* 4 February 1996, E14.

34. Hendricks, "Is It a Boy or a Girl?" 10.

35. Justine M. Schober, "Long Term Outcomes of Feminizing Genitoplasty for Intersex," in *Pediatric Surgery and Urology: Long Term Outcomes,* ed. Pierre Mouriquant (Philadelphia: W. B. Saunders, forthcoming).

36. Patricia Schroeder, "Female Genital Mutilation," *New England Journal of Medicine* 331 (1994): 739–40; Nahid Toubia, "Female Circumcision as a Public Health Issue," *New England Journal of Medicine* 331 (1994): 712–16.

37. Fran P. Hosken, *The Hosken Report: Genital/Sexual Mutilation of Females,* 4th ed. (Lexington, Mass.: WIN News, 1994).

38. Robin Morgan and Gloria Steinem, "The International Crime of Genital Mutilation," *Ms.,* March 1980, 65–67ff.

39. Mariella Furrer, "Ritual Agony," *Life,* January 1997, 38–39.

40. Pulitzer Prize Board, "Feature Photography: Stephanie Welsh," 1996. Available online at http://www.pulitzer.org/winners/1996/winners/works/feature-photography/.

41. Celia Dugger, "U.S. Grants Asylum to Woman Fleeing Genital Mutilation Rite," *New York Times,* 14 June 1996, A1; Celia Dugger, "New Law Bans Genital Cutting in the United States," *New York Times,* 12 October 1996, 1; Furrer, "Ritual Agony."

42. Dugger, "U.S. Grants Asylum"; Salem Mekuria, "Female Genital Mutilation in Africa: Some African Views," *Association of Concerned African Scholars Bulletin* (winter/spring 1995): 2–6.

43. Linda Burstyn, "Female Circumcision Comes to America," *Atlantic Monthly,* October 1995, 28–35.

44. Susan Jahoda, "Theatres of Madness," *Deviant Bodies,* ed. Jennifer Terry and Jacqueline Urla (Bloomington: Indiana University Press, 1995), 251–76.

45. Letter to the editor, *Ms.,* July 1980, 12.

46. Ruth Hubbard and Patrica Farnes, letter to the editor, *Ms.,* April 1980, 9–10.

47. Seble Dawit and Salem Mekuria, "The West Just Doesn't Get It," *New York Times,* 7 December 1993, A27.

48. Butler, *Gender Trouble,* 8.

49. Kessler, "Medical Construction of Gender," 25.

23

Mutilating Gender

Dean Spade

In "Mutilating Gender," legal activist and theorist Dean Spade uses the work of Michel Foucault to examine the relationship between gender normativity and technologies of gender-related bodily alteration. Although Spade is critical of medical discourse, practices, and institutions that undermine transgender access to body-modifying procedures, he side-steps some of the usual acrimony between service-seekers and service-providers by focusing instead on the regimes of normalization that inform both sides of the power-imbalanced, asymmetrical negotiations over bodily modification.

Spade makes explicit use Foucault's notion of power as a productive and enabling force, rather than merely a repressive one, as well as Foucault's view of governance and discipline as a mesh of power relations that increasingly insinuate themselves, in capillary fashion, into ever-more intimate aspects of life. Spade shows not only how certain social forces say "no" to transgender requests for bodily alteration in order to prop up a naturalized version of the sexual binary, but also how saying "yes" to such requests can likewise support and sustain standard forms of gender and embodiment. Such a move frustrates any simple attempt to link transgender activism, and the demand for increased availability of gender-related body-altering practices, with progressive, subversive, radical, or liberatory political ideals. Transgender consumers, as well as transgender service providers, are implicated in relations of power that produce and enforce the norms of gender.

In a rhetorical move of which Foucault would have approved, Spade combines intellectually legitimated forms of analysis and critique with a narrative account of his own quest for nonnormativizing body-alteration. His refusal to feign a disinterested distance from the topic of his analysis, his explicit articulation of his embodied stake in the matter at hand, and the knowledge gained from his own embodied situation all exemplify important methodological hallmarks of transgender studies.

> "How do you know you want rhinoplasty, a nose job?" he inquires, fixing me with a penetrating stare.
> "Because," I reply, suddenly unable to raise my eyes above his brown wingtips, "I've always felt like a small-nosed woman trapped in a large-nosed body."
> "And how long have you felt this way?" He leans forward, sounding as if he knows the answer and needs only to hear the words.
> "Oh, since I was five or six, doctor, practically all my life."
> "Then you have rhino-identity disorder," the shoetops state flatly. My body sags in relief. "But first," he goes on, "we want you to get letters from two psychiatrists and live as a small-nosed woman for three years...just to be sure."[1]

In 1958, a woman named Agnes presented her self to doctors at the Department of Psychiatry of the University of California, Los Angeles seeking plastic surgery to "remedy an apparent endocrine abnormality."[2] The doctors were engaged in a study of intersexed patients, and were interested to find that Agnes appeared a "feminine" woman, with female secondary sex characteristics, but also had a fully developed penis and atrophic scrotum. Agnes explained that she had been brought up as a boy, but had always felt she was a girl and had developed female characteristics at puberty. The medical team diagnosed Agnes with "testicular feminization syndrome," speculating that her feminine characteristics came from estrogens produced by her testes.[3] They performed surgery to remove her penis and testes in order to correct this "natural mistake."

Five years after Agnes obtained surgery, and eight years after first came to the UCLA clinic, she revealed to the doctors that she had not spontaneously developed female secondary sex characteristics, but had engineered a feminine appearance by taking her mother's estrogen beginning at the age of twelve. Hausman comments, "Agnes's 'passing' from man to woman turns out to have been based on another kind of 'passing' altogether."[4] Agnes achieved her surgical goals by fooling the doctors into believing that she was intersexed–the criteria for receiving such surgery in their program.

What is the significance of the necessity for and execution of Agnes's deception of the doctors? How should gender theorists, feminists, and trans people understand the long-standing practice amongst gender variant people of strategically deploying medically-approved narratives in order to obtain body-alteration goals?

This essay examines the relationship between individuals seeking sex reassignment surgery (SRS)[5] and the medical establishments with which they must contend in order to fulfill their goals. My starting point for this analysis is Foucault's understanding of power as productive rather than repressive, and of governance as occurring not primarily through repressive law but through disciplinary forces which exist in "diverse, uncoordinated agencies."[6] Using Foucault's models of power and governance, I look carefully at the diagnosis and treatment of Gender Identity Disorder (GID) from the perspective of persons seeking SRS, examining how the creation of the subject position "transsexual" by the medical establishment restricts individuals seeking body alteration and promotes the creation of norm-abiding gendered subjects.

Throughout this essay, I draw on my own experience of attempting to find low-cost or free counseling in order to begin the process of getting a double mastectomy. The choice to use personal narrative in this piece comes from a belief that just such a combination of theoretical work about the relationships of trans people to medical establishments and gender norms and the experience of trans people is too rarely found. Riki Anne Wilchins describes how trans experience has been used by psychiatrists, cultural feminists, anthropologists, and sociologists "travel[ling] through our lives and problems like tourists . . . [p]icnicking on our identities . . . select[ing] the tastiest tidbits with which to illustrate a theory or push a book."[7] In most writing about trans people, our gender performance is put under a microscope to prove theories or build "expertise" while the gender performances of the authors remain unexamined and naturalized. I want to avoid even the appearance of participation in such a tradition, just as I want to use my own experience to illustrate how the requirements for diagnosis and treatment play out on individual bodies. The recent proliferation of academic and activist work on trans issues has created the impression in many people (mostly non-trans) that problems with access to services for trans people are being alleviated, and that the education of many specialists who provide services to trans people has made available sensitive therapeutic environments for trans people living in large metropolitan areas who can avail themselves of such services. My unsuccessful year-long quest for basic low-cost respectful counseling services in Los Angeles, which included seeking services at the Los Angeles Gender Center, the Los Angeles Gay and Lesbian Services Center and Children's Hospital Los Angeles is a testament to the problems that still remain.[8] This failure suggests the larger problems with the production of the "transsexual" in medical practice, and with the diagnostic and treatment criteria that made it impossible for the professionals from whom I sought care to respectfully engage my request for gender-related body alteration.

I hope that the use of my experience in this paper will provide a grounding illustration of the regulatory effects of the current diagnosis-treatment scheme for GID and resist the traditional framing of transsexual experience which posits trans people as victims or villains, insane or fascinating. Instead, I hope to be part of a project already taken up by Riki Anne Wilchins, Kate Bornstein, Leslie Feinberg, and many others which opens a position for trans people as self-critical, feminist, intellectual subjects of knowledge rather than simply case studies.

I. GOVERNANCE: PASSING AS A TRANSSEXUAL

Here's what I'm after: a surgically constructed male-appearing chest, no hormones (for now—maybe forever), no first-name change, any pronouns (except "it") are okay, although when it comes to gendered generics I happen to really like "Uncle" better than "Aunt," and definitely "Mr. Spade."[9] *Hausman writes, "transsexuals must seek and obtain medical treatment in order to be recognized as transsexuals. Their subject position depends upon a necessary relation to the medical establishment and its discourses."*[10] *I've quickly learned that the converse is also true, in order to obtain the medical intervention I am seeking, I need to prove my membership in the category "transsexual"—prove that I have GID—to the proper authorities. Unfortunately, stating my true objectives is not convincing them.*

In their essay, "The Socio-Medical Construction of Transsexualism: An Interpretation and Critique," Billings and Urban examine the development of transsexualism as a disease, and sex-change surgery as its treatment. They argue that transsexualism is socially constructed by medical practice, and is maintained by profiteer doctors who gain wealth, fame, and surgical expertise through the diagnosis and treatment (which the authors call "mutilation") of a variety of sexual deviants incorrectly labeled "transsexuals."[11] Many of the conclusions of their essay contradict the basic premises of this paper: that sexual and gender self-determination and the expression of variant gender identities without punishment (and with celebration) should be the goals of any medical, legal, or political examination of or intervention into the gender expression of individuals and groups. However, many of their theoretical understandings of the operation of medical authority with regard to gender reassignment are valuable.[12]

Billings and Urban are concerned with the "domination of daily life and consciousness by professional authority . . . [and] the extent to which many forms of deviance are increasingly labeled 'illness' " as well the possibility that "[s]ex-change surgery privatizes and depoliticizes individual experiences of gender-role distress."[13] They argue that transsexualism is constructed by and only exists through medical practice, which has invented it as a psychological entity, a problem in the minds of patients. Instead, Billings and Urban suggest that "transsexualism is a relational process sustained in medical practice and marketed in public testimony."[14]

Billings' and Urban's critique of the invention of the "transsexual" as a medical anomaly, a mentally ill person requiring treatment, offers a useful point of departure for an analysis of the treatment and diagnosis of GID that questions the terms upon which individuals seeking body alteration may receive such care. Understanding physical and mental health care as social processes with regulatory effects, we can examine the standards by which such alteration is restricted.[15]

Foucault describes a notion of productive power that instructs a critical analysis of the regulatory effects of medical diagnosis and treatment. Foucault rejects what he terms "the repressive hypothesis" as a way of viewing the history of sexuality since the 16th century.[16] He argues that the history of sexuality is not characterized by repression, but by an "incitement to speak" about sex.[17] He describes how the imperative has been to speak about sex, to accumulate detailed knowledge of it, to identify and classify it, and to seek out the origins of sexual behavior and desire. Sexuality has become the locus of the "true self"—to know the self is to know one's sex, sexuality, and desire. In this model, sex is figured not as the thing that must not be spoken, but as a public problem needing to be managed by an increasingly large group of medical, psychiatric, and criminal justice specialists.[18]

Foucault demands that the project of asking whether approaches to sex are repressive or permissive be replaced by a project of examining how sex is put into discourse. His model of power as productive requires that power does not just say "no" and enslave free subjects, but rather produces knowledge, categories and identities that manage and regulate behavior. Foucault's favored example is the invention of homosexuality. He argues that the sexologists who first discussed homosexuality were not identifying a pre-existing identity, but rather were inventing the homosexual.[19]

Foucault's theory of power requires a conception of governance which goes beyond the a juridico-discursive model where power exists in law, which represses and forbids.[20] Instead Foucault demonstrates how governance occurs through disciplinary power, located in diverse, uncoordinated agencies, including educational, medical, and psychiatric institutions. Hunt and Wickham describe disciplinary power:

> Discipline, rather than being constituted by 'minor offences,' is characteristically associated with 'norms,' that is, with 'standards,' that the subject of a discipline comes to internalise or manifest in behaviour, for example standards of tidiness, punctuality, respectfulness, etc.... These standards of proper conduct put into place a mode of regulation characterised by interventions designed to correct deviations and to secure compliance and conformity... It is through the repetition of normative requirements that the 'normal' is constructed and thus discipline results in the securing of normalisation by embedding a pattern of norms disseminated throughout daily life and secured through surveillance... '[E]xercises' and the repetition of tasks characterise the disciplinary model of []power.[21]

Disciplinary, productive power constitutes governance in the sense that it "structures the possible field of actions of others."[22] A central element of this governance is the production, dissemination, and utilization of knowledge.[23] In this understanding of the workings of domination, law is replaced or supplemented by psychiatry, psychology and medicine, which create categories of dangerous individuals, subject positions that operate as regulatory instruments.

Foucault's model of power lends to a critique of the creation of categories of illness that serve, through diagnosis and treatment, to regulate gender expression. When such an analysis is applied to transsexuality, we must ask what will be the mediating principle behind the analysis. For Billings and Urban, the principle is that the treatment of distress in gender roles through surgery is fundamentally opposed to a liberating and politicized project of gender equality. They trace the invention of the category "transsexual" by doctors, examining how medical practice has established a childhood, a sexuality, a detailed life narrative for the "transsexual" that sexual deviants of many types have mimicked and/or internalized[24] as norms in order to relieve or explain gender distress. They correctly assert that this narrative shores up traditional notions of gender dichotomy and compulsory heterosexuality.[25] However, because their mediating principle is that body alteration is *always* a privatizing and depoliticizing response to gender role distress, they paint transsexuals as brainwashed victims who have failed to figure out that they are only undermining a revolution that seeks to save them. Billings and Urban arrive at this principle by creating an arbitrary line between technology and the body that they place at sex-change procedures. They fail to include in their analysis the fact that people (transsexuals and non-transsexuals) change their gender presentation to conform to norms with multiple other technologies as well, including clothing, make-up, cosmetic surgery not labeled SRS, training in gender-specific manners, body building, dieting, and countless other practices. Like other theorists "picknicking" on transsexual identity, their work to undermine trans alteration stabilizes exercises of normative gender production, even while they suggest that gender destabilization is their goal.

An approach that recognizes the possibility of a norm-resistant, politicized, and feminist desire for gender-related body alteration need not reject the critique of medical practice regarding transsexuality nor embrace the normalizing regulations of the diagnostic and treatment processes. An alternate mediating principle for a critical analysis is possible. Such an analysis requires seeing the problem not as fundamentally lying in the project of gender change or body alteration, but in how the medical regime permits only the production of gender-normative altered bodies, and seeks to screen out alterations that are resistant to a dichotomized, naturalized view of gender. An alternative starting point for a critique of the invention and regulation of transsexualism is a desire for a deregulation of gender expression and the promotion of self-determination of gender and sexual expression, including the elimination of institutional incentives to perform normative gender and sexual identities and behaviors. This understanding suggests that the problem with the invention of transsexualism is the limits it places on body alteration, not its participation in the performance of body alteration.[26]

Starting from this presumption, a Foucauldian critique of the diagnosis and treatment of transsexualism exposes how the invention of this "disorder" and its purported therapy do, indeed, function to regulate gender performance. Containing gender distress within "transsexualism" functions to naturalize and make "healthy" dichotomized, birth-assigned gender performance. It casts the critical eye on the gender performance of those transgressing gender boundaries, and produces a norm that need not be criticized. Similarly, this model establishes a structure for addressing violations of gender rules that individualizes, privatizes and depoliticizes the meaning of those transgressions. It is "in the minds of the ill" that gender problems exist, not in the construction of what is "healthy."

Similarly, the disciplinary power exercised by the gatekeepers (doctors, surgeons, psychiatrists, therapists) of SRS requires the repetitive, norm producing exercises to which Foucault refers. The "successful" daily performance of normative gender is a requirement for receiving authorization for body alteration.[27] Similarly, the successful recitation of the transsexual narrative in meeting after meeting with medical professionals, and in session after session with counselors and psychiatrists, is essential to obtaining such authorization. The next sections will deal specifically with these practices.

The next two sections look in detail at how some of the prerequisites for SRS serve to maintain normative gender performance and contain gender dysphoria in the realm of transsexuality. The final sections will examine the costs and benefits of strategic use of the transsexual subject position by persons seeking SRS, and question the meanings frequently assigned by non-trans theorists and medical practitioners to such strategic performances.

II. THE TRANSSEXUAL CHILDHOOD

"When did you first know you were different?"[28] *the counselor at the L.A. Free Clinic asked. "Well," I said, "I knew I was poor and on welfare, and that was different from lots of kids at school, and I had a single mom, which was really uncommon there, and we weren't Christian, which is terribly noticeable in the South. Then later I knew I was a foster child, and in high school, I knew I was a feminist and that caused me all kinds of trouble, so I guess I always knew I was different." His facial expression tells me this isn't what he wanted to hear, but why should I engage this idea that my gender performance has been my most important difference in my life? It hasn't, and I can't separate it from the class, race, and parentage variables through which it was mediated. Does this mean I'm not real enough for surgery?*

I've worked hard to not engage the gay childhood narrative—I never talk about tomboyish behavior as an antecedent to my lesbian identity, I don't tell stories about cross-dressing or crushes on girls, and I intentionally fuck with the assumption of it by telling people how I used to be straight and have sex with boys like any sweet trashy rural girl and some of it was fun. I see these narratives as strategic, and I've always rejected the strategy that adopts some theory of innate sexuality and forecloses the possibility that anyone, gender-troubled childhood or not, could transgress sexual and gender norms at any time. I don't want to participate in an idea that only some people have to engage a struggle of learning gender norms in childhood either. So now, faced with these questions, how do I decide whether to look back on my life through the tranny childhood lens, tell the stories about being a boy for Halloween, not playing with dolls? What is the cost of participation in this selective recitation? What is the cost of not participating?

Rachel Pollack writes:

> *What sense does it make to label some people as true transsexuals, and others as secondary, or confused, or imitation? Whom does such an attitude serve? I can think of no one but the gatekeepers, those who would seize the power of life and death by demanding that transsexuals satisfy an arbitrary standard. To accept such standards, to rank ourselves and others according to a hierarchy of true transsexuality, to try to recast our own histories to make sure they fit the approved model, can only tear us down, all of us, even the ones lucky enough to match that model.[29]*

Anne Bolin quotes an MTF she spoke with: "[Psychiatrists and therapists]...use you, suck you dry, and tell you their pitiful opinions, and my response is: What right do you have to determine whether I live or die? Ultimately the person you have to answer to is yourself and I think I'm too important to leave my fate up to anyone else. I'll lie my ass off to get what I have to."[30]

Symptoms of GID in the Diagnostic and Statistical Manual (DSM-IV)[31] describe at length the symptom of childhood participation in stereotypically gender inappropriate behavior. Boys with GID "particularly enjoy playing house, drawing pictures of beautiful girls and princesses, and watching television or videos of their favorite female characters.... They avoid rough-and-tumble play and competitive sports and have little interest in cars and trucks." Girls with GID do not want to wear dresses, "prefer boys' clothing and short hair," are interested in "contact sports, [and] rough-and-tumble play."[32] Despite the disclaimer in the diagnosis description that this is not to be confused with normal gender non-conformity found in tomboys and sissies, no real line is drawn between "normal" gender non-conformity and gender non-conformity which constitutes GID.[33] The effect is two-fold. First, normative childhood gender is produced—normal kids do the opposite of what kids with GID are doing. Non-GID kids can be expected to: play with children of the own sex, play with gender appropriate toys (trucks for boys, dolls for girls), enjoy fictional characters of their own sex (girls, specifically, might have GID if they like Batman or Superman), play gender appropriate characters in games of "house," etc. Secondly, a regulatory mechanism is put into place. Because gender nonconformity is established as a basis for illness, parents now have a "mill of speech,"[34] speculation, and diagnosis to feed their children's gender through should it cross the line. As Foucault describes, the invention of a category of deviation, the description of the "ill" behavior that need be resisted or cured, creates not a prohibitive silence about such behavior but an opportunity for increased surveillance and speculation,[35] what he would call "informal-governance."[36]

The Diagnostic Criteria for Gender Identity Disorder names, as a general category of symptom, "[a] strong and persistent cross-gender identification (not merely a desire for any perceived cultural advantages of being the other sex)."[37] This criterion suggests the possibility of a gender categorization not read through the cultural gender hierarchy. This requires an imagination of a child wanting to be a gender different from the one assigned to hir[38] without having that desire stem from a cultural understanding of gender difference defined by the "advantaging" of certain gender behaviors and identities over others. To use an illustrative example from the description of childhood GID symptoms, if a child assigned "female" wants to wear pants and hates dresses, and has been told that this is inappropriate for girls, is that decision free from a recognition of cultural advantages associated with gender? Since a diagnosis of GID does not require a child to state the desire to change genders, and the primary indicators are gender inappropriate tastes and behaviors, how can this be separated from cultural understandings of what constitutes gender difference and gender appropriateness? If we start from an understanding that gender behavior is learned, and that children are not born with some innate sense that girls should wear dresses and boys shouldn't like Barbie or anything pink, then how can a desire to transgress an assigned gender category be read outside of cultural meaning? Such a standard does, as Billings and Urban argue, privatize and depoliticize gender role distress. It creates a fictional transsexual who just knows in hir gut what man is and what woman is, and knows that sie is trapped in the wrong body. It produces a naturalized, innate gender difference outside power, a fictional binary that does not privilege one term.

The diagnostic criteria for GID produces a fiction of natural gender, in which normal, non-transsexual people grow up with minimal to no gender trouble or exploration, do not crossdress as children, do not play with the wrong-gendered kids, and do not like the wrong kinds of toys or characters. This story isn't believable, but because medicine produces it not through a description of the norm, but through a generalized account of the transgression, and instructs the doctor/parent/teacher to focus on the transgressive behavior, it establishes a surveillance and regulation effective for keeping both non-transsexuals and transsexuals in adherence to their roles. In order to get authorization for body alteration, this childhood must be produced, and the GID diagnosis accepted, maintaining an idea of two discrete gender categories that normally contain everyone but occasionally are wrongly assigned, requiring correction to reestablish the norm.

It's always been fun to reject the gay childhood story, to tell people I "chose" lesbianism, or to over articulate a straight childhood narrative to suggest that lesbianism could happen to anyone. But not engaging a trans childhood narrative is terrifying—what if it means I'm not "real"? Even though I don't believe in real, it matters if other people see me as real—if not I'm a mutilator, an imitator, and worst of all, I can't access surgery.

Transsexual writer Claudine Griggs' book takes for granted that transsexuality is an illness, an unfortunate predicament, something fortunate, normal people don't have to go through. She writes: "Fortunately, most people, though they strive to become a certain kind of woman or man, never question their foundational gender.... A person with gender dysphoria is crippled emotionally and socially, which accounts for part of the transsexual compulsion for body alteration."[39] On the first page of the preface she writes,

> *I am not an advocate of sex change procedures. I know that sex reassignment is necessary for some individuals with gender dysphoria in much the same way as a radical mastectomy is necessary for some individuals with breast cancer, but I hope that such treatment is undertaken only when no other effective prescription exists. The best recommendation, though pointless, is don't get cancer and don't be a transsexual.[40]*

This is precisely the approach I want to avoid as I reject the narrative of a gender troubled childhood. My project would be to promote sex reassignment, gender alteration, temporary gender adventure, and the mutilation of gender categories, via surgery, hormones, clothing, political lobbying, civil disobedience, or any other means available. But that political commitment itself, if revealed to the gatekeepers of my surgery, disqualifies me. One therapist said to me, "You're really intellectualizing this, we need to get to the root of why you feel you should get your breasts removed, how long have you felt this way?" Does realness reside in the length of time a desire exists? Are women who seek breast enhancement required to answer these questions? Am I supposed to be able to separate my political convictions about gender, my knowledge of the violence of gender rigidity that has been a part of my life and the lives of everyone I care about, from my real "feelings" about what it means to occupy my gendered body? How could I begin to think about my chest without thinking about cultural advantage?

III. CHOOSING PERSPECTIVE: PASSING "FULL-TIME"

From what I've gathered in my various counseling sessions, in order to be deemed real I need to want to pass as male all the time, and not feel ambivalent about this. I need to be willing to make the commitment to "full-time" maleness, or they can't be sure that I won't regret my surgery. The fact that I don't want to change my first name, that I haven't sought out the use of the pronoun "he," that I don't think that "lesbian" is the wrong word for me, or, worse yet, that I recognize that the use of any word for myself—lesbian, transperson, transgender butch, boy, mister, FTM fag, butch—has always been/will always be strategic is my undoing in their eyes. They are waiting for a better justification of my desire for surgery—something less intellectual, more real.

I'm supposed to be wholly joyous when I get called "sir" or "boy." How could I ever have such an uncomplicated relationship to that moment? Each time I'm sirred I know both that my look is doing what I want it to do, and that the reason people can assign male gender to me easily is because they don't believe women have short hair, and because, as Garber has asserted, the existence of maleness as the generic means that fewer visual clues of maleness are required to achieve male gender attribution.[41] This "therapeutic" process demands of me that I toss out all my feminist misgivings about the ways that gender rigidity informs people's perception of me.

Leslie Feinberg writes about the strategic use of gender categories, "Outside the trans communities, many people refer to me as "she," which is also correct. Using that pronoun to describe me challenges generalizations about how "all women" act and express themselves. In a non-trans setting, calling me "he" renders my transgender invisible."[42] Similarly, I do not want to forfeit the ability to utilize gender categories to promote social change. I want to keep open my ability to reject the use of some categories in some contexts because of the presumptions that underlie their definitions.

In "A 'Critique of Our Constitution is Colorblind,' " Neil Gotanda writes about how the terms of American dialogues about race are set by racism. He describes racial difference is understood through the rule of "hypodescent," which dictates that any person with a known trace of African ancestry is black. "[H]ypodescent imposes racial subordination through its implied validation of white racial purity." As a result, the uncritical proclamation "I am white" is a racist statement, because it reaffirms the definition of white that is grounded in a dichotomy of racial purity and impurity.[43] The terms of gender difference operate differently, but are similarly problematic–to declare membership in a static gender category affirms a regulatory system of dichotomous gender. What kind of "health" does such "treatment" restore me to, if it compels me to make such a declaration?

Perhaps the most overt requirement for transsexual diagnosis is the ability to inhabit and perform "successfully"[44] the new gender category. Through my own interactions with medical professionals, accounts of other trans people, and medical scholarship on transsexuality, I have gathered that the favored indication of such "success" seems to be the gender attribution of non-trans people. Because the ability to be perceived by non-trans people as a non-trans person is valorized, normative expressions of gender within a singular category are mandated.

Griggs' narrative exemplifies this paradigm of gender legibility. Her stories assume that gender identity is fundamentally about gender attribution: your *real* gender is the one that people can see on you. She argues that there is no "perceptual middle ground between male and female" which means that "transsexuals cannot fade gently" between genders.[45] For Griggs, the project of changing genders fundamentally concerns the perception of non-trans people that she is a born woman. She writes,

I have always had a feminine gender, yet I became a woman not because I changed my driver's license, took estrogens, applied makeup, grew long hair, or had genital surgery, but because on 1 July 1974, a man opened the door for me as I entered my 8:00 a.m. class.... Society must see a woman; otherwise, sex-change surgery or not, one cannot be a woman.[46]

Griggs fails to engage any feminist analysis of the act of accepting, uncritically, the entirety of the subject position "woman" (including the premises which underlie acts of chivalry). In door-opening story, the performance of coherent oppositional gender norms secures Griggs' own self-perception of femaleness. Griggs also tells a story about meeting a man at a bar who assumed her to be a man during a long conversation, and then discovered that she was a woman after the bartender addressed her. She describes that the rest of their interaction included him buying her drinks and saying things like

"Gee, I'm sorry...I feel terrible. Now that I see you, I don't know how I could possibly have thought...But maybe you shouldn't sit so rough, like. You have a beautiful figure...And if you didn't put your elbows on the bar, a guy could see.... And maybe,...a little makeup would soften you up...You could fix your hair."[47]

In response to this overt policing of her performance of femininity, Griggs writes, "After a while, even I began to wonder if I had carried the 'butch' thing too far."[48] Just like many medical practitioners, Griggs accepts that a successful transition hinges upon full participation in the normative, sexist, oppressive performance of "woman."

Judith Halberstam points out a similar operation in the desire of some female-to-male transsexuals (FTMs) and, I would add, of professionals "treating" FTMs, to distinguish FTMs from butch lesbians at any cost.[49] Halberstam describes that butch and FTM bodies are always read against and through each other—commonly through a continuum model that seeks to find a defining difference between the two.[50] She asserts that such a construction stabilizes butch lesbians as "women" and erases the disruptive work that butch identity engages on dichotomous gender categorization. She points to the lists of "passing tips" that are commonly shared between FTMs on the internet and at conferences.[51] Many such tips focus on an adherence to traditional aesthetics of masculinity, warning FTMs to avoid "punky" hair cuts that may make you look like a butch lesbian, and to avoid black leather jackets and other trappings associated with butch lesbians. A preppy, clean cut look is often suggested as the best aesthetic for passing. Again, this establishes the requirement of being even more "normal" than "normal people" when it comes to gender presentation, and discouraging gender disruptive behavior. The resulting image, with the most "successful" FTMs exiting as khaki-clad frat boy clones, leaves feminist gender-queer trannies with the question, why bother?

The "passing" imperative, which begins from the moment a SRS-seeker enters a medical office and is sized up by a professional who will decide hir "realness" and seriousness at least in part based on the success of the presentation of a gender norm, is an essential regulating aspect of the process of "transsexual" (and "non-transsexual") production. Wilchins notes:

Current practice in sex-change surgery assumes, even requires, "real-looking" genitals.... That is why so many doctors, while proudly showing off how "their vagina" can even fool OB/gyns, are reduced to muttering "no guarantees" and "we can't be certain" when asked about the pleasure potential of their work. It's also part of why many transwomen don't have a lot of erotic sensation after surgery.[52]

This framework erases the possibility that someone might not prioritize how their genitals will look to others, or might even wish for genitals that do not conform, aesthetically, to the culturally specified norms, is not even imagined in this framework. As Wilchins points out, an admission that a patient might want intersex genitals would fall on the deaf ears of doctors who only seek to produce genitals that fit into one of two narrowly-defined options.

What if the "success of transition was not measured by (non-trans) normative perceptions of true femininity and masculinity in trans people? I imagine that, like me, some people have a multitude of goals when they seek gender-related body alteration, such as access to different sexual practices, ability to look different in clothing, enhancement of a self-understanding about one's gender that is not entirely reliant on public recognition, public disruption of female and male codes, or any number of other things.[53] Some birth-assigned "men" might want to embody "woman" as butch lesbians—in a way that meant they enjoyed occasionally being "sirred" and only sometimes "corrected" the speaker. Some birth-assigned "women" might want to take hormones and become sexy "bearded ladies" who are interpreted a variety of ways but feel great about how they look. When the gatekeepers employ dichotomous gender standards, they foreclose such norm-resistant possibilities.

Marjorie Garber talks about how transsexuals see our bodies "theoretically." She describes how the FTM with a chest scarred by reconstruction sees a male chest.

> In spite of…unaesthetic results transsexual patients often go barechested, displaying what doctors call a "poor reality" sense along with their flattened chests. Another way of describing this, and a less condemnatory one, might be to say that the patient is regarding his new body *theoretically*; it is, he is, *male*, however attractive or unattractive the appearance.[54]

While I would argue that everyone sees their body theoretically, and everyone's self image is mediated through gender fictions and expectations, Garber's point describes a pleasure lost in the passing imperative. Most of the trans people I have talked to do not imagine themselves entering a realm of "real manness" or "real womanness," even if they pass as non-trans all the time, but rather recognize the absence of meaning in such terms and regard their transformations as freeing them to express more of themselves, and enabling more comfortable and exciting self understandings and images. However, recognizing that trans people make fine pleasures and benefits apart from the ability to conform to gender norms raises the threat discussed earlier that, indeed, trans people might be engineering ourselves.

The therapist asked me about "coming out" to my family about my surgery/GID. She was disconcerted when I described that my sister knew, but I doubted I would tell my foster parents any time too soon, and might not ever tell them, since it would likely be better for our relationship and they were not my intended audience. I felt there was nothing to gain by entering this conversation with them, and much to lose, and that any educational work that disclosure could achieve was best left with their understanding of me as a "lesbian." I'm skilled in dressing to downplay chest noticeability, so I imagined that for the time being, even after surgery, I would continue such a strategy when I saw them unless I decided it wasn't worth the benefits, or unless I decided to take hormones which would significantly change my appearance. This only further convinced her (we'd already covered my going by "Jane") that I lacked the proper commitment to this transition. How could I really need this surgery if I could stand to be perceived, for even a minute, to not have had it? "How do you know you want to do this? Why do you want to do this if it's not to pass as a man?" [I give some responses.] "Stop intellectualizing and tell me how you feel."

IV. MAYBE I'M NOT A TRANSSEXUAL

The counselor at the L.A. Free Clinic decided I wasn't transsexual during the first (and only) session. When I told him what I wanted, and how I was starting counseling because I was trying to get some letters that I could give to a surgeon so that they would alter my chest, he said, "You should just go get breast reduction." Of course, he didn't know that most cosmetic surgeons won't reduce breasts below a C-cup (I wouldn't even qualify for reduction), and that breast reduction is a different procedure than the construction of a male-looking chest. I also suppose that he wasn't thinking about what happens to gender deviants when they end up in the hands of medical professionals who don't have experience with trans people.

> *Some surgeons have strong reactions to transsexual patients, and often, if the surgery is done in a teaching hospital, the surgeon turns out to be a resident or staff member who is offended by the procedure. "In one case, with which I am familiar," writes a doctor, "the patient's massive scars were probably the result of the surgeon's unconscious sadism and wish to scar the patient for 'going against nature.'"[55]*

To this counselor, my failure to conform to the transsexuality he was expecting required my immediate expulsion from that world of meaning at any cost. My desire couldn't be for SRS because I wasn't a transsexual, so it must be for cosmetic surgery, something normal people get.

All my attempts at counseling, and all those experience of being eyed suspiciously when I suggested that I was trans, or told outright I was not by non-trans counselors, made me expect that I would get a similar reception from trans people in activist or support contexts. This has not been the case. I've found that in trans contexts, a much broader conception of trans experience exists. The trans people I've met have, shockingly, believed what I say about my gender. Some have a self-narrative resembling the medical model of transsexuality, some do not. However, the people I've met share with me what my counselors do not: a commitment to gender self-determination and respect for all expressions of gender. Certainly not all trans people would identify with this principle, but I think it makes better sense as a basis for identity than the ability to pass "full-time" or the amount of cross-dressing one did as a child. Wilchins posits an idea of identity as "an effect of political activism instead of a cause." I see this notion reflected in trans activism, writing, and discussion, despite its absence in the medical institutions through which trans people must negotiate our identities.

Feinberg writes:

> *Once I figured out that "transgendered" was someone who transcended traditional stereotypes of "man" and "woman," I saw that I was such a person. I then began a quest for finding words that described myself, and discovered that while psychiatric jargon dominated the discourse, there were many other words, both older and newer, that addressed these issues. While I accepted the label of "transsexual" in order to obtain access to the hormones and chest surgery necessary to manifest my spirit in the material world, I have always had a profound disagreement with the definition of transsexualism as a psychiatric condition and transsexuals as disordered people.[56]*

V. TELLING STORIES: STRATEGIC DEPLOYMENT OF THE TRANSSEXUAL NARRATIVE

Billings and Urban, when tracing the history of the invention of transsexualism and its diagnosis and treatment, describe how physicians in the 1970's began recognizing that "transsexuals had routinely and systematically lied."[57] One "expert" in treating transsexuality complained, "Those of us faced with the task of diagnosing transsexualism have an additional burden these days, for most patients who request sex reassignment are in complete command of the literature and know the answers before the questions are asked."[58] Billings and Urban describe:

> Since the reputable clinics treated only "textbook" cases of transsexualism, patients desiring surgery, for whatever personal reasons, had no other recourse but to meet this evaluation standard. The construction of an appropriate biography became necessary. Physicians reinforced this demand by rewarding compliance with surgery and punishing honesty with an unfavorable evaluation.[59]

A patient grape-vine emerged, through which patients informed each other of the best ways to pass the necessary requirements to surgery. There were even stories being passed between doctors of post-operative transsexuals posing as mothers of pre-ops in order to add credibility to the testimony of the patients in the eyes of the doctors.[60] Patients omitted information which would disrupt the version of normative femininity or masculinity that they were presenting to the doctors, including homosexuality and enjoyment of sex practices in the unaltered body.[61]

Billings and Urban describe that in response to the outbreak of stories of people lying to get SRS, the diagnostic structure was changed, so that the term "transsexual" was replaced with "gender dysphoria syndrome." However, they point out that this change was inconsequential, because "behavioral criteria" is still stressed by doctors. " 'Indeed, for prognosis, it is probable that the diagnostic category is of much less importance than the patient's pre-operative performance in a one-to-three year therapeutic trial of living in the gender of his choice.' "[62] Billings and Urban include an anecdote from a doctor who had performed over 100 sex-change operations, describing his method of verifying the "real-ness" of a patient's transsexuality. "[He] told us he diagnosed male-to-female transsexuals by bullying them. 'The 'girls' cry; the gays get aggressive.' ' They follow this up with the assertion that, based on information from their participant-informant at a gender clinic, "diagnosis in the post-Benjamin era remains a subtle negotiation process between patients and physicians, in which the patient's troubles are defined, legitimated, and regulated as illness."[63]

Billings and Urban argue that the screening and interviewing processes for SRS still function as a form of patient socialization, where diagnosis and treatment are linked to the performance of normative gender. Patients are aware of this, and utilize, to the extent that they can, their prior knowledge of the diagnostic criteria to convince doctors of their suitability to the "treatment" they seek.[64] For Billings and Urban, this is evidence of the evil of SRS—patients who are gender deviant are socialized by doctors to conform to gender norms.

I do not doubt that the existence of the transsexual narrative informs the self-understandings of many people, as it is part of an overall construction of normative gender that naturalizes dichotomous gender categories and labels transgression of such categories as illness. It likely leads some gender variant people to see their gender deviance through a depoliticized and privatized lens, as an individual illness rather than a commentary on the inhabitability of dichotomous gender. It also likely leads some people who understand themselves as not-transsexual to think that their adherence to gender norms is natural and healthy. Everyone is implicated in this narrative, not only trans people. However, I think that the image of SRS-seekers as solely victims of false consciousness is severely incomplete. A review of literature written by trans people, particularly the works less often cited by non-trans writers,[65] suggests a self-conscious strategy of deployment of the transsexual narrative by people who do not believe in the gender fictions produced by such a narrative, and who seek to occupy ambiguous gender positions in resistance to norms of gender rigidity.

After attending only three discussion group meetings with other trans people, I am struck by the naiveté with which I approached the search for counseling to get my surgery-authorizing letters. No one at these groups seems to see therapy as the place where they voice their doubts about their transitions, where they wrestle with the political implications of their changes, where they speak about fears of losing membership in various communities or in their families. No one trusts the doctors as the place to work things out. When I mention the places I've gone for help, places that are supposed to support queer and trans people, everyone nods knowingly, having heard countless stories like mine about these very places before. Some have suggestions of therapists who are better, but none cost less than $50/hr. Mostly, though, people suggest different ways to get around the requirements. I get names of surgeons who do not always ask for the letters. Someone suggests that since I won't be on hormones, I can go in and pretend I'm a woman with a history of breast cancer in my family and that I want a double mastectomy to prevent *it. I have these great, sad, conversations with these people who know all about what it means to lie and cheat their way through the medical roadblocks to get the opportunity to occupy their bodies in the way they want. I understand, now, that the place that is safe to talk about this is in here, with other people who understand the slipperiness of gender and the politics of transition, and who believe me without question when I say what I think I am and how that needs to look.*

VI. TRANSSEXUALS AS THE "EXEMPLARY ADHERENTS" TO GENDER NORMS

Garber writes about how trans people are more "invested in [the gender binary]" than everyone else.[66]

> The transsexual body is not an absolute insignia of anything. Yet it makes the referent ("man" or "woman") seem knowable. Paradoxically, it is to transsexuals and transvestites that we need to look if we want to understand what gender categories mean for persons who are neither transvestite nor transsexual. They are emphatically not interested in "unisex" or "androgyny" as erotic styles, but rather in gender-marked and gender-coded identity structures. Those who problematize the binary are those who have a great deal invested in it.

Prior to this point in the chapter, Garber refers to the biographies of famous transsexuals Renee Richards, Jan Morris, and, to some degree, Christine Jorgensen.[67] While Garber does stop to question why all the best-known transsexuals are MTFs and not FTMs, she does not question why the narratives of the transsexuals she uses as evidence are well-known, nor whether the "truths" about how transsexuals understand themselves and their gender identities that she collects from these biographies are at all strategically deployed. She asserts that trans people are more invested in dichotomous gender categories and are not interested in the in-between spaces of gender based on a few stories which 1) are likely the most popular stories of transsexualism among non-transsexuals because they affirm a transsexual narrative that reifies the naturalness of normative gender performance, and 2) may well have been strategically crafted by their narrators to achieve social acceptance/tolerance for transsexuals, which many people understand to be best sought through a model of innate transsexuality similar to the one deployed by Griggs. Her arrival at the conclusion that trans people are more invested in normative gender categories than non-trans people is facilitated by her failure to question the strategic value for trans people of adherence to gender normative notions of transsexuality. Absent from her analysis are the stories of trans people who work and live on the street, trans people of color, trans people who never strive to or never succeed in fitting into a vision of "successful" gender performance, with all of its racial and economic implications. Using a narrow set of famous examples, she comfortably arrives at an understanding of how trans people view gender that supports the way that non-trans people see trans people.

A similar move is made in Elsie Shore's case study of a "former transsexual," a birth-assigned male who sought SRS, was diagnosed with transsexuality, lived as a woman for a considerable period, and then decided days before surgery to return to male identity.[68] The author describes that when she met "Mickey," she had been "on female hormones for 21 months and . . . living exclusively in the female role for 14 months. Of medium height and build, dressed and made up in a realistic and nonflamboyant manner, Mickey presented as a convincing female. She [was] shy, lonely, and wanting to be loved and cared for."[69]

Shore attributes Mickey's change of heart about SRS and continuing life as a woman to his realization that his prior adherence to strict beliefs about what men needed to act like was not true. She says that when Mickey joined a church and met men who were "warm and caring without losing masculinity" he found out that "one is not required to be female to be kind and loving."[70] Additionally, Mickey fell in love with a woman in his new religion, and "felt a desire to protect and to possess her and conceptualized these feelings as those that a man experiences when in love with a woman."[71] Shore recognizes, also, that an influence on his decision might have been that the possibility of his feelings for this woman being understood as homosexual may have frightened him.

As Shore sorts through what Mickey's decision to return to the male role means, she rules out possibility of an original misdiagnosis of transsexuality. She believes the diagnosis was correct because the history Mickey presented to the gender clinic that admitted him was "consistent with the generally accepted picture of transsexual development."[72] Secondly, she believes that his success at living for two and a half years as a female attests to the fact that he was a "true transsexual," because "an individual with shallower cross-sexual identification will not" succeed at lasting a year in the new role.[73] Shore believes that Mickey was, indeed, a "true transsexual," but that his condition was in large part a result of the fact that he was a very nonaggressive person and had a highly stereotyped definition of "man" which led him to believe that he must be a woman. Shore cites other experts in transsexuality who have found that transsexuals have rigid notions of what masculinity is, and "confuse dependency feelings and lack of aggressiveness in social interactions with femininity and sexual behavior."[74] She concludes that therapeutic intervention directed at loosening rigid gender-role stereotyping might be a way to treat transsexuality without SRS.

Some contradictory presumptions underlie Shore's analysis. First, similar to Griggs, Shore sees the avoidance of SRS as a goal of treatment, and wants to keep SRS as a last resort option. Second, Shore accepts the diagnostic criteria and definition of transsexuality. She accepts that there is something about transsexuality that requires treatment of the individual transsexual to bring hir into a male or female role. These presumptions allow Shore to arrive at the conclusion that what requires treatment in transsexuals is their over-adherence to gender norms or stereotypes. Ironically, it is just this adherence that the diagnosis and treatment criteria require in order for people seeking SRS to achieve their goals. Shore's failure to critique the diagnostic criteria of transsexuality before coming to her conclusions creates a situation where SRS would be harder to get than ever: if the patient adopted the norm-based narrative of gender required by the diagnostic criteria, sie might still be refused treatment for precisely that.

Garber and Shore both assert that transsexuals are more deeply invested in gender norms than non-transsexuals without recognizing that the medical definition of "transsexuality" requires the performance of such an investment. Transsexuals are in a double bind—it is pathological not to adhere to gender norms, just as it is to adhere to them. The creation of the image of transsexuals as exemplary adherents to gender stereotypes requires an understanding of transsexuality that both fully accepts the medical definition of transsexual and ignores the multiple non-norm-adhering narratives that trans people produce outside of medical contexts.

VII. CONCLUSION

Personal narrative is always strategically employed. It is always mediated through cultural understandings, through ideology. It is always a function of selective memory and narration. Have I learned that I should lie to obtain surgery, as others have before me? Does that lesson require an acceptance that I cannot successfully advocate on behalf of a different approach to my desire for transformation?

An examination of how medicine governs gender variant bodies through the regulation of body alteration by means of the invention of the illness of transsexuality brings up the question of whether illness is the appropriate interpretive model for gender variance. The benefits of such an understanding for trans people are noteworthy.[75] As long as SRS remains a treatment for an illness, the possibility Medicaid coverage for it remains viable.[76] Similarly, courts examining the question of what qualifies a transsexual to have legal membership in the new gender category have relied heavily on the medical model of transsexuality when they have decided favorably for transsexuals.[77] A model premised on a disability- or disease-based understanding of deviant behavior is believed by many to be the best strategy for achieving tolerance by norm-adherent people for those not adhering to norms. Such arguments are present in the realm of illicit drug use and in the quest for biological origins of homosexuality just as they are in the portrayal of transsexuality as an illness or disability.

However, it is vital that the costs of such an approach also be considered. First, the medical approach to gender variance, and the creation of transsexuality, has resulted in a governance of trans bodies that restricts our ability to make gender transitions which do not yield membership in a normative gender role. The self-determination of trans people in crafting our gender expression is compromised by the rigidity of the diagnostic and treatment criteria. At the same time, this criteria and the version of transsexuality that it posits produce and reify a fiction of normal, healthy gender that works as a regulatory measure for the gender expression of all people. To adopt the medical understanding of transsexuality is to agree that SRS is the unfortunate treatment of an unfortunate condition, to accept that gender norm adherence is fortunate and healthy, and to undermine the threat to a dichotomous gender system which trans experience can pose. The reification of the violence of compulsory gender norm adherence, and the submission of trans bodies to a norm-producing medical discipline, is too high a price for a small hope of conditional tolerance.

NOTES

[1] RIKI ANNE WILCHINS, READ MY LIPS: SEXUAL SUBVERSION AND THE END OF GENDER 63 (1997).
[2] BERNICE L. HAUSMAN, CHANGING SEX: TRANSSEXUALISM, TECHNOLOGY, AND THE IDEA OF GENDER 1 (1995).
[3] *Id.*
[4] *Id.* at 2.
[5] I use this term in the broad sense, not just to signify the genital surgery which is often the legal criteria for achieving legal gender change. Specifically, I want to examine the types of surgery that are currently associated with "transsexualism" and therefore subject the person seeking them to the requirements of the Harry Benjamin standards of care. However, I also want to suggest a critical approach to the labeling of certain surgeries, such as mastectomy for people assigned "female" at birth or breast enlargement for people assigned "male" at birth, as surgery that changes gender expression or performance while other surgeries such as breast enlargement for people assigned "female" at birth or pectoral implants for people assigned "male" at birth are understood as innocuous "cosmetic" surgery.
[6] ALAN HUNT & GARY WICKHAM, FOUCAULT AND LAW: TOWARDS A SOCIOLOGY OF LAW AS GOVERNANCE 28 (1994).
[7] Wilchins, *supra* note 1, at 22.
[8] I was able to pay $10–20 weekly. I was qualified for services (stories of which are included in this paper) at the Children's Hospital because I was 21–22 throughout the year.
[9] My position on these questions has changed since I originally wrote this piece. I now go by "Dean" and "he." However, my aim is to capture the set of desires I had in the year in which I was seeking services in L.A. and finding myself outside of medical professionals' understandings of what it meant to be "trans." It was my failure to provide a gendered picture that they could recognize as cohesive and consistent that disabled them from providing me the services I sought.
[10] Hausman, *supra* note 2, at 3 (emphasis in original).
[11] Dwight B. Billings and Thomas Urban, *The Socio-Medical Construction of Transsexualism: An Interpretation and Critique*, 29 SOCIAL PROBLEMS 266, 276 (1982).
[12] As mentioned above, Billings and Urban understand SRS as "mutilation." They appear entirely opposed to SRS of any kind. In their understanding, persons who get sex change surgery are just sexual deviants whose possibility for a political response to their situation is being squelched because they are being sold a quick fix answer to their discomfort in gender or sex norms.

Among the transsexual patients we interviewed were ministers who embraced the label "transsexual" to avoid being labeled "homosexual"; sexual deviants driven by criminal laws against cross-dressing, or by rejecting parents and spouses, to the shelter of the "therapeutic state"; and enterprising male prostitutes cashing in on the profitable market for transsexual prostitutes which thrives in some large cities.

Id. at 276. Billings and Urban paint a picture of those seeking or receiving sex reassignment surgery as apolitical, needing to be educated rather than medically treated (mutilated) so that they can start a gender revolution. The revolution they imagine, however, has no place for body alteration to change gender presentation, and such activity can only represent for them, disempowering "commodification," "reification," and the reinforcement of traditional gender roles. While I agree with their assertion that the operation of medical authority in the diagnostic and treatment processes for transsexuality often does work to privatize and depoliticize the politics of gender conformity and deviance, I reject their narrow understanding of the potential political meanings of SRS, their ignorance of the politicized acts and identities of trans people, and the paternalistic and disrespectful approach to trans people they take throughout the paper, exemplified in moments when they refer to trans people like Christine Jorgenson using pronouns appropriate to their birth-assigned gender. *Id.* at 267.

[13] *Id.* at 266.

[14] *Id.*

[15] Forms of illness are always more that biological disease; they are also metaphors, bearing existential, moral, and social meanings. According to Taussig, "the signs and symptoms of disease, as much as the technologies of healing, are not 'things-in-themselves,' are *not only* biological and physical, but *are also* signs of social relations disguised natural things, concealing their roots in human reciprocity.
      Billings & Urban, *supra* note 10, at 276 (emphasis in original).

[16] MICHEL FOUCAULT, THE HISTORY OF SEXUALITY, VOL. 1: AN INTRODUCTION, 3–13 (1978).

[17] *Id.* at 18.

[18] *Id.* at 53–54.

[19] *Id.* at 43. "The nineteenth-century homosexual became a personage, a past, a case history, and a childhood…. the homosexual was now a species." *Id.*

[20] "Law is neither the truth of power nor its alibi. It is an instrument of power which is at once complex and partial. The form of law with its effects of prohibition needs to be resituated among a number of other, non-juridical mechanisms." MICHEL FOUCAULT, POWER/KNOWLEDGE: SELECTED INTERVIEWS AND OTHER WRITINGS 1972–1977, 141 (ed. Colin Gordon, 1980).

[21] Hunt & Wickham, *supra* note 6, at 49.

[22] Michel Foucault, *The Subject and Power*, in MICHEL FOUCAULT: BEYOND STRUCTURALISM AND HERMENEU-TICS 208, 221 (Herbert Dreyfus & Paul Rabinow eds. 1982).

[23] Hunt & Wickham, *supra* note 6, at 27.

[24] See, *infra*, section V, for a discussion of the strategic use of the transsexual narrative to gain access to SRS.

[25] The symptoms of GID described in the Diagnostic and Statistical Manual (DSM-IV) primarily focus on two elements: the failure to conform to gender stereotypes (particularly in children) or the desire for gender-related body altera-tion–SRS and hormone therapy (particularly in adults). *See infra*, section II, for a discussion of the construction of the transsexual childhood. Such a focus on gender conformity supports the conclusions of the Billings and Urban that the doctor-patient relationship in the transsexual situation is one in which the doctor is producing adherence to gender norms, and pathologizing gender non-conformity. However, the question arises as to whether the problem lies in the search for gender-related body alteration ("mutilation," as they would call it), or in the process by which permission for such self-engineering is obtained.

[26] Hausman acknowledges the resistant content possible in body alteration projects, and the ways that transsexual diag-nosis/treatment serves to contain that threat. "[T]he commonsense understanding of transsexualism as a 'disorder of gender identity' is a cover up for the potentially more threatening idea that transsexuals are subjects who choose to engineer themselves." Hausman, *supra* note 2, at 9.

[27] One doctor described the requirement: "Patients are expected to live in the new gender role…for 1 to 2 years in order to experience life in the new role and develop appropriate role behaviors." Elsie R. Shore, *The Former Transsexual: A Case Study*, 13 ARCHIVES OF SEXUAL BEHAVIOR 277 (1984).

[28] Feinberg writes about the search for origins of gender nonconformity as well, and answers this question: Who cares! As long as my right to explore the full measure of my own potential is being trampled by discriminatory laws, as long as I am being socially and economically marginalized, as long as I am being scapegoated for the crimes committed by this economic system, my right to exist needs no explanation or justification of any kind. LESLIE FEINBERG, TRANS LIBERATION: BEYOND PINK OR BLUE 32 (1998).

[29] Rachel Pollack, *The Varieties of Transsexual Experience*, 7 Transsexual News Telegraph 18, 20 (1997).

[30] CLAUDINE GRIGGS, S/HE: CHANGING SEX AND CHANGING CLOTHES 32 (1998). *See* section V, *infra*, for more discussion on strategic use of the transsexual narrative.

[31] AMERICAN PSYCHOLOGICAL ASSOCIATION, DIAGNOSTIC AND STATISTICAL MANUAL, 4th Edition 532 (1994).

[32] *Id.* at 533.

[33] *Id.* at 536. The difference is, apparently, that GID gender trouble "represents a profound disturbance of the individual's sense of identity with regard to maleness or femaleness." Personally, I never knew a tomboy or sissy who might not qualify as profoundly disturbed about their gender, especially in the eyes of their parents and teachers. The differential diagnosis of these kids from kids with GID seems like an afterthought in the writing–a quick way to try and make it not appear that all gender nonconformity is being pathologized by the generalized diagnosis which relies on an impossible norm–a child with no cross gender play habits or transgressive gender explorations. Since almost no child will state "I'm profoundly disturbed about my gender," this determination will always be left for parents, doctors, and teachers–the surveillance system kicks in.

[34] Foucault, *supra* note 15, at 21.

[35] Foucault uses the example of sexual discourse in the secondary schools of the 18th century. While the general impres-sion may be that the sexuality of children was hardly spoken of at these institutions, in reality an elaborate discourse about the danger of the sexuality of the schoolboy dominated. Every aspect of education was designed to contain the imagined danger. As Foucault describes, "the discourse of the institution–the one it employed to address itself" was consumed with concern, speculation, and attempted regulation of schoolboy sexuality. *Id.* at 28.

[36] Hunt & Wickham, *supra* note 6, at 27.

[37] APA, *supra* note 30, at 537.

[38]　I use the gender neutral pronouns "sie" (pronounced "*see*") and "hir" (pronounced "*here*") to promote the recognition of such pronouns, which resist the need to categorize all subjects neatly into male and female categories, at the suggestion of Leslie Feinberg. In this essay, I use these pronouns when discussing a hypothetical person, but when I am referring to people who have articulated a self-identification in a particular gender, I respect that choice by using pronouns which reflect it. Feinberg, *supra* note 24, at 1.

[39]　Griggs, *supra* note 29, at 10–13.

[40]　*Id.* at ix. Hausman posits a similarly helpless and afflicted view of transsexuals. "Ostensibly, the demand for sex change represents the desperation of the transsexual condition: after all, who but a suffering individual would voluntarily request such severe physical transformation?" Hausman, *supra* note 2, at 110. This presumption is a fundamental part of the medical approach to transsexualism. The therapists I've seen have wanted to hear that I hate my breasts, that the desire for surgery comes from desperation. What would it mean to suggest that such desire for surgery is a joyful affirmation of gender self-determination–that a SRS candidate would not wish to get comfortable in a stable gender category, but instead be delighted to be transforming–to choose it over residing safely in "man" or "woman"?

　　Griggs writes that there is no "perceptual middle ground between male and female" and that "transsexuals cannot fade gently" between genders. Griggs, *supra* note 29, at1. To this I would respond with a proverb that Feinberg quotes: "The person who says it cannot be done should not interrupt the person doing it." Feinberg, *supra* note 27, at 61.

[41]　MARJORIE GARBER, VESTED INTERESTS: CROSS-DRESSING AND CULTURAL ANXIETY 102 (1992).

[42]　Feinberg, *supra* note 27, at 19.

[43]　Neil Gotanda, A *Critique of "Our Constitution is Colorblind,"* in Critical Race Theory: The Key Writings That Formed the Movement 257 (Kimberle Crenshaw, et al. eds. 1995). "[U]nder the American system of racial classification, claiming a white racial identity is a declaration of racial purity and an implicit assertion of racial domination." *Id.* at 259.

[44]　Shaefer and Wheeler, chroniclers of Harry Benjamin's work, describe a "successful" transsexual:

　　With Benjamin's encouragement and the inspiration of Jorgensen's story, Janet took a more scientific and intelligent path toward fulfilling her dream. As with Inez, despite her generally masculine appearance and the late age at which she completed her surgery (in her late 50s), Janet's is a genuine success story. Freed from her lifelong gender struggle, her brilliant talent emerged. Janet and a business partner developed an invention sufficiently valuable to be sold eventually for millions of dollars.

　　Except for her closest and most intimate friends, no one in Janet's life knew that this loved and wonderful woman was not a genetic female. Although she died at 72 of lung cancer, Janet lived her last 25 years in great wealth and contentment.

　　Leah Cahan Schaefer & Connie Christine Wheeler, *Harry Benjamin's First Ten Cases (1938–1953): A Clinical Historical Note*, 24 Archives of Sexual Behavior 73 (1995) (individual pagination not available). The story illustrates the mediation of proper gender performance through capitalist values. I would assume that a patient who went on to have a career in sex work or food service would not be considered equally "successful." A similar trend was present in the story that begins section II, *supra*, where I describe the ways in which the therapeutic approach to my desire for body alteration necessitates a privileging of sexual or gender difference above all else, and an erasure of other aspects of my positionality. Such an occurrence falls in line with Foucault's analysis that the sexual self has become the true self–to confess your sex is to confess your self.

[45]　Griggs, *supra* note 29, at 1.

[46]　*Id.* at 17.

[47]　*Id.* at 21–22.

[48]　*Id.* at 22.

[49]　Judith Halberstam, *Transgender Butch: Butch/FTM Border Wars and the Masculine Continuum*, 4 GLQ 287 (1998).

[50]　*Id.* at 292.

[51]　*Id.* at 298. "[M]any of the tips focus almost obsessively on the care that must be taken not to look like a butch lesbian." *Id.*

[52]　Wilchins, *supra* note 1, at 121.

[53]　In some ways, some of these goals are similar to those of people who seek other kinds of cosmetic surgery. Perhaps the most notable difference between some instances of SRS and, say, breast enhancement, pectoral implants, or laser vaginal reconstruction is the ferociousness with which medical practitioners guard technologies which aid in enhancement of the femininity of birth-assigned men and the masculinity of birth-assigned women, and the easy pleasure with which they perform procedures to enhance the femininity of birth-assigned women and the masculinity of birth-assigned men. *See* Peter M. Warren, *A Cap and Gown–and New Breasts. Trends: In Time for High School Graduation, More Teens Are Getting Implants. Surgery on the Young Stirs Controversy.*, L.A. TIMES, May 21, 1999, at E1.

[54]　Garber, *supra* note 40, at 103 (emphasis in original).

[55]　*Id.* at 103.

[56]　Feinberg, *supra* note 27, at 63.

[57]　Billings and Urban, *supra* note 10, at 273.

[58]　*Id.*

[59]　*Id.*

[60]　*Id.* Doctors shared experiences of having patients later reveal, after the completion of surgery, that they had "tailor[ed] their views of themselves and their personal histories to prevailing 'scientific' fashions." *Id.* The director of Johns Hopkins University's gender clinic stated his concern, in 1973, about the possibility that many people "not qualified" for SRS were receiving such treatment through deception. "[T]he label 'transsexual' has come to cover such a 'multitude of sins.' Meyer acknowledged that among the patients who had requested and sometimes received surgery...were

sadists, homosexuals, schizoids, masochists, homosexual prostitutes, and psychotic depressives." *Id.* Doctors around the country shared a fear that they were losing control of the maintenance of the "transsexual" category as numerous deviants who did not perfectly conform to the formula cracked the code and received surgery through deception.

[61]   Such a strategy is present in Agnes's story as well. *Infra*, notes 2–4 and accompanying text. The sexual orientation of Agnes's boyfriend, Bill, was a location of great speculation and concern for the doctors treating Agnes. Their observations focused on whether Bill was homosexual or heterosexual, and whether Agnes and Bill had engaged in anal intercourse. "[T]he doctors…were constantly on the alert for signs of incipient homosexuality in their patient. Agnes's apparent heterosexuality was an essential component of her convincing self-representation as a woman." Hausman, *supra* note 2, at 6. The doctors were not willing to produce a woman who would have anal sex, or a homosexual boyfriend. Agnes's ability to be the most norm-abiding heterosexual intersexed person possible was essential to her achievement of SRS.

[62]   *Id.* at 275, *quoting* Dr. Donald R. Laub & Dr. Norman M. Fisk, *A Rehabilitation Program for Gender Dysphoria Syndrome by Surgical Sex Change*, 53 PLASTIC AND RECONSTRUCTION SURGERY 388, 401.

[63]   *Id..* at 275.

[64]   Of course, for some patients, the narrative doctors seek is the narrative they believe about themselves, and lying is not necessary for gaining access to SRS. However, for numerous others, tailoring stories and producing evidence of the expected symptoms of transsexuality is fundamental to achieving body alteration.

[65]   *See* section VI for a discussion some theorists' use of the biographies of famous transsexuals as evidence of transsexual adherence to gender stereotypes.

[66]   Garber, *supra* note 40, at 110.

[67]   Marjorie Garber, *Spare Parts: The Surgical Construction of Gender, in* Garber, *supra* note 40, at 93–117.

[68]   Shore, *supra* note 26, at 277.

[69]   *Id.* In this passage, Mickey's "realness" is linked to her "nonflamboyant" appearance. Just as FTM's are legitimated through a differentiation from butchness, MTFs are legitimated through a differentiation from drag queens and fags. Mickey's success at female identity is tied, in this description, to occupation of a stereotypical female identity that is separable from the "fake" femininity of female impersonators. A similar basis for Agnes's "realness" was used by her doctors.

"The most remarkable thing about the patient's appearance when she was first seen…was that it was not possible for any of the observers…to identify her as anything but a young woman.… Her hair, which was long, fine, and pulled back from her face across her ears, was touched a blonde-brown from its normal brown.… Her eyebrows were subtly plucked." She was dressed in a manner indistinguishable from that of any other typical girl of her age in this culture. There was nothing garish, outstanding, or abnormally exhibitionistic in her attire, nor was there any hint of poor taste or that the patient was ill at ease in her clothes (as is seen so frequently in transvestites and in women with disturbances of sexual identification).

Hausman, *supra* note 2, at 5.

[70]   *Id.* at 281.

[71]   *Id.*

[72]   *Id.* at 282.

[73]   *Id..*

[74]   *Id.* at 283.

[75]   Many trans people believe that a viable path to legal protection against discrimination on the basis of gender identity is through disability statutes. This possibility appeared somewhat truncated when the Americans with Disabilities Act (ADA) was passed including an explicit ban on coverage for transsexuals. See, 42 U.S.C.A. § 12100 et seq. (2000). However, recent state developments suggest that hope remains for anti-discrimination protection through disability statues. California trans activists recently celebrated after Governor Davis signed A.B. 2222. The bill provides that the California law may provide greater protection than the ADA. The bill extends protection to transsexuals and people with GID, which means that transgendered people who may be perceived to suffer from may be protected from discrimination in employment and housing on the basis of that perception. Additionally, the new law requires employers to enter into good faith negotiations with transgender employees who claim their transsexuality as a disability regarding "reasonable accommodations" for their disability.

[76]   Courts throughout the United States have arrived at different conclusions as to whether Medicaid coverage should include SRS. For a detailed account of the decisions and their reasoning, *see* Eric B. Gordon, *Transsexual Healing: Funding of Sex Reassignment Surgery*, 20 ARCHIVES OF SEXUAL BEHAVIOR 61 (1991).

[77]   *See Richards v. U.S. Tennis Ass'n*, 400 N.Y.S.2d 267 (1977); *R. v. Cogley*, [1989] V.R. 799; *M.T. v. J.T.*, 355 A.2d 204 (1975). However, it is important to note that "unpopular" conditions often considered disabilities associated with social deviance, including transsexuality, drug addiction, homosexuality, and voyeurism were intentionally excluded from coverage under the Americans with Disabilities Act. 42 U.S.C. §§ 12101, 12213 (1991). See Adrienne Hiegel, *Sexual Exclusions: The Americans with Disabilities Act As a Moral Code*, 94 COLUM. L. REV. 1451 (1994). This suggests that the disability model may not be reliable for achieving improved legal status for trans people, because it does not exclude the possibility that lawmakers can establish "deserving" and "undeserving" classes of disabled people.

IV

SELVES:
IDENTITY AND COMMUNITY

24

Body, Technology, and Gender in Transsexual Autobiographies

Bernice L. Hausman

In *Changing Sex*, Bernice Hausman historicizes the relationship between the discovery and synthesization of the so-called sex hormones, gender reassignment surgeries, and theories of gender identity. She asks how medical practitioners have justified the physical transformation of the transsexual body, and concludes that the theory of the gendered self originated precisely in the efforts of those practitioners to manipulate the sexed body. Transsexualism, rather than being a very marginalized and esoteric concern, thus is actually central to the development of contemporary Western notions of self, gender, body, and sex.

Hausman clearly believes that greater freedom of gender expression is a social good, yet she takes a remarkably conservative ethical perspective on bodily transformation. Unlike Janice Raymond, whose analysis she follows to a significant degree, Hausman does not presume that transsexual people are in themselves dangerous to women, but she starts from the premise that they reproduce gender stereotypes, which are quintessentially opposed to personal freedom and feminist progress. Consequently, her explicitly goal is to produce a compelling argument for the discontinuation of medical gender-reassignment procedures. In her advocacy of this position, she assumes that she, as a self-styled feminist scholar, should have greater authority over transsexual embodiment than transsexual people themselves.

In chapter 5, excerpted here, Hausman focuses on transsexual autobiographical narratives. She concludes that transsexual autobiographers construct a narrative space that contains the medical discourse but steps outside it, to claim a gender identity predicated on anatomical bodily difference, but different from the identity normally assigned. Despite her extensive review of the burgeoning literature on physical intersexuality and biological sex diversity, Hausman does not imagine that transsexual people can have anything other than a normatively sexed body. Hence, their autobiographical narratives are merely self-justifications that seek social acceptance for the drastic bodily alterations they desire.

Hausman validates a sense of transsexual agency in a somewhat circuitous manner, by claiming that transsexual autobiographical statements are the mechanisms that secure the acquiescence of physicians, surgeons, and psychiatrists in an ethically suspect practice that violates the integrity of the body. In making this claim, she sets herself in opposition to many transsexuals who feel that their relationships with service providers are often more adversarial than opportunistic. By imagining transsexuals to be peculiarly powerful in achieving their goals, Hausman fails to acknowledge the many forms of vulnerability to violence and discrimination that transsexual people actually face in society.

Thus far, my analysis has concentrated on medical discourses and practices, including the technologies that preceded and facilitated the conceptual production of "gender" as the psychological counterpart to biological sex. In this chapter, I shift gears somewhat and analyze discourses produced by transsexuals themselves about their experiences. My examination of transsexual autobiographies has two purposes: to demonstrate how "gender" discursively operates to mask the material construction of transsexuals through the technologies of medical practice and to show how transsexuals compromise the official understanding of "gender" as divorced from biological sex by their insistent reiteration of the idea that physiological intersexuality is the cause of their cross-sex identification. While the first point will allow us to see how "gender" works to contain transsexual accounts within the conceptual parameters of humanism, the second will make evident the extent to which official pronouncements of the medical establishment are not homologous to the understanding and experience of transsexuals concerning the origins and causes of their condition.

The purpose here is not to pit transsexual discourses against medical discourses in order to determine which most accurately represent the transsexual phenomenon. Rather, I am interested in marking discursive discontinuities in the context of which another story about transsexualism can be fashioned. If the story told in the first four chapters of this book is a subversive retelling of the official medical accounts concerning the emergence of transsexualism and the idea of gender, then the story told in this chapter is an attempt to subvert the official story put forth by transsexual autobiographers. Because I have thus far concentrated on the "official" history of transsexualism within medicine, here I use examples from the autobiographies of "official" transsexuals. All of the texts I examine in this chapter were published as books, many by well-established publishing houses. These texts (for the most part) do not document the stories of transients or sex workers—those marginalized subjects within an already marginalized subject formation—but tell the stories of celebrities or "public transsexuals" (that is, those made famous by their emergence as transsexuals, those who were already famous and had to account for their transformation, or those who chose to live publicly as transsexuals in order to set an example or work toward public acceptance of transsexualism).

This is not an insignificant issue, especially given the current popularity of media representations of the most marginalized transsexuals—*Paris Is Burning* comes to mind here. My decision to concentrate on the more mainstream accounts of transsexual experience—both within medicine and the transsexual community—is based on a desire to challenge these accounts with critical attention to their internal problematics. That is, instead of countering the official accounts of transsexualism—as well as the official accounts of gender—with evidence from more marginalized transsexual subjects (sex workers, for example), I have chosen to interrogate the official accounts themselves and demonstrate the extent to which they can be reread to tell another story. Ultimately, I believe, this kind of analysis will offer a more serious challenge to the hegemony of these discourses in the public sphere, where the spread of gender ideologies threatens to cover over other significant, and destabilizing, accounts of human subjectivity.[1]

The analysis of these "official" transsexual autobiographies is not unproblematic, however. Because most transsexuals do not write their life stories, those autobiographies authored by transsexuals cannot be taken to be representative of the "average transsexual." Yet books by transsexuals about sex change hold a significant position in contemporary transsexual culture. Mario Martino writes in *Emergence* that, as Marie, she was the first in her town to buy Christine Jorgensen's autobiography when it came out in 1967. In her autobiography, *Conundrum*, Jan Morris discusses the emotional significance of finding Lili Elbe's autobiography. *Man into Woman: An Authentic Record of a Change of Sex*, in a used-book store. Renée Richards found a copy of the same text at an important point in her life as Richard Raskind. Nancy Hunt writes in *Mirror Image*, "I can remember only once when my life has been altered by the printed word. That was upon reading an article in the *New York Times Magazine* on March 17, 1974.... It described the transition from man into woman of an English journalist now known as Jan Morris."[2] In addition, organizations such as the International Foundation for Gender Education (IFGE) sell all manner of books about transsexualism and transvestism, including transsexual autobiographies, as part of their educative outreach.

Thus, while transsexual autobiographies may not be representative of the experiences of many (or even most) transsexual subjects, they are indicative of the establishment of an official discourse (or set of discourses) regulating transsexual self-representations and, therefore, modes of transsexual subjectivity. The autobiographical texts help institute a certain discursive hegemony within a community whose members have a substantial investment in mimicking the enunciative modality of those who have been successful in achieving sex transformation. Collecting the autobiographies of successful transsexuals—either through personal contact or by print media—constitutes an important part of transsexual self-construction, self-education, and self-preparation for encounters with clinic personnel. As Sandy Stone writes in "The *Empire* Strikes Back: A Posttranssexual Manifesto": "[M]any transsexuals keep something they call by the argot term 'O.T.F.': The Obligatory Transsexual File.... Transsexuals also collect autobiographical literature."[3]

Transsexuals are a notoriously well-read patient population, primarily because their success in obtaining the medical treatments that they seek depends upon their ability to convince doctors that their personal history matches the officially sanctioned etiology.[4] In a context where telling the right story may confer legitimacy upon one's demand and the wrong story can foil one's chances for sex change, the autobiographies of those transsexuals who have successfully maneuvered within the strict protocols of the gender clinics constitute guide-books of no mean proportion. They also serve to assure would-be transsexual readers that they are members of a group and not as isolated as they may feel. This latter function helps individuals who often perceive themselves to be entirely alone and outside the cultural system to authorize themselves as deserving cultural subjects and is instrumental in their assumption of an identity as a transsexual.

All of this suggests that transsexual autobiographies serve to encourage and enable transsexual subjects to conform to the parameters of an established "transsexual personal history" in order to obtain the desired medical treatment. Certainly, I am not the first to suggest the limitations this tendency imposes on the construction of transsexual subjectivity. Sandy Stone argues that the instantiation of the "official transsexual history" necessary for approval for surgical and hormonal sex change produced a situation in which the potential "intertextuality" of transsexual subjectivity has been erased:

> [I]t is difficult to generate a counterdiscourse if one is programmed to disappear. The highest purpose of the transsexual is to erase him/herself, to fade into the "normal" population as soon as possible. Part of this process is known as *constructing a plausible history*—learning to lie effectively about one's past. What is gained is acceptability in society. What is lost is the ability to authentically represent the complexities and ambiguities of lived experience....Instead, authentic experience is replaced by a particular kind of story, one that supports the old constructed positions.[5]

In opposition to this tendency, she calls on transsexuals to resist passing, a behavior she claims is "the essence of transsexualism":

> I could not ask a transsexual for anything more inconceivable than to forgo passing, to be consciously "read," to read oneself aloud—and by this troubling and productive reading to begin to *write oneself* into the discourses by which one has been written—in effect, then, to become a (look out—dare I say it again?) a posttranssexual.[6]

Stone asks for this in order to alleviate the compromises of silence that she believes regulate transsexual subjectivity and keep an alternative, multifaceted, and potentially subversive story of gender, sex, and the body from surfacing in and through the culture at large. Stone asserts that this silence concerning the "lived experience" of transsexuals has a significant and damaging effect on their relationships with others: "Transsexuals who pass seem able to ignore the fact that by creating totalized, monistic identities, forgoing physical and subjective intertextuality, they have foreclosed the possibility of authentic relationships."[7]

"The *Empire* Strikes Back" is a powerful essay, representing the first attempt by a transsexual woman to argue as a lesbian-feminist and as a transsexual for the destabilizing potential of transsexualism within a cultural context that regulates the phenomenon into the relative safety of socially acceptable discourses about gender.[8] Nevertheless, Stone's argument stops short of recognizing gender as a category that might be fully deconstructed in its historical context. She claims that "the transsexual currently occupies a position which is nowhere, which is outside the binary oppositions of gendered discourse," and that consequently, "for a transsexual, *as a transsexual*, to generate a true, effective and representative counterdiscourse is to speak from outside the boundaries of gender, beyond the constructed oppositional nodes which have been predefined as the only positions from which discourse is possible."[9] The production of the concept of gender within research on intersexuality and transsexualism suggests, however, that the transsexual speaks fully within the cultural discourse of/on gender, not only because that discourse was produced precisely to account for intersexual and transsexual subjects' experiences, but also because the performance of transsexual subjectivity depends upon the expert manipulation of traditional gender codes. To be a transsexual is perhaps to be "in gender" more fixedly than other subjects whose gender performances are perceived to be "natural."

Stone suggests that a "true" transsexual discourse would problematize gender by destabilizing the official transsexual history of the "wrong body" and by introducing into discourse "disruptions of the old patterns of desire that the multiple dissonances of the transsexual body imply."[10] She wants to produce a more authentic history of transsexualism through a lifting of the silences necessary to secure the desired medical interventions and a destabilization of the official stories about transsexualism—in these goals she and I concur. In her discussion of transsexual autobiographies, she comments that the authors deny "mixture," what she understands as an acknowledgment of ambiguous gender: "Besides the obvious complicity of these accounts in a Western white male definition of performative gender, the authors also reinforce a binary, oppositional mode of gender identification. They go from being unambiguous men, albeit unhappy ones, to unambiguous women. There is no territory between."[11] Stone argues that in conjunction with medical discourses on transsexualism and the practices of the gender clinics, the transsexual autobiographies demonstrate these subjects' necessary capitulation to ideologies of gender difference and disambiguity.

Stone comments that while transsexuals maintain files that include autobiographical accounts, the medical gender clinics do not because "according to the Stanford gender dysphoria program...they consider autobiographical accounts thoroughly unreliable."[12] Indeed, a number of transsexual researchers comment on what Stone designates "constructing a plausible history," in other words, lying about one's past in order to obtain the desired medical treatment. Anthropologist Anne Bolin explains the situation in *In Search of Eve: Transsexual Rites of Passage*:

> Transsexuals have widespread networks extending nationwide. They keep tabs on what the caretakers are up to and on what their latest theories are. Transsexual lore is rich with information on manipulation and utilization of caretaker stereotypes. Transsexuals know what they can honestly reveal and what they must withhold. This lore consists of "recipes" for dealing with caretakers and the management of information that they know would discredit them in the eyes of their caretakers should it be revealed. They necessarily exploit caretakers' expectations for their own ends by presenting a transsexual identity in conformity with caretakers' conceptions of classic transsexualism.[13]

For Bolin, who advocates the depathologization of transsexualism and the equalization of power within the caretaker-patient relationship, the fact that a transsexual's lies "validate the caretakers' stereotypes about transsexuals" is a shame, given that this can "foster impressions of a homogeneous population" and lead to "a self-fulfilling prophecy and . . . a situation in which both caretakers and clients suffer."[14] Dwight Billings and Thomas Urban discuss this same issue, calling it "the con."[15]

For Robert Stoller, a psychoanalyst at the Gender Identity Clinic at the University of California, Los Angeles (which in the past has not provided surgery for transsexuals), transsexuals' lies about their personal histories have other implications. In discussing the criteria for a diagnosis of transsexualism, Stoller writes that "those of us faced with the task of diagnosing transsexualism have an additional burden these days, for most patients requesting 'sex change' are in complete command of the literature and know the answers before the questions are asked."[16] For Stoller, the discursive tangle of self-identified and self-diagnosed transsexualism is part of an overall problem in the clinical treatment of transsexual subjects, evidence of the lack of an adequate differential diagnosis. In his view, the production of the "plausible personal history" keeps clinicians from really understanding the phenomenon of transsexualism, and therefore from truly helping transsexual patients. Indeed, as Stone writes, "It took a surprisingly long time—several years—for the researchers to realize that the reason the candidates' behavioral profiles matched [Harry] Benjamin's so well was that the candidates, too, had read Benjamin's book, which was passed from hand to hand within the transsexual community, and they were only too happy to provide the behavior that led to acceptance for surgery."[17]

Is there a "true" or "authentic" history behind the autobiographical productions for the gender clinics—and behind other kinds of transsexual autobiographies? Where might we find it and of what use would it be? Sandy Stone and Anne Bolin believe that alleviating the silence around certain aspects of transsexual experience will result in a measurable change in current conceptions of transsexualism and the authenticity of transsexuals' lives. Significantly, both argue this issue with respect to transsexuals' sexual habits. Stone twice comments that a preoperative, masturbatory ritual of male-to-female transsexuals, "wringing the turkey's neck," is always excluded from transsexual self-representations, largely because the official etiology of male-to-female transsexualism denies for these subjects any kind of penile pleasure.[18] Bolin discusses the stereotype of heterosexuality that regulates the transsexual's pre- and postoperative sexual life and makes owning up to bisexuality or lesbianism (pre- or postoperatively) clinical suicide.[19] Both believe that allowing the suppressed stories to surface would be beneficial to both transsexuals and the public at large—Stone because she is interested in subverting culturally hegemonic narratives about gender, and Bolin because she wants to see transsexuals legitimated as a sexual minority rather than defined by the stigma of mental illness. Both suggest that the suppressed stories, the "truth" of the transsexual experience, are about sexuality; and both represent the power at work—the force that produces transsexual autobiography as singular and monolithic—as entirely repressive and negative, without any enabling function.[20]

Transsexual autobiographical narratives cannot merely be a part of the repressive structure of "official" transsexual experience, since they clearly enable others to identify themselves as transsexuals, thereby allowing a variety of individuals to actively construct themselves as transsexuals. This is evident in the autobiographies themselves, where the authors mention that finding texts by other transsexuals helped to authorize their own identifications. This suggests that a "true" or "authentic" transsexual experience is not necessarily repressed and excluded from the transsexual autobiographies, but rather, that transsexual experience is itself made possible by these discourses: that they involve certain necessary exclusions does not make them "inauthentic." Another way to examine these autobiographies is to use a Foucauldian model to analyze the statements made in transsexual autobiographies and thereby to examine the forms of subjectivity and experience made possible by those statements.[21] This approach would enable us to gauge the ways in which transsexual autobiographies function as enabling—and not merely repressive—narratives.

One important rhetorical strategy of transsexual autobiographers is to present arguments that resist open readings. This strategy is part of the overall structure of these autobiographies as what Judith Butler might call "constative performances." By "constative performances" she means those performances of identity that actively construct the identity they are taken to be expressions of. According to Butler, all performances that are understood as reflections of an essential identity or self are, in fact, constative performances. I call the constative performances of transsexual autobiographers "assertions" or "statements" since the latter terms suggest strategies of the written word.[22]

The statements about identity and sex that are made by the transsexual autobiographers are produced as implications of, supplements to, and corollaries for the texts' resistances to multiple interpretations. In other words, the closed nature of the texts is a central aspect of the production of discourse about transsexual personal experience. This can be linked to the kind of discursive strategies necessary for transsexuals to gain clinical treatment in the form of hormones and sex reassignment surgery. Whether the author produces a story that relies on a physiological rationale for transsexualism, or one that suggests a psychological (and therefore gender-oriented) origin of the desire to change sex, the assertions produced by the texts conform to the notion that the author was truly meant to be a member of the other sex, always has been a member of the other sex, and should be allowed to be recognized (legally and socially) as a member of the other sex.

What I find latent in these texts is not the possibility of an "authentic" account of the transsexual, nor a particularly subversive story about sexuality, but the idea of the transsexual subject as an engineered subject. The technological aspects of the transformations of "sex change" are rarely stressed in these autobiographies, and physical pain is often glossed over in favor of a quick remark concerning the "overwhelming success" of surgical and hormonal interventions. Those autobiographies that do offer representations of the plastic surgery and its aftermath suggest that the alternative narratives available in transsexual autobiography do not concern counterhegemonic discourses of gender, but rather accounts of human engineering through medical technology. The stories that detail sex conversion technologies highlight the physical pain that occurs as a result of medical intervention, and demonstrate that the "original" body exerts pressure against such change. They suggest that the demand for sex change is indicative of a desire to engineer the self as a subject without discontinuity or rupture, to produce oneself as a complete and total subject of gender. The tension between the two stories—the story of the subject as the other sex and the story of the methods used to make the subject represent the other sex—constitutes one central disjunction in transsexual autobiographical narratives.

Another disjunction occurs within the story of "gender" itself, insofar as transsexuals' claims to physiological transsexualism (a transsexualism based on intersexuality) disrupts the officially sanctioned narrative of aberrant gender identity formation (found in the entirely psychological accounts put forth by the American Psychiatric Association in the various editions of the *Diagnostic and Statistical Manual of Mental Disorders*). In some of the autobiographies, the two contradicting accounts—"transsexualism is caused by aberrant sexual physiology" and "transsexualism is caused by aberrant gender identity"—are put forth with equal stress; in others, one is privileged while the other is mentioned but not stressed. In all of the autobiographies the idea of a physiological transsexualism appears at least in the form of a passing comment.

As we saw in chapter 4, many physicians advocating "sex change" as treatment for transsexualism felt that in the future medical science would be able to find a somatic origin of cross-sex identification of the kind found in transsexual patients. A similar emphasis in the autobiographies may simply indicate a mirroring of the medical discourses as a way of legitimating autobiographical claims. However, it seems to me that something more significant is at stake in transsexuals' assertions of physiological intersexuality. These assertions, or the "clues" recounted in the autobiographies that offer hope to the writers that they may be physically akin to the other sex, reaffirm their sense that they already *are* the other sex and only need to be recognized as such. Such a belief suggests transsexuals' investment in the idea that identity resides in the body's tissues, regardless of the fact that the official medical story of transsexualism treats the body as contingent to the mind's identifications.

This is, of course, made manifest in the demand for "sex change," since demanding to be made into the other sex suggests that "being" at the level of the mind (gender) is not enough. But the claims to physiological aberration suggest as well that changing the body solely on the basis of gender identifications is not a comfortable transformation for many transsexuals—the assertion of partial physical identity as the other sex prior to sex reassignment is one way of arguing that "I was meant to be the other sex" all along. The discourses of gender, however tied to psychology and a constructionist perspective in the realm of psychiatry, maintain a connection to the idea of physiological sex through the transsexual phenomenon. As we will see, the relation between physiology and culture is both intimate and strained in the stories by transsexuals about their own "emergence."

In her "personal autobiography," Christine Jorgensen wrote:

> Neither my doctors nor I had ever advocated these procedures for other sexual breaches of Nature. Mine was a single, highly individual case and the doctors had proceeded along the lines they felt would be most beneficial to me alone, with my full knowledge, approval, and consent. Beyond that, I had no advice for anyone. If others had seen in me a false hope for their own problems, then surely it was "wrong" and "tragic," but help for others could only come from the acceptance and enlightenment of the public and the medical profession.[23]

Jorgensen attempted to refuse the symbolic status that she inevitably acquired as the Western world's first public transsexual by defining herself against transvestites and homosexuals, the two categories of sexual aberration most closely associated with transsexualism. The above statement underscores a central message of her autobiography, namely, that Christine Jorgensen's experience was unique, that her anomalous condition was in no way representative of other (sexually aberrant) individuals' experiences, that she was a model for no one but herself.

Her book, however, was (and continues to be) widely read among transsexuals.[24] Apparently, *Christine Jorgensen: A Personal Autobiography* was not so unique as to avoid reader identification. Mario Martino, for example, identified with Jorgensen's life story as well as Jorgensen's interpretation of her condition. As I suggested in chapter 4, Jorgensen faced a discursive difficulty in defining her case, since by the time she wrote the autobiography, the terminology used to discuss transsexualism had changed. In the autobiography, Jorgensen insisted on the (by 1967) outmoded discourse of intersexuality to identify and define her condition.[25] She herself had been enormously influenced by the "glandular thesis" presented by Paul de Kruif in his book *The Male Hormone*.[26] Jorgensen's representation of her transsexualism as a physiological condition is consistent with her insistence that as George her problem was not only *feeling* like a woman, but *appearing* to be a woman physically as well.[27] This is a theme that returns in many of the autobiographies.

The story, as Jorgensen related it, is of an "underdeveloped" but undoubtedly male subject who never really felt masculine and was unable to find a place in society where he could earn a living and move up in the world. As a child, George played often with girls, especially his sister, who was relegated the responsibility of looking after him and usually let him tag along with her and her friends. He felt that a "normal" social life was denied him because of his intense insecurity about his sexuality, as well as his acute shyness. He was underweight, unhappy, and uncertain about his sexual desires for men. The decision to change sex developed over a period of time, during which George attempted to gain insight into his problems as well as to earn a living. At a certain point, it became the overwhelming focus of his life, especially while he was a student at the Manhattan Medical and Dental Assistants School and while he saved money for his trip to Denmark. In Copenhagen, he became a research subject of Christian Hamburger and members of Hamburger's endocrinology lab, in return for which Jorgensen was granted surgical and hormonal treatment resulting in sex change in 1952. When the news of her transformation was leaked to the press, Christine Jorgensen became an international celebrity and in the book claims that of necessity she decided to go into show business because she felt she would never be able to live a private life anyway.[28] The overwhelming message of the autobiography is "I was meant to be a woman—see what a good woman I turned out to be, far more successful than my male self."

In the autobiography, Jorgensen supported the physiological perspective with reported speech from her doctors. For example, according to Jorgensen, Christian Hamburger told her the following: "I think the trouble is very deep-rooted in the cells of your body. Outwardly, you have many of the sex characteristics of a man. You were declared a boy at birth and you have grown up, so very unhappily, in the guise of a man. But, inwardly, it is quite possible that you are a woman. Your body chemistry and all of your body cells, including your brain cells, may be female. That is only a theory, mind you."[29] In another passage, Jorgensen claimed that "[a]lthough the term 'sex transformation' has been used by many people when referring to my case, even by me on occasion, mine was rather a process of revised sex determination, inspired by the preponderance of female characteristics."[30]

Christine Jorgensen is not the only subject whose claim to be the other sex was made almost entirely on physiological grounds—we saw a similar claim in Lili Elbe's autobiography, as well as in Michael Dillon's *Self: A Study in Ethics and Endocrinology*. Another person who underwent surgery a year before Jorgensen, Roberta Cowell, also used a physiological justification for her sex change. Indeed, Cowell was more aggressive than Jorgensen in arguing for her identity as an intersex subject, and she claimed that Jorgensen "was scientifically classified as a transvestite, a person with an irresistible urge to wear the clothing of the other sex."[31] Cowell, like Jorgensen, presented little actual physical evidence of intersexuality in her autobiography, relying instead on reported speech from her doctors and vague references to her "feminine characteristics."

A father of two, a fighter pilot during World War II, and a former race car driver, Cowell went through psychotherapy and various treatments in the postwar period until she found doctors who were struck by his "female" physical characteristics and agreed to sponsor his sex reassignment. He wrote: "In my own case, I was never either a transvestite or a homosexual. My sexual inclinations were normal until the period of hormonal imbalance began. While my body was undergoing changes, all [sexual] inclinations died. When they appeared again, they were re-oriented. But this re-orientation was normal, since I was then a woman."[32] According to Cowell, the doctors believed that there had been "an alteration in gland balance and perhaps in gland structure. The cause might possibly have been a series of emotional upsets. There seemed to be some degree of hermaphroditism present."[33]

Roberta Cowell described her physical condition by referring to stereotypes of feminine anatomy and posture. After a squash partner observed that he might want to wear a brassiere, Robert went to see a sexologist:

> A few days later I was in the Harley Street consulting-room of a famous sexologist. . . .
>
> He gave it as his considered opinion that my body showed quite prominent feminine sex characteristics: wide hips and narrow shoulders, pelvis female in type, hair distribution and skin female in type. Other female traits included the absence of laryngeal relief (no Adam's apple) and a tendency of the lower limbs to converge towards the knees.
>
> . . . Once I realized that my femininity had a *physical* basis I did not despise myself so much.[34]

Cowell's interpretation of bodily signifiers matches her presentation of the effects of hormone treatment. After taking hormones for a period of time, Robert Cowell found that "a definite change in the functioning of my mentality began to become apparent." According to her account, Robert was transformed (by hormones) into a stereotype of femininity:

> My mental processes seemed to be slightly slower, and at the same time I also showed signs of greatly heightened powers of intuition. It had been expected that the change of hormone balance might very well be manifested in changed mental processes, but I realized that it would be impossible to differentiate between the effects of mental and physical changes.
>
> Whatever the cause, I quite definitely began to be intuitive. . . .
>
> Sometimes when the telephone rang I would get the feeling that I knew who was calling, and I would be right.
>
> I also developed one super-feminine quality—the ability to blush. . . .
>
> Fiction, except for the works of P.G. Wodehouse, had rarely interested me. Now I found myself reading stories and novels of all kinds with sustained interest. . . .
>
> In general my nature was becoming milder and less aggressive.[35]

Despite the mental transformation, however, and even after the operation "to correct the congenital absence of vagina," an operation which left him "truly a complete female," Cowell felt that her "face was still fundamentally the same." She decided to have her "face drastically altered by surgery. This would remove all residual traces of masculinity and relieve me of the fear that I would be recognised. Incidentally, I could be made better-looking."[36]

The general discussion of her progress after surgery, however, recounts both the traits of femininity Roberta had to acquire consciously, and those which she unconsciously assumed (and therefore presumed to be naturally feminine). Roberta actively learned about feminine etiquette, hair and skin care, dieting, voice pitch, vocabulary, and cooking. She suggested at times the constructed-ness of her new self, as when she stated, "I always had to remember that I was building a new personality, and that I would have to curb undesirable tendencies as they arose while at the same time cultivating the traits which seemed most acceptable."[37] But she stuck steadfastly to her story that "spontaneous" feminization took place before she (as Robert) sought medical help. Then again, she was insistent that one can ascertain the existence of physiological factors from rather slim visual evidence: "A normal man or woman in the clothes of the opposite sex would look quite absurd, and either appearance or demeanor would make the masquerade easy to detect. It follows logically, therefore, that when an individual is able without any effort to pass, when properly dressed, as a member of the opposite sex, there must be some physical factor at work."[38]

Like Jorgensen, Cowell included in her autobiography a discussion of the medical theories concerning transvestism, embryonic sexual development, and endocrinology. Like Michael Dillon in *Self: A Study in Ethics and Endocrinology*, she presented "evidence" that supported the alleged facts of her own case. For example, Cowell wrote that

> Apart from legal, ethical and social considerations, a change from male to female is made more difficult by the fact that many of the male sex-characteristics are not reversible. . . . Unless the prospective patient is so feminine that he can pass for a woman *before treatment commences*, it is not likely that he can be helped. Presence of deep constitutional feminism is essential.[39]

She asserted, in addition, that it is easier to turn a woman into a man than a man into a woman (an assertion which has been proven false in the forty-odd years since her hormonal and surgical treatment).

Indeed, "medical science believes that on the very rare occasions when an apparent man turns into a woman it is because he has been a highly virilized woman all the time."[40]

In emphasizing intersexuality as the reason for their sex change, both Jorgensen and Cowell do not only represent the prevailing theories of the period during which their surgeries took place. While presenting their sex changes as being physiologically justified, either as cases of mistaken sex assignment or of spontaneously aberrant sexual development, these authors articulate one fundamental belief of most transsexual subjects—that the sense of being the other sex is an inborn and therefore irrefutable and unchangeable aspect of the self. One way of making that statement plausible is to argue that anything inborn must perforce be physiological.

More recent transsexual autobiographies continue to make gestures toward intersexuality as a rationale for cross-sex behaviors, but few rely as heavily on this reasoning as did Jorgensen and Cowell. What we will see in the other autobiographies are more sporadic representations of intersexuality in conjunction with a developing discourse about gender identity. The result is the elaboration of a common narrative concerning the identity of the self as a sex, a narrative that insists on the idea of a constitutional (inborn) identity as the other sex. The authors may present this constitutional identity as having been encouraged by circumstances and social learning. Like Jorgensen and Cowell, the other transsexual autobiographers set out to prove that "I was really meant to be a man/woman," but unlike Jorgensen and Cowell, later transsexuals used the discourses of gender, in addition to those of intersexual physiology, to substantiate their claims.

One advantage to this strategy is that the idea of an irrevocable core gender identity relies upon the implied presence of intersexuality in the register of the psyche. Conceived as a core or kernel of identity, gender metaphorically becomes a site of psychosocial sex, the center and origin of the body's sexual signifiers. Gender identity inherits the legacy of the glandular thesis by becoming the cause of sex in the body: if "natural" sexual physiology manifests in opposition to the gender identity at the core of the body's subjectivity, then another body is said to inhabit the external one. Thus, the idea of intersexuality remains central to the experience of transsexualism through the set of statements upon which transsexuals make their case in contemporary culture: "I am a man/woman inside," "I was meant to be a man/woman," or "I really am a man/woman on the inside." In the context of gender theory, all of these suggest an actual locatability of gender identity *in the body*, just as in the context of intersex theory they suggested the existence of cross-sex attributes and organs in the body. These statements undergird the autobiographical narratives, where each author interprets his or her experiences as examples of the facticity of an unambiguous relation between gendered behaviors and the body.

Emergence chronicles Marie Martino's confused youth and her journey toward sex reassignment as Mario, his organizing of a service for female-to-male transsexuals, and his two attempts at phalloplasty.[41] Like most transsexual autobiographers, Martino denies any identification as a homosexual, preferring to characterize his sexuality as "like any man's."[42] Martino insists throughout the narrative that he ought to have been born a boy and that indicators of his true sex were available throughout his life as Marie. Indeed, *Emergence* is perhaps the most aggressive of the autobiographies in its insistent assertions of the author's "true" identity as the other sex.

Marie Martino was born into a traditional Italian-American family, and all her life identified strongly with her father and older half-brother. Her sense of her maleness began very early, Martino recounts, and throughout the autobiography, he proudly presents incidents which seem to affirm the existence of this maleness. The pictures included in the autobiography are an apt example of this. For the author, these pictures undeniably document her childhood masculinity (as the captions confirm), yet both merely offer the reader images of a child whose sex is largely indicated by clothing. A three-year-old child with short hair is generally somewhat asexual; that is why children's, even infants', clothes are so conspicuously sex-coded. Some children maintain this sexlessness until puberty, when secondary sex characteristics can make identification of physical sex somewhat easier; others learn to produce themselves as visibly sexed subjects before puberty. But Martino presents these pictures as if their meanings were absolutely unambiguous, or rather, as if the ambiguity supports his claims to maleness.

The story Martino tells is of a female subject with a male core gender identity constantly repelled by the femininity forced on it by uncaring family, friends, and colleagues. Marie Martino tried twice to become a nun, attempts that were thwarted by her inability to control her sexual feelings toward the other novitiates.[43] In the autobiography, these feelings are always represented as being heterosexual, never indicative of lesbianism. Once he had completed his first series of surgeries, Martino married the woman he had been living with for nine years, legitimating the relationship as a heterosexual union and thereby reinventing its previous (lesbian) conditions. As a result of his experiences, Martino and his wife, both nurses, created "Labyrinth Services," a counseling and referral service for female-to-male transsexuals.

The book was produced out of this same desire to aid others who share a similar plight. The rhetoric of the text, its insistence on Martino's innate "maleness," stems from this purpose. Martino wants to leave nothing uncertain so that the (transsexual) reader may identify his or her own experience with those represented in the text, and may see in them a similar indisputability. Thus, if Christine Jorgensen's "personal" autobiography attempted to limit its scope by asserting her uniqueness as an individual case, in *Emergence* Mario Martino tries to open out his experience with his readers, to encourage identification or sympathy. This is perhaps one difference between the autobiography of a "public transsexual" (Martino) and the autobiography of a transsexual celebrity (Jorgensen).

The three autobiographies discussed thus far are more or less all closed texts, ones in which the reader is interpellated only as a fixed and passive presence whose function it is to verify the narration offered by the author. Alternate interpretations are at times suggested, but immediately foreclosed by the author. In each text there are totalizing interpretations attached to acts that imply, at least to a critical reader, a number of possible readings. The effect is multiple: on the one hand, for the reader interested in verifying his or her own gender confusions, these narratives provide ample opportunity for identification and mirroring. For a critical reader, on the other hand, the reading process can be confining, especially as the author makes blanket statements concerning sex, gender, and sexuality. The purpose of the narratives is to force the reader to comply with the author's experience, to begin to interpret his or her own life along the same trajectory. To resist this interpretive insistence in the face of these monolithic narratives is exhausting. But the authors want their readers to consider themselves only in relation to the theories of gender, sex, and the body espoused in each text—not in relation to alternative scenarios that might invalidate the author's own experience. Only in this way can the author verify his or her experience, by making gender a universal category and its signification through ordinary daily experiences unilateral and unambiguous.

Martino's *Emergence* presents the best example of this kind of closed narration. At one point in her life Marie Martino became a boarder at the home of a doctor and his family:

> Baby Jenny was about four months old when I moved in. The first time I changed her diapers, I forgot the plastic pants. Learning to make Jenny's Pablum, I must've used half of the box before getting the proper consistency. Between one thing and another, I knew I would not—could not—be a mother. I was not psychologically equipped for motherhood—I lacked the fortitude.[44]

Many mothers can, of course, relate experiences similar to those represented here. Getting the right consistency to Pablum is a learned experience and not something that comes "naturally." However,

Martino writes that as Marie she could never be a mother because she was not "psychologically equipped." Yet neither her inability to make Pablum nor her forgetfulness about plastic pants are psychological issues, and they are not questions of fortitude but of experience. Nevertheless, this explanation is never offered and Martino's summary "between one thing and another *I knew*" attempts to foreclose any other interpretation.

Martino relates another incident earlier in the text. Marie decided that she wanted to experience heterosexual intercourse and asked a male friend to "help" her:

> With a short grasping at my ample breasts, Bart had come to full measurement and was now thrusting, trying to penetrate my very tight vagina.
>
> "God, you are a virgin!" Perspiration was coating his body, and he was struggling.
>
> Why had there been no foreplay? It seemed funny now that I'd thought he could teach me a trick or two—why, I could teach him.
>
> No matter how high he elevated my lower torso, he could not penetrate and finally gave up. . . .
>
> That experience sealed my fate. I knew I could never live as a female, that I should never have been born one. It was all some horrendous mistake.[45]

The author suggests the possibility that Bart was simply not doing all he should to help Marie "open up," but then drops this interpretation. Sex, in this encounter, is engineered by the male partner, just as Marie would overpower her female lovers "as a man."[46] Martino's comment that the "experience sealed my fate" reveals the insistence with which this kind of incident is believed to have only one significant meaning, as well as how that significance is accepted as definitive for the subject's future. In both the passage concerning Baby Jenny and the one with Bart, the narrative ends with a statement with the operative term "I knew." The representation of experience that is immediately transformed into knowledge serves to close down interpretive options.

This element of interpretive foreclosure must be considered in relation to the clinical production of transsexualism in the dialogue between doctor and patient. There, the self-proclaimed transsexual must make clear to the doctor that there are no other diagnostic options apart from transsexualism that will make sense in his or her case. The subject's fixation on medically mediated sex change must be close to suicidal, and no other interpretive option can be made available to the doctor, who would then have just cause in denying the desired treatment. The transsexual's success in obtaining genital and hormonal sex change is therefore dependent upon his or her ability to direct the clinician's attention to specific areas of experience where the interpretation is clear and unambiguous. However, little of human experience admits of such unambiguous signification. It is therefore necessary to be able to present the interpretation in an unambiguous and assured manner, such that the interpretation becomes plausible to the doctor. The transsexual must also resist the gaze of the doctor into areas where meanings are not so clear and which might jeopardize his or her chances for sex reassignment. The autobiographies, then, mirror this function as it is forged in the clinical situation.

In the context of these autobiographies, gendered meanings are unilinear and very clear. The possibility that gender might pose a problem itself does not occur to the authors, who believe that all nontranssexual people experience gender as they do, only in the "right" bodies. This idea of the right or intended body has two sources: first, a belief that there is an organizing force to social existence, either Nature or God, and second, a belief that there is a direct connection between the body on the one hand and human behaviors, personality characteristics, and desires on the other hand. (Significantly, the "right bodies" are always considered to be heterosexual ones, in these autobiographies and in the medical literature.) In 1964 and 1968, Robert Stoller termed the latter a "biological force," which he believed to contribute substantially toward the acquisition of gender identity. He now believes this hypothesis to be questionable at best, claiming instead that clinical work overwhelmingly suggests that postnatal, cultural influences are the most significant factors in the formation of gender identity in humans.[47] Mario Martino, however, asserts a full and meaningful connection between physiology and psychology, offering a number of examples to substantiate his claims.

Martino takes whatever verification of his physiological masculinity that he can get: while working at a lab, the technicians practiced determining the 17-ketosteroid count with their own urine. Marie's turned out to be indicative of a 17-year-old male: "'I knew it: *I'm a guy!*' Everyone laughed at the idea. And I laughed louder and longer than anyone. This was just one more proof of my maleness. Something very definite to hang onto."[48] Yet, in discussing Marie's use of a dildo for intercourse with her lover, Martino comments that while it is a "venerable instrument used for intercourse," he "was unhappy resorting to this device." He writes that the experience "deepened my determination that my own destiny *was not to be set by biological patterns*."[49] And, in another twist, after reading Christine Jorgensen's autobiography, Marie considered the idea of intersexuality as it applied to herself:

> I toyed with the thought that I was an individual belonging to the highest degree of intersexuality, only my case was the reverse of Christine's since she had begun life as a boy. Then I was *not* too different! And there were tens of thousands all over the world with varying degrees of this same intersexuality.[50]

Martino's shifting reliance on the idea of biology as the basis of his transsexualism suggests a desire to have it both ways. He wants to defend the desire to change sex with the rhetoric of physiological intersexuality; he also wants to demand the construction of male sex organs. To have both, he needs to use biology and to repudiate it.

In the end, Mario Martino suggests a physiological rationale for transsexualism. While he acknowledges that "transsexuality…remains a rare and mystifying occurrence, its causal range as vast as the experience of life itself," he states:

> Parents often suffer guilt, wondering as to their own responsibility in this "difference." But, firm in their belief that the occurrence is inborn, many authorities discount parental practices as a factor. My own strongly held opinion is that *father and mother are not to be blamed*. We have only to look around at the number of less-than-perfect babies born every day to realize that sex disorientation is as possible, say, as a cleft palate, clubfoot, or other abnormality.[51]

None of the physical deformities he mentions, of course, email the kind of *cultural* dimension apparent in the transsexual phenomenon. The equivalence Martino suggests represents his own desire to make transsexualism *like any other physical difference*, to normalize it within the recognizable limits of physiological sex.

Nancy Hunt's *Mirror Image*, unlike the autobiographies discussed above, makes no overt claims about physiology as the cause of her transsexualism. Because of this, the text aptly represents the way a story about gender—that is, the subject's psychological orientation as a sex—can depend upon the idea of an inborn physiological tendency without really stating it as such Hunt presents the classic theories concerning transsexualism and gender identity early in the autobiography, finishing them off with the following comment: "It wasn't merely that I had cried more easily or hated fighting or thrown a ball like a girl, though these were all facts. It was a deeper difference. I wasn't like them [his male peers], and they sensed it, smelled it, and in consequence always kept me at a distance, as if I were a threat to them, as if I had been marked for punishment by the gods."[52] Poetic description of this sort pervades *Mirror Image* (as it does Jan Morris's *Conundrum*, discussed below), and serves to present only vague ideas about the causes of transsexualism. It is clear by the end of the autobiography that

Hunt really doesn't care what the causes of transsexualism might be—in her opinion, "By right of suffering and endurance and the Circuit Court of Cook County, I am Nancy."[53]

Yet the autobiography does present a theoretical position about transsexualism as a disorder of gender identity, perhaps best exemplified by this statement: "Women do differ from men, quite apart from anatomy. And I always sensed which one I was—again, quite apart from anatomy. I was not a man. I was a woman. And if my anatomy did not confirm this classification, then in the final event it was going to be easier to change my anatomy than to change myself."[54] This classic statement about transsexualism was not available to either Christine Jorgensen or Roberta Cowell, and (for whatever reason) was not used by Mario Martino. It is a statement that wholeheartedly addresses the gender theories, discounting any reliance on the notion that physiological intersexuality could be the origin of transsexualism. The contours of Hunt's story—the masculine pursuits at prep school and Yale, in the army, and as a reporter for the *Chicago Tribune* are represented as "masking" the author's true feminine interior—conform to this story of an internal gender identity finally allowed authentic expression as a woman.[55]

Hunt had no illusions about her original anatomical sex: "I knew well enough that I was not a girl—I had only to look at what my body had become: five feet ten inches tall, skinny as a fence post, muscles hard, beard growing, hair sprouting on chest and stomach. Secret dreams aside, I was locked in an undoubtedly male body, and like most adolescent male bodies it was bubbling with hormones and potent as a cocked pistol."[56] Throughout the text, she discusses her desire to be a woman as a psychosocial issue, and details her growing experiences as a woman with comments like the following: "After all the scientific explanations—whether physical or psychological, there remains the inexplicable fact that the male transsexual feels altogether more comfortable as a woman in a woman's world."[57]

Yet physiological allusions appear in *Mirror Image*. In discussing her children (of which she is the father), Hunt writes: "Until I became a parent, I assumed that sex-typed behavior is acquired, but my own children convinced me that it arises spontaneously. Certainly I did not teach manliness to my son; he simply exuded it from infancy. Similarly my daughters acquired femaleness from within themselves. I marveled at their innate femininity, their grace, the delicacy of their play."[58] Later, when Hunt began to take estrogenic hormones, he claims to have begun feeling the effects on the evening after the first injection: "Already the estrogens were affecting me physically. I could feel my genitalia shrinking in a way men commonly experience when they swim in cold water."[59] This, of course, was far too soon to feel any effects from hormonal treatment. On the following page, Hunt writes, "My shoulders, which once sloped steeply down from the neck, have assumed a feminine squareness; bra and shoulder-bag straps no longer slide off."[60]

These last two quotes are interesting insofar as they exemplify the transsexual's fantasy of hormonal power: the hormones work immediately, they change the shape of the entire body. Perhaps even more interesting is the idea that *square* shoulders are feminine; Hunt's utilitarian presentation of square-shouldered femininity (bra straps and shoulder bags don't fall off) belies the historicity of this concept. In the nineteenth century of course, it was the sloping shoulder that signaled femininity, and at the time that feature was believed to be the result of ovarian influence.

At one point Hunt mentions a conflict between her desire to become a woman and the sense that she still needed to "make her mark as a man," and this incident reveals the extent to which making a mark as a woman remained, for her, on a vastly different scale than making one's mark as a man. Hunt had been asked to become the *Tribune* "man in the Middle East." He did not want to go, but mused, "I was then forty-five. If I was ever going to make my mark as a man, it must be now." However, "I was more concerned with making my mark as a woman. Ellen [his second wife] and I were working on a fall suit for me: a rusty-orange plaid skirt with box pleats in front and a matching long-sleeved jacket. It was a difficult project, far beyond my own skills as a seamstress. It lay on top of the dining room sideboard, the pieces cut out but still pinned to the pattern paper. My instinct was to remain in paradise and finish my suit, but sensibly I knew that I must go to the Middle East. . . ."[61] The difference in scale here is startling. More significant, perhaps, is the way in which making a mark as a woman is presented in relation to fashion and fashioning. Hunt adheres to all the sex stereotypes of contemporary culture in her belief that to make oneself a woman is to engineer the perfect presence (or fashion the right effect), while to make one's mark as a man is to "do the right thing."

Canary: The Story of a Transsexual is reminiscent of Christine Jorgensen's autobiography, as well as Nancy Hunt's.[62] The narrative concerns Canary Conn's experiences as an "effeminate" and (as an adult) underdeveloped male (Daniel O'Connor) who grew up in the 1950s and 1960s, tried futilely to prove his masculinity throughout his adolescence, became a teenage rock music idol, married his girlfriend when she became pregnant, and eventually succeeded in obtaining sex change surgery at the age of twenty-three. The similarity to Christine Jorgensen rests largely in Conn's emphasis on other people's recognition of her effeminacy as Danny and her insistence that her male genitals were underdeveloped. These themes represent the physiological rationale that runs through the text. The autobiography is similar to Hunt's *Mirror Image* because of Conn's reliance on the theory of "masculinity as a mask" to explain anything that Danny did that was stereotypically masculine.

Interestingly, Canary Conn frames her account with a "medical" discussion of transsexualism: the first chapter delineates the outlines of gender identity theory, while at the end of the book she presents the possible biological aspects of the disorder. Thus, while in the first chapter she comments that "a transsexual is a person who is born one sex but who has a lifelong identity with the opposite sex. It's a problem of gender identity—genitals don't seem to match up with feelings inside," in the penultimate chapter she writes:

> Although there are many different factors involved, there are also biological bases for transsexualism. Because the fetus begins as a sort of tissue which is basically feminine, there are many possible ways that the necessary male hormones which differentiate the fetus might not be present at the time they are needed, or that unneeded male hormones are added to a fetus which is female by chromosomal makeup.[63]

She goes on to make the following claim, directly in opposition to the theories of gender identity that grew out of the protocols developed by Money and colleagues in the 1950s:

> "In order to illustrate," I said, "Let me ask you a question. If you, as a male, had become involved in an accident as an infant and your genitals were severed, your parents might have consulted with Dr. Lopez, or any one of the other doctors here, and decided to perform a sex change operation on you early in your life. They would then treat you as a normal female and rear you as one. How do you think you would feel? Would you feel like a boy or a girl?"
>
> "Well—uh—that is—well, I'd feel like a boy of course. I mean, I'd have to." The audience laughed, and the man sat down suddenly.
>
> "It stands to reason," I said, "that you would, indeed, feel as though something were wrong, at the very least. Your emotions, your physical makeup, even your sex drive toward what would be the opposite sex would all be important factors leading you to believe you were some-how in the wrong situation. . . . It's my theory that just such an accident happened to girls like myself—that we were somehow mutated in our prenatal development by drugs, diseases, etc."[64]

Conn's comments in this chapter seem to nullify her earlier claims about transsexualism as a gender identity disorder. However, in the context of these other autobiographies, all of which make some gesture toward a physiological basis for transsexualism, this position makes some sense. Transsexualism is perceived to be a gender identity disorder that (probably) has a physiological cause. What is interesting is the radical difference between this stand and that taken by Money and the Hampsons in their research on intersexuality in the 1950s, where they argued for the discontinuity between biological sex identity and a gender orientation that develops as a result of the original assignment of sex and social cues from parents and peers.[65]

It is in Jan Morris's autobiography, *Conundrum*, that we see the idea of transsexualism as a disorder of gender identity spun out in dazzling detail. Morris presents gender as the foremost identity of the subject, more important than sexual anatomy because it is closer to the spiritual. Morris's autobiography is the most consistently gender-oriented because in it there is almost no mention at all of physiology as a probable cause of transsexualism. Thus, while in the final chapter she states that "the transsexual urge, at least as far as I have experienced it, [is] far more than a social compulsion, but biological, imaginative, and essentially spiritual too," she never suggests elsewhere that she believes the cause of transsexualism to be rooted in the physiology of the body. Indeed, she writes, "That my conundrum actually emanated from my sexual organs did not cross my mind then [in childhood], and seems unlikely to me even now."[66]

Morris is no textbook case, however: her stint in the army, her marriage and five children, her success in the "masculine" pursuit of journalism—all of these testify to a personal history that deviates from the "official story" of total failure as a male subject. She maintains that she understood that she was "different" from an early age, that she knew at the age of three that she "had been born into the wrong body, and should really be a girl," but that she was determined to live life as a man until it became unbearable.[67] She regards her participation in all the traditional masculine activities as that of an outside, invited in for a moment but never really accepted as "one of the boys."[68] Morris presents her decision to change sex as a decision not to continue with a false life.

Conundrum is a frustrating book to read, if only because it says so little with so many words. As a professional writer, Morris has a facility with language that makes her discourse textually more interesting as well as rhetorically more manipulative. Morris's prose is overladen with expansive descriptions, in the course of which she philosophizes on the enigma of identity and its relation to sex. For Morris, the desire to change sex was connected to the idea that the self should be unified, having only one identity and representing that identity without rupture or discontinuity:

> In any case, I myself see the conundrum in another perspective, for I believe it to have some higher origin or meaning. I equate it with the idea of soul, or self, and I think of it not just as a sexual enigma, but as a quest for unity.

> [Gender] is the essentialness of oneself, the psyche, the fragment of unity.

> I was born with the wrong body, being feminine by gender but male by sex, and I could achieve completeness only when the one was adjusted to the other.

> All I wanted was liberation, or reconciliation—to live as myself, to clothe myself in a more proper body, and achieve Identity at last.

> I had reached Identity.[69]

Morris prefers the mystical to the material, and because of this, her discussion of transsexualism tends toward the indistinct. Nevertheless, some statements are made clearly enough: "I regarded sex merely as the tool of gender."[70] The vagueness of Morris's mystical spiritualism and the bluntness of her comments about gender are both the result of her refusal to think deeply about the matter: "During my years of torment, I generally found it safer...to approach my problem existentially, and to assume that it was altogether of itself, *sans* cause, *sans* meaning."[71] In effect, she has given herself license to say anything she wants about the matter. What she chooses to say is deeply indebted to the idea that psychology is the primary constituent of the self—thus sex can be a "tool of gender."

Besides Christine Jorgensen, Renée Richards is perhaps the most famous transsexual in the United States. She is famous largely because she fought the Women's Tennis Association in legal court in order to be allowed to play at WTA-sanctioned events as a woman. Otherwise, she might have remained as obscure as most transsexuals who attempt to "fade into the woodwork" of traditionally gendered society. Her autobiography, published in 1983, is a "play-by-play" account of her life as Richard Raskind—successful ophthalmologist, amateur tennis player, and transvestite—and her transformation into Renée—her alter ego or "feminine persona," whose subjectivity Raskind inhabited when dressed as a woman.

In a certain sense, there is much to recommend Richards's autobiography to the general reader—it is full of descriptive detail, juicy sex scenes, and hot sports cars, and contains little overt discussion of medical theory or specific ideas about the transsexual condition. There is, however, a lot of ad hoc psychologizing that Richards undoubtedly learned as his mother's son: Richards's mother was a psychiatrist and analyst. (Incidentally, this mother—as well as an older sister—are fingered as the "causes" of Richards's transsexual tendencies.) Richards provides a largely psychological narrative of her original inclinations to cross-dress and its development into transsexualism, and while her story does not coincide with all the aspects of the officially sanctioned medical history of transsexuality (she enjoyed too much heterosexual sex as Dick to be convincing as a failed man), it is a story largely about gender identifications gone awry. In this sense, *Second Serve: The Renée Richards Story* is an account aligned with the current medical conceptualization of transsexualism.

How interesting, then, to find the following comment at the beginning of the second chapter of the book (the first is dedicated to the story of Dick Raskind's birth, a harrowing tale of maternal courage as well as stubbornness, told with the edge of bitterness that accompanies all of Richards's recollections of her maternal parent):

> Another reason why [my childhood] remembrances are unsettling is that they seem so contrived. If I sat down to write a case history of an imaginary transsexual, I could not come up with a more provocative set of circumstances than that of my childhood. *The peculiar thing about this is that the cause of transsexualism may someday be proven to be biochemical.* If this happens, I can only conclude that fate has a sense of humor because my early life is strewn with unsubtle touches that beg to be seen as reasons for my sexual confusion. *If they aren't the true cause they ought to be.*[72]

The "unsubtle touches" referred to here include enforced cross-dressing, early morning closeness to the mother's body, competition with a tomboy sister, an absent and ineffectual father, an early association between voluntary cross-dressing and the lessening of anxiety, and the creation of an alternate female persona (Renée) who embodies all the femininity Dick excludes from his own behavior. In many ways, Richards's account presents her as a classic *transvestite* who becomes convinced that sex change was the only way to live out the contradictions of Dick's "sexual confusion."[73]

Richards's suggestion that transsexualism may well in the future be found to have a "biochemical" basis is the only reference to the possibility of a physiological cause of transsexualism in her book. Other than this brief mention, she sticks to the psychological account. There are clues in the text, however, that this account has been constructed specifically in relation to "official" medical discourses concerning transsexual etiology. For example, Richards relates her initial discussion (as Dick) with Harry Benjamin as follows:

> As [Dr. Benjamin] listened to me reviewing my history, he tilted his head first one way and then another, sometimes nodding agreeably. Occasionally, when I would grope for words, he would supply them so casually that I didn't notice at first. *Then I began to realize that this old man really did understand, so much so that he could probably have told the story without my help.* The childish exploits, the futile years of psychotherapy, the driving compulsion, the skulking around—all these constituted a familiar refrain that accompanied his daily work. He listened intelligently, and he understood almost as well as I did.[74]

Read in light of Sandy Stone's comment that transsexuals were presenting "classic Benjaminian" symptoms to their clinicians *because* they had been reading Benjamin's *The Transsexual Phenomenon*, Richards's account of Dick's visit to the great doctor's office becomes significant in a way clearly unintended by the author. Benjamin's "knowledge" of Dick's story—his ability to suggest words when Dick stumbled—demonstrates his ability to construct (or at least facilitate the construction of) the self-representations of his clients, who in going to see him usually knew what they wanted and what the doctor had the power to offer (hormone treatments and access to surgical sex change).[75]

Richards's narrative, like Morris's, falls mostly within the contemporary understanding of gender as a psychological construct disconnected from physiology. Few transsexual autobiographers adhere fully to the theories of transsexualism currently offered by clinicians: as we saw in the previous chapter, the American Psychiatric Association considers transsexualism to be a disorder of gender identity that has no physiological symptoms whatsoever.[76] The insistence of most of these autobiographers that transsexualism has its origin in the physiology of the body, then, represents a disjunction between the beliefs of transsexual autobiographers and those of the psychiatrists who refer transsexual subjects for surgery. To understand this disjunction fully, we would have to examine in detail the relation between psychiatry and the other medical specialties involved in the treatment of transsexualism, a task too large for the discussion here. What this disjunction suggests in terms of the transsexual population, however, is that the idea of a gender identity fully divorced from the body and its signification of sex is only rarely accepted by transsexual subjects.[77] For if gender was thought to float entirely apart from the semiotics of physical sex, sex reassignment surgery would be unnecessary. The fact that transsexuals request sex reassignment on the basis of cross-sex gender identity demonstrates the extent to which gender is thought to bear on the body.

The transsexuals' stories about gender identity are never seamless or completely convincing—in Jan Morris's case, the assertions of cross-sex gender identity can only be offered with mystical references and vague discussions about sexless sexuality.[78] What is most consistent in transsexuals' self-representations is the oft-repeated insistence that there must be something physical, measurable, materially detectable that motivates and justifies the desire to change sex. Because of this, the transsexual autobiographers feel sure that the body he or she achieves through sex reassignment is his or her "real body," the one he or she was meant to have, the one denied by some cruel trick of Nature or God.

Understandably, then, in only one of the autobiographies discussed above are the technologies of sex change presented as fundamental to the transsexual phenomenon. To think of sex conversion technologies as fundamental to transsexualism would be to acknowledge the tremendous physical transformation involved, and to acknowledge as well the impulse of the human body to resist such change. Instead, in most of the autobiographies the technologies of sex change are presented as the means to an end, the important but theoretically inconsequential treatments through which the transsexual subject may inhabit a body more appropriate to his or her felt gender identity. Thus, if transsexual subjects depend upon a network of technologies essential for their transformation into the other sex, they also depend upon an official effacement of the significance of those technologies to their very existence. The effect this has on the autobiographies is palpable, since the discussions of the mechanics of sex change invariably reveal tensions: how can a subject truly be the other sex if such extensive technological intervention is necessary to get him or her there?

In *Emergence*, Mario Martino documents in minute detail his two surgical attempts at phalloplasty. In another autobiography, *The Man-Maid Doll*, Patricia Morgan offers detailed comments about her surgeries to construct female genitalia from male. Canary Conn discusses the problems she faced during recovery at a clinic in Tijuana. Nancy Hunt, in a move uncharacteristic of the transsexual autobiographer, opens *Mirror Image* with a detailed discussion of the surgical theater and surgical procedure of male-to-female genital sex change. Later in her autobiography, Hunt describes her own painful recovery from a first, unsuccessful vaginoplasty. And Renée Richards describes the surgical procedure in detail in *Second Serve*, even focusing on the crucial role of the anesthesiologist, and discusses as well the painful first few days of postoperative recovery. These authors vividly portray their surgical experiences as painful and psychologically draining, thereby offering the reader information about the physical transformation and psychic consequences of genital plastic surgery. The effect of these passages is to bring the reader's attention to the immediate physicality of the procedures, and to undermine the text's primary argument that the subject was really meant to be the sex which he or she must be surgically fashioned into. This undermining occurs as the reader becomes aware of the level of pain incurred through the surgical procedures, which, in these narratives, is quite strikingly represented. The existence of representations of this intense pain serves to break up or unsettle the assured narrative confidence in the story of gender.

Mario Martino's description of then contemporary phalloplastic technique comprises a litany of unsuccessful practices that is, nevertheless, concluded by these comments: "These drawbacks, serious as they are, are minor when compared to the fulfillment phalloplasty brings. Its greatest value is the psychological uplift, and this psychological stimulation can heighten the physical excitement and pleasure. The neophallus is also, of course, a safeguard against exposure."[79] This statement comes after describing a "neophallus" that, while it may be "cosmetically good," will also be subject to "accidents with zippers or radiators" (because it lacks feeling), that is either permanently soft or always erect, and that probably will not be able to carry urine. In addition, phalloplasty "cannot produce an organ rich in the sexual feeling of the natural one."[80] This argument in favor of an operation with "serious technical drawbacks," but with immense "psychological benefits," is exactly that made by the medical team of Goin and Goin in their presentation of augmentation mammaplasty (discussed in chapter 2).[81]

After describing the possibilities for phalloplasty in general, Martino presents his own experiences. A surgeon with experience in phalloplasty on men injured in battle offered to operate on Martino. In a series of two operations, a penis-like tube-within-a-tube was constructed on his thigh (this is a variant of the famous tube pedicle pioneered by Harold Gillies during World War I). Martino writes that "the tube resembled a suitcase handle." The surgery was painful, but asking himself if it was "truly worth the male picture I'd fancied for myself?" he answered, "Yes, yes! If the surgery worked it would be the realization of a dream." This first attempt ended in infection. The doctor attempted to repair the damaged pedicle flap and was willing to continue the experiment, but Martino refused since the "underpart of the tube was eaten completely through and had formed a ridge in the middle. The tube was shrivelling, curling in on itself like a small snail. Instead of the handsome phallus I had expected to grow on my thigh for later relocation, I had a disintegrating suitcase handle." He comments that "I had come out of all this pain, expense, and time with a scarred thigh and not an inch of progress toward a phallus."[82]

Martino presents the most unsettling representation of the physical and psychological effects of phalloplastic surgery as he describes his second, "mostly successful," attempt to make a penis. The skin grafts were again "excruciatingly painful." But as he returned home from the hospital and made a side trip to visit a friend, Martino positioned his new penis up against his abdomen. He comments that "the blood supply was not sufficient to reach the tip of the penis, for within the week after the trip that area turned dark, signifying death of the tissue." The remedy for this included warm baths, but even these "would not save most of the head from turning black and foul-smelling. So, nightly, I sat in the tub and, very slowly, cut away the dead tissue."[83] This horrifying image of Martino sitting in a bathtub cutting away the head of his penis so that its putrid death will not jeopardize the health of the rest of the organ is only partially alleviated by his humorous comment "Talk about castration complex!" The passage is a reminder that the construction of a penis from nongenital flesh is a partial, and contingent, event. Martino ends up with "a respectable phallus—three-fourths perfect." Again, the painfulness of its creation is deferred by his final comments which emphasize the psychological benefits of the new organ:

> Now, I can tell myself, there is a new part of me—a part I have always conceived of myself possessing. It completes outwardly a picture of myself which I have always carried in my head. By day, whether working, driving, gardening, or relaxing, I sense always the presence of this outward acknowledgment of my maleness. And, by night, my new organ—for all its being less than perfect—is still deeply stimulating to both me and my mate, both psychologically and physically.[84]

For Martino, phalloplasty offers the female-to-male transsexual a real organ: "Whatever the technique employed, no longer must a transsexual use a *replica* at the most intimate of times."[85] The idea that the neophallus might be a replica is never considered; the penis made from the flesh of the thigh or abdomen is perceived to be the real thing, regardless of its inability to urinate or to become erect naturally. What is important is that it is of the body. Nevertheless, Martino recognizes that many female-to-male transsexuals "do not choose to have phalloplasty" due to the problems in procedure and outcome. He writes,

> They find that, after about six months on male hormones, the clitoris has usually grown too large to be contained within the protective lips or labia and now resembles a miniature penis. Resting on the outside of the labia, the clitoris is very quickly stimulated and even the feel of the dildo is sexually exciting: Any movement reminds the patient that *he has a semblance of the male organ.* So equipped and stimulated, the female-to-male transsexual realizes to some degree *the satisfaction of being male* and achieving climax. And even the artificial penetration of his mate add to his heightened sexual drive.
>
> Many patients are very nearly content with such an arrangement.... The combination of enlarged clitoris and dildoe [*sic*] or phalloplasty seems to us *an approximation of the normal male's response.*[86]

This passage suggests that both dildos and penises constructed through phallo-plastic surgery are replicas, since they can only approximate the physiology of a normal male. The passage also suggests that part of the pleasure of the transsexual man is the reminder that he is a man. Martino points out that either a dildo or neophallus can achieve this realization, although a dildo will only do so during sexual intercourse. As the passage cited previously suggests, since his phalloplasty Martino himself can experience the pleasure of this recognition twenty-four hours a day. This recognition, however, came at tremendous physical (and financial) cost.

If the destabilizing effect of the representations of physical pain and post-operative difficulties in Mario Martino's autobiography are immediately recovered by his assertions of the psychological benefits of phalloplasty, Patricia Morgan's portrayal of the corollary operations for the male-to-female transsexual are not so easily recuperated. This may be a result of the general outlines of her story, which represents her as a more marginal subject and therefore as being less subject to a normalizing narrative. Morgan portrays herself as a poor, effeminate, uneducated boy who always felt himself to be a girl and who had difficulty making a living once he left his mother's home. A male prostitute, he sought surgery partially as a way to have a more secure source of income: "[W]hen I found out that men wanted to buy my body as a woman, I said to myself, Wow! This could be even more prosperous and less hectic than running around seeking out fags."[87] After he found out about "the operation" from some other transvestite prostitutes, he began to save money. With introductions arranged by Harry Benjamin, he went to California for the surgery.

After the first surgery, Morgan writes that "I was a woman at last. But at the moment, I was just a glob of aching flesh." She continues: "Three days later, Dr. Belt returned to change my bandages. I was swathed from my waist through my crotch and around the hips. It was like being enclosed in a giant diaper. Dr. Belt took the scissors and started cutting the bandages away, throwing them on a tray on the adjoining bed. I just about got sick to my stomach at the sight and smell of all the blood and pus."[88] This first operation only removed Patricia's penis and placed her testicles in her abdomen.[89] After the operation to construct a vagina, the doctor placed a plastic form inside the new organ in order to keep it from closing:

> I just about went through the headboard when Dr. Belt and his son forced the new mole into me. I couldn't believe the pain. I grabbed the bars on the bed and gritted my teeth. The mole was tremendous. It was about nine inches long, but it felt like nine feet. They kept pushing it up and up and up inside my body. After about fifteen minutes, they finally got it in. But my body kept wanting to force it out again.
>
> I was in such pain that the nurse came in right away and gave me a shot to knock me out. I was just going under as Dr. Belt and his son started sewing the mole into my vagina.[90]

Morgan continues with the comment that for the next two weeks, the "pain remained unbearable." After being released and making another trip back to the doctor to have another mole sewn into her vagina, "I went home again and for days I was bleeding terribly." She adds that "the pain did not subside."[91]

Shortly after the second operation, while she still had a mole inside her vagina (although not one that was sewn in), Patricia Morgan was raped by a client of her prostitute roommate. She took the mole out so that the man would not discover her condition and would think that she was menstruating. Bleeding profusely, she put the mole back inside her and "tried to recover." A few days later, she and her roommate were arrested for prostitution, but she was bleeding so badly that she spent her thirty days in the prison hospital. After she got out, and subsequently underwent a third operation for an infection in her urethra, she finally engaged in voluntary sexual intercourse, during which she "bled like a red river. The bed was covered with my blood because I was still tender inside from the operation." Even after she returned to the East Coast, she "still wasn't fully recovered. There were days when I was perfectly all right and others when I ached all over."[92]

These vivid representations of genital plastic surgery are unique in the genre. For example, Christine Jorgensen writes that her penectomy "was not such a major work of surgery as it may imply.... Within a few days, I was resting well and had experienced little discomfort."[93] In describing her third surgical procedure, the vaginoplasty performed in the United States almost two years after her first operations in Denmark and against the clinical stance taken by her doctors in their 1953 article in the *Journal of the American Medical Association*, Jorgensen writes that the "extremely complicated operation took seven hours to perform. With skin grafts taken from the upper thighs, plastic surgery constructed a vaginal canal and external female genitalia. It was a completely successful procedure." The only problem she records were the facial burns she received due to the unforeseen need to use ether at the end of the lengthy operation.[94] While it is conceivable that her surgeries were less painful than Patricia Morgan's, and most probably more successful than Mario Martino's, all skin graft procedures entail some significant amount of pain. By not representing that pain, Jorgensen was able to deflect attention away from the actual surgical techniques that made her transformation into a woman possible; to treat them, in other words, as insignificant to the fact of her present existence as a woman.[95]

In an original and unexpected rhetorical move, Nancy Hunt begins *Mirror Image* with a description of the University of Virginia Medical Center, moving from outside to inside and finally to the operating room where "Elizabeth Johnson" is to undergo a "vaginal construction" that morning. Casually mentioning that she herself had undergone the same procedure six months before, Hunt describes the procedure, the patient's probable feelings, the attitudes of plastic surgeons, and finally, the surgery itself. From this she moves into a discussion of the possible causes of transsexualism and the reasons why psychotherapy generally fails to "cure" transsexuals of their compulsion to be the other sex ("No woman would abandon her psychological gender merely to accommodate herself to the circumstances of a biological accident. Certainly I would not. Let the biological accident be corrected, not me").[96]

This pleasant (albeit stark) introduction to transsexualism and surgical sex change does not square altogether with Hunt's own experience, which is recounted toward the end of the text. Hunt was startled by the results of her first surgical procedure (probably the castration and fashioning of the labia out of scrotal tissue; Hunt's penis would still be present): "Here was not classic mold of womanly beauty but rather a tattered mixture of the old and the new, the male and the female, the ugly and the beautiful. I was suspended halfway between two surgical procedures, neither man nor woman. I had not prepared myself for that spectacle, and I found it shocking."[97] Long after the second procedure, Hunt continued to feel pain and was told by a rather brusque gynecologist that her vagina would not be capable of heterosexual intercourse: it was too small and entered at the "wrong angle."[98] The diagnosis of the original surgical team was that there had been some stenosis, or shrinkage, during healing. Indeed, as Hunt reported her doctor saying, "When we got in there, we found a sort of pocket at the apex [of the vagina] that had been sealed off by the infection. We opened it up and did a skin graft, and you've got almost the full length of the original vagina." Another doctor was more graphic: "We cut in there,' he said, 'and this stuff like pus came spurting out.' " Hunt quotes from the surgeon's report: "Inspection was undertaken which revealed midline stenosis of the labia and absence of vaginal vault. The midline was sharply divided and as the stenotic vault was opened a pocket containing greenish somewhat grumous material was entered."[99]

In Canary Conn's account, her difficulties during and after her operations had to do with the ineptness of the hospital staff at the Tijuana clinic and their disdain for transsexuals. The problems she encountered demonstrate the necessity of attentive postoperative care, given the extent of the surgical intervention in sex conversion operations. After the first procedure, Conn's catheter was improperly inserted and she developed an addiction to the pain-killing drugs. The real problems came with the second procedure, which, due to Conn's financial situation, took place about two years after the first one. She reports her postoperative pain to have been excruciating, and that she did not receive medicine when she needed it. She continued to bleed, and the nursing staff did not change her sheets. Finally, bleeding profusely and fearful that no one would answer her cries, Conn recounts that she took a pair of scissors to attempt suicide. She blacked out before she was able to do anything, however, and the doctor arrived just in time to stop her bleeding.[100]

While Conn's experiences are told in a manner to heighten their dramatic impact, they exemplify some of the most significant issues in hospital social relations raised by transsexualism and sex conversion surgery. Surgical sex change is a costly and complicated procedure, necessitating intensive nursing care and the services of a team of attending physicians (surgeon, urologist, gynecologist, anesthesiologist, endocrinologist). While many writers speak of the generous and kind behavior of the staff that attended them, others like Canary Conn have less pleasant experiences. The postoperative care of the transsexual patient is part of the technology of sex conversion, and like the surgery itself, its quality and effect depend upon the human subjects who practice it. The success of the surgical procedure is, in some part, dependent on the kind of care the patient receives *after* the operation is completed. Conn's auto-biography, with its account of inadequate and hostile nursing care, points out that the technologies of sex change are not limited to hormonal treatments and the specific operative procedures of genital plastic surgery; they include as well the material practices of postoperative care, much of which is undertaken by the hospital or clinic nursing staff.

For Renée Richards, the pain of postsurgical recovery was a fit ending to her life as Dick Raskind: "It [the pain] was bad, but I asked for it, embraced it....it showed me that I was right in becoming Renée. If ever there was an opportunity for regret it came when I was quaking in the recovery room, yet that opportunity was not seized. At that moment I realized that I would rather have died in the attempt than live any longer in a nightmare of duality."[101] Richards provides details of the surgery and her recuperation, noting particularly the "dilator" necessary to maintain vaginal health in the absence of penile-vaginal intercourse.[102] Her narration in this section of the book is largely matter-of-fact, perhaps a consequence of her own training as a physician. At the end of this section, she writes, "By the end of my month's leave I was pretty well healed."[103] Overall, while the presentation of surgery is graphic enough in Richard's account, its significance to the rest of her story is downplayed. Surgical sex change is an experience to be gotten through, a means to an end, the techne of existence but not the stuff of it.

The discontinuity between the story of surgical sex change and the story of already being the other sex, like the discontinuity between the story of physiological intersexuality and that of gender, undermines the main assertions concerning the self as the other sex that transsexual autobiographers make and seek to maintain in these texts. Reading with attention to these discontinuities demonstrates that the statements made and supported by transsexual autobiographers concerning the primacy of gender and the innateness of the desire to become the other sex cover over other destabilizing narratives of self-construction. Reading for the subversions of technology, in other words, allows us to see how the normalizing narratives of gender work to obscure the radical discontinuities at the heart of the transsexual phenomenon.

This is not to suggest that transsexuals' accounts of their own experiences are wrong, or flawed; rather, it is to suggest that representations of transsexual experience are constructed within the parameters of a humanism that pervasively denies the existence of disruptive accounts of sex and sexuality. Feeling as if one is, truly, the other sex—all material evidence to the contrary—has been codified as a normalized sensibility within the theory of gender identity; it is no longer a culturally unintelligible narrative of subjectivity. Once we read for the discontinuities that the attention to technology and physiology affords, however, that intelligibility is compromised and can no longer sustain the story of gender as it proliferates in contemporary medical discourse and the society at large. Gender "deconstructs" because it can be shown to depend upon a relation to the body that it excludes definitionally.

Those of us who are not transsexuals may wonder what it is like to feel one-self "in the wrong body." These autobiographies reveal what it is like to want another body, understood as *the* other body, as a result of the subject's displacement of a radical abjection onto the body. The body, with its original sex, becomes abject through the inability of the transsexual subject to make that body signify appropriately within accepted gender codes. Reengineering the body is one way to avoid the sense of profound "outsiderness" expressed by all the transsexual autobiographers discussed above; becoming the other sex forces the body to signify according to traditional gender codes, enforcing cultural laws on the body's physiology. For these autobiographers, "sex change" makes their bodies (and experiences) intelligible at last.

It is this very intelligibility that is a problem for those who think critically about transsexualism. Sandy Stone, as discussed above, understands this intelligibility to constrain the possibility of telling the truth about transsexual experience. Yet the "true story" of transsexualism is already out, insofar as it is already at work in these autobiographies, helping to consolidate subjectivities around specifically marked parameters of behavior and narration. The official autobiography of the transsexual subject is part of the "true story" of transsexualism; without these texts we would not have the phenomenon that we have today, because within their narratives live the most important assertions—as well as the most destabilizing discontinuities—within which transsexual subjectivity is constituted. To understand transsexualism, we do not need to alleviate the suppression of an authentic story (as Sandy Stone suggests); rather, we need an analysis of the suppressive mechanisms that have constituted and continue to constitute the transsexual phenomenon in the twentieth century. And once we turn away from "gender" as the causal mechanism of transsexualism, we can recognize it as an authorizing narrative that works to ward off the disruptive antihumanism of technological self-construction.

NOTES

1. I would like to thank members of the Lesbian and Gay Studies Workshop at the University of Chicago, and especially Scott Mendel, for pointing out to me the necessity of addressing the significance of my choice to study "mainstream" discourses of transsexualism.
2. Mario Martino, with Harriet, *Emergence: A Transsexual Autobiography* (New York: Crown Publishers, 1977), 40; Jan Morris, *Conundrum* (New York: Harcourt Brace Jovanovich, 1974), 45; Niels Hoyer, ed., *Man into Woman: An Authentic Record of a Change of Sex*, trans. H. J. Stenning (London: Jarrolds, 1933); Renée Richards, *Second Serve: The Renée Richards Story*, with John Ames (New York: Stein and Day, 1983), 55; Nancy Hunt, *Mirror Image* (New York: Holt, Rinehart, and Winston, 1978), 137. I use the gendered pronoun appropriate to the sex of the subject at the time of the event being discussed.
3. Sandy Stone, "The *Empire* Strikes Back: A Posttranssexual Manifesto," in *Body Guards: The Cultural Politics of Gender Ambiguity*, ed. Julia Epstein and Kristina Straub (New York: Routledge, 1991), 285.
4. Anne Bolin, *In Search of Eve: Transsexual Rites of Passage* (South Hadley, Mass.: Bergin and Harvey, 1988), 64; Richard Green, *The "Sissy Boy Syndrome" and the Development of Homosexuality* (New Haven: Yale University Press, 1987), 7–8.
5. Stone, "The *Empire* Strikes Back," 295.
6. Ibid., 299.
7. Ibid., 298.
8. Sandy Stone names herself in the essay by referring to the 1970s controversy concerning her employment at Olivia Records, an all-woman recording company, as a sound engineer. She was the subject of a vociferous debate in a number of West Coast feminist publications, and of a chapter in Janice Raymond's *The Transsexual Empire* (Boston: Beacon Press, 1979). See Stone, "The *Empire* Strikes Back," 283–84.
9. Stone, "The *Empire* Strikes Back," 295.
10. Ibid., 299.
11. Ibid., 286.
12. Ibid., 285.
13. Bolin, *In Search of Eve*, 64.
14. Ibid., 64–65.
15. Dwight Billings and Thomas Urban, "The Socio-Medical Construction of Transsexualism: An Interpretation and Critique," *Social Problems* 29, no. 3 (February 1982): 273–74.
16. Robert J. Stoller, *The Transsexual Experiment*, no. 101 of the International Psycho-Analytical Library, ed. M. Masud R. Khan (London: Hogarth Press and the Institute of Psycho-analysis, 1975), 248n.
17. Stone, "The *Empire* Strikes Back," 291.
18. Ibid., 289, 292.
19. Bolin, *In Search of Eve*, 61–63.
20. For a discussion of "power" as a productive and enabling force, rather than one that is solely repressive, see Michel Foucault, *The History of Sexuality: An Introduction*, vol. 1, trans. Robert Hurley (New York: Vintage, 1978).
21. For a discussion of what constitutes a statement, as well as a discursive formation, see Michel Foucault, *The Archeology of Knowledge*, trans. A. M. Sheridan Smith (New York: Pantheon, 1972).
22. Judith Butler, *Gender Trouble: Feminism and the Subversion of Identity* (New York: Routledge, 1990).
23. Christine Jorgensen, *Christine Jorgensen: A Personal Autobiography* (New York: Paul Eriksson, 1967), 206.
24. She was consistently represented as the transsexual "prototype" or model for male-to-female transsexuals—the first of her kind—at "Coming Together/Working Together," International Foundation for Gender Education convention,

Denver, Colo. (April 1991).

25. According to Harry Benjamin, this perspective was not common in the United States. In *The Transsexual Phenomenon*, Benjamin wrote: "Biologically minded authors are likely to consider TVism and TSism as 'intersexual' phenomena, but those are almost exclusively European scientists. American writers…reserve the term 'intersexuality' exclusively for visual signs of disorders of sexual development, that is to say, for hermaphroditic and pseudo-hermaphroditic abnormalities. The Europeans, especially the Germans, use the term in a much wider sense, including not only transvestism and transsexualism as 'intersexual' but also homosexuality" (New York: Julian Press 1966), 71. This may explain Christine Jorgensen's doctors' use of "intersexuality" to define her condition.

26. It is fascinating that Jorgensen mentioned *The Male Hormone* as having had profound influence on her, since that text concentrates almost exclusively on the curative powers of testosterone, especially for "broken" or effeminate men. De Kruif discusses these curative powers as both psychological and physiological—testosterone could masculinize feminine men in both mind and body, as well as restore youthful energy to aging men. Yet Jorgensen writes that as George, she felt that she could not follow a masculinizing course (the one de Kruif focuses on in his book). Rather, Jorgensen became obsessed with the similarities between testosterone and estradiol (ovarian hormone): "'The chemical difference between testosterone and estradiol is four atoms of hydrogen and one atom of carbon.'…If Dr. de Kruif's chemical ratio was correct, it would seem then that the relationship was very close. That being so, I reasoned, there must be times when one could be so close to that physical dividing line that it would be difficult to determine on which side of the male-female line he belonged" (Jorgensen, Christine Jorgensen, 84–85). See also ibid., 78–80. See Paul de Kruif, *The Male Hormone* (New York: Harcourt Brace, 1945).

27. For instance, Jorgensen wrote, "But the recurring questions of what to do about my effeminate appearance continued to plague me. Even if it were possible to adjust my mind and attitudes to a more male outlook, I wondered what could be done about a 'masculine' mind in a feminine body" (*Christine Jorgensen*, 78).

28. Ibid., 203.

29. Ibid., 101–2.

30. Ibid., 207–8.

31. Roberta Cowell, *Roberta Cowell's Story* (New York: British Book Centre, 1954), 165. Vern Bullough and Bonnie Bullough remark that Cowell was a genetic male, suffering from adrenogenital syndrome (also known as testicular feminization syndrome). However, if this were the case, it would be highly unlikely that Cowell would have been able to "father" two children (Vern L. Bullough and Bonnie Bullough, *Crossdressing, Sex, and Gender* [Philadelphia: University of Pennsylvania Press, 1993], 255).

32. Cowell, *Roberta Cowell's Story*, 176.

33. Ibid., 99.

34. Ibid., 99–100.

35. Ibid., 120–21.

36. Ibid., 136. Cowell conveniently neglects to mention that surgery was also necessary to remove her male genital organs.

37. Ibid., 156.

38. Ibid., 177. This is reminiscent of Michael Dillon's comments in *Self: A Study in Ethics and Endocrinology* (London: Heinemann, 1946). See chapter 1.

39. Cowell, *Roberta Cowell's Story*, 194.

40. Ibid., 193. I believe that Roberta Cowell is the "Male with Female Outlook" discussed in Harold Gillies and Ralph Millard Jr.'s *Principles and Art of Plastic Surgery* (Boston: Little, Brown, 1957). Cowell does not name her plastic surgeon (or any of her doctors) in the autobiography. However, she says that she went to see a surgeon who was "world-famous" and that his "kindness was proverbial, but so was his way of being remarkably outspoken when he felt so inclined" (Cowell, *Roberta Cowell's Story*, 129). This description fits that offered by Reginald Pound in his biography of Gillies (Reginald Pound, *Gillies, Surgeon Extraordinary* [London: Michael Joseph, 1964]). Gillies believed that cosmetic surgery could lead to psychological benefit, a factor which helped to develop the possibility of sex reassignment surgeries. Finally, the discussion of the "Male with Female Outlook" in *The Principles and Art of Plastic Surgery* matches Cowell's autobiography almost exactly. There, Gillies quotes the endocrinologist's report of the examination of the patient's removed testes: "The general appearances are those of a postpubertal gonadotrophic suppression. It is known that the patient received prolonged oestrogenic and progesterone therapy, just before the orchidectomy. Although there are no controls with which these sections can be compared, it is considered unlikely that hormonal treatment alone could have caused the testicular atrophy. However, the lack of much information on the human subject means that this cannot be a dogmatic statement." Gillies also remarks that the patient's "nose was too big, [and] his lip abnormally long"—compare with Cowell's own comments: "The decision was to give me a new upper lip, reshape my mouth, and shorten my nose" (Gillies and Millard, *The Principles and Art of Plastic Surgery*, vol. 2, 385; and Cowell, *Roberta Cowell's Story*, 136–37).

41. The book is somewhat uncertain as to dates, although it more than makes up for that deficit in other details. Martino writes that she was in the eighth grade when the Christine Jorgensen story broke; since that story was first made public in December of 1952, that puts Marie's birth in 1939. She obtained surgical and hormonal treatments for sex change a few years after Jorgensen's autobiography was published in 1967—that is, in her early thirties. See Martino, *Emergence*, 40.

42. Martino, *Emergence*, 131.

43. Some of the passages describing Marie's experiences as a young novice are quite telling. For example, at the convent where Marie went to live during the first two years of high school, many of the nuns had men's (male saints) names:

Sister Clement, Sister Timothy, Sister Francis, etc. The second time Marie entered a convent, she took the name Sister Mary Dominick, after her older half-brother: "My first choice: Dom's name! It was like a new bond between my brother and me, almost placing me on par with him" (89). She became known to other nuns as "Dom," the same nickname her brother used. See Martino, *Emergence*, pp. 29–98.

44. Ibid., 121.
45. Ibid., 109–10.
46. Ibid., 130.
47. Robert Stoller, "A Contribution to the Study of Gender Identity," *Journal of the American Medical Association 45 (1964)*: 220–26; Stoller, *Sex and Gender: On the Development of Masculinity and Femininity* (New York: Science House, 1968), 65–85; Stoller, *Presentations of Gender* (New Haven: Yale University Press, 1985), 65–76.
48. Martino, *Emergence*, 114.
49. Ibid., 144. Emphasis added.
50. Ibid., 163. It is interesting that Jorgensen uses this comment to identify her own singularity, whereas for Martino it defines a commonality with others "all over the world."
51. Ibid., 244.
52. Hunt, *Mirror Image*, 43. See also ibid., pp. 23–42.
53. Ibid., 263.
54. Ibid.
55. This same discourse about masculinity as a "mask" is utilized by Roberta Cowell.
56. Hunt, *Mirror Image*, 59.
57. Ibid., 131.
58. Ibid., 83.
59. Ibid., 141.
60. Ibid., 142.
61. Ibid., 124–25.
62. Canary Conn, *Canary: The Story of a Transsexual* (Los Angeles: Nash Publishing, 1974).
63. Ibid., 6, 320. These final comments were ostensibly made by Conn to a group of doctors, an unlikely situation, as doctors do not consider transsexuals to be reliable purveyors of medical theory.
64. Ibid., 321.
65. See chapter 3. Money has since taken a more biologistic stance, characterized by the book he cowrote with Anke Ehrhardt (*Man and Woman, Boy and Girl: The Differentiation and Dimorphism of Gender Identity from Conception to Maturity* [Baltimore: Johns Hopkins University Press, 1972]). He likes to present this as a biosocial perspective that privileges neither biology nor culture in the construction of gender identity, but, as I discussed in chapter 3, his language belies an emphasis on the biological.
66. Morris, *Conundrum*, 173, 21.
67. Ibid., 3, 40–52.
68. Ibid., 27–39.
69. Ibid., 9, 25, 26, 104, 163.
70. Ibid., 104.
71. Ibid., 169.
72. Richards, *Second Serve*, 5. Emphasis added.
73. In Richard Docter's terminology, this would identify Renée Richards as a secondary transsexual, one who came to desire sex change after a period of time as a transvestite.
74. Ibid., 164. Emphasis added.
75. There is another moment that also suggests a story created to fit the theory—Richards claims she discussed her transvestism with her mother in her junior year at Yale (as Dick): "I thought it best to start out with the academic facts as I had learned them in Abnormal Psych.: 'Mother, as you know there are certain mental disorders that are characterized by gender confusion. Somehow, the individual has feelings and impulses that are characteristic of the opposite sex.' I quoted a good portion of the chapter on transsexualism with my mother nodding in agreement" (ibid., 87). At the time (1954 or 1955), neither "gender" nor "transsexualism" would have made it into a college textbook—the terminology was only then being codified into medical discourse. Clearly, Richards is inserting current theoretical conceptualizations back into her discussion with her mother.
76. American Psychiatric Association, *Diagnostic and Statistical Manual of Mental Disorders*, 3d ed. rev. (Washington, D.C.: American Psychiatric Association, 1987), 71–76. See also the third edition (1980), 263: "the presence of abnormal sexual structures rules out the diagnosis of Transsexualism."
77. If transsexuals routinely attribute their desire to change sex to the inconclusive domain of physiology, why is it that physicians, who have *never* documented any physiological reasons for transsexualism, accede to their demands?
78. "My more immediate physical delights were far more superficial and much easier to achieve. They were tactile, olfactory, visual, proximate delights–pleasures which, as it happened, I could handily transfer to inanimate objects too, within reason, so that I derived, though I tactfully kept the fact from my more intimate friends, a kindred sensual satisfaction from buildings, landscapes, pictures, wines, and certain sorts of confectionery" (Morris, *Conundrum*, 55).
79. Martino, *Emergence*, 255.
80. Ibid., 253–55.
81. John M. Goin and Marcia Kraft Goin, *Changing the Body: Psychological Effects of Plastic Surgery* (Baltimore, Md.: Wil-

liams and Wilkins, 1981), 191–92. See also chapter 2.

82. Martino, *Emergence*, 257–60.
83. Ibid., 262.
84. Ibid., 262–63.
85. Ibid., 255. Emphasis added.
86. Ibid., 264–65. Emphasis added.
87. Patricia Morgan, *The Man-Maid Doll*, as told to Paul Hoffman (Secaucus, N.J.: Lyle Stuart, n.d.), 29.
88. Ibid., 60.
89. Some physicians felt leaving the testicles might be important for male-to-female transsexual's sex drive. Harry Benjamin mentions two other reasons: "The reasons why some surgeons may wish to retain the testes is chiefly endocrine, based on the theory that the testes in transsexual men may produce more estrogen than they do normally…although they have as yet found no confirmation….Another reason for a surgeon's wish to preserve the testes is because of a legal technicality. He cannot be accused of a (possibly illegal) castration operation" (Benjamin, *The Transsexual Phenomenon*, 100–101).
90. Morgan, *The Man-Maid Doll*, 63. The use of the term "mole" here gives us a sense of the surgical technique Dr. Belt used with Morgan. A "mole" in this context fits with the dictionary definition of "a large, powerful machine for boring through earth or rock, used in the construction of tunnels." This suggests that Dr. Belt was attempting to encourage secondary epithelialization of the vaginal canal, since with the other procedures there would be no need to bore further into a canal that had been constructed of grafted tissue. With the secondary epithelialization technique, a hole is made in the perineum and then the walls of the hollow are encouraged to form an epithelial lining similar to that of a normal vagina.
91. Ibid., 63–65.
92. Ibid., 68–72.
93. Jorgensen, *Christine Jorgensen*, 136–37.
94. Ibid., 236–37.
95. Roberta Cowell's comments about her surgery were even more reticent, as she neglected to mention at all the need to remove her male genitals, concentrating instead on the surgery done to her face. See Cowell, *Roberta Cowell's Story*, 136. Jan Morris comments in *Conundrum* that "Dr. B—'s craftsmanship, though aesthetically brilliant, was functionally incomplete, and I underwent two further sessions of surgery in an English nursing-home" (145). While she does make some limited comments about the care in Dr. B—'s Moroccan clinic, in general she says little about the surgery. Does "functionally incomplete" mean that she couldn't urinate, or that Dr. B— had not constructed a vagina, or that the vagina could not function in penile-vaginal intercourse? Did she know she would have to undergo further procedures, or did she find out after the fact? Morris does not comment.
96. Hunt, *Mirror Image*, 12.
97. Ibid., 205.
98. Ibid., 219–20.
99. Ibid., 224, 225.
100. Conn, *Canary*, 194–97, 307–19.
101. Richards, *Second Serve*, 282.
102. Ibid., 286.
103. Ibid., 287.

25

A *"Fierce and Demanding" Drive*

Joanne Meyerowitz

In *How Sex Changed: A History of Transsexualism in the United States*, Joanne Meyerowitz authored a masterful account of the emergence of transsexualism over the course of the twentieth century. *How Sex Changed* was the first book-length work of transgender scholarship to rely on exhaustive archival research into primary source materials, and it thus relates the story of transsexualism with unprecedented authority. Meyerowitz relied not only on medical accounts, but also on media coverage and the views of transgendered people themselves, to craft a nuanced tale of how transsexualism helped reshape our culture's beliefs about the meaning—and interrelatedness—of biological sex, psychological gender, sexual orientation, and social gender role.

In the selection below, "A 'Fierce and Demanding' Drive," Meyerowitz describes how, in the wake of publicity about Christine Jorgensen's transsexual surgery, transsexuals and their doctors negotiated with one another to gain or grant access to medical procedures for altering the sex-signifying characteristics of the body. In much of the contemporary scholarship prior to Meyerowitz, notably in the work of Marjorie Garber and Judith Shapiro, transsexuals had been represented as passive vessels for their doctor's intentions, who merely parroted back the medical discourses espoused by their service providers, and who lacked real agency or critical awareness of their own embodied situation.

Meyerowitz's careful scholarship reveals the delicate politics involved in the 1950s and 1960s in creating the procedures, institutions and frameworks within which transgender people sought to address their needs, and over which doctors sought to exercise control.

In the 1950s and 1960s hundreds of people wrote to, telephoned, and visited doctors to inquire about sex-change surgery. A few may have asked for information on a whim or out of curiosity, and a few may have temporarily seen a change of sex as a way out of other personal problems. But most had what they described as deeply rooted, longstanding, and irrepressible yearnings, and they wanted medical treatment, sometimes with an urgency that bordered on obsession. For some of the prospective patients, the growing coverage in the press shaped their inchoate desires to transform their bodies. For others, the news stories renewed their hopes that doctors might actually respond to their already formulated requests. In the 1950s and afterward they used the press and the medical literature to label their longings, to place themselves in a recognizable category, and to find the names of doctors who might help them.

While the doctors and scientists debated the meanings of sex and gender, many transsexuals simply rejected the notion that the bodies they were born with represented their true or permanent sex. For many, the truth of sex lay in the sense of self, not in the visible body. One FTM remembered that as a young child he had refused to wear dresses because "something inside me just told me that I was a boy." Others acknowledged the common late twentieth-century perception that sex resided in the chromosomes. An MTF stated that "sex cannot be changed, and I am painfully aware of the fact." Nonetheless, she said, "external body appearance can be changed sufficiently that a person who is psychologically miserable any other way can safely, happily, and legally assume the status of woman and live and be accepted as such."[1] Sometimes they expressed their desires with the language of "being"—being the sex they knew they were. At other times they positioned their longings as matters of "becoming"—becoming the men or women they knew they ought to be. However they defined the quest, they laid claim to their own sense of authenticity and their own self-knowledge about whether they should or could live and count as women or men.

Their requests to alter their bodies resonated with other trends in modern American culture. In the mid-twentieth century Americans routinely encountered prescriptions for how they might remake themselves in pursuit of self-fulfillment. Humanist psychologists called for "self-actualization"; advertisements for cosmetics and diet aids invited people to refashion their faces and bodies; educators and book publishers promised to improve the minds of students and readers. Democratic ideals, however imperfectly practiced, suggested that all people had or should have equal opportunities to change their station in life, and twentieth-century liberal individualists increasingly insisted on the rights of "consenting adults" to determine their own course as long as they refrained from behaviors that might cause harm to others. In a society that valued self-expression and self-transformation, why not permit people to decide whether they wanted to live as men or as women, and why not allow them to change their bodies in the ways they desired?

In their interactions with doctors, transsexuals dreamed of the new possibilities created by medical science. But as they urged their doctors to enter uncharted territories of medical treatment, they bumped up against the power of medical gatekeepers, the costs of commodified medical care, and the limits of technology. In response, they learned that only persistence produced results. They needed the cooperation of doctors, but as they applied unsolicited pressure, they and their doctors ended up in conflict. It was in this troubled milieu that a few Americans entered the new terrain of "sex-reassignment surgery." In traditional medical histories, doctors often stand as pioneers in science. In the history of transsexuality, doctors, with a few exceptions, lagged behind, reluctant pioneers at best, pushed and pulled by patients who came to them determined to change their bodies and their lives.

In the mid-twentieth-century United States, Denmark looked like a liberal haven to people who hoped to change their sex. Jorgensen had found not one but several doctors who had rallied to her cause and seen her through her bodily change. Her doctors had taken her seriously, acknowledged her sanity, and used their authority and their technical expertise to change her life for the better. To Danish officials, however, Jorgensen stood as an isolated case. Her surgery, they said, would not serve as a precedent for future medical treatment. Although they still supported the Danish law permitting castrations, the officials at the Medico-Legal Council of the Danish Ministry of Justice, startled by a flood of requests for sex-change surgery, soon announced their decision to refuse the petitions of foreigners.[2]

Nonetheless, in the early 1950s transgendered people wrote repeatedly to the Danish endocrinologist Christian Hamburger, whose sympathetic treatment of Jorgensen had appeared in the American press. In less than a year after the Jorgensen story entered the public domain, Hamburger received "765 letters from 465 patients who appear to have a genuine desire for alteration of sex." Of the 465, 180 wrote from the United States. The letters, Hamburger wrote, ranged from "faulty attempts at presentation in writing" to "stylish masterpieces," from "almost undecipherable bits of paper" to "faultlessly typed reports of up to 60 foolscap pages." He read the letters as "a cry for help and understanding."[3]

Hamburger referred his American correspondents to doctors in the United States. Just one month after the Jorgensen story broke, he responded to a male-to-female correspondent who had already sent him "three letters...a collection of photos...and...Christmas greetings." He had received "several hundreds of letters," mostly, he said, from "men, suffering from the same disease as you." The letters impressed him, and he felt he had a "duty to help." He himself, however, could now help "persons of Danish nationality only." He told this correspondent and others to contact Dr. J. W. Jailer, an endocrinologist in New York.[4] Jailer, it turned out, had little interest in transsexual patients. Without providing any details, one MTF described her reply from Jailer as "distressing," and Harry Benjamin noted that others, too, had had "unfortunate experience[s]" with him. Within months Hamburger realized he had sent his correspondents to the wrong doctor. He began to advise them to "get in contact with Dr. Harry Benjamin." He told one letter writer: "If anybody can give you advice or help, it is Dr. Benjamin. I have referred several patients to him, and they have all found an understanding doctor or even friend in him."[5]

Into the 1960s, most roads led to Benjamin. Hamburger sent him patients, and so did the public transsexuals Christine Jorgensen and Tamara Rees, both of whom came under Benjamin's care. From the United States and abroad, other doctors also gave out his name, especially after he published his first articles on transsexualism. Dr. David O. Cauldwell, who coined the English word *transsexual,* and Dr. Walter Alvarez, who wrote a syndicated medical column, told letter writers to contact Benjamin, and later Dr. Robert Stoller, the psychoanalyst at the University of California at Los Angeles, sent him numerous patients. As his name appeared in the press as an expert on transsexualism and especially after his book came out in 1966, the letters snowballed in volume. New patients brought their friends and acquaintances to Benjamin's attention, and each new contact seemed to lead to others.[6]

Would-be patients traveled to meet Benjamin in his offices in New York City and San Francisco. He examined them, counseled them, and prescribed hormones, and he also engaged in voluminous correspondence with patients and nonpatients who asked for his help. The drag queen Margo Howard-Howard, who never seriously considered surgery, portrayed Benjamin as a "charlatan" who encouraged sex change for virtually anyone who crossed his door. "If Joe Lewis, champion fighter, had walked in for a routine examination," she wrote, "Benjamin would have told him he ought to be a woman." But more of Benjamin's patients appreciated his warmth, his concern for their well-being, his old-world charm, and the nonjudgmental way in which he accepted their unconventional desires. In her autobiography *Second Serve,* male-to-female Renée Richards, a doctor herself, remembered Benjamin, whom she first met in the 1960s, as "a likable fussbudget, very much in the tradition of the Old World general practitioner." At first she thought him "kindly and decent" but "hardly one to inspire unreserved confidence." Then she "began to realize that this old man really did understand." In her autobiography *Conundrum,* the journalist Jan Morris, also a male-to-female transsexual, expressed the same sentiment. She remembered Benjamin as "the first person I met who really seemed to understand."[7]

By all accounts, the prospective patients reflected the diversity of the population. They came from "all cultures, ethnic groups, and socioeconomic levels."[8] In one study of letters from 500 people requesting evaluation for surgery at Johns Hopkins Hospital in the late 1960s, 116 reported their race: 103 reported themselves as white, 13 as African Americans. Among 100 FTMs who participated in a counseling group in Yonkers, New York, in the late 1960s, the "ethnic groups" represented included "Irish, Italian, and German," followed by "English, Puerto Rican, Blacks, Polish, French, Greek, Spanish, Swedish, and Welsh," plus one "Canadian, Chinese, Columbian, Cuban, Danish, Hungarian, Indian, Rumanian, Russian, or Turkish" apiece. Case studies of patients in the West include several mentions of Mexican Americans.[9] The letters they wrote came from rural areas, small towns, and cities, and the jobs they mentioned spanned the spectrum from manual day labor and service work to working-class trades and clerical work to middle- and upper-class professions. Some had spent their entire lives in a single location; others had led rootless lives, drifting from job to job and from place to place. But the stories they told rarely dwelled on, and frequently failed to mention, the categories that sociologists tend to use to classify the population. There was no single plot to their stories, no single life trajectory from birth to transgendered adulthood to the request for surgery. But despite the wide disparities in social background, their stories reveal a few common patterns.

In their initial contacts with Benjamin and other doctors, many conveyed a sense of angst that hinted of suicidal despair. In a letter to Jorgensen, Benjamin described the "phone calls and letters" he had received as "frantic." An FTM wrote Benjamin from Florida: "I have reached the point where it is impossible for me to do much of anything constructive...Please forgive my extreme feelings of urgency, for I can truly not stand this feeling of being an impostor any longer. I have done all I can to help myself." An MTF wrote from the West Coast: "I find it increasingly difficult to go on living with myself. I am ready *now* to go to whatever extremes...necessary to have a 'sex change.' It is the only way I could ever hope of finding my peace of mind...I am tired and I am not willing to fight against my real desire any longer."[10]

They told of doctors who had offered every kind of treatment except sex-change surgery. One MTF had "been advised to have psycho therapy, [carbon dioxide] therapy, shock treatments, lobotomy, go out and live as a woman, join a homosexual colony, and commit myself to a mental sanitarium." Other MTFs encountered doctors who injected them with male hormones, and psychiatrists or psychologists who pushed them to relinquish their feminine ways. One FTM had "undergone everything from 'religious training' to self-hypnosis and shock treatments." Others reported lengthy psychoanalyses and months or years in mental institutions. Both MTFs and FTMs found doctors who promised operations and then backed away.[11]

In their exchanges with doctors and researchers, they tried to explain themselves, sometimes guilelessly and sometimes in ways patently calculated to convince doctors to recommend surgery. By the mid-1950s they had the label "transsexualism" to describe their longings, but they still needed to make themselves intelligible to doctors and others who dismissed them as insane. One MTF wrote her life history as a way to "clarify" her mind before she tried to persuade her doctor to recommend surgery. She understood her mission: "I have to make a person who is without doubt a normal person see my point of view as I, who am not normal, see it and I have to make my abnormal thoughts and conclusions seems as real and logical to him as they are to me."[12]

Many MTFs and FTMs recounted long and arduous journeys to change their assigned sex. Not all told tales of unremitting hardship, but most wrote sad, and sometimes desperate, letters emphasizing the difficulties of their lives, perhaps in part to impress upon doctors the seriousness of their requests. Some cast their lives in the plots they found in the popular press. Like Christine Jorgensen, they often portrayed themselves as pilgrims or pioneers who struggled against adversity. They vacillated between a persistent optimism in which struggle merited reward and a lurking pessimism in which insurmountable obstacles prevented them from moving on. From the 1950s on, they portrayed themselves as social beings whose outcast status excluded them from the sense of community for which they longed, and they also stressed personal freedom and presented themselves as individualists who asserted their right to live as they chose.

In recounting their lives to doctors, most emphasized a sense of difference that had begun in childhood. From an early age they had played with the toys and dressed in the clothes prescribed for the other sex. "I was eight," an MTF recalled, "when I announced myself a girl and demanded to play with dolls, dress in girl's clothes, and let my hair grow long." An FTM "had always felt that something was wrong." Since the age of four or five, he had "preferred male activities and toys."[13] As they had matured, their feelings had intensified. Some FTMs reported a sense of humiliation or "disgust" as their breasts developed and menstruation began, and some MTFs expressed a feeling of hatred or revulsion toward their genitals. They described a growing alienation from their own bodies, a sense that the body itself was a mistake. A young FTM explained: "Nothing about me seems abnormal, except I have the wrong body."[14]

Many reported years of ridicule for their unconventional presentations of gender. Their parents had misunderstood them, their siblings had teased them, and their peers had taunted and bullied them. One FTM from Arkansas told a doctor he had been "harassed" by "everybody" and called a " 'freak,' 'homo,' or 'hermaphrodite.' " His wife explained: "He was always considered a public freak. He has always been scorned, humiliated and ridiculed beyond all measure." A number of MTFs had joined the armed services in a futile attempt, as one described it, to "make a man of myself," but their peers in the military had not necessarily welcomed them. An MTF serving in the U.S. Army wrote Benjamin: "people disrespect and insult me constantly. I would rather die than be a man all my life. It is a life of torture."[15] The stories of ridicule included accounts of violence, "being hit, beat, raped … just really being punished."[16]

The police rarely offered protection. Both MTFs and FTMs told doctors about their "fear of arrest and persecution" at the hands of law-enforcement officials. Many worried about being arrested for crossdressing. Through the 1960s, some local governments used vagrancy and other statutes to regulate and restrain those who dressed in public as the other sex. In the early 1950s, for example, an MTF arrested in California served "six months probation. All because her drivers license said male." A friend of hers explained to Benjamin: "Now she is scared."[17] Publicity about arrests could lead to loss of jobs, as in the 1960s case of a male-to-female transvestite, an airline pilot, whose conviction for crossdressing cost him his job and pension a year before retirement. MTFs could expect harassment, and sometimes assault, when they were booked, and unless they went in the "queens' tank," the cells reserved for feminine men, time in jail could result in rape by other inmates. By the mid-twentieth century the police more frequently arrested male-to-female crossdressers, who appeared more shocking in dresses than FTMs appeared in pants. But FTMs who lived as men also knew, as one described it, "the apprehension of risking discovery and imprisonment." Another described his fears when using public restrooms: "In using a men's room, when dressed in male attire, I subject myself to possible apprehension as a 'male impersonator.' In using a women's room, other women there might possibly regard me as a man invading their privacy." He had, he said, "an insoluble and potentially dangerous problem."[18]

The doctors' records also report arrests for running away from home and other infractions. Transgendered youth sometimes tried to escape their unhappy pasts and to lose themselves in the anonymity of larger cities, where they might also find doctors and friends to help them. One FTM with "fanatic religious" parents was arrested en route from Tallahassee to San Francisco to meet with Harry Benjamin. Sometimes family members called in the police. The mother-in-law of another FTM had him arrested for taking money on false pretenses, but she objected primarily to his "unnatural" marriage to her daughter. The arrests often led to referrals to psychiatrists and sometimes to incarceration in jails or mental institutions.[19]

They might avoid such conflicts, but only, they said, at a psychic cost. The transsexual child, one MTF believed, had a choice: "whether to flaunt his desire … and launch himself on a defiant life of non-conformity and endless conflicts with society and the law—or to bury deeply his feminine inclination … no matter what the cost to mental well-being." Before her surgery, she chose to hide her femininity. She had, she said, "few friends," and her "tolerable world was the world of fantasy." She secretly dressed as a girl, and she had fantasies of "exotic surgical operations in which my brain would be transferred to the body of a beautiful girl." She contemplated suicide before eventually finding her way to doctors who agreed to help her.[20]

Whether they exposed themselves to ridicule and arrest or hid their desires protectively, they often portrayed themselves as misfits. Their stories, like Jorgensen's, were frequently tales of isolation, of people who may have had family and friends but still lacked and longed for a sense of belonging. By the 1960s more of them came to know and rely on other transgendered people, especially in the cities.[21] But even as they developed their own sense of community, they frequently presented themselves as seekers who looked for a place in the world where they might feel at ease and at home. Although they asked the doctors for surgery to change the insignia of sex, the quest itself was not solely or even primarily about breasts or ovaries or penises or testicles. In a letter to Robert Stoller, one FTM described it as "yearnings for release from...bondage." "A more complete transformation," he wrote, would provide "enough freedom to find...a real identity and a dignified existence." He did not want either "a temporary refuge" or a life "alone and apart."[22]

The request for surgery, though, was not just a strategy for self-protection or an attempt to escape from ridicule, violence, arrest, and isolation. It was also an active form of self-expression. Transsexuals often presented their personal quest as an overwhelming commitment to an unshakable sense of an authentic inner self. Increasingly they used a modernized variation of Ulrichs' nineteenth-century formulation, "a female soul in a male body." They spoke of "a female trapped in a male's body" or "a male entity...somehow imprisoned in a female body."[23] By the 1960s, this became a shorthand rendition for a particular life history in which the desire to change sex reflected the assertion of an inner self.

Among postmodern academics today, it is decidedly unfashionable to speak of a "true self," an "inner essence," or a "core" identity beneath a surface appearance. But transsexuals, like most people, had a deeply rooted sense of who they were. We need to attend, as psychoanalyst Lynne Layton reminds us, to "the specificity, construction, and experience of an individual's inner world and relational negotiations." Layton refers to a core identity as "something internal that recognizably persists even while it may continuously and subtly alter." For many late twentieth-century transsexuals, the "true" or "inner" or "trapped" self referred to this core identity and provided the dominant metaphor to summarize a "life-plot" of crossgender identification.[24]

Those who were more educated sometimes explained this sense of self with the modern language of psychology. Stephen Wagner referred directly to the "self-actualization" of postwar humanist psychology. He "had a hunch that the reason why some of us choose to become women is because of the basic pioneering spirit which is very essential in all of us...It is related very closely to the principle of nonconformity as well as to that of creativity." In this view, crossgender behavior and sex change were bold forms of self-improvement, creative acts of "individuality and individual freedom" that pushed against the limits of conventional mores. Others used the more traditional language of religion. The desire to change sex came from God or resided in the soul. An FTM told Robert Stoller: "God created me a girl, so maybe I should be. But I couldn't be, and which is more important, your mind or your body? God created my mind too, and if my mind is working that way, He created that." From a different spiritual angle, an MTF speculated on past lives and reincarnation and concluded, echoing Ulrichs, "maybe once in a great while a female spirit or soul accidentally incarnates in a male body."[25]

While some adopted the language of psychology and religion to express their understandings of themselves, more turned to biology to explain the source of their unconventional desires. Their crossgender identification felt so substantial and their desire to change their bodily sex so firmly rooted that most could not perceive the condition as anything but physical. Despite the publicity about Jorgensen, some transsexuals, especially FTMs, still presented themselves to doctors as hermaphrodites and pseudohermaphrodites. Several FTMs believed they had testicles hidden internally. One imagined his testicles in a lump in the groin and another in "swellings on either side of the vaginal outlet." They diagnosed themselves as biologically male and "rejected any other interpretation." To convince their doubting doctors, they sometimes requested (and occasionally underwent) exploratory surgery in an attempt to prove the existence of hidden male gonads.[26]

MTFs also favored a biological approach. Like FTMs, some portrayed themselves as intersexed, hoping perhaps, as one psychiatrist phrased it, to "substantiate a biological basis for their condition, and thus obtain the change of sex operation." A few who knew otherwise presented themselves as hermaphrodites because this seemed a more convincing story. "I realize my own condition perfectly," one MTF told Benjamin, "but to quite some few people...the idea of hermaphroditism is easier to explain and understand."[27] Others focused on hormones. One MTF explained herself to her children with the theory of bisexuality: "in each man and each woman there is a remnant of the opposite sex, and...the balance between the two is not always at the same point." Like Jorgensen, she explained her problem "in terms of hormones and ductless glands." Another MTF wrote to Benjamin: "All of us feel that there is something different about our chemical make-up."[28]

Some acknowledged the possibility that the desire to change sex was not a physical condition, but they insisted that the longing for transformation was too compelling and too authentic to eradicate. One MTF insisted: "I still feel that somehow...there must be a physical reason for the way I feel. It is such an overpowering feeling." Another MTF explained:

> At first I thought that there might be some organic cause or reason for my feelings, but now I'm not so sure. My family doctor and a psychiatrist that I went to told me that it was not organic but psychological. The psychiatrist wanted to rid me of the feelings but they are so strong and intense that I have no desire to change them...I can't imagine just why I feel as I do but the feelings are real and not put-on.

Another MTF "had no idea" why she had "always wanted to be a girl," but she considered it "a form of mental suicide," the death of her self, to abandon her femininity.[29]

As they related their life stories, they hoped for a sympathetic ear. For some, simply writing or talking to a humane doctor was "in itself a tremendous relief."[30] But usually they wanted more. Some sought doctors' advice on various treatment options, but many came already convinced that they wanted surgery. The surgery promised real benefits. They might live legally as they sex they desired without fear of arrest, assault, or exposure. "I want to work and live openly," one MTF told Benjamin, "with assurance of freedom from prosecution by law." Also, with bodily transformation, others might see and treat them as the men or women they knew or wanted themselves to be. An FTM who had lived as a man for twenty-three years explained to Benjamin: "I have to live in fear all the time...whenever it came to lite [sic] that I wasn't a man as they thought but a woman, then I would lose my job. I have suffered years of embarrassement [sic] and ridicule." With surgery, they hoped, they might "just liv[e] without the feeling of being a misfit."[31] But surgery was also symbolic. It was the coup de grâce that ended a "sham existence" or "a life of deceit." Surgery was not the only part or even the most important part of the quest for authentic self-expression. For some, however, it became a defining event. An MTF told Benjamin: "I think of nothing else but the operation."[32]

* * *

Operations, though, were not easy to obtain. First, they required money. In the American market economy, the quest for self-expression increasingly involved the purchase of goods and services that promised a better life. For the American transsexual, surgery was such a commodity, a desperately desired consumer item, available only to those who could afford it. The United States did not (and does not) have a national health plan that covered surgery, and private medical insurance would not cover "elective" procedures, especially ones that had not won the approval of mainstream doctors. Christine Jorgensen had found doctors who treated her for nothing as part of their medical research. Those who followed often hoped for similar treatment. "Maybe," one MTF said, "some doctor might want to operate...as a sort of experiment."[33] But transsexuals without substantial savings rarely found doctors in the United States or abroad who responded positively to requests for surgery. In 1955 Harry Benjamin wrote to urologist Elmer Belt: "Those who have no money or too little of it are simply out of luck. I feel a bit ashamed of the medical profession to allow such a state of affairs to exist." Ten years later Robert Stoller responded to a request for a "sex transfer": "I would say that your chances of getting such help are small, especially if you do not have a lot of money."[34]

Even patients with money had difficulty finding surgeons who would perform transsexual operations. Through the 1960s, the demand for sex-change operations well outpaced the supply. In 1966 Johns Hopkins Hospital announced its program to perform sex-reassignment surgery. Over the next two and a half years the doctors there received "almost 2000 desperate requests" for surgery. They turned almost all of them down, performing surgery on only 24 patients, just slightly more than one percent of the total.[35] In this bottleneck situation it took money, persistence, and unwavering will to find a doctor who would agree to surgery.

Facing obstacles at every turn, some transgendered people gave up. Stephen Wagner, for example, had searched for male-to-female surgery since the 1930s. After the publicity about Christine Jorgensen, he wrote Alfred Kinsey, "If I had the money, I would fly to Denmark at once!"[36] He renewed his efforts to find an American surgeon, corresponding with Christian Hamburger, Walter Alvarez, and Harry Benjamin, among others. Meanwhile, in his hometown of Chicago he visited doctors who he thought might offer operations. Dr. William S. Kroger, Wagner recounted, promised surgery and then changed his mind. According to Wagner, Kroger advised him "to move away from Chicago and live as a woman without...operations." Another doctor gave him injections of male hormones "to become more masculinized," which Wagner stopped against the doctor's wishes.[37] But aside from the doctors who failed to give him what he requested, Wagner expressed concerns of his own. When Harry Benjamin offered to see and treat him in New York, Wagner wondered how he would find a job and a home and worried how his sister and brother-in-law would react. He longed for operations to change his sex, but he also "hate[d]" himself "for being so overwhelmed by that horrible desire." And he did "not relish the idea of being a 'weak facsimile' of a woman." The lack of local doctors to help him conspired with his own anxieties and kept him from acting on his stated desires. In 1958 Harry Benjamin annotated his correspondence with Wagner: "Never met him. Not operated."[38]

For other transsexuals, the obstacles to surgery only strengthened their resolve. Debbie Mayne (pseudonym), an MTF with few financial resources, tried every possible avenue to find herself a surgeon. She wrote to Christian Hamburger, Harry Benjamin, and other doctors, convinced a reporter to help her find a surgeon in Europe, asked a transsexual friend to castrate her, and cooperated with the research of Drs. Frederic Worden and James Marsh in Los Angeles in the hope that they would recommend her for surgery. By the end of 1954 all her attempts had failed. Yet she told Benjamin: "I am *extremely confident* and determined...This drive is [so] fierce and demanding that it frightens me." She determined to "find me a quack in Mexico" who would perform the operation.[39] Others sought underground practitioners in the United States. An FTM had his breasts removed on his sister's kitchen table. According to one report, other transsexuals "resorted to abortionists, in the belief that these criminal operators would do anything for money."[40]

With or without surgery, transgendered people sometimes experimented with other forms of bodily change. Some FTMs bound their breasts to flatten their chests and decided to live fulltime as men. Tom Michaels (pseudonym), an FTM, described his transformation: "In a matter of months I progressed from my usual jeans and shirt to flannel slacks and tie to completely masculine attire and 'passing.' "[41] Some MTFs began the painful and lengthy process of electrolysis to rid themselves of their facial and body hair, and some crossdressed in public despite the risks of violence and arrest. Caren Ecker (pseudonym) lived for a while as a woman in Mexico City until the experiment ended "in disaster" when a "pawing drunk" discovered her secret. A few MTFs attempted other forms of self-induced physical change. In the mid-1960s one MTF bought "female hormone facial cream" and ate it, and also attempted "to push my testicle back up inside my body." Another attempted to create breasts by injecting "air, hand cream, mother's milk and water" into her chest.[42]

FTMs and MTFs usually took hormones under the care of doctors such as Harry Benjamin, but some managed to obtain solutions and tablets on their own. After a few months of testosterone injections, FTMs underwent visible, audible, and permanent changes. Their voices dropped to a lower pitch. Gradually their clitorises increased in size, their skeletal muscles developed, and their facial and body hair multiplied. Some FTMs also noticed weight gain, acne, a slight shrinking of the breasts, or male-pattern balding. As long as they took the hormone, it enhanced their libido and inhibited menstruation. It could also produce a surge of energy akin to the jolt from caffeine. For MTFs the visible changes were subtler. After taking estrogen, often combined with progesterone, MTFs noticed swelling in their breasts, sensitivity of the nipples, and sometimes softer hair and smoother skin. Their testicles atrophied, their libido declined, and their erections and ejaculations diminished or ceased. With prolonged doses, they experienced a more visible redistribution of subcutaneous fat and more pronounced growth of the breasts. For many, estrogen also seemed to have a soothing or calming effect. To quicken the process of change, some exceeded the recommended dosage, despite the risks of heart disease and liver damage for FTMs and thrombosis for MTFs. For this reason, Harry Benjamin warned against "self-medication."[43]

For some, binding their breasts or crossdressing or taking hormones was sufficient. Louise Lawrence, born in 1913, had lived fulltime as a woman since 1944. By the 1950s she saw surgery as one possible way of accommodating crossgender identification, but she did not seek it for herself. A friend said Lawrence considered herself "to [sic] old" for surgery, and Lawrence told a correspondent: "As in most everything else in life there are numerous ways of achieving a given result." Still, she recognized the urge to change sex and told Harry Benjamin: "I firmly believe that MOST transvestites have that same urge but in varying degrees and areas." She lived as a woman until her death in 1976, and under Benjamin's guidance she experimented with hormones.[44]

Others moved in fits and starts toward surgery. After he decided to don men's clothes, Tom Michaels spent years living as a man, some of them in "grossly anti-social behavior" with criminal associates, "the first social grouping which accepted me on my own terms." Ashamed of his life, he eventually decided to pursue "professional ambition" and earned a bachelor's degree in zoology. He reverted to living as a woman and spent a year in medical school. But he could not relinquish his desires. In the mid-1960s he contacted Robert Stoller in search of "a more complete transformation." It "would be infinitely easier," he wrote, "with medical help rather than opposition." He wanted the "necessary alterations" and also hoped for "moral support." He began taking testosterone and looked forward to surgery.[45]

* * *

For MTFs the search for surgery often began with castration. As doctors rebuffed them, some MTFs reached the point of desperation and cut off their own genitals. According to one review of the medical literature, published in 1965, 18 of 100 MTFs had attempted to remove their own testicles or penises, and 9 had succeeded.[46] At the age of forty-three, for example, Caren Ecker, now living in northern California, gave herself local anesthetic, removed her testicles, and, in her own words, "almost bled to death." Eventually Dr. Karl Bowman, of San Francisco's Langley Porter Clinic, recommended additional surgery to remove the penis. At the end of 1953 Dr. Frank Hinman Jr. performed the surgery at the University of California at San Francisco. As in cases of botched self-induced abortions, doctors sometimes felt more comfortable cleaning up afterward than providing medical care from the start.[47]

Annette Dolan (pseudonym) sent Harry Benjamin an autobiographical account of her self-surgery. (Later a different version of it appeared in print, under a pseudonym, in *Sexology* magazine.) "For years," she said, doctors had told her "there was no 'help' for me, and I accepted this [as] gospel." After Christine Jorgensen made the news, though, she made up her mind to undergo surgery. Initially hesitant, her doctor, probably Benjamin, eventually suggested she go abroad for castration, after which he could help her find a surgeon in the United States to perform the rest of the operations. Lacking funds for surgery overseas, she decided to perform the operation herself. She read medical texts outlining the operation and bought the surgical equipment needed to perform it. "I learned to ligate, suture and anesthetize," she said; "I studied the surgical procedure step by step and memorized its sequence." She excised her testicles successfully in an hour and later presented her doctor with the fait accompli. With any legal obstacles literally removed, she found a surgeon to complete the work. In 1954 Elmer Belt, a urologist at UCLA, performed the rest of her surgery, including construction of a vagina.[48]

Like many surgeons, Belt had a certain bravado. He took pride in his technical skills and saw new forms of surgery as a challenge to his expertise. He had, as he told Benjamin, "a strong sense of compassion for these poor devils" and also "an intense curiosity." He considered himself a "softie" who found it hard to turn away desperate patients.[49] In the 1950s he operated on other MTFs, including Barbara Richards Wilcox, who had made the news in the early 1940s when she had gone to court to change her legal gender status. Belt used a procedure in which he preserved the testicles, pushing them through the inguinal ring out of the scrotum and into the abdomen. He thought it medically best to preserve the testicles and the hormones they produced, and thereby managed to avoid whatever legal liability castration might potentially involve. At the end of 1954 Belt temporarily ceased his work when a committee of doctors at UCLA, including urologist Willard Goodwin and psychiatrist Frederic Worden, decided against the surgeries. In the late 1950s he quietly resumed his sex-reassignment practice, but in early 1962, under pressure from his wife, son, and office manager, he decided to stop for good. He complained about searching for hospitals that would let him perform sex-reassignment surgery, he feared that a dissatisfied patient would sue him and ruin his practice, and he groused about the impoverished patients who failed to pay their bills. When he learned that Dr. Georges Burou, a French surgeon with a clinic in Casablanca, was doing good surgery, he opted out.[50]

Other MTFs found a handful of other surgeons, mostly abroad, who would perform the operations. In 1954 and 1955 several of Benjamin's patients had operations in Holland. But European doctors were not as accepting as some transsexuals had imagined. After initial surgery in Holland and plastic surgery in Denmark, one MTF told Benjamin: "The 'favorable' doctors…are in the minority in Europe." And most of the "favorable" doctors refused American patients after 1955. In the mid-1950s other MTFs, including Debbie Mayne, went to Mexico for surgery with Dr. Daniel Lopez Ferrer. In the early 1960s Burou replaced Belt as the surgeon of choice for those who could afford his fees and the costs of international travel. For years afterward his widely acclaimed surgical skills brought him a steady stream of patients from Europe and the United States. In the early and mid-1960s operations were also occasionally performed "rather secretly," according to Benjamin, in the United States, as well as in Japan, Mexico, and Italy.[51] Dr. Orion Stuteville did "a few such procedures" in Chicago, as did Drs. Jaime Caloca Acosta and Jose Jesus Barbosa in Tijuana and Professor Francesco Sorrentino in Naples. By the end of the 1960s a few university hospitals—Johns Hopkins, University of Minnesota, Stanford, and University of Washington—had begun to provide surgery for a small number of MTFs.[52]

The techniques differed from place to place. Some surgeons removed only the testicles and penis, or one or the other, but most also performed plastic surgery to create labia, usually from the scrotum. Increasingly surgeons also created vaginas at the same time. Doctors had performed vaginoplasty since the nineteenth century, when they experimented with various methods for constructing vaginas for women born without them or for women with deformed or damaged ones. By the mid-1950s the most common method used skin grafts from the thigh, buttocks, or back. Occasionally surgeons used mucosal tissue from the intestine, but this entailed more-invasive surgery. By the late 1950s a few doctors preserved the sensitive skin of the penis, turned it inside out, and used it to line the vagina. In Morocco, Burou attracted patients by perfecting this method. In the late 1960s a handful of American doctors adopted his technique.[53]

The surgery itself was painful and harrowing. For Patricia Morgan, who underwent surgery with Elmer Belt in 1961 and 1962, the first operation lasted around eight hours. Belt removed the penis and pushed the testicles into the abdomen. When Morgan woke up, she saw "all the wires and tubes and catheters." "I was just a glob of aching flesh," she wrote later. After two and a half months Morgan returned for eight more hours of surgery to create a vagina. After the second operation, "the pain inside was even worse than before." After three days Belt removed the bandages. "I was sickened by the stench of the blood and the dead flesh," Morgan remembered. "There was swelling something fierce down there. I couldn't look." For two more weeks in the hospital, "the pain remained unbearable," and for a while after her release she still could not walk and bled profusely from her vagina.[54]

Before and after genital surgery, some MTFs sought other operations. Some wanted to enlarge their breasts. In New York in the 1950s Dr. Else K. La Roe, a German-born surgeon, gave breast implants to a few MTFs, including Charlotte McLeod. Other MTFs hoped to change the shape of their noses or shave off the more prominent cartilage on their "Adam's apples." Their goal in general was to appear as nontranssexual women, and the additional surgery often helped keep strangers from reading them as men. Faced with repeated requests for surgery, some doctors complained of "the tendency of these patients to desire polysurgery" and advised restraint in offering additional operations. But MTFs persisted, and occasionally their requests outstretched the medical technology. A few patients hoped that doctors could reduce their height or enable them to bear children. "In the most successful operation we ever had," Elmer Belt wrote, "the patient came in after all was done expressing dissatisfaction because there was not a uterus with tubes and ovaries...and she could therefore not have a baby." Another MTF approached Else La Roe in tandem with an FTM. They asked for "a mutual transplantation of their sexual organs," a request they may have borrowed from the realm of science fiction.[55]

* * *

Although doctors today usually posit equal numbers of FTMs and MTFs, in the 1950s and 1960s they believed that MTFs far outnumbered FTMs. The ratios (MTF:FTM) offered by various studies in Europe and the United States ranged from 8:1 to 2:1. They reflect the numbers of MTFs and FTMs that doctors encountered in their practices or in reviews of the medical literature. By the mid-1960s, for example, Benjamin had diagnosed and treated 152 MTFs but only 20 FTMs. At the end of the decade, when Johns Hopkins Hospital reported almost 2,000 requests for surgery, only one-fifth came from FTMs.[56] As a result of the numbers, some researchers considered transsexualism in the same way they considered fetishism or transvestism, as a largely, if not wholly, "male" condition. They sometimes speculated that sex differences in neuroendocrine development or in the psychodynamic processes in which the infant separated from the mother led to a skewed sex ratio in the prevalence of crossgender identification.[57]

For this reason, FTMs sometimes had trouble convincing doctors to take them seriously as candidates for surgery. In 1954, before he had FTM patients, Harry Benjamin did not know what to make of a correspondent who asked about female-to-male surgery. "There is no operation possible," he responded, "that would change a female into a male. In some rare cases a male has been operated on so that he later on resembles a female, but nothing like that is possible if the patient is a normal girl." At the end of the 1960s doctors at UCLA's Gender Identity Research Clinic debated privately whether FTMs even qualified as transsexuals. From 1968 to 1970 they held at least fifteen meetings devoted to FTMs. Robert Stoller wondered "whether there should be such a diagnosis as 'transsexualism' for females." After twelve years of treating FTMs, he could not find "etiological events which hold from case to case or even a very consistent clinical picture, other than the raging desire to become a male." His colleague Richard Green disagreed. He attempted "to convince the world (or at least our microcosm) of the existence of a syndrome of female transsexualism."[58] But the interest at UCLA was somewhat unusual. In the main, doctors focused their research and their attention on MTFs.

For their part, fewer female-to-male transgendered people asked doctors for surgery. They may not have seen examples in the press of successful surgical transformations, and they may have avoided a surgical solution that still could not produce a functioning penis. The subordination of women may also have played a role. Those who had grown up as girls may not have had the same sense of entitlement to medical services as did MTFs or the same insistent attitude with doctors, and those who lived and worked as women may have had fewer economic resources to finance medical intervention. The diverging constraints of masculinity and femininity may also have entered into their decisions. Female-to-males could dress as men with less risk of arrest. By midcentury, women frequently dressed in pants. On the streets, onlookers often treated a masculine or butch woman with hostility and contempt, but police rarely arrested her simply for her attire. Furthermore, in the postwar era some highly masculine women could find an accepting community in butch-femme working-class lesbian bar networks, but highly feminine men were increasingly reviled, even among gay men.[59] In addition, with hormone treatments most FTMs could live as men without arousing suspicions. If they grew facial hair they could usually expect casual observers to see them as men. For these and other reasons, female-to-male transgendered people often stopped short of surgery.

Still, some FTMs begged doctors for surgery and took it where they could find it. If they could not convince American doctors, they sometimes went to Europe or Mexico in search of operations.[60] In the early 1960s, for example, a twenty-six-year-old South American FTM came to the United States in search of surgery. In one "eastern medical center," operations were "advised but . . . not available"; in another, surgery was refused. He then "travelled to Denmark," where doctors refused to treat him because he "was neither a citizen nor a resident." Eventually he found doctors in New York who promised what he wanted. He began testosterone injections. In 1965 he underwent "bilateral mastectomy," and in 1967 he had "all internal genitalia" removed and his vagina closed.[61]

In most cases, surgery for FTMs meant removal of breasts and internal reproductive organs. These were procedures that surgeons performed routinely on women. They did not require unusual technical skills. Patients could sometimes convince doctors that painful menstruation, cysts, or other ailments justified the surgery. For many FTMs, mastectomy came first because breasts, especially large ones, made it difficult to live as a man. A 1968 study of six FTMs found that "they all hated their breasts and found them . . . mortifying." All six subjects gave "precedence to flat-chestedness over cessation of menstruation, much as they were repelled by the idea of having to menstruate."[62] Next they sought excision of the uterus, fallopian tubes, and ovaries, which would not only remove their reproductive organs but also end their menstrual periods (if they were not already taking testosterone) and eliminate their chief source of estrogen.

Through the 1960s, FTMs rarely underwent phalloplasty. The procedure was technically difficult, and few doctors attempted it. Surgeons first reported on phalloplasty after World War I, when they attempted to reconstruct penises for men whose had been amputated. By midcentury the favored technique was a "tube-within-a-tube," in which the internal tube served as the urethra. In the late 1940s the plastic surgeon Sir Harold Gillies described the technique, developed in part by others, in an article on men with "congenital absence of the penis."[63] In Britain, Gillies himself constructed a penis for at least one FTM in the late 1940s.[64] In the United States, though, there is no evidence of phalloplasty for transsexuals until the early 1960s, when Seth Graham (pseudonym) underwent surgery with Dr. D. Ralph Millard Jr. in Miami, Florida. Millard knew Gillies' work well: in the late 1950s they had coauthored a landmark book, *The Principles and Art of Plastic Surgery,* which included an illustrated description of the surgical procedure. In the case of Graham, Millard performed thirty operations over the course of three years as he attempted to perfect the penis and scrotum he had constructed. Eventually Graham refused to come back for more, even though Millard still wanted to "put a corona atop the terminus." By his own account, the medical treatment cost Graham around $10,000, only about $1,000 of which went directly to Millard. The remainder, he said, paid for two earlier unspecified operations, perhaps mastectomy and hysterectomy, and "the high cost of hospitals and drugs."[65] In the late 1960s surgeons at Johns Hopkins Hospital began performing phalloplasties on a handful of patients, and by the mid-1970s a few more surgeons, such as Ira Dushoff, in Jacksonville, Florida, and Donald Laub, at Stanford University, had experience with the operation.

As Seth Graham's account suggests, phalloplasty involved multiple stages of surgery, performed over a course of weeks, with unpredictable results. In the "tube-within-a tube" pedicle procedure, doctors created two tubes, usually from the skin of the abdomen. They incorporated the smaller tube, with skin surface turned inward, within the larger tube pedicle, with the skin surface outward. In a pedicle, the flap of skin, sutured into a tube, remained attached at both ends to the body, looking, as one FTM described it, like a "suitcase handle."[66] This supplied blood to the raised tissue, which was gradually moved end over end to its new position. Doctors implanted one end of the tube-within-a-tube on the clitoris and later freed the other end. The complicated procedure also involved skin grafts to the abdomen, and required extending the original urethra so it could reach the new urethra in the tube. Doctors aimed for "a satisfactory esthetic appearance...that would allow the patients to stand while voiding."[67] But even after multiple surgeries, the constructed penis did not necessarily look normal, and it sometimes failed to take. For erections, doctors might use cartilage or other implants to create a permanent stiffness, or they might leave the penis flaccid.

Some FTMs were "entirely pleased with the results of hormone therapy, breast amputation, and hysterectomy," but others hoped for genital surgery despite the dearth of doctors, the multiple surgeries, the expense, and the imperfect results. Without a penis, some continued to fear "discovery" and exposure.[68] But equally important, a penis, like a flat chest, provided one more sign that the body approximated the male sense of self. In the late 1960s Mario Martino took hormones and underwent operations to remove his breasts and reproductive organs, but he still wanted phalloplasty. "To have my body reflect my image of myself as a male," he wrote, "I would pay any price, do anything within honor." He had heard "vague rumors about surgeons...overseas" who created penises, but "nothing could be verified." Eventually he found a surgeon in the United States. The first attempt, from a tube pedicle on the thigh, failed because of infection. Four years later, Martino found another surgeon in the Midwest, who created a penis from a tube pedicle on the abdomen. Despite the pain and the problems, Martino expressed his satisfaction with the "new part of me," which he had "always conceived of myself possessing." "It completes outwardly," he said, "a picture of myself which I have always carried in my head." It served as "an acknowledgment" of his "maleness."[69]

Other FTMs sought additional forms of surgery. In 1969 Rob Dixon (pseudonym) began to live as a man while receiving hormone injections. A year later psychiatrist Richard Green reported: "This patient still insists on having surgery and feels that he hates the female aspects of his body." Dixon wanted "to have both breasts removed...as well as the uterus and ovaries." He also hoped for the surgery suggested by the UCLA urologist Willard Goodwin: an operation "to free up the enlarged clitoris and redirect the urethral orifice" as well as "insertion of prosthetic testes."[70] In the former operation, more common today, the doctor cuts the ligaments around the clitoris, enlarged by testosterone, to create an organ resembling a small penis. (It does not today involve repositioning of the urethra.) In the latter operation, the doctor constructs a scrotum from a skin graft and follows it up with implants in the shape of testicles. In 1960, for example, Lauren Wilcox, one of Benjamin's patients, had plastic testicles implanted at the time of hysterectomy. In a few cases doctors also closed the vagina when operating on FTMs. Of Benjamin's first twenty FTM patients, at least fourteen had some kind of surgery, but only one had his vagina closed.[71]

* * *

Before and after surgery, transsexuals engaged their doctors in a complicated give-and-take, fraught with trouble and conflict. On one side, patients felt angry at doctors who dismissed their desires for bodily change. The difficulty of finding surgeons who would perform the operations, the doctors' brusqueness, ignorance, or condescension, the expense of the treatment, and the complications attending surgery fed the frustrations of patients. On the other side, doctors bristled at the demands of patients who pressured them for treatment. They felt betrayed when patients tailored their stories in order to qualify for surgery and angry when patients failed to express gratitude for the risks taken on their behalf. More fundamentally, the conflicts brought up questions of control. Who could decide whether a person was or should be a man or a woman? Who could decide whether to change the bodily characteristics of sex? Transsexuals hoped to decide for themselves, but they needed the consent and cooperation of doctors.

The conflicts involved issues of knowledge and authority. Transgendered people often had more knowledge about their own condition than the doctors they approached. They had their firsthand stories of crossgender identification, and many of them had also read widely in the medical literature. They had their own compelling reasons to follow newspaper stories, track down case studies, and follow them up for leads on the impact of hormones and new surgical techniques. "Why," one MTF wondered, "did I know about the [sex-reassignment] procedure and doctors didn't?" Yet the doctors had the cultural authority, whether or not they had ever encountered, studied, or thought about transsexuality. Journalists turned to the medical profession to define the problem publicly and propose solutions. On a more personal level, doctors also had the power to determine exactly who would qualify for treatment. From the start, patients protested the clout of doctors "who do not know anything on the subject."[72]

In this situation, some transgendered people worked to educate the doctors. In San Francisco, Louise Lawrence devoted herself to teaching medical authorities and scientists about transvestites and transsexuals. From the mid-1940s, when she started to live as a woman, she worked with Karl Bowman at the Langley Porter Clinic to help doctors there understand transvestism. In the late 1940s she met Alfred Kinsey and began to send him letters, clippings, photos, books, and manuscripts. Eventually Kinsey paid her for her efforts.[73] He introduced her to Harry Benjamin, with whom she corresponded frequently to discuss reports in the medical literature and the popular press. Both Kinsey and Benjamin relied on Lawrence as a key source of information on transsexualism. Lawrence, for example, informed Benjamin of David O. Cauldwell's earlier writings on transsexuals. Benjamin, as two of his former colleagues noted, used her "as a sounding board for...many of his ideas." And Lawrence appreciated Benjamin as "one of the few medical men in this country who has any understanding of this problem."[74]

After the Jorgensen story broke, Lawrence redoubled her efforts. She saw the negative response of American doctors as an example of their "rigid attitude toward the acceptance of new and progressive ideas." In correspondence with an MTF, she speculated that the doctors who repudiated sex-change surgery had their own form of castration anxiety. "If only some of these American medical men could...not continually imagine that their own penis was removed when Christine's was, maybe we would see some sound thoughtful, imaginative progress made in this field." With Benjamin as her liaison, she corresponded and met with Jorgensen. She hoped to reply to the letters that Jorgensen did not have time to answer and to use them for scientific study. Jorgensen would not relinquish the letters, but she did refer some correspondents to Lawrence. Lawrence told one such letter writer that she was "trying to gather as much information...as possible in order that medical men...will be able to help people who come to them."[75]

The patients understood that they themselves provided the raw data that doctors and research-ers used to formulate their descriptions and their theories. Debbie Mayne told Benjamin that after reading his article "Transvestism and Transsexualism," her mother had commented, "why you have been telling me this right along." "Of course I have," Mayne said she replied; "where do you think the doctor gets his information?" For this reason many early transsexuals agreed, and even sought, to participate in research projects. In the late 1940s and early 1950s Alfred C. Kinsey took an avid interest in transvestites and transsexuals. With the encouragement of Louise Lawrence and Harry Benjamin, several transsexuals agreed to cooperate with him. Caren Ecker gave her life history to Kinsey "in hopes that any information...may in its small way eventually be of help to others of my kind." Like Ecker, others hoped to shape the scientific literature, with the longterm goal of increasing knowledge and public understanding. After reading *Sex and Gender,* an FTM wrote Robert Stoller: "perhaps in the same spirit one donates one's body to a medical school for the good of posterity, I would like to offer my psyche-soma to your group for what you could make of it."[76]

Caren Ecker referred to her educational efforts as "missionary work for our cause." While recover-ing from her surgery in San Francisco, she gave the curious doctors offprints of Benjamin's article, with the goal of "promoting interest and tolerance." Later she worked with Louise Lawrence for public education, and cooperated with Frederic Worden and James Marsh in their research project at UCLA. She was "trying to sell" Worden and Marsh, she said, "the true idea that I'm happy with my new life, and the idea that for suitable subjects it is right to make these changes."[77] These early, unorganized efforts to educate doctors and scientists were precursors to an organized transsexual rights movement that emerged in the late 1960s. From early on, though, transsexuals discovered how difficult it was to convince the doctors to treat them in the ways they wanted.

They quickly learned that researchers had their own agendas. For the MTFs interviewed by Worden and Marsh, the lesson came as a painful blow. In letters to Benjamin, four of the five subjects expressed outrage at their treatment. From the start, they resented the clinical attitude of Worden and Marsh, who wanted to test them but failed to listen to what they had to say. After psychological testing, Carla Sawyer (pseudonym) wrote: "I feel as if I have been flattened out, and rolled up and pushed through a knot hole and I told them so, too." When Marsh interviewed her, she said, he "didn't even seem to know about what my case concerned," and when Worden interviewed her, "he hadn't even taken the time to look at" a six-page letter she had given him. "I told them," she said, "I was getting pretty tired of it."[78]

Of the five MTFs interviewed, three had already had surgery, but two others, Carla Sawyer and Debbie Mayne, hoped their participation in the research would convince the doctors to recommend operations. Apparently Worden held out some possibility of surgery at UCLA. Despite her misgiv-ings, Sawyer stuck with the research project. She told Benjamin: "there is not much else that I can do except make myself available to them...the only thing I care anything about is having my sex changed."[79] Debbie Mayne, the most volatile of the group, spent a year working with Worden, waiting impatiently for approval for surgery. Louise Lawrence told her "NOT to blow [her] top." "I will agree," she wrote, "that Dr. Worden is probably a very young man who has a lot to learn...[but] for the sake of all of us try and hold your emotional reactions in check." With a heavy dose of paternalism, Harry Benjamin also tried to keep Mayne calm. "It isn't very wise and very diplomatic of you," he warned, "to antagonize Dr. Worden...Do try hard to give the impression of a well-balanced sensible person...you must not expect everybody...to understand this problem...do be a sensible girl." Not so easily reined, Mayne replied: "This girl is going to keep on raising hell until I get my operations." Ultimately, though, Worden refused to recommend surgery, leaving his subjects more frustrated and angry than before. Worden, Mayne concluded, "has never recommended anything for anybody...he doesn't know too much to begin with."[80]

Other participants in the research expressed their anger after Worden and Marsh published their article in 1955 in the *Journal of the American Medical Association*. They objected to the way the doctors had used their interviews to cast transsexuals in a negative light. The article, Janet Story (pseudonym) told Benjamin, "certainly was a cruel thing." Annette Dolan went into greater detail. She sent her objections to the *Journal of the American Medical Association*, Elmer Belt, and Harry Benjamin as well as to Frederic Worden. "In general," she said, "my words were twisted to suit their purpose." Point by point, she disputed their interpretations of her own responses and more generally of their understanding of transsexuals, and she wondered how they could draw conclusions from interviews with only five subjects. But mostly, she expressed her outrage at the cold approach and condescending tone of the researchers. Worden and Marsh, she wrote, had not "made a genuine attempt to establish a rapport with their subjects"; they had tried "to milk scientific information from them in the approximate manner laboratory animals are used." As she told Elmer Belt, she could "sense the subtle ridicule heaped by the authors on their subjects." Worden and Marsh had rewarded her willingness to participate in their research with a damaging portrayal of transsexual pathology, and she rightfully resented it.[81]

The episode with Worden and Marsh reflected ongoing conflicts. For decades to follow, both transsexuals and doctors confirmed the troubled relations between the patients who sought surgical sex change and the medical authorities who hesitated to recommend it. In the mid-1950s, Robert Stoller, then new to the field, "tried to reverse" Carla Sawyer's "sexual tendencies" and thereby "antagoniz[ed] the patient." Other doctors responded to would-be patients with the rankest of prejudice. In her autobiography, Vivian Le Mans remembered doctors "who threatened to have [her] arrested" for requesting sex-change surgery. "One doctor," she recalled, "even had his janitor chase me out of the office with a mop! He said he didn't want to contaminate his hands."[82]

In order to qualify for surgery, patients sometimes stuck, at least temporarily, with doctors whom they disliked and distrusted. In the late 1960s, Phoebe Smith went to a psychiatrist who attempted to kiss her to see, he said, how she would react and later tried to burn her with a cigarette to find out, he claimed, whether she would defend herself. Eventually she concluded that "the doctor had problems of his own." Around the same time, Mario Martino found a doctor who administered hormones and conducted monthly group therapy sessions where Martino gladly met other FTMs. But the doctor, Martino found, "took no real personal interest in me as a patient...nor in any of his patients." "One by one," Martino recalled, "his patients began to mistrust him," especially after the doctor could not refer them, as promised, to a surgeon. Martino began to wonder, "Was I patronizing a quack?" His skepticism rose as the doctor showed excessive interest in "sex and the sex act." Eventually Martino turned to other FTMs for the referrals, counseling, and advice he wanted.[83]

Increasingly, patients kept their guards up and avoided the kinds of self-disclosure that might damage their chances for surgery. Those who hoped for surgery had to tell their stories to doctors, but they soon learned to censor themselves as well. Patients tried to tell the doctors what they thought the doctors wanted to hear. Even with sympathetic doctors, they sometimes tailored their accounts to make themselves fit into the recognized diagnostic categories, to convince doctors that they were not just garden-variety homosexuals or transvestites, and to reassure doctors that they would not bring trouble after the operations were done. In order to impress their doctors with their need for surgery, MTFs attempted to demonstrate conventional femininity, and FTMs masculinity. They tried to persuade the doctors that they would lead "normal" and quiet lives after surgery. And they tried to convince doctors of their sense of urgency. "In order to get surgery," one MTF claimed, "you have to tell the doctor that if you don't get it you will commit suicide."[84]

Before the "sexual revolution" of the 1960s, many transsexuals refrained in particular from express-ing overt interest in sexual relations. After her surgery, Debbie Mayne told Harry Benjamin that she wanted "the sex life of the woman...I would not admit this before because I thought it might prevent me from getting the operation and I lied."[85] The surgeon may well have applauded Mayne's heterosexual interest, but she saw it as dangerous to mention any sexual interests at all. Transsexuals knew that "normal" meant heterosexuality after surgery, but if they expressed such interests, they might appear as overly interested in sex or they might come across, in the preoperative state, as homosexuals who did not qualify for surgery. This reticence about sexuality appeared in various records. Take, for example, the 1953 case study of an FTM, hospitalized against his will. "I never had any desire," he told a doctor. "I've never had any sex relations of any kind in my life. My wife said it never bothered her, that she could take it or leave it." He wanted "that operation," he said, but it did not have to do with sexuality. As if to underscore the point, he repeated later, "Sex isn't important to me." Or take the letter an MTF, hoping for surgery, wrote Harry Benjamin in 1955: "You can rest assured that all I ever want from life is something moral and right, and marriage and men are only minor things, because the really impor-tant thing is to dress as a woman and be accepted by society."[86] Perhaps these particular patients had little interest in sex, but maybe they saw the double bind and simply omitted, as did Debbie Mayne, the sexual acts or interests that they imagined would trigger the doctors' disapproval.

By the 1960s, doctors realized that their transsexual patients often structured their life histories to maximize their chances for surgery. The well-publicized story of "Agnes" served as a key case in point. In 1958, Agnes came to the UCLA Medical Center, seeking genital surgery. She met with a number of doctors, including Robert Stoller, and convinced them all that she qualified for surgery as an intersexed patient. She was, as the researchers recalled, "a 19-year-old, white, single secretary," living as a woman, but with male genitalia.[87] She had grown up as a boy in a Catholic working-class family, but she had always seen herself as a girl. During puberty, she had developed female secondary sex characteristics, including breasts, and at the age of seventeen, had begun to live as a woman. Earlier tests, conducted in Portland, Oregon, had shown that she had male (XY) chromosomes and neither a uterus nor ovaries nor a hypothesized tumor that might have produced estrogen. After exhaustive examinations, the doctors at UCLA recommended the surgery she sought. In 1959 a team of surgeons, including Elmer Belt, removed her male genitals and constructed labia and a vagina.

With her male genitals, feminized body, and high levels of estrogen, Agnes was wholly unlike any other intersexed patient that the doctors had encountered in their own observations or in the medical literature. The doctors pondered, publicly and privately, what she represented, and they used her case study in scholarly presentations and publications. Three medical doctors joined Stoller in authoring "Pubertal Feminization in a Genetic Male." They hypothesized that Agnes had "a diffuse lesion of the testis" which had produced the estrogen which had, in turn, produced her breasts. To Stoller, Agnes's bodily changes during puberty seemed to confirm the usually hidden "biological force" underlying gender identity. A congenital physical factor, which manifested itself later in the growth of her breasts, explained why "the core identity was female" even though "the child was an apparently normal-appearing boy and...also genetically male."[88] Stoller presented his findings on Agnes in 1963 at the International Psychoanalytic Congress in Stockholm and also published them in scholarly journals.

But all along, Stoller and his colleagues noted some suspicious evidence. During the seventy-odd hours of interrogation, Agnes refused to engage a number of topics, and she also refused to allow the doctors to interview her family. Furthermore, from the physical evidence gathered, the doctors had to acknowledge a "clinical picture that seemed to suggest the superimposition of an excess of estrogen upon the substratum of a normal male."[89] They discussed among themselves whether perhaps Agnes had given herself estrogen to induce the growth of her breasts. In the end, they convinced themselves that she had not. She herself denied that she had ingested estrogen. More important, her conventional feminine presentation impressed the doctors as genuine and ran counter to their stereotypes of "caricature" and "hostility...seen in transvestites and transsexualists." "It was not possible," they wrote, "for any of her observers, including those who knew of her anatomic state, to identify her as anything but a young woman."[90] Elmer Belt, impressed by the size of her breasts, remembered her in private correspondence as "very beautiful—well stacked."[91] The other doctors also suspended their disbelief in the face of contradictory anatomical evidence and convincing gender presentation.

Then, in 1966, seven years after her surgery, Agnes confessed. She told Stoller that her body had changed during puberty because she had taken estrogen tablets since the age of twelve. She had stolen the hormone from her mother, who had used it after her hysterectomy. As Stoller later reported, "The child then began filling the prescription on her own, telling the pharmacist that she was picking up the hormone for her mother and paying for it with money taken from her mother's purse." Posing as a unique example of an intersexed condition, Agnes had convinced her doctors to give her the surgery they routinely denied to male-to-female transsexuals. In the wake of her confession, Stoller wondered about his theories. Richard Green attempted to reassure him. "Do not despair about the biological force behind gender identity," Green wrote Stoller. "I am sure there is one somewhere and there are other cases to consider which are supportive of the idea."[92] Still, an embarrassed Stoller had to admit that Agnes "is not the example of a 'biological force' that...influences gender identity...rather, she is a transsexual."[93] He retracted his earlier findings at the International Psychoanalytic Congress in Copenhagen in 1967 and also published Agnes' revelations in 1968 in the *International Journal of Psycho-Analysis* as well as in his book *Sex and Gender.*[94]

The lesson was not lost on the doctors. Various researchers had already concluded that transsexuals were "unreliable historian[s]...unable to recall very well, or inclined to distort."[95] By the end of the 1960s, the medical literature on transsexuals regularly noted that transsexuals shaped their life histories and even fabricated stories that might convince doctors to help them. As a few more American doctors began to perform sex reassignment surgery, candidates less often portrayed themselves as intersexed, as had Agnes, but instead "as textbook examples of 'transsexuals.'" They presented "their personal histories," one article suggested, "to conform to the prevailing 'scientific' fashions." If they could prove to the doctors that the diagnosis fit, then perhaps the doctors might recommend the surgical treatment. As the doctors acknowledged the medical context that encouraged patients to coordinate their autobiographies with scientific accounts of transsexualism, they increasingly questioned "the extent to which the patient's stories and self-descriptions can be trusted."[96] In short, the patients mistrusted the doctors, and the doctors mistrusted the patients.

* * *

For transsexuals, the problems did not end when they convinced doctors to recommend and perform surgery. The fees, as Mario Martino remembered, were "staggering." In the mid-1950s, Harry Benjamin wrote: "I have my hands full with patients . . . who should have the operation but do not have the neces-sary funds." The funds needed varied, depending on the doctor and the surgeries performed, but in the 1960s, they generally ran a few thousand dollars. In some cases, disappointed patients, accepted for surgery but unable to afford it, talked of suicide or self-surgery. A number of MTFs engaged in prostitution to raise funds for their operations. Others tried to negotiate the costs. In the mid-1950s, with Benjamin's help, Debbie Mayne had the "extravagant fees" for her surgery in Mexico reduced and then agreed to pay on the installment plan. In 1970, Lyn Raskin convinced Georges Burou to reduce his $4000 fee to $1500.[97] Such arrangements required confrontations with doctors who generally did not expect patients to bargain with them for their services. The fees not only alienated the patients, but led, as one doctor described it, to "unpleasant experiences."[98]

In the doctors' offices and at the hospitals, wary patients observed the behavior of doctors and staff members who treated them unprofessionally. At Elmer Belt's clinic in Los Angeles, Annette Dolan sensed "an undercurrent of uneasiness caused by our presence." She also noted that her confidential records lay out on the business manager's desk, used, she said, "in the same manner as a best seller."[99] A few years later, at the same clinic, Aleshia Brevard remembered, Belt himself was "condescending and rude." In other cases, hospital staff treated the patients as oddities. When Mario Martino, with a full beard, entered the hospital for a hysterectomy, "everyone outside the department," he remembered, "lined up to take a look at the new specimen: *me*."[100]

Pain at the hands of doctors also heightened patients' discomfort. For months after surgery, MTFs had to dilate their vaginas frequently to keep them from closing. The first dilations were particularly painful. Carla Sawyer noted the "rough physical treatment" she received at the clinic of Elmer Belt, and a few years later, Patricia Morgan also recounted the pain. She said it took Elmer Belt and his son, also a doctor, fifteen minutes to force "a piece of plastic shaped like a man's penis" into her new vagina. "I grabbed the bars on the bed," she recalled, "and gritted my teeth."[101] While some patients accepted the pain as a necessary evil, others questioned the competence and motives of their doctors. The pain he endured during a routine pelvic examination made Mario Martino "suddenly apprehensive." He wondered: "Was this doctor as professional as he first appeared? Was he just impersonal? Or did he enjoy inflicting pain?"[102]

Given the less-than-perfect medical technology, the operations themselves often created addi-tional sources of frustration. For both MTFs and FTMs, there were infections, grafts that failed to take, and scar tissue that changed the appearance of the chest or labia. It was not unusual for new vaginas to close, new penises to wither, and urethras to constrict. FTMs who had phalloplasty regu-larly encountered post-surgical problems. In his first attempted phalloplasty, Martino reported how the tube pedicle failed: It "was shriveling, curling in on itself like a snail." In the second attempt, the head of the new penis "turned dark, signifying death of the tissue." Three months later he returned to the surgeon for another skin graft and "repairs."[103] Even after successful phalloplasty, FTMs often had "urinary problems in the form of fistulae, . . . infections, and incontinence." Frustrated patients, both FTMs and MTFs, returned to their doctors again and again with post-surgical problems. They sometimes underwent additional surgery to "correct a small vagina, a tender urethral stump, or a deformity of the labia," "to release strictures," to remove infected implants, or to attempt another graft after the first one had failed.[104]

The disappointments mounted when the bodily transformations did not have the appearance or the functions the patients wanted. One follow-up study on nine MTFs showed that all expressed "some dissatisfaction with the physical results of their surgery," especially with the size of the vagina or the "appearance of the labia and external genitalia." The doctors, aware of the limits of medical technology, acknowledged the "conflict with the surgeon." They admitted that "duplicating either sex in a perfect anatomical way is impossible."[105] Some tried to forewarn patients to lower their expectations about what the technology could accomplish. Harry Benjamin wrote one patient: "Please...do not expect either one-hundred per cent success, or one-hundred per cent happiness. There is no such thing."[106]

On top of it all, the patients knew that the doctors often saw them as mentally ill, irritating, or hostile. In the published medical literature, some psychiatrists, in particular, pathologized their transsexual patients. As Richard Green and Howard Baker noted, "the psychiatric literature is replete with deprecatory descriptions." Many doctors had, it seems, little experience with patients whose sense of urgency led them to insist on unusual forms of medical treatment. They seemed perplexed by the "extreme impatience" and the "anger" of patients who pushed them to stretch the boundaries of acceptable medical practice.[107] Accustomed to deference, they encountered patients whose determined demands surprised and annoyed them. Even the more sympathetic doctors sometimes lambasted their patients. In a letter to Willard Goodwin, Elmer Belt wrote: "These patients are simply awful liars. They lie when there is no need for it whatever." In letters to Harry Benjamin, he occasionally referred to his transsexual patients as "queers" or "nuts."[108] Robert J. Stoller considered MTFs "dissatisfied," "exhibitionistic and unreliable." "Some of these patients," he wrote to another doctor, "can be a real pain in the neck...even after surgery some of them can be quite persistent."[109] In his published writings, Harry Benjamin, the most sympathetic of the crew, wrote of the "selfishness, unreliability and questionable ethical concepts of some male and female transsexuals." A benevolent paternalist, he responded graciously to those who expressed "gratitude and loyalty" in response to his efforts.[110] But in a moment of pique, after a patient accused him of lying, he wrote, "You have been unappreciative and ungrateful."[111]

Those who underwent sex-change surgery encountered a range of daunting problems that went well beyond their dealings with doctors. Before and after surgery, they had to deal with families and friends who did not necessarily approve of the change of sex. They could choose to sever contact and move to a new life in which no one knew of their pasts, or else they could confront, and risk rejection by, anyone who knew their histories. They needed to find employment in their new gender status, often without the benefit of references from previous employers. They worried about the "apparent handicap they [had] in finding someone [who] will offer them employment," and they feared "being detected on the job."[112] As they changed their lives, a few transsexuals courted publicity, especially MTFs who hoped to follow in Jorgensen's footsteps, but most feared exposure in the press and also in daily life. Caren Ecker worried that the newspapers would print stories about her surgery. "I could see nothing of the financial good that came to Christine," she told Benjamin, "and only confusion to the plans I have made to continue my nursing career...publicity at this time would wreck all my chances." MTFs, in particular, worried about "passing," especially when their height, voices, facial features, or facial hair defied conventions of femininity. If they did not appear to be women, they risked the same harassment and arrest after surgery that they had faced before.[113]

The more sympathetic doctors did what they could to help their patients through the transition. Harry Benjamin tried to take care of "his girls." Aleshia Brevard, whom Benjamin treated in the early 1960s, remembered, "He really went to bat for me." Benjamin "talked to [her] parents" and "set up everything that there was to be set up, the meeting with the psychiatrist...all the legal rigmarole...it was all relatively painless because of him."[114] Benjamin, Belt, and others provided patients with letters attesting to the surgical change of sex. A typical letter, written by Elmer Belt in 1956, read: "This is to certify that a surgical operation performed for _____ has altered the genitalia of this patient, converting the sex from male to female, and that _____ in my opinion should legally be considered as belonging to the female sex."[115] The patient could show the letter to police if picked up for crossdressing or to skeptical bureaucrats who hesitated to change the name and sex on a driver's license, passport, or social security record. Benjamin also worried about the employment prospects of his patients and tried to encourage them in the job search. Mario Martino's surgeon hired him as a nurse, but few doctors went so far as to find jobs for their patients.

As the doctors advised their patients, they also inadvertently encouraged their dependence, which ultimately fueled frustrations. Benjamin and others urged post-operative patients to hide, and even to lie about, their past lives as the other sex. This placed the doctors among the few confidantes to whom the patients could turn. When the doctors failed to provide assistance, the patients felt betrayed. In Los Angeles in the mid-1950s, Annette Dolan, for example, hoped that Frederic Worden and Elmer Belt would help her and another MTF find jobs. "We are of the opinion," she wrote, "that an all out effort should have been made to give us a new start in life." When she asked Willard Goodwin for help, "he was," she said, "cold as ice."[116] Benjamin told her not to "expect anything from others" and also warned her that her "tactless" behavior might "rob" her "of some friends and sympathies." But she explained her sense of urgency: "What you fail to realize is that I literally am fighting for my life."[117]

For a few, the long struggle did not seem worth it in the end. In the available records, a handful of transsexuals expressed regrets about their new lives. One MTF failed to find employment as a woman and had to revert to living as a man. "I am not doing this," she told Belt, "because I desire to go back to an unhappy life, but I have to survive. It is a bitter pill, the bitterest I ever took, but there is nothing left to do." Another MTF decided after surgery that she had "a man's mind," that her "new body was all wrong." She made a good living as a "Latin Bombshell" stripper, but she disliked the aggressive men who expected her to have sex with them. She had lost her interest in sex with either men or women, and she found her life "lonely beyond belief."[118]

On the whole, though, those who managed to obtain surgery rarely regretted it. They overwhelmingly endorsed medical treatment, even though they had disappointments with the arduous process and imperfect results. Despite their persistent conflicts with doctors, they expressed their appreciation. In an article on FTMs, one doctor noted: "the patients demonstrate an attitude of extreme gratitude." In letters to Harry Benjamin, MTFs gave their thanks for the ways he had helped them fulfill "a life long dream" and find "peace of mind." "Nothing else in the world," one MTF wrote, "means or could ever mean so much to me as accomplishing this goal."[119] Surgery, of course, could not solve everything. "I guess that loneliness is the thing in this life that I now dread the most," Caren Ecker explained. "Still, I am grateful that my biggest problem is so well solved, that is, as well as it is possible to solve such a problem, and much better than I would have ever believed possible a few years ago."[120]

* * *

By the end of the 1960s, then, transsexuals had persuaded at least a few American doctors to move from theory to practice. They insisted that they could determine their own rightful sex and gender, and they convinced a handful of doctors to make their bodies accord with their minds. The request for bodily change distinguished them from other sexual "deviants." Homosexuals and transvestites did not have the same longings for medical intervention. For the most part, they wanted doctors to leave them alone. Doctors noted the differences, and so did transsexuals themselves. In the medical literature, the doctors engaged in and elaborated on the differential diagnoses that created the scientific classifications of sexuality, and in daily life, self-avowed transsexuals staked out their claims to identities of their own.

NOTES

1. Robert S. Redmount, "A Case of a female Transvestite with Marital and Criminal Complications," *Journal of Clinical and Experimental Psychopathology* 14:2 (June 1953), 95; K. G. autobiography, April 1964, no. 33 Diary Room, KI.
2. T. Sorensen and P. Hertoft, "Sex modifying Operations on Transsexuals in Denmark in the Period 1950–1977," *Acta Psychiatrica Scandinavica* (January 1980), 62–63.

3. Christian Hamburger, "The Desire for Change of Sex as Shown by Personal Letters from 465 Men and Women," *Acta Endocrinologica* 14:4 (1953), 363, 375.
4. Christian Hamburger to E. M., January 9, 1953, D. M. folder, box 6, Series IIC, HBC.
5. C. W. to Harry Benjamin, January 21, 1954; Benjamin to C. W., January 25, 1954, both in C. W. folder, box 8, Series IIC, HBC; Christian Hamburger to A. S., February 17, 1954, A. D. folder, box 4, ibid.
6. For examples of referrals, see Henrietta Thomas, "Harry Benjamin, M. D.: A Remembrance," *Chrysalis Quarterly* 1:5 (1993), 16; H. W. to Harry Benjamin, January 8, 1956, P. W. folder, box 8, Series IIC, HBC, B. S. to Harry Benjamin, June 11, 1954, B. S. folder, box 7, ibid; Robert J. Stoller to D.B., November 14, 1968, General, A-G, 1968–1969 folder, box 37, RSP.
7. Margo Howard-Howard with Abbe Michaels, *I Was a White Slave in Harlem* (New York: Four Walls Eight Windows, 1988), 78; Renée Richards with John Ames, *Second Serve: The Renée Richards Story* (New York: Stein and Day, 1983), 164; Jan Morris, *Conundrum* (New York: New American Library, 1975), 51.
8. Ira B. Pauly, "Adult Manifestations of Female Transsexualism," in *Transsexualism and Sex Reassignment*, ed. Richard Green and John Money (Baltimore: Johns Hopkins Press, 1969), 73.
9. John E. Hoopes, Norman J. Knorr, and Sanford R. Wolf, "Transsexualism: Considerations Regarding Sexual Reassignment," *Journal of Nervous and Mental Disease* 147:5 (1968), 513; Mario Martino with Harriet, *Emergence: A Transsexual Autobiography* (New York: Crown, 1977), 242. On Mexican Americans see, for example, Pauly, "Adult Manifestations of Female Transsexualism," 73.
10. Harry Benjamin to Christine Jorgensen, February 16, 1953, Documentation for CJ: A Personal Autobiog folder, box Clippings/Letters, CJP; R. W. to Harry Benjamin, March 19, 1956, R. W. folder, box 8, Series IIC, HBC; C.S. to Harry Benjamin [c. September 19, 1954], C. S. folder, box 7, ibid.
11. H. W. to Harry Benjamin [c. May 15, 1956], P. W. folder, box 8, Series IIC, HBC; P. K. to Harry Benjamin, September 23, 1968, P. K. folder, box 5, ibid. See also Gloria Marmar Warner and Marion Lahn, "A Case of Female Transsexualism," *Psychiatric Quarterly* 44 (1970), 478; S. W. to Harry Benjamin, July 2, 1954, S. W. folder, box 8, Series IIC, HBC; Pauly, "Adult Manifestations of Female Transsexualism," 59-87.
12. C. E., Life History [c. 1953], C. E. folder, box 4, Series IIC, HBC.
13. R. E. L. Masters, *Sex-Driven People: An Autobiographical Approach to the Problem of the Sex-Dominated Personality* (Los Angeles: Sherbourne, 1966), 224; Robert S. McCully, "An Interpretation of Projective Findings in a Case of Female Transsexualism," *Journal of Projective Techniques and Personality Assessment* 27 (1963), 436.
14. Warner and Lahn, "A Case of Female Transsexualism," 478; Robert J. Stoller, *Sex and Gender: On the Development of Masculinity and Femininity* (New York: Science House, 1968), 200.
15. Redmount, "A Case of a Female Transvestite," 95, 97; Harry Benjamin, *The Transsexual Phenomenon* (New York: Julian, 1966), 251; B. S. to Harry Benjamin, January 31, 1957, B. S. folder, box 7, Series IIC, HBC.
16. Interview with Regina Elizabeth McQuade by Susan Stryker, July 17, 1997, 1, transcript, GLBTHS.
17. H. W. to Harry Benjamin [c. May 15, 1956], P. W. folder, box 8; C. E. to Harry Benjamin, December 3, 1953, C. E. folder, box 4; both in Series IIC, HBC; Benjamin, *The Transsexual Phenomenon*, 138.
18. T. J. M. to Robert J. Stoller, November 1965, female Transsexualism section, box 9, RSP; Benjamin, *The Transsexual Phenomenon*, 242.
19. Harry Benjamin, handwritten note on R. W., April 5 [1956], R. W. folder, box 8, Series IIC, HBC; Redmount. "A Case of a Female Transvestite," 96.
20. Jane C. Doe (pseudo.), "Autobiography of a Transsexual," *Diseases of the Nervous System*, April 1967, 251, 252.
21. On the emerging sense of community, see Chapters 5 and 6.
22. T. J. M. to Robert J. Stoller, November 1965.
23. R.. W. B. to Harry Benjamin, March 27, 1967, R. W. B. folder, box 3, Series IIC, HBC; P. K. to Harry Benjamin, September 23, 1968, P. K. folder, box 5, ibid.
24. Lynne Layton, *Who's That Girl? Who's That Boy? Clinical Practice Meets Postmodern Gender Theory* (Northvale, N.J.: Jason Aronson, 1998), 11, 25; Jay Prosser, *Second Skins: The Body Narratives of Transsexuality* (New York: Columbia University Press, 1998), 158. Prosser argues, "it is the life-plot [of gender inversion] rather than actual somatic sex change that symptomizes the transsexual."
25. S. W. to Harry Benjamin, August 19, 1954, S. W. folder, box 8 Series IIC, HBC; L. C. to Harry Benjamin and Virginia Allen, April 10, 1971, L. C. folder, box 4, ibid.; Stoller, *Sex and Gender*, 200; Masters, *Sex-Driven People*, 248.
26. Pauly, "Adult Manifestations of Female Transsexualism," 76, 77. See also Karl M. Bowman and Bernice Engle, "Medicolegal Aspects of Transvestism," *American Journal of Psychiatry* 113:7 (January 1957), 587.
27. C. E. to Harry Benjamin, November 30 [1953], C. E. folder, box 4, Series IIC, HBC; see also Masters, *Sex-Driven People*, 244.
28. Ira B. Pauly, "Male Psychosexual Inversion: Transsexualism," *Archives of General Psychiatry* 13:2 (August 1965), 176; Nahman H. Greenberg, Alan K. Rosenwald, and Paul E. Nielson, "A Study in Transsexualism," *Psychiatric Quarterly* 34 (1960), 220; A. S. to Harry Benjamin, June 16, 1954, A. D. folder, box 4, Series IIC, HBC.
29. G. S. to Harry Benjamin, March 12, 1954, J. S. folder, box 7, Series IIC, HBC; R. B. to Harry Benjamin, October 24, 1953, R. B. folder, box 3, ibid; Doe, "Autobiography," 251, 254.
30. J. F. to Harry Benjamin, December 26, 1969, J. F. folder, box 4, Series IIC, HBC.
31. G. S. to Harry Benjamin, April 25, 1954, J. S. folder, box 7, Series IIC, HBC; M. G. to Harry Benjamin, March 12, 1969, M. G. folder, box 4, ibid; H. W. to Harry Benjamin [c. May 15, 1956], P. W. folder, box 8, ibid.
32. T. J. M. to Robert J. Stoller, November 1965; Hoopes, Knorr, and Wolf, "Transsexualism," 515; C. W. to Harry Benjamin. January 21, 1954.

33. Dean St. Dennis, "Boy Who Doesn't Want to Be One," San Francisco Chronicle, December 31, 1962, folder 33, box 15, Series IIIB, HBC.
34. Harry Benjmain to Elmer Belt, January 3, 1955, Correspondence file Harry Benjamin, KI; Robert J. Stoller to J. W., November 22, 1965, General, Q-Z, 1965–1966 folder, box 37, RSP.
35. Milton T. Edgerton, Norman J. Knorr, and James R. Callison, "The Surgical Treatment of Transsexual Patients," *Plastic and Reconstructive Surgery* 45:1 (January 1970), 38, 41.
36. S. W. to Alfred C. Kinsey, December 1, 952, Correspondence files S. W., KI.
37. S. W. to Harry Benjamin, July 2, 1954, S. W. Folder, box 8, Series IIC, HBC; S. W. to Alfred C. Kinsey, March 11, 1953, Correspondence file S. W., KI.
38. S. W. to Harry Benjamin, August 19, 1954; note to Harry Benjamin, February 1958, both in S. W. folder, box 8, Series IIC, HBC.
39. D. M. to Harry Benjamin, December 29, 1954, D. M. folder, box 6, Series IIC, HBC.
40. "Why More Men want to Change Their Sex" [n.p., c. 1955], 33, Blue Notebook, box 1/1 Scrapbook, VPC. On the FTM's surgery in his sister's kitchen, see D. B. M. to Harry Benjamin, October 26, 1965, D. M. folder, box 6, Series IIC, HBC.
41. T. J. M. to Robert J. Stoller, November 1965.
42. C. E., Life History [c. 1953], C. E. folder, box 4, Series IIC, HBC; "Transsexual," *Sexology* 31:6 (January 1965), 395; M. O. to Harry Benjamin, October 13, 1968, M. O. folder, box 6, Series IIC, HBC.
43. Benjamin, *The Transsexual Phenomenon*, 96. For recent accounts of the effects of hormones, see Rosemary Basson and Jerilynn C. Prior, "Hormonal Therapy of Gender Dysphoria: The Male-to-Female Transsexual," in *Current Concepts in Transgender Identity*, ed. Dallas Denny (New York: Garland, 1998), 277–296; Jerilynn C. Prior and Stacy Elliott, "Hormonal Therapy of Gender Dysphoria: The Female-to-Male Transsexual," in Denny, *Current Concepts*, 297-313.
44. Grace to Nancy, no. 13 [c. 1958], Grace-Nancy notebook; Louise Lawrence to B. S., June 7, 1954, Alfred C. Kinsey folder, LLC; Louise Lawrence to Harry Benjamin, April 24, 1953, TRNSV notebook, LLC.
45. T. J. M. to Robert J. Stoller, November 1965.
46. Pauly, "Male Psychosexual Inversion," 177.
47. C. E. to Harry Benjamin, October 5, 1953, C. E. folder, box 4, Series IIC, HBC. See also C. E. to Benjamin, December 3, 1953, ibid.; Louise Lawrence to Benjamin, December 29, 1953, TRNSV notebook, LLC; Bowman and Engle, "Medicolegal Aspects of Transvestism," 587.
48. Mary Smith, "They Said I was Courageous!" manuscript, A. D. folder, box 4, Series IIC, HBC. See also "Mary Smith," "Females in Male Bodies," *Sexology* 25:7 (February 1959), 428-433. The version in *Sexology* omits details of the operation and its success, presumably in an attempt to keep readers from copycat surgery. On Elmer Belt, see A. D. to Harry Benjamin, September 21, 1954, and February 13, 1955, A. D. folder, box 4, Series IIC, HBC.
49. Elmer Belt to Harry Benjamin, August 15, 1960, Elmer Belt, 1959–1962 folder; Belt to Benjamin, October 16, 1962-1965 folder, both in box 3, Series IIC, HBC
50. On Belt's surgical technique, see Elmer Belt to Alfonso de la Pena, April 25, 1960, Elmer Belt, 1959-1962 folder, box 3, Series IIC, HBC. On this decision to quit, see Elmer Belt to Harry Benjamin, October 16, 1962, Elmer Belt, 1962–1965 folder, box 3, ibid. On Barbara Richards Wilcox, see Leah Cahan Schaefer and Connie Christine Wheeler, "Harry Benjamin's First Ten Cases (1938–1953): A Clinical Historical Note," *Archives of Sexual Behavior* 24:1 (Befruary 1995), 80. Schaefer and Wheeler call Wilcox "Carol."
51. R. J. to Harry Benjamin, April 27, 1955, R. J. Folder, box 5, Series IIC, HBC; Benjamin, *The Transsexual Phenomenon*, 118.
52. Robert J. Stoller to D. B., November 14, 1968, General, A-G, 1968–1969 folder, box 37, RSP; Harry Benjamin to J. E.,
53. For a brief history, see Edgerton, Knorr, and Callison, "Surgical Treatment." See also James Fairchild Baldwin, "The Formation of an Artificial Vagina by Intestinal Transplantation," *Annals of Surgery* 40 (1904), 398–403; Howard W. Jones, "Operative Treatment of the Male Transsexual," in Green and Money, *Transsexualism and Sex Reassignment*, 313–317; Benjmain, *the Transsexual Phenomenon*, 102–104.
54. Patricia Morgan, as told to Paul Hoffman, *The Man-Maid Doll* (Seacaucus, N.J.: Lyle Stuart [c. 1973]), 60, 63.
55. Jones, "Operative Treatment," 316; Elmer Belt to B. O., September 5, 1956, B. O. folder, box 6, Series IIC, HBC; Else K. La Roe, *Woman Surgeon: The Autobiography of Else K. La Roe, M.D.* (New York: Dial, 1957), 359. On Else La Roe and breast implants, see Watson Crews, Jr., "The Full Facts about Sex Change," in *New York Sunday News*, March 22, 1964, 26. For an early fictional account, in which a doctor changed (and then rechanged) the sexes of a married couple, see I. S. (Isadore Schnedier), *Doctor Transit* (New York: Boni and Liveright, 1925).
56. Pauly, "Male Psychosexual Inversion," 179; Benjamin, *The Transsexual Phenomenon*, 119, 147; Edgerton, Knorr, and Callison, "Surgical Treatment, 39.
57. See, for example, Richard Green, "Change-of-Sex," *Medical Aspects of Human Sexuality* 3:10 (October 1969), 101.
58. Harry Benjamin to L. M., May 20, 1954, L. M. folder, box 6, Series IIC, HBC; Robert J. Stoller to Harry Guntrip, March 4, 1969, General, A-G, 1968–1969 folder, box 37, RSP; memorandum from Richard Green to Dr. Baker et al., February 7, 1970, Gender Clinic Meetings, 1962–970 folder, box 16, RSP.
59. On butch-femme working-class culture, see Elizabeth Lapovsky Kennedy and Madeline Davis, *Boots of Leather, Slippers of Gold: The History of a Lesbian Community* (New York: Routledge, 1993). On the declining vogue of "faries," see George Chauncey, *Gay New York: Gender, Urban Culture, and the Making of the Gay Male World*, 1890–1940 (New York: Basic Books, 1994), 358.
60. Benjamin, *The Transsexual Phenomenon*, 156.

61. Warner and Lahn, "A Case of Female Transsexualism," 478–480.
62. John Money and John G. Brenna, "Sexual Dimorphism in the Psychology of Female Transsexuals," *Journal of Nervous and Mental Disease* 147:5 (1968), 495–496.
63. Sir Harold Gillies, "Congenital Absence of the Penis," *British Journal of Plastic Surgery* 1 (1948), 8–28; see also John E. Hoopes, "Operative Treatment of the Female Transsexual," in Green and Money, *Transsexualism and Sex Reassignment*, 335-352; Edgerton, Knorr, and Callison, "Surgical Treatment," 40.
64. See Liz Hodgkinson, *Michael, Née Laura* (London: Columbus Books, 1989), chaps. 4–5.
65. S. G. to Harry Benjmain, November 8 and 18, 1963, S. G. folder, box 4, Series IIC, HBC.
66. Martino, *Emergence*, 261.
67. Edgerton, Knorr, and Callison, "Surgical Treatment," 44; see also Sir Harold Gillies and D. Ralph Millard Jr., *The Principles and Art of Plastic Surgery*, vol. 2 (Boston: Little, Brown, 1957), 376, 384.
68. Hoopes, "Operative Treatment," 341.
69. Martino, *Emergence*, 163, 191, 263.
70. Richard Green, Consultation Notes, November 20, 1970, Richard Green section, box 3, RSP.
71. Schaefer and Wheeler, "Harry Benjamin's First Ten Cases," 77; Benjamin, *The Transsexual Phenomenon*, 156.
72. Phoebe Smith, *Phoebe* (Atlanta: Phoebe Smith, 1979), 27; A. D. to Harry Benjamin, November 13, 1954, A. D. folder, box 4, Series IIC, HBC.
73. On Lawrence and Kinsey, see Joanne Meyerowitz, "Sex Research at the Borders of Gender: Transvestites, Transsexuals, and Alfred C. Kinsey," *Bulletin of the History of Medicine* 75:1 (Spring 2001), 72–90.
74. Schaefer and Wheeler, "Harry Benjamin's First Ten Cases," 81; Louise Lawrence to B.S., June 7, 1954, Alfred C. Kinsey folder, LLC. On Cauldwell, see Louise Lawrence to Harry Benjamin, October 28, 1953, TRNSV notebook, LLC. Lawrence appreciated recognition, but she published her own article under a pseudonym because the editors of the journal thought "it would be safer"; Louise Lawrence to Alfred C. Kinsey, June 4, 1951, Alfred C. Kinsey folder, LLC.
75. Louise Lawrence to E. E., April 14, 1953, TRNSV notebook, LLC; Louise Lawrence to B. S., June 1954.
76. D. M. to Harry Benjamin, November 3, 1953, D. M. folder, box 6, Series IIC, HBC; C. E. to Harry Benjamin, October 5 [1953], C. E. folder, box 4, ibid.; G.S. to Robert J. Stoller, February 1, 1970, General, Q-Z, 1969–1970 folder, box 37, RSP.
77. C. E. to Harry Benjamin, January 4, 1954, October 5 [1953], January 27 and Mary 9, 1954, C. E. folder, box 4, Series IIC, HBC.
78. C. S. to Harry Benjamin, November 21, 1954, C. S. folder, box 7, Series IIC, HBC.
79. Ibid.
80. Louise Lawrence to D. M., February 16, 1954; Harry Benjamin to D. M., March 14, 1954; D. M. to Benjamin, March 17, 1954; D. M. to Benjamin, December 18, 1954, all in D. M. folder, box 6, Series IIC, HBC.
81. J. S. to Harry Benjamin, May 15, 1955, J. S. folder, box 7, Series IIC, HBC; A. D. to Editor, *Journal of the American Medical Association*, June 13, 1955; A. D. to Elmer Belt [c. June 1955], both in A. D. folder, box 4, ibid.
82. Elmer Belt to Harry Benjamin, Dec. 5, 1955, C. S. folder, box 7, Series IIC, HBC; Vivien LeMans, *Take My Tool* (Los Angeles, Classic Publications,1968), 90.
83. Smith, *Phoebe*, 48-49; Martino, *Emergence*, 170–171, 188.
84. Mark Sulcov, "Transsexualism: Its Social Reality," draft of the Ph.D. diss., Indiana University, 1973, 2/15, KI Library.
85. D. M. to Harry Benjamin, April 17, 1955, D. M. folder, box 6, Series IIC, HBC.
86. Robert S. Redmount, "A Case of a Female Transvestite with Marital and Criminal Complications," *Journal of Clinical and Experimental Psychopathology* 14:2 (June, 1953), 108–109; B. S. to Harry Benjamin, July 2, 1955, B. S. folder, box 7, Series IIC, HBC.
87. Robert J. Stoller, Harold Garfinkel, and Alexander C. Rosen, "Passing and the Maintenance of Sexual Identification in an Intersexed Patient," *Archives of General Psychiatry* 2 (April 1970), 379.
88. Arthur D. Schwabe, David H. Solomon, Robert J. Stoller, and John P. Burnham, "Pubertal Feminization in a Genetic Male with Testicular Atrophy and Normal Urinary Gonadotropin," *Journal of Clinical Endocrinology and Metabolism* 22 (August 1962), *Journal of Psycho-Analysis* 45 (1964), 225. See also Harold Garfinkel, *Studies in Ethnomethodology* (Englewood Cliffs, N.J.: Prentice-Hall, 1967), 134.
89. Schwabe et al., "Pubertal Feminization," 843.
90. Stoller, Garfinkel, and Rosen, "Passing," 380.
91. Elmer Belt to Willard Goodwin, June 20, 1966, Male Transsexualism section, box 9, RSP.
92. Stoller, *Sex and Gender*, 136; Richard Green to Robert J. Stoller, June 15, 1966, Richard Green folder, box 34, RSP.
93. Stoller, *Sex and Gender*, 136.
94. After the Agnes episode, Stoller seemed to place less emphasis on the "biological force," which he now regarded only "as a possibility only in some extremely rare cases." See Robert J. Stoller to Saul I. Harrison, May 15, 1970, General, H-P, 1969-1970 folder, box 37, RSP.
95. Pauly, "Male Psychosexual Inversion, 175.
96. Lawrence S. Kubie and James B. Mackie, "Critical Issues Raised by Operation for Gender Transmutation," *Journal of Nervous and Mental Disease* 147:5 (November 1968), 435, 437.
97. Martino, *Emergence*, 173; Harry Benjmain to C. J., March 7, 1955, R. J. folder, box 5, Series IIC, HBC; Benjamin to D. M., December 22, 1954, D. M. folder, box 6, ibid.; Lyn Raskin, *Diary of a Transsexual* (New York: Olympia Press, 1971), 57, 84.
98. F. Hartsuiker to H. F., July 31, 1954, H. F. folder, box 4, Series IIC, HBC.

99. A. D. to Harry Benjamin, November 13 and December 23, 1954, A. D. folder, box 4, Series IIC, HBC.

100. Interview with Aleshia Brevard Crenshaw by Susan Stryker, August 2, 1997, transcript, 39, GLBTHS; Martino, *Emergence*, 213.

101. C. S. to Harry Benjamin, December 15, 1955, C. S. folder, box 7, Series IIC, HBC, Morgan, *Man-Maid Doll*, 63.

102. Martino, *Emergence*, 165.

103. Ibid., 260, 262.

104. Hoopes, "Operative Treatment," 342; Edgerton, Knorr, and Callison, "Surgical Treatment," 44.

105. Edgerton, Knorr, and Callison, "Surgical Treatment," 44; Norman Knorr, Sanford Wolf, and Eugene Meyer, "Psychiatric Evaluation of Male Transsexuals for Surgery," in Green and Money, *Transsexualism and Sex Reassignment,* 279.

106. Harry Benjamin to H. F., September 1, 1955, H. F. folder, box 4, Series IIC, HBC.

107. Howard J. Baker and Richard Green, "Treatment of Transexualism," *Current Psychiatric Therapies* 10 (1970), 88; Sanford R. Wolf, Norman J. Knorr, Jogn E. Hoopes, and Eugene Meyer, "Psychiatric Aspects of Transsexual Surgery Management," *Journal of Nervous and Mental Disease* 147: 5 (1968), 524.

108. Elmer Belt to Willard Goodwin, June 20, 1966; Belt to Harry Benjamin, July 26, 1965, and February 14, 1966, all in Elmer Belt, 1965-1971 folder, box 3, Series IIC, HBC.

109. Stoller, "Treatment of Transvestism and Transsexualism," 98; Robert J. Stoller to John Romano, February 28, 1968, General, Q-Z, 1967–1968 folder, box 37, RSP.

110. Harry Benjmain, "Newer Aspects of the Transsexual Phenomenon," *Journal of Sex Research* 5:2 (May 1969), 138. See also Harry Benjamin to Alfred C. Kinsey, December 3, 1954, Correspondence file to Harry Benjamin, KI.

111. Harry Benjamin to J.D., July 16, 1956, J.D. folder, box 4, Series IIC, HBC.

112. C. S. to Harry Benjamin, November 21, 1954, C. S. folder; G. S. to Harry Benjamin, April 2, 1954, J.S. folder, both in box 7, Series IIC, HBC.

113. C. E. to Harry Benjamin, January 22, 1954, C. E. folder, box 4, Series IIC, HBC.

114. Crenshaw interview, 31.

115. Elmer Belt to To Whom It May Concern, June 28, 1956, A. D. folder, box 4, Series IIC, HBC.

116. A. D. to Harry Benjamin, November 13 and 22, 1954, A. D. folder, box 4, Series IIC, HBC.

117. Harry Benjamin to A. D., December 3 and 22, 1954; A. D. to Harry Benjamin, December 23, 1954, all in A. D. folder, box 4, Series IIC, HBC.

118. M. H. to Elmer Belt, June 23, 1958, Elmer Belt, 1958–1959 folder, box 3, Series IIC, HBC; Latina Seville, "I Want to be Male Again," in Abby Sinclair, *"I Was Male!"* (Chicago: Novel Books, 1965), 90, 91, 94, 95.

119. Hoopes, "Operative Treatment," 346; A. D. to Harry Benjamin, February 2, 1955, A. D. folder, box 4, Series IIC, HBC; D. M. to Harry Benjamin, April 17, 1955, D. M. folder, box 6, ibid.; D. P. to Harry Benjamin, February 24, 1955, D. P. folder, box 7, ibid.

120. C. E. to Harry Benjamin, December 31, 1956, C. E. folder, box 4, Series IIC, HBC.

26

ONE Inc. and Reed Erickson

The Uneasy Collaboration of Gay and Trans Activism, 1964–2003

Aaron H. Devor and Nicholas Matte

With *Blending Genders* and *FTM*, his detailed and compassionate sociological studies of trans men and masculine women, Aaron Devor provided many female-to-male individuals with the sense of validity denied them in the only previous book-length study of their lives, Leslie Lothstein's 1983 *Female to Male Transsexualism*. One of the biggest problems facing trans men is the default assumption that they are "always already women," their histories always framed as an atypical facet of women's histories; They are either lesbians escaping their oppression as women, or women who cannot live with the social stigma of being lesbian. Along with the pioneering Lou Sullivan, Devor is one of the few writers who have worked to tell the story of an FTM individual in relation to the history of other men—particularly in relation to other queer men.

In this article, co-authored with his student Nicholas Matte, Devor goes beyond his usual approach to reclaim a piece of FTM history. Devor and Matte detail the life and contributions of Reed Erickson, a wealthy FTM who in the 1960s contributed massive, behind-the-scenes financial support to both the (predominantly male) homophile activists who founded the ONE Institute for Homophile Studies in Los Angeles, and to the Harry Benjamin Foundation, which evolved into the principal professional organization for medical and psychotherapeutic service providers specializing in transgender care. In reclaiming Erickson's accomplishments for the history books, Devor and Matte not only appropriately place his story in the context of other men's lives: they also offer a detailed account of uneasy alliances and suggestive tensions between homosexual and transgender communities and identities.

People who are today known as transgendered and transsexual have always been present in homosexual rights movements. Their presence and contributions, however, have not always been fully acknowledged or appreciated. As in many other social reform movements, collective activism in gay and lesbian social movements is based on a shared collective identity. Homosexual collective identity, especially in the days before queer politics, was largely framed as inborn, like an ethnicity, and based primarily on sexual desires for persons of the same sex and gender.[1] However, such definitions make sense only when founded on clearly delineated distinctions between sexes and genders. It becomes considerably harder to delineate who is gay and who is lesbian when it is not clear who is a male or a man and who is a female or a woman. Like bisexual people, transgendered and transsexual people destabilize the otherwise easy division of men and women into the categories of straight and gay because they are both and/or neither. Thus there is a long-standing tension over the political terrain of queer politics between gays and lesbians, on the one hand, and transgendered and transsexual people, on the other.

These boundary issues, with which recent gay and lesbian social movements have struggled, have been intrinsic to definitions of homosexuality since the concept of homosexual identity was first consolidated at the turn of the last century.[2] Early sexologists and their contemporaries commonly assumed that homosexuality was epitomized by females who seemed to want to be men and by males who seemed to want to be women.[3] For example, J. Allen Gilbert's 1920 article in the *Journal of Nervous and Mental Disease*, which described the 1917 gender transformation of Lucille Hart into Dr. Alan Hart, was titled "Homosexuality and Its Treatment."[4] Similarly, Radclyffe Hall's book *The Well of Loneliness* (1928), about a (transgendered) female who yearned to be a man, almost single-handedly defined lesbianism in the popular imagination for much of the twentieth century and is still widely acclaimed as a classic of lesbian literature.[5] It is not surprising, then, that many gays and lesbians who are not transgendered have been eager to make it clear that they are not, given that their societies commonly use gender transgressions to enforce homophobia. Yet others, eagerly seeking to valorize presumed homosexual people from the past, have adopted gender transgressiveness as a symbol of gay and lesbian pride. Nearly a hundred years since homosexuality was formally defined, news reports and gay and lesbian activists still routinely claim both historical and contemporary transgendered people as lesbian and gay.[6]

Only more recently have differently gendered people named themselves transgendered and transsexual and begun to build politicized organizations under self-defined banners.[7] During the last half century there also have been many examples of transgendered and transsexual people being shunned by gay and lesbian political organizations or having their histories expropriated. Despite this, many transgendered and transsexual people tried to persuade these organizations to embrace and endorse the fight for the rights of transgendered and transsexual people among and around them.[8] In this essay, after briefly expanding on this point, we tell the story of how one transsexual man was instrumental in the founding of one of the oldest and longest-running gay and lesbian groups in the United States. In doing so, we attempt to recoup a lost bit of the confluent histories of the transgendered and of the gay and lesbian social movements and to encourage the reexamination of how these two groups might work together more productively.

GAY/LESBIAN AND TRANSGENDER POLITICS

The modern gay and lesbian rights movement in the United States reached a milestone in the summer of 1969, when rioting broke out in New York City's Greenwich Village. The rioting, which lasted for several nights, began when female and male transgendered people resisted arrest at a gay bar, the Stonewall Inn.[9] Over the next few years, while gay and lesbian rights organizing expanded rapidly, the distinctive gifts and needs of transgendered people were often marginalized by the leadership of early gay and lesbian organizations. Bull daggers and drag queens, transgendered and transsexual people, were largely treated as embarrassments in the "legitimate" fight for tolerance, acceptance, and equal rights. Several incidents in the 1970s and 1990s were flash points for the smoldering tensions between homosexual people trying to attain social and political weight for themselves and others who hoped to achieve equal rights for all. These incidents illustrated the perception of some in the homosexual population that transgendered and transsexed people presented too great a challenge to mainstream society and thus discredited the endeavors of more "acceptable" gays and lesbians.

Lesbians and feminists have been more at the forefront of these struggles than gay men. In particular, some of the most hotly contested battles recently have been over the question of whether or not male-to-female (MTF) transsexuals are women for the purposes of inclusion in women-only organizations. Transgendered and transsexed people have posed the greatest challenges to gender definitions at a historical moment when women in general, and lesbians in particular, have begun only recently to feel that they exist as political players in their own right. Yet as lesbians and feminists have tentatively gained ground, transgendered and transsexual activists have argued that the identity categories of "lesbian" and "woman" do not exclude those with histories as men and that these categories are in fact a matter of subjective self-identification.[10] Many lesbian-feminist organizations and individuals nevertheless insist on a definition of womanhood that leaves no room for women who were born male.

Just such an interpretive clash occurred at Olivia Records in the 1970s. A women-only, lesbian-dominated recording company, Olivia was a source of pride to many feminists. Among the many challenges it faced in its early days was a paucity of women with well-honed recording skills who wished to work long hours, for little or no pay, in a women-only company with a questionable financial future. One such woman, Sandy Stone, who had been a recording engineer for A&M Records, was an MTF transsexual, a fact she never concealed from the other women at Olivia.[11] When it became more widely known that Stone was an MTF transsexual, some lesbian feminists were outraged, because they thought of her as a man who had infiltrated a women-only organization. The other women at Olivia initially resisted the pressure to request Stone's resignation, but in 1977 they succumbed when they believed that the company's very existence was at stake.[12]

Two years later, in *The Transsexual Empire*, lesbian-feminist Janice Raymond further publicized the story of Stone's tenure at Olivia and used it to support her case against transsexualism. Raymond vilified transsexualism as a "social tranquilizer" that was "*undercutting the movement to eradicate sex-role stereotyping and oppression.*"[13] The persistence of Raymond's theories about transsexualism became evident once again in a very public way in the early 1990s at the Michigan Womyn's Music Festival, a five-day women-only event run every year since 1976 on 650 acres of private land.[14] It is unclear when transsexual women began to attend it, but at least one, Nancy Jean Burkholder, had been to it once before 1991: in that year she was expelled for being transsexual. Over the next several years controversy raged over who should be allowed into the festival. Lesbian, gay, and feminist newspapers and magazines were barraged with letters to the editor. In 1994, 1995, and every year from 1999 to 2003 transgendered and transsexual activists set up an informational and protest "Camp Trans" outside the gates of the festival. Eventually, the organizers of the event, bowing to pressure from this coalition, said that anyone self-defined as a "womyn-born womyn" would be allowed into the festival.[15]

The combined gay and lesbian movement has also proved resistant to aligning itself with transgendered and transsexual people. Prior to the 1993 March on Washington for Lesbian, Gay, and Bi Rights, for example, transgendered and transsexual people worked to have the word *transgendered* added to the name of the march. Ultimately, the organizing committee decided to exclude the word from the title. Furthermore, when the decision was announced at an organizational meeting, cheers went up from some of those present.[16]

By 1997 more consistent progress toward unity had been made, with various gay and lesbian organizations expanding their mandate to include transgender perspectives. In September 1997 the National Gay and Lesbian Task Force amended its mission statement to include transgendered people.[17] Similarly, in September 1998 Parents, Families, and Friends of Lesbians and Gays voted to include transgendered people in their mission statement.[18] In April 2000 three transgendered activists were featured speakers at the Millennium March for Equality in Washington, DC, which drew hundreds of thousands of participants.[19] In March 2001 the Human Rights Campaign, which calls itself "America's largest gay and lesbian organization," amended its mission statement to include transgendered people.[20]

Nevertheless, there remains much work to be done to redress the longstanding rejection of trans-gendered and transsexual people by gays and lesbians. Part of this work is to make gays and lesbians aware of the important contributions of transgendered and transsexual people to the queer movement. This article seeks to share the story of one transsexual man who quietly ensured the survival of one of the first homosexual advocacy organizations, and now the oldest, in the United States. The article first looks at early gay activism in California in the 1950s; then it describes the context in which ONE Inc. and the Erickson Educational Foundation (EEF) began to work together to educate society about and to provide support to homosexual, transgendered, and transsexual people. It looks at the circumstances in which the two organizations developed, became partners, and eventually ended their relationship. Finally, it discusses the history of ONE after it lost the EEF's support and explains the importance of the organizations' partnership to contemporary queer activists and historians.

EARLY GAY ACTIVISM IN CALIFORNIA

Early efforts to represent and better the social position of sexual and gender minorities in the United States were initiated by people with firsthand knowledge of the pain of trans- and homophobia. They created organizations aimed at undoing the social stigma faced by LGBT people. So when the EEF and ONE began to work together in 1964, their goals and methods were similar in many ways. Nevertheless, the realities of the social stigmas faced by gays and lesbians, on the one hand, and by transgendered and transsexual people, on the other, could be quite different. Thus organizations whose purpose was to eradicate these stigmas also needed to be different in some respects. ONE's main focus was the experience of gay men, whereas the EEF's was that of gender-variant (particularly transsexual) people. Nevertheless, Reed Erickson, the foundation's founder, was keen to have the EEF work with gay and lesbian groups toward common goals. Therefore a brief introduction to the two organizations prior to their partnership is in order.

The early 1950s saw the creation of several groups whose aim was to improve social conditions for sexual minorities. The Knights of the Clock, one of the first homophile groups in the United States, was formed in Los Angeles in 1950 by Merton Bird and W. Dorr Legg. It continued to meet until the mid-1960s, and its function was to provide support for gay people in interracial couples.[21] The better-known, longer-lasting Mattachine Society, originally conceived as a political and civil rights discussion group for homosexual people, was also formed in Los Angeles in 1950, by Harry Hay. Other groups soon emerged in southern California, largely in response to the 1952 arrest of Dale Jennings, a member of the Mattachine Society, for soliciting an undercover police officer.[22] "A veritable flood of social protest" ensued after Jennings, who later accused the arresting officer of entrapment, admitted in court that he was homosexual but denied that this made him guilty of "lewd conduct."[23]

It was in this social climate that ONE, whose founders included Legg, Bird, Jennings, and Martin Block, another former member of the Mattachine Society, was incorporated in Los Angeles in October 1952. Taking its name from a famous quote by Thomas Carlyle, "A mystic bond of brotherhood makes all men one," the organization set about "to aid in the social integration and rehabilitation of the sexual variant."[24] To achieve its goals, which were primarily educational, ONE would produce publications, provide programs, and stimulate and support research.[25] The progress it made toward accomplishing these goals was impressive and swift.

For example, by January 1953 ONE had started to disseminate information about homosexuality by publishing *ONE Magazine*, the first publicly available prohomosexuality periodical in the United States. The magazine sold for twenty-five cents and was bravely hawked on the streets of Los Angeles, as well as distributed through the U.S. postal system.[26] By October 1954 the magazine had thousands of subscribers, but in that month the U.S. Post Office declared it obscene and unmailable and confiscated the issue. ONE promptly sued the U.S. Post Office for infringement of the constitutional right to freedom of the press. The case was not decided until 1958, when the U.S. Supreme Court ruled that gay and lesbian publications were not a priori obscene and could therefore be mailed legally through the postal system.[27] *ONE Magazine* continued to be published until 1967.[28] In 1958 ONE Institute also began to publish the first scholarly journal devoted to homophile studies, *ONE Institute Quarterly*, which today continues as the *Journal of Homosexuality* and as the online *International Gay and Lesbian Review*.[29] *ONE Institute Quarterly* was intended to stimulate further educational publications and research in "homophile studies," a field that ONE itself was pioneering.

While *ONE Magazine* and *ONE Institute Quarterly* both served as forums for gay-positive material and research, ONE Inc. also developed more traditional educational resources primarily through ONE Institute and its "extension division," which prepared short courses and events. For example, in January 1955 it began to offer a "Mid-Winter Institutes" series, the first of which was held at the Biltmore Hotel in Los Angeles. The one-day event consisted of meetings, discussions, a luncheon, and a dinner banquet and featured the psychiatrist Blanche M. Baker and the psychologist Evelyn Hooker. The second Mid-Winter Institute took place in January 1956.[30] The Mid-Winter Institutes, which continued into the 1980s, expanded to include scholarly talks, roundtable discussions, and theatrical presentations. Several hundred people attended these college-level, nondegree courses each year.

Through the extension division, ONE Institute also helped establish homophile studies and ONE Inc. chapters outside Los Angeles. Doing so often involved cooperating with other, local groups. For example, in 1957 ONE Institute offered a short course in conjunction with the Daughters of Bilitis at the home of Dr. Harry Benjamin in San Francisco. It also offered lectures in conjunction with local hosts in Denver (1959), San Francisco (1957, 1960), Chicago (1963, 1971), New York (1968), and Milwaukee (1973).[31] This Sunday-afternoon lecture series, which began in Los Angeles in 1958, has continued virtually uninterrupted ever since.[32] Through the lecture series and the Mid-Winter Institutes, ONE Institute offered a nondegree component comparable to what was done by extension divisions at community colleges and universities.

ONE Institute sought to provide still other formal educational opportunities. In October 1956 the ONE Institute of Homophile Studies was launched and held its first classes. The word *homophile* was chosen over the word *homosexual* because the founders of ONE Institute felt that *homosexual* implied medicalization and pathologization, whereas the more etymologically correct *homophile* was less encumbered by such negative connotations. The institute's goal was to become a degree-granting research institution in homophile studies.[33] The first course, in which fourteen students met for two hours per week for nine weeks to study homosexuality in biology and medicine, history, psychology, sociology and anthropology, law, religion, literature and the arts, and philosophy was simply called "An Introduction to Homophile Studies." By the 1957–58 term the institute had expanded its schedule to two nine-week semesters, and over the next thirty years it developed a plethora of more specific courses, including "Homosexuality in History," "Sociology of Homosexuality," "The Gay Novel," "The Theory and Practice of Homophile Education," "Homophile Ethics," "Psychological Theories of Homosexuality," "Counseling the Homosexual," "Law and Law Reform," and "Near Eastern Foundations of Biblical Morality" (31–47).

These early courses represent the beginnings of the multitude of college and university courses and programs now devoted to the study of lesbian, gay, bisexual, transgendered, and queer people. When ONE Institute began its pioneering work, however, the support network at colleges and universities for this area of study simply did not exist. The financial support for this work had to come entirely from private sources, and the social stigma associated with offering such support made trying to entice donors extremely difficult. Although ONE had clear goals and methods for accomplishing them, the organization was greatly hindered by its severe shortage of resources. In 1964, badly in need of an injection of funding, ONE Inc. met Reed Erickson.

REED ERICKSON AND THE EEF

Erickson had launched the EEF in June 1964 as a nonprofit philanthropic organization funded and controlled, despite having a board of directors, almost entirely by himself. The foundation's goals were "to provide assistance and support in areas where human potential was limited by adverse physical, mental or social conditions, or where the scope of research was too new, controversial or imaginative to receive traditionally oriented support."[34] A substantial part of the foundation's work, therefore, was funding what Erickson considered to be progressive projects. During the twenty years of its existence, the EEF made available millions of dollars from Erickson's personal wealth for the advancement of causes in which he believed. These fell into three main types, all of them related to social movements that remain important and relevant today. The three main social movements in which Erickson invested were those advocating on behalf of homosexuals, those advocating on behalf of transgendered (specifically, transsexual) people, and those developing what might now be called the "New Age" movement. He also funded a wide range of philanthropic projects outside of these major categories, such as the Interplast (International Plastic Surgery) project, which provided corrective plastic surgeries at no charge to impoverished children in Latin America and Africa.[35]

Because the EEF was run almost exclusively by Erickson, his personality was decisive both in the projects that the EEF supported and in the relationship between the EEF and ONE. Considering that his personal wealth sustained so many progressive projects, it is surprising that his vast contributions have not been more widely recognized. His fascinating life story bears on his interaction with ONE Inc. in important ways. Thus a biographical sketch is in order.

Reed Erickson was born as Rita Mae Erickson in El Paso, Texas, on October 13, 1917. Erickson's early years were spent in Philadelphia with his mother, father, and younger sister. After graduating from the Philadelphia High School for Girls, Erickson enrolled in a secretarial course at Temple University. Soon after, the family moved to Baton Rouge, Louisiana, where Erickson's father, Robert B. Erickson, had transferred his lead smelting business. In Baton Rouge, Erickson attended Louisiana State University and became the first woman graduate from its School of Mechanical Engineering. Erickson then returned briefly to Philadelphia to work as an engineer and lived as a lesbian in an intimate relationship for several years. There Erickson and a romantic partner took part in Henry Agar Wallace's 1948 campaign for the presidency on behalf of the Progressive Party and were part of a liberal social group that included many gays and lesbians, as well as civil rights activists and theater people. Their political involvement led to harassment by the FBI, and Erickson is rumored to have been blacklisted from several jobs as a result. By the early 1950s Erickson had returned once again to Baton Rouge to work in the family companies. At that time Erickson also started an independent company, Southern Seating, which produced and distributed stadium bleachers.

After Erickson's father's death in 1962, Erickson inherited the family businesses, Schuylkill Products Company Inc. and Schuylkill Lead Corporation, and ran them successfully for several years before selling them to Arrow Electronics in 1969 for around five million dollars. Erickson eventually amassed a personal fortune of over forty million dollars.

In 1963, as a patient of Harry Benjamin, Erickson began the process of masculinizing his body and living as Reed Erickson. That year he also married for the first time. Over the next thirty years he would marry three more times and become father to two children. In 1972 he moved with his wife and children and his pet leopard Henry to Mazatlán, Mexico, where he had built an opulent home, which he dubbed the "Love Joy Palace." Later he moved to southern California. By the time of his death in 1992 at the age of seventy-four, he had returned to Mexico, addicted to illegal drugs and a fugitive from U.S. drug indictments.

Before his tragic death Erickson had funded countless researchers and organizations in the fields of homosexuality, transsexualism, and "New Age" spirituality. While this article's focus is his contribution to the field of homosexuality, the EEF was also responsible for many projects in other fields. For example, it funded Harry Benjamin, John Money, Richard Green, and other pioneers of treatment and research connected with transsexualism. The EEF also provided its own services, acting as a referral agency, publicizing news about transgender issues, and giving support to isolated individuals throughout the United States and around the world. The EEF worked with local and national news agencies to make information about transgenderism available to the public. In addition, it provided information for college classes and sent speakers to lecture about their personal experiences of gender. As a clearinghouse for transgendered and transsexual information, the EEF was an essential community resource for transgendered people and their supporters, all of whom lived and worked in isolation during those years. The EEF's work was so valuable to those it benefited that many people have kept copies of the informational pamphlets produced by the EEF for decades after its demise. Working in still other fields, Erickson sponsored workshops and research in spirituality and funded the first printing of *A Course in Miracles*, a three-volume set of channeled spiritual guidance that has been translated into nine languages and has sold over one and a half million copies worldwide.[36] He also encouraged and funded John Lily's work in dolphin communication.

One of Erickson's initial interests was to have the EEF work with those in the field of homosexuality, presumably because of his experience as a lesbian and because in those early days of trans activism, Erickson would no doubt have seen the fights for gay and trans rights as naturally allied. The partnership with ONE was the first one undertaken by the EEF. Eventually, Erickson's long-standing support of ONE enabled it to embark on much more elaborate projects than it otherwise would have been able to do. Further, the patterns of his philanthropy evidence an uncanny ability to pinpoint individuals and organizations who, although still near the beginnings of their long careers, would later become highly successful at their endeavors. His relationship with ONE was no exception.

ONE AND THE EEF: BUILDING A RELATIONSHIP

By the time ONE Inc. and the EEF came together in 1964, the former had already established itself as an educational center, whereas Erickson was just starting his own organization and looking for substantial projects to fund. ONE could help Erickson do both, and Erickson could help ONE with much-needed financial resources. Further, both Reed Erickson, the man behind the EEF, and Dorr Legg, the driving force of ONE, had strong personalities that challenged and stimulated each other. As such, their partnership had the potential to be highly productive.

ONE Inc. had taken the unprecedented step of opening a business office in downtown Los Angeles in 1953, and the place had soon become a de facto gay community center and hotline. The staff answered thousands of calls from people all over the United States asking for help with problems ranging from housing to arrests to psychological distress. Such requests came from gay men; lesbian women; bisexual, transgendered, and transsexual people; parents; and teachers. Thus ONE, moving toward the fulfillment of its stated goals, had taken steps to obtain property and to promote the integration of homosexuals into society, but when its landlord put the building that housed the organization's offices up for sale shortly after ONE had moved in, all that ONE had achieved seemed at risk.[37]

It was through the financial appeal that went out to ONE's mailing list that Erickson saw his first potential major funding project. Having spent a frantic year finding the space at 2256 Venice Boulevard after an earthquake had rendered the organization's original offices on Hill Street in downtown Los Angeles unsafe, the staff at ONE had panicked. Not wanting to be out on the street again so soon, they decided that they needed to buy the building themselves and sent a request for donations to their entire mailing list. Few responded, partly because ONE, having sold *ONE Magazine*, had lost its nonprofit status and could no longer offer charitable tax receipts to donors, and partly because many potential donors feared being identified with ONE's high-profile homosexuality.[38] Erickson was one of those few, and his offer of assistance with ONE's larger mission stood out as both generous and eccentric.[39]

According to Legg, "[The] first response was from someone named Reed Erickson. He made numerous phone calls for extended conversation with me. This was in 1963 but went no further at the time."[40] Then in July 1964, only days after the EEF had been incorporated, Erickson asked Legg to see him in Baton Rouge. Legg remembered that "the people here had said, in regard to going down there, 'this is just a Southern queen who wants a date for the weekend and was willing to send an airplane ticket.'"[41] Nevertheless, Legg bought a new suit to wear in the stifling heat and humidity of Baton Rouge in July and boarded an airplane headed east. Legg recalled:

> I was to change in New Orleans and I got on this ancient flapping plane which just barely cleared the tree tops, flapping on to Baton Rouge from New Orleans. I got to the airport which was no kind of an airport at all, it was just a little shanty really with a wire fence. Eight or ten people got off. Here on the other side of the wire fence was what looked to me like a blonde high school kid. I said, "Are you Reed Erickson?" and he said, "Yes," I just said, "I was expecting somebody older." And I thought, "Uhoh, maybe they were right." And so we went out and got into this very large car with a built-in telephone. Well, those weren't all that common in 1964. So I thought, "Well there's money here."[42] ...
>
> During the drive into town I learned I would be put up at a motel. The room turned out to be a veritable presidential suite. Once seated there he said, "Tell me about ONE." After hours of talk with only an occasional question from him he said we would now go over to his house to meet his lover. Entering an old fashioned frame house by the kitchen we went through rooms with bare floors, Southern summer style. Here was what might be a Brancusi, there what might be a Matisse. Now we would meet Henry, his lover. Turning on the lights of a large glassed in porch revealed what looked to me like a ten foot leopard. My host went in and the two proceeded to tumble and roll around with great gusto. I was invited to pat the leopard's head which I most gingerly did. Back to the motel for a few more questions, then a laconic, "I'm very glad you have come." He would return in the morning for more talk. Still no inkling as to why I was there.
>
> Around noon the next day he said, "We have a small foundation and have been observing your *ONE Institute Quarterly* with interest. Do you have any projects you would like funded?" Did we have projects? However, I knew that "consulting engineer" on the letterhead meant that he was not interested in projects as a category but *a project* capable of being presented in detail right then. Fortunately the best talked over [project] had been our long desired bibliography of homosexuality. If this was to be funded by him, I was told, I must go back to my board and set up a foundation for which he would pay. When I reported back to ONE's board their skepticism may well be imagined. A blonde high school student who wrestled with leopards? Clearly the heat in the South had got the best of me. After some weeks of their amused dismissal of my wild story reluctant approval was given to go ahead with the foundation, I flew to New York to complete the details in his beautiful apartment hard by the United Nations building. Thus the "Bibliography Project" was then put in motion, and eventually completed as a two-volume opus of more than 12,700 entries, by far the largest of its kind even yet [in 1993].[43] For the next twenty years other projects were funded. One day without any special reason the scales fell from my eyes and I realized that our benefactor, the small blonde boy, was a female to male transsexual, ONE's first large contributor.[44]

A savvy businessperson, Erickson suggested a solution to ONE Inc.'s tax problem. Under his direction and at his expense, the Institute for the Study of Human Resources (ISHR), a nonprofit corporation, was founded in August 1964, a short six weeks after his first meeting with Legg, for the purpose of accepting charitable donations. It could then donate the money to ONE Inc. or the ONE Institute as it saw fit. Legg chose ISHR's name in recognition of the human resources lost when repressive social attitudes toward homosexuality stifled the human spirit.[45] The title also reflected what the EEF described in an early brochure as the EEF's aim: "to assist where human potential [was] limited by physical, mental, or social conditions, or where the scope of research [was] too new, controversial, or imaginative to receive traditionally oriented support."[46] ISHR's mission greatly resembled the EEF's, reading in part: "to promote, assist, encourage and foster scientific research, study and investigation of male and female homosexuality and various other types of human behavior; to advance education."[47] ONE Inc.'s research, social service, and educational work now shifted to ISHR, which allowed ONE Inc. the freedom to work unabashedly for homosexual law reforms.[48] ISHR's acting directors were Legg (who was also the secretary), Tony Reyes, and Don Slater, all of whom had been among ONE Inc.'s founders. Erickson was named president, and his soon-to-be wife, Aileen Ashton, was made a founding director, a position she held until 1975.

While Erickson was interested in promoting homosexual law reform and ONE's specific goals, he had his own ideas about the programs that should be offered and the ways that EEF projects and ONE projects could function together. Since he controlled the lion's share of the funding, he greatly influenced ONE's direction during these crucial developmental years. His first $2,000 donation went toward the cost of incorporating ISHR, and by October 1964, even before its bylaws had been drawn up, he had sent another $1,000.[49] In December 1964 a check for $10,000 arrived at ISHR as a first installment on a "Research Study Project in the Bibliography of Homosexuality."[50] By January 1965 ISHR was receiving $1,000 a month from the EEF.[51] From 1964 to 1976, and again from 1980 to 1983, Erickson's foundation provided 70–80 percent of ISHR's operating budget.[52] In total, ISHR recorded having received over $200,000 in direct grants.[53] These monies were channeled through ISHR to ONE Institute's educational programs, to the development of the Blanche M. Baker Memorial Library, and to various other educational and research projects.

Thus the establishment of ISHR allowed Erickson a vehicle through which to make tax-exempt charitable donations to support the activities of ONE. There were other donors to ISHR and to ONE, but without Erickson's extensive, committed, and regular support, many of ONE's activities, and perhaps even ONE itself, would not have been possible to the extent that it was with EEF money.

The projects undertaken by ONE after its partnership with the EEF make it clear that Erickson had a significant influence over the direction of ONE. While he may not have been involved in its day-to-day operations as was Dorr Legg, his financial support encouraged the direction those activities would take. For example, one of the first ONE Institute projects, and the lengthiest, that the EEF funded was the bibliography that Legg had mentioned to Erickson at their first meeting. Almost from its inception ONE had had plans to address the dearth of positive information on homosexuality by compiling an annotated bibliography on it, but the project could not get off the ground until Erickson came on the scene. He agreed to fund it for three years, and work began in late 1964 under Slater, later succeeded by Julian Underwood. By 1966 ONE had published the first version of *An Annotated Bibliography of Homosexuality.*

In 1970, after Underwood's untimely death, Vern L. Bullough, professor of history at California State University, Northridge, and vice president of ISHR, assumed responsibility for the bibliography.[54] Bullough had already gathered over a thousand entries on his own, and he also brought with him an additional several thousand entries that he had received from Gershon Legman. As an editor, he was joined by Legg and Barrett Wayne Elcano and by James Kepner Jr., who assisted in the editing process. A two-volume *Annotated Bibliography of Homosexuality* was published in 1976 by Garland Press. The completed work contained 12,794 entries and constituted an unprecedented contribution to the study of homosexuality.[55]

While the bibliography project came to Erickson for funding preconceived, several other projects involved Erickson's own particular interests. For example, in June 1974 a widely publicized three-day "Forum on Variant Sex Behavior," organized by Vern L. and Bonnie Bullough, took place in Los Angeles under the auspices of ISHR.[56] The goal of the meeting was to "give physicians, social workers, psychologists, counselors, clergy, teachers and other professionals a concentrated overview of up-to-date information and recent developments concerning some of the less well known types of behavior."[57] Research findings, workshops, and field trips covered issues concerning transsexualism, incest, transvestism, sadomasochism, and male and female homosexuality. The speakers included Vern L. Bullough; Zelda Suplee, director of the EEF; Virginia Prince, editor of *Transvestia* and widely recognized pioneer of transgender activism; Laud Humphreys, author of *Tearoom Trade: Impersonal Sex in Public Places*; Christopher Isherwood, widely acclaimed author; and Evelyn Hooker, author of the revolutionary 1957 study "The Adjustment of the Male Overt Homosexual."[58] Attendees remembered fondly how they were moved by Isherwood's warm and deeply emotional introduction of banquet speaker Evelyn Hooker.[59]

In March 1975 a second event, "Sex, Role, and Gender," took place, with similar goals and format. This event was particularly innovative in that one could receive one credit-hour from California State University, Northridge, in return for attending, making a field trip to a homosexual or transvestite establishment, and writing a report. The speakers at this event included a panel of people identified as transvestites and transsexuals. Perhaps the highlight of the event, which drew several hundred people, was the keynote speech, in which Christine Jorgensen spoke of her own experiences in changing her sex and gender.[60]

Clearly, the two events encompassed both the interests of ONE and the EEF, but the increased presence of transgender and other sexual minority topics on the agenda was undoubtedly related to Erickson's influence. The organizations' other collaborative projects focused on strictly homosexual topics while also representing an overlap of the goals and methods of social reform that both organizations outlined. For example, the social scientific study of homosexuals *by* homosexuals was unprecedented at the time. Through an ISHR grant from the EEF, ONE Institute developed a questionnaire that it distributed to its five-thousand-person mailing list and analyzed during several semesters of ONE Institute Sociology courses (1965–69). A first report of the results was presented by Underwood at the February 1969 Mid-Winter Institute, and commentary was provided by a sociology professor, a psychiatrist in private practice, and Richard Green, director of UCLA's Gender Identity Clinic. Oddly, although one thousand questionnaires had been returned, they were winnowed down, for Underwood's presentation, to four hundred completed by gay men.[61]

In another significant, although more oblique, contribution to homosexuality research that was funded by the U.S. National Institute of Mental Health (NIMH), Hooker tested expert clinicians to see if they could distinguish between the psychological projective test results of a nonclinical sample of homosexual men and those of a nonclinical sample of heterosexual men. Hooker's results, which showed that the clinicians could not distinguish between the two groups, laid the groundwork for a profound change in professional and public opinion about homosexuality.[62] It was the first empirical evidence that homosexual men were just as psychologically healthy as heterosexual men. In 1967 Hooker accepted a request to chair the NIMH's Task Force on Homosexuality. But the NIMH did not immediately publish the results of the task force's study. Hooker had delivered many lectures for ONE Institute over the years, and the organization was anxious to see her groundbreaking work made public. With Erickson's funding, ONE Institute published the "Final Report of the NIMH Task Force on Homosexuality" before it was officially published by the U.S. government.[63]

Although Erickson's interest and participation in projects such as the professional forums on sexual variance and the publications of prohomosexuality research varied, ONE's and the EEF's goals and methods overlapped significantly, which indicates the importance of their relationship to the development of both organizations. For example, both were interested in creating social change by addressing legal inequities. Erickson fully funded a one-month speaking tour of the United States by the British homosexual legal activist Antony Grey in 1967. Grey had been a key figure in the campaign to legalize homosexuality in Britain through the Albany Trust and the Homosexual Law Reform Society, of which he was secretary (1962–70). When these organizations were formed, male homosexuality was illegal in Britain; male homosexuals were liable for up to two years' hard labor for engaging in any act of "gross indecency," whether public or private, consensual or not. The report of the Wolfenden Committee, released in 1957 (having been commissioned in 1954 in response to a series of scandalous court cases concerning homosexuality), had recommended the legalization of homosexual acts between consenting adults in private. The Homosexual Law Reform Society had been set up in the spring of 1958 to pressure the government to act on the recommendation. The Albany Trust, a nonpolitical charitable arm of the society, had been established "to promote psychological health through research, education, and appropriate social action." Grey was widely acknowledged as a key player in spearheading the campaign that culminated, almost ten years after the Wolfenden report, in the passage of the 1967 Sexual Offences Act, which legalized homosexuality.[64]

Legg met Grey in England in 1966, shortly before the Sexual Offences Act was passed.[65] A visit from Erickson and his wife soon followed. Then, shortly after the act had passed, Legg invited Grey to visit the United States. Erickson had agreed to sponsor a one-month coast-to-coast speaking tour so that the U.S. homophile movement might benefit from Grey's knowledge of effective law reform tactics.[66] Grey arrived in New York City in late October 1967 and was immediately set to work by Zelda Suplee, an unforgettably dynamic woman who had become Erickson's indispensable adviser as well as the public face of the EEF and who acted as Grey's press secretary during his visit. During the next four weeks Grey spoke at more than twenty-five lecture, television, and radio events during what he later described as "the most hectic four weeks of my life."[67] He also met with editors, lawyers, psychologists, clergy, police, and homophile groups in New York City, Chicago, Los Angeles, San Francisco, and Washington, DC, and with various professional groups, including researchers at the Kinsey Institute for Research in Sex, Gender, and Reproduction in Bloomington, Indiana; the psychologist Wardell Pomeroy (who worked closely with Alfred Kinsey); the endocrinologist Harry Benjamin (who had brought transsexualism to the attention of the medical community); and the lawyer Morris Ernst (who had defended the work of both Havelock Ellis and James Joyce against censorship charges). Grey was accompanied on this exhausting but comfortably appointed tour by Dorr Legg, and the entire mission was funded by Erickson's EEF through ISHR.[68]

Both ONE and the EEF were interested in providing educational materials for social change. For ONE, this interest had led to a sharp focus on formal educational opportunities in homophile studies, which the EEF eagerly and generously supported. Perhaps ONE's proudest accomplishment came in August 1981, when it received authorization from the state of California to be the first U.S. institution of higher learning to offer master's and doctoral degrees in homophile studies. Courses began in October, and the first degrees were awarded on January 30, 1982, at the thirtieth-anniversary celebration of the founding of ONE Inc. On this auspicious occasion, over six hundred people gathered in the Wilshire Room of the Los Angeles Hilton Hotel saw Erickson and Isherwood awarded honorary doctorates.[69] Remarkably, although Erickson was already a degree holder, this was the first and only college degree that Isherwood had at that time yet received.

Soon after the creation of the ONE Institute graduate school, Erickson suggested that a campus should be found to house the school, its libraries, ONE's business and "community center" offices, and the EEF's offices. The foundation's offices in Baton Rouge and New York City, like ONE's business offices, played a key role as a place to which transgendered and transsexual people could go for education and support. The EEF also had mailing addresses in El Paso, Texas; Los Angeles and Ojai, California; Phoenix, Arizona; and Panama City. Thus the idea of having one centralized location from which to run all these operations (including ONE and its projects) seemed timely. The idea was attractive to ONE because, among other reasons, the owner of 2256 Venice Boulevard had neglected the building, and its maintenance problems were becoming desperate.[70] Late in 1982 Legg met with real estate agent James Dunham, who then helped Erickson negotiate the purchase of an impressive property called "the Milbank Estate," which Erickson had seen only in photographs.[71] Dunham recalled Erickson telling him. "I am buying this property for ONE; we will show the straight world what we can do."[72] Elizabeth Clare Prophet's Church Universal and Triumphant, which occupied the estate at that time, was planning to move its headquarters to Montana. After some wrangling, a sale price of $1.9 million was agreed upon. However, as the completion of the deal neared, there was some concern that the church would not go through with the sale if it knew that the property would be used by a homosexual organization. For this reason, and also because of tax considerations, the ownership of the property was made out to the EEF.[73] A down payment of $95,000 was made, with $1.4 million due at the closing on February 17, 1983, and another $400,000 to be paid out by Erickson over the next four years.[74]

A few days before the closing, the EEF's secretary informed the Church Universal and Triumphant that the $1.4 million would not be available until February 26, nine days later than agreed. The church threatened legal action if the payment was late.[75] So Erickson retrieved $1.4 million in South African krugerrands he had stashed in a bank vault. On February 17 representatives from the church came to his home in Ojai in two cars and a recreational vehicle, accompanied by security guards and a large dog, to collect the krugerrands. For more than three hours, two of the men counted the gold coins and brought them to other men waiting outside in a camper, who weighed them and put them into plastic coin holders. When everyone was satisfied that the amount was correct, the people from the church, the security guards, and dog all went to a Wilshire Boulevard coin dealership, where the coins were delivered and commemorative photographs were taken.[76] At this point the deal between Erickson and the church was complete, and the coins were the property of the church. However, the coin dealership would accept only a limited amount of gold per day, so a week passed before all of it had changed hands. At the beginning of that week gold was selling at $508 an ounce, but by the end of the week the price had dropped to $368. The church lost a considerable sum of money as a result, and Erickson, who took some pleasure in his business acumen, claimed to have personally driven the price of gold down through this one transaction.[77]

Over the next six weeks, a crew of people from ONE unearthed and moved its library, archives, and other possessions out of the building on Venice Boulevard, where the organization had been located for twenty-two years. ONE proudly proclaimed: "A landmark event will be celebrated here May 1 [1983] when ONE Institute announces its occupancy of the historic Milbank Estate as its permanent campus for Homophile studies, the first such campus of its kind in the world."[78] Eight months later, on January 29, 1984, ONE Institute held an open house and convocation ceremony at the Milbank mansion during which they awarded one master's and two doctoral degrees in homophile studies, the world's first in that discipline.[79]

ONE AND ERICKSON: THE UNRAVELING OF A RELATIONSHIP

Unfortunately, it seemed that no sooner had the ink dried on the contract for the Milbank purchase than the first signs of trouble in the relationship between Erickson and ONE began to surface. The deed to the property was supposed to have been turned over to ONE at a gala event on May 1, 1983, but the transfer was postponed until June 1, and then Erickson apparently abandoned the idea altogether.[80] The problems between ONE and Erickson resulted partly from the intrusion of Erickson's personal problems into the business partnership, partly from longstanding concerns about the relationship between trans and gay politics in the collaborative efforts of ONE and the EEF, and partly from Erickson's desire to use ONE to support projects unrelated to homosexuality.

Like many others, Erickson had experimented with illegal drugs during the previous decade. In the beginning, his use was purely recreational and did not interfere with his ability to conduct his business interests effectively. However, by the early 1980s he had developed a serious drug dependency. Erickson became a regular user of ketamine, a veterinary anesthetic that produced hallucinations in humans, and of cocaine.[81] In addition, he used other recreational drugs, although less extensively. By the time of the Milbank Estate purchase, the cumulative effects of Erickson's drug use were profound. He was frequently difficult to deal with and was often highly distrustful and suspicious of others, particularly those closest to him. He had become uncharacteristically inattentive to his business interests, forgetful, and increasingly unreliable.[82] This trend culminated in a series of arrests for drug offenses during the 1980s. Erickson's subsequent failures to appear in court eventually resulted in the forfeiture of several pieces of real estate and of large sums of money.[83] He was also suffering from bladder cancer, which left him unable to walk and semiconscious for days at a time.[84]

At the same time, tensions were increasing among ONE's leadership concerning the direction in which Erickson's funding was taking them. Jim Kepner later placed more of the blame for the break between Erickson and ONE on Legg than on Erickson. He recalled that Legg "went a little ways off of his rocker" when Erickson refused to turn over the deed to the Milbank estate. But the trouble had started even earlier:

> When ONE got the degree-granting privileges...Reed immediately wanted several of his metaphysical and other of his acquaintances, and probably some people involved with dope, to be given degrees. And Dorr flatly refused. Well, under the circumstances, since Reed was paying the bill, I would say Dorr made a serious blunder. Or he should have at least tried to keep negotiations open in some way....It [also] reached the point where I began to get kind of nervous: is ONE primarily a homophile organization, or is it a transsexual organization? I felt it got kind of out of balance. I felt that we support these people on our borders. If transsexuals define themselves as gay, well then, they're part of our community; if they define themselves as straight, well, we'll counsel them or help them or so on, but they're not really part of our community, by their own definition.[85]

Clearly, Erickson's ideas about who was "on the borders" were markedly different from Legg's and Kepner's. Additionally, Erickson's drug use and increasingly controlling support of ONE led to a growing confusion among ONE's leaders about ONE's role in relation to other EEF projects.

Less than two weeks before ONE was to hold the convocation and open house at Milbank, and three weeks after Erickson's first arrest for possession of illegal drugs, ONE received a letter from Erickson in which his growing mental instability was evident. In that letter he stated: "I find I can no longer support one of my long-time favorite projects. If you do not find funding within two weeks from today (I already discussed this with you about a week ago), I must sell the property."[86] Attempts to negotiate a tenancy for ONE quickly failed. By May 1984 Erickson was trying to evict ONE from the premises and had filed suit against ONE in state court.

In light of Erickson's aggressive actions (and of those whom he hired) and after having moved from a low-rent location on Venice Boulevard to the expensive Milbank property, ONE faced possible ruin. Losing Erickson's support was devastating to the organization. To protect its interests, ONE obtained a series of restraining orders and injunctions against Erickson and the EEF. The effort of defending their hold on the Milbank estate effectively paralyzed much of ONE's public operations.[87] By 1986 ONE Institute had ceased to be an authorized degree-granting institution under California State law.[88] It did, however, continue to publish the *ONE Newsletter*, keep the library open for researchers, and offer the ONE lecture series.[89]

The battle for Milbank raged from 1983 to 1993. At times, Erickson called in armed guards to restrict access to the grounds. He admitted other tenants to the upper two floors of one of the houses that ONE was not occupying. Members of his family also became residents. ONE's files were rifled, and items went missing. ONE's leaders presumed that it was Erickson's doing. Legg and Erickson filed suit against each other. Seventy years old and increasingly disabled by his medical conditions and drug problem, Erickson then fled to Mexico to escape arrest on drug charges. Legg, himself eighty years old, still proved an able fighter. He later recalled with great enthusiasm the various altercations between Erickson and himself in the battle for control over Milbank, claiming that on one occasion he had been trapped inside the estate when the gates were welded shut and that on another Erickson had directed contractors to weld Legg's hands to the gates if he refused to move them.[90]

Late in 1988, Erickson's daughter Monica, then twenty years old, was appointed conservator of his affairs due to Erickson's ill health. In conjunction with her mother, Erickson's ex-wife Aileen, she continued to fight for possession and ownership of the Milbank estate. But on April 4, 1990, the title to Milbank was conveyed by court order to ONE and ISHR. That order was overturned by an appellate court and a new trial was ordered.[91] Appeals launched on behalf of the EEF and Erickson, who died early in 1992, continued until October of that year, when Monica Erickson, now his executor, agreed to a settlement. The property was to be divided between Erickson's heirs and ISHR. Monica Erickson took possession of the Milbank house, the tennis courts, and the surrounding lands, whereas ISHR received the McFie house, also known as the Arlington house; the chauffeur's quarters; a meditation sanctuary; and a few smaller service buildings. ISHR agreed to but never mounted a plaque on the Arlington house that was to acknowledge it as a gift from Reed Erickson and rename it Erickson House.[92] In 1992 the assessed value of the property received by ONE was over one million dollars.[93] By August 1, 1993, ONE had vacated the portion of the estate awarded to Monica Erickson and had turned the keys over to her.[94]

ONE INC. AFTER ERICKSON

As the relationship between Erickson and ONE deteriorated, so too had the ability of ONE to function at full capacity. For a decade most of ONE's human and financial resources had been engaged in the fight for the Milbank property. Moreover, the organization's primary source of income, the EEF's grants to ISHR, had ceased. For the first few years, Dorr Legg, Professor Walter L. Williams of the University of Southern California, and a few others had continued to provide courses to a handful of graduate students, but by the late 1980s only Legg still taught at the ONE Institute graduate school. Although he continued to do so until his death in 1994,[95] the institute granted no more degrees.

ONE's monthly lecture series continued at the Milbank property during the dispute. At first, the lectures were presented on the main floor of the Milbank house. When that building passed out of ONE's possession, the series moved to the Arlington house. In March 1995 ONE sold the Arlington house both to repay debts incurred after Erickson's funding had stopped and to pay back taxes on the portion of the Milbank property that ONE had received in the settlement.[96] The lecture series then moved to the chauffeur's quarters. After that too was sold in early 1997, the University of Southern California agreed to sponsor the lecture series, but the response on campus was sporadic. In 1998 the series was incorporated as "Community and Conversation Groups" into the Los Angeles Gay and Lesbian Center. Meanwhile, ONE's library also moved from the Milbank house to the Arlington house to the chauffeur's quarters and finally to the University of Southern California.[97]

In January 1995 ONE regained prominence by merging with the International Gay and Lesbian Archives (IGLA) under the name ONE Institute.[98] ISHR, which still functions as a separate entity, supported the move with a donation of thirty-five thousand dollars and has continued to provide grants to ONE Institute.[99] The process of amalgamation was initiated and shepherded to completion by Walter L. Williams, who worked with ONE, IGLA, ISHR, and the University of Southern California to broker a deal that would strengthen all parties concerned. The newly reconstituted ONE Institute dedicated itself to several projects: the lecture series, educational outreach, ONE Institute Press, the new Center for Advanced Studies, and the maintenance of the combined ONE library and the IGLA collection.[100]

Currently, the main work of ONE Institute Press is the production of an online journal, the *International Gay and Lesbian Review*, which has published hundreds of book reviews of special interest to gay and lesbian readers.[101] ONE Institute Press also established the ONE Institute Web site, which provides valuable research resources. Finally, it publishes some of the work of the scholars supported by the ONE Institute Center for Advanced Studies, and other related items.

The Center for Advanced Studies supports scholars of lesbian, gay, bisexual, and transgendered studies from around the world while they use ONE Institute's library collections. For example, between 1994 and 1998, under Williams's direction, the institute provided research grants and housing to visiting scholars in a nineteen-unit residence at the University of Southern California. Similar grants, provided through ISHR twice a year, are funded with the interest on monies gleaned from the sale of ONE's portion of the Milbank property and from generous bequests made to ISHR or ONE by Hall Call, David G. Cameron, and others.[102]

ONE Institute's extensive library and archival collection is the largest collection of gay and lesbian resource material in the world.[103] It is itself the result of the merging of two collections. The first, the International Gay and Lesbian Archives, was built on a collection that Kepner started in 1942 and worked on until his death in 1997. In 1971 Kepner first opened the collection to the public as the Western Gay Archives. Over the years it was also known as the National Gay Archives and as the Natalie Barney/Edward Carpenter Library of the International Gay and Lesbian Archives.[104] The second component of the present library originated with ONE's collection. The combined collections house over twenty thousand books, pamphlets, and scripts; over three thousand videos of films and television programs; over six thousand periodicals; clippings files with over one million items; hundreds of audio recordings; and a small museum of ephemera.[105] After extensive negotiations spearheaded by Williams, a building at 909 West Adams Boulevard on the University of Southern California campus was extensively renovated, largely with the university's financial support, to house the library. In May 2001 a gala opening took place.[106]

Thus, although ONE had encountered both great support and great difficulty in its uneasy collaboration with Reed Erickson and the Erickson Educational Foundation, it has regrouped and joined forces with other organizations that share its vision. Further, it has found a new benefactor in the University of Southern California. However, while ONE Institute continues to accrue public recognition, the work of Erickson and the EEF has gone virtually unnoticed. The proceeds from Erickson's philanthropy quietly continue to fund gay and lesbian research almost forty years after he saw the need for this support and offered his wealth and his expertise to provide it. The custodians of his donations, ISHR's board of directors, have conservatively invested the profits from the sale of the Milbank property and use the income to make small grants in support of gay and lesbian research connected to ONE Institute.[107] In this way Erickson's contributions continue to provide support quietly behind the scenes. ONE Institute thrives once again because of the hard work of dedicated individuals and the financial contributions of many. Yet without the generosity of one crucial benefactor, ONE's success would most likely now be only a chapter in the history of gay and lesbian activism.

LOOKING BACK, MOVING ON

The relationship between ONE and Reed Erickson and the EEF ultimately ended in dissolution. A combination of factors was responsible, but several important points should be remembered. Both ONE and the EEF had common goals. They both sought to create social change through education, publicity, and the support of marginalized people. Both fostered research that contributed to the social acceptability of marginalized people and that was grounded in fact rather than in prejudice. Both recognized the need for substantial financial support of organizations working on such issues. Leaders of both organizations, mindful of their own experiences, strove to make the world a better place for others. Perhaps most significantly, both organizations recognized the need to work together as communities of marginalized people to effect significant and lasting change.

The story of the organizations' relationship is thus an important one not only for historians but also for activists and community members. The partnership, its problems, and its lessons provide us with valuable insights into the factors that can contribute to effective (or dysfunctional) relationships between transgender and homosexual groups. Since ONE has continued as an institution after the collapse of the EEF, the evidence we are left with and the versions of the story that remain in circulation are mainly from the perspective of ONE and its members. Erickson's personal and professional papers are much more difficult to trace than those of ONE, and many of his closest friends either are guarded in their comments or have died. It is thus unfortunate, both for Erickson and for gay, lesbian, bisexual, and transgender history, that a significant portion of the story remains as yet untold, and it is imperative that the contributions of transgendered and transsexual activists of the past do not go unnoticed.

Although ONE was a relatively unusual organization in the 1950s and 1960s, by the 1970s gay and lesbian social activism had proliferated rapidly. Other individuals and organizations had taken up the work of education and research about homosexuality; courses and programs of gay and lesbian studies had sprung up at many colleges and universities in Europe and North America. As of this writing, however, there are still no other U.S. institutions that offer graduate degrees in an area comparable to ONE's homophile studies.[108]

Much of the recent growth of gay and lesbian pride was built on an ethnic-like gay identity that necessarily defined inclusion by the exclusion of others. Gay and lesbian pride has been created at least partly to counteract a society that taught gays and lesbians to be ashamed of who they are.[109] As gays and lesbians have found their pride, many have retreated in shame from the transgendered and transsexual people who had always been among them. This shunning of transgendered and transsexual people remains a dark corner in the struggle for gay and lesbian rights. Transgendered and transsexual people have understood the need for alliances and have made many important contributions to the fight for lesbian, gay, bisexual, and transgendered rights.[110] Reed Erickson was only one of the untold numbers of unsung transgendered and transsexual people who have given generously to a movement that has not always appreciated their gifts. By making more people aware of this one transsexual man's tremendous contributions to the growth and development of a vital arm of the gay and lesbian movement, we hope to have contributed to a reappraisal of the value of a united lesbian, gay, bisexual, and transgender movement. The story of the relationship between ONE and the EEF reminds us of the challenges of creating and maintaining a unified movement. It is important that we recognize the need to work together toward common goals and that as we do so we remember that, as Erickson (and Carlyle) so rightly recognized, we are all one.

NOTES

1.   Joshua Gamson. "Must Identity Movements Self-Destruct? A Queer Dilemma," in *Queer Theory/Sociology*, ed. Steven Seidman (Cambridge, MA: Blackwell, 1996), 395–420; Steven Seidman, "Introduction," in Seidman *Queer Theory/Sociology*, 1–29.
2.   Jeffrey Weeks, *Sex, Politics, and Society: The Regulation of Sexuality since 1800* (London: Longman, 1981), 96–121.
3.   Ray Blanshard, "The Case for Publicly Funded Transsexual Surgery," *Psychiatry Rounds* 4, no. 2 (2000): 4–6; Richard von Krafft-Ebing, *Psychopathia Sexualis: With Especial Reference to the Antipathic Sexual Instinct,* trans. Franklin S. Klaf (New York: Stein and Day, 1965), 186–307.
4.   Gay and Lesbian Archives of the Pacific Northwest, "J. Allen Gilbert Papers," home. telport.com/~glapn/ar03012.html (accessed November 5, 2003).
5.   Esther Newton, "The Mythic Mannish Lesbian: Radclyffe Hall and the New Woman," *Signs* 9 (1984): 557–75: Jay Prosser, *Second Skins: The Body Narratives of Transsexuality* (New York: Columbia University Press, 1998), 135–69.
6.   Donna Minkowitz, "Love Hurts," *Village Voice*, April 19, 1994, 24–30; Kathleen Chapman and Michael Du Plessis, " 'Don't Call Me Girl': Lesbian Theory, Feminist Theory, and Transsexual Identities," in *Cross Purposes: Lesbians, Feminists, and the Limits of Alliance*, ed. Dana Heller (Bloomington: Indiana University Press, 1997), 169–85; Brigitte Eriksson, "A Lesbian Execution in Germany, 1721: The Trial Records," *Journal of Homosexuality* 6, nos. 1–2 (1981): 27–40; Nan Alamilla Boyd, "The Materiality of Gender: Looking for Lesbian Bodies in Transgender History," in *Lesbian Sex Scandals: Sexual Practices, Identities, and Politics*, ed. Dawn Atkins (New York: Haworth, 1999). 73–81. The Lesbian Herstory Archives listed transman Brandon Teena as among "lesbians" who had recently died in "In Memory of the Voices We Have Lost." *Lesbian Herstory Archives Newsletter*, January 1995, 7.
7.   The Erickson Educational Foundation (EEF) provided a panoply of support services for transgendered and transsexual people but did not frame itself as a political organization. Rather, it was constituted, as its name suggests, as an *educational* organization. Transgendered people were organizing as early as 1967 in San Francisco. See Members of the Gay and Lesbian Historical Society of Northern California. "MTF Transgender Activism in the Tenderloin and Beyond, 1966–1975: Commentary and Interview with Elliot Blackstone." *GLQ* 4 (1998): 349–72. By 1971 the EEF was funding some of the work of San Francisco's National Transsexual Counseling Unit, which had grown out of earlier activism. For current organizing of female-to-male transgendered people see FTM International, www.ftmi.org. For general transgender information see Gender Education and Advocacy, www.gender.org; and the International Foundation for Gender Education, www.ifge.org.
8.   Dallas Denny, "You're Strange and We're Wonderful: The Relationship between the Gay/Lesbian and Transgendered Communities." *TransSisters*, Autumn 1994, 21–23; Chryss Cada, "Issue of Transgender Rights Divides Many Gay Activists," *Boston Sunday Globe*, April 23, 2000, posted on Gender Advocacy Network News, "News Remail," April 26, 2000, www.tgender.net/news/gain.html.
9.   Martin Duberman, *Stonewall* (New York: Dutton, 1993).
10.   Gamson, "Self-Destruct," 408–11.
11.   "One of the first things I told them [Olivia Records] when we had our initial meeting and got to like each other very much," Stone says, "was that I was a transie. What I didn't tell them was that I was still in transition . . . simply because I felt it was personal information and I wasn't ready to share it. So at the time I started working at Olivia, I was actually preoperative. They didn't know that, and I didn't know it was volatile. I figured I would tell them at some point when we got to know each other better" (Davina Anne Gabriel, "Interview with the Transsexual Vampire: Sandy Stone's Dark Gift," *TransSisters*, Spring 1995, 17).
12.   "To the best of my knowledge," Stone recalls, "there was never a faction within Olivia that wanted to oust me. . . . When the boycott began to be threatened, we had to sit down and do some serious thinking. And there was a point where the collective said, 'Sandy, the reality of the situation is that if you don't leave, there's real danger.' And so I left" (Gabriel, "Interview," 18).
13.   Janice Raymond, *The Transsexual Empire: The Making of the She-Male* (Boston: Beacon, 1979), 129, 5.

14. *The Transsexual Empire* was reissued in 1994 by Teachers College Press with no changes other than the addition of a new introduction on transgenderism. See also Ann Cvetkovich and Selena Wahng, "Don't Stop the Music: Roundtable Discussion with Workers from the Michigan Womyn's Music Festival," *GLQ* 7 (2001): 131–51.

15. Nancy Jean Burkholder, "A Kinder, Gentler Festival?" *TransSisters*, November–December 1993. 4–5; Davina Anne Gabriel, "Mission to Michigan II: Exiles at Mecca." *TransSisters*, November–December 1993, 19–24, 27; Gabriel, "Mission to Michigan III: Barbarians at the Gates," *TransSisters,* Winter 1995, 14–23; Gabriel, "Mission to Michigan IV: No Room at the Information Table," *TransSisters*, Autumn 1995. 20–29; "In Your Face News Interview with Riki Anne Wilchins," August 25, 1999, www.camptrans.com/stories/interview.html.

16. Candice Elliot Brown, "The Gay, Lesbian, and Feminist Backlash,"www.transhistory.org/history/index.html (accessed March 13, 2000).

17. National Gay and Lesbian Task Force, "NGLTF Adopts New Mission Statements; New Board Co-Chairs and Members Named," September 23, 1997. www.ngltf.org/news/release.cfm?releaseID=105.

18. Parents, Families and Friends of Lesbians and Gays, "PFLAG Votes 'Yes' Overwhelmingly to Include Transgender in Mission," September 23, 1998, www.pflag.org/press/releases/923b.html.

19. The involvement of transgendered people in the Millennium March for Equality did not occur without difficulties. Much of the planning took place without their inclusion, and the transgendered speakers, Jamison Green, Dana Rivers, and Riki Anne Wilchins, were not allowed to speak for the agreed-on length of time (Penni Ashe Matz, editorial, posted on Gender Advocacy Network, "News Remail," listserv, May 10, 2000, www.gender.org/news/gain/html.).

20. Human Rights Campaign, "HRC and Gender Identity," March 2001, www.hrc.org.

21. W. Dorr Legg, introduction to *Homophile Studies in Theory and Practice*, ed. W. Dorr Legg et al. (Los Angeles: ONE Institute Press; San Francisco: GLB, 1994), 1–6.

22. C. Todd White, "Dale Jennings (1917–2000): ONE's Outspoken Advocate," in *Before Stonewall: Activists for Gay and Lesbian Rights in Historical Context*, ed. Vern L. Bullough (New York: Harrington Park, 2002), 85.

23. Legg, introduction to *Homophile*, 2.

24. Ibid., 3; ONE Inc., "Articles of Incorporation and By-Laws, 1953," in Legg, *Homophile*, 339.

25. The articles of incorporation state that ONE's purposes were "1. To publish and disseminate magazines, brochures, leaflets, books and papers concerned with medical, social, pathological, psychological and therapeutic research of every kind and description pertaining to sociosexual behavior. 2. To sponsor, supervise and conduct educational programs, lectures and concerts for the aid and benefit of all social and emotional variants and to promote among the general public an interest, knowledge and understanding of the problems of such persons. 3. To stimulate, sponsor, aid, supervise and conduct research of every kind and description pertaining to sociosexual behavior. 4. To promote the integration into society of such persons whose behavior varies from current moral and social standards and to aid the development of social and moral responsibility in all such persons. 5. To lease, purchase, hold, have, use and take possession of and enjoy any personal or real property necessary for the uses and purposes of the corporation."

26. The first out-of-state subscription check came from Alfred C. Kinsey (W. Dorr Legg, "Exploring Frontiers: An American Tradition," *New York Folklore* 19 [1993]: 228).

27. "40-Year Dedicated Activist Dorr Legg Dies at 89." *ONE-IGLA Bulletin*. Spring 1995, www.use.edu/isd/archives/onei-gla/bulletin/articles/LeggBio.html; Legg. *Homophile*, 17.

28. David G. Cameron. "ONE Institute" and "Architecture Notes" (flyer prepared for the Da Camera Society of Mount St. Mary's College on the occasion of the Chamber of Music in Historic Sites concert. March 25, 1984), International Gay and Lesbian Archives (IGLA) collection. At its height *ONE Magazine* had a circulation of eleven thousand (ONE, "ONE 1952-1982: Thirty Year Celebration; Program of Events," 1982, collection of Aaron H. Devor).

29. Legg, *Homophile*. 52–53; Walter L Williams, interview by Aaron H. Devor, tape recorded via telephone to Palm Springs, CA, May 12, 2000.

30. Legg, *Homophile*, 18.

31. Ibid., 32–50; ONE, "Program." According to Legg, the lectures in New York were given in 1968 *(Homophile*, 50); according to the "Program," they were given in 1966.

32. Reid Rasmussen, interview by Aaron H. Devor, tape recorded via telephone to Los Angeles, April 20, 2000; Walter L. Williams, interview by Aaron H. Devor, tape recorded via telephone to Palm Springs, CA, April 23, 2000. According to Legg, the lecture series began in 1958 *(Homophile*, 50); according to the ONE "Program," it began in 1956.

33. Legg, *Homophile*, 21—22.

34. Erickson Educational Foundation, brochure, collection of Aaron H. Devor.

35. *Erickson Educational Foundation Newsletter*, Spring 1983, 5.

36. "Introduction to a Course in Miracles," www.acim.org/about_acim_section/into_to_acim.html (accessed November 7, 2003).

37. Legg, *Homophile*, 16.

38. W. Dorr Legg to Evelyn Hooker, February 8, 1968, IGLA collection.

39. W. Dorr Legg, interview by Vern L. Bullough, Los Angeles, December 15, 20, and 29, 1993.

40. W. Dorr Legg to Thomas Hunter Russell, January 24, 1989, IGLA collection.

41. Legg interview.

42. Ibid.

43. Vern L. Bullough et al., eds., *An Annotated Bibliography of Homosexuality*, 2 vols. (New York: Garland, 1976).

44. Legg, "Frontiers," 233.

45. Ibid., 232.

46.   *Erickson Educational Foundation Newsletter*, Spring 1972, 1.
47.   ISHR, "Articles of Incorporation and By-Laws," n.d., IGLA collection.
48.   W. Dorr Legg to "Mort," February 14, 1968, IGLA collection.
49.   William Kraker to Reed Erickson, October 15, 1964, IGLA collection.
50.   W. Dorr Legg to William Kraker. December 23, 1964, IGLA collection.
51.   Taylor, Porter, Brooks, Fuller & Phillips to Chester A. Usry of the Internal Revenue Service, in response to Usry's letter of March 31, 1965. n.d., IGLA collection.
52.   David G. Cameron, interview by Aaron H. Devor, tape recording, Los Angeles, May 14, 1996: James Kepner Jr., interview by Aaron H. Devor, tape recording, Los Angeles, May 13, 1996.
53.   "A year by year listing of EEF funds received by ISHR and purpose for which they were spent," enclosure, Legg to Russell, IGLA collection. Kepner (interview) recalled that Legg had received additional checks made out to him personally and that other individuals who worked for ONE had received money directly from Erickson or the EEF, in addition to the grants listed by Legg as having been issued to ISHR.
54.   From 1964 to 1976 Bullough received sixty thousand dollars from Erickson for this project and for his other early work on (homo)sexuality (Vern L. Bullough, interview by Aaron H. Devor, tape recording, Los Angeles, May 30, 1996).
55.   Legg, *Homophile*, 53–56.
56.   Bullough interview.
57.   Legg, *Homophile*, 384.
58.   Laud Humphreys, *Tearoom Trade: Impersonal Sex in Public Places* (Chicago: Aldine, 1970); Legg, *Homophile*, 384–85; Evelyn Hooker, "The Adjustment of the Male Overt Homosexual," *Journal of Projective Technique* 21 (1957): 18–31.
59.   Legg, *Homophile*, 47.
60.   Ibid., 48, 386–87.
61.   Ibid., 128–30.
62.   Hooker, "Adjustment," 18–31.
63.   Legg, *Homophile*, 159.
64.   Antony Grey, interview by Aaron H. Devor, tape recording, London, August 23, 1999.
65.   Legg, *Homophile*, 60.
66.   Grey interview.
67.   *Erickson Educational Foundation Newsletter*, Spring 1968, 2, collection of Aaron H. Devor; Antony Grey, *Quest for Justice: Towards Homosexual Emancipation* (London: Sinclair-Stevenson, 1992), 142.
68.   Grey, *Quest*, 142–60.
69.   Legg, *Homophile*, 74–77: Legg interview. According to the ONE "Program," presentations at the banquet were also made by Lisa Ben, Del Martin, and Phyllis Lyon. Ben was publisher of *Vice Versa*, "the earliest known American periodical especially for Lesbians. Nine typewritten issues were privately distributed. June 1947–Feb. 1948." Martin and Lyon in 1955 had founded the Daughters of Bilitis, "the earliest lesbian emancipation organization in the U.S.…. dedicated to understanding of, and by, the lesbian" (Legg, "Frontiers," 235).
70.   Legg interview.
71.   The 3.5-acre property known as the Milbank Estate was named after Isaac Milbank, who had commissioned its creation in 1913. In that year Milbank, who had been a vice president and the general manager of the company that later became Borden Milk, was president of the corporation that developed the Country Club Estates area of Los Angeles, so named for its previous use as the Los Angeles Country Club. The Mediterranean-style twenty-seven-room mansion, designed by G. Lawrence Stimson, cost the then huge sum of thirty-five thousand dollars. It was joined by a smaller, but still grand, Georgian-style residence for Milbank's daughter Phila and his son-in-law Lyman McFie and by several lesser buildings used for recreation and service purposes. The Milbanks and the McFies lived in these homes until their deaths in 1976.
72.   *Erickson v. Legg*, C 499 120 (c/w C 520 792, C 541 097, C 693 216) U.S. p. 4 (n.d.). Trial brief and related cross-actions and consolidated actions. IGLA collection.
73.   Legg wrote to Erickson that "the idea of putting the Milbank property temporarily in the name of Erickson Educational Foundation seems to make good sense." W. Dorr Legg to Reed Erickson, January 14, 1983. IGLA collection; *Erickson v. Legg*, C 499 120 (c/w C 520 792, C 541 097, C 693 216) U.S. p. 5 (n.d.). Trial brief and related cross-actions and consolidated actions. IGLA collection; Walter Williams recalled that Legg objected to this arrangement but that Erickson insisted that it was the best way to proceed (Williams interview, May 12, 2000). Monica Erickson recalled that it was never her father's intention to give title to ONE (e-mail message to Aaron H. Devor, October 21, 2003).
74.   James Dunham, interview by Aaron H. Devor, tape recording, Los Angeles, June 12, 1996.
75.   Edward L. Francis to Reed Erickson, February 14, 1983, IGLA collection.
76.   Dunham interview; Helen Kleinstiver, interview by Aaron H. Devor, tape recording, Baton Rouge, LA, July 25, 1997.
77.   Kleinstiver interview.
78.   W. Dorr Legg, press release, April 20, 1983, IGLA collection.
79.   Legg, *Homophile,* 413.
80.   Zelda Suplee to W. Dorr Legg, August 17, 1987, IGLA collection; Zelda Suplee to Antony Grey, June 1984, quoted in Grey interview.
81.   Ketamine has more recently become a popular street and "club" drug also known as K, Ket, Special K, Vitamin K, and Kit Kat. For more information see the National Clearinghouse for Alcohol and Drug Information, www.health.org/pubs/qdocs/ketamine/index.htm.

82.   Monica Erickson, interview by Aaron H. Devor, tape recording, Los Angeles, June 3, 1996: Suplee to Grey, June 1984, quoted in Grey interview.

83.   Zelda Suplee to Antony Grey, September 26, 1985, quoted in Grey interview.

84.   Monica Erickson, handwritten declaration. April 25, 1984, IGLA collection: *California v. Erickson*, FY15759 U.S. 1 (1984). Declaration of Michael S. Pratter, IGLA collection.

85.   Kepner interview.

86.   Reed Erickson to ONE Institute, January 3, 1983 [*sic*], stamped received January 9, 1984. In January 1983 the Milbank property still belonged to the Church Universal and Triumphant. The correct date of the letter therefore is probably January 3, 1984.

87.   *Erickson v. Legg*, C 499 120 (c/w C 520 792, C 541 097, C 693 216) U.S. p. 8 (n.d.). Trial brief and related cross-actions and consolidated actions, IGLA collection.

88.   Jack L. Housden. of the State of California Council for Private Postsecondary and Vocational Education, to W. Dorr Legg, March 18, 1992. IGLA collection.

89.   Williams interview, May 12, 2000.

90.   Legg interview.

91.   *Erickson v. Legg*, B0 51473, CA LASC No. C 499 120, consolidated with C 502 792, C 541 207, C 693 216, CA2/7 4 (1991). Respondents' brief, IGLA collection. That the court order was overturned and a new trial ordered was confirmed by Monica Erickson, e-mail message to Devor.

92.   Thomas Hunter Russell to Michael S. Pratter and Alfred R. Keep, October 21, 1992, IGLA collection; Monica Erickson, e-mail message to Devor.

93.   County Assessor's Records, "Data Concerning the Milbank Estate," IGLA collection.

94.   W. Dorr Legg to Monica Erickson, August 1, 1993, IGLA collection.

95.   Williams interview, April 23, 2000.

96.   Westland Escrow, amended escrow instructions, March 8, 1995, collection of ISHR.

97.   Williams interview, April 23, 2000; Rasmussen interview.

98.   "ONE and IGLA Merge," *ONE-IGLA Bulletin*, Spring 1995, www.usc.edu/isd/archives/oneigla/bulletin/articles/ONE_IGLA_Merge.html.

99.   "ISHR Awards $35,000 to General Fund," *ONE-IGLA Bulletin*, Winter 1998, www.usc.edu/isd/archives/oneigla/bulletin/articles/ISHR.html; Rasmussen interview; Walter L. Williams to Aaron H. Devor, May 12, 2000.

100.   "ONE and IGLA Merge"; Ernie Potvin, "ONE Institute Organization and Activities," January 25, 1998, www.usc.edu/isd/archives/oneigla/organization_and_activities.htm.

101.   See *International Gay and Lesbian Review*, www.usc.edu/isd/archives/oneigla/onepress.

102.   Williams interview. April 23, 2000; Rasmussen interview.

103.   Williams interview, April 23, 2000.

104.   Ernie Potvin, "A Brief History of ONE Institute and the International Gay and Lesbian Archives (IGLA)," January 25, 1998, www.usc.edu/isd/archives/oneigla/background.html. According to Williams, Kepner provided the archives with an alternative name, the Natalie Barney/Edward Carpenter Library, as early as 1979. By 1985 that name was rarely used, and it was formally abandoned in 1994 (Williams to Devor).

105.   Potvin, "ONE Institute Organization"; www.oneinstitute.org.

106.   ONE Institute and Archives, "ONE's Grand Opening, May 6, 2001," www.usc.edu/isd/archives/oneigla/grandopening/page1.html (accessed July 25, 2001); Williams interview, April 23, 2000.

107.   Williams interview, April 23, 2000.

108.   John G. Younger, "University LGBT Programs, Lesbian, Gay, Bisexual, Transgender, and Queer Studies in the USA and Canada plus Sibling Societies and Study-Abroad Programs," March 28, 2000, www.duke.edu/web/jyounger/lgbprogs.html.

109.   Sally R. Munt, "Introduction," in *Butch/Femme: Inside Lesbian Gender*, ed. Sally R. Munt (London Cassell 1998) 1–12.

110.   Leslie Feinberg, *Transgender Warriors: Making History from Joan of Arc to RuPaul* (Boston: Beacon, 1996), 90–99.

27

"I Went to Bed With My Own Kind Once"

The Erasure of Desire in the Name of Identity

DAVID VALENTINE

DAVID VALENTINE IS AN ANTHROPOLOGIST whose doctoral fieldwork in New York City coincided with the emergence of "transgender" as an identity category, a tool for activism, and a label applied by medicine and social science. In this article, drawn from his fieldwork, Valentine argues that the conceptual distinction between sexuality and gender that underpins contemporary notions of heterosexual, homosexual, bisexual, and transgender identities fails to account for the specificity of erotic desire and sexual practice. He further claims that the "double binary" of homo/hetero and masculine/feminine, which presumably maps all possible sexual identity and gender identity positions, is a raced and classed construct that systematically renders unintelligible structures of desire and identification that take shape among many poor people, and many people of color.

Valentine's article revolves around a particularly instructive discussion recorded at the Alternative Lifestyles support group in Manhattan's Lower East Side in 1996. He recounts and interprets the discursive encounter between "transgender" as a concept wielded by social service institutions (represented in the person of a self-identified "transsexual heterosexual woman" who worked as a peer educator in a variety of social service agencies) and Miss Angel, whose narratives of personal identity and erotic desire could not be mapped easily onto the conventional grid of sexuality and gender, but who nevertheless resisted being called "transgender."

Valentine supports the cultural, political, and civil rights recognition afforded to many gender variant people through claiming the "transgender" label as a tool for activism and organizing, nevertheless, he contends that those who arguably have the greatest need for a progressive politics of gender and sexuality are precisely those who are most at risk of exclusion from identity-based movements, and identity-based models social service provision. This exclusion, he claims, occurs because the desires of these marginalized individuals are perceived by others to be confused, to the degree that they fail to accord with the ontological and epistemological assumptions that structure the contemporary categories of gender and sexuality themselves.

1. INTRODUCTION

What does it mean to talk about erotic desire? By this, I mean two inter-related things: what does it mean to talk about desire in a scholarly context; and what does it mean to talk about one's own desires? In the contemporary USA, popular discussions of erotic desire are drawn inevitably into a discussion of 'sexuality,' one which—again, inevitably—occurs against and invokes the binary of hetero/homosexual identity (troubled perhaps by the evidence of bisexuality, though even with bisexuality, desire is seen to lie discretely within the bounds of an identity category, namely 'bisexual'). Within queer, feminist, and anthropological scholarship, Foucault's famous point—that sexual identity has come to stand as the truth of who we are (Foucault, 1990[1980], pp. 51–73)—has been utilized to show how, since the late nineteenth century in the West, the erotic is not expressed as particular desires but, rather, as discrete identities. Foucault and others (e.g. Weeks, 1981; Katz, 1995) have pointed to the power of identity categories to both proliferate discourses about, and simultaneously restrain, talk of erotic desire as an experience which bears the name 'sexuality.' Erotic desires which fall outside the trinary of heterosexuality, homosexuality (either/or) and bisexuality (both/and), or which fail to make sense in terms of their basic logic of binary gender, are rendered unintelligible. Such 'unintelligible' desires present a unique opportunity for scholars to investigate the complexity of erotic desire, its expression in practice (linguistic and otherwise), and its relationship to identity categories.

Yet, despite the influence of Foucault, the troubling nature of desire-beyond-sexual identity has received relatively little attention. Since the early 1990s, many anthropologists have indeed pointed out that Western sexual identities and identity labels cannot make sense of—and indeed, are complicated by—non-Western sexual practices and desires (e.g. Blackwood, 1995; Donham, 1998; Johnson, 1997; Kulick, 1998). However, there has been little corresponding work which looks explicitly at the erratic connections between erotic desire and identity in US settings outside of immigrant communities (e.g. Manalansan, 1997). Most anthropologists of sexuality in the USA have tended to follow the basic anthropological tenet of using one's informants' categories to describe them. Consequently, gay men and lesbians—the usual subjects of discussions of 'sexuality' in the anthropological literature—are usually discussed in terms of those categories of identity which are meaningful to informants. As a result, the ontological assumptions which underpin these emic categories are left unexamined (e.g. Lewin, 1993; Shokeid, 1995; Weston, 1991). While attention to study subjects' self-categorization is clearly central to the anthropological enterprise, critical analyses of those categorizations is also vital to analysis.

If anthropology (and other social sciences) has neglected the ontological underpinnings of desire, there has been even less work in linguistics and linguistic anthropology which takes up the deeper implications of considering language and desire. As Kulick (2000) points out, much of the work that takes on the relationship between language and erotic desire has coalesced around a discussion of 'sexuality,' usually focusing on gay- and lesbian-identified (and occasionally transgender-identified) subjects. As with the studies I mentioned above, this work similarly depends for its analysis on a close identification with study participants' self-identity as gay and lesbian. But, as Kulick points out, there is a central flaw in much of this work, drawing as it does on a tautology: people who are lesbian and gay speak in a way that is defined as 'gay language'; and people who talk a 'gay language' are, thus, gay. Kulick argues that such studies continuously capitulate to a sexuality=identity formula. To move beyond this dynamic, Kulick proposes a reorientation of 'language and sexuality' studies from a focus on sexual identity to a focus on desire. He argues that a focus on desire will both complicate understandings of what 'sexuality' is and enable an examination of the relationship between linguistic practices and sexuality that is not constrained by identity categories.

Central to Kulick's argument is a critique of the essentialism implicit in much of the work on language and sexuality. This critique draws on a central tenet of contemporary social theory: that essentialized categories of identity obscure the crosscutting nature of social experience and identification. Being 'gay' or 'lesbian' for example, is experienced by different people in radically different ways depending on their racial identification, location, age, social class, personal history, and so forth. What is less clear, though, is that such categories of identity achieve a density of meaning through their reiteration, even in scholarly work that attempts to disrupt that meaning. By this I mean that even scholars who take a critical approach to essentialized identities require some baseline understandings about bodies and practices, about the relationship between signifier and signified, in order to mount a critique in the first place.

To take the examples of 'gay' and 'lesbian' once more, while we might accept that very different kinds of people may use these categories in identifying themselves, there are also some basic assumptions that flow from the organization of the categories themselves. Primary among these is that people who identify as 'gay' or 'lesbian' are understood as unambiguously men or women, and that they direct their desire to others who are, respectively, unambiguously men or women. That is, these categories rest implicitly on the logic of binary gender which underpins the homo/hetero identity structure, a structure which requires clearly gendered men and women to desire one another (or each other).

For those people who are not unambiguously gendered, the category 'transgender' has, since the early 1990s, become ubiquitous (by people so identified and in scholarly texts) to encapsulate this experience. 'Transgender' has become both a powerful tool of activism and a convenient label for social scientific research in bringing together a range of social and medicalized identities formerly seen as separate including, but not limited to, transsexuals, cross-dressers, drag queens,[1] and intersex people. Indeed, the power of the category is that it is actively seen as a collective term to gather in all non-normative expressions of gender, no matter how they are labeled. Another central element of contemporary discourses of 'transgender' is that transgender identities are seen to emanate from the experience of 'gender,' not 'sexuality.' In other words, transgender identities are conceptualized as quite distinct from homosexual identities, which are seen to have their source in 'sexuality.'

At the same time, it is important to note that even in discussions of transgender-identified[2] people, sexual desire is still generally encoded as either heterosexual or homosexual (or, indeed, bisexual). That is, sexual identity is usually claimed by transgender-identified people in accordance with their gender of identity. While most transgender-identified people insist on the differences between homosexuality and transgender identity (a significant point I will return to), many also identify as homosexual, based on their erotic and affective attraction to people who share the same gender category with which they identify. However, to reiterate, in contemporary scholarship and activism these identities are seen to flow from distinct kinds of ontological sources—transgender identity from 'gender,' and homosexual or heterosexual identity from 'sexuality.'

As such, this seems like a very neat system, which accounts both for gender identification and erotic desire within a double binary of homosexual/heterosexual and masculinity/femininity, with their roots respectively in yet another binary: that of sexuality and gender. But things are not always so clear cut, for frequently, as I will show, erotic desires expressed in speech can conflate, confuse, and contradict this neatness.

2. LANGUAGE AND DESIRE

As I noted above, 'talking about desire' in this paper refers not only to scholarly discussions of desire, but also points to the place where such an investigation might begin. One of the problems in 'talking about desire' (in a scholarly sense) is defining what 'desire' might mean; indeed there is a great difficulty in defining such an object, particularly for anthropologists, leery of psychological and individualistic explanations for human action (see Kulick, 2000, 2003). Here, however, I propose that one approach may be to simply listen to what people have to say about their desires without trying to account for them only in terms of identity categories. Indeed, my suggestion is to listen to talk-about-desire to see what that talk can tell us about identity categories. In paying attention to expressed erotic desire—whether in the intimacy of a particular encounter, reports of past experiences, or fantasies spoken out loud—the contradictions produced by categories of self-identity can become evident. By so doing, we may expose the complicated politics of the double binary (that is, homosexual/heterosexual and masculinity/femininity), enable a critical approach to the relationship between identity and desire, and a richer analysis of the binary of gender/sexuality that underpins them.

In what follows I will examine: (a) the way erotic desire is expressed in speech, in this case, reports of past experiences; (b) the ways that different kinds of desires are differently adjudicated as valid or invalid; and (c) the historical and cultural conditions that allow such adjudication to take place. Paying attention to what people say about their desire—and the ways such assertions are accepted or rejected—enables us to investigate the power of identity categories to obscure particular desires both in people's lives and in scholarly discussion of them. Moreover, this focus also points to a deeper epistemological issue, one which underpins both the question of language and desire but also much contemporary social theory: the relationship between gender and sexuality. In the data I present here, I want to show first that the use of particular kinds of identity categories disable certain kinds of desires from being validated. But second, I want to show that this process rests upon—and reproduces—a central analytic and political proposition in contemporary queer and feminist anthropology, as well as studies of language and sexuality: that those human experiences we call 'gender' and for 'sexuality' are distinct arenas of social practice, experience, and analysis (see Rubin, 1984). While the separation of gender and sexuality has been a theoretically productive tool, I will argue here that—ironically—this separation implicitly underpins the identity labels that feminist and queer scholars are at pains to deconstruct. Further, this theoretical framework, in which gender and sexuality are seen as separable human experiences, has implications beyond the study of gender and sexuality. My argument is that a progressive political and theoretical move to make a space for 'sexuality' as a field of investigation and activism has unwittingly produced a system whereby those who are already disenfranchised—through poverty and racism—cannot be fully accounted for in contemporary theorizations about gender and sexuality.

A focus on 'desire'—in the form of its expression through speech—enables us to consider the politics of categorizing certain experiences as 'sexual' and others as 'gendered.' To do so, I focus on two aspects of talk: first, the use of identity categories themselves; but second, and equally importantly, what people say about their erotic desires in ways that cannot be accounted for by these categories. The broader question is, therefore: what does the expression—and adjudication—of desire in talk tell us about the politics of sexual and gender identity in the contemporary USA?

3. THE ALTERNATIVE LIFESTYLES GROUP: 'SOMEONE LIKE ME'

The data I will discuss are drawn from an 'alternative lifestyles' support group at a Lower East Side community project in New York City in the Fall of 1996. I attended this group over the course of that Fall, and on one occasion I was able to tape record the proceedings.[3] The participants were a group of friends and acquaintances who came to the group weekly to talk about their experiences. As a group, they were united primarily by the fact that they all were tenants in low-income housing, for which this organization was a resource and gathering place. However, the core group consisted of mostly young African American or Latina/o people who could be described, or would describe themselves during the meeting as gay, lesbian, bisexual, and transgender (among other categories), even though, as I will show, these identifications were far from stable for all participants. Others came in and out over the weeks I was able to attend this group, and the one I describe here also included a young African American woman whose brother had come out to her as gay (and who was struggling to understand what this meant), as well as Sylvia, a very old white woman in a wheelchair who appeared to attend every group meeting at the center, whatever its topic.

The only outsiders in this group were myself—a white, gay-identified man—and Nora. Nora is Latina, a self-identified heterosexual transsexual woman, a former drug user, and now a peer educator for several NYC social service agencies. In conversation, Nora is explicit about her transsexual history, but refuses to accept that this makes her less of a woman. She has been in recovery from drug addiction since the early 1990s, and part of that recovery and personal growth has been working for social service agencies in New York. Through this experience, Nora has developed an understanding of 'transgender' which has been shaped in contexts of political and social service advocacy since the 1990s: that of a collective category which gathers into it any kind of non-normative gender expression, and which is distinct from homosexuality. This is evident from her explanation of what 'transgender' means to one of the group members early on in the meeting. Transgender, she said, is an

> umbrella term which includes [. . .] transsexuals, pre-op, post-op, uh, transvestites, drag queens, female impersonators [. . .] you know, it makes it much easier to define [. . .], a person or group or whatever.

Though Nora and the group participants shared common life experiences—of poverty, racism, drug addiction, and non-normative gender or sexual identity—the way they talked about themselves in this group was quite divergent, a difference underpinned precisely by Nora's experience in social service settings both as a client and as a counselor where she has learnt this usage of 'transgender.' It is this difference, in particular, the escalation of Nora's attempts to get one of the group members to identify as either transgender or gay that I will focus on in the analysis below.

At the beginning of this meeting, as we sat gathered around a conference table in an untidy meeting room, Nora introduced herself as follows: 'I'm Nora, I'm transsexual and I'm a woman and transsexual is my alternative lifestyle.' I introduced myself as 'a non-transgender gay man' which got a conversation going about what 'transgender' means (from which I have excerpted Nora's explanation, above). However, not everyone in the room professed such stable identities as Nora and I did. For example, when Ben, another core group member introduced himself, he said: 'I'm Ben, I'm just a male who enjoys. . . male companionship as well as female companionship.' Note that Ben did not refer to himself as 'bisexual' in this statement, though other group members did take on particular identity categories in talking about themselves.

One of them was Miss Angel. We had not been talking long when she entered the room, late as usual. Miss Angel—African American, a former drug user and sex worker—was one of the central participants in the group, the acknowledged linchpin of the core group of friends, who also worked as a chef at the community center. Upon her arrival, everything stopped and we waited as she took her place, made her observations, and came to rest. As she came in, so too did another participant, a woman I had not met before. As such, I introduced myself and explained my presence (and my tape recorder). Ben took this as a sign that I hadn't met Angel before, and he told her to introduce herself to me.

Excerpt A
1. Angel: Introduce ourselves? To whom?
2. Ben: Do you all know each other? [i.e. do Angel and I know each other]
3. A: Yes! These homosexuals know each other up in here! They better!

This brief excerpt is significant, particularly for what follows. In noting that we have met before, Angel grouped herself and me (identified to the group in this and earlier meetings as a gay man), as 'homosexuals.' While Ben's earlier cited statement to the group is interesting because he avoided identity categories in talking about himself, Angel's talk is notable because she did not: indeed during the rest of the meeting, she used a plethora of identity categories about herself, 'homosexual' being only the first. When Angel finally sat down and took command of the meeting (as she was wont to do), the following exchange took place:

Excerpt B

1. Angel: My name is Angel, I'm a pre-op transsexual. I dunno what I am, I'm a woman, simply . . . , OK? I'm HIV positive.
2. Nora: A genetic woman?
3. A: I'm a drug addict woman.
4. Interjection: Was!
5. Nora: Was still are.
6. Int: I hope!
7. A: No I was but I'm still, you know, they say you still supposed to say you're a drug addict.
8. Int: Well.
9. A: OK, still a drug addict .
10. N: It's up to you if you want to say that, you know, if you don't want to I mean [you don't have to].
11. A: Well whatever, look I'm telling the story right? Thank you. And I'm 31 years old and I'm a woman.

In this exchange, Angel makes several claims about herself—that she is a preoperative transsexual, a woman, a (former) drug addict, HIV positive and, moreover, that 'I dunno what I am.' In this support group, as indeed in many of this kind, the divulging of personal information such as HIV status or substance abuse history is not uncommon. Nora's question (Excerpt B, line 2), which is meant as a joke, leads Angel to provide another qualifier for 'woman': 'drug addict' (Excerpt B, line 3). This results in a discussion of Angel's history of drug addiction, and a discussion of what you are 'supposed' or 'don't have to' divulge about such details. In the end, Angel asserts her right to say who she is, and says simply: 'I'm 31 years old and I'm a woman.'

Given the distinction made in most contemporary theory and activism between homosexual and transgender/transsexual identity, Angel's claims to be (implicitly) homosexual (Excerpt A, line 3) and a transsexual woman (Excerpt B, line 1) are somewhat confusing; certainly they were confusing to Nora (and to myself), as is evident from an exchange that happened a few minutes later:

Excerpt C

1. Angel: I had to get to know new friends when I turned gay and it's not easy being gay.
2. Nora: How was your experience when you became a woman, a transsexual woman?
3. A: I was 13 years old when I did everything. 4 N: Was it even harder?
5. A: Was it harder? No.
6. N: Did it go from bad to worse?
7. A: No [. . .] Um, when I was 13. It was hard, I went to school-
8. Ben: With breasts.
9. A: The breasts.

This excerpt marks the first point in the conversation in which Nora attempts to disaggregate Angel's different self-identifications: as homosexual and as transgender/transsexual. Nora's questions to Angel above (Excerpt C, lines 2, 4, 6) are significant because Nora is implicitly proposing to Angel two different states of coming out: as 'gay' when she was 13, and as a 'transsexual woman' at a later date. Angel, however, does not make this distinction: she was 13 when she did 'everything.' To return to the conceptualization of desire and identity in the contemporary USA, the reason for this misunderstanding is, I would argue, based on different conceptual notions of personhood and identity: Nora, schooled in the language of 'transgender' through her work in social service agencies, sees a necessary division between experiences of being gay (the realm of 'sexuality') and experiences of being transgender (the realm of 'gender': 'how was your experience when you became a woman, a transsexual woman?'). Angel does not ('I was 13 years old when I did everything.')

This divergence in understandings became clearer still in a later exchange between them, as they discussed Angel's sexual history. Angel had informed us that she had had sex with straight and gay men, and with women (with one of whom she had had a child). However, all of Nora's questions—her implicit attempts, as in Excerpt C above, to elicit a stable identity from Angel—failed. A crucial point in the conversation occurred when Nora tried to pin Angel down on precisely how she labels herself after Angel made a seemingly oblique statement:

Excerpt D
1. Angel: I went to bed with my own kind. I tried it once.
2. Ben: How was it?
3. A: How was it?
4. B: Uh huh.
5. Nora: Now what is your own kind mean by definition, because you're always telling us—
6. A: I'm a woman, well you know.
7. N: You're a woman, transsexual, you're gay, you're homosexual.
8. B: A man.
9. A: Look, me, like me, someone like me. Someone like me....Someone like me.
10. N: [who] changes sexuality,[4] uh huh
11. B: With breasts.
12. A: With breasts.
13. N: OK.
14. A: I went out with someone like me. Her name was Billie Jean, she lives in Coney Island.

Here Nora finally tried to get Angel to define what her 'own kind' is. She listed the identity categories that Angel had used about herself in this meeting (woman, gay, homosexual, transsexual) implying that she cannot be all of these things. To this, Angel insisted: 'look, me, like me, someone like me. Someone like me.... Someone like me.' In the end Ben offered: 'with breasts' to which Angel affirmed 'with breasts,' and Nora left it there: 'OK.' However, while Nora's 'OK' indicates she was not willing to draw Angel any further on the topic, the import of her questions in excerpts C and D is that she was attempting to get Angel to channel her expressions (and experiences) of erotic desire—be it her desire for a woman, a man, or for 'someone like her'—through identity categories that cannot, in the end, account for them.

Both in excerpts C and D, Ben offers 'with breasts' by way of explanation of Angel's being, which Angel affirms (in Excerpt D, line 12). This reference to Angel's breasts—the result of hormone therapy—is the final word in both cases. The reference to her body is particularly instructive, for Angel's changing body shifts her—in contemporary progressive understandings—into the category of 'transgender' or more specifically, 'transsexual,' a category she indeed uses to describe herself. Yet, as is clear from the preceding conversation, Angel does not always stick to this definition of self. Indeed, Nora's attempts to pin her down on this point relates directly to the double binary I invoked earlier—Angel is conflating gendered and sexual identities, recounting desires which cannot be accounted for in a system which sees gender and sexuality as distinct.

Perhaps in response to this questioning, Angel tried to summarize her theory of sexuality and desire shortly after this exchange. She said:

> When it comes down to sex, I don't think... it's two men going to bed with each other, a man and a woman going to bed with it or pre-op or nothing like that. I just think it's just two people having sex, making love to each other, enjoying each other's company, enjoying each other's time, when we're together.

Here Angel is proposing a fluidity to sexual identity that neatly encapsulates a non-identitarian politics of sexual desire. A short while later, Nora made the following comment, which seems to support Angel's theory of desire:

> You label yourself what you want to label yourself. Other people don't label you, I mean unless you want to be labeled yourself, you know.

Yet Nora's questioning throughout this meeting points to the ways that such desires and passions are subject, always, to a rigorous system of labeling, whether or not someone wants to be labeled. Those desires that cannot be labeled—or which require different kinds of labels at different times—are produced as incoherent, or, at the very least, the product of confusion.

Later in the group, Nora tells of her days of sex work when non-transgender men who were her clients would ask her what their desire for her meant for their own sexual identity:

Excerpt E
1. Nora: And they're attracted to that [a feminine person with a penis]. So they would tell me, 'well what am I?' I said 'well I can't tell you what you are unless you know and I can't not tell you this is what you are and this is what you're gonna be, you know, because it's not my life.' My life, I know what I am.
2. Angel: I'm a woman with a large clit.
3. N: I know what I am.

In this excerpt, Nora states 'I know what I am' and her statements of self never vary: she is a heterosexual transsexual woman. Nora's claim overlaps yet another assertion by Miss Angel—this time that she is 'a woman with a large clit'—which joins the other categories she has taken on during the meeting: gay, homosexual, and transsexual. In contrast to Nora's clear sense of knowing 'what I am' above, Angel claims 'I dunno what I am' (Excerpt B, line 1), an observation that Nora implicitly draws on in asking Angel to adhere to one of them.

I would argue that Nora's attempts to get Angel to pick just one of the definitions of self that she has used during the meeting fail not because Angel cannot account for 'what she is,' but rather because she can account for herself in many different ways. Nora, as I have noted, shares much of Angel's history and experience as a former drug user, sex worker, and person of color. However, Nora differs from Angel in that she has an understanding of gender and sexual identity gained through her contact with the social service agencies she works for, and defined by a distinct split between gay identities on the one hand and transgender identities on the other. Angel has no such model of personhood, and these distinctions do not seem to signify much to her. All she can say when Nora requests a definition of what 'my own kind' might mean is: 'someone like me.'

At the end of the group, Nora said: 'In the long run, as long as you know the truth that's really all that matters.' But what is the truth? And what operations of power—and requirements for asserting identity to make sense of one's desire—make some kinds of desires more true—and more coherent—than others? The ways these different kinds of knowledge are assessed, within this group and within a broader system of identity, complicates how such assertions of self and expressions of desire—which are expected to be congruent with such identities—are seen as being 'truthful.' Nora's inability to tell her former clients—or to ascertain about Angel—'what' they are points to the place where desires escape identity and become unnamable and, consequently, unrepresentable.

4. GENDER, SEXUALITY, AND THE NAMING OF DESIRE

The interactions that occurred at the Alternative Lifestyles group and the conceptual mismatches they illustrate only make sense if one considers the history of the last quarter of the twentieth century, in which gay and lesbian (and later, bisexual and transgender) people made their mark in American society. By the end of the 1960s, when the now almost-mythical Stonewall rebellion was about to take place, homosexuality had long been pathologized. But it was also differently conceptualized than it was in the late 1990s when this group meeting took place. Homosexuality was seen in medical and popular understandings as a failure of gendered identity and desire, a phenomenon which produced homosexual men as feminine and homosexual women as masculine. That is, in the pre-Stonewall era, the dominant understanding of homosexuality was that it was caused by—and was manifested in—gender variance. In 1972, Esther Newton, could write that '[d]rag and camp are the most representative and widely used symbols of homosexuality in the English speaking world.' (Newton, 1979[1972], p. 100).

Thirty years later, it would be harder to make such an argument. It is interesting to note that Nora, in her description of 'transgender', includes drag queens in her list of identities that are captured by 'transgender' (as do I in my own list; see note 2). While images of drag still figure large in media representations of male homosexuality, nowadays it is far more likely to see both gay men and lesbians in both news and entertainment media as gender normative professionals and citizens: lawyers, teachers, and even parents. These images are the result of decades of gay and lesbian activism in which the link between homosexuality and gender variance have been at least partly replaced by the image of gay men and lesbians who adhere to time-honored white, middle-class American values. This activism has gone hand-in-glove with a call for gay and lesbian civil rights, based on the claim that gay and lesbian Americans are responsible citizens whose sexuality—coded as private in American culture—should not be the purview of public scrutiny or regulation. This schema opposes a still-powerful US American folk model of homosexuality which sees it as a gendered inversion, and, in Urvashi Vaid's words, works to make a claim that 'homosexual sexuality is merely the queer version of heterosexuality' (Vaid, 1995, p. 44). In particular, accommodationist gay and lesbian politics has increasingly worked with a model of 'gay' which implicitly foregrounds the similarity of gay and lesbian people to heterosexual people (and, implicitly, an adherence to white middle class American-ness) while, at the same time, highlighting its difference from gender variance. This accommodationist politics took the forefront in many public campaigns for civil rights in the late 1980s and 1990s, and was articulated in high profile debates about homosexuals in the military, adoption, and marriage rights (for the purest examples of this kind of accommodationist politics, see the work of neo-conservative gay scholars and writers such as Andrew Sullivan, 1995, and Bruce Bawer, 1993).

During the same period, from the early 1990s, 'transgender' emerged in contexts of activism and social service provision as a collective category to provide a voice for those who were no longer capable of being accounted for in terms of 'homosexuality.' To be sure, the differences between gender-normative gay men and lesbians and those with variant expressions of gender are not new and the connection between gender variance and homosexual desire has been contested for almost as long as homosexuality has existed as a category (see Chauncey, 1994; Meyerowitz, 2002). However, the advent of gay and lesbian activism in the 1970s resulted in a radical shift in medical and popular understandings of homosexuality, bringing the gender-normative model of homosexuality to the fore. These understandings rest, implicitly, on a theory of gender and sexuality that sees these two experiences as distinct in the sense that one does not have to be—indeed, in the language of much post-Stonewall gay activism, is not—gender variant just because one diverges from the heterosexual norm. This insistence on distinguishing between gender and sexuality allowed for the emergence of a new category, 'transgender', in the 1990s which rests precisely on this assumed distinction.[5]

So, in the past 30 years in the USA a newly emerging model of gender and sexuality as distinct arenas of social experience and analysis has resulted in the inability of Nora (representative here of larger institutional discourses and practices) to make sense of Miss Angel's expressed desires, because of the requirement that erotic desire be made sense of through sexual identity categories that are distinct from gendered identity categories.

This is not to say that this system is absolute. For one, the folk model of gender and sexuality which see gender and sexuality as intrinsically linked is far from dead. Moreover, activists and scholars have challenged the politics of neo-conservative writers and groups (e.g. Vaid, 1995; Warner, 1999); and feminist and queer scholars continue to query the relationships between 'gender' and 'sexuality' (e.g. Wieringa and Blackwood, 1999; Jolly and Manderson, 1997). Yet at the same time, the explanatory force of this heuristic separation has gained institutional force in the very use of identity category labels—underpinned by that separation—to talk about sexual desire. That is, as 'transgender' becomes a category of personhood but also of activism, politics, and in academic debates, the theoretical distinction between gender and sexuality becomes solidified as fact in every iteration of that category (and the category to which it is opposed: homosexuality). And as such, Miss Angel's voice and her desires are rendered as nonsensical.

Miss Angel's claim to be 'gay', 'transsexual' and 'transvestite' may be seen, by people like Nora and others (e.g. see Plummer, 1992) to hark back to an earlier (and implicitly, outmoded and false) model of homosexuality which conflated sexuality and gender. Yet, Angel's professions of identity and desire are not unique. Among many African American and Latino communities in NYC, such claims are frequently made. In the communities in which I did fieldwork where primarily young, poor, people of color predominated—drag balls , bars, sex work strolls—the category of 'transgender' is rarely used. Rather, categories such as 'fem queen' (another category Angel sometimes used about herself), 'butch queen' (a category that I—as a non-transgender identified gay man—was frequently classed under), and 'butches' (masculine female-bodied people), as well as a range of others, were all seen as united by the overarching category of 'gay.' While the borders between these identity categories were strictly monitored in these communities, as categories generally are, the source of their commonality was never denied, and was seen to flow from a complex nexus between those experiences which, in contemporary social theory, we call 'gender and sexuality.'

In other words, to be 'gay' in these contexts is not necessarily marked by gender normativity. Rather, in those communities, it is the difference from heteronormativity—rather than the difference between 'gay' and 'transgender'—which underpins the organization of gender and sexuality. Yet, their unity as 'gay' people, defined by another set of characteristics—the conjunction of their disenfranchisement in terms of both class and racial memberships and their non-normative genders/sexualities—precludes them from membership in the contemporary mainstream understanding of 'gay.'

As such, these desires and senses of self which cannot be made to fit into certain identity categories are confusing. Early on in the meeting, Angel had demanded her right to tell her own story ('look I'm telling the story right?' Excerpt A, line 11), but she also recognized the power of institutions to form what one should say about oneself ('they say you still supposed to say you're a drug addict.' Excerpt A, line 7). In the end, Nora cannot push Angel to use a unitary category that makes sense in Nora's conceptualization of gendered and sexual identity, so Angel does get to tell her own story in her own words. But Angel's words, like many of her peers', are also subject to discourses and practices which produce those stories as incoherent. In a conversation with one social worker to whom I related the conversation I discuss here, she argued that Angel was a victim of 'false consciousness' and that she should be educated into a more enlightened understanding of identity. In other words, to paraphrase Miss Angel, 'they say you supposed to say you're transgender.'

For this social worker, and for many other social service providers, activists, and scholars, a model of gender and sexuality as separate experiences underpinning discrete identities is implicitly a truth, and no longer simply an analytic or an activist move. Yet ironically, as I have tried to show here, the practices and politics that have resulted from this shift have, in part, reproduced a set of social relationships whereby those who arguably have the most need for a progressive politics of sexuality and gender are excluded from its explanatory purview by being made to seem confusing and confused.

There are two related theoretical points which can be drawn from this analysis, which map onto the questions I asked at the outset: what does it mean to talk about desire, both in scholarly contexts and in talking about one's own desire? First, I have suggested that the use of identity labels, conceptualized through a binary understanding of 'sexuality' and 'gender,' reproduce a system where desires that span these experiences—and are narrated as such—are difficult to make sense of, or can be dismissed as a kind of 'false consciousness.' Secondly, though, paying attention to such desires, rather than dismissing them, gives us a way of focusing on the practices and desires which underpin the complex lives of human beings, unrestrained as they are experientially by how such desires come to be accounted for. As such, a focus on desire expressed in talk enables a complication of the categories that have gained such force and power in academic, activist, and increasingly, popular understandings of what counts as 'sexuality.'

Looking at what people say about what they desire, who they desire, and how they act upon those desires can highlight for us the political nature of desire and the ways such yearnings are shaped by the identity categories through which they are forced to speak if they wish to get a hearing. Such a focus can enable us to look more closely at the seemingly neutral categories of 'gender' and 'sexuality,' and complicate the relationship between them. And, most usefully, it requires us to not simply assume that desire is self evidently explained by the categories 'gender' and 'sexuality' in using them to talk about the complexity of erotic lives.

ACKNOWLEDGMENTS

My thanks to Nora, Miss Angel, Ben, and the other members of the Alternative Lifestyles group for allowing me to tape record and make use of their words in this paper. Thanks also to Don Kulick for his comments and suggestions on this paper. Finally, thanks are due to a core group of readers—Bambi Schieffelin, Henry Goldschmidt, and Ben Chesluk—whose comments are always supremely helpful. I am also indebted to Dr. Barbara Warren and Rosalyne Blumenstein for facilitating my research. The research upon which this paper is based was assisted by a fellowship from the Sexuality Research Fellowship Program from the Social Science Research Council with funds provided by the Ford Foundation.

NOTES

1. The inclusion of 'drag queen' in this list is a particular choice on my part, and not one that all transgender-identified people —or drag queens —might agree with. Indeed, I include it here, somewhat reluctantly, only because many of my informants do so in their explanations of what 'transgender' encompasses. As will become apparent later in this paper, 'drag queen' is a central category in thinking about the relationship between identity and desire.

2. I use the construction 'transgender-identified' to mark the ways in which people both take on the category transgender as something meaningful about themselves; as well as the sense of being identified by others to fall into a category. This is a useful way of dealing with the conceptual mismatches I will be talking about in this paper, but it also speaks to the ways that self identity and identification by others of the self are not separate but complexly related phenomena.

3. I had, initially, intended my fieldwork to revolve around a linguistic anthropological methodology, and intended to record extensive periods of conversation and talk in a variety of settings to aid my analyses. However, it became clear to me from early in my project that the politics of taping among the people with whom I conducted fieldwork was fraught. Given the nature of social scientific involvements with transgender-identified people's lives (see Valentine, 2003), many people were deeply suspicious of my research goals, and refused to be taped, even when I had gained their trust. Group settings, such as the one I describe here, were particularly difficult because of the number of people present and the fluidity of the group over time. As such, the transcripts from the group meeting I have included here represent virtually the only taped conversation I was able to record in my 18 months of fieldwork; even during this meeting, I had to turn the recorder off and on to accommodate the wishes of one participant. However, the conclusions I draw from this material were confirmed frequently through my ethnographic research, as I discuss elsewhere (Valentine, 2000).

4. Given my argument, one might imagine that Nora would have said 'gender' rather than 'sexuality' here. At the same time, however, her use of 'sexuality' indicates the slippage between these categories in talk and practice, and points to the gaps produced by needing to talk about desire in discrete categories.

5. This argument does not intend to draw away from the organizing and advocacy engaged in by transgender-identified people in claiming this category; nor is it intended to contest the political gains achieved under this category. My goal here is to point to a particular cultural logic that underpins contemporary understandings of both gender variance and homosexuality in order to consider the deeper implications of these politics.

REFERENCES

Bawer, B., 1993. *A Place at the Table: The Gay Individual in American Society.* Poseidon Press, New York.

Blackwood, E., 1995. Falling in love with an-Other lesbian: reflections on identity in fieldwork. In: Kulick, D., Willson, M. (Eds.), *Taboo: Sex, Identity, and Erotic Subjectivity in Anthropological Fieldwork.* Routledge, New York, pp. 51–75.

Chauncey, G., 1994. *Gay New York: Gender, Urban Culture, and the Makings of the Gay Male World.* Basic Books, New York.

Donham, Donald L., 1998. Freeing South African: the 'modernization' of male-male sexuality in Soweto. *Cultural Anthropology* 13 (1), 3–21.

Foucault, M., 1990 [1980]. *The History of Sexuality. Volume 1: an Introduction* [trans. by Robert Hurley]. Vintage, New York.

Johnson, M., 1997. *Beauty and Power: Transgendering and Cultural Transformation in the Southern Philippines.* Berg, New York.

Jolly, M., Manderson, L., 1997. Introduction: sites of desire/economies of pleasure in Asia and the Pacific. In: Manderson, L., Jolly, M. (Eds.), *Sites of Desire, Economies of Pleasure: Sexualities in Asia and the Pacific.* University of Chicago Press, Chicago, pp. 1–26.

Katz, J.N., 1995. *The Invention of Heterosexuality.* Dutton, New York.

Kulick, D., 1998. *Travesti: Sex, Gender, and Culture among Brazilian Transgendered Prostitutes.* University of Chicago Press, Chicago.

Kulick, D., 2000. Gay and lesbian language. *Annual Review of Anthropology* 29, 243–285.

Kulick, D., 2003. Language and desire. In: Holmes, J., Meyerhoff, M. (Eds.), *The Handbook of Language and Gender.* Blackwell, Oxford.

Lewin, E., 1993. *Lesbian Mothers: Accounts of Gender in American Culture.* Cornell University Press, Ithaca, NY.

Manalansan, M.F., 1997. In the shadows of Stonewall: examining gay transnational politics and the diasporic dilemma. In: Lowe, L., Lloyd, D. (Eds.), *The Politics of Culture in the Shadow of Capital.* Duke University Press, Durham, pp. 485–505.

Meyerowitz, J., 2002. *How Sex Changed: A History of Transsexuality in the United States.* Harvard University Press, Cambridge.

Newton, E., 1979 [1972]. *Mother Camp: Female Impersonators in America.* University of Chicago Press, Chicago.

Plummer, K., 1992. Speaking its name: inventing a lesbian and gay studies. In: Plummer, K. (Ed.), *Modern Homosexualities: Fragments of Gay and Lesbian Experiences.* Routledge, New York, pp. 3–25.

Rubin, G., 1984. Thinking sex: notes for a radical theory of the politics of sexuality. In: Vance, C. (Ed.), *Pleasure and Danger: Exploring Female Sexuality.* Harper Collins, New York, pp. 267–319.

Shokeid, M., 1995. *A Gay Synagogue in New York.* Columbia University Press, New York.

Sullivan, A., 1995. *Virtually Normal: An Argument About Homosexuality.* Alfred A. Knopf, New York.

Vaid, U., 1995. *Virtual Equality: the Mainstreaming of Gay and Lesbian Liberation.* Doubleday, New York.

Valentine, D. 'The calculus of pain': violence, anthropological ethics, and the category transgender. *Ethnos* 66(2) (in press).

Valentine, D., 2000. 'I Know What I Am': the Category 'Transgender' in the Construction of Contemporary US American Conceptions of Gender and Sexuality. PhD dissertation, Department of Anthropology, New York University.

Warner, M., 1999. *The Trouble with Normal: Sex, Politics, and the Ethics of Queer Life*. The Free Press, New York.

Weeks, J., 1981. *Sex, Politics, and Society: the Regulation of Sexuality since 1800*. Longman, London.

Weston, K., 1991. *Families We Choose: Lesbians, Gays, Kinship*. Columbia University Press, New York.

Wieringa, S., Blackwood, E., 1999. Introduction. In: Blackwood, E., Wieringa, S. (Eds.), *Female Desires: Same-sex Relations and Transgender Practices Across Cultures*. Columbia University Press, New York, pp. 1–38.

28

Bodies in Motion
Lesbian and Transsexual Histories

NAN ALAMILLA BOYD

HISTORIAN NAN BOYD EXAMINES THE RELATIONSHIP between citizenship and the intelligibility of the body in this essay exploring several transgender controversies in the 1990s. Boyd argues that the body is not a natural fact, but rather "a highly politicized, unstable, and symbolic structure, intimately connected to the state." She contrasts the "state"—the locus of statutory power—with the "nation"—an imagined community that struggles to align itself with the power of the state. Notions of community and identity thus become critical for understanding the dynamics of social movements that seek political redress for social injustices through acts of state power.

Boyd examines the way that "transsexual bodies" complicated and challenged notions of a "lesbian nation" in the 1990s in the United States. She discusses historical figures such as Babe Bean, Lou Sullivan, Billy Tipton, and Brandon Teena, as well as the controversy surrounding transsexual participation at the Michigan Women's Music Festival, to reveal the political stakes involved in particular historical constructions of lesbian and transgender identity.

Boyd claims that transsexual bodies unsettle familiar historical narratives of identity, and reterritorialize national geographies. In doing so, they risk becoming unintelligible, and thus vulnerable to a loss of citizenship. At the same time, the very outlaw status of the transsexual body can be figured as a space of radical possibility, a new way for bodies to matter.

> *Here on the gender borders at the close of the twentieth century, with the faltering of phallocratic hegemony and the bumptious appearance of heteroglossic origin accounts, we find the epistemologies of white male medical practice, the rage of radical feminist theories and the chaos of lived gendered experience meeting on the battle field of the transsexual body: a hotly contested site of cultural inscription, a meaning machine for the production of ideal type.*
> —Sandy Stone, "The Empire Strikes Back: A Posttranssexual Manifesto"

> *My point of departure is that nationality . . . nationness, as well as nationalism, are cultural artifacts of a particular kind. To understand them properly we need to consider carefully how they have come into historical being, in what ways their meanings have changed over time, and why, today, they command such profound emotional legitimacy.*
> —Benedict Anderson, *Imagined Communities*

This essay concerns the relationship between bodies and nations, and more specifically, transsexual bodies and lesbian nations.[1] It explores how visible, intelligible, and legible bodies come to reflect, define, and regulate the nation as a boundaried political geography.[2] I suggest that the naturalized body is not simply a duped or docile subject; nor is it free to determine its own form.[3] Rather, the body remains a highly politicized, unstable, and symbolic structure, intimately connected to the state, and as a result, it reflects both nationalism and resistant social movements.

In many ways, the connection between nationalism's history and the body's relationship to the state remains obscure.[4] However, as Michel Foucault explains, while divinely ordained monarchies crumbled in the face of late nineteenth-century West European republicanism and the concomitant rise of state nationalism, state-sanctioned punishments (law) helped transform the body into a political anatomy.[5] Not only did the materiality of the body gain meaning as it became *subject to* new laws and regulations, but paradoxically the body became the *subject of* the state as a (perhaps interchangeable) physical representation of republican ideology.[6] In other words, the body begins to imagine itself meaningfully autonomous and individual only in relation to the collective: the republican state. Thus, the body's subjectivity—its social and political agency—remains linked to its physicality, to the social meaning of human corporeality. In this way, through the nineteenth century, as *individuals* began to participate more dynamically in the body politic, the body through its social and political gestures, indeed its social and political embodiments, began to participate more efficiently in its own regulation and prohibitions.

While the body becomes self-regulating as respectable or heteronormal, for example, in order to affirm an empowered relationship to the state, the body's intelligibility incorporates it within the nation. The nation, as Benedict Anderson argues, functions as "an imagined political community," a community that will never completely know itself—it will never know all its constituents—but it learns to recognize its members (even sight unseen) as part of a limited, boundaried, and sovereign entity, "a deep, horizontal comradeship."[7] The nation functions differently than the state in that the state emerged as the political invention of the Age of Revolution and Enlightenment, as a political geography sovereign through its own efforts and imaginings rather than its God-ordained nobility or territorial sweep. The nation, however, emerged as the state's cultural artifact and constant companion. The nation and nationalism, if Anderson's arguments are correct, claim cultural legitimacy for the state insofar as nationalism replaced religious and dynastic symbols with a secular semiotics of political representation.[8] However, as this essay will demonstrate, while nationalisms reflect, reinforce, and reinvigorate the state, contemporary social and political movements also invoke the language of nationalism in order to resist and restructure the state. In other words, while late eighteenth-century revolutionary movements engineered the hegemony of the modern nation/state in order to resist monarchial and/or colonial tyranny, contemporary resistant movements (anticolonial, socialist, antiracist, queer) often imagine themselves within a cultural system—nationalism—that reinscribes the foundations of state capitalism.

These notes help us understand the body's relationship to both the nation (nationalism) and the state (law), particularly since some bodies matter more than others. Bodies that inhabit or enact naturalized states of being remain culturally intelligible, socially valuable, and as a result, gain and retain the privilege of citizenship and its associated rights and protections. Bodies that matter, as Judith Butler argues, are worth protecting, saving, grieving.[9] Some bodies, however, are less intelligible or unintelligible and are not instrumental or valuable to the state; in fact, these bodies undermine in many different ways the recognition or comradeship central to nationalism's purpose. It makes no difference if these bodies die or if no one grieves them because, as Butler explains, abject bodies—bodies transgressive of borders and boundaries—do not matter. They do not function intelligibly as matter, and they do not have value. How then does the materiality or morphology of the body influence its social value, its political purchase? Do abject or queer bodies retain inchoate or inherently resistant positions vis-à-vis the state? Is it necessary to transition (or pass) from abject to intelligible in order to function within the state (or in order to resist a state-sanctioned, rights-based economy of value)? How do bodies that do not matter become bodies that matter?

Despite twentieth-century antihumanist and anti-essentialist gestures away from the body, the material body continues to influence contemporary social and political movements. For instance, as queers begin to visibly take up public space and imagine themselves part of a larger political community, they often do so around a system of meanings that transforms bodies into specific, cohesive, and authentic identities. Gay men, lesbians, bisexuals, and transsexuals, as increasingly viable subjects in relation to the state, police their own borders, regulating the social territories they inhabit, including their bodies, in an effort to secure and protect limited political entitlements. For example, in June 1994 the Human Rights Campaign Fund (HRCF), a U.S. gay and lesbian lobbying organization, brought antidiscrimination legislation to Congress through several key representatives. If adopted, this legislative package, known as ENDA (the Employment Non-Discrimination Act), would protect lesbians, bisexuals, and gay men in the United States from "job discrimination or special treatment on the basis of sexual orientation."[10] In an effort to speedily secure the bill, however, HRCF refused to use language that would also protect the transgendered from job discrimination.[11] When confronted by transgender activists who argued that ENDA failed to protect the "visibly queer," HRCF countered that trans-inclusive language would set back the legislative process and could cost ENDA twenty to thirty potential congressional votes.[12] In other words, in order to forge a relationship with the state, particularly around legal protections, the lesbian and gay nation regulates its borders and disciplines its body to project an intelligible picture of itself, one with clear boundaries around not just the sexual identity of its constituents but the unambiguous gender (and genital status) of those who might be protected by this legislation. With this move, the queer body becomes coherent and self-regulating in relation to the state, not queer at all, in fact.[13] It becomes, instead, disciplined and intelligible within a state-sanctioned language about appropriately gendered "lesbian," "gay," and perhaps "bisexual" bodies. While the struggle over queer antidiscrimination legislation continues, other theaters of struggle showcase the ambivalent relationship between subject and state, body and nation.[14]

THE THEATER OF HISTORICAL RECUPERATION

History, as this story unfolds, is a battleground, an intellectual territory that serves political purposes, and lesbian, feminist, and transgender communities share a common but sometimes hostile relationship to overlapping historical geographies. In contemporary lesbian history, butch drag or female-to-male cross-dressing has signaled the presence of lesbians. Indeed, in a working-class context, butch iconography was lesbian iconography, and masculine gender codes when worn on an anatomically female body stood in for or advertised lesbian desire and sexuality.[15] However, because of the historical relationship between butchness and lesbian sexuality, lesbian histories often conflate "cross-dressing" (anatomical females sporting masculine appearance for the purpose of advertising lesbian sexuality) with "passing" (anatomical females donning masculine appearance for the purpose of being perceived as men).[16] Lesbian history, for example, particularly in its earlier phase, often documented the history of passing women as a method for bringing lesbians into history because these individuals (when "discovered" to be women) were the most visible and publicly accessible historical subjects.[17] However, transsexuals and transgender community historians and activists take a different approach to the historical recuperation of female-to-male cross-dressers. They argue that anatomical females who passed as men in public might just as easily be recuperated as transgendered men than passing women or cross-dressing lesbians in that their perceived gender identity was male rather than female.

In this way, lesbian and transgender communities construct a usable past around the recuperation of many of the same historical figures.[18]

The slide show *She Even Chewed Tobacco,* for example, discusses cross-dressing and passing women in U.S. Western history. Created in 1979, it introduces the character Babe Bean, a "passing woman" who lived in Stockton, California, from 1897–98, and places Bean within a narrative about women's history that suggests that passing women functioned as a cultural precursor to contemporary butch lesbians.[19] The slide show's introductory segment states that in the nineteenth century, "a small but significant group of American women rejected the limitations of the female sphere and claimed the privileges enjoyed by men. They worked for men's wages, courted and married the women they loved and even voted. They did so by adopting men's clothing, hiding their female identities from most of the world and passing as men." *She Even Chewed Tobacco* uses passing women as liminal characters to highlight the gulf between male privilege and female oppression. It positions them within a late-1970s feminist discourse that stresses labor equity, suffrage rights, and lesbian love. Moreover, it tells a Horatio Alger-esque story, embedding a nationalist trope of success within feminist discourse: successful cross-dressing produced women who, as citizens, could vote. In this way *She Even Chewed Tobacco* gives nineteenth-century female-to-male cross-dressers a history as women within the rubric of contemporary lesbian and feminist concerns. No mention is made of cross-gender identity, and the only conclusion one might make about the lives of passing women is that if they lived at a time when they could enjoy economic freedom, political rights, or sexual love for women as a woman, they would not choose to masquerade as men. Indeed, it is this concept of masquerade that underscores the argument that nineteenth- and twentieth-century female-to-male cross-dressers were really women and, in fact, probably lesbians.

Babe Bean is a complicated historical figure, however, because for a short period of time Bean straddled the boundary between man and woman. In August 1897, Bean was arrested in Stockton, California, for cross-dressing. After the arrest s/he stayed in Stockton for approximately a year and became something of a local celebrity. Bean continued to dress entirely in men's clothing, lived alone on a houseboat, and attended meetings at the local Bachelor's Club. However, Bean communicated only through writing and refused to speak aloud, which shrouded the truth of her/his sex. In other words, even though Bean admitted to having a female body, her/his self-presentation was so consistently masculine that some of the citizens of Stockton remained unconvinced of Bean's sex. "The mystery is still unsolved as to whether 'Babe' Bean is a boy or girl, a man or a woman," one news article reported, dubbing Bean "the mysterious girl-boy, man-woman."[20]

In 1898, Bean left Stockton for San Francisco and joined the U.S. military, serving in the Philippines during the Spanish-American War. Bean returned to San Francisco after the war, his arms covered with elaborate tattoos, and he adopted the name Jack Garland. At this time in San Francisco, 1903, cross-dressing was made illegal by city ordinance. And although Garland spent the rest of his life in San Francisco, working as a male nurse and a free-lance social worker, he was not arrested again. However, when Jack Garland died in 1936, after almost forty years of living as a man, his "true sex" was revealed to be female. Jack Garland was born in 1869, daughter of José Marcos Mugarrieta, San Francisco's first Mexican consul, and Eliza Alice Garland.

The late Lou Sullivan, a female-to-male (FTM) transsexual and also an active member of San Francisco's Gay and Lesbian Historical Society (GLHS), published a biography of Jack Garland in 1990 entitled *From Female to Male: The Life of Jack Bee Garland,* which retextualizes Babe Bean's life as the life of Jack Garland. Sullivan states in his introduction that "Jack Garland demonstrated, through his lifelong adherence to his male identity, that his reasons for living as a man were more complex than just his dissatisfaction with the way society expected women to dress. [Jack Garland] was a female-to-male transsexual."[21] Furthermore, while many histories of female-to-male cross-dressers tell the story of how passing women were able to pursue the women they loved under the protective cover of male dress and, perhaps, male identity, this was not the case for Jack Garland. Garland preferred the company of men. Sullivan notes that "he dressed and lived as a man in order to be a man among men," which further unhinges any direct connection between cross-gender behavior and sexuality. In the memoirs he left behind, Jack Garland states that "Many have thought it strange that I do not care to mingle with women of my own age, and seem partial to men's company. Well, is it not natural that I should prefer the companionship of men? I am never happy nor contented unless with a few of 'the boys.' "[22]

While Sullivan rewrites lesbian history to produce a history of visible transsexuals, one cannot overlook Garland's racial, class, and national passings. The turn of the century was a period of intense racial, ethnic, and national consolidation which marked the rise of Anglo-Saxonism, the production of a nationalist discourse of U.S. exceptionalism, and intensified U.S. colonization. Garland's gender certainly did not exist independent of these circumstances. For instance, Garland chose Anglo names for himself, which signals a movement toward white-ethnic or Anglo-American identifications. Moreover, while his silence in Stockton masked, most obviously, the feminine tenor of his voice, it also hid any Spanish language affects that would have destabilized his ethnic and national crossings. Also, for the last decades of his life, Garland wandered the streets of San Francisco and lived in poverty. Here, gender remains inseparable from class—while Garland's maleness allowed for late-night street wandering and urban rescue work, the very public and class-specific nature of his activities reinforced his gender. Finally, Garland's participation in the Spanish-American War and his service to the U.S. military wrapped a cloak of nationalist allegiance around his political subjectivity, highlighting both his masculinity and Americanness. Clearly, the story of Babe Bean/Jack Garland exceeds a singularly recuperative narrative.

Billy Tipton, the jazz pianist and saxophonist whose so called true sex was revealed when he died in Spokane in 1989, provides another example of a historical subject claimed by both lesbian/feminist and transgendered communities. Like Jack Garland, Billy Tipton lived his adult life as a man, over fifty years. Born in Kansas City, Missouri, in 1914, at the age of eighteen he applied for a social security card under his brother's name, Billy, and hit the road as a musician. He formed the Billy Tipton Trio in 1954, recorded two albums, and toured the West until he settled in Spokane in the 1960s. Through these years, Tipton married several times but, according to his lovers, never revealed his female anatomy. Betty Cox, Tipton's lover from 1946–53, claims that Tipton must have used "sexual devices" when making love: "I know it sounds incredible, but I'm a normal healthy woman who enjoys her man ... [a]nd if that little Billy was alive today, well, I'd still enjoy him."[23] On the other hand, Kitty Oakes, Tipton's third wife, claims that they didn't have sex during their eighteen-year marriage. She notes that Tipton had been injured in an auto accident, explaining "—there was an attraction between us, but it wasn't sexual."[24] Over the course of their relationship, Tipton and Oakes adopted and parented three sons.

Tipton did not have surgery or openly identify as a transsexual; instead, he represented himself, even to his closest friends and family, as a man. Clearly, Billy Tipton's gender identity was male. Still, critics and enthusiasts have recuperated Tipton as an example of the kind of extreme measures women must undergo to pursue equitable economic opportunities. "[Tipton] apparently began appearing as a man to improve her chances of success as a musician," one reporter noted.[25] Jason Cromwell, a sociologist specializing in female-to-male transsexual identities, refutes this idea. "You don't die from a treatable medical condition if you are simply a woman living as a man so you can take advantage of male privileges."[26] (Tipton died of an untreated bleeding ulcer.) A print graphic published in several transgender community newsletters and magazines takes this idea one step further. It positions a simple "trivial pursuit" question in the center of the page with statements swirling around it; the question reads: "Billy Tipton was a (choose one): a. woman, b. lesbian, c. crossdresser, d. man." A check is placed next to answer d, indicating that the correct answer is that Tipton was a man. Statements protectively encircling the ad read:

> Billy Tipton was a jazz musician. When he died, in 1989, television and newspaper sources proclaimed him to have been a woman who had lived as a man in order to be a jazz musician. "He gave up everything," they said. They were wrong. He didn't give up anything, for he wasn't a woman. They gay community was quick to proclaim Billy as a lesbian. They were wrong, too. Billy wasn't a lesbian, either. Billy was married, with three adopted sons. His family did not know of his female anatomy, but they knew something the newspaper and television and gay press didn't—that Billy Tipton was a man.

In smaller print, in the bottom right corner, a more provocative statement reads, "Billy Tipton was transsexual.... His life was not an imposture, and the notion that he was anything less than a man is a denial of everything that he was. Hands off! He's one of ours!"[27] Like Jack Garland, the recuperation of Billy Tipton's life exceeds a simple narrative about women's economic opportunities or lesbian sexual identity. Instead, without denying labor inequity or lesbian history, Tipton's life evidences the uneasy fit between unintelligible bodies and contemporary (recuperative) historical practice.

More recently, Brandon Teena, a twenty-one-year-old who, despite his female body, lived as a man and dated women, was murdered on December 31, 1993, in Humboldt, Nebraska. Three months earlier he had moved from his hometown, Lincoln, to Falls City, where, it was noted, he was "popular with the girls." After a misdemeanor arrest, however, police revealed his anatomical sex to the local press, who published it. This information angered two men, who disrobed Brandon Teena at a Christmas Eve party ostensibly to prove to his girlfriend that he was "actually a female." Early the next morning, on December 25, 1993, Brandon Teena was abducted, beaten, and raped by the same two men; they "threatened to silence her permanently" if he went to the police. A week later, after Brandon Teena filed charges, the same two men murdered him and two of his friends.[28]

The murders attracted a great deal of national attention, particularly after Brandon Teena's family asserted that the murders would not have occurred had the rape and battery been prosecuted by the local police.[29] Meanwhile, in the gay press, coverage of Brandon Teena's death evolved into a discussion about lesbian and gay civil rights. Pat Phelen of Citizens for Equal Protection, Nebraska's gay and lesbian rights organization, stated that "this incident underscores the need for the state to pass laws protecting the rights of Gays and those perceived as Gay."[30] The National Gay and Lesbian Task Force (NGLTF), San Francisco's Citizens United against Violence (CUAV), and New York City's Anti-Violence Project (AVP) similarly asserted that Brandon Teena's death exemplified the worst kind of violence against women and lesbians:

> Brandon Teena was raped and then murdered for being a woman who broke the rules: she presented herself as a man, dated the prettiest girl in town, and was not sexually involved with men.... For all these transgressions, as a woman and as a lesbian, she was murdered.[31]

Because gay press coverage of the events leading to Brandon Teena's death pointedly represented him as lesbian or female, these articles obscure his transgendered identity, erasing its specificity.

For example, Donna Minkowitz's *Village Voice* coverage of Brandon Teena's murder evades a direct analysis of transgender experience in order to buttress lesbian visibility and political subjectivity. While Minkowitz notes repeatedly that Brandon did not identify as a lesbian and that he talked frequently to his lovers and friends about being transsexual, Minkowitz nevertheless identifies Brandon Teena as a confused but sexy cross-dressing butch lesbian:

> From photos of the wonder-boychic playing pool, kissing babes, and lifting a straight male neighbor high up in the air to impress party goers...Brandon looks to be the handsomest butch item in history—not just good looking, but arrogant, audacious, cocky—everything they, and I, look for in lovers.[32]

Minkowitz's article ultimately functions as a cautionary tale about violence against lesbians, but it doubles back on itself in a gesture of "blame the victim." Minkowitz's article explains that if Brandon had only found someone to talk to about "her" latent homosexuality, to counsel "her" through "her" intense self-hatred as a lesbian, "she" would not have gotten so embroiled in the pattern of deceit that sealed "her" fate. As the final lines of Minkowitz's article explain, "The frustration she had felt for so long had finally frustrated others, and the fury she could not express was ultimately expressed on her. By men."[33]

Minkowitz's narrative places the facts of Brandon Teena's life, indeed his own statements about himself, within a lesbian and gay paradigm that stresses visibility, pride, and coming out of the closet. Minkowitz understands Brandon Teena's insistence that he was not a lesbian to be the words of an unrealized, homophobic young woman who, had she greater access to social services, might have adjusted to lesbian life.[34] In this light, as Jordy Jones argues in an article for *FTM*, a newsletter produced by and for female-to-male transsexuals, "Brandon Teena was not killed because *she* was a Lesbian, *he* was transgendered. This is neither more or less horrific than if he had been killed for lesbianism, but it is different." Jones continues that "If the queer community makes of Brandon a martyr to a cause, so be it. But if he is to be canonized in any way, it should be done in such a way that respects his right to self-definition."[35] Self-definition is often difficult to pin down where no written sources point to a transsexual or transgendered identity per se, but through his survivors, Brandon Teena speaks clearly. Brandon Teena's mother notes that he never identified as a lesbian but instead wanted to be a man. And his girlfriends, who identified as heterosexual, understood him, if they had knowledge about his genital status, as a preoperative transsexual. Lana Tisdel remembered, "He said he was born female, is a female, but wants to be a male," and another girlfriend recalled that Brandon Teena, "was a woman outside but felt like a man, and...was going to have an operation."[36]

Self-definition is central to the recuperation and, perhaps, appropriation of historical figures for presentist means. But gender cannot continue to function as a slippery subset of sexuality, as evidence for a history of sexual outlaws that obliterates the possibility of gender outlaws and erases transgender history and experience. As Jason Cromwell notes in an article on Billy Tipton,

> I know that as an FTM many within our community would like to claim Billy as one of our own. We have so few role models, even though history is filled with females who lived and passed as men. Billy did not have surgery to alter his sex, and he certainly lived during a time when it was available. However, this is true for many FTMs, because the results are not very good and quite costly. Billy left no written explanation for the actions of his life. He left us instead with a life lived for over 50 years as a man. Does his life as a man have no meaning?[37]

What is the meaning, then, of cross-gender behavior and identity? What are the facts of gender when, upon the death of an anatomical female who lived his entire adult life as a man, his so called true identity is revealed to be female and his sexuality is recuperated as lesbian? What is the material substance that determines the truth of one's gendered or sexual identity: written articulation, daily practice, or, finally, genitalia?[38] Clearly, in the last instance—in these cases, hospital beds and autopsies—genitals remain the material fact of gender for many historians, and when gender (which often doubles back as biological sex) determines sexual identity, historical recuperation becomes a tricky political contest indeed. Yet these touchy and not so new questions about the materiality of gender are rarely addressed except by transsexuals and, not surprisingly, in lesbian S/M literature, where a discourse about the body remains central to community life. It is here that a relationship between lesbian and transsexual communities is more articulately fleshed out.

THE THEATER OF SOCIAL SPACE

In the first issue of *Venus Infers*, a magazine for lesbian sadomasochists, Pat Califia poses the question, "Who is my sister?" and outlines some controversies that were raised at the 1992 Powersurge Conference, a conference for leather-dykes that had as its goal the creation of "lesbian only space." The Powersurge Conference was located in Seattle, hosted by the Outer Limits, a Seattle-based women's leather and S/M group. Its program advised that a "lesbian is a WOMAN who considers herself to be a lesbian." Furthermore, it cautioned that the conference organizers would not "be the gender police," so participants should respect this policy, noting that "Because gender lines are bending and fading in these changing times we also have a further clarification for attendance...: If you can not slam your dick in a drawer and walk away, then the Amazon Feast and the Dungeon parties are not available to you." However, despite the graphic imagery, two floating signifiers ("lesbian" and "WOMAN") refused to contain themselves during the conference, and the admission policy generated for Powersurge 2 in 1993 changed its tone, specifying that the conference "is open to and welcomes women born women leatherdykes (chromosomal [XX] females only)."[39]

Like the admission policies generated by the Michigan Womyn's Music Festival and the 1991 National Lesbian Conference in Atlanta, which banned "non-genetic women," the 1993 Powersurge Conference policy was generated in response to the participation of transsexuals. However, as Califia observes, this policy excluded lesbian-identified male-to-female transsexuals while it continued to include ex-lesbian female-to-male transsexuals, despite their male appearance and identity, because they remain "chromosomally correct" according to the 1993 admission policy. This raises some peculiar questions about the relationship between bodies and nations—questions that have indeed generated some creative responses (like chromosomal admission tests).[40]

Califia's article stresses the pressing need to address the conflicted relationship between ex-lesbian FTMs, lesbian-identified MTFs, and leatherdykes. Califia articulates her discomfort with continued FTM participation at lesbian (leather) events, particularly while lesbian-identified MTF transsexuals have been excluded. While maintaining the right to self-determination (including the right to identify as a male-to-female transsexual lesbian *or* a female-to-male transsexual lesbian), Califia nevertheless encourages FTMs to take responsibility for their chosen gender. She states that "If someone is taking male hormones, letting their facial hair grow, has taken a male name, changed their legal documents to say they are male, and expects to be addressed by a male name and male pronouns, I can't really visualize that person as being a lesbian."[41] She notes her discomfort as she watches a roomful of lesbians listen respectfully to FTM "leatherdykes" describe how they want to "cut off their tits," while MTF leatherdykes who "love their tits" are not allowed to participate in Powersurge. Thus, on the one hand, while Califia argues that the material that informs gender springs from a number of life experiences and choices (legal identity, hormonal therapy, facial hair, etc.), she concludes that the relationship one determines with her or his physical body ultimately underscores the social fact of gender. In other words, Califia argues that a line between genders does exist, and male-identified individuals, despite their chromosomes, socialization, or genital status, cannot be lesbians. FTMs must place themselves on a continuum that realistically and by choice pulls them into the category "man"—and out of "women only" spaces. So, while the precise boundary between genders remains unclear, the regulatory function of gender boundaries remains uncontested.

Controversies surrounding the Michigan Womyn's Music Festival's entrance policies frame these questions from a different angle. This festival, which has been in existence for twenty years, is a weeklong event where thousands of women gather in a Michigan forest to camp, socialize, attend workshops, and enjoy an impressive line-up of mostly lesbian musicians. Until 1991 the festival had no explicit policy with regard to the attendance of transsexuals (or exactly who "womyn" are), but in 1991 Nancy Jean Burkholder was expelled from the festival after one day of attendance because she was suspected of being a transsexual. Burkholder was not the first transsexual woman to enter the festival. In fact, she had attended the year before, but for some reason in August 1991, security tightened, and Burkholder was expelled because even though this policy remained absent from 1991 festival literature, a security guard asserted that "transsexuals were not permitted to attend the festival."[42] Before she left, however, Chris, the security guard and contact person for the producers, asked Burkholder whether she had had a sex change operation. Burkholder said Chris could look at her genitals, but Burkholder maintained that her surgical history was her own business.[43] This information signals the ambiguity of the festival's policy. Burkholder was being ejected, but was it because of her genital status, her surgical history, her consciousness, or her chromosomes? Chris stated that the festival had a "no transsexuals" policy, and while this may be true, her curiosity about Burkholder's surgical history suggests that morphology may, indeed, have something to do with gender, or in this case with "womyn."

As a result of these events, the 1992 Michigan Womyn's Music Festival's literature got clearer about its policies, stating that the festival was open to "womyn-born-womyn" only. Although no transsexuals were expelled from this festival even though there were several in attendance, the 1993 festival saw the expulsion of four MTF transsexual lesbians and the birth of "Camp Trans," a quasi-refugee colony that pitched tent just outside the entrance to the festival. From this venue transsexuals and friends continued to distribute literature about the festival's exclusionary policy in an attempt to gauge whether the producers' policies matched those of the festivalgoers. Through the next year, the protesters pressured the festival producers, Lisa Vogel and Barbara Price, to state explicitly that their "womyn-born-womyn only" policy really meant that the festival was open to non-transsexual women only, which would raise the stakes not only to the level of explicit discrimination but closer to the body where one might measure one's transsexualness against surgical or hormonal intervention. However, the festival producers refused to change their "womyn-born-womyn" policy and in August 1994 "Camp Trans, for humyn born humyns" reseated itself, hosting a wealth of extracurricular activities, again just outside the entrance of the festival.

In 1994, however, the scab fell off the uneasy peace between S/M and non-S/M dykes as Tribe-8, a raucous band of musicians, performed amid controversy about their ostensibly violent lyrics and stage presence. At the same time, the Lesbian Avengers gathered momentum inside the festival in defense of excluded (transsexual) Lesbian Avengers on the outside. On the sixth day of the festival, after a group of protesters walked to the front gate and challenged the festival's entrance policy with a variety of differently sexed and gendered bodies, the producers agreed to allow transsexuals to enter the festival but still under the rubric of "womyn-born-womyn."[44] This constituted a victory for the protesters in that the meaning of gender was placed within the realm of self-definition, but questions of morphology continued to plague the policing of borders as it remained unclear whether non- or pre-operative MTF transsexuals might enter the festival or whether FTMs at any stage remained within the rubric of "womyn-born-womyn." In other words, how much or in what ways did the body constitute consciousness? Could consciousness exist irrelevant to the body's contours? Could individuals with penises be "womyn-born-womyn"? Might individuals with vaginas be men?

At this point, the compromise/victory engineered at the 1994 Michigan Womyn's Music Festival sounds a lot like Califia's fluid boundary whereby in the end, despite your body hair, legal identity, genital status, or surgical history, you place yourself as a result of your consciousness at any particular point in time on a bipolar gender continuum that admits the existence of a boundary between men and women, male and female. You decide for yourself what you are and whether or not you can, in good faith, enter a gender-bound social space. Even with this fluid and self-determining approach to the meaning and function of gender difference, gender remains foundational to the articulation and function of community. Bodies take on social meaning in relation to, for instance, the lesbian nation only if they can fix themselves in time and space as one gender or another. Despite mutating morphology, or the potentially revolutionary transformation of the body in response to oppressive gender constructs, the ability to articulate oneself intelligibly as one gender or another remains central to the function of community, social identity, political formation, and ultimately the forging of a relationship to the state in the name of separatism or civil rights protections.

DISCUSSION

In order to pose an alternative and more provocative perspective, one that does not necessarily reinscribe a boundary between male and female, I return to Powersurge's "slam your dick in a drawer" policy. This policy provides an example of a community that encourages gender play as an integral part of its practice but simultaneously struggles to maintain some kind of anatomy-based exclusionary policy around which the dyke part of the term "leatherdyke" continues to make sense. In this case the problem is not male-identification, self-definition, or surgical history but the function of the penis itself. In other words, dykes may have any variety of chromosomal configurations, shifting gender identifications, and most certainly ambiguous bodies, but Powersurge leatherdykes by definition cannot have functioning or particularly sensitive penises—or penises large enough to slam in a drawer. This policy, which remained in effect even though Powersurge 1995 dropped its "women-born-women" requirements, seems to be something of an innovative and practical solution to a theoretical conundrum (although it certainly raises a whole different set of problems). In many ways the "slam-your-dick-in-a-drawer" policy leaves a traditional sex/gender system behind in that sexuality (or dykeness) remains independent of gender and birth bodies. Dykeness has nothing to do with gender, is not something you are born with, nor is it a product of socialization or self-definition. Dykeness becomes a brute manifestation of one aspect of the body rather than an expression of genetic female same-gender or even cross-gender sexuality. Certainly, dykeness in this instance resonates loudly as lack, but because it is read from the body's immediate material form, gender's relationship to sexuality is erased and gender is innovatively excused from the picture.

Along a similar line, in a roundtable discussion, a number of FTMs challenge a sex/gender system that leaves no room for lesbians who are men or men who retain a lesbian history. Mike, for example, reveals that "I never really identified as female, but I identified as a lesbian for a while." He continues,

> Being a dyke gave me options. I knew I wasn't straight; I tried it, and it didn't work. I wanted to be with women. But the more I was out in the lesbian community, and the more I was out into S/M, the more I came to realize that, hey, I didn't fit there either, exactly. For me, it's not about being a man or being a woman, cuz there is some fluidity in there. I identify primarily as male, but I still have roots with the women's community that I don't want severed. I'm thankful that I was socialized female.[45]

Sky, another FTM, similarly unsettles an intuitively clear relationship between gender and sexual identity: "My emotional affinities are still very clearly with queer women. I'm forty years old, and I've been involved with dykes for more than half of my life. I'm not going to give that up...the dyke community is home."[46] According to these statements, Mike and Sky's lived practice as women (or lesbians) had become a historical anchor and the material fact of gender (or sexuality) despite their male bodies and male gender identities.[47] These statements suggest a paradigm in which sexual identity has social meaning beyond or outside gender, so that men might, at times, be lesbians—and women, gay men.[48]

These reconfigurations do not necessarily provide evidence for a third sex or third gender, nor do they indicate a postmodern proliferation of genders and sexualities. Instead, the tension between transsexual bodies and lesbian nations suggests a site where sex and gender no longer combine to flesh out culturally intelligible bodies. As Max Valerio argues, "Transsexuals are freaks, outsiders and outlaws in this world. We have lived the unthinkable. Are privy to information and experiences that most people have little conception of. This is our power, our damning glory."[49] Valerio's statement calls attention to the specificity of transsexual experience. He, along with sociologist Henry Rubin and literary critic Jay Prosser, argues that it is the materiality (the daily practice) of transsexual embodiment that confounds and displaces bipolar gender and sexual nationalism.[50] These observations resonate in response to gender and queer theory's appropriation of transsexual bodies as potentially revolutionary cultural artifacts.[51] They also resonate in response to a (lesbian) feminist critique and condemnation of transsexuality.

Most famously, Janice Raymond has argued that MTF transsexuals are dangerous to women and by extension lesbians because they not only colonize femaleness through embodiment, but they provide material for a medical-psychiatric empire to resolve a contemporary gender identity crisis by trading one set of gendered stereotypes for another. Raymond argues that through MTF transsexuals, doctors invade women's social spaces (as well as their bodies) and market the future of gender.[52] Bernice Hausman, in a more recent book, makes a similar claim. She argues that the contemporary concept of gender, as distinct from biological sex, is relatively new and emerged as a psychiatric response to medical technologies employed through the mid-twentieth century to "solve" the problem of intersexuality (or hermaphroditism). With the birth of new technologies such as endocrinology and plastic surgery, doctors found that they could reshape the genitals of an intersexed individual, usually a child, into something less ambiguous. The idea of a core gender identity grew out of these practices because some surgically altered individuals continued to express themselves as the "wrong" gender despite hormonal and surgical intervention. Gender, some psychiatrists reasoned, seemed to be fixed within the body rather than the product of socialization or an immediate expression of morphology. More surprisingly, the body's exterior began to seem more plastic than its interior. However, in Hausman's narrative, the agents of these inimical social changes shift from doctors to transsexuals in that through the late 1950s, as a response to the celebrity of Christine Jorgenson, transsexuals began to use the language of core gender identity to demand genital reconstruction. Thus, through the development and gradual acceptance of sex reassignment surgery as the appropriate medical intervention or cure for "gender dysphoria," transsexuals helped stabilize and naturalize the relatively new concept of gender identity. So while Hausman charts new territory in the history of medicine and its impact on feminist theory, she ultimately (like Raymond) blames transsexuals for normalizing, naturalizing, and codifying a bipolar gender system, fixing biological women into a feminine frame.[53]

As this essay illustrates, however, the meaning of gendered bodies, particularly transgendered bodies, remains complicated by and dependent on the territories (nations) bodies inhabit. Transsexuals do not fix gender in time and space, nor do they always already undermine its insipid naturalization. Rather, in the examples cited above, transsexual bodies reconfigure historical narrative and reterritorialize social space. Contrary to Raymond and Hausman's assertions, these actions upset a fixed relationship between sex, gender, and sexuality. In fact, while this essay does not intend to disrupt or deny the value of separatist practice, it illustrates (through the lens of lesbian nationalism) the function of intelligible bodies to the body politic. It argues that the body politic (the nation) exists for intelligible bodies, and despite anti-essentialist gestures to the contrary, contemporary sex/gender politics often document the absolutely desperate reiteration of bipolar gender as a foundation for sexual nationalism. Finally, this essay poses the specter of the outlaw (particularly as it takes the form of unruly, unreadable, inconsistent, but nevertheless material bodies) and suggests that outlaw bodies sharpen a boundary not between men and women, male and female, or even transsexual and non, but between abject and intelligible. This distinction evidences the possibility that while most bodies, even transgendered bodies, fit neatly or fold back into the body politic as readable, comprehensible, and intelligible, some retain or reclaim a fleeting moment of social and cultural unintelligibility, inhabiting a queer space, I would argue, outside, beyond, invisible to, and perhaps, as a result, in confrontation with the state.

NOTES

The author thanks CLAGS, the Center for Lesbian and Gay Studies, for the generous Rockefeller Fellowship that made the production of this essay possible. Thanks also go to Michael Du Plessis, Elizabeth Freeman, Ben Singer, and especially Alex Harris for insight and support through the writing process.

1. While it is important to distinguish between the terms "transsexual" and "transgender," particularly since access to medical technologies and state entitlements (i.e., change of name, alteration of birth certificate) are often dependent on a medical diagnosis of "transsexualism," this essay uses these terms somewhat interchangeably in order to broaden the category transsexual. For instance, if the term "transsexual" is used to signify a body that has entered into a formal relationship with doctors and the state with regard to "sex reassignment" (with the stated goal of eventually completing "the surgery"—a nonsense term with regard to female-to-male transsexuals who experience a series of surgeries, if any), many pre- and nonoperative transsexuals, particularly female-to-males, fall out of the category "transsexual" and can only be understood as "transgendered." For diagnostic categories, see the American Psychiatric Association's *Diagnostic and Statistical Manual of Mental Disorders,* 4th ed. (1994); for a more comprehensive discussion of the term "transgender" and its relationship to transsexuality, see Susan Stryker, "My Words to Victor Frankenstein above the Village of Chamounix," *GLQ* 1:3 (1994) 251–52; for more information about FTM surgeries, see James Green, "Getting Real about FTM Surgery," *Chrysalis: The Journal of Transgressive Gender Identities* 2:2 (1995) 27–32.
2. As this essay will explore further, the concept of nationalism ("the nation") refers to both the creation and reiteration of world political and economic borders (i.e., the post–World War II consolidation of the nation-state as the legitimate international political form, most obviously visible in the creation of the United Nations) *and* the contemporary emergence and articulation of resistant, deterritorialized, subcultural, and political movements. While Black Nationalism functions as the most resilient form of state-resistant nationalisms in the United States, more recently one can speak of the Lesbian Nation, the Queer Nation, and the Transgender Nation. See Michael Warner's introduction and Lauren Berlant and Elizabeth Freeman, "Queer Nationality," in *Fear of a Queer Planet,* ed. Michael Warner (Minneapolis: Minnesota University Press, 1993); Eve Kosofsky Sedgwick, "Nationalisms and Sexualities in the Age of Wilde," in *Nationalisms and Sexualities,* ed. Andrew Parker, Mary Russo, Doris Sommer, and Patricia Yaeger (New York: Routledge, 1992); David Evans, *Sexual Citizenship* (New York: Routledge, 1994), particularly his chapter "Trans-Citizenship: Transvestism and Transsexualism."
3. For more on the naturalized body, see Michel Foucault, *Discipline and Punish: The Birth of the Prison* (New York: Vintage, 1979), particularly "Docile Bodies," 136–69.
4. See George Mosse, *Nationalism and Sexuality* (New York: Howard Fertig, 1985) for an account of the rise of state nationalism through the construction of sexually respectable bodies.
5. Foucault, *Discipline and Punish.*
6. See Elizabeth Grosz, *Volatile Bodies: Toward a Corporeal Feminism* (Bloomington: Indiana University Press, 1994); Robyn Wiegman, *American Anatomies: Theorizing Race and Gender* (Durham: Duke University Press, 1995); Thomas Laqueur, *Making Sex: Body and Gender from the Greeks to Freud* (Cambridge: Harvard University Press, 1990); Anne Fausto-Sterling, *Myths of Gender: Biological Theories about Women and Men* (New York: Basic Books, 1985); *Representations* 14 (spring 1986), particularly Catherine Gallagher, "The Body Versus the Social Body in the Works of Thomas Malthus and Henry Mayhew," 83–106. See also Jennifer Terry and Jacqueline Urla, eds., *Deviant Bodies* (Bloomington: Indiana University Press, 1995); Judith Halberstam and Ira Livingston, eds., *Posthuman Bodies* (Bloomington: Indiana University Press, 1995).
7. Benedict Anderson, *Imagined Communities* (New York: Verso, 1991), 5–7.
8. Anderson argues that "print culture" and "print capitalism," particularly the publication and distribution of the popular novel and newspaper, weakened and ultimately replaced historically sacred symbols. *Imagined Communities,* 9–46.
9. Judith Butler, *Bodies That Matter: On the Discursive Limits of "Sex"* (New York: Routledge, 1993), 16.
10. Doug Hattaway, "The Employment Non-Discrimination Act," *HRCF Quarterly* (summer 1995): 6–7.

11.   "Trans Community Protests Human Rights Campaign Fund," *AEGIS News* (June 1995): 11.

12.   "HRCF Kicks Transfolk Out of National Anti-Discrimination Bill!" *TNT: Transsexual News Telegraph* 5 (summer 1995): 8; Susie Day, "ENDA Discrimination," *Lesbian & Gay New York*, Sept. 17, 1995, 9.

13.   Here I stress Michael Warner's use of the term "queer" as an identity that functions to both disrupt the minoritizing logic of toleration and assert a critique of heteronormalcy. See introduction to *Fear of a Queer Planet*, ed. Warner, vii–xxxi.

14.   As Foucault notes, in the age of Enlightenment "there will be hundreds of tiny theaters of punishment" where specific territories or functional sites, like HRCF's Employment Non-Discrimination Act, aid the production of disciplined bodies. Michel Foucault, *Discipline and Punish: The Birth of the Prison* (New York: Vintage, 1979), 113.

15.   Joan Nestle, *A Restricted Country* (Ithaca, N.Y.: Firebrand, 1987); Joan Nestle, ed., *The Persistent Desire: A Femme-Butch Reader* (Boston: Alyson, 1992); Elizabeth Lapovsky Kennedy and Madeline D. Davis, *Boots of Leather, Slippers of Gold: The History of a Lesbian Community* (New York: Routledge, 1993).

16.   Judith Halberstam provides a historical account of lesbian masculinities in "Female Masculinities: Tommies, Tribades and Inverts," and "Lesbian Masculinity or Even Stone Butches Get the Blues" (unpublished manuscripts).

17.   Esther Newton problematizes the slippage between masculinity and lesbianism in "The Mythic Mannish Lesbian: Radclyff Hall and the New Woman," *Signs* 9:4 (1984): 557–75. Nestle's and Kennedy and Davis's recent work (cited above) also clarify the distinction between passing women and butch lesbians by articulating in rich detail the function of butch gender codes as a component of lesbian desire and representation.

18.   Jason Cromwell, "Default Assumptions, or The Billy Tipton Phenomenon," *FTM* 28 (July 1994): 4–5; Susan Stryker, "Local Transsexual History," *TNT: Transsexual News Telegraph* 5 (summer–autumn 1995): 14–15.

9.   Originally produced by the San Francisco Lesbian and Gay History Project (1979), *She Even Chewed Tobacco* is currently distributed in video form by Women Make Movies. See " 'She Even Chewed Tobacco': A Pictorial Narrative of Passing Women in America," in *Hidden from History: Reclaiming the Gay and Lesbian Past*, eds. Martin Duberman, Martha Vicinus, and George Chauncey, Jr. (New York: Penguin, 1989).

20.   Louis Sullivan, *From Female to Male: The Life of Jack Bee Garland* (Boston: Alyson Press, 1990), 31.

21.   Sullivan, *From Female to Male*, 3.

22.   Sullivan, *From Female to Male*, 4.

23.   Betty Cox, quoted by Cindy Kirshman in "The Tragic Masquerade of Billy Tipton," *Windy City Times*, March 1, 1990, 17.

24.   Doug Clark, "Billy Tiptop: An Improvised Life," *Seattle Spokesman Review*, January 21, 1990. See also Cindy Kirshman, "The Tragic Masquerade"; Ann Japenga, "A Jazz Pianist's Ultimate Improvisation," *Los Angeles Times*, February 13, 1989.

25.   Linda Lee, "Women Posing as Men Pursued Better Opportunities," *Seattle Post Intelligence: What's Happening*, September 10, 1989, 11. While the initial flurry of mainstream press coverage echos this analysis (see "Musician's Death at 74 Reveals He Was a Woman," *New York Times*, February 2, 1989; "Autopsy: Musician Was a Woman," *Newsday*, February 2, 1989), follow-up articles argued that Tipton's sexual or gender identity had more to do with his cross-dressing than his desire to succeed as a musician. See Kirshman, "The Tragic Masquerade"; Clark, "Billy Tipton: An Improvised Life"; and Japenga, "A Jazz Pianist's Ultimate Improvisation."

26.   Jason Cromwell, "Default Assumptions, or The Billy Tipton Phenomenon," 4–5.

27.   "Billy Tipton Was a (Choose One):" *TNT: Transsexual News Telegraph* 1 (summer 1993): 22. A smaller version of this "advertisement" also appeared in *Engender* 2 (July 1993).

28.   "2 Men Held in Slaying of 3 at Humboldt," *Omaha World-Herald*, January 2, 1994; "Rape Report Tied to Killings: Family Says Slaying Were Preventable," *Lincoln Journal-Star*, January 4, 1994; "Woman Who Posed as a Man Is Found Slain with 2 Others," *New York Times*, January 4, 1994; "Her Fatal Deception?" *New York Newsday*, January 5, 1994; "Charade Revealed Prior to Killings," *Des Moines Register*, January 9, 1994; "Questions in Triple Homicide," San Francisco Chronicle, March 17, 1994.

29.   "Rape Report Tied to Killings."

30.   Kristina Campbell, "Transsexual, Two Others Murdered in Nebraska," *The Washington Blade*, January 14, 1994, 19; Mindy Ridgway, "Queers Have No Right to Life—In Nebraska," *San Francisco Bay Times*, January 13, 1994, 7.

31.   Terry A, Moroney, letter to Anthony Marro, editor, *New York Newsday*, January 5, 1994. See also AVP press release, "Anti-Violence Project Calls for Bias Classification in Nebraska Lesbian Murder," January 5, 1994.

32.   Donna Minkowitz, "Love Hurts," *Village Voice*, April 19, 1994.

33.   Minkowitz, "Love Hurts."

34.   In fact, Minkowitz is so sure Brandon Teena was a lesbian that she wonders why Brandon Teena moved from Lincoln, a city with a visible gay community, to Falls City, an even more remote Nebraska town, rather than San Francisco or Denver, "the gay mecca of choice for corn belters." Clearly, Minkowitz can not see the events of Brandon Teena's life and death outside a gay lens. Perhaps Brandon Teena wanted to evade *misrecognition* as a lesbian and as a result chose a city with heightened gender codes so to more effectively live as a man.

35.   Jordy Jones, "FTM Crossdresser Murdered," *FTM* 26 (Feb. 1994): 3.

36.   Campbell, "Transsexual, Two Others Murdered in Nebraska," 19; "Charade Revealed Prior to Killings," 4B; "Her Fatal Deception?" See also Denise Noe, "Why Was Brandon Teena Murdered?" *Chrysalis* 2:2 (1995): 50.

37.   Cromwell, "Default Assumptions, or The Billy Tipton Phenomenon," 5.

38.   See Grosz, *Volatile Bodies*, for a discussion of the materiality of subjectivity.

39.   Pat Califia, "Who Is My Sister: Powersurge and the Limits of Our Community," *Venus Infers* 1:1 (summer 1993): 4–5.

40.   Renee Richards, for example, was asked (but refused) to submit to a Barr body test in which cells from the inside of the cheek are examined to reveal chromosomal distributions. See Bernice Hausman, *Changing Sex: Transsexualism, Technology, and the Idea of Gender* (Durham: Duke University Press, 1995), 12.

41.   Califia, "Who Is My Sister," 6.

42.   Nancy Jean Burkholder, "A Kinder, Gentler Festival?" *TransSisters* 2 (November–December 1993): 4.

43.   Burkholder, "Kinder, Gentler Festival?" 4.

44.   Davina Anne Gabriel, "Mission to Michigan III: Barbarians at the Gates," *TransSisters* 7 (winter 1995): 14–32; Riki Anne Wilchins, "The Menace in Michigan," *Gendertrash* 3 (winter 1995): 17–19.

45.   "FTM/Female-to-Male: An Interview with Mike, Eric, Billy, Sky, and Shadow," in *Dagger: On Butch Women,* ed. Lily Burana, Roxxie, and Linnea Due (Pittsburgh: Cleis Press, 1994), 155.

46.   Sky, in "FTM/Female-to-Male," 158.

47.   On the other hand, Henry Rubin argues in a study of FTM identity formation that FTMs often consolidate their gender identities around a vehement disidentification from butch lesbians. Henry Samuel Rubin, "Transformations: Emerging Female to Male Transsexual Identities" (Ph.D. diss. Brandeis University, 1996). See also Ben Singer, "Velveteen Realness" (paper delivered at the CLAGS Trans/Forming Knowledge Conference, May 2, 1996).

48.   C. Jacob Hale, "Dyke Leatherboys and Their Daddies: How to Have Sex without Men or Women," paper delivered at the Berkshire Conference on the History of Women, June 8, 1996).

49.   Max Wolf Valerio, "Legislating Freedom," review of *The Apartheid of Sex* by Martine Rothblatt, *TNT: Transsexual News Telegraph* 5 (summer–autumn 1995): 26.

50.   Henry Samule Rubin, "Transformations: Emerging Female to Male Transsexual Identities"; Jay Prosser, "No Place Like Home: The Transgendered Narrative of Leslie Feinberg's *Stone Butch Blues,*" *Modern Fiction Studies* 41 (fall–winter 1995).

51.   For an overview of feminist and queer theory's approach to transsexual identities, see Kathleen Chapman and Michael du Plessis, " 'Don't Call Me *Girl*': Feminist Theory, Lesbian Theory, and Transsexual Identities" in *Cross Purposes: Lesbian Studies, Feminist Studies, and the Limits of Alliance*, Dana Heller, ed. (Bloomington: Indiana University Press, 1997); and Ki Namaste, " 'Tragic Misreadings': Queer Theory's Erasure of Transgender Subjectivity," in *Queer Studies: A Lesbian, Gay, Bisexual, and Transgender Anthology,* Janice G. Raymond, *The Transsexual Empire: The Making of the She-Male* (Boston: Beacon, 1979).

53.   Hausman, *Changing Sex.*

29

Manliness

Patrick Califia

When prolific author, sex activist, and psychotherapist Pat Califia became Patrick Califia at the age of forty-five, it was a surprise to much of the lesbian community in which he had been a foremost public figure. Although in 1997 he had published *Sex Changes*, a commentary on transgender politics, his personal decision to undergo gender transition was still unexpected in many quarters. Four years later, in this article originally published by the San Francisco sex shop, Good Vibrations, Califia reflected on his experience of manhood and masculinity.

Califia finds the label "man" inadequate to describe his experience, since his history and knowledge of the world had been so different from men who were biological males raised as boys. He suggests that manhood in its conventional form has little in common with the way he had chosen to be in the world. He also acknowledges that his own understanding of manhood resonates with that of many women, and was shaped by his history of living—however uncomfortably—as a woman for most of his life. In making these admissions, Califia brings into public discussion topics that have circulated more privately for some time among transgender men. Some FTMs feel that perhaps it is not possible to "be a man" without a lifetime's socialization in the role of man. Moreover, socially dominant forms of masculine personhood—even if they could be attained—are often not even desired by individuals with female life histories, particularly if those individuals have feminist leanings and lesbian histories.

Califia raises the issue of "female masculinity" in this provocative opinion piece, and raises as well the question of any attendant political obligation to reshape social and cultural understandings of masculinity. His article is perhaps most relevant for FTM men who have come out of the lesbian-feminist community, who have retained the values of that community and who have forged an even closer sense of community with each other through their transitions. It should also be of interest, however, to a broader audience of gender scholars seeking critical vantage points on the social construction of manhood, masculinity, and maleness.

"Why are blonde jokes so short?"
"So men can remember them."

"Why do sperm have such a short way to swim?"
"Because if they had to stop to ask directions, they'd never make it."
—Anonymous Internet humor

I'm home recuperating from chest surgery. It has taken me four years of therapy, 55 doses of testosterone, innumerable conversations with friends, a lot of soul-searching, and two months working for a gay men's mental health service to get to this point. In the end, what it came down to was that I could not progress in my exploration of masculinity and male identity without the help of a plastic surgeon. Despite a deeper voice, a redistribution of body fat, and a fuzzy face, in order to pass I had to wear a ridiculously bulky jacket and limit my social interactions to gender-naïve people. It had gotten harder, not easier, to assert my preference for male pronouns. Even when there was polite compliance, I felt like the other person's eyes were flicking from my chest up to my face, and inside they were silently saying, "Yeah, right."

I still don't quite know what to call myself. It is hard to claim the word "man"; easier to simply define as FTM (female-to-male) or transgendered. I had accumulated 45 years of history operating in the world as a woman, albeit a very different sort of woman, before I transitioned. Those habits of thought, self-image, movement, expression are hard to break, no matter how deep my dissatisfaction. I am more than a little jealous of "primary transsexuals" who can honestly say they feel like men who were born into the wrong bodies; that they are correcting an error of nature. My gender dysphoria has had more to do with feeling that there is something wrong when other people perceived or treated me as if I were a girl. Not wanting to be female, but not having much enthusiasm for the only other option our society offers.

My therapist keeps reminding me that it's possible to be both male and female, or to create an individual synthesis of gender expression that is a path between these dichotomies. I don't know if this is where I will be for the rest of my life, or if getting more facial hair will tip the balance and send me with more determination into the territory of manhood. (It feels silly to even say these words.) But something has changed, with the new shape of my torso. I was afraid I would feel mutilated or injured, and I don't. I feel relief. I feel lightness of being and hope and optimism. It feels right to have smaller nipples, a chest that tells grocery store clerks and people behind the counter at the post office to call me sir instead of ma'am.

I know that some of my reluctance to embrace manliness wholeheartedly comes from a twisted relationship with my father, who seemed determined to beat any resistance to femininity out of me. Through physical ordeals that were scripted as games or sports, he offered me one chance after another to prove to him that I wasn't a girl. Boxing. Football. Shooting. Wrestling. Hiking. Hunting and fishing. Of course, none of these contests were fair.

All I had to do to lose was to show pain, lose my temper, or give up—let alone cry. My father's idea of what it meant to be a man was based on the insane standards of a Wild West show or a World War II action movie. He embodied a crazy amount of physical courage, strength, and stamina, a spooky skill in woodcraft, knowledge about wildlife, and an appetite for alcohol and women that made him a small-town legend. He was an intelligent and unscrupulous sadist who nevertheless possessed great charm, charisma, and sentimental tenderness. I always knew that my father was quite capable of killing another man. This was supposed to make me feel safe, since one of the tasks of a real man is to protect his wife and children, but it seemed to me that what I mostly needed was to be protected from him, and nobody was equal to that chore.

When I was equivocating about whether to keep taking testosterone or not, asking myself if I liked it just because it gave me an excuse to stick a needle full of a drug into my body, I tripped over an amazingly deep well of shame about maleness, and antipathy toward it. The jokes at the start of this column come from that place. Everybody, even men, know that they are at best stupid, wrong, and backward; at worst, evil. The good people, the people who will transform the world and make it a safer, better place, are women. The hero of today is not Superman. She is a 16-year-old cat/woman-of-color on a motorcycle, or an 18-year-old blonde martial artist who patrols graveyards with a sharp wooden stake in one hand. I love "Dark Angel" and "Buffy the Vampire Slayer." Amazons are still necessary. The archetype of the female warrior offers something reparative to 21st-century souls. But if I am no longer a dyke, no longer an Amazon, what/who am I? Are men good for anything at all?

I've asked as many straight women as I know about this, figuring that since they sleep with men and even live with them, they ought to know what valuable qualities they possess. It seems to be an embarrassing question. A couple of times, my het girlfriends have admitted that they like cocks or that boyfriends are useful for picking up heavy things and changing the oil in the car. One woman mentioned that her male lover was the only person who would watch "Beavis and Butthead" with her, and laugh as hard as she did. Another said that watching her boyfriend move around the apartment was like watching her big dog run through the park. There was something unselfconscious about his physicality that made her love him.

Where are the toeholds I could use to scale the wall into the castle of manliness? I like penetration, and I think I'm pretty good at it, but my dick is not a biological organ; there's no way to skirt around that deficit. I'm disabled, so I hardly ever pick up heavy things, and what I know about cars could be written on the inside of a matchbook cover in 20-point type. Physical grace is a rare and valuable experience. Most of the time I live in my head, or in a book, or in somebody else's head. My macho is in my intellect; my sharpest weapon is my tongue; my biggest muscle is my brain. I get inside other people's sexual places by understanding them, by being willing to see and accept aspects of their fantasies or needs that are usually repressed.

In a world where women are supposed to feel and men are supposed to act, I stand in the middle and comprehend what both of them are doing, and why. But I remain a stranger in each of these territories.

When I crave a seamless male image, what I'm mostly longing for is consistency and invisibility, the social convenience of passing without being questioned or challenged. It's dangerous to confuse other people about your gender. There's a lot of transphobic rage on the street, looking for a target. Why "normal" people should be so angry about someone else's deviance is an interesting question, but it's not one I want to confront every time I go out to buy a sandwich or walk through a museum. I have been an outsider all my life, and sometimes I get weak and long for the simpleminded pleasure of belonging, just being one more horned beast in the herd.

Maybe the problem is that I am trying to find a different rationale for living or a different code of virtue for men and women, when in fact we all ought to be judged according to a single standard. Things like compassion, honesty, the ability to nurture, independence, self-care, vulnerability, friendship, desire, creativity, assertiveness, or industry are worthwhile qualities for both men and women to possess. It's no longer acceptable for men to claim exemption from housework or the emotional reciprocity it takes to maintain intimacy because of their willingness to compete, fight, or die in dangerous occupations or emergencies. Still, I keep thinking there must be something unique about being a man, something fit to be celebrated in ritual and mythology, the stuff of a spiritual mystery teaching. Or is this desire the root of the oppression of women—the need to cordon off certain activities or experiences and say "Only we can do this and women may not," because we must have a source of pride and uniqueness in order to have meaningful lives?

Perhaps transition will be an ironic experience for me, and I will discover that I remain the same person, having changed only my physical appearance. Now, that's a depressing thought! I wonder if I can talk about what I like about being a man and disliked about being a woman without being attacked for being sexist? Can I make a few generalizations with the understanding that there will always be individual exceptions? I'm not trying to say one gender is better than the other or ought to have power over the other. I have no idea if the experience of genetic men resembles mine. But taking testosterone has given me some clues about the differences between the sexes.

It's harder to track psychological or emotional changes due to taking testosterone than it is to notice the physical differences. But I think the former actually outweigh the latter. It isn't that testosterone has made me a different person. I always had a high sex drive, liked porn and casual sex, couldn't imagine giving up masturbation, was able to express my anger, and showed a pretty high level of autonomy and assertiveness. But all of these things have gotten much more intense. During the first six months on T, every appetite I had was painfully sharp. A friend of mine expressed it this way: "When I had to eat, I had to eat right fucking now. If I was horny, I had to come immediately. If I needed to shit, I couldn't wait. If I was pissed off, the words came right out of my mouth. If I was bored, I had to leave." My body and all the physical sensations that spring from it have acquired a piquancy and an immediacy that is both entertaining and occasionally inconvenient. Moving through the world is even more fun, involves more stimulation than it used to; life is more here-and-now, more about bodies and objects, less about thoughts and feelings.

This is especially true of sexuality. I always liked visual erotic material, but it can take me over now in a way that it didn't before. This applies to dirty magazines, X-rated videos, billboards that feature girls with cleavage, and any person on the street who seems attractive. Before taking T, I never bought into the bullshit about women's sexuality being "whole-body" rather than genital; I knew where my orgasm came from. Now I feel a much stronger, localized concentration of reaction and need. I can absolutely understand why men can (and must!) pay $40 for a blowjob on the way home from work, or get caught jacking off in public toilets. There's something about having genitals that visibly change when you get aroused that makes the sexual experience more palpable. It makes the fact that I desire something or someone seem much more real.

Casual sex has changed. When I want to get off, my priority is to find somebody who will do that as efficiently as possible, and while I certainly would rather have a pleasant interaction with that person, I don't think a lot about how they were doing before they got down on their knees, and I don't care very much how they feel after they get up and leave. It's hard to keep their needs in mind; it's easier to just assume that if they wanted anything, it was their responsibility to try to get it. I always preferred to take sexual initiative, and that has become even more ego-congruent. Part of what I like about men is their willingness to put it out there, so to speak—to take responsibility for running the fuck. While this can be a rather obnoxious quality, it's also true that if sex is going to happen, somebody has to be the one to say, "Let's do it."

It's easier to make decisions. I don't get so caught up in agonizing about what I should do. I just want to make a choice so I can move on and get something done. What I do matters less than the fact that I'm able to get busy, feel that I'm making progress. My hand-eye coordination has improved. (I'm not kidding. I never used to be able to catch things that were thrown at me, and parallel parking was a nightmare. Now I don't even think about doing these tasks.) Working with other people has also, for some weird reason, gotten better. I don't fret about hierarchies or teamwork. It just seems to happen, to fall into place. Of course, that may be because I am mostly doing things with groups of men, and we don't have to engage in that endless crap about reaching consensus, or punish each other if somebody dares to excel. Men seem able to form teams or squads more easily than women. There's less bullshit about leadership or taking orders.

As bitterly as I've hated my father, I also spent much of my childhood admiring his physical adeptness and longing for his approval and love. (Isn't this a song that every man sings into his beer?) There was a good person in there. If he hadn't been troubled by a mother who made him feel guilty for being smart and healthy (unlike his brother, who had Down's syndrome), a bad marriage to a religious fanatic, a life-threatening job that crushed his body and soul, and clinical depression, we would have had a very different relationship.

Despite the terrifying responsibility of trying to provide for a wife and six kids on a coal miner's salary, he was capable of memorable acts of care and enchantment. He pulled every one of my baby teeth, and was so quick about it, so good at making me laugh, that I can't remember feeling any pain at all. Whether he was giving me nasty-tasting cold medicine or putting ointment in my eyes, he was gentle and sweet to me when I was sick. He was always bringing home amazing things from underground—rocks that glowed when you put them under a blacklight, fossilized ferns and dinosaur footprints, quartz crystals and agates, plain egg-shaped rocks that contained glittering wonders when they were cracked in half. My love of wildlife and my ability to navigate and survive outdoors are not small gifts, and they are things that my mother certainly would never have tried to instill in me.

Being a fag or a third-gender person is a way for me to try to salvage the good that I saw in my father, the virtues that I see in ordinary men, without being damaged by the ugliness, the unbridled rage, the hatred of homosexuals, the racism, the arrogance that made me wary of my dad. I loved him because he couldn't shoot our sick old dog, but I hated him because he could clobber me every day and never think twice about how it felt to me or whether it was fair. He was not able to be consistent. He was able to shoulder the crushing responsibility of being a breadwinner and a man's man, but he couldn't engage in enough introspection to calculate the cost of that, or flexible enough to look for other solutions to life's big problems. Still, even in his capacity for violence, I am able to see something worthwhile. I'm not a pacifist. I can't believe that there will ever be a time when human beings won't need hunters or soldiers. What we need to find (or regain) is a sense of grief or loss when animal or human life is taken, and a profound humility about whether we are worthy to effect such a profound change, even if our intentions are to serve life and protect the people we love.

There are altars to goddesses all over my house. A few statues and posters of Shiva, Ganesha, Cernunnos, and Pan have crept in as well. I have a silver picture of Sulis, a Celtic god of healing springs, that I wear around my neck. I'm glad there are pagan gods who are phallic because they represent pleasure or wisdom or the ability to unite with the female principle, not because they are domineering or murderous. Gods who represent the wild world, who guard as well the feral part of human beings. Divine heroes like Gilgamesh and Enkiddu, men who loved each other.

It seems so much more difficult for men to approach one another in a spirit of equality and desire than it is for women to bond erotically and romantically. But I think that is where most of the transformation of manhood and masculinity is taking shape. Few insults can carry as much scorn as the word "cocksucker." When I hear somebody spit out this slur, I am struck not just by the antigay hatred behind it, but also the self-hatred.

Men are going to despise themselves, their bodies, and their genitals until they learn how to express their maleness in an honorable and respectful way. Despite our imperfections, our limitations, how do we become worthy of self-care, and mutual affiliations? This question has far-reaching spiritual and political implications. I expect it may take the whole second half of my life to figure out even a partial answer. But I believe someday I will hear the word "cocksucker," and know that it's said with awe, with admiration, to designate a holy person, a state of priesthood, a healer, a hero.

30

selection from
Lesbians Talk Transgender

ZACHARY I. NATAF

IN *LESBIANS TALK TRANSGENDER*, FEMALE-TO-MALE TRANS MAN ZACH NATAF addresses the complex relationship of lesbians with both MTF and FTM transgender people. In the section of his book reprinted below, Nataf explores how lesbian feminists have reacted to the impact on lesbianism of visible and viable transgender identities.

Nataf begins by raising a crucial issue in the debate: if gender roles and sexuality categories become blurred, where does that leave lesbians? Through skillfully editing voices originating among transgender people and non-transgender lesbians, Nataf addresses the fears of the lesbian feminist community. He acknowledges the essential authenticity of the female body experienced in lesbian relationships, and the seemingly natural gender divisions that are themselves essential to a gender-based sexuality (and which, as such, are the basis of the inequalities against which lesbian feminists are fighting.) Nataf notes a new sophistication within contemporary lesbian feminism, that builds on the historical foundations of the tradition, but which is also willing to accept a new diversity of lesbian identities, and new movements within the transgender communities. This historical evolution has enabled some lesbians to listen to transgender voices, and to reconsider the bio-determinist accusations and arguments that have taken place between the two communities.

Nataf concludes by questioning who can best claim that "biology is not destiny." He points out that if any group has taken that argument to its literal conclusion, it is transgender people. And yet, he does so in a way that creates the space in which transgender and lesbian communities can both communicate their fears and dreams, to create an opening for dialogue, and to suggest that the two groups are really not that far removed in their political aspirations.

Some lesbians have anxiety and fear about how easy it is to alter the body. Its mutability and the irreversible nature of the changes resulting from the hormones, even before any surgery, are terrifying when we have a sense of the entity of the body as certain and inviolable and fixed. Other major fears expressed by lesbians are to do with gender and sexuality categories blurring or breaking down, impacting upon their sense of lesbian community. What are transsexuals really? The effect on the identity of partners of TSs, the impact on butch identity, the alienness of the constructed genitals of MTFs all have resonances for lesbians. Resistance to dealing with one's own sense of fear, discomfort, ambivalence and prejudice, and feeling forced to change one's safe, familiar view of the world, also contribute to anxiety.

More transsexuals also now exist who do not pursue a complete change. Increasing numbers of individuals utilize some but not all of the available sex-change technology, resulting in 'intermediate' bodies, somewhere between female and male...Some of these may not want to leave their lesbian communities, and they should not be forced to do so. They may cause confusion, repelling some lesbians and attracting others. But if community membership were based on universal desirability, no one would qualify...Our society should be as inclusive, humane, and tolerant as we can make it.

—Gayle Rubin, 'Of Catamites and Kings'

Male-to-female transsexuals feed into that fear, in for example Jan Raymond's book, that scientists are going to create a race of perfect women.

—Alison Gregory

The question is what are these people going to be when they've changed sex? That is what threatens. When it's a lesbian becoming a man, what they really want to know is who are they going to sleep with? Are they going to sleep with straight men, gay men, straight women, lesbians? It's that bit that bothers them because in terms of lesbian identity, I think there's a huge identification issue. And where does this lesbian go? Do we just lose them into the abyss out there because they change sex?

—Annette Kennerley

The FTM presence at Powersurge (the leather dyke conference in Seattle) last year made me uncomfortable. A lot of this is my personal garbage. I am afraid that the visibility of FTMs will change the definition of what's butch until women will feel they have to take male hormones to make them masculine enough to be butch. I am afraid other people will judge my own strategies for dealing with gender dysphoria... [T]he leather dyke community is very competitive. Labels are important to us and we stigmatise women who don't meet our expectations of the roles we have assigned them... I'm afraid of not qualifying, not counting, being second-rate. Being uncomfortable is not necessarily a bad thing. Any time I try to absorb some new information, I have to tolerate a period of ambivalence and ambiguity.

—Pat Califia, 'Who is my Sister?'

[O]ur mere presence is often enough to make people sick. Take that great scene in the film, *The Crying Game*...The revelation of Dil's gender ambiguity called into question both the sexual orientation (desire) and the gender identity of Fergus. His vomiting can be seen as much as a sign of revulsion as an admission of attraction, and the consequential upheaval of his gender identity and sexual orientation...heretofore unquestioned states of very personal identity.

—Kate Bornstein, *Gender Outlaw*

I'd met a male-to-female transsexual. And that freaked me out and I thought, no I can't cope with this. In essence your body is still male, even with the operation. S. told me what the operation involved. And I guess if she hadn't told me that—that it is the penis and it's been inverted—then maybe I wouldn't have reacted the way I did. But my reaction was, 'Oh my God, that is a cock.' And I just didn't want to be anywhere near it.

—Kacha

LESBIAN FEMINIST POLITICS

Feminists struggled to reclaim lesbianism from the oppressive designation of pathology created by nineteenth-century sexologists and its persistence as a listed mental disorder in the American Psychiatric Association's *Diagnostic and Statistical Manual* (till 1973). Feminists sought to purify the category of lesbian. A pure lesbianism was fashioned and boundaries drawn to determine who was to be included and who was not. The characteristic of sameness based on common experience of oppression due to the social status of women became conflated with biological/anatomical sameness, exacerbating the biological link to gender.

For cultural feminism the source of an authentic woman's consciousness had its roots in the female body as testament and 'truth'. Radical feminism mapped women's territory within those boundaries which grew out of that 'truth'. Revolutionary feminism, which pointed out that the system of patriarchy was upheld by the actions of individual men, meant that it became even more critical to be able to designate who was a man and who was a woman in order to distinguish oppressor from oppressed. The commonsense belief that it was self-evident what a man/woman was meant the categories themselves were not questioned.

> Hiking Dykes, a walking group, split over the issue of whether a transsexual could join the group or not. The feminist argument against allowing transsexuals to be part of a woman only group was that they don't have a woman's past. They weren't brought up as women and because so much of the women's movement was premised on personal experience and sharing that experience and theorising out of that, feminists argued for exclusion of transsexuals. The other reason is the practical experience of actually being in groups with transsexuals. It's probably unfair to judge all transsexuals on the ones that one has come across. But it's very difficult for people to lose the habits of their gender upbringing. Male-to-female transsexuals in women's groups dominate, in my experience. In this society women have little enough space and time for their voices to be heard. So if they form a group so that they can have women's voices heard they don't really want to have a man there.
>
> —Rosemary Auchmuty

> It was weird for me to sit in a room full of dykes and watch them listen respectfully while FTMs talked about wanting to cut off their tits. But when the handful of MTFs who had come to the workshop dared to speak out, the hostility toward them was palpable. FTMs take male hormones so they can look as masculine as possible. They wear penile prostheses in their pants and crossdress. Most of them would have surgery to give themselves penises if they could afford it and if the surgery could create a fully-functional male sex organ. Why do these folks qualify as 'leather dykes' when MTFs don't? MTFs take female hormones, love their tits, often undergo painful surgery to create female genitals, and live full-time as females and as dykes. It made absolutely no sense to me that FTMs were welcome at a [leather dyke conference] when MTFs were not.
>
> I think MTF dykes have earned the right to be part of my community. Not every MTF is my close personal friend or somebody I'd want to sleep with, but they certainly are not the enemy.
>
> —Pat Califia, 'Who is my Sister?'

Even socialist feminism, which looks at the material circumstances of oppression, assumes that 'natural' gender divisions are the basis of inequality and disempowerment.

> Neither gender is a bit of a difficult concept to crunch in a society which structures identity through gender. What does it mean? There would be an enormous shift in the mode of structuring identity. I don't know if the proliferation of gendered identities is deconstructive or not. I suspect it's no more or less deconstructive than if you just have gay people hanging around. I don't think it's going to make any amount of difference to the way the dominant figures. In terms of the strategy in relation to gender, transgendered people tend to fit more into a reactionary strategy than a radical strategy. A radical strategy wouldn't accept a biological argument for human domination and subordination.
>
> —Paula Graham

Transgender is seen by feminists to be politically reactionary and an individual solution to what is a collective problem.

> I don't see male-to-female and female-to-male transsexuals as equivalent in any way. I don't define male-to-female transsexuals who become lesbians, as lesbians. I don't think they should be in women only spaces because I don't think they are women. A male-to-female will always be a man whether he's had his penis cut off and breasts put there or not. As far as I'm concerned, he is a man. Men are brought up with much more status than women. He hasn't been brought up with the same oppressions as women. I wouldn't trust him and I wouldn't want to have anything to do with him.
>
> In terms of female-to-male transsexuals, it's different because, yes, they've been brought up as a woman but, no matter what individual reasons they feel there are for doing it, they become part of the class of oppressors. There are a lot of advantages to living that way. It's a complete fucking cop out. In a lot of ways it would be easier for us all to bloody live as men. They have got so many more privileges. To me it's an individual solution to the collective oppression of women. And that's why it enrages me because I don't think we can ever find solutions on an individual basis to a society that absolutely fucks women over. I am suspicious of those women because I think they are making alliances with men and taking privileges that men have but still wanting to be part of the support system that they get from women. In fact they want the best of both worlds. I would exclude those women from the lesbian community.
>
> —Hilary McCollum

> I think there's becoming less and less affirmation of women being attracted to women. It seems now that the only really sexy lesbian sexuality is one that's very phallocentric. What does that say about us as women, that we have to take on a masculine body to attract women?
>
> —Inge Blackman

Feminism questioned the content of gender roles, demanding expansion of them and changing the balance, claiming that gender shouldn't matter any more and that it was a false constraint. Although, for some, lesbian is a separate gender category to woman, when political lines against patriarchy are drawn the binary is reinvoked. This may be necessary as a strategy but what are the consequences as a description of reality? The fact that some women, some lesbians, actually fell on the border or beyond as well as on either side of the line failed to provoke a dissolution of the categories altogether.

> What is it that makes you want to go further into something much more to do with gender, not about being a lesbian or being butch? I think there's got to be another element, because you can be as butch as you like and why do you need to do anything more? But it's interesting that in a more liberal climate there are still butch lesbians who want to have a sex change. This is something more than lesbian politics can encompass and I think that's what is threatening people.
>
> —Annette Kennerley

Separatists have re-entrenched behind the view of gender as bi-polar, policing the borders. Not only do multiple genders seem unthinkable in separatist lesbian feminism, they are simply not the issue. But at a time in our culture when gender is a burning issue, separatism seems an obsolete tool for making sense of the world. All difference, not just men, maleness and patriarchy, has become a target of suppression. Inevitably the unique and complex experiences of and the differences between lesbians cannot be subsumed within the boundaries of the 'pure lesbian'.

> I think lesbian separatist feminist politics has had its day now. Maybe it was necessary at the time. There's always a reason for separatism in any political movement, but ultimately you come back out of that. I think

men have the potential to change. You've got to believe that really. The best way to do it is by contact and influence and being brought up as boys by people who are committed to that. And if women are becoming men, they'll make very different men than a lot of the ones around. Maybe that's the argument to reclaim male power. We've tried to get power and be equal to men in so many ways, why not have their bodies and experiences too? The ultimate way to take power off them is to create a new man. What better way to do it than out of our own bodies?

—Annette Kennerley

Robin Morgan is interesting because she actually precedes Daly in the argument that if a lesbian-identified transsexual sleeps with another lesbian woman and doesn't mention their sexuality, then it's rape. Because it's deceit.

—Roz Kaveney

First, class differences expressed in terms of female masculinity and butch/femme were duly excommunicated. Then race and ethnicity raised conflicts when black lesbian feminists refused to give up the common struggle against racism with the men in their communities, even if that meant criticising racist white feminists, making it very clear that all women are not the same. With no discussion, male-to-female transsexual lesbian feminists were vilified and expelled as infiltrators, followed by s/m, queers and now the new Other: female-to-male transsexuals and transgenderists. The latter are seen as tainted by mixing with gay men. Rad fems cite lesbians working with gay men around Clause 28 and AIDS issues as the latest reason why lesbian feminism is losing the support of lesbians, not the expulsions or constraints with which they exclude most lesbians who don't tow their line.

I think the reason that transgender is coming into the lesbian community is because of our increased association with gay men. That partly came out of Clause 28, which was a turning point where lesbian feminism lost its support in the lesbian community.

I think female-to-males who identify as gay men are to do with the way gay male culture has become glorified within the lesbian community in the past ten years. And Cherry Smyth's kind of line, 'a chick with a dick', the playing on dildos and dicks and fucking gay men and getting into the whole body beautiful culture, that is gay men. It's something that's taken over the lesbian community in the past seven or eight years. And so I don't think it's that surprising that lesbians are having sex changes to become gay men.

—Hilary McCollum

I find FTMs becoming gay men the most understandable element of it really because you're not leaving a gay construct. But why you would go to all that trouble to remain within a gay construct, is slightly mysterious. I see it as having to do with the mystique of the phallus, which permits one to appropriate a male position without entering into relations of domination with women. It's a perfect solution in a way to the power imbalances. You can have your dick and eat it too.

—Paula Graham

Outside the separatist enclave of lesbian feminism, at the grassroots, other lesbians get on with their lives, bringing lesbian feminism to a maturity which reflects the real diversity among lesbians now, even if this does not add up to a coherent community.

I do think that [separatist feminists] are only a small group of women. I think they were always a small group of women. I think that they were just vocal. Queers do want the feminist label but I don't think we've been so interested in identifying as lesbians. They were trying to stake out a territory that was specifically lesbian and they did it very successfully. And, now, if you're interested in women-identified-women,

women-loving-women, you know where to go. Coffee-shops, bookstores, etc. I just hope that the gender community comes up with something that's a little more confrontational and not as separatist.

—Judith Halberstam

Like any other social group, transsexuals and other transgendered people exhibit the social and political range, from reactionary and conservative to progressive and radical. Some FTMs want male privilege and power and are sometimes overcompensatingly sexist in their treatment of women. Others want male bodies but feel that male stereotypes are oppressive for themselves and others and fight to deconstruct male privilege.

I think it's easy for me to challenge other men on sexism, being very out as gay. I'm almost expected to confront them on what's going on. Maybe if I was straight I would find it more difficult.

—Martin

I find there's no excuse for misogyny and I do hear it among FTMs. Sometimes it's those guys who haven't gone through lesbian feminism. But sometimes with the younger ones there's a lack of consciousness. I still think that trying to emulate what the culture considers to be male is a waste of an opportunity to go beyond that.

—David Harrison

Some MTFs do want to be the dependent bit of fluff draped over a man's arm and want to obey him and reinforce his power. Others are feminists and lesbians and don't want to have anything to do with men because they have been abused by men, individually or by the system of patriarchal power.

I suppose the worst part of my life was when I went through the period of going with men. I was naive and men exploited me, they just wanted to find out what their own sexuality was and they used me to do that. The reason I'm so angry with men is a hangover from that. I felt very used and exploited.

—Josephine Asher

Ironically, as a marginalised and disempowered group, transgendered people seem to have some inordinate power to uphold and maintain the gender system. This allows us to be blamed for gender: because we alert people to the fact that gender is not natural, gender somehow becomes the fault of transgendered people.

Trans-people become society's gender trash that it wants to sweep under the carpet and forget. Seeing the diversity of transgendered people and not just the stereotypes is how feminists, lesbians and gays, differently abled people and other oppressed or marginalised people will recognise trans-people as allies instead of opponents.

Transgender politics is raising the consciousness of transsexuals and other gender-challenged people, helping us to find pride and solidarity and so to heal the trauma of growing up transgendered in a culture that stigmatises and pathologies that experience. In this way the stereotypes and bi-polar gender itself are being challenged, the need to pass is being challenged, and the need to create lies about one's past and one's status as transgendered becomes less compelling and even counterproductive. But that also requires educating and challenging non-transgendered people around one.

I think that each movement gets to a new layer in deconstructing gender. Feminists thought they could do it. Bisexuals argued they could, lesbian and gay, then queer and now transgender...If only they could be brought together and things would change. But I don't think history works like that. It's so much more haphazard and random.

Is Kate [Bornstein] a failed transsexual because she says I'm neither a man or a woman? Did it not work for her or is that what we're all going towards? She had to go through the surgery to come to that position. You can't say I can be neither from this point of view. You have to go through it. And that's what a lot of people find difficult. If you really believe in the possibility of being non-gendered, multigendered, then why change? That's where most feminists get lost in the argument.

—Cherry Smyth

But still for some TSs whose gender identity is completely transposed, the dissonance of identity and physical body is unbearable, aggravated by others attributing the wrong gender to them because their body presents something else. This means that some TSs will continue to need to change their bodies by surgery to approximate something closer to their sense of self. For other transsexuals and transgendered people, only partial modification with hormones is necessary and in milder cases of gender dysphoria cross-dressing might be sufficient.

Some people just want to explore, experiment or play with gender, pushing against the rigid categories, stereotypes and norms, blurring, bending and fucking with gender expectations. Very few people can cross-live, get employment successfully and be safe in the streets without hormones and some surgery. Many feminists see the choice of hormones and surgery as politically deluded because of risks to the individual's health and the dependency on a patriarchal medical establishment, but also because it is seen as collusion and has implications that other gender 'aberrant', rebellious people, especially children, could be forced to undergo similar treatment to bring them in line with the status quo. There is also a notion of the natural—of bodily integrity being tampered with and violated—and of colluding with consumer capitalism's misogynist body image fashions.

A feminist argument proposes that it's actually in the government's interest to provide these operations, because they would rather have people living the gender role they want to than have people who are one sex, but stretching the limits of that sex beyond what they would want. In other words, they would rather have transsexuals than lesbians and gays. They would rather have people fitting into heterosexual society.

—Rosemary Auchmuty

Surgery is seen as self-mutilation and the result of some form of deep self-hatred or hysteria. Rad fems in their arrogance believe they know best what's good for other people. They don't seem to listen or hear when transgendered people say they are healing themselves and choosing the best options to turn around dysfunctional lives, fully accepting the health risks of the surgery (which is radical and intrusive) and hormones (which increase the likelihood of breast cancer in MTFs and liver cancer in FTMs, among other conditions). It is worth the risks to live their lives as themselves and as they choose, not as someone else chooses for them.

Self-mutilation is the abusive action of someone who hates themselves. I don't deny that, and it engenders further self-dislike often by incurring the distaste of others. Gender reassignment surgery, on the other hand, is to change the body in ways that will enable the person to be more comfortable in themselves. Which in my opinion is completely the opposite.

—Gerry

The UNITY and Inclusion benefit for Camp Trans, a watershed event which may change the direction of lesbian feminism beyond the issue of transsexual inclusion, was held at the Lesbian and Gay Community Centre on 29 June 1994. The benefit was to raise funds to support a camp that would offer workshops on transgender to women attending the Michigan Womyn's Music Festival, which has a 'women-born-women' policy and excludes MTF TSs. Speakers and performers at the event included Amber Hollibaugh, Minnie Bruce Pratt, Holly Hughes, Kate Bornstein, Leslie Feinberg and Riki Ann Wilchins.

> The lesbian feminists who spoke at the Camp Trans benefit, by reclaiming the fight against gender oppression as central to feminist activism, have claimed taking responsibility for construction of one's own identity and desire— which may mean by choosing to take sexual risks—as a feminist act. This runs counter to both the 'pure, safe haven' concept of women's community and to the concept of conformity to a collective standard instead of one's own conscience. It also reflects a new maturity on the part of lesbian feminists, a security in the strength of our woman-centered lives amidst a patriarchal society.
>
> —Beth Elliott, 'AND? AND? AND?'

> My argument is that a biological determinist policy is harmful and could set back the entire women's movement, theoretically affect it and skew its direction. But that a policy of 'all women welcome' is really going to revitalise the women's movement and I'm finding a very receptive ear.
>
> —Leslie Feinberg

IS BIOLOGY DESTINY?

> One is not born, but becomes a woman. No biological, psychological, or economic fate determines the figure that the human female presents in society: it is civilization as a whole that produces this creature, intermediate between male and eunuch, which is described as feminine.
>
> —Simone de Beauvoir, *The Second Sex*

> In some cases, some transsexuals, some transgendered people do jump from one box into the other and are reinforcing the binary. But fewer and fewer true feminists who are really looking for gender freedom are buying that. They're listening to what transgendered people have to say and a lot of transgendered people these days are saying, 'No I'm not a man, no I'm not a woman. I'm something else under the sun.' And that is so much less threatening to feminists who are in fact struggling against the same binary we're struggling against. We are in fact this new wave of transgendered people, holding up the same 'biology is not destiny' button that feminists have been holding up for a long time. I agree with Sandy Stone and Riki Ann Wilchins when they say that this transgender movement is simply the next logical phase of feminism.
>
> —Kate Bornstein

Lesbian feminists and transgendered people each accuse the other of taking a bio-determinist view of gender. Transsexuals in particular are seen to uphold society's gender status quo by changing their bodies to fit desired gender roles, as if they were having sex conversion surgery in direct response and as a solution to rigid gender roles and not because of their compelling experience of transposed gender identity. But radical lesbian feminism seems, to transgendered people, to invest in the same dominant discourse of dimorphic sex and binary gender as the hetero-patriarchy. Feminism may be in opposition to patriarchy, but it seems to accept the basic premise and agree to the terms of essentialised gender in creating its oppositional view.

> I do tend to see transgender as reactionary in the sense that much of the discourse around it is biologist and it has a tendency to reinforce that notion that gender is biological. It fits in basically with the reactionary forces which are attempting to stem the flow of gender change.
>
> —Paula Graham

It's almost like saying gender is fixed if I feel like a man trapped in a woman's body or a woman trapped inside a man's body. That I've got to change the external to fit the internal, not challenge the external. There are different types of women; some women can be hairy, have beards, can be aggressive. There are some men who can be passive, almost prototype feminine, but have an external masculine body. There's nothing really that actually challenges that so far, that I've seen. But at the same time, an FTM that I know has gone through radical changes; he's become more confident and become somehow more at peace with himself. Individually, people have turmoil that they feel can only be changed by surgery, and that is a personal journey, but I'm looking at it in a wider context and what that says about gender.

—Inge Blackman

The man trapped in a woman's body metaphor, and vice versa, inaccurately describes the experience of most transgendered people, yet it has become an easy one for the mainstream media to latch on to and it persists. It is a short-hand used by transgendered people when avoiding long discussions with a traditionally gendered person, especially if s/he is a bigot or basically not prepared to think about the issues. Many transgendered people feel they are not the gender they were assigned and are not comfortable with their birth sex; beyond that, they feel varying degrees of identification and belonging to another gender category. Most often gender is fluid and identity evolves. The achieved anatomy is a way of relieving the confusion and anxiety, and the body is a point of reference, not a nature.

Minnie Bruce-Pratt has written this book *S/He*. She talks about how she was brought up in the south and was made to see whiteness as natural and how that always seemed to her completely wrong and she got a real sense of injustice. And her position on that reminds her of her position around transgender, that she thought gender was natural. And she's had to completely reconstruct everything she thought.

—Cherry Smyth

When confronted with transsexuality, radical feminism reverses Simone de Beauvoir's 'anatomy is not destiny' insight, with claims that our gender reality and destiny are bound by chromosomes. This sets back the course of feminism, aligning it with the establishment it is critiquing.

Even chromosomal sex is not an absolute. There are occurrences which are neither XX or XY and, in conjunction with other factors like hormones can yield unexpected anatomical combinations. Assignment would seem to be the site of determining power which fundamentally affects gender, rather than the invisible factors of biological sex. It is morphology that is the basis of that assignment. But when anatomical sex is altered because of errors in assignment or surgical conversion, the search by others for the true sex of those altered individuals reinforces biology over ideology.

Even XX chromosome women can fail the Barrbody test, used to test athletes, because the appropriate number of Barrbodies which need to be present to indicate femaleness, when counted under a microscope, is not consistent from one day to the next. What methods will lesbians use, in spaces that exclude all but XX chromosome women, to determine the gender status of women attending?

I used to be much more essentialist than I am now. I believed that men were genetically deficient and I believed that I was born butch. When I lived in Israel and I had to be in the closet I suddenly became much more social determinist. In my MA thesis, I tried to prove through the history of biology and physiology that biological sex is an absolute continuum. And it's a completely artificial divide. There's no medical way whatsoever of proving who is a man and who is a woman. Which is why they have all these problems at the Olympics. I wish that it was really no more significant than the colour of your eyes. I've never felt like it was anybody's business what my gender was. But you can't exist without a gender for political reasons and I always identify as a woman for that reason.

—Spike Pittsberg

There are, in addition to the XX and XY pairs, some other commonly-occurring sets of gender chromo-somes, including XXY, XXX, YYY, XYY, and XO. Does this mean there are more than two genders?

Let's keep looking. What makes a man—testosterone? What makes a woman—estrogen? If so, you could buy your gender over the counter at any pharmacy. But we're taught that there are these things called 'male' and 'female' hormones; and that testosterone dominates the gender hormone balance in the males of any species. Not really—the female hyenas, for example, have naturally more testosterone than the males; the female clitoris resembles a very long penis – the females mount the males from the rear, and proceed to hump. While some female humans I know behave in much the same manner as the female hyena, the example demonstrates that the universal key to gender is not hormones.

—Kate Bornstein, *Gender Outlaw*

Transsexuals are usually certain about their subjective experience of gender, their gender identity. It is their anatomical sex, sex assignment and attribution by others that are in contradiction to that subjective sense of themselves. Gender could be said to be destiny for transsexuals (Judith Shapiro, 'Transsexualism'). The goal is corrected attribution of gender. It seems to be a liberation from what is, for most, the physical fate of what they were born with. This disconnection of identity, attribution, social role from anatomical sex as the foundation and 'natural' sex as the only reality of gender, puts gender up for grabs—what it is, who has it and in what form or combination, seem to make trans-gender the heir to the 'anatomy is not destiny' legacy.

What if transsexuality was found conclusively to have a biological basis?

I would say that if transsexualism was found to have a biological basis, that would be seen as maintaining heterosexuality, and that's a problem for lesbians and gays because it would put lesbians and gays more out on a limb as people who were resisting the need for men to be like this and women to be like this. We're actually saying that a man and a woman should have the chance to be like anything and then you wouldn't need to have surgery and that is the society I'd like to work towards. The other thing I would be worried about is that there would be pressure on gays and lesbians to have surgery as well. There would be some kind of argument that 'X and Y and Z were able to convert to being men, why don't you do that? And then we'll all be happier. If you want to wear trousers why don't you become a man?"

—Rosemary Auchmuty

NOTED

Originally published in *Lesbians Talk Transgender* by Zachary Nataf (London: Scarlett Press, 1996) pp. 36-47.

31

Gender Without Genitals
Hedwig's Six Inches

Jordy Jones

In his first academic publication, long-time artist, activist, and transgender trend-setter Jordy Jones, currently a doctoral candidate in Visual Studies at the University of California, Irvine, discusses the identity politics at play in the film version of John Cameron Mitchell's popular *Hedwig and the Angry Inch*. Mitchell's film has become a flashpoint for divergent and sometimes conflicting understandings of gender and embodiment among members of a gay, lesbian, bisexual, and transgender community often assumed by outsiders to have a more unified point of view.

Although many viewers consider Hedwig to be a celebratory expression of gender diversity, Jones articulates the ambivalence many transsexuals feel toward the film. He argues that Hedwig is not a transsexual, and characterizes the story as a gay male coming out narrative that uses transsexualism as a metaphor. Jones links the film's (mis)representations to issues of ethnicity and race, in order to reveal an unexpectedly conservative politics of identity at work beneath the film's appealing visual surface.

Though limiting his analysis to a single recent film, the concerns Jones raises in his article are equally applicable to many other well-known filmic representations of transgender lives, such *The Crying Game* or *The Adventures of Priscilla, Queen of the Desert*. The problems Jones sees in Hedwig—and the dissent its generally warm reception has stirred in some quarters of the transgender community—have less to do with strictly aesthetic considerations than they do with the production, circulation, and reception of mass media representations of transgender issues that largely bypass any significant input from transgender people themselves, and thus, more often than not, reproduce and perpetuate misperceptions.

In queer and transgender theories of the late twentieth and early twenty-first centuries, the construction that is commonly called "the gender binary"[1] has come under attack. Critics fault it for failing to explain adequately, and to allow for, the full range of lived genders experienced by living gendered subjects. In place of a black-and-white binarism, a sort of "rainbow flag" of gender is sometimes proposed. Gender, according to this new trope, is not a binary, but rather a spectrum. How useful is this idea of a (linear) spectrum for understanding multiple and diverse genders? It certainly provides for more positions, and more livable ones, than does a binary structure. A spectral analysis, however, locks a multiplicity of positions into absolute relation to one another as well as to the extremes, which, while they may be arbitrary, nevertheless remain opposites. In the absence of theories of gender that allow for the potentially infinite proliferation of specificities, eccentric subjectivities are forced into preformed genres, and important differences are abolished in favor of a provisional intelligibility. This often results in categorical collapse, "border wars,"[2] and unfortunate cases of mistaken identity.

In *Hedwig and The Angry Inch*³, Hansel, a "slip of a girlyboy from communist East Berlin,"⁴ who hopes to escape to a rock-and-roll lifestyle in The West, undergoes, at the urging of his single mother and his African-American G.I. lover, a "sex-change operation [that gets] botched."⁵ Abandoned by the G.I. in a Kansas trailer park, Hansel, now renamed Hedwig, seduces the born-again teenage son of an U.S. Army general, and schools him in the art of rock. When this boy, now renamed Tommy Gnosis, leaves Hedwig to become a star by performing the songs they wrote together, the scorned and vengeful Hedwig stalks him. In seedy dives located in the shadows of the coliseums where Tommy performs, Hedwig plays with "The Angry Inch"—the band named in arch tribute to the stump of her (almost) excised penis. Between musical numbers she tells her life story to a sparse and mostly disinterested audience.

Hedwig, which has established a reputation as a transgender film, and more specifically as a film about a transsexual, features a main character who has been largely misrecognized. The character of Hedwig is not actually a transsexual woman, nor is John Cameron Mitchell, the man who created the character Hedwig, and who has played her on stage and screen. Hedwig is, rather, an overt citation of a transsexual woman, and Mitchell, as Hedwig, is a non-transsexual gay man *in drag as his fantasy of a transsexual woman*. Through the figure of transsexuality, Mitchell explores his own relation to male femininity through an identity other than his own. He explains:

> To be gay, is to be free of a lot of bullshit. It's a privilege that you have to take advantage of…I enjoy Hedwig's being a mask—I can explore things that are meaningful to me through a personality and a history that's not mine.⁶

In *Bodies That Matter*, Judith Butler reads heterosexually-produced drag films like *Tootsie*, *Victor/Victoria* and *Some Like It Hot* as containment narratives in which the threat of queerness is "both produced and deflected" and in which "homophobia and homosexual panic are negotiated."⁷ I would like to suggest that rather than articulating transsexual subjectivity or even drag subjectivity, *Hedwig* narrates a male homosexual negotiation of transsexual panic by means of the idiom of drag. This panic is fuelled by the collapse in popular consciousness of the categories of woman, homosexual man, transsexual woman, and drag queen.

In pointing out that Hedwig is neither transsexual nor a woman, I certainly do not intend to invoke a gender binary in which male is definitively opposed to female, or man opposed to woman, or to suggest that gender is somehow deterministically sutured to sex. My intention, rather, is to insist upon a specificity of sex/gender subjectivity. Transsexuality is not a fixed or closed category. Transsexual subjectivity however, as I am using it here, can be minimally defined as the articulation of a transsexual desire—and it is desire, more than anything else, that defines transsexuality. The transsexual considers him or herself a member of the sex "opposite" to his or her original physical embodiment and/or wishes to be or to become a member of the sex into which he or she was not assigned at birth. The beautiful boy Hansel, who eventually becomes Hedwig, never articulates a desire to become a woman. His transformation is certainly not his idea, nor is it freely chosen. In discussing the Berlin Wall as a metaphor for the divide between the sexes, Mitchell says: "Hedwig undergoes an operation she never wanted in order to escape to the West only to wind up a poor divorcee in Kansas a year later, listening to reports of the fall of the Wall."⁸ Transsexuality in *Hedwig* is used as a device for the author to confront the horror and fascination of phallic lack, to visit both sides of the received binary gender divide, and to emerge psychically transformed yet physically intact.

The title of this article cites two works explicitly, and refers to others more obliquely. In the song "Angry Inch," the character Hedwig describes the "botched sex-change operation" that left her with a truncated stump where her penis once was, and which ostensibly turned her into a woman, in the following way: "Six inches forward; five inches back. I've got an angry inch." In this article, I have used the "inches" to structure the several arguments I am make regarding the complex queer subjectivities of the character Hedwig and of her creator, John Cameron Mitchell. The inches are both absent and present. The absence of the five lends motive to the anger of the one remaining, and fuels the ultimate return to originary embodiment. The narrative of Hedwig is one of loss and redemption, and follows a fairly linear structure, although that linearity is curved, and thus circles back to its point of origin. Hedwig's lost inches are ultimately returned, and through their return are proved to never have been missing at all. As a story of a spiritual journey undertaken through the flesh, the lost inches have both the volume of matter and the weight of metaphor.

The title of this article, "Gender Without Genitals," is taken from a list of definitions of "Camp" written by Phillip Core. In this definition, he foreshadows the arguments of queer theorists such as Gayle Rubin and Judith Butler, who argue that sex and gender, to be properly understood, ought not be conflated. Since many of the popular readings of Hedwig hinge on just these sorts of conflations, (i.e.: Hedwig has no penis, therefore she must be a woman) my use of the term is intended to underscore the need to analyze sex and gender as separate, although not unrelated, phenomena.

INCH 1: ORIGINS: WHAT WENT WRONG?

Hedwig is a story of origins and endings. The origin is the split, the cut, the sexual divide, the wall thrown up to keep the Other out. The origin launches a tale that sets the ego-shattered lover searching for his sundered half. This origin lies between "one" and "two," in the horrifying ellipsis that implies infinite potential proliferation. The story of origins poses the traumatic question: "What went wrong?" If the sex/gender system is as "natural," inevitable, and secure as it is purported to be, why does it break down with such frequency, and why does it require such vigilance to maintain? The origin ends at the ultimate destination: the halves made whole, the sexes united, the wall thrown down, the panic of self-loss through merger with the Other successfully managed, the transcendent self redeemed, the answer found, the One triumphant.

Hedwig recounts how, when she was the boy-child Hansel, her mother told him Aristophanes' story of the origin of love, recorded in Plato's *Symposium*.[9] The story of the three original sexes, and their division, becomes more than an improbable bedtime story; it becomes the guiding metaphor of Hansel's life. According to Aristophanes, the original sexes were not two, but three, reflecting respectively the man/sun, the woman/earth and the man-woman/moon. These original humans were round, resembling two contemporary humans merged back to back. They had four arms, four legs, two faces and two sets of genitals:

> There was man, woman and the union of the two, having a name corresponding to this double nature, which had once a real existence but is now lost, and the word 'Androgynous' is only preserved as a term of reproach. These original beings were powerful and challenged the gods. Zeus conceived of a plan to humble their pride and improve their manners…(to) cut them in two and then they will (be) diminished in strength and increased in numbers.[10]

Aristophanes goes on to describe how the affections of the split beings tended towards that from which they had been split. In his story, the origin of love is one and the same as the origin of the sexes, and of the origin of the sexualities. In this version of creation, original androgyny was associated with what would eventually be called heterosexuality, and the original binary sexes became the homosexual beings. He explains:

Men who are a section of that double nature which was once called Androgynous are lovers of women…the women who are a section of the woman do not care for men, but have female attachments…but they who are a section of the male follow the male, and while they are young, being slices of the original man, they hang about men and embrace them, and they are themselves the best of boys and youths because they have the most manly nature.[11]

Aristophanes' version of the origin of the homosexual impulse in the creation story of the sexes and of love is clearly recalled in Eve Kosofsky Sedgwick's discussion of two polar theories of same-sex object choice. She points out the contradiction between seeing it "as a matter of liminality or transitivity between genders, and seeing it on the other hand as reflecting an impulse of separatism…within each gender."[12] Since in Aristophanes' story, it is the heterosexuals who bear the remnants of an originary androgyny, Hansel expresses confusion as to his identity; as Hedwig, s/he eventually chooses to identify with these "children of the moon," rather than with the male homosexual "children of the sun." In effect, Hedwig/Hansel sutures Sedgwick's transitivity back onto Aristophanes' theory. Hedwig sings of those androgynous beings who would become heterosexual after the god's cut:

And the children of the moon
Looked like a fork shoved on a spoon.
They were part sun, part earth.
Part daughter, part son.[13]

The story from *The Symposium* precipitates a crisis for the young Hansel, and sets him upon a quest. Understanding himself to be divided, he fixes his energy on the goal of reintegration with his lost other/self. Understanding that the sexes and the sexualities originated contemporaneously with love itself, the adult Hedwig explains to her audience:

It is clear that I must find my other half. But is it a he or a she? Is it Daddy? He went away. Or Mother? …What does this person look like? Identical to me? Or somehow complementary? …And what about sex? Is that how we put ourselves back together again? Is that what Daddy was trying to do?[14]

Hansel had been sodomized by his father, who eventually abandoned his family. His incestuous abuse both asks and answers the question "What went wrong?" Hansel's mother is as tainted by her political choices as Hansel's father is by his sexual ones; she fled to the East rather than the West when the Berlin Wall was erected. In the cramped confines of their squalid flat, she forces Hansel, in a macabre reenactment of German fairy tales and holocaust history, to 'play in the oven' with his radio, his head and his toys all stuffed inside. A flash-forward scene early in the film shows the post-operative adult Hedwig with her head back inside the oven, surrounded once again by toys, including, in the foreground, a stuffed black tar-baby-like doll. A licorice-sweet, sticky stereotype, the place of the racially tainted childhood toy will soon be filled by Luther Robinson, the big black sugar daddy who will fulfill Hansel's fantasy of escaping to the West, by facilitating Hansel's transformation into Hedwig.

The question "What went wrong?" was once central to discussions of homosexuality, and is sometimes still asked. The search for the "gay gene" testifies to this; no similar quest exists for the origin of heterosexuality. Etiological questions remain central to the popular pathologization of transsexuality. No one asks, or would think to ask, "what went wrong" with the gender of a boyish boy or a girlish girl. Since in such cases nothing is seen as wrong or askew, the question of origins never arises. It's only "gender trouble" that provokes the question. Fem boys, sissy boys, tomboys, and other ambiguously gendered children must answer to the question of cause. Transsexuals, in order to access the means to medically transition, are also generally expected to produce origin narratives on demand.

Although the question remains whether Hansel's father raped him 'because' he was fem or whether he became fem and later trans as a result of the assault, the connection between childhood trauma and gender non-conformity is made clear. The atypical gender is a wound that exists prior to the cut that makes Hedwig of Hansel. If he was fem first, his femininity may have provoked the assault. If he became fem only as a result of the molestation, a traumatic cause is identified at the origin of an unacceptable variation of proper manhood. The child Hansel's rape by the father splits him, names him, and sets him on a negative Oedipal journey[15] wherein he must become his mother (the original Hedwig who becomes his namesake) in order to reunite eventually with his father and put himself back together. Did his failure to perform 'boy' adequately invite the repeated acts of girling? Butler asserts: "If a man can identify with his mother, and produce desire from that identification…he has already confounded the psychic description of stable gender development."[16]

As Aristophanes told it, the homosexual double-beings were purely male or female; it was the heterosexual beings who were androgynous. Soranus, however, a Greek physician of the second century, associated characteristics of women with male homosexuals. He anticipated Sedgwick's theory of transitivity, but with a decidedly negative slant. Soranus tied the desire to assume the receptive or passive role in anal intercourse with a failure of virility.[17] Early sexology echoed and elaborated this account. Michel Foucault described the theories of Carl von Westphal as shifting the practice of sodomy onto the person of the homosexual, thus creating a new category of personhood, where previously only acts (without attached identities) had existed. Foucault further described von Westphal's new homosexual person as being seen to possess "a kind of interior androgyny, a hermaphrodism of the soul."[18] The 19th century "third sex" theories of homosexual advocate Karl Ulrichs anticipated this view, holding that the body of the male homosexual contained the soul of a woman, and conversely that the female homosexual body held the soul of a man. The same idea was later recapitulated by the "trapped in the wrong body" origin story of transsexual identity. Ulrichs' defense of homosexuality as natural was soon elaborated into theories of hereditary degeneracy and of pathologies demanding cures.

Tommy Gnosis, Hedwig's young born-again Christian lover, is as obsessed with origins and separations as Hedwig is, and his stories of origin offer instructive comparison to hers. In a pivotal scene, Tommy bursts into Hedwig's trailer just as she begins to lose herself in a fantasy of finally merging with the lost other. Tommy is angry with his father the General, and he frames his anger in sexualized biblical interpretations. He says:

> "Oh, Hedwig. Oh God. When Eve was still inside Adam, they were in Paradise. When she was separated from him, that's when Paradise was lost. So when she enters him again, Paradise will be regained!"[19]

Tommy hates his literal father, and transfers this Oedipal rage towards God the Father. In speaking of his rather heterodox personal relationship with his savior, the Christian boy explains:

> "You know what He saved us from was his fucking father. I mean, what kind of God creates Adam in his image, pulls Eve out of him to keep him company, and then tells them not to eat from the Tree of Knowledge?"[20]

Tommy expresses sympathy with the knowledge-seeking Eve, whom he associates with his new lover, and he asks Hedwig to "give [him] the apple."[21] Although Tommy's origin stories are biblical and Hedwig's pagan, they are similar in positing an idyllic and atavistically desirable prehistory in which the sexes were united.[22] They are also similar in holding that a traumatic event occurred in which the figure of the Father, whether as Jehovah or Zeus, ripped into merged original beings and separated them forever. Hedwig will eventually find her other half, though not, as she had expected, in the person of a lover, but within herself. When this finally happens, the fantasy that is Hedwig will dissolve. Hansel will be reborn with the knowledge that Hedwig is the feminine within himself. Once he integrates this lost Other into his own person, he is able to turn away from the fantasy of trans-sexuality, and towards a normative male homosexuality.

INCH 2: AFFINITIES: IDENTIFICATIONS AND AMBIVALENCE

Nineteenth-century theories of inversion, perversion, and degeneracy maintain a tenacious hold on the twenty-first-century popular imagination. The homosexual slides almost effortlessly into the transsexual. The effeminate boy Hansel need never claim the soul of a woman, need never articulate a desire to change—but with a flip of the wrist, a slip of the tongue, and a flick of a knife, the narrative performs an easy but incomplete and imaginary transformation. The "angry inch" of penile stump referred to in the work's title makes the possibility of vaginal penetration impossible; it facilitates an imaginary identification with being-female, without its physical realities. Hedwig sings:

> When I woke up from the operation
> I was bleeding down there…
> …My first day as a woman
> and already, it's that time of month.
> But two days later
> the hole closed up…
> …and I was left with a one inch mound of flesh
> where my penis used to be
> where my vagina never was.[23]

Genitally, Hedwig is neither male nor female. "All I got" she says, "is a Barbie Doll crotch."[24] To the extent that 'trans-' connotes going through, across or beyond, and 'un-' connotes being cut off, void, and negated, Hewig is not transsexed, but rather unsexed.[25] She may nevertheless be transgendered, for although she lacks a sex, she does not lack gender. Indeed, she campily performs "gender without genitals" in her stage show.[26] The sutures removed, the signs of sex gone, the character of Hedwig freely embarks on a journey of female masquerade. In working through the homosexual territory where the receptive male dissolves into the apparent female, the unmanly son of the missing father works his way through the stations of the cross-female to emerge in the end as wholly male, fully human, entirely redeemed. A question: can *Hedwig* be read as manhood ritual?

Hansel is castrated, and in being castrated, becomes Hedwig, a fantasy of that which is always already castrated. S/he retains enough of her penis for it to be angry, if not necessarily envious, or enviable. Do transsexual women have penis envy? Can one be envious of that which one voluntarily relinquishes? But Hedwig is never really transsexual, and is never really a volunteer. It was a case of mistaken identity all along. Hedwig both 'is' and 'has' the phallus—S/he is both castrated and super-phallusized. Butler suggests that a "yearning to have penis-envy" is supposed by a masculine identity because the phallus is "already elsewhere," and, further, that "to assume the feminine position is to take up the figure of castration."[27] Perhaps taking up the figure of castration is to be free of the fear of castration. Leo Bersani suggests just such an anti-Oedipal potential in male homosexual desire:

> An exclusively heterosexual orientation in men…may depend on a misogynous identification with the father and a permanent equating of femininity with castration. The male's homosexual desire, to the extent that it depends on an identification with the mother, has already detraumatized sexual difference

(by internalizing it) *and* set the stage for a relation to the father in which the latter would no longer have to be marked as the Law, the agent of castration.[28]

When the boy Hansel is born and named "Hansel" he is "boyed"[29] by that act of naming, but quickly enough the borders of the child's gender stability begin to dissolve and break down, as he is subjected to the corrosive caprices of the adults entrusted with his care. Without agency of his own in the world, it is only in the imaginary that he can deploy any power. Hansel's gender crisis speaks through his ambivalent identity. For the 'girlyboy,' the question of whether the other half is a he or a she is complicated by the question of whether he himself is a he or a she. Carol Clover notes, "The helpless child is gendered feminine; the autonomous adult is gendered masculine; the passage from childhood to adulthood entails a shift from feminine to masculine."[30] For any boy, growing up to be a man is not a certainty. For a feminine boy, it is even less certain. He might reject the being-masculine, but this course comes with a threat. As Butler states, "if a man refuses too radically the 'having of the phallus' he will be punished with homosexuality."[31]

Radically split long before the literal/imaginary castration, Hansel's quest for his other half becomes the quest for, and return to, the phallus that was symbolically taken from him. To retrieve it he must negotiate transsexual panic: the threat of—mixed with desire for—becoming woman, becoming Other. In seeking the other, outside of himself, he finds himself. Hansel, in becoming Hedwig, faces the horror of reiterative castration. He finally triumphs, rectifies the phallic lack, and escapes the imaginary to join the world of the symbolic.

Butler writes that "the Oedipal threat depends for its livelihood on the threatening power of the threat, on the resistance to the identification with masculine feminization and feminine phallicization."[32] In willfully occupying, albeit temporarily and fantastically, the position of masculine feminization, Hansel/Hedwig shares a space with the transsexual woman, a figure who continually resists the resistance to the identification with masculine feminization. Unlike the ambivalent Hansel/Hedwig, the transsexual woman actively desires this identification and acts as a counterforce to the constant pressure brought to bear on the (un)marked male to be manly.

INCH 3: MAKING HEDWIG OF HANSEL: THE "MAGIC NEGRO" WAVES HIS WAND

To quote Butler yet again, "Identification is always an ambivalent process,"[33] and, it might be added, it is never a single process, but rather many intersecting and overlapping ones. In negotiating his difficult identification with his mother, Hansel must negotiate not only the question of sexual difference, but also questions of national, cultural, political, and religious identity. Specifically, the transition from Hansel to Hedwig encodes a complex negotiation of German-ness and Jewishness, Nazism and the Holocaust (explored in the following section), as well as the relationship of these elements to the hegemonic presence of the United States in Europe—personified in *Hedwig* by American G.I. Luther Robinson.

As noted earlier, when the adult Hedwig was the boy Hansel, the East German apartment that he and his mother lived in was so tiny that, in a grim echo of Germany's Nazi past, he had to play while crouching on the floor with his head stuffed inside the oven. Meanwhile, his artistic mother sculpted —in the shower. Hansel dreamed of escape to a fantasized West, which he knew only from listening to pop music on American Armed Forces Radio broadcasts. For the precocious boy, the attraction of the West was less political than cultural. His heroes were the sexually ambiguous rockers: David Bowie, Iggy Pop, Lou Reed. In recounting his musical inspirations, Hansel also mentions female pop icons Toni Tenille, Debby Boone and Anne Murray. The play and the slippage here are between heterosexual womanhood and male crypto-homosexuality. Icons of butch heterosexual masculinity such as Jim Morrison, Bruce Springsteen and Eric Clapton are absent from Hansel's pantheon of rock gods.

The Berlin Wall separates the Hansel of the East from the Hedwig of the West. Ambiguously identified, split down the middle, constantly in search of her other half, Hedwig is like Germany, and she shares her birthday with the Berlin Wall: August 13, 1961. Unable to find his other half in the East as a man, Hansel is ready to try it in the West as a woman. At twenty-six, Hedwig explains, Hansel was aware of a frustrated homosexual desire: "I had never kissed a boy and I was still sleeping with mom. The search for my other half on this side of the Wall had proved futile. Might it be found on the other?"[34]

Although subjected to life-long 'girling,' Hansel does not, however, enact positive transsexual desire, and he does not imagine castration as an option until the arrival of the "Magic Negro,"[35] African-American soldier Luther Robinson. The "Magic Negro" is a black filmic figure who possesses extraordinary powers—these may be spiritual, moral, or intellectual, often literally magical and occasionally also physical—which he or she uses to effect some transformation in the white main character. Rita Kempley explains: "It isn't that the actors or the roles aren't likeable, valuable or redemptive, but that they are without interior lives. For the most part, they materialize only to rescue the better-drawn white characters."[36] In Hansel's case, Luther will literally effect his transformation into Hedwig.

At their first meeting, Luther discovers Hansel sunbathing nude—face down in a bomb crater near the Wall—and calls out, "Girl, I sure don't mean to annoy you. My name is Corporal Luther Robinson."[37] Hansel turns over, revealing his "little bishop in a turtleneck."[38] Luther is surprised but undeterred by this revelation of biological sex, and tells him: "Damn, Hansel, I can't believe you're not a girl, you're so fine."[39] Luther courts Hansel with candy Gummy Bears, offering to him the "panting faces of every imaginable color, creed and non-Aryan origin fogging up the bag like the windows of a Polish bathhouse."[40] Hansel chooses "a single clear bear from the bag of multi-colored treats." Hedwig reminisces: "It is the biggest one I've ever seen…I suddenly recognize the flavor in my mouth. It's the taste of power. Not bad."[41] The power that Hansel tastes here for the first time is the virginal awakening of awareness of his sexual appeal to, and power over, this ostensibly more powerful man. It is also the strong draw of what that powerful man represents. The man is the way out, a way for Hansel to get away from himself, to head West to Hedwig. The uncolored candy bear clearly represents for him a complex fantasy of freedom: not just the freedom to cross the Wall into the mythic West of American pop music, but also a freedom from the burdens of a body marked or colored by race or sex.

Luther is more a plot device than a character. It is he who first suggests that Hansel wear women's clothing. He addresses Hansel and his mother, the elder Hedwig, as "ladies" when he proposes marriage, and it is he who suggests the change of sex. He explains that the Army will require a physical examination of his new "wall-bride." He says "To walk away, you've got to leave something behind. Am I right, Mrs. Schmidt?"[42] Mrs. Schmidt agrees, saying: "Hansel, to be free, one must give up a little part of oneself. And I know just the doctor to take it."[43] In the semi-forced feminization that follows, Luther Robinson not only shows Hansel what he has presumably unconsciously wanted all along, but allows him access to his conscious desire for the West. Waving his big black magic wand over and into the beautiful German boy, it is Luther who makes Hedwig of Hansel, and then makes Hedwig into a Dorothy in reverse, sweeping her away not to Oz, but to Kansas—she's definitely not in East Germany anymore. A cliché of the trifling black man, Luther then fulfills his stereotypical role as amoral "Mack Daddy" and exits the story by leaving Hedwig (or it Hansel?) for another boy.

Although Luther is a man who has sex with men, he isn't gay, per se. Rather, he is "on the down low." To be both Black and gay is to be marked (at least) twice. Enormous pressures are brought to bear on the doubly-marked to choose sides and declare a primary affiliation. The insistent question, "Well, what are you—*really*?" is violent in that any answer requires the suppression of part of the self, and the fracture of the whole. A perception exists in the mainstream gay and Black communities, respectively, that gay men aren't supposed to be Black and Black men aren't supposed to be gay. Commenting on this predicament, and suggesting the simple, yet profoundly courageous stance needed to counter such outrageous demands, Tim'm T. West and Juba Kalamka of the homo-hop crew *Deep Dickollective* declaim, "Don't let faggots call you nigger. Don't let niggers call you faggot."[44]

Mitchell misses an opportunity to use Luther to present a more complex image of American diversity; the marginalized racial and sexual spaces invoked by his presence remain unexplored. Why is a descendent of slaves cast ironically as the promise of the Free World? How is he magically enlarged to stand in for America, while being simultaneously reduced to the figure of Black Phallus? Luther threatens not only white European womanhood, but also, for different reasons, white European manhood. Luther as America emasculates Eastern Europe; he carries out the threat of castration while promising liberation. Luther has his own cultural walls to contend with, but they are not addressed within the narrative; they are merely hinted at as Luther helps Hansel cross his.

The date is November 9th, 1989. Sitting alone drinking vermouth on the rocks, Hedwig recounts her feelings to the audience, counting her transformation among her misfortunes. "I sit in my mobile home, and on bootleg cable, watch the Wall come down. Divorced, penniless, a woman. I cry, because I will laugh if I don't."[45] Butler writes: "To identify with a sex is to stand in some relation to an imaginary threat, imaginary and forceful, forceful precisely because it is imaginary."[46] Where is the identification here, and where, and what, is the threat? Did Hansel want Luther? How does Hansel's capitulation to an imagined superior masculinity relate to, and possibly reiterate, his earlier capitulation to his father? Did Hedwig want Luther? How are Hedwig's desires different from Hansel's? Did Hansel desire his castration? Does Hedwig desire to become a woman? The virginal child of the sun becomes the experienced child of the moon. A dress and a head-wig complete the transformation.

INCH 4: ANOTHER OTHER: TAKING IT UP THE YITZHAK

The complex negotiation of cultural, ethnic, and national identities played out in the relationship between Hansel/Hedwig and Luther Robinson is further elaborated in the relationship between Hedwig and Yitzhak, a minor character in both stage and screen versions, who is curiously central to the logic of both works. Relationships between characters, as well as casting choices and the author's biography, call attention to the singularity of Yitzhak's role in *Hedwig*. John Cameron Mitchell wrote and starred in the original theatrical productions of *Hedwig and the Angry Inch*[47] and also wrote, starred in, and directed the film adaptation. Mitchell, more than anyone, *is* Hedwig. Hedwig came out of Mitchell in much the same way that Tommy Gnosis describes Eve coming out of Adam: she is made of his material. Tommy, like Mitchell, is a general's son, and thus, in his fictional teenage daily life, echoes Mitchell's lived one.[48] Hedwig can also be said to have created Tommy Gnosis, to the extent that she orchestrates her young lover's transformation from General's son to rock idol. In much the same way, Mitchell himself is transformed by playing Hedwig on stage and screen. She is, to some extent, his Magic Tranny. The peculiar collapse of characters still apparent in the film was even more evident in the stage play, where Mitchell played all of the characters except for one, Yitzhak, who was played by a woman, Miriam Shor, in both the stage and screen productions. Only Yitzhak—another Other, a specifically Jewish and biologically female Other—is represented by another actor.

Yitzhak is literally a marginal character, hovering in the wings of the story's action. He is a scraggly-haired, lightly bearded roadie who hovers around the edge of the stage during Hedwig's entire monologue, sometimes muttering curses under his breath, sometimes singing plaintively to Hedwig, occasionally drawing moderate insults and threats from her. In the film version, Yitzhak's relationship to Hedwig is left entirely unexplained and unmotivated. Though he is clearly presented as some type of transgender character, who and what he might be is left unspecified, and he remains unassimilated within the narrative of psychic reintegration that structures *Hedwig*. In the stage version, however, Hedwig identifies Yitzhak as her husband, explaining:

> We met during my Great Croatian Tour of the early mid-nineties. He was the most famous drag-queen in Zagreb. Phyllis [Phyllis Stein, Hedwig's manager] thought he would make a great opening act. Billed as "The Last Jewess in the Balkans" he lip-synched something from *Yentl* under the name Krystal Nacht.[49]

The clues to Yitzhak's former life as a Balkan drag queen are shown only through the subtlest of gestures. He gazes longingly at Hedwig's wigs, and occasionally makes a half-hearted attempt to secure his own time at the microphone. Most often, though, Yitzhak simply hangs about, too present to be a minor character, too vague to be a co-star. And perhaps that is how Hedwig wants it. She sees in him a threat to her monopoly of the spotlight, and she recapitulates her own castration in taking from him the thing that makes him most himself: his drag. Again, in the stage version only, Hedwig relates:

> He was good. He was too good. His applause drowned out my introduction and I refused to go on. But on my way out, he begged me to take him with me. My face might have been my mother's, it was so still. I said to him, 'Krystal, to walk away, you gotta leave something behind. I'll marry you on the condition that a wig never touch your head again.' He agreed and we've been inseparable ever since. And we'll continue to be. Right, Yitzhak? (pointing into the house) Look, Yitzhak, immigration! (Yitzhak doesn't look.) Barbra Streisand! (nothing) You're no fun, go back to your hole. (Yitzhak goes.)[50]

This information is vital for understanding the character; unfortunately it is missing entirely from the film version of *Hedwig*. That it is necessary to rely so heavily on absent information in order to analyze the character exemplifies the trouble the character represents in the first place. Yitzhak is at once vital and incidental. In the end, however, his marginality trumps both his vitality and his visibility, and the back-story we need to understand him is deemed dispensable. But if Hedwig's story is important, and Yitzhak's not, why then, on stage, is Yitzhak's role given the unique privilege of a separate actor, when far more important characters are represented through Hedwig's storytelling and never appear "in the flesh?" This Jewish "man" played by a Jewish "woman" is the lone supporting player for the gentile "woman" played by a gentile "man." Yitzhak's story (though not his character) is edited out of the film entirely. Could it be that the story of the woman, and the story of the Jew, are so ultimately unknowable (so Other) in the imagination of the gentile man, that any attempt to tell them is considered futile?

The references to Barbra Streisand raise further questions. Streisand is a favorite of lip-synch performers, of course, but Yitzhak is specific; while still in Zagreb, he chose to perform songs from *Yentl*, the film in which Streisand cross-dresses as a nineteenth-century Eastern European youth in order to become a yeshiva student. While this refers explicitly to the casting of the female Shor as Yitzhak, there is never any hint as to the reasons behind this choice. Female-to male (FTM) performance artist Lazlo Perlman notes:

> The cross-gender casting of Yitzhak (was) gratuitous in both the play and the movie…(it) seemed merely a nod at the fact that there is more to gender play than drag queen, and more to transgendered identity than MTF or Tranny Girl. As an idea I applaud that, but that's all it was—an idea. Who Yitzhak was wasn't explored. Neither was "why" "he" was. Was he supposed to be FTM? Was he supposed to be a drag king? We're not told. Only Hedwig is explored. Keeping the story about Hedwig is a fine choice—they should have stuck to it. I didn't need the nod to other kinds of gender variant people, myself, not if all they're going to do is stand there in the figurative corner, anyway.[51]

Yitzhak does more than stand in the corner, but only a little bit more. Mainly, he acts as Hedwig's comedic straight man and dramatic buffer. He becomes the target of her misplaced rages against her father, Luther Robinson, and Tommy Gnosis. Yitzhak loves Hedwig, or loves something about her, but like a victim of Stockholm Syndrome, he allows her abuse while simultaneously catering to her, hating her, and resenting her power over him. A self-absorbed narcissist, Hedwig can see Yitzhak only as Other, never as (another) subject. She uses him sexually, using her penile stump to perform shallow penetrative intercourse upon his motionless body as they silently lie spooned together at night, his body impassive and his eyes staring into the darkness. She refuses to face him just as Tommy refuses to face her. Here we see a glimmer of the ultimate return of Hedwig to the male body of Mitchell, and of Yitzhak to the female body of Shor. Foreshadowing the ultimate redemption of "naturally" sexed bodies, Hedwig hints at her own once and future virility when *she* takes *him*.

That Yitzhak is Jewish can be inferred from his name, just as John Cameron Mitchell's status as an American gentile can be inferred from his. We know for a fact that Hedwig is German. The ghost of the Holocaust haunts Hedwig's relationship to Yitzhak, and that of anti-Semitism haunts Mitchell's relationship to his work. The Holocaust was not a fluke. It was not a random mutation of the 20th century, but rather the product of centuries of European anti-Semitism. I am not suggesting that Mitchell, or even Hedwig for that matter, is an anti-Semite, but rather that historical anti-Semitism runs so deeply through the gentile psyche as to be virtually inextricable from its makeup. Freud associated the contempt of the gentile man for the Jew with his contempt for women. In his analysis of "Little Hans," he attributes the roots of anti-Semitic feelings to the boy's conflation of circumcision and castration, and further links this with his relationship to women. He writes:

> The castration complex is the deepest unconscious root of anti-Semitism; for even in the nursery little boys hear that a Jew has something cut off his penis—a piece of his penis, they think—and this gives them the right to despise Jews. And there is no stronger unconscious root for the sense of superiority over women.[52]

Raped by her father and coerced into an unwanted castration by her mother and her lover, Hedwig is both a survivor and a victim—and as a victim, Hedwig re-victimizes. Yitzhak is Hedwig's uncanny double, recapitulating not only the act of castration, but also the narratives of marriage, migration, and loss. He is the Jew to her German.[53] He is also, paradoxically, both man to her woman and woman to her man. When Hedwig penetrates Yitzhak, she evokes the male physicality of Mitchell. The circumcised Yitzhak and the female (that is, castrated) Shor collapse into a body penetrable even by the partially penectomized Hedwig. Playing the role of the war bride, Yitzhak gives up his identity and his independence for a green-card marriage. Later, he masochistically facilitates Hedwig's National Socialist play-acting. Careening through one of the cheap American restaurants where she performs, perched atop a food service trolley pushed along by the Jewish Yitzhak, the German Hedwig delivers a Nazi salute to the audience.

As a Jew, Yitzhak represents an extreme of otherness to the German Hedwig, who is envied, feared, suppressed, and abused. Tobaron Waxman points out the incongruity of Yitzhak's over-determined Jewishness in the context of his supposed Balkan origin. He notes that the name "Yitzhak" is specifically Hebrew and is not equivalent to the more secularized "Isaac," saying:

> "Yitzhak" is a specifically Hebrew name. Most Russians did not grow up with religion, and so do not have Jewish names. This is true across Eastern Europe, unless you were educated underground. Even those whose families sent them to yeshivas underground have a secular/Christian name, and another name they use amongst Jews, or in a religious context. So it seems he (Mitchell) really wants you to see and

hear this Hebrew language association, while the character is a catch all for the harsh, bereft, depressive life of Eastern Europe.[54]

Hedwig is associated strongly with a divided Germany and the Berlin Wall. The Jewish figure of Yitzhak evokes other divides, and other walls—specifically Jewish walls that mirror many of the metaphorical functions of Hedwig's. In traditional synagogues, the Mechitza divides men and women during prayer. In Jerusalem, Jews visiting the Western Wall to pray are divided upon approach. Military security insures that the sexes are split; the regulation of gender at the Wall is literally policed. Describing his experience visiting the wall during early transition, FTM transsexual writer Ali Cannon notes: "Walking down that path to the Wall, I knew that I was crossing the great binary divide of Jewish law and regulated social religious space...I was also aware that I was not "supposed" to be there."[55]

The experience of TJ Michels, a transgender butch, is stranger still. When she attempted to follow her sisters to the women's section of the Western Wall, a guard who mistook her for a teenage boy forced her to go to the men's section instead, and she disappeared unnoticed into the mass of men. Her initial excitement over unexpectedly "passing" as a man quickly gave way to discomfort. When she insisted upon going into the women's section, after glimpsing her sisters through a gap in the mechitza, she was visually inspected and finally grudgingly allowed to cross over, but only at the cost of becoming conspicuous among those of her "own" sex. She related the unsettling sense of disappearance: "I phenomenologically vanished. I had absolutely no identity to cling to, my body was rendered meaningless...as my gender ceased to be intelligible."[56]

I include these first-person narratives of the experiences of transgender Jews at the Western Wall to highlight the existence of other transgender embodiments and other walls, and to suggest the ways in which they haunt the narrative of Hedwig. There is a strong parallel between Michel's experience of phenomenologically vanishing at the wall and the filmic disappearance of the character Yitzhak (along with the subjective positions he represents). He and they are both there and not there.

Like Luther, Yitzhak functions primarily to move Hedwig's story along, but he also brings into play yet another cutting father, to join the Zeus of Aristophanes and the Gnostic God of Tommy Gnosis. The Bible tells of Abraham, father of Isaac (Yitzhak), who is commanded by God to sacrifice his son upon a stone altar, now enshrined beneath the Dome of the Rock, at the very place where the Western Wall still stands. Abraham prepares to comply, but is stopped by the hand of God; his willingness makes the actual sacrifice unnecessary. Yitzhak is honored in the monotheistic religions as a preempted human sacrifice—the son's neck pressed always to the blade, the blade forever in the hand of the father, the earthly father subject to the eternal Law of the Father, to the law of God in Heaven.[57]

Tiring of Hedwig's continual abuse, Yitzhak seeks a way out. When he secures a part in a production of *Rent* that is being staged in Guam, Hedwig withholds his passport, restaging the scene in which Luther and the elder Hedwig arrange her castration, marriage and emigration. An abusive lover again evokes the passport as a tool to fix an unwilling partner into a coerced identity. She makes good on her threat of inseparability, holding her reluctant husband hostage. Unable to love Yitzhak, she is also unwilling to let him go.

INCH 5: SITUATIONS: HEDWIG SCHMIDT-ROBINSON, NEÉ MITCHELL

In the greater *Hedwig* phenomena, character, performance, and person slip: Mitchell has become a popular and sought-after speaker on transgender issues. At issue is the slippage between character and actor in the *persona* of the star. The naïve spectator is asked to disregard the distinctions between the actor/laborer, the star *persona*, and the screen character. How can one criticize the assumption of an identity without resorting to essentializing rhetoric? Kobena Mercer provides a clue when he notes that "the observation that *different readers make different readings* of the same cultural texts is not as circular as it seems: I want to suggest that it provides an outlet onto the dialogic character of the political imaginary of difference."[58] Of course a transsexual will read Hedwig differently than will a non-transsexual gay man. A black man will read Luther Robinson differently than a white man will. Different transsexuals will read Hedwig differently than one another and different black men will read Luther Robinson differently as well. Sedgwick points out the obvious but too often overlooked axiom: "People are different from each other."[59]

Does the text have any responsibility to the reader? Neither reading nor writing is a politically neutral activity. The burden of representation is heavy. One rock-and-roll drag queen should certainly not have to bear it all. Mercer notes that: "where subordinate subjects acquire the right to speak only one at a time, their discourse is circumscribed by the assumption that they speak as representatives' of the entire community from which they come."[60] How many transsexual rockers does one world need? And what does it mean when the *one* representative does not actually come from the community represented? "Google" searches of the terms "transsexual" plus "rock-and-roll" bring up thousands of mentions of *Hedwig*—and little else. After *Hedwig*, the next most frequent search return is another drag production: *The Rocky Horror Picture Show*. Rare are the mentions of such real-life transsexual rockers as Jayne County, Shawna Virago and The Deadly Nightshade Family, Lipstick Conspiracy, Christine Beatty of Glamazon, All The Pretty Horses, Nicole McRory, Bridgette Bratt, Jennifer Convertible, or The Transisters.

Singer Veronica Klaus, herself a transsexual, says simply that *Hedwig* is "not Mitchell's story to tell."[61] Mitchell wrote Hedwig, so of course, at one level, it *is* his story to tell. But Klaus has a point. Mitchell, in helping himself to the cultural *cachét* of transsexuality, in some ways recapitulates Tommy Gnosis' theft of Hedwig's song-writing output. Mitchell needs metaphorical material to develop his character. As Gnosis' career could not have soared as it did without Hedwig, Mitchell's similarly could not have done so without the combined output of trans cultural production.

In his transgender explorations, Mitchell uses Hedwig, and he uses drag. Butler notes that "There is no necessary relation between drag and subversion" and she "calls into question whether parodying the dominant norms is enough to displace them."[62] Mitchell's Hedwig drag is denaturalized. It is aggressively artificial, intentionally distant from its referent, and secure in a tradition of drag in which the gap between the object and the subject of the performance gapes wide. Realness is neither sought nor delivered. Hedwig doesn't pass and doesn't want to pass; to do so would be to miss the point. Hedwig's drag is a double citation: it cites "woman" in general, and "transsexual woman" specifically. "Woman," untheorized, is "natural;" it is the subject that animates human female flesh. Of course, she is never *really* natural, but the notion of natural womanhood is thinkable; indeed it is over-thought. A transsexual woman, on the other hand, is artificial by definition—a self-made woman who is never natural, always constructed. Nevertheless, she has her norms. A marginal figure, she is still well enough established in mainstream cultural awareness that there are certain stereotypical notions attached to her. Common clichés of the transsexual woman include the following. She is an extreme form of drag queen. She is a man in a dress. She is the ever-popular tranny prostitute, the she-male pro, and of course the sick man who cuts "it" off.[63] She is the battling transsexual of daytime television; *Jerry Springer Show* headlines blare: "Your girlfriend is a MAN!" In the early history of transsexuality, the figure of Christine Jorgenson dominated the media as a sexually exotic version of the classic blond bombshell. Hedwig cites *all* these norms.

Butler suggests that "an economy of difference is in order in which the matrices, the crossroads at which various identifications are formed and displaced, force a reworking of that logic of non-contradiction by which one identification is always and only purchased at the expense of another."[64] Is an abundant economy of identities possible in which Mitchell can explore the feminine to find the other half within himself, and do it with camp and wit and style, and with no suspicion that it might be at the expense of another? Does such an economy actually exist? Many 'feminized fags'[65] know what it is to be girled. Even heterosexual men can understand the experience of 'girling.' It is the constant threat of punishment for the wrong glance in the locker room, the wrong gait when walking, the wrong choice of shirt, the wrong hand gesture. The threat and promise of feminization is both terrifying and, at times, desirable. Leo Bersani has written at length about the seductive draw towards ecstatic ego dissolution that is the province of both women and anally receptive men. He writes: "[It] is an image with extraordinary power…a grown man, legs high up in the air, unable to refuse the suicidal ecstasy of being a woman."[66]

The slippage between gay man/drag queen/transsexual woman/biological female is inevitable given the exclusion of all of them from the normative category "man." Of course a gay man is a man, but he is also not a man. His manhood is constantly in question because, to put it crudely, "men" do not take it up the ass. This slippage may be inevitable, but the insistence on specificity is also crucial. Butler notes the importance of critical reflection "in order not to replicate at the level of identity politics the very exclusionary moves that initiated the turn to specific identities in the first place."[67] It is exclusionary to insist upon a space of difference. But is it also always violent? Is it not also violent to insist upon entry?

Butler asks: "Is 'assuming' a sex like a speech act? Or is it, or is it like, a citational strategy or re-signifying practice?"[68] Butler emphasizes that the sexed position ("gender") is only secured by being "repeatedly assumed" or reiterated. The boy Hansel slips into being Hedwig not only by the slip of the knife but also by repeated girling. For Mitchell, imagining a literal castration facilitates the process of imagining his character. Mitchell as Hedwig attempts a contestation of the symbolic through "the domain of the culturally impossible, the domain of the imaginary,"[69] but he ultimately capitulates to the law of the symbolic when he recuperates, and is recuperated within, his masculinity. Of course it is a homosexual masculinity, and therefore it is never completely secure. Mercer says: "certain kinds of performative statements produce different meanings not so much because of what is said but because of who is saying it."[70] Mitchell might slip again, might become Hedwig again at any moment. Indeed, he does become Hedwig over and over again, through the literal reenactment on the stage at every performance, and on film at every screening.

INCH 6: FULL CIRCLE: THREE HAVES MAKE A WHOLE

At the conclusion of *Hedwig and the Angry Inch*, male and female become one. The search is over. The violent rupture of the origin of love is healed as halves unite; the Other and the Same integrate; and opposites, which are always said to attract, finally merge. Symbolically enacting both the mythic reunification of the children of the moon, and the historic reunification of Germany in the closing years of the cold war, Hansel/Hedwig's queer body is healed in a metaphysical staging of (oddly enough) heterosexual desire, the merging of the male and female.

Hansel was marked male at birth, and marked feminine male in childhood. When Hedwig is eventually marked as woman, she is specifically marked a transsexual woman. Hedwig both is and is not transsexual. If the 'botched sex-change' is the measure of transsexuality, she is. If psychical identity as woman and physical feminization beyond castration and clothing is the measure, she is not. If transsexual desire is the measure, she most certainly is not. Hansel never expressed a desire for re-embodiment. His desire was for his other half, and for the West. Becoming-Hedwig was a strategy for Hansel to find and merge with the other half, elsewhere. For Mitchell, Hedwig is merely a trope, his way of exploring metaphysical questions through identification with an Other. Retaining the root of her penis, Hedwig is literally a phallic woman. The angry inch is a trace of the male precursor mark. She is re-marked male at the film's conclusion—when the body returns to a state fantasized as unmarked. Butler notes that (for Lacan) "Sex is that which marks the body prior to its mark, staging in advance which symbolic position will mark it"[71] and notes further that "It is the first mark that prepares the body for the second one"[72] Hansel's performed effeminacy, and his molestation, prepared his body for the next mark—the mark of castration through which he is able to fulfill his desire to cross the Wall, and to imagine the crossing of the sexual divide. Hansel's 'punishment' enacts his desire. Hedwig the character begins with Hansel's dismemberment. When Hedwig the character as well as *Hedwig* the story come to an end, Hansel is—literally—remembered. It is between the dismembering and the remembering of Hansel that the fantasy of Hedwig, a fantasy of gender without genitals, is enacted.

Towards the end of *Hedwig*, immediately preceding her redemption and her ultimate, impossible, return to male embodiment, it seems that she has finally hit bottom. Having lost everyone - her father, her mother, her first husband Luther, her lover Tommy, her agent, and her second husband Yitzhak—she is alone. Abandoned by her band, she is reduced to prostitution, to strolling an alley for trade. She does not, however, experience the real-life dangers of "walking while trans." As a fantasy, Hedwig is immune from the hazards of authenticity; nothing of the real touches her. Transsexual rocker and activist Shawna Virago has written of a common real-world experience of transsexual street prostitutes, and of those transsexual women, who, merely walking, are taken to be prostitutes:

> Hey, Bitch, up against the hood…I can tell you're up to no good
> Just gimme some lip…I'll arrest you for bad make-up.
> Hey, Bitch that's a pretty big dick…for an All-American chick
> I might just let you walk…if you suck my cock [73]

Hedwig is briefly inspected, but passed over by an Orthodox Jewish passer-by who is cruising for trans sex. He appears strangely drag-like himself in his frum gear. From the depths of the alley, Tommy Gnosis' limousine mysteriously emerges, and he picks Hedwig up, tearfully admitting her ownership of his lyrics. They enjoy a brief reunion—drinking, taking drugs, singing and kissing—before crashing into a truck. The accident is reported in the sensationalistic press, and Tommy's career plummets in the wake of his public association with a "transsexual." The film veers into its final, somewhat chaotic, scenes.

Hedwig, who is now mysteriously reunited with her band, is shown receiving great acclaim and performing to a wildly enthusiastic audience. She passes her wig to Yitzhak, who dons it, instantly transforming from a "sullen male roadie"[74] to a radiant, smiling and buxom woman in a tight dress and bright-red, high-heeled, "fuck-me" pumps. Is this Krystal Nacht? It hardly seems possible. This new woman bears none of the camp gaps that signify drag, but seems thoroughly if rather over-abundantly female. He, now she, is passed grinning from hand to hand over the heads of the cheering crowd. Hedwig rips off her own dress, revealing her male body…and collapses. She, now he, is nearly naked, clearly whole, and wholly male. The reunion is complete; the return of Hedwig as an artist coincides with the return and redemption of Hansel as a man. The trans bodies of the characters disappear, returning to the 'natural' sexes of the actors. The tropes dissolve. From some imaginary space off-screen, Tommy sings:

> Forgive me,
> For I did not know.

'Cause I was just a boy
And you were so much more
Than any god could ever plan
More than a woman or a man.[75]

Hedwig rises, revealing her male body. Hansel is revealed, and re-membered. But *is* it Hansel? It *looks* like Hansel. Could it be Tommy? His forehead bears the shining silver cross that Hedwig painted on it when she christened Tommy "Gnosis" in her mobile home in Kansas so long before. Mitchell explains:

On stage, she becomes Tommy so there's more to kind of chew on. That was the hardest thing in the film, what to do with that scene. And in a way, I really didn't know. Tommy was telling her that she had to rethink the way "the origin of love" is interpreted. He's saying maybe there is no other half, and you have to look within.[76]

This new Tommy sings that there is "nothing in the sky but air."[77] Thus Gnosis becomes Agnosis; Yitzhak becomes a babe, and Hedwig returns to being Hansel or Tommy—or might it be Mitchell? Whoever he is, he is presented *au natural,* crouching wet and naked in the alley behind the nightclub where he has just finished performing, any hint of the apparent woman apparently rinsed away by the rain. The male and the female halves of the animated original androgyne reappear and merge, the halves made whole, the masculine and feminine integrated into the symbol of the fantasy of the remarked/unmarked body. In noting that the ostensibly happy ending provided both a conclusion and a disruption, transgender film theorist Kam Wei Kui notes that it:

disturb[ed] the sense of belonging for both gays and trans (what is Hedwig 'really'? gay or transwoman?), and of course by undoing the trans visuality, the transwoman became invisible or just simply vanished, while a new gay guy re-emerge[d] on the scene.[78]

Mercer says that: "the question of agency in cultural practices that contest the canon and its cultural dominance suggests that it really does matter who is speaking.[79]

Who is speaking here? Is it a new being or the original? It may be both. The 'happy ending' coincides with the trans characters returning to the sexes of their birth,[80] and the Christian boy abandoning God: all phantasms disappear. For Mitchell, there is little of the political attached to this. It is his artistic interrogation of his own feminine side, a specifically male homosexual experience of the feminine. The interrogation of male femininity is important work. Transformed irrevocably by his journey, he is the same, but different.

While *Hedwig* may be largely apolitical for Mitchell, it is not and cannot be completely apolitical for certain others. There are those who see it as an unacceptable infringement on hard-won trans cultural turf. From this point of view, Mitchell's appropriation of the mask of transsexuality constitutes a trespass at best, and at worst a theft and transmogrification of a subject position, though a practice not unlike blackface on a white actor. Even those who take the position that, as a bit of camp fun, *Hedwig* shouldn't be taken too seriously express some leeriness at the flippancy with which important psychological, social and political questions are treated. Kui continues:

This film was not made to represent "real" transgender lives: it was a piece of entertainment. It used transgender as trope, in this aspect…a person out of control, but at the same time…(showing) how strong survivors can be… (but) I am a bit wary of the obligatory fun, outrageousness and extravaganza that go along with transgender as trope.[81]

It can be argued, of course, that all representation is political. And in the art of the actor, the assumption of a role implies that the actor takes on that which is not otherwise his or hers. Acting is necessarily a sort of identity theft. The question of whether some particular representation is "good" or "bad" for a particular community is not one that particularly interests me, and is not what I hope to have accomplished here. *Hedwig* is an important film, and it is an important cultural phenomena. It has quickly secured a place in the queer film canon, and it continues to establish a devoted underground following and fan base among high-school and college age youth, mainly queer, who exhaustively analyze its minutiae, and who, in some cases, use it as a basis for developing their personal philosophies of life.[82] As an important cultural phenomenon, *Hedwig* deserves serious attention, including critical and political analysis. That is what I have attempted to do here, and I hope that this effort will open the door to further critical attention.

Hedwig has been consistently referred to as a transgender film. This it well may be if the broadest definition of transgender is used, one in which drag, male femininity, cross-gender role-play, psychic bisexuality, et cetera are all included. Easily included within that definition would be *Hedwig* as a gay male rite of passage narrative, one that uses the figure of the transsexual to represent the path not taken—because it is the wrong path. It is important to note, however, that it is the wrong path specifically for Mitchell. There are many paths, and for others, transsexuality is definitely the right one. It is of utmost importance—socially, politically and spiritually—that the various paths remain open, unobstructed and viable so that each may pass in safety to his or her own proper destination.

In closing, I would like to turn briefly to the idea of abundance. Tensions over identities and border wars are attributable at least in part to a perception, sometimes justified and sometimes not, that resources are limited. In pointing to a possible line of escape from a mindset of scarcity towards one of becoming-abundant, I conclude with a quote from *Anti-Oedipus,* the book Foucault described as an "Introduction to the Non-Fascist Life."[83]

> Making love is not just becoming one, or even two, but becoming as a hundred thousand. Desiring-machines or the nonhuman sex: not one or even two, but *n* sexes. The…slogan of the desiring-revolution will be first of all: to each its own sexes.[84]

NOTES

Many thanks to those who have provided valuable insight into and productive readings of this project: Catherine Greenblatt, C. Jacob Hale, Juba Kalamka, Veronica Klaus, Kam Wei Kui, Bliss Lim, Lazlo Pearlman, James Singer, Susan Stryker, Shawna Virago, Tobaron Waxman, Cecile Whiting.

1. The "Gender Binary" can be understood more accurately as a binary of sex/gender, in which the two are imagined as necessarily coupled and ascribed largely separate realms: Male/Man ≠ Female/Woman. For an analysis of the sex/gender system in which the two are uncoupled and analyzed separately see:
     Rubin, Gayle. 'The Traffic in Women: Notes on the 'Political Economy' of Sex,' in *Toward an Anthropology of Women*, ed. Rayna R. Reiter (New York: Monthly Review Press, 1975), 157–210. and 'Thinking Sex: Notes for a Radical Theory of the Politics of Sexuality,' in *Pleasure and Danger: Exploring Female Sexuality*, ed. C. Vance and Paul Kegan (London: Routledge, 1984) pp. 267–319.
2. Judith Halberstam and C. Jacob Hale, "Butch/FTM Border Wars: A Note on Collaboration," *GLQ 4* (1998), pp. 283-85.
3. John Cameron Mitchell (text) and Stephen Trask (music and lyrics) *Hedwig and The Angry Inch* (Woodstock and New York, Overlook Press: 1998), p. 43. The "botched sex-change", which is coerced, results in the "angry inch" of the title and becomes, eventually, the name of Hedwig's band.
4. Ibid., p. 19.
5. Ibid., p. 43.
6. John Cameron Mitchell to D.L. Alvarez: Interviewed for Planet Out – online, 2001.
7. Judith Butler, *Bodies That Matter: On the Discursive Limits of Sex* (New York and London, Routledge: 1993), p. 126.
8. Mitchell to Steel: *The Advocate*, 2001.

9.   Plato, *Symposium*, trans. Benjamin Jowett (Indianapolis, Library of Liberal Arts: 1945).

10.   Ibid., p. 31.

11.   Ibid., p. 32.

12.   Eve Kosofsky Sedgwick, *Epistemology of the Closet* (Berkeley & Los Angeles: University of California Press, 1990), pp. 1–2.

13.   Mitchell and Trask, *Hedwig and The Angry Inch*, p. 27.

14.   Ibid., p. 32.

15.   Kaja Silverman, *Male Subjectivity at the Margins* (New York and London, Routledge: 1992), pp. 339–388. For a sustained discussion of Freud and the Negative Oedipal Complex as it relates to formation of ego organization in feminine male homosexuals see her chapter on "A Woman's Soul Enclosed in a Man's Body: Femininity in Male Homosexuality"

16.   Butler, *Bodies That Matter*, p. 99.

17.   Vern L. Bullough, *Homosexuality: A History* (New York and Scarborough, Ontario: Meridian, 1979), p. 4.

18.   Michel Foucault, *The History of Sexuality Volume 1: An Introduction* trans. Robert Hurley (New York: Vintage Books, 1978), p. 43.

19.   Mitchell and Trask, *Hedwig and The Angry Inch*, 66.

20.   Ibid., 61.

21.   Ibid., 61.

22.   These 'fission' myths of the origin of sexual difference are distinct from scientific understandings of sex, in which sex proper begins with the fusion of genetic material from two genetically different sources.

23.   Mitchell and Trask, *Hedwig and The Angry Inch*, p. 45.

24.   Ibid., p. 43.

25.   MTF Transsexual R&B singer and songwriter Veronica Klaus points out that when male-to-female genital surgery goes wrong, the results are generally not angry inches but shallow holes. Personal conversation with the author, March 2001.

26.   Phillip Core, *Camp: The Lie that Tells the Truth*, (New York: Delilah Press, 1984)

27.   Butler, *Bodies That Matter*, pp. 101–102.

28.   Leo Bersani, *Homos*, (Cambridge, MA and London: Harvard University Press, 1995), p. 58.

29.   From Judith Butler's discussion on the originary "girling" of the girl through the act of naming - in *Bodies That Matter*, pp. 7–8.

30.   Carol J. Clover, *Her Body, Himself: Gender in the Slasher Film* in *The Dread of Difference: Gender and the Horror Film*, ed. Barry Keith Grant (Austin, University of Texas Press: 1996) p. 95.

31.   Butler, *Bodies That Matter*, p. 103.

32.   Ibid. p. 97.

33.   Ibid. p. 126.

34.   Ibid, p. 36.

35.   Many thanks to Juba Kalamka of *Deep Dickollective* and *Sugartruck Recordings* for introducing me to the filmic figure of the "Magic Negro."

36.   Rita Kempley. "Too Too Divine; Movies' 'Magic Negro' Saves the Day, but at The Cost of His Soul", *Washington Post*, June 7, 2003.

37.   Mitchell and Trask, *Hedwig and The Angry Inch*, p. 36.

38.   Ibid., p. 36.

39.   Ibid., p. 38.

40.   Ibid., p. 38.

41.   Ibid., p. 38.

42.   Mitchell and Trask, *Hedwig and the Angry Inch*, p. 43.

43.   Ibid., p. 43.

44.   Deep Dickollective, *Bougie Boho Post-Pomo Afro Homo* (San Francisco: Sugartruck Recordings/Sevenleft Nanomedia, 2001).

45.   Ibid., p. 46.

46.   Butler, *Bodies That Matter*, p. 100.

47.   John Cameron Mitchell wrote the script and Stephen Trask wrote the music and the lyrics of the theatrical version of *Hedwig and The Angry Inch*. It was originally presented at the Westbeth Theatre Center on February 27, 1997 and opened off-Broadway at the Jane Street Theatre on February 14, 1998. In the original theatrical production, all of the action is described by Hedwig during conversational interludes between songs and the cast is minimal, consisting only of John Cameron Mitchell as Hedwig/Tommy Gnosis, Miriam Shor as Yitzhak and (Stephen Trask's band) Cheater as The Angry Inch. In the film version, the cast is filled out, and while Hedwig still "describes" the action, we are taken into a filmic imaginary space where we see her descriptions.

48.   Mitchell has commented on this in interviews in which he has said that the character of Hedwig was inspired by an East German babysitter employed by his family to look after a younger sibling when the family was stationed in Berlin, where his father was Stadt-Commandant. Hedwig meets Tommy when she is working as a babysitter for his baby brother.

49.   Mitchell and Trask, *Hedwig and the Angry Inch*, p. 54.

50.   Mitchell and Trask, *Hedwig and the Angry Inch*. p. 56.

51.   Lazlo Pearlman, in conversation with the author, March, 2002.

52.   Sigmund Freud. "Analysis of a Phobia in a Five-Year-Old Boy," 1909. in *The Standard Edition of the Complete Psychologi-*

cal Works of Sigmund Freud, Volume 10. Ed. and trans. James Strachey and Anna Freud. (London: Hogarth, 1955), pp. 198–99.

53. Towards the end of the stage play, Mitchell makes this explicit. Hedwig attempts to make up to Yitzhak, apparently briefly considering him as a possible other half. She says to him: "You and me. Singing back up in our oven. Couple of survivors. The German and the Jew. Think of the symmetry. Think of the power. Think of the publicity. The gods would be terrified." She attempts to kiss him and he spits in her face. Mitchell and Trask, *Hedwig and the Angry Inch*, p. 68.

54. Tobaron Waxman is a performance artist. His work includes elements of traditional Jewish texts and philosophy, as well as politics and desire. He uses technologies of photography and video, choreography, liturgy, internet and performance to interrogate concepts of 'Gender', 'Conflict', 'Consent', 'Other', and 'Israel'. In conversation with the author, 2004.

55. TJ Michels and Ali Cannon "Whose Side Are You On? Transgender at the Western Wall" in *Queer Jews*, ed. David Shneer & Caryn Aviv. (New York & London, Routledge 2002), p. 87.

56. Ibid. p. 91.

57. Tobaron Waxman, in conversation with the author, 2004.

58. Kobena Mercer, *Skin Head Sex Thing: Racial Difference and the Homoerotic Imaginary* in *How Do I Look? Queer Film and Video*, eds. Bad Object-Choices (Washington, Bay Press: 1991), 193–194.

59. Sedgwick, *Epistemology of the Closet*, p. 22.

60. Kobena Mercer, *Skin Head Sex Thing*, p. 205.

61. Veronica Klaus, Personal conversation with the author, March 2001.

62. Butler, *Bodies That Matter*, p. 125.

63. The idea that transsexual women are created through the act of 'cutting it off' remains popular although it is an inaccurate description of MTF gender reassignment surgery. Its persistence is likely tied to the notion of the woman as castrated, defined by lack.

64. Butler, *Bodies That Matter*, p. 118.

65. Ibid., p. 103.

66. Leo Bersani, "Is the Rectum a Grave," in *October*, No. 43 [Winter 1987], p. 212.

67. Butler, *Bodies That Matter*, p. 118

68. Ibid,. p. 108. –Butler is speaking here about the process of assuming a sex in a presumably lifelong sense, not of assuming a 'different' sex for a temporary duration, as in a drag performance.

69. Ibid., p. 111.

70. Kobena Mercer, *Skin Head Sex Thing*, p. 193.

71. Butler, *Bodies That Matter*, p. 97.

72. Ibid., p. 98.

73. Shawna Virago, *Johnny Law*, unpublished song lyrics, 2001.

74. Mitchell and Trask, Hedwig and The Angry Inch, p. 13.

75. Ibid. p. 73.

76. Mitchell to D.L. Alvarez: Interviewed for Planet Out - online

77. Mitchell and Trask, *Hedwig and The Angry Inch*, p. 74.

78. Kam Wei Kui, Executive Director of the Netherlands Transgender Film Festival, in conversation with the author, 2002, from Amsterdam.

79. Kobena Mercer, *Skin Head Sex Thing*, p. 181.

80. When asked the meaning of this, Mitchell replied: "I used to be more the kind of person who needed everything to be clear. Some people found the last 20 minutes, which is similar to on stage, to be unclear as opposed to ambiguous. Unclear is more pejorative than ambiguous...which is a good thing. Right?" (Mitchell to D.L. Alvarez: Interviewed for Planet Out - online)

81. Kam Wei Kui, in conversation with the author, 2002.

82. The reception of *Hedwig* is something of which I have not gone into any detail here. My sources for this assertion, however, include personal conversations, on-line fan-club records sites and chat rooms. For anyone wishing to take this area of analysis further, I would recommend starting with a visit to the "Hedwig in a Box" site at: http://www.hedwiginabox.com/

83. Gilles Deleuze and Félix Guattari, *Anti-Oedipus: Capitalism and Schizophrenia*, trans. Robert Hurley, Mark Seem and Helen R. Lane, (Minneapolis: University of Minnesota Press, 1983), p. xiii.

84. Ibid., p. 296.

V

TRANSGENDER MASCULINITIES

32

Of Catamites and Kings
Reflections on Butch, Gender, and Boundaries[1]

Gayle Rubin

Gayle Rubin is justly famous for her articles "The Traffic in Women" and "Thinking Sex"—the latter often cited as a foundational text of queer theory. A lesser-known piece, reproduced below, shows every bit as much of Rubin's trademark brilliance in its thoughts on the varieties of female masculinity.

Writing in 1992, Rubin offers a candid assessment of the extent of gender dysphoria in lesbian communities, and suggests that issues of gender variance and what later came to be called female masculinity were "strangely out of focus in lesbian thought, analysis, and terminology." In breaking this silence, and in pointing out the areas of overlap between lesbian and transgender concerns, Rubin helped chart the course of transgender scholarship in the decade ahead.

Perhaps the most striking feature of Rubin's article is her call for lesbian communities to tolerate the presence of FTM transsexuals, rather than expel them, during their transition from woman to man. Categories like woman, man, butch, lesbian and transsexual, Rubin contends, are all "imperfect, historical, temporary, and arbitrary. We use them and they use us.... Instead of fighting for immaculate classifications and impenetrable boundaries, let us strive to maintain a community that sees diversity as a gift and anomalies as precious."

WHAT IS BUTCH?

Conceptions and Misconceptions of Lesbian Gender

Attempting to define terms such as *butch* and *femme* is one of the surest ways to incite volatile discussion among lesbians. "Butch" and "femme" are important categories within lesbian experience, and as such they have accumulated multiple layers of significance. Most lesbians would probably agree with a definition from *The Queen's Vernacular*, that a butch is a "lesbian with masculine characteristics."[2] But many corollaries attending that initial premise oversimplify and misrepresent butch experience. In this essay, I approach "butch" from the perspective of gender in order to discuss, clarify, and challenge some prevalent lesbian cultural assumptions about what is butch.

Many commentators have noted that the categories "butch" and "femme" have historically served numerous functions in the lesbian world. Describing the lesbian community in Buffalo from the 1930s through the 1950s, Elizabeth Kennedy and Madeline Davis comment that

these roles had two dimensions: First, they constituted a code of personal behavior, particularly in the areas of image and sexuality. Butches affected a masculine style, while fems appeared characteristically female.

Butch and fem also complemented one another in an erotic system in which the butch was expected to be both the doer and the giver; the fem's passion was the butch's fulfillment. Second, butch-fem roles were what we call a social imperative. They were the organizing principle for this community's relation to the outside world and for its members' relationships to one another.[3]

While I do not wish to deny or underestimate the complexity of its functions, I will argue that the simplest definition of butch is the most helpful one. Butch is most usefully understood as a category of lesbian gender that is constituted through the deployment and manipulation of masculine gender codes and symbols.

Butch and femme are ways of coding identities and behaviors that are both connected to and distinct from standard societal roles for men and women.[4] Among lesbian and bisexual women, as in the general population, there are individuals who strongly identify as masculine or feminine as well as individuals whose gender preferences are more flexible or fluid. "Femmes" identify predominantly as feminine or prefer behaviors and signals defined as feminine within the larger culture; "butches" identify primarily as masculine or prefer masculine signals, personal appearance, and styles. There are also many lesbians (and bisexual women) with intermediate or unmarked gender styles. In the old days, terms such as *ki-ki* indicated such intermediate or indeterminate gender styles or identities. We appear to have no contemporary equivalent, although at times, *lesbian* and *dyke* are used to indicate women whose gender messages are not markedly butch or femme.[5]

Butch is the lesbian vernacular term for women who are more comfortable with masculine gender codes, styles, or identities than with feminine ones. The term encompasses individuals with a broad range of investments in "masculinity." It includes, for example, women who are not at all interested in male gender identities, but who use traits associated with masculinity to signal their lesbianism or to communicate their desire to engage in the kinds of active or initiatory sexual behaviors that in this society are allowed or expected from men. It includes women who adopt "male" fashions and mannerisms as a way to claim privileges or deference usually reserved for men. It may include women who find men's clothing better made, and those who consider women's usual wear too confining or uncomfortable or who feel it leaves them vulnerable or exposed.[6]

Butch is also the indigenous lesbian category for women who are gender "dysphoric." *Gender dysphoria* is a technical term for individuals who are dissatisfied with the gender to which they were assigned (usually at birth) on the basis of their anatomical sex. Within the psychological and medical communities, gender dysphoria is considered a disorder, as were lesbianism and male homosexuality before the American Psychiatric Association removed them from its official list of mental diseases in 1973.[7] I am not using *gender dysphoria* in the clinical sense, with its connotations of neurosis or psychological impairment. I am using it as a purely descriptive term for persons who have gender feelings and identities that are at odds with their assigned gender status or their physical bodies. Individuals who have very powerful gender dysphoria, particularly those with strong drives to alter their bodies to conform to their preferred gender identities, are called transsexuals.[8]

The lesbian community is organized along an axis of sexual orientation and comprises women who have sexual, affectional, erotic, and intimate relations with other women. It nevertheless harbors a great deal of gender dysphoria.[9] Drag, cross-dressing, passing, transvestism, and transsexualism are all common in lesbian populations, particularly those not attempting to meet constricted standards of political virtue.[10]

In spite of their prevalence, issues of gender variance are strangely out of focus in lesbian thought, analysis, and terminology. The intricacies of lesbian gender are inadequately and infrequently addressed. *Butch* is one of the few terms currently available with which to express or indicate masculine gender preferences among lesbians, and it carries a heavy, undifferentiated load.[11] The category of butch encompasses a wide range of gender variation within lesbian cultures.

Within the group of women labeled butch, there are many individuals who are gender dysphoric to varying degrees. Many butches have partially male gender identities. Others border on being, and some are, female-to-male transsexuals (FTMs), although many lesbians *and* FTMs find the areas of overlap between butchness and transsexualism disturbing.[12] Saying that many butches identify as masculine to some degree does not mean that all, even most, butches "want to be men," although some undoubtedly do. Most butches enjoy combining expressions of masculinity with a female body. The coexistence of masculine traits with a female anatomy is a fundamental characteristic of "butch" and is a highly charged, eroticized, and consequential lesbian signal.[13]

By saying that many lesbians identify partially or substantially as masculine, I am also not saying that such individuals are "male identified" in the political sense. When the term *male identified* was originally used in early seventies feminism, it denoted nothing about gender identity. It described a political attitude in which members of a category of generally oppressed persons (women) failed to identify with their self-interest as women, and instead identified with goals, policies, and attitudes beneficial to a group of generally privileged oppressors (men). Though such women were sometimes butch or masculine in style, they might as easily be femme or feminine. One typical manifestation of male identification in this sense consisted of very feminine heterosexual women who supported traditional male privilege. On a more contemporary note, some of the feminine right-wing women whose political aims include strengthening male authority in conventional family arrangements could also be called male identified.

There are many problems with the notion of male identified, not the least of which are questions of who defines what "women's interests" are in a given situation and the assumption of a unitary category of "women" whose interests are always the same. But the point here is not a political critique of the concept of male identification. It is simply to register that a similarity in terminology has often led to a conflation of political positions with gender identities. A strongly masculine butch will not necessarily identify politically with men. In fact, it is sometimes the most masculine women who confront male privilege most directly and painfully, and are the most enraged by it.[14]

VARIETIES OF BUTCH

The iconography in many contemporary lesbian periodicals leaves a strong impression that a butch always has very short hair, wears a leather jacket, rides a Harley, and works construction. This butch paragon speaks mostly in monosyllables, is tough yet sensitive, is irresistible to women, and is semiotically related to a long line of images of young, rebellious, sexy, white, working-class masculinity that stretches from Marlon Brando in *The Wild One* (1954) to the character of James Hurley on "Twin Peaks" (1990). She is usually accompanied by a half-dressed, ultrafeminine creature who is artfully draped on her boots, her bike, or one of her muscular, tattooed forearms.[15]

These images originate in the motorcycle and street gangs of the early fifties. They have been powerful erotic icons ever since, and lesbians are not the only group to find them engaging and sexy. Among gay men, the figure of the outlaw leather biker (usually with a heart of gold) has symbolically anchored an entire subculture. During the late seventies, similar imagery dominated even mainstream male homosexual style and fashion. There are many rock-and-roll variants, from classic biker (early Bruce Springsteen) to futuristic road warrior (Judas Priest, Billy Idol) to postmodern punk (Sex Pistols). The contemporary ACT UP and Queer Nation styles so popular among young gay men and women are lineal descendants of those of the punk rockers, whose torn jackets and safety pins fractured and utilized the same leather aesthetic.

Within the lesbian community, the most commonly recognized butch styles are those based on these models of white, working-class, youthful masculinity. But in spite of the enduring glamour and undeniable charm of these figures of rebellious individualism, they do not encompass the actual range of lesbian masculinity. Butches vary in their styles of masculinity, their preferred modes of sexual expression, and their choices of partners.

There are many different ways to be masculine. Men get to express masculinity with numerous and diverse cultural codes, and there is no reason to assume that women are limited to a narrower choice of idioms. There are at least as many ways to be butch as there are ways for men to be masculine; actually, there are more ways to be butch, because when women appropriate masculine styles the element of travesty produces new significance and meaning. Butches adopt and transmute the many available codes of masculinity.[16]

Sometimes lesbians use the term *butch* to indicate only the most manly women.[17] But the equation of butch with hypermasculine women indulges a stereotype. Butches vary widely in how masculine they feel and, consequently, in how they present themselves. Some butches are only faintly masculine, some are partly masculine, some "dag" butches are very manly, and some "drag kings" pass as men.

Butches vary in how they relate to their female bodies. Some butches are comfortable being pregnant and having kids, while for others the thought of undergoing the female component of mammalian reproduction is utterly repugnant. Some enjoy their breasts while others despise them. Some butches hide their genitals and some refuse penetration. There are butches who abhor tampons, because of their resonance with intercourse; other butches love getting fucked. Some butches are perfectly content in their female bodies, while others may border on or become transsexuals.

Forms of masculinity are molded by the experiences and expectations of class, race, ethnicity, religion, occupation, age, subculture, and individual personality. National, racial, and ethnic groups differ widely in what constitutes masculinity, and each has its own system for communicating and conferring "manhood." In some cultures, physical strength and aggression are the privileged signals of masculinity. In other cultures, manliness is expressed by literacy and the ability to manipulate numbers or text. The travails of Barbra Streisand's character in *Yentl* occurred because scholarship was considered the exclusive domain of men among traditional Orthodox Jews of Eastern Europe. Myopia and stooped shoulders from a lifetime of reading were prized traits of masculinity. Some butches play rugby; some debate political theory; some do both.

Manliness also varies according to class origin, income level, and occupation. Masculinity can be expressed by educational level, career achievement, emotional detachment, musical or artistic talent, sexual conquest, intellectual style, or disposable income. The poor, the working classes, the middle classes, and the rich all provide different sets of skills and expectations that butches as well as men use to certify their masculinity.[18]

The styles of masculinity executive and professional men favor differ sharply from those of truckers and carpenters. The self-presentations of marginally employed intellectuals differ from those of prosperous lawyers. Classical musicians differ from jazz musicians, who are distinguishable from rock-and-roll musicians. Short hair, shaved heads, and Mohawks did not make eighties punk rockers more studly than today's long-haired heavy-metal headbangers. All of these are recognizably male styles, and there are butches who express their masculinity within each symbolic assemblage.

Butches come in all the shapes and varieties and idioms of masculinity. There are butches who are tough street dudes, butches who are jocks, butches who are scholars, butches who are artists, rock-and-roll butches, butches who have motorcycles, and butches who have money. There are butches whose male models are effeminate men, sissies, drag queens, and many different types of male homosexuals. There are butch nerds, butches with soft bodies and hard minds.

BUTCH SEXUALITIES

Thinking of butch as a category of gender expression may help to account for what appear to be butch sexual anomalies. Do butches who prefer to let their partners run the sex become "femme in the sheets"? Are butches who go out with other butches instead of femmes "homosexuals"? Does that make femmes who date femmes "lesbians"?

Butchness often signals a sexual interest in femmes and a desire or willingness to orchestrate sexual encounters. However, the ideas that butches partner exclusively with femmes or that butches always "top" (that is, "run the sex") are stereotypes that mask substantial variation in butch erotic experience.[19]

Historically, butches were expected to seduce, arouse, and sexually satisfy their partners, who were expected to be femmes. During similar eras, men were expected to inaugurate and manage sexual relations with their female partners. Both sets of expectations were located within a system in which gender role, sexual orientation, and erotic behavior were presumed to exist only in certain fixed relationships to one another. Variations existed and were recognized but were considered aberrant.

Though we still live in a culture that privileges heterosexuality and gender conformity, many of the old links have been broken, bent, strained, and twisted into new formations. Perhaps more importantly, configurations of gender role and sexual practice that were once rare have become much more widespread. In contemporary lesbian populations there are many combinations of gender and desire.

Many butches like to seduce women and control sexual encounters. Some butches become aroused only when they are managing a sexual situation. But there are femmes who like to stay in control, and there are butches who prefer their partners to determine the direction and rhythms of lovemaking. Such butches may seek out sexually dominant femmes or sexually aggressive butches. Every conceivable combination of butch, femme, intermediate, top, bottom, and switch exists, even though some are rarely acknowledged. There are butch tops and butch bottoms, femme tops and femme bottoms. There are butch-femme couples, femme-femme partners, and butch-butch pairs.

Butches are often identified in relation to femmes. Within this framework, butch and femme are considered an indissoluble unity, each defined with reference to the other; butches are invariably the partners of femmes. Defining "butch" as the object of femme desire, or "femme" as the object of butch desire presupposes that butches do not desire or partner with other butches, and that femmes do not desire or go with other femmes.

Butch-butch eroticism is much less documented than butch-femme sexuality, and lesbians do not always recognize or understand it. Although it is not uncommon, lesbian culture contains few models for it. Many butches who lust after other butches have looked to gay male literature and behavior as sources of imagery and language. The erotic dynamics of butch-butch sex sometimes resemble those of gay men, who have developed many patterns for sexual relations between different kinds of men. Gay men also have role models for men who are passive or subordinate in sexual encounters yet retain their masculinity. Many butch-butch couples think of themselves as women doing male homosexual sex with one another. There are "catamites" who are the submissive or passive partners of active "sodomites." There are "daddies" and "daddy's boys." There are bodybuilders who worship one another's musculature and lick each other's sweat. There are leather dudes who cruise together for "victims" to pleasure.[20]

FRONTIER FEARS: BUTCHES, TRANSSEXUALS, AND TERROR

No system of classification can successfully catalogue or explain the infinite vagaries of human diversity. To paraphrase Foucault, no system of thought can ever "tame the wild profusion of existing things."[21] Anomalies will always occur, challenging customary modes of thought without representing any actual threat to health, safety, or community survival. However, human beings are easily upset by exactly those "existing things" that escape classification, treating such phenomena as dangerous, polluting, and requiring eradication.[22] Female-to-male transsexuals present just such a challenge to lesbian gender categories.

Although important discontinuities separate lesbian butch experience and female-to-male transsexual experience, there are also significant points of connection. Some butches are psychologically indistinguishable from female-to-male transsexuals, except for the identities they choose and the extent to which they are willing or able to alter their bodies. Many FTMs live as butches before adopting transsexual or male identities. Some individuals explore each identity before choosing one that is more meaningful for them, and others use both categories to interpret and organize their experience. The boundaries between the categories of butch and transsexual are permeable.[23]

Many of the passing women and diesel butches so venerated as lesbian ancestors are also claimed in the historical lineages of female-to-male transsexuals. There is a deep-rooted appreciation in lesbian culture for the beauty and heroism of manly women. Accounts of butch exploits form a substantial part of lesbian fiction and history; images of butches and passing women are among our most striking ancestral portraits. These include the photographs of Radclyffe Hall as a dashing young gent, the Berenice Abbott photo of Jane Heap wearing a suit and fixing an intimidating glare at the camera, and Brassaï's pictures of the nameless but exquisitely cross-dressed and manicured butches who patronized Le Monocle in 1930s Paris.

Some of these women were likely also transsexuals. For example, several years ago the San Francisco Lesbian and Gay History Project produced a slide show on passing women in North America.[24] One of those women was Babe Bean, also known as Jack Bee Garland. Bean/Garland later became the subject of a biography by Louis Sullivan, a leader and scholar in the FTM community until his recent death from AIDS. Sullivan's study highlighted Garland's sex change in addition to his relations with women.[25] It is interesting to ponder what other venerable lesbian forebears might be considered transsexuals; if testosterone had been available, some would undoubtedly have seized the opportunity to take it.

In spite of the overlap and kinship between some areas of lesbian and transsexual experience, many lesbians are antagonistic toward transsexuals, treating male-to-female transsexuals as menacing intruders and female-to-male transsexuals as treasonous deserters. Transsexuals of both genders are commonly perceived and described in contemptuous stereotypes: unhealthy, deluded, self-hating, enslaved to patriarchal gender roles, sick, antifeminist, antiwoman, and self-mutilating.

Despite theoretically embracing diversity, contemporary lesbian culture has a deep streak of xenophobia. When confronted with phenomena that do not neatly fit our categories, lesbians have been known to respond with hysteria, bigotry, and a desire to stamp out the offending messy realities. A "country club syndrome" sometimes prevails in which the lesbian community is treated as an exclusive enclave from which the riffraff must be systematically expunged. Everyone has a right to emotional responses. But it is imperative to distinguish between emotions and principles. Just as "hard cases make bad law," intense emotions make bad policy. Over the years, lesbian groups have gone through periodic attempts to purge male-to-female transsexuals, sadomasochists, butch-femme lesbians, bisexuals, and even lesbians who are not separatists. FTMs are another witch-hunt waiting to happen.[26]

For many years, male-to-female transsexuals (MTFs) have vastly outnumbered female-to-male individuals. A small percentage of MTFs are sexually involved with women and define themselves as lesbian. Until recently, lesbian discomfort was triggered primarily by those male-to-female lesbians, who have been the focus of controversy and who have often been driven out of lesbian groups and businesses. Discrimination against MTFs is no longer monolithic, and many lesbian organizations have made a point of admitting male-to-female lesbians.

However, such discrimination has not disappeared. It surfaced in 1991 at the National Lesbian Conference, which banned "nongenetic women."[27] Transsexual women became the *cause célèbre* of the 1991 Michigan Womyn's Music Festival. Festival organizers expelled a transsexual woman, then retroactively articulated a policy banning all but "womyn-born-womyn" from future events.[28] After decades of feminist insistence that women are "made, not born," after fighting to establish that "anatomy is not destiny," it is astounding that ostensibly progressive events can get away with discriminatory policies based so blatantly on recycled biological determinism.

The next debate over inclusion and exclusion will focus on female-to-male transsexuals. Transsexual demographics are changing. FTMs still comprise only a fraction of the transsexual population, but their numbers are growing and awareness of their presence is increasing. Female-to-male transsexuals who are in, or in the process of leaving, lesbian communities are becoming the objects of controversy and posing new challenges to the ways in which lesbian communities handle diversity. A woman who has been respected, admired, and loved as a butch may suddenly be despised, rejected, and hounded when she starts a sex change.[29]

Sex changes are often stressful, not only for the person undergoing change but also for the network in which that person is embedded. Individuals and local groups cope with such stress well or badly, depending on their level of knowledge about gender diversity, their relationships with the person involved, their willingness to face difficult emotions, their ability to think beyond immediate emotional responses, and the unique details of local history and personality. As a community goes through the process of handling a sex change by one of its members, it evolves techniques and sets precedents for doing so.

Though some lesbians are not disturbed by FTMs, and some find them uniquely attractive, many lesbians are upset by them. When a woman's body begins to change into a male body, the transposition of male and female signals that constitutes "butch" begins to disintegrate. A cross-dressing, dildo-packing, bodybuilding butch may use a male name and masculine pronouns, yet still have soft skin, no facial hair, the visible swell of breasts or hips under male clothing, small hands and feet, or some other detectable sign of femaleness. If the same person grows a mustache, develops a lower voice, binds his breasts, or begins to bald, his body offers no evidence to contravene his social signals. When he begins to read like a man, many lesbians no longer find him attractive and some want to banish him from their social universe. If the FTM has lesbian partners (and many do), they also risk ostracism.

Instead of another destructive round of border patrols, surveillance, and expulsion, I would suggest a different strategy. Lesbians should instead relax, wait, and support the individuals involved as they sort out their own identities and decide where they fit socially.

A sex change is a transition. A woman does not immediately become a man as soon as she begins to take hormones. During the initial states of changing sex, many FTMs will not be ready to leave the world of women. There is no good reason to harass them through a transitional period during which they will not quite fit as women or men. Most FTMs who undergo sex reassignment identify as men and are anxious to live as men as soon as possible. They will leave lesbian contexts on their own, when they can, when they are ready, and when those environments are no longer comfortable. It is not necessary for gender vigilantes to drive them out. Some FTMs will experiment with sex change and elect to abandon the effort. They should not be deprived of their lesbian credentials for having explored the option.

The partners of FTMs do not necessarily or suddenly become bisexual or heterosexual because a lover decides on a sex change, although some do eventually renegotiate their own identities. An attraction to people of intermediate sex does not automatically displace or negate an attraction to other women. Dealing with their sex-changing partners is difficult and confusing enough for the lovers of transsexuals without having to worry about being thrown out of their social universe. Friends and lovers of FTMs often have intense feelings of loss, grief, and abandonment. They need support for handling such feelings, and should not be terrorized into keeping them secret.

In the past, most FTMs were committed to a fairly complete change, a commitment that was required for an individual to gain access to sex-change technologies controlled by the therapeutic and medical establishments. To obtain hormones or surgery, transsexuals (of both directions) had to be able to persuade a number of professionals that they were determined to be completely "normal" members of the target sex (that is, feminine heterosexual women and masculine heterosexual men). Gay transsexuals had to hide their homosexuality to get sex-change treatment. This has begun to change, and transsexuals now have more freedom to be gay and less traditionally gender stereotyped after the change.

More transsexuals also now exist who do not pursue a complete change. Increasing numbers of individuals utilize some but not all of the available sex-change technology, resulting in "intermediate" bodies, somewhere between female and male. Some FTMs may be part women, part men—genetic females with male body shapes, female genitals, and intermediate gender identities. Some of these may not want to leave their lesbian communities, and they should not be forced to do so. They may cause confusion, repelling some lesbians and attracting others. But if community membership were based on universal desirability, no one would qualify. Our desires can be as selective, exclusive, and imperious as we like; our society should be as inclusive, humane, and tolerant as we can make it.

LET A THOUSAND FLOWERS BLOOM

In writing this essay, I have wanted to diversify conceptions of butchness, to promote a more nuanced conceptualization of gender variation among lesbian and bisexual women, and to forestall prejudice against individuals who use other modes of managing gender. I also have an underlying agenda to support the tendencies among lesbians to enjoy and celebrate our differences. Lesbian communities and individuals have suffered enough from the assumption that we should all be the same, or that every difference must be justified by a claim of political or moral superiority.

We should not attempt to decide whether butch-femme or transsexualism are acceptable for anyone or preferable for everyone. Individuals should be allowed to navigate their own trails through the possibilities, complexities, and difficulties of life in postmodern times. Each strategy and each set of categories has its capabilities, accomplishments, and drawbacks. None is perfect, and none works for everyone all the time.

Early lesbian-feminism rejected butch-femme roles out of ignorance of their historical context and because their limitations had become readily obvious. Butch and femme were brilliantly adapted for building a minority sexual culture out of the tools, materials, and debris of a dominant sexual system. Their costs included obligations for each lesbian to choose a role, the ways such roles sometimes reinforced subservient status for femmes, and the sexual frustrations often experienced by butches.

The rejection of butch-femme was equally a product of its time. Feminism has often simply announced changes already in progress for which it has taken credit and for which it has been held responsible. The denunciation of butch-femme occurred in part because some of its premises were outdated and because lesbian populations had other tools with which to create viable social worlds.

Yet wholesale condemnation of butch-femme impoverished our understandings of, experiences of, and models for lesbian gender. It subjected many women to gratuitous denigration and harassment, and left a legacy of confusion, lost pleasures, and cultural deprivation. As we reclaim butch-femme, I hope we do not invent yet another form of politically correct behavior or morality.

Feminism and lesbian-feminism developed in opposition to a system that imposed rigid roles, limited individual potential, exploited women as physical and emotional resources, and persecuted sexual and gender diversity. Feminism and lesbian-feminism should not be used to impose new but equally rigid limitations, or as an excuse to create new vulnerable and exploitable populations. Lesbian communities were built by sex and gender refugees; the lesbian world should not create new rationales for sex and gender persecution.

Our categories are important. We cannot organize a social life, a political movement, or our individual identities and desires without them. The fact that categories invariably leak and can never contain all the relevant "existing things" does not render them useless, only limited. Categories like "woman," "butch," "lesbian," or "transsexual" are all imperfect, historical, temporary, and arbitrary. We use them, and they use us. We use them to construct meaningful lives, and they mold us into historically specific forms of personhood. Instead of fighting for immaculate classifications and impenetrable boundaries, let us strive to maintain a community that understands diversity as a gift, sees anomalies as precious, and treats all basic principles with a hefty dose of skepticism.

NOTES

1. I am indebted to Jay Marston for the conversations and encouragement that led me to write this essay, and to Jay Marston, Nilos Nevertheless, Allan Berube, Jeffrey Escoffier, Jeanne Bergman, Carole Vance, and Lynn Eden for reading the drafts and making innumerable helpful suggestions. Kath Weston kindly shared some of her work in progress. Thanks to Lynne Fletcher for ruthless editing (my favorite kind). I am, of course, responsible for any errors or misconceptions. I am out on this particular limb all by myself, but I am grateful to them all for helping me get here.

2. "**Butch.** 1. lesbian with masculine characteristics, see **dyke.** 2. non-homosexual man whose virile appearance both draws and repels the [male] homosexual. Syn: all man; butch number…stud. 3. [gay male who is] manly in speech, in fashions and in bed; submission impossible. **Butch it up.** warning [to gay man] to act manly in the presence of friends who 'don't know' or the police who do. **Butch queen.** homosexual man whose virile activities and responsibilities make him hard to detect." Bruce Rodgers, *The Queen's Vernacular: A Gay Lexicon* (Straight Arrow Books, 1972), p. 39; see also **dyke,** pp. 70–71.

3. Elizabeth Lapovsky Kennedy and Madeline Davis, "The Reproduction of Butch-Fem Roles: A Social Constructionist Approach," in *Passion and Power: Sexuality in History,* edited by Kathy Peiss and Christina Simmons, with Robert A. Padgug (Philadelphia: Temple University Press, 1989), p. 244.

4. In this essay, I am taking for granted a number of things that I will not directly address. I am assuming two decades' worth of sustained critique of categories of sex and gender, including the argument that gendered identities, roles, and behaviors are social constructs rather than properties intrinsic to or emanating from physical bodies. Gender categories and identities are, nevertheless, deeply implicated in the ways in which individuals experience and present themselves. I am also aware of the many critiques that make straightforward use of terms like *identities* difficult. In this article, however, I am less interested in a rigorous use of terminology or theory than I am in exploring lesbian folk beliefs regarding gender, and aspects of gender experience among lesbian and bisexual women. I do not intend to exclude bisexual women by speaking mostly of lesbians. Many bisexuals have similar issues and experiences.

   In addition, I am not interested in engaging the argument that butch-femme roles are a noxious residue of patriarchal oppression or the claim that butch-femme roles are uniquely situated "outside ideology" and embody an inherent critique of gender. For a statement of the first position, see Sheila Jeffreys, "Butch and Femme: Now and Then," *Gossip* 5 (London: Onlywomen Press, 1987), pp. 65–95; for the latter, see Sue-Ellen Case, "Towards a Butch-Femme Aesthetic," *Discourse* 11 (Winter 1988–1989): 55–73. Oddly, Jeffreys and Case pursue similar agendas. Each argues that lesbianism in some form is a road to philosophical or political salvation. For Jeffreys, this can be accomplished only by the lesbian couple who "make love without roles" (p. 90) while for Case it is the butch-femme couple that lends "agency and self-determination to the historically passive [female] subject" (p. 65).

   Case's approach is far preferable to that of Jeffreys. However, both analyses are overblown and place an undue burden of moral gravity on lesbian behavior. Like lesbianism itself, butch and femme are structured within dominant gender systems. Like lesbianism, butch and femme can be vehicles for resisting and transforming those systems. Like lesbianism, butch and femme can function to uphold those systems. And nothing—not "mutual, equalitarian lesbianism" and not butch-femme—escapes those systems completely. Butch and femme need no justification other than their presence among lesbians; they should not be judged, justified, evaluated, held accountable, or rejected on the basis of such attributions of significance.

5. *Androgynous* is also sometimes used to indicate women somewhere between butch and femme. Androgynous used to mean someone who was intermediate between male and female, and many traditional and classic butches were androgynous in the sense that they combined highly masculine signals with detectably female bodies. Those who cross-dressed enough to successfully pass as men were not androgynous. This older meaning of *androgynous* is lost when the term is used to refer to individuals whose self-presentation falls somewhere between butch and femme.

6. I should make it clear that I do not consider any behavior, trait, or mannerism to be inherently "male" or "female," and that my operating assumption is that cultures assign behaviors to one or another gender category and then attribute gendered significance to various behaviors. Individuals can then express gender conformity, gender deviance, gender rebellion, and many other messages by manipulating gender meanings and taxonomies.

7. Ronald Beyer, *Homosexuality and American Psychiatry: The Politics of Diagnosis* (New York, Basic Books, 1981). There was opposition to classifying homosexuality as a disease before the 1973 decision and there are still some therapists who consider homosexuality a pathology and would like to see the 1973 decision revoked. Nevertheless, the removal of homosexuality from the *Diagnostic and Statistical Manual III* remains a watershed.

8. For an overview of gender issues, including some aspects of transsexuality, see Suzanne J. Kessler and Wendy McKenna, *Gender: An Ethnomethodological Approach* (Chicago: University of Chicago Press, 1978). For female-to-male transsexuals, see Lou Sullivan, *Information for the Female to Male Cross Dresser and Transsexual*, 3rd edition, (Seattle: Ingersoll Gender Center, 1990); and Marcy Scheiner, "Some Girls Will Be Boys," *On Our Backs 7*, no. 4 (March–April 1991): 20–22, 38–43.

9. Not all lesbians are gender dysphoric, and not all gender dysphoric women are lesbian or bisexual. For example, there are manly heterosexual women who sometimes attract (and confuse) lesbians. There are female-to-male transsexuals who are erotically drawn to women and identify as heterosexual men (even when they have women's bodies), and there are female-to-male transsexuals who are attracted to men and consider themselves male homosexuals.

10. For a discussion of "mannish lesbians" in the historical context of the early twentieth century, see Esther Newton, "The Mythic Mannish Lesbian: Radclyffe Hall and the New Woman," in *Hidden from History: Reclaiming the Gay and Lesbian Past*, edited by Martin Bauml Duberman, Martha Vicinus, and George Chauncey, Jr. (New York, New American Library, 1989).

11. Older lesbian culture had many terms in addition to *butch. Bull, bull dyke, bulldagger, dagger, dag, diesel dyke, drag butch,* and *drag king* are among the expressive terms that were once more commonly in circulation. See Rodgers, *The Queen's Vernacular*, pp. 70–71.

12. For discomfort with the association of female-to-male transsexuals (FTMs) with butch lesbians, see a fascinating exchange that appeared in several issues of *FTM*, a newsletter for female-to-male transsexuals and cross-dressers. It began with an article in issue 12, June 1990, p. 5, and continued in the letters columns in issues 13, September 1990, p. 3, and 14, December 1990, p. 2. A related exchange appeared in issue 15, April 1991, pp. 2–3.

13. See Judith Butler, *Gender Trouble* (New York: Routledge, 1990), especially p. 23. For a study of butch-femme that contains a critique of Butler, although not on this point, see Kath Weston, "Do Clothes Make the Woman? Gender, Performance Theory, and Lesbian Eroticism," unpublished manuscript, 1992.

14. The concept "woman identified" explicitly links sexual orientation and certain kinds of "political" behavior (Radicalesbians, "The Woman Identified Woman," in *Radical Feminism,* edited by Anne Koedt, Ellen Levine, and Anita Rapone [New York, Quadrangle, 1973]). The concept of the woman-identified-woman presents problems beyond the scope of this discussion. But while it equated feminism with lesbianism, "woman identified" did not at that time mean femininity or female gender identity. In contrast to "male identified," it is rarely taken as a synonym for "femme," although it has often been used as a synonym or euphemism for lesbianism. Although the apparent relationships between feminism and lesbianism were exciting and trailblazing when this essay first appeared in 1970, much of what has gone awry within feminist politics of sex can be traced to a failure to recognize the differences between sexual orientations, gender identities, and political positions. Sexual preference, gender role, and political stance cannot be equated, and do not directly determine or reflect one another.

15. See, for example, *On Our Backs,* 1984–1991; *Outrageous Women,* 1984–1988; and *Bad Attitude,* 1984–1991. For a look at the evolution of lesbian styles in the eighties, see Arlene Stein, "All Dressed Up, But No Place to Go? Style Wars and the New Lesbianism," *Out/Look* 1, no. 4 (Winter 1989): 34–42, reprinted in this volume.

16. See Butler, *Gender Trouble,* p. 31. In addition, not only butches play with symbols of masculinity. Lesbian femmes can play with male attire, as do heterosexual women, for a variety of reasons. A suit and tie do not necessarily "make the butch."

17. This is similar to gay male usage. Gay men use *butch* to refer to especially masculine men (Rodgers, *The Queen's Vernacular*). For a humorous send-up of gay male notions of butch, see Clark Henley, *The Butch Manual* (New York: Sea Horse Press, 1982).

18. Several well-known butches of classic lesbian fiction exhibit some of the class spectrum of butch masculinity. Beebo Brinker is exemplary of white, working-class butchness (Ann Bannon, *I Am a Woman* [Greenwich, Conn.: Fawcett Gold Medal, 1959]; *Women in the Shadows* [1959]; *Journey to a Woman* [1960]; and *Beebo Brinker* [1962]). Randy Salem's Christopher "Chris" Hamilton is an educated, middle-class, white butch (Randy Salem, *Chris* [New York: Softcover Library, 1959]). Two of the upper-class, aristocratic cross-dressers are Jesse Cannon (Randy Salem, *The Unfortunate Flesh* [New York: Midwood Tower, 1960]) and, of course, Stephen Gordon from *The Well of Loneliness* (Radclyffe Hall,

The Well of Loneliness [New York: Permabooks, 1959]). And butch takes many more forms than these few examples can express.

19.   For a discussion of the differences between erotic roles such as "top" and "bottom," and gender roles such as butch and femme, see Esther Newton and Shirley Walton, "The Misunderstanding: Toward a More Precise Sexual Vocabulary," in *Pleasure and Danger: Exploring Female Sexuality,* edited by Carole S. Vance (Boston: Routledge & Kegan Paul, 1984).

20.   Lesbians, in turn, provide models for other permutations of gender, sex, and role. I know a technically heterosexual couple that consists of a lesbian-identified woman whose primary partner is an effeminate, female-identified mostly gay man. The woman once told me she has "lesbian sex" with the "girl" in him.

21.   Michel Foucault, *The Order of Things* (New York, Pantheon, 1970).

22.   Mary Douglas, *Purity and Danger: An Analysis of the Concepts of Pollution and Taboo* (Boston: Routledge & Kegan Paul, 1966).

23.   Transgender organizations directly address issues of variant gender and how to live with it, understand it, and customize it. Some lesbian and bisexual women gravitate to such groups to sort out their gender questions in a context that provides a more sophisticated awareness of the subtleties of gender diversity than is currently available within most lesbian communities.

24.   San Francisco Lesbian and Gay History Project, ' "She Even Chewed Tobacco': A Pictorial Narrative of Passing Women in America," in *Hidden from History: Reclaiming the Gay and Lesbian Past,* edited by Martin Bauml Duberman, Martha Vicinus, and George Chauncey, Jr. (New York, New American Library, 1989).

25.   Louis Sullivan, *From Female to Male: The Life of Jack Bee Garland* (Boston: Alyson, 1990). In addition to the Garland biography, Sullivan wrote prolifically on transsexual issues and edited the *FTM* newsletter from 1987 to 1990.

26.   It is interesting to speculate about how gay men will deal with FTMs who are gay male identified. Traditionally, gay male communities have dealt relatively well with male-to-female transvestites and transsexuals, while lesbian communities have not. But gay men are now faced with women becoming men, who may or may not have male genitals whose origins are undetectable.

27.   "Genetic Lesbians," *Gay Community News,* May 19–25, 1991, p. 4.

28.   "Festival Womyn Speak Out," *Gay Community News,* November 17–23, 1991, p. 4. It is interesting to note that S/M was not a big issue at Michigan in 1991, nor was there controversy over S/M at the National Lesbian Conference. It saddens me that lesbians, from whom I expect better, appear so prone to need a target for horizontal hostility.

29.   And if a woman who was disliked starts a sex change, the sex change becomes a convenient pretext to get rid of her/him. Obnoxious behavior that would be tolerated in a butch will often be considered intolerable in an FTM. Like other groups of stigmatized individuals, transsexuals are often subjected to particularly stringent standards of conduct.

33

The Logic of Treatment

Henry Rubin

Sociologist Henry Rubin uses two distinctive methodologies often considered antithetical to one another—phenomenology and Foucaultian discourse analysis—to investigate how female-to-male transsexuals achieve and embody their identities as men. In doing so, he attempts to account for the "external" historical and cultural conditions that create the conditions of possibility for the subjects of his study, while at the same time attempting to acknowledge that the "internal" experience of having an identity is rarely perceived as historically contingent.

In the selection below, Rubin offers a genealogical account of the "logic of treatment" articulated within the medical model for the care of transgender men that developed over the course of the twentieth century. He outlines the "pre-history" of treatment in discussions of endocrinology, and the related but short-lived and little-known field of organo-therapy. This pseudo-scientific practice involved injecting humans with nonhuman primate hormones, or transplanting chimpanzee testicles to humans, in an attempt to prolong life or increase sexual function. One of organo-therapy's chief proponents and practitioners was the pioneering advocate for transsexualism, Dr. Harry Benjamin.

Rubin makes a useful contribution to transgender scholarship by detailing how, from an early date, the logic of treatment was different for female-to-male and male-to-female individuals—a difference made especially clear in his close reading of the theory of gender and personality developed by FTM medical doctor Michael Dillon in *Self: An Essay on Ethics and Endocrinology.*

The category of "transsexual" is a relatively recent achievement of culture and not a transhistorical phenomenon. Harry Benjamin, long considered the father of modern transsexualism, writes

> The phenomenon of gender-role disorientation, that is…anatomic females feeling themselves to be men and wanting to change sex has existed in rare individuals since time immemorial and was, in more modern days, occasionally described by psychologists as "total sex-inversion," or with similar designations. *Its clinical picture, however was never seen as a definite, recognizable entity*, rare in the general population, fascinating for the science of sexology, and impressive in its often tragic consequences for the individual (Benjamin 1969, I; emphasis added).

As Benjamin suggests, until quite recently, the clinical picture of transsexuals had gone unrecognized or had been subsumed within other categories, such as "sex-inversion." Sexuality (sexual instinct with a particular object choice) had not been distinguished from gender (one's psychosocial outlook), which were both neatly tied to one's sex (anatomy, morphology, and physiology). Disorders of any one of these always implied a totally disordered system called "sex-inversion." Benjamin's modification of this diagnosis with the adjective "total" implies that, from his perspective in 1969, these disorders could now present themselves as *partially* disordered systems of sexuality, gender, sex, or any combination thereof.

Benjamin's claims are unusual for a medical practitioner because he does not abide by the positivism that traditionally guides medical histories. Benjamin acknowledges that transsexuals did not exist until a medical diagnosis and a logic of treatment took shape. Prior to these developments, there may have been individuals who felt that their bodies did not represent their gendered subjectivity, but these were not transsexuals. A history of the emergence of female-to-male transsexualism can be told as the medicalization of inversion and the making available of medical techniques appropriated from both the emerging science of endocrinology and the surgical treatment of war veterans.

This chapter is a Foucauldian genealogy of these techniques and of the systems of thought about gender, sex, and sexuality that such techniques generated and within which they are embedded. A positivist history of transsexuals would assume that they have existed throughout time, and would return to the historical record to locate transsexuals who had previously been misidentified as lesbians, passing women, or some other misnomer. Genealogy suggests instead that positivist moments of "misidentification" are not merely due to poor science or clumsy history, but rather to the historic variability of the categories that organize our understanding of bodies and identities. Where a positivist assumes that better science or more nuanced history could accurately identify and distinguish between categories of sexuality or gender, a genealogist refuses the assumption that individuals exist apart from the historically changing categories that make them.

GENEALOGY OF FEMALE-BODIED INVERSION

The substance of Foucault's work included a genealogy of the emergence of the homosexual man as a new species of man (Foucault 1980, 43). Although Foucault did not pursue a genealogy of female-bodied inversion, this task has been picked up by historians of gay and lesbian social formations, like George Chauncey Jr., who use genealogy as a method for documenting the emergence of "deviant" female-bodied categories of identity. Chauncey has developed a genealogical account of the emergence of female homosexuality from the late nineteenth century through the first third of the twentieth century. In his article "From Sexual Inversion to Homosexuality: The Changing Medical Conception of Female 'Deviance,' " Chauncey points out that late nineteenth-century medical models assumed that gender inversion, in forms such as cross-dressing, smoking, or dislike for needlework, was the necessary criterion for female-bodied "deviance." Loving another woman was considered *secondary* to the more salient gender inversion. By the 1920s, Chauncey argues, this had changed so that anyone who desired someone of the same sex was considered "homosexual."

> "Sexual inversion" referred to a broad range of cross-gender behavior (in which males behaved like women and vice-versa) of which homosexual desire was only a logical but indistinct aspect, while "homosexuality" focused on the narrower issue of sexual object choice. The differentiation of homosexual desire from cross-gender behavior at the turn of the century reflects a major reconceptualization of the nature of human sexuality, its relation to gender, and its role in one's social definition (Chauncey 1989a, 88).

At the end of his article, Chauncey suggests that the process of separating gender from sexuality is far from a *fait accompli* and is, in fact, a project that continues. The goal of these first two chapters is to continue the genealogy of female-bodied "deviance." The chapters focus on the emergence of the category "female-to-male transsexual" as a distinct socio-cultural subject position, separate from, yet still dependent upon, female homosexuality.

PRE-HISTORY OF EXPERIMENTAL ENDOCRINOLOGY

> Our salvation, the preservation of our youth and activity and of the harmonious equilibrium of all our functions can only be ensured if we can find the means to come to the help of the noble cells of our organs. Therein lies the most logical solution of the tormenting problem of our downfall, of our old age.... Nature...has provided us with a wonderful source of energy.... Such is indeed the role of the genital glands.... These glands elaborate the elements of future life, which are destined to fecundate the ovule in order to give birth to a new being and to transmit to the species the creative energy, held by the individual. At the same time, however, they secrete a liquid which, passing direct into the blood, carries to all the tissues the stimulus and the energy necessary to the individual himself. In this we are able to observe a marvelous manifestation of the design of creation. In a single organ Nature has united the source of the life of the individual and that of the species. This is confirmed by the fact that the emasculated male loses both powers at the same time (Voronoff 1928, 44).

From one perspective, the birth of endocrinology was a reincarnation of the search for the fountain of youth and everlasting life. Endocrinology promised to isolate the physiology of life in the ductless glands and their "internal secretions." This search led first to the isolation of sex glands as the source of virility and fertility in men. Then sex hormones were discovered. These new discoveries were each seen, in turn, as the determining factor of body morphology, anatomy, and psychosexual outlook in men and women. This triad of vitality, virility, and fertility propelled endocrinology into the study of pathological conditions and gave shape to the scientific paradigm from which female-to-male trans-sexualism would emerge.

Thomas Kuhn, a historian of science, explains how a new scientific paradigm functions. He writes that a scientific paradigm "define[s] the legitimate problems and methods of a research field for succeeding generations of practitioners." A useful paradigm breaks new ground and is "sufficiently unprecedented to attract an enduring group of adherents away from competing modes of scientific activity. Simultaneously, it is sufficiently open-ended to leave all sorts of problems for the redefined group of practitioners to resolve" (Kuhn 1970, 10). The endocrinological paradigm that developed in the nineteenth and twentieth centuries was built on three essential tenets: (1) The normal functioning of sex glands and sex hormones affects anatomy and secondary sexual characteristics; (2) all humans have a hermaphroditic bedrock; and (3) hermaphroditic deviations are natural, treatable conditions. These tenets emerged from decades of endocrinological experiments.

The late eighteenth century witnessed endocrinology's first experiments. John Hunter established a "remote sympathy" between the sex glands of animals and their sexual characteristics through experiments on pigeons, cocks, hens, pigs, and cows. This "remote sympathy" was a causal relationship between the gonads and traits that were not visibly connected, such as plumage color, size of male organ, lactation, and fertility. Hunter demonstrated this relationship by removing and transplanting the male and female gonads. In his *History of Endocrinology*, Victor Cornelius Medvei suggests the importance of Hunter's early work to endocrinology:

> It should be made clear at this point that Hunter's transplant experiments of the spurs in fowl and of the testes in cocks...were intended to study the 'vital principle,' assumed to be responsible for the union of the graft with the host, and for the survival and growth of the graft. This 'vital principle' was supposed to work independently of the nervous system and humoral mechanisms acting as integrating factors in the body. These experiments were, therefore, not carried out with any underlying endocrine speculations...they happened to fit—subconsciously, as it were—into the endocrine framework of a later era (Medvei 1982, 196).

Hunter's own words suggest contained only a passing reference to the sexual significance of his experiments. "Here is the testicle of a cock, separated from that animal and put through a wound made for that purpose, into the belly of a hen, which mode of turning hens into cocks is much such an improvement for its utility as that of Dean Swift when he proposed to obtain a breed of sheep without wool" (Hunter, in Medvei 1982, 197). Hunter did not see much use-value resulting from this experiment. He could hardly have anticipated that individuals in the twentieth century would draw upon his work to enact a female-to-male sex change, but transsexual sex changes are built upon the early endocrine experiment whose original purpose was to isolate a "vital principle."

Hunter speculated on the effects of the gonads on sexual power and on the direction of that sexual instinct. He believed the gonads, the testes in particular, were responsible for the sex drive but its direction was independent of the gonads. These brief comments set the stage for twentieth century debates on hormone treatments.

In 1849, A. A. Berthold, a German experimental endocrinologist, made the link that Hunter had noted between the gonads and the sex characteristics of animals explicit. While Hunter had wanted to know whether gonads could be transplanted and what vital force lay within them, Berthold was interested in the effects of transplants on sexual nature. Berthold experimented with the castration of cocks and found that castration caused the comb to atrophy. He hoped to reverse the effects of castration with transplantation. Experiments like Berthold's were pursued in the later decades of the nineteenth century and in a form of treatment in the early twentieth century called "organotherapy." As a result of his experiments, Berthold speculated that the sympathy between the gonads and the sexual characteristics might rely on an intermediary source running through the blood stream, but it was only later that hormones were found to be that missing link. In the meantime, organotherapy was all the rage.

ORGANOTHERAPY: A USE-VALUE FOR INTERNAL SECRETIONS

Organotherapy was the use of sexual glands or glandular tissue as a therapeutic means of restoring what the patient lost in aging. The claim to have found the vital principle and to be able to treat the weak and infirm by means of it was received with both skepticism and enthusiasm. The skeptics thought the results were due to autosuggestion, while enthusiasts believed the rejuvenating effects were genuine. From the organotherapeutic experiments of Charles Brown-Séquard in the 1890s to the work of Serge Voronoff in the 1920s, organotherapy was as closely followed by medical journals and the popular press as was the cloning of sheep in the 1990s. The discovery of hormones led to the dismissal of organotherapy as quackery and nonsense.

Brown-Séquard and Voronoff both challenged a basic law of nature: bodies always exhaust their resources. They sought an effective means of countering the aging process. Although men (and women, though they were of a lesser interest to these practitioners) had always aged and eventually died, they thought that organotherapy could force this law to succumb to human control.

> From the period of my observations among the eunuchs in Egypt, which revealed to me the importance of the internal secretion of the interstitial glands, I was haunted by the idea that it might be possible to gain control over this wonder potential force, and *utilize it for our needs, when as we advance in age, its natural source begins to show signs of exhaustion* (Voronoff 1928, 63; emphasis added).

Voronoff and the others established organotherapy as the means of overcoming the law of exhaustion. Organotherapists viewed science as an unproblematic means of surpassing nature. Voronoff compared endocrinology to the science that allowed humans to "fly" higher than birds, and "swim" to the depths of the sea by submarine. These beliefs accelerated the race for individual immortality and the survival of the species.

Endocrinology had found a use-value for its knowledge about internal organs and hormones. Voronoff and the organotherapists also believed that ovarian tissue held a woman's vital principle and suggested that she also be treated with gonad transplants or extracts. They observed that a woman's vitality decreased with the onset of menopause and argued that she would benefit from ovarian treatments.

Voronoff began his research and treatment using monkey glands. In 1919, Voronoff's harvesting of glands from the bodies of monkeys literalized the French colonization of the Algerian body politic. Like his colonialist stance toward Algerians, Voronoff thought monkeys were "almost human," standing on the evolutionary scale below Western, white men. They seemed like perfect subjects for the experimental trials of organotherapy. However, transplanting monkey glands into humans, even for the purpose of rejuvenation, proved too threatening. The scientific community and the public, concerned about inter-species mixings, produced such an outcry that Voronoff abandoned his Algerian monkeys. However, it took more time for the French to grow uncomfortable with their harvest of the Algerian body politic.

Voronoff turned to public perceptions of Egypt to justify his research and organotherapeutic treatments. The Egyptian "other" was a deathly danger to Western achievements. The fate of the Egyptian eunuch, who had lost all vitality, was to be avoided at all costs. In Voronoff's eyes, Egypt served as the outline of the pathology that could befall aging Westerners. Voronoff's Egypt is one where he "was constantly in touch with eunuchs, and . . . present at the [early] deathbed of several of them" (Voronoff 1928, 58). The organotherapeutic logic of treatment was based on aversion to a figure that represented the antithesis of the West's ideal man. In their eagerness to avoid the fate of eunuchs, who were essentially feminized men, Westerners were willing to use glandular therapy to revitalize themselves, bolster their masculinity, and increase their fertility.

Nationalism also plays its part in the logic of organotherapy. Brown-Séquard, a Frenchman, and Eugene Steinach, an Austrian, each had patriotic stakes in the rejuvenation of their men. Brown-Séquard was actually born in England, but became a naturalized citizen of France. The social construction of national identity informed Brown-Séquard's scientific beliefs about overcoming the natural limits of life. If national identity and national membership were a social matter, and not conferred automatically by birth, then other "natural" phenomena, such as life and death, could also be a matter of culture. If national identity was really a modifiable social phenomenon, then it seemed possible to manipulate other things, such as gender and sex. Steinach's nationalist agenda was determined by his location in Austria. His work on rejuvenation in the interwar period was consistent with themes of German regeneration. Hitler was not supportive of his later work, however, and the German occupation of Austria made Steinach an exile in Switzerland.

Steinach, Voronoff, and Brown-Séquard each mobilized nationalist themes and fears of the East to increase the appeal of organotherapy. To fight against popular and medical fears of inter-species mixing, Voronoff marshaled white fears of the East and nationalist dreams of revitalization to promote his elixir of life. The transplanting of monkey glands to human bodies seemed scandalous, but the call to revitalize oneself was successful because of a fear of Egyptian eunuchs. Where Hunter, Berthold, and the early organotherapists who used animal transplants failed to overcome popular opinion, the use of nationalist ideals allowed later scientists to continue their work in organotherapy.

SYNTHESIZING HORMONES, MAPPING THE NORMAL HERMAPHRODITIC BEDROCK

The shift from organotherapies to hormonal therapies began in 1905. Early genetic theory had posited the gene as the determining factor of sex, but biochemical endocrinology claimed that hormones were the supplementary agents that finished the task of becoming a sex. One of endocrinology's main projects in the 1920s and 1930s was the isolation of sex hormones. Along with its goal of mapping the normal hormonal constitution, endocrinology produced synthetic hormones that could be used with greater success in treatments for sexual "dysfunction."

The isolation and classification of natural estrogens proceeded at a more rapid pace than did testosterone. Animal urine, especially from pregnant mares, became a source for estrogenic products, while testosterone was more expensive, time-consuming, and complicated to collect. Twenty-five thousand liters of male urine generated a mere fifty milligrams of testosterone in 1931. In the 1930s, endocrinology began collecting testosterone from the urine of captive populations—soldiers or prisoners—for male hormone treatments, but until then, testosterone was not available in the same quantities as estrogens. Nelly Oudshoorn documents the difficulties of obtaining enough specimens to produce any marketable treatments of male sex hormones:

> The first standardized preparation of male sex hormones was not put on the market by Organon until 1931;
> five years after the equivalent drug for women. . . . Technical problems further delayed the actual marketing
> of the first standardized male sex hormone preparation. The major problem was how to produce a highly
> purified hormone preparation free from other substances of similar solubility, and in particular free of
> female sex hormones (Oudshoorn 1994, 98).

Oudshoorn claims that the emerging field of gynecology was already medicalizing women's bodies. Men's bodies were not subject to regular examination in the same way. This sped up the isolation of estrogens and provided a use-value for female sex hormones.

These asymmetries delayed the investigation into the nature or function of testosterone and its utilization as a treatment. Without the possibility of testosterone treatment, nascent FTMs remained unrecognizable as transsexual subjects. Although the synthetic production of testosterone was achieved in 1936, slightly earlier than estrogens, natural estrogenic preparations were obtained earlier and with greater technical ease than testosterone. The slower process of isolating and categorizing "male" hormones explains a delay in the use of testosterone as a treatment for FTMs. It also explains the slower historical emergence of an FTM identity.

During the zigzag process of isolating and synthesizing hormones, endocrinologists were also at work mapping the normal hormonal state of men and women. Endocrinology surprised itself by discovering the presence of "male" hormones in normal females in 1931 and "female" hormones in normal males in 1934 (Oudshoorn 1994, 25–26). These discoveries created the possibility of sex change treatments.

These results challenged the dualistic model of sex, which dictated that men be treated exclusively with "male" hormones and women be treated only with "female" hormones. Oudshoorn's study of endocrinology details the decline of the dualistic model and the rise of a new endocrinological paradigm.

> In the 1920s, there emerged a lively dispute in the scientific community about the dualistic assumption
> that sex hormones are strictly sex-specific in origin and function. A growing number of publications ap-
> peared contradicting the pre-scientific idea of a sexual duality located in the gonads and underlying the
> concept of the sexual specificity of sex hormones (Oudshoorn 1994, 24).

The dualistic model of sexed bodies assumed that men and women were two completely distinct types of human beings whose bodies were homologous. This dualism assumed that androgens were exclusively male and estrogens were exclusively female.

The discovery of hormones discredited the dualistic model of sex that viewed male and female as exclusive categories. It challenged the notion that there was any ascertainable site of male and female essences. Instead, these chemical agents were free-flowing and hard to pin down. The isolation of hormones indicated that men and women have both "male" and "female" hormones.

By the 1930s, endocrinology had replaced the dualistic model with a hermaphroditic model. According to this model, all people have a hermaphroditic bedrock of hormones. Men and women each have both kinds of hormones. In the normal condition, there is a proper balance of male and female hormones and the anatomical manifestations of sex are unambiguously male or female.

> Instead of locating the essence of femininity or masculinity in specific organs, as the anatomists had done, sex endocrinologists introduced a quantitative theory of sex and the body. The idea that each sex could be characterized by its own sex hormone was transformed into the idea of relative sexual specificity (Oudshoorn 1994, 38).

The pathologies that the endocrinologists now categorized were deviations of degrees.

> The model suggested that, chemically speaking, all organisms are both male and female....In this model, an anatomical male could possess feminine characteristics controlled by female sex hormones, while an anatomical female could have masculine characteristics regulated by male sex hormones (Oudshoorn 1994, 39).

Normal men and women were latently hermaphroditic, while the ill and the treatable were manifestly hermaphroditic.

Textbooks demonstrate the adoption of this new model at the clinical level. In a chapter called "Sex Glands" from the 1924 book *Organotherapy in General Practice,* there are several mentions of the basic principle of the new model of sex—latent hermaphroditism.

> Biedl assumes that there is always present a *hermaphroditic ground work....* "It is only by the assumption of a *hermaphroditic primitive genital trace,* together with the dependence of the somatic and psychic sex characteristics upon the *internal secretory activity of the genital glands,* that we can explain those cases in which complete alteration of single sex characteristics, or even of the entire sexual character, takes place during the life of the individual" (G.W. Carnick Co. 1924, 136; emphasis added).

The experimental endocrinologist Arthur Biedl, quoted in this passage, identifies a latent hermaphroditic bedrock and the role of hormones as key factors in human development. The notion of a hermaphroditic bedrock gained strength throughout the 1930s, becoming the basis for a new logic of treatment for sexual pathologies in the 1940s and 1950s.

The assumption that all bodies were a combination of male and female hormones provided an epistemological space for nascent transsexuals to lay claim to sex change technologies. In the older, dualistic model of sex, paradoxical treatments (male sex hormones in female bodies) were contra-indicated because of fears about cross-sex contamination. The new hermaphroditic model had no way to block paradoxical treatments because both men and women were already in possession of estrogens and androgens. With the discovery of "paradoxical hormones" in all men and women, a way opened up for transsexuals to appropriate hormones to transform their bodies.

CURES FOR INVERSION: A NEW USE-VALUE FOR INTERNAL SECRETIONS

From the 1930s through the 1950s, endocrinology treated inverts with hormones. Though there was a general consensus that inverts could benefit from hormones, clinicians and experimenters disagreed about which hormones were appropriate for particular bodies. Which hormones would cure inversion?

The treatment protocol constructed in the 1940s and 1950s is one of the cleaving knives that cut up the category of "inversion." Physicians started their treatment by deciding if a case was acquired or innate. If it was acquired, it was possible to treat the condition with homo-sexual hormones. The term "homo-sexual hormones"—estrogens for females and testosterone for males—relies on the old dualistic paradigm according to which only men have testosterone and only women have estrogens. Like organotherapy, homo-sexual hormones were designed to balance a patient's sexual accounts.

If a case of inversion was considered innate, it was deemed resistant to homo-sexual hormone treatments. Innate homosexual inverts could be treated with hetero-sexual hormones—testosterone for females and estrogens for males. The use of hetero-sexual hormones came from the newly discovered paradoxical finding that female bodies had "male" hormones and male bodies had "female" hormones. The purpose of treatments of hetero-sexual hormones was to hormonally castrate inverts and prevent them from acting out their pathological natures. The use of estrogens in cases of innate male inversion was justified by locating an innate, incurable illness in their bodies. By anchoring inversion in the body, male-bodied inverts began to qualify for heterosexual hormones (estrogen). Hetero-sexual hormone treatments for female-bodied inverts, however, was still contra-indicated by a particularly gendered and sexualized logic of treatment. This resulted in an asymmetry in the treatment of male- and female-bodied inverts.

Many inverts were treated against their will. This practice is a black stain on the history of endocrinology. These same events are significant to the history of transsexualism because they mark some of the first uses of hetero-sexual hormones to alter the character or the body of inverts. These events have two historical trajectories; one is homosexual and the other is transsexual. The homosexual history is about unwanted treatments and the removal of the homosexual diagnosis from the *Diagnostic and Statistical Manual* of the American Psychological Association in 1974. Without a doubt, the end of unwanted treatments is a success story. The transsexual history is a record of the logic that paved the way for desired treatments. This history is also a success story, but its end is the creation, rather than the removal, of a diagnosis. With this diagnostic category, transsexuals became recognizable and treatments were made available.

Endocrinologists held the belief that inversion was as much a disorder of sex and gender as it was a disease of sexuality. Such disorders were all wrapped into one ball of wax. This belief system is summarized with hindsight by historian of science Dr. Heino F. L. Meyer-Bahlburg in 1984:

> The general rationale underlying these studies [in the 1940s and 1950s] was derived from the well-known relationships of testosterone and other androgens to masculine body characteristics and in animals, to certain aspects of masculine behavior, as well as from the analogous relationships of estrogens to feminine somatic and behavioral characteristics. Accordingly, the expectation was that male homosexuals would show a deficiency of testosterone and/or other androgens, and/or an excess of estrogens whereas female homosexuals would show the reverse. Other endocrine disorders were thought to be possibly associated with the sex hormone abnormalities as cause or consequence (Meyer-Bahlburg 1984, 376).

This account shows the belief that inversion was a deficiency of hormones that a dose of homo-sexual hormones would cure. The earliest studies exhibit the hope that homo-sexual hormones would correct the direction of the inverts' desires as well as their gender presentation. C. A. Wright was one of the early advocates for treating male homo-sexual inverts with testosterone and female inverts with estrogen.

> The sex attraction of the true congenital homosexual is based on an endocrine imbalance....In as much as the gonadotropic factor governs development and the normal functioning of the sex glands, it seems indicated to use [testosterone] in the treatment of these cases in the male. It is probable that the addition of estrin...is indicated in women (Wright 1938, 449–52).

Out of the twelve cases reported by Wright in his original study, nine showed an improvement in hormone levels, a return to heterosexual behavior, and a concomitant reform of their psychosocial outlook. Four case reports on male inverts from Dr. Louis A. Lurie of Cincinnati, Ohio in 1944 were typical of the period. Lurie's discussion divides homosexual inverts into two categories, innate and acquired, the endocrine factor was crucial in the former type. Treatments with testosterone were virilizing in such cases. Only one of the four boys in this series was "overtly" homosexual; he had had homosexual experiences. Lurie noted with confidence that the other three were latent homosexuals. The boys' gender inversion was being treated as much as their sexual "disorder."

> In general, the physical examination was negative.... The endocrine picture was very suggestive. The boy was of average height but 15 pounds overweight. The fat distribution was principally of the mons-mammary-girdle type. There was no hair on the face.... The genitalia were small. It was noted that C. was very effeminate. He talked in a high-pitched girlish voice and walked with a mincing gait. His face was round and his cheeks were rosy. He was extremely neat about his person and always looked clean and well dressed. He did not engage in any rough play with the other boys. He was very easygoing and very seldom asserted himself.... He had a huge appetite and drank a great deal of water between meals. He always asked for milk. He appeared extremely phlegmatic and very sleepy. He yawned constantly.... He preferred being by himself.... He appeared to daydream a great deal (Lurie 1944, 181).

Lurie found no genital irregularities, but he read this boy's body as hormonally deficient. His appetite and yawning were symptomatic of his testosterone deficiency and indicated the necessity for revitalization. He, like the other boys in Lurie's study, was "successfully" treated with homo-sexual hormones—testosterone. His body changed, as it would have anyway in the case of this thirteen-year-old adolescent, and he joined the armed forces.

These early accounts were countered by Glass and Johnson's "Limitations and Complications of Organotherapy in Male Homo-sexuality."

> Insofar as homosexuality is concerned organotherapy failed to influence the psychosexual behavior in eight of the subjects but seemed to benefit the other three.... Among the eight who failed to respond favorably, [five] complained of an actual intensification of the homosexual drive so that further treatment was withheld or abandoned by them (Glass and Johnson 1944, 541–42).

The endocrinologists were disappointed that the treatments exacerbated their patients' homosexuality. It became apparent to them that testosterone could affect the power but not the direction of the sex drive.

Heller and Maddock point out the other treatment options available in 1947: "Diametrically opposed to this type of therapy is the use of castration in over 100 cases of sexual perversion and homosexuality reported by Sand and Okkels (1938) who note that the results have been gratifying in all but one case" (Heller and Maddock 1947, 420). This review of the literature in 1947 concludes:

> The *power* of the human sex drive is largely dependent on *physiological* factors, i.e. proportional to the amount of circulating androgen (or estrogen in the female). On the other hand, the *direction* of the human sex drive seems to be largely dependent upon *psychological* factors, which are conditioned by the early environment and sexual experiences of the individual. It would seem to follow that vigorous androgenic treatment would tend to increase the power of the sex drive in both the normal and homosexual male without influencing the direction of the sex drive in either case. Similarly, castration will markedly diminish, but not abolish, the power of the sex drive, and the diminished drive in the case of normals will continue

in the direction of heterosexuality, whereas the small drive remaining in the homosexual will continue in the direction of homosexuality (Heller and Maddock 1947, 422).

In 1947, physicians decided that male inverts could not be "cured" of their homosexual inversion, but they could be rendered *sexually inactive*. Libido reduction, through estrogen treatments, was the next best thing to a true change of sexual object choice.

The clinical literature of this period ignores female inverts, in part because medicine assumed that females were the mirror of the male inverts. It was also clear that estrogen was an ineffectual treatment for females with sexual direction disorders and testosterone treatments were contra-indicated due to their virilizing effects. The association of testosterone with virility justified homo-sexual hormone treatments for male inverts with deficient masculine desires or gender presentation. This same equation of virility and testosterone foreclosed testosterone treatments for nascent FTMs.

In the 1940s, female inversion was considered medically untreatable. Their condition did not respond to estrogen. Testosterone was not yet available to female inverts because of the belief that it would virilize them and increase their libido. Male inverts might be treated with testosterone, to virilize them, or estrogens, to castrate them. This asymmetry of treatment options delayed the recognizability of female inverts *qua* FTM transsexuals.

BECOMING TREATABLE: TWO TYPES OF INVERSION

Without a treatable physical abnormality, the care of female inverts would pass into the domain of the psychologists. Dr. Michael Dillon's 1946 book, *Self: Ethics and Endocrinology*, was an attempt to make a case for the hormonal treatment of female inverts. Dillon had changed his sex from female to male in the 1940s, first his birth certificate and then his body. Though he does not mention his own sex change, the argument in *Self* might represent the logic he used to convince his physicians to do what he wanted. His text positions people like himself as a special kind of invert.

Dillon starts off by suggesting that there are several grades of sex, from male to female, and intersexuals of all kinds in between: "[T]hese intersexes...have the primary characteristics of male or female, i.e. the gonads, the ovary or testis; but they display also the secondary characteristics of the other, including the temperament. This state is known as homosexuality" (59). Dillon tries to establish inverts as homosexuals who need treatment like intersexuals.

Dillon then outlines a typology of the different types of these "homosexuals." He starts with a standard distinction between permanent and transient homosexuality. Adolescent exploration is the transient type, whereas other types are not bound by either time or geography. Both male and female homosexuals exist. The rest of his article explores the female types.

Dillon's next distinction is between permanent homosexuals whose disorder stems from endocrine imbalances and those whose disorder is psychological in nature. In order to determine which homosexuals belong within the domain of endocrinology, Dillon separates mannish inverts, whose disorders are acquired or deliberate, from masculine inverts, whose disorders are innate.

> It is not a new distinction but it is one that is all too frequently overlooked. The difference is that of the deliberate adoption and imitation of the habits, interests and dress of the other sex...and of the natural acquisition of them as the result of the innate possession of the mental outlook and temperament of the other sex (44).

Dillon notes that psychologists do not make a distinction between mannish and masculine inverts and he believes this to be a flaw in their typologies.

Yet, there is a clear distinction. Where the one imitates and acquires, the other seems to develop naturally along the lines of the other sex. Invariably, [the latter] cry "I have always felt as if I were a man." In these instances the body may approximate in essentials to one sex...but the personality is wholly peculiar to the opposite one (51).

Dillon then claims that Radclyffe Hall's 1929 novel, *The Well of Loneliness*, portrays a girl of the innate masculine type.

Dillon closes by arguing for medical treatments for masculine female homosexuals. Psychologists are of no use to this type, he says, as some hidden physical condition must dictate their nature. Until this factor can be discovered, these special inverts should be treated with testosterone. Dillon argues, "Surely where the mind cannot be made to fit the body, the body should be made to fit, approximately, at any rate to the mind" (53). With a discussion of the moral blamelessness of homosexuals, Dillon makes a final recommendation that these victims should be given care free of charge.

Dillon clearly believes that there are similar features among female types—what they were, what they did, and what their bodies were like. By parsing the categories of homosexuals, he *repositions* one type of female invert as the cousin of intersexuals. Although the people he refers to as "masculine inverts" are like other homosexuals, they are more like intersexuals, and are deserving of testosterone treatments. This repositioning was necessary because of a lack of treatment protocols that could justify testosterone injections for female inverts in the 1930s and 1940s. Dillon asserts that those of his type are more like intersexuals so that they can remain in the hands of the endocrinologists.

MORE LIKE HERMAPHRODITES: TREATMENT FOR BODILY DISORDERS

In his chapter, "Hermaphrodism," Dillon makes the second move that repositions masculine inverts closer to intersexuals and provides the dominant logic of treatment for the group soon to be known as female-to-male transsexuals. As in his previous chapter on homosexuals, Dillon makes no explicit mention of his own transsexualism. He is still on a course that approaches, but does not directly name the condition. This he leaves for Cauldwell in 1949. In lieu of a name and a diagnosis, Dillon draws on types of intersexual conditions to develop a logic of treatment for others like him.

Intersexuals were usually classified as either true or pseudo-hermaphrodites: "[T]rue hermaphrodism does not depend upon the shape or existence of the external organs, it is the presence of both ovary and testis in the abdomen that makes for it" (59). Dillon emphasizes that hermaphrodites do not necessarily have external, visible anomalies. By establishing this fact, he could suggest that doctors should treat people like himself despite their apparently normal bodies. Intersexual pathologies were hidden in the abdomen and undetectable to the naked eye. Scientific progress would eventually be able to find the physiological basis for inversion, but for now, abnormalities like his were hidden.

Dillon moves from the "hidden pathology" analogy to examples of intersexed individuals who have incompletely formed or entirely absent penises. This condition, known as hypospadias, is seen as legitimating medical intervention. Usually, he notes, these individuals are mistaken for girls at birth and reared as girls until puberty when male secondary sexual characteristics emerge. Of all the intersexed conditions, the hypospadic comes closest to the phallic lack of FTMs.

There is, in addition, sometimes complete lack of a penis altogether, and this and the undescended testicles cause the parents to suppose that their child is a girl. As such, therefore, he is brought up—with disastrous results when the error is discovered a puberty, for at that time the voice may break, the muscles develop and the skeletal growth assumes adult male proportions. Sometimes, however, *the changes are not so evident* that the individual may live for some years under the delusion he is a female unless his instincts gain the upper hand (61; emphasis added).

Lack of a penis or a small penis due to a gonad failure is treatable, and, Dillon argues, should be treated, but only in the cases where the individual's psychosexual outlook does not correspond to the sex assigned at birth.

> Certain patients who have realized that they were not the same, physically, as other girls, have been horrified to discover that in reality they were men, undeveloped males. Some such cases on record refused treatment, preferring to go on living as women, and, being without external genitalia, they are outside the scope of the law and have a perfect right to do as they wish (62).

These women are hypospadic pseudo-hermaphrodites with feminine psychosexual outlooks. In such cases, Dillon claims it would be inappropriate to intervene. However, if the hypospadic individual has a masculine psychosexual outlook, Dillon argues that it is in their best interest to be treated.

Though Dillon does not mention the types of treatment he has in mind, he refuses to call this treatment a "sex change" because the term causes sensational media coverage. He also says that it does an injustice to the psychosexual outlook of the patient. Dillon emphasizes that, since the body is unremarkably female, claims to manhood may seem outlandish to others. Because they view these patients as women, others can make sense of the desired treatment only as a "change" of sex.

> [I]t is not surprising that his statements are met with some incredulity. . . . They may never have been given real cause before to doubt his sex was female, why should they alter their view now? Far easier to assume that, by pure perversity, he has wanted to "change his sex" and that by some curious means he has managed to accomplish a pseudo-alteration (63).

Despite the assumptions made by others, these individuals have only changed their bodies to conform to their psychosexual outlook. They have not changed their sex. "Sex confirmation" may be a better term for what Dillon has in mind, though he does not use this phrase.

The remainder of Dillon's chapter on intersexuals is devoted to the role of genetics in inversion. Dillon hoped to pinpoint the cause of inversion at a deeper, microscopic level of the body in order to strengthen the proposed kinship between intersexuals and inverts of the innate/masculine type. "There is no reason to suppose that sex variations of character are less able to be [genetically] transmitted than those of the body" (71).

Dillon's logic of treatment for intersexuals and some inverts rests upon two principle assumptions about embodiment and subjectivity. The first of these is in line with traditional medicine, but the second seems counter-intuitive. First, a body shall not be treated unless there is an obvious and identifiable physiological or anatomical pathology. Failure to find such an anomaly precludes treatment or engenders a more penetrating search for bodily errors.

Second, the mind, not the body, should indicate the appropriate type of treatment. The correct course of treatment depends on the patient's psychosexual outlook. This unusual diagnostic protocol continues to be a point of conflict among physicians.

PSYCHOLOGICAL TREATMENT OF FTM TRANSSEXUALS

The logic of treatment put forth by Dillon was reflected in the scattered case studies in the medical literature in the 1950s (Cauldwell 1949; Hamburger 1953; Benjamin 1954), but his efforts were ultimately only partially successful. The treatment of female-bodied inverts was remanded to the psychologists who favored psychoanalysis or aversion therapy.

It is possible to trace the consolidation of the logic of treatment by examining the reasons psychologists employed to reject medical treatment. The psychologists viewed nascent FTMs as a type of female homosexual with internalized homophobia. They disregarded their patients' claims of intersexuality. According to psychologists in the 1950s and 1960s, such patients had a mind problem, not a body problem. Each of these case reports summarizes the physical condition of the patient and concludes that there are no observable anatomical anomalies and therefore no justification for hormone treatments. Throughout the cases, there is evidence that these patients tried to establish their similarity to intersexuals and their difference from female homosexuals. The case reports demonstrate that FTMs magnified these differences and grew insistent on their similarities to intersexuals. As medical treatments became less available, their claims of difference from homosexuals and similarity to intersexuals grew stronger.

In 1956, Bowmen and Engle reported on a case of a man and a wife, each of whom were "transvestic." "Transvestism" was the preferred term of psychologists who categorized transsexuals as an extreme type of cross-dressing homosexual. They focused on social presentation, especially clothes, and sexual object choice, rather than on bodies, in order to assert their control over these patients. They conclude, "according to psychological explanations, transvestitism is the result of intense castration fears, as are homosexuality, exhibitionism, and fetishism" (Bowmen and Engle 1956, 587). They conceded that no psychological treatments have proven successful. However, Bowmen and Engle counsel psychological intervention over medical treatment because the latter "does not really solve the problem" (Bowmen and Engle 1956, 587) and can be the cause of legal mayhem.

A 1959 report on fifty cases (thirteen FTMs and thirty-seven MTFs) emphasizes the "homosexual" desires of these patients and dismisses the notion that transvestites and transsexuals had physiological anomalies like intersexed patients.

> There was no evidence of genital dysplasia or male anatomical conformation.... With one notable exception the female patients were homosexually oriented. These 12 women [sic] had experienced homosexual attachments, and the wish to take the male role in sexual intimacy with a Lesbian partner was the predominant and expressed reason advanced by those who wished for trans-sexualization" (Randell 1959, 1450).

The one exception was an FTM in a partnership with an MTF. In an effort to bolster his theory that transsexuals are a type of homosexual, Randell goes on to cite a 1955 study that "failed to discover abnormal gonadal status in transvestite patients.... [Worden and Marsh] believe that such patients are in conflict over strong, but unacceptable sexual urges and feel threatened by all sexual activity whether hetero-, homo-, or masturbatory" (Randell 1959, 1451). Of his thirteen FTM cases, and the entire series of fifty, Randell asserts, "no convincing evidence of anatomical intersexuality was found" (Randell 1959, 1451).

Until the 1980s, "true" female-bodied transsexuals had feminine women as their preferred sexual object choice. Psychologists argued that female-bodied gender inverts with sexual desires for men were, by definition, not true transvestites.

> Heterosexual [sic] individuals with transvestitism are generally psychopaths who want to attract attention. That variety is not considered genuine transvestitism....Consequently, sexuality among genuine transvestites is mostly homosexual along the conventional lines. Accepting Dukor's theory that genuine transvestitism is the final consequence...of a female, active type of homosexuality it will hardly be possible to include the absence of desire for homosexual contacts in the characteristics of true transvestitism since from their own point of view their sexual contacts with individuals of the same somatic sex are heterosexual (Hertz and Westman 1961, 291).

Psychologists recommended psychotherapy for inverts with homosexual desires and transvestic presentation. They believed that medical intervention was contra-indicated.

Within these same reports are scattered references to how the FTM patients viewed their situations. Almost all of the reports make references, in belittling tones, to the patient's claim to have a physiological disturbance, or to be intersexed. Throughout these reports, psychologists choose to use the female pronouns to emphasize their belief that the FTMs really were women. Bowmen and Engle make this comment about the "wife" in the case of the transgendered couple: "His wife took a man's name, dressed as a man, and worked outside the home as a man. She had for some time taken testosterone and felt that a lump in her groin was a testicle" (Bowmen and Engle 1956, 587). This report, with its use of the female pronoun, demonstrates the mocking tones of the psychologists. It also shows how FTMs actively constructed their situation in terms that would be most likely to secure medical treatments. By claiming to have a testicle, this patient could locate his condition in his body and indicate that his true sex was male. These two claims made medical treatment more likely.

Likewise, a case report from 1961 describes the case of a twenty-five-year-old who claimed "she had had no menstruation for 13 months. She pointed out that her appearance had gradually assumed more masculine features. Her voice had become deeper, her breasts smaller, her musculature had developed, her feet and hands had grown. She had observed a weak growth of beard and she had started shaving" (Hertz et al. 1961, 289). This report echoes Dillon's description of the hypospadic hermaphrodite who, having been brought up as female, goes through a surprise male puberty with all the attendant physical changes.

The FTMs also asserted that they were not homosexuals. Hertz writes, "She stated that she had a distinct feeling that in some way she was a man. In consequence of this idea she did not consider the above-mentioned woman [the patient's partner] a homosexual person, nor did she admit that she herself was homosexual. 'A homosexual woman would be repugnant to me' " (Hertz et al. 1961, 290). These refusals to be categorized as homosexual or to have his partner categorized as a lesbian are counter-discourses that these FTMs marshaled against the psychological discourses that foreclosed medical treatments. In another report, a psychologist called in to ascertain the sanity of an FTM accused of a crime writes, "she has been continually harassed throughout her life by 'everybody,' and labeled a 'freak,' 'homo,' or 'hermaphrodite.' A.C. always thought these derogations were unjust. She considered herself to have always been masculine and knew that her wife felt about her and accepted her as such" (Redmount 1953, 95).

Similar reports indicated that it was not at all unusual for FTMs to present themselves as intersexed, and that some even took additional steps to secure this representation of themselves by gaining access to and self-administering hormones. One psychologist reports, "The rationale she offered was that she was a pseudo-hermaphrodite. She was noncommittal about a prior bilateral mastectomy, though admitted having taken male hormones over a period of time" (McCully 1963, 437). This patient "admitted" to taking hormones, an act which was obviously a crime to the psychologist. This psychologist is well aware that the patient's claims to being hermaphroditic would legitimate the desired course of treatment and suggests that these claims are made for that very purpose: "Putting herself across as an hermaphrodite would achieve one of her ends, an operation. She grudgingly accepted that she had some physical female anatomy, giving that much lip service to reality since it furthered her goals. She herself believed that she had functioning male sexual organs" (McCully 1963, 437). On the one hand, this psychologist believes that the patient had deliberately presented his case in a way that would guarantee the desired surgery. On the other hand, the psychologist summarizes the patient's belief system as delusional.

This choice, between viewing the patient's claims as delusional or strategic, is found in many of the accounts, but nowhere as starkly as in the aforementioned report on an FTM criminally accused by his mother-in-law of fraudulent financial affairs. Dr. Robert Redmount concludes his remarks on this case with this pithy summary: "Her life-long adjustments seem to represent *less an attempt to accept reality and more of a protest against it*" (110; emphasis added). Redmount hardly concurs that this protest is viable. His ultimate aim would be to help the patient avoid "her own self-destruction" (111). The use of the female pronoun throughout these cases, plus the ubiquitous comments on the normal physiological condition of these patients, indicates the psychologists' beliefs that these patients are delusional. Endocrinologists might defer to the patient's desire for treatment based on the likelihood that a physiological etiology for their condition would eventually be uncovered. The psychologists could only view their patients as at worst deluded, and at best strategic.

SURGICAL LOGIC OF TREATMENT: RECONSTRUCTIVE VERSUS COSMETIC

The history of plastic surgeries and their use-value for nascent FTMs depends upon a similar logic of treatment whereby some bodies are made treatable and others are considered healthy and not treatable. With a firm grasp on this logic of treatment, it will be relatively easy to understand how surgeries became available to nascent FTMs.

Yet the history of surgical procedures is more complex because there are many different surgeries that FTMs pursue. In popular belief systems, "sex changes" are thought to be a one-stop procedure, like walking through a machine in a doctor's office. This perception relies on the assumption of the primacy of the phallus. In actuality, sex reassignment/confirmation has always been a multi-stage process consisting of life-long hormone treatments and multiple surgeries including chest reconstruction, phallic reconstruction, scrotal reconstruction, and partial or total hysterectomies.

For a variety of reasons, FTMs pursue surgery less vigorously than they do testosterone. The multiple surgical procedures, although highly desired by FTMs, are out of financial reach for many and are considered inadequate, functionally and aesthetically, by most. Hormones have carried greater importance than surgeries for the history of the emergence and consolidation of an FTM identity.

History of Surgical Techniques

Both chest reconstruction and hysterectomy have their roots in the medical treatment of "disorderly" female bodies. Mastectomies were performed as early as 1669 (Maliniac 1950, 6) for hypertrophic, pendulous breasts which put women physically at risk. These early plastic surgeries were as risky as the condition itself. Anesthesia, advances in blood flow control, and antiseptic all contributed to the safety and success of surgery, especially non-critical procedures, in the nineteenth and twentieth centuries. From the 1890s onward, improvements were made in the techniques of mastectomy, leading to better results for nipple grafting or transposition, minimization of scarring, and increased sensation. Aside from pendulous breasts, mastectomies were often performed during the twentieth century for women diagnosed with cancerous lumps or illnesses related to the mammary glands. These female bodies commanded surgical attention because they were ill bodies.

The practice of hysterectomies has a long history as well. In 1809, Ephraim McDowell reported on a case in which he removed the ovaries and fallopian tubes of his patient. In 1869, Robert Battery did an ovariotomy that he later used on unspecified "abnormal females." By 1878, the first total hysterectomy had been performed (Dally 1991, 141). Hysteria, originally believed to result from a "loose womb," was most frequently treated by hysterectomy.

Phalloplasties, unlike mastectomies and hysterectomies, were first developed for male bodies. Veterans injured during World War I received the first phalloplasties. John Hoopes's 1969 review article provides an overview of the development of these techniques. Harold Gilles, a British surgeon who was instrumental in the formation of plastic surgery as a field of medicine, created an "abdominal flap" procedure in 1916. This most popular technique creates a "suitcase handle" attached at both ends to the abdomen and eventually released on one end.

Surgeons struggled with two functional difficulties presented by phallic reconstruction—urinary and sexual. Hoopes (1969) reported that, in the 1940s, Frumkin, Maltz, and Gilles all tried various means for constructing a urethra that would not be eaten away by the toxicity of urine. The problem of producing a phallus that could become rigid enough for sexual intercourse and flaccid for everyday life remains unsolved. Various attempts from 1940 onward have included rib cartilage grafts and synthetic materials. Preservation of sensation for FTMs was improved by the use of the enlarged clitoris as the "peg" upon which the phallus is constructed (Munawar 1957).

Scrotum was first grafted for men in 1957 by Gilles. As late as 1969, Hoopes wrote about FTMs: "utilization of the labia majora would seem an appropriate procedure...however they do not provide tissue of sufficient bulk to construct an acceptable scrotum" (Hoopes 1969, 344). More recently, techniques have been developed for expanding the labial tissue and inserting saline implants not unlike the procedures for female breast augmentation.

Reconstruction or Cosmetic Surgery?

Kathy Davis writes that plastic surgery became more oriented to *cosmetic* improvements than to its original goals of *reconstruction*. Cosmetic surgery, from rhinoplasty to breast augmentation, has been questioned from the start because of the moral problem of judging beauty. Since standards of beauty are considered conventional, rather than immutable, the choice to pursue cosmetic surgery has been considered suspect.

Reconstructive surgeries were not morally problematic in this way. Especially because many of the reconstructive surgeries discussed above were related to illness, war, or industrial accidents, these procedures and the patients who wanted them were considered morally innocent in a way that cosmetic procedures and patients were not.

Cosmetic surgery was considered a voluntary procedure that was merely motivated by psychological unhappiness with one's appearance in the world. This discontent was a mind problem that needed to be addressed psychologically. Just as the psychologists considered transvestic inversion to be a mind problem, cosmetic requests indicated an unhealthy mental adjustment to a physical reality. Reconstructive surgeries, by contrast, were not considered voluntaristic or vain. They were mandated, instead, by disobedient bodies that were unhealthy to the patient. This illness model located the problem in the body in order to justify medical intervention within its proper domain of action.

From the start, cosmetic surgeries were more popular among women than among men (Davis 1995). Reconstructive surgeries were developed in response to industrial and war-time activities, which affected more men than women. There is not only a moral distinction between reconstructive and cosmetic surgeries, but also a gendered distinction between them. In light of these distinctions, it is unsurprising that nascent FTMs invoked the reconstructive, rather than the cosmetic, logic of treatment. In order to obtain surgeries while minimizing the stigma attached to their lives, nascent FTMs sank their problems deep into their flesh.

In ethnographic interviews, FTMs uniformly use the language of reconstruction to discuss the procedures they want or have had. For example, instead of "mastectomy," they say they had "chest reconstruction surgery." Instead of a "sex change," they had a "sex confirmation" surgery that *repaired* their bodies in much the same way as a man might have a reconstructive surgery after an industrial accident or a war. By positioning themselves as innocent accidents of nature, they located their problems in their bodies and deferred the stigma associated with voluntary surgery. This made them treatable bodies, like other men who were heroic and manly victims deserving of medical attention.

CONCLUSIONS

The history of the emergence of an FTM subject position is the history of the "proliferation of perversions" in the twentieth century. Inversion, a category that referred to both gender/sex and sexual "deviance," split into discrete categories, each with its own diagnosis and logic of treatment. Endocrinology played a crucial role in this process. The growth and legitimacy of this field were established by studying the normal and pathological effects of "internal secretions" on sexual characteristics.

Some scholars of transsexualism have suggested that medical gatekeepers forced transsexuals to develop a purely strategic justification that deceived physicians in order to gain access to hormones and surgeries. While transsexuals had to marshal new discourses in order to make themselves recognizable as transsexuals, this was not a purely tactical claim. Though some transsexuals have instrumentalized the logic of treatment in order to qualify for treatments, chapters three and four present evidence these FTMs have written this story not only for that instrumental purpose, but also for their own sense of themselves. For example, the belief that they have a hidden male physiology, a chromosome out of place, or a hormonal imbalance, is not only instrumental, but also provides a narrative that makes sense of their identities. As much as these claims substantiate the logic of treatment and provide a rhetorical justification for treatments, they also represent FTMs' attempts to theorize the circumstances that confront them, to put their enigmatic existence into words, and to relieve themselves of the constant queries about who and what they are.

The development of a differential diagnosis for transsexualism helped to constitute an FTM subject position, but identities are not reducible to their diagnoses, nor to the discourses of the medical and psychological experts who have treated these bodies. George Chauncey writes:

> [I]t would be wrong to assume, I think, that doctors created and defined the identities of "inverts" and "homosexuals" at the turn of the century, that people uncritically internalized the new medical models. . . . Such assumptions attribute inordinate power to ideology as an autonomous social force . . . they belie the evidence of *preexisting subcultures and identities* contained in the literature itself (Chauncey 1989a, 87–88).

The same can be said of the emergence of female-to-male transsexualism. While there is considerable value in a genealogy of medical discourses, the emergence and consolidation of an FTM identity cannot be reduced to the development of a diagnosis without simultaneously reducing these subjects to "medical dupes."

Because of the interdependence of transsexuals and their medical care providers, the tendency to overemphasize the role of the doctors is not easy to resist. However, because transsexualism is both more and less than a medical condition, history must also acknowledge the sub-cultural discourses that contributed to the production and maintenance of these identities. Therefore, it is necessary to examine the tension between male-identified inverts and the subcultural discourse of the lesbian-feminist revolution during the 1970s.

34

Look! No, Don't!
The Visibility Dilemma for Transsexual Men

J AMISON G REEN

J AMISON G REEN, ONE OF THE FOREMOST FTM TRANSSEXUAL ACTIVISTS in the United States since the early 1990s, writes here of the doubly ironic "visibility dilemma" experienced by many transsexual men. Transsexual experience becomes invisible, he claims, in direct proportion to the success of appearing to others as a member of one's subjectively experienced gender; conversely, to the extent that one reveals a transsexual life course to others, one risks undermining the achieved gender status.

Most transsexuals, like most other people, wish to be seen as belonging to the sex or gender to which they considered themselves to belong. This is why they suffer the risks, pain, and social stigma of transitioning. Historically, this desire has been the basis for decisions by many transsexuals to remain silent about their past lives in other genders. But as a new wave of transgender activism took root in the 1990s, activists such as Green felt compelled to be visible publicly as "out and proud" transsexuals. Borrowing a concept from the gay liberation movement, Green argues that the "closet" induces a heavy burden on transsexual people, and is itself supported by the very social conventions that lead to prejudice and discrimination.

Green describes how "out" transsexuals experience more "gender policing," (i.e., expressed judgments of the acceptability or authenticity of the transsexual's identity). But he also notes that the more congruent transsexuals' identities and bodies become through the process of transition, the less interesting they tend to become to the public, and the less illustrative their lives are of the diversity of gender experience—and therefore the more difficult it becomes for them to remain effectively "out." Green concludes that despite the ironies, transsexual visibility is crucial to expanding general awareness of the great range of difference contained within social norms of gendered embodiment.

Transsexual people usually wish to be perceived and taken seriously as members of the gender class in which they feel most comfortable. Transsexual men are able to integrate into mainstream society through employment and social relationships; their natural masculinity (enough by itself in many cases), combined with the external effects of testosterone, renders them virtually undetectable in most social situations. Cultural tolerance for a wide variety of adult male 'looks' (appearance styles) and behaviours is also a factor in the success of many transitional men. Billy Tipton is just one modern example of a transgendered person who was accepted as a man among his peers without benefit of hormones or surgery. But what happens to the transsexual man who 'comes out' and admits to having been born female?

Many of us have been 'outed' because of unfortunate medical situations or indiscreet friends or family members. A few of us have been used as grist for the insatiable media mill as we have fought to retain employment in places where we originally represented ourselves as female, or have been sued by disgruntled ex-spouses. And some of us have chosen to make ourselves visible as FTMs—men who were born with female bodies, not 'women who became men'—because we have realized that the isolation individual men like ourselves experience can lead to poor self-esteem and ill-informed choices with respect to treatment in medical, legal and social arenas.

I am one of the growing cadre of men who have chosen to make ourselves available to assist transsexual and non-transsexual people in understanding the experience of transsexual men. I have inched my way out of the transsexual closet with considerable trepidation, and many people in my life have no idea of my transitional past because I choose not to disclose it to them. I have found that when a man elects to reveal his transsexual history or status, results are mixed, varying according to situation—but generally the experience has struck me as being somewhat like joining another species.

I started doing educational work regarding gender and transgender issues in 1989 at the request of Steve Dain and Lou Sullivan, both of whom were too busy (and, in Sullivan's case, too ill) to continue to do some of the college and university classroom lectures and question-and-answer sessions they had been doing regularly for several years. There was no remuneration for these sessions, which would last an hour or sometimes two, and with travel time could often take three or four hours. I soon realized that taking time away from my employer to give classroom lectures meant that I was actually losing money in the service of education. In other words, we sometimes pay for the privilege of telling our stories. Sullivan also referred me to a speaker's bureau operated by a large San Francisco transvestite club, through which I participated in numerous panel presentations for classes in which the professor wished to clarify the difference between transvestites and transsexual people. Through these panels I learned that these presentations can be a valuable form of therapy. It can be worth every penny it costs to receive the validation I feel when I am sincerely thanked for sharing my personal story, especially when the exchange has proven enlightening for even one person in the audience. And yet, as I listen to each panel of cross-dressers, transgenderists and transsexual people reciting our oh-so-similar litanies of struggle and change, there seems to be a self-centeredness, even a pathetic quality of self-justification to so many of our public 'confessions'. We say we want to be invisible, yet we beg to be acknowledged. Stepping in front of the class we become laboratory rats, frogs in the dissection tray, interactive multimedia learning experiences.

> 'How old were you when you first realized you were a frog, Mr. Green?'
> 'How did your parents react when you told them you were a frog?'
> 'Do you date? Do you tell your partners you're a frog?'
> 'So, how does it work? I mean, uh, can you, like, do it?'

No one has really ever suggested that I am an actual frog—but these are essentially the questions that are most frequently asked. Of course, these questions are expected. I often sit in the audience as if I were a student until the professor announces that apparently the guest speaker will be late or has forgotten (unless the class is so small that the professor recognizes me as a stranger and quizzes me with her eyes, hoping I am there to take this class period off her hands, or unless my visit is a repeat performance and the professor knows me on sight). Then I rise up from within their midst, students gasping and murmuring around me: 'It was sitting next to me and I didn't know!' 'Oh, my God.' 'I never would have guessed.' 'He looks so normal!' It's fun to fool them, at first. It's validating, reassuring. It's educational. I get to show them that they never know who might be transsexual, that transsexual people are just like anyone, just like them. I am an object lesson.

I started out, like most transsexual speakers, just telling my story and leaving time for questions. Over the years I learned the most effective way to tell my story quickly, whetting the students' appetites, planting certain concepts in their minds and leaving more time to respond to their questions rather than lecturing. I do this because when they see me think on my feet, when I can use spontaneous humour, when I am vulnerable to them, then they see me most completely as a human being. They come to trust me. I find this trust ironic because it grows very quickly out of their original expectations that I will not be what I seem, or that they would be able to tell that I am trying to be something that I am not. When I am successful, it is because they let go of their preconceptions and their prejudices, they realize that they can exist without those crutches of belief, that they can move through the world without fear and without certainty and still the world goes on. Nothing really changes when they acknowledge the existence of transpeople (transsexual and transgender people) and realize that we are not inherently monsters or perverts. Nothing really changes except that their compassion quotient expands exponentially. Nothing really changes except each of the students goes away with a little piece of me that they can own and mould and reinterpret as they wish.

I lose a bit more control of the use of my own story every time I tell it. Every time I lecture a class of 200 students, 200 more people in the world know—or think they know—something about my genital organs, even if I never talked about them. They learn more about me in one hour than my co-workers who see me every day will ever know—unless my co-workers sign up for Human Sexuality.

It's one thing to confine one's public confessions to the educational arena (as a guest lecturer), a world contained within the ivy-covered walls and ivory towers of inquiry and theoretical exploration (unless you are seeking tenure). It's quite another to venture into the political arena where theory and practice become one and there is little tolerance for exploratory gestures. Here you must act, advance, thrust and parry, and be prepared to compromise. There is no hanging back, no way of just checking in and then retiring. Once you have stepped into the ring, it's you and the bull: there is no escape without everyone knowing you did not have the spine for it. And they'll know why you didn't have the spine: regardless of what you tell them, it will be because you are a trans person. It's one thing to present yourself to a university class—where they know they must behave themselves in front of their professor, where they know they can be critical in private, on paper, in their intellectual analysis of some mutilated creature's pathetic display of narcissistic neediness. It's quite another to offer yourself up, uninsulated, as fodder for politicians and journalists who have no reservations about expressing their distaste for our ilk, and no reason whatsoever to care about us or our issues. It will take much more than a personal story and an attitude of 'specialness' for having lived on both sides of the gender fence to find any compassion in these hardened souls.

And why should we even be trying to talk to politicians and journalists? Such behaviour is completely at cross-purposes with the stated goals of medical and psychological treatment for transsexual people. That treatment is supposed to make us feel normal. We are not supposed to want attention as transsexuals; we are supposed to want to fit in as 'normal' men. We are supposed to pretend we never spent 15, 20, 30, 40 or more years in female bodies, pretend that the vestigial female parts some of us never lose were never there. In short, in order to be a good—or successful—transsexual person, one is not supposed to be a transsexual person at all. This puts a massive burden of secrecy on the transsexual individual: the most intimate and human aspects of our lives are constantly at risk of disclosure. Every time a transsexual man goes into a public (or even private) toilet he is aware of his history; every time he makes love with a partner; every time he seeks medical care; whenever he is at the mercy of a governmental body or social service agency, he is aware of his history—or aware of any anomalies in his body—and must consciously be on guard against discovery. And this is supposed to be the optimal ground of being for a successful person? I think not.

This burden of secrecy is reinforced by myriad social conventions and institutions that support rather than challenge individual prejudice concerning the existence of transsexual people. There are doctors who will not admit they provide services to us. Insurance companies deny medical coverage for conditions relating to 'sex reassignment' or 'surgical sex change' (which can be extrapolated to mean any medical condition once one's transsexual status is known). Some governments or governmental agencies will not allow us to change our identity records to ease our passage through life. Employers are free to dismiss us because they feel that who we are is just too 'disruptive'. It is easy to see how a non-transsexual could feel justified in treating transsexual people with disdain or disgust. So long as their ignorance and prejudice protect them from expressing basic human courtesy to transpeople, non-transsexuals will continue their persecutions.

Yet all these obstacles have not stopped us. All this disapproval has not prevented—will not prevent—the existence of transsexual men and women. It is easy to see how transsexual people are typically justified in their desire to circumscribe knowledge of their past or present lives. And yet as more of us become visible, those whose livelihoods or relationships depend on maintaining secrecy may feel tempted to disclose themselves and take a stand, while they are simultaneously alienated from those who are doing so because their own circumstantial constraints compel them not to act. This inner conflict may breed the very same low self-esteem that activists are attempting to alleviate. The individual who is not able to reconcile his desire to help the nascent trans community with his own need for confidentiality and security may isolate himself further from the only people who share his experience, or he may actively oppose community-oriented efforts.

Can one accomplish anything for the trans community while remaining closeted? I do believe so, certainly. But I think many—not all—transpeople who want to remain hidden will resist making any blatant pro-trans noises for fear of calling attention to themselves. Having stepped out of the transsexual closet myself, I occasionally wonder when certain of my friends—both trans and non-trans—will feel the pressure of my growing notoriety and decline to be seen with me. I wonder who knows about my transsexual past, and who doesn't. Have my co-workers seen me on television? Have acquaintances seen my photo on the cover of San Francisco's queer community newspaper when it was on the streets for two weeks? Would they say anything about it if they had? Have my friends told their friends about me; is that why people seem so eager to be introduced to me? Are they kind, or are they curious? Is it me that people seem attracted to, or is it the exotic trans phenomenon?

Walking down the street in San Francisco or New York City, Boston, Atlanta, Portland, Seattle, London, Paris, Rome, no one seems to take any special interest in me. I am just another man, invisible, no one special. I remember what it was first like to feel that anonymity as testosterone gradually obliterated the androgyny that for most of my life made others uncomfortable in my presence. It was a great relief to be able to shake off layers of defensive behaviours developed to communicate my humanity from inside my incategorizability. It was a joy to be assumed human for a change, instead of stared at, scrutinized for signs of any gender. Now, whenever I stand up in front of a class or make any public statement in support of transgender or transsexual people, I am scrutinized for signs of my previous sex, knowing my gender is reinforced by my male appearance. No one notices me on the street, yet I have been on television and in films, my photograph has appeared in several national (US and internationally distributed) magazines, and I have been asked for commentary and interviews that have appeared in many more publications. In some cases I am identified as transsexual, and in others there is no indication as to my transsexual status. In some cases, my appearance in a publication has had nothing whatsoever to do with transsexualism (I do have other areas of expertise). And I have a lurking suspicion that I would not receive the attention I do (for non-transsexual-related accomplishments) if I still retained the androgynous appearance that I had for the first 40 years of my life. In fact, I know that androgynous people such as I was have often been passed over as subjects and spokespersons on such topics as women in non-traditional jobs because we didn't appear acceptably gendered, and this applies equally to pre-transition female-to-male people and post-transition male-to-female people.

Now, however, people are quite comfortable with my male presentation. My psyche seems to fit nicely into male packaging: I feel better; people around me are less confused, and so am I. So why tell anyone about my past? Why not just live the life of a normal man? Perhaps I could if I were a normal man, but I am not. I am a man, and I am a man who lived for 40 years in a female body. But I was not a woman. I am not a woman who became a man. I am not a woman who lives as a man. I am not, nor was I ever a woman, though I lived in a female body, and certainly tried, whenever I felt up to it, to be a woman. But it was never in me to be a woman. Likewise, I am not a man in the same sense as my younger brother is a man, having been treated as such all his life. I was treated as other than a man most of the time, as a man part of the time, and as a woman only rarely. Certainly I was treated as a little girl when I was young, but even then people occasionally assumed I was a little boy. I always felt like something 'other'. Can I be just a man now, or must I always be 'other'?

The tremendous sense of relief that transitioning men feel marks what is probably one of the most satisfying periods of their lives. While immense challenges arise during transition, and while there may be a sense of urgency to complete the process that can obliterate all other external concerns, the sense of growing into one's self—of really becoming who one is at last—is so rewarding that it may erase the long-standing pain of being misunderstood concerning one's gender. The transition itself opens so many windows on the gender system that we may be compelled to comment on our observations, which could not be made from any other vantage point than a transsexual (or sometimes transgender) position.

An even further irony is that once a man is no longer visibly transsexual—that is, once his previous androgyny has been transformed to unquestionable masculinity—he may no longer be of interest to the press. I have had reporters at public events look right through me when directed to me as an expert or knowledgeable source. They do not wish to interview me because I do not look like a transsexual. Only after they somehow find out that I am a trans person are they interested in me, and then not for my expertise, but for the tingling quizzicality they can enjoy while they stare at me, hardly hearing a word I say, and wonder how someone so male ever could have been a woman.

Seeking acceptance within the system of 'normal' and denying our transsexual status is an acquiescence to the prevailing binary gender paradigm that will never let us fit in, and will never accept us as equal members of society. Our transsexual status will always be used to threaten and shame us. We will always wear a scarlet T that marks us for treatment as a pretender, as other, as not normal, as trans. But wearing that T proudly—owning the label and carrying it with dignity—can twist that paradigm and free us from our subordinate prison. By using our own bodies and experience as references for our standards, rather than the bodies and experience of non-transsexuals (and non-transgendered people), we can grant our own legitimacy, as have all other groups that have been oppressed because of personal characteristics.

Transgendered people who choose transsexual treatment, who allow themselves to be medicalized, depend on a system of approval that grants them access to treatment. That approval may be seen as relieving them of their responsibility—or guilt—for being outside the norm. They then become either the justification for the treatment by embodying the successful application of 'normal' standards; or they become the victims of the treatment when they realize they are still very different in form and substance from non-transsexual people, and they still suffer from the oppression they wished to escape by looking to doctors to make them 'normal'. By standing up and claiming our identity as men (or women) who are also transpeople, by asserting that our different bodies are just as normal for us as anyone else's is for them, by insisting that our right to modify our bodies and shape our own identities is as inalienable as our right to choose our religion (though not nearly as inexpensive or painless), we claim our humanity and our right to be treated equally under law and within the purviews of morality and culture.

Gender and genitals comprise a stronghold of control binding all people to a social order that has serious difficulty tolerating diversity or change. Somebody's got us by the balls and they don't want to let go. Who is that somebody? Who is so afraid of losing control? What are they going to lose control of? What is preserved by denying the legitimacy of transsexual (and transgendered) people? What is destroyed by acknowledging us? Is it the right of succession? Is it the right to own property? Is it the ability to know whether to treat another as an equal, an inferior, or a superior human being?

In the introduction to the 1994 edition of *The Transsexual Empire*, Professor Janice Raymond postulates the reason why 'there are not as many female-to-constructed male transsexuals'. She writes that for women:

> the construction of gender dissatisfaction has been medicalized through promotion of breast implants, hormone replacement therapy, infertility hormones and reproductive procedures, and plastic surgery. (Raymond, 1994: xiv)

She also points out that:

> Maleness is not so easy to come by, especially because the majority of vendors (professionals) are males themselves and more discomfited in giving it away. (*ibid.*: xv)

These are very female-centred positions, and don't allow any space for variant opinions. Raymond states that the medicalization of transsexualism prevents the destruction of stereotypical gender roles and reinforces sexism (*ibid.*: xvii). It is Raymond herself (in collusion with some of the doctors she so vehemently objects to) who has put us into gender boxes. Her dogmatic insistence that it is impossible to change sex and that transsexuals never move beyond gender roles are blatant reactionary responses to what she perceives as threats to female bodies, feminism and feminist politics—everything upon which she bases her own identity concept. Raymond's brand of feminism cannot survive without rigid gender roles, and especially not without the objectification and vilification of men as actors in either male or female roles.

Bernice Hausman (1995) also takes on the medicalization of gender, asserting that transsexuals are expert at the arts of impersonation, producing gender as the real of sex, though gender does not 'exist' (Hausman, 1995: 193). She claims that transsexuals are unable to accept and accommodate themselves to the sexual meanings of their natural bodies, and the demand for treatment is made to accommodate a cultural fantasy of stable identity (*ibid.*). She even takes gender away from homosexual people by claiming that 'gender is a concept meaningful only within heterosexuality and in advocacy of heterosexuality' (*ibid.*: 194). Yet, as Judith Halberstam has pointed out, '. . . lesbians are also turned on by gendered sexual practices and restricted by the limiting of gender to bio-binarism'. (Halberstam, 1994: 225). Refreshingly, Halberstam states:

> The breakdown of genders and sexualities into identities is in many ways…an endless project, and it is perhaps preferable therefore to acknowledge that gender is defined by transitivity, that sexuality manifests as multiple sexualities, and that therefore we are all transsexuals. (*ibid.*: 226)

Halberstam goes so far as to say that 'There are no transsexuals'. And while I believe this last remark to be nobly intended, I must disagree with it if for no other reason than to acknowledge my own transformation. At least Halberstam's position gives us all individual voices. While Raymond wants us to take sides and rage against each other until someone dies, Hausman's effort to obliterate the discussion by dismissing the entire concept of gender renders us all speechless.

Gender is a form of communication, a language that we all use to express and interpret each other socially. For most practical purposes, however, the majority of our society have not learned how to separate sex from gender, and the use of the terms interchangeably (most commonly the substituting of gender for sex in an effort to avoid intimations of impropriety) only muddies the waters. The middle-of-the-road American sees a masculine woman or a feminine man, and he doesn't care who they actually sleep with. He's already figured out that they're queer, and he's ready to kill to protect mom and apple pie. The signifiers that matter are not necessarily the clothing, or the genitals (which are not visible), or the sex partner (who may not be present or apparent), but the qualities of character and non-genital physicality, as well as aspects of personal expression that may be cultivated or innate, that give the 'reader' an idea of the subject's masculinity or femininity, which the reader then may choose to apply to his understanding of the subject's maleness or femaleness, extrapolating further to define the subject's sexual orientation or activity. Thus gender is both expressed and interpreted, but it may not be interpreted as gender when the signals are mixed, that is when the body and the gender do not conform to the reader's expectations. Everyone uses gender to communicate, as much as we use our clothing, our posture, our vocabulary, our tone of voice. The fact that gender is problematic for some theorists as well as some transpeople is no justification for an attempt to mandate it out of existence.

Like Raymond, Hausman uses the fact of sex reassignment surgery as part of her argument against it, citing descriptions of surgery and post-operative pain in transsexual autobiographies. Hausman notes that the admission of pain serves 'to undermine the text's primary argument that the subject was really meant to be the sex he or she must be surgically fashioned into' (Hausman, 1995: 167). The implication is that if there is pain, then there is something unnatural about the body's situation. More faulty logic. Not all transsexual people experience undue pain with their surgeries. Not all non-transsexual people are pain-free, whether or not they have had any surgery. To embrace another two arbitrary extremes that can also co-exist in one physical body, both athletes and disabled people can attest to the pain that sometimes accompanies self-actualization. I don't see how the quality of being pain-free confers a greater veracity on a subject's experience.

Hausman says that to advocate the use of hormones and surgery in the service of gender identity: 'one must accede to the facticity of gender and its status as the master signifier of sex. In other words, one must believe in the simulation as real' (ibid.:193). The abstraction from broad experience that makes this kind of theory possible is reinforced by the exercises in self-justification that are most transsexual autobiographies (Denny, 1994).[1] The distance established by the printed page still allows most readers to perceive the transsexual subject as object, as less than human, or certainly dismissible. Rarely do transsexual people represent themselves as active agents in their own transformations. They are compelled to change. They always knew something was wrong. There's that binary thinking again: if something is wrong, it must be made right. Is it so surprising that transsexual people would seem to apologize for themselves in a world that has vilified and ostracized them?

What we need to understand, and why female-to-male visibility is necessary in order to bring the point home, is that what we experience is not something wrong, but something different. If Hausman sees gender as the mirage doppelgänger of sex, and sex as 'the real', she can have no context in which to comprehend those of us who experience our own reality differently. To me, my gender never was the signifier of my sex; my gender was, and is, the social expression of myself that I was unable to change to conform to the expectations others had of my sex. I tried hard to be a non-conforming woman. I believed the feminist line that biology is not destiny. Now I feel as if I'm being told by Gender Studies theorists that biology is not destiny unless you are transsexual. I cannot say that I was a man trapped in a female body. I can only say that I was a male spirit alive in a female body, and I chose to bring that body in line with my spirit, and to live the rest of my life as a man. Socially and legally I am a man.

And still, I am a different kind of man. I am not trying to encroach on the identities (or physical space) of women (so Raymond's argument holds no weight, especially her position that maleness is hard to come by). I am not worried about 'passing' for male or 'getting caught'. I am not concerned that men won't accept me, because my experience has been that they do. I am not worried about fabricating a past: I accept my past. I have continuity in my body, and the 'real of sex' for me is the way I express myself, as both a gendered and a sexual body.

Look! No, don't! Transsexual men are men. Transsexual men are men who have lived in female bodies. Transsexual men may appear feminine, androgynous or masculine. Any man may appear feminine, androgynous, or masculine. Look! What makes a man a man? His penis? His beard? His receding hairline? His lack of breasts? His sense of himself as a man? Some men have no beard, some have no penis, some never lose their hair, some have breasts. All have a sense of themselves as men.

Look! No, don't! Don't notice that I am different from other men unless you are ready to acknowledge that my uniqueness is the same difference that each man has from any other man. If transsexual men want to disappear, to not be seen, it is because they are afraid of not being seen as men, of being told they are not men, of being unable to refute the assertion that they are not men. All men fear this. In this way, all men—trans and non-trans—are the same. Many non-trans men have never thought about it because they have never had occasion to conceive of a situation in which their manhood would be called into question. But if they stop to think about it, I would venture to guess that all men would cling tenaciously to their self-concept as men, even if they lost their penis (though the loss of this unique organ would very likely be a serious threat to a man who had not examined his sense of self). One thing all men understand is that they are not women. This is also true for transsexual men, even though they have lived in female bodies. As soon as a transsexual man reveals his trans status, he is examined for vestiges of 'woman' that may then be used to invalidate his maleness, his authenticity, his reliability. Look! No, don't! What is true, what is false? What is a 'real' man?

I am real; I am an authentic and reliable man. I am also a transsexual man. I am a man who lived for 40 years in the body of a woman, so I have had access to knowledge that most men do not have. Invisibility has been a major issue in my life. Throughout my childhood and young adulthood I—my identity—was, for the most part, invisible. I was always defined by others, categorized either by my lack of femininity, or by my female body, or by the disquieting combination of both. The opportunity to escape the punishing inadequacy imposed on me by self-styled adjudicators of sex role performance was one I could not ignore. I simply will not accept a similar judgement of my masculinity. And I have yet to meet someone who could look me in the face, who could spend any time at all in conversation with me, who would deny my masculinity now the way they would dismiss it before as 'just a phase' or 'inappropriate behaviour for a girl'.

The fact is that the known biological aspects of sex difference—which we call natural and think of as immutable—are no more immune to change than the psychosocial manifestations of sex difference—which we call gender and cultural, and understand to be mutable (Hubbard, 1998: 46). One of the most difficult things for me to reconcile about my own transition was my movement out of a place in lesbian culture and into a white heterosexual embodiment. Let me emphasize: Not all transsexual men have lesbian histories, and not all transsexual men are heterosexual. Nonetheless, my personal politics are quite closely aligned with queer culture, so I am again a different sort of heterosexual man. I am not afraid of homosexuality, though I do not practice it. Many gendered and heterosexist social constructs collapse like cardboard sea-walls against the ocean of my transsexual reality.

Academics are afraid of being called essentialists,[2] but I am not afraid of saying that as an artist and as a human being I am motivated to express both the core and essence of my being-ness, and I will stand by the truth of my experience and the logic of my analysis. If phrases like 'male energy' are too vague and ethereal (Raymond, 1994: xxi), what are we to do with phrases like 'the real of sex'? My experience of myself, corroborated by other functioning, self-actualized adults (both heterosexual and gay and lesbian) who have known me much or all of my life, is that I seem far more comfortable to myself as a man, more 'natural', and more acceptable to them. Not that they didn't love or accept me before my transition to manhood, because they did. Some of them were resistant, even fearful concerning my change. But they rode the wave, and most of us have landed together, still friends, still relatives, still intrigued by the possibilities in life.

There: was that the self-justification part, or was it evidence, testimony on behalf of myself and other transsexual men? When I state the facts of my experience, listeners or readers get to choose whether or not the tone they perceive is one of self-justification. It all comes down to attitude. In my transition I lost only two friends. I have gained countless more since then. And I have learned something about responsibility, about duty, and about what civil rights really means. I've learned how discrimination really works, and how class, race, sex—and gender—distinctions are used to empower some and dis-empower others. I've learned that power is relative, while strength is internal. Before my transition I was just a middle-class white transgendered female, ostensibly a woman and therefore lesbian (in my sexual intimacy), trying to make my way in the world, climbing the career ladder, building my rela-tionships, enjoying my hobbies and pastimes, hoping that someday I would be recognized as a literary, musical, and photographic artist. During my transition I learned about shame, fear and hatred. I also learned what courage is. Since my transition I am just a middle-class white man, ostensibly male, who happens to be heterosexual (in my sexual intimacy), trying to make my way in the world, climbing my own career trellis, building my relationships, enjoying my hobbies and pastimes, working towards someday being recognized as a literary, performing, and photographic artist.

Look! No, don't! It all comes down to attitude. If you accept me–if you can acknowledge that I am a man, even a transsexual man— then you can accept that life has variation, life is rich, you don't control it, you experience it. You can still analyse concepts, you can still have opinions, you can even disagree with me. And if you don't accept me, well, then you don't. But as you go through life categorizing and qualifying, judging and evaluating, remember that there are human beings on the other end of the stick you're shaking, and they might have ideas and feelings and experiences that are different from your own. Maybe they look different from you, maybe they are tall women with large hands, maybe they are men who have given birth to their own children, maybe the categories you've delineated won't work in all cases. Look! No, don't! Transsexual men want to disappear because we are tired of being forced into categories, because we are beyond defending ourselves.

Look! No, don't! Transsexual men are entering the dialogue from more perspectives, more angles, than were ever theorized as being possible for them. Maybe if we are ignored we will go away. Maybe if we are continually not permitted to speak, not allowed to define ourselves, not given any corner of the platform from which to present our realities, then we will disappear and refrain from further complicating all the neat, orderly theories about gender and sex. Maybe if no one looks at us we will be safe.

At first I thought my transition was about not being looked at any longer, about my relief from scrutiny; now I know it is about scrutiny itself, about self-examination, and about losing my own fear of being looked at, not because I can disappear, but because I am able to claim my unique difference at last. What good is safety if the price is shame and fear of discovery? So, go ahead: Look!

NOTES

This chapter was written in 1996 and presented at the Second International Congress on Sex and Gender Issues, King of Prussia, PA, on 21 June 1997.

1. I must admit that I have not read many autobiographies by male-to-female transsexual people, but I have read every one published through 1996 (by commercial publishers) written by female-to-male transsexual people, and I have been almost uniformly disappointed to find that every explanation sounds like self-justification, like a liturgy of cause and effect, like rationalization, even when it's the truth. People doubt, people wonder. People who cannot imagine the experience transsexuals have will probably always think of it as something false or deluded. This is why I have found educational public speaking to be so effective: people have a direct experience of my physical presence and my gender expression, and it becomes true for them in a visceral way they do not easily dismiss or forget.
2. Raymond reacts against such charges (1994: xx–xxi).

REFERENCES

Denny, D. (1994) 'Review: two transsexual autobiographies', *Journal of Gender Studies*, Summer.

Halberstam, J. (1994) 'F2M: the making of female masculinity'. In L. Doan, (ed.), *The Lesbian Postmodern*. New York: Columbia University Press.

Hausman, B.L. (1995) *Changing Sex: Transsexualism, Technology, and the Idea of Gender*. Durham, NC: Duke University Press.

Hubbard, R. (1998) 'Gender and genitals: constructs of sex and gender'. In D. Denny (ed.), *Current Concepts in Transgender Identity*. New York: Garland.

35

Queering the Binaries

Transsituated Identities, Bodies, and Sexualities

Jason Cromwell

Writing as an anthropologist and as a female-to-male trans man, Jason Cromwell begins "Queering the Binaries" by reviewing the literature on transsexual sexuality, which he then critiques in reference to the lives of trans men and their partners. Cromwell uses qualitative research methods, including participant observation, to enable female-to-male transsexuals and their partners to speak for themselves. In doing so, his subjects reveal a range of complexities within the sexualities of FTM men.

Cromwell finds that trans men make conscious, strategic choices about how they address the apparent incongruities of their lives. They and their intimate partners frame for themselves what it means to be masculine, or to be a man. They often deploy socially normative concepts of manhood, which nonetheless become "queered" by the context in which they are used. In queering masculinity, Cromwell contends, many FTMs reverse conventional ontological processes to reconstruct the cultural boundaries that delimit their subjective experience, using language to assert a sense of self that can be grasped by others. The articulation of a transgender self-identity is an active and ongoing process that begins through apposite use of language, and may or may not ultimately involve a decision to modify the body through hormones and surgery.

Cromwell's book is one of the first academic studies by a trans man on trans men, and as such it offers insights and interpretations that have been largely inaccessible to other researchers. His work is especially useful in countering the distortions and silences often present when trans people discuss their sexual practices with non-transgender audiences.

"If I identify as an FTM, and if I have sex with a gay man who identifies as a woman, are we a straight couple?" asks Jack Hyde. For most people the answer to that question would be yes. But such a response would be superficial and limited to bodily configurations (i.e., a female-bodied person paired with a male-bodied person) and leave out the dynamics of trans-subjectivity. The "ontological premise" (Mageo 1995:284) of such a response is based on biological determinism. Transpeople and people with nonheterosexual identities queer the Western binaries of body-equals-sex-equals-gender-equals-identity as well as the binary of heterosexual and homosexual.

Jack's query was meant to bring into question these very binarisms. I have known Jack for more than a decade and have seen him shift from stone butch to FTM transsexual to transgender to amorphous shape-shifter to something else. Although he prefers to be referred to with male pronouns, he is also comfortable with female ones. In the final analysis, Jack is what Jack chooses to be, whenever and however he chooses.

If, as Steele asserts, "human sexuality is constructed" (1996:167), then construction sites that are left out of the picture or constructed as nonexistent are those of transbodies, transsexualities, and transidentities. This chapter will explore further the terrain of queering the binaries within transsituated identities, bodies, and sexualities. By "queering the binaries," I mean that they are made peculiar, seem bizarre, and spoil the effectiveness of categories.

Traditionally, both the homogeneous portrait and the etiological constructs were a moral discourse that proscribed and, too frequently still proscribes, how transpeople were and are to identify (including their personal histories) and how they are supposed to feel (past and present) and behave (past, present, and future).[1] Although nineteenth-century sexologists were concerned more with "aberrant" females than with males, once the "transsexual" category was established their vision became almost myopic, to the near-exclusion of female-bodied people.[2]

THE ETIOLOGICAL CONSTRUCTION OF FTMS AND TRANSMEN

> Transsexuals make a big scrap heap out of everybody's tidy life. If they can file us some place they are happy, but when they can't they are tormented.
>
> —Vern, cited in Martin 1992:104

Beginning with the first literature on transsexuals, specific characteristics, behaviors, identities, and sexualities have been attributed to them. All individuals were to have fit within these attributions, which became diagnostic criteria and were considered the etiological factors in the diagnosis of "true" transsexualism.[3] FTMs and transmen, if included at all, classically were described as having masculine behaviors and interests by age three or four. They were said to possess no femininity, be physically active and aggressive, and play only with boys' toys. They were described as inventing a male name by the age of seven or eight and openly stating a desire to be a boy and then a man. By adolescence they were insisting on being treated as, and dressing as, boys. They hated the onset of puberty, especially the development of breasts and menses. By adulthood they were passing as and being accepted as men and were employed only in masculine occupations. Furthermore, as children they were not considered beautiful or feminine by their parents. The mother was distant and depressed, and the father was masculine but unsupportive of the mother's depression. He did not encourage the child's femininity, whereas both parents encouraged the child's masculinity. FTMs and transmen were said to be attracted only to feminine, nonhomosexual females (Stoller 1972:48, 1973:386, 1975:223–27; see also Benjamin 1964, 1969; Ehrhardt, Grisanti, and McCauley 1979; Lothstein 1983; Money and Brennan 1968; Pauly 1974a, 1974b).

Clear distinctions were made between lesbians, masculine women, and FTMs and transmen (Ehrhardt, Grisanti, and McCauley 1979; Lothstein 1983; Money and Brennan 1968; Pauly 1974a, 1974b; Stoller 1972, 1973). Lesbians desired other lesbians, masculine women desired heterosexual men, and transmen/FTMs desired heterosexual women. FTMs/transmen avoided being touched or touching their own genitalia, whereas masculine women and lesbians did not (Pauly 1969:68, 76, 82).[4] Finally, transmen/FTMs wanted to be husbands and fathers but lesbians and masculine women did not (Lothstein 1983:27).

Regardless of their expressed desires, transgendered people in general—transsexuals specifically—were denied sexuality, and, by implication, so were their partners (cf. Whittle 1996:207). Medico-psychological practitioners insisted that "true transsexuals" had low libidos, were asexual or autoerotic, or were only able to engage in sexual relationships (homosexual or heterosexual) by using intense fantasies of themselves as women (if MTFs/transwomen) or as men (if FTMs/transmen).[5] They were also said to feel disgust and abhorrence for their sex organs (Benjamin 1977[1966]:27, 36).

Although many practitioners still maintain that is the case, by the late 1970s some, not all, were becoming aware that transpeople are sexual beings. Feinbloom, for example, recognized that MTFs not only identified as heterosexuals but also as bisexuals and as lesbians (1976:31). Stone, too, noted with some irony that "Benjamin's subjects did not talk about any erotic sense of their own bodies. Consequently nobody else who came to the clinics did either" (1991:291).[6] Benjamin's book 1977[1966] became the bible of transbehavioral characteristics. All subsequent published works by practitioners perpetuated the stereotype of transsexuals as nonsexual or as disgusted by sex and genitalia.

Some, if not most, transsexuals have been complicit in denying their sexuality. Most intentionally presented themselves to practitioners as if they fulfilled all the stereotypes in order to gain the services the clinics provided (Bolin 1988:64–65; see also Walworth 1997). As early as 1975, Stoller was aware of that complicity and noted, "Those of us faced with the task of diagnosing transsexualism have an additional burden these days, for most patients requesting 'sex change' are in complete command of the literature and know the answers before the questions are asked" (248). By the 1980s most practitioners assumed that all transsexuals "distort their autobiographies" and "tend to be less than honest about their personal histories" (Lothstein 1983:46, 160). Nonetheless, they continue to use the same diagnostic criteria.

Although only a few gender identity clinics still exist, some clinics and numerous private practitioners continue to withhold hormones and deny surgeries if a transperson identifies as gay or lesbian (pre- and post-transition); is incapable or unwilling to pass as "normal" and nontransgendered; refuses to behave or dress in stereotypical ways; and does not want complete sex reassignment or states they want some surgical procedures but not all (Denny 1996:40).[7]

TRANSSUBJECTIVITIES

What is oppressive in our society is the linking of biological sex (female or male) to gender identity (woman or man).

—MacGowan 1992:318

As a "dynamic map of power" the moral discourses both constitute and erase, deploy and paralyze transsituated identities, bodies, and sexualities (Butler 1993:117). Based on limited case studies, practitioners, as gatekeepers, determined what constituted a "true transsexual." Transsubjectivities were defined and subject to control by moral discourses. Gatekeepers elevated and regulated transidentities (cf. Butler 1993:117), forcing those who did not and could not take those positions to seek elsewhere. "My pretransition 'presentation' was pretty feminine," observes Arthur Freeheart. "My life-style, as full-time parent, was pretty 'female.' All the gender professionals I've dealt with have said they never met an FTM like me. So they were rather reluctant to take me seriously or think that I had much of a chance of being perceived as male. My struggle to get hormonal and surgical alterations was made much more difficult by that." Despite his difficulties with clinicians, Arthur now successfully lives as a man.

Both FTMs/transmen and MTFs/transwomen were treated similarly. At another clinic, Margaux was told that she would "have trouble passing" and was rejected as a candidate for hormones but the clinicians would help her accept herself as a homosexual. When she protested that she was not a homosexual she was told, "We're not here to negotiate! You've heard our terms. Take them or leave them" (cited in Denny 1992a:15). Identities framed within a medicalized border effectively negated individual identity and erased those whose histories, identities, bodies, and sexualities did not fit within the criterial boundaries of "true transsexual."

Furthermore, identity as a transperson was to be paralyzed and erased, left in an operating room, whereupon, following recovery, a "new man" or "new woman" was to emerge. "That treatment [hormones and surgeries] is supposed to make us feel normal. We are not supposed to want attention as transsexuals; we are supposed to want to fit in as 'normal' men. We are supposed to pretend we never spent fifteen, twenty, thirty, forty plus years in female bodies, pretend that the vestigial female arts some of us never lose were never there. In short, in order to be a good—or successful—transsexual person, one is not supposed to be a transsexual person at all" (Green 1996:7). Consequently, a "true" transidentity was constituted and deployed as legitimate only if the individual either denied they had ever been a transsexual or had ever identified as such—one had to become normal (i.e., heterosexual and identify solely as a male/man or a female/woman).

Although normal should be in the eye of the beholder, frequently it is a moral command: "Normal does not mean what people do, on the average, but what they ought to do" (Money 1986:4). Medico-psychological practitioners and the literature they generated were (and still are to a large extent) moral discourses with "ethical prescriptions" that tell transsexuals how they should behave in order to receive the diagnosis of transsexual (Mageo 1995:285).

What the clinicians fail to realize is that "identifications are multiple and contestatory" (Butler 1993:99). Butler discusses the power positions that disallow non-normal (i.e., nonheterosexual) identities and identifications. From a legal standpoint (and possibly from her philosophical perspective) such positions are illegitimate. In everyday life, however, the non-normal occurs with great frequency. Although those in positions of power continually try to erase subject-positions outside of what is viewed as culturally legitimate (and consequently normal and viable), people who live those subject-positions continue to attempt to articulate them. As they find their tongues, they subvert the concept of identity and the binary construction of bodies, sexes, genders, and sexualities.

IDENTITIES SUBVERSIVE

> I'm sort of fluid, and it varies with who I'm with.
> —Vern, cited in Martin 1992:105

Although the moral discourses perpetuated by the medico-psychological practitioners have attempted to prevent the articulation of transidentities outside their prescribed borders, transpeople have persisted. Unable to articulate or "expunge the censured dimension of the sel[ves] from 'their' behavior[s]" (Mageo 1995:291) or from the realities of their lives, transpeople have begun to develop other discourses. "For the record," says Del La Grace Volcano, "I see myself as FTM. 'Inter' rather than 'trans' sexual. Though this hardly matters in terms of how I am treated. I see myself as BOTH (male and female) rather than NEITHER (male nor female). In my case, the two add up to something non-numerical. I am simply gender-variant."

Transidentity in some cases is "an identity distinct from male and female—a combination of the two *plus* everything excluded by them" (Roscoe 1995:449, emphasis in the original). Transgender and transsexual are genders that exist outside the binary of two. That has become more evident since more and more individuals are retaining the labels, and subsequently the identities, of transpeople, however they may define themselves. Grace (1996:60) has said, "I call myself a 'hermaphrodyke' for now, which I like to think of as my own custom gender blend. . . . I see myself as BOTH male and female; 'either/or' rather than 'neither/nor.'" And, as I have observed to someone asking about how I define myself,

> I don't know that I've ever really felt like a man. I'm not even sure I, as a transperson can feel that way. I [did] not have most, if any, of the experiences that boys growing into manhood have. I am most comfortable and really only able to present to the world as a man. I am not comfortable, although I'm probably

capable of, presenting as androgynous. It was, and still is, impossible for me to present as a woman. I do not identify as a man. I identify as an "other," as a transman. What I've come to realize over the years is that regardless of what others think of me, whether I take hormones or not, I am what I am. For appearances sake, I am a man. But I'm not an ordinary man. Never could be and never will be.

What we both have expressed is the awareness that we are not like other men. Many transpeople acknowledge that their histories, identities, bodies, and sexualities are different from nontransgendered men and women. Their partners also recognize the difference.

I don't find all FTMs attractive. There are those still stuck in a state of arrested penis envy—you know, "If I just had a penis, I'd be a real man and all my problems would be over." Those guys are defining themselves and their masculinity from the outside in—they're letting the outside world be their judges. What I find incredibly attractive and sexy are those FTMs who have defined themselves from the inside out. They've integrated into their personalities everything about themselves that "fits" them and the hell with what *you* think. To me, these guys are the essence of masculinity. (Bonnie C.)

I'm attracted to the yin/yangness—polarity is sexy to me. TSmen have an otherness, a differentness, that I like. (Amy H.)

Transsituated identities disrupt the binary notions of male and female as opposites.

I certainly don't fit the "man trapped in a woman's body" or any other stereotyped idea of what a "real transsexual" is like. I'd be just as bored with being a manly man all the time as I was being a girly girl. Truthfully I look much better in hot pink sheer tops now than I did as a girly girl. (Joshua Goldberg)

I don't force myself to identify with one or the other but explore both my male and my female sides. It is okay to feel/be male with a feminine side. I think that what makes me/us so special is that we are aware of both sides of our persona and we can express them. (Chris K.)

Disruption occurs because an individual is capable of articulating an identity founded upon both/and as well as neither/nor and either/or.

BODIES SUBVERSIVE

> Gender *per se* is not the problem.
>
> —MacGowan 1992:318

For convenience sake, most transpeople present to the world as men or women. Although passing as nontransgendered is almost always a reflection of identity, it is also safer than presenting as gender-ambiguous or androgynous. After all, "fitting in is less work than dealing with the fallout from not fitting in" (Vern, cited in Martin 1992:109). Consequently, passing also includes being erased as transgendered. "For transsexual men who self-identify solidly and nonproblematically as men, and especially if they don't self-identify as FTMs or as trans," C. Jacob Hale observes, "I would guess that there's no sense of erasure in 'passing' as a non-ts man, indeed that they would not think of it as 'passing' at all but rather just showing the world who they really are. That's not me, though."

However much they may pass, transpeople, whether they identify as trans or not, are always aware of their transness—an awareness situated in their bodies.[8] "I cannot say that I was a man trapped in a female body. I can only say that I was a male spirit alive in a female body, and I chose to bring that body in line with my spirit, and to live the rest of my life as a man" (Green 1996:18). Transpeople, especially those who take hormones and have had surgeries, are aware that their bodies are or have been transsexed or reconstructed. As I have written to a correspondent,

> At one point, I recall thinking seriously about buying what was then a popular slogan t-shirt for pregnant women. It read, "under construction" with an arrow pointing downward. I was entering the first-stage of a three-to four-stage groin-flap phalloplasty. My body, at least my genitalia, at that time, was under construction. Prior to that surgery I had a bilateral mastectomy to remove my breasts. I had my chest reconstructed into a more male-appearing one.
>
> Surgeries allowed me to reconstruct my body, just as bodybuilding allows me to construct my body. Surgeries allowed removal of parts or the addition of parts. Bodybuilding is a similar removal and addition. Removal of fat, addition of muscle. The point is my body has been constructed to better suit my self-image as a man.

According to Butler, "Thinking the body constructed demands a rethinking of the meaning of construction itself" (1993:xi). Technology, whether surgical or hormonal, has enabled transpeople "to exert control over the body" (Boddy 1995:135) and to reconstruct them, albeit within the parameters maintained by medico-psychological practitioners. "I think FTMs who do hormones and, perhaps, surgical alterations end up with inter-sexed bodies." Arthur Freeheart has said, "whether they want to or not. But if you SAY you want an intersexed body, it's next to impossible to get professional support and services."

Many, if not all, practitioners will refuse to perform surgeries on anyone who does not declare a desire for all the procedures. In practice, many transpeople, especially FTMs and transmen, do not return for all of the surgeries deemed necessary for complete sex reassignment. "The phalloplasty was not successful," Jack Watson reports, "and I did not proceed past the first stage. This left me with a pedicle flap penis that has no sensation and is non-erectile, that is, it is a nonfunctioning penis (although it does function as a pants-filler). Over the years I've thought about having it removed, but it has become a part of me." Or people stop short of having surgeries at all. "I'm a guy without a dick," Mitch G. says. "I have a vagina. That's my reality. I don't think anyone could truly relate to me as a woman even seeing me naked anyway. I don't look like a woman and I don't act like a woman."

The body is the site on which individuals "erect a reliable sense of self" (Boddy 1995:135). Those who choose nonsurgical or limited surgery routes use their sense of self, their experiences, and their bodies to determine what is normal rather than the senses of self, the experiences, and the bodies of nontransgendered people (cf. Green 1996:12).

Nontransgendered people can and do have transsituated perspectives when it comes to the bodies of their partners.

> My partner has a dick. He isn't "missing" anything—he has a complete, wonderful, sexy body. (Bonnie C.)

> I am very comfortable with his body. Sometimes I forget that male bodies can look any other way. (Amy C.)

> Prior to his having surgery I had no problem with him having breasts.
> After surgery I realized that I had a veil in my mind, it acted as a filter. After surgery the filter was no longer necessary. His chest was now in reality what it had always been in my head. (Kristen K.)

Many transpeople and many of their partners reconstruct transbodies as both normal and different. To acknowledge transbodies as normal is a disruption of the binary body-equals-sex.[9] What is disrupting is the pairing of opposite-sexed parts in one body. A normal transbody may well have both a penis and breasts. Another normal transbody will bear the marks from chest surgery, and a penis may not be present but an enlarged clitoris (probably renamed) may be.[10] A woman, that is, can be other than female-bodied and a man can be other than male-bodied. "I feel that I have a great deal of choice in how I express my gender and that I am blessed rather than cursed," observes Del La Grace Volcano.

Another disruption occurs in the binary of feminine and masculine. "I can't identify with the cultur-ally normative notions of male or female," says Justin M. "But I id[entify] as male, because to me there is a big difference between being considered female with a strong masculine side and being considered male with a strong feminine side. I am not a butch woman. I am a feminine gay man." Contrary to the medico-psychological practitioners (and many others within mainstream Western society), these bodies (and experiences and identities) are not wrong. They are different (cf. Green 1997:18).[11]

SUBVERSIVE SEXUAL DESIRES

> The body's structure, physiology, and functioning do not directly or simply determine the configuration or meaning of sexuality.
>
> —Vance 1989:7–8

Because transsituated identities and bodies are different, sexual desires likewise defy the binary of heterosexual and homosexual and play havoc with the concept of bisexual. These "categories and terms always assume a nontransgendered paradigm—nontrangendered people's subjectivities and embodiments are always the reference points for these categories" (Hale 1997b:39). By attempting to fit everyone into a nontransgendered paradigm, medico-psychological practitioners have attempted to desexualize transpeople.

Within the narratives made available through the medico-psychological literature (and, for that matter, through published autobiographies), both MTF and FTM transsexuals are disgusted by and hate their genitalia, and, by implication, sexual acts of any kind are considered equally disgusting and abhorrent. Some theorists go beyond making implications and state emphatically that "disgusted by their genitals, transsexuals masturbate rarely and indulge less in sexual relations with others" (Stoller 1975:173; see also Pauly 1974:501).[12] As Arthur Freeheart says, "Sexuality is a subject that many gender professionals have problems with. It seems that having a sex life and/or being able to take pleasure in your own sexual feelings 'presurgery' is either seen as a 'cure' for gender discomfort or proof that you must not have enough body hate and body repulsion to be transsexual."

In fact, most clinicians have been dumbfounded by learning of transpeople using genitalia for sexual reproduction. Regarding an FTM/transman, Lothstein stated incredulously, "What was remarkable was that Barbara was willing to allow herself to be penetrated, to enact the role of a woman and have sex with a man" (1983:103).[13] Many would be even more astounded by those who derive pleasure from genitalia, including vaginal penetration.

> I am one of those who "enjoy my cunt" but still see myself as male. I do not identify as a lesbian or a dyke. I am a sexual being and will be sexual with the organs I have. (Rich)

> I'll use the equipment I've got. To me, that's a sign of strength, of my manhood. (Mark Craig)

In most of the literature, FTMs/transmen are allowed sexuality, albeit a very limited one in which a heterosexual paradigm prevails. They supposedly are attracted only to "feminine, heterosexual women with no homosexual drives visible or present in history, women who desire pregnancy and motherhood, and who like male bodies" (Stoller 1975:224; see also Pauly 1969:72).

> After I fell in love with Jack I was confused for about a week. Then I decided I am a dyke in love with an FTM. I didn't fall in love with a gender, but with a person. (Kristen K.)

> Het[erosexual], bi[sexual], lesbian don't work. Nothing mainstream does. I'm an "other" lover. (Bonnie C.)

Just as medico-psychological practitioners assume that FTMs/transmen are attracted only to heterosexual, feminine women, they also assume that those women also identify as heterosexual.[14] It is possible that like FTMs/transmen themselves, their partners are complicit in perpetuating such beliefs.

Nonetheless, although it has recognized that transmen and FTMs have partners, most of the literature has denied them actual physical sexuality. Stoller asserts that FTMs/transmen are "cut off" from sexual pleasure because masturbation makes the individual aware "of the femaleness of the genitals, no matter how powerful the fantasies of being a male." Relations with women are also viewed as undesirable because only an abnormal (i.e., a lesbian) would want to touch a transman's/FTM's genitals. A heterosexual ("normal") woman would not want to do so and "would not be permitted to do so anyway" (Stoller 1973:387). Pauly, too, maintains, "Because they do not wish to be exposed as females, they avoid genital contact themselves. Their satisfaction comes in being accepted as men, and even after prolonged, intimate contact, their female partners are not aware of their *true* identities" (1969:86, emphasis added; see also Stoller 1972:48).[15]

"When I was being seen as a butch dyke I was stone in that the only contact my partners had with my genitalia was through the transference of pleasure my dildo could convey," says Spencer Bergstedt. "However, once I came out as male and my then-partner acknowledged that she saw me as male, it became much easier for me to allow myself the pleasure of relating to my genitalia." Counter to Stoller's claim that FTMs/transmen "make every effort to keep [their female bodies] secret" (1973:387), Kristen K. reports, "I go down on both cocks. I can suck his dick [dildo] off or I can suck off what medically would be his clit, but I see both of them as cocks."

According to the literature, both FTMs/transmen and MTFs/transwomen are reported to deny any homosexuality and to avoid contact with homosexuals because if homosexuals desire transsexuals they are announcing a preference for same-sexed (and concomitantly same-gendered) bodies. Such desire is viewed as a threat to the transsexuals' body image (Benjamin 1977[1966]:34; Stoller 1975:224). "With my current partner, the changes in my body due to the T[estosterone]—facial and body hair, chest surgery, etc—have been instrumental to me in feeling that she sees me as a man rather than as the butch dyke she used to know," Bergstedt notes. "The fact that my dick has grown (and for me, I use the terms dick, cock, neo-phallus—I don't call it a clit—but that's my choice—others choose differently) is more like a bonus."

Many FTMs and transmen before identifying as a transperson have (or have had) relationships with lesbian women. Some of these relationships survive the identity transition from butch dyke to transman/FTM. The female partners may or may not shift their identity from lesbian to straight or bisexual or queer woman.[16]

> I think of myself as more or less a dyke. But the word lesbian now seems too confining. Mostly I just think of myself as queer. Whatever I am, I ain't straight. (Amy H.)

> I have been a queer/lesbian. I'm viewed as heterosexual when I go out in the world, but I have always identified as queer. (Allie H.)

Not only do transmen and FTMs have relationships with lesbian-identified women but they also do so with men. Most clinicians remained unaware of this, however, until the late 1980s. For example, Stoller declares that FTMs/transmen are "repelled by the idea of sexual relations with males" (1973:386), and Feinbloom hesitantly states, "I am unaware of any female to male transsexuals who consider the possibility of male homosexuality" (1976:31).

> I look for men who I describe as fluid in their sexual orientation. The men I've had the most fun with are the men for whom their identity, their orientation, is not an issue. (Harrison, cited in Nataf 1996:33)

> If a guy wants to be with me because he likes my looks *and* my parts, then why should it bother me? I also don't think that it makes a guy "ungay" because he likes being with one of us. Attraction is on many levels with genitals being only one of those. (Mitch G.)

Men, whether they identify as straight, gay, or bisexual, are attracted to FTMs/transmen and have sexual relations with them.[17]

> I met a handsome man who I wanted to get to know. Then I was told that he is not just a man but an FTM man. He is still the same attractive and quality person I met. (Gabriel M.)

> The hot, sexy wetness when my FTM partner is turned on makes my knees weak (and other things strong)! I also love to get fucked once in awhile, but I'm not too fussy about what device is used. Feels the same either way. (Erik K.)

Transpeople also have sexual relationships with other transpeople.

> I am a transman (FTM) in a relationship with another transman. I am an FTM who has not, as yet, had surgery. [My lover] sees past what I see in the mirror every day. We utilize every body part, nothing is off limits. We are two men exploring all the possibilities that we can with each other. (Anderson 1997:23)

> What is it when a transfag and a transdyke get together and make magic together with their bodies and hearts? It's beauty and delight and peacefulness and excitement and . . . . Whatever else it is, it isn't lesbian or gay or bisexual or heterosexual, because all of those miss the crucial fact that his transsexuality and queerness, her transsexuality and queerness, are a major part of what gets them together in the first place and keeps it fun and exciting and hot and lets it pass into beauty. (C. Jacob Hale)

Contrary to Califia's view (1997:217), such relationships are not strategies for avoiding the problems inherent in having relationships with nontranspeople, nor do they make passing more problematic. They are one of the multiple ways in which transpeople have relationships.

> With a heterosexual man I can be their best nightmare fantasy in the shape of a boy hustler. With a heterosexual woman I can be a pretty hetero male; or if I perceive her as a fag hag, I can be a faggot with bi tendencies. With a lesbian top femme I can be a high heel worshiping boy bottom or a third sex butch, a lesbian man. With a gay man I can be a cock worshiping catamite or a fisting top. With gender ambiguous bi men and women and sexually ambiguous transgendered people maybe I can just be myself. (Nataf 1996:32)

These strategies or constructions are "queer gender play," within which the people involved commit to what Hale refers to as a "recoding":

Genitals, sex toys, voices, body shapes, and much more, are recoded in ways fairly commonly understood within these worlds, and specific recodings, even ones unusual within these worlds, are fairly easily communicated between two sex partners. This kind of recoding only works when the recoding of a specific element of gender categorization is done in concert with recodings of other specific elements of gender categorization in such a way as to produce an internally consistent whole, understood and allowed—not disrupted—by both partners.

As descriptive truth, then, this view works by creating a culture of two (or more) in which the elements of the dominant cultural gender categorizations are not ignored but reorganized. (1995:16)

Transsexualities are grounded within a paradigm that uses transsituated language to express multiple ways of being identified, of being embodied, and of being sexual.

TRANSSITUATED STRATEGIC DISCOURSE

> We can't be whole, balanced people if we are living a lie.
>
> —Green 1994b:8

Transpeople's acknowledgment of identities, bodies, and sexualities as different rather than wrong is the creation of strategic discourse. Those take what was defined as wrong, whether bodies, identities, or sexual desires, and reframe them as different based on experience. The reframing is a subversion of the dominant paradigm and its discourses. Part of the reframing occurs in the renaming of body parts, or in framing them with mental veils, or in having body parts reconstructed to match mental images.

My use of the term *reconstructed* is deliberate. Transpeople both construct and reconstruct their bodies, identities, and sexualities. Through medical interventions body parts are added on (e.g., breast implants and some genitoplastic procedures) and subtracted or relocated/repositioned (e.g., vaginoplasties [vaginal reconstructions], chest constructions, and other genitoplastic procedures). But long before medical interventions may occur most transpeople have constructed and reconstructed their bodies in many different ways. For some, the construction is a process of disassociation and disconnection. That construction has been viewed by medico-psychological practitioners as a mentally disordered process labeled *gender dysphoria,* although more accurate terms would be *body dysphoria* or *body-part dysphoria.* These constructions and reconstructions, at least the stated desire for them, are made the chief criteria for diagnosis as a transsexual. Most medico-psychological practitioners still view transpeople as needing, and being obsessed with, surgical interventions.

"THE PROBLEM—NO PENIS"

The problem as stated in the subheading—and the attitudes the statement reveals—infuriates many FTMs and transmen.[18] For them, not having a penis is not a problem because what they do have, no matter how configured, are fully functional genitalia that give them and their partners great pleasure. The problem is the attitude that without surgically constructed penises they are not real men or even able to be categorized as such. The prevailing attitude (and what constitutes a further problem) is the reduction of maleness to specific genitalia (Rubin 1996:175). "One of the things that was really hard for me," recalls C. Jacob Hale, "was that I knew I didn't fit classical definitions of 'transsexual' and I didn't think I had much interest in genital surgery. What helped me a lot was to stop asking 'What am I?' and to start asking instead, 'What changes do I need to make to be a happier person?' For me, that included testosterone and elective breast removal/chest reconstruction."

Transmen and FTMs (as well as the transwomen and MTFs who also see the surgical imperative as a problem) realize that reconstructing their bodies is not what makes them a whole person. For them, all things carry equal value: body, identity (spiritual, as well as personal and social), and sexuality. That is the reconstruction—reassociation and reconnection with the body—whereby a transperson becomes a whole person.

Medico-psychological literature is inevitably presented with practitioners' subjective perspective but is presented as objective, leaving false impressions of what transpeople were or could be or want to be. So long as medico-psychological practitioners control the discourses about transsubjectivity, and as long as transsexuals remain complicit, the binaries remain seemingly intact. Once transpeople begin articulating their own transsubjectivities, however, new discourse, and thus the expansion of binaries, can begin.

Transsituated discourses are produced by transpeople whose identities, bodies, and sexual desires fall outside of the dominant discourses and even outside of the available lesbian and gay discourses. Available discourses are inadequate because they "cannot communicate about our gendered sexual desires and practices" (Hale 1996:118n8). "Maybe it's so far beyond our words that we don't know how to talk about it," Hale says. "Maybe male and female provide the parameters or limits or constraints, embedded as male and female are in our bodies and subjectivities. But maybe the core is that our distance from male and female, painful and alienating though our distance can be at times, lets us get at something more bound up in being human, lets us touch the purely human places in one another in ways specific to our transness."

Transsituated discourses reverse ontological premises. While such premises try through moral discourse to "condemn alternative experience to obscurity" (Mageo 1996:291), transsituated discourses begin the process of reordering the order of things (Foucault 1970). By articulating their experiences and identities, by affirming their bodies as their own and as viable, and by revealing their sexualities, transpeople and their partners disallow themselves "to be distorted," "consigned to silence," or prejudicially interpreted. "It's not the act or the partner, it's the identity," says Mike Hernandez. "For instance, sex involving a penis penetrating a vagina is not determinate of orientation. If it's a straight man and woman and that's how they identify, it's het[erosexual] sex. If the penis happens to be a dildo and the parties happen to be dykes, it's lesbian sex. If it's a gay man and a transfag, it's gay sex. If it's a fag and a dyke, it's queer sex."

Everyone has an identity and a body and—to paraphrase Erchak (1992:55)—anyone is sexy. The possibilities open in unexpected and multiple ways. For many within the mainstream of society, the reordering of things and the expression of that reordering in transsituated discourses are threatening and subversive. Nonetheless, transsituated identities, bodies, and sexual desires exist and will continue to queer the binaries.

NOTES

1. The etiological factors sound suspiciously like those postulated for lesbianism over the course of the history of homosexuality. For example, Stoller states that all types of masculinity in females (including butch lesbians, masculine women, and FTM/transmen) are caused by a mother who is distant during the child's infancy and childhood; the mother does not encourage the child's femininity; and the father, if present, encourages the child's "masculine" behaviors and activities (Stoller 1973:391; see also Pauly 1974a:497–98).

2. For example, Benjamin (1977[1966]) has one chapter of thirteen pages; Stoller (1975) includes one chapter with twenty-one pages; and Green and Money (1969) have three chapters (sixty-four pages) devoted exclusively to FTMs/transmen. It would not be until Lothstein (1983) that an entire volume would be purportedly about that topic. An additional fourteen years would pass before another would appear (Devor 1997).

3. MTFs/transwomen classically were described as devoid of masculine behavior and interests. They are thought to have had feminine behaviors since early childhood and to be pretty children. They are commonly dressed in girls' clothing

by an important family member (usually the mother). They talk of wanting to be a girl. They are smothered by their mothers, whose husbands are passive and barely present. Their physical body is a source of great discomfort, and they want surgery to turn them into women (Stoller 1975:74).

Clear distinctions were made between effeminate homosexuals, transvestites, and transsexuals. Homosexuals were said to wear female clothing as parody or to attract other homosexual men; transvestites are believed to be erotically excited by women's clothes; and MTFs only wear such clothing as an expression of their identity. Homosexuals and transvestites are comfortable in male roles, MTFs are not. Transvestites are employed in masculine endeavors; their behaviors, mannerisms, and other gender cues are masculine when cross-dressing is not involved. MTFs/transwomen are employed in female occupations and are feminine in attire; they also have feminine behaviors and mannerisms. Homosexuals and transvestites develop masculine identities, MTFs/transwomen do not. Homosexuals and transvestites alternate between masculinity and femininity, MTFs/transwomen do not. Homosexuals and transvestites are effeminate, MTFs/transwomen are feminine. Homosexuals desire other homosexuals as partners, transvestites may be bisexual but are usually heterosexuals married to women. MTFs/transwomen desire only masculine, heterosexual males as partners. Homosexuals and transvestites like and want their own penises, MTFs/transwomen do not (Stoller 1975:130–47).

4. Clearly, Pauly (and presumably others as well) did not know about stone butches.
5. Although a few practitioners still deny transpeople sexuality (cf. Denny 1996:40), attitudes began to change during the late 1970s and early 1980s. The shift appears to have occurred when practitioners began to realize that some transsexuals changed their sexual preference (Bullough and Bullough 1998:21).
6. The majority of practitioners and most of the early research on transsexuals took place within gender identity clinics (Lothstein 1983:83).
7. The first gender identity clinic was established at Johns Hopkins University in 1965–66 (Bullough and Bullough 1998:20; Denny 1992b:10). During the late 1960s and early 1970s, more clinics were started at university medical schools (e.g., the University of Minnesota, University of California at Los Angeles, University of Virginia at Charlottesville, and University of Washington, and at Vanderbilt, Stanford, Case Western Reserve, and Duke Universities). Eventually, there were at least forty clinics in the United States and Canada (Denny 1992b:10). Although many transpeople went for treatment, most clinics were research-oriented and considered transsexualism and treatments related to it experimental. Most were staffed by medico-psychological practitioners who were seldom trained in sexuality but were interested in research (Denny 1992b:11–12). Clinics began closing following the closure of the Johns Hopkins Clinic in 1979. Those which survived (there were fewer than twelve in the late 1990s) are no longer affiliated with universities (19).
8. This is the case no matter what. How else can one explain the existence of an Internet list closed to non-FTM/transmen and to transmen/FTMs who identify as transgendered? Members of this exclusive list are female-to-male transsexuals who do not want nontranspeople to know they are transsexuals yet feel the need to talk with others who have the same or similar experiences and the same desire to be closeted. While lurking I have observed individuals deny that they were ever female, even to the point of denying that their families treated them like girls. I have also seen statements such as "I was transsexual, now I'm just a man" and "I had a female body, now I have male body." Those who post to the list insist that being trans was or is unimportant. As such it is hard to fathom why they join other Internet lists as well as bulletin boards and chat rooms. What is ironic about their presence in these venues is their insistence that they must cease being trans and go into the world as "just men," which they seem incapable of doing.
9. Whittle (1996:205) argues that transpeople not only challenge the crossing of morphological boundaries but also challenge the notion that boundaries ever really existed.
10. See Hale (1997a) for a discussion of the renaming of body parts.
11. Cameron's book of photographs (1996) is testimony to the increasing visibility of transpeople (especially transmen/FTMs).
12. I have never heard an FTM or a transman express disgust or repulsion for their genitalia. I have heard mild expressions such as "didn't like" or "don't like" and that they "don't belong" or "aren't mine." These are hardly expressions of revulsion or disgust, however.
13. This example also serves another purpose in that it illustrates how adamantly some clinicians were in maintaining sex and gender paradigms as well as reifying the body. Lothstein (as did many others) refused to use his clients' preferred names or pronouns. He (as do others) also strongly maintains that transsexuals or anyone who presented themselves to a clinic as such suffered from a "disorder of the self-system involving an early childhood developmental arrest, disturbances in ego functions, and stemming primarily from borderline personality and narcissistic disorders" (1983:10).
14. Stoller asserts (1972:48n2) that FTMs/transmen's partners had prior failed heterosexual relationships and none of the partners enjoyed penetrative sex. He also claims that nonlesbians would reject FTMs/transmen, whose bodies are female. FTMs/transmen would be able to find lovers only among lesbians but would be rejected by them as well (Stoller 1973:386). Unfortunately, too many FTMs and transmen believe that to be the case.
15. Pauly's (and others) framework reifies the body such that the true identity is, of course, the body.
16. The word *queer* is used as an encompassing term for anyone who does not identify as heterosexual. Many avoid the term and use lengthy expressions such as "lesbian, gay, bisexual, transgendered, and friends" (LGBTF) (cf. Queen and Schimel 1997:19).
17. Specialized terms have arisen for nontranspeople who are attracted to and have sexual relations with transpeople: *trannytrollop, t-bird, transhag, transfaghag,* and *trannyhawk.* The latter term has a negative connotation and refers to men who fetishize and prey upon MTFs/transwomen.
18. "The Problem—No Penis" was a slide presented by Donald Laub, a plastic surgeon, during the First FTM Conference of the Americas, August 1995, San Francisco (see also Rubin 1996 and Hale 1997a).

36

selections from

"Spoiled Identity"

Stephen Gordon's Loneliness and the Difficulties of Queer History

HEATHER K. LOVE

IN "SPOILED IDENTITY," HEATHER LOVE re-examines Radclyffe Hall's celebrated and notorious novel, *The Well of Loneliness*, and its central character Stephen Gordon, in light of recent developments in queer and transgender studies. While paying careful attention to the different ways that Hall's work has been both claimed and disavowed by lesbian as well as transgender audiences and critics, Love focuses on the difficulties inherent in contemporary attempts to reclaim a "queer" heritage, as identity categories shift across the terrains of history and memory, and as different affective responses to queerness fall in or out of favor.

Love usefully summarizes and comments on the arguments of three recent critics of Hall's novel—Teresa de Lauretis, Judith Halberstam, and Jay Prosser, all of whom examine the meaning of Gordon's melancholic "female masculinity." Whereas de Lauretis sees Gordon's gender dysphoria as a form of Freudian fetishism, a longing for her "lost" femininity, Prosser finds the roots of Gordon's unhappiness in a thwarted transsexual desire for male embodiment; Halberstam understands Gordon's misery to be the product of neither feminine lack not masculine failure, but rather of society's inability to recognize and accommodate masculinity in a female form.

Love argues that while Stephen Gordon's masculinity has recently received overdue critical attention, interpreters of Hall's novel have continued to misrecognize Gordon's feelings of inadequacy, longing, and shame. Since the rise of a homosexuality-affirming Gay Pride discourse in the 1960s, she argues, such negative feelings have been relegated to a pre-liberation period, and their salience for the present disavowed. Love contends that without the painful recognition of shameful continuities between characters like Stephen Gordon and contemporary queer identities, we cannot fully come to terms with the role of shame in supporting and sustaining the homophobic social oppression of queer difference. The rhetoric of celebrating diversity gets us only so far, she claims; we must also risk looking back, and not avoid experiencing the grief of what we may see there.

I sometimes have a queer feeling, I think: "Something very like this has happened before." The nasty things must not be repeated though.

— Radelyffe Hall to Evguenia Souline, 30 July 1937

"Those who are failures from the start, downtrodden, crushed—it is they, the weakest, who must undermine life among men."[1] Nietzsche's diatribe against the "born failure" in *The Genealogy of Morals* anticipates a common reaction to the heroine of Radelyffe Hall's 1928 novel *The Well of Loneliness*.

A few months after the novel's obscenity trial, a verse lampoon titled *The Sink of Solitude* appeared, mocking the fate of "pathetic post-war lesbians."[2] The following year Janet Flanner, writing more coolly in the *New Yorker*, quipped that Hall's "loneliness was greater than had been supposed."[3] From the moment of its publication, readers balked at the novel's melodramatic account of what Hall called "the tragical problem of sexual inversion."[4] But the readers who have reacted most adversely to the novel's dark portrait of inverted life are those whose experience Hall claimed to represent. *The Well*, still the most famous and most widely read lesbian novel, is also the novel most hated by lesbians themselves. Since gay liberation Hall's novel has been singularly out of step with the discourse of gay pride. One reader, voicing a common reaction, said that she "consider[ed] this book very bad news for lesbians."[5] According to a model of readerly contagion not unlike the poisoning effect of ressentiment that Nietzsche traces in the *Genealogy*, Hall's account of Stephen Gordon's life is a depressing spectacle that must undermine life among lesbians.

With its inverted heroine and its tragic view of same-sex relations, *The Well* has repeatedly come into conflict with contemporary understandings of the meaning and shape of gay identity. During the 1970s the novel was attacked primarily for equating lesbianism with masculine identification; in the years of the "woman-loving-woman" its mannish heroine, its derogation of femininity, and its glorification of normative heterosexuality were anathema. While the recent recuperation of butch-fem practices and the growth of transgender studies have sparked renewed interest in the book, Hall's embrace of the discourse of congenital inversion is still at odds with the antiessentialism of contemporary theories of sexuality. The dissemination of the Foucauldian notion of "reverse discourse" has also led some critics to reconsider Hall's embrace of the language of inversion, but for many, such revisionism fails to exonerate the novel. Though Hall does make congenital inversion "speak in its own name," her use of the term cannot absorb the stigma associated with this medical discourse. In this sense, *The Well* might be said to give reverse discourse a bad name.[6]

Behind such arguments over the novel's ideology one senses discomfort with the extreme sadness of *The Well*. Its association with internalized homophobia, erotic failure, and a stigmatizing discourse of gender inversion has allowed the novel to function as a synecdoche for the worst of life before Stonewall. So accepted is the link between *The Well* and this history of suffering that critics have found it convenient to refer to the "self-hating Radclyffe Hall tradition."[7] In her influential article "Zero Degree Deviancy" Catharine Stimpson takes *The Well* as the primary example of the tradition of "the dying fall," which she defines as "a narrative of damnation, of the lesbian's suffering as a lonely outcast." Such a narrative, Stimpson writes, "gives the homosexual, particularly the lesbian, riddling images of pity, self-pity, and of terror—in greater measure than it consoles."[8] Stimpson's attention to the text's "riddling" effects on the reader is typical of responses to the novel. Many readers understand Hall's dark portrait of lesbian life as not only an effect but a cause of lesbians' difficult history. Thus Blanche Wiesen Cook, writing in 1979, fantasized about what it would have been like to grow up not having read *The Well*: "Unrequited love, tearful abandonment, the curse of it all might never have existed."[9]

* * *

THE TURN TO SHAME

One of the central paradoxes of queer studies is that its dreams for a better future are founded on a history of suffering, stigma, and violence. Like any transformative criticism, queer historiography always has a somewhat hostile relationship to the past it takes as its object. "Oppositional" criticism opposes not only existing structures of power but the very history that gives power meaning. Opposing the past does not mean dispensing with it; insofar as the losses of the past motivate us and give meaning to our current experience, we are bound to memorialize them ("We will never forget"). But we are equally bound to overcome the past, to escape its legacy ("We will never go back"). Negotiating this double bind has proved difficult for queer critics and historians, who have worked to preserve the past even as they have turned to face the political future.

* * *

A QUEER FEELING

In a discussion of Nietzsche, Foucault draws a distinction between curative and redemptive approaches to history: "The purpose of history, guided by genealogy, is not to discover the roots of our identity, but to commit itself to its dissipation. It does not seek to define our unique threshold of emergence, the homeland to which metaphysicians promise a return; it seeks to make visible all of those discontinuities that cross us."[10] The redemptive approach to history is informed by a need to shore up our own identity in the present; it is thus a close relative of what I have called affirmative history, which seeks to confirm contemporary gay and lesbian identity by searching for moments of pride or resistance in the past. A curative approach to history, by contrast, seeks out the "discontinuities" in the past in order to disrupt the stability or taken-for-granted quality of the present.

The spectacle of Stephen Gordon's "spoiled identity" can function as just such a discontinuity. In her experience of suffering, her self-hatred, and her romantic failures, Stephen is the opposite of a role model for contemporary readers. She is not who we want to be; she represents more nearly what we fear becoming. Because it interrupts their affirmative identificatory responses, readers might think of *The Well* as queer, as effectively countering (or crossing) the consolidation of gay and lesbian identity in the present.

Analyzing the production of such powerful disidentifications with the queer past, Christopher Nealon argues for the importance of historical affect both in twentieth-century texts and in our reaction to them. Nealon suggests that the "activity of reception is a kind of organic historiography" and adds that "affect is not only historical (of course it is), but... historiographical:... our feelings, characters' feelings, and our feelings about characters' feelings are themselves theories of history:... thinking about homosexuality as a kind of historiographical-theoretical labor, produced in and through feeling, gets us further than thinking about homosexual 'identity.' "[11] Nealon stresses the importance of attending to the representation of negative affects in such "outmoded" texts. In such encounters we find the clues to understanding the social, corporeal, and affective difficulties of queer existence.

Nealon implies that attention to the feelings that queer texts from the past inspire may help contemporary critics turn their focus from identity to the history of queer experience. Yet identity's "dissipation" is not quite the same as its disappearance. Nor does queer criticism aim to "do away" with identity in any definitive sense. The critique of identity in queer theory has often been misunderstood as a diatribe against identity. It would be a mistake to think that we can do away with the discourse of identity altogether. Nor can we ignore the powerful identifications that bind us to the spectacle of Stephen Gordon's suffering. But such identifications are always partial, ambivalent, and mixed.

While the historical situation of "people like Stephen" has changed radically since the publication of the novel, the continuity between this earlier "shameful" moment in queer history and our own has yet to be accounted for by queer criticism. Thinking through our partial, ambivalent identification with Stephen's suffering might offer us a way to reckon with the difficulties of queer history. We cannot use Stephen's history in any straightforward sense, because it is a history that has "gone bad." But the very spoiling of identity turns our critical attention to the experience of queer subjectivity, both in the past and in the present.

One sign that we have not fully encountered the difficulties of the past is that we do not have ready to hand a critical vocabulary for describing the destitutions and embarrassments of queer existence.

Yet *The Well* itself offers a stunningly rich account of such experiences. Critics of *The Well* have paid little attention to Hall's careful account of Stephen's experience; instead, they have sought to unmask the novel's various ideologies of misogyny and homophobia. While such critiques are important, they have deflected attention from the novel's representation of homophobia and feeling. As Althusser reminds us, it is impossible to remove ideology from the realm of experience: "When we speak of ideology we should know that ideology slides into all human activity, that it is identical with the 'lived' experience of human existence itself."[12] In Stephen, critics encounter the image of a queer subject who lives out ideology's effects in a particularly painful way; the novel is unrelentingly specific about this experience. *The Well* offers a meticulous account of the outrages, failures, and disappointments that attend gender and sexual nonconformity in a homophobic world.

In her portrayal of Stephen's loneliness, then. Hall offers us a study of a complex, historically specific structure of feeling. In *Marxism and Literature* Raymond Williams defines the latter term as follows:

> We are talking about characteristic elements of impulse, restraint and tone; specifically affective elements of consciousness and relationships: not feeling against thought, but thought as felt and feeling as thought: practical consciousness of a present kind, in a living and interrelating continuity. We are then defining these elements as a "structure": as a set, with specific internal relations, at once interlocking and in tension. Yet we are also defining a social experience which is still in process, often indeed not yet recognized as social but taken to be private, idiosyncratic, and even isolating, but which in analysis (though rarely otherwise) has its emergent, connecting, and dominant characteristics, indeed its specific hierarchies.[13]

While Williams proposes that the term *structure of feeling* may have special relevance for literature, it has also proved crucial for queer studies, in which the analysis of uncodified subjective experiences is an important supplement to the study of the history of formal laws, practices, and ideologies. The saturation of experience with ideology is particularly important to queer critics, because the ideologies of homophobia and heterosexism do so much of their work on the level of experience. Thus there can be no antihomophobic inquiry without sustained attention to the intimate effects of homophobia. We are used to discussing shame only as a sign of false consciousness, but a queer analysis of shame is crucial, because quite often shame is the modality in which homophobia is lived. Hall's abject portrait of pre-Stonewall life is far from useless; rather, in describing Stephen's loneliness, Hall offers us insight into how homophobia is lived out as a social, affective, and corporeal reality.

While loneliness is a traditional feature of twentieth-century gay novels, it is normally closely associated with the condition of being in the closet. For Hall, loneliness only secondarily has to do with the condition of "having a secret." Judith Halberstam notes in this connection that Stephen's extreme visibility in the novel displaces questions of sexual secrecy and knowledge: "Stephen Gordon in no way lives her life as an open secret, and she in fact represents the unmistakable visibility of female sexual perversion when it appears in male clothing."[14] The novel is studded with incidents recounting Stephen's painful visibility in public.[15] As a result, loneliness in the novel is not primarily a question of epistemology but one of ontology. It afflicts Stephen's being; it is deeply inscribed in her body. Rather than be contained by the closet, Stephen attempts to work out the difficulties of her vexed being, but she is thwarted. Loneliness in the novel is literally about being alone, about being an exile, about bearing a stigmatized identity. But at the same time it describes a condition of singularity, of occupying an unprecedented and uncharted place in the order of creation. Hall understands loneliness as a state of desolation, a deeply felt psychic and corporeal state of abandonment, refusal, and loss. It describes not only a way of life but a social experience insistently internalized, felt to be both essential and permanent.

Critics tend to regard Hall's deployment of the discourse of inversion as a mistake or an unfortunate consequence of her historical situation. But this essentialist discourse was extremely useful to Hall in her attempt to articulate loneliness as a structure of feeling. In the novel Stephen's intimate and social alienation is underwritten by an ideology of failure. Loneliness is an effect of her experiences of public and private refusal; Hall traces how social experiences line up with the discourse of inversion and become sedimented in both the psyche and the body. In adopting this medical model of difference, Hall can describe the way that negative social experiences are somatized. Stigma, though a social experience, appears to emanate, as if naturally, from Stephen's body. Thus, as her experience of refusal becomes part of the intimate landscape of the self, Stephen takes up the burden of representing larger social losses for those around her.

INTOLERABLE BIRTHRIGHT

Stephen Gordon is a disappointment from the start. Hall describes her existence as an aberration, one of nature's mistakes; she underlines her difference by framing Stephen against a background of conventional perfection. The novel opens with a view of Morton, the family estate where Stephen is born:

> Not very far from Upton-on-Severn—between it, in fact, and the Malvern Hills—stands the country seat of the Gordons of Bramley: well-timbered, well-cottaged, well-fenced and well-watered, having, in this latter respect, a stream that forks in exactly the right position to feed two large lakes in the grounds.
>
> The house itself is of Georgian red brick, with charming circular windows near the roof. It has dignity and pride without ostentation, self-assurance without arrogance, repose without inertia; and a gentle aloofness that, to those who know its spirit, but adds to its value as a home. (11)

The appearance of this well-appointed estate in the first sentence of *The Well* establishes a central contrast. While the stream "forks in exactly the right position to feed two large lakes," the disturbing split in Stephen's gender renders her neither fully masculine nor fully feminine. Her gender transgression results in an incompleteness ultimately unassimilable by the world of Morton. Thus in this novel of dispossession Stephen will lose much more than a house; the loss of Morton comes to stand for the crushing psychic effects of exile.

Hall's conservatism and nationalism are evident in her lament for the perfection of "such an homestead" (11).[16] *The Well* mourns the personal and social losses that all inverts face because of society's hatred of them: not the least of such losses for Hall, however, was that of class privilege. What Stephen stands to inherit, besides Morton, is the sacred trust of the aristocracy: she, like her father, is fair-minded, honorable, and generous; she acts perfectly the part of the country gentleman—scholar, sportsman, and lover of nature. Barred from her inheritance both by her sex and by her gender nonconformity, Stephen is forced into a life of bohemian wandering. In contrast to the uncertainties of her life in London and Paris, Morton remains the sign of absolute value, the privileged site of continuity, human connection, and moral rectitude. Its brick-and-mortar impassivity exists in an endless narrative present; it seems to watch over the rest of the novel. While Stephen uses her wealth to set up house elsewhere, her exile is clearly irreversible. Throughout *The Well* Hall describes inverts as radically unhoused: wanderers in the no-man's-land of sex, they are exposed to the unmitigated hostility of the "so-called normal" world (301).[17]

As the opening passage progresses, it seems less a description of an English country manor than an inverted portrait—a photographic negative—of queer subjectivity. With Morton, Stephen loses a way of life enabled by stability, permanence, and social acceptance. Her exile and subsequent public exposure lead to a split in her subjectivity. She becomes less expressive, stonier, as she attempts to provide in her person a substitute for the sheltering indifference of the house. But at the same time she is cast adrift, subjected to the shifting tides of emotion. Thus she loses access to feelings associated with Morton, "dignity and pride without ostentation, self-assurance without arrogance, repose without inertia." Though Stephen is not a purely desperate or lonely character—she experiences happiness, pride, joy, desire, and interest—she never approaches the tranquil self-respect that Morton projects. This deprivation is not without its pleasures: the novel is filled with descriptions of the voluptuous pride that Stephen takes in her appearance, her strength, and her abilities. But even at such moments the abyss of shame into which she regularly plunges is precariously near.

In her dispossession Stephen loses not only Morton but her parents, who initially seem as perfect as their house. Sir Philip is "exceedingly well-favoured," "a lover and a dreamer" (12); Lady Anna is the "archetype of the very perfect woman, whom creating God has found good" (11). Such exquisite beings are practically guaranteed conjugal bliss: "Seldom had two people loved more than they did; they loved with an ardour undiminished by time; as they ripened, so their love ripened with them" (12). In the midst of this perfection, however, a note of yearning is retroactively introduced by Stephen's conception: "Sir Philip never knew how much he longed for a son until, some ten years after marriage, his wife conceived a child; then he knew that this thing meant complete fulfilment, the fulfilment for which they had both been waiting" (12). While Sir Philip and Lady Anna once seemed to provide each other with complete happiness, the promise of a son rewrites the history of their marriage as a time of waiting for, rather than possession of, fulfillment.

Without considering that his firstborn might be a girl, Sir Philip names the child after Saint Stephen and dreamily maps out his heir's education and upbringing. Lady Anna suppresses her misgivings in deference to her husband; in time, she too begins to fantasize about playing with this phantom son in the meadows surrounding their house. When Stephen turns out to be a girl, their only consolation is ultimately a bitter one: though biologically female, Stephen bears the impress of her parents' desire. This "wide-shouldered, narrow-hipped tadpole of a baby" (13) is born with a significant strain of masculinity, which only becomes more apparent with time. Stephen's arrival heralds not Sir Philip and Lady Anna's "complete fulfilment" but a reign of incompleteness, discomfort, and loss in their lives. Thus Stephen is a kind of supplement, a third term that exposes what is lacking in their union.[18]

As if to manifest the logic of the supplement, Stephen arrives as a failed or imitation boy. Lady Anna brings forth not the perfect copy of her husband that they both desire but what she calls "a blemished, unworthy, maimed reproduction." Stephen closely resembles Sir Philip—her sensitive mouth, auburn hair, and hazel eyes are his—but she exaggerates the signs of physical lack in him, for instance, the replica "tiny cleft in her chin, so small that just at first it looked like a shadow" (13–14). Each outward resemblance between father and daughter reinforces Lady Anna's disappointment over the difference between them. Though she tells herself that she ought to be "proud of the likeness," her child appears to her a caricature, an imitation "most unnatural and monstrous" (15).

Though bitterly disappointed that his wife has borne him a daughter, Sir Philip never expresses his anguish openly. Seeing Lady Anna's grief, he "hid[es] his chagrin" (13) and insists that they call the child Stephen anyway. He raises her as a boy, encouraging her to ride astride, hunt foxes, lift weights, and read Greek; without question or comment, he comforts her on the many occasions when neighbors, playmates, servants, and her mother laugh at or deride her cross-gendered appearance. Sir Philip takes pleasure in Stephen's "masculine" qualities, denying both her female body and the problems that her gender nonconformity causes her, and she incorporates her father's pride in her masculine pursuits and his belief that she is part of nature. His protestations that she is, in her own way, perfect anticipate Stephen's self-justifications; over and against the evidence of monstrosity, she too will insist that she is part of nature's scheme.

The novel suggests that Stephen has inherited from her parents not only her strange gender identity but her great capacity for negative feeling. Her childhood is permeated with sadness from the outset. Immediately following the birth,

> Anna Gordon held her child to her breast, but she grieved while it drank, because of her man who had longed so much for a son. And seeing her grief, Sir Philip hid his chagrin, and he fondled the baby and examined its fingers.
>
> "What a hand!" he would say. "Why it's actually got nails on all its ten fingers: little, perfect, pink nails!"
>
> Then Anna would dry her eyes and caress it, kissing the tiny hand. (13)

Stephen incorporates the feelings of scorn and disappointment that her mother feels for her in her youth; they surface later as intense shame and self-hatred. One might also trace Stephen's feeling of exclusion to her mother, who refuses to interact with her directly but instead routes her attitudes toward Stephen through her concern for Stephen's father. At the same time, Stephen inherits her mother's habit of grief; crying while she feeds her, Lady Anna initiates Stephen into a lifetime of suffering.

Stephen's sense of self is keyed throughout to a series of experiences of love granted and withdrawn. Lady Anna shrinks from her infant touch, and Stephen's most intimate experience is structured by this refusal. Thereafter Stephen finds it difficult to maintain a gendered sense of self. When her love goes unreciprocated, her gender inversion migrates toward abjection; with no one to perform her masculinity for, her loneliness becomes even more acute. In this sense, to be desired is, for Stephen, *to be*.

In her first traumatic encounter with failed romantic love, Stephen "enters…a new world" that turns "on an axis of Collins," the housemaid (18). To impress Collins, Stephen dresses up in the outfits of famous men from history, which leads "to much foraging in the nursery rag-bag, much swagger and noise, much strutting and posing, and much staring in the mirror" (19). The very possibility that her love might be returned sends Stephen into a frenzy of narcissistic self-display. Her confidence with Collins is impressive, as Stephen tells the house staff gravely, "Yes, of course I am a boy" (19). Through the powerful agents of costume, performance, and fantasy, Stephen effectively transforms herself into a cocky young man.

But Stephen's romance comes to a bitter conclusion when she sees Collins kissing Henry, the footman. For several days Collins has been ignoring her; finally, Stephen happens upon the pair in the garden, where "a really catastrophic thing" happens:

> Henry caught Collins roughly by the wrists, and he dragged her towards him, still handling her roughly, and he kissed her full on the lips. Stephen's head felt suddenly hot and dizzy, she was filled with a blind, uncomprehending rage; she wanted to cry out, but her voice failed completely, so that all she could do was splutter. But the very next moment she had seized a broken flower-pot and had hurled it hard and straight at the footman. It struck him in the face, cutting open his cheek, down which the blood trickled slowly. (28)

The passage, attentive to the roughness of the kiss, seems to mirror Stephen's perspective. Not only does the scene expose Collins's preference for Henry; it also offers Stephen her first glimpse of adult sexuality. Her position as unwanted third is paradigmatic: throughout the novel her desire is thwarted by a woman's turn toward a man. But her reaction to seeing this kiss in the garden is not simply a jealous one. Rather, she experiences the incident as a referendum on her very being. Collins has been indulging Stephen's belief that she is a boy: she has been an attentive audience for Stephen's performances and has flirted with her in an offhanded way. When Stephen sees Collins kiss Henry, her precariously constructed masculinity comes crashing down, and she throws a jagged piece of pottery at him, leaving a wide gash from which blood slowly trickles down his face. In this recasting of the primal scene, Stephen symbolically castrates the footman. At the same time, she identifies with him; the version of masculinity that she takes up in the scene operates under the threat of such a castration. In later life Stephen wears this threat emblazoned on her body, in the scar on her own cheek.

Immediately after this scene Sir Philip tells Stephen that he is going to treat her like a boy. Hall ends the chapter with a description of the quasi-contractual character of this shared disavowal of Stephen's gender. After Sir Philip tells Stephen not to speak to her mother about such incidents but to come to him instead. Stephen looks at him: "Sir Philip saw his own mournful eyes gazing back from his daughter's tear-stained face. But her lips set more firmly, and the cleft in her chin grew more marked with a new, childish will to courage. Bending down, he kissed her in absolute silence—it was like the sealing of a sorrowful pact" (29). While the scene with Collins has pointed up the tragic impossibility of Stephen's desires. Stephen here takes comfort from her father by adopting his strategy of fetishistic disavowal. Father and daughter mutually deny the fact that she is not a boy and that as a result, she will be systematically barred from erotic and affective satisfaction.

The apparent contrast that Hall draws between the Gordons' perfection and Stephen's freakishness does not hold up under scrutiny. Rather, Stephen seems to inherit the longing, the sense of incompleteness and lack, that her parents feel at her birth. By repetition Stephen magnifies the flaws of this "most perfect" family. When she finally leaves Morton, Stephen takes the sexological texts hidden in her father's study, "as though in a way they were hers by some intolerable birthright" (233). The novel suggests that this "intolerable birthright"—her patrimony of loss, lack, and grief—comes from both God and the Gordons.

DESOLATE BODY

Stephen's cross-gender identification is a particular site of shame and confusion for her and for her latter-day readers. In queer criticism her gender identity is the primary terrain where debates about her abjection or her sufficiency play out. With her avowed desire to be a man, her powerful gender dysphoria, and her romantic failure, Stephen represents the melancholic image of the butch lesbian that critics and activists have tried to overcome in recent years.

The stereotype of the melancholic butch—freak of nature, failed woman or failed man, rejected lover—is so powerful and so affectively charged that debates about cross-identification in queer and lesbian circles are often drawn irresistibly to it. Particular questions about Stephen's abjection center on her masculine identification and her desire to be a man. Such a desire is nearly taboo in contemporary lesbian discourse, though it has been addressed recently by transgender and transsexual critics. With the easing of phobic pressures on the figure of the masculine woman, critics have been more willing to accept and engage with Stephen's masculinity.

But even critics who have recognized Stephen's masculinity have consistently misrecognized her felt experience of inadequacy, longing, and lack. Reading Stephen retrospectively into happier narratives of cross-gender identification, these critics have failed to attend to Hall's descriptions of Stephen's intensely negative feelings. Their strongly idealist rereadings imagine a perfectibility belied both by Stephen's experience and by contemporary queer experience. An understanding of Stephen's loneliness is inseparable from an understanding of her aversive experience of her own embodiment.

Recent analyses of Stephen's experience of her body have turned on the novel's "mirror scene," first explored in depth by Teresa de Lauretis in *The Practice of Love* and later taken up by Halberstam and Jay Prosser. Returning home from a shopping trip, having been rebuffed by her lover Angela Crossby, Stephen contemplates her naked image in the mirror:

> Even as she did so she hated her body with its muscular shoulders, its small compact breasts, and its slender flanks of an athlete. All her life she must drag this body of hers like a monstrous fetter imposed on her spirit. This strangely ardent yet sterile body that must worship yet never be worshipped in return by the creature of its adoration. She longed to maim it, for it made her feel cruel; it was so white, so strong, and so self-sufficient; yet withal so poor and unhappy a thing that her eyes filled with tears and her hate turned to pity. She began to grieve over it, touching her breasts with pitiful fingers, stroking her shoulders, letting her hands slip along her straight thighs—Oh, poor and most desolate body! (186–87)

Stephen's confrontation with her own image proves intensely alienating. Unlike the child in Lacan's mirror scene, who sees an ideal or complete image, Stephen sees one that is aversive, lacking, and divided against itself. This "desolate body" exists for Stephen as an object of pity rather than of admiration.

De Lauretis, in her avowedly "perverse" reading, interprets the scene in terms of Freudian fetishism. Explicitly resisting the "traditional reading of Stephen's masculinity complex," de Lauretis locates in this scene a moment of Stephen's longing for the lost female body: "Because it is not feminine, this body is inadequate as the object of desire, to be desired by the other, and thus inadequate to signify the female subject's desire in the feminine mode; however, because it is masculine but not male, it is also inadequate to signify or bear the subject's desire in the masculine mode." Stephen's problem is not the absence of the phallus but, de Lauretis argues, the presence in her body of the paternal phallus, "which renders the female body (the mother's, other women's, and [her] own) forever inaccessible to Stephen."[19] What is essential in de Lauretis's theory of desire is to have a body that the mother desires.[20] Given the conundrum of Stephen's identity, de Lauretis proposes a theory of "lesbian fetishism," which describes how a lesbian fetish—"any object, any sign whatsoever, that marks the difference and the desire" (228) between lesbian lovers—substitutes for the phallus.

In *Second Skins* Prosser argues that every effort to read *The Well* as a lesbian novel has been "a case of trying to fit a square peg into a round hole." In "configuring inversion as a metaphor for homosexuality," he argues, "we have left out what sexual inversion in sexology and in Hall's novel are most literally about:…gender inversion, cross-gender identity." Prosser imagines gender inversion as a precursor to transsexual subjectivity, a longing for biological, psychic, and sexual transformation not yet medically available to the subjects in the case histories. Like Stephen herself, Prosser understands Stephen's gender trouble as "a failure to be real," her difficulties as a matter of "gender ontology" rather than social acceptance.[21] Prosser treats Stephen sympathetically, taking her descriptions of her experience at face value. By interpreting *The Well* as, in effect, a case history, Prosser avoids reading Stephen's experience as a question of "false consciousness" and provides a counterbalance to the dominant mode of response to the novel.

According to Prosser, de Lauretis's theory of lesbian desire erases Stephen's explicit, deep longing for masculinity. Prosser insists that "the mirror scene is not a moment of sexual perversion—the perverse desire of the mannish lesbian—but of sexual inversion" and that what Stephen sees in the mirror is "the inverted body of the pretransition female-to-male transsexual." For Prosser, the scene brings Stephen face to face with her ontological lack: the mirror shatters her illusion of her maleness and reflects back to her "the reality of her failure to be a real man."[22] Though Prosser's approach to *The Well* is important for countering dismissive or censuring responses to Stephen's masculinity, his literal interpretation of her desire "to be a real man" blinds him to the larger place of gender in the novel. Though Stephen understands herself as castrated or physically lacking, the people around her often understand her as *insufficiently* castrated, because she does not accede to a feminine role. Her mother seems most often outraged not by Stephen's failure to be a man but by her overt masculinity—her failure to be a "normal woman." In taking Stephen's self-description at face value, and in reading *The Well* as a case history of inversion. Prosser treats that self-description as if it were not inflected by ideology.[23]

In *Female Masculinity* Halberstam also critiques de Lauretis's failure to acknowledge Stephen's desire to be masculine. But Halberstam avoids Prosser's literalism and his understanding of gender ontology in the novel. For her, "social disapproval," not the lack of authentic (i.e., biological) maleness, causes Stephen's loneliness. Halberstam also takes issue with what she understands as de Lauretis's biologism. De Lauretis's theory of fetishism is itself an effort to explain how the female body can and does bear desire in the masculine mode; I understand de Lauretis to be describing Stephen's experience of her gender rather than making a definitive statement on the structure of female (masculine) desire. But Halberstam adamantly resists the notion that Stephen is lacking in relation either to femininity or to masculinity. She asserts that "nowhere... does the narrative even hint at... the inadequacy of Stephen's masculinity" and argues for the sufficiency of the female body to bear desire in a masculine mode.[24]

For Halberstam, the mirror scene is a sign not of Stephen's hatred of the sight of her body but of her disidentification with femininity and nakedness. In diametric opposition to Prosser's claim that for Stephen, "neither looking like nor feeling like constitute being," Halberstam argues that the novel is structured by an "epistemology of the wardrobe," "a dressing that is not exactly cross-dressing and that positions itself against an aesthetic of nakedness."[25] Through such means, Halberstam suggests, Stephen performs her nonontological but nonetheless satisfying and real female masculinity. Through Halberstam's reading is an important interruption of received notions about the sadness or inadequacy of the butch lesbian, it does not account for Stephen's constant and deep sense of lack. Even if Stephen feels like a loser because of social disapproval, she experiences her loneliness as a bodily lack. Halberstam's desire to affirm the possibility of successful and satisfying female masculinity draws attention away from Stephen's affective and corporeal experience.

Prosser suggests, finally, that it is the "repeated failure of lesbian relations more than any other feature that thwarts the attempt to read the novel as lesbian." Crucially, he acknowledges Stephen's lack and the pain associated with it, but he is able to do so, perhaps, only because he has another narrative in mind for her. Confronted with Stephen's ontological problem, Prosser suggests an ontological cure: the technological modification of Stephen's being. He takes the novel's failure to provide a happy lesbian ending as its failure to be a lesbian novel. (Might one also argue, then, that *Romeo and Juliet* is not about straight people?) Prosser further suggests that narratives that "don't quite fit, which exceed or resist their homosexual location... might find belonging in a transsexual context." Despite his understanding of Stephen's divided self and her difficulty in existing between sexes, Prosser assimilates her story to a redemptive narrative that, through the modern technology of sexual reassignment surgery, solves her problem in the present. Thus his own critical practice works in concert with the genre of transsexual autobiography, in which "all life events... seem to lead toward the telos of the sex-changed self. This gendered coherence is inextricable from the narrative coherence of the genre."[26] Prosser admits that such a tidy tale of progress is a back-formation, a kind of order possible only in retrospect, but that is precisely what allows him to rewrite Hall's novel as a body narrative of transsexuality.

Put off by the darkness of Hall's account of Stephen's gender trouble, each of these critics attempts to assimilate her narrative to a later, happier narrative of gendered existence. But Stephen is beyond the reach of such redemptive narratives. Throughout she struggles with the question of how to give and receive love, a question inseparable from the unresolvable nature of her gender identity. Stephen cannot steer a clear course between the masculine and the feminine; any attempt to resolve her sense of nonfit into a longing for either masculinity or femininity misses a crucial aspect of her experience. Of course these feelings are ideological, but they are also real. Stephen is doomed to experience her own body as essentially unlovable. In one sense, this failure is crushingly specific: it has everything to do with being a mannish woman in rural, quasi-aristocratic prewar England. Yet no change in circumstances would render Stephen perfectly happy or satisfied. Despite our present sense of expanding possibilities for gendered embodiment, the melancholia in Stephen's experience of herself is impossible to wish away.[27]

UNWANTED BEING

The relationship between gender formation and loss is at the heart of Butler's work on the melancholy of gender. In the introduction to *The Psychic Life of Power*, Butler underscores the crucial role of loss in subject formation and the assumption of gender:

> Is there a loss that cannot be thought, cannot be owned or grieved, which forms the condition of possibility for the subject? Is this what Hegel called "the loss of the loss"...? Is there not a longing to grieve—and, equivalently, an inability to grieve—that which one never was able to love, a love that falls short of the "conditions of existence"? This is a loss not merely of the object or of some set of objects, but of love's own possibility: the loss of the ability to love, the unfinished grieving for that which founds the subject.[28]

Butler considers "the loss of the loss" primarily in connection with her theory of heterosexual gender melancholia, in which she posits the foreclosure of same-sex attachments as the basis of normative gender identifications. This theory, which follows from Freud's reflection on melancholic incorporation in *The Ego and the Id*, allows Butler to consider the founding loss at the heart of both normative and non-normative gender identifications. Such an understanding of the tenuous nature of all gender identifications accords, as we have seen, with Hall's representation of gender identity in *The Well*; Hall repeatedly links Stephen's abject experience of gender to the gender anxieties and failures of the "so-called normal." But in *The Well* such anxieties, once activated, transform Stephen into a despised creature. We might think of Butler's attempt to resituate such losses at the foundation of normative gender identity as a way of easing the burden of stigmatization that attaches to people like Stephen.

Though she has considered the relationship between the performativity of drag and heterosexual gender melancholia at length, Butler hesitates to extend this theory to a description of cross-gender identification. As Butler herself points out, there is a risk in speaking of gender melancholia in relation to figures who are already so closely allied in the popular imagination with melancholia. Discussing the figure of "the melancholic drag queen," Butler writes:

> Where there is an ungrieved loss in drag performance (*and I am sure that such a generalization cannot be universalized*), perhaps it is a loss that is refused and incorporated in the performed identification, one that reiterates a gendered idealization and its radical uninhabitability. This is neither a *territorialization of the feminine by the masculine* nor an "*envy*" *of the masculine by the feminine*, nor a sign of the essential plasticity of gender. What it does suggest is that gender performance allegorizes a loss it cannot grieve, allegorizes the incorporative fantasy of melancholia whereby an object is phantasmatically taken in or on as a way of refusing to let it go.
>
> *The above analysis is a risky one* because it suggests that for a "man" performing femininity or for a "woman" performing masculinity (the latter is always, in effect, to perform a little less, given that feminin-

ity is often cast as the spectacular gender) there is an attachment to and a loss and refusal of the figure of femininity by the man, or the figure of masculinity by the woman. Thus, it is important to underscore that drag is an effort to negotiate cross-gendered identifications, but *that cross-gendered identification is not the exemplary paradigm for thinking about homosexuality*, although it may be one.[29]

In this passage one can hear Butler speaking back to a series of stigmatizing narratives about queer and transgendered people. She is anxious for her theory of gender melancholia to disrupt rather than reinforce the habitual association of cross-gender identification, homosexuality, and melancholy.

The narratives that Butler resists here sound strikingly like her own theory of gender melancholia. In her theory of blocked identifications there is a surprising and persistent echo of received understandings of the melancholy of both homosexuality and cross-gender identification. Butler's theory that gender is founded on loss and foreclosed desires chimes in particular with pathologizing descriptions of butch subjectivity. "The stone butch," as Halberstam writes, "has been characterized as more blocked, more lacking, and more rigid than all other sexual identities."[30] But rather than pursue the connections between the melancholic drag queen or the sad stone butch and her theory of gender melancholia, Butler explores the melancholia of all gender identifications, both normative and nonnormative. Her aim is a reversal of terms, so that heterosexual identifications will be understood as the most blocked, lacking, and rigid. "In this sense," she writes, "the 'truest' lesbian melancholic is the strictly straight woman, and the 'truest' gay male melancholic is the strictly straight man."[31]

While the political importance of her attempt to disrupt the association between cross-gender identification and melancholy is clear, Butler refuses to consider how gays and lesbians actually live out the melancholy of gender. Stephen's subject formation is a painfully slow-paced and explicit account of such an experience. In a crucial scene Hall describes Stephen's reaction, directly after she has been betrayed by Angela and lacerated by her mother for her "unnatural" desires, to another shattering experience of refusal:

> As though drawn there by some strong natal instinct, Stephen went straight to her father's study; and she sat in the old arm-chair that had survived him; then she buried her face in her hands.
>
> All the loneliness that had gone before was as nothing to this new loneliness of spirit. An immense desolation swept down upon her, an immense need to cry out and claim understanding for herself, an immense need to find an answer to the riddle of her unwanted being. All around her were grey and crumbling ruins, and under those ruins her love lay bleeding; shamefully wounded by Angela Crossby, shamefully soiled and defiled by her mother—a piteous, suffering, defenceless thing, it lay bleeding under the ruins. (203)

The study is a particularly charged site of meaning in the novel. Sir Philip has spent late nights there reading the books on inversion that he has locked away from his wife and daughter; later, when he is crushed under a tree, he is taken to his study to die, unable at the end to utter the secret that is so much on his mind. Stephen's occupation of the study in this scene underscores her continuing identification with her father and her disidentification with her mother—which is, according to the copy of Krafft-Ebing that she is about to discover, precisely her "problem." That Stephen is drawn to the study by a "strong natal instinct" indicates that her melancholy is not only a symptom of delayed mourning for her father but a preexisting structure of gender melancholia activated by his death and her mother's refusal. In addition, the scene's rhetoric of encryption evokes Stephen's melancholic incorporation of the image of her dead father. Her discovery of her secret nature in her father's study is apt, because it is there that he has brooded most over the image of Stephen's—and his own—failed masculinity.

Stephen's confrontation with her mother is a curious restaging of the oedipal crisis. While Stephen has desired her mother with relative impunity, it is only after the death of Sir Philip that Lady Anna herself forbids Stephen access to her. While the Gordon family scene reproduces the oedipal geometry—with Stephen in the starring role of son—Lady Anna's prohibition here runs counter to the oedipal logic of prohibition. The mother is not forbidden to Stephen on account of the taboo against incest; rather, Stephen here again encounters the foreclosure of a mode of desire. Lady Anna's "No" is articulated as a homosexual prohibition: she denies Stephen access to Angela and, by implication, to herself, telling Stephen that she has always been disgusted by her touch. But this homosexual prohibition is articulated primarily as a prohibition against gender inversion. "Above all," says Lady Anna, "this thing is a sin against the father who bred you, the father whom you dare to resemble" (200). The relocation of the homosexual prohibition in Stephen's gender identity anchors lack securely in her body, which readily produces itself as the site of loss and castration.

On the one hand, the difficulties presented by Stephen's loneliness are epistemological: she feels "an immense need to find an answer to the riddle of her unwanted being." But, on the other, with the resonant phrase *unwanted being* Hall underlines the ontological aspect of Stephen's loneliness. The phrase both describes the experience that she has just weathered—her rejection by Angela and her mother—and points to a more general social fact: Stephen bears an unwanted identity, a social subjectivity constituted by public refusal and scorn. Her public and private experiences of refusal are reinforced by the ontological language of inversion, the pathologizing discourse that renders her very being excessive. The word *unwanted* resonates throughout the novel, for it describes how personal rejections are internalized, so that they form the core of Stephen's being. A description of a transitory event becomes a fixed quality, an essential aspect of identity. Unwanted from birth, Stephen becomes an "unwanted being": it is her utter abandonment by all those who might have recognized or desired her that makes her loneliness so acute. Such an experience is dictated as well by a more general social logic. The refusals that Stephen undergoes follow from the assumption that she is unfit for love and life. Thus Lady Anna and Angela reject her as a matter of course. For Stephen, however, the sting of erotic rejection casts her even further into despair because it coincides with a general expectation of failed love.

Importantly, Hall stages Stephen's total abjection against a backdrop of "grey and crumbling ruins." Neither public nor private, this allegorical landscape figures the catastrophic collapse of the distinction between two spheres. Ruins stand in for the experience of refusal and for Stephen's ruined subjectivity. The landscape of ruins evoked in this passage recalls a moment from Butler's discussion of gender melancholia: "In melancholia, not only is the loss of an other or an ideal lost to consciousness, but the social world in which such a loss became possible is also lost. The melancholic does not merely withdraw the lost object from consciousness, but withdraws into the psyche a configuration of the social world as well."[32] In this scene Stephen's interior world is revealed as the site of just such a devastated social landscape. Significantly, Hall moves from a discussion of Stephen's self to a description of "her love": "A piteous, suffering, defenceless thing, it lay bleeding under the ruins." The antecedent to this *it* is buried earlier in the passage: in this final. uncanny moment, not only Stephen's love but Stephen herself is pinned under the ruins. Naming Stephen an it, Hall enacts her abjection linguistically, metamorphosing her into a piece of crushed flesh.

For queer subjects, the loss disavowed in heterosexual gender melancholia is lived as a real social and affective experience. Butler's speculation about the constitutive loss at the heart of all gender identifications resonates remarkably with the phenomenology of Stephen's "unwanted being." In the landscape of ruins surrounding her heroine. Hall offers an image of the crushing convergence of social, psychic, affective, and corporeal factors that determine Stephen's inability to be loved. Butler's project allows us to understand gender melancholia as a condition associated not only with nonnormative gendered embodiments but with gender as such. The antihomophobic charge of this project is undeniable. Yet such a project is incomplete without an account of what it feels like to live out the melancholia structuring all gender.

* * *

In charting our course by the lights of our forerunners, we are often tempted to disavow their suffering. We tend to read history according to the successes of the past and to see in its failures only ideology at work. Proceeding in the mode of affirmation, we construct a genealogy that steps from stone to stone, looking for high points of pride, gender flexibility, and resistance. Of course, such wishful thinking can be effective in bringing about political transformation. As Elizabeth Grosz writes in connection with feminism, "Any oppositional political movement...involves a disavowal of social reality so that change becomes conceivable."[33] But political change can happen not only through disavowing loss but also through cleaving to it.

We need a genealogy of queer affect that embraces the negative, shameful, and difficult feelings central to queer existence. We have been used to thinking of such affect as waste, the inevitable by-product of our historical tough luck. But as long as homophobia structures our public and private lives, and books like *The Well* continue to be so eerily familiar, we cannot do without an analysis of the intimate effects of homophobia. While it is painful to recognize our continuity with figures like Stephen Gordon, it is through such shaming acts of identification that we come to terms with the difficulty of queer history and its legacy in the present. Without such a reckoning we cannot remember history's failures or do justice to our own experiences. Celebration gets us only so far, for pride itself can be toxic when it is sealed off from the shame that has nurtured it.

In a recent essay Christopher Castiglia suggests that individual and collective acts of memory are central to queer existence. His argument captures the ambivalence of memory for queer communities, which are strengthened by acts of retrospection but often are burdened by a legacy of loss. "To look back," Castiglia concludes, "is, after all, to refuse the imperative laid down at the destruction of Sodom."[31] The significance of Castiglia's invocation of this story is made evident by the story itself: "Then the Lord rained on Sodom and Gomorrah sulfur and fire from the Lord out of heaven; and he overthrew those cities, and all the Plain, and all the inhabitants of the cities, and what grew on the ground. But Lot's wife, behind him, looked back, and she became a pillar of salt" (Gen. 19.24–26 NRSV). Lot's wife looks back on a scene in which all of her past attachments have been destroyed. In doing so, she refuses the imperative of the Law and responds instead to the call of what the Law has destroyed. The fear, of course, is that in looking backward, we will be paralyzed by grief, and grief will overwhelm politics. But grief is politics, to the extent that politics is inseparable from history.

NOTES

I would like to thank Laura Doan. Rita Felski, Jonathan Flatley, Susan Fraiman, Judith Halberstam, David M. Halperin, Eleanor Kaufman, David Kurnick, Derek Nystrom, Aoibheann Sweeney, and Bryan Wagner for their careful and engaged readings of this piece.
Originally published in *GLQ* 7:4 pp. 487–519. Copyright © 2001 by Duke University Press.

1.   Friedrich Nietzsche, *The Genealogy of Morals*, trans. Walter Kaufmann (New York: Vintage, 1989), 122.
2.   Quoted in Diane Souhami, *The Trials of Radclyffe Hall* (New York: Doubleday, 1999), 238.
3.   Janet Flanner, "Paris Letter." *New Yorker*, 4 October 1930, 84.
4.   Quoted in Souhami, *Trials of Radclyffe Hall*, 158.
5.   Quoted in Rebecca O'Rourke, *Reflecting on "The Well of Loneliness"* (London: Routledge, 1989), 127.

6. The reconsidering of Stephen's masculinity in *The Well* began with Esther Newton's groundbreaking article "The Mythic Mannish Lesbian: Radclyffe Hall and the New Woman," *Signs* 9 (1984): 557–75. In recent years Judith Halberstam's work (*Female Masculinity* [Durham: Duke University Press, 1998]) and Jay Prosser's transsexual reading of *The Well* (*Second Skins: The Body Narratives of Transsexuality* [New York: Columbia University Press. 1998]) have been crucial to this reassessment. Several critics in the 1980s began to rethink *The Well* in terms of Foucauldian reverse discourse: see esp. Newton. "Mythic Mannish Lesbian"; Sonja Ruehl. "Inverts and Experts: Radclyffe Hall and the Lesbian Identity," in *Feminism, Culture, and Politics*, ed. Rosalind Brunt and Caroline Rowan (London: Lawrence and Wishart, 1982), 15–36; and Jonathan Dollimore. "The Dominant and the Deviant: A Violent Dialectic," *Critical Quarterly* 28 (1986): 179–92.

7. Blanche Wiesen Cook, " 'Women Alone Stir My Imagination': Lesbianism and the Cultural Tradition," *Signs* 4 (1979): 721.

8. Catharine Stimpson, "Zero Degree Deviancy: The Lesbian Novel in English," *Critical Inquiry* 8 (1981): 364, 369.

9. Cook, " 'Women Alone Stir My Imagination,' " 719.

10. Michel Foucault, "Nietzsche, Genealogy, History," in *Aesthetics, Method, and Epistemology,* vol. 2 of *Essential Works of Foucault, 1954–1984*, ed. James D. Faubion, trans. Donald F. Bouchard and Sherry Simon (New York: New, 1998), 386–87.

11. Christopher Nealon, "Invert-History: The Ambivalence of Lesbian Pulp Fiction," *New Literary History* 31 (2000): 747.

12. Louis Althusser, *Lenin and Philosophy*, trans. Ben Brewster (New York: Monthly Review Press, 1971), 223.

13. Raymond Williams, "Structure of Feeling," in *Marxism and Literature* (Oxford: Oxford University Press, 1977), 132.

14. Halberstam, *Female Masculinity*, 98–99.

15. Whether Stephen "faces the guns of Bond Street" (165) or sits in a fashionable restaurant in Paris, her appearances in public are narrated as hostile stares and taunts ("Look at that! What is it?" [165]). Her neighbor, Ralph Crossby, annoyed at Stephen for hanging around his wife, comments casually, "That sort of thing wants putting down at birth" (151). Stephen's most intimate relations and friends reinforce her experiences of refusal. Her mother keeps her at a distance from earliest infancy and, having found out about her affair with Angela Crossby, seconds the world's opinion, telling Stephen that she would rather see her "dead at my feet than standing before me with this thing upon you" (200).

16. On Hall's conservatism see Laura Doan, *Fashioning Sapphism: The Origins of a Modern English Lesbian Culture* (New York: Columbia University Press, 2001).

17. "If I were asked to name the chief benefit of the house," Gaston Bachelard writes, "I should say: the house shelters day-dreaming, the house protects the dreamer, the house allows one to dream in peace" (*The Poetics of Space*, trans. Maria Jolas [Boston: Beacon. 1964], 6). Hall is likewise concerned with the protecting function of the house, but for her, the inwardness of dreaming is not the first priority. Rather, the house provides a vital link between the inward and the outward: it offers a publicness lined with and enabled by acceptable forms of domestic privacy. For Stephen, Morton signifies public acceptance and recognizability guaranteed by the institutions of property, inheritance, and social hierarchy. It also offers an intimate space in which the orderly domestic relations that such publicness presumes can flourish.

18. The distinction that Judith Butler elaborates between melancholia and narcissism aptly describes the gap between expectation and outcome that structures Stephen's birth. Butler considers Freud's formulation that in melancholia the shadow of the object falls on the ego; she then contrasts it with Lacan's understanding of narcissism, in which the shadow of the ego falls on the object. While in narcissism one encounters one's own plenitude in the object, Butler writes, "in melancholia this formulation is reversed: in the place of the loss that the other comes to represent, I find myself to be that loss, impoverished, wanting. In narcissistic love, the other contracts my abundance. In melancholia, I contract the other's absence" (*The Psychic Life of Power: Theories in Subjection* [Stanford: Stanford University Press, 1997], 187). While the Gordons understand their desire for a son as narcissistic, as a desire for a copy that will reflect their image, Stephen's birth recasts this desire as melancholic. The Gordons hope to transfer their plenitude to a son who is Sir Philip's mirror image; instead, they find themselves inscribed at the site of Stephen's loss: they contract her absence.

19. Teresa de Lauretis, *The Practice of Love: Lesbian Sexuality and Perverse Desire* (Bloomington: Indiana University Press, 1994), 212–13.

20. According to de Lauretis, Stephen can gain the mother's love only by satisfying her narcissistic desire for a daughter who is feminine. But there is no reason that the mother's desire for Stephen should work exclusively along such lines. Several factors in *The Well* broaden the spectrum of the mother's desire for Stephen: her prenatal expectations of a boy, Stephen's chivalrous attitude toward her mother, and her close resemblance to her father. Part of what makes Lady Anna's attitude toward Stephen so difficult is that she fluctuates between disappointed desire for Stephen as a daughter and outraged and ambivalent desire for her to be a son.

21. Prosser, *Second Skins*, 168, 161–62.

22. Ibid., 161.

23. Stephen's very longing for masculinity has disturbed feminist critics since the novel's publication. Vera Brittain, who valued Hall's representation of the experience of the inverted, nevertheless criticized her "overemphasis of sex characteristics" in the novel, arguing that she had confused the distinction between "what is 'male' or 'female' or what is merely human in our complex make-up." Brittain's 1928 review in *Time and Tide* is reprinted in Brittain, *Radclyffe Hall: A Case of Obscenity?* Halberstam, *Female Masculinity*, 104.

24. Prosser, *Second Skins*, 161; Halberstam, *Female Masculinity*, 99.
25. Prosser, *Second Skins*, 166, 168, 116.
26. Thanks to Rita Felski for thinking through this question with me in connection with her work on tragic women.
27. Butler, *Psychic Life of Power*, 24.
28. Judith Butler, *Gender Trouble: Feminism and the Subversion of Identity* (New York: Routledge, 1990), 235; emphasis added.
29. Halberstam, *Female Masculinity*, 112.
30. Butler, *Gender Trouble*, 235.
31. Butler, *Psychic Life of Power*, 181.
32. Elizabeth Grosz, *Space, Time, and Perversion: Essays on the Politics of Bodies* (New York: Routledge, 1995), 153.
33. Christopher Castiglia, "Sex Panics, Sex Publics, Sex Memories," *boundary* 2 27, no. 2 (2000): 175.

37

Transsexuals in the Military
Flight into Hypermasculinity

GEORGE R. BROWN

IN THIS ARTICLE, U.S. AIR FORCE PSYCHIATRIST GEORGE BROWN seeks to explain his clinical findings that the military has a greater incidence of male-to-female transsexualism than the general population. He argues that many MTF individuals seek refuge from the initial distress associated with their transgender identification by pursuing hypermasculine careers.

Transsexual adults in Brown's empirical study reported that they became aware at a very young age of the stigma attached to transgender phenomena, and consequently denied, suppressed, and kept their transgender feelings secret for as long as possible. Brown observes that many male-to-female transsexuals use negative reinforcement to conceal their feelings, and to support their own rejection of these feelings. Many take up vocations—such as military service—that are broadly perceived as masculine, and make commitments to the social role of "man"—such as becoming a husband or father—that are subsequently difficult to alter. In doing so, they find a temporary relief from their gender distress but also create a series of obstacles that delay the eventual resolution of their conflict through a process of gender transition.

Based on this interpretation of his data, Brown suggests that the distinction drawn in much of the clinical literature between "primary" transsexuals (who persistently express transgender feelings and behaviors from an early age) and "secondary" transsexuals (who make a gender transition later in life) is not related to the strength or authenticity of transgender feelings, but rather to individual ability or opportunity to act on those feelings.

To be a boy is to be macho, to have weapons, to be a fighter, and to kill, at first in play, then maybe later in a war. (Money, 1980)

INTRODUCTION

The concept of hypermasculinity, described in part by Money in the quote above, has been variably described throughout this century as "make-believe masculinity" (Fenichel, 1945), "masculine protest" (Adler, 1923/1955) "macho personality" (Chodoff, 1982), and "Man's Man" or "Ladies' Man" (Glass, 1984). Hypermasculinity has multiple facets with sexual and gender implications and inventories have been developed to assess its features (Mosher and Sirkin, 1984). Characteristics include foolhardiness, overcompetitiveness, bellicosity, fragile hardiness, and equations of "violence as manly" and "danger as excitement" (Glass, 1984; Mosher and Sirkin, 1984).

Cultural factors are important in a consideration of hypermasculinity, as the term may have inappropriate, judgmental connotations depending on its usage. Masculinity itself is not a unitary construct;

the line separating mature masculinity from hypermasculinity can be drawn in different places on a continuum of male gender roles depending on cultural context. Role behavior that is deemed hypermasculine in middle-class, Caucasian, American culture may be considered mature masculinity in a Hispanic society (Goldwert, 1985). This clinical investigation accepts the general definitions of hypermasculinity as indicated by the previously cited authors as they apply to the cultural contexts of the patients in the group to be described.

Three major theoretical constructs have been applied to the induction of a hypermasculine adaptation in males: repudiation of feminine aspects of the self, defense against homosexual anxiety, and early/middle childhood parental influences (Glass, 1984; Ovesey, 1969; Mosher and Sirkin, 1984). Most relevant to a consideration of gender-dysphoric males is the first of these constructs. Stoller and Herdt (1982), in their cross-cultural contribution to the study of masculinity, noted that the repudiation of feminine aspects of the self in a sexually dichotomized society can become a "frantic preoccupation". It is clear that the transsexual drive for sex reassignment surgery and hormones qualifies as "frantic preoccupation" and, had we seen these very same patients while they transverse their rocky hypermasculine terrain, one can readily speculate the same would have applied.

As an active duty military psychiatrist at a major medical center I have had the special opportunity of studying such patients in the midst of their "rocky hypermasculine terrain." The Air Force base is situated in the mid-western United States in a community of about 300,000 military members, dependents, retirees, and civilians; all individuals who have, or have had, a connection to any branch of the U. S. military service are entitled to psychiatric care at this facility.

Intuitively, one would assume that the prevalence of severe gender dysphoria and, specifically transsexualism, would be low in the military—certainly lower than in the civilian population. Surely, a male who is gender dysphoric and engages in cross-gender activities and possibly sexual activity with other males would not voluntarily submit himself to a system known for its staunch intolerance of deviancy in any form, whether it be homosexuality, long hair, or wrinkled uniforms. Furthermore, given an incidence of transsexualism of between 1:37,000 and 1:100,000 males (Roberto, 1983), the likelihood of seeing *any* transsexual patients in the general adult outpatient clinic or the 30-bed inpatient unit at this medical center over a 3-year time span is low. It seems especially unlikely in the absence of any specialty clinics dealing with sexual or identity problems or any interest in studying problems believed by many not to exist in this system.

During the past 3 years I have evaluated 11 biologic males with severe gender dysphoria, all of whom meet DSM-III (American Psychiatric Association, 1980) criteria for a diagnosis of transsexualism. Three had had no military experience. Eight had had extensive active duty military experience; only one was drafted, then chose to enlist. The other seven joined voluntarily at a time when no draft existed or other options were readily available to them. All branches of service were represented; three were on active duty at the time of evaluation, one was a Department of Defense employee, and four were veterans. Ages ranged from 20 to 44 years. Three were officers. All were Caucasian and six had been married. All were requesting cross-gender hormones and/or sex reassignment surgery.

Of the three civilian patients evaluated, one had received written and verbal recommendations from his internist to "join the Army, go to boot camp, and learn how to run over trees with a tank" as treatment for his transsexualism. This advice was rejected.

A striking similarity was noted in the histories of nearly all of the military gender dysphorics: They joined the service, in their words, "to become a real man." Representative quotes from taped interviews include:

I tried to do things to make me feel more masculine, like joining the Navy and getting married.

I joined the Navy hoping maybe the problem would go away. It did for a while, but it's still here.

I joined the Air Force as a cover. In uniform, my masculinity would not be questioned—I was above reproach.

The following two cases are representative of the group.

CASE A

L. B., a 37-year-old, single, Caucasian, biological male, was abandoned by his natural mother at birth and adopted by a middle-income childless couple at 2 weeks of age. He showed an interest in cross-gender activities throughout childhood, including doll play and extensive nonfetishistic cross-dressing beginning at age 6. He was the object of ridicule by boys his age, especially when he wore unisex clothes to school. Adolescence was particularly tumultuous and after graduating from high school, he enlisted in the Air Force. He believed basic training and military discipline "would make a man out of me" and "make my [adoptive] father proud of me." After successfully completing basic training, he became a laboratory technician at a base in Germany and lived in the male barracks. The only period of his life he did not cross-dress was during the first half of his tour of duty. Concurrently, he took up avocations that involved significant personal risk: mountain climbing in the Alps and high-speed race car driving. He masturbated for the first time at age 19 and began dating women. During the peak of hostilities in Southeast Asia, he applied for combat helicopter training. He completed his 4-year tour of duty without incident and went to college, during which he experienced increasing gender dysphoria (which had reemerged before his discharge from the military), substance abuse, and depressive symptomatology. These symptoms prompted multiple requests for hormones and surgery and an evaluation at a Gender Identity Clinic 9 years ago. At the time of the current evaluation, he had been taking prescribed female hormones and living successfully in the cross-gender role for over a year as a female nursing student. He has not participated in dangerous sports for many years and dates exclusively heterosexual men. He has no medical or surgical problems and no personality disorder.

CASE B

L. N., a 26-year-old single, Caucasian, biological male, was the youngest of three sons born to a farming family from the Midwest. His father retired after serving 20 years in the Air Force, and was described as emotionally distant and physically absent during L. N.'s entire childhood. He cross-dressed privately beginning at age 7 and would pray nightly, asking God to let him wake up the next morning as a girl. He was quiet, withdrawn, and socially awkward as an adolescent. After graduation from high school, he went to college where he joined a fraternity, lived in a male dormitory, cut his hair short, and began dating women. He discontinued all cross-gender activities and enrolled in an Air Force program as an officer candidate. After 2 years, he became disillusioned with the military and questioned his original motives for joining ("I thought it would make a man out of me"). He intentionally failed a college course in order to be dismissed from the Air Force. He resumed his cross-gender activities and went on to work in the male role at a major Air Force base as a Department of Defense employee handling sensitive information requiring a security clearance. He had been taking female hormones, binding his genitals, and growing his hair long for 8 months prior to evaluation and he cross-dresses in all environments outside of work. He has no medical or surgical problems and, although he displays schizoid and avoidant traits, no personality disorder is diagnosable.

FLIGHT INTO HYPERMASCULINITY

The transsexual "flight into femininity" is well-described by Steiner *et al.* (1978) as a possible phase observed in middle adulthood applicants for sex reassignment surgery. It is clear that in the cases above, and in others I am aware of anecdotally (e.g., 6 transsexual fighter pilots; Lothstein, personal communication, 1986), a diametrically opposed phenomenon may be occurring: a "flight into hypermasculinity." For some, the mere act of enlisting was not enough. In the first case described above the patient deliberately chose the path of greatest danger while in the service: He elected to leave the relative safety of his laboratory technician job and apply for combat helicopter pilot training at the peak of the Viet Nam war, when this was an extremely high-mortality position. Another patient in this sample graduated second in his class at Officer's Candidate School. He volunteered for Special Warfare School, became a Green Beret, and saw extensive combat in Viet Nam and Thailand, completing 4 years of active duty in the Army. In addition to these cases, the military experiences of several well-known transsexual individuals are well-documented in their autobiographies (Cowell, 1954; Jorgensen, 1967; Morris, 1974; Richards, 1983).

Gershman (1986) has stated that the development of identity is an example of a continuum within an individual and evolution is continuous around a central core. Although core gender identity is believed to be largely established by 18 months, other maturational levels of development are operational throughout childhood and adolescence, with attainment of a mature gender identity/role in early adulthood in many individuals (Gershman, 1968).

Levine *et al.* (1975) described a "role transformation" in the 12 male transsexuals they studied. Military history was not specified. The succession of roles they observed was as follows: role ambivalence, transsexual homosexuality, "drag queen," adult transsexual. The 8 patients in this military population seem to have undergone a succession of identities and roles as well, although my observations fit more closely with the evolution delineated in Fig. 1.

The gender-disordered child has, at most, an awareness of the self as different from the societal dictates of his anatomy. He does not know what a transsexual is and feels confused about his identity/role. According to Stoller (1974; 1975), a lack of symbiosis anxiety as a protective shield against femininity may contribute to early overidentification with an engulfing mother, unimpeded by the proverbial absent, unreliable, and inconsistent father. Whether or not this theory is widely applicable, the pre-transsexual adolescent does not possess the ego strength to withstand the social ostracization and ridicule of adopting the cross-gender role. Furthermore, he cannot tolerate his growing awareness of the mismatch between his anatomy and sense of self. In the prevailing adolescent atmosphere of

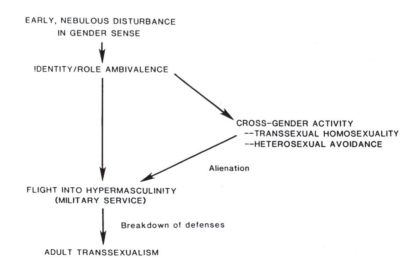

Figure 37.1 Transsexual role transformation.

individualized conformity, "fitting in" is the means of securing psychological supplies and bolstering a flagging self-esteem. Even non-gender-dysphoric adolescents are readily rejected by their peers for minor aberrations in behavior and appearance. The "solution" (adaptation) to this dilemma may be withdrawal into schizoid isolation and fantasy, a well-known clinical variant among applicants for sex reassignment (Meyer, 1974). Alternatively, he may attempt to "force a fit" by the unconscious and conscious "selection" of a hypermasculine adaptation. Inadequate, faulty object relations and a high prevalence of borderline personality organization (Levine and Lothstein, 1981) obviate a consideration of a more moderate, androgynous approach. Androgyny or integration are not *rejected*, they merely do not exist as choices for the untreated transsexual.

For the hypermasculine phase gender-dysphoric male in late adolescence, "the first order of business of being a man is: don't be a woman" (Stoller and Herdt, 1982). Benefits theoretically accrued from such a hypermasculine flight include: (i) Panacea for a variety of anxieties, e.g., homosexual anxiety, anxiety over loss of love of family and friends. (ii) Recoup of lost of love and respect from significant others, especially parents (de-alienation). (iii) Trial identifications with hypermasculine figures interpreted as more socially acceptable and readily available in the mass media. (iv) Seemingly safe haven away from intense cross-gender feelings: More masculinity is seen as less femininity and less problematic (requires purge of all aspects of the femme self).

This hypermasculine flight coincides chronologically with the age most men enter military service, either voluntarily or via the draft. The military places a high premium on virility, stoicism, machismo, assertiveness, and all that is, by definition, hypermasculine. It seems that active duty is a natural choice for the gender-dysphonic male in the hypermasculine phase who is attempting to make a last ditch effort to take the path of least resistance vis-à-vis society and family. He sees a chance to maximize his ambivalently present masculine self while de-integrating and purging his feminine self, all in the service of adaptation and accommodation. In an all-volunteer force (the situation that has pertained since 1973), the prevalence of gender-dysphoric, initially hypermasculine males could very well be much higher than in the civilian population as a result of this mechanism, which clearly relies heavily on reaction formation for its unconscious components.

OUTCOME

What is the outcome of the gender-dysphoric soldier? An answer to this question can be, at best, educated speculation given the size of this sample and the general selection for more severely disturbed individuals. Literature is almost entirely lacking on the subject, with the exception of a single paper detailing the military's management of five cases of gender dysphoria and one case of physical intersex in a soldier's spouse (Jones *et al.*, 1984). A consideration of the eight patients in the present sample and the five reported by Jones and co-workers indicates four possible outcomes:

1. Early (less than 1 year) breakdown in hypermasculine defenses with premature discharge;
2. Later (after 1 year) breakdown with premature discharge from service;
3. Completion of tour(s) of duty subsequent to breakdown in hypermasculine defenses;
4. Completion of tour(s) of duty with hypermasculine defenses intact; self-referral later in life as veteran.

Half of the patients in this sample evidenced the first outcome; one each for outcomes 2 and 3; two for outcome 4. The five cases described by Jones *et al.* assorted one case to outcomes 1, 3 and 4 and two cases to outcome 2. Completion of all tours of duty or a 20-year career subsequent to a breakdown in hypermasculine defenses accompanied by adoption of a cross-gender in hypermasculine defenses accompanied by adoption of a cross-gender identity/role is the least likely outcome of the 13 cases listed, while early discharge at less than 1 year of service is the most likely outcome, initiated by the individual or by the military system. This is not surprising given that hypermasculinity is itself a form of gender disorder, specifically a disorder of gender role in response to a primary disorder of core gender identity. These component disorders conflict with each other, creating a self-imposed mismatch between core gender identity and gender role. The resolution of this conflict necessitates abolition of the hypermasculine role and defensive structure and evolution towards the adult transsexual phase with its concomitant quest for hormones and surgery.

MILITARY POLICY

Current military policy regarding gender-dysphoric service members is sketchy and appears to be applied on a case-by-case basis. The military's formal position as applied to transsexuals who are self- or service-identified is often the same as in cases of homosexuality and bisexuality as defined in Department of Defense memorandum 1332.14, dated 28 January 1982: Homosexuality and bisexuality are incompatible with military service and their presence "adversely affects the ability of the Armed Services to maintain discipline, good order, and morale" (Jones *et al.*, 1984). Transsexuals can be considered as homosexual or bisexual by military definition if they engage in, or desire to engage in, bodily contact for the purposes of sexual gratification with a person of the same anatomic sex. This results in prohibition from enlistment or separation from service through administrative (nonmedical) channels, usually with an Honorable Discharge.

Heterosexual transsexuals, as defined by a desire for sexual contact with the anatomically other sex (DSM-III; American Psychiatric Association, 1980), pose a more difficult problem. Their gender disorder cannot be ignored or relegated to irrelevancy in this unusual situation. Policy is still evolving in this area.

For those who receive sex reassignment, irrespective of sexual orientation, medical arguments have been used successfully to support both prohibition from enlistment and separation from service (*Doe v. Alexander*, 1981). A more recent legal opinion prepared for the U. S. Air Force supports the use of medical arguments (i.e., the probable need for specialized medical, surgical, and psychiatric care is incompatible with worldwide deployment) over the vague, general grounds for discharge as applied to homosexuals in Air Force regulations AFM 39-12 and AFR 36-2 (OpJaGAF 1982/24, 1984).

The above considerations are usually circumvented entirely by the medical authorities, possibly due to these vagaries, and patients are diagnosed with personality disorders (usually Borderline) and administratively discharged as "unadaptable to military service" on that basis. The matter is far from resolved and largely untested. The legal opinion cited previously summarizes the military's precarious position:

> The short of the matter seems to be that if we propose to base the policy of discharging members who undergo sex change operations on promotion of good order, discipline, morale, or other similar virtues, we must prepare for a challenge on the ground that there is no empirical evidence that transsexuals have an adverse impact on those values. (OpJAGAF 1982/24, 1984).

Given that gender dysphoria is an all-pervasive disorder and not an "off-duty" idiosyncrasy or alternative life-style, it seems that the adaptability of some cross-gendered servicemen is predicated upon intact hypermasculine defenses. Without a significant breakdown in these defenses, they do not come to the attention of the system and are not identified as "deviant." For the majority, whose hypermasculine flight falls far short of a complete tour of duty, military life itself becomes yet another mismatch. The difficulties they experience in nearly all facets of military life (*after* evolving beyond this phase) leads first to their identification as deviant and, second, to mandatory evaluation for confirmation of that suspicion. At this point, both the patient and military system are happy to part and go their separate ways. On the other hand, it is conceivable that a significant number of higher functioning transsexuals without severe character pathology could traverse the military system undetected, as did four of the veterans in this sample.

CONCLUSION

A phase of hypermasculinity seems to be experienced by the gender-dysphoric males in this sample, usually during middle to late adolescence and variably sustained into young or middle adulthood. As a caricature of mature masculinity, the hypermasculinity adaptation in these males necessitates a way of being that is staunchly nonfeminine; risk-taking behaviors, machismo, and a facade of power are prized. While some patients choose hypermasculine pursuits limited to contact sports, race car driving, or mountain climbing, an unknown number choose military service as the quintessential hypermasculine environment in which to purge their cross-gender identifications.

The prevalence of transsexualism in the armed forces may actually be much higher than in the civilian population. This potentially increased loading of transsexuals in uniform may be due to the hypermasculine phase adaptation described and possibly to existing military policies. For example, it has been previously hypothesized that the number of homosexuals in the military is actually increased by military policies that exclude women from the draft and concentrate on late adolescent males (Harry, 1984). This theory is predicated on the finding that the homosexual men who enlisted or were drafted at age 17 or 18 did not yet "know" they were gay, as the median age of "coming out" (i.e., assuming a homosexual role) is 19 or 20 years (Dank, 1971; Harry and DeVall, 1978). As military policies, formal and informal, serve to reaffirm values of masculinity and heterosexuality, they also serve as an enticement for the hypermasculine phase gender-dysphoric male who is frequently in this very age group.

There are numerous other motivations, overt and covert, underlying the decision to enlist in the military service. Many of these may have little or nothing to do with hypermasculinity, e.g., patriotism, desire to be in close quarters with other males, economic pragmatism in a difficult job market, method of escape from a malignant home environment. It is unclear what role these factors may play in the gender-dysphoric male population, in addition to the proposed hypermasculine defensive structure.

More study is warranted on the prevalence of gender disorders in the military environment. Awareness of these problems, especially in the active duty force, is essential for the provision of optimal mental health care in the context of the mission of the Department of Defense. While information on the natural history of male gender dysphorics in the military is sparse, data on the prevalence of gender disorders in women who choose military careers is entirely lacking. This, too, could be a fruitful avenue of inquiry in future studies of gender dysphoria in the military.

ACKNOWLEDGMENTS

The author thanks Sandra Dinwoodie for preparation of the manuscript; Lynda Collier, Lt. Colonel, Ret., for assistance in data collection; and Leslie Lothstein, Ph.D., for helpful comments on the manuscript.

REFERENCES

Adler, A. (1955). *The Practice and Theory of Individual Psychology*, translated by P. Rabin (original work published 1923). Routledge and Kegan Paul, London.
American Psychiatric Association. (1980). *Diagnostic and Statistical Manual of Mental Disorders* (3rd ed.), APA, Washington, DC.

Chodoff, P. (1982). Hysteria and women. *Am. J. Psychiat.* 139: 545–551.

Cowell, R. (1954). *Roberta Cowell's Story,* William Heinermann Ltd., London.

Dank, B. (1971). Coming out in the gay world. *Psychiatry* 34: 180–197.

Doe v. Alexander (1981). 510 F. Supp 900, D. Minn.

Fenichel, O. (1945). *The Psychoanalytic Theory of Neurosis,* Norton, New York.

Gershman, H. (1968). The evolution of gender identity. *Am. J. Psychoanal.* 28: 80–90.

Glass, L. L. (1984). Man's man/ladies' man: motifs of hypermasculinity. *Psychiatry* 47: 260–278.

Goldwert, M. (1985). Mexican machismo: the flight from femininity. *Psychoanal. Rev.* 72: 161–169.

Harry, J. (1984). Homosexual men and women who served their country. *J. Homosex.* 10: 117–125.

Harry, J., and DeVall, W. (1978). *The Social Organization of Gay Males, Praeger,* New York.

Jones, F. D., Deeken, M. G., and Eshelman, S. D. (1984). Sexual reassignment surgery and the military: Case reports. *Milit. Med* 149: 271–275.

Jorgensen, C. (1967). *A Personal Autobiography,* Paul S. Erikson, New York.

Levine, E. M., Shaiova, C. H., and Mihailovic, M. (1975). Male to female: The role transformation of transsexuals. *Arch. Sex. Behav.* 4: 173–185.

Levine, S. B., and Lothstein, L. M. (1981). Transsexualism or the gender dysphoria syndromes. *J. Sex. Marit. Ther.* 7: 85–113.

Meyer, J. K. (1974). Clinical variants among applicants for sex reassignment. *Arch. Sex. Behav.* 3: 527–558.

Money, J. (1980). *Love and Love Sickness,* Johns Hopkins University Press, Baltimore.

Morris, J. (1974). *Conundrum,* Harcourt Brace Jovanovich, New York.

Mosher, D. L., and Sirkin, M. (1984). Measuring a macho personality constellation, *J. Res. Pers.* 18: 150–163.

OpJAGAF 1982/24 (1984). *Med. Services Dig.* 35: 2.

Ovesey, L. (1969). *Homosexuality and Pseudohomosexuality,* Science House, New York.

Richards, R. (1983). *The Renee Richards Story: Second Serve,* Stein and Day, New York.

Roberto, L. G. (1983). Issues in diagnosis and treatment of transsexualism. *Arch. Sex. Behav.* 12: 445–473.

Steiner, B. W., Satterberg, J. A., and Muir, C. F. (1978). Flight into femininity: the male menopause? *Can. Psychiat. Assoc. J.* 23: 405–410.

Stoller, R. J. (1974). Symbiosis anxiety and the development of masculinity. *Arch. Gen. Psychiat.* 30: 164–172.

Stoller, R. J. (1975). *Perversion: The Erotic Form of Hatred,* Pantheon, New York.

Stoller, R. J., and Herdt, G. H. (1982). The development of masculinity: A cross-cultural contribution. *J. Am. Psychoanal. Assoc.* 30: 29–61.

The views expressed herein are those of the author and do not necessarily reflect those of the Department of Defense or the United States Air Force.

VI

EMBODIMENT: ETHICS IN TIME AND SPACE

38

What Does It Cost to Tell the Truth?

Riki Anne Wilchins

Gender provocateur Rikki Anne Wilchins, who founded the protest group Transexual Menace as well as the reform-oriented GenderPAC advocacy group, is one of the best-known voices in the contemporary transgender movement. Wilchins has a talent for turning the complicated formulations of scholars and theorists of gender and sexuality into pithy, efficacious, and politically charged sound bites.

In "What Does it Cost to Tell the Truth?," Wilchins offers a transgender-specific reply to a question posed by Michel Foucault, about the necessity of making oneself an object of knowledge for others. Wilchins describes with characteristically biting humor how the meaning of her body, as well as the bodies of her transsexual friends, changed as they underwent their gender transitions. In doing so, she is able to comment on various cultural schemas of bodily intelligibility that become visible only when transgendered subjects transform the shape and appearance of their flesh.

More important, however, is the critique Wilchins offers of the entire process of investing meaning in the bodies of others. Why, as a culture, are we compelled to read the embodiment of others, and make judgments about that person based on that reading? In grappling with that question, Wilchins helps point the way to linking anti-transgender discrimination with other body-based rationales for social oppression such as body size, reproductive capacity, disability, and race.

I was twenty-six when I learned I was very tall. For most of my life I had been considered normal height. But at twenty-six, suddenly, strangers in elevators began leaning toward me conspiratorially and asking, "How tall are you, anyway?" as if we'd been having a conversation on the subject. There were delivery men who inquired, "You play roundball?" and even one man on a motorcycle who slowed alongside me to exclaim, "You must be a volleyball player!"

Although I had never before worried about my height, I began studying myself in mirrors. I began *seeing* myself as tall. In short order, I became self-conscious about the length of my body. I stooped fashionably while walking down the street, tried not to stand up too straight in bars or at parties, and leaned against walls and pillars when speaking so I wouldn't appear to be towering over shorter people.

WELCOME TO GENDERHELL

I learned a lot of other things about my body as well. My voice was unnervingly deep. My hands were too large, my shoulders too broad, my hips too narrow, and my feet much too big. The same size basketball sneakers I'd been wearing for over ten years suddenly looked ridiculous, even to me. People made public jokes about my "boats." I stopped wearing them, even stopped shooting hoops. Although I'd been slender for decades, since I was now "too big," I stopped working out at the gym as well.

I was obsessed with how I looked and was perceived. I became a ferocious shopper, lusting after any clothing that would hide my height and shoulders. I bought winter gloves and dress shoes a size too small. My pinched hands and feet went along with the higher voice I practiced when speaking on the phone.

Over a terrifyingly short period of only one year, my entire perception of my body changed to match the social truths everyone else read there. The mirror, formerly a friend, turned into a deadly enemy. I felt humiliated, ashamed, each time I looked in it, weeping quietly in dressing rooms and loudly at home. I appeared ridiculous to myself because I was seeing what I was told was there: this absurdly tall person with large hands, ungainly feet, wide shoulders, a deep voice, and a masculine manner. Need I go on? What is most remarkable is that I had been about the same size and shape since I was fifteen.

READ ANY GOOD WOMEN LATELY?

What had happened was that I'd started being read by others "as a woman."

That my body became the site of all kinds of social inspection and pronouncements didn't surprise me. But the virulence did. I was accosted from every direction: from the men who hissed at me on street corners; to the man on the train who leaned over and said, "Nice tits," as I boarded; to the construction workers who whistled or yelled, "Faggot!"; to the driver who rolled down his window at a crowded intersection, the very first time I went out in a dress, to shout, "God, you sure are uuug-ly!"

In many ways I imagine that what happened to me is not much different from what happens to many teenagers once their bodies hit puberty and are seized by the cultural machine. In my case, though, I already had a stable body image, and I was an adult, fully aware of what was going on. It shocks me to this day how quickly I learned to make my body over, to embrace the various social truths about it, and to see on it what I was told. I knew what people were thinking when they looked me up and down, stared at my body parts, and inspected my face.

TELL ME HOW I LOOK

"People being introduced to me no longer make eye contact—they make crotch contact," a friend, just starting to be read as a woman, told me.

My body, like hers, heretofore just a place to put food, carry out certain operations of pleasure, and get me from point A to point B, had overnight become an armed camp which I surveyed at my peril. It hurt to be me, and it hurt to see me.

I am reminded of a recent meeting with a transsexual female friend of mine. She had begun living full-time as a woman, and eagerly showed me pictures of herself in make-up and various outfits. Again, this is much like any teenager would do. What particularly struck me was that, as she anxiously scanned my face for a reaction, she said, "I have to depend on other people to tell me how I look because I don't know how to see myself yet."

How strange that she was soliciting this information from someone who customarily walks around with a short, butchy haircut, wearing no make-up, dressed in blue jeans, sneakers, and a large black Transsexual Menace T-shirt. Which is to say that I do not, at first blush, inspire confidence as the best possible judge of such matters. I could not care less how either of us is read by nontranssexuals.

NO ADMISSION TO LIFE WITHOUT A VALID GENDER ID

> How does it happen that the human subject makes himself into an object of possible knowledge, through what forms of rationality, through what historical necessities, and at what price? My question is this: How much does it cost the subject to be able to tell the truth about itself?
>
> Michel Foucault, "How Much Does It Cost to Tell the Truth?"[1]

Foucault asked about the necessity of making one's self an object of possible knowledge, to be learned and memorized. For genderqueers, that necessity is survival. The purpose of a gender regime is to regulate these meanings and to punish those who transgress them. In order to survive, to avoid the bashings, the job discrimination, and the street-corner humiliations, my friend will be forced to place herself as a site of *truth* to be mastered. That knowledge will come from others. She must know how others see her so she can know how to see herself; otherwise, she enters society at her peril.

She will gradually learn how she looks and what her body means. She will carry this knowledge around, producing it on demand like pocket ID when she enters a subway car, applies for a job, approaches the police for directions, uses a women's room, or walks alone at night past a knot of men. Summoning up the image in her mind's eye, she will recall the truth of her looks, checking it quickly to determine if anything is "wrong," feeling shame at her shortcomings and pride in her attractive features.

Like me, she may find herself growing further and further from direct sensation, so that in small, gradual steps it becomes successively less important what her body *feels like* than how she *feels about* it. As the source of what her body means becomes more firmly lodged in the perceptions of others, she may experience a curious and distressing sense of dislocation and vulnerability. This ID that she carries—her body—will be continually subjected to being displayed, stamped, and judged.

Since her status and legitimacy as a woman will always be at risk, always be determined by and dependent upon others, she may find that her lack of contact with sensation grows along with a nagging sense of bodily disorientation. She will wake one day to find herself lost within the unfamiliar landscape of her own body, like a nomad in some strange and foreign desert, surrounded by unknown landmarks and inhabited by those whose alien features, and distant ways, she can no longer recognize.

What does it cost to tell the truth?

A DACHSHUND PONDERS WIENER-PEOPLE

Someone out there is undoubtedly saying, "Well, all this is very moving, but there *is* a reality to bodies and you can't get around it. For starters, compared to other women, you are tall." Such a comment highlights my point.

We like to think, in Judith Butler's memorable phrase, that physical features exist somewhere out there "on the far side of language."[2] But if even a feature as fundamental and measurable as my "tallness" can only be derived through your reviewing a population of bodies, perceiving some normative measure, and then carrying out (albeit unconsciously) an operation of comparison, then that tallness looks suspiciously to me like something you read on me instead of some innate feature in me. My measurable height may not be arguable; what it *means* is.

Characteristics of mine that are truly innate, that originate "on the far side of language," ought to be totally apparent to you whether you'd ever seen another human being or not, even if you'd only seen me mounted like the gendertrash insect I am, even if you were a Martian seeing your first humanoid, or a wiener-dog viewing its first vertically challenged primate. Any other readings of my body are culturally relative, contingent upon the context in which you locate me. Hence, if we lived among the Munchkins, you'd argue I was naturally a giantess, while if we lived among the New York Knicks, you'd insist I was somewhat short.

The response to deconstructing the body in this way is frequently to offer up counterexamples, of which skin color is the most common. That line of reasoning goes like this: "Perhaps you're right. Perhaps *some* things about bodies are culturally constructed. But some features are simply there. For instance, what about race? Surely color is just color and not some cultural by-product."

Not so, I say, for while skin color itself may be on the far side of language, nearly everything else we can know about it and all that is culturally resonant is not. Such resonances are often specific to particular subcultures. *Black*, for example, is a peculiarly American phenomenon. White Americans often see only "African-American" or "black" when they look at someone who appears darker-hued than they are. This perception unconsciously follows the notorious "one drop rule,"[3] a bizarre invention of white America which historically held that "one drop" of African blood made a person black. Yet most black Americans are able to see the complex range and variety of shades in which skin color can come. Since being white has been supremely privileged, and therefore required no further qualification, specific shades of brown or black have held tremendous significance and implications for surviving within a racist system.

EVERYONE'S ANSWER IS THE ONLY ANSWER

Each era in history considers its own embrace of the body's features as "natural" and eternal. But bodies, like all cultural products, go through periods, phases, and even fashions. Consider the breast in the recent American landscape. Only a few decades ago the duckbilled breast, as shaped by the tortured duckbill-shaped bra, was the standard of beauty. Shortly thereafter, large full breasts were seen as beautiful and the height of femininity. In just the next generation, with bras burning across the land, small breasts were "naturally" feminine and those "cursed" with big, full breasts found themselves "too big."

For another hoot, consider how definitions of masculinity and muscularity have changed. Look at George Reeves of the old black-and-white *Superman* TV show. His stomach stuck out beyond his chest; his arms had no noticeably defined muscles. Compare him to Christopher Reeve of the modern *Superman* movies, who was sculpted like a body-builder. Both generations find their models "naturally" manly. Both would find the other's model incomprehensible.

For that matter, you would think at least that cherished staple, the Big Dick, would have a stable cultural identity. I mean, more is always better, right? Not necessarily. Thomas Laqueur[4] relates that the ancient Greeks, from whom we inherit much of our aesthetics, found small penises masculine and attractive. Large dicks were considered animal-like, and often the butt (sorry) of public jokes. Men with big dicks learned shame and began to "tuck," just like any sensible drag queen. A transmale friend who recently returned from a trip to Greece told me how comfortable he'd felt. Everywhere he went, all the statues and pictures had small, manly dicks—just like his.

OH YEAH? WELL, MY MOM SAYS YOUR BODY IS JUST A DISCURSIVELY PRODUCED EVENT BASED ON HIGHLY VARIABLE CULTURAL NORMS

As I sat down next to my seatmate on the bus leaving the National Women's Music Festival in Bloomington, Indiana, she said quickly, "Please pardon my fat hips." I was nonplused, not having noticed her hips. Foucault's questions came to mind: What kind of system bids us each make of our bodies a problem to be solved, a claim we must defend, or a secret we must publicly confess, again and again?

Since she and I were stuck together for the next two hours, we proceeded to discuss some of these questions, in particular, why she had felt obliged to apologize to me, a complete stranger.

"Oh, I know, I shouldn't think of them that way," she said. "My feminist friends tell me I should think of them as *nurturing* and *material*."

"Oh, no," I exclaimed, "that's the same thing. It just means this time the jury came back with a different verdict. You're still in the dock awaiting judgment—either way they decide, you'll still have been radically disempowered. The question really should be, what is the original cultural concern with your pelvis and body fat that *requires* us to recognize and agree on a meaning in the first place? In other words, whose agenda is it that demands your hips must be gendered with a particular meaning, or to even have any meaning at all?"

"The body," said Simone de Beauvoir, "is a situation."[5] In order to grasp our bodies, to think of them as well as to understand the cultural gaze that fixes upon them, we must construct what our bodies can be said to mean and to look like.

We rely upon other members of our speech community to do this, since it is in the meanings reflected back at us through culture that we find *truth*. Almost everything about bodies is discovered through comparison from the collection of meanings stored in a common language: pretty, fat, plain, masculine, short, light-skinned, wrinkled, feminine, broad, sleek, ugly, athletic, deformed, slim, rotund, buxom, old, delicate. The litany traps and enfolds each body.

For some of us, the meanings culture drapes upon our bodies are extremely painful and depressing. Worse still, a gender system tends to enforce monolithic meanings. Big breasts must mean one thing, hairy backs another, wrinkles yet another still, providing us little or no room to construct our selves and create alternatives.

Simply having our bodies exposed to social judgment can be painful and disturbing to some people. I remember my sixty-five-year-old friend who said, "You know, when I first look at myself in the mirror, I look fine. I think, *Well, all right!* But I look once again, harder, imagining how people must see me, and then I see only the fat and wrinkles and I feel just awful."

What does it cost to tell the truth?

I guess if your sense of self matches closely with the cultural grid of what you should mean, and you find those meanings pleasing, then the "truth" doesn't come too expensive. For the rest of us, though, it can cost a great deal.

NOTES

1. Michel Foucault in *Bodies That Matter: On the Discursive Limits of Sex* by Judith Butler (New York, Routledge, 1993), p. 93.
2. Judith Butler, *Gender Trouble* (New York: Routledge, 1990), p. 114.
3. Kathy Russell, Midge Wilson, and Ronald Hall, *The Color Complex* (New York: Anchor Books, 1992), p. 14.
4. Thomas Laqueur, *Making Sex: Body and Gender from the Greeks to Freud* (Cambridge, MA: Harvard University Press, 1990), p. 31.
5. Simone de Beauvoir, *The Second Sex* (New York: Vintage, 1983), p. 301.

Read at a transsexual speak-out held at New York's Lesbian and Gay Community Center in 1993 in honor of the fortieth anniversary of Christine Jorgensen's sex-change surgery.

39

Transmogrification
(Un)Becoming Other(s)

Nikki Sullivan

Nikki Sullivan, a critical theorist of body modification practices, examines similarities and differences between transsexual surgeries and other forms of bodily modification such as piercing, branding, tattooing, cosmetic surgery, and self-demand amputation. Sullivan contends that all such practices can be considered "trans" practices, and that, conversely, transsexual body modification can be considered simply one particular type of a wider class of phenomena.

Sullivan is especially concerned with how, across a wide range of discourses, various critics tend to perpetuate moral judgments about what constitutes "good" rather than "bad" body modification practices. She elucidates the way that dominant cultural formations tend to validate body modification practices that affirm cultural norms, and to disparage countercultural forms of bodily modification. Likewise, she points out how in various critical contexts, body modifications that mark an antithetical relationship to the dominant culture are celebrated while normalizing procedures are condemned. She then surveys a few of the ways that proscriptions emanating within both critical and conventional moralities play out with regard to transgender body modification practices.

Central to Sullivan's argument is her development of the concept of "transmogrification," usually defined as a strange or grotesque transformation characterized by distortion, exaggeration, and "unnatural combinations." Rather than seeing transmogrification as a negative process that produces disavowed and abjected monstrous others, she sees it as the expression of a fundamental human condition, part of the process through which we all negotiate the boundary between self and other, and through which we perpetually transform ourselves in relation to an Other. In seeking to articulate an analytics of transmogrification rather than a moral condemnation of the monstrous and strange, Sullivan calls for an "intercorporeal ethics" that recognizes and welcomes our own strangeness as well as the strangeness of others. This ethical practice simultaneously seeks out common norms and modes of interpersonal engagement, and never loses sight of the notion of justice.

A number of critical theorists have, of late, posited connections between transgender body modification(s) and other modificatory practices such as tattooing, branding, piercing, and so on. Drawing similar analogies, others have discussed the ambiguous and often fraught relationship with surgery that (some) transsexuals, transgenderists, and those who undergo 'cosmetic' and/or modificatory procedures more generally, may experience. Perhaps at bottom, what procedures as diverse as mastectomies, penectomies, hormone treatments, tattooing, breast enhancement, implants, corsetry, rhinoplasty, scarification, branding, and so on, have in common, is that they all function, in varying ways and to varying degrees, to explicitly transform bodily being—they are all, in one sense at least, 'trans' practices.

However, whilst it may be possible and even useful to identify similarities between 'trans' practices and 'trans' bodies and/or subjectivities (in the broadest sense of the term), it is nevertheless crucial that we pay close critical attention to the differences between such practices, the bodies they transform or inform, and the ways in which these are interpreted, evaluated, situated, and lived. The question, then, is how to begin such a task. Obviously there are many possible ways to approach the differences between modified (or 'trans') bodies, but something that seems common to much of the current work done in this area is the tendency to set up a dichotomy between 'good' and 'bad' forms of embodiment. This is apparent in some accounts of the differences between transsexualism and transgender, and some analyses of the supposed distinction between 'non-mainstream body modification' and cosmetic surgery. In short, the assumption seems to be that forms of body modification that do not *explicitly* set themselves up in opposition to so-called 'normative' ideals and ways of being are politically suspect.

Rather than simply interpreting and evaluating different kinds of modified bodies in terms of their presumed capacity to radically challenge the norm, my aim in this paper is to explore both the difficulties and the implications of doing so. My analysis will proceed via a focus on transmogrification—that is, strange or grotesque transformation: transformation that is characterized by distortion, exaggeration, extravagance, and, as the *Shorter Oxford English Dictionary* puts it, 'unnatural combinations'. In and through the juxtaposition of diverse examples of transmogrification I will raise the question of what such bodies do (at least in a particular historico-cultural context), how they function, what effects they produce, what connections they make with other bodies and with particular bodies of knowledge, why, and to what ends.

TRANSGENDER, COSMETIC SURGERY, 'NON-MAINSTREAM' BODY MODIFICATION: COMPARATIVE PRACTICES?

In *Sex Changes: The Politics of Transgenderism*, and in *Lesbians Talk Transgender*, Patrick Califia and Zachary Nataf respectively both claim that so-called sex-reassignment procedures could be thought of, and are often experienced as, similar to other forms of body modification, such as tattooing, piercing, and branding.[1] What underlies these claims is the belief that transgenderism as its currently understood and experienced, is significantly different from transsexualism as it seems to have been conceptualized and lived prior to the rise of postmodernism, queer theory, transgender theory and activism, and so on. Here 'trans' practices and procedures are not a means by which one moves from one sex/gender to the 'opposite' sex/gender. Rather, they are a (rather explicit or literal) example of the many ambiguous and complex ways in which bodies are continually changed and changing. Given this, Judith Halberstam has suggested that rather than considering sex reassignment procedures as the surgical answer to a gender dysphoria problem that needs to be resolved, 'we consider what we're now calling transsexual surgery as cosmetic' surgery. In and through such a conceptual shift

> maybe we would take the stigma [of transsexual surgery] away. Maybe we wouldn't see it as the complete, pathological rearrangement of identity.... Maybe we'd begin to see it as a way or organizing your body to suit your image of yourself. And then we wouldn't have this whole therapeutic intervention, where people are saying 'Why do you want to become a man? What's wrong with you?' You could say, 'Because I prefer the way a penis looks on my body to the way a vagina looks on my body'.[2]

In short, there is a sense in the work of Nataf, Califia, and Halberstam that the association of transgender practices and procedures with other forms of body modification (tattooing, piercing, branding, cosmetic surgery) does, or at least might, enable a move away from essentialized, essentializing and/or pathologizing theories of trans embodiment and the social and political implications of such.

'NON-MAINSTREAM' BODY MODIFICATION *VS.* COSMETIC SURGERY

Not everyone, however, conceives of the relation between cosmetic surgery and other 'non-mainstream' forms of body modification (which, if we agree with Halberstam, Califia, and Nataf, might include transgender practices and procedures), in as positive a way as does Halberstam. In fact, for many writers and theorists, particularly those interested or involved in what might loosely be called 'modern primitivism', the relation is a purely oppositional one.[3]

In a paper entitled "Embodying Desire: Piercing and the Fashioning of 'Neo-butch/femme' Identities"[4] Lisa Walker critically examines dichotomous accounts of 'non-mainstream' body modification (such as tattooing, piercing, branding, scarification) and cosmetic surgery, in which the latter is understood as a form of compliance to normative gendered standards of beauty, and the former is represented as a radical political practice. This sort of position, as Walker notes, is taken by Andrea Juno the editor of *Modern Primitives*—a text which, for many, represents the Holy Writ of the so-called modern primitive movement—by Kather Acker, who Juno interviews in *Angry Women*,[5] and is perhaps presented most clearly in the 1991 documentary *Stigmata: The Transfigured Body*, in which both Juno and Acker appear. Here Acker states that women who get plastic surgery "are just looking to come as close as possible to norms that they've internalized", whereas women who get pierced, tattooed, cut, or branded "are actively searching for who to be and it has to do with *their own* pleasure, *their own* feeling of identity...they're not *obeying* the normal society...its very different".[6] Similarly, Juno describes 'non-mainstream' body modification as a creative and liberatory form of self-reclamation, whereas cosmetic surgery—at least as she sees it—involves the surrendering of one's creativity, one's individuality, one's body, to the mandates of a male-defined system.[7] In fact, throughout *Stigmata*, as Walker notes, cosmetic surgery is equated with false-consciousness, lack of agency, conformity, abuse, and the internalization of hetero-patriarchal norms, values, and conventions.

Walker claims that another dichotomy—that is, butch/femme—is often mapped onto this alleged distinction between 'non-mainstream' body modification and cosmetic surgery, the implication being that butchness is (all too often) understood as an anti-normative reinscription of 'female' embodiment and gender-codes, whereas femme is regarded as a reaffirmation of feminine (read normative) modes of bodily being, even in its most extreme forms—in cases of what Lisa Duggan and Kathleen McHugh describe as a 'perverse proliferation of femininity'.[8] Not only has this limited understanding of butch/femme been (convincingly) called into question by theorists such as Joan Nestle,[9] Biddy Martin,[10] and Ann Cvetkovich,[11] but moreover, Walker demonstrates that the conflation of butchness with 'non-mainstream' modificatory practices and thus with transgression, and femmes with 'cosmetic surgery' and thus with gender conformity, is misguided to say the least. Walker makes the fairly obvious point that many femmes are tattooed, pierced, branded, and so on, and then seems to turn her argument back on itself, claiming that nevertheless practices like tattooing are more often than not gendered in ways that may not be immediately evident.[12] For example, femmes, she says, often choose to tattoo different parts of the body than do butches, and tend to select significantly different (that is, less conventionally 'masculine') tattoo designs, and body jewelry.

In effect then, what Walker's article demonstrates is that the distinction posited by Acker and those like her, between 'non-mainstream' body modification and cosmetic surgery, and, by association, between transgression and conformity, is questionable since 'non-mainstream' body modification tends to be practiced, experienced, or explained in gendered ways. 'Non-mainstream' modificatory practices , she writes, "do not necessarily indicate the fluidity of gender identity, but [more often than not] express gendered identities that we experience as integral to who we are, rather than as purely conscious choices we make about how to define ourselves".[13]

Whilst Walker's work does destabilize the distinction between gender conformist and non-conformist 'non-mainstream' modificatory practices, and also questions one's capacity to simply reinscribe one's (gendered) bodily being in totally open ended ways, it does not, however, explicitly challenge the association of cosmetic surgery with conformity to hetero-patriarchal ways of knowing and of being. So, whilst Walker's paper is useful in all sorts of ways, it doesn't manage (although this is not its aim) to provide what it is that I have been searching high and low for: that is, a critique of the all too often unquestioned conflation of cosmetic surgery with conformity.

RECLAIMING COSMETIC SURGERY?

In her work on cosmetic surgery, feminist theorist Kathy Davis, attempts to complicate the commonly held association between cosmetic surgery and patriarchal ideals, and to understand women's[14] participation in these practices as something more than passive, mindless, conformity. She argues that rather than simply trying to achieve feminine beauty ideals, the majority of women who undergo surgery do so in order to 'feel at home in their bodies', to become who they really are, to alleviate the pain and suffering associated with feeling monstrous. Thus she suggests that the recipient of cosmetic surgery experiences her embodied being in much the same way as the transsexual does, and that in both cases surgery can play a reparative role despite its association with oppressive institutions such as the medical profession.[15]

What interests me about Davis' analysis is not so much her rethinking of cosmetic surgery—which tends to be fairly conservative and (at least inadvertently) patronizing, but rather, the fact that the link she makes between cosmetic surgery and transsexualism has the opposite effect to what Halberstam hoped or imagined such an association might have. In effect, the association as Davis makes it reinscribes the trans-body as the body of a poor unfortunate victim whose suffering can (hopefully) be eliminated once-and-for-all in and through surgical intervention. Sex-reassignment surgery, like cosmetic surgery, will, according to this way of thinking, enable the displaced person to finally feel at home in his/her body, to become whole. Of course, there are all sorts of problems with this paradigm, not least of all the question of the (im)possibility of such an ideal form of embodied being.

In a paper entitled "'My Body is my Art': Cosmetic Surgery as Feminist Utopia?",[16] Davis again implies a connection between transgenderism and cosmetic surgery when she cites the French performance artist Orlan who claims "I am a woman-to-woman transsexual act".[17] Orlan, whose body functions as the raw material for what she describes as her 'carnal art' has, since 1990, undergone a series of videotaped surgical operations to transform herself into a new being whose chin is modeled on Boticelli's *Venus*, lips on Moreau's *Europa*, nose on Geromes' *Psyche*, eyes on Fontainbleau's *Diana*, and brow on daVinci's *Mona Lisa*. Orlan has also had temple implants inserted as part of a project entitled *Omnipresence*, and in her *Self-Hybridization* series uses computer graphics to enter "into the skin of the other" and to create an "appearance which is alien to our customs and civilization".[18] But in this instance, becoming 'other' in and through what one might call a 'perverse proliferation of femininity' is read as (at least potentially) politically radical since Orlan, who Davis implies is a critically informed postmodern performer, *intentionally* "turns the tables and uses surgery as a medium"[19] through which to challenge normative notions of gender identity. In short, then, the distinction between conformity and transgression that Davis (at least implicitly) posits in this paper is founded on the notion of intent—the idea that a practice is radical if it is consciously undertaken by a self-transparent and seemingly autonomous subject who explicitly defines his or her transformation in these terms. The most obvious problem with this position is that it negates the political potential of a practice that is not seemingly self-consciously undertaken for transgressive purposes. Moreover, such an interpretation involves taking a person at their word, that is, accepting their account of their motives as unambiguous and as true—something many feminist critics of cosmetic surgery have great trouble doing. What Davis seems to forget, and what Sandy Stone and Judith Shapiro have pointed out in their work on transsexualism, is that we embody a range of (often conflicting or contradictory) discourses and tend to reiterate particular paradigms to explain or justify our actions in accordance with the context in which we are being questioned.

THE BODY FOR OTHERS, OR THE LIMITS OF SELF-AUTHORIZATION

But it is not enough, I'd argue, to claim that one's actions simply signify what one intends them to signify, or, by extension, that one's identity is self-defining. What Janice Raymond's work on trans-sexualism illustrates most profoundly is that other people will not always read one's actions and/or one's embodied being in the same way as one might understand one's own, and that there are all sorts of very real material effects which occur in and through such a disjunction. Sandy Stone's account of the ways in which transsexuals who require surgery must prove, in accordance with an established set of criteria not of their own making, that they *are* in fact 'transsexuals', and that they therefore fit the eligibility criteria for surgery, demonstrates that identity is never autonomous, but rather, is constituted in and through relations with others and with a world. This 'intercorporeality' if you like, is illustrated in interesting ways in "Facing the Dilemma" in which Kathy Davis recounts numerous responses to her work from colleagues, friends, and other academics whom she has encountered at conferences.

As Davis tells it, as a result of her attempts to understand women's participation in cosmetic surgery as something other than the passive acceptance of patriarchal exploitation, she has been accused, on numerous occasions, of being too liberal, of advocating cosmetic surgery (which she staunchly denies she does), and of not being a 'good feminist'. Even her more supportive (postmodern) colleagues have suggested that she write instead about more appropriate and less contentious forms of perverse embodiment such as female body-building, or cross-dressing. These anecdotes interest me because they illustrate, I would suggest, that it is not only the explicitly modified body that is up for debate in accounts of trans(formative) practices. Rather, it is also the case that the status of the embodied subject who speaks/writes in particular ways, and about particular practices and identities, is fiercely patrolled. In other words, in and through the practices mentioned, and the debates regarding those practices, the body of the one who speaks, as well as the one who is spoken about, is (re)inscribed, is caught up in the process(es) of marking and being marked, of becoming and unbecoming, that are integral to subjectivity and sociality.

Given all this, it seems valid to claim that the notion of intent is a rather shaky rock upon which to build a theory of various forms of body modification and the similarities and differences between them. This claim is further illustrated by Kathryn Pauly Morgan's approach to what she describes as the rapid development of genetic engineering: that is, of cosmetic surgery, transsexual surgery, and the technological transformation of other aspects of human life including reproduction, and death. For Morgan, it seems that contemporary culture is hell-bent on creating new species of 'woman-monster[s]' (or Robo Women) with artifactual bodies that serve to imprison rather than liberate, and to support patriarchy rather than undermining it.[20] In fact, Morgan claims that it is becoming increasingly im-perative that we all participate in modificatory practices which, we are told, will improve our bodies and our lives, but, which Morgan claims will only bind us evermore tightly. A similar fear regarding the technological imperative to alter one's body is evident in Califia's (significantly more self-reflective) account of his response to the FTM presence at a leather dyke conference held in Seattle. Califia, writing prior to his own gender transition, says:

> The FTM presence at Powersurge…made me feel uncomfortable. A lot of this is my personal garbage, I am afraid that the visibility of FTMs will change the definition of what's butch until women will feel they have to take male hormones to make them masculine enough to be butch.[21]

But, as Califia goes on to add, being uncomfortable is not necessarily a bad thing, at least not if one acknowledges one's dis-ease and attempts to analyze where it might come from, what function it plays, and so on. This kind of self-reflexivity, however, does not seem to occur in Morgan's work. Rather, Morgan attempts to disavow and to overcome the feelings of discomfort, the threat posed by the (modified) body of the other, by defining that body as monstrous, as 'other', thereby creating a distinction between self and other and seeking to keep the border between the two firmly drawn. But, unfortunately for Morgan, Rosi Braidotti lets the cat out of the bag when she explains that 'the monstrous other is both liminal and structurally central to our perception of normal human subjectivity'.[22]

MONSTROUS OTHERS

This figure of the monster plays a similar role in the critiques of (or is it just out-and-out attacks on?) transsexualism developed by Mary Daly and Janice Raymond. The monster, a surgically created yet fleshly being, is, for Daly and Raymond, a symptom of (patriarchal) power gone mad, and if that isn't bad enough, some women (perhaps even some feminists) have been seduced, they argue, into becoming monsters, or at least into offering hospitality to monsters, rather than responding with the kind of (metaphoric) violence that such a situation calls for, at least in their scheme of things. But, given Braidotti's insight, we could read these incredibly vitriolic outpourings as examples of an all too common response to being faced with one's nemesis, one's shadow, the uncanny personification of justice and retribution.

Taking a position similar to that of Raymond and Daly, Sheila Jeffreys, in an outraged response to Halberstam's account of transgender bodies in her reading of *Linda/Les and Annie*, argues that such a body (Linda/Les' body) is a symptom of self-hatred, and that it should be read as evidence of the internalization and perpetuation of patriarchal abuse in the form of self-mutilation.[23] And here I can't help but be reminded of Janice McLane's reading of the marks of 'self-mutilation' as a voice on the skin, a voice that cannot express what the abuse-survivor has been forbidden to speak. McLane says:

> This voice is so appalling that even the self speaking in wounds cannot stand to hear it. For who can really bear to be their own torturer? Who can look into their own eyes and see the three-headed-baby nature of themselves, such a freak that they carve their own body into wounds? Some people can look into a mirror and call their own wounding tattoo-art, body piercing, religious ecstasy, a drug trip … But these terms themselves are an artful arranging of cooked bits on a plate to disguise the fact that one is eating pieces of bloody dead animal.[24]

So for McLane too, the body (and in some sense the subjectivity) of the person who participates in (particular) modificatory practices is monstrous.

This conflation of body modification with monstrosity raises the question of whether or not monstrosity is always, and by definition, a negative thing? Transgender activist Susan Stryker has 'reclaimed' the figure of the monster in her well-known paper "My Words to Victor Frankenstein

Above the Village of Chamounix", which is subtitled 'Transgender Rage'. For Stryker, the monstrous body/the transsexual body with "its flesh torn apart and sewn together again", is an unnatural and strange creation, an, "assemblage of incongruous anatomical parts", that haunts the Law (of propriety), interrupting its edicts, spreading dis-unity and dis-cord, heralding the warning that an investigation of one's nature may well result in the discovery of 'seams and sutures in yourself'.[25] In one sense at least, what Stryker's paper suggests is that all bodies are unnatural, created, formed and transformed in and through modificatory processes and procedures of one sort or another. However, as we've seen, this inter-subjective relation of marking and being marked, of becoming and unbecoming (whether literally or otherwise), is more often than not disavowed in and through the projection of all that is commonly held to be 'negative' onto the marked body of the other, the monster.

I will return to this point in a moment, but first I want to mention Stryker's claim that despite the conservative and normalizing aims of the medical profession, the bodies that it 'creates' with its scalpels and sutures, its injections and implants, nevertheless "are something more and something other than the creatures our makers intended us to be".[26] As Stryker goes on to explain, the subjectivity shaped in and through the (un)becoming processes of transsexual embodiment "is no more the creation of the science that refigures its flesh, than the monster's' entire being is the creation of Dr Franken-stein".[27] But at the same time, neither is it the case that the monstrous subject is the author of its own (un)becoming. Rather, as Stryker puts it, "phallogocentric language, not its particular speaker, is the scalpel that defines our flesh.... [And] though I may not hold the stylus myself, I can move beneath it for my own deep self-sustaining pleasures'.[28] In short, Stryker points to the intersubjective character of corporeal inscription and of the process of (un)becoming other.

Given the connections, similarities, overlaps, resonances, and intersections, noted thus far between transgenderism, cosmetic surgery, and 'non-mainstream' forms of body modification, perhaps we could bring Stryker's insights to bear on the debate regarding the status of such practices, and in particular their relation to the question of agency. Perhaps we could acknowledge, for example, that the medical profession may tend, for the most part, to have normalizing aims but that this does not mean, for example, that women who undergo breast augmentation are necessarily and simply passive victims of patriarchy. Nor would it any longer be possible, if we took seriously Stryker's account of the ambiguous, unpredictable, and open-ended character of embodiment as necessarily trans-forma-tive, to represent the tattooed, scarified, pierced, branded, subject as the heroic author of his/her own (counter-cultural, and thus transgressive) self-transformation.

Whilst I think Stryker's article is fascinating and insightful, and, as I've said, potentially useful for any attempt to rethink body modificatory practices more generally, I'm nevertheless concerned that some practices and forms of perverse embodiment may be more open to reinscription than others, particularly in specific contexts.

What a quick scan of the material available on transgenderism, 'non-mainstream' body modifica-tion, and cosmetic surgery shows, is that the first of these is most often discussed (at least in contemporary academic/theoretical circles) by what we might call queer theorists; the second ('non-mainstream' body modification) appears most often to be the object of attention of counter-culturalists on the one hand, and criminologists and psychologists on the other; whereas cosmetic surgery is examined almost solely by feminists of one persuasion or another. In saying this I do not mean to suggest, for example, that queer theorists can't be feminists, and so on. Rather, my point is that for the most part, the ways in which these issues are approached seems to be tied to a particular discursive (theoretical and political) history and to specific conventions that at times function, much like a drag anchor.

TRANS-FORMATION OR 'SELF-MUTILATION'?

In order to explore this claim in more detail I want to turn now to the notion of 'self-mutilation'. Whilst I am aware that there are some writers who would argue that transgender practices constitute a form of self-mutilation,[29] these theorists seem to me to be in the minority, at least, as I've said, in contemporary theoretical/academic circles. This is less the case when it comes to 'non-mainstream' body modification, and less still when it comes to cosmetic surgery which almost always seems to be understood as a problematic form of (self-)mutilation.

'Non-mainstream' body modification is frequently read by (some) psychologists,[30] criminologists,[31] and sociologists[32] as 'self-mutilation', and thus as the symptom of a mental health problem, and/or of self-loathing associated with a history of abuse. It is also often associated with other forms of so-called 'anti-social' behavior such as drug addiction, sex-work, and crime in general. In more liberal accounts of 'self-mutilation', such as the work of McLane whom I mentioned earlier, the person who participates in practices which mark, wound, open, the body is often represented as a victim, as someone who is in need being healed. Further, 'self-mutilation' is frequently cited as a problem most commonly found amongst women and girls. Lists of 'feminine' forms of 'self-mutilation', which include cutting, burning, anorexia, bulimia, drug-abuse, and 'plastic surgery' are also common—as is the association of such practices with the figure of Princess Diana, the fairytale feminine victim of a system that ultimately brought about her complete annihilation.

Despite the fact that those who participate in 'non-mainstream' forms of body modification almost always state, when given the opportunity, that they are enacting new forms of embodiment, that they are defining themselves, that they are enjoying transgressive pleasures, that they are reclaiming their bodies, or that they are making counter-cultural statements with their bodies, such self-interpretations or (re)inscriptions are all too often negated or silenced in and through what Victoria Pitts refers to as mutilation discourse—a body of knowledge that has institutional legitimacy.[33] The following quote which Pitts cites is an example of mutilation discourse. It appears in an article on branding in which the writer interviews a clinical psychologist, a figure endowed with institutional authority. The psychologist says: "They [people who are branded] may think it's adornment, and I'm sure they think its OK, but I would be really interested to find out about their home lives. It's my belief that they're running from something".[34] Given that the article is framed in terms of the question of whether branding is art or simply self-mutilation, the use of the opinion of a so-called 'expert' frustrates, silences, and/or renders illegitimate the claims made by those who practice this particular form of body modification. The implication is, as Pitts notes, that the body modifier is a misguided victim who cannot, and should not, be taken at their word. Thus any claim of agency on the part of the body modifier is rendered at best invalid, and at worst as an attempt to rationalize self-harming desires. The conclusion then is that those who participate in modificatory practices are sick and that the reasons they offer for their behavior are really just rather pathetic and transparent attempts at disavowal.

Similar claims have been made about cosmetic surgery and those who choose to go under the surgeon's knife in order to 'feminize' their bodies. Kathryn Pauly Morgan, for example, claims that what the voices of women who undergo cosmetic surgery *appear* to be saying, and what they are *really* saying, are two entirely different things. Consequently, Morgan's task is to interpret the truth that the unreliable voice of the modifier attempts to disavow. Morgan continues to deny the modifier any subjective agency when, drawing on the assumptions that inform mutilation discourse, she states that the rhetoric of choice conceals the mechanisms of patriarchal exploitation, and that the term 'elective' surgery thus 'performs a seductive role in facilitating the ideological camouflage of the *absence* of choice'.[35]

However, *not* undergoing cosmetic surgery does, in Morgan's terms, consist of making a choice, as her discussion of what she describes as the feminist 'response of refusal' illustrates.[36] If this is so then it is not so much that subjects in general do not have choice because choice is an abstract concept that is founded on a (flawed) humanist model of the subject and of social relations. Rather, the situation is that some women (namely feminists, or at least those who choose *not* to undergo 'cosmetic procedures'—whatever that term might include) can and do make informed choices, whereas other women (namely those who get cosmetic procedures done, and who are, by definition, *not* feminists) might think that they do, but in fact they don't. Or, if the latter do have some sort of agency they choose not to exercise it—a choice which in itself surely involves some level of agency and thus undermines Morgan's claim.

In these 'holier-than-thou' approaches to 'non-mainstream' body modification and cosmetic surgery that I've referred to briefly thus far, the (body of the) other is constituted *as* other: is interpreted, evaluated, and categorized in accordance with the criteria established by the one who seems to have the backing of legitimized institutional discourses. In each case, the voice of the explicitly modified other is silenced, and the relation between self and other, the ways in which these bodies necessarily mark and are marked by one another and by myriad other bodies of knowledge and of flesh, is veiled over and/or disavowed. What we find here are attempts to inscribe and to circumscribe being; attempts to claim, once-and-for-all that I (the subject, the author) am not a victim of patriarchy, of my past, of false-consciousness, unlike the marked other whose flesh is a literal confession of his/her unenlightened being.

This leads me to think that whilst drawing connections between cosmetic surgery, 'non-mainstream' body modification, and transgender practices might have the potential to depathologize the transgender body in *some* theoretical contexts it may well *not* have such a positive effect in others—in particular, in a feminist context (whatever that might mean). On the other hand, articulating some sort of (non-essential and shifting) connection(s) between these various modes of trans-formative embodiment might enable us to bring some of the insights developed by queer or transgender theorists working on transgender bodies to bear on feminist attempts to rethink cosmetic surgery and/or practices and procedures which 'feminize' the body.

BEING/(UN)BECOMING

In an article entitled "Revolting Bodies: The Monster Beauty of Tattooed Women", Christine Braunberger articulates a form of body aesthetics that she calls 'monster beauty'. For the most part I disagree with Braunberger's analysis which relies on a distinction between tattooing, which she claims is a transgressive or 'revolting' aesthetic for women, and cosmetic surgery. But what I do find interesting and useful about the article is, that drawing on the work of Robert Bogden, Braunberger argues that monster beauty is a way of thinking, of presenting; it is a set of (critical) practices rather than the characteristic of an individual.[37] Whilst Braunberger uses this notion of monster beauty as a critical practice to argue that insofar as the aesthetics of monster beauty is concerned with 'becoming monstrous' rather than with 'becoming normal' it is opposed, to cosmetic surgery, I think that it might be possible to use the trope of monstrous (un)becoming in significantly different and more productive ways.

Before I go on to discuss this in more detail, I want firstly to say something more about the tendency apparent in a number of the works that I've discussed thus far, to presume that there are 'good' and 'bad' forms of modification and/or embodiment. As is no doubt clear by now what is considered 'good' and what is regarded as 'bad' is often decided on the basis of how transgressive and/or liberating or, alternatively, how conformist and/or oppressive a practice or way of being appears to be.

Moreover, it is almost always the case that in anti-normative academic analyses, particularly those which one might associate with queer theory, feminism, and/or counter-culturalism, conformity is assumed to be bad and transgression good. There are a number of objections that one could make here however. Firstly, it seems unlikely, as Walker has argued, than any kind of modificatory practice is intrinsically radical or conformist, and, by extension, that any identity is purely 'counter'-cultural. Secondly, it is not enough to unquestioningly assume that conformity is bad and transgression is good or to presume that such categories are stable, discrete, identifiable, and unambiguous. And lastly, as Halberstam points out, despite celebratory claims to the contrary, "the experience of transgression itself is often filled with fear, danger, and shame, rather than heroic self-satisfaction"[38] particularly in contexts other than academia.

Consequently, one could argue that it is impossible to achieve some sort of consensus regarding the political, ethical, or ontological status of a particular practice and/or identity—and this paper is by no means an attempt to do that. What I want to suggest is that rather than setting up oppositions—between, for example, transsexualism and transgender, cosmetic surgery and 'non-mainstream' body-modification, tattooing and face lifts, 'femme' tattoos and 'butch' tattoos, transgender mastectomies and breast augmentations such as those undergone by Lolo Ferrari—that we ask ourselves whether, in one sense at least, all of these forms of embodiment could be said to constitute and to be constituted by, transmogrification: that is, a process of (un)becoming strange and/or grotesque, of (un)becoming other.

TRANSMOGRIFICATION

The word 'strange' connotes a sense of something 'other', something unknown and unaccountable, something that incites wonder. Similarly the term grotesque is often used when referring to a piece of art, a sculpture, or a body that consists of the dis-junction and interweaving of polyvalent elements that somehow resist unification into a singular and 'sensible' whole. One could conclude from this that transmogrification as a process of (un)becoming strange and/or grotesque, is both transgressive and conformist, and simultaneously, is neither of these things. But this is not quite the argument that I want to run here.

What I want to suggest is that the trope of transmogrification might allow us to acknowledge important similarities, overlaps, resonances, and intersections between a range of modified bodies. And that recognizing and theorizing these connections might be helpful to any attempt to rethink trans-embodiment. Perhaps, by extension, it might also allow us to begin to acknowledge and to theorize the ways in which all bodies mark and are marked; to rethink the ways in which bodies are entwined in (un)becoming rather than presuming that they are simply mired in being unless they undergo explicit, visible, and identifiable transformational procedures.

At the same time, however, it seems to me that it's equally important that we pay close critical attention to the *different* ways in which bodies of flesh, bodies of knowledge, and the relations between them, could be said to transmogrify. Obviously mapping these similarities and differences would be a huge task and one that I cannot even begin to undertake in anything like a satisfactory manner in this paper. It is a project that could be approached in a myriad different ways and from an infinite number of angles, and it is a project which, as Halberstam's mapping and theorizing of the similarities and differences between transgender butch and FTM's shows, is already well underway.[39]

In *Female Masculinity*, in a response to Jay Prosser's critique of her earlier essay "F2M: The Making of Female Masculinity," Halberstam states:

> We are not all transsexual, I admit, but many bodies are gender strange to some degree or another, and it is time to complicate on the one hand the transsexual models that assign gender deviance only to trans-sexual bodies and gender normativity to all other bodies, and on the other hand, the hetero-normative models that see transsexuality as the solution to gender deviance and homosexuality as a pathological perversion.[40]

What Halberstam identifies here is two diametrically opposed dichotomies that, as we've seen, inform much of the work produced on transgender bodies and, in fact, on body modification more gener-ally. The first of these involves the (at least implicit) claim that transgender embodiment constitutes a *becoming strange* that is inevitably non-normative, whereas non-transgender embodiment is equated with simply *being normal*: so the opposition between what is transgressive and what is conformist is framed in terms of *becoming strange* versus *being normal*. This sort of argument appears with monotonous frequency in accounts of 'non-mainstream' body modification (and the identities such practices generate) as radical and as opposed to either 'normal' 'unmarked' bodies, or to those which are presumed to have been normalized in and through cosmetic surgery. On the other side of the same theoretical coin we find a distinction being posited between *becoming normal* and *being strange*. This position, found most commonly in pseudo-medical accounts of transsexualism as well as in a significant number of transsexual autobiographies, tolerates body-modificatory practices only insofar as they (supposedly) enable a move away from strangeness and towards normalcy. This sort of posi-tion is also apparent in Kathy Davis' defense of cosmetic surgery against charges of self-mutilation or psycho-somatic colonization, on the grounds that it can alleviate the pain of being strange and engender a process of becoming 'normal'.

What bothers me about the logic that informs both of these positions is that it serves ultimately to set up not only a (false) opposition between the normal and the strange, between conformity and transgression, between being and becoming, and between self and other, but also, an impasse, a dead-end, a wall against which one seems forced to bang one's head repeatedly in the hope of dislodging something. But, as John Caputo points out in his discussion of the work of Jacques Derrida, this aporia is also what drives, impels, sets into motion the desire for something else, for forms of strangeness and/or grotesqueness that I can not pin down nor judge, but whose very incalculability "requires that we calculate, that we enter into legal and political battles".[41]

In an interesting attempt to deconstruct the kind of (humanist) logic of which I have been critical throughout this paper, and, ultimately, to reconfigure identity and difference as always already inter-relational, and in process, Margrit Shildrick[42] suggests that

> the singularity of…subject bodies is…constructed and reiterated by regimes of normalization that defer the slippage of excessive embodiment, [and that this] is obscured by the insistence that monstrosity is radically other.[43]

What Shildrick means by this is that the monstrous other simultaneously defines the limits of the singular embodied subject *and* reflects its fundamental instability and/or vulnerability. The monstrous other, she argues, demonstrates that the relation between self and other, between bodies of flesh and bodies of knowledge is, as Maurice Merleau-Ponty would put it, chiasmatic or fundamentally inter-twined.[44] Or, one could say that body modification alerts us to what Shildrick describes as "the crisis at the boundaries of the body which is never one"[45], because it articulates, literally, the chiasmatic process of transmogrification, of (un)becoming strange, of (un)becoming other. And this brings me to the point that I've been laboring towards for the entirety of this paper—that is, that the connec-tions I've articulated between the different forms of body modification which I've brought together (although not, I hope, in a unifying way) under the heading of transmogrification, might not only function to contest the epistemological and ontological boundaries of bodies of flesh and bodies of knowledge, but, perhaps more importantly, might, by extension, help to (re)configure an ethics—in the Levinasian sense—of intercorporeality. And it might, with any luck, enable a reformulation of the relationship between body modification and justice that acknowledges or is informed by an ethics of intercorporeality. Let me explain what I mean by this.

In much of the recent work on transsexual/transgender bodies, and in many of the accounts of cosmetic surgery that do not wish to simply banish such practices and procedures on the grounds that they are inherently hetero-patriarchal, the claim is that access to modificatory procedures is a matter of justice. Justice here becomes a matter of tolerating difference, of being liberal minded, of allowing the other to claim and to exercise his/her rights, in particular, if s/he is suffering. But as I've demonstrated throughout the paper there are a plethora of problems with this sort of approach, founded, as it is, on the kind of humanist logics that I, like Shildrick, am critical of. Following Derrida, I want to suggest that justice "is not a thing. [It] is not a present entity or order, not an existing reality or regime; nor is it an ideal"[46] towards which we can plot a path. Rather, justice solicits us. Justice is strange, it is a singular call from a future that we cannot know; it is the call of the other who is never separate from the self. Justice, as Caputo so nicely puts it, is

> the relation to the other, the dis-juncture that opens the space for the incoming of the other [the stranger].... Justice haunts us … disturbs the assured distinction between what is and what is not.[47]

Perhaps we could say then, that justice is monstrous, that it is a shape-shifting, a haunting, that not only disturbs humanist logic, but also simultaneously, and necessarily, generates an opening onto alterity, to *différance,* to a future, or futures, yet to come. As Derrida puts it, all experience open to this incalculable, unpredictable and uncontainable future "is prepared or prepares itself to welcome the monstrous *arrivant.*"[48] If this is so, then rather than judging, attempting to define, to know, the modified (body of the) other, we too might welcome (un)becoming other(s). And in this we may begin to engender an ethics of transmogrification.

NOTES

1. Califia, Pat [Califia, Patrick]. (1997) *Sex Changes: The Politics of Transgenderism*, San Francisco: Cleis Press, p.224; Nataf, Zachary (ed.) (1996) *Lesbians Talk Transgender*, London: Scarlet Press, p. 55.
2. Halberstam, Judith (1996) in Nataf (ed.) *Lesbians Talk Transgender*, London: Scarlet Press, pp. 55–6.
3. See, for example, MacKendrick, Karmen (1998) "Technoflesh, of 'Didn't That Hurt?'", *Fashion Theory*, 2:1, pp. 3–24.
4. Walker, Lisa (1998) Embodying Desire: Piercing and the Fashioning of 'Neo butch-femme' Identities", in Sally Munt (ed.) *Butch/Femme: Inside Lesbian Gender*, London: Cassell, pp. 123–32.
5. Juno, Andrea (2000) *Angry Women*, London and San Francisco: RE/Search Publications.
6. See Leslie Asako Gladsjo's (1991) *Stigmata: The Transfigured Body*.
7. See the introduction to Juno, Andrea & V. Vale (1989) *Modern Primitives*, London and San Francisco: RE/Search Publications.
8. Cited in Halberstam, Judith (1998) "Between Butches", in Sally Munt (ed.) Butch/Femme: Inside Lesbian Gender, London: Cassell, p. 60.
9. Nestle, Joan (ed.) (1992) *The Persistent Desire: A Femme/Butch Reader*, Boston: Alyson Press.
10. Martin, Biddy (1996) *Femininity Played Straight: The Significance of Being Lesbian*, London and New York: Routledge.
11. Cvetkovich, Ann (1995) "Recasting Receptivity: Femme Sexualities", Karla Jay (ed.) *Lesbian Erotics*, New York: New York University Press, pp. 125–46.
12. Walker (1998) p. 131.
13. Ibid., p. 131.
14. Davis' work on cosmetic surgery is concerned only with women, and she does not question the possible limits of this conceptual category.

15.   Davis, Kathy (1998) "Facing the Dilemma", in P. D. Hopkins (ed.) *Sex/Machine: Readings in Culture and Technology*, Bloomington: Indiana University Press, p. 304, n. 3.

16.   Davis, Kathy (1999) "'My Body is my Art': Cosmetic Surgery as Feminist Utopia", in Janet Price and Margrit Shildrick (eds.) *Feminist Theory and the Body*, Edinburgh: Edinburgh University Press, pp. 454–65.

17.   Ibid., p. 57.

18.   Orlan, cited in Ayers, Robert (2000) "Serene and Happy and Distant: An Interview With Orlan", Mike Featherstone (ed.) *Body Modification*, London: Sage Publications, pp. 177–8.

19.   Davis, (1999), p. 459.

20.   Morgan, Kathryn Pauly (1995) "Women and the Knife: Cosmetic Surgery and the Colonization of Women's Bodies", in Dana E. Bushnell (ed.) *"Nagging" Questions: Feminist Ethics in Everyday Life*, Boston: Rowman & Littlefield Publishers Inc., p. 313.

21.   Cited in Nataf (1996) pp. 36-7.

22.   Braidotti, Rosi (1996) "Signs of Wonder and Traces of Doubt: On Teratology and Embodied Difference", in Nina Lykke and R. Braidotti (eds.) *Between Monsters, Goddesses, and Cyborgs: Feminist Confrontations with Science, Medicine, and Cyberspace*, London: Zed Press, p. 141.

23.   Jeffreys, Sheila (1998) "Heterosexuality and the Desire for Gender", in D. Richardson (ed.) *Theorising Heterosexuality: Telling it Straight*, Buckingham: Open University press, p. 81–2.

24.   McLane, Janice (1996) "The Voice on the Skin: Self-Mutilation and Merleau-Ponty's Theory of Language", *Hypatia*, 11:4, p. 111.

25.   Stryker, Susan (1994) "My Words to Victor Frankenstein Above the Village of Chamounix: Transgender Rage", *GLQ* Vol.1, particularly p. 240.

26.   Ibid., p. 242.

27.   Ibid., p. 242.

28.   Ibid., p. 250.

29.   See for example, Jeffreys (1998); and Greer, Germaine (2000) *The Whole Woman*, London: Anchor Books.

30.   See, for example, Grumet, G. W. (1983) "Psychodynamic Implications of Tattoos", *The American Journal of Orthopsychiatry*, 53:3, pp. 482–92; Favazza, Armando (1996) *Bodies Under Siege: Self-Mutilation and Body Modification in Culture and Psychiatry*, 2nd ed., Baltimore: Johns Hopkins University Press.

31.   See, for example, Post., Richard (1968) "The Relationship of Tattoos to Personality Disorders", *Journal of Criminal Law, Criminology, and Police Science*, no. 59, pp. 516–24.

32.   Walsh, Barent and Paul Rosen (1988) *Self-Mutilation: Theory, Research and Treatment*, New York: Guilford Press; Hewitt, Kim (1997) *Mutilating the Body: Identity in Blood and Ink*, Bowling Green, OH: Bowling Green State University Popular Press.

33.   Pitts, Victoria (1999) "Body Modification, Self-Mutilation and Agency in Media Accounts of Subculture", *Body & Society*, 5:2-3, pp. 291–303.

34.   Cited in Pitts (1999) p. 299.

35.   Morgan (1995) p. 318.

36.   Ibid., p. 321–4.

37.   Braunberger, Christine (2000) Revolting Bodies: The Monster Beauty of Tattooed Women", in *NWSA Journal* 12:2. p. 8.

38.   Halberstam (1998) p. 59.

39.   Halberstam, Judith (1998) *Female Masculinity*, Durham: Duke University Press.

40.   Halberstam, Judith (1994) "F2M: The Making of Female Masculinity", Laura Doan (ed.) *The Lesbian Postmodern*, New York: Columbia University Press, pp. 210–28.

41.   Caputo, John (1997) *Deconstruction in a Nutshell: A Conversation with Jacques Derrida*, New York: Fordham University Press, p.140

42.   Shildrick, Margrit (1999) "This Body Which Is Not On: Dealing With Differences", Mike Featherstone (ed.) *Body Modification*, London: Sage, pp. 77–92.

43.   Ibid., p. 90

44.   See, Merleau-Ponty, Maurice (1968) The Visible and the Invisible, Evanston, IL: Northwestern University Press, and Shildrick, Margrit (2002) *Embodying the Monster: Encounters With the Vulnerable Self*, London: Sage.

45.   Ibid., p. 90.

46.   Cited in Caputo (1997), p. 131–2.

47.   Ibid., 154–5.

48.   Derrida, (1995) 'Passages – From Traumatism to Promise', in E. Weber (ed) *Points…Interviews, 1974–1994*. Stanford: Stanford Uni press, p. 307.

40

Fin de siècle, Fin du sexe
Transsexuality, Postmodernism, and the Death of History

Rita Felski

Over the past decade it has become commonplace to consider transsexualism and other transgender phenomena to be a symptom of "postmodernism." Rita Felski provides a useful way of thinking about the meaning of this claim by asking, "What is the connection between discourses of the end of history and the end of sex?" Perhaps surprisingly, Felski finds that our cultural imaginings of historical time are related to our understanding of gender difference—and she suggests that the ferment of attention to transgender issues in the 1990s was related to Western culture's fascination with the calendrical event known as Y2K, the impending year 2000.

Felski takes the epigram of her article from the late nineteenth-century French artist Jean Lorrain, who used the phrase "*fin de siecle, fin de sexe*" to describe what he considered to be the historical exhaustion of European culture more than a century ago. Felski contrasts the apocalyptic view of Jean Baudrillard, who sees in the figure of the transsexual the end of all meaning, with the more utopian vision of Donna Haraway, whose implicitly transgender figure, the cyborg, offers the prospect of finding radically new forms of meaning and significance.

Felski concludes with a brief discussion of how transgender issues have been taken up in recent feminist theorizing. She cautions against transgenderism becoming yet another way of effacing the specificity of female and women's experience, yet she is excited by the prospect of using transgender phenomena to better understanding the complex reconfiguration of embodied subjectivity in the new techno-scientific environment of the emerging twenty-first century.

When and how did history die? Was its passing a climactic and catastrophic one, tied to the unspeakable horrors of Auschwitz and Hiroshima which shattered, once and for all, any lingering belief in the redemptive power of Western myths of progress? Or did it dissolve slowly and invisibly into a phantasmagoria of media images, into glossy simulations of a rapidly receding, ever more unknowable past? At what point in time did the idea of history itself become history, did it become possible to say, "that was then, this is now?" And how does this perception of a temporal gulf between "then" and "now," between the era of past history and posthistoire, tally with the claim that we no longer possess a historical consciousness? Is it history that has died, or merely the philosophy of history, and is there a difference? And finally, and most importantly for my present purposes, what is the connection between discourses of the end of history and the end of sex? How do our cultural imaginings of historical time relate to changing perceptions of the meaning and nature of gender difference?

I begin some tentative responses to these questions by noting the pervasiveness of images of transsexuality within much postmodern and poststructuralist thought. For example, in *The Transparency of Evil*, Jean Baudrillard writes, "the sexual body has now been assigned an artificial fate. This fate is transsexuality–transsexual not in any anatomical sense but rather in the more general sense of transvestism, of playing with the commutability of the signs of sex... we are all transsexuals."[1] Here transsexuality, or perhaps more accurately, transgenderism, serves as an overarching metaphor to describe the dissolution of once stable polarities of male and female, the transfiguration of sexual nature into the artifice of those who play with the sartorial, morphological, or gestural signs of sex. The media visibility of such celebrities as Madonna, Michael Jackson, and La Cicciolina becomes symptomatic for Baudrillard of a fascination with the exaggeration, parody, and inversion of signifiers of sexual difference which pervades the entirety of contemporary Western culture. Contemporary critical theory itself both echoes and intensifies such practices of gender bending and blending in its sustained conceptual challenge to the ontological stability of the male/female divide. While male theorists like Derrida, Deleuze, and Baudrillard himself profess their desire to "become woman" by aligning themselves with a feminine principle of undecidability and masquerade, so feminists are in turn increasingly appealing to metaphors of transvestism to describe the mutability and plasticity of the sexed body. Two of the most influential feminist theorists of recent times, Donna Haraway and Judith Butler, have both sought in different ways to break out of the prison house of gender by reconceptualizing masculinity and femininity as performative, unstable, and multiply determined practices.

"Fin de siècle, fin de sexe": the epigram coined by the French artist Jean Lorrain to describe the symbolic affinity of gender confusion and historical exhaustion in the late nineteenth century seems even more apt for our own moment.[2] An existing repertoire of fin-de-siècle tropes of decadence, apocalypse, and sexual crisis is reappropriated through self-conscious citation, yet simultaneously replenished with new meaning, as gender emerges as a privileged symbolic field for the articulation of diverse fashionings of history and time within postmodern thought. Thus the destabilization of the male/female divide is seen to bring with it a waning of temporality, teleology, and grand narrative; the end of sex echoes and affirms the end of history, defined as the pathological legacy and symptom of the trajectory of Western modernity. Ineluctably intertwined in symbiotic relationship, phallocentrism, modernity, and history await their only too timely end, as a hierarchical logic of binary identity and narrative totalization gives way to an altogether more ambiguous and indeterminate condition. Indeed, this idea that history has come to an end has become perhaps the most ubiquitous and least questioned commonplace of postmodern thought, even as particular expressions of this motif vary in register from the nostalgic to the celebratory.

My aim in this paper is not to prove or disprove such claims—the end of history is clearly not a thesis that is amenable to empirical adjudication—but to investigate further the rhetorical mechanisms of their deployment and their varying political agendas. What does it mean exactly to talk about the death of history? To what extent does such a claim tacitly reinscribe the very logic of temporality that it seeks to negate? And to what extent does a perspective sensitive to gender issues either affirm or complicate the thesis of the end of history and the end of sex? Through a brief discussion of the work of Baudrillard and Haraway, two of the most influential diagnosticians of the postmodern moment, I will suggest that their writings are in fact imbued with large-scale visions of historical time which are in turn allied to their diverging views of the transgendered subject as either apocalyptic or redemptive metaphor. I then turn to the work of Italian philosopher Gianni Vattimo, which usefully explores the inevitable historicity of postmodern thought, though I will also argue that it fails to address adequately the different meanings and political valences accruing to particular manifestations of this historicity. Finally, I will consider the significance of discourses of the end of history and the end of sex from the standpoint of feminist theory.

(TRANS)GENDERED HISTORIES: BAUDRILLARD AND HARAWAY

Baudrillard's relentless polemic against the pathology of Western culture depicts a world overflowing with meaning and thus empty of it, a teeming promiscuity of information/communication that is obscene in its total transparency. Media saturation, computerization, the imperatives of consumerist and cybernetic logics conspire to create a hallucinatory limbo of the hyperreal which has no exteriority, no point outside the network. Notions of history, reality, and linear time live on only as exo-skeletal traces, fossilized remains endlessly replayed on the screens of our video terminals. Post 1968, politics has been revealed as a self-delusory project; all forms of liberation—sexual, political, aesthetic—engender only an escalation of networks of simulation which subsume, neutralize, or dissolve all meaning. Increasingly, the model of the code gives way in Baudrillard's work to that of the virus, signaling the invasive yet invisible multiplication of contagious signifiers engaged in constant proliferation.

In Baudrillard's later work, questions of gender and sexuality centrally define this nightmarish vision of an epidemic of signification. *The Transparency of Evil* mourns the reduction of sexuality to "the undifferentiated circulation of the signs of sex" (*TE* 12) as the erotic falls prey to the logic of simulation through its own ubiquitous presence as spectacle. "After the demise of desire," Baudrillard writes, "a pell-mell diffusion of erotic simulacra in every guise, of transsexual kitsch in all its glory" (*TE* 22). In Baudrillard's relentlessly heterosexual and sexist universe, this loss of desire is attributed to the disappearance of sexual difference; we have become "indifferent and undifferentiated beings, androgynous and hermaphroditic" (*TE* 25), creatures without gender and hence without sex. Bio-technological research heralds a brave new world of cloning and parthogenesis, of serial reproduction by celibate machines replicating like protozoa. Feminists in turn accelerate this confusion of gender categories by reducing the once inescapable destiny of being male or female to a matter of preference and rights. The figure of transsexuality thus becomes for Baudrillard a privileged metaphor of a general social process of implosion and de-differentiation which renders all terms commutable and indeterminate. The end of sex echoes and affirms the end of history, understood both as a problem of agency (the eclipse of the subject by the sovereignty of the object) and also of knowledge (the impossibility of imputing any meaning or direction to temporal processes).

Yet, even as he insists that narrative has become impossible, Baudrillard's writings inscribe a metahistorical fiction of the first order, articulating a powerfully nostalgic narrative of the fall. Harking back to an imagined era of referential plenitude, they emplot an exemplary parable of the decline of Western civilization from the standpoint of the latecomer, the one who comes after. At one point, Baudrillard writes, "we are merely epigones. . . . The highest level of intensity lies behind us. The lowest level of passion and intellectual illumination lies ahead of us."[3] Such a melancholic vision of cultural decadence is of course a recurring trope within the modern, the faithful and constant shadow of the overarching myth of historical progress. On the one hand, Baudrillard denies the possibility of a meaningful future, claiming that linear and progressive time no longer exist in an imploding universe where history turns back on itself in a necrophilic spiral of infinite regression. In the mythic no-time of TV that we all inhabit, history is flattened out into a smorgasbord of endlessly recycled images of the past. On the other hand, this very diagnosis explicitly posits a history that once was and is no more, expressing a profoundly historical sense of the current impossibility of history. Even as he insists that linear time has been replaced by reversibility and repetition, Baudrillard reinscribes a temporal schema structured around the triadic relation of a disappearing present, an absent future, and an authentically self-present, if no longer knowable past.

This point can be highlighted by considering Donna Haraway's very different emplotment of historical time. Like Baudrillard, Haraway insists on the radical transformation of social relations engendered by cybernetic systems, biotechnological innovation, and an all-pervasive dissemination of media networks. She too argues that old oppositions of masculine and feminine, along with their corollary distinctions of private versus public, mind versus body, culture versus nature, no longer hold in the new world system that she entitles the informatics of domination. In this context she introduces her resonant symbol of the postmodern cyborg, a hybrid blend of male and female, organism and machine, that emblematizes the contemporary fusion and intermingling of previously distinct categories. We are all cyborgs now, she states; "the cyborg is our ontology, it gives us our politics."[4] Haraway's transgendered cyborg, however, bears little kinship to Baudrillard's transsexual subject. An ironic and polyvalent symbol of both matrices of domination and possibilities of resistance, it gestures resolutely toward the future rather than gazing toward the past. Instead of demonizing technology and taking refuge in a nostalgic vision of an organic feminine, Haraway argues, feminists need to explore the new possibilities, pleasures, and politics made possible by transgressed boundaries and fragmented selves. The cyborg serves as a feminist icon for the postmodern era, an unruly child of technological systems that it simultaneously exploits and contests.

How, then, do cyborgs embody or subvert existing patterns of historical time? Haraway explicitly refuses the redemptive frame of Western progress narratives as well as the organicist myth of the fall. The cyborg, she declares, is outside salvation history and has no origin story; it rejects the seductions of vanguard politics and teleological notions of agency. Yet even as it weaves its way among multiple perspectives, Haraway's manifesto (a quintessentially modernist genre which her text both ionizes and reproduces) expresses a deeply historical awareness of the irreversible and linear nature of time. Drawing upon Fredric Jameson's tripartite scheme of capitalist development, her argument insists on both the distinctiveness of our own epoch and the impossibility of returning to an earlier moment. "We cannot go back ideologically or materially," she writes; "it's not just that 'god' is dead, so is the 'goddess'" (204). The "Manifesto for Cyborgs" is a text permeated by a strong sense of its own temporality, of the irrevocable historical transformation of our material and conceptual universe by cybernetic and biotechnological logics which have definitively severed us from our own past. Without minimizing the logics of domination shaping our own era, Haraway seeks nonetheless to recuperate both political agency and the redemptive promise of the future. Coding the transgendered subject of the postmodern as liberating icon rather than nightmarish catastrophe, she sees new and unimagined possibilities in hybrid gender identities and complex fusions of previously distinct realities. In its expectant and hopeful gesturing toward a "not yet" that may liberate women from the naturalized oppressions and dichotomies of the past, Haraway thus carves a resolutely utopian, forward-looking temporality out of social conditions often identified with the dwindling of political possibilities.

The texts of Baudrillard and Haraway, then, exemplify two very different political and philosophical responses to the de-differentiation of sexual difference as postmodern trope. Transsexuality, as Sandy Stone observes, currently functions as a hotly contested site of cultural inscription; this contestation expresses itself not simply in ongoing disputes between doctors, feminists, and transsexuals themselves, as Stone argues, but also in the more general cultural appropriations of the figure of transsexuality as a semiotically dense emblem in the rhetoric of fin de millenium.[5] Interpreted as historical symptom or philosophical symbol, this figure inspires a multiplicity of claims and counterclaims regarding its liberatory or catastrophic meanings. Nowhere is this more apparent than in two recent anthologies on gender and the postmodern body edited by Arthur and Marilouise Kroker, *Body Invaders* and *The Last Sex*.[6] Here celebrations of transsexuality as perverse artifice couched in the vocabulary of postmodern feminism and queer theory are juxtaposed alongside dark apocalyptic imaginings of docile bodies completely inscribed by intersecting grids of commodification and biotechnological control. While *Body Invaders* inclines toward a more pessimistic reading of the aestheticized body as a dystopian symbol of the omnipresent tyranny of simulation, *The Last Sex* euphorically celebrates

this same free-floating aestheticism as the necessary precondition for a future transgender liberation and the emergence of a third sex. Thus the editors rhapsodically gesture toward a "new sexual
horizon" that is "post-male and post-female"; their goal, they write, is to achieve the indeterminate
state of "female, yet male, organisms occupying an ironic, ambivalent and paradoxical state of sexual
identity."[7] If ends of centuries serve as privileged cultural moments for articulating highly charged
myths of death and rebirth, senescence and renewal, in our own era such hopes and anxieties are writ
large across proliferating representations of the transgendered body.

THE PARADOX OF HISTORICITY: GIANNI VATTIMO

What interests me in these various writings, then, is not just the weighty yet conflicting meanings
assigned to transsexuality in recent theories of the postmodern, but also the paradoxical reinscription
of historicity in the very act of its disavowal. Even as they subvert conventional structures of sociological realism and philosophical narrative through fragmented and multiperspectival forms, the texts I
have discussed simultaneously reveal a profound sense of locatedness in time, positioning themselves
in relation to past and future histories that are richly endowed with both redemptive and dystopian
meanings. This paradox is explored in some detail by a contemporary theorist of the condition of
posthistoire, Gianni Vattimo. According to Vattimo, the defining feature of the modern is its narrative
structuring of time as the progressive realization of an ideal of human emancipation; modernity is
epitomized by a project of Hegelian overcoming which assumes the emancipatory value of the new
as a means of transcending the errors of the past. Vattimo thus agrees with Lyotard and others that
postmodernity signals the dissolution of such a unilinear narrative of history with its corollary notions
of progress and overcoming. What has come to an end, Vattimo insists, is not simply a certain set of
ideas about history, but history itself, insofar as history is inseparable from its rhetorical articulation
as a metaphysically driven narrative.[8]

Yet Vattimo also recognizes the contradictory nature of such a claim; the elevation of the postmodern
over the modern reproduces precisely that same gesture of historical overcoming, the valorization of
the new and the now over the inauthentic past, that is endemic to the logic of the modern itself. The
critique of history and modernity thereby reveals itself to be inexorably enmeshed within the very
Enlightenment narrative that it seeks to contest. As many writers have noted, the announcement of
the end of metanarratives thus becomes another metanarrative, which assigns an ontological reality
to history in the very act of its negation. Here Vattimo takes Lyotard to task for seeking to ground
his own account of the postmodern through unproblematic procedures of historical legitimation. To
argue that Auschwitz, or the terrors of Stalinism, have irrevocably dissolved the project of modernity
is to endow such events with world-historical significance and hence to reaffirm the very philosophy
of history that is ostensibly being called into question.[9] Vattimo's aim here is not to minimize the tragic
and unspeakable events of the twentieth century, but merely to note that they cannot in themselves
prove or disprove a progress narrative without recourse to a competing account, such as a view of the
modern as exemplifying a historical logic of escalating domination. Similarly, Lyotard's insistence on
the unrepresentability and singularity of Auschwitz as signaling the definitive dissolution of Western
progress narratives would itself be seen by Vattimo as a profoundly historical affirmation of the irreversible change of consciousness brought about by a particular event. These events, in turn, never
speak to us in their raw actuality, but always involve multilayered processes of mediation, interpretation, and emplotment.

According to Vattimo, then, the heritage of history and modernity cannot simply be transcended,
because any such project of going beyond history must remain trapped in the very logic of overcoming that it seeks to contest. While archaism and progressivism, the idealization of the past and of the

future, are both revealed as philosophically bankrupt positions, Vattimo simultaneously insists that we cannot transcend metaphysics but can at best begin to recover from it as if from a sickness. Thus he advocates an alternative of Heideggerian *Verwindung*, a resigned and self-conscious acceptance of one's own necessary implication within historicism which thereby seeks to deflect much of its force. Yet Vattimo is himself, I would argue, insufficiently self-conscious in his philosophical emplotment of the *Bildung* of a metahistorical subject which has lost its previous unconditional belief in the universal truth of history. First of all, such a sweeping narrative ignores alternative voices and traditions within the history of modernity itself; one might consider, for example, the ambiguous yet often contestatory relationship of nineteenth-century feminist discourses to dominant male-centered philosophies of history.[10] The repeated inscription of a single linear trajectory from modern totality to postmodern plurality within much contemporary theory simply reaffirms a reified and ultimately problematic construction of the homogeneity of the past. Secondly, this same narrative is in turn insufficiently attuned to the nonsynchronous relations of various social groups to the condition of historicity in our own time. Thus the present explosion of women's texts exploring issues of memory, temporality, tradition, and change seemingly contradicts the bland assertion that "we" no longer live historically. To assume that because history is not pure event, it can only be defined philosophically, to reduce the question of history to a problem in the self-critique of Western metaphysics, is surely to fall prey to a disabling theoreticism unable to address the multiple discursive sites at which the category of the historical is constituted as a social and pragmatic concern. Indeed, from a sociological perspective, one might speak not of the death of grand narratives but the proliferation of them, as ever more subordinate groups identify themselves as historical actors in the public domain.

Thus second-wave feminism, for example, has given rise to diverse and conflictual fashionings of historical time. One of its most familiar stories emplots the historical *Bildung* of the female subject as she liberates herself from the manacles of tradition and the constraints of the past in order to enter and transform the world as an autonomous, self-determining, modern individual. An opposed and equally influential feminist narrative appropriates and rewrites the myth of the fall, situating an authentic femininity in a nondifferentiated prelapsarian condition (nature, the organic, the pre-Oedipal) prior to the alienating subject-object split of modernity. Both of these competing stories have come to appear increasingly problematic in their construction of a historical metanarrative grounded in a normative ideal of femininity, as poststructuralist feminists have been eager to point out. Yet, as my discussion of Haraway suggests, such critiques in turn engender their own developmental stories and binary oppositions in describing how the naive essentialisms and binarisms of early feminist thought have given way to the more enlightened, sophisticated, and theoretically self-conscious perspectives of the present. Indeed, as M. J. Devaney has recently argued, the discourse of legitimation of much postmodernist thought often invokes a relatively uncomplicated idea of progress in its claims to refute the past errors of a univocal and monolithic entity variously defined as modernity/Enlightenment thinking/the Western metaphysical tradition.[11]

Rather than seeking simply to "transcend" narrative or teleology, then, feminism can perhaps more usefully acknowledge both its own inevitable enmeshment within rhetorics of emplotment and their changing forms, meanings, and effects. To argue that the evident failure of Western myths of progress renders any further appeal to history terroristic and totalizing is surely to remain trapped within a logic of identity which subsumes the changing uses and elaborations of a particular paradigm within the binary logic of either/or: *either* metanarrative and hence a reactionary because totalizing politics, *or* linguistic fragmentation and (by questionable analogy) social freedom. One might insist at this point that Western feminist metanarratives, however problematic in certain respects, *mean* differently from those of liberalism or Marxism, because of their own historically particular and relatively fragile relationship to institutional power and authority.[12] The politics of big historical stories is not, after all, given in their form, but depends upon the specific mechanisms of their deployment, circulation, and institutionalization. Such stories may, for example, help to engender symbolic solidarities and affiliations within disadvantaged groups eager for enabling myths of origin or inspiratory utopias, even as they may in turn become regulatory mechanisms of exclusion and totalization. Which of these will turn out to be the case can surely only be answered in contingent rather than absolute terms.

In his recent work, Vattimo both acknowledges yet minimizes the force of such oppositional voices in noting that the new visibility of social movements and minorities has irrevocably pluralized, and hence dissolved, the category of history. For Vattimo, like Baudrillard, the proliferation of histories signals the death of history, leaving only multiple images of the past projected from different points of view.[13] Yet this is surely to construct an over-simple relationship between the universal and the particular, as if the histories being written by women or postcolonial peoples, to take just two examples, comprised nothing more than a random plurality of local narratives, whose various truth claims remained inaccessible to meaningful adjudication. Yet many of these histories seek to contest and transform our view of the past by discovering its exclusions, oppressions, and hidden triumphs, to rewrite and extend, rather than negate, history. The discourses of contemporary social movements such as feminism often seem in this respect to blur the clarity of the ubiquitous distinction between *grands* and *petits récits*. As narratives engendered by a profound sense of exclusion from conventional Oedipal genealogies, they question rather than affirm the notion of a universal subject of history; yet they also seek to reconfigure our understanding of both past and present in a manner that transcends the local. From the perspective of those whose view of historical knowledge is indissolubly linked to the pragmatics of everyday life and contestatory politics in the public arena, Vattimo's own metatheoretical pronouncements may speak more eloquently of the European philosopher's crisis of faith in a particular metaphysical tradition than of the status of history as such. As Judith Roof has noted, such a strategy does not undermine intellectual authority so much as reinscribe it; the truth that there is no truth, the knowledge that history no longer exists, becomes the new locus of the certainty, identity, and will to power that is ostensibly being displaced.[14]

CONCLUSION

This in turn brings me back to my starting point: the figure of transsexuality or transgenderism as the site of deeply invested and symbolically charged rewritings of history and time. In counterposing the differing temporalities shaping the work of Baudrillard and Haraway, I do not seek to make them represent "male" versus "female" versions of the postmodern; any such move would oversimplify diverse and often conflicting representations of history on both sides of the gender divide. Yet particular cultural affiliations and identifications undoubtedly shape our imaginings of temporal processes; the obsessive relationship to a past historicity that marks the texts of Marxist and post-Marxist theorists such as Baudrillard, Jameson, Lyotard, and Vattimo engenders a narrative of loss that is by no means as universal as these writers often assume. Thus even a cursory glance at recent feminist writings reveals an array of rather different temporalities when it is woman, rather than man, who is envisioned as the imaginary subject of history. Even as they call into question existing Oedipal stories, such texts insist on the relevance of history as an ongoing concern rather than a defunct problematic for many women. Furthermore, as evidenced by my discussion of Haraway, the questioning of sexual difference does not inevitably signal a waning of the historical imagination; rather, it may help to generate powerful new feminist stories of possible futures, fueling imaginative projections of new worlds and alternative genealogies.

Such a claim itself, of course, paradoxically undermines the trope of transgenderism by drawing attention to the particular gender-political affiliations shaping the formation of cultural narratives of beginnings and ends. The end of sex is an idea whose truth is self-evidently symbolic rather than literal, yet even as metaphor it captures only one aspect of the contemporary cultural imaginary. Not all social subjects, after all, have equal freedom to play with and subvert the signs of gender, even as many do not perceive such play as a necessary condition of their freedom. As Arjun Appadurai has argued in a different context, we cannot grasp the complex cultural dynamics of our own time in terms of a single logic of either increasing homogeneity or heterogeneity; rather, we need to consider the diverse and often simultaneous movements between de-differentiation and redifferentiation that are played out across the force fields of cultural worlds.[15] Thus even as gender distinctions are irrevocably denaturalized through economic, political, and technological changes, so in turn the very question of women's specificity and difference has come to the fore as never before. The erosion of gender remains indissolubly linked to the affirmation of particular gendered identities, such that a conventional opposition of "equality" and "difference" feminism reveals itself as an illusory and misleading antithesis.

In this sense, transgenderism remains a necessarily ambiguous figure for feminist theorists. I have questioned the view that symbols of gender crisis are inextricably linked to a loss of historicity and agency; in both the last fin de siècle and our own, this seems much more true of the feminized male than of the masculinized woman, whose ambiguous gendering is frequently charged with historical purpose and an exhilarating sense of new possibilities rather than with decadence and exhaustion. Thus the remarkable influence and impact of the Harawayan cyborg on the feminist imaginary undoubtedly bears witness to a widespread desire for inspiratory icons which do not simply reproduce extant images of idealized femininity. Yet Susan Bordo introduces a useful note of caution into the feminism/postmodernism debate, suggesting that such celebrations of multiple and shifting identities may merely serve once again to elide the particularity of women and to deny the specificity of gendered embodiment. Furthermore, the very prominence of metaphors of transvestism and cross-dressing within contemporary feminism has been called into question by Eve Sedgwick and Michael Moon, who argue that this often careless appropriation works to elide the particularities of actual transvestite cultures and practices, including their intimate and ongoing linkage to the history of homosexuality.[16] The same is of course true of transsexuality; its elevation to the status of universal signifier ("we are all transsexuals") subverts established distinctions between male and female, normal and deviant, real and fake, but at the risk of homogenizing differences that matter politically: the differences between women and men, the difference between those who occasionally play with the trope of transsexuality and those others for whom it is a matter of life or death.

Gender, in this sense, remains both essential and impossible for feminism, which shifts between a radical questioning of the ontology of femininity and an insistence upon its real effects. Neither the idealization nor the demonization of recent theories of transvestism and transsexuality, it seems to me, does adequate justice to feminism's always already conflictual relationship to the male/female divide. A similar oscillation between affirmation and negation also typifies the condition of history, which flickers persistently on our horizon in a movement of simultaneous doing and undoing. Clearly, our present imaginings of time differ markedly from nineteenth-century depictions of the purposeful unfolding of the laws of history. Yet in conceding the demise of Victorian evolutionism we do not negate, but rather affirm, our own sense of historicity, our recognition that certain assumptions and vocabularies are now no longer possible. The waning of nineteenth-century models of history does not necessarily signal a loss of locatedness in time or of the desire to imbue cultural phenomena with meaning by locating them within larger temporal frames. The distinction lies, perhaps, in the fact that we have become more aware of the speculative nature of our stories, and of their inevitable plurality, rather than in the fact that we have gone "beyond" them. Narratives of the end of history are, I have suggested, in this sense symptomatic of the very historicity they seek to disavow.

To put it another way, the signifier "history" has more than one referent. Often, as in the case of Baudrillard and Jameson, the proliferation of diverse histories in our own era is acknowledged only in order to be negated. It is only because we no longer have access to a true history, the argument runs, that we are increasingly surrounded by impoverished simulacra of the historical. Quite apart from the epistemological problems posed by such sweeping distinctions between authentic and inauthentic forms of representation, this nostalgic narrative works to erase the power-laden logics of previous histories, including, I would insist, their problematic relationship to women and questions of gender. In renouncing this unilinear trajectory from the presence to the absence of history, we leave ourselves free to ask other kinds of questions. How do current apprehensions of historical time either appropriate, transform, or contest those of earlier eras? To what extent do these diverse apprehensions bear witness to conflicting visions of the politics of history on the part of particular cultural groups? How can we remain attentive to disjuncture and nonsynchrony in the experience of temporality while simultaneously acknowledging systematic connections and relations among discrete cultural practices? From such a standpoint, the thesis of the end of history merely repeats rather than subverts the ongoing myth of a universal history.

NOTES

Originally published in *Centuries' Ends, Narrative Means*, edited by Robert D. Newman (Stanford University Press, 1996). No portion of this text may be reproduced without the express permission of the publisher.

1. Jean Baudrillard, *The Transparency of Evil* (New York, 1993), pp. 20–21; hereafter cited in text as *TE*.
2. Cited in Will L. McLendon, "Rachilde: *Fin-de-Siècle* Perspectives on Perversity," in *Modernity and Revolution in Late Nineteenth-Century France*, ed. Barbara T. Cooper and Mary Donaldson-Evans (Newark, Del., 1992), pp. 52–61.
3. Jean Baudrillard, *Cool Memories* (London, 1990), p. 149.
4. Donna Haraway, "A Manifesto for Cyborgs: Science, Technology and Socialist Feminism in the 1980s," in *Feminism/Postmodernism*, ed. Linda Nicholson (London, 1990), p. 191; hereafter cited in text.
5. Sandy Stone, "The *Empire* Strikes Back: A Posttranssexual Manifesto," in *Body Guards: The Cultural Politics of Gender Ambiguity*, ed. Julia Epstein and Kristina Straub (New York, 1991), p. 294. I am grateful to Andrew Parker for providing me with a copy of this text.
6. Arthur Kroker and Marilouise Kroker, *Body Invaders: Panic Sex in America* (New York, 1987) and *The Last Sex* (New York, 1993).
7. Arthur and Marilouise Kroker, "Scenes from the Last Sex: Feminism and Outlaw Bodies," in *The Last Sex*, pp. 18–19.
8. Gianni Vattimo, *The End of Modernity: Nihilism and Hermeneutics in a Postmodern Culture* (Baltimore, 1988).
9. See Gianni Vattimo, "The End of (Hi)story," in *Zeitgeist in Babel: The Postmodernist Controversy*, ed. Ingeborg Hoesterey (Bloomington, Ind., 1991), pp. 132–41.
10. See Rita Felski, *The Gender of Modernity* (Cambridge, Mass., 1995), ch. 6.
11. M. J. Devaney, "'Since at Least Plato' and Other Postmodernist Myths," unpublished doctoral dissertation, University of Virginia, 1994.
12. Susan Bordo also makes this point. See her "Feminism, Postmodernism and Gender-Scepticism," in *Feminism/Postmodernism*, pp. 133–56.
13. Gianni Vattimo, *The Transparent Society* (Baltimore, 1992), p. 3.
14. Judith Roof, "Lesbians and Lyotard," in *The Lesbian Postmodern*, ed. Laura Doan (New York, 1994), p. 59.
15. Arjun Appadurai, "Disjuncture and Difference in the Global Cultural Economy," in *The Phantom Public Sphere*, ed. Bruce Robbins (Minneapolis, 1993), pp. 269–95.
16. Bordo, "Feminism, Postmodernism and Gender-Scepticism," pp. 144–45; Eve Kosofsky Sedgwick and Michael Moon, "Divinity: a Dossier, a Performance Piece, a Little Understood Emotion," in Eve Sedgwick, *Tendencies* (Durham, N.C., 1993), pp. 219–24.

41

Skinflick

Posthuman Gender in Jonathan Demme's *The Silence of the Lambs*

Judith Halberstam

THE STATEMENT "IDENTITY IS ONLY SKIN DEEP" sums up Judith Halberstam's analysis of Jonathan Demme's controversial film, *The Silence of the Lambs*. She addresses late-twentieth-century angst over body manipulation and modification, and looks beyond available categories of gendered personhood and sexed embodiment to develop a new, potentially post-human, construct of the self.

In her discussion of the psychopathic killer "Buffalo Bill," Halberstam deftly circumvents then-current criticisms of queer activists who dismissed Demme's film as a "negative representation" of gay issues. Buffalo Bill is neither homosexual nor transsexual, Halberstam contends, despite his wish to be contained within a woman's skin. Rather, he is an emblem of the discomfort we all feel with our bodies in postmodern societies. The monstrosity he represents is not one that is readily reduced to and contained within his individual body, but is instead the effect of a social process—a set of banal, impersonally menacing, bureaucratic operations that constantly work on and transform all of our bodies. Figures like Buffalo Bill, and like the figure of the transsexual, speak to broader concerns with the meaning of embodiment in a culture obsessed with dieting, working out, tattooing, piercing, or otherwise modifying our flesh.

Halberstam has made many powerful contributions to transgender studies, queer theory, and feminism—most notably her widely adopted turn-of-phrase, "female masculinity." Her work has been especially influential because it provides a common ground upon which a broader intellectual community can better appreciate the relevance of specific issues emerging within transgender scholarship, while simultaneously helping transgender scholars contextualize their own work within broader currents and trends in contemporary critical inquiry.

The monster, as we know it, died in 1963 when Hannah Arendt published her "Report on the Banality of Evil" entitled *Eichmann in Jerusalem*. Adolf Eichmann, as the representative of a system of unspeakable horror, stood trial for "Crimes Committed Against Humanity." Arendt refused, in her report, to grant the power of horror to the ordinary looking man who stood trial. While the press commented on the monster who hides behind the banal appearance, Arendt turned the equation around and recognized the banality of a monstrosity that functions as a bureaucracy. She writes:

> [The prosecutor] wanted to try the most abnormal monster the world had ever seen . . . [The Judges] knew, of course, that it would have been very comforting indeed to believe that Eichmann was a monster, even though if he had been Israel's case against him would have collapsed. . . . The trouble with Eichmann was

precisely that so many were like him, and that the many were neither perverted nor sadistic, that they were, and still are, terribly and terrifyingly normal.[1]

Arendt's relegation of Eichmann from monster dripping with the blood of a people to the conformist clerk who does his job and does not ask questions suggests that crime and corrupt politics and murder all demand complicit and silent observers. Eichmann's crime was that he was no monster, no aberration from the norm.

What exactly is the comfort of making Eichmann or others like him into monsters? Monsters confirm that evil resides in specific bodies, particular psyches. Monstrosity as the bodily manifestation of evil makes evil into a local effect, not generalizable across a society or culture. But modernity has eliminated the comfort of monsters because we have seen, in Nazi Germany and elsewhere, that evil works often as a system, it works through institutions and it works as a *banal* (meaning "common to all") mechanism. In other words evil stretches across cultural and political productions as complicity and collaboration.

Modernity makes monstrosity a function of consent and a result of habit. Monsters of the nineteenth century—like Frankenstein, like Dracula—certainly still scare and chill but they scare us from a distance. We wear modern monsters like skin, they are us, they are on us and in us. Monstrosity no longer coagulates into a specific body, a single face, a unique feature, it is replaced with a banality that fractures resistance because the enemy becomes harder and harder to locate, and looks more and more like the hero. What were monsters are now facets of identity; the sexual other and the racial other cannot be separated from self. But still, we keep our monsters ready.

Horror lies just beneath the surface, it lurks in dark alleys, it hides behind a rational science, it buries itself in respectable bodies, so the story goes. In a postmodern horror movie, *The Silence of the Lambs* (1991) by Jonathan Demme, fear no longer assumes a depth/surface model; after this movie (but perhaps all along) horror resides at the level of skin itself. Skin is at once the most fragile of boundaries and the most stable of signifiers; it is the site of entry for the vampire, the signifier of race for the nineteenth-century monster; skin is precisely what does not fit, Frankenstein sutures his monster's ugly flesh together by binding it in a yellow skin, too tight and too thick. When, in the modern horror movie, terror rises to the surface, the surface itself becomes a complex web of pleasure and danger; the surface rises to the surface, the surface becomes Leatherface, becomes Demme's Buffalo Bill, and everything that rises must converge.

Demme's film weaves its horror and its pleasure around the remains of other horror films and literature. It quotes from Alfred Hitchcock's *Psycho*, from Brian De Palma's *Dressed To Kill*, from William Wyler's *The Collector* and it features a reincarnation of Bram Stoker's insane Renfield, the murderous idiot savant of *Dracula*. This film, indeed, has cannibalized its genre, consumed it bones and all and reproduced it in a slick and glossy representation of representations of violence, murder, mutilation, matricide and the perverse consequences of gender confusion. *The Silence of the Lambs* is precisely never silent, it hums with past voices, other stories; it holds the murmur of vampires, the outrage of the monster's articulations, the whispers of the beasts who were told but never got to tell. The viewer is now a listener, a listener to the narrative of the monster.

But, in *The Silence of the Lambs*, the monster is everywhere and everyone and the monster's story is not distinguishable from other textual productions validated within the film. *The Silence of the Lambs* skillfully pits Jodie Foster as FBI agent Clarice Starling against the charismatic intellect of ex-psychiatrist and serial murderer Dr. Hannibal "the Cannibal" Lecter played by Anthony Hopkins. Starling goes to visit Lecter in his maximum security cell in order to engage his help in tracking down a serial killer. The murderer has been nicknamed Buffalo Bill because he skins his female victims after murdering them.

Starling is no match for Lecter and he manipulates her by insisting upon "quid pro quo" or an equal exchange of information. In return for information about Buffalo Bill, Lecter demands that Starling tell him her nightmares, her most awful memories of childhood, her darkest fears. As she reveals her stories to Lecter's scrutiny, Starling is forced to relinquish the authority invested in her position as detective. Suddenly, with only the glass separating the two, Starling seems no more free than Lecter; both are incarcerated by knowledge or lack of, by memory, by power structures, by violence, by the unnameable menace of Lecter the Intellecter.

Dr. Hannibal Lecter is considered an unusual threat to society not simply because he murders people and consumes them, but because as a psychiatrist he has access to minds. He is someone "you don't want inside your head," Starling's boss warns her; of course you don't want him inside your body either and you certainly don't want to let him put you inside his! Boundaries between people (detective and criminal, men and women, murderers and victims) are all mixed up in this film until they disappear altogether, becoming as transparent as the glass that (barely) divides Lecter and Starling. Lecter illustrates to perfection the spooky and uncanny effect of confusing boundaries, inside and outside, consuming and being consumed, watching and being watched. He specializes in getting under one's skin, into one's thoughts and he makes little of the classic body/mind split as he eats bodies and sucks minds dry.

The subplot in *The Silence of the Lambs* involves the tracking of murderer-mutilator Buffalo Bill. Buffalo Bill, we find out, skins his victims because he suffers a kind of gender dysphoria that he thinks can be solved by covering himself in female skin; in fact, he is making himself a female body suit, or "a woman suit" as Starling puts it, and he murders simply to gather the necessary fabric. Buffalo Bill, of course, is no Lecter, no thinker, he is all body, but the wrong body. Lecter points out that Buffalo Bill hates identity, he is simply at odds with any identity whatsoever; no body, no gender will do and so he has to sit at home with his skins and fashion a completely new one. What he constructs is a posthuman gender; a gender beyond the body, beyond human, a carnage of identity.

Buffalo Bill symbolizes the problem of a kind of literal skin disease but all the other characters in the film are similarly, although not necessarily pathologically, discomforted. Skin, in this movie, creeps and crawls, it is the most fragile of covers and also the most sticky. Skin becomes a metaphor for surface, for the external; it is the place of pleasure and the site of pain, it is the thin sheet that masks bloody horror. But skin is also the movie screen, the destination of the gaze, the place that glows in the dark, the violated site of visual pleasure.

In a by now very influential article, Laura Mulvey writes "sadism demands a story." "Visual Pleasure and Narrative Cinema," of course, attempts to develop a theory of spectatorship that addresses itself to questions of who finds what pleasurable.[2] Such questions become all too pertinent when we consider that audiences change through history even as monsters do. Women were once the willing audience of the literature of horror, Gothic indeed was written for female consumers, but now women watch horror films, with reluctance and with fear, reluctant to engage with their everyday nightmares of rape and violation, fearful that the screen is only a mirror and that the monster may be sitting next to them as they watch. Films that feature sadistic murderers stalking unsuspecting female victims simply confirm a certain justified paranoia which means that women aren't crazy to be paranoid about rape and murder but rather they are crazy not to be.

For the female spectator of the horror movie, pleasure has to do with identification. Do we identify, in other words, with the detective or the victim, with the murderer persecuted by his gender markings or with the disembodied intellect of the imprisoned psychiatrist? This film allows us the pleasure of many different identifications and refuses to reduce female to a mess of mutilated flesh. The woman detective or female dick alters traditional power relations and changes completely the usual trajectory of the horror narrative. So does Dr. Hannibal Lecter when he refuses to answer Starling's questions until she has answered his. His story requires her story, and hers depends upon his. Each role in this narrative is now fraught with violence, with criminality, with textuality; no role is innocent, no mind is pure, no body impenetrable. Each role demands and produces a narrative, a text, about violence and evil, about the painful things people do to each other. Like the skin that Buffalo Bill attempts to suture into identity, stories in *The Silence of the Lambs* cover the nakedness of fear and fashion it into horror. The camera glances at mutilation and then frames it within more stories, more sadism, more silence. The silence of the lambs of course is no silence at all but rather a babble of voices fighting to be heard.

I resist, then, the temptation to submit Demme's film to a feminist analysis that would identify the danger of showing mass audiences an aestheticized version of the serial killing of women. I resist the temptation to brand the film as homophobic because gender confusion becomes the guilty secret of the mad man in the basement. I resist indeed the readings that want to puncture the surface and enter the misogynist and homophobic unconscious of Buffalo Bill, Hannibal the Cannibal and Clarice Starling. The film indeed demands that we stay at the surface and look for places where the surface stretches too thin. We cannot look to the ruptures to reveal the truth of pleasure or the pleasure of truth but we can look to the places where skin becomes transparent and see that nothing is hidden. Gender trouble, indeed, is not the movie's secret, it is a confession that both Starling and Buffalo Bill are all too willing to make.

And yet, the gender trouble that Buffalo Bill represents, as he prances around in a wig and plays with a poodle called Precious, cannot be simply dismissed. It seems to me that *The Silence of the Lambs* emphasizes that we are at a peculiar time in history, a time when it is becoming impossible to tell the difference between prejudice and its representations, between, then, homophobia and representations of homophobia. In the example of *The Silence of the Lambs*, I would agree with Hannibal Lecter's pronouncement that Buffalo Bill is not reducible to "homosexual," or "transsexual." He is indeed a man at odds with gender identity or sexual identity and his self-presentation is a confused mosaic of signifiers. In the basement scene he resembles a heavy metal rocker as much as a drag queen and that is precisely the point. He is a man imitating gender, exaggerating gender and finally attempting to shed his gender in favor of a new skin. Buffalo Bill is prey to the most virulent conditioning heterosexist culture has to offer. He believes that anatomy is destiny.

A film like *The Silence of the Lambs* creates disagreement not just between those who see it as homophobic and those who don't, but between the lesbian and heterosexual feminists who were thrilled to see a woman cast as a tough detective character, and the gay men who felt offended by Buffalo Bill. It also divides sentiment along gender lines: I think *The Silence of the Lambs* is a horror film that, for once, is not designed to scare women, it scares men instead with the image of a fragmented and fragile masculinity, a male body disowning the penis.

Buffalo Bill, we may recall, uses female skin to cover his pathological gender dysphoria. He is a seamstress, a collector of textiles and fabrics and an artist who fashions death into new life and in so doing he divorces sex from murder. This is a new kind of killer. Buffalo Bill is not interested in getting in women, he never rapes them, he simply wants to get them out of a skin that he perceives as the essence of female. Buffalo Bill reads his desire against his body and realizes that he has the wrong body, at least externally. He is a woman trapped in a man's skin but no transsexual. Hannibal's remark to Starling that this man is not a transsexual and not a homosexual suggests that if he were the first, Buffalo Bill would be simply confused about his genitals; if he were the second, he would be confused about an object choice. Neither is the case.

The "case" is precisely the problem and Buffalo Bill's case becomes Starling's as she tracks him to his sewing room. Buffalo Bill thinks he is not in the wrong body, but the wrong skin, an incorrect casing.

He is not interested in what lies beneath the skin for skin is gender for the murderer just as skin, or outward appearance, becomes the fetishized signifier of gender for a heterosexist culture. Buffalo Bill's sewing machine treats gender as an outfit made of natural fibers. Skin becomes the material which can be transformed by the right pattern into a seamless suit. But the violent harvest that precedes Buffalo Bill's domestic enterprise suggests that always behind the making of gender is a bloodied female body cut and measured to the right proportions.

And the case is also Hannibal the Cannibal's for he knows Buffalo Bill as a former case history and he knows what he is doing and why. Hannibal was once Buffalo Bill's psychiatrist, Buffalo Bill was once his case. Hannibal, however, created a monster as an inverted model of his own pathology. Inversion in this film depends upon two terms always and neither one can function as a norm. If homosexuality is an inversion of heterosexuality, this assumes that heterosexuality is the desired term. But in *The Silence of the Lambs* inversion reduces norm and pathology, inside and outside to meaningless categories: there is only pathology and varying degrees of it, only an outside in various forms. Buffalo Bill is an inversion of Hannibal the Cannibal, and Hannibal inverts his patient's desire because what Hannibal wants to put inside of himself, Buffalo Bill wants to dress in.

Buffalo Bill is Starling's case and when a new body is found in Clay County, West Virginia, Starling's home state, she flies home with her boss to conduct the autopsy. The corpse laid out on the table, of course, is a double for Starling, the image of what she might have become had she not left home, as Lecter points out, and aspired to greater things. This scene, in many ways, represents a premature climax of the horror in the movie. We see laid out for us exactly what it is that Buffalo Bill does to his victims. Prior to the autopsy, the camera has protected the viewer from close-ups of photographs taken of victims' bodies. Similarly, when Starling is being taken to Lecter, she is shown a photographic image of what Lecter did to a nurse. He attempted to bite her face off but the image of that hideous unmasking is kept hidden from the viewer. In the autopsy scene, the camera reveals all that it had promised to spare us: it lingers on the green and red flesh, the decayed body with two regular diamonds of flesh cut from its back.

The autopsy scene, indeed, resolves the drama of identification for the female spectator who found herself torn between detective and victim. After this scene the gaze is most definitely Starling's. The narrative has seemed to implicate Starling with the victim by identifying the two women in relation to their backgrounds and ages, and so there is some tension as Starling enters the morgue to begin the examination of the body. But Starling quickly establishes the difference between herself and the body in the body bag by setting herself up as an authority. She begins her visual analysis of the corpse and at first, as her voice trembles and her hands shake, as her body gives her away, the camera watches her from a position below the corpse—the spectator is positioned with the victim on the table. "What do you see, Starling?" asks Crawford. "She's not local," she replies, "her ears are pierced three times and there's glitter nail polish. Looks like town to me." Unlike Starling, then, the victim is not a hometown girl. The camera moves now to a position above the body and the gaze of the camera abruptly becomes Starling's gaze as we look down upon a mottled arm rotting and covered with dead leaves and other traces of the river she was hauled out of. Starling's examination of the corpse becomes more sure and the tension of identification between detective and victim is relieved for the moment.

Starling, like the viewer, seemed inclined to look away from the corpse, horrified perhaps by the nakedness of violence so plainly detailed before her. But, the corpse finally becomes object, thing, post-human when Starling looks at a photograph of its teeth and sees something in the throat. Before the photograph, her gaze, like our gaze, begins to linger. Turning back to the corpse moments later, Starling surveys the undignified flesh and speaking into a tape recorder, she begins to piece the body together, rebuild the mutilated body, and learn what the body has to tell.

The camera itself has done a kind of violence to whatever humanity remained upon or within the body—this is no longer a body framing an inner life, the body is merely surface, a picture. The camera has framed the victim in much the same way as Buffalo Bill does as he prepares his lambs for the slaughter. Keeping his victim naked in an old well shaft, he addresses her as "it" when he must talk to her. And the camera also enables Starling to turn the corpse into a case, a case that she must solve even as the victim has become a case that Buffalo Bill will wear. This hideous wake, then, foreshadows the scenes in Buffalo Bill's basement gender factory and the autopsy becomes a site of trauma in terms of the film's narrative about gender—the corpse is no woman, it has been degendered, it is postgender, skinned and fleshed, it has been reified, turned at last into a fiction of the body.

We know from what happened to Buffalo Bill that Hannibal's patients go on to lead illustrious careers and so it is an ominous finale in the movie when Starling, Lecter's fledgling patient and the FBI's fledgling agent, steps up to accept her graduation certificate from the FBI: different degree, same profession—crime. As a camera captures her moment of graduation, the flash bulb is reminiscent of that earlier moment, that prior photograph of the victim's teeth in the autopsy lab. As she becomes a "real" agent, Starling is framed as victim, as a lamb in wolf's clothing. As if to capitalize on the decline of Starling's authority, a phone call interrupts her graduation celebration. It is from the now escaped Hannibal; he tells her not to worry, he will not pursue her. Hannibal and Starling are both loose, both free, both out and about. The scene shows Hannibal on a Caribbean isle watching his psychiatrist from his prison days. Hannibal tells Starling, "I'm having an old friend for dinner," and he adjusts his clothes elegantly. Hannibal is dressed to kill. Buffalo Bill, of course, kills to dress and only one costume will do.

Hannibal Lecter feeds upon both flesh and fiction. He needs Starling's stories as much as he needs to track down his next victim. "Quid pro quo," he tells Starling; he wants a fair rate of exchange. Hannibal demands that no one be innocent and Starling must have a story to match the story he will sell her. Starling's story is a fiction of her power that is revealed in the process as no power at all but only the difference between two sides of the glass. Hannibal determines the limits of a carceral system. He is not disciplined by his imprisonment nor punished because as long as there are people around him he can cannibalize their stories. The ever hungry mind, Hannibal analyzes people to death. He whispers all night to the man in the cell next to him and by morning the man, Multiple Miggs, has swallowed his own tongue; Hannibal enacts murders through bars and cages, through minds. Prisons come in all shapes and sizes and while Hannibal's is a restricted area equipped with a screen playing a TV evangelist at high volume, Starling is stuck inside her head, her body and the disturbing memories that Hannibal insists are not buried far beneath the power suit but quite present at the surface, on the top, visible and readable.

Starling's narrative of her childhood flight from her aunt and uncle's house becomes as terrifying as any other aspect of the horror narrative. The pieces of her past cohere slowly as Hannibal extracts each one surgically and then confronts her with it. The secret of her past that threatened all along to be some nasty story of incest or rape is precisely not sexual. Clarice Starling is the girl who wanted to save the lambs from the slaughter, who could only carry one at a time and who finally could not support the weight. Clarice Starling is the girl who freed the lambs from the pen and then watched in horror as they refused to leave it. Starling saves others in order to save her own skin.

Hannibal stays imprisoned until there is no longer a story to hear. The installments that Starling gave him of her life maintained his interest just as each new killing maintains the FBI's interest in Buffalo Bill. The serial killing, indeed, like the psychoanalytic session, promises interminable chapters, promises to serialize, to keep one waiting for an ever deferred conclusion. Serial murders have something of a literary quality to them: they happen regularly over time and each new one creates an expectation; they involve a plot, a consummate villain and an absolutely pure (because randomly picked) victim; they demand explanation; they demand that a pattern be forced onto what appears to be "desperately random" (as Hannibal Lecter tells Starling). "Sadism demands a story," I noted earlier, quoting Mulvey. And, the story that sadism demands is the Gothic story embedded in the heart of a consumer culture *and* the realistic story embedded deep within Gothic culture. Lecter's Gothic sadism demands Starling's benign story, and Starling's innocence demands the Gothic tale that she as much as Lecter chooses to tell about a series of "desperately random" killings.

Serial killings, like chapters in a periodical, stand in need of interpretation and interpreters (like the police, the tabloids, the public, the detective, the psychologist, the critic) produce the story that the bodies cannot tell. Starling and the FBI insist that there be a reason, a concrete explanation for the skinning of women, and Lecter complies but only as long as Starling recognizes that she also is complicit in the narrative, she too must tell and be told. Telling does not mean finding a story in the unconscious that fits, it means inventing the unconscious and inventing the unconscious so that it can lie well enough to keep up with the fiction of everyday life.

Like some monstrous parody of nineteenth century Gothic, these two characters mimic the vampire and Frankenstein's monster. Franco Moretti describes Shelley's monster and Stoker's vampire as "dynamic, *totalizing*, monsters" who "threaten to live forever, and to conquer the world."[3] Buffalo Bill and Hannibal are also totalizing and each consumes other lives in order to prolong his own. Buffalo Bill combines in one both Frankenstein and the monster; he is the scientist, the creator and he is the body being formed and sculpted, stitched and fitted. Like Frankenstein, Buffalo Bill must search abroad for the body parts he needs and bring them back to the laboratory. The "filthy workshop of creation" is now a basement sweatshop and new material is stored in a well in the form of a woman who Buffalo Bill is starving out of her skin. Buffalo Bill, however, is pickier than his predecessor; he demands particular human remains, size 14 to be precise, no one size fits all.

"Is he a vampire," a policeman asks Starling as she is on her way to pay Hannibal a final visit. "There's no word for what he is," she replies. Of course, he is a vampire, and a cannibal, a murderer and a psychopath. He is also a psychiatrist who drains minds before he starts on the bodies and perhaps he makes no distinction between the two. Hannibal is, Starling might have answered, a psychoanalyst, a doctor in the most uncanny of sciences. Freud predicted Hannibal when he noted in "The Uncanny": "Indeed, I should not be surprised to hear that psycho-analysis, which is concerned with laying bare these hidden forces, has itself become uncanny to many people. . . ."[4] Hannibal and Buffalo Bill play out the doctor/patient dynamic that has precisely become uncanny, homoerotic (heimoerotic), transferential in the most literal way. Buffalo Bill leaves Hannibal his first victim, an ex-lover, in the form of a severed head. This is totem or taboo or something more than oedipal/edible. Not exactly father and son, certainly not a professional relationship, the two "monsters" bond in the business of death and divorce death once and for all from sexuality. Murder is no romance in *The Silence of the Lambs*, it is a lesson in home economics—eating and sewing.

Hannibal the Cannibal and Buffalo Bill are Dr. Jekyll and Mr. Hyde as much as they are Dracula and Frankenstein. Jekyll, of course, produced Hyde from within his own psyche and he cannibalizes him when the pressure is on. Hyde is an incredibly close relative to Buffalo Bill—he too is "hide-bound," trapped in his skin, hidden by his hide, hiding from the law.[5] Like Buffalo Bill, Hyde performs his ritualistic crimes for his other half; he murders for Jekyll, he carouses for Jekyll, he indulges perverse desire for Jekyll. The homoerotic dyad bound to one body, hiding one self in the other, allows one self to feed off the others' strengths and weaknesses. No longer homosexuals, they are simply victims of modern science: psychiatry, a mind fuck.

Criticism has psychologized horror, made it a universal sign of humanity or depravity: horror, supposedly, is what we *all* fear in our oedipal unconscious. It is archetypal and yet individual, a condition of language or separation from the mother, a fragmentation or unspeakable desire. Now, in *The Silence of the Lambs*, horror is psychology, a bad therapeutic relationship, a fine romance between the one who knows and the one who eats, the one who eats and the one who grows skins; the one who castrates and the one who enacts a parody of circumcision. Psychology is no longer an explanation for horror, it generates horror, it founds its most basic fantasies and demands their enactment in the name of transference and truth.

It is no surprise that psychoanalysis and cinema have replaced fiction as the privileged locus of the horror/pleasure thrill. Psychoanalysis, writes Foucault, is "both a theory of the essential relatedness of the law and desire, and a technique for relieving the effects of the taboo where its rigor makes it pathenogenic."[6] Psychoanalysis uncovers and prohibits and in its prohibition lies the seeds of a desire. The moment of uncovering, of course, the moment when the skin is drawn back, the secrets of the flesh exposed, that moment is cinematic in its linking of seeing and knowing, vision and pleasure, power and punishment. The making visible of bodies, sex, power and desire provokes a new monstrosity and dares the body to continue its striptease down to the bone. Hannibal Lecter elicits Starling's poor little flashbacks only to demonstrate that stripping the mind is no less a violation than stripping the body and that mind and body are no longer split: Starling's memories are peeled back even as Buffalo Bill prepares his next lamb for the slaughter; and the raw nerve of Starling's memory is as exposed as the corpse that she dissected.

As a curious trademark, Buffalo Bill leaves a cocoon of the Death Head Moth in his victims' throats after he has killed them. Starling first finds one of the cocoons during the postmortem when she notices something is lodged in the corpse's throat. Later, we discover that Buffalo Bill collects butterflies and hatches moth cocoons. While the skull and crossbones markings on the moth are an obvious standard of the horror genre, the cocoon and the moth symbolize Buffalo Bill's particular pathology. Buffalo Bill and his victims are both cocoon and moth, larva and imago. Buffalo Bill is the cocoon holed up in a basement waiting for his skin to grow, for his beautiful metamorphosis to take place, and he is the moth that lives and breeds in clothes. Lecter calls Buffalo Bill's crime "transformation"—he knows that Buffalo Bill is waiting in the dark for his beautiful gender suit to grow.

Buffalo Bill's victims are also cocoon and moth, they must shed their skins and fly on to death. Or, they are the moths, the producers of material. By placing the cocoon in his victims' throats, Buffalo Bill marks the difference between moth and larvae, outside and inside as no difference at all. The cocoon is inside the victims and the victims have shed their cocoons, the covering is internal and outside there is nothing but raw flesh. The blocked throat, of course, symbolizes the silence of the lambs to the slaughter. A woman who has been reduced to a size 14 skin has no voice, no noise coming from inside to be heard outside. The voice, "the grain of the voice," is the last signifier of something internal to the body.

But Hannibal too attempts a transformation. In order to escape from his prison cell, Hannibal murders two police men. He cuts the face off one of them and covers himself with it and dresses in his clothes. When help arrives, Hannibal is taken out of the facility on a stretcher. By draping the bloody face over his own, Hannibal tears a leaf out of Buffalo Bill's casebook. Identity again proves to be only skin deep, and freedom depends upon appropriate dress. But even when he was in the cage, Hannibal was not bound by his chains, indeed he seemed only to be there because he wanted to be, because he wanted to hear the end of Starling's story. Sitting calmly behind the bars, his hands on his knees, his mouth open, the story of Starling's personal horror issuing from his lips, Hannibal resembles a Francis Bacon "Face." His features are blurred, his flesh resembles meat and his mouth, open to tell, forms the image of a scream that is felt not heard. But another Bacon painting also provides a fitting backdrop to this baconesque film. His "Figure with Meat" blurs human flesh into animal flesh and makes the slaughterhouse a central image of human cruelty. The abattoir, of course, was at the center of Starling's childhood nightmare and it becomes the setting for Buffalo Bill's sartorial activities. The figure with meat, in this narrative, is Starling but also Lecter and Buffalo Bill. The horrific human figure sits framed by the dripping flesh of what he will eat, a skinned animal with a recyclable hide, a carcass no longer worth saving.

Like the mythical moth that flutters too close to the flame, Buffalo Bill both covets and fears light. He keeps himself entrapped in the darkness and stalks his victims by night using infrared glasses. Like Buffalo Bill, the viewer of *The Silence of the Lambs* can also see in the dark. In the climatic hunting scene towards the end of the film, when Buffalo Bill plays hide and seek with Clarice Starling, the spectator watches through Buffalo Bill's eyes. Clarice's clarity deserts her and again, as she was in relation to Hannibal Lecter, Clarice is reduced to a listener. We see Clarice stumbling around through the infrared of Buffalo Bill's bloody vision. But even as we see with Buffalo Bill, it would not be accurate to say we, as spectators, are simply identified with his murderous gaze. We are in fact divided between the gaze of the camera that frames its object (here it is Starling) into still life or thingness and Starling's blindness that manages to direct a gun straight at the camera. Starling has been framed and blinded—but blindness (like silence) has a power all its own. To be blind is to avoid being trapped by appearance, it confers the freedom to look back.[7] Her shot in the dark hits Buffalo Bill and blows out a window, letting the light in. Starling has not only returned the gaze she has destroyed it and remade it.

As a final point of contact with posthuman gender and the cinematic gaze, I want to examine one more manifestation of transformation in the film. Starling traces her clues to the house of the first murder victim and she goes into the victim's bedroom that has been kept exactly as Frederika left it. The camera looks over Starling's shoulder as she picks over the dead woman's belongings—a jewelry box, a romance novel called *Silken Threads*, a diet book. The room is decorated with butterfly wallpaper, a tailor's dummy and in the closet hangs material with paper diamonds pinned to it, ready to cut out. In Frederika's room, Starling finally realizes Buffalo Bill's sartorial pathology. Later, in Buffalo Bill's basement, the camera again lingers upon the signifiers of the crime—textiles, threads, needles, cocoons, a sewing machine and tailor's dummies. The two rooms are collapsed into one momentarily as the next victim's screams bleed through from the cellar. Buffalo Bill, of course, has become Frederika just as Frederika has become Buffalo Bill—he wears her, she is upon him, he is inside her. Victim and murderer are folded into each other as Starling enters gun in hand to attempt to fix boundaries once and for all.

Buffalo Bill's misidentify forced him to assume what we might call a posthuman gender. He divorces once and for all sex and gender or nature and gender and remakes the human condition as a posthuman body suit. Buffalo Bill kills for his clothes and emblamatizes the ways in which gender is always posthuman, always a sewing job which stitches identity into a body bag. Skin, in this film, is identity itself rather than the surface of an interior identity. Buffalo Bill, in other words, is a limit case for gender, for identity, for humanness. He does not understand gender as inherent, innate; he reads it only as a surface effect, a representation, an external attribute engineered into identity. Buffalo Bill is at odds with identity because he is willing to kill to get one, he commits violent acts in order to stabilize his condition. While we are repelled by Buffalo Bill for what he does to women, while the female spectator must ultimately look away from his experimentation, nonetheless Buffalo Bill represents a subtle change in the representation of gender. Not simply murderer-monster, Buffalo Bill challenges the heterosexist and misogynist constructions of the humanness, the naturalness, the interiority of gender even as he is victimized by them. He rips gender apart and remakes it as a mask, a suit, a costume. Gender identity for Buffalo Bill is not the transcendent signifier of humanity, it is its most efficient technology.

Hannibal Lecter, with his own masks and dissemblings, is the image of a violence that cannot be kept in a cage; he is not evil incarnate, but a representation of the evil that spreads across discourse, sound and sense; across people, bodies and minds; across behaviors, actions and passivities; across systems, bureaucracies and institutions. Monstrosity in *The Silence of the Lambs* in fact is an effect of the surface, a ripple across fields of criminality, surveillance and discipline. Monstrosity, in this film, cannot be limited to a body, even a body that kills in order to clothe itself, or a body that cannibalizes in order to feed. Monstrosity is now a disembodied and disembodying force, reduced to silence, to blindness, to surface.

Horror is the relation between carcass and history, between flesh and fiction. The destruction of the boundary between inside and outside that I have traced here marks a historical shift. *The Silence of the Lambs* equates history with cannibalism; aesthetic production with a sacralized meal, Gothic horror with the abject form of that cannibalism leaving the body. *The Silence of the Lambs* has cannibalized nineteenth-century Gothic, eaten its monsters alive and thrown them up onto the screen. The undead, the monsters who threaten to live forever find eternal life in the circularity of consumption and production that characterizes Hollywood cinema.

NOTES

1. Hannah Arendt, *Eichmann in Jerusalem* (New York: Penguin Books, 1963) 276.
2. See Laura Mulvey, "Visual Pleasure and Narrative Cinema," *Screen* 16.3 (Autumn 1975): 14.
3. Franco Moretti, *Signs Taken For Wonder: Essays in the Sociology of Literary Forms*, trans. Susan Fischer, David Forgacs and David Miller (London: Verso, 1983) 84–5.
4. Sigmund Freud, "The Uncanny" (1919) in *On Creativity and the Unconscious*, intro. Benjamin Nelson (New York and London: Harper and Row, 1958) 151.
5. In the novel *The Silence of the Lambs* by Thomas Harris (New York: St. Martin's Press, 1988), Buffalo Bill works for a leather company called Mr. Hide.
6. Michel Foucault, *The History of Sexuality I: An Introduction*, trans. Robert Hurley (New York: Vintage Books, 1980) 129.
7. As an interesting note on the theme of blindness as a fear blocker, in another film made from a Thomas Harris novel, *Manhunter* (1988), the female would-be victim is also blind and her blindness also aids her in her escape from a murderer. In this film, the murderer's predilection is to take posed photographs of his victims after he has killed them. He works in a dark room developing film, furthermore, and this is where he meets the blind woman. Obviously, Harris is making connections between vision and the production of horror—what you cannot see will not hurt you seems to be the message, and the dark is always to the woman's advantage. This may be read as a kind of postmodern rewriting of the feminist slogan "take back the night."

42

Genderbashing

Sexuality, Gender, and the Regulation of Public Space

Viviane K. Namaste

With this article, Viviane K. Namaste, a Montreal-based transsexual activist and theoretician, helped call attention to the role of gender in acts of violence commonly known as "gaybashing." She demonstrates that most targets of violence are victimized not because of their sexual orientation, but because of the way their visible gender presentation is perceived to be threatening to male and heterosexual domination of public space. She renames this form of violence "genderbashing" to more accurately reflect its basic motivating force, and to better capture the sense of who is most at risk for violence of this sort.

Namaste carefully teases apart the many strands of assumption that contribute to vastly greater-than-average instances of violence experienced by male-to-female transgender sex-industry workers of color. She delineates the role of anti-woman violence in policing public space as a space for men, and the role of anti-homosexual violence in policing public space as a space for heterosexuals. She goes beyond this analysis, however, to show how falling outside the hetero/homo binary, and the man/woman dichotomy, creates further vulnerabilities for the people who occupy those spaces—a vulnerability often compounded by stigma inflicted by racism, the disparagement of prostitution, and AIDS phobia. Namaste demonstrates as well how genderbashing was geographical spatialized in the city of Montreal at the time of her writing.

Namaste's work is neither strictly empirical nor wholly impressionistic, but rather blends a sense of personal and political urgency with a cogent analysis of the broader social circumstances in which transgender people live. It offers a compelling example of the way in which trans scholarship is often rooted in the particular problematics of transgender lives and transgender political activism, and thus calls attention to dimensions of society that might otherwise remain unobserved by other people.

In chapters 4 and 5, I examined the effacement of transsexual and transgendered people through the micrological work of discourse and rhetoric. Chapter 4 illustrated how gendered discourse undermines transsexual identities, while chapter 5 explored the concept of erasure in terms of the reduction of TS/TG people to the merely figural, a reduction that makes transsexuality literally impossible. This chapter provides a different lens through which to consider the obliteration of transsexual and trans-gendered people, taking up the question of violence against sexual and gender minorities.[1]

The chapter has two aims: (1) a critical reflection of the conceptual relations between gender and sexuality within the realm of violence against sexual and gender minorities, and (2) an analysis of how the documents produced by activists, the police, and policy makers are used in specific institutional sites to frame particular understandings of violence. A case study of antiviolence activism in Montréal exposes the effacement of transsexual and transgendered people in lesbian/gay community-based discussions of violence. The stated goals of this chapter, of course, are related. Reflection on how violence is conceptualized can raise important questions about the oversights within the institutional policies and practices designed to respond to violence against sexual and gender minorities.

In North America, violence against lesbians, gay men, and bisexuals is escalating at an alarming rate. A survey conducted in 1986–87 by the Philadelphia Lesbian and Gay Task Force reports that violence against lesbians and gay men in that city had doubled since 1983–84.[2] The United States National Gay and Lesbian Task Force (NGLTF) documents that incidents of violence against sexual minorities increased 127 percent from 1988 to 1993.[3]

Though scholars[4] and community activists[5] have increasingly addressed the issue of violence against lesbians and gay men, there remains very little reflection on the function of gender within these acts of aggression. In this chapter, I argue that a perceived transgression of normative sex/gender relations motivates much of the violence against sexual minorities, and that an assault on these "transgressive" bodies is fundamentally concerned with policing gender presentation through public and private space. I also consider the implications of this research for transsexual and transgendered people. Given that the perception of gender dissidence informs acts of queerbashing, we can deduce that those individuals who live outside normative sex/gender relations will be most at risk for assault. Finally, I examine some of the ways in which educational strategies on violence separate gender and sexuality, and thus prevent a political response that accounts for the function of gender in queerbashing. Specific examples are taken from briefs presented in November 1993 to the Québec Human Rights Commission's public hearings in Montréal on violence and discrimination against lesbians and gay men.[6] I demonstrate the ways in which gender and sexuality are separated, and thus how the issue of gender is foreclosed by certain gay male community activists.

These briefs occupy central roles in defining the issue of violence against sexual minorities within a Québécois context. They coordinate how violence is understood, and therefore the kinds of strategies, interventions, and programs needed to adequately respond to the situation. Although antiviolence activists in Québec had claimed that the issue of violence against sexual minorities was by no means new, the public consultations held in 1993 were the first official recognition of this phenomenon by the state. Because agencies such as the Québec Human Rights Commission make use of these texts to organize their activities, these briefs are much more than political position papers: they function to order our understandings, and actions, of violence against sexual and gender minorities. As Canadian sociologist Dorothy Smith claims, such texts are central to the ongoing, practical work of governments:

> The relations of ruling in our kind of society are mediated by texts, by words, numbers, and images on paper, in computers, or on TV and movie screens. Texts are the primary medium (though not the substance) of power. The work of administration, of management, of government is a communicative work. Organizational and political processes are forms of action coordinated textually and getting done in words. It is an ideologically structured mode of action—images, vocabularies, concepts, abstract terms of knowledge are integral to the practice of power, to getting things done.[7]

If, as Smith argues, texts are central to the coordinating activities of government, a critical examination of some of the texts presented to the Québec Human Rights Commission provides an opportunity to examine the social relations of gender in one institutional site. My analysis is particularly concerned with how transsexual and transgendered people are rendered invisible by key texts that ignore violence against transsexual and transgendered people. In this regard, the circulation of these briefs in the institutional world represents one of the ways in which the erasure of transsexual and transgendered people is textually coordinated. I use the term "erasure" to designate a conceptualization of gender that excludes the bodies and experiences of transsexual and transgendered people, and that informs the taken-for-granted work of institutions. "Erasure" refers to the conceptual and institutional relations through which transsexual and transgendered individuals disappear from view.

GENDER AND SEXUALITY

The relations between gender and sexuality figure centrally in this chapter, and it is necessary to clarify how they can at once intersect and diverge. The theoretical work of Gayle Rubin is useful for this purpose.[8] In 1975, Rubin wrote a by-now famous anthropological essay on women and kinship. Taking up Claude Lévi-Strauss's notion of exchange,[9] in which one's social status is achieved in part through the exchange of gifts, she remarks that it was always women who were exchanged by men. Rubin argues that this defines women in terms of their reproductive capabilities, thereby making biology a social phenomenon and consolidating a heterosexual contract. In 1984, however, Rubin revised her statement, at least in terms of its application within Western societies. She notes that her earlier work had confused gender and sexuality:

> In contrast to my perspective in "The Traffic in Women," I am now arguing that it is essential to separate gender and sexuality analytically to more accurately reflect their separate social existence.[10]

Because gender and sexuality are not the same thing, Rubin suggests, scholars interested in theorizing sexuality should not assume that feminist theory is the perspective best able to account for the social organization of erotic life:

> I want to challenge the assumption that feminism is or should be the privileged site of a theory of sexuality. Feminism is the theory of gender oppression. To automatically assume that this makes it the theory of sexual oppression is to fail to distinguish between gender, on the one hand, and erotic desire, on the other.[11]

In 1992, Rubin offered a further clarification of the relations between gender and sexuality: while it is certainly true that gender and sexuality are not the same thing, it is also true that they intersect in quite significant ways. Rubin considers the question of FTM transsexuality, remarking that there is a great deal of common ground between butch lesbians and FTMs. Despite these similarities, lesbian communities are often openly hostile to transsexuals: "A woman who has been respected, admired, and loved as a butch may suddenly be despised, rejected, and hounded when she starts a sex change."[12] In Rubin's analysis, lesbian communities should not instantly reject an FTM transsexual, because this individual elaborates a unique vision of gender. Rubin reminds her readers that sexual and gender outlaws share a common history: "Lesbian communities were built by sex and gender refugees; the lesbian world should not create new rationales for sex and gender persecution."[13]

The development of Rubin's thinking on the relations between gender and sexuality provides an occasion to reflect on the difficulties involved in theorizing this question. In certain social, cultural, and historical contexts, a separation of gender and sexuality seems impossible. In other locations, however, they appear markedly distinct. One of Rubin's most important contributions in this area is the acknowledgment that these issues change over time. In her discussion of lesbian communities, for instance, she observes that bars that catered to lesbians were also havens for transsexuals. Ruben even notes that many "butch" women who are embraced as important figures in lesbian history could also, and in some instances more accurately, be labeled transsexual.[14] To appreciate the ways in which gender and sexuality intersect historically, as Rubin does, is to demand a critical examination of more contemporary relations between these issues. While Rubin discusses the expulsion of transsexuals from lesbian communities, she highlights the ways in which lesbian sexuality is defined in exclusive relation to a "naturalized" gender category rooted in biology. Lesbian identity is secured through the invocation of a sexual category, not a label of gender. Rubin observes how contemporary lesbian identity forces a separation of gender and sexuality, despite the fact that they were entwined historically.

Throughout this chapter 1 will explore the insights of Rubin in an attempt to develop an effective response to violence against sexual and gender minorities. What role does gender play in attacks against lesbians and gay men? Is violence against transsexuals common, and is it of a different order than that against sexual minorities? Does the response to violence offered by gay male communities actually prevent activists and educators from addressing the needs of women and transgendered people? How are gender and sexuality linked, or juxtaposed, within a problematic of "queerbashing"? This chapter hopes to shed light on several issues: how violence affects TS/TG individuals; how the notion of gender is frequently eclipsed within discussions on violence against gays and lesbians; how we can develop appropriate responses to this problematic; and how we can go about gathering and interpreting data on the relations between gender and violence.

The chapter is primarily a theoretical one: I do not present the results of comprehensive empirical research on violence against TS/TG people. Nevertheless, it is my hope that the chapter will clearly illustrate the value of careful theoretical reflection on the issue of violence in the development of appropriate solutions to this problem. Drawing on the kind of poststructuralist sociology I propose in chapter 3, I am interested in examining several related issues with respect to violence: the every-day social world; the production and/or effacement of transgendered people within that world; the development of appropriate interventionist political strategies; and a reflexive sociological practice, which understands how different theories construct, legitimate, and/or obliterate their objects. But this chapter is only a beginning: although I try to illustrate how transgendered people are erased within select community discourses on violence, and although I use this insight to consider more appropriate ways for scholars and activists to collect and analyze data, I do not offer an empirical study herein. The present chapter, then, ought to be interpreted in light of these strengths and limitations.

I use the term "violence" to refer to a variety of acts, mannerisms, and attitudes. It can range from verbal insults (e.g., calling someone a "fag"), to an invasion of personal space (e.g., throwing a bottle at a lesbian as she walks by), to intimidation and the threat of physical assault. "Violence" also includes the act of attacking someone's body—whether through sexual assault (rape), beating, or with weapons like baseball bats, knives, or guns. The question of violence is obviously linked to that of discrimination: in the case of queerbashing, the denial of same-sex insurance benefits, for example, privileges heterosexual relationships over homosexual ones, and thus fosters an atmosphere of intolerance of sexual minorities. The NGLTF reports a marked rise in violence against sexual minorities in Colorado immediately following the passage of Amendment 2, a state ordinance prohibiting antidiscrimination legislation on the basis of sexual preference.[15] While violence and discrimination support each other, this chapter focuses on the notion of violence as defined above.

LIMITS OF TOLERANCE: GENDER NORMS AND GENDER TRANSGRESSIONS

"Gender" refers to the roles and meanings assigned to men and women based on their presumed bio-logical sex.[16] It is a social function, neither timeless nor historical. For example, we generally associate the color pink with girls and femininity and the color blue with boys and masculinity. There is noth-ing inherent in either of these colors that links them to a particular gender: pink, or turquoise, could just as easily designate masculinity. Gender is also about what men and women are supposed to do in the world—men wear pants, have short hair, can grow beards, and are considered more physically aggressive than women. Women can wear skirts, have longer hair, wear makeup, and are judged to be emotional. In Western societies, it is thought that there are only two genders—men and women.[17]

"Sexuality," in contrast, refers to the ways in which individuals organize their erotic and sexual lives. This is generally categorized into three separate areas: heterosexuals—individuals who have sexual relations with members of the opposite sex; homosexuals—those who have sexual relations with members of the same sex; and bisexuals—people who relate erotically to both men and women.[18]

In Western societies, gender and sexuality get confused. For example, when a fifteen-year-old boy is assaulted and called a "faggot," he is so labeled because he has mannerisms that are considered "effeminate." He may or may not be gay, but he is called a "queer" because he does not fulfill his expected gender role. A young girl can be a tomboy until the age of eleven or so, but she must then live as a more "dainty," "feminine" person. If she does not, she may be called a "dyke"—again, regardless of how she actually defines her sexual identity. In both examples, the presentation of gender determines how these youths are received by their peers. When people shout "faggot" at a fifteen-year-old boy, they really mean that he is not a "masculine" man. Gender and sexuality are collapsed. As Rubin points out, the merging of gender and sexuality enables some feminist theorists to write about erotic desire.[19]

The fusion of gender and sexuality has distinct implications for the problematic of violence. The connotations of the pejorative names used against individuals who are assaulted—names like "sissy," "faggot," "dyke," "man-hater," "queer," and "pervert"—suggest that an attack is justified not in reaction to one's sexual identity, but to one's gender presentation. Indeed, bashers do not characteristically inquire as to the sexual identity of their potential victims, but rather make this assumption on their own. On what basis do "queerbashers" determine who is gay, lesbian, or bisexual?

Joseph Harry's research suggests that gender be considered an important variable in queerbashing incidents.[20] Harry found that groups of assailants involved in these crimes relied on gender cues to ascertain sexual identity. If they judged a potential victim to be "effeminate," for example, he was subject to attack. A related study confirms this hypothesis: 39 percent of men surveyed who behaved in a "feminine" manner had been physically assaulted, compared with 22 percent of men who were "masculine" and only 17 percent of men who conducted themselves in a "very masculine" fashion.[21] According to this survey, males who are classified as "effeminate" are more than twice as likely to experience physical violence than males whose gender presentation corresponds to social norms. A study of anti-lesbian abuse in San Francisco indicates that 12 percent of lesbians surveyed had been punched, kicked, or otherwise physically assaulted.[22] Significantly, the only justification offered relates to gender:

> [F]ourteen of the women said that the only explanation for incidents they had experienced was the fact that they had short hair and were wearing trousers and in most cases were in the company of another woman.[23]

Women and men who transgress acceptable limits of self-presentation, then, are among those most at risk for assault. Assaults against men judged to be "effeminate" or women deemed "masculine" reveal the ways in which gender and sexuality are intertwined. Gender is used as a cue to locate lesbians and gay men. Though the perceived transgression of gender norms motivates bashing, this affects men and women differently. The gendered construction of space—both public and private—figures centrally in these acts of aggression.

GENDERED SPACE AND THE PUBLIC/PRIVATE DICHOTOMY

One of the remarkable things about the study of violence against sexual minorities is the way in which such aggression can be linked to commonsense assumptions of what constitutes "public" space, who has the right to occupy it, and how people should interact therein. The gendered dimension of the public space has been examined by many feminist scholars.[24] Shirley Ardener remarks that the presence of men is used to define a particular place as "public."[25] This means that women are confined to the private sphere. A public/private, masculine/feminine opposition has deep historical roots. In *Prostitution and Victorian Society*, Judith Walkowitz notes that society sanctioned the presence of men in the streets as well as public establishments such as taverns and gambling houses. Women who were found in these same sites, however, had violated middle-class notions of what "decent" women did and did not do, and the places they frequented. Walkowitz provides an elaborate analysis of the ways in which prostitutes came to be labeled "public" women.[26]

In this light, attacks against lesbians and gay men can be interpreted in terms of a defense of the "public" as that domain that belongs to men—heterosexual men, to be more precise. Entrance into the public sphere is secured through the enactment of a sanctioned gender identity, preferably within the context of a heterosexual dyad. Couples who violate this prescription, and perhaps especially transgendered people who walk alone, pose a fundamental challenge to public space and how it is defined and secured through gender.

Empirical data support such statements. Social scientists like Comstock and Valentine have recently explored the gender and geographic differences in cases of anti-lesbian abuse and anti-gay assault. It is argued that while both lesbians and gay men are attacked, lesbians are assaulted in "ordinary" public spaces. Gay men, in contrast, are habitually beaten in areas known to be gay—ghettoes, parking lots of gay bars, or public parks where men have sex with other men. For instance, in Comstock's study, 45 percent of lesbians were queerbashed in public lesbian/gay spaces, 42 percent in nonlesbian/gay areas, 30 percent in the home, and 17 percent in the school. In contrast, 66 percent of gay men were attacked in gay areas, only 29 percent in "ordinary" public space, 26 percent in the home, and 24 percent in the school. Thus, men "experience more violence in lesbian/gay areas and in secondary school settings," while women "experience more violence in straight-identified, domestic, and higher-education settings."[27] The presence of women in public who are not accompanied by men is a threat to the implicit masculine dimension of public space. It is for this reason that lesbians, and other females perceived to be a threat to normative hetero-sexuality, are assaulted in the streets. The issues become even more complex when variables of race are examined: in Comstock's empirical study, 20 percent of people of color surveyed were assaulted in lesbian/gay space, compared with only 9 percent of white lesbians and gay men.[28] This data suggests that geographic areas known to be gay villages and/or cruising grounds are most dangerous for men of color. Conversely, women (especially those who are perceived to be lesbians or "masculine") are most at risk in everyday locations that assume the "naturalness" of heterosexuality.[29]

Comstock demonstrates that gay men are usually attacked when alone (66 percent of survey respondents), while lesbians are often attacked in pairs (44 percent of respondents).[30] It is noteworthy, however, that these numbers are drastically reduced when men and women walk together: only 8 percent of women respondents were physically assaulted when they were with a man. The figure drops to 1 percent for men accompanied by women. The safety secured through an opposite-sex partner seems to hold regardless of the public space that one occupies (i.e., lesbian/gay or "ordinary" space).

This research underlines the importance of gender as a variable in the issue of violence. Gay men can avoid assault within a space designated as gay by having a woman with them, while lesbians can escape physical harm in the "everyday" (i.e., heterosexual) world by having a man with them. Both of these strategies rely on implicit assumptions about who men and women are and how they should interact in public. As G. Valentine expresses it,

> Heterosexuality is ideologically linked to the notion of gender identities (masculinity and femininity) because the notion of opposite-sex relationships presumes a binary distinction between what it means to be a man or a woman.[31]

Valentine articulates a position similar to that of Rubin: gender and sexuality are intertwined, such that "masculinity" and "femininity" appear to be the "natural," complementary extremes of heterosexuality. Homosexuality, then, is associated with gender inversion. Furthermore, heterosexual men and women can walk together safely in the streets; gay men and lesbians, in contrast, must negotiate the threat of violence each time they enter the public realm—particularly if they walk with a same-sex partner.

The gendered nature of both public and private space upholds a binary opposition between men and women and thus bolsters the ideological workings of heterosexual hegemony. Individuals who are perceived to be—or who declare themselves as—lesbian, bisexual, or gay are among those most likely to be attacked, given a cultural conflation between gender and sexuality. Yet the issue is much deeper than perpetrators using gender cues to identify potential victims. A more profound question centers around the ways in which men and women should interact in public. The demarcation of public space is intimately related to the articulation of culturally sanctioned gender identities.[32]

TRANSSEXUAL AND TRANSGENDERED PEOPLE AND VIOLENCE

The perceived violation of gender norms at the root of many instances of assault, harassment, and discrimination affects all males and females—not just those whose sexual identity is located outside of heterosexuality. By emphasizing the function of gender in queerbashing, research can help develop education and activist programs that are relevant to people of all sexual and gender identities. A stress on the intersection of gender and violence demonstrates that the issue of queerbashing profoundly affects heterosexuals, insofar as the threat of violence polices one's gender presentation and behavior.

Although this research is desperately needed and must be strongly encouraged, it should be supplemented with an investigation of the everyday experiences of people who live outside normative sex/gender relations. An attention to people who call themselves transsexual and/or transgendered can provide more insight into the relations between gender and violence.

Despite the variety of gender identities available in transgender networks, and despite the prevalence of transgendered people in other cultures, most people in Western societies assume that there are only two sexes (males and females) and two genders (men and women).[33] For transsexual and/or transgendered people, this poses a significant problem: a person must choose the gender to which he/she belongs and behave accordingly. Because most people believe that there are only "men" and "women," transgendered people need to live as one or the other in order to avoid verbal and physical harassment. In transgendered communities, this is known as the need to pass. Passing is about presenting yourself as a "real" woman or a "real" man—that is, as an individual whose "original" sex is never suspected.[34] Passing means hiding the fact that you are transsexual and/or transgendered. Most people go to extraordinary lengths to live undetected as transsexuals. Electrolysis, voice therapy, the binding of breasts, mastectomy, and plastic surgery are some of the more common means employed to ensure that people pass successfully.

The necessity of passing is directly related to the cultural coding of gender. In their ethnomethodological study of the implicit ways in which gender operates, Suzanne Kessler and Wendy McKenna demonstrate that social meanings are grafted onto bodies in order to give them one of two binary sexes. The researchers presented 960 students with representations of many different bodies. For example, they showed a picture of a body with long hair, breasts, and wide hips, and asked the participants in the study to tell them if the person was a "man" or a "woman." Kessler and McKenna found that the interpretation of sexed bodies was overwhelmingly skewed in favor of masculine referents. If a penis was present, a "male" gender attribution was made 96 percent of the time. Yet in order for a figure to be considered "female" more than 95 percent of the time, it needed to have a vagina *and* two other cues indicating femininity (e.g., long hair, breasts).[35]

This research has profound implications for the study of violence and gender. If gender ambiguity is habitually resolved within a masculinist frame of reference, then genetic males who live as women will be among those most at risk for assault. Simply put, within Western societies, it is easier for females to pass as men than for males to pass as women. Ethnographic research on gender confirms this hypothesis: in Holly Devor's study of "gender-blending" females, she notes that several of the women she interviewed felt free enough to walk down dimly lit streets late at night, given that they were perceived to be men.[36] Furthermore, many genetic females can live full-time as men without plastic surgery and/or male hormones. Conversely, many genetic males need to take female hormones in order to pass successfully as women.

Although nonpassing transsexuals would seem to be foremost among those at risk, other individuals experience similar harassment, such as nontranssexual people with seemingly transsexual characteristics. Tall women with broad shoulders and men with wide hips and little facial hair are among those most likely to be mistaken for transsexuals.

Given the cultural coding of gender into a binary framework, a high incidence of violence directed against TS/TG people is not surprising. Although there is very little data available on transgendered people as victims of violence, a 1992 study showed that 52 percent of MTF transsexuals and 43 percent of FTM transsexuals surveyed in London, England, had been physically assaulted.[37] Contrast these numbers with data from a 1989 American telephone poll, which revealed that 7 percent of lesbians and gay men were victims of assault in the previous year.[38] Although these samples represent two different countries, the statistical difference of violent incidents against gay/lesbian and transgender individuals is remarkable and certainly suggests that gender plays a crucial role in the attacks generally referred to as "gaybashing."

Although gender plays a central role in incidents of queerbashing, a collapse of gender and sexuality precludes a consideration of how this violence specifically affects transgendered people. Dorian Corey notes that contemporary gay antiviolence activists do not recognize the different ways aggression is, and has historically been, directed against transgendered people and gays:

> When the closet doors were shut [for gays, in the past], drag queens, of course, were out there anyways. We never had a closet. Let's face it, when you put on a dress and hit the world, you're declaring what you are . . . . These children that are supposedly straight looking, they're the ones getting bashed, so now [in the 1990s] they're protesting. The girls were always getting their asses kicked. It's just a thing of who you are and what you are.[39]

Transsexual activists have suggested that one of the ways we can respond to the function of gender in violence is by naming it directly. As an activist button proclaims, "transsexuals get queerbashed too." Activists also insist that we need to speak of *genderbashing*, not gaybashing. This discourse separates gender and sexuality, since their collapse prevents an appreciation of the specificity of violence against transsexual and transgendered people.

TRANSSEXUAL/TRANSGENDERED PEOPLE AND PUBLIC SPACE

If lesbians and gay men are attacked differently according to the public space they occupy, how can we think about the relations between space and gender for transgendered people? Despite the lack of empirical research on this phenomenon, we can stipulate that transsexual and transgendered people are at risk in known lesbian/gay areas, as well as in "ordinary" public spaces. An MTF transsexual in a gay village, for example, may be perceived as a gender outlaw by a homophobic assailant and attacked as a "faggot."[40] Analogously, an FTM transsexual walking on an "ordinary" street may be perceived as a threat to masculine, heterosexual public space, especially if he does not completely pass as a genetic male. The issue of passing is especially complex in the case of many FTMs, who are often perceived to be young, slightly effeminate boys.[41] To pass as a man, in such an instance, can involve the dangers associated with a public gay identity. Yet the issues become even more complex if it is discovered that the person being attacked is transgendered, not (or not only) lesbian, gay, or bisexual. When FTMs are assaulted, for instance, rape is a routine part of the violence they endure.[42] This suggests that gender functions not merely as a cue to identify potential victims. FTMs who are raped are told, through the act of sexual assault, that they are "really" women, and they will be treated as such. Biology is destiny. The rape of an FTM declares that "women" have no right to be out in public—especially when unaccompanied by a man—and that these individuals have no right to act "as if" they are men. This instance of violence is more than a mere attack on someone perceived to be a gay man; it is fundamentally about policing one's gender presentation in public sites. The act of rape functions as an aggressive reinscription of the FTM individual's biological sex and social gender.

The division of public and private spaces, which relies upon and reinforces a binary gender system, has profound implications for people who live outside normative sex/gender relations. Transgendered people are in jeopardy in both "ordinary" public spaces and in those designated as lesbian/gay. While one must address the workings of gender in these sites, an investigation of violence against TS/TG people would also account for the emergence of TS/TG public space.

SEX WORK AND TRANSSEXUAL/TRANSGENDERED PUBLIC SPACE

"Transsexual and transgendered public space" refers to urban areas known for their transsexuals and transvestites, such as the Meat District on the border of New York's Greenwich Village, Santa Monica Boulevard in Los Angeles, or the Tenderloin in San Francisco. While gay male public space is defined through the presence of gay businesses and bars, transsexual public space reflects the areas of the city frequented by transsexual and transvestite sex workers.

Since gender and sexuality are not the same, it is not surprising that most cities have separate geographic areas known for transgendered people and lesbians/gays. Pat Califia articulates the differences between gay ghettoes and sex worker areas:

> Gay ghettos operate differently than other types of sex zones. They are more likely to be residential districts for gay men as well as places where they can find entertainment. Although johns still enter gay ghettos in quest of pleasurable activities not available within the nuclear family, they have better luck scoring if they camouflage themselves as residents of the area.[43]

Because transgender areas are not tied to a notion of a resident (as in the case of gay ghettos), the ways in which the space can be defined varies. Although certain sections of the city are known for their transsexuals and transvestites, these people are usually only visible at night. New York's Meat Market District is so named because of its many meat-packaging warehouses. When these businesses close at the end of the day, transgendered sex workers come out to earn their livelihoods, and thus transform the meaning of the term "meat" into one with explicit sexual connotations. Time of day and geographic space converge to establish a public transgender identity. For example, a Toronto sex worker interviewed in David Adkin's film *Out: Stories of Lesbian and Gay Youth* refers to the area where transgender prostitutes solicit clients as "trannie town."[44]

As Califia demonstrates, the recent emergence of gay ghettos has separated sexual minorities from transsexual prostitutes. Although bars catering to transgendered people are extremely rare, they are usually located in sex worker districts rather than in gay villages. In Montréal, for example, the transsexual/transvestite bar Café Cléopâtra is situated near the corner of Sainte-Catherine and Saint-Laurent streets, in the heart of the red-light district.[45] The bar is widely known for its prostitutes—it is a space not only where transgendered people can socialize, but where they can also earn their livings. Montréal police observe the establishment regularly. While recent years have not witnessed any official raids on the bar, it is common for officers to walk in, "do the rounds," and inspect bar patrons, sex workers, and their prospective clients.[46]

This police harassment of transgendered people relates to the laws against prostitution. In Canada, prostitution is entirely legal, but soliciting clients is not.[47] Individual officers have enormous scrutiny in the interpretation of what constitutes "solicitation": it may be a verbal agreement about sexual acts in exchange for financial compensation, or it may be a smile or glance directed at an undercover officer. While the latter instance would probably not be considered "solicitation" in a court of law, officers still have the power to charge individuals with the crime and place them in custody for a night. The crime of "soliciting" sex, of course, is fundamentally concerned with the regulation of public space, and it implicitly assumes that independent women have no right to be on the street at night.[48] It is the communication of sexual desire that is criminalized in Canada, not sexual desire or its enactment per se. Not surprisingly, this legislation does not affect all sex workers equally. Cathy, the operator of an escort service, remarks that street prostitutes—those most visible in the public eye—are most affected by this law: "escort services . . . have enjoyed . . . tolerance as we go tiptoeing around in the night, not bothering communities because we're not standing in people's front yards."[49] Research indicates that police use the soliciting law to harass prostitutes, following them down the street in a patrol car or stopping to talk with them during their work.[50]

LIMITS OF ANTIVIOLENCE ACTIVISM: OPPOSING GENDER AND SEXUALITY

The preceding discussion has emphasized some of the ways in which gender is fundamental to a conceptual organization of violence, most especially violence in public space: that males judged to be "effeminate" are subject to verbal abuse and physical attack; that lesbians are subject to a lesser degree of aggression in public when they are with a male partner as opposed to a female; and that more than half of MTF transsexual respondents in one survey reported being victims of a physical attack. The final section of this chapter considers the conjuncture of gender, violence, and public space, with a particular concern for how community-based responses to violence against sexual and gender minorities can actually eclipse the realities of violence against transsexual and transgendered prostitutes.

Much of the activist response to violence against sexual and gender minorities has centered on the gay village of a particular city.[51] As most gay men are assaulted in areas demarcated as "gay," this focus is useful. Yet such a strategy forecloses an investigation of gender and ignores the different experiences of lesbians, bisexual women, and transgendered people with respect to public space and violence. By emphasizing sexual identity, this discourse establishes an antiviolence agenda that is, at best, only somewhat useful. Consider the text of an educational poster produced by Montréal's police department (Service de police de la communauté urbaine de Montréal, or SPCUM): "Being lesbian, gay, or bisexual is not a crime. Bashing is." The slogan—which also appears on buttons produced by antiviolence activists in Toronto—addresses the perpetrators of violence directly, and in that, it is to be commended. Despite this direct address, however, the poster does not engage the cognitive processes at work that perpetrators use to determine who is gay, lesbian, or bisexual. In this discourse, identity is mobilized as the ground upon which acts of violence are established. People are bashed because they are gay, lesbian, or bisexual. But we have already seen that bashing occurs due to the perception of potential victims, and that compulsory sex/gender relations figure centrally in these acts of interpretation. In this light, educational materials that address the perpetrators of violence should focus on the interpretive processes these people use to locate queerbashing victims. Because gender is the primary mechanism through which this takes place, there is a desperate need for posters, pamphlets, and presentations that outline the ways in which a binary gender system is upheld, as well as the power relations concealed within it. Through a stress on being, rather than on the perception of doing, the SPCUM poster reifies sexual identity and prevents a proper investigation of gender in the problematic of violence.

Implicitly, gender and sexuality are juxtaposed. This opposition can be witnessed in the brief presented by the SPCUM to the Québec Human Rights Commission in association with its public hearings on violence and discrimination against lesbians and gay men (November 1993). The relationship between sexual minorities and the police figured centrally in the public consultation. Only three years earlier, the SPCUM had publicly *assaulted* lesbians, bisexuals, and gay men during a raid on Sex Garage, an underground warehouse party raided by the MUC police. Activists also expressed ongoing concern about the possibility of a serial murderer in Montréal who targeted gay male victims. In addition to these issues, activists charged that the SPCUM had little knowledge of, or interest in, the increased violence against sexual minorities—particularly the assaults that occurred in the gay village.[52]

In their brief to the commission, the SPCUM presented data on the prevalence of crime in District 33—the geographic area that includes (but is not limited to) the gay village. The borders of the village (René-Lévesque and Ontario, Amherst and Papineau) were compared to a similar section of the city—that demarcated by the streets René-Lévesque and Ontario (north/south axis) and Amherst and Saint-Laurent (east/west). The SPCUM was interested in comparing these two sections of District 33 in order to evaluate the frequency of violent incidents (thefts, sexual assault, harassment). The areas are proportional in size, each comprising about 20 percent of the district. Moreover, they share certain similarities in terms of the businesses, bars, and people present:

> Tous deux sont dans l'axe de la rue Ste-Catherine, rue très fréquentée de jour comme de nuit et où l'on retrouve divers commerces, restaurants, bars et salles d'amusement. On y retrouve également des activités reliées à la vente et la consommation de stupéfiants, à la prostitution masculine et féminine contrôlée, en partie, par deux groupes de motards criminels. [Both include Sainte-Catherine street, which is busy both day and night, and where one can find a variety of businesses, restaurants, bars, and amusement halls. One can also find activities related to the sale and consumption of drugs, as well as male and female prostitution, which is controlled, in part, by two groups of criminal bikers.][53]

The SPCUM data indicates that between November 1991 and October 1993, a total of 1,454 crimes were recorded for the gay village—approximately 18 percent of the total number of reported crimes in District 33.[54] Given that the gay village comprises 20 percent of the district, the study implies that incidents of violence and crime correspond proportionately to geography. (However, the brief does not address the population of the gay village in relation to that of the entire district, thus associating violence with city space rather than demographics.)

The SPCUM offers comparative data to legitimate this figure. The section of District 33 to which the gay village is compared indicates 2,774 incidents of violence over the same time period, a statistic that amounts to 34 percent of the violence in the total district.[55] Since the comparison territory is relatively equal in size to that of the gay village, it is suggested that violence and crime occur more frequently in this area than in the section of the city known to be populated by gay men. By demonstrating the ways in which crime in the gay village is statistically *below* the proportional incidents of violence in District 33, the SPCUM attempts to dismiss activists who point to increased instances of bashing in Montréal's gay village. (The results of the SPCUM study are presented in figure 1.)

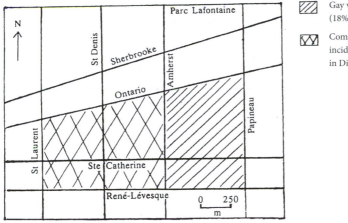

Gay village, 1454 incidents
(18% of total crimes in District)

Comparison territory, 2774
incidents (34% of total crimes
in District)

Figure 42.1 Incidents of violent crimes in two section of Police District 33, Montreal, November 1991–October 1993 (source: SPCUM 1993, 10–11).

There are, of course, tremendous differences in the data on violence collected by police departments and that collected by lesbian and gay community groups.[56] What is perhaps even more remarkable about the research presented by the SPCUM, however, is the way in which it forces a separation between sexuality and gender in terms of public space. The comparative section of District 33—that area bordered by Saint-Laurent, Amherst, Ontario, and René-Lévesque—is well-known as the city's sex worker district. The city's only transsexual/transvestite bar is located here, and streets in this region are also frequented by TS/TG prostitutes. Although the SPCUM maintains that both the gay village and this comparative section are homes to prostitution, they do not account for the gendered breakdown of this activity. Field research conducted in the summer of 1993 indicates that most male prostitutes work in the gay village, toward Papineau; directly on its borders (Parc Lafontaine, located just above Amherst and Ontario); or in an adult cinema at the corner of Sainte-Catherine and Amherst. In contrast, most female prostitutes work on the corner of Saint-Laurent and Sainte-Catherine, on Saint-Denis, or on side streets in the vicinity. Transgendered prostitutes can also be found in this area. (The geographic location of sex workers in District 33 is depicted in figure 2.)

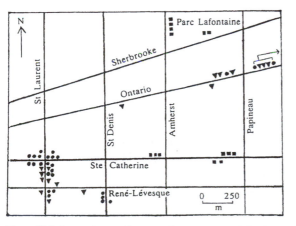
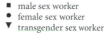

■ male sex worker
● female sex worker
▼ transgender sex worker

Figure 42.2 Sex-worker presence according to gender in Police District 33, Montreall, November 1991–October 1993 (source: field research). Note: more sex workers can be found further east on Ontario.

Regarding incidents of violence, most TS/TG prostitutes work in an area with a much higher frequency of criminal acts than the gay village (34 percent versus 18 percent). Although these statistics do not necessarily indicate that more transgendered people (proportionally) are victims of violence than gay men, it is certainly fair to stipulate that they work in an area known for criminal activities. To present this region as a comparative sample against the gay village is, then, to juxtapose gender and sexuality. While the SPCUM attempts to dispel fears about the high incidence of violence in gay space, it offers no examination of the role gender plays either in this site or its comparative territory. Because gender is not signaled as a factor in the discussion of District 33—along with other variables including poverty and homelessness—the SPCUM assumes that crime does not vary according to the gendered dimension of public space. The focus accorded to sexuality and the gay ghetto makes it impossible to address the violence that is directed against TS/TG people—whether they are in the gay village, a sex worker zone, or elsewhere.

It is important to understand the ways in which gender and sexuality can work against each other in the issue of violence. Because many of Montréal's gay male activists decried an increase in anti-gay violence within the city's gay village, the police department responded by documenting violent crimes committed in this area and contrasting the results with a comparison territory in the same district. Gay activists fused sexuality and geography, and did not account for the ways in which gender functions in queerbashing. The SPCUM, in turn, responded to the discourse established by gay male activists (violence against gay men in the village) and used comparative data to refute the proposed frequency of these instances. Both strategies relied on a separation of gender and sexuality, and thus prevented a political coalition among gay men, women, lesbians, and transsexuals.[57]

The brief presented by the SPCUM is significant precisely because of its refusal to address the gendered nature of violence. It serves to define the problematic of violence against sexual minorities (against gay men, more specifically), but it eclipses questions of gender and therefore cannot address the realities of women and transsexuals. The SPCUM document, as a response to an activist position on violence against men in the gay village, exemplifies the erasure of TS/TG people in the institutional world. The conceptualization of violence and public space offered by certain gay male activists relies upon a gendered understanding of public space and forecloses an adequate appreciation of violence directed against TS/TG individuals. The SPCUM brief subsequently takes up this conjuncture between gender and public space in order to refute the claims of the significant number of aggressive incidents against men in the gay village of Montréal. In this manner, transsexual and transgendered people are obscured both within a gay male activist discourse and within the police response to this position. A conceptual association among gender and geography makes transsexuals disappear from public space. This conceptual problematic is taken up in the administration of the everyday world. This effacement marks one instance of an institutional erasure of transsexual and transgendered people.

A separation of gender and sexuality becomes more complicated when we consider the ways in which gender, sexuality, and prostitution overlap in specific public spaces. While most TS/TG prostitutes in Montréal are visible in the vicinity of Saint-Laurent and Sainte-Catherine, many of these people also frequent Ontario est—a street that falls within the border of the gay village. Despite its location in a gay area, sections of Ontario est (between Panet and Dufresne) are known for transgendered prostitution—particularly at night. In the summer of 1993, residents of this sector (Centre-Sud) protested the presence of prostitutes and intravenous drug users. Groups of citizens harassed and assaulted sex workers in the area, intimidated their clients, and vandalized an apartment known to be a piquerie, or shooting gallery.[58] A community group was established to continue this pressure, although it officially distanced itself from the violent tactics employed. At one meeting I attended, residents discussed various strategies that could be employed to evict sex workers from the area. One man stood up and spoke out about his plan to take a baseball bat and assault two Haitian transgendered prostitutes, known to work on the corner of Ontario and Panet Streets. Like many perpetrators of queerbashing who target black gay men as easy victims,[59] this attacker viewed black transgendered women as those least likely to retaliate and most worthy of assault. Notwithstanding the fact that such violence occurs within the gay village, it cannot be explained as an instance of homophobia. Rather, this proposed assault emphasizes the importance of accounting for gender, race, class, and public space in an analysis of violence. An investigation of gender and space cannot merely accept an area known as a gay ghetto to be monolithic, but must examine the ways in which subsections of this region can be claimed, or contested, as transgendered locations.[60] These differences can be subtle, changing from one block to the next and varying with the hour of the day (or night) and the passage of time more generally. Once the definition of TS/TG public space is acknowledged, we can examine the complexity of the violence that occurs within these sites, accounting for the specificity of violence against TS/TG individuals. That people of color are singled out for attack in TS/TG public spaces parallels the increased violence they face within gay villages.[61]

CONCLUSION

Taking up the kind of poststructuralist sociology proposed in chapter 3, this chapter reflects on the issue of gender and violence. The erasure of transgendered people from the social text is amply illustrated by the antiviolence discourse proposed by gay male activists in Montréal and subsequently adopted by the Montréal police. One of the political arguments to be made from this insight is not that transgendered people experience more violence than lesbians and gay men (although that may be a valid observation). Rather, I consider how a gendered knowledge on violence—one that presupposes men's bodies—ignores and excludes the bodies and experiences of transsexual and transgendered people. Since such an exclusion is made possible by a collapse between gender and sexuality, a careful theoretical reflection on the relations between these terms is warranted. This theoretical reflection can in turn inform both how we gather data on the issue, as well as the political responses we develop. Such a reflexive sociology appreciates how an object of inquiry is constructed in and through a process of research.

The theoretical issues presented here, especially the relations between gender and sexuality, raise additional questions as to the collection and interpretation of evidence on gendered violence. What implications does the presence of TS/TG people in public space hold in terms of violence? Do bashers drive into these areas, looking to assault a transsexual woman or a transvestite prostitute, as they often drive into gay villages in search of queerbashing victims?[62] Are transgendered people of color assaulted more frequently than those who are white? What happens when transgender prostitutes enter areas demarcated as "gay"? Are these people subject to assault because of an association between prostitution and AIDS, and if so, how does this relate to increased violence against those perceived to be HIV-positive?[63] Since much of the data on queerbashing indicates that it is often perpetrated by young males, usually in groups,[64] are transgendered youth most at risk for assault? What are the specific methodological difficulties involved in collecting data on violence against transgendered people? Will these people be reluctant to report the assaults they experience to the police, as are many lesbians, gay men, and bisexuals? Given that transsexuals are incarcerated according to their "original," biological sex (e.g., an MTF person is placed in an all-male jail), can we expect transsexuals to consider police and law enforcement officials in a favorable light?[65] Do transgendered people even inform gaybashing hotlines when they are assaulted, or do they not consider themselves part of these communities? How can we record incidents of genderbashing for the collection of hate crime statistics?[66] These are only a few of the questions that a more detailed, empirical study of violence against transgendered people would address.

In recent years, the issue of violence has received increased attention in the communities of the sexually marginalized, as well as within the academy. Although some of the research emphasizes the role of gender in violence,[67] it has yet to explore the implications of this issue for transgendered individuals and communities. The definition of public space is intimately linked to culturally sanctioned gender identities. This has profound implications for people who live outside normative sex/gender relations: "ordinary" public space as well as regions known as gay ghettoes are sites where the potential of being verbally abused, and/or physically assaulted, is remarkably high. Furthermore, although gender and sexuality are conventionally confused, such that "effeminate" men and "masculine" women are "gaybashed" irrespective of their sexual identities, the variables of gender and sexuality can also be juxtaposed. Such an opposition can be quite explicit, as when middle-class gay men struggled to evict transgendered prostitutes from Vancouver's West End.[68] A separation of gender and sexuality can also be more subtle, as in the discourse on violence proposed by many gay male activists that privileges sexuality over gender, and hence develops a political response that is only valid for urban, middle-class gay men.

Taking up the issue of violence against sexual and gender minorities, this chapter has attempted to illustrate how some of the responses to violence preclude an adequate conceptualization of gendered aggression. Through a literature review on gender and violence, as well as a preliminary analysis on the geographic location of Montréal prostitutes in 1993, I have argued that the discourse of violence against sexual minorities excludes transsexual women. Furthermore, the briefs presented to the Québec Human Rights Commission offer an engaging case study of how the social relations of gender are textually coordinated in one institution, such that transsexuals are beyond consideration.

If TS and TG individuals are rendered invisible through the daily work of institutions, the generation of knowledge that makes sense of this effacement is crucial. While this chapter outlines some theoretical reflections concerning this problematic, the following chapters broaden this inquiry by engaging in a process of empirical research.

NOTES

1. The chapter limits itself to the literature on violence against lesbians and gay men, as well as a case study of antiviolence activism in Montréal. The scholarship on violence against non-transsexual women is not considered by analysis.
2. Quoted in G. Valentine, "(Hetero)Sexing Space: Lesbian Perceptions and Experiences in Everyday Spaces," *Environmental Planning D: Society and Space* 11 (1993): 409.
3. National Gay and Lesbian Task Force, *Anti-gay/lesbian Violence, Victimization, and Defamation in 1993* (Washington, D.C.: NGLTF Policy Institute, 1994), 1.
4. Valentine, "(Hetero)Sexing Space"; Gary Comstock, *Violence Against Lesbians and Gay Men* (New York: Columbia University Press, 1991); and B. von Schultess, "Violence in the Streets: Anti-lesbian Assault and Harassment in San Francisco," in *Hate Crimes: confronting Violence Against Lesbians and Gay Men*, ed. G. Herek and K. Berril (London: Sage, 1992), 65–75.
5. Michael Hendricks, "Lesbian and Gay Community Relations with the M[ontréal] U[rban] C[community] Police," brief presented for the group Lesbiennes et Gais contre la violence to the Québec Human Rights Commission, November 1993.
6. Brief presented to the Québec Human Rights Commission include Hendricks, "Lesbian and Gay Community Relations,"; Irène Demczuk, "Des droits à reconnaître. Hétérosexisme et discrimination envers les lesbiennes"; David Pepper, "Community Based Responses to Bias Crimes: Some Critical Steps;" SPCUM, "Mémoire sur la discrimination et la violence envers les gais et les lesbiennes"; and Ki Namaste, "Transgenders and Violence: An Exploration" (brief upon which this chapter was based). Copies of these briefs are available from the Commission des droits de la personne et de la jeunesse, 360 Saint-Jacques, Montréal, Québec, H2Y 1P5 Canada.
7. D. Smith, *The Everyday World as Problematic: A Feminist Sociology* (Toronto: University of Toronto Press, 1987), 17.
8. "The Traffic in Women: Notes on the 'Political Economy' of Sex," in *Toward an Anthropology of Women*, ed. R. Reiter (New York: Monthly Review Press, 1975), 157–210; "Thinking Sex: Notes Towards a Radical Theory of the Politics of Sexuality," in *Pleasure and Danger: Exploring Female Sexuality*, ed. C. Vance (Boston, Routledge and Kegan Paul, 1984),

267–319; and "Of Catamites and Kings: Reflections on Butch, Gender, and Boundaries," in *The Persistent Desire: A Femme-Butch Reader*, ed. Joan Nestle (Boston, Alyson, 1991), 466–82.

9. Lévi-Strauss, *Les Structures élémentaires de la parenté* (Paris: Presses universitaires de France, 1949).
10. Rubin, "Thinking Sex," 308.
11. Ibid., 307.
12. Rubin, "Of Catamites and Kings," 475.
13. Ibid, 477.
14. Ibid, 474.
15. NGLTF, "Anti-gay/lesbian Violence," 16.
16. Marlene Mackie, *Exploring Gender Relations* (Toronto: Butterworths, 1983).
17. S. Ortner and H. Whitehead, eds. *Sexual Meanings: The Cultural Construction of Gender and Sexuality* (Cambridge: Cambridge University Press, 1981).
18. A. Kinsey, W. Pomeroy, and Clyde E. Martin, *Sexual Behavior in the Human Male* (Philadelphia: W. B. Saunders Company, 1948).
19. Rubin, "Thinking Sex," 307.
20. Joseph Harry, "Conceptualizing Anti-gay Violence," *Journal of Interpersonal Violence* 5 (1990): 350–58; Harry, "Derivative Deviance: The Cases of Extortion, Fag-Bashing and the Shakedown of Gay Men," *Criminology* 19 (1982): 546–63.
21. Harry, "Derivative Deviance."
22. Von Schultess, "Violence in the Streets."
23. Valentine, "(Hetero)Sexing Space," 409.
24. See, for instance, Shirley Ardener, *Defining Females: The Nature of Women in Society* (London: Croom Hem, 1978); e. Garmonikow, D. Morgan, J. Purvis, and D. Taylorson, *The Public and the Private* (London: Heineman Educational Books, 1983); R. Sydie, *Natural Women, Cultured Men: A Feminist Perspective on Sociological Theory* (Toronto: Methuen, 1987); and Judith Walkowitz, *Prostitution and Victorian Society: Women, Class, and the State* (Cambridge: Cambridge University Press, 1980).
25. Ardener, *Defining Females,* 10.
26. Walkowitz, *Prostitution and Victorian Society,* 5.
27. Comstock, *Violence Against Lesbians and Gay Men,* 49.
28. Ibid, 49-50.
29. See Valentine, "(Hetero)Sexing Space," 410.
30. Comstock, *Violence Against Lesbians and Gay Men,* 65.
31. Valentine, "(Hetero)Sexing Space," 410.
32. While queerbashing is centrally concerned with policing the public presentation of gender and sexuality, it is noteworthy that many lesbians and gay men who are victims of violence have the personal property destroyed. For instance, in Kansas City, Kansas, the word "fag" was spraypainted on eight cars parked near a gay bar (NGLTF, *Anti-gay/lesbian Violence*, 24). In Ovett, Mississippi, local residents objecting to the presence of a feminist and lesbian retreat verbally harassed the women, placed a dead dog on their mailbox, and threatened their physical safety (ibid., 37). Despite the sanctity of private property within capitalist democracy, sexual minorities risk having their cars, homes, and possessions vandalized—an act of violence that attempts to regulate sexuality and gender within the *private* sphere.
33. Feinberg, *Transgender Warriors*; Ortner and Whitehead, *Sexual Meanings*; Gilbert Herdt, ed., *Third Sex, Third Gender: Beyond Sexual Dimorphism in Culture and History* (New York: Zone Books, 1994); Holly Devor, *Gender Bending: Confronting the Limits of Duality* (Bloomington: Indian University Press, 1989); Bullough and Bullough, *Cross Dressing, Sex, and Gender*.
34. The issue of "passing" has been examined from an ethnomethodological perspective within sociology. See Harold Garfinkel, *Studies in Ethnomethodology* (Englewood Cliffs: Prentice-Hall, 1967); and Kessler and McKenna, *Gender: An Ethnomethodological Approach*.
35. Kessler and Mckenna, *Gender: An Ethnomethodological Approach,* 151–52.
36. Devor, *Gender Bening,* 133.
37. Brian Tully, *Accounting for Transsexuality and Transhomosexuality* (London: Whiting and Birch, 1992), 266.
38. NGLTF, *Anti-gay/lesbian Violence.*
39. Quoted in A. Enigma, "Livin' Large: Dorian Corey," *Thing* 8 (1992): 35–36.
40. The confusion of gender and sexuality manifests itself at the level of semantics, such that "faggot" is an insult with which many MTF transsexuals are familiar. The NGLTF report on violence includes the following incident: "A [MTF] transsexual activist for the homeless and people with AIDS was verbally abused in a hospital. As she sat in a wheelchair with a 103 degree fever, a doctor and several hospital employees repeatedly called her an 'AIDS carrying fucking faggot'" (NGLTF, *Anti-gay/lesbian Violence*, 26).
41. See Devor, *Gender Blending;* Bullough and Bullough, *Cross Dressing, Sex, and Gender.*
42. For example, Brandon Teena, a FTM transsexual murdered in Humbolt, Nebraska, was assaulted and raped on week before his death. Details of this incident are discussed in the NGLTF, *Anti-gay/lesbian Violence*, 18. Also see, Aphrodite Jones, *All She (sic) Wanted* (New York: Pocket Books, 1996). For insightful analyses of how U.S. lesbian and gay communities have misrepresented Brandon Teena to be a lesbian rather than an FTM transsexual, consult Kathleen Chapman and Michael du Plessis, "Don't Call me *Girl*': Lesbian Theory, Feminist Theory, and Transsexual Identities," in *Cross-Purposes: Lesbians, Feminists, and the Limits of Alliance*, ed. Dana Heller (Bloomington: Indiana University Press, 1997), 169–85; and C. Jacob Hale, "Consuming the Living, Dis(re)membering the Dead in the Butch/FTM Borderlands," *GLQ: A Journal of Lesbian and Gay Studies* 4, no. 2 (1998): 311–48.

43. Pat Califia, "The City of Desire: Its Anatomy and Destiny," *Invert* 2, no. 4 (1991): 14.

44. David Adkin, *Out: Stories of Lesbian and Gay Youth* (Montréal: National Film Board of Canada, 1993).

45. For more on the geographic area of Montréal's red-light district, see Daniel Proulx, *Le Red Light de Montréal* (Montréal: VLB, 1997); Danielle Lcasse, *La Prostitution féminine à Montréal, 1945–1970* (Montréal: Boréal, 1994); and Limoges, *La Prostitution féminine à Montréal*.

46. Montréal police entered Café Cléopâtra with a video camera, for instance, on November 13, 1997. See Namaste, *Évaluation des besoins*, 61.

47. *Pocket Criminal Code of Canada* s. 195.1 (Toronto: Carswell, 1987), 118–19.

48. Valerie Scott, "C-49: A New Wave of Oppression," in *Good Girls/Bad Girls: Sex Trade Workers* and *Feminists Face to Face*, ed. Laurie Bell (Toronto: Women's Press, 1987), 100–103.

49. Cathy, "Unveiling," in *Good Girls/Bad Girls*, 88–91.

50. Nakins and Gendron, *Project Prostitution*, 4.

51. See, for instance, Hendricks, "Lesbian and Gay Community Relations with the MUC Police."

52. Ibid., 3.

53. SPCUM, "Mémoire sur la discrimination et la violence envers les lesbiennes et les gais," 10. English translation mine.

54. Ibid., 10–11.

55. Ibid., 11.

56. See Cornstock, *Violence Against Lesbians and Gay Men*; NGLTF, *Anti-gay/lesbian Violence.*

57. The human rights hearings were intended to address violence against lesbians and gay men. Many lesbians, however, felt that the issues that concerned them as women were not addressed within a gay male setting—a feeling that led to the formation of a lesbian caucus (see Demzcuk, "Des droits à reconnaître"). Following the hearings, the lesbian caucus officially withdrew from the community coalition, the *Table de concertain des lesbiennes et des gais du grand Montréal*. The caucus cited a lack of understanding of gender issues on the part of gay men as the primary reason for their departure. (Remarkably, neither lesbian or gay male activists met with representatives of transsexual communities to address the question of violence.)

58. These tactics parallel those of citizens in Vancouver who, in the mid-1980s, organized to evict sex workers from the city's prestigious West End. See S. Arrington, "Community Organizing," in *Good Girls/Bad Girls*, 104–8. For an excellent analysis of the ways in which right-wing extremists mobilized residents of *Centre-Sud*, consult the brief prepared by the Comité contre le racisme d'Hochelaga-Maisonneuve for the Québec Human Rights Commission. At one of their demonstrations, chants progressed from "dehors les putes" [whores out] to "dehors les gauchistes" [leftists out] to "plus de tapettes dans netre quartier" [no more fags in our neighborhood]. Comité contre le racisme d'Hochelaga-Maisonneuve, "Mémoire depose à la Commission des droits de la personne dans la cadre de la consultation publique sur la discrimination et la violence envers les gais et les lesbiennes," brief presented to the Québec Human Rights Commission, Montréal, 1993.

59. Comstock, *Violence Against Lesbians and Gay Men*, 49–50.

60. See Arrington's insightful comments on the geopolitical situation in Vancouver's West End in the mid-1980s, when property-owning gay men instigated a drive to remove prostitutes (transgendered people among them) from residential area. Arrington, "Community Organizing," 104–8.

61. Comstock, *Violence Against Lesbians and Gay Men*, 49–50.

62. Ibid., 49.

63. NGLTF, *Anti-gay/lesbian Violence*, 29.

64. Comstock, *Violence Against Lesbians and Gay Men*, 65.

65. For more on transgendered people in prison, see James Tee, *Health Issues of the HIV + MTF Transgendered Prison Population* (Toronto: PASAN—Prisoner's AIDS Support Action Network [489 College St., Suite 405, Toronto, Ontario, M6G 1A5, 416-920-9567], 1997); Maxine Petersen, Judith Stephens, Robert Dickey, and Wendy Lewis, "Transsexuals within the Prison System: An International Survey of Correctional Services Policies," *Behavioral Sciences and the Law* 14 (1996): 219-29; and Ann Scott, "A Brief on HIV/AIDS in the Transgendered Prison Population," presentation at the International Foundation for Gender Education conference, Toronto, March 27, 1998. Also see Ann Scott and Rick Lines, "HIV/AIDS in the Male-to-Female Transsexual and Transgendered Prison Population: A Comprehensive Strategy. A Brief from PASAN" (Toronto, May 1999).

66. Documenting hate crimes against gays and lesbians is difficult because the violence must be clearly accompanied by anti-gay epithets. For instance, if a man is stabbed in the gay village his wallet stolen, he will be considered the victim of robbery unless the assailants called him a derogatory insults relating to his perceived sexuality (see SPCUM, "Mémoire sur la discrimination et la violence envers les gais et les lesbiennes"). In the case of violence against transgendered people, this criteria for documentation is questionable, since many MTF transsexuals are called "faggot." Programmatically, we should not have to wait until bashers decry transgendered people with the proper vocabulary before we have an adequate manner of recording such genderbashing incidents.

67. See Valentine, "(Hetero)Sexing Space"; von Schultess, "Violence in the Streets"; and Harr, "Conceptualizing Anti-gay Violence."

68. Arrington, "Community Organizing," 104–8.

43

From the Medical Gaze to Sublime Mutations

The Ethics of (Re)Viewing Non-normative Body Images

T. BENJAMIN SINGER

IN THIS ARTICLE, ADAPTED FROM FREQUENT CONFERENCE AND MEDICAL SCHOOL PRESENTATIONS, gender theorist and transgender healthcare activist Ben Singer articulates the relationship he sees between aesthetic judgment and quality of service-provision. Singer contends that the affective response of care-providers who are unable to comprehend the complex configurations of transgender bodies and identities often results in poor health care for transgender people. His remarks are made with specific reference to healthcare delivery in the United States, which does not have a standardized national healthcare system.

Singer draws on disability-rights discourse as well as queer theories of visuality to develop his notion of a "transgender sublime" through the analysis of photographic representations of non-standard bodies, including transsexual and intersex bodies. His materials range from anonymous and depersonalized representations in medical textbooks through the self-representative work of trans-identified photographers Loren Cameron and Del LaGrace Volcano.

Singer concludes his article by contrasting the idea of gender complexity that he finds in a popular transgender healthcare training model with a "rhizomatic" model borrowed from poststructural theorists Gilles Deleuze and Felix Guattari. The latter, Singer contends, more fully captures the unexpected nature of the transgender complexity that induces disorienting encounters with the sublime, which in turn affects the quality of transgender health care.

This article uses the aesthetic concepts of the "beautiful" and the "sublime" to explore the politics of representation in images of non-normative bodies across contexts that range from medical textbooks to work by artists exploring their own sense of embodied difference. It begins with photographs from medical textbooks that, since the nineteenth century, have been used as documentary evidence of the moral depravity of various types of individuals deemed different from a valued norm: homosexuals, criminals, and people with atypical anatomy. Medicine and criminology have colluded in a common aesthetic impulse: to locate the sight/site of deviance on the bodies of a wide array of social outcasts. The nineteenth-century technology of photography emerged as a privileged medium for situating the truth of deviance, so much so that an article in the popular medical journal *The Lancet* once commented that:

> Photography is so essentially the art of Truth—that it would seem to be the essential means of reproducing all forms and structures which science seeks for delineation.[1]

Through mechanical reproduction, photography powerfully generates the aura of an unmediated reality. According to William Mitchell in the *Reconfigured Eye*, photography has an "apparent Kryptonite connection to the referent" that is "automatic, physically determined, and therefore presumably objective." Mitchell goes on to say that photography shares with scientific methodologies like random sampling and double blind clinical trials the appearance of "a guaranteed way of overcoming subjectivity and getting at the real truth" (28).[2]

What follows is a series of images concerned with lingering issues of representation regarding people with non-normative anatomy. As will be seen, image-making practices have significant social, political and material consequences for those with atypical embodiment. They are not "merely" representational, but also resonate deeply with the social and material circumstances of life. As such, my analysis reconnects the severed relationship between representational strategies, on the one hand, and, on the other hand, the ethical and social dimension of non-normative-bodied-people's existence.

My critical concern parallels Raymond William's observation in his entry on "Aesthetic" in *Keywords* that:

> "[aesthetic] is an element in the divided modern consciousness of *art* and *society*: a reference beyond social use and social valuation which, like one special meaning of *culture*, is intended to express a human dimension which the dominant version of *society* appears to exclude. The emphasis is understandable but the isolation can be damaging, for there is something irresistibly displaced and marginal about the now common and limiting phrase 'aesthetic considerations', especially when contrasted with *practical* or *utilitarian* considerations, which are elements of the same basic division" (32).[3]

For the purposes of this analysis, the "damaging isolation" of "aesthetic considerations" from "practical" ones negatively impacts on how medical providers are trained to see and interact with non-normative-bodied people. Such separation severely impedes quality health care delivery for people with atypical anatomy. If ways of seeing are intimately linked to social practices, then deconstructing the medical gaze reveals the practical as well as ethical stakes in what upon cursory inspection seems a strictly aesthetic matter.

Photographs, particularly photographs of human bodies, have a profoundly ethical dimension. Through their codes and conventions, styles of lighting and modes of address, photographs literally *show* us how to relate to another person, which is of course also the central concern of ethics: *a proper regard for the other's legitimate claims for recognition*. Consequently, after critically commenting on how different-body-ness can be viewed in opposition to the medical gaze, I will draw upon my ethnographic work on the regulation of transsexuality through public health, to re-view the medical model that renders atypical embodiment pathological. The resulting analysis suggests that an aesthetic shift away from notions of beauty, and toward the concept of subliminity, shows us a more ethical way to relate to non-normative-bodied people in medical contexts.

As seen in these side-by-side images of people with intersex condition [Fig. 43.1], atypically embodied individuals represented in medical textbooks are often shown with bars across their eyes.[4] Protecting the confidentiality of patients in medical settings requires that anonymity be ensured, and thus at first glance the bar would seem to indicate respect for the privacy of the person pictured. However, even as it ensures anonymity, it also creates the effect of scientific objectivity through de-sexualizing, de-familiarizing, and ultimately depersonalizing the represented figure. This visual strategy makes clear that these are medical photographs, rather than pornography, or snapshots for a family album.

Despite legitimate concerns about confidentiality, such photographs ultimately strip away not only

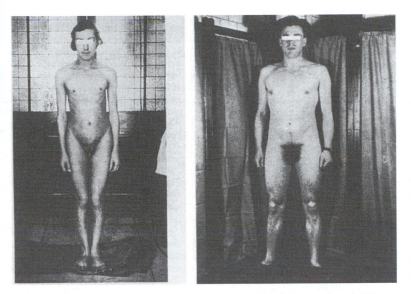

Figure 43.1 From L.R. Broster et al., eds., *The Adrenal Cortex and Intersexuality.* Chapman and Hall, 1938. Reprinted in *Stolen Glances: Lesbians Take Photographs.* Tessa Boffin and Jean Fraser, eds., London: Pandora Press, 1991 (16).

the clothing, but also the inherent personhood of their subjects. They create anonymous character types and specimens of physical pathology, rather than images of people with uncommon bodies. While the notion of "personhood" is open to anti-humanist critique, the eye bars are a clinical shadow cast across a face that might otherwise be recognized as belonging to a fellow human being. Thus we are compelled to question the kind of culture that needs to create anonymized photographs of physical pathology.

In this image of an adult with an intersexed condition [Fig. 43.2], a portion of the accompanying caption reads: "Adult with testicular feminization . . . These individuals are usually taller than average and tend to have a very attractive 'female' physique."[5] The full-figured "Marilyn Monroe" body-type

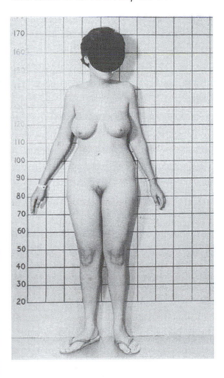

Figure 43.2 "Adult with testicular feminization (XY, but with an insensitivity to androgen). These individuals are usually taller than the average female and tend to have a very attractive 'female' physique." (From J. Money and A. Ehrhardt, *Man and Woman, Boy and Girl* (Baltimore: Johns Hopkins Press, 1972). Copyright 1972 by the Johns Hopkins Press. Reprinted by permission.)

pictured, something that came into and went out of vogue over the latter half of the twentieth century, offers an apt reminder that body-image is always subject to the shifting representational politics of sex and gender, and that there are fashions in bodies as much as in clothing and hairstyles.[6] Unpacking the aesthetics of this photograph further, as a product of the medical gaze it carries the stamp of documentary truth, realism, authenticity, and authority. The viewer imagines this to be an unmediated vision of medically detected pathology, yet a closer inspection reveals instead a carefully constructed and highly codified image. Notice, for example, the grid in the background that evokes a police line-up of criminal suspects. The numbered scale along the left side of the photograph, along with the two-dimensional grid, both rely on the visual conventions of criminology as well as medical taxonomy, two new sciences of the nineteenth century that arose about the same time that photographic technology was perfected for portraiture and documentary purposes.

The collusion of the medical gaze with the criminological project is a residue of the way photography was used by police and medical professionals alike to establish visual evidence of physical pathology and criminal deviance. That this image was published in the 1970s suggests how persistently the project of scientific objectivity has linked criminality with deviance. In this image, as in the others, the colonizing eye of authority, what Griselda Pollack terms the "mastering eye/I," is mapped onto people with nonstandard bodies via the medium of photography.[7] The result encourages uncritical viewers to adopt a point of view that reduces the personhood of those with nonstandard bodies to a medical disorder or criminal character type, the "truth" of which, as the previous quotation from *The Lancet* suggests, is located in the depicted body, rather than in the staging of the image.

Knowing that these images have been constructed by the medical gaze raises further questions about the importance of context for interpretation. How is it that we know these images are not intended to be pornographic? Perhaps it is because the posture of the body does not seem to invite intimacy, or because the middle of the face is obscured by a large black dot; perhaps it is because none of these bodies meet the culturally normative standards of ideal physical beauty that are most typically eroticized. The fact that these images are located in a medical textbook instead of *Playboy* magazine cues the viewer to see these images in a specific way. The context compels one to consider what qualifies as a "normal" body in comparison to those that are "different."

Photographs of transsexual people are almost as common in medical texts as photographs of people with intersexed bodies. Here [Fig. 43.3] we see an image with the accompanying caption: "The results of surgical and hormonal transformation of a male-to-female transsexual" (137).[8] The style of attire dates this image to the 1970s; while the grid-like background that characterized the other photographs has dropped away, the depersonalizing dot creating the effect of an anonymous character type still persists. Compare this image with that of Marsha P. Johnson [Fig. 43.4], a veteran of the Stonewall riots who fought back against the police during the 1969 disturbances that helped launch the contemporary gay, lesbian, bisexual, and transgender movements (130).[9] Notice that Johnson appears quite different from the figure in the roughly contemporaneous image in the medical textbook. Notably, she looks directly at the camera so that her eyes meet the gaze of the viewer. Through this look she asserts her subjectivity and resists objectification. The image has a snapshot quality, a photographic convention often used by "amateurs" rather than "experts" to capture a fleeting moment, rather than a premeditated or carefully staged event. Johnson's photograph also significantly differs from the medical images because it locates her in a social setting—people are visible in the background, at what appears to be a street fair or parade. Unlike the medical photographs of anonymous bodies, this picture is of a specific individual who is integrated into a social network in a public space. This alone communicates to viewers that trans people's lives have significant social, and not just medical, contexts.

In the 1920s, sexologist Magnus Hirschfield, a leading figure in the pre-Nazi-era homosexual eman-

Figure 43.3 The results of surgical and hormonal transformation of a male-to-female transsexual. Note feminization of body contours and posture. (From J. Money, "Prenatal hormones and postnatal socialization in Gender Identity Differentiation," in J.K. Cole and A Dienstbier (ocs). *Nebraska Symposium on Motivation*, 1973 (Lincoln: University of Nebraska Press, 1974). Copyright 1974 by the University of Nebraska Press. Reprinted by permission.

Figure 43.4 Marsha P. ("Pay it no mind!") Johnson. From *Transgender Warriors*. Photographed by Andrew Holbrooke. Printed by permission of the artist.

cipation movement in Europe, established photographic archives at the Institute of Sexual Science in Germany. According to Tessa Boffin and Jean Fraser, writing in the introduction to *Stolen Glances*:

> "…while (other) sexologists used their photographic records to establish their subjects' status as deviant people whose bodies exhibited signs of degeneracy, Hirschfield inverted this equation. His photographic records were collected to assert the visibility and thus the *viability* —of a social group, which Hirschfield termed an intermediate or third sex."[10]

Boffin's and Fraser's observation about Hirschfield's archive is suggestive for several reasons. Quite apart from the manner in which individual photographs worked to assert the visibility and viability of otherwise pathologized subjects, the archive itself powerfully demonstrated that individuals typically

Figure 43.5 Loren Cameron, God's Will ©1995 from *Body Alchemy*. All
Rights Reserved. Printed by permission of the artist.

seen in isolation had lives grounded in collective social structures; they were part of their broader
society's historical and cultural fabric. Presumably, groups whose documentation has been gathered
into an archive exists in other contexts as well, spaces not limited to the clinic or the prison.

Another alternative to the medical gaze is a self-portrait by Loren Cameron [Fig. 43.5], an artist
who began his photographic career by documenting his transition from female to male.[11] In "God's
Will," Cameron asserts control over the image-making process, showing the shutter release bulb in
his left hand while injecting body-modifying testosterone with the syringe in his right hand. The
image is provocatively self-representational, simultaneously connecting his material and aesthetic
manipulation of his own body. Cameron's self-portrait refutes the Frankensteinian logic of medical
expertise that puts the doctor and the medical establishment in the role of creator; it recasts the sense
of sacrality and power typically associated with the concept of God as an expression of self-actualization and self-determination, rather than as subjection to an inscrutable external force. While the
medical model asserts that Cameron is a product of medical intervention—or even invention, and thus
a proper subject of the medical gaze—this self-image represents him as an active moral and ethical
agent assuming responsibility for his own embodiment.

Cameron's self-portrait draws upon the representational conventions of body-building magazines
by using chiaroscuro lighting, an effect that starkly contrasts light and dark to cast deep shadows and
create a highly defined, sculptural surface effect.[12] This technique enhances the visual appearance of
musculature. Caught in a polarized field of light and dark, his form is intersected by, yet resists, simple
aesthetic dichotomies, just as his gender identity and embodiment are irreducible to familiar social
binaries. The end result is an idealized, muscular, masculine beauty—further distancing Cameron's figure from the determinedly un-idealized images of transsexual bodies found in medical textbooks.

Of all the images in Cameron's *Body Alchemy*, "God's Will" best exemplifies "the beautiful," an
aesthetic category Dick Hebdige identifies as foundational to "the birth of formal aesthetics in the
Enlightenment when the categories of the Sublime and the Beautiful were first used to differentiate the
varieties of aesthetic experience" (47–48).[13] The beautiful in this sense is not only something regarded

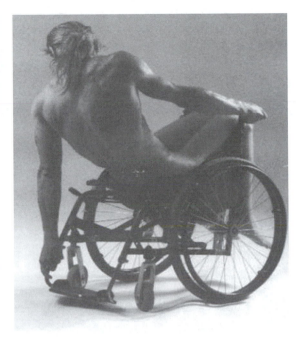

Figure 43.6 "If only I didn't have these skinny legs!"—
Peter—Reprinted from "Completely Unperfect," Mainstream:
Magazine of the Able-Disabled (23) Februrary 1997.

as conventionally attractive, but also something that enacts the notions of "unity" and "totality" that were central to nineteenth-century European aesthetics. The beautiful is something that can be apprehended in its entirety, such as a framed painting; the frame itself draws attention to, and creates a boundary for, the subject contained within it. In *"God's Will,"* Cameron presents a unified portrait of physical beauty, his body held in a classic body-building physique pose, framed by an empty, black, negative space. The stark relief creates the impression of a living Greek statue.

Figures 43.6–43.8 also draw upon the aesthetic of the beautiful, and use similar photographic techniques such as idealized poses and dramatic lighting to create an overall aesthetic unity. They are from the photo essay "Perfectly Imperfect," published in *Mainstream: Magazine of the Able-Disabled*. Although the images adopt visual codes from high fashion photography that promote unrealistic images of conventional beauty, the aesthetic choices function as a *legitimizing strategy,* as they do in Cameron's work, to produce beautiful, humanizing portraits of bodies normally considered monstrous or ugly. In this way, bodies normally regarded as culturally unintelligible become momentarily legible as a comprehensible unity.

More is at play here, however, than just the visual aesthetics of the beautiful. These images also have a textual voice. Contrary to the documentary fallacy, photographs do not "speak a thousand words" unless we have been trained to hear their voices. Ways of seeing are deeply embedded in culture, and images by themselves are hard-pressed to alter their conditions of visual reception. Visual perceptions of non-normative bodies, in particular, have been shaped through countless structured acts of viewing, in contexts that range from talk show spectacles to case studies of medical pathology. Consequently, supplementary narratives often accompany contemporary images of non-normative bodies. Captioned commentary counters the tyranny of the visual and helps redirect the spectator's pre-conditioned gaze.

In "Perfectly Imperfect" the self-representational images of non-normative-bodied people are accompanied by statements written by the subjects themselves. For example, in Fig. 43.7 we not only see Didi's body, but also see his words:

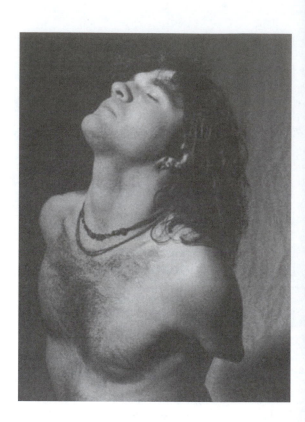

Figure 43.7 "The human body is beautiful. Beauty is a matter of taste and has no norm…"—Didi—
Reprinted from "Completely Unperfect," Mainstream: Magazine of the Able-Disabled (23) February 1997.

> The human body is beautiful. Beauty is a matter of taste and has no norm. Isn't my body beautiful enough to be shown? Just because there are limbs missing or differently grown… Am I expected to hide myself only because I don't live up to the ideal of beauty created by society?[14]

This caption reverses the primacy of the visual by critically commenting on the operation of a normatively structured (and structuring) gaze. According to Mitchell, in general, "if an image follows the conventions of photography and seems internally coherent, if the visual evidence that it presents supports the caption, and if we can confirm that this visual evidence is consistent with other things that we accept as knowledge within the framework of the relevant discourse, then we feel justified in the attitude that seeing is believing" (43).[15] In the case of these images, however, the "visual evidence" does not so much "support" the caption, because the caption enacts a reversal; rather, the photograph's "voice" critiques the visual norms of standardized beauty and directs viewers to read the pictured body differently.

While these images could be criticized for asserting traditional standards of beauty featuring nonnormative bodied models, the accompanying voice resists such an interpretation. Furthermore, these photographs are not only visually confrontational—the subject looks back without a bar across their eyes—but they also engage the viewer through direct textual address. For example, Dany in Fig. 43.8 attempts to literally reposition the viewers' eyes, saying: "For goodness sake!' Why are you always staring at my short arms? Why don't you look at me as I am? From top to bottom. All that is me!"[16] As limited as this captioning strategy is, it is effectively didactic. The voice instructs viewers in how to re-view the image, how to look differently at the body represented, and thus it forces into question the social norms of ideal physicality along with their photographic representational conventions. This technique calls attention, by comparison, to the profound silence and passivity of medical photographs

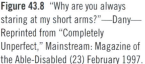

Figure 43.8 "Why are you always staring at my short arms?"—Dany— Reprinted from "Completely Unperfect," Mainstream: Magazine of the Able-Disabled (23) February 1997.

of non-normative bodies. Recalling the caption for Fig. 43.3, "(t)he results of surgical and hormonal transformation of a male-to-female transsexual," we see how medical discourses remain uncritical of the image and collude with the pathologizing gaze. The direct address of the captioned images in "Perfectly Imperfect," on the other hand, implicate the viewer in the act of looking, and disrupt the complacent voyeurism inscribed within the medical gaze. Because the photographic subject looks back, and *talks* back, viewers cannot hide behind the fetishistic unidirectionality of their look. Their privilege of seeing without themselves being seen has been subverted.[17]

The self-representational photographs of non-normatively-embodied people that most interest me all attempt to represent the social situation of non-normative embodiment. Thus, none of the images attempt to entirely displace the medical gaze, or to eliminate the circus sideshow role people with nonstandard bodies play in a spectacle-driven popular culture, for this too is an important component of their social context. Far from making social stigma simply disappear, they enact the *ambivalence* of living in a nonstandard body that is constantly bombarded by prurient medical, talk show, or pornographic gazes.

In "Jester," [Fig. 43.9] another Loren Cameron self-portrait from *Body Alchemy*, we see and hear Cameron addressing his own ambivalence about placing his body in front of the camera:

Every time I tell someone I am transsexual, I have a turbulent series of emotions. At first, I am afraid that whomever I'm telling will have a negative response, that they will somehow be repelled and become hostile or in some way reject me. .... But then, if I've been given a positive reception, I begin to spill it all with myopic enthusiasm, answering every question, which always encourages another. People are naturally curious, and some have a real need to know. By revealing myself, I have consensually invited their voyeurism; they can't help but watch as I make a spectacle of myself.... In the end, when I have spilled my guts or exhausted their interest, I begin to retreat a little. A grayness falls over me, and I realize that I feel unsafe. I feel naked. Self-doubt starts to poke holes in my ego, and I begin to think I have exploited myself: I am ashamed of my exhibitionism. I promise myself not to tell anyone ever again.[18]

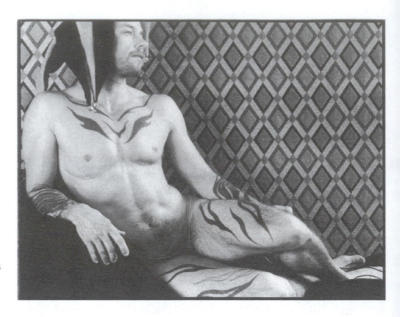

Figure 43.9 Loren Cameron, Carney
© 1995 from *Body Alchemy*. All Rights
Reserved. Printed by permission of
the artist.

Contradiction and tortured ambivalence characterize this work in part because Cameron has no way to be seen strictly on his own terms, within a social context where his body and identity are culturally intelligible. His image and the accompanying autobiographical narrative suggest that his ambivalence is located socially and spatially, not just subjectively. Within the medical gaze, trans embodiment, subjectivity, authority, and expertise are always already in the process of being structurally undercut. The result is both internal (psychic) and external (social or spatial) ambivalence. Quite literally, two valences—two values moving in two directions, affirmative and negative, or visible and invisible—operate at the same time. In the end, such a doubled and conflicted predicament allows for only a very circumscribed social space.

In *Vision and Difference*, Griselda Pollack writes about the relationship between gender and social space as she examines the situation of nineteenth-century women painters. She argues that the aesthetic distinctiveness of their work from that of male artists was not a matter of biological sex difference, but rather was created by a rigidly stratified gender structure. She observes that women artists were confined to working in "spaces of femininity," thus depicting subjects in drawing-rooms and private gardens, whereas men painted figures in bars and brothels. Differences in particular ways of seeing and representing were "the product of a lived sense of social locatedness, mobility and visibility, in the relations of seeing and being seen." She goes on to note that gendered social spaces, because they are shaped "within the sexual politics of looking," demarcate a "particular social organization of the gaze," which works "to secure a particular social ordering of sexual difference. Femininity is both the condition and the effect" (66).[19]

To the extent that gender and a "particular social organization of the gaze" are mutually constitutive, Pollack's argument about subjectivity, artistic production, and space can be applied to another Cameron self-portrait from a triptych titled "Distortions" [Fig. 43.10]. Here we see Cameron literally framed or boxed in, like a criminal or a caged animal, by transphobic cultural discourses. In this case, transphobia is represented in Pollack's terms as both the "condition and the effect" of Cameron's social existence. With his hand held to side of his head, and wearing a look of pained consternation, Cameron is ringed by contradictory statements such as: "Sorry, but I don't like men," followed by "You're not a man--you'll never shoot sperm." This series of transphobic accusations narrates subjectivity under

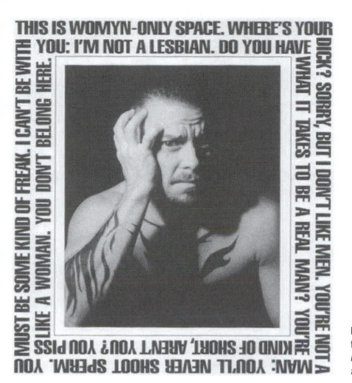

THIS IS WOMYN-ONLY SPACE. WHERE'S YOUR DICK? SORRY, BUT I DON'T LIKE MEN. YOU'RE NOT A MAN: YOU'LL NEVER SHOOT SPERM. YOU MUST BE SOME KIND OF FREAK. I CAN'T BE WITH LIKE A WOMAN. YOU DON'T BELONG HERE. YOU: I'M NOT A LESBIAN. DO YOU HAVE WHAT IT TAKES TO BE A REAL MAN? YOU'RE KIND OF SHORT, AREN'T YOU? YOU PISS

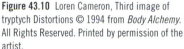

Figure 43.10 Loren Cameron, Third image of tryptych Distortions © 1994 from *Body Alchemy*. All Rights Reserved. Printed by permission of the artist.

erasure, and at the same time undercuts any viable discursive or social position that Cameron, its subject, might occupy. The non-locatable aspect of his body-identity-image is verbalized in the final poignant command: "You don't belong here"(31).[20]

Though Cameron's images are as mediated, constructed, and codified as the medical photographs, they offer a glimpse of social stigma from a subjective and spatial—that is, an *embodied*—point of view. They permit the representation of a particular, specifically located subjectivity. The medical gaze creates the illusion of anonymous bodies, suspended in time and placed outside of any habitable social world, and thus disallows the very possibility of subjectivity. Cameron's work challenges this desubjectification and pathologization, not by promoting naïvely celebratory images in an attempt to make stigma vanish; but rather, by restaging and re-presenting the ambivalence experienced by a person trapped, not in a wrong body, but in the wrong cultural context.

Recent work by photographer Del LaGrace Volcano [Fig. 43.11] exemplifies a third type of gaze, that of "the sublime."[21] His *Sublime Mutations* is a retrospective collection of images taken over twenty-five years that includes people with nonstandard bodies and atypical expressions of gender. Like Cameron, Volcano controls the gaze by turning the camera around and framing the image (of) himself, thus thwarting spectatorial voyeurism by returning the gaze of the viewer--something the symbolically "blindfolded" subjects of the medical gaze can never do. In *Female Masculinity*, Judith Halberstam writes of photographer Catherine Opie's "insistence that her portraits 'stare back,'" thus creating a "power dynamic between both photographer and model, but also between image and spectator" that "challenges the spectator's own sense of gender congruity, and even self" (35).[22] In these photographs the subject's look is an essential challenge to the viewer's sense of complacency in their own stable subjectivity. This same reversal of the look is evident in Volcano's work. Volcano adopts a series of different guises, which he calls "sublime mutations," all shot against a background of bathroom tiles

Figure 43.11 Del LaGrace Volcano, "Del Boy," 2001. "Gender Optional: Mutating Self Portraits" from *Sublime Mutations*. Printed by permission of the artist.

that evoke the objectifying grid that maps disordered character types in criminological and medical photography. The tiles also suggest that Volcano is photographing himself in the bathroom mirror, a privileged, often private site/sight for "making up" a gendered identity. This activity in the mirror enacts an inside/outside process of transformation that, according to Jay Prosser in *Second Skins*, echoes traditional transsexual "trapped in the wrong body" narratives that turn the "invisible-inside" into the "visible-outside" through radical bodily transformation.[23]

"Daddy Del" [Fig. 43.12] is an image from the "Mutating Self Portraits" series through which Volcano explores time, futurity, physical maturity, and visual imagination. In this image, Volcano goes beyond the notion that a hidden gender identity must be physically liberated.[24] Instead, he "puts on" the age of another, perhaps future self, in order to imagine what he might look like as he grows old.[25] Another

Figure 43.12 Del LaGrace Volcano, "Daddy Del," 2001. "Gender Optional: Mutating Self Portraits" from *Sublime Mutations*. Printed by permission of the artist.

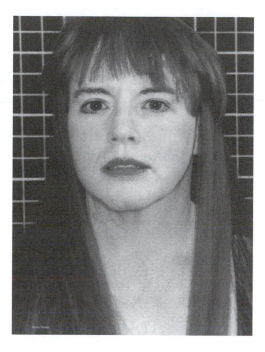

Figure 43.13 Del LaGrace Volcano, "Debra Would," 2001. "Gender Optional: Mutating Self Portraits" from *Sublime Mutations.* Printed by permission of the artist.

portrait, "Debra Would" [Fig. 43.13], offers a powerful counterpoint to "Daddy Del."[26] In this image, whose title puns Volcano's birth-assigned name, "Debra Wood," we see a hypothetical vision of a self who might have been, but never was—a Volcano who never did transition from female to male. This deliberate play with the signifiers of time and aging, the juxtaposition of a (foreclosed) virtual self-image with a probable (future) one, takes Volcano's portraiture out the realm of traditional drag, in which the clothing and gestures of one gender are displayed on the body of the "opposite" sex. Rather than merely camping on gendered signifiers, Volcano engages the elements of time, space, and identity-as-process to show, with sublime effect, that sex and gender are much like aging and other embodied processes. His layering of gender identity, body, and life-trajectory (present/past/future) though highly stylized, artistically fashioned, and *fictional*, are in many ways more *truthful* images of identity and embodiment than can be captured by the supposed objectivity of medical photography.

In a final image by Volcano, "Andro Del," [Fig. 43.14] we see a figure that is perhaps inhuman, super-human, or post-human, a figure characterized by a whiteness that appears both hyper-racialized yet somehow attempts to point beyond race.[27] This image of transgender whiteness is inherently ambivalent, defying any definitive reading in terms of gender or race. As a picture of androgyny, screened on a non-biological, zinc-like surface, it conjures up notions of a "world without gender."[28] In a public talk at the Trans-Art symposium in San Francisco, Judith Halberstam commented that: "this is a very interesting shot for the way it is able to wash gender out. It would be quite difficult to pin some sort of gender identity upon this figure, and I think that has something to do with the blurring of whiteness with androgyny. Here (Del) is making his own whiteness very clearly a platform for building androgyny upon." Halberstam then compared this to an image by Robert Mapplethorpe of one of his Black models, to argue that the spectator can see "that same conjuring up of some kind of androgyny, but it's as if Black masculinity cannot be rendered androgynous; the hyperbolic function and representation of Blackness in conjunction with masculinity means that you literally can't wash gender out of the mix on certain bodies."[29] In this case, race, or more precisely, skin tone, works to focus our attention on gendered detail; it has an engendering effect. "Andro Del" ironically represents

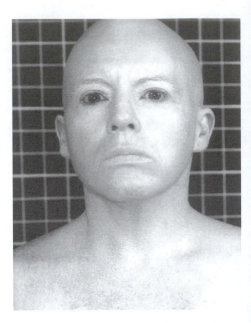

Figure 43.14 Del LaGrace Volcano, "Andro Del," 2001. "Gender Optional: Mutating Self Portraits" from *Sublime Mutations*. Printed by permission of the artist.

(hyper) whiteness as an inhuman trait that erases gender, whereas white skin, within a racist imaginary, typically is the only marker of full humanity. At the same time, dark skin represents less than white status, while also rendering male bodies as hyper-masculine gendered threats to the social order.

While this photograph could appear complicit with the medical gaze that strips familiar human qualities from non-normative bodied people, the viewer is confronted, once again, with a return look that suggests no matter how pernicious, the effect of the medical gaze will not go unchallenged. Asserting authority through visual defiance, Volcano creates a metaphor for the social predicament of people with non-normative bodies by using a combination of disturbing physical attributes with a powerfully wielded return gaze. This is the ultimate "sublime mutation" staring back at a viewer no longer able to hide behind the privilege of their assumed normalcy.

Whereas Cameron's photograph "God's Will" uses the aesthetic strategy of "the beautiful," to make possible the social assimilation of an abjected difference or otherness, Volcano's series, in contrast, offers an encounter with the sublime, which, unlike the beautiful, surpasses bounded meaning and remains resistant to easy interpretation. According to Hebdige:

> …following Burke, a distinction can be made between the sublime and the beautiful. Whereas the form of the beautiful is said to consist in limitation (contemplation of a framed picture, a bounded narrative, etc.), the sublime challenges the act of judgment itself by suggesting the possibility of limitlessness. The sublime mixes pleasure and pain, joy and terror, and confronts us with the threat of the absolute Other—the limitations of our language and our capacity to think and judge, the fact of our own mortality. In Burke's and Kant's category of the sublime, reason is forced to confront its incapacity to deal rationally with the infinite (51). [30]

Deconstructing the medical gaze in this article is important because it unearths hidden ethical considerations in what, on the surface, seems a strictly aesthetic matter. Just as the medical photographs inhibit "a proper regard for the other," the medical model that categorizes atypical embodiment as pathology achieves the same result. I developed my analysis of the images discussed in this article in the broader context of ethnographic research on the regulation of transsexuality through public health policies and discourses. Through this research I became a participant-observer in a paradigm shift from a model of medical pathology to a "trans-health" model of care that parallels the shift from the "medical gaze" to "sublime mutations " that I have outlined above. In what follows, I will focus on one particular aspect of this paradigm shift to demonstrate how the sublime plays out in the context of health care.[31]

Healthcare Paradigm Shift

Pathology Model	Trans-health Model
Normative bodies and Genders	Nonstandard Bodies and Genders –
M/F – only two types	Spectrum of body types and genders
Institutional Regulation	Harm Reduction and Advocacy
Gate-keeping (meeting standard criteria)	Informed Consent
Experts and Providers in Control	Peer Expertise and Community Partnering
Pathologization	Self-determination
Gender Identity Disorder	Non-disordered Gender Complexity

During my fieldwork I documented specific barriers to health care in public health contexts that erase the subjectivity and lived experiences of trans people within medical systems structured on exclusionary sex/gender binaries.[32] I also identified a simultaneous effort, most pronounced among lesbian and gay medical care advocates in U.S. urban areas such as San Francisco, New York, Philadelphia, and Boston, to include transsexual and transgender public health issues as part of a progressive political effort to address the "T" in an "LGBT" movement. Instead of finding *only* an erasure of trans presence within medical and public health programs, I also found a simultaneous proliferation of concerns about the inclusion of trans people.

This sense of "proliferation" follows Foucault's argument in the *History of Sexuality*, that discourses can both enforce repressive social controls while also operating at the same time as a "reverse discourse." Foucault claimed that "homosexuality began to speak in its own behalf, to demand that its legitimacy... be acknowledged, often in the same vocabulary, using the same categories by which it was medically disqualified" (101).[33] The same can be said of transsexuality, which emerged in the 1950s as a medical term that served to regulate non-normative gender identities and bodies, but which became, by the 1990s, part of the "umbrella" category "transgender," a term developed to counter the discourse of medical pathologization. The term "transgender" turned up frequently in my research in U.S. public health contexts, and somewhat surprisingly has been institutionalized in medical programs. That resistant discourses like those mobilized by the category "transgender" can be appropriated into medical contexts fits with Foucault's understanding of power as not merely repressive, but also productive—implicated and enmeshed everywhere with bodies, identities and pleasures. These two seemingly contradictory impulses of erasure and proliferation work in concert with one another—the very proliferation of trans-inclusion activities itself becomes a specific barrier to health care, by contributing to genuine confusion and cognitive crisis on the part of well-intentioned service providers. This is because they lack the cultural competency to understand and adequately care for the burgeoning variety of identities and bodies gravitating toward, and generating from, trans-specific health care initiatives.[34]

This state of affairs is reminiscent of Marjorie Garber's concept of a "category crisis" within the binary gender system,[35] yet the crisis provoked by trans inclusion is not limited to the concept of gender itself; it involves as well the destabilizing pressure unruly bodies and genders exert on other recognizable categories and institutional practices. The crisis is precipitated by the ever-expanding range of trans bodies and genders that resist institutional assimilation, coupled with the concomitant ethical demand created by the (quasi)recognition of the term "transgender" within medical institutions. The sheer variety of trans bodies and genders exceeds providers' cognitive capacity to comprehend them. This very excess is the enabling condition of the sublime. To grasp how the provision of adequate health care for trans people requires that service providers risk an encounter with the sublime, it is necessary to shift the focus of analysis from ethical concerns to aesthetic categories.

What I mean by this can be demonstrated concretely by the work of trans-health trainer Samuel Lurie, whose cultural competency trainings are designed to sensitize providers to important issues concerning trans-health access. In his very effective public presentations, Lurie begins with the "Traditional Binary Gender Model," in which we can see foundations of the medical model represented as binaries: male/female bodies, masculine/feminine gender expressions and (hetero)sexual orientation, that are all traditionally *supposed* to flow causally, one to the other, in normative fashion.[36] He then introduces the "Continuum Gender Model" to demonstrate the non-binary range of bodies, genders and sexualities. Finally, he introduces his "Revolutionary Gender Model," which builds on the continuum principle, but adds to it the complexity of interrelationships between different axes of identity.[37] Lurie's graphic representation of large numbers of possible combinations of bodies, gender expressions and sexual orientations borders on the sublime—it confronts us all with a vision of potentially infinite specific possibilities for being human.

When Lurie presented these heuristic models of gender diversity at the *Third Annual Philadelphia Trans-health Conference* [2004], he paused upon introducing the "Revolutionary Gender Model," scanned the crowd, and noted the profound effect it had on the audience by saying, "I see many of your eyes glazing over."[38] I have witnessed the same information-overload when using Lurie's slides in my own workshops. This visceral reaction on the part of the training participants is the same physical and affective response that providers in trans-health contexts experience on a routine basis. Feeling overwhelmed is a sensory dimension of the experience of the sublime—and shutting down is a form of psychical protection against the terror of boundary collapse at the edge of limitlessness. With the ever-increasing proliferation of trans body-types, identities, discourses, communities, and experiential worlds, it is hardly surprising that one very well intentioned doctor I interviewed confessed, "For the most part I am learning a lot and really enjoy this work, but some days I'm like, *please, just for today—enough, okay?*" Her being intellectually overwhelmed by the range and variation of identities and bodies she encountered manifested in that moment as palpable emotional distress.

This incident was not the only time during my ethnographic fieldwork that I encountered the poorly-recognized phenomenon of a conceptual limit to a service-provider's ability to recognize the legibility and meaning of trans identities and bodies. This limit creates an additional barrier to trans care over and above the many material forms of erasure trans people experience within normative social systems as a result of binaristic models of human personhood, and the pernicious institutionalized transphobia of many medical and psychotherapeutic spaces. This limit generates uncertainty and confusion even on the part of sympathetic and well-intentioned providers to the extent that it constitutes the sublime experience of "*reason (being) forced to confront its incapacity to deal rationally with the infinite*." The sublime effect of exceeding the cognitive limit is produced, to a significant degree, by the collapse of the medical gaze's epistemological frame. In that sublime moment of rupture, bodies that literally and metaphorically exceed two-dimensional medical images step into a new social context, and make new ethical claims.

Acknowledging the cognitive-conceptual limit for providers that creates barriers to health care for people with non-normative bodies does not excuse those providers from their ethical responsibility to grapple with their limits. They still need to achieve cultural competency. But trans people, particularly trans-health educators, have a corollary responsibility to witness and respect the provider's encounter with the sublime, so that it may become a transformative experience that results in better health care for all.

In my own trainings, I have introduced Lurie's "Revolutionary Gender Model" with the intent to precipitate a sublime crisis of comprehension, and possibly the experience of terror, among training participants. I use their response to this information as teaching moment, and ask: "Is anyone confused?" Usually, at least one timid hand will go up, and that person will admit to being overwhelmed by the content of the diagram. After that, others will also voice their experience of confusion. Then I say: "Great! It *is* confusing. Confusion is inherent in this process. Your response is exactly what can be expected when beginning to provide trans-specific services." This reassurance usually results in visible relief registered on participants' faces. At this point, my objective is to teach providers how to deal with their confusion, and how to live in the uncomfortable zone of the unknown. To do this, I discuss particular strategies to reduce ambiguity, including how to ask someone about their gender identity or body in ways that do not alienate them. I also use this moment to un-teach something they may have heard before: "Make no assumptions." I tell them this is impossible, because we are always making assumptions to navigate an increasingly complex world. Instead, by pointing out the seeming limitlessness of trans bodies and genders and social worlds, I encourage them to believe *many* things are possible, more than they ever imagined. I challenge them to become intimate with sublimity, instead of trying to eradicate it in the course of performing their work.

As providers rise to this challenge, training environments still require use of conventional pedagogical techniques, including lists and diagrams. As demonstrated by the "Revolutionary Gender Model," such tools can represent the potential combinatorial complexity of gender components. However, to borrow a term from critical theorists Gilles Deleuze and Felix Guattari, all "arborescent" schema that map phenomena into tree-like logical structures, such as the Revolutionary Gender Model, ultimately fail to capture the fact that it is not complexity alone, but rather another form of difference from the expected, that elicits the sublime. When working in training contexts, I often become frustrated when trying to explain why trans identities, bodies, and even use of language consistently fall outside even the complex branching patterns of the Revolutionary Gender Model; it is because transgender phenomena often sprout up seemingly from nowhere, and shoot off into wild and inexplicable directions. This rootless, unpredictable, and circuitous variability is precisely what Deleuze and Guattari call "rhizomatic." The rhizome:

> should not be confused with the lineages of the arborescent type, which are merely localizable linkages between points and positions. Unlike the tree, the rhizome…operates by variation, expansion, conquest, capture, offshoots…[and] is always detachable, connectable, reversible, modifiable…. In contrast to centered (even polycentric) systems with hierarchical modes of communication and pre-established paths, the rhizome is an acentered, nonhierarchical, nonsignifying system without…an organizing memory or central automaton, defined solely by a circulation of states. What is at question in the rhizome is a relation to sexuality…that is totally different from the arborescent relation. [39]

Deleuze and Guattari note that rhizomes encompass "all manner of becomings." Transgender sublimity likewise can be said to encompass all manner of becomings, in the sense that being overwhelmed and even transformed by it does not follow simply from calculating the possible combinations of potential bodies and genders in the world. Instead, it arises from a dimension that evades quantitative operations. A rhizomatic view of gender moves us closer to a more profound understanding of the qualitative aspect of gendered embodiment and subjectivity, and better explains the radically transformative effect an encounter with the transgender sublime can precipitate.

It is my hope that by seizing the moment of sublime recognition of the limitless possible bodies, genders and sexualities in trans worlds, and by confirming the potential terror of being faced with the great unknown, that a more ethical way to relate to trans people can emerge in the training of medical service providers. To deny or to try to eliminate the sublime aspect of trans-health is to miss an opportunity to create strategies that accommodate both the needs of providers and the needs of those accessing care. The paradigm shift from a medical pathology to a trans-health approach provides us with a context for such ethical relationships to emerge.

It may be naïve, or even utopian, to think that a paradigm shift in medical practices can have a profound impact on gendered social relations, or even on relationships between doctors and patients. However, mobilizing the power of "sublime mutations" to alter the field of vision allows us to identify, and enact, corresponding shifts in medical practice. This aesthetic and ethical practice demands that a proper regard for others sometimes means meeting an/other on its own terms, even if those terms are sublimely disorienting at first glance.

NOTES

I am indebted to Susan Stryker for incisively guiding this essay through various stages of embodiment. I also want to thank David Valentine for his unfailing intellectual and moral support. Heather Love and the GASWorks group at the University of Pennsylvania provided helpful feedback on an earlier draft. Research for this essay was supported by a fellowship from the Sexuality Research Fellowship Program of the Social Science Research Council with funding from the Ford Foundation.

Every reasonable attempt was made to secure permission for all photographs reproduced in this article; any errors or omissions will be corrected in subsequent editions of this volume upon written notification to the publisher.

1. *The Lancet,* 22 January 1859, vol. 1, p. 89, quoted by John Tagg in 'Power and Photography' in *Screen Education*, no. 36, 1980 (41).
2. William Mitchell, *Reconfigured Eye: Visual Truth in the Post-Photographic Era*, Cambridge: MIT Press, 1992 (28). In *Reconfigured Eye* Mitchell discusses how we have learned to accept photosensitive emulsion-on-paper as having an unmediated, direct, relationship to the referent, and how this convention is challenged by digital imagery. While much of the book focuses on technical aspects of image-making, his critique of visual and epistemological "truth-making practices" is relevant to the underlying impulse of my article: demystifying the scientific objectivity-effect of the medical gaze in representations of non-normative bodies.
3. Raymond Williams, *Keywords*, London: Fontana, 1973 (28).
4. From L.R. Broster et al., eds., *The Adrenal Cortex and Intersexuality*. Chapman and Hall, 1938. Reprinted in *Stolen Glances: Lesbians Take Photographs*. Tessa Boffin and Jean Fraser, eds., London: Pandora Press, 1991 (16).
5. From Rhoda K. Unger, *Female and Male: Psychological Perspectives*, New York: Harper and Row, 1979 (121). Originally from J. Money and A. Ehrhardt, *Man and Women, Boy and Girl*, Baltimore: Johns Hopkins Press, 1972. (Copyright 1972 by the Johns Hopkins Press.)
6. The ethics and aesthetics of body-style have been commented on by other theorists. See, for example, Marcia Ian, who suggests in "How Do You Wear Your Body: Bodybuilding and the Sublimity of Drag," (*Negotiating Lesbian and Gay Subjects*, eds. Monica Dorenkamp and Richard Henke, New York and London: Routledge, 1995) that the body itself is drag, a fact starkly demonstrated through the physical excess of bodybuilding which results in "the tightest fitting bodysuit imaginable, a suit made of veins and translucent skin that looks like the inside worn on the outside" (83). Ian links bodybuilding and the sublime, saying: "[b]odybuilding is about the body's self-loathing, its horror at its own repulsive beauty, and is therefore sublime" (72). Ian locates this notion of the sublime in the body or in ones' relationship to their body, whereas in the analysis I develop later in this argument, it is the *situation* of trans people inside/outside healthcare settings that creates the sublime.
7. Griselda Pollock, *Vision and Difference: Femininity, Feminism and Histories of Art*, London and New York: Routledge, 1998. In *Vision and Difference*, Pollack discusses "the conventions of geometric perspective which had normally governed the representation of space in European painting since the fifteenth century," saying "...this mathematically calculated system of projection had aided painters in the representation of a three-dimensional world on a two-dimensional surface by organizing objects in relation to each other to produce a notional and singular position from which the scene is intelligible. It establishes the viewer as both absent from and indeed independent of the scene while being its mastering eye/I" (64). In a similar sense, medical photographs, relying on the three-dimensional "reality" of the referent, represent depicted bodies on a two-dimensional grid and at the same time "establish the viewer as both absent from and indeed independent of the scene" while "being its mastering eye/I."

8. From Unger, *Female and Male*, 137. The history of the medicalization of transsexuality supports this observation. See, for example, Joanne Meyerowitz, *How Sex Changed: History of Transsexuality in the United States*, Cambridge and London: Harvard UP, 2002. Meyerowitz documents that nineteenth- and early twentieth-century European doctors proposed a theory of "bisexuality" to explain transsexuality. This theory was not about sexual orientation, as being attracted to two different sexes, rather, it was a notion that transsexual people had a mixture of male and female physical characteristics. By contrast, American doctors favored the concept of a psychological disorder to explain the etiology of what was considered primarily a mental disease. If not about the body, then, representing transsexuals with clothing on in an American medical text is consistent with this history.

9. Image from Leslie Feinberg, *Transgender Warriors: Making History from Joan of Arc to RuPaul*, Boston: Beacon Press, 1996. According to Feinberg, "Marsha was found floating in the Hudson River near the piers in New York City shortly after 1992 Pride March. The police 'investigation' reportedly consisted of two phone calls, and they ruled her death a suicide. A people's postering campaign dug up reports that Marsha had been harassed near the piers earlier that evening" (image 130, 131).

10. Tessa Boffin and Jean Fraser, eds., *Stolen Glances: Lesbians Take Photographs*, London: Pandora Press, 1991 (17).

11. Loren Cameron, *Body Alchemy: Transsexual Portraits*, San Francisco: Cleis Press, 1996. Image from "God's Will" series, 1995 (27).

12. It is interesting to note that film *noir* uses similar lighting techniques commonly regarded by film theorists to represent both beauty and danger.

13. Dick Hebdige, "The Impossible Object: Towards a Sociology of the Sublime," in *New Formations*, 47–48.

14. "Completely Unperfect" in *Mainstream: Magazine of the Able-Disabled*, San Diego: Exploding Myths, Inc., February 1997 (23).

15. Mitchell, *Reconfigured Eye*, 43.

16. *Mainstream*, 21.

17. The techniques of direct address and captioned voice are commonly used when photographs of transsexual people are shown. See, for example, "How Shall I Address You? Pronouns, Pussies and Pricks—Talking to Female-to-Male Transsexuals," in the lesbian sex magazine *On Our Backs*, San Francisco: Blush, Jan/Feb. 1995 (18–23). Included in this feature article are several images of unclothed transsexual men and women. Next to each photo is a captioned quote by the person pictured. A sidebar image of Susan Stryker, looking directly at the camera, hand on hip, is titled: "Looking at You, Looking at Me." In her accompanying narrative Stryker confrontationally addresses viewers, saying: "Ask yourself—why do you look when we transsexuals make spectacles of ourselves? Is it the curiosity of the freak show, the same voyeuristic desire mixed with dread and titillation that makes you scan the asphalt for gobs of red as you drive slowly past the accident scene?" (21). This mix of horror, fascination and even titillation strongly suggests an element of sublime in the exchange set up by this combination of image and text.

18. "Carney" from self-portrait series in Cameron, *Body Alchemy* (image 14, 15).

19. Pollock, *Vision*, 66.

20. "Distortions" from triptych in Cameron, *Body Alchemy* (31).

21. "Gender Optional: Mutating Self Portraits, London 2000," in Del LaGrace Volcano, *Sublime Mutations*, Konkursbuch 2000 (173).

22. Judith Halberstam, *Female Masculinity*, Durham and London: Duke UP, 1998 (35).

23. Jay Prosser, *Second Skins: The Body Narratives of Transsexuality*, New York: Columbia UP, 1998.

24. Volcano, *Sublime*, 174.

25. Author's interview with Volcano, San Francisco, May 2001.

26. Volcano, *Sublime*, 178.

27. Volcano, *Sublime*, 176

28. A "world without gender" was a popular activist slogan of the Transgender Movement in the 1990s.

29. "Complications," Panel Discussion, Trans-Art, GLBT Historical Society, San Francisco May 20th, 2001.

30. Hebdige, "Impossible," p. 51.

31. Research funded by the Social Science Research Council's Sexuality Research Fellowship Program, 2002–2003. The trans-health model is drawn from ethnographic research data. While represented as schematically divided chart, this diagram serves a heuristic function only. The social situation is more complex and in some contexts elements found on one side can be listed on the other.

32. For an influential book that analyzes the phenomenon of erasure see: Viviane Namaste, *Invisible Lives: The Erasure of Transsexual and Transgendered People*, Chicago/London: U. of Chicago Press, 2000. Namaste examines Canadian healthcare practices and asserts that "…(trans) individuals are excluded from the institutional world through specific administrative policies, procedures and practices. Demonstrating the thesis of this book that transsexuals are *erased in the everyday social world*, the concept of erasure here designates the exclusion of TS/TG people from the institutional site of health care" (159, emphasis added). Her argument about a comprehensive erasure is compelling, especially considering the operation of social spaces wherein binary gender practices dominate like healthcare and prison systems. However, here and in other unpublished work ("The Trans Sublime in Public Health"), I critique Namaste's research as being historically specific to a time when trans-health was in its controversial infancy. Her thesis has limited explanatory value regarding healthcare systems wherein *inclusion* is increasingly promoted by use of the category "transgender." "Transgender" facilitates access for people who do not fit standard gender categories, and, paradoxically, creates a newly stable category of personhood that impedes access for anyone not fitting its expanded gender parameters.

33.   Michel Foucault, *History of Sexuality Volume 1: An Introduction*, New York: Vintage Books, 1980.
34.   "Cultural competency" emerged in my ethnographic research as a common buzzword among social service and medical care networks. This term corresponds to a belief that cultural differences impede access to services, and that understanding these differences make providers more sensitive, thus leading to "lowering the threshold" of systemic barriers to care. In these settings, while "culture" often pertains to categories of "race and ethnicity," it is also sometimes applied to categories of difference such as "gender, class and sexual orientation."
35.   Marjorie Garber, *Vested Interests: Cross-Dressing and Cultural Anxiety* (New York: Routledge, 1992) p. 16.
36.   Samuel Lurie, "Four Steps to Providing Health Care for Transgender People" (self-published training handout, 2004). Inclusion of these slides is not intended to call into question Lurie's considerable training expertise. A distinction should be made between the use of these models in training contexts where certain pedagogical techniques are conventional, and my analysis of these slides to explain the "transgender sublime." My use of these models is to demonstrate the *effect* they have on training participants; their heuristic truth-value is not germane to this discussion.
37.   Lurie, "Four Steps."
38.   *Third Annual Philadelphia Trans-health Conference*, Philadelphia, PA (March 2004).
39.   Gilles Deleuze and Felix Guattari, *A Thousand Plateaus: Capitalism and Schizophrenia* (Minneapolis: University of Minnesota Press, 1987; trans. Brian Massumi), pp 7–21.

44

From Functionality to Aesthetics
The Architecture of Transgender Jurisprudence

Andrew Sharpe

ANDREW SHARPE HIGHLIGHTS ONE OF THE MAJOR THEORETICAL PROBLEMS in transgender and transsexual legal reform—determining the moment at which legal recognition, and legal rights, will be afforded to a transgender person who has adopted a new gender role.

In almost all jurisdictions, Sharpe points out, both statute and case law determine the only possible point of change to be genital surgery (which is far more of a defining moment for male-to-female transsexuals than for female-to-male transsexuals, who typically either have several genital surgeries, or none). What has changed over time, however, are the criteria that determine whether the genital transformation successfully accomplishes a "change of sex." Previously, the criterion had been "functionality," that is, whether the surgical result allowed the person operated upon to assume a heterosexual role in the act of intercourse. Increasingly, the criterion has been an aesthetic one: what cultural norm (man or woman) does the person look like?

Sharpe argues that legal definitions of gender, and the rationale for determining legally when gender changes, are closely tied to homophobia and the fear of gay marriage. This anxiety is discernible in the judicial enquiry into, and assessment of, the sexual practices of pre-operative transsexual people, the classification of their desire, their gender performance, their capacity to participate in heterosexual intercourse, and the aesthetics of the post-operative body. As a result, the law continues to determine the primarily psychological and subjective matter of gender identity by requiring the physical body to submit to visual and behavioral scrutiny.

INTRODUCTION

1. This article will consider the significance of the New Zealand decision of *Attorney-General v. Otahuhu Family Court* [1] in the context of a developing transgender jurisprudence. It will highlight how, in one respect, this case represents a significant departure from prior, law reform oriented, decisions. That is to say, and for the purposes of determining the sex claims of transgender persons, the case deemphasises a concern over the sexual functioning of the body. While this is to be welcomed it also serves to foreground the bodily aesthetics of law that prior transgender jurisprudence has partially masked through a preoccupation with (hetero) sexual capacity. In other words, the decision highlights how transgender jurisprudence is underscored by a concern with the 'monstrosity' of bodies as much as, and perhaps more than, law's phallocentric imperative. Moreover, it is important not to overstate the departure that *Attorney-General v Otahuhu Family Court* represents. On the contrary it will become clear that a focus on a shift from functionality to aesthetics, from substance to form, belies an important commonality, other than a continued requirement for surgical intervention, that

621

links the New Zealand decision to prior transgender jurisprudence oriented toward reform. This link is, as we shall see, to be found in judicial anxiety over proximity to the homosexual body. Before considering the shift from functionality to aesthetics within transgender jurisprudence it is first necessary to refer to the landmark English decision of *Corbett v Corbett* [2] which provides a context to situate transgender law reform.

THE BIRTH OF A JURISPRUDENCE

2. The English decision of *Corbett v Corbett,* more than any other, inaugurated transgender jurisprudence in the common law world. In this case the petitioner, Mr Arthur Corbett, sought to have his marriage to April Ashley, a male to female transgender person who had undergone sex reassignment procedures, declared a nullity. While the practical effect of such a finding related to questions of maintenance the key legal question required a determination as to the sex of April Ashley for marriage purposes. In answering this question Ormrod J held that "sex is determined at birth" and by a congruence of chromosomal, gonadal and genital factors.[3] According to this (bio) logic April Ashley was determined to be a male person. The decision has been subject to sustained and almost universal criticism within academic and law reform circles.[4] Despite this the Corbett decision has been followed consistently by the English courts[5] and has been influential throughout the common law world. Judicial thinking in relation to transgender persons it would seem always commences with Corbett. That is to say, the development of transgender jurisprudence is to be understood through its relation with Corbett. Thus for the body of reform oriented transgender jurisprudence, traceable most notably to the New Jersey decision of *MT v JT,*[6] a point of unity has been to think beyond this English decision. However, we shall see that a further unifying theme of law reform jurisprudence, culminating in *Attorney-General v Otahuhu Family Court,* is to be found in judicial anxiety over proximity to the homosexual body. Interestingly, this commonality links not only law reform judgments, but transgender jurisprudence more generally given that Corbett itself is riddled with homophobic anxiety.[7]

FROM (BIO) LOGIC TO FUNCTIONALITY

3. The first superior court decision to depart from the (bio) logic that is given expression in Corbett was the New York case of Re Anonymous.[8] In this case, which involved an application by a male to female transgender person to have her birth certificate changed to reflect surgical intervention, Pecora J held the applicant to be female because her anatomy had been brought into conformity with her psychological sex. Unlike the Corbett analysis the decision created a legal space for the post-operative transgender body while it simultaneously drew a clear distinction between that body and pre or non-surgical transgender bodies. Moreover, and importantly in the present context, the judgment appears to understand 'harmony' as dependent on post-operative vaginal capacity for (hetero) sexual intercourse. It is especially difficult to account for this requirement in a case concerning an application to change a birth certificate. In this context, a legal concern over the adequacy of the vagina would seem to be explicable only in terms of phallocentric and performativist assumptions about the female body.

4. The 'psychological and anatomical harmony' test formulated by Pecora J. in Re Anonymous was consolidated in *MT v JT.*[9] In this case the New Jersey Supreme Court considered valid a two year marriage between a biological man and a post-operative male to female transgender person. Handler J. distinguished the earlier New York decisions of *Anonymous v Anonymous* and *B v B,*[10] where the court had denied transgender sex claims for marriage purposes, on the basis that the transgender persons in those cases were pre-operative and were therefore incapable of (hetero) sexual intercourse.

While reference was made to the fact that MT could no longer "function as a male sexually either for purposes of recreation or procreation", [11] the court placed particular emphasis on her post-operative sexual capacity and desire:

> Implicit in the reasoning underpinning our determination is the tacit but valid assumption of the lower court and the experts upon whom reliance was placed that for purposes of marriage under the circumstances of this case, it is the sexual capacity of the individual which must be scrutinized. Sexual capacity or sexuality in this frame of reference requires the coalescence of both the physical ability and the psychological and emotional orientation to engage in sexual intercourse as either male or female.[12]

The reference to the "psychological and emotional orientation to engage in sexual intercourse" is significant. It suggests that the creation of a 'functional' vagina, while essential, is, in and of itself, insufficient for the purposes of legal recognition of male to female transgender sex claims. Rather, recognition for the purposes of marriage proves to be dependent on the additional requirement of heterosexual desire. In this regard, the legal regulation of MT's body is concerned with more than her submission to genital reconstruction. Law desires to know her desire, to know that it is heterosexual, and to be assured through that knowledge as to the 'authenticity' of MT's transsexuality.

5. In relation to MT's sexual functioning the court explored in some detail her genital topography. Drawing on the evidence of Dr. Ihlenfeld, MT's medical doctor, Handler J. noted that MT had "a vagina and labia which were adequate for sexual intercourse and could function as any female vagina, that is, for traditional penile/vaginal intercourse".[13] There is no reference in the judgment or the medical evidence as to any sexual pleasure that MT might derive from her vagina.[14] Rather, law seeks reassurance that MT's vagina can function as a site of heterosexual male pleasure. The functionality of MT's vagina in this regard finds further expression in the evidence of Dr. Ihlenfeld, who pointed out that MT's vagina had been "lined initially by the skin of [her] penis", that it would, in all likelihood, later take on "the characteristics of normal vaginal mucosa", and that though at "a somewhat different angle, was not really different from a natural vagina in size, capacity and the feeling of the walls around it".[15]

6. This judicial emphasis on (hetero) sexual capacity is again apparent in the US case of *Richards v United States Tennis Association*.[16] Here the Supreme Court of New York held Renee Richards, a male to female transgender person, to be female for the purposes of competing in the US Tennis Open because of "overwhelming medical evidence" that she was female.[17] The concern with functionality is evident in Ascione J's assertion that transsexuals "desire the removal of...[their genital] apparatus and further surgical assistance in order that they may enter into normal heterosexual relationships".[18] Here not only is heterosexual functioning scripted as a prerequisite to legal recognition. Rather, sexual function is understood as the end to be realised through the means of sex reassignment surgery. Here the value and meaning of surgery lies in the male to female body's capacity to be sexually penetrated. Moreover, Ascione's anxiety over this matter is assuaged by medical testimony that "[f]or all intents and purposes, Dr. Richards functions as a woman".[19]

7. More recently, the test of 'psychological and anatomical harmony' has found favour in the Australian context. In *R v Harris and McGuiness*[20] the New South Wales Court of Criminal Appeal held Lee Harris, a post-operative male to female transgender person convicted of procuring 'another' male person to commit an act of indecency, to be female for the purposes of criminal law.[21] However, legal recognition proved dependent on what Mathews J described as 'full' sex reassignment surgery as distinct from the mere fact of surgical intervention.[22] While Mathews J. pointed out that surgery had deprived Lee Harris of "the capacity to procreate or to have normal heterosexual intercourse in her original sex",[23] and while the prospect of having a sexually/procreatively functional male classified

as female concerned the court, these forms of irrevocable loss do not ground the decision. Rather, it is the capacity for (hetero) sexual intercourse which 'full' sex reassignment provides that proves crucial. In this regard the reasoning of Handler J. in *MT v JT* is replicated.

8. The requirement of functionality becomes particularly clear in the context of the judicial reasoning adopted toward the fact that Lee Harris was unable to have sexual intercourse as a female due to the closing-up of her vagina post-surgically. In refusing to treat as significant this inability Mathews J placed emphasis on its 'temporary' nature. That is to say, it is assumed that this inability will be surgically corrected. It would seem that a permanent inability to engage in (hetero) sexual intercourse would fall short of 'full' sex reassignment. It is, perhaps, curious that capacity for (hetero) sexual intercourse should have any bearing upon determining sex for the purposes of the criminal law. This is especially so given the facts of, and the charges brought in, Harris and McGuiness. That is to say, it is difficult to see the relevance of vaginal capacity in relation to the practice of fellatio.[24]

9. The legal analysis in Harris and McGuiness received further judicial endorsement in Australia in *Secretary, Department of Social Security v HH*.[25] In this case the Administrative Appeals Tribunal upheld a decision of the Social Security Appeals Tribunal that a male-to-female post-operative transgender person was a woman for the purposes of section 25 (1) of the Social Security Act 1947 (Cth) and was therefore entitled to an age pension at sixty, rather than sixty-five. While unanimous that the sex of HH was female for the purposes of section 25 (1) the panel of three (O'Connor J., Muller and Brennan) produced two distinct judgments. However, for present purposes it is sufficient to point out that the primary judgment (O'Connor J. and Muller) endorsed the story of 'psychological and anatomical harmony'.

10. As in Harris and McGuiness the decision in HH is significant for the way in which it foregrounds heterosexual capacity as a condition of legal recognition. Thus O'Connor J and Muller insist that anatomy must be the overriding factor in sex determination if "overwhelmingly contrary to the assumed sex role".[26] This contention that the female sex role can only be properly fulfilled with the 'right' anatomical parts, specifically a vagina, assumes that the role requires penetrative sex. This phallocentric view of the female sex role finds further expression in the assertion that after reassignment surgery the male-to-female transsexual is "functionally"[27] a member of her 'new' sex. As in Re *Anonymous and R v Harris and McGuiness*, it is far from clear that vaginal capacity has any relevance to the subject matter of the litigation, namely, an age pension. Indeed, it is the complete lack of relevance in relation to the case facts which serves to emphasise the centrality of heterosexual capacity within transgender jurisprudence.

11. This view finds further support from O'Connor J and Muller in what appears to be a direct quotation from *Richards v United States Tennis Association*:

> Transsexuals are not homosexual. They consider themselves to be members of the opposite sex burdened with the wrong sexual apparatus. They desire the removal of this apparatus and further surgical assistance in order that they may enter into heterosexual relationships.[28]

As in the previous cases cited heterosexual capacity proves to be more than an essential precondition of legal recognition. It is through an analysis around functionality that law comprehends and makes sense of the desire for and the fact of sex reassignment surgery. In this regard law conflates gender identity and sexual desire in thinking about transgender persons. Further, the analysis adopted in HH reproduces a view of heterosexual relations as realisable only through penetrative sex. Moreover, the statements that "transsexuals are not homosexual" and that they desire "surgical assistance in order that they may enter into heterosexual relationships", apart from and through erasing gay, lesbian and other non-heterosexual transgender subjectivities, serve once again to bring to the surface judicial anxiety over proximity to the homosexual body when dealing with transgender sex claims. The view that the production of heterosexual capacity is central to this line of reform oriented jurisprudence finds further expression by the Federal Court of Australia in *Secretary, Department of Social Security v SRA*.[29] This case concerned a pre-operative male to female transgender person who had been recognised as female by the Administrative Appeals Tribunal for the purposes of a Wife's Pension. The tribunal departed from the test of 'psychological and anatomical harmony' relied on in prior reform oriented jurisprudence preferring instead a test of 'psychological, social and cultural harmony' thereby dispensing with anatomical considerations.[30] On appeal the Federal Court rejected this approach emphatically rearticulating the 'psychological and anatomical harmony' line. In the process the court stressed that SRA, unlike a male to female post-operative transgender person, was not "[f]unctionally...a member of her new sex and capable of sexual intercourse".[31]

12. The test of 'psychological and anatomical harmony' has also been adopted in New Zealand in the case of *M v M*.[32] More pertinently, this decision represents the first in Australasia to extend the analysis to marriage. In *M v M* Aubin J. upheld the validity of a 12 and a half year marriage between a post-operative male to female transgender person and a biological male. In considering M to be female for marriage purposes Aubin J. declined to follow Corbett. In rejecting biological factors as determinative of the issue, and in allusions to the judgments of Ormrod J. in Corbett and Nedstadt J. in the South African case of *W v W*,[33] Aubin refused to view M as a "pseudo-woman", [34] as a "pastiche"[35] or as an "imitation".[36] Rather, and in purporting to follow the Australian criminal law decision of *R v Harris and McGuiness*,[37] Aubin took the view that, although the question of sex cannot be decided "merely upon sympathetic or compassionate grounds",[38] a change of sex, "in a real sense"[39] had occurred in the case of M.

13. The reference to change "in a real sense" maps Mathews J's insistence in Harris and McGuiness on the need for 'full' sex reassignment surgery. Thus Aubin J states that "the proper inference to be drawn from the evidence available to me is that the applicant undertook all medical procedures that it was possible for her to take to change her sexuality from that of a man to that of a woman"[40] and that "as a result sexual intercourse is possible and [the applicant] states that she actually achieves a sexual orgasm on occasion".[41] Moreover, while the medical report on which he relied was five years old Aubin J found that there was "nothing in the evidence to suggest that there was any change"[42] and concluded that "sexual intercourse was possible throughout this marriage".[43] Further, while the marriage ultimately failed, hence the proceedings, Aubin noted that "Mr M [the respondent] did not attribute its failure...to sexual difficulties within the marriage" and that had that been the case "it seems very improbable that the marriage would have lasted as long as it did".[44] In view of the fact that "[a] valid marriage in New Zealand law does not require that sexual intercourse takes place"[45] and that "[t]here is now no legal means of ending a marriage merely for non-consummation"[46] the significance of Aubin's multiple references to heterosexual capacity cannot be accounted for by their legal relevance. Rather, they point to the centrality of function in judicial attempts to comprehend the resexing of the body. In *M v M*, as in the earlier cases considered, knowledge of heterosexual capacity and practice of the transgender body serves to reduce judicial anxiety over proximity to homosexuality.

14. This anxiety over homosexuality is evident in Aubin's judgment in another respect. Thus, Aubin J. asks rhetorically whether the surgery undertaken by M amounted to "no more than some ultimately futile attempt to change her from an anguished Mr Hyde into a well-adjusted Mrs Jekyll, producing a kind of hermaphroditic mutant unable to enter into a valid marriage with a man, or indeed with a woman".[47] This passage is revealing irrespective of, and perhaps despite, the fact that Aubin J. did not view M's sex reassignment surgery as futile. The literary reference to Jekyll and Hyde invokes the

notion of the monstrous body. Moreover, it is clear from the reference to "an anguished Mr Hyde" that it is the pre-operative body that Aubin views as monstrous. This invocation of the figure of the monster is interesting, and perhaps revealing, given the etymology of the term 'monster'. While there is some debate about the term it would appear to come from monere, to warn, or monstrare, to show forth or demonstrate.[48] Both these words, then, and importantly, refer to signs as well as defective births or malformations. It is contended that one sign that the pre-operative body emits before the legal gaze is the sign of homosexuality. In particular, the male to female pre-operative body is imagined as the locus of sodomy. Thus it is not merely that the coupling of the words "hermaphrodite" and "mutant" represent a heightened moment of insensitivity toward transgender and intersexual persons or that Aubin J.'s resort to the "hermaphroditic mutant" serves to remind us that law cannot, and will not, think sex in any other than binary, oppositional and genitocentric terms that calls for attention. Rather, the invocation of the monstrous serves to issue forth the spectre of homosexuality. This negation of the sex claims, and the homosexualisation, of the pre-operative body serve as prelude to the moment of departure from Corbett. That is to say, the depiction of the pre-operative body as monstrous serves to reduce anxiety with regard to the (re) sexing of M's body which the court subsequently sanctions.

FROM FUNCTIONALITY TO AESTHETICS

15. Before turning to the decision of *Attorney-General v Otahuhu Family Court*[49] it is first necessary to return to the judgment of the Federal Court of Australia in *Secretary, Department of Social Security v SRA*.[50] For it is here that the shift from function to aesthetics within transgender jurisprudence is first evident. After expressing satisfaction with regard to post-operative male to female heterosexual capacity, Lockhart J. contended that:

> The female-to-male transsexual is probably in a rather different situation because even successful surgery cannot cause him to be a fully functional male, although he can be given the appearance of male genitals.[51]

This view is both curious and problematic. In the first place, judicial comparison of female to male and male to female transgender bodies serves to highlight law's reproduction of the active/passive sexual dichotomy. The 'inadequacy' of the female to male transgender body is inextricably tied to a legal assumption about the (hetero) sexual practices it is to perform. Further, because law reads the vagina as absence or lack it is easier for the judiciary to be satisfied as to the post-surgical sexual functioning of the male to female transgender body.[52] The penis is clearly viewed as a more complex organ, one considerably more difficult to replicate.

16. However, in the present context the significance of Lockhart J's statement that "successful surgery cannot cause [a female to male transgender person] to be a fully functional male" lies in the fact that this in no way precludes legal recognition for the purposes of social security provisions. That is to say, Lockhart J. makes it quite clear that the post-surgical female to male transgender body is to be regarded as male irrespective of a capacity for heterosexual intercourse.[53] It is less clear whether the same view is taken with regard to the male to female transgender body as Lockhart J. places emphasis here on post-surgical vaginal capacity for heterosexual intercourse. Thus, at least, in relation to the female to male transgender body the decision in SRA differs from *MT v JT* and Harris and McGuiness, where legal recognition and heterosexual capacity were viewed as inextricably connected. To the extent that these obiter statements in SRA depart from these decisions, that departure might be explicable in terms of a view of social security legislation as being beneficial in character.

17. In *Attorney-General v Otahuhu Family Court* this analysis is applied to the case facts. This is perhaps especially significant in that the case is concerned with marriage, an area of law traditionally

most resistant to transgender sex claims. Moreover, it is clear that the decision applies to both male to female and female to male transgender persons. Prompted by the case of *M v M* the Attorney-General made an application on behalf of the Registrar of Marriages for "a declaration as to whether two persons of the same genetic sex may by the law of New Zealand enter into a valid marriage where one of the parties to the proposed marriage has adopted the sex opposite to that of the proposed marriage partner through sexual reassignment by means of surgery or hormone administration or both or by any other medical means".[54]

18. In deciding the case the New Zealand High Court purported to follow the legal analyses in *MT v JT, Harris and McGuiness* and *M v M* insisting that legal recognition of sex claims for marriage purposes was dependent on sex reassignment surgery. The court made it clear that bodily change brought about through hormone administration or other medical means was insufficient in this regard:

> There is clearly a continuum which begins with the person who suffers from gender dysphoria (a state of mental unease or discomfort) but who has not chosen to cross-dress on a regular basis and has embarked on no programme of hormonal modification or surgery, through to the person who has embarked on hormone therapy and perhaps had some minor surgical intervention such as removal of gonads, through to the person who undergoes complete reconstructive surgery…in order for a transsexual to be eligible to marry in the sex of assignment, the end of the continuum must have been reached and reconstructive surgery done.[55]

Thus, like other common law decisions, the pre or non-surgical transgender body is constructed as necessary 'outside' to a resexed transgender body that is given a presence within law. However, it would be misleading to suggest that the decision in Otahuhu followed, in any simple way, previous decisions articulating the test of 'psychological and anatomical harmony'. While Otahuhu shares much with prior transgender jurisprudence recognising sex claims there is a striking difference. In *MT v JT, Harris and McGuiness* and *M v M* the judiciary had insisted that legal recognition was dependent on, not merely sex reassignment surgery, but also, post-operative capacity for heterosexual intercourse. In Otahuhu however, while Ellis J. stated "that in order to be capable of marriage two persons must present themselves as having what appear to be the genitals of a man and a woman"[56] he insisted that they did not "have to prove that each can function sexually"[57] for "there are many forms of sexual expression possible without penetrative sexual intercourse".[58]

19. The uncoupling of sex reassignment surgery from the capacity for heterosexual intercourse is significant as it serves to highlight law's concern over bodily aesthetics. While an aesthetic concern over bodies is a consistent theme of transgender jurisprudence it is usually masked, at least partially, by a preoccupation with heterosexual capacity. In the judgment of Ellis however, law's anxiety over bodily aesthetics is foregrounded. Irrespective of sexual functioning, and guided by an obvious genitocentrism, Ellis J. seeks, and finds, reassurance in the fact that the male to female post-operative body "can never appear unclothed as a male"[59] and that the female to male post-operative body "can no longer appear unclothed as a woman".[60] Absent a concern over sexual functioning law's view of phallic female, and vaginaed male, bodies as monstrous becomes all the more evident as does the homosexual sign they emit in the legal imaginary. These monstrous bodies are required to undergo "a risky surgical procedure"[61] if they are to accord with law's aesthetic sensibility and to reduce homophobic anxiety.

20. The decision in Otahuhu is significant in another crucial respect. While Ellis J. emphasised that "the declaration sought is to resolve the capacity to marry and is not intended to resolve questions that arise in other branches of the law such as criminal law, and the law of succession"[62] he departed from previous transgender jurisprudence expressing the opinion that:

> It may be that for other legal purposes, a transsexual who has not had reconstructive surgery or only minimal surgical intervention (such as removal of the testes) could be classified in his or chosen sex for certain purposes such as the employment law, criminal law and the law of inheritance.[63]

In other words, Ellis J., at the very least, held out the possibility that a superior court might dispense with the requirement of anatomical change. However, while this aspect of the judgment is, perhaps, to be welcomed the potential for differential treatment of transgender bodies across legal subject matters serves to redraw attention to the bodily aesthetics of law. That is to say, why is it that law can entertain the possibility of creating a legal space in the areas of employment, crime and inheritance for the monstrous body of marriage law? or to put it another way, why is it that law's aesthetic sensibility cannot be compromised in the marriage context? Such questions might be responded to in a number of ways. One possible explanation might invoke a visibility/invisibility distinction. That is to say, the genital region of the body, which law seeks to police, while visible to parties to a marriage, is not visible in the other contexts referred to by Ellis J. While such an argument may have some explanatory power it appears dubious in the criminal law context where a number of sexual offences would locate the genitalia of non or pre-surgical transgender bodies on the visibility side of the distinction.

21. It is my contention that a more convincing explanation for differential treatment of transgender bodies in the marriage context lies in the sexual significance genitals have in/for law. In other words, and as we have already seen, legal anxiety over homosexuality surfaces whenever parties whose genitals are not dissimilar, and therefore not 'complementary', assert heterosexual identity and desire. In sex reassignment surgery law finds, at least some, assurance that marriage, the institution of heterosexuality, will be insulated from the spectre of the homosexual body. In this sense law produces heterosexuality not only as identity or sexual practice, but as an effect of the present, and of course 'oppositional', anatomical form of the parties to desire.

22. The concern over proximity of the homosexual body to marriage finds expression in other portions of Ellis' judgment. Thus in a passage that evinces a concern that law should not hinder the heterosexualisation of transgender bodies effected by sex reassignment surgery, Ellis J. expressed the view:

> If the law insists that genetic sex is the pre-determinant for entry into a valid marriage, then a male to female transsexual can contract a valid marriage with a woman. To all outward appearances, such "marriages" would be homosexual marriages. The marriage could not be consummated.[64]

Anxiety over the prospect of "homosexual marriages" is evident in the fact that Ellis J. problematises the word "marriages" even though such marriages are quite clearly lawful. Moreover, the homophobia of the judgment is further evidenced by Ellis' assertion that such a marriage "could not be consummated". It is curious why reference to consummation should be made given its obvious irrelevance to the law of marriage in New Zealand, a point rendered abundantly clear by Ellis J. in other portions of the judgment.[65] Rather, it would seem that the idea of consummation is deployed against what Ellis J. sees as the transgender homosexual body in order to 'denaturalise' that body and its desires. This concern over the proximity of the homosexual body to marriage manifests itself in yet another regard:

> From a practical point of view, sex change procedures are unlikely to be undertaken by legitimate medical personnel in New Zealand without the individual having first obtained a dissolution of his or her marriage in the original sex. There is always the possibility that a person could undergo such procedures with less ethical professionals.[66]

This passage of the judgment is revealing. While it is true that psychiatrists are reluctant to refer married persons for sex reassignment procedures and surgeons reluctant to perform those procedures on married persons,[67] that attitude is premised on a view of homosexual desire, a desire which medicine, not unproblematically, inscribes onto married bodies, as inconsistent with transgender. It is significant that Ellis J. finds it necessary to delegitimise and to characterise as unethical medical practitioners who might be capable of imagining non-heterosexual transgender identities and desires.

CONCLUSION

23. This article has highlighted how sex reassignment surgery and heterosexual capacity have operated as preconditions of legal recognition in reform oriented transgender jurisprudence. In departing from Corbett this body of law has not merely abandoned chromosomes in favour of anatomical form. Rather, it is the sexual workings of the body that the judiciary have scrutinised. Indeed, it would seem that it is precisely post-operative sexual functioning that has enabled the judiciary to comprehend the desire for surgical intervention. Against this background the New Zealand decision of *Attorney-General v Otahuhu Family Court* proves significant. The importance of the case lies in its deemphasis of sexual function in determinations of transgender sex claims.

24. While *Attorney-General v Otahuhu Family Court* might be viewed as a 'progressive' decision removing a further obstacle to legal recognition it also serves to foreground the bodily aesthetics of law that prior transgender jurisprudence has partially masked through a preoccupation with (hetero) sexual capacity. In other words, the decision highlights how transgender jurisprudence is underscored by a concern with the 'monstrosity' of pre-operative bodies especially in the marriage context. Importantly, this view of the pre-operative body as 'monstrous' is explicable in terms of judicial anxiety over proximity to the homosexual body. In the final analysis functionality and aesthetics, as means through which to resolve the question of legal sex, find their unity in keeping the homosexual body at bay.

NOTES

[1]   [1995] 1 *NZLR* 603.
[2]   [1970] 2 *All ER* 33.
[3]   Ibid at 48.
[4]   For previous discussion and criticism of the Corbett decision see, for example, D. Green (1970) 'Transsexualism and Marriage' *New Law Journal* 120:210; E.S. David (1975) 'The Law and Transsexualism: A Faltering Response to a Conceptual Dilemma' *Connecticut Law Review* 7:288; A. Samuels (1984) 'Once a Man, Always a Man; Once a Woman, Always a Woman – Sex Change and the Law' *Medicine and Science Law*, 163; J. Dewar (1985) 'Transsexualism and Marriage' *Kingston Law Review* 15:58; and J. Taitz (1986) 'The Law Relating to the Consummation of Marriage where one of the Spouses is a Post-Operative Transsexual' *Anglo-American Law Review* 15:141.
[5]   See Dec C.P 6/76 National Insurance Commissioner Decisions; *E.A. White v British Sugar Corporation* [1977] *IRLR* 121; Social Security Decision numbers R (P) 1 and R (P) 2 [1980] National Insurance Commissioner Decisions; *R v Tan* [1983] QB 1053; *Peterson v Peterson* The Times 12 July 1985; *Franklin v Franklin* [1990] The Scotsman, 9 November; *Collins v Wilkin Chapman* [1994] EAT/945/93 (Transcript); *S-T (formerly J) v J* [1997] 3 *WLR* 1287, [1998] 1 *All ER* 431.
[6]   355 A 2d 204 [1976] 206.
[7]   See A Sharpe (1997) 'Anglo-Australian Judicial Approaches to Transsexuality: Discontinuities, Continuities and Wider Issues at Stake' *Social and Legal Studies* 6 (1): 23–50.
[8]   293 NYS 2d 834 [1968].
[9]   355 A 2d 204 [1976] 206.
[10] *Anonymous v Anonymous* 67 Misc. 2d 982; 325 N.Y.S. 2d 499 (Sup. Ct. 1971); *B v B* 78 Misc. 2d 112, 355 N.Y.S. 2d 712 (Sup Ct. 1974).
[11] MT v JT 355 A 2d 204 [1976] at 206.
[12] Ibid at 209.
[13] Ibid at 206.
[14] Indeed, a concern with one's own sexual pleasure is not typically read as a sign of 'authentic' transsexual identity within the medical arena. See H. Benjamin (1966) *The Transsexual Phenomenon*, NY: The Julian Press, Inc at 13–14, 54; J.

Money and C. Primrose, 'Sexual Dimorphism and Dissociation in the Psychology of Male Transsexuals', in Green and Money (eds) *Transsexualism and Sex Reassignment*, Baltimore: The Johns Hopkins Press (1969) p121–122; R.J. Stoller (1973) 'Male Transsexualism: Uneasiness' *American Journal of Psychiatry* 130: 536–9.

[15]   355 A 2d 204 [1976] at 206.

[16]   [1977] 400 NYS 2d 267.

[17]   Ibid. In this case the United States Tennis Association had required Renee Richards to pass the Barr (chromosomal) body test in order to be eligible to participate in the women's singles of the United States Open. The Supreme Court held that requirement to be "grossly unfair, discriminatory and inequitable, and violative of her rights under the Human Rights Law of this State" (at 272).

[18]   Ibid at 271.

[19]   Ibid per Dr. Money.

[20]   [1989] 17 *NSWLR* 158.

[21]   Section 81A NSW Crimes Act 1900 (now repealed).

[22]   *R v Harris and McGuiness* [1989] 17 *NSWLR* 158 at 193.

[23]   Ibid at 194.

[24]   Lee Harris and Phillis McGuiness had been approached by a vice squad officer who had requested oral sex.

[25]   13 AAR 314.

[26]   Ibid at 320.

[27]   Ibid.

[28]   Ibid at 317.

[29]   [1993] 118 ALR 467.

[30]   [1992] 28 ALD 361.

[31]   *Secretary, Department of Social Security v SRA* [1993] 118 *ALR* 467 at 493.

[32]   [1991] *NZFLR* 337.

[33]   [1976] 2 *SALR* 308.

[34]   [1991] *NZFLR* 337 at 344.

[35]   Ibid.

[36]   Ibid.

[37]   *R v Harris and McGuiness* [1988] 35 *A Crim R* 146.

[38]   [1991] *NZFLR* 337 at 348.

[39]   Ibid. Interestingly, uncertainty as to whether the determination of sex involves a question of law or fact is apparent in Aubin J's judgment. This is particularly evident in references to the Australian case of *R v Cogley* [1989] VR 799. In *R v Cogley* the Victorian Court of Criminal Appeal unanimously held that the determination of sex was "a question of fact to be determined by the jury". For a discussion of this case and the law/fact distinction in the context of transgender sex claims see A. Sharpe (1994) 'The Precarious Position of the Transsexual Rape Victim' Current Issues in *Criminal Justice* 6 (2): 303–7.

[40]   Ibid at 339.

[41]   Ibid at 340.

[42]   Ibid.

[43]   Ibid.

[44]   Ibid at 339.

[45]   *Attorney General v Otahuhu Family Court* [1995] 1 *NZLR* 603 at 612.

[46]   Ibid.

[47]   *M v M* [1991] *NZFLR* 337 at 347.

[48]   See J. Epstein, (1995) *Altered Conditions: Disease, Medicine and Storytelling*. Routledge. P91.

[49]   [1995] 1 *NZLR* 603.

[50]   [1993] 118 *ALR* 467.

[51]   Ibid at 493.

[52]   This view of the female body is traceable to a body of liberal theory and perhaps most notably to the writings of Immanuel Kant (*The Metaphysics of Morals*). See Ngaire Naffine (1997) 'The Body Bag' in N. Naffine and R. Owens (eds) *Sexing the Subject of Law*. Sweet and Maxwell. p79–93.

[53]   Ibid.

[54]   *Attorney-General v Otahuhu Family Court* [1995] 1 *NZLR* 603 at 604.

[55]   Ibid at 614–615.

[56]   Ibid at 612.

[57]   Ibid.

[58]   Ibid at 615.

[59]   Ibid at 607.

[60]   Ibid at 615.

[61]   Ibid at 614.

[62]   Ibid at 607.

[63]   Ibid at 615. While such a view was articulated by the Social Security and Administrative Appeals tribunals in the Australian decision of *Secretary, Department of Social Security v SRA* (above note 30) the judgment of Ellis J represents its first airing by a superior court within a common law jurisdiction.

[64]   Ibid at 629.
[65]   Ibid at 612. Of course, the shift from sexual function to bodily aesthetics evident in *Attorney-General v Otahuhu Family Court* is perhaps unlikely to be followed in common law jurisdictions where consummation continues to play an important role in determining marriage questions.
[66]   Ibid at 619.
[67]   See D. King (1993) above note 21. Indeed, the famous transsexual Jan Morris went to Casablanca for her surgery in 1972 after she was told she must divorce her wife in order to receive surgery in the UK (Jan Morris (1986) *Conundrum: An Extraordinary Narrative of Transsexualism*. NY: Holt).

VII

MULTIPLE CROSSINGS: GENDER, NATIONALITY, RACE

45

selections from

The Chic of Araby

Transvestism and the Erotics of Cultural Appropriation

Marjorie Garber

In *Vested Interests*, her influential study of "cross-dressing and cultural anxiety," Harvard literary critic Marjorie Garber[1] made a major contribution to the field of transgender studies in the early 1990s by calling attention to the pervasiveness of themes of cross-dressing and shifting sexual identities in a wide range of Western cultural texts. In "The Chic of Araby," Garber demonstrates how gender-crossings and cross-cultural exchanges often collapse into one another in the Western cultural imagination. She addresses a central feature in Eurocentric discourses on the "Orient," namely that the Orient, as the West's Other—is feminine, whereas the West is masculine. This gendering of geography creates a situation where crossing a cultural or national boundary becomes symbolically invested with anxieties about gender's instability and lack of fixity.

Garber specifically discusses several popular films and texts, such as T. E. Lawrence in *Lawrence of Arabia* or Rudolph Valentino's role in the silent film classic *The Sheik*, both of which conflate the wearing of traditional Arab robes, scarves, and sandals by Western men with gendered cross-dressing. Similar themes play out in the history of Isabelle Eberhardt, the daughter of a Russian aristocrat who posed as an Arab boy in her nineteenth-century travels in the Middle East.

In a startling dramatic moment in David Lean's *Lawrence of Arabia* (1962) an Arab chieftain loyal to the old ways confiscates and smashes the camera of an American reporter because he thinks the reporter has captured his image. This incident, which may feel assaultive to the audience imagining itself behind the *other* camera, the movie camera, testifies not only to differences in religious belief, East and West, but also to a historical moment of technological intervention: the moment when the image of T.E. Lawrence, dressed in the flowing skirts of an Arab prince, captured the imagination of the newspaper-reading public.

The photograph is in its material form a "negative," a phantom or ghost, an inverse or inverted image of what it will, when "developed," come to represent. The photograph, in other words, is a "film" that presents itself in order for the viewer to believe that some reality lies *behind* it. Here, indeed, is its specific if figural relevance to Middle Eastern representation: for the photograph is, in these particulars, very like the veil. And it is the veil, a garment that simultaneously conceals and reveals, the material embodiment of the literal striptease, that is the most characteristic adornment of the transvestite of "Araby."

Lawrence once wrote that he adopted the costume of the desert Arabs—skirt, headdress and sandals—at the invitation of his chosen Arab leader, Emir Sherif Feisal, whose regal good looks reminded him of his childhood hero, Richard I, the Lionhearted.[2] "Suddenly Feisal asked me if I would wear Arab clothes like his own while in the camp. I should find it better for my own part, since it was a comfortable dress in which to live Arab-fashion as we must do. Besides, the tribesmen would then understand how to take me."[3]

The robes in which he was originally dressed by his Arab friends were "splendid white and gold-embroidered wedding garments which had been sent to Feisal lately (was it a hint?) by his great-aunt in Mecca" (*Seven Pillars*, 129).[4] In David Lean's superb film, Peter O'Toole, in the title role, cavorts with increasing delight in these white and gold garments, bowing to his shadow in the sun like an Arabian Malvolio, while the troops look on in amused pleasure. Feisal's wedding garments are the costume of a bridegroom, but in Western translation, as in O'Toole's inspired promenade through the sands, they are emblematically transformed into the white dress and veil of an Occidental bride. Indeed, Lawrence himself returns again, offhandedly but with a characteristic self-irony, to this figure of the wedding dress and its cross-cultural cross-gendering; on the Roman road to Damascus, he reports, "Rain came and soaked me, and then it blew fine and freezing till I crackled in armour of white silk, like a theatre knight; or like a bridal cake, hard iced" (*Seven Pillars*, 508).

Throughout *Seven Pillars of Wisdom* Lawrence reports, again not without a certain pleasure, that British army officers repeatedly either snickered or sneered at his costume, finding it not only offensively "Oriental" but (what may have seemed the same thing) feminizing. Arriving at Suez with the astounding news of the capture of Akaba, he was first given the cold shoulder at the Sinai Hotel because of his dress, and challenged as to his military and national identity: "they looked at my bare feet, white silk robes, and gold head–rope and dagger. Impossible!" (*Seven Pillars*, 327)

In his account of his first encounter with General Allenby, Lawrence reports with amused self-regard that the General, although adapting rapidly to less traditional modes of warfare, "was hardly prepared for anything so odd as myself—a little barefooted silk-skirted man" (*Seven Pillars*, 33). Later, as he is supervising the long-overdue cleansing of the fetid Turkish hospital at Damascus, "a medical major strode up and asked me shortly if I spoke English. With a brow of disgust for my skirts and sandals he said, 'You're in charge?' Modestly, I smirked that in a way I was, and then he burst out, 'Scandalous, disgraceful, outrageous, ought to be shot. . . .'" (*Seven Pillars*, 682)

What is noteworthy in all of these instances is not so much the narrow imaginations of the expatriate English as it is Lawrence's own almost sensual delight in both his appearance and their consternation. In Lean's film this is underscored by the fact that the scandalized major shortly encounters Lawrence once again at military headquarters, this time dressed in orthodox army garb, and begs the honor of shaking his hand. Asked drily by Lawrence whether they haven't met before, he fulsomely replies, "Oh, no, sir. I should remember *that!*"

To the Arab troops, however, Lawrence was a unique figure of a different kind, and also in part because of his costume. That the whiteness of his garments was part of their symbolic allure is evident from his account of his bodyguards, who "dressed like a bed of tulips, in every colour but white; for that was my constant wear, and they did not wish to seem to presume" (*Seven Pillars*, 475). "My clothes and appearance were peculiar in the desert," he reports with some pride. "It was notoriety to be the only cleanshaven one, and I doubled it by wearing always the suspect pure silk, of the whitest (at least outside), with a gold and crimson Meccan head-rope, and gold dagger. By so dressing I staked a claim which Feisal's public consideration of me confirmed."

What is the claim he here boasts of staking? Not only—I want to suggest—that of the English Arab chieftain, the Western prince of the desert, the white-skinned Arab soldier—but also that of Feisal's chosen, the clean-shaven Englishman whom, long ago, the Prince had dressed in wedding clothes.

Lawrence recalls in *The Seven Pillars of Wisdom* an intimate scene in Feisal's retreat at Aba el Lisan. The two men having discussed at leisured length "histories, tribes, migration, sentiments, the spring rains, pasture," Lawrence happens to mention that Allenby has given them the magnificent gift of two thousand camels, the means of victory. "Feisal gasped and caught my knee saying, 'How?' I told him all the story. He leaped up and kissed me." When Lawrence remarks that after the victory he can leave them, Feisal "protested, saying that I must remain with them always" (*Seven Pillars*, 541–42). The "magnificent gift" bestowed, paternally, by a superior officer; the grasp of the knee; the kiss—these iconographic indicators of fellowship are presented in a style at once artless and compelling. He wears, by design and designation, a costume based on wedding clothes intended for Feisal; he brings with him as Allenby's gift (a kind of "dowry") a vast number of camels, priceless contributions to the war effort; Feisal expresses the wish to have Lawrence remain with them (him) always. Lawrence seems oblivious to the iconography of marriage here, but its multiple inscription calls attention to itself repeatedly. Indeed, his own blindness to this recurrent thematic of his narrative adds to the sense of unwitting self-revelation that is a constant textual effect of his prose, and part of its considerable seductive power.

Lawrence's sexual ambivalences are clearly expressed throughout his memoirs, and have been much commented upon by biographers.[5] In his admiration for the "Eastern boy and boy affection which the segregation of women made inevitable," friendships that "often led to manly loves of a depth and force beyond our flesh-steeped conceit," and in which, "If sexuality entered, they passed into a give and take, unspiritual relation, like marriage," he idealizes the male companionships of the desert, describing one of his youthful servants as the "love-fellow" of the other, kneeling in appeal, "all the woman of him evident in the longing" (*Seven Pillars*, 244). And in his report of the confrontation at Der'a with the Turkish Bey, whose homosexual advances he spurned, he describes the experience of "a delicious warmth, probably sexual, . . . swelling through me" (*Seven Pillars*, 454) in the midst of the savage beating administered by the Bey's men.

His faltering confession of his pleasure at the hands of his torturers at Der'a marks a key turning point in *Lawrence of Arabia*, as it does in John Mack's psychologically compelling biography. Lawrence's discovery of sexual pleasure in the infliction of pain led to the elaborate arrangements for flagellation at the behest of an imaginary "uncle," who was punishing him for equally imaginary crimes: actually, for Lawrence's own guilt at his masochistic pleasure. The beatings he had sustained at the hands of his mother, whom he adored, the fact that he and his four brothers were illegitimate sons of a British peer—these may have played a part in opening his sensory responsiveness to the allure of pain and discipline. The ineluctable cycle of pleasurable punishment, guilt, punishment for that guilt, pleasure in the punishment, guilt again, and so on, dominated his final years.[6] Like many exceptional and brilliant individuals, Lawrence's personal power came also from a sense of personal limitation; swerving, in effect, to avoid the "normal" social world of his Oxford upbringing, he displaced his enormous energies onto other, more global and more exotic realms where the family romance could be deployed to political as well as personal ends.[7]

For the adult Lawrence of *Seven Pillars* women occupy only a marginal and mysterious role. In a letter to a friend in the House of Commons he later wrote, "Women? I like some women. I don't like their sex: any more than I like the monstrous regiment of men. There is no difference that I feel between a woman and a man."[8] This offhand evocation of John Knox's Reformation-era tirade against women in authority (*The First Blast of the Trumpet against the Monstrous Regiment of Women*, 1558) will suggest something of the pressures Lawrence felt himself to be under in a world of sexuality and sociability. Without question, he was more comfortable with men than with women, and with "the plain man" rather than "the elaborated man," describing the sexual lives of such "plain men" (here, English soldiers in barracks), significantly, in terms of costume: "Sex, with them, is something you put on (and take off) with your walking-out dress: on Friday night, certainly: and if you are lucky on Saturday afternoon, and most of Sunday. Work begins on Monday again, and is really important."[9]

Throughout his life he seems to have been most comfortable in societies of men (his four brothers; his all-male school; his fellow archaeologists on a dig at Carchemis in Turkey; his army companions; his Arab associates). In this context, his own assumption of Arab dress, the white, flowing robes and gold headdress prescribed for him by Feisal, at once the sign of a warrior prince and a bride, paradoxically manly, even heroic, despite (or because of) his silk skirts—all this seems a mode of self-expression for Lawrence. He sees himself as at once self-demonstrative and self-denigrating, an apt guise for a complicated man who could write that he "liked the things underneath me and took my pleasures and adventures downward. There seemed a certainty in degradation, a final safety" (*Seven Pillars*, 581).

It is intriguing, in light of his later involvement with conventions of dress that cross boundaries of culture, gender, and class, to note that T.E. Lawrence's one attempt at a conventional male-female relationship itself began with a scene of cross-dressing. His one proposal of marriage—to a woman who would reject him in favor of his younger brother, and marry someone else when that brother was killed in the War—was made to an early childhood friend whom he initially mistook for a boy.

Janet Laurie had been the Lawrences' neighbor from 1894 to 1896, and later was sent to boarding school in Oxford to be near them. She and Lawrence saw a great deal of one another when he was an undergraduate, but the basis of their affection was begun in childhood. She was a tomboy, and he tended to tease her for "not being a boy" (Mack, 64). Laurie's own account of their first meeting, as recorded by John Mack, offers a fascinating point of entry into this scenario of courtship and mis-prision: "Her parents had wanted another son and so kept her hair short and dressed her like a boy. She was in church, and behind her were two or three Lawrence brothers with their nanny, Florence Messham. She heard one of the boys, who proved to be Ned, say to Miss Messham, 'What a naughty little boy to keep his hat on in church.' She turned around and put out her tongue and said, 'I'm not a boy, I'm a girl.' She overheard Miss Messham ('I took a great dislike to her') say, 'Well, she may not be a little boy, but she's a very rude little girl. Thus the friendship began."[10]

So it seems that T.E. Lawrence's one serious attempt at a heterosexual relationship, the failure of which, some of his friends and biographers maintain, enforced his decision to live asexually among men, began in a moment of childhood cross-dressing and the misreading of children's dress codes. The one woman to whom Lawrence proposed was a woman he first met when she was dressed like a boy.

The *figure* of dress plays an important role, rhetorically as well as imaginatively, in Lawrence's writing. We have seen that he refers to sex, and sexual desire, as "something you put on (and take off) with your walking-out dress"—if you are so lucky as to be, unlike Lawrence himself, a "plain man." At another moment he speaks eagerly of a key meeting with superior officers, including Allenby, as an opportunity for "seeing the undress working of a general's mind" (*Seven Pillars*, 553). That he is *in* costume—that his robes are both naturalized and masquerade—is a constant theme of his letters to friends. "It's a kind of foreign stage, on which one plays day and night, in fancy dress," he wrote to an old Oxford schoolmate. "You want apparently some vivid colouring of an Arab's costume, or of a flying Turk, and we have it all, for that is part of the mise en scène...Disguises and prices on one's head, and fancy exploits are all part of the pose."[11]

Lawrence's flair for self-theatricalization, his self-conscious awareness of his "silk-skirt[s]" and "fancy dress," are evident in the photographs of him taken in that period. Yet "I loathe the notion of being celluloided," he later wrote to Robert Graves. "My rare visits to cinemas always deepen in me a sense of their superficial falsity.... The camera seems wholly in place in journalism: but when it tries to re-create it boobs and sets my teeth on edge. So there won't be a film of me."[12] This spectacularly false prediction records his success at persuading Alexander Korda to abandon plans for a projected film of Lawrence's life.

It was Lowell Thomas who popularized the Lawrence legend in New York and London, Thomas who concocted the film-and-lecture shows that made "Lawrence of Arabia" a household name in the U.S. in 1919 even before he was celebrated in Britain. Lawrence was, characteristically, ambivalent about Thomas's glorification of him, and though he initially collaborated with the publicity effort, he came to resent it, calling Thomas "vulgar," a popularizer who indulged in "red-hot lying."[13]

He wrote to a man named Greenhill whom he had known in the desert campaign in Saudi Arabia, "For Lowell Thomas: I don't bear him any grudge. He has invented some silly phantom thing, a sort of matinee idol in fancy dress, that does silly things and is dubbed 'romantic.' Boy scouts and servants love it."[14] Boy scouts and servants; the class inflection, self-ironized, here underscores Lawrence's ambivalence toward his own "phantom" personae as officer and enlisted man. After the war he sent a letter to another acquaintance, disclaiming the heroics with which Lowell Thomas had credited him: "Only I was in fancy dress, & so I made a good 'star' for his film."[15] And to E. M. Forster, who had taken on the task of reviewing Thomas's book *With Lawrence in Arabia*, he wrote to correct the author's "rubbish," which he dismissed as "either invention or gossip": "I was never disguised as an Arab (though I once got off as a Circassian & nearly got on as a veiled woman!)" (*Selected Letters*, 283).

This tantalizing glimpse of a deliberately cross-dressed Lawrence, who "nearly got on as a veiled woman," remains itself a phantom, hovering at the margins of the legend. But the matinee idol, the "star," the European hero in Eastern "fancy dress," ambivalently sexual, masochistic, full of controlled violence: *this* phantom of the chic of Araby would be "celluloided," over and over again, in the years that immediately followed Lowell Thomas's famous footage of the Palestinian campaigns. The celebrity of Lawrence, the spectacular success of his story, that played to packed houses at Madison Square Garden in New York City in the spring of 1919, and the Royal Opera House in Covent Garden in the fall of the same year, itself contributed to the vogue for romantic films about "Arabia" that swept the U.S. in the twenties. In many ways Lawrence is the phantom presence behind the figure of the Western aristocrat in exotic "fancy dress," the sheik of Araby. And the incarnation of that fantasy was to be found in the spectacular success of an Italian-born actor, dressed in Arab robes, on the Hollywood screen.

RADICAL SHEIK

No single figure in the history of film has been more closely identified with passionate eroticism than Rudolph Valentino, whose appearance as Ahmed Ben Hassan in *The Sheik* (1921) set off a frenzy of response among (largely female) filmgoers. The story of the sheik's abduction of Lady Diana Mayo, whom he plucks from her horse and carries off to his tent, is full of the cartoon-like energy of sexual sadism. "Lie still, you little fool," the Sheik tells Lady Diana, and when she asks "Why have you brought me here?," he sneers, "Are you not woman enough to know?" The fantasy of abduction-turned-to-passionate-love in the desert made Valentino a star, and a love god.

Sheet-music vendors seized the moment to popularize *The Sheik of Araby*, Sheik fashions were worn by both women and men, men slicked their hair with Vaseline, and, in the sincerest form of flattery, imitation Sheik films quickly followed: *Arabian Love* starring John Gilbert, *Arab* with Ramon Navarro, and *Song of Love* with Edmund Carewe. "Shriek—For the Sheik Will Seek You Too!" invited the posters for Valentino's film, making sure audiences knew how to pronounce the new term—which promptly entered the dictionary with a second, slang meaning of "romantically alluring man" to second the original "Moslem religious official" and "leader of an Arab family, village, or tribe."[16]

The association of Valentino's role with unbridled sexual passion continues today in the merchandising of an appropriate tie-in product: the Sheik condom, now available in a number of styles—traditional

Non-Lubricated Sheik (with the picture of a brooding Mediterranean-handsome man in halftones on the box), Ribbed Sheik, Sheik Elite, and—the cross-dresser's special—new She's Sheik, still presumably to be worn by a male, but with larger-print warnings about the prevention of pregnancy and disease to recommend it to the prudent female customer.

One of the most curious, and yet predictable, features of *The Sheik*'s screenplay—based on a near-pornographic novel by an Englishwoman, Edith M. Hull, writing under the unisex initials E.M.—was that the Sheik himself turned out, in the course of the plot not to be an Arab at all, but a Scot—in fact, the Earl of Glencarryl, a Scottish nobleman who had been abandoned in the Sahara as a baby. This fortunate turn of events "legitimized the relationship between Lady Diana and the Sheik, transforming an intended rape into a suitable love match; the family romance again, as so often, prevented interracial mixture, and preserved the honor of the "white" race. At the close of the film the lovers are en route "back to civilization on their honeymoon," according to *Exhibitors Trade Review*, which carried a synopsis of the plot.[17] A similar romance plot is found in Edgar Rice Burroughs's *Tarzan*, where the hero is discovered to be "really" Lord Greystoke—and, not incidentally, in the story of T.E. Lawrence, "Lawrence of Arabia," the illegitimate son of Sir Thomas Chapman. Thus Valentino (born Rodolpho Guglielmi) as Sheik Ahmed had all the advantages of desert attire, including a dazzling tan, a curving scimitar, and (incongruously but crucially) a cigarette holder, without the necessity of a correlative racial inferiority.

The sequel, *Son of the Sheik* (1926), based on Hull's book *Sons of the Sheik* but conflating the two "sons" in one—Valentino, who also played his own father in the film, thus rendering himself self-authored and doubly irreplaceable—adds elements of masochism to the already heady erotic brew. At one point Valentino is stripped to the waist and beaten (here we might recall the torture scene in *Lawrence of Arabia*, and Lawrence's own elaborately staged private beatings). The main plot involves, again, an abduction, but this time motivated by revenge rather than by love. His lovemaking, clearly as much desired as feared by his captive (Vilma Banky), is calculatedly cruel and explicitly misogynistic: as he lights his inevitable cigarette and strips off his robe and jeweled belt, he tells her, "All the beauties of the Arabian Nights being unveiled could not get a look from me."

In a famous still photo from *The Sheik*, Valentino's cigarette holder is counterpoised by a revolver held in the hand of Agnes Ayres, as Lady Diana; the tacit switch of power tools underscores the riskiness of gender semiotics out of which the Sheik crafts his particular sexual appeal. Valentino's clean-shaven, boyish face, like his cigarette holder, became objects of defensive scorn for many self-identified "red-blooded-American-male" movie-goers, and sexual magnets for women—as well as for some men. As for Lady Diana, she is not just any old captive woman, but a militant feminist (again, see the gun) in pants. Once abducted by Ahmed, however, she quickly changes her tune, and her clothes, replacing her riding breeches with a skirt at his behest. Hull's novel describes her outfit and her sexual situation with lavish precision:

> Diana's eyes passed over him slowly till they arrested on his brown, clean-shaven face, surmounted by crisp, close-cut brown hair. It was the handsomest and the cruellest face that she had ever seen. Her gaze was drawn instinctively to his. He was looking at her with fierce burning eyes that swept her until she felt that the boyish clothes that covered her slender limbs were stripped from her, leaving her beautiful white body bare under his passionate stare. She shrank back, quivering, dragging the lapel of her riding jacket together over her breast with clutching hands, obeying an impulse that she hardly understood. "Who are you?" she gasped hoarsely.
> "I am the Sheik Ahmed Ben Hassan . . ."

Theorists of the gaze need look no further for its transfixing role in early film. *The Sheik* picked up on these plain hints, to foreground the elements of gender-and wardrobe-switching (Valentino in robes, Agnes Ayres in jodhpurs, both in eyebrow pencil and mascara), and added a spice of Middle Eastern pederasty—disclaimed, of course, by the closet-Scots hero. "You make a charming boy," the Sheik declares [and here the camp resonances of "boy" are to a modern audience unmistakable], "but it was not a boy I saw in Biskra."[18] The association of Araby with homoeroticism and boy love here has come full circle, as the "Lady" in pants displaces the "boy" as the object, at least the overt object, of the culturally cross dressed, apparently "Oriental" Sheik's desire.[19]

* * *

THE TRANSVESTITE AS "BON GARÇON"

In a satiric episode in a play called *New Anatomies* by contemporary playwright Timberlake Wertenbaker, five women, four of them cross-dressed, appear in a cabaret bar. One is costumed as a man for "professional" reasons; she is a singer. Others explain their men's clothes as motivated by sexual orientation, or merely by willful choice.[50] All four, in a way, mirror the extraordinary life of the play's protagonist, Isabelle Eberhardt, a European woman who dressed like an Arab man, lived with the tribes of the North African desert, and manufactured for herself a new identity.

Isabelle Eberhardt was the illegitimate daughter of an aristocratic Russian woman and of the tutor engaged to care for her older children. Born in 1877, reared in exile in the outskirts of Geneva, Eberhardt was brought up like a boy, her hair cropped, her clothes boys' clothes, following Bakunin's instruction that "every child of either sex should be prepared as much for a life of the mind as for a life of work, so that all may grow up equally into complete men."[51] Educated bilingually in French and Russian, she learned Latin, Arabic, Italian, and a little English, and read Voltaire, Rousseau, Zola, and the Russian novelists. But her passion, following that of her biological father, Alexander Trophimowsky, was for Islam. By the age of sixteen she could read the Koran in Arabic, and inscribe classic Arabic calligraphy. She was enchanted by the Orientalism of Pierre Loti; the Near and Middle East and North Africa, which for the French was "the Orient," became her ideal fantasy place and then her home during a short, nomadic life that ended at 27 when her body, dressed like an "Arab cavalryman," was recovered from a flash flood in southwest Algeria.

Eberhardt's situation seems overdetermined both psychoanalytically and culturally. An illegitimate child, a girl, an exile relocated in a European country itself divided in language and cultural traditions, she early developed a fantasy parentage and a family romance: "As the daughter of a Muslim Russian father and Christian Russian mother," she wrote in a letter to a newspaper in 1903, a year before her death, "I was born a Muslim and have never changed my religion. My father having died shortly after my birth in Geneva, where he lived, my mother lived on in that city with my old great-uncle [Trophimowsky], who brought me up absolutely like a boy."[52] Her most recent biographer compares her, significantly, to T.E. Lawrence, another illegitimate child who was captivated by the East and the Arabs—and by their dress.

Eberhardt initially identified herself with her brother Augustin de Moerder, who was also, in all probability, Trophimowsky's child. Together they conceived the dream of going to North Africa. But Augustin, weak-willed and early addicted—as Eberhardt would later become—to drugs, continually disappointed his sister's expectations. Thus on the eve of moving her family to Algeria in 1895 she found Augustin missing and her mother ill. Instead of the journey to North Africa, Eberhardt was forced to settle, this time, for a trip to a photographer's studio.

The portrait photographer Louis David, a family friend, took two pictures which would become part of the Eberhardt legend: a full-length portrait of the young Isabelle in "Arab" costume, odds and ends from David's cupboard of Orientalist wares: a burnous, Turkish slippers clearly too large for her feet, an ornamented vest and dagger; and a close-up of herself in the costume of a sailor, wearing a hat with the name of the ship "Vengeance"—signifying, as she would remark to a friend and later inscribe in her diary, "the sacred aim of my life: revenge" for the injustices she felt had been wrought upon the de Moerder family.[53]

Cross-dressing for Isabelle Eberhardt thus became both a way of *obeying* the paternal and patriarchal law (Trophimowsky permitted her to go into Geneva only if she dressed as a boy) and a way of *subverting* it. "My life here is quite funny," she wrote to Augustin. "Just imagine—I go around dressed as a sailor, even in town, right under the noses of agents" (Kobak, 38). Dressed in this fashion, and drinking with friends, she made a bet with her companion, a married man five years older, that she would dare to kiss him in public. The "boy" in the sailor suit won the bet. Later, in North Africa, she took on the persona of a young Arab man, taking the name "Mahmoud Saadi." Under that name she spent her happiest years in the desert and in the town of El Oued, dressed in the traditional garb of the Tunisians: a burnous worn over a voluminous silk shirt, baggy trousers, white stockings, and yellow slippers. Her head was shaved completely, in the Muslim style, and she wore a tasseled fez. Casual acquaintances took her, unsurprisingly, for a young man.

Eberhardt appears to have taken a certain pleasure in gender indeterminacy. While she was still in Geneva and writing under a male pseudonym, "Nicholas Podolinsky," one of her correspondents—a Greek artillery officer—wrote to her with irritation, "I didn't know and still don't know what kind of a person I'm dealing with, what their real name is and to what sex or nationality he or she belongs. Meanwhile I haven't the time to write to unknown people behind diverse pseudonyms."[54] Another correspondent, the editor of a French journal who was to become a lasting friend, wrote in 1897: "Dear Mademoiselle and *confrère*, I easily forget in reading your letters whether you're a girl or a boy. If it weren't for your feminine handwriting, I'd believe the latter supposition more easily. In any case this proves you have an unusual virility.... Don't ever be completely masculine because a superior woman is superior to her masculine colleague... [don't get] too close to that other part of the human species that is egoism personified."[55]

Passing, while it was clearly a logistical asset for her in North Africa, was an option—in fact, an intermittent reality—for Eberhardt even in Geneva. A visitor to her family's home in 1897 reported that she observed "a young fellow of about sixteen...sawing wood in the courtyard. His delicate, elegant hands should have told us his sex, but we had no idea. It was only on the third visit that Monsieur Trophimowsky revealed the disguise to us. I warmed to the young lady, who was so gifted and so well-educated."[56] (It is interesting to speculate—given the dissymmetries of gender preconception—on whether the visitor would have warmed so readily to a young man she had mistaken for a young woman.)

A North African with whom Eberhardt had been corresponding under the name of Mahmoud—and who had seen and been struck by the photograph of her as a sailor—had a similar response when he met her for the first time at her family's new home in Algeria: "I shan't attempt to describe my astonishment on the quayside when, instead of shaking hands with a Mahmoud, I found myself in the presence of a young girl, very elegantly dressed" (Kobak, 54). The elegant female dress was Eberhardt's choice, deliberately putting in question her correspondent's assumptions, or, as she put it, his "prejudice[s]" (Kobak, 54). "*Bon garçonisme,*" tomboyishness, is how she herself described to him the "mask" she wore toward the outside world, so full of "*pseudo-semblables, so dissemblables*" (Kobak, 55).

Later, in 1899, she again broke through her gender disguise, this time of necessity, since her passport described her as female; she therefore presented herself to the head of the Arab Bureau in Biskra, dressed as an Arab man, but announcing herself as a woman. Once more the doubleness of her gendered persona, the wearing and then the doffing of the mask, intrigued and attracted her associate; the colonel in charge invited her to lunch at his house, and then to dinner. Self-difference here is figured in the sequence *semblable/pseudo-semblable/dissemblable*, in which *all* of the subject positions are occupied by Isabelle Eberhardt.

When in men's clothing, Arab or Western, she was often "read," like many cross-dressing women, as a "boy" rather than a man. Her "dainty hands"[57] and smooth complexion gave her away. Eberhardt seems sometimes to have believed that she was traveling incognito, or passing, when her Arab companions apparently knew of her "real" gender and were too polite, or too indifferent, to remark upon it: "Si Larbi never suspected that I was a woman, he called me his brother Mahmoud, and I shared his nomadic life and his work for two months," she wrote, with some complacency (Kobak, 97).

Eberhardt switched back and forth from male to female and from European to Arab costume throughout her life, largely in response to perceived political necessity, but also as a concession to her lovers' preferences. A Turkish diplomat to whom she was briefly engaged before her sojourn in North Africa wrote her requesting that she let her cropped hair grow out ("as I've let my beard grow") before their marriage.[58] Even the man she married, Slimène Ehnni, a young Arab officer from a regiment in El Oued, was at times ambivalent about her masquerade, fearing for her safety, and at one point she abandoned her male garb to dress in Arab women's clothes at his request.

When an assassination attempt upon her necessitated her appearance in court, the question of appropriate costume became an issue for debate between husband and wife. Slimène felt that European clothing would make a better impression, and she wrote back to him in some heat:

> You absolutely *must not buy European clothes, because you've no idea how much it costs and I formally forbid* you to contract a centime of debts. You know me and know very well that I'm prepared to obey you in everything, except when you're talking nonsense. One can tell you know nothing of what it *costs* to dress *not well*, but at least passably as a Frenchwoman: a wig (this costs, for a shaved head like mine, some 15 to 20 francs, because a simple plait won't do), a hat, underwear, corset, petticoats, skirts, stockings, shoes, gloves and so on. All I will concede is to stop *dressing as an Arab*, which is anyway the only thing which would prejudice the authorities against me. I shall therefore dress *as a European* [man], now that I'm properly equipped. I swear to you, *it's not for the pleasure of dressing up as a man*, but because it's *impossible* for me to do otherwise. At court-martial…they always said to me, 'We quite understand that you wish to wear men's clothes, but why don't you dress as a European?' Anyway, that's all I have to say to you on the subject. It's impossible for me to do otherwise.…I don't care if I dress as a *workman*, but to wear ill-fitting, cheap and ridiculous women's clothes, no, never…(Kobak, 167)

In this letter, full of energetic underlinings and denials, class, gender, and nationality are deployed as categories that contain, or define, cultural anxieties. Eberhardt asserts her desire to present herself as a European—which is to say, a European man—as a strategic choice prescribed by economic and political factors. To dress as an Arab man is politically unwise, to dress as a Frenchwoman, economically impossible. The passionate rhetoric of the letter almost succeeds in repressing any more personal desire. But, like the delicate hands or *imberbe* face that give her away, the letter reveals what it seeks to conceal: "I swear to you, *it's not for the pleasure of dressing up as a man*."

Eberhardt was apparently willing to regard all of these categories as in play except one: willing, indeed apparently eager, to present herself as European or Arab, male or female, aristocrat or workman, depending upon the context, she was militant in her assertion of Muslim faith. As she wrote in an open letter to the *Dépêche Algerienne*:

> The investigating magistrates have repeatedly expressed their surprise at hearing me describe myself as a Muslim and an initiate of the Kadriya brotherhood at that; they also have not known what to make of my going about dressed as an Arab, sometimes as a man, and at other times as a woman, depending on the occasion, and on the requirements of my essentially nomadic life. . . .
>
>   In order to avoid giving the impression…that in donning a costume and adopting some religious label I might be inspired by some ulterior motive, I wish to state unequivocally that I have not been baptised

and have never been a Christian; although a Russian citizen I have been a Muslim for a very long time in fact.[59]

This emphatic declaration, which privileges religious faith so strongly over gender and nationality ("I have been a Muslim for a very long time"; "dressed as an Arab, sometimes as a man, and at other times as a woman, depending on the occasion, and on the requirements of my essentially nomadic life"), suggests that the mechanism of displacement may be at work, substituting for an element of "high psychical value"[60] (here, gender identity) one of comparatively low value (religion), so that what makes the writer most anxious is veiled, distorted, or censored, and replaced by something that provokes less anxiety. As we have noted, Eberhardt's situation was itself quintessentially that of multiple displacement; she is a "displaced person" in virtually every sense. In fact, her cross-dressing seems to mark and make legible the condition of category crisis itself. For Eberhardt is, in a sense, an example of the *personification of displacement*.

Lacan, following Roman Jakobson, associated displacement with metonymy, the chain of signification which "eternally stretch[ed] forth towards the *desire for something else*—of metonymy. Hence its 'perverse' fixation at the very suspension-point of the signifying chain where the memory-screen is immobilized and the fascinating image of the fetish is petrified."[61] Eberhardt's own desire for the towns and peoples of North Africa has inevitably been transmuted by her biographers, then and now, into a fetishizing activity of which cross-dressing was the sign. "Is what thinks in my place, then, another I?" Lacan asked, reading Freud's enigmatic "*Wo es war, soll Ich werden*." "Who, then, is the other to whom I am more attached than to myself, since, at the heart of my assent to my own identity it is still he who agitates me? His presence can be understood only at a second degree of otherness, which already places him in the position of mediating between me and the double of myself, as if it were with my counterpart" (Lacan, 171–72). For Eberhardt "Si Mahmoud Saadi," constructed of Arab cloth, was the self as *another* other, *semblable* and *dissemblable* at once, the one who mediates between: the transvestite. Thus a French Algerian writer records his first meeting with "two strangers in native costume":

> One of the strangers was very dark-skinned and sickly-looking, but with regular and appealing features. He was called Si Slimane (sic) Ehnni.... His companion, elegant and slim, was a cavalier in a *haik* and a fine, immaculately white burnous.... "May I introduce Si Mahmoud Saadi," the dark visitor said, "that is his *nom de guerre*; in fact it is Mme. Ehnni, my wife."[62]

Slimène's rhetorical certainty—"in fact it is...my wife" is nicely contrasted with his acceptance of the other person who is also there, and who takes pride of place when being introduced: "Si Mahmoud Saadi" "his" *nom de guerre*. The diary Eberhardt began on the first of January 1900—the beginning of a new century—referred to herself regularly in the masculine gender [*je suis seul*], occasionally changing to the feminine. And a French brigadier-general wrote glowingly of her double-gendered persona:

> We understood each other very well, poor Mahmoud and I, and I shall always cherish exquisite memories of our evening talks. She was what attracts me most in the world: a rebel [*réfractaire*]. To find someone who is really *himself*, who exists outside all prejudice, all enslavement, all cliché, and who passes through life as liberated as a bird in space, what a treat![63]

Through the shrewd manipulation of borders, identity papers, names and roles, Eberhardt, displaced and out of place in Geneva, became (at least for the popular press, and to a certain extent for herself) in effect a *spirit of place* in North Africa. The figure of clothing was for her a palpable sign; on January

1, 1900 she wrote in her diary that she wanted "to reclothe myself in that cherished personality, which in reality is the true one, and to go back to Africa again" (Kobak, 107).

Her critics tend to read her transvestism as the most vivid evidence that Eberhardt was "matter out of place," pollution, or dirt, in Mary Douglas's classic formulation,[64] but by animating the trope of displacement she reversed the paradigm. It is striking, for example, that the French journalist quoted above comments on the *cleanliness* of her garments.

When she participated in a desert *fantasia*, perhaps the only European woman to have done so, she described herself, tellingly, in a letter to her brother Augustin. For writing to this biological brother (who, though almost surely also the illegitimate child of Trophimowsky, had been given—unlike his sister—the "legitimate" family surname of de Moerder), Isabelle Eberhardt here triumphantly produces a family romance in which transvestite costume becomes the sign of recognition and decipherment. "You will see there," she wrote,

> a cavalier mounted on a fiery little horse, wearing a gandoura and white burnous, with a high white veiled turban, a black rosary around his neck, and his right hand bound with a red cloth to hold the bridle better, and it'll be Mahmoud Saadi, adoptive son of the Great White Sheikh, son of Sidi Brahim.[65]

* * *

THE EROTICS OF CULTURAL APPROPRIATION

In July 1972, James Morris, the noted British travel writer and foreign correspondent booked himself a round-trip ticket to Casablanca, where he would visit the clinic famous Dr. B—and undergo the surgery that transformed him from a man into a woman Morris had been approved for surgery at home, in England, at the Charing Cross Hospital in London. In the narrative of this transformation, *Conundrum*, the woman who is now Jan Morris explains that the London surgeon would have required that James Morris divorce his wife before undergoing the operation, and that Morris, although willing to get a divorce eventually, resisted doing so as a condition of his surgery.

It seems clear, however, that for Morris, who had journeyed so extensively in Africa, North and South, Casablanca was a special, liminal place, the geographic counterpart of his/her psychological and physiological condition. S/he required a more exotic setting than Charing Cross for this most exotic of crossings. "I sometimes heard the limpid Arab music, and smelt the pungent Arab smells, that had for so long pervaded my life, and I could suppose [Casablanca] to be some city of fable, of phoenix and fantasy, in which transubstantiations were regularly effected, when the omens were right and the moon in its proper phase."[72]

For Renée Richards, another transsexual who traveled to Casablanca for the surgery the city's exoticism evoked an opposite response; twice Richards, at that point still a man, went to the door of the Casablanca clinic, this "fantasy place" whose address he had long known by heart, and twice he left without entering (Richards, 246). When Dr. Raskin finally had the operation it was at home, in New York, on familiar ground. But for Jan Morris the lure of Casablanca was part of the process of transformation.

In the long period of probation before his surgery, when he took female hormones to change the contours and chemistry of his body, Morris imagined his indeterminate gender identity as a veil. "I first allowed my unreality to act as its own cloak around me, she writes, "or more appositely perhaps as the veil of a Muslim woman, which protects her from so many nuisances, and allows her to be at her best or her worst inside" (Morris 113). For her, cross-gender is also imagined as cross-culture. What she describes as "our pilgrimage to "Casablanca" (Morris, 172; where the plural denotes "mine and that of other transsexuals," but the implication of "James's and Jan's" remains latently powerful) is a literalization of a cultural fantasy that played itself out in cross-dressing as well as in homo- and bisexual relations between East and West, European and Arab.

"Paradoxically," writes Elizabeth Wilson in her book *Adorned in Dreams*, "in Islamic cultures women wear trousers and men robes."[73] The paradox, of course, is seen through Western eyes; it is likely that Western dress conventions seem equally paradoxical when viewed from some vantage points in Kabul or Algiers. Nonetheless, this simple reversal of expectation has enabled, in that part of the world often called the West (in practice, certain regions of Western Europe and North America), a wide range of transvestic practices and behaviors, from disguise to drag, from passing to protest.

That Jan Morris's pilgrimage should have as its ultimate destination not the heights of Eastern exoticism but a "flat in Bath" (Morris, 156) underscores the fundamentally ideological nature of the "conundrum" which she describes in biographical and biological terms. Morris is only exotic, magical, set apart, in the middle stages of the journey, as neither man nor woman, when the hormones have arrested and even reversed signs of age, have produced the illusion of a kind of Fountain of Youth or Shangri-La. Once transformed, returned from Casablanca, Morris no longer inhabits that exhilarating no man's land. The biological clock, its works tinkered with but replaced, begins again to tick, and Morris finds herself, to her delight, transformed into a middle-aged suburban matron, who "wear[s] the body of a woman" (Morris, 159).

What seems so striking to me, though, is that James Morris sought to realize his dream in Casablanca. Transsexualism here presents itself as a literalization of the Western fantasy of the transvestic, pan-sexualized Middle East, a place of liminality and change.

APPOINTMENT IN MOROCCO

There is, in fact, more than a little appropriateness to the fact that Marlene Dietrich's signature costume of top hat and tails, the costume that signifies cross-dressing not only for her, in her own subsequent films and performances, but also for the legions of female impersonators who have since "done Dietrich" in drag, made its first appearance in a film called *Morocco*. Why cross-dressing in Morocco? Because the one was already, in European as in North American eyes, the figure for the other. Araby was the site of transvestism as escape and rupture.

Joseph von Sternberg's 1930 classic is the scene of multiple transvestic motifs—motifs that insistently put the sartorial rhetoric of gender in question. Dietrich, as the nightclub singer Amy Jolly, elegantly attired in her men's clothes, casually leans down to kiss a woman in the audience on the lips, and then reappears for her next stage turn dressed "as a woman," in a bathing suit and a feather boa. Her nightclub act is introduced by a bumbling male impresario in formal dress sporting a large hoop earring. Gary Cooper, as legionnaire hero Tom Brown, tucks a rose—Dietrich's gift to him—behind his ear. The master of ceremonies in his tuxedo begins to look like a drag version of Dietrich. So—although in a different tonal register—does Adolph Menjou when he comes to her dressing room in white tie and tails. The question of an "original" or "natural" cultural category of gender semiotics here is immediately put *out* of question. There is in the nightclub in Morocco nothing *but* gender parody.

The apparition of a woman in men's formal clothes (a spectacle that makes it clear that such "civilized" dress is *always* in quotation, no matter who wears it) is in this landmark film combined with a place, Morocco, and an object of clothing, the veil, that together constitute an interposition or disruption. The veil is to clothing what the curtain is to the theater. It simultaneously reveals and conceals, marking a space of transgression and expectation; it leads the spectator to "fantasize about 'the real thing' in anticipation of seeing it."[74]

The veil as a sign of the female or the feminine has a long history in Western culture, whether its context is religious chastity (the nun, the bride, the orthodox Muslim woman) or erotic play (the Dance of the Seven Veils). But presuppositions about the gendered function of the veil—that it is worn to mystify, to tantalize, to sacralize, to protect or put out of bounds—are susceptible to cultural misprision as well as to fetishization. Thus a German ethnologist who traveled for six months with the Tuareg of the North African desert felt called upon to report that there was "nothing effeminate about these Tuareg nobles…on the contrary, they are shrewd, ruthless men with a look of cold brutality in their eyes."[75] Although the Tuareg were known as fierce warriors, the fact that their men wore veils at all times while Tuareg women freely showed their faces was clearly a puzzle. The men's eyes, however, were still visible through a slit in the veil, and could be construed, at least by those who expected or hoped to find such a thing, as showing "cold brutality"—in other words, manliness. This Eurocentric obsession with the veil as female—with what is veiled as "woman"—is established early in *Morocco* as itself a mystification and a coded sign.

At the beginning of the film Arab women unveil themselves flirtatiously at Gary Cooper from the tops of city buildings. On shipboard en route from Europe Dietrich wears a fashionable *Western* veil of sheer black netting attached to a perky black hat, before making her appearance in male formal dress. Her sexual rival, the wife of the adjutant (superbly named "Madame Caesar" although—or because—she is emphatically *not* above suspicion), disguises herself in a Moroccan robe and veil in order to pursue Cooper. The distinction between the two women is both gendered and nationalized, though Madame Caesar's "Arab" costume is manifestly a kind of adventurer's fancy-dress, a colonial appropriation, not an acknowledgment of cross-national (or cross-racial) sisterhood. In the famous final scene, kicking off her sandals and tying her stylish neck-scarf around her head like a peasant kerchief, Dietrich joins the Arab women in the trek across the desert. Class markers are thus tied both to gender and to race; Dietrich "descends" from upper-class white tie and tails—the sign of the male, the aristocrat, or the high-style lesbian—to the status of a native camp follower. But what is most striking is the way in which von Sternberg's film puts the signification of gender in question, and does so in a particular locale.

Thus, in von Sternberg's *Morocco*, the "Foreign Legion," that colonial fantasy of amnesic brotherhood in which a recruit is permitted to put his past under erasure, is another version of this medial space. And so too is the boat that brings "Amy Jolly," the quintessential *jolie amie*, to Casablanca. That Amy Jolly's journey is twinned historically with Dietrich's (and von Sternberg's) passage from Germany to Beverly Hills underscores the transitional moment marked and encoded in the film. For Hollywood *was* Morocco, *was* Casablanca, as cross-dressing itself became, in the years that followed, nothing less than the radical of representation in film.

In cinematic representation the word "film" interposes itself, *like* a veil, as a space of multiple meaning: membrane or covering; photographic transparency; motion picture. The veil is a film, the film is a veil. What is disclosed *is* what is concealed—that is, the fact of concealment.

Here it is useful to recall not only Jacques Lacan's figure of the veil as a sign of latency,[76] but also the observations of Heinz Kohut, the pioneer theorist of narcissism, on theater and reality. Kohut notes that people "whose reality sense is insecure" resist abandoning themselves to artistic experiences because they cannot easily draw a line: "They must protect themselves, e.g., by telling themselves that what they are watching is 'only' theater, 'only' a play." So too with the analysand; only analysands "whose sense of their reality is comparatively intact will…allow themselves the requisite regression in the service of the analysis"—a regression that "takes place spontaneously, as it does in the theater."[77] This fear of blurring the line, of not being able to distinguish "reality" from "theater," this susceptibility to fantasy—to *cultural* as well as to intra-psychic fantasy—is, precisely, the stage (stage in both senses, both the process and the playing space) of the transvestite.

* * *

MAN AND OMAN

I want to conclude this articulation of an abiding cultural fantasy and its effects by taking note of at least one Middle Eastern society in which cross-dressing has played a crucial defining role. As will be clear shortly, my interest in the Omani *xanith* is not so much in determining the precise social function this personage performs for his own culture as in the ways the *xanith* has recently come to signify something particular in, and for, a discourse of "third gender" roles in the United States and in Britain.

The association of the Middle East with transvestism and sexual deviance, and particularly with male homosexuality, reached what might be thought of as a theoretically inevitable stage with the discovery by an anthropologist, in 1977, of an Arabic culture that seemed to institutionalize the transsexual male as a third gender role. Writing in the British anthropological journal *Man*, Unni Wikan described the *xanith* of coastal Oman, effeminate males who wore pastel-colored *dishdashas*, walked with swaying gait and "reeked of perfume," who functioned as house servants and/or homosexual prostitutes, and who associated on most formal and informal occasions not with the men in this rigidly segregated Muslim society, but with the women. At a wedding Wikan observed *xanith* singing with the women, eating with them, even entering the bride's seclusion chamber and peeping behind her veil.

Wikan identified these *xanith* as "transsexuals," a term she defined as "a socially acknowledged role pattern whereby a person acts and is classified as if he/she were a person of the opposite sex for a number of crucial purposes." (This definition, which she attributed to Drs. Harry Benjamin and Robert Stoller, was later to be one of many points on which she was challenged.) The transsexuals of this Omani society—which she located in and around the small coastal town of Sohar, "reputed home of Sinbad the Sailor"—occupied, said Wikan, an intermediate role between men and women, a third position that was clearly demarcated by their dress.

> The transsexual . . . is not allowed to wear the mask [which covers forehead, cheeks, nose, and lips of Omani women from about the age of 13], or other female clothing. His clothes are intermediate between male and female; he wears the ankle-length tunic of the male, but with the tight waist of the female dress. Male clothing is white, females wear patterned cloth in bright colours, and transsexuals wear unpatterned co-loured clothes. Men cut their hair short, women wear theirs long, the transsexuals medium long. Men comb their hair backward away from the face, women comb theirs diagonally forward from a central parting, transsexuals comb theirs forward from a sideparting, and they oil it heavily in the style of women. Both men and women cover their head, transsexuals go bareheaded. Perfume is used by both sexes, especially at festive occasions and during intercourse. The transsexual is generally heavily perfumed, and uses much make-up to draw attention to himself. This is also achieved by his affected swaying gait, emphasized by the close-fitting garments. His sweet falsetto voice and facial expressions and movements also closely mimic those of women.[100]

The transsexuals in Omani society, unlike women, according to Wikan, are deemed capable of representing themselves in a legal capacity; juridically, they are men, as they are grammatically, be-ing referred to in the masculine gender. They are punished if they attempt to wear women's clothes. *Xanith*, biologically male, serve as passive homosexual prostitutes. If they wish to and can afford to, however, they may marry, and if they succeed in "perform[ing] intercourse in the male role"

(Wikan, 308), and giving the traditional proof of defloration of the bride, they cease to be *xanith* and become men.

Thus Wikan suggests that it is the sexual act, and not the sexual organs, that defines gender in the society. Should he wish to, a *xanith* who has married may return to his former status, as some older *xanith*, once widowed, sometimes do; this change he signals by a public action (like singing at a wedding) that declares him to be no longer a man. The *xanith* can continue throughout his life to change from the role of "woman" to that of "man." Wikan explains the social necessity of this third gender role by the high standard of purity imposed upon Omani women; prostitutes are necessary, though held in low repute. *Xanith* are often "sexual deviants," who are attracted to their own sex; this the society accepts, though it does not approve. The Omani system thus protects women, while severely restricting their freedoms, and accommodates sexual variation as well as male sexual appetite by establishing a triad of gender roles, woman, man, and transsexual. About one in fifty males in Sohar become *xanith*.

The appearance of Wikan's article in the pages of *Man*—a journal whose complacent nineteenth-century title lent an unacknowledged irony to the succeeding exchanges—led to immediate and heated debate. The situation of the *xanith*, it was suggested by one scholar, was more likely the result of economic than of innate gender characteristics; a "man" is one who has the wherewithal to buy "himself" a bride—something, for example, that "dominant lesbian women" in a similar society of Muslims in Mombasa, Kenya, had perceived, choosing to have dependents rather than to be one. Poverty, not the demands of the male role, might be the cause of the *xanith*'s lifestyle.[101] Another correspondent accused Wikan of being "doggedly ethnocentric," and ignoring comparative materials from other cultures in order to make a claim for singularity in the case of the *xanith*. Citing articles on transsexuals in Aden, Australia, and Polynesia, as well as in the streets of Naples and Sydney, he urged anthropologists to come out of the closet and study the scene around them in the major cities of the West.[102]

Wikan retorted sharply, again in *Man*, flinging the charge of ethnocentrism back at her first critic; the argument that marriage creates an inequality in the status of women vis-à-vis men is "nothing less than straightforward and fashionable ethnocentricity," she declared. Indeed this epithet, which is clearly the worst possible insult to an anthropologist, surfaced yet again in Wikan's stinging reply to a *second* letter from the same critic ("less readiness to reshape…reality with ethnocentric—or Mombasa—concepts would protect her from pursing so many odd and fruitless tangents").[103] Citing the British explorer Richard Burton on the subject of pederasty among the Arabs and faulting Wikan for "assuming that in a sex act between men one partner is always a substitute woman," Gill Shepherd of the London School of Economics again contended that Wikan was overemphasizing gender and ignoring economic and class factors.

The controversy continued to occupy *Man* and its readers. A further pair of correspondents queried Wikan's use of the term "Oman"—which covers a wide variety of communities, all different from one another—suggested that (presumably like Margaret Mead) she "may possibly have been misled by her female informants," and challenged the notion of "intermediate gender" in particular and the role analysis mode of theorization in general.[104] And another writer challenged Wikan's use of the term "transsexual," pointing out that her definition (given above) differed sharply from Stoller's description of transsexuals as those who "contend from earliest childhood that they are really members of the opposite sex." "Anthropologists," the writer asserted, "would perhaps be better off just using ethnic labels in the analysis of cross-gender and sexual behaviour in other societies. Sufficient cross-cultural data are not yet available to make sound judgements as to how well Western *clinical* categories fit these behaviours in non-Western societies."[105]

This, in point of fact, seems to be not only a key problem in Wikan's argument but also a key factor raising the temperature (and the stakes) in the exchange that it provoked. How possible is it to take a term like "transsexual," coined in 1949 to describe the condition of certain European and Anglo-American men, and translate it back into a culture which had been closed to the outside world (by Wikan's account) until 1971? What are the *ideological* and *political* implications of this cross-cultural labeling, and what if anything does it have to do with the constructed role of the Middle East itself as an "intermediate" zone, a place where pederasty, homosexuality, and transsexualism are all perceived (by Western observers) as viable options? If a Shangri-La for transsexualism as a "natural" development, a "third gender role" crucial to the social economy, were to be discovered *anywhere*, we should not perhaps be surprised to find that it is located in Oman, in the "reputed home of Sinbad the Sailor."

Nor should we be surprised that, whatever the methodological shortcomings of Wikan's research, or the unexamined implications discerned in it by feminists, Marxists, or comparative anthropologists, her argument for the *xanith* should be welcomed, uncritically, by another interested group; the editors, and presumably the readers, of *TV-TS Tapestry: The Journal for Persons Interested in Crossdressing and Transsexualism*. An article by "Nancy A.," entitled "Other Old Time Religions," cites Wikan's research extensively and straightforwardly, describing the dress and customs of the *xanith in Omani* society, and noting as well other transvestite or transsexual societies mentioned by Wikan or her various correspondents: the *berdache* of the Plains Indians, virtually the locus classicus of transsexualism in anthropology, and inevitably mentioned in survey studies of cross-dressing;[106] the *mahu* of Tahiti, who serves as a symbolic marker in his village, against which men can define their own role ("Since I am not the '*mahu*,' I must be a man," as Nancy A. puts it, though her source in the pages of *Man* is less liberally inclined; *his* imagined Tahitian villager says to himself, "this is what I am not and what I must not become"[107]).

At one point, after noting that *xanith* who wear women's clothes are imprisoned and flogged, the author comments in a somewhat wistful parenthesis "(I guess it's not so great after all)"—a reminder that "Nancy A." herself is a male-to-female cross-dresser. The final paragraph makes it clear that the *xanith* and the *mahu* are for *Tapestry*'s readers nothing less than role models, examples of societies in which the cross-dresser and transsexual have a crucial defining place. "I'm not sure," she concludes, "if these examples tempt you to fly to Tahiti or Oman . . . but at least you can see other societies' responses to a common phenomenon. Although we can't be as open as we would like, we can get out and help others understand and be more accepting. We have no clearly defined role, set rigidly in the society we live in, as do the others we have mentioned, so we have to make our own way."

Nancy A.'s article manifestly illustrates many of the dangers warned against by Unni Wikan's critics. Obviously a lay commentary and an unsophisticated one at that, completely unscholarly in style and method, it generalizes with unwarranted broadness and collapses distinctions that the warring anthropologists on the battlefields of *Man* are at great, and important, pains to draw. The ultimate epithet, "ethnocentric," could again be deployed against it, if so big a club is needed to swat so small a fly. Yet the very ethnocentricity of the piece is its political strength. Nancy A. espouses what might be described as an ethnocentric pluralism. The *xanith*, the *berdache*, and the *mahu* are her brothers—or her sisters. Her aims are frankly political and oppositional, her subject position as social marginal is her license to generalize and indeed to omit what does no suit her purposes. For example, she takes the title of Wikan's article, "Man Becomes Woman: Transsexualism in Oman as a Key to Gender Roles," and masterfully abbreviates it, in the manner of the *National Enquirer*, as "Man Becomes Woman," so that she can say, without overt irony, that Unni Wikan notes such-and-such "in her article, 'Man Becomes Woman' in the anthropological journal *Man*." This is a tour-de-force of titles and gender roles, and if *Man* does not become *Woman* as a result of such efforts, perhaps it ought to. Certainly the kind of -centrism indicated by *Man*'s nineteenth-century title is at least a little decentered in the course of these exertions, and feminists who cavil about welcoming male-to-female transsexuals in their midst might take note of the effectiveness of an interested critique from a position so culturally disadvantaged ("we can't be as open as we would like") that it mandates outreach as a condition for existence ("we can get out and help others understand and be more accepting"; "we have to make our own way").

The strictly veiled, strictly masked, strictly segregated women of the Sohari region of Oman, Wikan reasoned, were the precondition for the development of the *xanith* role. Men needed sex, women needed companionship, both needed servants; the *xanith* needed money, or sex, or acceptance, or all of these. The triadic structure she suggested, and that came under such sharp attack in part because it did posit a social logic, a story of positions and positionality, is a cultural reading of a social phenomenon, a reading clearly influenced, whether before or after the fact, by Wikan's discovery of a clinical literature of transsexualism. This move did not fully satisfy either anthropologists or clinicians. But it provided a necessary template for transsexuals and transvestites themselves—*some* transsexuals and transvestites, U.S. transsexuals and transvestites, not the *xanith*—to analyze and interpret the possibilities and dignities of their own social role.

This is another side to Orientalism; more than one kind of Western subject looks East, and sees himself/herself already inscribed there. What, finally, does the controversy around *Man* and Oman have to do with "the chic of Araby"? The *xanith* provided an uncanny "role model" for some observers specifically concerned with gender dysphoria and gender roles, and offered yet one more extraordinary example of the complex ways in which some Westerners have looked East for role models and for deliberate cultural masquerade—for living metaphors that define, articulate, or underscore the contradictions and fantasies with which they live.

NOTES

1. In the Introduction to *Vested Interests*, Garber writes, "Many names have been given to this 'third sex' or 'third term'.... The 'third' is that which questions binary thinking and introduces crisis—a crisis which is symptomatized by *both* the overestimation *and* the underestimation of cross-dressing. But what is crucial here—and I can hardly underscore this strongly enough—is that the 'third term' is *not* a term. Much less is it a *sex*, certainly not an instantiated 'blurred' sex as signified by a term like 'androgyne' or 'hermaphrodite', although these words have culturally specific significance at certain historical moments. The 'third' is a mode of articulation, a way of describing a space of possibility. Three puts in question the idea of one: of identity, self-sufficiency, self-knowledge."
2. T.E. Lawrence, *Secret Dispatches from Arabia*, ed. Arnold Lawrence (London: Golden Cokrell Press, 1939), 37–38 (from *Arab Bulletin* 1, 32 [November 26, 1916], 482).
3. T.E. Lawrence. *Seven Pillars of Wisdom* (London: Jonathan Cape, 1935; rpt. Harmondsworth: Penguin Books, 1986), 129.
4. In a strong essay published after I had completed this chapter, Kaja Silverman also notes the telling detail of the wedding clothes, which she regards as an aspect of Lawrence's "double mimesis," his insertion of himself into the structural positions occupied by certain Arabs (like Feisal) who became ego ideals for him, and with whom he aligned his own "fantasmatic." "To wear [Feisal's wedding garments] is to be in a position to love that image of the Other's virility which has become the 'self' " (Silverman, 26). Where my reading of the white wedding costume differs from hers is in my sense that Lawrence (and by "Lawrence" I mean here, on the one hand, the author of *Seven Pillars*, and on the other, the protagonist of David Lean's film) could simultaneously regard himself as Feisal's "other" and as his *bride*. Silverman, whose chief interest is in the transformation of Lawrence's "reflexive masochism" into "feminine masochism" after the rape and beating incident at Der'a, does not see the early Lawrence of the Arabian campaign as "feminized." Yet, as I have been arguing, there is no necessary inconsistency between a hyper-virilized and a feminized position *from the point of view of the reader or viewer* regarding a cross-dressed subject. Silverman, "White Skin, Brown Masks: The Double Mimesis, or With Lawrence in Arabia," *differences* 1, 3 (Fall 1989), 3–54.
5. Richard Aldington, *Lawrence of Arabia: A Biographical Enquiry* (London: Collins, 1955), and, especially, the fine biography by John E. Mack, *A Prince of Our Disorder: The Life of T.E. Lawrence* (Boston: Little, Brown, 1976).
6. Searching his personal history for earlier beatings that might have given pleasure, Mack finds that it was Lawrence's mother, not his father, who beat him, since his father was apparently too tender-hearted to do so. But with his mother, who was in many ways as strong-willed as Lawrence himself, he enjoyed an extremely affectionate relationship, and seems to have had a relatively happy boyhood, despite the stain of illegitimacy that marked him and his four brothers. Indeed—and this is the point—he seems in some ways never to have progressed beyond boyhood into an adolescence of courtship and awakening sexuality, hetero- or homosexual. His adventures in the East, his archaeological researchers,

his remarkable success with the Arab revolt, were in a way a translation of his boyhood fascination with the medieval world, the crusades, and Richard I, the Lionhearted.

7. One of the major displacements in his life was, apparently, that of the sexual object . C.F.C. Beeson, a close friend in his years of adolescence, reports that Lawrence showed no interest in girls; Arnold Lawrence, T.E.'s youngest brother, claimed that he died a virgin (Mack, *A Prince*, 25; 67).

8. To Earnest Thurtle, *The Letters of T.E. Lawrence*, ed. David Garnett (London: Cape, 1938), p. 649. This droll reference to John Knox's *First Blast of the Trumpet against the Monstrous Regiment of Women* (1558), punning on the military sense of "regiment" as well as Knox's primary sense of "rule," is characteristic of Lawrence's deployment of his extraordinarily wide reading.

9. To James Hanley, 1931. *Letters of T.E. Lawrence*, 728.

10. Mack, *A Prince*, 20. Interview with Janet Laurie Hallsmith, March 25, 1965.

11. Letter to Vyvyan Richards, July 15, 1918. Malcolm Brown, *T.E. Lawrence, The Selected Letters* (New York: Norton, 1989), 149, 151.

12. Letter to Robert Graves, February 4, 1935, *Selected Letters*, 520.

13. Letter to E.M. Forster, June 17, 1925. *Selected Letters*, 283.

14. Letter to Greenhill, March 20, 1920. Humanities Research Center, University of Texas, Austin. Mack, *A Prince*, 277.

15. Letter to Miss Fareedah El Akle, January 3, 1921. *Selected Letters*, 183.

16. *American Heritage Dictionary* (Boston: Houghton Mifflin, 1973), 1193. The current fashion among TV newscasters to pronounce this world "shake" rather than "sheek" is not a correction of an earlier vulgar error on the part of American filmgoers, but—at least according to the dictionary—an alternative, and equally (but no more) correct pronunciation. That Dan Rather and others would rather say "shake" than "sheek," however, seems to me to suggest that they want to distance themselves, and today's Middle Eastern dignitaries, from the Hollywood image made so popular by Valentino.

17. *Exhibitors Trade Review*, November 19, 1921, 1763. There is a new star in heaven... Valentino: *Biographie, Filmographie, Essays*, ed. Eva Orbanz (Berlin: Verlag Volker Spiess, 1979).

18. Alexander Walker, *Rudolph Valentino* (London: elm Tree Books/Hamish Hamilton, 1976), 43-51, 110-23. On Valentino's life and films, see also Jack Scagnetti, *The Intimate Life of Rudolph Valentino* (New York: Jonathan David, 1975), 30–36, 106–18, 138–40; Noel Botham and Peter Donnelly, *Valentino: The Love God* (London: Everest Books, 1976), 70–75, 102–8, 194–206; Orbanz, *There is no star in heaven.*

19. For a valuable discussion of Valentino from the point of view of cinematic spectatorship, see Miriam Hansen, "Pleasure, Ambivalence, Identification: Valentino and Female Spectatorship," *Cinema Journal* 25, 4 (Summer 1986): 6–32. Hansen's article, which came to my attention after I had written the analyses of Valentino that appear both in this chapter and in Chapter 13, argues from a similar vantage point about his gender re-coding and the way it is inflected by class and race.

20. Virginia Woolf, *Orlando: A Biography* (1908) (London: Penguin, 1970), 108.

21. To Lady -----, Adrianopole, April 1, 1717. *Embassy to Constantinople: The Travels of Lady Mary Wortley Montagu.* ed Christopher Pick (London: Century Hutchinson, 1988), 97–98.

22. To Lady Mar, Adrianople, April 1, 1717. *Embassy to Constantinople*, 108–9.

23. Terry Castle, *Masquerade and Civilization: The Carnivalesque in Eighteenth Century Culture and Fiction.* (Stanford: Stanford University Press, 1986), 72–73.

24. Frank W. Wadsworth, "Hamlet and Iago: Nineteenth-Century Breeches Parts," *Shakespeare Quarterly* 17 (1966): 129–39.

25. Mary Edwards Walker, *Hit* (New York, 1871), 62–63.

26. *The London Journal of Flora Tristan, 1842, or The Aristocracy and the Working Class of England*, trans. Jean Hawkes (London: Virago, 1982), 58.

27. Prevesa, November 12, 1809. *Bryon's Letters and Journals*, ed. Leslie A. Marchand (Cambridge: Belknap Press of Harvard University Press, 1973–82), 1:228.

28. Hobhouse found the demonstration "beastly"; Byron's response, Crompton notes, is not recordered. Louis Crompton, *Bryon and Greek Love* (Berkeley: University of California Press, 1985), 143–44. Leslie A. Marchand, *Bryon: A Biography* (New York: Alfred A. Knopf, 1957), 1:243.

29. Isaac Disreali, *The Literary Character of Men of Genius*, 3rd. ed. (London: John Murray, 1822), 101–2.

30. John Hindley, *Persian Lyrics, or Scattered Poems from the Diwan-i-Hafiz* (London: E. Harding, J. Debrett, and West & Hughes, 1800), 33n.

31. The identity of "Thyrza," given Bryon's celebrity and reputation for amorous amplitude, was a subject of highly interested dispute; Lady Falkland, whom Byron had assisted financially but did not know, wrote him passionately asserting that she must be "Thyrza," and Byron's contemporary biographer, Thomas Moore, was at pains to describe Thyrza as not a real person at all, but a myth.

32. July 5, 1807. Marchand, *Bryon's Letters and Journals*, 1:124.

33. Byron, *The Letters and Journals*, ed. R.E. Prothero (London: John Murray, 1989), 2:116n.

34. R.C. Dallas, *Correspondence of Lord Byron with a Friend* (Paris: Galignani, 1825), 3,41–42. This and the previous quotation are cited by Crompton, to whose fascinating book on Byron's bisexuality and its political consequences I am much indebted.

35. *Medwin's Conversations of Lord Byron* (1824), ed. E. J. Lowell, Jr. (Princeton: Princeton University Press, 1966), 67. Crompton 110, 209, 243.

36. George Gordon, Lord Byron, *Don Juan*, ed. T.G. Steffan and W.W. Pratt (London: Penguin Books, 1987). Byron wrote to Henry Drury, "I see not much difference between ourselves and the Turks, save that we have foreskins and they have none—that they have long dresses and we short, and that we talk much and they little." May 3, 1810. Marchand, *Byron's Letters and Journals*, 1:238.

37. In an essay on cross-dressing and the politics of gender in *Don Juan* Susan Wolfson notes that Byron's relation to his own mother gives biographical plausibility to Juan's role as phallic woman, and observes that the real power of transvestite transformation lies in the other major transvestic figure in the poem, the woman cross-dressed as a man, the Duchess of Fitz-Fulke. "'Their She Condition': Cross-Dressing and the Politics of Gender in *Don Juan*," *ELH* 54,3 (Fall 1987): 611.

38. William Hazlitt, "Lord Byron," *The Spirit of the Age* (1925), reprinted in *The Complete Works of William Hazlitt*, ed. P.P. Howe, 21 vols. (London: J.M. Dent, 1930–34), 11:75.

39. 'The Tale of Kamarr al Zamamn," 216th Night. *The Book of the Thousand and One Nights and a Night*, trans. and annotated by Richard F. Burton (rpt. New York: Heritage Press, 1943), 2:1150–52.

40. "The Tale of Ali Shar and Zumurrud," 326th Night. Burton, *Nights*, 3:1475.

41. Vern L. Bullough, in *Sexual Variance in Society and History* (Chicago: University of Chicago Press, 1976), sees this as a probable echo of the mameluke period, "when the slave (*mameluke* means 'owned') who became the favorite of a ruling Sultan could expect to advance rapidly" (226).

42. Burton, "Terminal Essay," *Nights*.

43. Koran, trans. Mohammed Marmaduke Pichthall (New York: New American Library, 1953), 7 (The Heights): 25. Ali ibn Bakr, Burhan al-Din, al-Marghinani, *The Hedaya or Guide: A Commentary on the Mussulman Laws*, trans. Charles Hamilton, preface and index by Stanish Grove Grady, ed. (rpt. Lahore, West Pakistan: Premier Book House, 1957), 4:597 (Book 54, sec. 2).

44. The nineteenth-century Egyptologist William Edward Lane reported that boys about to undergo the rite of circumcision were dressed in girls' clothing. Among the Muslims of Egypt Lane describes females impersonators called *khawals*, "dancers" (and others, called *gink*, "a term that is Turkish, and had a vulgar signification which aptly expresses their character"), who wore their hair long and braided, plucked out the hair of their beards, applied kohl and henna to their eyes and hands in imitation of women, and danced to the accompaniment of castanets. Their costumes, "as if to prevent their being thought to be really females," were "partly male and partly female: it chiefly consists of a tight vest, a girdle, and a kind of petticoat." When walking in the streets, these men frequently veiled their faces, "not from shame, but merely to affect the manners of women." W.E. Lane, *Manners and Customs of the Modern Egyptians* (1860; rpt. London: Everyman's Library, 1963), 551, 388–89. Vern Bullough noted in 1976 that boys were still sometimes dressed as girls in Egypt to avoid the evil eye, since boys were thought more vulnerable to the "eye" than girls. *Sexual Variance*, 233.

45. Burton, "Terminal Essay," *Nights*.

46. Edward Rice, *Captain Sir Richard Francis Burton* (New York: Scribners', 1990), 181, 184.

47. Charles Montagu Doughty's *Arabia Deserta* chronicles Doughty's arduous trip through the Arabian peninsula in 1876–78. Doughty, an ardent Evangelical Christian, criticized Burton, and Burton's *Personal Narrative of a Pilgrimage to El-Medinah and Meccah*, for accepting Islam, and with it the comforts of Arab hospitality. Doughty's account records his suffering from the hardships of the desert, the heat, and the cruelty of the Bedawin.

48. E. Burgoyne, ed, *Gertrude Bell—From her personal papers* (London: E. Benn, 1958–61), 2:296–97.

49. Gertrude Bell, *The Desert and the Sown* (London: William Heinemann, 1907; rpt. Boston: Beacon Press, 1987), Preface (unpaged).

50. Sarah Graham-Brown, "Introduction" to Bell, *The Desert and the Sown*, ix.

51. Mel Gussow, "A Sexual Cover-Up in 'New Anatomies,'" *New York Times*, February 22, 1990.

52. Cited in Anne Kobak, *Isabelle: The Life of Isabelle Eberhardt* (New York: Alfred A. Knopf, 1989), 16.

53. Letter to *La Petite Gironde*, 1903. Kobak, *Isabelle*, 29.

54. Diary, January 18, 1900; quoted in Kobak, *Isabelle*, 33.

55. Christos Christidi, 1896; quoted in Kobak, *Isabelle*, 39.

56. J. Bonneval, January 1897; quoted in Kobak, *Isabelle*, 43.

57. Mme. Casson, quoted in Kobak, *Isabelle*, 49.

58. Recall the advice of *Information for the Female-to-Male Crossdresser and Transsexual*, 2nd ed. (San Francisco: L. Sullivan, 1985), 24.

59. Ahmed Rachid, letter to Eberhardt, July 5, 1898, quoted in Kobak, *Isabelle*, 71.

60. *The Passionate Nomad: The Diary of Isabelle Eberhardt*, trans. Nina de Voogd (Boston: Beacon Press, 1987), 53.

61. Sigmund Freud, *The Interpretation of Dreams* (1900), *SE* 4: 307.

62. Jacques Lacan, "The Agency of the Letter in the Unconscious, or Reason Since Freud," *Ecrits*, trans. Alan Sheridan (New York: W.W. Norton, 1977), 167.

63. Robert Randau, *Notes et souvenirs* (Algiers: Charlot, 1945), quoted in Kobak, *Isabelle*, 195.

64. General Herbert Lyautey, letter to Victore Barrucand. Quoted in Kobak, *Isabelle*, 212.

65. Mary Douglas, *Purity and Danger* (London: Routledge and Kegan Paul, 1966), 40.

66. Letter to Augustin de Moerder, November, 1900, quoted in Kobak, *Isabelle*, 139–40.

67. Michael Vieuchange, *Smara: Chez Les Dissident du Sud Marocain et du Rio de Oro*, ed. and introduction by Jean Vieuchange (Paris: Librairie Plon, 1932), xxi. Translated by Fletcher Allen, *Smara: The Forbidden City* (New York: E.P. Dutton, 1932; rpt. New York: Ecco Press, 1987).

68. I was very anxious to take a photograph of Al. Akhsas, probably never photographed before. I made a first effort; but,

once up, and having the three men around me, they suddenly became afraid [that his identity might be detected] and forced me to sit again. So I sat down and waited for half an hour. Them I fixed two pins so that my blue veil would not move, and I could operate beneath it without being seen…for the second time, Larbi and El Mahmoul presses so much against me, jostling me, that the shutter worked before I was ready. It was the last on the spool, so there was no remedy…bad night…I took a considerable risk trying to get that photograph, and I misfired. I should have been so glad to get it. (*Smara*, 44).

69.   Rhea Talley Stewart, "Afghanistan Lifted the Veil Decades Ago," *New York Times*, May 22, 1989, A16.

70.   Paul Bowles, *The Sheltering Sky* (New York: Vintage Books, 1949; 1990). In the scene of transvestic transformation, Kit pulls on the "full soft trousers" and the "loose vests and the flowing robe" her lover provides for her "with growing delight," noting that "she looked astonishingly like an Arab boy" (290–91).

71.   Nancy Collins, "Winger on the Wild Side," *Vanity Fair*, October 1990, 194.

72.   Dr. George Burou. Morris's omission of suppression of "Dr. B—'s" surname, whether motivated by discretion of stylistic verve, makes the whole episode into a novelistic adventure with something or an eighteenth-century flavor.

73.   Jan Morris, *Conundrum: An Extraordinary Narrative of Transsexualism* (New York: Henry Holt and Company, 1974;1986), 136. Renée Richards, with Jack Ames, *Second Serve* (New York: Stein and Day, 1983).

74.   Elizabeth Wilson, *Adorned in Dreams: Fashion and Modernity* (Berkeley: University of California Press, 1985), 162.

75.   Ludmilla Jodanova, *Sexual Visions: Images of Gender in Science and Medicine between the Eighteenth and Twentieth Centuries* (Madison: University of Wisconsin Press, 1989), 90.

76.   Peter Fuchs, *The Land of Veiled Men*, trans. Bice Fawcett (New York: Citadel Press, 1956), 49.

77.   Jacques Lacan, "The Signification of the Phallus," in *Ecrits: A Selection*, trans. Alan Sheridan (New York: W.W. Norton, 1977), 287–88.

78.   Heinz Kohut, *The Analysis of the Self* (Madison, Connecticut: International Universities Press, 1971; 1987), 210–11.

79.   For example, René Girard, "Scandal and the Dance: Salome in the Gospel of Mark," *New Literary History* 15, 2 (Winter 1984): 311–24, and in the same issue, Françoise Meltzer, "A Response to René Girard's Reading of Salome"; Linda Seidel, "Salome and the Canons," *Women's Studies* 2 (1984): 29–66; Françoise Meltzer, *Salome and the Dance of Writing: Portraits of Mimesis in Literature* (Chicago: University of Chicago Press, 1987), 13–46.

80.   Huysmans's Des Esseintes finds in Salome "the symbolic incarnation of undying Lust, the Goddess of Immortal Hysteria,…the monstrous Beast, indifferent, irresponsible, insensible." Joris-Karl Huysmans, *A Rebours*. Translated as *Against Nature* by Robert Baldick (Baltimore: Penguin, 1959), 66.

81.   Françoise Meltzer, *Salome and the Dance of Writing*, 46.

82.   In a passage that has been allusively linked to Salome, describing the power of Dance upon the spectator, Mallarmé makes the connection between femininity and textuality explicit, while retaining the emphasis upon the poet as gazing subject and the dancer as "illiterate" (*illettrée*), "unconscious" (*inconsciente*) object of the gaze, who becomes the catalyst for the male poet's creativity:

par un commerce dont paraît son sourire verser le secret, sans tarder elle te livre à traverse le voile dernier qui toujours reste, la nudité de tes concepts et silencieusment écrira ta vision à la façon d'un Signe, qu'elle est.

[through a commerce whose secret her smile appears to pour out, without delay she delivers up to you through the ultimate veil that always remains, he nudity of your concepts and silently begins to write your vision in the manner of a Sign, which she is.]

Steohane Mallarmé, *Oeuvres completes* (Paris: Pleiade, 1946), 307. Translated by Barbara Johnson, in her essay, "Les Fleurs du Mal Armé: Some Reflections on Intertextuality," *A World of Difference* (Baltimore: the Johns Hopkins University Press, 1987), 127.

83.   Edward Said, *Orientalism* (New York: Vintage Books, 1978), 187.

84.   Joseph A. Boone, "Mappings of Male Desire in Durrell's *Alexandria Quartet*," *South Atlantic Quartley* 88, 1 (Winter 1989): 81.

85.   Gustave Flaubert, *Flaubert in Egypt: A Sensibility of Tour*, ed. and trans. Francis Steegmuller (London: Bodley Head, 1972), 39.

86.   Oscar Wilde, Salome, *A Tragedy in One Act*, trans. Alfred Douglas (New York: Dover Publications, 1967), 64.

87.   Richard Ellmann, *Oscar Wilde* (New York: Alfred A. Knopf, 1988), 344.

88.   Russell's film is clearly indebted to the earlier Alla Nazimova silent film version of Wilde's play, a clear case of camp *avant la lettre*.

89.   Lacan, "The Signification of the Phallus," 287.

90.   Cornelia Otis Skinner, *Madame Sarah* (New York: Paragon House, 1966) 63, 123–23, 260-70. Ellmann, *Oscar Wilde*, 371. After his arrest in 1895 Wilde sent a friend to ask her to assist him by paying four hundred pounds for the rights to *Salome*, but although she expressed sympathy, she delayed and did nothing. Ellmann, *Oscar Wilde*, 458; Skinner, *Madame Sarah*, 123–24.

91.   [Walford] Graham Robertson, *Time Was: The Reminiscences of W. Graham Robertson* (London, 1931; New York: Quartet Books, 1981), 125–27. Ellmann, *Oscar Wilde*, 372.

92.   The "typical response" to Bev Francis's body, according to *Newsweek*, was "that *can't* be a woman." Charles Leerhsen and Pamela Abramson, "The New Flex Appeal," *Newsweek*, May 6, 1985, 82. See also Laurie Schulze, "On the Muscle," in *Fabrications: Costume and the Female Body* (New York: Routledge, 1990), 59–78.

93.   Ernest Jones, *The Life and Work of Sigmund Freud*. Edited and abridged in one volume by Lionel Trilling and Steven Marcus (New York: Basic Books, 1961), 377.

94. Angela Livingstone, *Salomé, Her Life and Work* (Mt. Kisco, New York: Moyer Bell, 1984), 18.

95. Sigmund Freud, "Lou Andreas-Salomé" (1937), trans. James Strachey. *SE* 23:297.

96. Peter Gay, *Freud: A Life for Our Time* (New York: W.W. Norton, 1988; Doubleday Anchor, 1989), 193.

97. Letter to Freud, October 17, 1917, in Ernst Pfeiffer, ed., *Sigmund Freud and Lou Andreas-Salomé, Letters*, trans. Williams and Elaine Robson-Scott (New York: W.W. Norton, 1966), 66–67.

98. Letter to Freud, November 6, 1927. In Pfeiffer, *Letters*, 168.

99. Letter from Rilke to Lou Andreas-Salomé, 1898, quoted in Andrea Livingstone, *Salome, Her Life and Work*, 126.

100. Letter from Freud to Andreas-Salomé, November 10, 1912, Pfeiffer, *Letters*, 11.

101. Unni Wikan, "Man Becomes Woman: Transsexualism in Oman as Key to Gender Roles," *Man* NS 12 (1977): 307. Reprinted in a somewhat expanded form as "The *Xanith*: A Third Gender Role?" in Unni Wikan, *Behind the Veil in Arabia: Women in Oman* (Baltimore and London: The Johns Hopkins University Press, 1982), 168–86.

102. Gill Shepherd, "Transsexualism in Oman?" (letter), *Man* NS 13 (1978): 133–4.

103. Robert Brain, *Man* NS 13 (1978): 322–23.

104. Shepherd, "The Omani *xanith*," *Man* NS (1978), 663–71; Wikan, response, 667–71.

105. G. Feurstein and S. al-Marzooq, *Man* NS 13 (1978), 665–67.

106. J. M. Carrier, "The Omani *xanith* controversy," *Man* NS 15 (1980): 541–42.

107. For example, Peter Ackroyd, *Dressing Up* (New York: Simon and Schuster, 1979) 37. Ackroyd classifies the *berdaches* with Tahitian, Brazilian, Aztec and Inca tribal transvestites as members of an "honorary third sex" in a section of his book called "Transvestism Accepted." Nancy A., "Other Old Time Religions," *The TV-TS Tapestry Journal* 40: 70–72.

108. The example of the *mahu*, from Robert I. Levy, "The Community Function of Tahitian Male Transvestism: A Hypothesis," *Anthropological Quarterly* 44 (1971), 12–21, is cited in Brain's letter to *Man*.

46

Transgender Theory and Embodiment
The Risk of Racial Marginalization

KATRINA ROEN

IN THIS ARTICLE, FEMINIST SCHOLAR KATRINA ROEN takes the transgender theorizing of the 1990s to task for its noted blindness to issues of racial and ethnic difference, and she questions the extent to which transgender theory can be usefully applied in cross-cultural contexts.

Roen notes that transgender theorizing has launched a critical dialogue that productively reworks the limitations of early queer theory in dealing with questions of gender diversity, but she remains skeptical that current transgender theory, originating largely in the United States and Western Europe, is equipped to deal with the lived experiences of "gender liminal" individuals in non-Western cultures. The crux of Roen's concern is the extent to which the medicalized notions of bodily change known as "transsexualism" function, through the operations of colonization and modernization, to efface other cultural responses to gender liminality in colonized geographical locations.

Drawing specifically on her fieldwork among South Pacific Islanders, Roen offers various examples of indigenous frameworks for understanding embodied gender that do not correlate to Eurocentric transgender theorizing. She calls for a next generation of transgender scholarship that would pay greater attention to cultural and historical specificity, that would explicitly recognize race as well as gender as a significant component of embodied difference, and would resist making sweeping theoretical claims that marginalize non-Western experience.

INTRODUCTION

Queer theories have been variously criticised for their ethnocentrism (Hennessy, 1995; Goldman, 1996; Lee, 1996; Walters, 1996) and their lack of careful attention to the lived realities of transsexual and transgendered people (Namaste, 1996). In the course of this decade, a forum is being established through the publication of transgender theorists' work, where transgender theorists may rework 'queer'. But, how well does this reworking address concerns about ethnocentric theorising? Where are people of racial 'minorities' situated in queer and transgender theories? Despite the claims of inclusiveness of both transgender and queer writings, do perspectives of whiteness continue to resonate, largely unacknowledged, through transgender and queer theorising?

In this paper, I present a critique of the medicalisation of transsexuality which foregrounds cultural identity rather than gender identity. In doing this, I challenge concepts of queer and transgender, usually revered for their all-inclusiveness, as to how well they work cross-culturally. I illustrate the points made in this paper by drawing from interviews with gender liminal people (that is, people who live between genders, live as a third gender, or are undergoing a transgendering process) who live in

New Zealand and who belong to cultures indigenous to the South Pacific. Although I am basing my argument on details that apply to this specific geo-political context, the implications of this challenge to ethnocentrism in queer and transgender theorising extend well beyond the South Pacific.

Through this paper, I pose questions about the role of queer and transgender theories in providing discursive alternatives to western medical constructions of transsexuality. Because of the complex language that is required to discuss the intersections of these topics discussed here I ask you, the reader, to allow me some flexibility in my uses of the terms queer, trans, transpeople, transgender, and gender liminal.

I am reluctant to subsume Maaori [1] (indigenous New Zealand) transpeople within the same terminology as Pakeha [2] (white New Zealand) transpeople, especially in cases where there is obviously a desire to foreground Maaori political and cultural identities over (trans)gender identities, and where pursuing those Maaori political goals includes developing a critique of Pakeha conceptions of the relationship between sexed bodies and lived gender. Because I am loathe to simply refer to these Maaori people as transgendered, I employ the term used by some anthropologists working in this area: gender liminal (see Besnier, 1994, p. 287, for further explanation of this decision about terminology).

Throughout this paper, I tend to refer to 'race' rather than 'ethnicity'. The factors influencing this decision are discussed in Alice's (1991) article: *Whose Interests? Decolonising 'Race' and 'Ethnicity'*. Alice argues that while the term ethnicity:

> allows diversity, it...ignores the demands of indigenous peoples to recognise their *decolonised identities*. The problem is that 'ethnicity' denies the preference of some indigenous peoples to use a language of 'race' which legitimates their first-nation status, a status quite different from other 'ethnic' minorities. (p. 65)

It therefore seems more appropriate to write of 'race' rather than 'ethnicity' for a paper which challenges transgender and queer theorising to address questions of race, indigeneity, and colonisation. Despite this justification, I acknowledge problems with the term 'race' in that it, arguably, refers to a category which is entirely mutable and unidentifiable. This paper works from the understanding that it is necessary to work with (while critiquing) such problematic categories as 'race' and 'gender'.

Anthropological research documents numerous examples of non-western cultures where concepts of gender liminality are accommodated through available gender roles (e.g., Roscoe, 1987, 1991; Nanda, 1990; Besnier, 1994). The relationship between this aspect of anthropological study and research on transsexuality and transgenderism has complex implications for the various parties involved. On the one hand, a romanticised version of third-gender acceptance within non-western cultures can provide images of hope for transgendered people fighting gender oppression. Besnier (1994), critical of such romanticising of Polynesian acceptance of gender liminality, comments on the risk of assuming that gender-phobic attitudes are purely colonial phenomena. He writes: 'explaining violence against liminal individuals as the sole result of emergent modernity in the Pacific Islands presupposes a romanticized view of Polynesia that has no validity outside the western imagination' (p. 560, note 47).

On the other hand, through the processes of westernisation (via colonisation, it is now not uncommon for gender liminal persons to seek sex reassignment surgery even though they live within a cultural context where their gender liminality might formerly have been understood in terms of a gender role for which bodily change was not considered an issue. For some gender liminal people, however, it is important to maintain 'traditional' cultural values by resisting identification with (contemporary western) medical discourses on transsexuality. For other gender liminal people, particularly in contexts where little detailed historical information about sexuality and gender remains decades after colonisers' attempts at assimilation and annihilation, it is not simply a case of reclaiming cultural values around gender liminality, but of creating gendered ways of being that satisfy aspects of both racial and (trans)gendered politics.

TRANSGENDER THEORISING

Stryker (1994) outlines two strands of meaning associated with 'transgender'. The first, which she describes as the original meaning, refers to people who cross genders without seeking sex reassignment surgery. The second depicts transgender as a far more diverse and expansive umbrella term 'that refers to all identities or practices that cross over, cut across, move between or otherwise queer socially constructed sex/gender boundaries' (p. 251, note 2). Stryker claims some cultural diversity for transgender in explaining that it 'includes, but is not limited to, transsexuality, heterosexual transvestism, gay drag, butch lesbianism, and such non-European identities as the Native American berdache or the Indian Hijra' (p. 251, note 2). In the same essay, Stryker situates transsexuality as a 'culturally and historically specific transgender practice/identity through which a transgendered subject enters into a relationship with medical, psychotherapeutic, and juridical institutions in order to gain access to certain hormonal and surgical technologies for enacting and embodying itself' (pp. 251–252, note 2). In this paper, my working definition of 'transsexual' is similar to Stryker's, but I question how well 'transgender' might operate as the expansive and culturally diverse term Stryker describes.

Some transgender writings (e.g., Stone, 1991; Stryker, 1994; Prosser, 1998) offer inspiring readings of and challenges to medical constructions of transsexuality that prescribe possible modes of sexual embodiment, and that collaborate with legal institutions to selectively endorse certain gendered ways of being. These concerns about the medicalisation of transsexuality are held not only by transgenderists for whom gender may be highlighted relative to questions of racial politics. Some transpeople also seek to challenge medical approaches to transsexuality on the basis that these approaches represent a violation of cultural values and beliefs about the relationship between sexed embodiment and lived gender. Here, I will draw from three specific transgender texts and pose questions which resonate through the following discussion of the medicalisation of gender liminality among indigenous peoples of the South Pacific.

Sandy Stone's *Posttranssexual Manifesto* presents the possibility of subverting dominant discourses on gender which medical science endorses. Rather than being complicit in the discourses of 'the traditional gender frame', Stone argues that it is preferable to 'seize upon the textual violence inscribed in the transsexual body and turn it into a reconstructive force' (Stone, 1991, p. 295). She proposes that transsexuals who live to pass (and pass to live) be 'recruited' from their lives of invisibility where they strive to maintain 'plausible histories' to effect the growth of 'the genre of visible transsexuals' (p. 296). It is the deconstruction of the man/woman binary and the possibility of identifying visibly as transsexual, that Stone describes as posttranssexuality. For Stone, posttranssexuality provides a means of expanding the bounds of culturally intelligible gender.

Judith Halberstam, in *F2M: The Making of Female Masculinity*, poses a transgendered challenge to the concept of gender, describing gender as a fiction and a postmodern mixing and matching of body parts. In her writing about gender as a fiction, Halberstam breaks down the notion that there is any 'crossing' to be done in moving between/among genders. According to Halberstam, there are a number of ways in which we all—transsexual or otherwise—live this fiction. She writes: 'masculinity or femininity *may* be simulated by surgery, but they can also find other fictional forms like clothing or fantasy. Surgery is only one of many possibilities for remaking the gendered body' (Halberstam, 1994, p. 225). Halberstam defines her concept of 'gender fictions' as 'fictions of a body taking its own shape, a cut-up genre that mixes and matches body parts, sexual acts, and postmodern articulations of the impossibility of identity' (1994, p. 210).

It is through this notion of gender as a fiction, that Halberstam develops her argument about the concept of 'trans', and attempts to break down the barriers which put the 'trans' in 'transsexual'. Reflecting on Stone's *Posttranssexual Manifesto*, Halberstam writes: 'The *post* in posttranssexual demands...that we examine the strangeness of all gendered bodies, not only the transsexualized ones and that we rewrite the cultural fiction that divides a sex from a transsex, a gender from a transgender' (Halberstam, 1994, p. 226).

Susan Stryker takes up aspects of Stone's call for transsexual visibility, and Halberstam's claim about the 'strangeness of all gendered bodies', in her writing on transgender rage. Through the particularly emotive expression of her transgender rage that takes the form of an article published in 1994, Stryker performs a crafty reclaiming of monstrosity—a subversive identification with Frankenstein's monster— writing: 'As we rise up from the operating tables of our rebirth, we transsexuals are something more, and something other, than the creatures our makers intended us to be' (p. 242). Stryker is specifically concerned with the relationship between the motivations of medical science and transsexual agency, and uses the reclaiming of monstrosity as a means of affirming that it is possible to invest in medical processes of transsexing without being complicit in the maintenance of the gender binary. She also acknowledges the oppressive effects of medical science that 'seeks to contain and colonise the radical threat posed by a particular transgender strategy of resistance to the coerciveness of gender: physi- cal alteration of the genitals' (p. 244). Stryker argues that despite the conservative and normalizing motivations of medical science, there is no guarantee of 'the compliance of subjects thus embodied with the agenda that resulted in a transsexual means of embodiment' (p. 242).

Stryker's expression of transgender rage, with its specifically corporeal features, comes to a cre- scendo when she writes:

> Rage colors me as it presses in through the pores of my skin, soaking in until it becomes the blood that courses through my beating heart. It is a rage bred by the necessity of existing in external circumstances that work against my survival. (p. 244)

That she is coloured by rage is explicit. How she is coloured by race is not.

'TRANSGENDER' VOICES?

How might queer and transgender politics and theories work (or not work) for people whose primary political affiliation is with their racial or cultural identity group? In order to explore this question, I will draw on interviews with fa'afafine [3] (Samoan males who live as a 'third gender') and transsexuals conducted in New Zealand in 1996 as part of my doctoral research. Although the interviews were not focused primarily on questions of cultural identity or politics, I did seek research participants from a diverse range of cultural backgrounds, and some of these people talked about their politics and identities in ways which have prompted and informed the current discussion. The three inter- viewees whose voices will be heard here are: Don, a 45-year-old Samoan fa'afafine; Pat, a 32-year-old pre-operative female-to-male Maaori man; and Tania, a 36-year-old pre-operative male-to-female Maaori transsexual. (All names are pseudonyms chosen by the interviewer or the interviewee at the time of the interview. References to research participants as a 'man', a 'fa'afafine', and a 'transsexual' draw from those interviewees' own ways of describing themselves.)

Don provides an example of reclaiming a traditional sexuality/gender subject position which is very distinct from, but in some respects resembles, transgenderism. He talks about the importance of fa'afafine in Samoan culture, and how his own sense of self-esteem relates to being fa'afafine. To begin with, he describes the relationship between his Samoan and fa'afafine identities by saying: 'for me culture is always first and then sexuality', and 'any interaction I have with anybody, the two things I want them to find out about me is the fact that I'm Samoan first and foremost and... [secondly] that I'm fa'afafine'. In stating his priorities thus, Don sets himself in sharp relief to queer and transgender stances which often highlight gender and sexuality to the point of obscuring race altogether. Elaborating on this contrast Don describes how, to him, fa'afafine simply 'means like a woman', whereas:

> All the Palagi [4] [English] terms: gay, faggot, queer... [they're] awful... [Those terms] actually tell you how that society views that person. My culture just views it 'like a woman'. And it's like a special woman. It's a knowledgeable woman but recognised [as]... anatomically male. (Don, interviewed: May, 1996)

He describes being taught from an early age that to be fa'afafine was to be valued and respected, despite shifting to New Zealand as a child and having to learn that fa'afafine were far less tolerated there.

> I was never put down or anything... I grew up with this really arrogant opinion of myself: for some reason the world is rather special with me in it! Being fa'afafine was really special. Jesus, when I came to New Zealand that was soon cut out!... I remember my mother saying: 'You mustn't walk like that, Don'; I said: 'Why not?' [and she replied:] 'Well, they don't do that in New Zealand'. . . . That's something I never ever accepted. (Don, interviewed: May, 1996)

For Don, cultural identity precedes gender/sexuality identity in political importance, but the two are intrinsically linked: one does not make sense without the other.

Although he plays an active role in his local gaylesbitrans support networks, he is highly sceptical about the Palagi system of dividing and labeling sexualities and genders, preferring to espouse a more holistic approach. He is also critical of Palagi attempts to reclaim words such as queer, suggesting that this only reflects Palagi cultures' intolerant attitudes towards sexuality and gender variance. Don points out that the division-by-labels of sexuality and gender categories makes it hard to talk about concepts of fa'afafine and holism, for the language assumes categories which obscure the importance of the inclusivity of fa'afafine.

For Don, being fa'afafine does not imply dissatisfaction with sexed embodiment nor does it make specifications about partner-gender: fa'afafine is constructed across sexuality and gender. However, he echoes his elders in expressing concern about younger fa'afafine being attracted by the glamour and lifestyle of cities where they come to think of themselves more in terms of western transvestite and transsexual identities, rather than according to traditional understandings of fa'afafine. Some of these young fa'afafine opt for sex reassignment surgery. Don hastens to add that he is not simply opposed to sex reassignment surgery: he has some older fa'afafine friends who have waited years, ensuring that they are making the right decision, before going ahead with surgery. Nevertheless, he is concerned about the general westernization and subsequent degradation of fa'afafine identities, saying: 'I know of some of the traditional fa'afafines and each time I've gone back to Samoa it's always been the case "Oh gosh, we're being reduced to a... cock in a frock"'.

Don's willingness to accept that some of his fa'afafine friends seek sex reassignment surgery, accompanied by his concern for younger fa'afafine who are completely seduced by Palagi understandings of sexuality and gender, remind me of Besnier's comment: 'Further discussion of gender liminality in Polynesia cannot take place without locating the category in a specific historical context and must address its relationship to modernization and change' (1994, p. 328). To this I add that discussion of transgenderism would benefit from further consideration of the effects of westernisation on gender liminality: not for the sake of a simplistic reclaiming of a 'third gender' [5] status, but for the sake of contextualising transgender theorising with respect to cross-cultural understandings of gender as those understandings change over time.

Some aspects of Don's reclaiming fa'afafine as a highly esteemed way of being and challenging Palagi approaches to sexuality and gender seem to me to work along similar lines to queer and transgendered critiques of psycho-medical discourses on transsexuality. He describes fa'afafine as inclusive and expansive in a way that is reminiscent of some authors' descriptions of queer (Goldman, 1996; Walters, 1996). He describes fa'afafine as encompassing gender-crossing possibilities similar to those discussed by some transgender authors (e.g., Stryker, 1994). Given that there are these parallels between Don's discourse on fa'afafine ways of being and some queer and transgender discourses, how might they inform one another more fruitfully? How might queer be theorised to better take into account Don's perspective of putting culture first and gender/sexuality second? Must there be such a prioritising for issues of racism, homophobia and transphobia to be effectively combated?

Perhaps fa'afafine identities provide an example of a crossing that can be sanctioned (for Don, if not for all fa'afafine) because family ties and the knowledge of cultural history are still sufficiently intact. This is different in cultural contexts where such historical ties have been lost. As Besnier points out, with the possible exceptions of New Zealand and Hawai'i,

> Polynesian societies were generally not subjected to systematic annihilating efforts on the part of colonizing populations…[so w]hile North American berdache traditions died out with the contexts that supported them, the cultural setting in which Polynesian gender liminality is embedded never disappeared. (p. 559, note 36)

Therefore, how might Don's perspective on gender liminality differ from those of people for whom such historical, cultural connections have been largely lost? What recourse do these people have for reclaiming culturally specific understandings of gender crossing?

Some Maaori transpeople are attempting to map discursive pathways for the purpose of reclaiming both cultural and queer identities. They juggle Maaori and transgendered identities in their attempts to hold specific forms of racialised gender liminality in high esteem. Issues of specific concern are: the lack (or inaccessibility) of knowledges about pre-colonial concepts of gender and sexuality; the relative facility of accessing western psycho-medical discourses as ways of understanding experiences of gender liminality; the possible contradictions between medical and Maaori discourses on (transsexual) bodies; and the current power differential between Maaori and Pakeha which enables New Zealand laws (and therefore transsexuals' legal rights) to be dictated primarily by Pakeha (medical) understandings of sexed embodiment. According to New Zealand legislation at the time of writing this paper, it was possible for documentation relating to passports and marriage certificates to carry the post-transition gender marker (M or F) only after sex reassignment surgery had taken place (Alston, 1998a, b).

Tania provides an example of some of the dilemmas faced by Maaori gender liminal people. Whilst she is aware of queer and transgender critiques of compartmentalizing of gender and sexuality, and she has developed her own strident criticisms of the medicalisation of transsexuality, she finds it convenient at this early stage of her transition to use the idea of a 'transsexual' identity as somewhere to 'belong'. Like Stryker's monster, Tania is choosing to go through with medical procedures, while being critical of contemporary western conceptions of the body/psyche relationship upon which medicalised perspectives on transsexuality are based. On principle, she disagrees with the suggestion that she must have sex reassignment surgery to attain the legal rights of a woman, arguing that this reduces 'woman' to a vagina. In practice, she has decided to opt for sex reassignment surgery, a decision which she describes as relating partly to the current legal situation of non-operative transpeople in Aotearoa/New Zealand [6]. Tania finds it useful to think of sex reassignment surgery as a goal: something tangible to aim for.

Tania describes herself as moving in predominantly Maaori circles, and talks about Maaori women in general, and a Maaori male-to-female transgendered friend in particular, serving as role models in her development of her self as a woman. According to Tania, her transgendered friend appears to have been accepted by local Maaori insofar as she has authority as a woman during traditional gender-specific cultural rituals and practices. (Incidentally, this friend of Tania's is non-operative.) Tania talks about this person as very vocal and assertive in demanding acceptance as a woman within traditional Maaori contexts. Perhaps following her friend's lead, Tania has developed various arguments herself which validate her transsexuality and depend upon the assertion of her identity as Maaori. To explain this, she draws on the Maaori conception of identity as something which is never based in the individual alone but relates to the extended family (whaanau) and to genealogy (whakapapa). She argues that to deride her for being transsexual would be to denigrate her entire ancestral line: a far more risky and grave action than merely discriminating against an 'individual'.

Theorising transgender and queer more specifically to address race, indigenousness and colonisation might provide more discursive pathways for indigenous people struggling to live in gender liminal ways. For this purpose, it is vital to theorise queer so that it is more relevant and open to people for whom gender/sexuality identities come second to racial identities, and to theorise queer so that it is open to cross-cultural interpretations of the relationship between sexed embodiment and lived gender. By this means, the important work being done by transgenderists and queers who challenge medical definitions of sexualities and genders, may be accessible to a more racially diverse range of people who might otherwise find no recourse but to invest in medical discourses on transsexuality.

The other interviewee who talked about seeking ways to validate his Maaori identity and make sense of his gender liminal experiences is Pat. Unlike Tania, Pat invests strongly and relatively uncritically in medical discourses on transsexuality. He is concerned with 'paving the way' for others who try to access female-to-male surgery as well as wanting to pass in every possible way as a heterosexual man. Whilst thinking of himself as a heterosexual man and wishing to masculinize his body as much as possible, Pat does not quite go so far as to maintain at all costs the 'plausible history' described by Stone. He is willing to be publicly visible as trans in order to change people's attitudes, but wishes that he had simply been born 'in the right body' to start with. He repeated time and again how dissatisfied he is with his body, describing the enormous efforts he and his partner have made to access the medical services he wants. Both Pat and his partner explained their intense scepticism about the skills and attitudes of medical professionals in response to transsexuals, and said that it was important for them both to do as much research as they could to make sure that he was getting the best treatment possible.

The transgender rage which motivates Stryker to subvert medical discourses, for Pat is directed towards taking as much control over the medical process as possible: ensuring that he progresses as speedily and safely as possible towards the imagined 'male' body. Having been on hormones for some time, Pat is concerned about the effects of having hormones without surgery, suggesting that 'getting testosterone pumped into your body every three weeks' but 'missing the main part...[that] I should have been born with it in the first place' is only adding to his sense of not being fulfilled. For Pat, there is no room for ambiguity and therefore medical discourses suit his purposes well—if only the surgery he wants becomes available to him.

From being adopted and growing up in a family where there was little chance of developing pride in his cultural heritage, Pat has found a niche where both his Maaori and his transgender identities can be respected and valued, though he sees himself ultimately moving toward just being a heterosexual man.

The area of Pat's life where he describes most enthusiastically the meeting of his trans and Maaori identities is in the kapa haka (cultural performance) group to which he belongs. When he and his partner initially joined this group they were received unquestioningly as a heterosexual couple by the other group members, many of whom were gay men and women and 'queens'. As Pat describes it, he eventually became tired of the queens always taking centre-stage and decided to out himself as trans. In his words: 'everybody loves the queens...and here I am amongst all these queens and [eventually, I say] "OK, OK, you're queens, I'm King!"'. Upon realising that Pat, too, was trans, one of the queens who is skilled in Maaori tattoo art designed some tattoos to be drawn over his mastectomy scars for performances during which he and the other men are topless.

In Pat's talk about his life, there is a tension between the simultaneous honouring of his Maaori and trans identities, and his striving towards simply being a heterosexual man (which he perceives to be achievable only through medical means). The only time Pat talked about transgender identity as something to be held in high esteem was when he talked about it in conjunction with his Maaori identity in the context of the kapa haka group. However, he spent a great deal of the interview talking about his frustration with medical professionals, his disappointment about the inaccessibility of the surgery he would like to have, and his desire to pass in all aspects of life as a heterosexual man. Unlike Halberstam, Pat neither embraces the idea of gender as a fiction nor wishes to live with his current mixing and matching of body parts. Unlike Stryker's monster, Pat does not imagine himself rising from an operating table having found a way to be other than a medically constructed transsexual, or a conservatively defined heterosexual male.

If more [strong and healthy] images of Maaori gender liminal people were available to Pat, how might his relationship to medical discourses on transsexuality be different? How can Pat's sense of dissatisfaction with his body and frustration with medical processes be contrasted with Tania's critical investment in medical discourses and Don's complete distancing from western understandings of the relationship between sexed anatomy and lived gender? What other discursive means might Maaori gender liminal people employ to challenge the corporeal colonisation that is transsexuality? How can queer and trans academics and activists work race into theorising without making simplistic assumptions about indigenous cultures who can call on 'third gender' traditions, but by making queer theorising useful to indigenous people who seek culturally appropriate alternatives to medical discourses on transsexuality?

For Pat, becoming comfortable with his body, and with himself, may well mean reclaiming his cultural identity (hence the importance of the kapa haka group to him). In reclaiming his Maaori identity while striving to fit into the medical requirements for sex reassignment surgery, he is straddling two worlds that are potentially at odds with one another. If transgender theories were more inclusive of racialised Others, then Pat might be able to reclaim his cultural identity while reclaiming his (trans)gender identity, without having to straddle two conflicting worlds.

Transgender theorising offers important critiques of restrictive ways of understanding gender. Those critiques are necessarily culturally specific. In this paper, I seek to alert readers to the danger of championing transgenderism as offering cross-culturally applicable challenges to the medicalisation of transsexuality. I also present a discussion of empirical research that challenges the fantasy of the acceptance of gender liminality among indigenous Pacific peoples and that contributes a racialised component to transgenderists' descriptions of sex reassignment surgery as corporeal colonisation.

CONCLUSION

If we review transgender writings through lenses that disallow racial identity to be [completely obscured by the passionate outpourings of transgender rage,] how might transgender theorising come to 'look' different? If we think of colonisation as a process of rendering racialised bodies monstrous, how might we approach differently the reclaiming of transsexual bodies as monstrous? How might the postmodern strategy of mixing and matching of body parts be differentially available with regard to racialised bodies? How might investing in aspects of current transgender discourse amount to complicity with the colonising culture of which medical discourses are only a small part? How can transgender theorising be critical of its own racialised politics in a way that is productive for those who place race first and gender second? Perhaps Pat, performing topless in the kapa haka group—mastectomy scars overlaid with Maaori tattoo art—provides an illustration of how transgender and racial politics do not need to be approached in an either/or fashion, but can be worked together.

The questions I raise in relation to the living and theorising of gender liminality in a post-colonial context are inspired by, but not limited to, the concerns of gender liminal indigenous persons. Indeed, most of these issues are felt across transpeople of many racial identities, such as the on-going battles surrounding legal rights of transpeople, issues about accessibility and cost of medical procedures, and questions around the position of transsexuality within psycho-medical discourses. What I have chosen to highlight, however, is how these issues might require different subversive strategies, and different theoretical workings, according to the racial positioning of the transpeople concerned. My purpose in doing this is to critique the way perspectives of whiteness [7] echo, largely unacknowledged, through transgender (and queer) theorising and to thus inspire more critical thinking about the racialised aspects of transgender bodies and gender liminal ways of being.

ACKNOWLEDGMENT

I would particularly like to thank Nicky Green and Karen Nairn, for their encouragement and their critical readings of my work, and Niko Besnier for offering feedback on an earlier draft of the paper. I would also like to thank Victoria Grace and Rosemary DuPlessis for their on-going support, and the Feminist Studies Department of the University of Canterbury for providing an office-with-a-view and a friendly working environment.

NOTES

Originally published as Roen, Katrina. "Transgender Theory and Embodiment: The Risk of Racial Marginalization" from *Journal of Gender Studies* 10:3 (2001) pp. 253–263. Reproduced with permission from Taylor and Francis.

[1]   Maaori, also spelt Maori, is the collective name which refers to the various indigenous tribes of Aotcaroa/New Zealand. I privilege the former spelling because it highlights the long vowel sound and appears to be the preferred spelling in Maaori language texts.
[2]   Pakcha is the Maaori word referring to the white people who colonised Aotearoa/New Zealand during the nineteenth century, and their descendants.
[3]   Fa'afafine is the Samoan word, literally meaning 'like a woman', that refers to anatomical males who live outside of the masculine gender role and take on feminine attributes and roles.
[4]   Palagi is the Samoan word referring to white people.
[5]   Besnier (1994) critiques the notion of fa'afafine as a third gender: pp. 320, 326–327.
[6]   The legal situation referred to here is that: without sex reassignment surgery Tania would be ineligible for a passport or other such legal documentation identifying her as female; were she sentenced to prison she would be sent to a men's prison; and were she to be dismissed from her place of employment on the grounds of her (trans)gender identity there would be little legal precedent and no definitive legislative ground upon which she could claim unfair dismissal. This may be contrasted with discrimination on the grounds of sexual identity which is explicitly prohibited by the Human Rights Act (1993).
[7]   For an inspiring model of writing whiteness overtly into texts, so that it is articulated as a racialised position rather than being normalized, see Frankenberg (1996).

REFERENCES

ALICE, L. (1991) Whose interests? Decolonising 'race' and 'ethnicity', *Race, Gender, Class*, 11/12, pp. 64–69.
ALSTON, A. (1998a) Legal aspects of gender reassignment, *Journal of Law and Medicine*, 5(3), pp. 279–287.

ALSTON, A. (1998b) *Transgender Rights as Legal Rights*. Unpublished paper presented at: International Conference on Gender, Sexuality and the Law, Keele University, England.

BESNIER, N. (1994) Polynesian gender liminality through time and space, in: G. HERDT (Ed.) *Third Sex, Third Gender: Beyond Sexual Dimorphism In Culture and History* (New York, Zone Books).

FRANKENBERG, R. (1996) When we are capable of stopping, we begin to see, in: B. THOMPSON & S. TYAGI (Eds) *Names We Call Home: Autobiography on Racial Identity* (London and New York, Routledge).

GOLDMAN, R. (1996) Who is that queer queer? Exploring norms around sexuality, race, and class in queer theory, in: B. BEEMYN & M. ELIASON (Eds) *Queer Studies: A Lesbian and, Gay, Bisexual, and Transgender Anthology* (New York and London, New York University Press).

HALBERSTAM, J. (1994) F2M: the making of female masculinity, in: L. DOAN (Ed.) *The Lesbian Postmodern* (New York; Columbia University Press).

HENNESSY, R. (1995) Queer visibility in commodity culture, in: L. NICHOLSON & S. SEIDMAN (Eds) *Social Postmodernism: Beyond Identity Politics* (Melbourne; University of Cambridge).

LEE, J.Y. (1996) Why Suzie Wong is not a lesbian: Asian and Asian American lesbian and bisexual women and femme/butch/gender identities, in: B. BEEMYN & M. ELIASON (Eds) *Queer Studies: A Lesbian and, Gay, Bisexual, and Transgender Anthology* (New York and London, New York University Press).

NAMASTE, K. (1996) 'Tragic misreadings': queer theory's erasure of transgender subjectivity, in: B. BEEMYN & M. ELIASON (Eds) *Queer Studies: A Lesbian and, Gay, Bisexual, and Transgender Anthology* (New York and London, New York University Press).

NANDA, S. (1990) *Neither Man Nor Woman: The Hijras of India* (Belmont, CA, Wadsworth Publishing Company).

PROSSER, J. (1998) *Second Skins: The Body Narratives of Transsexuality* (New York, Columbia University Press).

ROSCOE, W. (1987) Bibliography of Berdache and alternative gender roles among North American Indians, *Journal of Homosexuality*, 14, pp. 81–171.

ROSCOE, W. (1991) *The Zuni Man-Woman* (Albuquerque, NM, University of New Mexico Press).

STONE, S. (1991) The Empire Strikes Back: a posttranssexual manifesto, in: J. EPSTEIN & K. STRAUB (Eds) *Body Guards: The Cultural Politics of Gender Ambiguity* (New York, Routledge).

STRYKER, S. (1994) My words to Victor Frankenstein above the village of Chamounix: performing transgender rage, *GLQ: A Journal of Gay and Lesbian Studies*, 1, pp. 237–254.

WALTERS, S.D. (1996) From here to queer: radical feminism, postmodernism, and the lesbian menace (or, why can't a woman be more like a fag?), *Signs: Journal of Women in Culture and Society*, 21(4), pp. 830–869.

47

Romancing the Transgender Native
Rethinking the Use of the "Third Gender" Concept

Evan B. Towle and Lynn M. Morgan

Anthropologists Towle and Morgan examine the concept of "third gender" in U.S. anthropological scholarship over the past quarter-century. They find it to be a useful and popular, though problematic, term precisely because its inherent ambiguities are well-suited to its historical moment; at a time when large segments of the U.S. population are encountering cultural differences from around the globe, "third gender" signals both tolerance for diversity and an adherence to Western categories of personal identity. The authors note that, increasingly, in social science literature, the term "third gender" is being replaced by or conflated with the newer term "transgender." Towle and Morgan are also interested in popular texts by and for members of North American transgender communities that treat "third gender" natives of other cultures as part of their own imagined communities. The authors acknowledge that thinking about "third genders" elsewhere has been a powerful way to envision emancipatory possibilities within Euro-American contexts, but they consider this practice to be fraught with pitfalls. Specifically, they consider popular transgender writing on "third genders" to make several errors. To begin with, it falsely places other cultures in an idealized "primordial location," a Garden of Eden where gender diversity flourished before the Fall into Western modernity. It tends to reduce the complexity of non-Western gender configurations to a single "third gender" status and to ignore other forms of gender diversity in a given culture that cannot be relegated to the culturally specific "third" term. Furthermore, "third gender" terms necessarily commit typological errors by reifying gender categories and ignoring the range of differences that can exist within any given identity category. They tend to treat non-Western societies as static, while imagining Eurocentric societies to be dynamic—"they" have culture, while "we" have history. Finally, this inconsistent application of the concept of culture fosters a "West versus the rest" mentality that contributes to the misrecognition of others, and complicates any potential political alliance across the boundaries of cultural difference.

Towle and Morgan note that the dialog between contemporary U.S. transgender communities and discourses, and gender communities and identities elsewhere, is in an early stage of formulation. The authors justifiably insist that U.S. transgender writers not caricature other cultures to advance their own local interests and agendas; they should, however, take equal care not to caricature U.S. transgender writers and activists (for example, Anne Ogborn, a transsexual woman who has spent considerable time participating in hijra communities in India, and who receives considerable attention in the article below) who make conscientious, ethically self-reflexive attempts to encounter, recognize, and interact with members of other cultures. At this early stage of the dialog, it is important to encourage, rather than silence, people willing to engage in an important conversation.

This essay offers a critical examination of how "third gender" concepts are used in popular American writing by and about transgendered people. Over the past decade there has been an increase in the popular use of cross-cultural examples to provide legitimacy to transgender movements in the United States. Descriptions of the "transgender native" are often drawn from ethnographic portrayals of gender variation written by anthropologists for American audiences. Introductory anthropology textbooks commonly cite the *hijra* of India, the *berdache* of native North America, the *xanith* of the Arabian peninsula, the female husbands of western Africa, and the Sambia (a pseudonym) boys of Papua New Guinea who engage in "semen transactions."[1] Such examples are often glossed together under the "third gender" rubric.

"Third gender" roles and practices were once regarded by most Western readers as exotica, with little relevance to our "modern" societies. These days, however, anthropological accounts of "third gender" variation are used frequently by popular writers such as Kate Bornstein and Leslie Feinberg, and by contributors to periodicals such as *Transgender Tapestry* and *Transsexual News Telegraph*, to buttress the argument that Western binary gender systems are neither universal nor innate. Paradoxically, this rise in popularity comes just when some anthropologists are finding serious fault with the "third gender" concept.[2] This essay explores its appeal as well as recent critiques of it. We illustrate the critiques with excerpts taken from several popular academic and nonacademic works whose authors write about transgender theories and experiences, and we point out some of the analytic paradoxes, contradictions, and dangers inherent in invoking the transgender native.

We come to this discussion from anthropological experience as well as from personal transsexual experience. As the self-conscious subjects of our own inquiry into how anthropologists and trans-identified individuals alike use transgender-native models, we are ultimately invested in ensuring careful, responsible representation of individuals outside our culture. We are simultaneously committed to supporting transgender/transsexual scholarship, representation, and activism. If a common complaint among trans individuals is that their lives and identities are violated and misrepresented for the goals of scholarship, then it behooves us to make sure that we do not commit the same offense against others for the goal of political advancement.

Although our examples are drawn from popular, widely read texts about transgenderism, our purpose is not to criticize the authors' intentions or even the products of those intentions. We understand that these texts rise to popularity because they are immeasurably helpful and meaningful to many readers searching for support and guidance. They carry weight because they inform not only the trans individuals themselves but also their therapists, doctors, family members, partners, and coworkers. One text that we discuss briefly, *True Selves*, is commended in numerous glowing reviews, such as the following:

> I've read a number of books describing transsexualism, hoping to find the right one to give to people as I tell them about my own transition. When I read this one, I knew this was it, and I told my parents about myself within the week. They have since told me that this book was essential to their understanding of my condition. I believe the authors have provided an invaluable resource for anyone whose life is touched by knowing a transsexual person.[3]

Twenty-seven similar reviews on Amazon.com, as of this writing, attest to the book's value to its wide readership. Our goal in this essay is to facilitate constructive critical inquiry into how we imagine ourselves and the place and time in which we live. In the process, we ask about the ramifications of such inquiry for the cultures considered to offer positive gender models as well as for the cultures (especially our own) implicated in the critiques.

Disagreements among anthropologists about using "third gender" concepts show that the issue need not be who holds "better" or "more accurate" or "more significant" knowledge. Anthropological knowledge is based on the conviction that examining a situation from slightly outside it can expose meanings that the participants might miss. (As Bornstein quotes an anonymous source, "I'm not sure who discovered water, but I'm pretty sure it wasn't a fish.")[4] And "member" knowledge is based on the conviction that members have a right to represent themselves, both to inspire others and to resist hostile and repressive political forces. But the politics of membership are complex. Do transgender natives, speaking for themselves, merit a place in the literature? What if they elect to be silent or invisible? Ideally, knowledge circulates freely and continually among scholars, laypeople, policy makers, activists, and theorists, any or all of whom might belong to or ally themselves with member communities. A contradiction emerges, however, when members appropriate scholarly accounts for their own ends and then deny others a voice, or vice versa. The argument about dominant knowledge might better address how knowledge is produced, deployed, and consumed within a given set of power relations.

Despite our commitment to the value of ethnographic comparison, we are skeptical of the utility of the generic transgender native in the popular literature. Understanding of other cultures is not enhanced by broad, decontextualized transcultural surveys or by accounts that encourage readers to take cultural features out of context. We do not believe that the goal of dismantling gender oppression and the binary gender system should seek legitimacy in narrow or sanctified appropriations of non-Western cultural histories or practices, although this method is used both in anthropology and in the popular literature. Rather, analysis should center on the meanings, ideologies, disputes, and practices that situate gender dynamics in specific historical and cultural contexts.

A BRIEF HISTORY OF "THIRD GENDER" CONCEPTS IN ANTHROPOLOGY

One longtime goal of anthropologists has been to document the diversity and meanings of human cultural practices. Historically, anthropology has been the Western discipline with the greatest access and sensitivity to non-Western cultural practices and with the greatest authority in writing about them. Well before Michel Foucault restored historicity to the study of sexuality, anthropologists had provided ethnographic accounts of gender practices in various cultures.[5] One of the most important analytic contributions was the sex/gender distinction, which made it possible to argue that biological features did not "naturally" correspond to sexual practice, sexual orientation, gender identity, or sexual desire. The sex/gender distinction itself has been confounded and criticized over the years, with critics arguing that anatomical sex as well as sexuality and gender can be socially constructed.[6] Subsequent theories have resulted in an increasingly complex understanding of the intersections among biology, identity, performance, power, and practice.

In the 1980s anthropology underwent a so-called crisis of representation, in which anthropologists began to come to terms with the realization that supposedly objective descriptions of non-Western cultures were infused with ethnocentric assumptions and colonial privilege. This realization, in combination with postcolonial studies and the emergence of gay and lesbian social movements, led anthropologists to redirect the anthropological gaze toward the Western societies from which many of them came. There they began to scrutinize the social construction of Western gender dichotomies and sexual forms of expression.[7]

The term *third gender* was apparently introduced in 1975 by M. Kay Martin and Barbara Voorhies, who employed it to draw attention to the ethnographic evidence that gender categories in some cultures could not be adequately explained with a two-gender framework.[8] This revelation had profound implications for feminist and gender theory as well as for social movements and political activists in the United States, because it allowed them to think outside a dichotomous gender system. *Third gender* began to be applied to behaviors that transcended or challenged dyadic male-female codes or norms. It was also applied to societies (most of them non-Western) that seemed to provide institutionalized "intermediate" gender concepts and practices.

Gilbert H. Herdt, one of anthropology's most ardent and widely read proponents of the "third gender" concept, has used the term to discuss gender and sexuality among the Sambia, a New Guinea group that practices "semen eating" (in which young boys perform fellatio on older men) and, more generally, to open the discursive space for analyzing nondichotomous gender categories. But a close reading of Herdt's work suggests that he is motivated to use *third gender* more by his own dissatisfaction with dualistic theories than by any conviction that the term is ethnographically accurate or adequate. In short, he uses it as a heuristic device, for illustrative purposes. In his preface to *Third Sex, Third Gender* Herdt cautions the reader that the word *third* should not be taken too literally; rather, it is "emblematic of other possible combinations that transcend dimorphism."[9] Like his colleague Will Roscoe, who has written extensively about "alternate gender roles" in Native North America, Herdt has been influential in introducing non-Western perspectives into the gay rights and transgender movements in the United States.[10] Articles written by Herdt and Roscoe allow transgender activists to argue, loaded with ethnographic ammunition, that they were "born [not into the wrong body but] into the wrong culture."[11]

Anthropologists make an important contribution to contemporary discussions of gender by pointing out that the two-gender system is neither innate nor universal. For many transgender activists and their allies, the cross-cultural perspective provides a welcome alternative to the heavily psychologized, medicalized, and moralistic analyses previously invoked in the West to explain gender variation. Using cross-cultural comparison—a tried-and-true strategy—for deconstructing and challenging many supposed cultural truths—anthropologists have argued against the biological basis of race, just as they have against the biological basis of gender: "What began as a critique of universals and a search for factors of cross-cultural comparison has become instead a critical inquiry into the assumptions of Western scientific models of sexuality and folk ideologies of the classification of individuals."[12] Anthropologists demonstrate the cultural logic of seemingly aberrant practices, showing, for example, how female-to-female marriage may function to perpetuate patrilineal social organization or how performing fellatio can be interpreted to promote the virility of young men.[13] Such examples provide ethnographic evidence to people working to challenge binary gender-based social arrangements in the West.

In recent years, the term *transgender* has sometimes replaced *third gender* to designate "gender roles and practices which are not definable in terms of local understandings of gender normativity," but the substitution has not necessarily rectified the attendant epistemological problems.[14] David Valentine argues that the concept of "transgenderism," and the corresponding social movements, arose recently and rapidly in the United States out of specific, identifiable developments in the cultural politics of sexuality. The birth of transgenderism responded to the sentiment among gay and lesbian rights advocates that one's sexual orientation does not reflect on one's gender; that is, "you can be a man and desire a man … without any implications for your gender identity *as* a man," and the same is true if you are a woman (190). This envisioning of gays and lesbians, who are to be seen as identical to heterosexuals in all ways but private sexual practices, removed many individuals—drag queens, butch lesbians, cross-dressers, and others—from the categories "gay" and "lesbian." These individuals, who are different from heterosexual and gender-normative people in other, possibly more conspicuous ways, are left to assume the category "transgender(ed)" (191–93).

The word *transgender* is a trendy signifier. But Valentine argues that it should not be applied incautiously to nonnormative gender practices elsewhere:

> If… "transgender" has a specific history and set of meanings which implicitly mark it in terms of its difference from USAmerican understandings of "gay," then labeling *bantut* [Philippines] or *travesti* [Brazil] as "transgender" is just as problematic. That is, despite the sensitivity to local practices and beliefs, the use

of "transgender" in these ethnographic texts actually relies on the same ontologies of gender and sexuality presupposed by the category "gay" which these authors [Mark Johnson and Don Kulick] so assiduously avoid.[15]

Anthropologists are not immune from the temptation to use the word transgender as a shorthand gloss. Despite the care they often take to "mark out a cultural specificity to the gender and sexual practices of their informants and to avoid 'gay' in the USAmerican or European sense," Valentine points out that they sometimes sweep a variety of nonnormative gender identities under the heading of "transgender" (91). He cites the subtitles (although not the substance) of Kulick's *Travesti: Sex, Gender, and Culture among Brazilian Transgendered Prostitutes* and Johnson's *Beauty and Power: Transgendering and Cultural Transformation in the Southern Philippines*, as well as Evelyn Blackwood and Saskia E. Wieringa's edited volume, *Female Desires: Same-Sex Relations and Transgender Practices across Cultures*, as examples of this trend.

Valentine is interested—and deeply implicated, by his own admission—in the ways that anthropologists are complicit in creating the very categories they seek to understand and deconstruct. The appearance of selected books by anthropologists on transgender reading lists is a way for "transgender-identified people [to] draw on such anthropological texts to talk about themselves and others as transgender."[16] Yet certain anthropological texts are inevitably passed over, while others find an avid readership. Valentine suspects that the key to the popularity of these texts is the extent to which the ethnography in them seems to condone or reinforce, if it does not actively contest, "the categories of [U.S.-based] identity politics" (90). For example, ethnographic accounts of Native American two-spirit (formerly *berdache*) peoples such as Roscoe's *Zuni Man-Woman* and Sabine Lang's *Men As Women, Women As Men* may resonate with a U.S. readership because they are consistent with social movements that promote gay and transgender rights, autonomy, and self-determination for first-nation peoples, as well as New Age spirituality. The phenomenon of appropriation shows how widely anthropologists are recruited (sometimes willingly and deliberately, sometimes unknowingly) to participate in projects of identity formation. By the same token, when anthropologists use the "transgender" concept to discuss "non-normative genders and sexualities cross-culturally," they "are complicit with those activists who imagine 'transgender' as a universal category of gender difference" (199).

EMANCIPATORY POSSIBILITY MEETS ANALYTIC PARADOX

For a society steeped in a binary gender ideology, the notion of "third gender" is intriguing and revelatory on many levels. It has been instrumental in sparking theoretical reflection about the "nature" and, especially, the social construction of gender. As Suzanne J. Kessler and Wendy McKenna said over twenty years ago, "Studying gender categories in other cultures…makes gender problematic, that is, uncovers our taken-for-granted belief in the facticity of gender which prevents us from seeing gender as a social accomplishment."[17] "Third gender" ideas build on our long-standing cultural fascination with societies that are allegedly less inhibited than our own. "A common and more or less clearly articulated motivation in this corpus of work," Niko Besnier writes, "is to demonstrate that preindustrial societies are more 'tolerant,' 'accepting,' 'approving,' or 'accommodating' of erotic diversity and gender variation than 'the West.'"[18] Thus the "third gender" concept set the stage for celebrating non-Western societies while disparaging Western ones.

This concept opens up creative possibilities for reimagining the "natural" expression and performance of identity and desire. After all, why should we be constrained by binary gender assumptions if the full range of human desire and behavior is substantially broader? Examples of societies that accept "third gender" roles justify the argument that homophobia and other forms of social opprobrium are unnecessary and even wrong, which in turn justifies antidiscrimination legislation and other legal protections. Carolyn Epple points out that ethnographic evidence of multiple genders has obvious emancipatory potential, for it "is clearly central to many social goals (deliverance from biology as destiny) and political agendas (disruption of the masculine, heterosexist hegemony)."[19]

Marjorie Garber constructed her influential book on cross-dressing, *Vested Interests*, around the idea that "thirds" are analytically useful because they upset the binary and encourage flexibility. She rejects the idea that the "third" is principally a word, sex, or specific referent of any kind. It is, rather, "a mode of articulation, a way of describing a space of possibility." Garber is especially interested in the ability of multiple kinds of "thirds" to disrupt multiple binary categories and symmetries by placing them in larger, messier contexts. In this sense, the "third" is good to think. Throughout *Vested Interests* Garber uses the notion of cross-dressing "thirds" to explore "the extraordinary power of the transvestite as an aesthetic and psychological agent of destabilization, desire, and fantasy."[20] According to Valentine, Garber insists that "crossdressing (and by extension, transexualism)should be understood on its own terms, not simply in terms of the 'twoness' of male and female."[21] This analysis allows gender variability and performance to be positioned at the center (rather than on the fringes) of social theorizing about gender and sexuality, and in this way Garber's perspective is useful and potentially empowering. But the free-ranging creativity that gives *Vested Interests* its popular allure (the book is good to think) also leaves Garber vulnerable to criticism from those who prefer their research subjects to be located in ethnographic, historical, and political contexts.

In his study of transvestite beauty pageants and the transformation of gender and culture in the Philippines, for example, Johnson criticizes Garber for reducing transvestitism "to the realm of literary or aesthetic psycho-sexuality, [to] that which escapes cultural categories but which makes their reformulation possible." It is vital, he argues, to examine the experiences of actual people as they negotiate gender, sexuality, and identity in contexts of cultural and political transformation. Johnson objects to two dimensions of Garber's analysis. First, the "space of possibility" she indexes by the "third" cannot exist outside, or prior to, "the repressive constraints and generative power of culture." If transvestites, hermaphrodites, and other transgender categories occupy a space of desire and possibility, of undecidability, then they do so no less as socially and historically constituted subjects than as those who inhabit the conventional space that Garber claims they interrupt.[22]

Second, Johnson "questions[s] the usefulness and validity of universalizing psychoanalytic semiotics in cross-cultural analysis." In this sense, he says, Garber's argument is predicated on culture-bound assumptions, because it assumes that the "transvestite figure inhabits a cultural world where identity, including sex and gender, is premised on dualism and where transactions between persons are conceptualized in terms of opposition and distinction."[23] Johnson, underscoring the need for a culturally sensitive analysis, shows that these assumptions do not pertain to Southeast Asian cosmologies.

The "third gender" is a uniquely Western concept produced by a society just beginning to grapple with the theoretical, social, political, and personal consequences of nondichotomous gender variability. It is thus an apt rhetorical and analytic device for the current historical moment, because it can accommodate contradictory social impulses; it signals both tolerance for cultural diversity and adherence to Western categories. Rather than accept uncritically the need for a "third" gender category, though, we should ask how "our" narratives about "them" (cultural others) reflect our own society's contradictory agendas concerning sexuality, gender, and power.[24]

In spite of the obvious imaginative and political potential created by the awareness of gender diversity across cultures, several flaws emerge in the utilization of "third gender" concepts. In the remainder of this essay we enumerate and illustrate these flaws, which we organize as follows:

1. The primordial location. "Third gender" societies are accorded a primordial, foundational location in our thinking, as though they underlay or predated Western gender formulations.
2. Reductionism and exclusionism. The "third gender" concept lumps all nonnormative gender variations into one category, limiting our understandings of the range and diversity of gender ideologies and practices.
3. Typological errors. By identifying "third gender" types, the concept ignores the diversity of experience within categories and glosses over the often contentious processes through which social formations, relations, and hierarchies are created, lived, negotiated, and changed.
4. Inconsistent use of the culture concept. Does culture facilitate or delimit social change?
5. The West versus the rest. "Third gender" concepts may isolate the West, for analytic purposes, from other societies, thereby reinforcing our ethnocentric assumptions; inhibiting us from forging alliances across national or cultural borders; and inducing us to focus on diversity between cultures while ignoring diversity, or the complexities of social change, within them.

The reader will find the figure of the transgender native woven throughout the discussion. This figure is a literary trope often used in transgender testimonial writing to invoke longing for the other. It serves in several texts as a generic, seductive figure who lives an idealized existence in a utopian place and time. The transgender native is portrayed not as a normal, fallible human being living within the gender constraints of his or her own society but as an appealing, exalted, transcendent being (often a hero or healer). He or she can be imagined (e.g., as a transgender ancestor), discovered (e.g., on a trip to a foreign land), enacted (e.g., as one's own persona), or simply cited to justify one's own argument. The transgender native surfaces in several of the following examples as an object of desire.

THE PRIMORDIAL LOCATION

Many contemporary transgender authors give "third gender" examples a primordial place in their narratives.[25] Primordialism works in two ways, often simultaneously. First, accounts of historical and non-Western gender variability are used to suggest that our contemporary (trans)gender variability is both ancient and natural. (Some authors even conflate time and place, collapsing historical with distant situations.) Second, summaries of historical and non-Western gender variability often appear at the beginnings of texts, suggesting that "old" and/or "other" forms of gender variation provide the foundation for the modern forms.[26] Bornstein, a playwright, a male-to-female activist, a performance artist, and author of the influential book *Gender Outlaw*, invokes the transgender native in the form of her assumed primordial ancestors, whom she imagines living in an age before oppressive gender ideologies were invented: "My ancestors were performers. In life. The earliest shamanic rituals involved women and men exchanging genders. Old, old rituals. Top-notch performances. Life and death stuff. We're talking cross-cultural here. We're talking rising way way way above being a man or a woman. That's how my ancestors would fly. That's how my ancestors would talk with the goddesses and the gods. Old rituals."[27] Bornstein recalls an idealized past at the same time that she positions non-Western societies as superior to Western societies ("We're talking cross-cultural here"). This rhetorical strategy is intended to create a kind of collective magic, to summon for the reader a pleasant and supportive, if imaginary, community. Yet the danger of portraying the transgender native in this way is that it can perpetuate stereotypes about non-Western societies, with their "shamanic rituals" and panoply of gods.

The beginning of *True Selves* asserts that "transsexualism exists and has always existed." The authors, Mildred L. Brown, a clinical sexologist and therapist, and Chloe Ann Rounsley, a writer, journalist, and marketing consultant, add the following description of our cross-dressing ancestors: "Shamans and medicine men were thought to hold special powers and were considered 'twin souled,' with knowledge of both male and female secrets. As such, they typically played prominent roles in ancient rituals, fertility rites, religious festivals, medieval folk ceremonies, and seasonal celebrations. These individuals were typically men who dressed in elaborate skirts, feathers, makeup, and ornamentation. Most cultures had at least one such individual, who held a unique position within the group."[28] Brown confesses that one of her motivations for writing the book was years of work with transsexual patients who would "search in vain for materials that would help them communicate *the* transsexual experience" (2; emphasis added). This is certainly a laudable goal, and we would not suggest that every book written on the subject must withstand academic scrutiny. Yet Brown misleads her readers by suggesting that there is a single, universal transsexual experience, as well as a single "third gender" experience characteristic of all people who lived in other places or times.

The primordial transgender native who is invoked as a symbol of healing in the past can also portend healing for the future. In this sense, the past becomes the future: "Older, so-called primitive societies usually valued their transgendered people as special beings. They were given roles of healers, visionaries, spiritual leaders, mediators, teachers, and guides. These powers are a natural outgrowth of harmonizing the masculine and feminine energies within. There are even some who are now saying that more and more transgendered people are being born into this world to help our troubled planet."[29] Another example of how crosscultural gender variation plays a foundational role in explaining modern transgenderism crops up in *Transsexual Workers*, whose author, Janis Walworth, offers the following response to a question about how to explain a worker's transsexualism to international clients: "Transsexualism is a worldwide phenomenon. In many parts of the world, traditional cultures have provided a place in society for transgendered people, whether or not they have made any surgical modifications to their bodies. In some cultures, including Native American cultures, transgendered people were not only accepted but revered."[30] In other words, international clients should need no explanation of the transsexual phenomenon, presumably because many already know and accept gender variation in their own societies. While we applaud Walworth's willingness to consider what others may think or know in cross-cultural encounters, she commits several oversights. For example, we question her assertion that a gender variant found in one part of the world necessarily holds constant (i.e., takes the same shape or has the same meaning) across countries and cultures. Walworth lumps the wide diversity of "Native American cultures" into one category and further assumes that familiarity with gender variation translates into acceptance, which, unfortunately, it often does not. For instance, while the *hijras* in India are well known, they are not universally revered or even accepted. Walworth might have posed her assumption as a question: Would it be a good thing if an Indian businessperson familiar with *hijras* regarded an American transsexual as similar and deserving of similar treatment? The answer is by no means clear.

A more ambitious way to introduce the transgender native to Western readers is to find him or her. Our search has turned up the following journalistic travelogue, in which American seekers visit foreign lands in search of the transgender native. In *Transgender Tapestry* Nancy Nangeroni writes about her journey to the Hawaiian island of Molokai "in search of *māhū*" (a Polynesian term for a genderliminal person). With the goal of "meeting and interviewing some transgender people who [had] been fortunate enough to grow up in a climate that was more accepting of gender difference than was ours," Nangeroni and a photographer set out to find the people whose "spirits...follow similar paths" to theirs.[31] After a good deal of asking and searching, they manage to track down a *māhū* named Moana who runs a hula school and drives a school bus. Having "introduced themselves and [given] her copies of Mariette's [the photographer's] book, *Transformations: Crossdressers and Those Who Love Them*, as well as a recent copy of *Transgender Tapestry* magazine," they waited as Moana,

Moana's sister, and another *māhū* named Jody "looked the materials over"; they "seemed suitably impressed" by them (27). Nangeroni's action can be seen as a simple act of generosity, yet it can also be interpreted as having encouraged the *māhūs* to view themselves as akin to mainland American transgendered people, like the presumed readers of Nangeroni's article. But it is not at all clear that Nangeroni and Moana shared an understanding of what either *māhū* or *transgendered* meant. When Moana used the word *māhū*, she referred to effeminate men. She did not use it to refer to more broadly defined transsexuals, such as those who are biologically male but wish to live as women or those who see themselves as neither male nor female. Moana later referred to herself as a homosexual, not as a transsexual, indicating that the local understanding of *māhū* reflects presumed sexual practices rather than internalized gender identities. But Nangeroni does not dwell on the subtleties of identity, practice, or semantics;[32] the reader learns no more about them.

At one point Nangeroni was denied further interviews with Moana because parents (presumably of students at the hula school) asked Moana not to talk with reporters. Yet when Nangeroni approached Moana at the airport to say that she would send her a draft of the article to approve before publication, Moana replied, "Just print it," which prompted Nangeroni to say that she "knew that we are of a common soul, engaged in the same struggle for simple human dignity and respect." Although Nangeroni shifts in the middle of the story from "enjoying [the] island visit to feeling like subversive intruders in a precarious paradise," she leaves the reader with the firm idea that *māhūs* and transsexuals are essentially the same; their identities may be at different stages of cultural evolution, but they are nonetheless interchangeable.[33]

Many American readers became familiar with another transgender native, the *hijra*, through the anthropologist Serena Nanda's popular ethnography, *Neither Man nor Woman*. Anne Ogborn took the project a step farther when she traveled to India and adopted this identity. Her account tells of her life in a community of *hijras*: "For as long as I have been out as a transsexual woman, I have been in a cycle. First to be healed by the community, then [to] heal the community. I applied this to my voyage to India. I didn't go to study *Hijras*, but to be with them, and as it turns out, to become one. I am not an anthropologist or a student of comparative religion. I'm a transsexual woman. I wanted to have a new experience of that."[34] Ogborn was on a spiritual journey in search of belonging. She was looking not for scholarly understanding but for fulfillment as a transsexual woman. She went to India armed, one suspects, with a superficial knowledge of a "third gender" utopia there. She wants to equate Indian *hijras* with American transsexuals, but the comparison is a crude one. To her, life as a *hijra* is merely an elaboration on the American theme of transsexuality, but in India *hijras* exist in a completely different context and constellation of meanings. Repeating the problem seen in the above examples, Ogborn assumes that the enactment and interpretation of identities formulated in one cultural context will remain stable when transferred to another context.

Ogborn's simplistic interpretation of the meaning of "third gender" categories may be the result of how gender variability is presented to American readers. Books and articles about transgenderism in the United States often begin with brief, superficial reviews of gender variability in other times and places. This is true of Feinberg's widely read *Transgender Warriors*, which, while generally ignored as a work of history, has enjoyed great popularity because it is accessible, romantic, inclusive of a wide range of gender variability, and optimistic. Feinberg has packaged a message that people want to hear. One young man from Perth, Western Australia, writes:

> I'm a 20-year-old female-to-male transsexual. Five years ago, I didn't even know other people like me existed. Now, thanks to this book, I know people like me have been around as long as human beings from the more ordinary walks of life . . .

Leslie presents a very personal history of transgenderism. Hir short autobiography echoes that of the many people who don't fit into the male OR female ONLY roles society has pushed us into over the centuries. . . .

. . . I want to major in History now. ::grin::[35]

Feinberg's story of self-realization in the book offers readers a vision of a primordial, eternal community of "transgender warriors" that extends much farther than the title suggests. "Have all societies recognized only two sexes?" asks Feinberg. "Have people who traversed the boundaries of sex and gender always been so demonized? Why is sex-reassignment or cross-dressing a matter of law?" "How," she wonders, "could I find the answers to these questions when it means wending my way through diverse societies in which the concepts of sex and gender shift like sand dunes over the ages? And as a white, transgender researcher, how can I avoid foisting my own interpretations on the cultures of oppressed peoples' nationalities?" [36] Much to her credit, Feinberg acknowledges the ethical and political complexities of appropriating cross-cultural information for selfish purposes. Paradoxically, however, her argument requires that she appropriate other cultural models of gender or, more specifically, an interpretation of cultural models that says, "Our ancestors lived in societies that enjoyed much more humane social relations than we do" (121). "I am heartened," Feinberg continues, "by the realization that hatred of sex and gender variation is not rooted in human nature. The more I dig, the more I find that although what we think of as gender today has been expressed differently in diverse historical periods, cultures, regions, nationalities, and classes, there appears to have always been gender diversity in the human population" (121).

After a speedy review of gender-related practices and beliefs among non-Western peoples, Feinberg suddenly calls a halt to the exercise, explaining that she intends to focus on the West to avoid participating in the "campaigns of hatred and bigotry that are today woven into the fabric of Western cultures and have been imposed on colonized peoples all over the world."[37] Her relationship to crosscultural evidence is ambivalent, however, because she also admits that she "found the key to a vault containing information [she] had looked for all [her] life" during her first visit to the Museum of the American Indian in New York City (21). But although the cross-cultural examples she found there were pivotal to her selfawareness, Feinberg warns the reader that studying non-Western societies (or even discussing them in any detail) may amount to Western imperialism. One wonders whether she intends her own life story to serve as a model for young, American "gender warriors" so they will not feel the need to explore treacherous crosscultural terrain themselves.

To relegate non-Western societies to the primordial slot is deeply problematic. Primordialism implies that ancient history lives on in the contemporary lives of non-Western peoples, who are then called on to exemplify "our sacred past" (the title of Feinberg's chapter on commonly used ethnographic examples of gender variability in non-Western societies). It further implies that there is (or was) a single pancultural genealogy from which all humans evolved (although some presumably evolved farther than others). The question of whether "diverse [non-Western] societies" are closer to a collective ancient cultural heritage than we are was long ago rejected by most scholars, who do not accept the social Darwinian notion that the world's societies can be ranked on a hierarchy of evolutionary stages from "barbaric" to "modern" (even when the goal is to glorify the former). Anthropologists and postcolonial scholars insist that all living human beings and cultures are equally contemporary and thus equally far removed from a panhuman cultural past.

Assigning non-Western accounts primordial status would seem to suggest that other cultures can (and should?) provide us with our own history. This assumption, evident in the literature that gives prominent attention to the Native American *berdache*, implies that gender variation among peoples who once lived on what is now American soil should be more relevant to American gender discourse than distant cultures. Could we say, for example, that accounts from precolonial North America are somehow more relevant to contemporary Americans than accounts from Papua New Guinea or Oman? Even some scholarly studies, including Kessler and McKenna's often cited *Gender* and the History Project's *Improper Bostonians*, introduce examples of Native American *berdaches* to show that gender shifting and homosexuality were once accepted on what is now American land.[38] These authors would certainly agree that in the case of North America there is little cultural continuity between native peoples and Europeans, because the colonizers so effectively destroyed the native peoples and their customs. Yet if geographic proximity or occupation of the same land is no guarantee of cultural affinity, what justifies the popular fascination with the *berdaches*?

Feinberg's great success is attributable to her ability to tap the understandable desire of marginalized and oppressed people to imagine and derive meaning from stories of a proud past. It is clear why she would want to reclaim a history that was strategically denied her: "It's time for a fresh look at history and this time, I don't intend to be left out."[39] The danger, however, is that our "fresh look at history" might lead us to violate or misconstrue other peoples' histories and experiences. Feinberg wants to draw on the work of anthropologists and historians only for raw data with which to advance specific, highly controlled political agendas. She herself keeps her distance from academic anthropologists, at once criticizing their characterization of Native American gender systems but using anthropological data, however loosely, to support her world history of transgenderism. Much is lost in the process, including the voices of Native American peoples, ethnographic details that might make their gender ideologies comprehensible to outsiders, and an appreciation of the need to look for meaning closer to home. To avoid the pitfalls of primordialism and to understand better the roots of gender oppression and the possibilities for gender liberation, we need more investigations of our own society's gender politics and histories.[40]

REDUCTIONISM AND EXCLUSIONISM

The "third gender" concept is by nature flawed because it subsumes all non-Western, nonbinary identities, practices, terminologies, and histories. Thus it becomes a junk drawer into which a great non-Western gender miscellany is carelessly dumped. Ethnographic examples can come from distinct societies located in Thailand, Polynesia, Melanesia, Native America, India, western Africa, and elsewhere and from any point in history, from ancient Greece to sixteenth-century Brazil to nineteenth-century England to contemporary North America. Popular authors routinely simplify their descriptions, ignoring or, worse, conflating dimensions that seem to them extraneous, incomprehensible, or ill suited to the images they want to convey. In her description of life as a *hijra*, for instance, Ogborn admits that "I haven't the faintest idea what the religious tenants [*sic*] of this place are. They [the other *hijras*] told me I should ask Ratnaa [her guru] about God every day, but my Hindi isn't good enough to talk about abstruse things. So I just sing the praises of Allah and I'm happy. It's a simple, Franciscan sort of thing to do."[41] Ogborn has already told us that she is not a student of comparative religion, yet we doubt that one can begin to understand *hijra* existence or to communicate *hijra* experience to Western readers without referring to "abstruse things." Ogborn does not mention the social and political contexts that gave rise to the current condition of *hijras*, or the complicated relationship in India between Islamic and Hindu faiths and cultures, or the caste system, probably because they are beside the point she wants to make. Her message is simply that transgendered individuals (as well as the category of "third gender") are mobile across cultures and have affinities that transcend language and cultural barriers. In this sense, Ogborn gives primacy to what she imagines as transcultural gender similarity, placing it above all other kinds of difference and giving, as Valentine puts it, "little attention to the specific historical and political conditions, or ontological assumptions, underlying it."[42]

Paradoxically, the "third gender" concept can constrain and narrow—as well as expand—our ability to imagine different kinds of gender variability. By focusing on *hijras*, for example, American readers may be less inclined to inquire about or to investigate other Indian discourses around sex and gender.[43] The "third gender" concept encourages students to think that "the natives" must have only one alternative to the dichotomous gender system available to them.

Leaving aside the question of how to sort and make sense of the contents of the overburdened "third gender" category, we should ask whether it functions to protect "first" and "second" categories from becoming analytically muddled or contaminated. The existence of the "third" category might imply—wrongly, in our view—that "first" and "second" categories are inviolable and unproblematic, at least for the purposes of exploring gender variability. But while critics argue that gender categories should not be limited to two,[44] simply adding one more accomplishes little. One danger is the tendency to believe that adherence to a three gender system would necessarily be less oppressive. "The greater the number of genders," cautions Agrawal, "the greater their oppressive potential as each may demand the conformity of the individual within increasingly narrower confines."[45] The role of *hijra*, for instance, is quite narrow, she argues, noting that locals insist that a "real *hijra*" is a castrated individual and not "just" an effeminate or crossdressing male (292–93). The alternate gender roles cited in the literature are not necessarily more open or accommodating than binary gender roles; Agrawal's example shows that "third gender" systems, too, can be rigid and intolerant.[46]

Ethnographic examples of gender variability can uphold, or can be interpreted as upholding, the tired two-gender ideology, although some ethnographic cases show that this interpretation can be profoundly mistaken. For example, Kulick's compassionate study of Brazilian *travestis* attempts to understand why homosexual men who "live their lives in female clothing, call one another by female names, and endure tremendous pain in order to acquire female bodily forms" reject the suggestion that they want to be or to become women.[47] Among *travestis*, gender identity is understood to derive from sexual practice rather than from anatomy. It is determined by "the role [that] genitals perform in sexual encounters" (227), and *travestis* understand and position themselves as having the same gender as women (233). In this sense, Kulick argues that *travestis* solidify a normative binary gender system, but not the Euro-American system that makes gender contingent on anatomical sex. The "third gender" concept would have prevented a researcher from reaching this conclusion, he says, because "there is a real danger that theories of third gender in fact radically naturalize and reinforce traditional understandings of sexual dimorphism" and thus "[leave] the traditional male-female binary intact" (230). Epple, writing about the Navajo *nádleehí*, makes the same point from another ethnographic location: "Casting [Navajo *nádleehí*] as [an alternate gender role] does not subvert but reifies—indeed is based upon—the very system it is intended to dismantle: the binary gender system and its assumed natural coherence among sex, gender, and desire."[48] The term *third gender* does not disrupt gender binarism; it simply adds another category (albeit a segregated, ghettoized category) to the existing two. It is ironic, Epple observes, that the "third gender" concept "sets gender incongruence apart, keeps the meanings of 'man' and 'woman' safe from its disruptive influences" (273).[49]

TYPOLOGICAL ERRORS

The "third gender" concept focuses attention on the classification of types and on the functional interactions among people as they assign and act out social roles. In such schemes, one type of gender variation is posited per nation or per culture: India has its *hijra*, Tahiti its *māhū*, the Arabian peninsula its *xanith*, Thailand its *kathoey*, Native America its *berdache*, and so on.[50] Roscoe, coeditor of *Boy-Wives and Female-Husbands: Studies in African Homosexualities* and *Islamic Homosexualities:Culture, History, and Literature*, editor of *Living the Spirit: A Gay American Indian Anthology* and *Queer Spirits: A Gay Men's Myth Book*, and author of several other popular works, argues that some cultures do recognize and label specialized gender "types."[51] These, he says, are the products of material histori-cal conditions, including the division of labor and means of production. His point is well taken: the "third gender" concept draws attention to just such examples. One flaw of the typological framework, however, is that it reinforces the all-too prevalent tendency to pigeonhole people and therefore to prejudge their identity, behavior, and interactions. Creating a normative template of the presump-tive alternate gender role has the unfortunate effect of privileging certain narrowly defined cultural scripts over others and ignoring the possibility of diversity within roles. Typologies also encourage static thinking: are the *hijras* timeless and unchanging? Typologies can be heuristically useful, but only to a point, for ultimately they yield an unchanging model that seems paradoxically antithetical to many transgender political aims.

Contemporary gender theories include many alternatives to typological models. Poststructuralist and performance theories show how gender identities and relations are discursively produced, ne-gotiated, enforced, resisted, and transformed as power shifts in a society.[52] These theories tend to emphasize the dynamism and malleability of gender identities without overlooking the hegemonic and regulating effects of medicine, jurisprudence, and the state on gender formation and preservation. Theories of gender performativity, for example, can take account of the popular American temptation to manipulate and disrupt conventional gender norms.[53] The ability consciously and deliberately to disrupt gender conventions, we argue, is vital to transgender political projects, but in this context it is important to analyze the dynamic social change that occurs in non-Western societies as well as at home.

INCONSISTENT USE OF THE CULTURE CONCEPT

We have written this essay because we are uncomfortable with how non-Western examples are used in some popular transgender literature. All too often, such examples convey the image of a transgender Shangri-la elsewhere; they encourage us to think that the mere existence of "third" gender categories allows difference to flourish and be accepted. Yet this utopianism is flawed not only on empirical grounds, as anthropologists have shown, but on epistemological grounds. An argument that relies on cross-cultural evidence of gender variation elsewhere to support the possibility of radical change at home is illogical: if gender is determined by culture elsewhere, then it must be determined by cul-ture at home, too. If gender and sexual expression are shaped by culture, then they can only ever be changed through collective social action, not through simple acts of will.

All societies demand a certain degree of gender consistency and conformity to the prevailing norms. One prevailing norm in the United States is that gender is both binary and adopted for life. That this expectation is not universal does not mean that other societies allow individuals to put on, take off, or exchange gender identities or behaviors on a whim. Yet Feinberg says, again, that there are "diverse societies in which the concepts of sex and gender shift like sand dunes over the ages" and uses this interpretation to claim that gender warriors should be able to adopt whatever identity they desire whenever they choose. In other words, if one culture has a role for X and another culture accepts the practice of Y, then we should be able to have (and be, and do) whatever we want. The problem is that while culture is malleable, it also constrains gender norms and behaviors; societies hardly ever allow individuals to transgress their norms freely and publicly. The existence of categories such as *hijra*, *berdache*, and *māhū* shows that cultures can create what one might interpret as alternatives to a binary gender system, but it does not support Feinberg's hope that the United States will achieve gender norms that are completely open-ended or unaffected by cultural constraints, because these alternative social positions do not tend to behave in the emancipatory ways they are portrayed. Instead, these categories work in specific relation to their cultural contexts. In several cases, this means upholding a rigid gender system by formalizing variations.

Ironically, the emphasis on "third gender" types may also diminish the richness and complexity of other peoples' lives, flattening their lived realities. This effect is evident in the tendency to romanticize, to assume that people living in societies that recognize "third genders" must enjoy greater gender liberation and freedom. When Ogborn relates her typical day as a *hijra*, the careful reader can find numerous inconsistencies between the events she describes and her upbeat interpretation of how *hijras* are received. Ogborn quotes one Indian woman as saying, "We are poor, but at least we have the *Hijras* living with us," and does not seem to understand that the woman might have meant, "At least we are not as badly off as the *Hijras*." In another instance, Ogborn reports that "everyone stops and watches as we go by, even though we do this three or four days a week."[54] Ogborn interprets both events as signs that *hijras* are regarded as nobility, although she has just finished describing her harassment at the hands of a gang of children: "They shout 'Gandu, Gandu' ('Butt fucker') at my back. Later they realize I speak only broken Hindi and instead yell, 'Faggot, faggot.' They ring the doorbell and throw rocks at my door when I am home" (20). Here local knowledge does not separate gender identity and sexuality, as do American transgender (and gay and lesbian) activists; what is and what is done may not be meaningfully distinct. The children's actions can tell us quite a bit about what it means to be a *hijra* or a non-*hijra* participant in that society. They demonstrate that knowledge about *hijra* sexual practices is widespread (whether the information is accurate is an interesting question, given that *butt fucker* implies an active role in penetration and *hijras* are known to be castrated), that a biologically male person in female clothing is first criticized for homosexual acts, and that such an individual is not given the freedom to choose a sexual partner.

When her group of *hijras* is not given enough money for a performance at a wedding or birth, Ogborn is one of the first to expose her genitals. To a man who cannot pay enough, Ogborn threatens, "If you want your son to have children, I'd take up a collection." (She is referring to the rumor that *hijras* kidnap and castrate boys to add to the *hijra* population.)[55] Ogborn prefers to think that she enjoyed a high status in her adopted *hijra* identity. Yet the relationship between *hijras* and the general population is complicated, involving scorn, fear, and derision as well as a complex form of appreciation.[56]

The "grass is always greener" phenomenon that presumably drew Ogborn to India is perhaps inevitable, but the misery she may have experienced at home had nothing to do with the possibility of her acceptance elsewhere. Popularizers tend to ignore or minimize the harassment, ridicule, discrimination, and violence sometimes directed at those who live as alternate-gendered individuals.[57] The presence of alternate gender categories does not necessarily mean that people living in such societies enjoy greater freedom to choose their own gender identities or forms of sexual expression, or that alternate gender roles are accorded social respect. To find out whether they do and are, we need to investigate the lived quotidian realities of people in various settings. Few ethnographic accounts of such realities appear even in the anthropological literature. The omission is significant, because it implies that Western readers are interested in others' lived realities only insofar as they suit our fantasies or political aims. Happily, ethnographers have begun to document lived transgender and gender-variant experiences. Nanda's work with *hijras* was an early example; more recent ethnographies are filling in the gap.[58] In a society with no cohesive transgender community, a society that does not routinely accept gender expression outside prescribed norms, it is understandable that community is sought where it is presumed to be, outside the here and now. In the lived realities of isolation, a mythical transgender community is ever present and ever supportive, although in our own society transsexual and transgendered individuals argue about whether we experience similar or comparable oppressions, about the value of passing, about surgeries and standards of care, and about degrees of disclosure. In short, our identities are consistently contested. In our communities and discussions we experience conflicts that do not seem to afflict these other individuals, who, we assume, do not argue about their identities, which are fixed.

THE WEST VERSUS THE REST

Gender ideologies and relations evolve in highly politicized, ever-changing cultural landscapes whose boundaries will not necessarily coincide with geopolitical boundaries and should not be assumed a priori. If on some level we know that being Indian does not "cause" *hijra* identity, then what factors do explain its emergence? Distinguishing "the West" from "the rest" does not advance our understandings of the historical and political contexts in which gender ideologies are negotiated. Does gender variability flourish under conditions of victimization, for example, or of resistance? Is it authorized by spiritual intercession? Do material conditions (such as hunger or affluence) affect whether it is tolerated? To what extent does it result from the exercise of state power or technological capacity? How is it affected by the interpretations of biology or the requirements of kinship? For example, in Japan's famous Takarazuka theater, young Japanese women perform all the roles, including those of romantic Western male sex symbols. One interpretation of this state-sanctioned exercise of gender discipline is that it directs heterosexual female desire toward figures who will not threaten the normative heterosexual family. The Takarazuka theater, in combination with the geisha tradition (which can likewise be seen to preserve the institution of marriage), also provides a cultural script for the *onnabe* phenomenon, in which biological females act out ideals of American chivalry to straight women in bars for money.[59] The distinction between "Western" (oppressive) and "non-Western" (potentially liberatory) gender systems has the unfortunate effect of essentializing other cultures and keeping us from examining other conditions of possibility.

Setting the West apart from the rest can result in old-fashioned American ethnocentrism, specifically, the assignment of who gets to name and represent "the transgender community." When the American critic Jody Norton reviews a book on transgenderism written by the British social psychologist Richard Ekins, she criticizes him for forwarding an interpretation that contradicts her own. The issue is whether male-to-female "transgenders" should be regarded as male or as female. Norton writes: "First, Ekins declares that 'male femalers' are men (as indeed, his term for m-t-f transgenders suggests[)]. Ekins is not writing about transgender as it has been embodied in many historical cultures (hura [*sic*], *xanith*, *māhū*, *berdache*/two-spirit) at all. Similarly, many *American* m-t-f transgenders do not understand ourselves as fundamentally male."[60] That is, Norton criticizes Ekins not only for not using cross-cultural examples but for not putting American interpretations of gender transgression at the center of his analysis. Norton wants us to see that the American form of transgenderism, as advanced by popular American authors, is the descendant of the cross-cultural examples and is the standard bearer for worldwide transgenderism. Norton exacerbates, in our view, the very problem that transgender politics should aim to solve, namely, how to create a society that does not force individuals to conform to others' expectations of them. Invoking "third gender" examples in an oversimplified way or citing them out of context to underwrite Western social agendas is an unwitting kind of neocolonial (or at least ethnocentric) appropriation that distorts the complexity and reality of other peoples' lives.

CONCLUSION

We join an increasing number of anthropologists who caution against using caricatures of other cultures to advance locally situated arguments. The "third gender" concept encourages Westerners to make poorly informed assumptions about the meaning and significance of gender dynamics in non-Western societies. Epple warns us to beware of re-creating the worlds of other cultures "to suit our own intentions."[61] Rather than rely on superficial understandings of "third gender," we would prefer to examine the content and complexities of gender in each specific cultural setting.

The issues we raise in this essay ask whose knowledge is authorized and legitimated in the struggle for greater freedom and knowledge. Debates over appropriate gender behavior have not always included the input of gay, lesbian, bisexual, and transgendered individuals and collectivities, but the rise of social movements has made space for these voices. Norton even claims that the voices of transgendered people themselves should be granted greater legitimacy than those of academic scholars: "The most *significant* 'expert' knowledge and theory is [*sic*] generated by members (. . . Feinberg, [etc.])."[62] The questions, of course, are, "Significant for whom?" and "Expert on what?" Our ability to comprehend the complexity of others' lives is jeopardized when the power to represent them is placed in the hands of those who stand to gain from misrepresenting them. Under this scenario, a member or native can relegate the social scientist expert to providing incidental raw data correctly interpreted only by the member or native. The danger inherent in this strategy is that the other becomes merely a rhetorical device for forwarding the identity of the self.

The complex relationship between member, lay, and expert knowledges (to use Ekins's terms) and participants has yet to be satisfactorily explored in the context of popular transgender literature. We know, for example, that popular literature (such as *Transgender Warriors*) influences the views of transgenderism that are held by clinicians, supporters, and transgendered people themselves. Such influence should go hand in hand with the responsibility of promoting the appropriate use of cross-cultural examples. Unfortunately, the popularization of "third gender" concepts often contributes to ethnocentric assumptions about other cultures, even when the authors' intentions are liberatory, progressive, and transcendent.

Transgender and transsexual activists need not invoke mythical gender warriors to support the idea that individuals should be free to express and embody themselves as they see fit or to justify their existence. (If warriors are sought, they are here.) Nor do they need to look elsewhere for acceptance. (Acceptance comes through understanding and mutual respect.) The potential that trans bodies and trans lives have to shed light on normative gender relations is immense. Who else has the opportunity to live these questions: What is the difference between women and men? Through what acts are gender identities communicated? What does failing to communicate a gender identity mean for social interactions?

Some use this potential to enable the study of gender "transgressions" in the United States to help illuminate what it means for everyone to inhabit gendered bodies. As Valentine and Riki Anne Wilchins write: "Bodies which are suspect, whether because they are wearing T-shirts that proclaim 'Transexual' or because they have big Adam's apples, or because they are born with genitalia that cannot be classified as either male or female, are not what have to be explained. Rather, the requirement that they explain themselves should itself be investigated." [63] Research that positions the trans body and life as foundational to the study of gender allows for the possibility of our (transgender/transsexual) greater freedom and also for greater knowledge about how we, collectively, have come to this point in the social life of bodies.

Rather than reify or romanticize presumed gender variability in non-Western societies, we would prefer to see greater attention given to the historical and social contexts in which gendered and sexualized bodies and relationships are produced, reproduced, and transformed.[64] The examination of context should include a critical interrogation of the circumstances under which other cultural examples are brought into American gender discourse. Why are such examples salient now? To what end have they become so? When we look at gender variability in other cultures, whom do we see and not see, and why? What are those individuals doing, and how are their actions constrained or facilitated by their social, political, and religious milieus? How much wishful thinking is evident in the way that cross-cultural evidence is mobilized and popularized in the United States? Is such evidence used to legitimate certain gender agendas (e.g., bodily reconfiguration through hormones or surgery) over others (e.g., symbolic or spiritually based gender reassignment)? These contexts will increasingly be transnational because of the heavy traffic across borders in images, bodies, ideas, technologies, and transgender political activism. What new social movements are created by connections made across cultural and national borders? What new possibilities for social and political solidarity might be fostered? The sensitivity with which we address these questions will depend on our ability to understand the limits of "third gender" thinking.

NOTES

We wish to thank the Stonewall Center at the University of Massachusetts at Amherst for calling this essay into being, and also Carol Cohen, Constance Johnson, Don Kulick, Andrew Lass, Ellen Lewin, Beth Notar, Susan Shaw, Eleanor Townsley, Jim Trostle, David Valentine, and the members of the Amherst-based Five College Faculty Seminar on Sexuality—Barbara Cruikshank, Lisa Henderson, Margaret Hunt, Janice Irvine, Jackie Urla, and Nancy Whittier—who generously provided feedback and suggestions to improve the essay. We are grateful to Jill Sady and Pat Kuc for their able editorial assistance.

1.   See Serena Nanda, Neither Man nor Woman: The Hijras of India (Belmont, Calif.: Wadsworth, 1990); Sabine Lang, Men As Women, Women As Men: Changing Gender in Native American Cultures, trans. John L. Vantine (Austin: University of Texas Press, 1998); Will Roscoe, The Zuni Man-Woman (Albuquerque: University of New Mexico Press, 1991); Roscoe, Changing Ones: Third and Fourth Genders in Native North America (New York: St. Martin's, 1998); Unni Wikan, Behind the Veil in Arabia: Women in Oman (Baltimore: Johns Hopkins University Press, 1982); Ifi Amadiume, Male Daughters, Female Husbands: Gender and Sex in an African Society (London: Zed, 1987); Gilbert H. Herdt, Guardians of the Flutes: Idioms of Masculinity (New York: McGraw-Hill, 1981); and Herdt, The Sambia: Ritual and Gender in New Guinea (New York: Holt, Rinehart and Winston, 1987).
2.   See Anuja Agrawal, "Gendered Bodies: The Case of the 'Third Gender' in India," Contributions to Indian Sociology, n.s., 31 (1997): 273–97; Niko Besnier, "Polynesian Gender Liminality through Time and Space," in Third Sex, Third Gender: Beyond Sexual Dimorphism in Culture and History, ed. Gilbert H. Herdt (New York: Zone, 1996), 285 –328; Deborah A. Elliston, "Erotic Anthropology: 'Ritualized Homosexuality' in Melanesia and Beyond," American Ethnologist 22 (1995): 848 –67; Carolyn Epple, "Coming to Terms with Navajo Nádleehí: A Critique of Berdache, 'Gay,' 'Alternate Gender,' and 'Two-Spirit,'" American Ethnologist 25 (1998): 267–90; Mark Johnson, Beauty and Power: Transgendering and Cultural Transformation in the Southern Philippines (New York: Berg, 1997); Don Kulick, Travesti: Sex, Gender, and Culture among Brazilian Transgendered Prostitutes (Chicago: University of Chicago Press, 1998); Ki Namaste, " 'Tragic Misreadings': Queer Theory's Erasure of Transgender Subjectivity," in Queer Studies: A Lesbian, Gay, Bisexual, and Transgender Anthology, ed. Brett Beemyn and Mickey Eliason (New York: New York University Press, 1996), 183–203; Kath Weston, "Lesbian/Gay Studies in the House of Anthropology," Annual Review of Anthropology 22 (1993): 339–67; and Saskia E. Wieringa and Evelyn Blackwood, Introduction to Female Desires: Same-Sex Relations and Transgender Practices across Cultures, ed. Evelyn Blackwood and Saskia E. Wieringa (New York: Columbia University Press, 1999), 1–38.
3.   xydonna@aol.com, "The Best Book of Its Kind," 2 February 1998, accessed on 5 April 2002 at www.amazon.com/exec/obidos/tg/stores/detail/-/books/0787902713/customer-reviews/3/ref=cm_rev_next/104-4278502-4690310?show=-submittime.
4.   Kate Bornstein, My Gender Workbook: How to Become a Real Man, a Real Woman, the Real You, or Something Else Entirely (New York: Routledge, 1998), 7.
5.   For a review of the literature see Weston, "Lesbian/Gay Studies." 6. See Anne Fausto-Sterling, Sexing the Body: Gender Politics and the Construction of Sexuality (New York: Basic, 2000).
7.   See Carole S. Vance, "Anthropology Rediscovers Sexuality: A Theoretical Comment," Social Science and Medicine 33 (1991): 875–84.
8.   M. Kay Martin and Barbara Voorhies, "Supernumerary Sexes," chap. 4 of Female of the Species (New York: Columbia

University Press, 1975), 23. Agrawal cites Karl Ulrich as the person who coined the term third sex ("Gendered Bodies," 279 n. 8), although it is unlikely that he used it to refer to cross-cultural gender categories. See Elizabeth Lapovsky Kennedy and Madeline D. Davis, Boots of Leather, Slippers of Gold: The History of a Lesbian Community (New York: Routledge, 1993); Besnier, "Polynesian Gender Liminality," 338; and Suzanne J. Kessler and Wendy McKenna, Gender: An Ethnomethodological Approach (New York: Wiley, 1978), 23. 9. Gilbert H. Herdt, "Introduction: Third Sexes and Third Genders," in Herdt, Third Sex, Third Gender, 20.

10. Roscoe uses the terms third gender and fourth gender somewhat idiosyncratically: for him, third gender refers to "male berdaches and sometimes male and female berdaches, while 'fourth gender' always refers to female berdaches" (Changing Ones, 7). The basic idea, however, follows Herdt: nondichotomous, institutionalized genders can be analytically gathered and enumerated as "third" and "fourth" genders.

11. Riki Anne Wilchins, Read My Lips: Sexual Subversion and the End of Gender (Ithaca, N.Y.: Firebrand, 1997), 30.

12. Herdt, "Introduction: Third Sexes and Third Genders," 441.

13. Amadiume, Male Daughters, Female Husbands; Herdt, Guardians of the Flutes.

14. David Valentine, "'I Know What I Am': The Category 'Transgender' in the Construction of Contemporary U.S. American Conceptions of Gender and Sexuality" (Ph.D. diss., New York University, 2000), 90.

15. Ibid., 91.

16. Ibid., 89.

17. Kessler and McKenna, Gender, 22.

18. Besnier, "Polynesian Gender Liminality," 316.

19. Epple, "Coming to Terms with Navajo Nádleehí," 273.

20. Marjorie Garber, Vested Interests: Cross-Dressing and Cultural Anxiety (New York: Routledge, 1992), 11, 71.

21. Valentine, "'I Know What I Am,'" 68. Valentine deliberately uses the nontraditional spellings transexual and transexualism throughout his work. The usage follows that of his study participants, who seek to depart from the medicalized discourse about transsexuality (vii).

22. Johnson, Beauty and Power, 24–25.

23. Ibid., 25.

24. See Besnier, "Polynesian Gender Liminality."

25. See Kate Bornstein, Gender Outlaw: On Men, Women, and the Rest of Us (New York: Routledge, 1994); Mildred L. Brown and Chloe Ann Rounsley, True Selves: Understanding Transsexualism…for Families, Friends, Coworkers, and Helping Professionals (San Francisco: Jossey-Bass, 1996); Randi Ettner, Confessions of a Gender Defender: A Psychologist's Reflections on Life among the Transgendered (Evanston, Ill.: Chicago Spectrum, 1996); Leslie Feinberg, Transgender Warriors: Making History from Joan of Arc to RuPaul (Boston: Beacon, 1996); Tiffany Elisabeth Jordan, "Tiffany Elisabeth's Ballet Studio," accessed on 19 September 1999 at www.geocities. com/WestHollywood/Heights/4519/ tiff_tgx.html; and Janis Walworth, Transsexual Workers: An Employer's Guide (Los Angeles: Center for Gender Sanity, 1998).

26. See Brown and Rounsley, True Selves; Ettner, Confessions of a Gender Defender; Jordan, "Tiffany Elisabeth's Ballet Studio"; and Walworth, Transsexual Workers.

27. Bornstein, Gender Outlaw, 143.

28. Brown and Rounsley, True Selves, 25, 26.

29. Holly Boswell, quoted in Jordan, "Tiffany Elisabeth's Ballet Studio."

30. Walworth, Transsexual Workers, 89.

31. Nancy Nangeroni, "In Search of Māhū⁻," Transgender Tapestry, no. 85 (1998): 24. For a discussion of the problematic definition, history, and etymology of māhū see Besnier, "Polynesian Gender Liminality."

32. See Deborah A. Elliston, "Negotiating Transnational Sexual Economies: Female Māhū⁻and Same-Sex Sexuality in 'Tahiti and Her Islands,'" in Blackwood and Wieringa, Female Desires, 232–52.

33. Nangeroni, "In Search of Māhū⁻," 29.

34. Anne Ogborn, "Saheli!" Transsexual News Telegraph 3 (1994): 20.

35. trentboy@mindless.com, "Trans* People Have a History Too," 8 October 1997, accessed on 19 September 1999 at www. amazon.co.uk/exec/obidos/tg/stores/detail/-/books/ 0807079413/customer-reviews/026-5989269-0429268.

36. Feinberg, Transgender Warriors, xi–xii.

37. Ibid., xii.

38. Kessler and McKenna, Gender, 21; History Project, comp., Improper Bostonians: Lesbian and Gay History from the Puritans to Playland (Boston: Beacon, 1998), 8.

39. Feinberg, Transgender Warriors, 59.

40. For an excellent example of queer history that does not rely on an idealized past see Kennedy and Davis, Boots of Leather, Slippers of Gold.

41. Ogborn, "Saheli!" 29.

42. Valentine, "'I Know What I Am,'" 64.

43. See Mary E. John and Janaki Nair, "Sexuality in Modern India: Critical Concerns," Voices for Change 3 (1999): 4– 8. Accessible at www.hsph.harvard.edu/grhf/SAsia/ library/libraryframe.html.

44. Anne Fausto-Sterling, "The Five Sexes: Why Male and Female Are Not Enough," Sciences 33, no. 2 (1993): 20–25; Fausto-Sterling, Sexing the Body.

45. Agrawal, "Gendered Bodies," 294.

46. See also Kulick, Travesti.

47. Ibid., 5–6.

48. Epple, "Coming to Terms with Navajo Nádleehí," 273.

49. See also Agrawal, "Gendered Bodies," 292–93; Bornstein, Gender Outlaw, 132–35; Gert Hekma, "'A Female Soul in a Male Body': Sexual Inversion As Gender Inversion in Nineteenth-Century Sexology," in Herdt, Third Sex, Third Gender, 213–39, 234; and Rosalind Morris, "Educating Desire: Thailand, Transnationalism, and Transgression," Social Text, nos. 52–53 (1997): 53–79, 62–65.

50. Of course, Native America consists of many distinct nations, and berdache is a colonial term that glosses over and erases the gender variability among these nations.

51. Will Roscoe, pers. com. with Lynn M. Morgan, 1999.

52. See Sue-Ellen Case, Philip Brett, and Susan Leigh Foster, eds., Cruising the Performative: Interventions into the Representation of Ethnicity, Nationality, and Sexuality (Bloomington: Indiana University Press, 1995); Samuel Delaney, "Aversion/Perversion/Diversion," in Negotiating Lesbian and Gay Subjects, ed. Monica Dorenkamp and Richard Henke (New York: Routledge, 1995), 7–34; Cathy Griggers, "Lesbian Bodies in the Age of (Post) Mechanical Reproduction," in Fear of a Queer Planet: Queer Politics and Social Theory, ed. Michael Warner (Minneapolis: University of Minnesota Press, 1993), 178–92; Marcia Ian, "How Do You Wear Your Body? Bodybuilding and the Sublimity of Drag," in Dorenkamp and Henke, Negotiating Lesbian and Gay Subjects, 71–92; Rosalind Morris, "All Made Up: Performance Theory and the New Anthropology of Sex and Gender," Annual Review of Anthropology 24 (1995): 567–92; and Stephen Whittle, "Gender Fucking or Fucking Gender? Current Cultural Contributions to Theories of Gender Blending," in Blending Genders: Social Aspects of Cross-Dressing and Sex-Changing, ed. Richard Ekins and Dave King (New York: Routledge, 1996), 196–214. We would like to thank Susan Shaw for pointing us to these references.

53. See Judith Butler, Gender Trouble: Feminism and the Subversion of Identity (New York: Routledge, 1990).

54. Ogborn, "Saheli!" 21.

55. Ibid., 23.

56. See Agrawal, "Gendered Bodies."

57. See ibid., 292; Kessler and McKenna, Gender, 29; and Kulick, Travesti.

58. See Nanda, Neither Man nor Woman; Holly Devor, FTM: Female-to-Male Transsexuals in Society (Bloomington: Indiana University Press, 1997); Johnson, Beauty and Power; Kulick, Travesti; Annick Prieur, Mema's House, Mexico City: On Transvestites, Queens, and Machos (Chicago: University of Chicago Press, 1998); and Valentine, " 'I Know What I Am.'"

59. See Jennifer Robertson, Takarazuka: Sexual Politics and Popular Culture in Modern Japan (Berkeley: University of California Press, 1998).

60. Jody Norton, review of Male Femaling: A Grounded Theory Approach to Cross-Dressing and Sex-Changing, by Richard Ekins, Transgender Tapestry, no. 84 (1998): 23; emphasis added.

61. Epple, "Coming to Terms with Navajo Nádleehí," 275.

62. Norton, review of Male Femaling, 23; emphasis added.

63. David Valentine and Riki Anne Wilchins, "One Percent on the Burn Chart: Gender, Genitals, and Hermaphrodites with Attitude," Social Text, nos. 52–53 (1997): 221; see also Kulick, Travesti. On Valentine and Wilchins's use of the nontraditional spelling transexual see n. 21 above.

64. See Namaste, "'Tragic Misreadings,'" 194.

48

Unsung Heroes
Reading Transgender Subjectivities in Hong Kong Action Cinema

Helen Hok-Sze Leung

Vancouver-based media studies scholar Helen Hok-Sze Leung, in her article on transgender subjectivity in Hong Kong action cinema, interrogates two recent Chinese films. She asks a set of theoretical questions that have emerged within European and North American transgender theorizing, and simultaneously advocates increased research into gender-variant phenomena outside of Euro-American contexts. In doing so, she calls attention to the anxiety she perceives in the field of transgender studies, that the notion of "transgender" itself may become an exclusionary narrative rooted in the experiences of Europeans and North Americans, one that is detrimental to understanding other forms of gender difference in cultures of non-Western origin.

Leung notes the tendency in recent criticism of Hong Kong cinema to treat the theme of gender atypicality as either a symbolically subversive queer destabilization of gendered spectatorship, or else as a metaphor for other types of dissidence. She proposes instead to treat the magical sex-change Dongfang Bubai in Ching Sui Tung's 1992 *Swordsman II*, and the butch gangster Thirteen in Raymond Yip's 1998 *Portland Street Blues*, not merely as symbols, but rather as agents enacting culturally specific transgender narratives of desire, identity, and embodiment. By asking what these previously invisible but now intelligible subject-positions might signify, she poses the question of what conditions permit these transgender subjects to appear on-screen in the first place.

Leung's nuanced "transgender" readings of *Portland Street Blues* and *Swordsman II* allow her not only to address ethnocentric misreadings of sexuality and gender in these films and their respective gangster and martial arts genres, but also to critique the implicit Eurocentrism of much transgender theorizing. Her article makes a valuable contribution to an emergent trans-Pacific, cross-cultural dialog about the utility of the "transgender" rubric for understanding Asian gender practices and cultural formations.

INTRODUCTION: TRANSGENDER THEORY AND HONG KONG CINEMA

In her introduction to the "transgender issue" of the journal *GLQ*, Susan Stryker offers a definition of *transgender* that captures the nuance and complexity of the term:

> ... I use *transgender* not to refer to one particular identity or way of being embodied but rather as an umbrella term for a wide variety of bodily effects that disrupt or denaturalize heteronormatively constructed linkages between an individual's anatomy at birth, a nonconsensually assigned gender category, psychical

identifications with the sexed body images and/or gendered subject positions, and the performance of specifically gendered social, sexual, or kinship functions.[1]

In Stryker's formulation, *transgender* is not a single identification or embodiment. It is an umbrella concept that refers to all "bodily effects" that trouble the assumed coincidence between our anatomy at birth, the gender assignment that is imposed on us (i.e. the "M" or "F" on the birth certificate), and our own subjective identifications. *Transgender* includes transsexuality in its rubric but is not reducible to it. The emergence of transgender theory—a growing body of knowledge that deploys *transgender* as at once a descriptive, analytical, and deconstructive category—has significantly reconfigured the debates on gender and sexuality.[2] It has challenged feminist theory to examine its history of transphobia, while igniting a resurgence of interest in the sexed body and its vexed relation to gender.[3] For gay and lesbian studies, transgender theory has complicated the discourse of sexual orientation and the notion of same-sex desire, both of which rely on a categorical distinction between male and female bodies. At the same time, transgender theory has inspired new critical intersections with gay and lesbian work on alternative gender practices and with theories of bisexuality.[4] Most importantly, the academic presence of transgender theory, which would not have been possible without the ongoing activism of transgender advocates in legal, social, and medical battles, is also starting to challenge the hitherto exclusive authority of medical expertise on transgender lives.[5] At the very least, no consideration of transgender issues can now go unchallenged without a recognition of both the diversity of transgender experiences and the agency of transgender subjects.

More recently, there is increasing recognition that more research on transgender phenomena outside of the Euro-American context is needed. This is the result of an anxiety in the field that the notion of "transgender" itself may be in danger of reifying into an exclusionary narrative that is rooted only in the experiences of Europeans and North Americans. The response to this call for diversity has been especially keen in Asian Studies, resulting in the recent establishment of the Transgender Asia Research Centre and a growing number of works by emergent scholars from a variety of disciplines.[6] The recent release of films with transgender themes from locales as diverse as Singapore (*Bugis Street*, dir. Yongfan, 1997), Thailand (*Iron Ladies,* dir. Yongyoot Thongkongtoon, 2001), Sri Lanka (*Flying With One Wing*, dir. Asoka Handagama, 2002) and China (*Enter The Clowns*, dir. Cui Zi'en, 2001) also attests to the vitality of transgender cultural expressions in Asia. Hong Kong cinema similarly provides a rich source of material for the consideration of transgender issues. From Stanley Kwan's 1996 documentary *Yin ± Yang: Gender in Chinese Cinema* to the recent works of critics such as Yau Ching and Natalia Chan, there has not been a lack of insight and critical interest in issues of gender variance and gender transgression in Hong Kong cinema. Yet, as I will argue in more details in the rest of the article, there is a tendency in the critical works to date to view cross-gender expressions largely as symbolic subversion: as a disruption of the binary gender system, as queer destabilization of gendered spectatorship, or as a vehicle for dissident sexuality. Not enough attention has been paid to the formation of transgender *subjectivity*—i.e. the conditions in which transgender subjects may emerge on screen, not as symbols but as agents of his or her specific narrative of transgender embodiment. In this article, I would like to trace the contours of two possible transgender subject-positions through a re-reading of two films in the action genre. What does the hitherto invisibility and now intelligibility of these subject-positions signify for the gendered structure of the genre? In particular, what would the recognition of transgender subjects mean for the coding of masculinity in these genres, so commonly assumed to be the exclusive expression of genetically male bodies? By the same token, what implications does such recognition have for the coding of the male-born body that wilfully gives up its access to masculinity or even its embodiment of maleness?

TRANSSEXUAL EMERGENCE: *SWORDSMAN II* AND
THE TRANSFORMATION OF DONGFANG BUBAI

Swordsman II [*Xiao'ai jianghu II zhi Dongfang Bubai*] (dir. Ching Siu-Tung, 1992) is the second install-ment of a series of films loosely adapted from Jin Yong's 1963 novel, *The Smiling, Proud Wanderer* [*Xiao'ao jianghu*]. The film features one of the most memorable villains in Jin Yong's *oeuvres*: Dongfang Bubai, an ambitious swordsman who has castrated himself in order to acquire an awesome form of martial art. There is a dramatic difference between the novel's and the film's treatment of this remarkable character. In the space of this difference, it is possible to locate the emergence of a transsexual subjec-tivity, one which has critical implications for the status of masculinity in the martial arts genre.

In the afterword to the 1980 edition *The Smiling, Proud Wanderer*, Jin Yong recalls the anxious political climate under which he wrote the serialized novel. The intense power struggle between warring factions in China, which at that time was teetering on the brink of the Cultural Revolution, inspired some of the major themes in the novel.[7] The character Dongfang Bubai, whose name literally means "undefeated in the east,"[8] is a cunning parody of Mao Zedong's self-appellation as the "red sun in the east" and a pointed allusion to his megalomaniacal appetite for power. The critical force of Jin Yong's allusion, however, derives from a transphobic understanding of the gendered body. In the novel, the extremity of Dongfang Bubai's thirst for power is marked by his willingness to castrate himself. This trope of castration-as-desire-for-power recalls a historiographic cliché: the contention that many of the political disasters in imperial China can be attributed to the usurpation of power by eunuchs.[9] Jin Yong stretches this symbolic equation even further. The monstrosity of power corruption is symbolized not only in the fact of castration but in the very process of bodily transition from male to female. When Dongfang Bubai appears in the novel for the first time, her enemies are confounded. They remember *him* as "an awe-inspiring and fearsome fighter" who has "usurped the leadership of the Sun-Moon Holy Sect and reigned supreme in the martial world for twenty years" (1282). *She* now appears in front of them, "beardless, rouged, and wearing lurid clothes that appear to be neither masculine nor feminine" (1282). She sits embroidering in a perfumed chamber, "having lost all previous appetite for women" and become completely devoted to a man and obsessed with becoming a woman (1291). Dongfang Bubai has become, in the words of the novel's heroine Yingying, "not a human, but a monster" (1293). The novel disposes of Dongfang Bubai within one chapter but its anxiety over the "monstrosity" of sex change continues. One of the most important narrative development hinges on the secret of an elder swordsman and his son-in-law, both of whom have self-righteously persecuted the novel's hero, Linghu Chong, who is being wrongfully blamed for a series of crime. The novel subsequently reveals the two men to be the real criminals. Hungry for power, they have been practising the same dark art that has transformed Dongfang Bubai. The physical changes in the elder swordsman are described through his wife's observations. She chillingly starts to notice the change in the pitch of her husband's voice, the shedding of his beard, and the loss of his (hetero)sexual appetite (1468). These are not, of course, medically accurate symptoms of castration nor literal descriptions of transsexual transitions. Rather, the horror of power corruption is projected, through the wife's terrified observations, onto a sex-changed body. The novel allegorizes transsexuality, likening the somatic transition from male to female to a process of moral degeneration. Such transphobic understanding of ultimate villainy as a form of literal emasculation reveals the novel's own anxiety about the free-spirited and hermetic masculinity it celebrates in its hero Linghu Chong.[10] In the afterword, Jin Yong suggests that Linghu Chong never achieves the true freedom that he desires, *not* because of worldly political struggles that have entangled him throughout the novel, but because of his committed love first for Yue Lingshan and later for Yingying. According to Jin Yong, Linghu Chong is "imprisoned" when he returns a woman's love, and most free in "Yilin's unrequited love for him" (1690). Apparently, a man is only free in a relationship with a woman if he does not return her love and thus escapes the "prison" of her influences! Jin Yong's remarks betray an acute anxiety about feminine sexuality and its constricting effects on the masculine freedom he envisions for Linghu Chong. Jin Yong's anxiety becomes *literalized* on the villainous male bodies: Dongfang Bubai and the other corrupted swordsmen are portrayed to be literally and monstrously bounded by their feminizing bodies. Ironically, it is exactly at the moment that these swordsmen are becoming feminized that they lose their sexual desire for women, thus escaping from the very influences that Jin Yong identifies as constraining for masculine freedom.[11] In this light, the novel's transphobia actually reveals an underlying crisis in the genre's conception of masculinity and freedom. On the one hand, an idealized masculinity is perceived to be vulnerable to the constraints of heterosexual desire. On the other hand, the ultimate freedom from heterosexual desire is inevitably coded in metaphors of castration (which, in this novel, is further imagined as a form of sex change) and, by implication, the *loss* of masculinity. This contradiction may explain why Jin Yong, even as he laments Yingying's constraining influences, does not end the novel differently, with Linghu Chong wandering free and unfettered by heterosexual desire. To do so would, I suspect, bring Linghu Chong too monstrously close to Dongfang Bubai, who in fact represents what is both most abhorred and most desired in the novel's conception of masculinity and freedom.

If such a critique of the novel simply reveals the ideological limits of its times, then the dramatic transformation of Dongfang Bubai on the screen in 1992 owes something to the first stirrings of queer politics in Hong Kong. The debates over the decriminalization of homosexuality throughout the 1980s had resulted not only in the emergence of gay and lesbian identities and organized activism around those identities, but also a new discursive space where issues of sexual and gender transgressions can be openly voiced.[12] *Swordsman II* was made at this time, feeding the public's newfound fascination with queer subject matters while reinvigorating a gender-bending tradition that has arguably always existed in Chinese cinema.[13] One of the film's most glaring departures from the novel's treatment of Dongfang Bubai is the centrality it accords to the novel's villain. While Dongfang Bubai dies within one chapter in the four-volume novel, she occupies the most prominent role in the film, usurping even the limelight of Linghu Chong (Jet Li), not unlike the way she has usurped the leadership of the Sun-Moon sect in the novel. The film also invents an erotic relationship between Linghu Chong and Dongfang Bubai, further blurring the line between hero and villain. Most unexpectedly, Brigitte Lin was cast in the role of Dongfang Bubai. The box office success of the film would later revitalize Lin's sagging career and instigate a trend of gender-bending roles that distinguish the careers of actors like Leslie Cheung, Anita Yuen, Anita Mui and, most prominently, Lin herself. The casting of Lin, an actress famous for her immense beauty, is significant. No longer represented as a castrated half-man, Dongfang Bubai remerges on screen as a (transsexual) woman. The film's inclusion in the Netherlands Transgender Film Festival in 2001, almost ten years after its initial release, completes Dongfang Bubai's remarkable transformation. Conceived as a symbol of masculinity-under-threat by a transphobic imagination during the 1960s, Dongfang Bubai is emerging in the new millennium as a transsexual icon.[14] However, the film has not always enjoyed such enthusiastic critical reception. In fact, it was routinely criticized in the first wave of queer critical writing to emerge from Hong Kong in the 1990s. This critical gap in the film's reception reveals an interesting contradiction between queer theorizing and transsexual subjectivity.

In the introduction to *Seconds Skins: the Body Narratives of Transsexuality*, Jay Prosser calls our attention to queer theory's foundational reliance on the figure of transgender. As a body of knowledge that takes as its point of departure the "queering"—i.e. the destabilization and displacement—of established categories of gender and sexuality, it is no surprise that queer theory finds the trope of crossing and traversing genders immensely valuable to its theoretical enterprise. Prosser suggests, however, that the queer appropriation of transgender privileges only a particular segment of the conceptual umbrella represented by the term transgender: "Crucial to the idealization of transgender as a queer transgressive force in this work is the consistent decoding of 'trans' as incessant destabilizing movement between sexual and gender identities."[15] Prosser argues that the formulation "transgender = gender performativity = queer = subversive" results in a conceptual split between queer and *transsexual*. The transsexual subject position, as Prosser shows, does not necessarily value fluidity, movement, and performativity but rather "seek[s] quite pointedly to be nonperformative, to be constative, quite simply to *be*" (32). Prosser's subsequent articulation of a theory of transsexual embodiment delineates a specifically transsexual experience of the body that is not easily reconciled with the queer imperative. While queer theory celebrates disruptions and instability as transgressive forces, the transsexual subject in Prosser's formulation is invested in gender transitivity not in and of itself, but as a process that eventually *arrives* at a more stable form of gendered embodiment. It is not surprising, then, that critics who turn to *Swordsman II* for a queer reading are often disappointed. In one of the earliest pieces of queer criticism on Hong Kong cinema, Chou Wah-Shan offers a scathing critique of the film. He takes issue in particular with the casting of Brigitte Lin: "Dongfang Bubai and Linghu Chong are clearly homosexual lovers. Casting the beautiful actress Brigitte Lin in the role completely takes away the shock and anxiety a male actor would inspire in playing that role."[16] Chou is especially irked by one scene: Dongfang Bubai asks her concubine Sisi to substitute for herself while making love to Linghu Chong in the dark. Chou interprets this scene as the film's final reinscription of heterosexuality: the only sexual scene in the film occurs unambiguously between a man and a woman. In a much more complex and nuanced reading, Yau Ching shifts the interpretive focus and locates queer pleasure in the spectatorial gaze. Yau argues that the film in fact offers its spectators "layered and diverse paths to project their desire" and the character Dongfang Bubai "allows us to refuse identification through sexual difference."[17] For Yau, the spectator's simultaneous recognition of the actress' female body and the character's male body means that identification with the character demands a (temporary) suspension of seamlessly gendered identification. Thus, as the gender discrepancy between actress and character becomes less intelligible—i.e. as Dongfang Bubai's transition progresses—the queer pleasure of the film also diminishes: "When Dongfang Bubai becomes more and more like a woman, the spectatorial pleasure of the female audience also becomes less radical and more conservative, until they finally only see the reflection of their own gender identification."[18] Both critics, in their very different readings, view Dongfang Bubai as a subversive character only in so far as s/he remains a symbol of gender instability. Chou prefers to see Dongfang Bubai played by a male actor, thus displaying a feminized male body and serving as an object of homosexual desire for Linghu Chong. Yau relishes the casting of Brigitte Lin, as long as a queer discrepancy is maintained between Lin's (meta-textual) female body and Dongfang Bubai's (textual) male body. Both critics become disappointed when they are confronted with what is arguably Dongfang Bubai's subjective emergence: i.e. as a transsexual woman who challenges Linghu Chong's (and our) demand to *tell the difference* of transsexuality. In this light, the scene that has appeared so *un*queer to critics, can be re-read as an inscription *not* primarily of heterosexuality, but of transsexual agency.

Prior to the seduction scene, Dongfang Bubai has just told her concubine Sisi about her somatic changes, citing them as the reasons for their recent lack of physical intimacy. At that moment, Linghu Chong enters the compound and asks Dongfang Bubai, known to him only as a beautiful stranger, to run away together from the turmoil of worldly affairs. Dongfang Bubai extinguishes the lights and asks Sisi to substitute for her. She then pushes Sisi into Linghu Chong's arms and the two make love in the dark. Later on in the film, Linghu Chong discovers the true identity of Dongfang Bubai and fights alongside his allies against her. Yet, when she is about to die, he tries to save her life, repeatedly asking if it was really *her* with whom he has spent that memorable night. In fact, he begs her to confirm that it was indeed her. Dongfang Bubai neither confirms nor denies, telling him that he "will never know, and will always regret this moment" (presumably the moment of her death). She then lets herself fall into the bottom of the cliffs, leaving Linghu Chong none the wiser. Why does Dongfang Bubai offer Sisi to Linghu Chong? And what is her motive for "deceiving" Linghu Chong until the very end? Chou, who insists on reading Dongfang Bubai as "rightfully" a gay man, argues that it is the film's way of "avoiding an explicit male-male sex scene."[19] Yet, Chou has already critiqued the casting of Brigitte Lin as a heterosexualization of the relationship between Dongfang Bubai and Linghu Chong. Why would her recognizably female body be in danger of suggesting a homosexual scene? The substitution in fact only makes sense as part of a transsexual narrative. In his discussion of transsexual embodiment, Jay Prosser theorizes the transsexual subject's relation to his or her transitioning body through Didier Anzieu's notion of the "skin ego." Anzieu's reworking of psychoanalytic theories departs from the emphasis Lacan and his followers place on language as the defining structure of ego formations. Instead, Anzieu returns to Freud and the importance he attributes to the body, especially its surface, in the formation of the ego.[20] It is from this *tactile* origin of the psyche that Prosser derives his theory of transsexuality:

> Writing against the grain of most poststructuralist theories of the body informed by psychoanalysis, Didier Anzieu suggests the body's surface as that which matters most about the self. His concept of the "skin ego" takes the body's physical skin as the primary organ underlying the formation of the ego, its handling, its touching, its holding—our experience of its feel—individualizing our psychic functioning, quite crucially making us who we are.[21]

Prosser goes on to explain the untouchability, or "stoneness," of the pre-transition body—a recurrent motif in transsexual narratives—as a feeling of a non-coincidence between "the contours of body image" and the material body, a "description simply of the refusal of body ego to own referential body."[22] Dongfang Bubai's refusal of sexual intimacy, both with Sisi and with Linghu Chong, can be explained in Prosser's scheme as precisely this wilful non-recognition of the (transitioning) body that is not (yet fully) her own. Furthermore, as Prosser suggests, it is this "dis-ownership of sex ... [that] maintains the integrity of the alternatively gendered imaginary."[23] In other words, Dongfang Bubai's refusal to be sexualized during physical intimacy as either "not quite man" (by Sisi) or "not quite woman" (by Linghu Chong) is her means to maintain her subjectively gendered imaginary of being a woman. However, she does not simply stop there. She literalizes this alternative gendered imaginary, through Linghu Chong's desire for her, *on* Sisi's body. Prosser deploys Oliver Sacks's work on neurology to draw a parallel between the way amputees feel and animate their prosthetic limbs through a phatasmatic memory of their real limbs and the way transsexuals experience their post-surgical bodies. In place of actual memory, Prosser suggests that transsexuals experience their surgically transformed bodies through *nostalgia*, for an idealized body that *should* have existed:

> The body of transsexual becoming is born out of a yearning for a perfect past—that is, not memory but nostalgia: the desire for the purified version of what was, not for the return to home per se (*nostos*) but to the romanticized ideal of home.[24]

Sisi's body represents for Dongfang Bubai the idealized gendered body that she longs to become/ return to. In substituting for Dongfang Bubai, unbeknown to Linghu Chong, Sisi is serving as a phatasmatic extension of Dongfang Bubai's body. By denying Linghu Chong the power to tell the difference,

Dongfang Bubai has in effect closed the gap between her subjectively embodied gender and Linghu Chong's actual experience of her body. The price of Dongfang Bubai's subjective emergence in this erotic encounter is, of course, the erasure of Sisi. In this scene, she is disowned from her own body, which has become a phantom limb possessed by both Dongfang Bubai (through identification) and Linghu Chong (through desire). It is thus fitting that the figure of the concubine returns with a vengeance in the film's sequel, *The East is Red* [*Dongfang Bubai zhi fengyun caiqi*] (Dir. Ching Siu-Tung, 1993). In the latter film, one of Dongfang Bubai's former concubines Xue Qianxun (Joey Wong) refuses to be abandoned like Sisi. In a scheme to lure Dongfang Bubai (not dead after all) out of hiding, she impersonates her former lover and embarks on a killing spree, thus sending the entire martial world on a search for the real Dongfang Bubai. Xue's scheme is similar to Dongfang Bubai's deception of Linghu Chong in one important way: successfully disguised as a transsexual woman, Xue challenges the world to "tell the difference" of transsexuality, with the confidence that they, like Linghu Chong (and the audience) would be unable to do so.

My reading of Dongfang Bubai as a transsexual subject does not mean to suggest that she presents a "positive image" of transsexual femininity. After all, she is a brutal, cunning and power-driven villain. What I appreciate in the film, in contrast to the character's treatment in the novel, is the intelligibility of Donfang Bubai as a transsexual woman, who is moreover an agent of her own actions. Her power, though awesome and terrifying, is worthy of her enemies' respect. Most of all, she is no longer a symbol of damaged masculinity, to be conquered by Linghu Chong's free-spirited heroism. Instead, she has fully emerged into her self-chosen subject position as a woman. Unlike the novel, the film is not primarily about masculinity under siege. Rather, it offers a spectacular display of transsexual femininity that has successfully eclipsed the centrality of masculine heroism in the genre.

TRANSGENDER BUTCH BLUES: HEROIC MASCULINITY AND HOMOEROTICISM IN *PORTLAND STREET BLUES*

The transsexual narrative that I trace, through Jay Prosser's theory of transsexual embodiment, in Swordsman II is by no means the only possible articulation of transgender identity. While the transsexual trajectory tends to be marginalized within queer theory, it is by contrast the dominant expression of transgender identity within the medical discourse of gender dysphoria, which views transgender people pathologically as patients in need of treatment. The "treatment" offered is a rigid process of sex reassignment that follows strict medical protocols, prescribed and monitored by medical and mental health professionals. A "cure" is understood to be the patient's successful reassignment from one sex to another.[25] Until very recently, narratives of transgender embodiment that do not conform to, or consciously reject, this grammar of binary gender transitions are viewed with suspicion and hostility by the medical community. Since the 1990s, thanks to the continual efforts of transgender activists, the medical establishment has been relinquishing some of its exclusive claim to expertise on transgender lives. With increasing input and participation of activists, academics and cultural producers who are themselves the consumers of transgender care, a much more complex and diverse picture of the experiences and needs of transgender people is starting to emerge, both in the medical community and in mainstream culture.[26] Leslie Feinberg's 1992 novel Stone Butch Blues, for instance, has brought a new visibility to transgender narratives that explicitly departs from the transsexual trajectory. The protagonist Jess has first lived as a butch lesbian, then taken hormones and undergone surgery and lived as a man, while finally realizing that neither of those identities fully encompasses who s/he is. Towards the end of the novel, Jess asks this poignant question:

I felt my whole life coming full circle. Growing up so different, coming out as a butch, passing as a man, and then back to the same questions that had shaped my life: woman or man?[27]

The novel deliberately refrains from answering the question. In the end, Jess stops passing and resolves to live as s/he is: neither man nor woman but transgendered in hir own way. All of Feinberg's subsequent writing, as well as the works of authors like Kate Bornstein and Riki Wilchins, are committed to a sustained critique of the binary conception of gender at the same time that they demonstrate the diversity of transgender lives.[28] In my reading of *Portland Street Blues* [*Hongxing shisan mei*] (dir. Raymond Yip, 1998), I would like to trace, in the protagonist Sister Thirteen [*Shisan mei*], a form of transgender subjectivity that does not conform to the transsexual trajectory. Previously overlooked by critics, the possibility of reading Thirteen as a transgender character also has critical implications for the debates on homoeroticism in the gangster genre.

Portland Street Blues is the fourth installment of the *Young and Dangerous* series, which are blockbuster films adapted from a comic book series about young Triad gangsters. The film documents how Sister Thirteen (Sandra Ng), leader of the Portland Street branch of the Hung Hing Triad, rises to power. From her first appearance in the opening scene where she is dressed in a classy black suit, with her hair slicked back and a cigarette between her lips, Thirteen perfectly embodies the heroic masculinity made famous by Chow Yun-Fat's characters in John Woo's films from the 1980s. In the *Young and Dangerous* series, this tradition of heroic masculinity is modulated and reinvented through the youthful characters played by Ekin Cheng and Jordan Chan.[29] What is Thirteen's subjective relation to this/ her masculinity? The first flashback sequence in the film is initiated by a scene of mourning. While Thirteen burns incense in front of a portrait of her late father (Ng Man-Tat), she explains to her Triad brother: "I've always thought of myself as a man. Do you know why?" A dissolving shot cuts from the late father's portrait to the past where the father is playing mah-jong with Triad bosses who use him as a pawn in the game. The narrative of Thirteen's transgender identification is thus visually linked to her father, a man who has never been able to live up to the heroic masculinity glorified in the genre. As a result, he is harassed and bullied and eventually dies in brutal humiliation. Thirteen's masculine identification thus also signals her identification with Triad power. However, the desire for Triad power alone does not explain Thirteen's transgender identification, only the *type* of masculinity she embraces. Her masculinity is not simply "functional": it is not just a means to gain Triad power. Subsequent flashback sequences show that long before her Triad ambitions, Thirteen was already a tomboy in her youth. Scenes of Thirteen and her girlhood companion A Yun (Kristy Yeung) playing, smoking, joking, and cuddling in bed together consciously echoes what would be recognized in the Hong Kong lesbian lexicon as a TB/TBG (literally "tomboy/ tomboy girl" and signifying butch/femme) relationship, even in the absence of any explicit sexual relations between the two. Thirteen is what Judith Halberstam would call a "transgender butch." Halberstam first formulates this category in order to challenge the overlapping, often blurry but frequently contested "borders" between butch and FTM (female-to-male transsexual) identities:

There are real and physical differences between genetic females who specifically identify as transsexual and genetic females who feel comfortable with female masculinity. There are real and physical differences between female-born men who take hormones, have surgery, and live as men and female-born butches who live some version of gender ambiguity. But there are also many situations in which those differences are less clear than one might expect, and there are many butches who pass as men and many transsexuals who present as gender ambiguous and many bodies that cannot be classified by the options transsexual and butch.[30]

The category of "transgender butch," which emphasizes a cross-gender identification (transgender) while retaining a reference to a masculine form of femaleness (butch) that is distinct from either "man" or "woman," provides a more flexible category for those who inhabit the borderland between butch and FTM. I describe Thirteen as a transgender butch to signify her masculine identification and masculine presentation as well as to underscore the fact that she does not seek to pass as a man or transition physically. This specificity is important to my reinterpretation of the film's sexual dynamics.

The romantic plot of *Portland Street Blues* is full of twists and turns and offers an especially interesting example of the way transgender theory complicates the discourse of sexual orientation. Throughout the film, Thirteen suspects that A Yun is in love with Coke (Alex Fong), a hit man from the rival Dong Sing Triad. To Thirteen's surprise, A Yun admits towards the end of the film that the true object of her love has always been Thirteen. Her apparent desire for Coke is, like her many scheming acts of seduction earlier on in the film, simply a weapon of manipulation. In retrospect, it becomes clear that she seduces Coke in order to keep him away from Thirteen who, in a further twist of the romantic plot, greatly admires Coke and later betrays an intense affection for the man. Thirteen also runs a prostitute ring, cruises young women, and is widely known to be a lesbian. Yet, the only emotionally charged and intimate encounter she has in the film is with Coke. As a result, many reviewers are puzzled by the film's sexual dynamics. The veteran film critic Sek Kei, for instance, ends his review of the film with this question: "... moreover, is the Sandra Ng character [Sister Thirteen] actually homosexual or heterosexual? This was never made very clear."[31] Sek Kei wants to know, once and for all, whether Thirteen is "actually" lesbian or straight. What Sek Kei, or any other critic for that matter, fails to take into account is Thirteen's transgender identification and its implication for our understanding of her sexuality. If we read Thirteen not simply as a woman but more specifically as a transgender butch—i.e. as a *masculine* figure—then her desire for Coke is neither lesbian nor straight, but *gay*. Admittedly, my use of the term "gay" here is tongue-in-cheek, as the word inevitably invokes a discourse of sexual orientation that categorizes desire according to the sex of the desiring bodies, regardless of their gender presentation. Yet, if we take transgender identifications seriously, then sexual orientation may be much more complex than what the binary scheme of heterosexuality and homosexuality can describe. Is Thirteen's desire for Coke still heterosexual if she does not identify as feminine? In fact, since she is attracted to Coke as a self-identified *masculine* woman, would it not be more accurate to describe this attraction as *homoerotic*? This latter suggestion makes particular sense in the scene where Thirteen and Coke show immense tenderness for each other. The two are reunited for the first time after many years. They reminisce and make sexual jokes, in ways that are typical of male-male camaraderie. Then, all of a sudden, the mood shifts and Thirteen awkwardly asks Coke for a hug and he obliges, tentatively but tenderly. The film critic Shelly Kraucer has observed that during the exchange, the editing consistently violates the 180 degree rules, which means that from our perspective, the two characters keep switching position from left to right, continually replacing one another in placements.[32] The editing of the sequence recalls John Woo's famous manoeuvre in *The Killer*. In a formal analysis of the film, David Bordwell describes the ways in which Woo "cuts across the axis of action" to make the two heroes John and Li (Chow Yun-Fat and Danny Lee) "pictorially parallel":

> Thereafter John and Li are compared by every stylistic means Woo can find: crosscutting, echoing lines of dialogue, and visual parallels ... He intercuts tracking shots in John's apartment to make Li literally replace John, and he will have them face off again and again, in a dizzying series of variant framings, while telling the blind Jenny they're childhood friends. Woo violates Hollywood's 180-degree cutting rule in order to underscore graphic similarities between the two men.[33]

In the scene from *Portland Street Blues*, the "quotation" of Woo is significant in two ways: it anchors Thirteen's transgender identification in the mirror of Coke's masculinity at the same time that it represents an intense intimacy between two masculine figures. In a later scene when Thirteen arrives at the place where Coke has been shot dead, she grieves for him in a highly masculinized gesture: she picks up three burning cigarettes, lays them down on the ground together like three burning sticks of incense, and then kneels down to pay respect to Coke. Furthermore, in another implicit romantic subplot between Thirteen and her Triad partner Han Bin, who awkwardly tries to give her a ring to express his affection, the relationship is also coded in generic images of male-male camaraderie rather than heterosexual romance. The bonding scenes between the two show them getting drunk together while heading out to cruise women, expressing mutual respect for each other's abilities, and loyally watching each other's back amidst Triad power intrigue. All of these scenes typically occur between male characters in the genre. Thus, Thirteen never once steps out of her role as masculine hero, even—in fact, especially—in her romantic relations with men. What, then, is the significance of Thirteen's appropriation of this hitherto exclusively male homoeroticism (now understood as eroticism between two masculine-identified figures, regardless of their assigned birth sex)? In order to answer this question, it is necessary to turn, for a moment, to the debates on homoeroticism in Hong Kong action cinema.

In Jillian Sandel's analysis of John Woo's pre-Hollywood films, she suggests that the implicit homoeroticism in Woo's films signifies a repudiation of femininity, heterosexual desire and the burden of family, all of which threaten the hero's ideal of individualism and freedom.[34] However, this homoerotic tension is never allowed explicit expression in the films and is instead resolved in an aestheticized excess of violence inflicted on the male bodies. For Sandel, the homoerotic relationships in Woo's films are impossible to sustain because they articulate a form of freedom that the films associate with capitalism which, for Sandel, is an economic system that only permits competitive relations between individuals. Sandel's analysis is quite compelling but it is premised upon an overly hasty identification of femininity and the family with Chinese tradition. Violently masochistic masculinity is, by contrast, linked to capitalism, with the unresolved homoerotic relations between men as its (impossible) fantasy of freedom. In another reading of the films' masculinity, Mikel J. Koven reverses Sandel's argument in an equally problematic move. Koven contends that the discussion of homoeroticism in gangster films is a Western "misreading" of "traditional Chinese masculinity" which he characterizes as more openly expressive of emotions. For Koven, the intense affective investment in honour, duty, and loyalty commonly experienced by Chinese men are misrecognized as eroticism by Western critics.[35] Both Sandel and Koven, in their rush to set up a Chinese vs. Western dichotomy, are unable to see the interconnections, rather than oppositions, between homoeroticism, masculine freedom, and "traditional Chinese masculinity." While Sandel insightfully links the homoeroticism in Woo's films with the repudiation of femininity and family, she overlooks the possibility that the masculine freedom idealized in these homoerotic relationships is not necessarily an embrace of capitalist individualism and a repudiation of Chinese tradition. Rather, it is a nostalgic reconstruction of traditional masculinity, precisely in response to the competitive individualism of capitalism which eclipses such relations. Kovel, by contrast, recognizes the action genre's investment in traditional masculinity but is unable, or unwilling, to understand it as anything but categorically heterosexual.[36] Contrary to Kovel's assumption, homoeroticism abound in pre-modern in Chinese culture and is far from incompatible with "traditional Chinese masculinity."[37] As I have argued earlier on in the article, there is a crisis in the conceptualization of masculinity in the martial arts genre. While heterosexual desire is perceived, on the one hand, to be a constraint on masculine freedom, the repudiation of heterosexuality, on the other hand, seems to lead dangerously to feminization and homosexuality. While Jin Yong alleviates this crisis with an expression of transphobia, Woo represses it by offering a homoerotic subtext that is forever deferred by outbursts of violence, thus never in danger of developing into homosexuality.

Just as *Swordsman II* provides an intriguing variation on the theme of masculinity in Jin Yong's novel, so *Portland Street Blues* provocatively modulates the homoeroticism in Woo's genre films. The film attempts to imagine a male-female relationship that departs from the generic portrayals of heterosexuality. The "homoerotic" relationship between Thirteen and Coke (or Han Bin) is unfettered by the burden of family and free from feminine influences. It is built upon loyalty and mutual respect. Yet, for such relationships to be intelligible within the gender dynamics of the genre, the film must fully articulate Thirteen's transgender identification as a masculine subject. This portrayal, which in effect concedes that masculinity is not the exclusive property of male bodies, is simply too threatening to be accommodated fully in a genre film. In a discussion of the cross-dressing opera diva Yam Kim-Fai, Natalia Chan argues that Chinese culture seems to have more tolerance for women who cross-dress as men than vice versa, because a cross-dressing female performer like Yam Kim-Fai, who embodies a "tragic" version of feminized (*yinrou*) masculinity, does not pose a real threat to the tradition of tough, strong (*yanggang*) masculinity.[38] Thirteen's decidedly *un*feminine masculinity in *Portland Street Blues* certainly departs from this tradition of feminized masculinity exemplified by Yam. More importantly, unlike Yam, the role of Thirteen is not a cross-dressed performance. Sandra Ng is not playing a male character as Yam was in Cantonese operas. Rather, Thirteen *is* a masculine character who has announced her transgender identification and who embodies a masculinity that rivals that of any other male characters in the film. She even forges a homoerotic relation with another hero. As such, she represents a far greater threat to the gendered structure of power than the examples of cross-dressed masculinity in Chan's analysis. The film's concluding scene exposes the anxiety of the genre towards this threat, which ironically is the fruit of its own production. After Thirteen has avenged the death of Coke, a mass of young gangster led by Ho-Nam, the hero of all the early *Young and Dangerous* films, congregate around her. This show of mass collectivity is a signature scene in all the films in the series. As Thirteen grieves Coke's death, Ho-Nam remarks coolly, "She is a woman after all." Here, Ho-Nam speaks the anxious conservative voice of the genre in this sudden attempt to tame the transgender butch, who has until this moment been its shining star. However, his remark sounds oddly disingenuous as the sight of a masculine hero grieving for another man is a commonplace in gangster films. Ho (Ti Lung) grieving (far more emotionally than Thirteen) for Mark (Chow Yun-Fat)'s death at the end of *A Better Tomorrow*, for instance, would not have shown him to be "a woman after all." Ho-Nam's insistence on Thirteen's "difference" is the film's anxious last-minute disavowal of her transgender identification, but the remark also ends up undermining the film's own innovative reworking of generic masculinity.

UNSUNG HEROES

My analysis of the two films is meant to provoke future work on other unsung heroes who have been overlooked as transgender subjects in Hong Kong cinema. I also hope to have shown that insights from transgender theory can significantly complicate our understanding of sexual desire. Furthermore, exploring different forms of transgender subjectivity and the context of their emergence in these two films has revealed an intriguing crisis in the representation of masculinity in the martial arts and gangster genres. The most idealized forms of masculinity in these genres involve a repudiation of heterosexuality and feminization; yet such repudiation also threatens to expose the repressed homoerotic roots of this masculine ideal. In *Swordsman II* and *Portland Street Blues*, transgender portrayals are a means to resolve this crisis. Yet, they end up reconfiguring the fundamental gender and sexual dynamics underlying the genres. *Swordsman II*'s bold transformation of Dongfang Bubai substitutes the novel's anxiety of emasculation with an abandonment of masculinity altogether. In the film, it is the heroic *femininity* of a transsexual woman that triumphs over the restrained masculinity of Linghu Chong. In *Portland Street Blues*, a butch woman's successful embodiment of masculinity and appropriation of homoerotic desire has disrupted the seemingly natural association of heroic masculinity with genetic male bodies. Still, despite the box-office success of these films, they remain exceptional examples. There have not yet been another transsexual woman or transgender butch on screen storming the martial or gangster world in heroic glory. I believe a critical recognition of these characters *as* transgender subjects is a necessary first step towards their continual existence on the big screen.

Just as exploring transgender subjectivities in film can lead to reconceptualizations of generic formulations of gender and sexuality, so the social and political recognition of transgender subjects may lead to changes in public attitudes towards gender and sexual variance. At the time of writing, following the recent suicide of Leslie Cheung on April 1, 2003, there has been an unprecedented surge of public appreciation for his brilliant cross-gender performances on screen and on stage. On May 7, just a little over a month after Cheung's death, the much less publicized but equally heartbreaking suicide of Lin Guohua, a transgender woman from Taiwan, has also prompted much public reflection on the urgent need to respect, support, and protect transgender lives.[39] It is my hope that contributing to cultural work that respects the complexity of transgender experience and the agency of transgender subjects will, in its own modest way, contribute to the ongoing social and political struggles for gender and sexual diversity.

NOTES

Earlier drafts of this article were presented during 2002 at Inside Out: The 12th Toronto Gay and Lesbian Film and Video Festival, the "Intersecting Asian Sexualities" conference at the University of British Columbia, and the "Queer Visualities" conference at SUNY-Stony Brook. I have benefited enormously from the thoughtful responses to my work at these events. I am also grateful to Kam Wai Kui, whose rich experience in transgender activism and continual love of Hong Kong cinema have illuminated endless conversations that ultimately shaped many of my best ideas.

1. Susan Stryker, "The Transgender Issue: An Introduction," *GLQ* 4:2 (1998), 149.
2. In addition to the works cited in the article, the growing scholarship that is defining the emergent field of transgender theory includes, amongst others, the works of Kate Bornstein, Jacob Hale, Kate More, Vivien Namaste, and Riki Wilchins.
3. One of the earliest critiques of transphobia in feminism is Sandy Stone's now classic rebuttal to Janice Raymond in "The Empire Strikes Back: A Posttranssexual Manifesto," revised 1993 version, http://www.sandystone.com/empire-strikes-back. See also Pat Califia, *Sex Changes: The Politics of Transgenderism* (San Francisco: Cleis, 1997), 86–119.
4. For an account of gay studies' relation to transgender theory, see Califia, 120-162. For works that intersect lesbian gender practices and transgender theory, see Minnie Bruce Pratt, *S/he* (New York: Firebrand, 1995) and Joan Nestle, *A Fragile Union* (San Francisco: Cleis, 1998). For the intersection between transgender theory and bisexuality, see Claire Hemmings, *Bisexual Spaces: A Geography of Sexuality and Gender* (New York: Routledge, 2002), 99–144.
5. In 1997, the Harry Benjamin International Gender Dysphoria Association (HBIGDA), the professional organization of health specialists in transgender care, elected transgender individuals to sit on its board of directors for the first time. See Stryker, 146.
6. For a description of the aims and activities of the Centre, as well as links to recent scholarly works on transgender issues in Asia, visit the Centre's web site at http://web.hku.hk/~sjwinter/TransgenderASIA/.
7. Jin Yong [Louis Cha], *Xiao'ao Jianghu* [The smiling, proud wanderer] Vol. 4 (Hong Kong, Minghe she, 1980), 1690. Subsequent references to this text will be given parenthetically after quotations. All translation of Chinese that appears in the article is my own.
8. Dongfang Bubai has also been variously translated as "Master Asia" or "Asia the Invincible" in the film's English subtitles and other English-language publications on the film.
9. For a discussion of this historiographic "use" of the eunuch, see Samshasha [Xiaomingxiong], *Zhongguo tongxing'ai shilu* [History of homosexuality in China], revised ed. (Hong Kong: Rosa Winkel Press, 1997), 348–9.
10. For a discussion of the role of the hero-hermit in martial arts fiction, see Chen Pingyuan, *Qiangu wenren xiakemeng: wuxia xiaoshuo leixing yanjiu* [The literati's chivalric dreams: narrative models of Chinese knight-errant literature] (Taipei: Rye Field Publishing, 1995), 187–228. See, also, Kam Louis's study of the archetypes of masculinity in Chinese culture, *Theorising Chinese Masculinity: Society and Gender in China* (Cambridge: Cambridge UP, 2002).

11. I am indebted to one of the anonymous reviewers of the book for pointing out this intriguing relation between feminization and freedom from female sexuality in the martial arts genre.

12 For an analysis of the relation between the decriminalization debates and the emergence of gay identity in the 1980s-1990s, see Petula Sik-Ying Ho, "Policing Identity: Decriminalisation of Homosexuality and the Emergence of Gay Identity in Hong Kong" (Ph.D. Diss., University of Essex, 1997).

13. See Stanley Kwan's documentary *Yin ± Yang: Gender in Chinese Cinema* [*Nansheng Nuxiang*] (1996) for a provocative look at transgressive gender representations throughout Chinese cinema.

14. The description of the film in the festival catalogue celebrates Dongfang Bubai's "ease with this newly acquired gender identity as a woman." http://www.transgenderfilmfestival.com/2001/_GB/article_swordsman.html

15. Jay Prosser, *Second Skins: The Body Narratives of Transsexuality* (New York: Columbia UP, 1998), 23.

16. Chou Wah-Shan [Zhou Huashan], *Tongzhi lun* [On tongzhi] (Hong Kong: Tongzhi yanjiu she, 1995), 300.

17. Yau Ching [You Jing], *Lingqi luzao* [Starting another stove] (Hong Kong: Youth Literary Bookstore, 1996), 165.

18. Ibid., 166.

19. Chou, *Tongzhi* 300.

20. Didier Anzieu, *The Skin Ego: A Psychoanalytic Approach to the Self*. Trans. Chris Turner (New Haven: Yale University Press, 1989). For a discussion of Anzieu's notion of the "self" in the context of the development of psychoanalytic theory, see Barbara Socor, *Conceiving the Self: Presence and Absence in Psychoanalytic Theory* (Madison and Connecticut: International Universities Press, 1997), 253–260.

21. Prosser, 65.

22. Ibid., 77.

23. Ibid.

24. Ibid., 84.

25. Updated versions of the Harry Benjamin International Gender Dysphoria Association Standards of Care for Gender Identity Disorders are available from http://www.hbigda.org/soc.html.

26. For an account of transgender activism that challenges thse medical discourse of transsexuality, see Califia, 221–244.

27. Leslie Feinberg, *Stone Butch Blues* (Milford, CT: Firebrand, 1992), 301.

28. See, especially, Leslie Feinberg, *Trans Liberation: Beyond Pink or Blue* (Boston: Beacon, 1998), Kate Bornstein, *My Gender Workbook* (London: Routledge, 1998), and Joan Nestle, Clare Howell, and Riki Wilchins, eds., *Genderqueer: Voices From Beyond The Sexual Binary* (Los Angeles, Alyson, 2002).

29. For a detailed analysis of the *Young and Dangerous* series in relation to the gangster genre in Hong Kong cinema, see Lisa Odham Stokes and Michael Hoover, *City On Fire: Hong Kong Cinema* (London: Verso, 1999), 79–86.

30. Judith Halberstam, *Female Masculinity* (Durham: Duke UP, 1998), 142–173.

31. Sek Kei, *Shi Qi yinghua ji* [*Collected Reviews of Sek Kei*]Vol 4 (Hong Kong: Subculture, 1999), 39.

32. Shelly Kraucer, email correspondence, May 28, 2002.

33. David Bordwell, *Planet Hong Kong* (Cambridge, MA: Harvard UP, 2000), 108–109.

34. Jillian Sandel, "A Better Tomorrow: American Masochism and Hong Kong Action Film," *Bright Lights Film Journal*, No. 13 (1994). Reprinted on http://www.brightlightsfilm.com/31/hk_better1.html.

35. Mikel J. Koven, "My Brother, My Lover, My Self: Traditional Masculinity in the Hong Kong Action Cinema of John Woo," *Canadian Folklore* 19.1 (1997), 55–8.

36. Ibid., 56.

37. For a beautifully written account of the homoerotic tradition [*nanfeng*] in pre-modern Chinese literature and culture, see Kang Zhengguo, [*Aspects of Sexuality and Literature in Ancient China*] (Taipei: Rye Field Publishing, 1996), 109–166.

38. Natalia Chan [Luo Feng], *Shengshi bianyuan* [*City on the Edge of Time*] (Hong Kong: Oxford UP (China), 2002), 41–2.

39. The Gender/Sexuality Rights Association in Taiwan has created a memorial website for Lin. See http://www.gsrat.org/.

49

Whose Feminism Is It Anyway?
The Unspoken Racism of the Trans Inclusion Debate

Emi Koyama

Emi Koyami, a grass-roots activist, author, and academic in Portland, Oregon, works on transgender and intersex issues, sex-worker rights, queer domestic violence, and anti-racism. In this article she delivers a stinging rebuke of both lesbian-feminists and transgender activists who have participated in the heated debates about the inclusion of transgender women in women's only space. Both groups, she contends, historically have predicated their arguments on racist practices and assumptions.

Koyami pays particular attention to the controversy surrounding transsexual attendance at the Michigan Women's Music Festival, which has played an influential role in shaping the debate on the status of transsexualism within feminist politics in the United States. She is sharply critical of a group of white, middle-class post-operative transsexual women who issued a statement in 2000 that supported a "no-penises" policy at the festival. This policy would allow these women to attend the festival, while barring their transsexual sisters who could not afford expensive genital surgeries not covered by health insurance. This group specifically noted that their proposed policy was disadvantageous to transgender women of color and poor people, but nevertheless considered their proposal the best compromise position available. Koyami has equally harsh words for the lesbian-feminists whose rationale for excluding transsexual women from women-only space recapitulated the logic of similar justifications within identity-based political movements for the exclusion or marginalization of women of color and the poor.

Koyami concludes her article by calling attention to the assimilationist argument for transsexual inclusion in feminist and women's movements espoused by many middle-class white transsexuals, that is, that "except for our history of embodiment we're just like you." She claims this argument, which parallels the liberal movement for gay and lesbian social inclusion, necessarily whitewashes the crucial question of difference within identity-based political communities. It is precisely by denying the importance—or even the very existence—of difference within an identity group that people in unmarked positions of privilege (such as white or middle-class status) gain the ability to falsely universalize from their own experience, and marginalize and exclude those in less privileged circumstances.

I.

I have never been interested in getting myself into the mud wrestling of the whole "Michigan" situation (i.e. the debate over the inclusion of trans people in Michigan Womyn's Music Festival). But I have become increasingly alarmed in the recent months by the pattern of "debate" between white middle-class women who run "women's communities" and white middle-class trans activists who run trans movement. It is about time someone challenged the unspoken racism, which this whole discourse is founded upon.

The controversy publicly erupted in 1991, when organizers of the Michigan Womyn's Music Festival expelled a transsexual woman from the campground, or "the Land," announcing that the festival is open only to "womyn-born-womyn," a category designed to exclude transsexual women. Next year, a small group of transsexual activists gathered in front of the Festival entrance to protest the policy. According to Davina Anne Gabriel, then the editor of *TransSisters: The Journal of Transsexual Feminism*, the "stated intent [of the protest] from the very beginning was to persuade the organizers to change the festival policy to allow postoperative—'but not preoperative—'male-to-female transsexuals to attend." [1] Based on the survey Gabriel and others conducted in 1992, they argued that majority of festival participants would support such a policy change, while the same majority would oppose inclusion of "pre-operative" transsexual women. [2]

If that was the case in 1992, the debate certainly expanded by 1994, when the protest came to be known as "Camp Trans." "In the first Camp Trans, the argument wasn't just between us and the festival telling us we weren't really women. It was also between the post-ops in camp telling the pre-ops they weren't real women!" says Riki Anne Wilchins, the executive director of GenderPAC. According to an interview, Wilchins advocates the inclusion of "anyone who lives, or has lived, their normal daily life as a woman" including female-to-male trans people and many "pre-operative" transsexual women. [3] Or, as Gabriel alleged, Wilchins made a "concerted effort" to "put herself in charge" of the protest and to "force us ['post-operative' transsexual women] to advocate for the admission of preoperative [male-to-female] transsexuals." Gabriel reported that she "dropped out of all involvement in the 'transgender movement' in disgust" as she felt it was taking the "hostile and belligerent direction" as symbolized by Wilchins. [4]

For several years since its founding in 1994, GenderPAC and its executive director Wilchins were the dominant voice within the trans movement. "Diverse and feuding factions of the transgender community were brought together and disagreements set aside for the common good," JoAnn Roberts describes of the formation of the organization. But like Gabriel, many initial supporters of GenderPAC became critical of it as Wilchins shifted its focus from advocating for rights of transgender people to fighting all oppressions based on genders including sexism and heterosexism. Dissenters founded alternative political organizations specifically working for trans people's rights. [5]

Similarly, five transsexual women including Gabriel released a joint statement just few days before the Michigan Womyn's Music Festival 2000 criticizing both festival organizers and Wilchins as "untenable, anti-feminist, and ultimately oppressive of women, both transsexual and non-transsexual." Wilchins' tactics were too adversarial, confrontational and disrespectful to women, they argued. Non-transsexual and "post-op" transsexual women alike "deserve the opportunity to gather together in a safe space, free of male genitals," because "male genitals can be so emblematic of male power and sexual dominance that their presence at a festival…is inappropriate." They further stated that "people with male genitals who enter the Festival risk offending and oppressing other attendees." [6]

"We acknowledge that a post-op only/no-penis policy is not perfect," admitted the writers of the statement. "This policy cannot address issues of race and class: specifically, the exclusion of women, especially women of color, who are not able to afford sex reassignment surgery." But it nonetheless is "the best and fairest policy possible," they argue, because it "balances inclusion of transsexual women with legitimate concerns for the integrity of women's culture and safe women's space." [7] Their pretence of being concerned about racism and classism betrayed itself clearly when they used it as a preemptive shield against criticisms they knew they would encounter.

As for the gender liberation philosophy of Wilchins, they stated that they agreed with her position that "freedom of gender expression for all people is important." Yet, "as feminists," they "resent anyone attempting to co-opt" the "love and creativity of the sisterhood of women" for "a competing purpose" such as Wilchins'. [8] The pattern is clear: when they say "feminism" and "sisterhood," it requires any important issues other than "the celebration of femaleness"—'i.e. racial equality, economic justice and freedom of gender expression—'to be set aside.

Jessica Xavier, one of the statement signatories, once wrote: "We too want the safe space to process and to heal our own hurting. We too want to seek solace in the arms of our other sisters, and to celebrate women's culture and women's music with other festigoers." [9] Has it never occurred to her that her working-class and/or non-white "sisters" might need (and deserve) such "space" at least as much as she does?

II.

While it was Maxine Feldman who performed openly as a radical lesbian feminist musician for the first time, it was the success of Alix Dobkin's 1973 album *Lavender Jane Loves Women*, that proved that there "was a wide audience for such entertainment" and helped launch the unique culture of "women's music." [10] "My music comes from and belongs to women experiencing women. So does my life... Long live Dyke Nation! Power to the women!" declared Dobkin in the cover of her debut album. [11]

The history of the trans inclusion/exclusion debate within women's music culture is almost as old as the history of women's music culture itself. Olivia Records, the "leader in women's music," was founded in 1973, which stimulated the nationwide proliferation of highly political large annual women's music festivals, modeled after the hippie be-ins of the 1960s. [12] It was only three years later that Olivia came under heavy attack for refusing to fire the recording engineer who was found to be a male-to-female transsexual lesbian. The series of "hate mail, threats of assault, and death threats" intensified especially after the publication in 1979 of Janice Raymond's *The Transsexual Empire: The Making of the She-Male*, which described the engineer as a dominating man, eventually forcing her to leave the collective. [13]

Feminist objections to the inclusion of transsexual women in the women-only space are, on the surface, rationalized on the basis that transsexual women are fundamentally different from all other women due to the fact they were raised with male privilege. Because of their past as boys or men, they are viewed as a liability for the physical and emotional safety for other women. When radical feminism viewed sexual violence against women not as isolated acts by a small number of criminals, but as a social enforcer of male dominance and heteronormativity, a woman's concern for her safety became almost unquestionable. [14] The effectiveness of Raymond's malicious argument that "all transsexuals rape women's bodies by reducing the female form to an artifact" was no surprise, given the context of the building momentum for the feminist war against violence against women. [15]

Defenders of the "womyn-born-womyn" policy argue that transsexual women who truly value the women's movement and culture should respect the festival policies by refraining from entering the Land. "Just as many Womyn of Color express the need for 'room to breathe' they gain in Womyn-of-Color space away from the racism that inevitably appears in interactions with a white majority, womyn born womyn still need and value that same 'room to breathe,'" argued Lisa Vogel, the owner of the Michigan Womyn's Music Festival. [16] This exact pattern of argument is extremely common in lesbian and/or feminist publications—complete with the comment about how much they as white women respect women of color spaces and how transsexual women should do the same for "womyn-born-womyn." "I've spent years educating other white festigoers about honoring the workshops and spaces that are planned for women of color only... It grieves me to see 'progressive' folks attacking an event that is sacred space for women-born-women" wrote a reader of *Lesbian Connection*, for example. [17]

However, another reader of *Lesbian Connection* disagrees with this logic: "If women born with vaginas need their space, why can't Michigan provide 'women-born-women' only space the way they provide women-of-color only space" instead of excluding transsexual women from the entire festival? [18] Logically, it would not make any sense to exclude an entire subgroup of women from a women's festival unless, of course, the organizers are willing to state on the record that transsexual women are not women.

Another flaw of the "respect" argument is that "women of color only" spaces generally welcome women of color who happen to have skins that are pale enough to pass as white. If the inclusion of pale-skinned "women of color" who have a limited access to white privilege is not questioned, why should women who may have passed as boys or men?

Radical feminism, in its simplest form, believes that women's oppression is the most pervasive, extreme and fundamental of all social inequalities regardless of race, class, nationality, and other factors. [19] It is only under this assumption that the privilege transsexual women are perceived to have (i.e. male privilege) can be viewed as far more dangerous to others than any other privileges (i.e. being white, middle-class, etc.)

But such ranking of oppressions and simplistic identity politics is inherently oppressive to people who are marginalized due to multiple identities (e.g. women of color) or creolized identities (e.g. mixed-race people). Cherríe Moraga wrote: "In this country, lesbianism is a poverty—as is being brown, as is being a woman, as is being just plain poor. The danger lies in ranking the oppressions. The danger lies in failing to acknowledge the specificity of the oppression." [20] Susan Brownmiller's failure to acknowledge how rape charges are historically used as a political weapon against the black communities and Andrea Dworkin's uncritical acceptance of the popular stereotypes about Hispanic communities being characterized by "the cult of machismo" and "gang warfare" illustrate this danger well. [21]

Combahee River Collective, the collective of Black lesbians, discussed the problem with the feminist identity politics in its famous 1977 statement. They wrote: "Although we are feminists and lesbians, we feel solidarity with progressive Black men and do not advocate the fractionalization that white women who are separatists demand... We reject the stance of lesbian separatism because it is not a viable political analysis or strategy for us." [22] It is not simply that white radical feminists happened to be racist; rather, the series assumptions behind radical lesbian feminism (e.g. women's oppression is the most pervasive and fundamental) was faulty as it privileged "those for whom that position is the primary or only marked identity." [23]

Decades of protests by women of color failed to educate those who have vested interest in maintaining this racist feminist arrogance. Here is an example: Alix Dobkin wrote as recently as 1998 "fresh scare tactics were essential to turn a generation of 'Lesbians' and 'Dykes' against each other... when that failed to wipe us out, they tried 'racist.'" [24]

In other words, Dobkin attributed the accusation of racism to the patriarchy's attempt to "wipe" lesbians out and *not* to the legitimate concerns of women of color, effectively accusing these women of color of conspiring with the patriarchy. "What is the theory behind racist feminism?" asked Audre Lorde. [25] She argued, "many white women are heavily invested in ignoring the real differences" because "to allow women of Color to step out of stereotypes... threatens the complacency of those women who view oppression only in terms of sex." [26]

III.

I used to think that feminists' reluctance to accepting transsexual women was arising from their constant need to defend feminism against the patriarchy as well as from the plain old fear of the unknown. I confess that I have given transphobic feminists far greater benefit of the doubt than I would to any other group of people exercising oppressive and exclusionary behaviors, and I regret that my inaction and silent complacency contributed to the maintenance of the culture that is hostile to transsexual people.

This realization came to me, ironically, during a panel presentation in spring 2000 by Alix Dobkin and several other lesbian-feminists about sharing "herstory" of lesbian feminism. The room was packed with women in their 40s and up, and nearly all of them appeared white and middle-class. I was already feeling intimidated by the time the presentation began because everyone seemed to know everyone else except for me, but my level of fear and frustration kept piling up as the evening progressed.

The presentation was all about how great the women's community was back in the 70s, when it was free from all those pesky transsexuals, S/M practitioners and sex radicals (or so they think). I heard the room full of white women applauding in agreement with the comment that "everyone trusted each other" and "felt so safe regardless of race," clearly talking about how she as a white woman did not feel threatened by the presence of women of color, and it nauseated me. Another women talked about how great it was that a private women's bar she used to hang out in had a long stairway before the door to keep an eye on potential intruders, and I felt very excluded because of my disability. I had never felt so isolated and powerless in a feminist or lesbian gathering before.

The highlight was when the sole Black women stood up and said that she felt like an outsider within the lesbian-feminist movement. The whole room went silent, as if they were waiting for this uncomfortable moment to simply pass without anyone having to take responsibility. Feeling the awkward pressure, the Black woman added "but it was lesbians who kept the American discussions on racism and classism alive," which subsequently was met with a huge applause from the white women. I kept wanting to scream "It was lesbians of color and working class lesbians who kept them alive, and you white middle-class lesbians had less than nothing to do with it" but I did not have the courage to do so and it deeply frustrated me. [27]

Obviously, many lesbian-feminists—'the same people who continue to resist transsexual people's inclusion in "women's" communities—'have not learned anything from the vast contributions of women of color, working class women, women with disabilities, etc. even though they had plenty of opportunities to do so in the past few decades. It is not that there was not enough information about women of color; they simply did not care that they are acting out racism, because they have vested interest in maintaining such a dynamic. The racist feminism that Audre Lorde so eloquently denounced is still alive.

I no longer feel that continued education about trans issues within women's communities would change their oppressive behaviors in any significant degree, unless they are actually willing to change. It is not the lack of knowledge or information that keeps oppression going; it is the lack of feminist compassion, conscience and principle that is.

Speaking from the perspective and the tradition of lesbians of color, most if not all rationales for excluding transsexual women are not only transphobic, but also racist. To argue that transsexual women should not enter the Land because their experiences are different would have to assume that all other women's experiences are the same, and this is a racist assumption. The argument that transsexual women have experienced some degree of male privilege should not bar them from our communities once we realize that not all women are equally privileged or oppressed. To suggest that the safety of the Land would be compromised overlooks, perhaps intentionally, ways in which women can act out violence and oppressions against each other. Even the argument that "the presence of a penis would trigger the women" is flawed because it neglects the fact that white skin is just as much a reminder of violence as a penis. The racist history of lesbian-feminism has taught us that any white woman making these excuses for one oppression have made and will make the same excuse for other oppressions such as racism, classism, and ableism.

IV.

As discussed earlier, many lesbian-feminists are eager to brag how much respect they have toward the needs of women of color to hold "women of color only" spaces. But having a respect for such a space is very different from having a commitment to anti-racism. The former allows white women to displace the responsibility to fight racism onto women of color, while the latter forces them to confront their own privileges and racist imprinting.

Do white feminists really understand why women of color need their own space? They claim they do, but judging from the scarcity of good literature written by white feminists on racism, I have to wonder. "It was obvious that you were dealing with non-european women, but only as victims" of the patriarchy, wrote Audre Lorde in her famous letter to Mary Daly. White women's writings about women of color frequently lose "sight of the many varied tools of patriarchy" and "how those tools are used by women without awareness against each other." [28] Many white feminists happily acknowledge ways in which white men's racism hurt women of color (through poverty, prostitution, pornography, etc.) to pretend that they are advocates of women of color, but often use it to absolve their own responsibility for racism. It is, then, no wonder that those who claim to "respect" the space for women of color simultaneously employ oppressive rhetoric against transsexual people without having to face their own contradictions.

Similarly, the transsexual women who wrote the statement supporting "no penis" policy did not see any contradiction in expressing concerns about racism and classism in one sentence and endorsing the racist and classist resolution in the next. Like white middle-class feminists, these transsexual women felt perfectly justified to absolve their responsibility to confront racism and classism and then call it feminist.

To make thing more complicated, some trans activists who are politically more savvy support "womyn-born-womyn" policy or at least regard it as an acceptable feminist position. Kate Bornstein, for example, "encourages everyone to engage in mutually respectful dialogue, without specifying what outcome might be desirable or possible," because "exclusion by lesbian separatists" cannot be considered oppressive when lesbians do not have very much "economic and social resources." [29] Another transsexual woman, in a private conversation, told me that she would rather be excluded from the Land altogether than risk the possibility of a male entry under the pretence of being transsexual. [30] While I appreciate their supposedly feminist good intentions, I must remind them that their arguments support and reinforce the environment in which white middle-class women's oppression against women of color and working class women are trivialized or tolerated. I must remind them that it is never feminist when some women are silenced and sacrificed to make room for the more privileged women.

V.

White middle-class transsexual activists are spending so much of their energy trying to convince white middle-class lesbians that they are just like other women and thus are not a danger to other women on the Land. "We are your sisters," is their typical plea. Supporters of transsexual women repeat this same sentiment: "As a lesbian who has interacted with the local trans community, I can assure you that womyn-born-womyn have nothing to fear from [male-to-female] transsexuals," wrote one woman. [31] But it is time that we stop pretending that transsexual women are "just like" other women or that their open inclusion will not threaten anybody or anything. The very existence of transsexual people, whether or not they are politically inclined, is highly threatening in a world that essentializes, polarizes and dichotomizes genders, and the Michigan Womyn's Music Festival and lesbian-feminism are not immune from it.

The kind of threat I am talking about is obviously not physical, but social, political and psychological. It is the same kind of threat bisexual and pansexual politics present to gay identity politics and mixed-race people present to Black Nationalism. Much has been written about the transformative potential of transsexual existence—how it destabilizes the essentialist definitions of gender by exposing the constructedness of essentialism. [32]

In the "women's communities," transsexual existence is particularly threatening to white middle-class lesbian-feminists because it exposes not only the unrealiableness of the body as a source of their identities and politics, but also the fallacy of women's universal experiences and oppressions. These valid criticisms against feminist identity politics have been made by women of color and working class women all along, and white middle-class women have traditionally dismissed them by arguing that they are patriarchal attempts to trivialize women's oppression and bring down feminism as Dobkin did. The question of transsexual inclusion has pushed them to the position of having to defend the reliableness of such absurd body elements as chromosomes as the source of political affiliation as well as the universal differences between transsexual women and non-transsexual women, a nonsensical position fraught with many bizarre contradictions.

It is my feeling that transsexual women know this intrinsically, and that is why they feel it is necessary to repeatedly stress how non-threatening they really are. By pretending that they are "just like" other women, however, they are leaving intact the flawed and unspoken lesbian-feminist assumption that *continuation of struggle against sexism requires silent compliance with all other oppressions*.

Like Gloria Anzaldúa's "New Mestiza," transsexual people occupy the borderland where notions of masculinity and femininity collide. "It is not a comfortable territory to live in, this place of contradictions." But speaking from the borderland, from its unique "shifting and multiple identity and integrity," is where transsexual activists will find the most authentic strength.

The borderland analogy is not meant to suggest that transsexual people are somewhere between male and female. Rather, the space they occupy is naturally and rightfully theirs, as the actual Texas-Mexico borderlands belong to Chicano/as, and I am merely calling attention to the unnaturalness of the boundary that was designed to keep them out. "A borderland is a vague and undetermined place created by the emotional residue of an unnatural boundary," Anzaldúa wrote, "it is in a constant state of transition. The prohibited and forbidden are its inhabitants." [33] The fact that many transsexual women have experienced some form of male privilege is not a burden to their feminist consciousness and credibility, but an asset—that is, provided they have the integrity and conscience to recognize and confront this and other privileges they may have received.

In her piece about racism and feminist identity politics, Elliott Femyne bat Tzedek discusses how threatening boundary-crossings are to those in the position of power and privilege. "Think about the phrase...'You people make me sick.' Think of how the person screaming this phrase may commit physical violence against what so disturbs him/her...those in power do actually feel sick, feel their lives being threatened...Men protecting male power have a much clearer view than Feminists do of exactly how threatening crossing gender is." [34]

By the same token, feminists who are vehemently anti-transsexual have much better understanding of how threatening transsexual existence is to their flawed ideology than do transsexual people themselves. The power is in consciously recognizing this unique positionality and making connections to the contributions of women of color and other groups of women who have been marginalized within the feminist movement. With this approach, I am hopeful that transsexual women, along with all other women who live complex lives, will be able to advance the feminist discussions about power, privilege and oppression.

NOTES

1. Davina Anne Gabriel, from an open letter to *Lesbian Connection* dated Jan. 27, 2000. Distributed on-line.
2. Phrases "pre-operative" and "post-operative" are put inside quotation marks (except when it is part of someone else's quote) because it is my belief that such distinction is irrelevant, classist and MtF-centric (i.e. disregards experiences of FtM trans people). I believe that such over-emphasis on genital shape is deeply oppressive to trans people and contributes to the suppression and erasure of intersex people.
3. *In YourFace* Interview of Riki Anne Wilchins. Distributed as a press release from GenderPAC on Aug. 18, 1999.
4. Gabriel, from the open letter.
5. JoAnn Roberts, *The Next Wave: Post-Reform Transgender Activism* (2000), distributed on-line.
6. Beth Elliott et al., *The Michigan Women's Music Festival and Transsexual Women: A Statement by Transsexual Women* (2000). Distributed on-line.
7. Ibid.
8. Ibid.
9. Jessica Xavier, *Trans Am: The Phantom Menace at Michigan* (1999), distributed on-line.
10. Lillian Faderman, *Odd Girls and Twilight Lovers: A History of Lesbian Life in Twentieth-Century America* (1991).
11. Alix Dobkin, from the cover jacket of her album, *Lavender Jane Loves Women* (1973), as reprinted in the re-mastered CD edition.
12. Faderman, *Odd Girls*.
13. Pat Califia, *Sex Changes: The Politics of Transgenderism* (1997).
14. Susan Brownmiller, *Against Our Will: Men, Women and Rape* (1975).
15. Janice G. Raymond, *The Transsexual Empire: The Making of the She-Male* (1979).
16. Michigan Womyn's Music Festival press release on Aug. 24, 1999.
17. From *Lesbian Connection*, Jan./Feb. issue, 2000.
18. Ibid.
19. From introduction to Barbara A. Crow, ed., *Radical Feminism: A Documentary Reader* (2000).
20. Cherríe Moraga, *La Güera*, in *This Bridge Called My Back* (1981) ed. by Cherrie Moraga and Gloria Anzaldúa).
21. Hester Eisenstein, *Contemporary Feminist Thought* (1983).
22. Combahee River Collective, *A Black Feminist Statement* (1977), from Moraga and Anzaldúa, *This Bridge*.
23. Lisa Duggan, *Queering the State*, from *Sex Wars* (1995).
24. Alix Dobkin, *Passover Revisited, Chicago Outlines* April 15, 1998.
25. Audre Lorde, from 1979 speech *The Master's Tool Will Never Dismantle Master's House*, published in *Sister Outsider* (1986).
26. Audre Lorde, from 1980 speech *Age, Race, Class and Sex*, published in *Sister Outsider*.
27. These comments were made at a "herstory sharing session" hosted by Lesbian Community Project in Portland, Oregon in early May.
28. Audre Lorde, *An Open Letter to Mary Daly*, published in *Sister Outsider*.
29. Kate Bornstein, *Gender Outlaws: On Men, Women, and the Rest of Us*, cited by Califia, *Sex Changes*.
30. From private conversation.
31. From *Lesbian Connection*.
32. For example, see Marjorie Garber, *Spare Parts: The Surgical Construction of Gender*, from *Differences: A Journal of Feminist Cultural Studies*, no.3, 1989.
33. Gloria Anzaldúa, *Borderlands/La Frontera: The New Mestiza* (1987).
34. Elliott Femyne bat Tzedek, *Identity Politics and Racism: Some Thoughts and Questions*, from *Rain and Thunder: A Radical Feminist Journal of Discussion and Activism*, issue 5, 1999. Personally, I was surprised to find this article in a radical feminist publication, especially since the same issue of *Rain and Thunder* also published a very hurtful column by Alix Dobkin that appear to endorse violence against transsexual women in women's restrooms.

50

Transgendering the Politics of Recognition

Richard M. Juang

In "Transgendering the Politics of Recognition," Richard Juang argues that anti-transgender discrimination and violence are often accompanied by racial and ethnic discrimination, and conversely, that situations interpreted as instances of racial and ethnic injustice often also involve a policing of gender and sexual boundaries. He calls particular attention to the synergy of injustices that result from the combination of racialized gender stereotypes with sexualized racial stereotypes.

Juang notes that the equal valuation of persons is the basis for a liberal democratic politics of rights; this is not to claim that all difference should be eliminated through the universal enforcement of a homogenizing norm, but rather that differences such as race, ethnicity, sex, sexuality, gender, or physical ability should never provide a basis for disrespect, domination, and oppression. After theorizing the concept of "transgender recognition" through a close reading of Patricia William's *The Alchemy of Race and Rights*, Juang turns his attention to two specific hate crimes—the negligent homicide of African-American transgender woman Tyra Hunt, and the to beating death of non-transgender Asian-American Vincent Chin—to demonstrate the ways he understands racism and transphobia to be mutually constituitive.

Juang contends that rigorously critical and ethical cross-cultural or multi-cultural analyses of gender, sex, and sexuality should play a vital role in advancing the recognition of transgender people as proper subjects of civil rights discourses in democratic societies. He concludes his article with a set of guidelines for engaging in ethically responsible cross-cultural investigations of gender difference. Juang feels that cross-cultural comparisons should always elaborate the historical context in which they take place, carefully define their purpose for being made, be reciprocal rather than parasitical, and exhibit an understanding of what is at stake in the struggles and choices of people different from oneself.

Being recognized within a liberal democracy means being valued, having one's dignity protected, and possessing some access to public self-expression. The struggle for recognition's key components—value, dignity, and self-expression—is a cornerstone of modern U.S. political, social, and cultural activity. Despite its unquantifiability, recognition's importance can be measured by the consequences of its absence: an unvalued person readily becomes a target or a scapegoat for the hatred of others and begins to see him or herself only through the lens of such hatred. An existence restricted to purely private expressions of the self, to the closet, becomes a corrosive situation.

The only acceptable vision of a just society includes equal recognition for transgender and non-transgender persons alike. While short-term, tactical compromises in the struggle for our rights are inevitable (for example, allowing employers to require a consistent gender presentation in order to gain the right to determine for oneself what that gender presentation will be), a society in which we finally settle for anything short of the full array of rights and privileges enjoyed by non-trans citizens will remain an unjust society. Such an ethical horizon is not a utopian fantasy, but is inherent in the very idea of justice. As John Rawls observes, inherent to a concept of justice is the principle that "Each person possesses an inviolability founded on justice that even the welfare of society as a whole cannot override. For this reason justice denies that the loss of freedom for some is made right by a greater good shared by others. It does not allow that the sacrifices imposed on a few are outweighed by the larger sum of advantages enjoyed by many."[1]

To encompass all trans persons, a robust transgender politics of recognition should address the discriminations and prejudices targeted not only against gender, but against racial and ethnic differences. Present discussions of transgender issues in the classroom, mass media, and everyday conversation separate out transphobia, heterosexism, and misogyny from racism, ethnocentrism, and Eurocentrism. This separation misrepresents how oppressive forces intersect in practice: racism is frequently gendered, while gender discrimination is often shaped by racism. In the first half of this essay, I hope to outline some of the ways that anti-transgender discrimination and violence are often accompanied by racial and ethnic discriminations, and conversely, situations interpreted as instances of racial and ethnic injustice often also involve a policing of gender and sexual boundaries. Rather than provide a wide survey of examples, I will focus [attention] on two seemingly unconnected events separated by over a decade: the deaths of Tyra Hunter and Vincent Chin. In turn, our ability to address hate violence more generally depends on an expanded politics of recognition.

Articulating a web of connections does not mean that we ignore the complex differences among identities and forms of discrimination. Indeed, accuracy demands that we attend to the different origins, histories, and consequences of structures of oppression. While strategically useful in many instances, the representation of broad ranges of racial and gender identities under rubrics such as "persons of color" and "transgender" risks ignoring substantial cultural and economic realities that define and shape identities. One risks, in essence, the very kind of non-recognition that a politics of recognition intentionally seeks to avoid. While this essay cannot offer an overarching strategy for a robust transgender politics of recognition, it will close in on a narrower question raised by an intersectional analysis: the use of cross-cultural comparisons in asserting the legitimacy of transgender identities. A self-critical, multiculturalist ethics may be useful in avoiding an "imperializing" politics of recognition. In terms of a broader political strategy, I would simply note that direct political and cultural efforts toward recognition have been and will probably continue to be as heterogeneous as transgender persons and communities themselves.

I. RECOGNITION AND INTERSECTIONALITY

Conventional discussions of rights and equality, including sex equality, have excluded transgender persons as aberrant cases, and a simple assimilation of trans persons into existing paradigms for civil equality is inadequate; put crudely, it has not been enough, historically, to claim in theoretical terms that transgender persons are deserving of rights because we are "just like everyone else," when the definition of "everyone" has been established, in practice, through the exclusion of transgender persons.

A politics of recognition consists of more than just the dissemination of positive images for a group. For Charles Taylor, recognition is shorthand for how value is attributed to both persons and groups. Its conceptual origins are in the classical liberal philosophies of the eighteenth century that predicated political life on a principle of equal dignity. Ideally, such a principle accords value to persons by virtue of their individual humanness, rather than by exterior considerations such as family, social rank, or wealth.[2] At stake in the contemporary idea of recognition is not the complete elimination of differences. Such assimilation would mean the forcible repression or purging of human difference and diversity in favor of a single idealized norm. Rather, the goal of much of the contemporary politics of recognition is to make illegitimate the use of racial, cultural, sexual, or physical difference as a basis for stigmatization and inequality.

The emergence of democracy as a political system, Taylor notes, "has ushered in a politics of equal recognition, which has taken various forms over the years, and has now returned in the form of demands for the equal status of cultures and of genders."[3] Taylor's use of "genders" rather than "men and women" is telling in its open-endedness. Although he does not seem to intentionally include transgender persons, the openness of Taylor's language fits well with an understanding of democratic politics that demands a constant vigilance against a priori exclusions from the realm of rights and civic participation. One should not have to "earn" a conferral of equal value. Rather, the equal valuation of persons is the *basis* for a democratic system of politics and rights. Furthermore, the assigning of unequal status as a precondition for civic and political participation, as in the case of racially segregated systems of education, is illegitimate.

Critical to a politics of recognition is both an attention to material conditions of inequality and to the semiotics of inequality. In regard to *Brown v. Board of Education,* Charles Lawrence has argued that "Read most narrowly, the case is about the rights of Black children to equal educational opportunity. But *Brown* can also be read more broadly to articulate a principle central to any substantive understanding of the equal protection clause, the foundation on which all anti-discrimination law rests. This is the principle of equal citizenship. Under that principle, 'Every individual is presumptively entitled to be treated by the organized society as a respected, responsible, and participating member.'"[4] *Brown*, Lawrence argues, is simultaneously about ending unequal access to education and about dismantling the systems of signification that sanction white racial supremacy. Systems of meaning and valuation interact with material and economic practices in ways that complement, reinforce, or even guide those practices: "*Brown* held that segregation was unconstitutional not simply because the physical separation of Black and white children is bad or because resources were distributed unequally among Black and white schools. *Brown* held that segregated schools were unconstitutional primarily because of the *message* segregation conveys–the message that Black children are an untouchable caste, unfit to be educated with white children."[5]

Analytically, the concept of recognition is useful as a starting point, but not as an end in itself. The refusal of recognition is often not simply the consequence of a single form of discrimination, but often precedes or extends out of a constellation of social forces. Indeed, as Frank Wu observes, for opponents of desegregation, *Brown* "was thought to be the harbinger of a sexual calamity," with, for example, Judge Thomas Brady of Mississippi "predict[ing] that white Southern men would fight to the death to preserve racial purity, defined as whiteness and the honor of their women."[6] For understanding such ideologies, Kimberlè Crenshaw's concept of intersectionality becomes useful. Crenshaw provides a way of articulating how constellations of forces operate such that racial hierarchies can both define and be defined by sexual policing. Analytically distinctive structures of oppression and privilege can manifest, in practice, simultaneously in complex patterns of collusion and antagonism.[7] For Crenshaw and subsequent critical race theorists, analyzing an instance of injustice as *solely* racial, gendered, or economic in nature is likely to result in an inadequate understanding of causes, injuries, and solutions. Sumi K. Cho observes that "In light of the prevalent and converging racial and gender stereotypes of Asian Pacific American Women as politically passive and sexually exotic and compliant, serious attention must be given to the problem of racialized sexual harassment.... The law's current dichotomous categorization of racial discrimination and sexual harassment as separate spheres of injury is inadequate to respond to racialized sexual harassment."[8] Stereotypes such as the hyper-femininity and sexual submissiveness of Asian-American men and women, for example, are not merely a problem of negative images that can be remedied by creating more positive portraits. When a belief in the sexual submissiveness of Asian-Americans is taken to imply a broader social submissiveness, Asian-Americans are not simply misrepresented, but become more readily the target of sexual harassment and employment discrimination because perpetrators believe that we are unlikely to fight back. Alternately, one might see the intersectional translation of racial privilege into heterosexism and male privilege when whiteness appears to entitle young men to engage in homophobic violence as an extension of their masculinity ("boys will be boys") in situations where racial supremacist violence would be far less tolerated, such as in schools, and where violence by men of color would be interpreted as an indication of simple criminality.

Crenshaw's work has at least three further implications. First, specific constellations of racial and gendered discrimination result in unique kinds of physical and representational violence. Second, seemingly disparate acts of violence and discrimination may also be linked to one another by what Cho observes as the pattern of "synergism" that "results when sexualized racial stereotypes combine with racialized gender stereotypes".[9] Third, no one particular form of oppression, for example sexism, is necessarily the root cause for, or automatically more urgent to address than another.

II. THEORIZING TRANSGENDER RECOGNITION:
PATRICIA WILLIAMS'S *THE ALCHEMY OF RACE AND RIGHTS*

In the United States, the history and structures of anti-black racism stand as an intellectual touchstone for understanding how and why recognition is refused. This necessarily leads to the question, what is the connective tissue between transphobia and racism? A sufficient answer to the question is more subtle than simply saying that both are forms of unjust discrimination. In her ground-breaking work, *The Alchemy of Race and Rights*, Patricia Williams writes of meeting S., a white transsexual woman and law student. Intending to transition, S. "wanted to talk to me before anyone else at the school because I was black and might be more understanding. I had never thought about transsexuality at all and found myself lost for words."[10] Williams's ambivalent silence should not be read, I think, as a signal of unconscious transphobia, but as the sign of an important experiential difference between the racism experienced by non-trans persons of color and the transphobia faced by white transgender persons.

Not surprising, S. was met, Williams recalls, with antagonism over what bathroom she should use; her fellow students asserted their proprietorship over public facilities, over the meaning of those facilities, and even over the significance of S.'s body when she enters "their" space:

> After the sex-change operation, S. began to use the ladies' room. There was an enormous outcry from women students of all political persuasions, who "felt raped," in addition to the more academic assertions of some who "feared rape." In a complicated storm of homophobia, the men of the student body let it be known that they too "feared rape" and vowed to chase her out of any and all men's rooms. The oppositional forces of men and women reached a compromise: S. should use the dean's bathroom. Alas, in the dean's bathroom no resolution was to be found, for the suggestion had not been an honest one but merely an integration of the fears of each side. Then, in his turn the dean, circumspection having gotten him this far in life, expressed polite, well-modulated fears about the appearance of impropriety in having students visit his inner sanctum, and many other things most likely related to his fear of a real compromise of hierarchy . . .
>
> At the vortex of this torment, S. as human being who needed to go to the bathroom was lost. Devoured by others, she carved and shaped herself to be definitionally acceptable. She aspired to a notion of women set like jewels in grammatical mountings, fragile and display-cased. She had not learned what society's tricksters and its dark fringes have had to learn in order to survive: to invert, to stretch, meaning rather

than oneself. She to whom words meant so much was not given the room to appropriate them. S. as "transsexual," S. as "not homosexual," thus became a mere floating signifier, a deconstructive polymorph par excellence.[11]

Through their phobic responses, S.'s fellow students and their dean transform bathrooms from a ubiquitous public convenience into extensions of their own genders, sexualities, and institutional positions. S., Williams observes, attempted to adapt to the phobic "logic" of the situation by protesting that she was not homosexual, and thus not a sexual threat. However, this attempt at accommodation fails. The conceptual framework erected against S. denies her claim to self-definition in the first place by prohibiting her access to a public space in which the self-definition of one's sex is a symbolic part of the act of entry.

It might seem strange, then, that in arrogating such power to themselves, S.'s fellow students would then imagine themselves the *victims* of sexual assault. But in conceiving of bathroom spaces as extensions of their sexed personhood, S.'s fellow students transform the bathrooms from a place of passive "urinary segregation," in which entry and exit occur with minimal thought, into spaces requiring a vigilant and active patrolling of sex definition and their own bodies. In the transphobic imagination, the bathroom becomes the extension of a genital narcissism (which could be expressed, roughly, as "my body is how sex should be defined for all other bodies" and "the presence of other kinds of body violates the sex of my own body").

At the same time, being black and non-trans is not the same as being transsexual and white, and the privileges of whiteness have a complicated relationship to the encounter with transphobia. We see in Williams's account at least three levels of complication. The structures of racism and transphobia do not emanate from the same historical space or set of ethical assumptions; non-trans persons who would likely balk at racial restrictions on bathroom use often see no problem with excluding persons based on their gender expressions or transgender identity. At the same time, among the privileges of whiteness in predominantly white institutions is the ability to take inclusion for granted; it is, arguably, this sense of automatic belonging that S. finds betrayed by her fellow students. Lastly, the simple projection of kinship threatens an act of *mis*recognition in which Williams would be reduced to the status of a pure victim while her racial identity is enlisted into S.'s search for legitimacy: "Initially it felt as if she were seeking in me the comfort of another nobody; I was a bit put off by the implication that my distinctive somebody-ness was being ignored—I was being used, rendered invisible by her refusal to see all of me."[12] The incautious use of the gains made by persons of color into furthering the social and political inclusion of white persons demands a certain degree of critical skepticism. In the context of LGBT political organizing, Allan Bérubé notes,

> dramatic race-analogy scenarios performed by white activists beg some serious questions. Are actual, rather than "virtual," people of color present as major actors in these scenarios, and if not, why not? What are they saying or how are they being silenced? How is their actual leadership being supported or not supported by the white people who are enacting this racialized history?[13]

The need for caution does not deny the existence of a connective tissue, however. For Williams, the link between herself, a black non-trans woman and law professor, and S., a white transsexual woman and student, lies in the ideological framework revealed by the refusal of material and symbolic recognition:

> In retrospect, I see clearly the connection between S.'s fate and my being black, her coming to me because I was black. S.'s experience was a sort of Jim Crow mentality applied to gender. Many men, women, blacks,

and certainly anyone who identifies with the term "white" are caught up in the perpetuation and invisible privilege of this game; for "black," "female," "male," and "white" are every bit as much properties as the buses, private clubs, neighborhoods, and schools that provide the extracorporeal battlegrounds of their expression. S.'s experience, indeed, was a reminder of the extent to which property is nothing more than the mind's enhancement of the body's limitation...[14]

To Williams, S. was cut off from the natural act of claiming an identity (linguistically, one might imagine such an act as the simple but foundational grammatical act of speaking in the first person: "I am..."). The persons around S. relegated her a priori to the status of a non-person; they laid claim to an exclusive ownership of gendered and sexual identities. For Williams, her connection to S. extends out of the understanding that ideologies of segregation work through both material and symbolic exclusions. Segregation is material in nature insofar as public spaces are physically cordoned off and defended as the private reserve of certain privileged subjectivities. Segregation is also symbolic insofar as the material act of exclusion attempts to convey the message and bolster the illusion that the boundaries of proper identities and the attribution of value, and dignity are fully and solely in the hands of those privileged subjects.

In spirit, if not explicitly, transgender scholars have followed Williams's work by providing increasingly nuanced analyses of the differences in identities and experiences *among* trans persons. In Williams's account, the students who decried student S. as a "rapist" echoed a long-standing stereotype of transsexual women as secret sexual predators. Judith Halberstam has argued that trans men and masculine women are, in contrast, more likely to be imagined as targets than as threats. Halberstam notes that "The codes that dominate within the women's bathroom are primarily gender codes; in the men's room, they are sexual codes."[15] In turn, gender policing in bathrooms intersects with the asymmetries that structure the cultural ideals of the divide between public (coded as a space of masculine sexual privilege) and private (coded as feminine domesticity). Because of these intersections, "The perils for passing FTMs in the men's room are very different from the perils of passing MTFs in the women's room. On the one hand, the FTM in the men's room is likely to be less scrutinized because men are not quite as vigilant about intruders for obvious reasons. On the other hand, if caught, the FTM may face some version of gender panic from the man who discovers him, and it is quite reasonable to expect and fear violence in the wake of such a discovery. The MTF, by comparison, will be more scrutinized in the women's room but possibly less open to punishment if caught."[16] Masculine and androgynous women in the women's room receive intensified scrutiny and face the demand by law enforcement to confirm their sex in ways that feminine men or androgynous persons in the men's room typically do not. These are, of course, interpretively useful generalizations, not absolutes. One can refine the analysis of gender policing further by exploring the ways that persons are scrutinized also for skin color, class, age, body art, and other features.

Susan Stryker describes our contemporary moment as a "wild profusion of gendered subject positions, spawned by the rupture of "woman" and "man" like an archipelago of identities rising from the sea: FTM, MTF, eonist, invert, androgyne, butch, femme, nellie, queen, third sex, hermaphrodite, tomboy, sissy, drag king, female impersonator, she-male, he-she, boy-dyke, girlfag, transsexual, transvestite, transgender, cross-dresser."[17] This proliferation does not mark a momentary cultural confusion that will subside into some more simple model of sex, gender and sexuality later; on the contrary, such nuanced self-definitions indicate that such complexity is, as C. Jacob Hale argues, phenomenologically real.[18] What is politically critical is the understanding that no single type of gender policing is exemplary of all other forms at the same time that these multiple experiences of gender policing are also experientially real, and function as preludes to the denial of recognition.

III. SOCIAL DEATH: TYRA HUNTER AND VINCENT CHIN

On August 7, 1995, Tyra Hunter, a black transgender woman, was struck by a car. As the emergency medical technician at the scene began to administer aid, he suddenly exclaimed, "This bitch ain't no girl…it's a nigger, he's got a dick!" and walked away. Witnesses later reported that, while Hunter was possibly still conscious, the EMT stood, "laughing and telling jokes" with his fellow technicians for several minutes. Tyra Hunter would subsequently die of her injuries at Washington, DC General Hospital.[19]

On June 19, 1982, Vincent Chin, a non-transgender Chinese-American, was clubbed to death by Ronald Ebens and his stepson, Michael Nitz. In a national and local atmosphere poisoned by the media's heavy-handed Japan-bashing, Chin's attackers blamed him for taking away "American" jobs. Both men were charged with manslaughter and released on probation with a three-thousand-dollar fine. Wayne County Circuit Court chief justice Charles Kaufman defended his light sentencing by noting that: 'We're talking here about a man who's held down a responsible job with the same company for 17 or 18 years, and his son who is employed and a part-time student. These men are not going to go out and harm somebody else. I just didn't think that putting them in prison would do any good for them or for society. You don't make the punishment fit the crime; you make the punishment fit the individual."[20]

These two instances of discriminatory behavior seem separated by different kinds of conduct, perpetrators, victims, and motives. Nevertheless, they are, I would suggest, two faces of one ideological coin. The deaths of a black transgender woman and a non-trans Chinese-American man are connected through acts of injustice predicated on gross refusals of civil and human recognition. In the first instance, the EMT's marked hostility toward women as a whole—"this bitch"—colluded, in his eyes, with Hunter's "failure" to meet his sexualized and gendered expectations of a black woman. Misogyny, racism, homophobia, and transphobia are all *simultaneously* audible in the EMT's statement. Regarded as an "it," Hunter is rendered socially dead, such that, lying injured on the ground, she is left to die, treated by the technicians at the scene as if she were *already* dead.[21] The display of callousness and arrogance on the part of the perpetrators is not incidental; rather it arises from their implicit belief that they possessed the right to either withhold or grant recognition in the form of medical care according to racialized, gendered, and sexual criteria.

In the second instance, a similar arrogance is visible in Judge Kaufman's explanation of his light sentencing. In effect, he absolves Chin's attackers of their violent racism because they were "responsible" family men. Kaufman imagines himself as the defender not of racist killers, but of well-employed, heterosexual heads-of-households whose personal well-being and society's welfare are imagined to be one and the same: "I just didn't think that putting them in prison would do any good for them or for society." Kaufman gives voice to a discourse that equates whiteness with middle-class heterosexual masculinity and with society in general. For Kaufman, a challenge to Ebens's and Nitz's racially motivated violence, legible as an assertion of supremacism, would threaten their socially sanctioned gender and class roles. In turn, Chin, while also employed and about to get married, has no standing as a man, a worker, or as a properly familial heterosexual. Although there is no clear reason why another attack on an Asian-American would *not* occur, Vincent Chin and Detroit's Asian-American community are dismissed from view as merely "somebody else," a referent without content.

My contention that these two instances of injustice are connected through their enactment of an exclusionary and *simultaneous* policing of race, gender, and sexuality, may seem overbroad. Nonetheless, I would suggest that neither Hunter's nor Chin's deaths are intelligible without reference to broader patterns of bias and exclusion. Barbara Perry has argued that hate crimes, understood as assaults against the communities to which an individual appears to belong, are significantly oriented toward creating a *spectacle* of subordination, as well as physical harm. Hate crimes, Perry argues, are intended as a message to the *communities* who bear witness, as well as the immediate victims, to get back "in their place."[22] The "messages" conveyed by acts of hate violence are not idiosyncrátic personal expressions, but attempts to reinforce publicly available discourses that support the subordination of historically marginalized groups. In short, even though the bulk of hate crimes are *not* committed by organized hate groups, acts of transphobic or racist violence are nonetheless attempts to turn beliefs in transgender deviance or white supremacy into concrete realities.

Tyra Hunter and Vincent Chin faced different historical legacies, to be sure. The intense demand to be "properly" gendered imposed on Tyra Hunter might be reckoned, in part, to be one of the consequences of the nineteenth-century construction of "womanhood" as white and centered in the domestic sphere; in contrast to such a standard, Cheryl Harris argues, "Black women functioned as important regulatory symbols: by representing everything that "woman" was not. . . . Indeed, through the rigid construction of the virgin/whore dichotomy along racial lines, the conception of womanhood was deeply wedded to slavery and patriarchy and the conduct of all women was policed in accordance with patriarchal norms and in furtherance of white male power."[23] Vincent Chin and Asian-Americans stand in the shadow cast by a different history. As Ronald Takaki notes, we have been painted as "perpetual foreigners" whose presence in the United States is regarded as transitory or even parasitical. These historical differences do not mean that Hunter's and Chin's deaths are isolated from one another, however. Taken together, the EMT's regard of black trans women as sexually deviant and socially dead and Judge Kaufman's claim that white heterosexual family men are preeminently valuable are interlocking and mutually reinforcing. As a mass of beliefs, they echo historically enduring hierarchies of racial, gender, and sexuality.

Here, it becomes important to address the distinction between a politics of recognition and economic or redistributive justice. The severe economic vulnerability of trans persons makes us vulnerable to abuse in many settings, from the workplace to the criminal justice system. Non-discrimination laws alone are simply inadequate. In historical perspective, as Derrick Bell has argued, the gains made toward racial equality since *Brown* have been regularly undermined by the structuring of economic interests in parallel with racism. Economic justice remains a necessary part of civil and human rights struggles, Bell argues, stressing the need to develop strategies that will "dilute both the financial and psychological benefits" of discriminatory behavior.[24] Recognition is, generally, an insecure achievement when it relies on the largesse of those with the power to grant or deny it or when it pits self-interest against moral persuasion.

Yet, to the extent that discriminatory actions have their roots in phobic beliefs that are *not* economically motivated, an emphasis on recognition remains essential. Hate violence does not correlate readily to economic disparities and "hatemongers are not all alienated deprived youth. It is also the case that hate crimes knows no class boundaries . . . Hate crime is increasingly likely to occur in places of privilege such as the workplace and college campuses."[25] The beliefs surrounding Tyra Hunter's or Vincent Chin's deaths, or student S.'s exclusion from bathrooms, had less to do with economic disparities than with the systematic devaluation of their personhoods and communities. Such devaluation took place in terms of cultural and social, rather than material worth. In all three cases, the question that became visible was not whether they could afford fair treatment, but whether or not they deserved fairness in the first place. Economic equality, whether measured in terms of income or more complex quality-of-life measurements, does not safeguard against the perception that one's life, identity, psychological integrity, and communities are of no *inherent* value.

Transphobia and Hate-Motivated Violence

Hate-motivated violence deserves an extended consideration insofar as it is one of the areas in which an expansion of our current politics of recognition is particularly needed. From the schoolyard thug to the thug with a badge, both opportunistic violence and state-sanctioned violence are a barbed-wire cage that keeps us from fully participating in the culture, society and political life around us. While violence is by no means the only civil rights concern of trans persons or persons of color, it is, nonetheless, the most direct means by which we have been warded off from attempting to make rights claims or pointing out unjust inequalities.

The relationship between the refusal of recognition and hate violence is multi-layered. Most evidently, non-recognition promotes hate crimes by allowing perpetrators to regard victims as targets who "deserve" to be hated. Beneath this causal relationship are at least three other pernicious consequences of non-recognition. Non-recognition renders invisible the frequency of those crimes. For example, neither transgender persons nor perceptions of gender identity appear as categories of persons or motives in the FBI's hate crimes statistics.[26] Non-recognition further leads to a dismissive attitude by the criminal justice system, the media, and the public toward the consequences of hatred for its victims and to victims being blamed for "bringing it on themselves." Most perniciously, perhaps, when victims receive inadequate support, it becomes possible to accept such attitudes and to resign oneself to the "inevitability" of being hated. Often then, the consequence is that hate crimes then go unreported and unaddressed, thus creating a cycle of suppression and silence.

Trans persons are systematically misrepresented both within the mass media and within the criminal justice system. We are regarded as persons whose identities are not simply "deviant," but actively deceptive and criminal. As I write this essay, a mistrial has occurred in the prosecution of Gwen Araujo's killers. Araujo was a seventeen-year-old trans woman was tortured and strangled by four men. Even when, because of pressures brought by family, friends, and transgender activists, the attention of the media and criminal justice system are sympathetic to the victims of anti-transgender hate crimes, trans persons can end up represented in ways that undermine the equal recognition implicit in hate crimes laws. Both prosecution and defense relied upon rhetorical ploys that have no actual ethical or legal basis. To the prosecutor, Araujo had committed "the sin of deception"[27] even as he closed his case by arguing that "the provocation [for murder] did not flow from Eddie [Gwen] Araujo."[28] The defense, in its turn, accused Araujo of "sexual fraud."[29]

The mass media bears a significant responsibility for misrepresenting trans persons and the scale of violence that we face. Trans activists have changed, to be sure, the quality of non-LGBT press coverage, especially since Brandon Teena's murder. We are less frequently represented as exotic perverts in order to create sensationalistic copy. Nonetheless, reporters still have trouble with names, genders, and, most important perhaps, context. (Indeed, I should note that the significance of turning Brandon Teena's life into a movie, *Boys Don't Cry*, remains to be seen; I have met a number of persons who, after seeing the film, did not know that he was an actual person.) In September of 2003, for example, *Newsweek* reported sympathetically on the murders of Ukea Davis, Bella Evangelista, Kiera Spaulding, Stephanie Thomas, and Mimi Young over a one-year period. However, the tendency to blame the victim for the crime still persisted; Bella Evangelista is implied to have been complicit in her death by deceiving unsuspecting heterosexual men: "[Evangelista] occasionally resorted to an especially risky form of prostitution–soliciting straight men on the street without telling them her true gender." The chilling larger context of violence against trans persons is relegated to a parenthetical comment: "Evangelista's killing was gruesome, but it wasn't unique. In the past year, four other transgender men have been found brutally murdered in the Washington area. Another was attacked and narrowly survived. Police say that so far, they have found no connection between the crimes...(Nationwide, nine other transgenders have been murdered in the past 12 months, according to Remembering Our Dead, a San Francisco-based activist group.)"[30] Among the consistent features of non-LGBT reporting on anti-trans hate crimes is the tendency for journalists to portray such crimes as a shocking new development or a sudden surge. In fact, it would have been more accurate to describe the violence in Washington as the continued expansion of an epidemic. Kylar Broadus observes that roughly two killings a month of trans persons are recorded each year. Furthermore, any number taken from currently available sources is likely to be *low* due to a combination of underreporting and misreporting, "because the individual victim is not identified as transgendered–because [authorities] will ignore the victims' transgender name and identity and state, 'It was a man,' or say, 'It was a gay man in drag' that was killed."[31]

Turns-of-phrase such as "sins of deception" and "sexual fraud" have no ethical or legal basis; they are strictly rhetorical strategems. Their effectiveness rests not only on widespread stereotypes and misconceptions, but on an a priori negation of transgender identity. Just as persons of color in the nineteenth century were excluded from testifying against white persons in court because their color presumptively negated the legitimacy of their testimony in a white supremacist juridical context, transgender persons are rendered "unreal" in a rigidly binaristic and heterosexist cultural environment.

IV. TOWARD A CRITICAL MULTICULTURALISM

The need for portraits of subjectivity that do not simply assimilate existing culturally dominant standards of normalcy and that enable a critical assessment the United States' particular sex-gender system has lead many to search for alternative sex-gender systems in which gender non-conformity is valued. Indeed, I recall reading Walter Williams's influential *The Spirit and the Flesh* for the first time as an undergraduate. With embarrassing hubris, I walked into Robert Warrior's office, the professor for my Native American literature class, and asked why gender and sexuality were not more prominent topics in the class? Gently but firmly, he asked me if I had learned anything yet about water rights, education issues, or sovereignty. The question made clear that while gender and sexual identity were not unimportant areas of inquiry, they should not be detached from the concerns over survival and justice for the communities in which those systems of gender and sexuality emerged.

What are the benefits and risks of writing about apparently transgender aspects of cultures "outside" the West as a source of cultural legitimacy in the United States? This question might seem an odd departure from my explorations of Williams's and Crenshaw's works and the deaths of Tyra Hunter and Vincent Chin. However, as Derrick Bell and others have noted, U.S. black and Native American struggles over rights and self-determination were watched intensely by those engaged in decolonization in Africa, Asia, Latin America, and the Caribbean. For some observers, U.S. civil rights struggles were an extension inwards of anti-colonialism. No less, whether or not early transgender activists considered themselves part of a broader liberation movement, they were part of a milieu steeped in racial civil rights struggles, labor organizing, anti-war and peace movements, and second-wave feminism. One might argue that post-war civil rights struggles generally cannot be read in terms of strictly national beliefs and actors.

This broader historical intersectionality requires us to attend to one of the key strategies of legitimation in transgender politics: the representation of cultures in which apparently "third sexes or genders" have a positive role and of cultures with different taxonomies for embodiment and sexual life more generally. The precedent such intellectual work has been set by feminist and, more recently, gay and lesbian historians and anthropologists who have sought world-views in which gender relations are not organized around patriarchy and domesticity, and sexuality is not defined in terms of mutually exclusive heterosexual and homosexual identities. Indeed, as Patrick Califia-Rice has noted, the archive of cross-cultural comparisons of gender and sexuality often undermines attempts to demarcate cleanly between transgender and gay-lesbian historiography.[32]

Transgender writers have referred to cultural systems in which so-called "third" genders or sexes have an established role in order to develop a critique of the fixity and universality of contemporary Western taxonomies of gender and sex.[33] One relatively moderate argument that can be made based on cross-cultural comparisons is that transgender identities do not herald the decay and end of civilization, but is simply one of many cultural possibilities. The existence of other cultural taxonomies is part of a larger body of evidence supporting the claim that Western models of sex, gender, and sexuality do not reflect some bedrock cultural necessity, but is one of several roads of historical development that is open to future change. For trans persons, knowledge of other cultural systems lends credence to the idea that transphobia and rigid gender roles are neither a permanent nor an organic feature of societies, and offers the possibility that there might well be a future in which transgender persons possess cultural and social legitimacy despite or even because of their identity.

The benefits of cross-cultural comparisons entail an equivalent degree of ethical danger. At the outset, transgender or third sex/gender are labels that might well be rejected or culturally unintelligible if applied. The act of misrepresentation or mistranslation is not trivial. In prioritizing sex or gender over other dimensions of cultural reality or in isolating sex and gender from their cultural milieu, it is easy to treat other cultures and persons in a fashion similar to the way that U.S. trans persons have been regarded by, for example, medical and psychiatric institutions that have tended to be interested in us primarily as case studies of a 'condition.' When transgender writers are located within the United States, the danger of misrepresentation is compounded by the problem of taking on an imperialistic approach to political and intellectual work. To be sure, trans persons typically have neither the financial nor the cultural capital to be a neocolonial vanguard; there is nothing to be gained by rehearsing the facile metaphors central to Janice Raymond's vitriolic *Transsexual Empire*. What is risked in using other cultures as a means to our own political ends, is an erosion of ethical consciousness in which we come to regard both "trans" and non-trans persons as mere instruments in struggles that they have had little voice in shaping and whose fruits they are unlikely to share.

By no means is the problem of cross-cultural representation faced by transgender writers alone. How transphobia intersects with the act of cross-cultural representation in the so-called mainstream of Western mass media is instructive about the uses to which the representations of other cultures can be put. One cornerstone of transphobic representation works through a radical constriction of the norms against which sex and gender expressions are interpreted and evaluated. Take, for example, a short review of a travel book from *The Economist*:

> It is, one imagines, every sex-tourist's nightmare: the go-go bar, the tuk-tuk, the hotel room and then…the discovery that there is rather more to the lovely lady than had been bargained for. Thailand's ladyboys have struck again.[34]

Within a few brief sentences, *The Economist* above imagines transgender subjectivity as nothing more (or less) than a threat to heterosexual genital security. "Thailand's ladyboys," Thai *kathoeys*, are depicted strictly with regard to whether they conform to the desires of the heterosexual European sex-tourist, presented here as the standard of normalcy and the "one" whose subjectivity should be "imagined" by the reader. Whether or not Thai *kathoeys* are represented in a positive or negative light in this instance is, to some extent, irrelevant; more important, I think, is the fact that *kathoey* identity is represented as dependent on, and subordinate to the presumptive gender expectations and heterosexuality of the narrator. The *kathoey* becomes nothing more or less than the extension of a sexual "nightmare." At the same time, the author invokes the common stereotype of the devious and cunning Asian: in effect, *kathoeys* are Fu Manchu posing as Madame Butterfly.

Writing for the *New Internationalist*, Urvashi Butalia offers an alternative and far more expansive mode of representation in a profile of Mona, an Indian *hijra*:

> Mona Ahmed's visiting card currently lists five names. Apart from Mona, which is how I know her, there is Ahmad Bhai, Saraswati, Ahmed Iqbal and Radharani. These names are a mix of Hindu (Saraswati, Radharani), Muslim (Ahmed Bhai, Ahmed Iqbal) and Christian (Mona), but they also combine different genders. Mona, Saraswati, and Radharani are female names. Ahmed Bhai and Ahmed Iqbal are male names. This is entirely appropriate–with Mona it's difficult to tell from one moment to the next which gender she will assume . . .
>
> As a eunuch she has limited ways of making a living: eunuchs live on the fringes of Indian society and can't easily find jobs. The group to which she belongs make their living by blessing newborn children in return for money–an act which plays on people's fear of the "evil eye" and is the reason families willingly oblige . . .
>
> There are times when Mona yearns to be what she calls "normal." But that normality doesn't have to do with sex. Instead, it's a longing to be a part of mainstream society. It has to do with acceptability, with respect–all of which elude her simply because she cannot be classed as one or other of the two genders available us. At other times she laughs at the trap of "normal" society. Years ago she adopted a little girl when she felt a strong urge to motherhood which for her has nothing to do with biology.[35]

The difference here is qualitative, not merely quantitative. Mona's identity cannot be reduced to either her physicality or her gender, but must be seen within the cultural, religious, and economic structures that are specific to India as a modern nation. Mona's identity, while understood relationally, is not represented as a subordinate extension of another's reality. Celebratory representation need not be a central concern here. Rather, the "positive" quality of Butalia's representation of Mona extends from the manner in which she depicts Mona's reality as composed through the complex relationships among her personal agency, the social and economic possibilities surrounding her, and the larger, evolving communities and histories within modern Indian society.

On the one hand, when portrayed as strange and deviant, different systems of sex and gender relations can be used to reaffirm the belief that the West's culturally dominant understanding of sex and gender identity is natural and superior. On the other hand, placed in a broader cultural and historical context, the depiction of a different sex and gender system can also be used to demonstrate that the binary and heterocentric understanding of "normal" sex and gender identity in the United States is not a fact of nature, but the product of a specific historical legacy, one that is reinforced not by the force of nature but by relations of privilege and exclusion. The desire to engage in comparative thought should not be dismissed merely as a search for Shangri-La. Instead, the use of cross-cultural comparisons as a strategy of legitimation requires a heightened awareness of the ethical stakes involved.

A multiculturalist ethics provides a useful vantage point. In the United States, multiculturalism has been, typically, an attempt to challenge ethnocentrism through education after the demise of overt racial and ethnic supremacism. At its weakest, multiculturalism descends into the tokenistic and easily forgotten celebration of cosmetic cultural differences. Ideally, more serious changes in ways of thinking can take place through a rigorous, critical multiculturalism in which education focuses "on the material historical productions of difference rather than on 'culture' as a ready-made thing,"[36] and explore how specific systems of identification, discrimination, and privilege become forged over time.

A critical multiculturalist approach toward the representation of cultural differences in transgender intellectual work has at least three dimensions: the elaboration of historical context, the need to define the purposes and limits of cross-cultural comparison, and establishing reciprocity rather than parasitism. The representation of Native American cultures by trans persons, particularly the idea of two-spiritedness, provide a useful vantage point. When speaking of gender systems, the idea of a system or a structure should not be mistaken as meaning historical immobility or indicating a machine-like creation of identity categories. In the case of Navajo categories of gender, Wesley Thomas argues that "gender formulation and reformulation are ongoing processes that have been affected by the influence of Euro-American cultures. The Navajo world has always evolved by synthesizing traditional ideas and practices with new ones."[37] Cultures should be recognized not as templates, but as dynamic systems containing internal debates, tensions, and contradictions. Awareness of this internal autonomy and self-reflexivity is analytically vital. Robert Warrior notes that: "American Indian intellectual discourse can now ground itself in its own history the way that African-American, feminist, and other oppositional discourses have … far from engaging in some new and novel practice that belongs necessarily to the process of assimilating and enculturating non-Native values, we are doing something that Natives have done for hundreds of years–something that can be and has been an important part of resistance to assimilation and survival."[38] Second, information about another culture constitutes a critical vantage point from which to see one's own culture from a different perspective; it does not enable one to claim those identity categories as one's own. As Gary Bowen observes, "There are many 'magpies' who are drawn to latch onto the bright shiny aspects of Native culture, who misappropriate Native culture, customs, and artifacts in the belief that they are 'honoring' Native people by imitating them without understanding them."[39] Finally, substantive cross-cultural work demands that one understand and value that the stakes present in struggles beyond one's own.

NOTES

1. John Rawls, *A Theory of Justice* (Cambridge, MA: Harvard University Press, 1999), 3.
2. Charles Taylor, *Multiculturalism: The Politics of Recognition*, ed. Amy Gutmann (Princeton: Princeton University Press, 1994), 27.
3. Ibid., 27.
4. Charles Lawrence III, "If He Hollers Let Him Go: Regulating Racist Speech on Campus," in *Words that Wound: Critical Race Theory, Assaultive Speech, and the First Amendment*, [ed. Mari J. Matsuda and Charles Lawrence III], 59 (Boulder: Westview, 1993).
5. Ibid., 59.
6. Frank H. Wu, *Yellow* (New York: Basic Books, 2002), 265–6.
7. Kimberlè Crenshaw, "Beyond Racism and Misogyny: Black Feminism and 2 Live Crew," in *Words that Wound: Critical Race Theory, Assaultive Speech, and the First Amendment*, [ed. Mari J. Matsuda and Charles Lawrence III], 111–132 (Boulder: Westview, 1993). Crenshaw distinguishes among three kinds of intersectionality: structural, "to refer to the way in which women of color are situated within overlapping structures of subordination"; political, "to refer to the different ways in which political and discursive practices relating to race and gender interrelate, often erasing women of color"; and representational, "referring to the way that race and gender images, readily available to our culture, converge to create unique and specific narratives deemed appropriate for women of color. Not surprisingly, the clearest convergences are those involving sexuality, perhaps because it is through sexuality that images of minorities and women are most sharply focused" (114–6).
8. Sumi K. Cho, "Converging Stereotypes in Racialized Sexual Harassment: Where the Model Minority Meets Suzie Wong," in *Critical Race Feminism*, ed. Adrien Katherine Wing, 212 (New York: New York University Press, 1997).
9. Ibid., 205.
10. Patricia J. Williams, *The Alchemy of Race and Rights* (Cambridge, MA: Harvard University Press, 1991), 123.
11. Ibid., 123–4.
12. Ibid., 124.
13. Allan Bérubé, "How Gay Stays White and What Kind of White it Stays," *The Making and Unmaking of Whiteness*, eds. Birget Brander Rasmussen, Eric Klinenberg, Irene J. Nexica, and Matt Wray, 245–6 (Durham, NC: Duke University Press, 2001).
14. Williams, *Alchemy*, 124.
15. Judith Halberstam, *Female Masculinity* (Durham, NC: Duke University Press, 1998), 24.
16. Ibid., 25.
17. Susan Stryker, "The Transgender Issue: An Introduction," *GLQ* 4, no. 2 (1998): 148.

18. C. Jacob Hale, "Leatherdyke Boys and Their Daddies: How to Have Sex Without Women or Men," *Social Text* 52, no. 3 (1997): 230.

19. Scott Bowles, "A Death Robbed of Dignity Mobilizes a Community," *Washington Post,* December 10, 1995.

20. Judith Cummings, "Detroit Asian-Americans Protest Lenient Penalties for Murder," *New York Times,* April 26, 1983.

21. In his comparative study of systems of slavery, Orlando Patterson argues that slaves are regarded as "socially dead," insofar as they are considered by the slave-owning culture to be cut off from family, kinship and community, and lack both honor and power. *Slavery and Social Death* (Cambridge, MA: Harvard University Press, 1982), 1–3.

22. Perry emphasizes the ideological and semiotic dimension of hate crimes, and argues that a hate crime "involves acts of violence and intimidation, usually directed toward already stigmatized and marginalized groups. It attempts to re-create simultaneously the threatened (real or imagined) hegemony of the perpetrator's group and the "appropriate" subordinate identity of the victim's group. It is a means of marking both the Self and the Other in such a way as to reestablish their "proper" relative positions, as given and reproduced by broader ideologies and patterns of social and political inequality." Barbara Perry, *In the Name of Hate: Understanding Hate Crime* (New York: Routledge, 2001), 10.

23. Cheryl I. Harris, "Finding Sojourner's Truth: Race, Gender, and the Institution of Property," *Cardozo Law Review* (18 November 1996): 315.

24. Derrick Bell, *Faces at the Bottom of the Well: The Permanence of Racism* (New York: Basic Books, 1992), 61.

25. Perry, *In the Name of Hate,* 38.

26. Federal Bureau of Investigation, *Uniform Crime Report,* Hate Crimes Statistics, 2002. http://www.fbi.gov/ucr/hate-crime2002.pdf.

27. Chris Lamiero as quoted by Michelle Locke, "Prosecutor: Transgender Teen 'Executed,' " Associated Press, Wednesday, April 14, 2004 11:01 PM. http://www.guardian.co.uk/uslatest/story/o,1282,-3978164,00.html

28. http://www.nbc11.com/news/3378630/detail/html.

29. Ibid.

30. Holly Bailey, "Targeting Transgenders," *Newsweek,* September 8, 2003, 53.

31. Quoted in Cei Bell, "Danger Across Genders" *The Philadelphia Enquirer,* April 14, 2003. http://www.philly.com/mld/inquirer/news/editorial/5627384.html.

32. Patrick Califia-Rice, *Sex Changes: The Politics of Transgenderism* (San Francisco: Cleis, 1997).

33. Leslie Feinberg, *Transgender Warriors: Making History from Joan of Arc to RuPaul* (Boston: Beacon Press, 1996).

34. "Skirting Pain." Review of *The Third Sex: Kathoey, Thailand's Ladyboys,* by Richard Totman. *The Economist* (June 14–20, 2003): 82.

35. Urvashi Butalia, "The Third Sex," *New Internationalist* (October 2002), 5.

36. David Palumbo-Liu, "Multiculturalism Now: Civilization, National Identity, and Difference Before and After September 11th," *Boundary 2* 29, no. 2 (2002): 110.

37. Wesley Thomas (Navajo), "Navajo Cultural Constructions of Gender and Sexuality," in *Two-Spirit People: Native American Gender Identity, Sexuality, and Spirituality,* eds. Sue-Ellen Jacobs, Wesley Thomas, and Sabine Lang, 169 (Urbana, IL: University of Illinois Press, 1997).

38. Robert Warrior (Osage), *Tribal Secrets: Recovering American Indian Intellectual Traditions,* (Minneapolis: University of Minnesota Press, 1995), 2.

39. Cited in Leslie Feinberg, *Trans Liberation: Beyond Pink or Blue,* (Boston: Beacon Press, 1998), 66.

REFERENCES

Goldberg, David Theo. 1994. Introduction: Multicultural conditions. In *Multiculturalism: A critical reader,* ed. David Theo Goldberg. Oxford: Blackwell.

Young, Iris Marion. 1998. Unruly categories: A critique of Nancy Fraser's dual systems theory. In *Theorizing multiculturalism: A guide to the current debate,* ed. Cynthia Willett. Oxford: Blackwell.

Permissions

Benjamin, Harry. "Transsexualism and Transvestism as Psycho-Somatic and Somato-Psychic Syndromes," from *American Journal of Psychotherapy*, Vol. 8, pp. 219–230, 1954. Reprinted by permission of the Association for the Advancement of Psychotherapy.

Bornstein, Kate. "Gender Terror, Gender Rage" *Gender Outlaw: On Men, Women, and the Rest of Us.* (New York: Routledge, 1994) pp. 71–85. Reprinted with permission.

Boyd, Nan Alamilla. "Bodies in Motion: Lesbian and Transsexual Histories" from *A Queer World: The Center for Lesbian and Gay Studies Reader*. Duberman, Martin, ed. (New York: N.Y.U., 1997) Copyright © 1997 Nan Alamilla Boyd. Reprinted with permission.

Brown, George. "Transsexuals in the Military: Flight into Hypermasculinity" from *Archives of Sexual Behavior*. Volume 17, #6, pp. 527–537 (1988). Reprinted with permission from the International Academy of Sex Research.

Butler, Judith. "Doing Justice to Someone: Sex Reassignment and Allegories of Transsexuality," in *GLQ: a Journal of Lesbian and Gay Studies*, Vol. 7, No. 4, pp. 621–636. Copyright © 2001, Duke University Press. All rights reserved. Used by permission of the publisher.

Chase, Cheryl. "Hermaphrodites with Attitude: Mapping the Emergence Intersex Political Activism," in *GLQ: a Journal of Lesbian and Gay Studies*, Vol. 4, No. 2, pp. 189–211. Copyright © 1998. Duke University Press. All rights reserved. Used by permission of the publisher.

Cromwell, Jason. "Queering the Binaries: Transsituated Identities, Bodies, and Sexualities," from *Transmen and FTMs: Identities, Bodies, Genders, and Sexuality.* (Champaign: University of Illinois Press, 1999) pp. 122–136. Reprinted with permission.

Devor, Aaron H. and Matte, Nicholas. "ONE Inc. and Reed Erickson: The Uneasy Collaboration of Gay and Trans Activism," in *GLQ: a Journal of Lesbian and Gay Studies*, Vol. 10, No. 2, pp. 179–209. Copyright © 2004. Duke University Press. All rights reserved. Used by permission of the publisher.

Felski, Rita. "Fin de siècle, Fin du sexe: Transsexuality, Postmodernism, and the Death of History" from *New Literary History* 27, no. 2 (Spring 1996) pp. 337–349. Reprinted with permission from The Johns Hopkins University Press.

Garber, Marjorie. "The Chic of Araby: Transvestism and the Erotics of Cultural Appropriation" from *Vested Interests: Cross-Dressing & Cultural Anxiety* (New York: Routledge, 1997) pp. 304–352. Reprinted with permission.

Suggestions for Further Reading

Adams, Rachel. "Masculinity without Men." *GLQ: A Journal of Lesbian and Gay Studies* 6: 3 (2000), pp. 467–478.

Amadiume, Ifi. *Male Daughters, Female husbands: Gender and Sex in an African Society*. London ; Atlantic Highlands; N.J. : Zed Books, 1987.

Atkins, Dawn, ed. *Looking Queer: Body Image And Identity In Lesbian, Bisexual, Gay, and Transgender Communities*. New York: Haworth Press, 1998.

Benjamin, Harry. *The Transsexual Phenomenon*. New York: Julian Press, 1966.

Billings, Dwight B. and Thomas Urban. "The Socio-Medical Construction of Transsexualism: An Interpretation and Critique." *Social Problems* 29 (1981): 266–82.

Blackwood, Evelyn and Saskia Wieringa, eds. *Female Desires: Same-sex Relations and Transgender Practices Across Cultures*. New York: Columbia University Press, 1999.

Blanchard, Ray "Clinical Observation and Systematic Studies of Autogynephilia." *Journal of Sex and Marital Therapy* (1991) 17/4, Winter: 235–251.

Bloom, Amy. *Normal: Transsexual CEOs, Cross-Dressing Cops, Hermaphrodites With Attitude*. New York: Random House, 2002.

Bolin, Anne. *In Search of Eve: Transsexual Rites of Passage*. South Hadley, MA: Bergin and Garvey, 1988.

Bullough, Bonnie, Vern L. Bullough and James Elias, eds. *Gender Blending*. Amherst, MA: Prometheus Books, 1997.

Bullough, Bonnie, Vern L. Bullough and James Elias and Bonnie Bullough. *Crossdressing, Sex, and Gender*. Philadelphia: University of Pennsylvania Press, 1993.

Butler, Judith, *Gender Trouble: Feminism and the Subversion of Identity*. New York: Routledge, 1990.

———. *Bodies That Matter: On the Discursive Limits of "Sex."* New York: Routledge, 1993.

———. *Undoing Gender*. New York: Routledge, 2004.

Califia, Pat. *Sex Changes: The Politics of Transgenderism*. San Francisco: Cleis Press, 1997.

Cameron, Loren. *Body Alchemy*. San Francisco: Cleis Press, 1996.

Chapman, Kathleen, and Michael du Plessis. "Don't Call Me 'Girl'": Feminist Theory, Lesbian Theory, and Transsexual Identities." In *Cross Purposes: Lesbian Studies, Feminist Studies, and the Limits of Alliance*, Dana Heller, ed. Bloomington: Indiana University Press, 1997.

Chase, Cheryl. "Affronting Reason." In *Looking Queer: Image and Identity in Lesbian, Bisexual, Gay, and Transgendered Communities*, Dawn Atkins, ed. Bighamton, NY: Haworth, 1998. 209–235.

Coleman, Eli, Walter Bockting, and Louis Gooren. "Homosexual and bisexual identity in sex- reassigned female-to-male transsexuals." *Archive of Sexual Behavior*. (1993) Feb22(1): 37–50.

Currah, Paisley. "The transgender rights imaginary." *Georgetown Journal of Gender and the Law* 4 (2003) 705–720.

———, Shannon Minter, and Richard Juang, eds. *Transgender Rights: History Politics, Culture*. (Minneapolis: University of Minnesota Press, 2006).

Dekker, Rudolph. M. and Lotte C. van de Pol. *The Tradition Of Female Transvestism In Early Modern Europe*. Hampshire: The Macmillan Press Ltd. 1989.

Denny, Dallas, ed. *Current Concepts in Transgender Identity*. New York: Garland, 1998.

Detloff, Madelyn. "Idealized, Debased, and Ordinary: Gender in (Post)Modern Circuits of Desire." *Modern Fiction Studies* 47:4 (Winter 2001), 977–985.

Devor, Holly. *Gender Blending: Confronting the Limits of Duality*. Bloomington: Indiana University Press, 1989.

———. *FTM: Female-to-male Transsexuals in Society*. Bloomington: Indiana University Press, 1997.

Docter, Richard. *Transvestites and Transsexuals: Toward a Theory of Cross-Gender Behavior*. New York: Plenum Press, 1988.

Dreger, Alice Domurat. *Hermaphrodites and the Medical Invention of Sex*. Cambridge, Mass.: Harvard University Press, 1998.

Ekins, Richard. *Male Femaling: A Grounded Theory Approach to Cross-Dressing and Sex-Changing*. London, New York: Routledge, 1998.

Elliot, Patricia. "A Psychoanalytic Reading of Transsexual Embodiment." *Studies in Gender and Sexuality* 2, no. 4 (2001): 295–325.

Elliot, Patricia and Katrina Roen. Transgenderism and the question of embodiment. *GLO: A Journal of Lesbian and Gay Studies*, (1998). 4 (2): 231–261.

Ellis, Havelock. *Studies in the Psychology of Sex*. Vol. 7, *Eonism and Other Supplementary Studies*. Philadelphia: F.A. Davis, 1928.

Epstein, Julia and Kristina Straub, eds., *Body Guards: The Cultural Politics of Gender Ambiguity*. New York: Routledge, 1991.

Fausto-Sterling, Anne. *Sexing the Body: Gender Politics and the Construction of Sexuality*. New York: Basic Books, 2000.

Feinberg, Leslie. *Transgender Warriors: Making History from Joan of Arc to Ru Paul*. Boston: Beacon Press, 1996.

Feinbloom, Deborah Heller. *Transvestites and Transsexuals*. New York: A Delta Book, 1976.

Feinbloom, Deborah Heller, et al., "Lesbian/Feminist Orientation Among Male-to-Female Transsexuals," *Journal of Homosexuality* 2 (Fall 1976).

Ferris, Lesley, ed. *Crossing the Stage: Controversies on Cross-Dressing*. New York, London: Routledge, 1993.

Foucault, Michel. *Herculine Barbin: Being the Recently Discovered Memoirs of a Nineteenth-Century Hermaphrodite*. New York: Pantheon, 1980.

Freud, Sigmund. "Some Psychical Consequences of the Anatomical Distinctions between the Sexes." In *The Complete Psychological Works of Sigmund Freud*, Vol. 18. Translated by James Stratchey. New York: Norton, 1976 [1925].

Gamson, Joshua. *Freaks Talk Back: Television Talk and Sexual Nonconformity*. Chicago: University of Chicago Press, 1998.

Green, Jamison. *Becoming a Visible Man*. Vanderbilt University Press, 2004.

Green, Richard. *The "Sissy Boy Syndrome" and the Development of Homosexuality*. New Haven: Yale University Press, 1987.

Green, Richard and John Money, eds., *Transsexualism and Sex Reassignment*. Baltimore: Johns Hopkins University Press, 1969.

Grosz, Elizabeth. *Volatile Bodies; Toward a Corporeal Feminism*. Bloomington: Indiana University Press, 1994.

Halberstam, Judith. *Female Masculinity*. Durham and London: Duke University Press, 1998.

———. *In A Queer Time And Place: Transgender Bodies, Subcultural Lives*. New York: New York University Press, 2005.

———. "Mackdaddy, Superfly, Rapper: Gender, Race, and Masculinity in the Drag King Scene." *Social Text* 52/53 (1997):104–131.

Halberstam, Judith and Ira Livingston, eds. *Posthuman Bodies*. Bloomington: Indiana University Press, 1995.

Hale, C. Jacob. "Leatherdyke Boys and Their Daddies: How to Have Sex without Women or Men." *Social Text* 15, nos. 3-4 (1997): 225–238.

———. "Tracing a Ghostly Memory in My Throat: Reflections on Ftm Feminist Voice and Agency" *Men Doing Feminism*, ed. Tom Digby. New York: Routledge, 1998. 99–129.

Hamburger, Christian. "The Desire for Change of Sex as Shown by Personal Letters from 465 Men and Women." *Acta Endocrinologica* 14 (1953): 361–75.

Haynes, Felicity and Tarquam, McKenna, eds. *Unseen Genders: Beyond the Binaries*. New York: Peter Lang, 2001.

Hemmings, Clare. "From Lesbian Nation to Transgender Liberation: A Bisexual Feminist Perspective." *Journal of Gay, Lesbian, and Bisexual History* 1, no. 1 (1996): 37–59.

Herdt, Gilbert, ed. *Third Sex, Third Gender: Beyond Sexual Dimorphism in Culture and History*. New York: Zone Books, 1994.

Heyes, Cressida. "Feminist solidarity after queer theory: The case of transgender." *Signs*, (2003)28 (4):1093–1120.

Hird, Myra J. "For a Sociology of Transsexualism," *Sociology* 36(3): 577–595.

Hodgkinson, Liz. *Michael Nee Laura: The Story Of The World's First Female To Male Transsexual*. London: Columbus Books Ltd., 1989.

Irving, Janice. *Disorders of Desire: Sex and Gender in Modern American Sexology*. Philadelphia: Temple University Press, 1990.

Jackson, Peter A. "Thai Research on Male Homosexuality and Transgenderism and the Cultural Limits of Foucaultian Analysis." *Journal of the History of Homosexuality* 8, no. 1 (1997): 52–85.

———. "Pre-Gay, Post-Queer: Thai Perspectives on Proliferating Gender/Sex Diversity in Asia." *Journal of Homosexuality* 40, nos. 3/4 (2001): 1–25.

Jackson, Peter A. and Nerida M. Cook, eds. *Genders and Sexualities in Modern Thailand*. Chiang Mai, Thailand: Silkworm Books, 1999.

Jacobs, Sue-Ellen, Wesley Thomas, and Sabine Lang, eds. *Two-Spirit People: Native American Gender Identity, Sexuality, and Spirituality*. Urbana: University of Illinois Press, 1997.

Jeffreys, Sheila. "FTM Transsexualism and Grief." *Lesbian Network*, (2002) No. 64: 16–17.

Johnson, Mark. *Beauty and Power: Transgendering and Cultural Transformation in the Southern Philippines*. Oxford: Berg, 1997.

———. "Global Desirings and Translocal Loves: Transgendering and Same Sex Sexualities in the Southern Philippines." *American Ethnologist* 25, no. 4 (1998):695–711.

Kessler, Suzanne J. *Lessons from the Intersexed*. New Brunswick: Rutgers University Press, 1998.

Kessler, Suzanne J. and Wendy McKenna. Who Put the "trans" in Transgender?: Gender Theory and Everyday Life, *The International Journal of Transgenderism* (2000) 4, 3: http://www.symposion.com/ijt/gilbert/kessler.htm

King, Dave. "Social Constructionism and Medical Knowledge: The Case of Transsexualism." *Sociology of Health and Illness* 9 (1987): 351–377.

———. *The Transvestite and the Transsexual: Public Categories and Private Identities*. Aldershot: Avebury, 1993.

Kroker, Arthur and Marlilouise Kroker. *The Last Sex: Feminism and Outlaw Bodies*. New York: St. Martin's Press, 1993.

Kulick, Don. *Travesti: Sex, Gender, and Culture among Brazilian Transgendered Prostitutes*. Chicago: University of Chicago Press, 1998.

Lacan, Jacques. "On a Problem Preliminary to Any Possible Treatment of Psychosis." In *Écrits: A Selection*. Trans Alan Sheridan. New York: Norton, 1982 [1958]. 179–225.

Lang, Sabine. *Men As Women, Women As Men: Changing Gender In Native American Cultures*. Austin: University of Texas Press, 1998.

Laqueur, Thomas. *Making Sex: Body and Gender from the Greeks to Freud*. Cambridge, MA: Harvard University Press, 1990.

Lothstein, Leslie Martin. *Female-to-Male Transsexualism: Historical, Clinical, and Theoretical Issues*. Boston: Routledge and Kegan Paul, 1983.

Mackie, Vera. "The Trans-sexual Citizen: Queering Sameness and Difference." *Australian Feminist Studies* 16, no. 35 (2001): 185–192.

Mageo, Jeanette-Marie. "Samoa, on the Wilde Side: Male Transvestism, Oscar Wilde, and Liminality in Making Gender." *Ethos* 24, no. 4 (1996).

MacKenzie, Gordene Olga. *Transgender Nation*. Bowling Green State University Press, 1994.

Manalansan, Martin F. "Disaporic Deviance/Divas: How Filipino Gay Transmigrants 'Play with the World.'" In *Queer Diasporas*. Cindy Patton and Benigno Sánchez-Eppler, ed. Durham: Duke University Press, 2000. 183–203.

McLelland, Mark. "The Newhalf Net: Japan's 'Intermediate Sex' On-Line." *International Journal of Sexuality and Gender Studies* 7, nos. 2/3 (July 2002): 163–175.

Millot, Catherine. *Horsexe: Essay on Transsexualism*. New York: Autonomedia, 1990.

Minter, Shannon. "Do transsexuals dream of gay rights? Getting real about transgender inclusion in the gay rights movement."*New York Law School Journal of Human Rights*, (2000)17 (2): 589–623.

Money, John and Anke A. Ehrhardt. *Man and Woman, Boy and Girl: Differentiation and Dimorphism of Gender Identity from Conception to Maturity*. Baltimore: Johns Hopkins University Press, 1972.

Money, John, Anke A. Ehrhardt, John Hampson, and Joan Hampson, "Hermaphroditism: Recommendations concerning assignment of sex, change of sex, and psychologic management."*Bulletin of the Johns Hopkins Hospital* (1955b) 97: 284–300.

Money, John, Anke A. Ehrhardt, John Hampson, and Joan Hampson. "Imprinting and the establishment of gender role." *Archives of Neurology and Psychiatry*, (1957)77: 333–336

More, Kate, and Stephen Whittle, eds. *Reclaiming Genders: Transsexual Grammars at the Fin de Siècle*. London: Cassell, 1999.

Moricl, Liora. 1999. "Dana International: A Self-Made Jewish Diva." *Race, Gender & Class*, 6: 4 (1999), 110 Money, John, Anke A. Ehrhardt, John Hampson, and Joan Hampson 124.

Namaste, Viviane K. *Sex Change, Social Change: Reflections on Identity, Institutions, and Imperialism*. (Toronto: Women's Press, 2005).

Nanda, Serena. *Neither Man nor Woman: The Hijras of India*. Belmont, CA: Wadsworth Publishing, 1990.

Nestle, Joan, ed. *The Persistent Desire: A Femme-Butch Reader*. Boston: Alyson Publications, 1987.

Newton, Esther. "The Mythic Mannish Lesbian: Radclyffe Hall and the New Woman." *Signs* 9 (1984): 557–575.

Nicholson, Linda. "Interpreting Gender." *Signs*, (1994). 20 (1): 79–105.

Norton, Jody. "Transchildren and the Discipline of Children's Literature." *The Lion and the Unicorn*. 23:3 (September 1999), 415–436.

Pathy-Allen, Mariette. *The Gender Frontier*. Heidelberg: Kehrer Verlag, 2003.

———. *Transformations: Cross-Dressers and the People Who Love Them*. London: Dutton, 1989.

Pauly, Ira B. "Female transsexualism: Part I." *Archives of Sexual Behavior*. (1974) Nov: 3(6): 487–507.

———. "Female transsexualism: part II." *Archives of Sexual Behavior*. (1974) Nov: 3(6): 509–526.

Pillard, Richard and Weinrich, J. D. "Periodic table model of gender transpositions: Part I. A Theory Based on Masculinization and Defeminization of the Brain." *Journal of Sex Research*, (1987). 23 (11): 425–454.

Prieur, Annick. In *Mema's House, Mexico City: On Transvestites, Queens, and Machos*. Chicago: University of Chicago Press, 1998.

Prosser, Jay. "No Place Like Home: The Transgendered Narrative of Leslie Feinberg's *Stone Butch Blues*." *Modern Fiction Studies* 41 (Fall-Winter 1995): 483–514.

———. "'Some Primitive Thing Conceived in a Turbulent Age of Transition': The Transsexual Emerging from *The Well*." In *Palatable Poison: Critical Perspectives on* The Well of Loneliness *Past and Present*. Eds. Laura Doan and Jay Prosser. New York: Columbia University Press, 2002. 129–144.

———. "Transsexuals and the Transsexologists: Inversion and the Emergence of Transsexual Subjectivity." *Sexology in Culture: Labeling Bodies and Desires*. Ed. Lucy Bland and Laura Doan. Oxford: Polity Press, 1998. 116–132.

Ramet, Sandra P., ed. *Gender Reversals and Gender Cultures: Anthropological and Historical Perspectives*. New York: Routledge, 1996.

Reich, June L. "Genderfuck: The Law of the Dildo." *Discourse* 15, no. 1 (1992): 112–127.

Reis, Elizabeth. "Impossible Hermaphrodites: Intersex in America, 1620–1960." *Journal of American History* 92:2 (September 2005), 411–441.

———. "Teaching Transgender History, Identity, and Politics" *Radical History Review* 88 (Winter 2004), 166–177.

Rosario, Vernon A. "The Biology of Gender and the Construction of Sex?" *GLQ: A Journal of Lesbian and Gay Studies*. 10: 2 (2004), 280–287.

———. "Trans [Homo] Sexuality? Double Inversion, Psychiatric Confusion, and Hetero-Hegemony." In *Queer Studies: A Lesbian, Bisexual, Gay, Transsexual Anthology*, ed. Brett Beemyn and Mickey Eliason, 35–51. New York: New York University Press, 1996.

Roen, Katrina. "'Either/Or' and 'Both/Neither': Discursive Tensions in Transgender Politics." *Signs: Journal of Women in Culture and Society* 27, no. 2 (2002): 501–522.

————. "Technologies of Trans-sexing: Discursive Tension and Resistance Within Psycho-medical and Transgendered Theorising of Transsexual Bodies." In *Theoretical Issues in Psychology*, Ed. John Morss, Niamh Stephenson, and Hans Van Rappard (Kluwer Academic Publishers, 2001): 35–45.

Roscoe, Will. "How to Become a Berdache: Toward a Unified Analysis of Multiple Genders." In *Third Sex, Third Gender: Beyond Sexual Dimorphism in Culture and History,* edited by Gilbert Herdt, 329-72. New York: Zone Books, 1994.

————. "Was We'wha a Homosexual?: Native American Survivance and the Two-Spirit Tradition." *GLQ: A Journal of Lesbian/Gay Studies* 2(3) (1995): 193–235.

————. *The Zuni Man-Woman.* Albuquerque: University of New Mexico Press, 1991.

Rothblatt, Martine Aliana. *The Apartheid Of Sex: A Manifesto On The Freedom Of Gender.* New York: Crown Publishers, 1995.

Rottnek, Matthew, ed. *Sissies and Tomboys: Gender Nonconformity and Homosexual Childhood.* New York: New York University Press, 1999.

Roughgarden, Joan. *Evolution's Rainbow: Diversity, Gender, and Sexuality in Nature and People.* Berkeley: University of California Press, 2004.

Rudacille, Deborah. *The Riddle of Gender: Science, Activism, and Transgender Rights.* New York: Pantheon. 2005.

Salamon, Gayle. "The Bodily Ego and the Contested Domain of the Material." *differences: A Journal of Feminist Cultural Studies* Volume 15, Number 3, Fall 2004, pp. 95–-122.

San Francisco Lesbian and Gay History Project. "'She even chewed tobacco': A Pictorial Narrative of Passing Women in America." In *Hidden from History: Reclaiming the Gay and Lesbian Past,* ed. Martin Duberman, Martha Vicinus, and George Chauncey, Jr. New York: Penguin, 1989. 183–194.

Sinnott, Megan J. *Toms and Dees: Transgender Identity and Female Same-Sex Relationships in Thailand.* Honolulu: University of Hawaii Press, 2004.

Sharpe, Andrew, *Transgender Jurisprudence: Dysphoric Bodies of Law.* London: Cavendish Publishing Ltd., 2002.

————. "Transgender Jurisprudence and the Spectre of Homosexuality." *Australian Feminist Law Journal* vol 14 (March 2000) pp. 23–37.

————. "Transgender Performance and the Discriminating Gaze: A Critique of Anti- Discrimination Regulatory Regimes," *Social and Legal Studies: An International Journal* Vol 8(1) (March 1999): 5–24.

———— with Leslie J. Moran, "Policing the Transgender/Violence Relation," *Current Issues in Criminal Justice* Vol 13(3) (March 2002): 269–285.

Sloop, John M. "Disciplining the Transgendered: Brandon Teena, Public Representation and Normativity." *Western Journal of Communication* 64 (2000): 165–189.

Stoller, Robert J. *The Transsexual Experiment.* Vol. 2 of *Sex and Gender.* London: Hogarth: 1975.

Stone, Allucquére Rosanne. *The War of Desire and Technology at the Close of the Mechanical Age.* Cambridge, MA: MIT Press. 1996.

Straayer, Chris. *Deviant Eyes, Deviant Bodies: Sexual Re-Orientations in Film and Video.* New York: Columbia University Press, 1996

Stryker, Susan. "Sex and Death Among the Cyborgs," *Wired* (May, 1996), 134–136.

————, ed. *The Transgender Issue. GLQ: A Journal of Lesbian and Gay Studies* 4:2 (1998).

————. "Transgender Studies: Queer Theory's Evil Twin." *GLQ: A Journal of Lesbian and Gay Studies* 10:2 (Spring, 2004), 212–215.

————. "Transsexualism: The Postmodern Body and/as Technology," in David Bell and Barbara Kennedy, eds., *The Cybercultures Reader.* New York: Routledge, 2000, pp. 588–597.

Sullivan, Louis G. *From Female to Male: The Life of Jack. B. Garland.* Boston: Alyson Press, 1990.

Swedenburg, Ted. "Saida Sultan/Danna International: Transgender Pop and the Polysemiotics of Sex, Nation, and Ethnicity on the Israeli-Egyptian Border." *The Musical Quarterly,* 81, no. 1(1997): 81–108.

Taylor, Melanie. "Peter (A Young English Girl): Visualizing Transgender Masculinities." *Camera Obscura.* 19:2 (2004), iv–45.

Terry, Jennifer. *An American Obsession: Science, Medicine, and Homosexuality in Modern Society.* Chicago: University of Chicago Press, 1999.

Terry, Jennifer and Jacqueline Urla, eds., *Deviant Bodies.* Bloomington: Indiana University Press, 1995.

Tully, Brian. *Accounting for Transsexualism and Transhomosexuality.* London: Whiting & Birch Ltd, 1992.

Turner, Stephanie S. "Intersex Identities: Locating New Intersections of Sex and Gender." *Gender and Society* 13 (1999): 457–479.

Tyler, Carole-Ann. "Boys Will Be Girls: The Politics of Gay Drag." In *Inside/Out: Lesbian Theories, Gay Theories,* ed. Diana Fuss. New York: Routledger, 1991. 32-70.

————. "The Supreme Sacrifice? TV, 'TV,' and the Renée Richards Story." *Differences: A Journal of Feminist Cultural Studies* 1, no. 3 (1989): 160–86.

Valentine, David. "'The calculus of pain': violence, anthropological ethics, and the category transgender." *Ethnos* 66, no. 1 (2003): 27–48.

————. "We're not about gender": the uses of "transgender." In *Out in theory: Tthe emergence of lesbian and gay anthropology.* Ellen Lewin and William L. Leap, eds. Urbana: University of Illinois Press, 2002, pp.222–245.

———— and Riki Anne Wilchins. "One percent on the burn chart: gender, genitals, and hermaphrodites with attitude." *Social Text* 52/53 (1997):215–222.

Vidal-Ortiz, S. "Queering Sexuality and Doing Gender: Transgender Men's Identification with Gender and Sexuality." *Gendered Sexualities (Advances in Gender Research)* (2002). Volume 6: 181–233.

Wallace, Lee. "*Faʻafafine: Queens of Samoa* and the Elision of Homosexuality." *GLQ: A Journal of Lesbian and Gay Studies* 5:1 (1999): 25–39.

Walsh, Margaret A. "The Geography of Gender: Transgender Experiences Revise the Map." In *The Problems of Resistance: Studies in Alternate Political Cultures*. Ed. Steve Martinot and Joy James. Amherst, NY: Humanity Books, 2001. 110–118.

Whittle, Stephen. *Respect and Equality: Transsexual and Transgender Rights*. London: Cavendish Publishing, 2002.

———. *The Transgender Debate: The Crisis Surrounding Gender Identities,* South Street Press: 2000.

———. "The Trans-Cyberian Mail Way." *Journal of Social and Legal Studies*, 7, no. 3 (1998): 389–408.

Whittle, Stephen and Tarryn Witten. TransPanthers: The Greying of Transgender and the Law, *Deakin Law Review* (2004), Vol 4 No 2: 503–522.

Wickman, Jan. *Transgender Politics: The Construction and Destruction of Binary Gender in the Finnish Transgender Community*. ÅBO: Åbo Akademi University Press, 2001.

Witten, Tarryn M. "Aging and Gender Diversity." *Social Work Today*, 4:4 (2004), 28–31.

Witten, Tarryn M. and A. Evan Eyler, "Hate crimes and violence against the Transgendered," *Peace Review*, 11:3 (1999), 461–468.

Witz, Anne. "Whose Body Matters? Feminist Sociology and the Corporeal Turn in Sociology and Feminism." *Body and Society* 6 (2000): 1–24.

Worth, Heather. "Bad-Assed Honeys with a Difference: South Aukland *Faʻafine* Talk about Identity." *Intersections* 6 (August 2001).

Zhou, Jiang-Ning, et al. "A Sex Difference in the Human Brain and its Relation to Transsexualism" *Nature* Vol. 378 (2 November 1995): 68–70.

Zita, Jacqueline. "Male Lesbians and the Postmodernist Body." in Claudia Card, ed. *Adventures in Lesbian Philosophy*. Bloomington and Indianapolis: Indiana University Press, 1994, pp. 112–132.

Index

Page numbers in italics refer to Figures or Tables.